D1428967

THE PENGUIN RHYMING DICTIONARY

Rosalind Fergusson

MARKET HOUSE BOOKS LIMITED

VIKING

VIKING

Penguin Books Ltd, Harmondsworth, Middlesex, England
Viking Penguin Inc., 40 West 23rd Street, New York, New York 10010, U.S.A.
Penguin Books Australia Ltd, Ringwood, Victoria, Australia
Penguin Books Canada Ltd, 2801 John Street, Markham, Ontario, Canada L3R 1B4
Penguin Books (N.Z.) Ltd, 182–190 Wairau Road, Auckland 10, New Zealand

First published 1985

Copyright © Market House Books Ltd, 1985

All rights reserved. Without limiting the rights under
copyright reserved above, no part of this publication
may be reproduced, stored in or introduced into a
retrieval system, or transmitted, in any form or by
any means (electronic, mechanical, photocopying,
recording or otherwise), without the prior written
permission of both the copyright owner and the
above publisher of this book.

British Library Cataloguing in Publication Data

The Penguin rhyming dictionary.
  1. English language—Rhyme—Dictionaries
  I. Fergusson, Rosalind
  423′.1   PE1519

  ISBN 0-670-80036-8

Library of Congress Catalog Card Number
84-51880

PREFACE

Milton, in his preface to *Paradise Lost*, complained of the 'troublesome and modern bondage of rhyming . . . the invention of a barbarous age, to set off wretched matter and lame metre'. Yet many creators of superb matter and lilting metre, both before and since 1668 (when these words were written), have felt it necessary to make their verses rhyme. Some poets have relied on their heads to satisfy this need, others have resorted to rhyming dictionaries. *Walker's Rhyming Dictionary*, for example, has been in continuous publication for 150 years. According to its preface, it has 'been a friend in need to generations of poets and rhymesters from Byron downwards'. But when John Walker, a retired schoolmaster, compiled his *Rhyming Dictionary* in 1775, he had to do so without the benefit of a computer.

Had he had access to modern technology, the main part of his *Rhyming Dictionary*, in which the words are listed in reverse alphabetical order (working from the last letter of each word back to the first), would have been relatively simple to produce from the headword list of any standard dictionary. However, this list alone does not provide the poet seeking a rhyme for, say, *trite*, with any of the perfect rhymes: *sight*, *indict*, *Fahrenheit*, *acolyte* or *apartheid*. On the other hand, it throws together as if they rhymed those classic examples of English spelling inconsistency: *bough*, *cough*, *though*, *rough* and *through*.

To compile the *Penguin Rhyming Dictionary*, a list of words together with their phonetic transcriptions was extracted from a standard dictionary data base. The computer was programmed to sort these words, working from the end of the phonetic transcription back to the beginning, into phonetic order. Unsuitable and unrhymable words were then discarded and the remainder of the list was sorted into rhyming groups. The result it that homophones (phonetically identical words of different meaning), such as *sight*, *cite* and *site*, are now grouped together, and such rhymes as *stipulation* and *manipulation*, rather than being buried in an alphabetical list of *-ation* words, appear side by side.

With its ability to scan through a complete list of phonetic transcriptions in a matter of minutes, the computer is an incomparably more versatile rhymester than the live poet with his dying brain cells and deteriorating memory. This dictionary offers to the poet the fruits of the computer's labour, providing him or her with all the words that one would expect to find in a standard English dictionary, including a selection of proper names. There is only one condition of entry for a word: that there should be at least one other word that rhymes with it. Because poetry is not only a question of rhymes – and because poets may wish to know what their verses mean – a short gloss is provided for the more obscure words.

RF
1984

v

HOW TO USE THE DICTIONARY

1. To find the rhymes for any particular word, first look in the index, which forms roughly the second half of the book.

2. The index will refer the user either to a group number (e.g. **15**) or a subgroup number (e.g. **15.3**) in the first part of the book.

3. Find the word you have looked up in the group or subgroup to which you have been referred. The words closest to this word will be its closest rhymes.

4. If you have been directed to a group rather than to a subgroup, you will find several separate paragraphs under the group heading. The first paragraph contains monosyllabic words, the second paragraph disyllabic words, and so on.
   Example: To find the closest rhymes to **ballet**, look this word up in the index. The reference **2** means that it will be found in the group headed **2**. Because it has two syllables it will be found in the second paragraph. The words that follow it – **Calais, callais, palais, chalet**, etc. – are its closest rhymes.

5. Note that **ballet** can be made to rhyme, with varying degrees of closeness, with all the words in group **2** and its subgroups. This applies to all the words in all the groups (see note (b), below).

6. Within each paragraph, whether in a main group or in a subgroup, the words given are listed in phonetic order, working from the end of the word to the beginning. The basis of the phonetic order is given on page ix. However, in most cases, paragraphs are short enough for a word to be located by quickly scanning it, rather than by trying to work out its position in the phonetic order.

7. If the index directs you to a subgroup rather than to a group, you will find a list of close rhymes that have been picked out and placed in a subgroup because it would not have been possible to place them next to each other in a main group. (This usually means that some of the words in the subgroup contain different numbers of syllables.)

   Example: To find the closest rhymes to **atmosphere**, go as directed by the index to subgroup **6.1**, where all the words ending in **-osphere** are listed – from **biosphere** to **magnetosphere**.

The following points should be noted:

(a) All the words in the lists contained in the first part of the book are included in the alphabetical index in the second part of the book.

(b) The rhyming words are arranged in the numbered groups under one-syllable headings, such as *-ite*, *-ank*, and *-oe*. These headings are broad guides to the final

vii

sound of the words in the groups. For example, the *-oe* groups contains **potato**, **although**, and **show** as well as **hoe** and **roe**.

(c) Some group headings are followed by a guide to further rhyming possibilities, often in the form of a cross-reference. Unless otherwise stated, these cross-references apply to all the subgroups of both the group in which they appear and the group to which they refer. For example, the cross reference from group **5** to group **16** applies also to the subgroups **5.1** to **5.24** and subgroups **16.1** to **16.406**.

(d) The glosses that follow difficult words are intended as brief guides to their meanings or to the field in which they are used; they do not constitute full dictionary definitions. The italicized labels – *US, Scot, Austral*, etc. – indicate that the word is an American, Scottish or Australian synonym, often informal, for the given gloss. Thus (*Welsh* mountain) means 'a Welsh word for mountain'. However, (Welsh mountain) means 'a mountain in Wales'.

PHONETIC ORDER

a as in *sat*
ar as in *card, half*
ay as in *day, rail*
e as in *bed*
err as in *err, fern*
air as in *pair, rare*
ee as in *meet, teach*
ear as in *veer, fear*
i as in *win*
ie as in *tie, bite*
ire as in *fire*
o as in *pot*
or as in *form, talk*
oor as in *moor*
oy as in *boy, coil*
oe as in *toe, boat*
ow as in *town, foul*
our as in *hour*
u as in *mug*
oo as in *foot*
ue as in *true, tool*
er as in *water* and other unstressed
    vowel sounds
b as in *big*
k as in *kite, car*

ch as in *chip*
d as in day
f as in *fall, phone*
g as in *gate*
j as in *job, page*
h as in *hat*
l as in *lean*
m as in *mope*
n as in *neat*
ng as in *sing*
p as in *pearl*
qu as in *quick*
r as in *ripe*
s as in *soon*
sh as in *sheep, nation*
zh as in *treasure*
t as in *team*
th as in *thing*
dh as in *bathe*
v as in *vase*
w as in *wool*
x as in *box, works*
y as in *yoke*
z as in *zoo, reason*

RHYMING DICTIONARY

1 -ar

are, ah, bar, baa, Ba (soul in Egyptian mythology), car, scar, char, dah (sound in Morse code), fa, far, Ga (African people), gar (freshwater fish), jar, ha, haar (North Sea fog), lah, blah (silly talk), mar, ma, maar (volcanic crater), knar (knot in wood), parr, par, pa, spar, spa, Kwa (language group), Ra, bra, Kra (isthmus of Thailand), Fra (title of Italian monk), Saar (European river), shah, ta, tar, tahr (goatlike mammal), Ptah (Egyptian god), star, var (unit of power), moire, schwa (unstressed vowel sound), pya (Burmese coin), tsar.

aa (volcanic rock), toea (Papua New Guinea coin), baba, Sabah (Malaysian state), durbar (native ruler's court), oba (African chief), drawbar (metal bar on tractor), crowbar, towbar, Pooh-Bah, subah (province in Mogul empire), Akbar (Mogul emperor of India), rollbar, unbar, Dunbar, facebar (wrestling hold), disbar, crossbar, kasbah, busbar (electrical conductor), fracas, markka (Finnish currency), taka (Bangladeshi currency), Neckar (West German river), shikar (big-game hunting), trocar (surgical instrument), chukar (partridge), sidecar, calcar (spurlike projection), railcar, Shankar, eschar (dry scab on skin), streetcar, boxcar (US closed railway van), cha-cha, kwacha (Zambian currency), morcha (Indian anti-government demonstration), Dada, radar, sirdar, numdah (coarse Indian felt), Gondar (Ethiopian city), sofar (marine location system), shofar (ancient Jewish horn), afar, sol-fa, gaga, Degas, Hagar (Old Testament character), durgah (tomb of Muslim saint), nougat, Elgar, kanga (African woman's cotton garment), koftgar (Indian goldsmith), ajar, nightjar, Lehár, Doha (capital of Qatar), Zohar (Jewish mystical work), hoo-ha, belah (Australian tree), nullah (Indian stream or drain), moolah (Slang money), kiblah (direction of Mecca), dobla (medieval Spanish coin), éclat (brilliant success), verglas (thin film of ice), hoopla, Omagh, summa (medieval scholastic compendium), grandma, Sennar (region of the Sudan), dinar, thenar (palm of the hand), Donar (Germanic god), sonar, Dahna (Arabian desert), faux pas, papa, culpa (act of neglect), oompah, grandpa, COSPAR (Committee on Space Research), feldspar, Berar (region of India), Kura (Asian river), hurrah, Accra, Biskra (Algerian town), mudra (Hindu religious dancing movement), Stranraer, presa (musical term), paisa (Indian coin), pulsar, orgeat (drink made from barley), Qatar, ta-ta, guitar, sitar, hectare, kantar (unit of weight), qintar (Albanian coin), daystar (the sun), lodestar (star used in navigation), Telstar, instar (stage in insect development), sunstar (starfish), earthstar (woodland fungus), navar (aircraft-navigation system), Avar (former European people), louvar (whale-like fish), dvandva (compound word), halvah (Middle Eastern sweet), boulevard, boudoir, couloir (mountain gully), armoire, memoir, Renoir, mirepoix (mixture of sautéed vegetables), octroi (duty on goods), voussoir (wedge-shaped stone), bourgeois, patois, Magyar, cholla (spiny cactus), Konya (Turkish city), gunyah (*Austral* bush hut), quasar, Isar (European river), bizarre, Mizar (multiple star), beaux-arts, hussar.

antiar (Javan tree), caviar, Cantuar. (of Canterbury), handlebar, turbocar, judoka (judo expert), Halakah (traditional Jewish literature), motorcar, advocaat, la-di-da, deodar (Himalayan cedar), tahsildar (Indian tax collector), havildar (Indian noncommissioned officer), zamindar (Indian landowner), Kandahar (Afghan city), Omaha, almemar (raised platform in synagogue), Tsushima (Japanese islands), Charminar (16th-century Indian monument), seminar, Achernar (star), Tanana (Alaskan river), jaçana (long-legged bird), grandpapa, Peckinpah, fluorspar, akhara (Indian gymnasium), Amen-Ra (Egyptian sun-god), registrar, commissar, Manisa (Turkish city), collapsar (black hole), Aisha (Mohammed's favourite wife), langue de chat, Parashah (reading in synagogue), coup d'état, pietà, Bogotá, Janata (Indian political party), avatar (manifestation of Hindu deity), superstar, colcothar (jeweller's rouge), bolivar (Venezuelan currency), cultivar (cultivated plant), chihuahua, pesewa (Ghanaian coin), Aduwa (Ethiopian town), tous-les-mois (plant with edible tubers), peau de soie (silk or rayon fabric), escritoire, remontoir (device in a watch), polynya (water surrounded by ice).

Mauna Kea (extinct Hawaiian volcano), justiciar (medieval king's deputy), Mauna Loa (active Hawaiian volcano), Jogjakarta (Indonesian city), Kathiawar (large Indian peninsula), petit bourgeois.

1.1
debar, millibar (unit of atmospheric pressure), Zanzibar.

1.2
Calabar (Nigerian port), Malabar (Indian coastal region), coolabah, cinnabar (chief ore of mercury), isobar, isallobar (line on map).

1.3
doodah, Üsküdar (Turkish town).

1.4
cigar, Chandigarh (Indian city), budgerigar.

1.5
aha, ha-ha, brouhaha.

1.6
Bihar (Indian state), Cooch Behar (Indian city), pakeha (non-Maori).

1.7
à la, fa-la, Lala (Indian form of address), tra-la, Haleakala (Hawaiian volcano).

1.8
zila (Indian administrative district), Shangri-la.

1.9
galah (Australian cockatoo), escolar (spiny-finned fish), Agartala (Indian city).

1.10
Armagh, Hama (Syrian city), Toyama (Japanese city).

1.11
cymar (woman's short jacket), Waldemar (Danish king), Kohima (Indian city).

1.12
mama, Shema (basic Jewish doctrine), jacamar (tropical bird), Palomar (Californian mountain observatory), Beach-la-Mar (Pacific trading language), grandmama, Panama.

1.13
hoorah, tempura (Japanese food).

1.14

mara (South American rodent), Pará (Brazilian state), Tambora (Indonesian volcano), baccarat, agora (Israeli coin), Aymara (South American Indian people).

1.15

Navarre, baklava (rich cake), samovar (Russian tea urn).

1.16

peignoir, rouge et noir (card game).

1.17

abattoir, repertoire, conservatoire.

1.18

devoirs (compliments), reservoir.

1.19

bazaar, alcazar (Moorish palace in Spain), Balthazar, kala-azar (tropical disease), superbazaar (Indian department store).

2 -ay

eh, ay, bay, bey (Turkish form of address), Kay, cay (low island or bank), day, dey, fay, fey, gay, jay, hey, hay, hae (*Scot* have), lay, clay, flay, fley (*Dialect* be afraid), gley (bluish-grey soil), play, splay, slay, sleigh, May, may, neigh, nay, née, nae (*Scot* no), Neagh (Northern Irish lake), pay, Spey, spay, spae (*Scot* foretell), qua (in the capacity of), re, ray, bray, brae, cray (*Austral* crayfish), dray, fray, Frey (Norse god), frae (*Scot* from), grey, Gray, spray, tray, trey, stray, say, Tay, tay (*Irish* tea), stay, they, weigh, whey, way, wae (*Dialect* woe), ngwee (Zambian coin), sway, yea.

plié (ballet posture), mouillé (phonetics term), foyer, abbé, Torbay, cube (tropical plant), sickbay, Bombay, bombé (having projecting swollen shape), rosebay (type of rhododendron), parquet, Les Cayes (Haitian port), okay, croquet, tokay (small lizard), bouquet, Biscay, risqué, heyday, Mayday, pay-

day, urdé (heraldic term), bidet, Friday, coudé (describing type of telescope), workday, weekday, midday, half-day, someday, Mande (language group), Monday, sundae, Sunday, noonday, washday, birthday, Thursday, Tuesday, doomsday, café, parfait (frozen dessert), au fait, Hofei (Chinese city), buffet, margay (catlike mammal), reggae, nosegay, deejay, Mahé (island in Seychelles), ballet, Calais, callais (Neolithic ornamental stone), palais, chalet, Male (capital of the Maldives), vale (farewell), waylay, melee, Pelé, relay, Islay, au lait, olé, piolet (type of ice-axe), coulee (flow of molten lava), bouclé, bouclée (support for billiard cue), pipeclay, soufflé, reflet (lustre), agley (*Scot* awry), inlay, unlay (untwist), replay, foreplay, wordplay, swordplay, endplay, screenplay, gunplay, display, misplay (play badly), horseplay, mislay, bobsleigh, outlay, lamé, Niamey (capital of Niger), semé (heraldic term), gourmet, dismay, nene (Hawaiian goose), fine (musical term), chiné (mottled), mornay, pince-nez, frappé, épée, prepay, repay, Taipei (capital of Taiwan), Hopeh (Chinese province), coupé, Hupeh (Chinese province), Nupe (Nigerian people), toupee, Gaspé (peninsula in Quebec), jaspé (variegated), strathspey (Scottish reel), parkway, walkway, beret, ciré, Shiré (African river), foray, moray, Fauré, Kure (Japanese port), hooray, chambray (fine woven cloth), hombre (*US* man), defray, affray (noisy fight or disturbance), passé, Tigré (Ethiopian province), in re (in the matter of), sunray, stingray, cy pres (legal term), respray, betray, portray, entrée, estray (stray domestic animal), distrait, astray, ashtray, Vouvray (dry white wine), x-ray, essay, per se, lycée, plissé, hearsay, assay, gainsay, unsay, soothsay, cliché, broché (woven with raised design), crochet, bouchée (vol-au-vent), touché, dragée, Roget, projet

3

(draft of proposed treaty), congé, satai (spiced barbecued meat), pâté, pattée (describing type of cross), Leyte (Philippine island), jeté, conté (artist's hard crayon), Changteh (Chinese port), Chengteh (Chinese city), mainstay, outstay, backstay (nautical term), jackstay (nautical term), Cathay, pavé (paved surface), névé (mass of ice), survey, corvée (forced labour), duvet, purvey, chevet (part of church), inveigh, convey, airway, fairway, stairway, leeway, freeway, seaway, clearway, doorway, Norway, throughway (*US* motorway), subway, hatchway, archway, headway, Medway, speedway, skidway (*US* platform for logs), midway, tideway (strong tidal current), Broadway, roadway, halfway, maguey (fibre-yielding plant), railway, spillway (channel carrying surplus water), Solway, Galway, hallway, tramway, someway, Anhwei (Chinese province), sternway (ship's movement), Conway, runway, gangway, slipway, shipway (shipbuilding structure), paceway (*Austral* racecourse), Kweisui (Chinese town), gateway, outweigh, footway (pedestrian path), beltway (*US* ring road), pathway, driveway, causeway, cruiseway (canal for recreational purposes), soignée, passepied (17th-century minuet), blasé, Laotze (ancient Chinese philosopher).

holiday, everyday, unbirthday, Wednesday, coryphée (leading ballet dancer), merengue (Caribbean dance), popinjay, cassoulet, underclay, cor anglais, teleplay, underplay, interplay, overplay, animé, consommé, résumé, Dubonnet (*Trademark*), cloisonné (type of enamel work), Hogmanay, Massenet (French composer), underpay, overpay, Kol Nidre (Jewish prayer), émigré, Castlereagh (British statesman), divorcé, fiancé, Colonsay (Hebridean island), recherché, écorché (anatomical figure), ricochet, negligee, protégé,

Fabergé, décolleté, overstay, naiveté, Milky Way, alleyway, anyway, taxiway, Camagüey (Cuban city), cableway, Hemingway, expressway (*US* urban motorway), Rambouillet (breed of sheep), sommelier, atelier, Parmentier (cookery term).

Marinduque (Philippine island), Hiroshige (Japanese artist), Tenzing Norgay, Oriente (Cuban province), companionway (stairway on ship), ukiyoe (school of Japanese painting), summa cum laude (highest achievement in examination).

2.1
Rainier, Fourier, dossier, métier, boulevardier, Du Maurier, couturier, Olivier.

2.2
Douai (French city), roué, Niue (Pacific island).

2.3
Benue (Nigerian state), tatouay (large armadillo), habitué.

2.4
obey, mangabey (monkey), disobey, Iskander Bey (Albanian patriot).

2.5
flambé, harambee (East African work chant).

2.6
piqué, appliqué.

2.7
decay, tourniquet, sobriquet, communiqué.

2.8
today, workaday, Faraday, Saturday, yesterday, alackaday.

2.9
Santa Fe, auto-da-fé (ceremony of Spanish Inquisition), Morgan le Fay.

2.10
Haringey, Fotheringhay.

2.11
belay (make secure), delay, gilet (bodice resembling waistcoat), Millais, relay, roundelay (medieval dance), virelay (old French poem).

2.12
allay, Malay, Pelée (volcano in Martinique), Rabelais, Mandalay (Burmese city), Charollais (breed of cattle), brise-soleil (structure protecting window), underlay, beaujolais, interlay, overlay, cabriolet.

2.13
roble (oak tree), paso doble.

2.14
carnet, KaNgwane (South African homeland).

2.15
matinée, ratiné (coarse cloth), in nomine (musical term).

2.16
barré (guitar-playing procedure), Le Carré.

2.17
mare (plain on moon's surface), moiré, soiree, Whangarei (New Zealand port), ricercare (musical term).

2.18
bourrée, purée, de jure (according to law).

2.19
array, cabaret, disarray, Monterey (Californian city), Monterrey (Mexican city).

2.20
assay, chassé (ballet step), bio-assay (biology term), immunoassay (immunology technique).

2.21
Ruse (Bulgarian city), repoussé (raised design), retroussé.

2.22
cachet, sachet, attaché, papier-mâché.

2.23
maté (tree cultivated for caffeine), écarté (card game), Hakodate (Japanese port).

2.24
sauté, Obote, cenote (natural well in limestone), chayote (tropical climbing plant), chicalote (type of poppy).

2.25
velouté, kachang puteh (Malaysian roasted nuts).

2.26
byway, highway, superhighway (*US* fast dual carriageway).

2.27
noway, Ogooué (African river).

2.28
aweigh, away, flyaway, throwaway, stowaway, breakaway, takeaway, hideaway, foldaway, Alloway, Galloway, rollaway (mounted on rollers), mulloway (Australian fish), Stornoway, caraway, faraway, straightaway, waterway, motorway, cutaway, counterweigh, castaway, Hathaway, overweigh, areaway (passageway between buildings).

2.29
ridgeway, carriageway, steerageway (nautical term), passageway.

2.30
Bizet, frisé (fabric with long nap), Champs Elysées.

2.31
rosé, San Jose (Californian city), exposé.

3 -err
err, Ur, burr, bur, birr (make whirring sound), cur, Kerr, skirr (move rapidly), chirr (make shrill sound), fur, fir, her, blur, slur, myrrh, murre (type of guillemot), knur (knot in tree trunk), per, purr, spur, br'er, sir, shirr, stir, were, whirr, 'twere.

voyeur, recur, occur, incur, concur, Frondeur (French rebel), coiffeur, defer, refer, prefer, infer, confer, transfer, millefleurs (floral design in textiles), demur, longspur (songbird), hotspur (impetuous person), Hotspur, larkspur, cockspur (type of grass), masseur, chasseur, douceur (a tip or bribe), deter, hauteur, inter, bestir, astir, aver, prie-dieu, milieu, seigneur, poseur.

butterbur (flowering plant), cocklebur (coarse weed), underfur, connoisseur, force majeure, voyageur (Canadian woodsman), rapporteur (person who prepares report), disinter, raconteur, Richelieu, écraseur (surgical cutting device).

entrepreneur, carillonneur (bell-ringer).

3.1
saboteur, littérateur (professional writer), restaurateur.

4 -air
air, heir, e'er, Ayr, ere, bare, bear, care, scare, chair, dare, fare, fair, hair, hare, lair, blare, Clare, flair, flare, glare, glair (egg-white), mare, mayor, Khmer (former Cambodian civilization), ne'er, snare, pear, pare, pair, spare, quare (*Irish* remarkable), square, rare, prayer, share, tear, tare, stair, stare, there, their, they're, vair (medieval fur trimming), wear, ware, where, swear.

tuyère (nozzle in blast-furnace), howe'er, forebear, forbear, Flaubert, threadbare, Rambert, highchair, wheelchair, armchair, pushchair, midair, Kildare, Mayfair, warfare, fieldfare, welfare, fanfare, infare (*Dialect* wedding reception), unfair, funfair, mohair, unhair (remove hair from hide), horsehair, éclair, declare, Sinclair, commère (female compere), nightmare, plein-air (art term), whene'er, Bonaire (West Indian island), ensnare, au pair, ampere, impair, compere, compare, despair,

foursquare (firmly), headsquare, where'er, confrère (fellow member of profession), corsair, torchère (stand for holding candelabrum), ploughshare, parterre (formally-patterned garden), Altair (star), Voltaire, Basse-Terre (West Indian island), Astaire, Lothair (German king), trouvère (medieval French poet), seaware (large seaweed), nowhere, neckwear, hardware, redware (seaweed), stemware (stemmed glasses), firmware (computer term), somewhere, treenware (wooden utensils), tinware, stoneware, glassware, forswear (reject with determination), elsewhere, unswear (retract), sportswear, nightwear, footwear, software, liveware (personnel working with computers), menswear, Gruyère, meunière (cookery term), Robespierre, misère.

overbear, Medicare (*US* health insurance programme), aftercare, Aberdare, nom de guerre, maidenhair (tropical fern), De la Mare, doctrinaire (theoretical and impractical), abampere, portecochere (covered entrance for vehicles), fourragère (ornamental cord on uniform), solitaire, Finisterre (Spanish headland), Finistère (French department), tableware, kitchenware, ironware, earthenware, ovenware, basaltware (black stoneware), chargé d'affaires.

4.1
premiere, derrière (buttocks), portière (curtain hung in doorway), rivière, jardinière, boutonniere (flowers worn in buttonhole), son et lumière.

4.2
carfare (*US* bus fare), savoir-faire.

4.3
affair, thoroughfare, chemin de fer.

4.4
bêche-de-mer (marine organism), coco de mer (palm tree), Weston-super-Mare.

4.5

debonair, questionnaire, legionnaire, billionaire, millionaire, concessionaire, commissionaire, multimillionaire.

4.6

repair, prepare, disrepair.

4.7

beware, anywhere, everywhere.

4.8

aware, underwear, Delaware, well-aware, chinaware, unaware, lustreware (pottery with lustre decoration), otherwhere, silverware.

4.9

knitwear, agateware (ceramic ware resembling agate), graniteware (enamel-coated iron vessels).

5 -ee [see also **16**]

be, bee, quay, key, ski, Dee, fee, ghee (clarified butter), gie (*Scot* give), gee, he, lea, Leigh, lee, li (Chinese unit of length), ley (line of prehistoric track), flea, flee, glee, plea, mi, me, mee (Malaysian noodles), knee, pea, pee, re, Brie, bree (*Scot* thin soup), Cree, scree, dree (*Scot* endure), free, spree, tree, three, see, sea, Hsi (Chinese river), she, tee, te, tea, thee, wee, we, twee, Twi (Negroid people), ye, zee (*US* zed).

drawee, cooee, bawbee (former Scottish coin), Frisbee (*Trademark*), ackee (tropical fruit tree), Bacchae (priestesses of Bacchus), Torquay, trochee (metrical foot), latchkey, turnkey, passkey, Volsci (ancient Latin people), ash-key, lychee, Kochi (Japanese port), Penchi (Chinese city), Chaldee, grandee, standee (person who stands), vendee, spondee, Dundee, fundi (East African mechanic), thuggee (practices of Indian thugs), lungi (Indian loincloth or turban), Meiji (period in Japanese history), burgee (ship's identification flag), gee-gee, squeegee, ogee (architectural moulding), Fuji, algae, Belgae (ancient Celtic people), pongee (silk fabric), mallee (shrubby eucalyptus tree), bailee, Philae (island in Upper Egypt), Orly, Thule, Eastleigh, mamey (tropical fruit tree), thermae (ancient Roman public baths), gimme, Cannae (ancient Italian city), Pawnee, Shawnee, koine (a common language), donee (receiver of gift), townee, whangee (bamboo grass), rappee (English snuff), tapis (tapestry or carpet), tepee, cowpea (tropical climbing plant), rupee, Tupi (South American Indian people), yippee, chickpea, boree (Australian acacia tree), Horae (Roman goddesses), Puri (Indian port), decree, machree (*Irish* my dear), carefree, grigri (African talisman), agree, Capri, esprit, shoetree, ridgetree (timber along roof ridge), gumtree, crosstree (nautical term), farci (stuffed), Parsee (member of religious sect), precis, sycee (silver ingots), emcee (master of ceremonies), Shansi (Chinese province), Shensi (Chinese province), Kiangsi (Chinese province), sightsee, Clichy (industrial Parisian suburb), specie, chichi, buckshee, banshee, shoji (Japanese rice-paper screen), bougie (catheter), settee, titi (South American monkey), coatee, goatee, suttee (Hindu custom), bootee, tutee, stacte (Old Testament incense spice), draftee, Santee (US river), grantee, mustee (person of mixed parentage), trustee, moolvie (Muslim learned man), peewee, ennui, étui, razee (sailing ship), fusee (spindle in watch).

Savaii (island in Western Samoa), employee, diploë (bone in skull), Meroë (ancient Sudanese city), honeybee, bumblebee, heitiki (Maori neck ornament), Waikiki, Didache (early Christian treatise), Cherokee, après-ski, hydroski (hydrofoil on seaplane), debauchee, Tweedledee, Sekondi (Ghanaian port), refugee, takahe (New Zealand bird), appellee (accused person), parolee, infulae (ribbons on bishop's mitre), internee, Mycenae, calipee (edible part of turtle), Principe (island west of Africa), cap-a-pie (from head to foot), Kayseri (Turkish city), conferee (conference participant), disagree, doubletree (horizontal bar on vehicle), saddletree (frame of saddle), whiffletree (crossbar in harness), trestletree (ship's timber), manteltree (lintel over fireplace), axletree (carriage axle), Sadducee, fricassee, undersea, oversee, Marshalsea (former English court), licensee, garnishee (legal term), repartee, allottee, deportee, picotee (type of carnation), legatee (recipient of legacy), manatee (whale-like mammal), devotee, inductee (*US* military conscript), appointee, El Misti (Peruvian volcano), peccavi, vis-à-vis, ach-y-fi (Welsh expression of disgust), eau de vie, ratatouille, fedayee (Arab commando), cuir-bouilli (hardened leather), bourgeoisie, devisee (legal term), jalousie, Zuider Zee, chimpanzee.

Kauai (Hawaiian island), evacuee, interviewee, Wu-lu-mu-ch'i (Chinese city), chincherinchee (South African plant), fiddle-de-dee, bahuvrihi (linguistics term), satyagrahi (exponent of nonviolent resistance), Maebashi (Japanese city), recognizee (legal term).

5.1
lei, payee, Danaë (Greek mythological character), Pompeii.

5.2
torii (gateway to Japanese temple), reliquiae (fossil remains), facetiae (witty sayings), minutiae, exuviae (layers of shed skin), amicus curiae (legal adviser to court).

5.3
marquee, maquis (Mediterranean shrubby vegetation), raki (strong aromatic drink), bidarkee (Eskimo canoe).

5.4
chickadee (small songbird), Pasargadae (ancient Persian city).

5.5
pledgee, Himeji (Japanese city).

5.6
gidgee (small acacia tree), mortgagee, obligee (creditor), perigee.

5.7
agee (*Scot* awry), apogee.

5.8
pili (Philippine tree), jubilee, Galilee, galilee (medieval church porch), Rosie Lee.

5.9
alee, Tralee, libellee, fleur-de-lis, Omphale (Greek mythological queen), shiralee (*Austral* swagman's bundle), Peterlee, Trincomalee (Sri Lankan port), Thermopylae.

5.10
Wad Medani (Sudanese town), bouquet garni, maharani, Liliuokalani (queen of Hawaiian islands).

5.11
trainee, distrainee (legal term), detainee.

5.12
jinni (Muslim mythological spirit), nominee, examinee, Mnemosyne (Greek goddess), Euphrosyne (Greek goddess).

5.13
Chinee, assignee (legal term), consignee.

5.14
Guarani (Paraguayan currency), Kootenay (US river), alienee (legal term), abandonee (legal term).

5.15
kepi, escapee.

5.16
topee, épopée (epic poem).

5.17
Marie, sirree, jamboree, chickaree (red squirrel), referee, transferee, sangaree (spiced drink), dungaree, kedgeree,

rapparee (17th-century Irish soldier), camporee (local Scout meeting), gaucherie, Sault Sainte Marie (Canadian inland port), chinoiserie.

5.18
degree, pedigree, filigree, mistigris (joker in poker game).

5.19
lessee, addressee.

5.20
promisee, Tennessee, Pharisee, felo de se (person who commits suicide).

5.21
foresee, endorsee, divorcee.

5.22
remittee, Hippolyte (queen of the Amazons), typothetae (*US* printers collectively).

5.23
amputee, distributee (legal term).

5.24
guarantee, warrantee, absentee, patentee, covenantee.

6 -eer

ear, bier, beer, kier (vat in bleaching process), cheer, deer, dear, fear, sphere, gear, jeer, here, hear, leer, Lear, Leah, clear, mere, smear, near, sneer, peer, pier, spear, queer, rear, sear, sere, cere (swelling on bird's beak), ser (Indian unit of weight), sheer, shear, tear, tier, steer, stere (unit for measuring timber), veer, weir, Wear, we're, year.

Aïr (region in the Sahara), Zaïre, Meir, gambier (astringent obtained from plant), fakir, Bashkir (Mongoloid people), voir dire (legal term), nadir, mudir (local governor), killdeer (US plover), reindeer, endear, mandir (Hindu temple), ensphere, headgear, footgear, Aegir (Norse god), Tangier, cohere, adhere, menhir, inhere, mishear, unclear, emir, Vermeer, Mimir (Norse

mythological giant), Ajmer (Indian city), Thirlmere, Grasmere, besmear, Kashmir, cashmere, Izmir (Turkish port), compeer (person of equal status), Shakespeare, lequear (ceiling with sunken panels), eyrir (Icelandic coin), career, Fenrir (Norse mythological wolf), uprear, Asir (region of Saudi Arabia), Aesir (chief Norse gods), Landseer, sincere, cashier, Ayrshire, Cheshire, Berkshire, Yorkshire, Shropshire, Hampshire, Wiltshire, Flintshire, wheatear (small songbird), haltere (insect's modified hind wing), frontier, austere, wasteweir (channel carrying surplus water), Goodyear, vizier.

Aboukir, belvedere, bayadere (Hindu dancing girl), bombardier, Agadir, brigadier, balladeer, grenadier, commandeer, interfere, hemisphere, barysphere (central portion of earth), bathysphere, overhear, Cordelier (Franciscan friar), chandelier, cameleer, fusilier, bandoleer (soldier's shoulder belt), gondolier, gasolier (fitting for gaslights), pistoleer (soldier armed with pistol), cavalier, chanticleer, Tirich Mir (Pakistani mountain), insincere, Derbyshire, Denbighshire, Lancashire, Radnorshire, Leicestershire, Gloucestershire, Worcestershire, Warwickshire, Brecknockshire, Pembrokeshire, Staffordshire, Bedfordshire, Hertfordshire, Oxfordshire, Cambridgeshire, Monmouthshire, racketeer, rocketeer (rocket engineer), musketeer, profiteer, gadgeteer (lover of gadgetry), muleteer, pamphleteer, sonneteer, puppeteer, corsetier, gazetteer, volunteer, oversteer.

Diyarbakir (Turkish city), Buckinghamshire, Nottinghamshire.

isodiaphere (type of atomic nucleus), Merionethshire.

6.1
biosphere, ecosphere, thermosphere (atmospheric layer), atmosphere, troposphere (lowest atmospheric layer),

aerosphere (earth's entire atmosphere), hydrosphere (earth's watery regions), centrosphere (central part of earth), mesosphere (atmospheric layer), stratosphere, photosphere (visible surface of sun), lithosphere (earth's crust), exosphere (highest atmospheric layer), rhizosphere (soil around plant's roots), ionosphere, ozonosphere (region of stratosphere), magnetosphere.

6.2
chimere (bishop's sleeveless gown), Vladimir, epimere (part of embryo), cassimere (woollen cloth), antimere (biology term), kerseymere (woollen cloth).

6.3
amir (former ruler of Afghanistan), Windermere, centromere (part of chromosome), metamere (animal's body segment), Buttermere, blastomere (embryonic cell), Rothermere (British newspaper magnate), actinomere (biology term).

6.4
veneer, engineer, domineer, scrutineer, mutineer, mountaineer, carabineer (soldier armed with carbine).

6.5
pioneer, Bikaner (Indian city), buccaneer, chiffonier (tall chest of drawers), sloganeer, cannoneer, auctioneer, pontonier (military bridge builder), souvenir, gonfalonier (medieval Italian magistrate), electioneer.

6.6
appear, reappear, diapir (geological fold), disappear.

6.7
cuirassier (16th-century mounted soldier), xerosere (ecology term), adipocere (waxy substance from corpses).

6.8
Breconshire, Lincolnshire, Huntingdonshire, Cardiganshire, Northampton-

shire, Carmarthenshire, Caernarvonshire.

6.9
privateer, charioteer.

6.10
megathere (extinct sloth), dinothere (extinct elephant-like mammal), isothere (line on map), chalicothere (extinct horse-like mammal), titanothere (extinct horse-like mammal), uintathere (extinct rhinoceros-like mammal).

6.11
revers, revere, severe, Bedivere, Guinevere, persevere, Guadalquivir (Spanish river).

7 -ie
I, ay, aye, eye, bye, buy, by, Skye, sky, die, dye, fie, guy, hi, high, hie (to hurry), lie, lye (alkaline solution), Bligh, fly, ply, sly, my, nigh, nye (flock of pheasants), snye (side channel of river), pie, pi, spy, wry, rye, cry, scry (divine by crystal-gazing), dry, fry, pry, spry, try, sigh, shy, tie, Thai, taille (former French tax), sty, thigh, thy, vie, why, Wye, swy (*Austral* gambling game).

shiai (judo contest), aye-aye, kowhai (New Zealand tree), rabbi, thereby, whereby, hereby, nearby, flyby (flight past), forby (*Scot* besides), Dubai, goodbye, Sakai (Japanese port), cockeye (squinting eye), rocaille (decorative rock work), sockeye, Tokay (Hungarian sweet wine), buckeye (US tree), pinkeye (acute conjunctivitis), bronchi, deadeye (nautical term), redeye, goldeye (US fish), Sendai (Japanese city), hi-fi, sci-fi, bigeye (tropical fish), gilgai (*Austral* natural water hole), nilgai (Indian antelope), Songhai (West African people), magi, fungi, Weihai (Chinese port), Pohai (inlet of Yellow Sea), Shanghai, shanghai, Tsinghai (Chinese province), ally, Alai (Russian mountain range), Eli, walleye (divergent squint), mayfly, firefly, blowfly, shoo-fly, blackfly, catchfly (plant with sticky parts), gadfly, sandfly, gallfly, greenfly, horsefly, housefly, botfly, imply, comply, demy (size of paper), Katmai (Alaskan volcano), Panay (Philippine island), Menai, mooneye (US freshwater fish), Brunei, Sinai, charpai (type of bedstead), porkpie, magpie, espy, potpie (meat and vegetable stew), decry, descry, retry, assai (musical term), asci (botany term), Kasai (African river), Masai (African people), Pasay (Philippine city), Versailles, nisi, loci, bonsai, workshy, cockshy (target in throwing games), shuteye, necktie, recti (straight muscles), hogtie (*US* tie limbs together), untie, pigsty, Levi (Old Testament character), oxeye, cocci (bacteria), Veii (ancient Etruscan city), banzai (Japanese patriotic cheer).

Haggai (Old Testament prophet), alibi, syllabi, lullaby, passer-by, overdye, argufy, satisfy, ultrahigh, jai alai (Spanish game), jus soli (legal term), butterfly, overfly, damselfly, dragonfly, dobsonfly (large insect), haeremai (Maori expression of welcome), decani (musical term), Iceni (ancient British tribe), goldeneye (diving duck), Philippi, occupy, counterspy, samurai, Madurai (Indian city), prophesy, lex loci (law of the place), Hokusai, chigetai (Asian wild ass), Paraguay, Uruguay, tiger's-eye.

locus standi (legal term), dissatisfy, preoccupy, decree nisi.

certiorari (legal term), corpus delicti (facts constituting an offence), dramatis personae.

7.1
radii, bindi-eye (Australian plant), nuclei, genii, Falerii (ancient Italian city), Helvetii (Celtic tribe), pons Varolii (nerve fibres in brain).

7.2
Mackay, Malachi.

7.3
defy, deify, reify (make real), rubefy (make red), speechify, preachify, Frenchify, ladyfy, edify, modify, codify, dandify, salify (mix with salt), jellify, stellify (change into a star), vilify, nullify, uglify, amplify, simplify, ramify, mummify, tumefy (swell up), carnify (medical term), unify, cockneyfy, magnify, damnify (injure), tepefy (make tepid), typify, stupefy, liquefy, aerify (change into a gas), scarify, rarefy, horrify, torrefy (dry with intense heat), scorify (refine by smelting), glorify, purify, chondrify (change into cartilage), metrify (translate into poetic metre), petrify, vitrify, nitrify (treat with nitrogen), putrefy, countrify, basify (make basic), casefy (become cheese-like), specify, versify, ossify, crucify, calcify, falsify, Nazify, certify, prettify, citify, fortify, mortify, notify, brutify (brutalize), beautify, fructify (bear fruit), sanctify, stultify, quantify, testify, mystify, justify, vivify (bring to life).

syllabify, alkalify, exemplify, saponify (change into soap), personify, reunify, indemnify, solemnify, transmogrify, electrify, diversify, intensify, denazify, acetify (convert into vinegar), identify, demystify, revivify, detoxify, oversimplify.

7.3.1
nidify (build a nest), rigidify, solidify, humidify, lapidify (change into stone), acidify, dehumidify.

7.3.2
jollify, mollify, qualify, disqualify.

7.3.3
dignify, lignify (make woody), signify, presignify.

7.3.4
clarify, saccharify (convert into sugar).

7.3.5
terrify, verify, esterify (chemistry term).

7.3.6
gasify, classify, pacify, declassify.

7.3.7
dulcify (sweeten), demulsify (separate an emulsion), emulsify.

7.3.8
ratify, gratify, stratify, beatify, interstratify (geology term).

7.3.9
rectify, objectify (represent concretely), subjectify (interpret subjectively).

7.4
assegai (sharp light spear), anthropophagi (cannibals).

7.5
belie, quillai (South American tree), rely, villi (finger-like projections), morbilli (measles), locus sigilli (position of document seal).

7.6
July, vox populi, lapis lazuli.

7.7
ally, alkali, underlie, Lorelei, overlie, antalkali.

7.8
reply, multiply.

7.9
apply, supply, misapply.

7.10
deny, Gemini, anno Domini.

7.11
sori (spore-producing structures), tori (*plural of* torus), a priori, a fortiori, memento mori, a posteriori.

7.12
awry, serail (harem), Terai (Indian marshland), caravanserai.

7.13
Mira Ceti (star), arbor vitae (coniferous tree), aqua vitae, curriculum vitae.

8 -ire [see also **17.4**]
ire, byre, dire, fire, gyre (circular movement), hire, lyre, mire, pyre, spire, quire, choir, squire, sire, shire, tire, Tyre, tyre, wire.

sapphire, backfire, wildfire, hellfire, shellfire, camphire (henna), samphire (Eurasian plant), bonfire, gunfire, misfire, crossfire, spitfire, portfire (device for firing rockets), foxfire (glow emitted by fungi), bemire, admire, quagmire, pismire (*Dialect* ant), vampire, empire, umpire, respire, transpire, inspire, conspire, expire, acquire, inquire, enquire, esquire, Bushire (Iranian port), satire, retire, attire, saltire (heraldic term), entire, haywire, rewire, tripwire, desire.

retrofire (firing of retrorocket), retrochoir (space behind cathedral altar), Molly Maguire (Irish secret society member).

8.1
afire, melaphyre (type of basalt), granophyre (granitic rock), lamprophyre (igneous rock).

8.2
aspire, perspire, suspire (to sigh), acrospire (botany term).

8.3
require, antechoir (part of church).

9 -or
or, oar, ore, o'er, awe, boar, bore, caw, corps, core, score, chore, chaw (*Dialect* chew without swallowing), door, daw (jackdaw), dor (dung beetle), four, for, fore, gore, jaw, hoar, whore, haw, lore, law, lor (exclamation of dismay), claw, flaw, floor, splore (*Scot* a revel), more, maw, mor (acidic humus), nor, gnaw, snore, paw, pore, pour, spore, squaw, roar, raw, braw (*Scot* excellent), craw, draw, drawer, straw, soar, saw, sore, shore, Shaw, pshaw, tor, tore, taw (large marble), torr (unit of pressure),

store, thaw, Thor, Waugh, war, wore, swore, yaw, your, yore.

forbore, Gabor, chokebore (shotgun), smoothbore, markhor (Himalayan goat), décor, ichor (blood-like fluid), encore, threescore, fourscore, stridor (high-pitched breathing sound), moidore (former Portuguese coin), sudor (sweat), jackdaw, bandore (16th-century stringed instrument), landau, vendor, indoor, Indore (Indian city), condor, outdoor, ephor (ancient Greek magistrate), therefore, wherefore, guffaw, Roquefort, Balfour, nagor (African antelope), rigor (medical term), Bogor (Indonesian city), gewgaw (showy trinket), algor (chill), nylghau (Indian antelope), pledgor, crackjaw (difficult to pronounce), lockjaw, Tanjore (Indian city), heehaw, Hawhaw, Johore (Malaysian state), Lahore (Pakistani city), abhor, bylaw, folklore, dewclaw, scofflaw (US habitual lawbreaker), Danelaw, deplore, implore, explore, coleslaw, outlaw, claymore (two-edged sword), Seymour, Timor, Broadmoor, ignore, rapport, forepaw, pawpaw, Cawnpore (Indian city), downpour, southpaw, furor, withdraw, uproar, bedstraw, lessor, Esau, seesaw, eyesore, Mysore, foresaw, Warsaw, bowsaw, tussore (Indian silk), bedsore, handsaw, jigsaw, whipsaw (saw with flexible blade), footsore, seashore, foreshore, ashore, bashaw (important person), kickshaw (worthless trinket), rickshaw, Bradshaw, offshore, scrimshaw (shell or ivory carving), cumshaw (tip or gift), inshore, onshore, longshore, Utah, lector (university lecturer), Choctaw (American Indian people), cantor (leading singer in synagogue), grantor, Nestor (Greek mythological character), restore, drugstore, prewar, postwar, hacksaw, bucksaw (woodcutting saw), Luxor (Egyptian town), señor, signor, bezoar (hairball).

hellebore (poisonous plant), usquebaugh (Irish liqueur), Maribor (Yugoslavian city), underscore (to stress), overscore (cross out), battledore (former racket game), theretofore, heretofore, obligor (debtor), underfloor, son-in-law, overslaugh (military term), Barrymore, Baltimore, Aviemore, Mount Rushmore, Mackinaw (US short coat), Tengri Nor (Chinese salt lake), assignor (legal term), Elsinore, Koko Nor (Chinese lake), millepore (coral-like organism), nullipore (red seaweed), madrepore (coral), Singapore, blastopore (embryology term), archespore (spore-making cell), overawe, overdraw, windlestraw (Dialect dried grass stalks), promisor, Arkansas, wappenshaw (gathering of Scottish clansmen), alongshore, Wichita, Ouachita (US river), legator (person making bequest), Minotaur, guarantor, warrantor, patentor, williwaw (US state of turmoil), man-of-war.

daughter-in-law, sister-in-law, father-in-law, mother-in-law, brother-in-law, imperator, recognizor (legal term), caveat emptor.

9.1
Dior, Melchior, Gwalior (Indian city), excelsior, Confiteor (Catholic prayer).

9.2
macaw, zoochore (botany term), albacore (variety of tunny), isochor (line on graph), esprit de corps, anemochore (botany term).

9.3
louis d'or (former French coin), humidor (humid tobacco-storing container), cuspidor (spittoon), corridor, stevedore, Corregidor (Philippine island), lobster thermidor.

9.4
adore, picador, Mogador (Moroccan port), commodore, Ecuador, mirador (balcony or turret), Labrador, comprador (agent of foreign enterprise), mata-

dor, Salvador, toreador, conquistador, El Salvador, San Salvador.

9.5
before, petit four, hereinbefore.

9.6
afore, trochophore (invertebrate's larva), lophophore (minute organism's tentacles), semaphore, ctenophore (marine invertebrate), pinafore, gonophore (biology term), carpophore (botany term), carrefour, sporophore (spore-bearing organ), photophore (light-producing organ), siphonophore (marine invertebrate), ommatophore (eye-bearing stalk), chromatophore (zoology term), pneumatophore (biology term), gametophore (plant part).

9.7
Tagore (Indian poet), Chandernagore (Indian port).

9.8
galore, Vellore (Indian town), roquelaure (man's hooded cloak), Bangalore, Mangalore (Indian port).

9.9
hackamore (*US* rope halter), sycamore, sophomore, sagamore (American Indian chief), mattamore (subterranean storehouse), furthermore, evermore, nevermore, forevermore.

9.10
diaspore (mineral), zoospore, endospore, megaspore (botany term), microspore (botany term), tetraspore, exospore (outer layer of spore), teliospore, aeciospore, chlamydospore, aplanospore.

9.11
Chickasaw (American Indian people), stegosaur, dinosaur, pterosaur, hadrosaur, vavasor (baron's vassal), plesiosaur, ichthyosaur, ankylosaur, megalosaur, elasmosaur, tyrannosaur, titanosaur.

9.12
mentor, centaur, stentor (loud-voiced person), bucentaur (Venetian state barge).

9.13
herbivore, carnivore, omnivore, insectivore.

10 -oor
boor, Boer, dour, Gur (language group), lur (Bronze Age musical horn), Moore, Moor, moor, poor, spoor, Ruhr, sure, tour, you're, cure, lure, Muir, pure.

Niebuhr (German historian), tambour, pandour (18th-century Croatian soldier), Darfur (Sudanese province), Uigur (Mongoloid people), Kungur (Chinese mountain), langur (monkey), adjure, abjure, conjure, velours, Namur (Belgian province), Sedgemoor, unmoor, Dartmoor, Exmoor, Nippur (ancient Babylonian city), Jaipur (Indian city), Nagpur (Indian city), Kanpur (Indian city), parure (set of jewels), hachure (lines drawn for shading), brochure, assure, cocksure, unsure, detour, contour, Guntur (Indian city), procure, obscure, ordure (excrement), bordure (outer edge of shield), endure, rondure (curvature), ligure (Old Testament precious stone), doublure (decorative lining inside book), armure (silk or wool fabric), immure, demure, tenure, inure, conure (small parrot), manure, purpure (heraldic purple), guipure, impure, couture, nervure (biology term), gravure (method of printing).

troubadour, pompadour (18th-century women's hairstyle), kieselguhr (type of rock), Damanhûr (Egyptian city), Kohinoor, Nishapur (birthplace of Omar Khayyám), Jamshedpur (Indian city), Lyallpur (Pakistani city), Jabalpur (Indian city), Bhagalpur (Indian city), commissure (tissue linking two organs), embouchure, reassure, plat du jour, Thanjavur (Indian city), dasyure (small marsupial), clair-obscure (art term), Réaumur, confiture (fruit preserve), prefecture, calenture (mild tropical fever), cynosure (centre of attraction).

somatopleure (embryonic tissue), Chota Nagpur (East Indian plateau), Kuala Lumpur, photogravure, rotogravure.

10.1
amour (love affair), Amur (Asian river), paramour.

10.2
ensure, insure, reinsure, coinsure.

10.3
liqueur, secure, pedicure, manicure, sinecure, epicure, insecure.

10.4
allure, colure (circle on celestial sphere), velure, craquelure (cracks on old paintings), cannelure (groove around bullet).

10.5
mature, armature (moving electrical part), premature, immature, crenature (notch in scalloped edge), overture, caricature, magistrature.

11 -oy
boy, buoy, coy, Fowey, joy, hoy (freight barge), cloy, ploy, poi (Hawaiian food), Roy, Troy, soy, toy.

carboy (bottle for corrosive liquids), dayboy, playboy, highboy (*US* tallboy), choirboy, hautboy (strawberry), doughboy (boiled dumpling), lowboy (*US* table with drawers), cowboy, ploughboy, linkboy (torch carrier in streets), pageboy, bellboy, callboy, smallboy (steward's assistant), tallboy, schoolboy, tomboy, houseboy, potboy (employee in public house), footboy (boy servant), liftboy, postboy, kikoi (African banded cloth), decoy, Khoikhoi (language group), McCoy, Sainte Foy (suburb of Quebec), enjoy, ahoy,

Namhoi (Chinese city), alloy, deploy, employ, Amoy (Chinese port), Hanoi, annoy, charpoy, sepoy (Indian soldier serving British), teapoy (table with tripod base), Rob Roy, viceroy, destroy, Tolstoy, travois (American Indian sled), savoy, Savoy, envoy, renvoi (legal term), convoy, borzoi.

maccaboy (rose-scented snuff), sonobuoy (buoy detecting underwater noises), paperboy, attaboy, stableboy, didicoy (type of gypsy), overjoy, permalloy (iron–nickel alloy), redeploy, Illinois, Iroquois, corduroy, cunjevoi (tropical plant).

hobbledehoy, paduasoy (silk fabric).

11.1
alloy, kumbaloi (worry beads), hoi polloi, saveloy.

12 -oe
owe, oh, beau, bow, Chou (Chinese dynasty), dough, doe, doh, foe, go, Joe, ho, hoe, lo, low, blow, flow, floe, glow, slow, sloe, mow, mo (*short for* moment), mot (witty remark), know, no, snow, Poe, po (chamber pot), Po (Italian river), row, roe, crow, fro, froe (cutting tool), grow, pro, throw, sew, sow, so, soh, show, toe, tow, stow, though, whoa, woe, Vaud (region of Switzerland), zo (Tibetan cattle).

Rouault (French artist), duo, Abo (*short for* Aborigine), jabot, Garbo, oboe, hobo (*US* a vagrant), bubo (a swelling), elbow, flambeau (torch), mambo (dance), crambo (word game), combo, rainbow, longbow, crossbow, oxbow (curved lake), psycho, Tycho (crater on moon), bucko (*Irish* young fellow), stucco, milko (*Austral* milkman), wilco, salchow (ice-skating jump), Glencoe, plonko (*Austral* alcoholic), bronco, Moscow, gaucho, poncho, shadow, eddo (Asian plant), meadow, Bordeaux, dildo, rondeau (poem), rondo (musical work), Sappho,

Defoe, UFO, nympho, info, ergo, Virgo, doggo, forego, sorgo (fodder crop), bongo, Congo, mongo (Mongolian currency), drongo (tropical bird), outgo, Glasgow, banjo, heigh-ho, coho (Pacific salmon), Soho, halo, Gwelo (Zimbabwean town), furlough, kyloe (Scottish cattle), Lilo (*Trademark*), silo, Shiloh, rouleau, tableau, pueblo, deathblow, airflow, inflow, outflow, whitlow, Oslo, Hounslow, ammo, demo, memo, trumeau (architectural term), Sumo (Japanese wrestling), Malmö, lino, rhino, wino, mono, tonneau, foreknow, dunno, Gounod (French composer), Juno, capo (guitar attachment), chapeau (hat), hippo, hypo, typo, tempo, burrow, furrow, scarecrow, Velcro (*Trademark*), escrow (legal term), hydro, Afro, aggro, outgrow, hedgerow, Monroe, repro, metro, retro (*short for* retrorocket), de trop (superfluous), Cointreau, intro, Castro, bistro, maestro, Jethro, peso, verso, torso, whoso (whoever), Rousseau, trousseau, CUSO (Canadian voluntary service organization), Tussaud, also, fatso, scherzo, schizo, sideshow, peepshow, ditto, Shinto (Japanese religion), tiptoe, bestow, gusto, although, bravo, servo, Provo, galvo (*short for* galvanometer), salvo, Volvo (*Trademark*), Oyo (Nigerian state), yo-yo, Tokyo, ouzo, muso (*Austral* musician).

Bilbao, cacao, sirocco, Morocco, morocco (leather), Monaco, touraco (African bird), fiasco, Tabasco, gazpacho, quebracho (South American tree), foreshadow, aboideau (Canadian dyke), tournedos, commando, tally-ho, bibelot (trinket), Fontainebleau, overflow, Alamo, dynamo, piano, volcano, Huguenot, pompano (Atlantic fish), Llandudno, Limpopo, status quo, quid pro quo, Diderot (French philosopher), bordereau (insurance invoice), Cicero, allegro, overgrow, semipro, in vitro,

overthrow, Curaçao, oversew, so-and-so, calypso, concerto, undertow, hammertoe, de facto, tick-tack-toe (*US* noughts and crosses), mistletoe, octavo (book size), proviso.

continuo (musical term), La Rochefoucauld (French writer), Acapulco, overshadow, fortepiano (type of piano), Avogadro (Italian physicist).

12.1
K.O., Mayo (Irish county), carabao (water buffalo), Galileo, Bulawayo (Zimbabwean city).

12.2
guyot (submerged mountain), Leo, Cleo, Rio, Krio (African language), trio, con brio (musical term), absente reo (legal term).

12.3
radio, audio, rodeo, studio, cameo, Romeo, Borneo, Scipio (Roman general), Scorpio, stereo, cheerio, curio, vibrio (bacterium), embryo, Lashio (Burmese town), nuncio (papal representative), patio.

Pinocchio, capriccio (lively musical work), adagio, solfeggio (musical term), arpeggio, seraglio (harem), intaglio (engraving), Ontario, etaerio (class of fruit), Ajaccio, pistachio, mustachio.

braggadocio (boasting), oratorio, ex officio.

12.3.1
video, presidio (Spanish military establishment).

12.3.2
billyo, punctilio (strict etiquette).

12.3.3
olio (miscellany), folio, polio, portfolio, imbroglio (confused situation).

12.3.4
Roneo (*Trademark*), Antonio.

12.3.5
Rosario (Argentine port), scenario, Lothario (libertine), impresario.

12.3.6
ratio, fellatio.

12.4
Io (satellite of Jupiter), ngaio (New Zealand tree), noyau (nut liqueur), Ohio.

12.5
Ibo (African people), placebo, gazebo, Essequibo (South American river).

12.6
bimbo (*Slang* fellow), limbo, akimbo.

12.7
umbo (small hump), gumbo (thick stew), jumbo, nelumbo (aquatic plant), Colombo, mumbo jumbo.

12.8
squacco (European heron), shako, whacko (*Slang* exclamation of delight), tobacco.

12.9
echo, dekko, gecko, secco (wall painting), re-echo, Art Deco, El Greco.

12.10
chico (US shrub), Nikko (Japanese town), picot, pekoe, beccafico (European songbird), Puerto Rico.

12.11
tricot (knitted fabric), medico, calico, coquelicot (corn poppy), haricot, Jericho, portico, Mexico, magnifico, simpatico (pleasant), politico.

12.12
cocoa, coco (*short for* coconut), loco, smoko (*Austral* teabreak), poco (musical term), rococo, con fuoco (musical term), Orinoco.

12.13
flamenco, Lysenko (Russian geneticist), Timoshenko (Russian general).

12.14
fresco, Enesco (Rumanian musician), UNESCO, alfresco, Ionesco (French dramatist).

12.15
disco, Frisco (*short for* San Francisco), cisco (fish), Morisco (Spanish Moor), San Francisco.

12.16
mikado, Barnardo, Dorado (constellation), bravado, avocado, El Dorado, Colorado, desperado, muscovado (raw sugar), amontillado, aficionado, incommunicado, Llano Estacado (region of Texas).

12.17
dado, gambado (leather stirrup), Toledo, tornado, strappado (form of torture), bastinado (form of torture), carbonado (industrial diamond).

12.18
lido, speedo, credo, libido, Toledo, torpedo, teredo (mollusc), tuxedo.

12.19
widow, aikido (Japanese self-defence system), comedo (blackhead), do-si-do, Bushido (code of the samurai).

12.20
Dido, Hokkaido.

12.21
dodo, Jodo (Buddhist sect), Komodo (East Indian island), Quasimodo.

12.22
udo (Oriental plant), judo, ludo, Trudeau, pseudo, escudo (Portuguese currency), testudo (Roman military manoeuvre).

12.23
bandeau (headband), Brando, Orlando, glissando (musical term), scherzando (musical term), sforzando (musical term), ritardando, San Fernando, rallentando.

12.24
kendo (Japanese sport), crescendo, innuendo, diminuendo (musical term).

12.25
window, tamarindo (tamarind).

12.26
argot, Argo, cargo, largo, magot (Oriental figurine), embargo, Chicago, galago (bushbaby), virago, farrago (hotchpotch), botargo (fish roe), Santiago.

12.27
sago, Tobago, lumbago, plumbago (graphite), imago (adult insect), San Diego, Winnebago (US lake), solidago (plant genus), pichiciego (Argentine armadillo).

12.28
ego, gigot (leg of mutton), Vigo (Spanish port), amigo, Montego, superego, alter ego.

12.29
chigoe (tropical flea), Bendigo (Australian city), indigo, vertigo, Abednego.

12.30
Sligo, serpigo (skin disease), prurigo (skin disease), lentigo (freckle), intertrigo (chafed skin), impetigo.

12.31
logo, Togo (African republic), à gogo.

12.32
Hugo, colugo (flying lemur), aerugo (verdigris), lanugo (covering of fine hair).

12.33
ago, undergo, sapsago (Swiss cheese), archipelago.

12.34
NALGO, hidalgo (Spanish nobleman).

12.35
mango, quango, tango, fandango, Durango (Mexican state), contango (stock exchange term).

12.36
bingo, dingo, jingo, lingo, gringo, stingo (strong beer), flamingo, eryngo (a plant), Santo Domingo (capital of Dominican Republic).

12.37
Idaho, Navaho, Arapaho.

12.38
aloe, callow, fallow, hallow, mallow, sallow, shallow, tallow, marshmallow.

12.39
Carlow (Irish county), Harlow, Marlowe, Monte Carlo.

12.40
bellow, cello, fellow, felloe (part of wooden wheel), jello (US jelly), hello, mellow, yellow, niello (compound used in engraving), duello (duelling), bordello, bedfellow, Longfellow, morello, Martello, Othello, Novello, Punchinello (clown), ritornello (musical term), saltarello (Italian dance), violoncello.

12.41
kilo, Iloilo (Philippine port).

12.42
below, billow, pillow, willow, furbelow, pomelo (grapefruit), tupelo (tree), Murillo (Spanish painter), peccadillo (trivial misdemeanour), armadillo, cigarillo, Michelangelo.

12.43
follow, hollow, wallow, swallow, Apollo.

12.44
bolo (a knife), kolo (Serbian folk dance), Jolo (Philippine island), polo, solo, criollo (type of cocoa), palolo (marine worm), Marco Polo.

12.45
alow (nautical term), hallo, cembalo (harpsichord), cymbalo (dulcimer), piccolo, pedalo (pedal boat), buffalo, brigalow (Australian acacia tree), gigolo, bungalow, tangelo (tangerine–grapefruit hybrid), tremolo, bummalo

(Bombay duck), cattalo (breed of cattle), diabolo (game with spinning top).

12.46
aglow, afterglow, counterglow (glow in sky).

12.47
Imo (Nigerian state), primo, supremo.

12.48
Eskimo, ultimo (last month), proximo (next month), Geronimo, centesimo (monetary unit), fortissimo, bravissimo, pianissimo, generalissimo.

12.49
Como, Nkomo, homo, duomo (cathedral), major-domo.

12.50
machismo, verismo (type of opera), gran turismo.

12.51
Arno (Italian river), Kano (Nigerian state), Carnot (French physicist), llano (South American grassland), guano (excrement of sea birds), Meccano (*Trademark*), Nagano (Japanese city), Romano (type of cheese), soprano, Cinzano, San Stefano (Turkish village), oregano.

12.52
meno (musical term), tenno (Japanese emperor), steno (*US* shorthand typist), Renault (*Trademark*), ripieno (musical term).

12.53
journo (*Austral* journalist), Pernod (*Trademark*), inferno.

12.54
beano, kino (dark red resin), keno (US game of chance), chino (*US* cotton twill cloth), fino (dry sherry), leno (fabric weave), Reno, vino, albino, bambino, zecchino (gold coin), ladino (white clover), amino, merino, neutrino (elementary particle in physics), casino, Latino (*US* Latin American), Trevino, maraschino, cappuccino, Borodi-

no (Napoleonic battle site), palomino, Filipino, solferino (reddish-purple colour), San Marino (European republic), concertino (musical term), andantino (musical term), Valentino, San Bernardino (Californian city).

12.55
minnow, winnow, domino, topminnow (small fish), Maginot.

12.56
kimono, kakemono (Japanese wall hanging).

12.57
Apo (Philippine mountain), da capo (musical term), Gestapo.

12.58
depot, Aleppo (Syrian city).

12.59
kakapo (parrot), apropos, malapropos.

12.60
arrow, barrow, farrow, Jarrow, Harrow, harrow, marrow, narrow, sparrow, tarot, yarrow, handbarrow, wheelbarrow, restharrow (woody plant).

12.61
claro (cigar), taro (Asian plant), Pissarro (French painter), saguaro (giant cactus), Pizarro (conqueror of Peru), Utamaro, Kilimanjaro.

12.62
Pharaoh, faro (card game), ranchero (*US* rancher), bolero, primero (card game), pampero (South American wind), torero (bullfighter), Herero (African people), sombrero, montero (Spanish hunting cap), cruzeiro (Brazilian currency), caballero (Spanish gentleman), banderillero (bullfighter's assistant).

12.63
hero, Nero, Pierrot (French pantomime clown), cero (Atlantic fish), zero, Pinero (English dramatist), subzero, antihero, superhero, Rio de Janeiro.

12.64
Biro (*Trademark*), Cairo, giro, tyro (novice), autogiro (aircraft).

12.65
borrow, morrow, morro (rounded hill), sorrow, tomorrow.

12.66
duro (silver peso), Douro (Spanish–Portuguese river), Truro, bureau, maduro (cigar), Politburo, chiaroscuro (art term).

12.67
Negro, Montenegro (region of Yugoslavia).

12.68
basso (bass singer), Picasso, sargasso (seaweed), El Paso (Texan city).

12.69
gesso (white plaster), expresso.

12.70
so-so, nitroso (chemistry term), maestoso (musical term), grandioso (musical term), mafioso (member of the Mafia), virtuoso, oloroso (sherry), doloroso (musical term), amoroso, capriccioso (musical term).

12.71
mezzo (musical term), Arezzo (Italian city), intermezzo.

12.72
bateau (flat-bottomed boat), gateau, plateau, chateau, mulatto, annatto (tropical tree).

12.73
dato (Philippine chief), rubato (musical term), spiccato (musical term), Waikato (New Zealand river), staccato, legato, sfumato (art term), tomato, esparto, vibrato, castrato, pizzicato, obbligato (musical term), ostinato (musical term), moderato, inamorato (lover).

12.74
Cato, jato (jet-assisted takeoff), Plato, NATO, potato.

12.75
ghetto, stretto (musical term), zucchetto (skullcap), stiletto, palmetto (small tropical palm tree), libretto, neutretto (hypothetical particle in physics), falsetto, terzetto (vocal trio), cavetto (architectural moulding), amoretto (cupid), vaporetto (Venetian steamboat), Tintoretto, lazaretto (ship's locker), allegretto.

12.76
Quito (capital of Ecuador), keto (chemistry term), Leto (mother of Apollo), Pitot (French physicist), Tito, veto, coquito (palm tree), mosquito, graffito, bonito (small marine fish), magneto, Negrito (member of Asian people), Hirohito, sanbenito (garment worn by heretics), incognito.

12.77
Otto, Giotto, lotto, blotto, motto, potto (short-tailed mammal), grotto, Watteau, ridotto (musical entertainment), risotto.

12.78
auto, quarto, Oporto.

12.79
koto (Japanese musical instrument), photo, Kyoto (Japanese city), con moto (musical term), in toto, telephoto, Kumamoto (Japanese city).

12.80
couteau (a knife), Pluto, Maputo (capital of Mozambique), prosciutto (Italian cured ham), tenuto (musical term), ritenuto (musical term), sostenuto (musical term).

12.81
recto, perfecto (cigar).

12.82
alto, Rialto, contralto.

12.83
canto, manteau (a cloak), panto, portmanteau, Taranto (Italian port), quo warranto (legal term), Esperanto, Espíritu Santo (Pacific island).

12.84

lento, cento (type of poem), memento, pimento, Sorrento, pentimento (art term), Sacramento, Benevento (Italian city), Risorgimento (Italian political movement), divertimento (musical work), pronunciamento (manifesto).

12.85

conto (Portuguese currency), pronto, Toronto.

12.86

presto, manifesto.

13 -ow

ow, bow, bough, cow, scow (boat), chow, ciao (Italian greeting), dhow (Arab sailing boat), Dou (Dutch painter), how, Lao (Asian people), plough, Slough, slough (bog), mow (grimace), now, pow, row, brow, Frau, prow, sow, sough (make sighing sound), thou, vow, wow.

meow, Cracow, Foochow (Chinese port), Soochow (Chinese city), Changchow (Chinese city), Hangchow (Chinese port), Moldau, endow, hoosegow (*US* jail), know-how, somehow, pilau, allow, snowplough, Mau Mau, eyebrow, highbrow, lowbrow, hausfrau, kowtow, Paotow (Chinese city), avow, bow-wow, powwow.

disendow, anyhow, disallow, middlebrow, disavow.

14 -our

our, hour, bower, cower, scour, dower (widow's inheritance), Gower, gaur (Asian wild cattle), lour (look menacing), flour, flower, glower, power, paua (New Zealand shellfish), sour, shower, tower, stour (*Dialect* turmoil).

embower, Glendower (Welsh chieftain), deflower, safflower, Mayflower, wallflower, cornflower, cornflour, sunflower, moonflower (night-blooming plant), willpower, empower, manpower, horsepower, watchtower, devour.

Eisenhower, gillyflower, cauliflower, passionflower, hydropower, superpower, overpower.

15 -oo

ooh, boo, coo, coup, chew, do, goo, Jew, who, loo, blue, blew, clue, clew (ball of yarn), flu, flew, flue, glue, plew (fur trade term), slew, Shluh (North African people), moo, gnu, pooh, rue, roux, roo (*Austral* kangaroo), brew, crew, Crewe, cru (wine-producing region), screw, drew, grew, sprue (tropical disease), shrew, true, strew, through, threw, Sioux, sue, sou (coin), shoe, shoo, choux (type of pastry), chou (type of cabbage), too, to, two, woo, Wu (Chinese dialect group), ewe, you, yew, queue, cue, Kew, kyu (judo grade), skew, due, dew, few, phew, hue, hew, lieu, mew, smew (diving duck), knew, new, pew, spew, stew, thew (muscle), view, zoo.

zebu (type of ox), bamboo, cuckoo, Manchu (Chinese dynasty), eschew (avoid), hairdo, redo, Urdu, kudu (African antelope), hoodoo, voodoo, Hindu, undo, outdo, snafu, Corfu, kung fu, ragout (stew), juju, boohoo, Wuhu (Chinese port), yoo-hoo, yahoo, igloo, canoe, Vishnu (Hindu god), coypu, hoopoe, pooh-pooh, shampoo, Nehru, guru, Hebrew, ecru (yellowish-grey colour), aircrew, accrue, airscrew (propeller), woodscrew, thumbscrew, unscrew, corkscrew, withdrew, Andrew, Renfrew, untrue, bestrew, construe, lasso, shih-tzu (breed of dog), fichu (scarf), cashew, cachou (type of sweet), snowshoe, gumshoe, Honshu, horseshoe, bijou, Attu (island off Alaska), battue (hunting term), tattoo, thereto, whereto, hereto, Hutu (African people), tutu, Bantu, Mantoux (French physician), into, onto, unto, bayou (marshy stream), debut, imbue (instil), fescue (a grass), rescue, miscue, askew, subdue, mildew, vendue (*US* public sale), endue (endow), fondue, undue, sundew, curfew, argue, ague, value, curlew, purlieu (outlying area), emu, genu (knee), menu, venue, non-U, foreknew, anew, issue, tissue, pursue, ensue, statue, virtue, Matthew, nephew, purview (scope), preview, revue, review, Jesu.

caribou, bunraku (Japanese puppet theatre), Katmandu, derring-do, Dien Bien Phu (Vietnamese battle site), kinkajou, sapajou (capuchin monkey), ballyhoo, misconstrue, overthrew, jujitsu, overshoe, acajou, Lissajous (French physicist), passe-partout, cockatoo, thitherto, hitherto, Timbuktu, thereinto, whereinto, hereinto, rendezvous, I.O.U., barbecue, curlicue (decorative curl), autocue, feverfew (medicinal plant), Montague, clerihew (humorous verse), devalue, revalue, ingénue (naive girl), impromptu, interview, overview.

Machu Picchu (ruined city of Incas), Mogadishu (capital of Somali Republic), tu-whit tu-whoo, undervalue, Bartholomew, cock-a-doodle-doo.

15.1
taboo, peekaboo, bugaboo (source of fear), marabou (African stork), marabout (Muslim holy man).

15.2
teledu (Asian badger), billet-doux (love letter), didgeridoo.

15.3
ado, to-do, amadou (fungal tinder), well-to-do, overdo.

15.4
Lulu, Sulu (Philippine archipelago), Zulu, Gazankulu (South African homeland), Honolulu.

15.5
halloo, trou-de-loup (pit dug for defence), toodle-oo, calalu (Caribbean edible leaves), ormolu (gilt decoration), Port-Salut (French cheese), Peterloo, Waterloo, Tuvalu (group of Pacific islands), hullabaloo, Kinabalu (Malaysian mountain).

15.6
buroo (*Dialect* unemployment benefit), Karoo (South African plateau), Peru, jackeroo (*Austral* trainee sheep-station manager), buckaroo (*US* cowboy), switcheroo (*US* unexpected change), wanderoo (Indian monkey), kangaroo, wallaroo (large kangaroo), Timaru (New Zealand port), Brian Boru (medieval Irish king).

15.7
bedew (cover with dew), honeydew, residue.

15.8
adieu, overdue.

15.9
renew, sinew, detinue (legal term), retinue, continue, avenue, revenue, discontinue.

15.10
bazoo (*US* mouth), kazoo, razoo (*Austral* coin), Kalamazoo.

16 -y [This is the unstressed syllable at the end of such words as *baby*, *charity*, and *autonomy*.
Rhymes dependent on this syllable alone are unsatisfactory and should be avoided. Further rhymes for **16.112–16.209** may be created by adding *-ly* to appropriate adjectives. See also **5**.]
rugby, busby, Grimsby, Trotsky, hardly, homely, scarcely, costly, lively, paisley, acme, pygmy, chimney, chutney, scampi, debris, laundry, foundry, sundry, belfry, angry, hungry, paltry, poultry, sultry, pastry, Chelsea, Nazi, safety, ninety, empty, sixty, earthy, lengthy, filthy, swarthy, ivy, envy, clumsy, Swansea.

panoply, calumny, industry, bankruptcy, dynasty.

16.1
ai (three-toed sloth), Bahai (member of religious group), Lanai (Hawaiian island), lanai (Hawaiian veranda), Molokai (Hawaiian island).

16.2
Hawaii, Mordecai (Old Testament character).

16.3
doughy, joey, blowy, Chloe, snowy, showy, toey (*Austral* nervous), shadowy, billowy, willowy.

16.4
chewy, phooey, gooey, hooey, louis, Louis, bluey (*Austral* blanket or bundle), gluey, screwy, tui (New Zealand songbird), dewy, Dewey, Brahui (Pakistani language), Drambuie (*Trademark*), Rapa Nui (Easter Island), Wanganui (New Zealand port).

16.5
abbey, cabby, scabby, gabby (talkative), flabby, crabby, shabby, tabby, Newtonabbey.

16.6
Babi (Persian religious heretic), carby (*Austral* carburettor), Derby, Mugabe, Punjabi, Wahhabi (member of Muslim sect), kohlrabi, Abu Dhabi, Hammurabi (ancient Babylonian king).

16.7
baby, gaby (simpleton), maybe, crybaby, bushbaby.

16.8
plebby, webby, Entebbe.

16.9
Kirkby, herby.

16.10
Phoebe, phoebe (US bird), Hebe (Greek goddess), freebie, Galibi (American Indian people).

16.11
bobby, dobby (loom attachment), hobby, lobby.

16.12
obi, Kobe (Japanese port), dhobi, goby, Gobi, Toby, adobe, Nairobi, Okeechobee (lake in Florida).

16.13
chubby, hubby, clubby (sociable), rabi (Indian crop), scrubby, grubby, shrubby, tubby, stubby.

16.14
booby, jube (gallery in church), looby (foolish person), ruby.

16.15
wallaby, Araby, sassaby (African antelope).

16.16
Philby, trilby, astilbe (flowering plant).

16.17
Djambi (Indonesian port), namby-pamby.

16.18
Tshombe (African statesman), zombie.

16.19
baccy, lackey, tacky, wacky.

16.20
khaki, kaki (Asian fruit tree), charqui (dried meat), parky, saki (monkey), sake (Japanese liquor), Saki (Scottish author).

thearchy (government by gods), diarchy, triarchy, malarkey (nonsense), nomarchy (modern Greek province), menarche (first occurrence of menstruation), gynarchy (government by women), eparchy, Iraqi, squirearchy, autarchy (unrestricted rule), autarky (economic self-sufficiency), pentarchy, heptarchy.

hagiarchy (government by saints), matriarchy, patriarchy, oligarchy, hierarchy, trierarchy (Athenians providing state triremes), Nagasaki, Kawasaki, sukiyaki, teriyaki (Japanese cookery term).

16.21
laky (reddish), flaky, snaky, quaky, shaky, headachy.

16.22
checky (heraldic term), recce, Shimonoseki (Japanese port).

16.23
jerky, murky, perky, quirky, turkey, Turkey, Albuquerque.

16.24
cheeky, leaky, cliquey, sneaky, peaky, squeaky, creaky, freaky (*Slang* strange), streaky, tiki (Maori amulet), dashiki (loose-fitting Negro garment), cock-a-leekie.

16.25
dicky, hickey (gadget), quickie, tricky, sticky, garlicky, gimmicky, panicky, finicky, entelechy (philosophy term), parastichy (botany term), orthostichy (botany term).

16.26
spiky, crikey, psyche, Psyche (Greek mythological character), Tyche (Greek goddess).

16.27
cocky, jockey, hockey, gnocchi, rocky, stocky, outjockey (outwit by deception), jabberwocky.

16.28
balky (inclined to stop suddenly), chalky, Gorky, gawky, porky (obese), pawky (*Scot* having dry wit), talkie, stalky, Milwaukee, walkie-talkie.

16.29
Loki (Norse god), smoky, poky, croaky, hokey cokey, okey-dokey.

16.30
ducky, lucky, clucky (*Austral* pregnant), plucky, mucky, truckie (*Austral* truck driver), yukky, unlucky, Kentucky.

16.31
bookie, cookie, hooky, rookie, Gurmukhi (Punjabi script), cleruchy (Athenian colony).

16.32
kooky, fluky, spooky, kabuki (Japanese drama), Saluki, bouzouki.

16.33
stomachy (paunchy), anarchy, synarchy (joint rule), monarchy, schipperke (breed of dog), synecdoche (figure of speech), sciamachy (fight with imaginary enemy), theomachy (battle among the gods), logomachy (argument about words), tauromachy (bullfighting), Andromache, gigantomachy (battle fought by giants).

16.34
milky, silky.

16.35
bulky, sulky.

16.36
hanky, lanky, manky, cranky, swanky, hanky-panky, Killiecrankie (Scottish battle site).

16.37
inky, kinky, dinky, slinky, pinkie, Malinke (African people), Helsinki.

16.38
donkey, wonky.

16.39
chunky, funky, junkie, flunky, monkey, spunky.

16.40
pesky, kromesky (type of croquette).

16.41
risky, frisky, whisky.

16.42
dusky, husky, musky, Russky.

16.43
Dostoevsky, Alexander Nevski (Russian prince).

16.44
Tchaikovsky, Stokowski (US conductor), Malinowski (Polish anthropologist).

16.45
Nijinsky, kolinsky (Asian mink).

16.46
catchy, snatchy (disconnected), patchy, scratchy, fratchy (quarrelsome), Apache.

16.47
starchy, hibachi (portable brazier), Karachi, vivace, mariachi (Mexican street musicians).

16.48
sketchy, stretchy, tetchy.

16.49
itchy, bitchy, pitchy, semplice (musical term).

16.50
botchy, blotchy, veloce (musical term), sotto voce, viva voce.

16.51
Bauchi (Nigerian state), grouchy.

16.52
duchy, touchy, archduchy.

16.53
duce, Baluchi (Muslim people), penuche (coarse Mexican sugar), Vespucci, Mizoguchi (Japanese film director).

16.54
Ranchi (Indian city), Comanche.

16.55
paunchy, raunchy.

16.56
bunchy, punchy, crunchy.

16.57
baddie, caddie, caddy, daddy, laddie, Paddy, paddy, sugar daddy, finnan haddie.

16.58
cadi (Muslim judge), khadi (Indian cotton cloth), hardy, Mahdi (Sudanese military leader), mardy (*Dialect* spoilt or irritable), tardy, foolhardy, Matadi (Zaîrese port), Takoradi (Ghanaian port).

16.59
lady, cedi (Ghanaian currency), shady, charlady, milady, landlady, maravedi (Spanish coin).

16.60
eddy, heady, neddy, Pedi (member of African people), ready, thready, steady, already, unready, unsteady.

16.61
birdie, sturdy, wordy, Makurdi (Nigerian port), hurdy-gurdy.

16.62
beady, needy, speedy, reedy, greedy, seedy, weedy, tweedy.

16.63
biddy, kiddy, giddy, midi, middy (midshipman), Zebedee, perfidy, raggedy, tragedy, remedy, comedy, Kennedy, subsidy, accidie (apathy), chickabiddy (term of endearment), tragicomedy.

16.64
bridie (*Scot* meat pie), tidy, vide, untidy, mala fide, bona fide.

16.65
body, noddy (tropical sea-bird), poddy (*Austral* hand-fed calf), shoddy, toddy, waddy (Aborigine's wooden club), wadi (watercourse), embody, dogsbody, anybody, everybody, antibody, busybody, underbody, afterbody (discarded part of rocket), disembody, Irrawaddy (Burmese river).

16.66
bawdy, gaudy, Geordie, lordy (exclamation of surprise).

16.67
Cody, toady, tody (West Indian bird), petalody (botany term), staminody (botany term), polypody (type of fern).

16.68
dowdy, Gaudi (Spanish architect), howdy, cloudy, rowdy, Saudi, pandowdy (*US* fruit pie), howtowdie (Scottish chicken dish).

16.69
buddy, cuddy (small cabin in boat), bloody, muddy, nuddy, ruddy, study, fuddy-duddy, understudy.

16.70
goody, woody, goody-goody.

16.71
Judy, moody, broody, shrewdie (*Austral* shrewd person), camoodi (anaconda).

16.72
nobody, Lombardy, somebody, Picardy, malady, melody, psalmody, threnody (ode of lamentation), monody (solo in Greek tragedy), hymnody, jeopardy, dipody (metrical unit), tripody (metrical unit), parody, prosody, rhapsody, bastardy, custody, Mahanadi (Indian river), tetrapody (metrical unit), chiropody.

16.73
alcalde (Spanish mayor), Vivaldi, Fittipaldi (Brazilian motor-racing driver).

16.74
wieldy, unwieldy.

16.75
Grimaldi, Garibaldi, garibaldi.

16.76
oldie, mouldy.

16.77
Andy, bandy, candy, Kandy (Sri Lankan city), dandy, Gandhi, handy, pandy (school punishment), randy, brandy, sandy, sandhi (linguistics term), shandy, bandy-bandy (small Australian snake), jaborandi (tropical shrub), onus probandi (burden of proof).

16.78
bendy, trendy, Wendy, effendi (Turkish title of respect).

16.79
bhindi (Indian vegetable), Hindi, Sindhi (inhabitant of Pakistan), shindy, windy, Rawalpindi.

16.80
Fundy (Canadian bay), Lundy, mandi (large Indian market), Grundy (narrow-minded critical person), aliunde (from another source), salmagundi (mixed salad dish), jaguarundi (feline mammal).

16.81
Burgundy, organdie, Ormandy (US conductor), Normandy.

16.82
daffy, NAAFI, Taffy, taffy (*US* chewy sweet).

16.83
furphy (*Austral* rumour), Murphy, surfie (*Austral* male surfer), turfy.

16.84
Ife (Nigerian town), beefy, leafy.

16.85
jiffy, Liffey (Irish river), miffy (easily upset), sniffy (contemptuous), spiffy (*US* smart or stylish), squiffy, salsify.

16.86
coffee, toffee.

16.87
trophy, strophe, Sophie, Sophy (title of Persian kings).

16.88
chuffy (*Scot* chubby), huffy, fluffy, snuffy (unpleasant), puffy, scruffy, toughie, stuffy, dandruffy.

16.89
goofy, Sufi (member of Muslim sect), Newfie (inhabitant of Newfoundland).

16.90
atrophy, exstrophy (medical term), pansophy (universal knowledge), teleg-

raphy, tachygraphy (shorthand), calligraphy, epigraphy (study of ancient inscriptions), stratigraphy (study of geological history), scintigraphy (medical diagnostic technique), lexigraphy (system of writing), hypertrophy, anastrophe (rhetorical device), catastrophe, monostrophe (type of poem), apostrophe, phototelegraphy (telegraphic transmission of photographs), radiotelegraphy.

16.90.1
tenorrhaphy (surgical repair of tendons), herniorrhaphy (surgical repair of hernia), staphylorrhaphy (repair of cleft palate).

16.90.2
biography, zoography (branch of zoology), cacography (bad handwriting or spelling), chalcography (copper or brass engraving), zincography, discography, glyphography (printing process), stylography (engraving with stylus), xylography (printing from wooden blocks), holography, thermography, tomography (x-ray technique), filmography, seismography, cosmography, scenography (depicting in perspective), pornography, phonography (representing sounds by symbols), ethnography (branch of anthropology), typography, topography, cerography (engraving on waxed plate), xerography, pyrography (creating design by burning), orography (mapping mountain relief), chorography (mapping regions), micrography, hydrography (mapping oceans and rivers), reprography, petrography (classification of rocks), nosography (written classification of diseases), cartography, glyptography (engraving gemstones), cryptography (study of codes), lithography, orthography.

lexicography, selenography (mapping moon's surface), iconography.

autobiography, phototypography, palaeontography (description of fossils), chromolithography, photolithography.

16.90.2.1
geography, cardiography, radiography, ideography (using written symbols), hagiography, palaeography (study of ancient handwriting), bibliography, stereography (study of geometrical solids), areography (description of Mars), choreography, physiography (physical geography), biogeography, zoogeography, historiography, electrocardiography.

16.90.2.2
pyelography (x-ray examination of kidneys), metallography (branch of metallurgy), dactylography (study of fingerprints), crystallography, encephalography.

16.90.2.3
demography, anemography (recording wind measurements).

16.90.2.4
planography (printing from flat surface), stenography, organography (description of biological organs), uranography (mapping of stars), oceanography.

16.90.2.5
dittography (unintentional repetition), hyetography (study of rainfall distribution).

16.90.2.6
photography, chromatography (chemistry term), telephotography, astrophotography, cinematography.

16.90.3
dystrophy, epistrophe (rhetorical device), antistrophe (section of choral ode).

16.90.4
theosophy (religious or philosophical system), philosophy, anthroposophy (mystical doctrine).

16.91
baggy, jaggy (jagged), flaggy (limp), quaggy (marshy), ragi (cereal grass), craggy, scraggy, shaggy.

16.92
leggy, dreggy (full of dregs).

16.93
piggy, ciggy, twiggy.

16.94
boggy, doggy, foggy, froggy, groggy, soggy, demagogy.

16.95
corgi, porgy (Atlantic fish).

16.96
bogey, bogie (wheels on railway coach), dogie (*US* motherless calf), fogy, logy (*US* dull or listless), stogy (*US* long cheap cigar), yogi, judogi (judo costume).

16.97
buggy, muggy, shuggy (*Dialect* fairground swing).

16.98
boogie, boogie-woogie.

16.99
romaji (alphabet for transliterating Japanese), argy-bargy.

16.100
cagey, stagy (theatrical).

16.101
edgy, fledgy (feathered).

16.102
clergy, theurgy (divine intervention), chemurgy (branch of chemistry), zymurgy (study of fermentation processes), micrurgy (microscopic technique), dramaturgy.

16.103
widgie (*Austral* unruly young woman), prodigy, effigy, elegy, strategy, syzygy (position of celestial body), Murrumbidgee (Australian river), apophyge (architectural term).

16.104
bodgie (*Austral* unruly young man), dodgy, splodgy, podgy, stodgy, pedagogy (teaching principles and practice).

16.105
orgy, Georgie.

16.106
anagoge (allegorical interpretation), apagoge (logic term), paragoge (linguistics term), isagoge (academic introduction to topic).

16.107
budgie, smudgy, pudgy.

16.108
eulogy, anergy (lack of energy), energy, synergy, liturgy, lethargy.

16.108.1
geophagy (eating soil), theophagy (sacramental eating of god), omophagy (eating raw food), anthropophagy (cannibalism).

16.108.2
allergy, mammalogy (study of mammals), analogy, tetralogy (four related literary works), metallurgy, genealogy, mineralogy, pyrometallurgy, electrometallurgy.

16.108.3
trilogy, brachylogy (concise style), antilogy (contradiction in terms).

16.108.4
ology, symbology, ecology, tocology (obstetrics), oncology (study of tumours), conchology (study of shells), paedology, pedology (study of soils), graphology, psephology (study of elections), nephology (study of clouds), morphology, ufology, algology, typhlology (study of blindness), haplology (omission of syllable), hoplology (study of weapons), gemology, zymology (chemistry of fermentation), pomology (fruit cultivation), homology, nomology (science of law), seismology, cosmology, oenology (study of wine), menology (ecclesiastical calendar), penology

(punishment of crime), rhinology, Sinology (study of Chinese), technology, ichnology (study of fossil footprints), hymnology, limnology (study of lakes), hypnology, ethnology, carpology (branch of botany), typology (theology term), tropology (use of figurative language), aerology (study of the atmosphere), serology, virology, hierology (sacred literature), orology (mapping mountain relief), horology, urology, neurology, necrology (list of dead people), hydrology, dendrology (study of trees), agrology (study of soils), petrology (study of rocks), metrology (study of measurement units), patrology (writings of Church Fathers), gastrology, astrology, misology (hatred of reasoning), nosology (classification of diseases), scatology, cetology (study of whales), tautology, otology, proctology, histology, Christology, pathology, ethology (study of animal behaviour), anthology, sexology, doxology.

amphibology (ambiguity of expression), pteridology (study of ferns), methodology, angelology, enzymology, potamology (study of rivers), entomology, ophthalmology, iconology, immunology, herpetology (study of reptiles), Scientology (religious cult), helminthology (study of parasitic worms).

geomorphology, palaeethnology (study of prehistoric man), dialectology, psychopathology, neuropathology, phytopathology (study of plant diseases).

16.108.4.1
geology, rheology (branch of physics), theology.

archaeology, stoichiology (branch of biology), radiology, ideology, audiology (study of hearing), ophiology (study of snakes), hagiology (writings about saints), teleology, speleology, craniology, balneology (study of therapeutic baths), Mariology, embryology, glaciology, sociology, aetiology (study of causes), deltiology (collecting picture postcards), osteology, ichthyology, axiology (study of values), phraseology, physiology, museology (science of museum organization).

astrogeology, dysteleology (philosophy term), venereology, soteriology (doctrine of salvation), bacteriology, ecclesiology (study of Christian Church).

epidemiology, phytosociology (study of plant communities).

16.108.4.2
biology, myology (study of muscle diseases), bryology (study of mosses), cryobiology, psychobiology, microbiology, agrobiology, radiobiology, sociobiology.

16.108.4.3
oology (study of bird's eggs), zoology, protozoology (study of protozoans), palaeozoology (study of fossil animals).

16.108.4.4
trichology (study of hair), codicology (study of manuscripts), myrmecology (study of ants), synecology (ecological study of communities), gynaecology, autecology (ecological study of individuals), lexicology (study of vocabulary), toxicology, musicology.

16.108.4.5
phycology (study of algae), mycology (study of fungi), psychology, parapsychology, metapsychology.

16.108.4.6
cacology (bad choice of words), malacology (study of molluscs), pharmacology.

16.108.4.7
pharyngology, laryngology, otolaryngology.

16.108.4.8
philology, syphilology, dactylology (manual sign language), vexillology (study of flags).

16.108.4.9
anemology (study of winds), etymology, epistemology (theory of knowledge).

16.108.4.10
phenology (study of recurring phenomena), phrenology, palynology (study of pollen), selenology (study of the moon), terminology, criminology, phenomenology, biocenology (branch of ecology).

16.108.4.11
phonology, chronology, lichenology, volcanology, organology, demonology, campanology, oceanology, geochronology (ordering of geological events), dendrochronology.

16.108.4.12
apology, topology, escapology, anthropology, palaeoanthropology.

16.108.4.13
chorology (geography term), acarology (study of mites), futurology, numerology (divination by numbers), martyrology, meteorology, gastroenterology.

16.108.4.14
phytology (botany), cytology, sitology (study of nutrition), parasitology.

16.108.4.15
eschatology (branch of theology), grammatology (study of writing systems), dermatology, haematology, thaumatology (study of miracles), somatology (study of the body), stomatology (study of the mouth), rheumatology, pneumatology (branch of theology), erotology, geratology, teratology (study of monsters), systematology, symptomatology.

16.108.4.15.1
climatology, primatology (branch of zoology), microclimatology, palaeoclimatology (study of past climates).

16.108.4.16
ontology (philosophy term), deontology (branch of ethics), gerontology, palaeontology, micropalaeontology (study of microscopic fossils).

16.108.4.17
cryptology (study of codes), Egyptology.

16.108.4.18
lithology (study of rocks), mythology, ornithology.

16.109
mangy, rangy.

16.110
bingey (*Austral* the stomach), dingy, mingy, stingy, lozengy (heraldic term).

16.111
scungy (*Austral* miserable), gungy, spongy.

16.112
alley, bally, kali (salt-marsh plant), dally, galley, Halley, pally, rally, sally, Sally, sallee (Australian eucalyptus tree), challis (lightweight fabric), tally, valley, wally (*Scot* made of china), tomalley (lobster's liver as food), reveille, trevally (marine fish), teocalli (truncated Aztec pyramid), dilly-dally, soapolallie (Canadian fruit drink), shillyshally, peelie-wally (*Scot* looking unwell).

16.113
Bali, barley, Kali (Hindu goddess), Charlie, Dali, Mali, parley, quale (essential quality), Gurkhali (language of Gurkhas), Somali (African people), tamale (Mexican food), finale, Umtali (Zimbabwean city), triticale (wheat–rye hybrid), Mexicali (Mexican city), Rub' al Khali (Arabian desert).

16.114
Bailey, bailey, bailie (*Scot* municipal magistrate), ceilidh, scaly, daily, gaily, paly (heraldic term), Old Bailey, Bareilly (Indian city), Israeli, Disraeli, ukulele, jus naturale (Roman natural law).

16.115
belly, Kelly, skelly (Lake District fish), Delhi, deli, jelly, smelly, nelly, Shelley, telly, Leadbelly, potbelly, Grappelli, underbelly, vermicelli, tagliatelle, Machiavelli, Tirunelveli (Indian city).

16.116
early, Burghley, burly, burley (thin-leaved tobacco), curly, girlie, hurley (stick used in hurling), pearly, surly, wurley (Aboriginal hut), hurly-burly.

16.117
barely, fairly, squarely, rarely.

16.118
Ely, dele (symbol for deletion), Healey, Lely (Dutch portrait painter), mealy (powdery), freely, Greeley (US political leader), steely, stele (upright stone slab), wheelie, Swahili, sapele, Ismaili (follower of Aga Khan), Matabele (African people), campanile (bell tower), jus civile (Roman civil law).

16.119
dearly, merely, nearly, really, yearly, sincerely, biyearly.

16.120
billy, skilly (thin soup), Chile, chilly, chilli, dilly (*Slang* remarkable person), filly, gillie (*Scot* huntsman's attendant), ghillie (laced shoe), hilly, lily, frilly, Scilly, silly, Tilly.

Cybele (Phrygian goddess), hillbilly, readily, steadily, bodily, Caerphilly, gingili (sesame oil), family, simile, homily, merrily, verily, Sicily, Chantilly.

cantabile, rockabilly (type of rock music), Piccadilly, piccalilli, subfamily, facsimile, willy-nilly, lilly-pilly (Australian tree), willy-willy (*Austral* cyclone or duststorm).

superfamily (biological classification), sal volatile.

16.120.1
primarily, ordinarily, necessarily, momentarily.

16.121
phyle (ancient Greek tribe), highly, Riley, wily, corpus vile (worthless object of experiment), heterostyly (botany term).

16.122
collie, colly (*Dialect* soot or grime), dolly, folly, golly, jolly, holly, lolly, Molly, molly (tropical fish), Polly, poly, brolly, trolley, volley, wally, wolly (*Dialect* pickled cucumber), loblolly (US pine tree), Barbirolli.

16.123
Chorley, Morley, squally, Crawley, sorely, Warley (English town), Macaulay, Bengali, Nepali, creepy-crawly.

16.124
poorly, surely, purely, Kalgoorlie (Australian city).

16.125
oily, doily, roily (cloudy or muddy).

16.126 [see also **16.164**]
coley, choli (short-sleeved bodice), coly (African bird), goalie, holy, holey, lowly, slowly, moly (Greek mythological magic herb), soli (musical term), aïoli (garlic mayonnaise), unholy, pinole (type of flour), ravioli, guacamole (dish using avocados), roly-poly.

16.127
hourly, sourly.

16.128
cully (*Slang* pal), gully, mulley (having no horns), sully.

16.129
bully, fully, pulley, woolly, patchouli (tree yielding fragrant oil), fearfully, awfully, dreadfully, hopefully, frightfully.

16.130
coolie, schoolie (*Austral* schoolteacher), Julie, truly, duly, muley (having no

horns), newly, Grand Coulee (US dam), unruly, guayule (bushy shrub), unduly, douroucouli (monkey).

16.131
neighbourly, emboly (embryology term), Kimberley (South African city), Stromboli (island with active volcano), broccoli, rascally, Wycherley (English dramatist), orderly, elderly, argali (Asian wild sheep), soldierly, gingerly, scholarly, formerly, normally, mannerly, finally, signally, equally, neroli (brown fragrant oil), thoroughly, Thessaly, cicely (aromatic plant), partially, specially, leisurely, Italy, quarterly, utterly, masterly, westerly, easterly, systole, sisterly, fatherly, weatherly (nautical term), northerly, motherly, brotherly, southerly, gravelly, Beverly, Tivoli, overly, miserly.

usually, hyperbole, epiboly (embryology term), melancholy, disorderly, anomaly, unmannerly, naturally, generally, literally, severally, especially, officially, initially, diastole, northwesterly, southwesterly, northeasterly, southeasterly.

materially, macrocephaly (abnormal largeness of skull), microcephaly (abnormal smallness of skull), hydrocephaly, macrencephaly (abnormal largeness of brain), universally, incidentally.

16.131.1
virtually, actually, effectually, eventually.

16.131.2
beggarly, splenomegaly (abnormal enlargement of spleen), acromegaly (chronic disease), cardiomegaly (abnormal enlargement of heart).

16.131.3
marginally, originally.

16.131.4
personally, occasionally.

16.131.5
Tripoli, tripoli (porous rock), Gallipoli.

16.131.6
properly, monopoly, oligopoly (economics term), Trichinopoly (Indian city).

16.131.7
latterly, philately.

16.132
drably, chablis.

16.133
pebbly, trebly.

16.134
ghibli (hot North African wind), glibly, scribbly.

16.135
knobbly, wobbly.

16.136
bubbly, doubly, stubbly.

16.137 [further rhymes may be derived from **228.16**]
probably, terribly, horribly, passably, possibly, presumably.

16.138
trembly, Wembley, assembly, subassembly.

16.139
humbly, crumbly, grumbly.

16.140
darkly, clerkly, Berkeley.

16.141
meekly, treacly, weakly, weekly, biweekly, triweekly.

16.142 [further rhymes may be derived from **228.23**]
quickly, prickly, sickly, thickly, radically, tragically, publicly, typically, basically, drastically, physically, specifically, strategically, emphatically, dramatically, diametrically.

16.143
likely, unlikely.

16.144
blankly, frankly.

16.145
Hinckley (English town), wrinkly, crinkly.

16.146
badly, gladly, madly, Bradley, sadly.

16.147
deadly, medley.

16.148 [further rhymes may be created by adding -ly to the past participle of appropriate verbs]
fiddly, Ridley (English bishop), tiddly, markedly, fixedly, decidedly, allegedly, ashamedly, concernedly, resignedly, assuredly, confessedly, repeatedly, admittedly, reportedly, advisedly, supposedly, confusedly, unashamedly, unconcernedly, unadvisedly.

16.148.1
deservedly, reservedly, unreservedly.

16.149
oddly, godly, ungodly.

16.150
lordly, broadly.

16.151
cuddly, Dudley.

16.152
cowardly, niggardly, dastardly, inwardly, outwardly.

16.153
worldly, unworldly, otherworldly.

16.154
friendly, unfriendly.

16.155
kindly, blindly.

16.156
roundly, soundly, profoundly.

16.157
secondly, jocundly.

16.158
chiefly, briefly.

16.159
snuffly, roughly.

16.160
giggly, niggly, wiggly.

16.161
ugli, ugly, smugly.

16.162
googly, Hooghly (Indian river).

16.163
singly, shingly, tingly.

16.164 [see also **16.126**]
wholly, solely.

16.165
gamely, lamely, namely.

16.166
seemly, extremely, unseemly.

16.167
timely, sublimely, untimely.

16.168
comely, glumly.

16.169
manly, Stanley, unmanly, Osmanli (relating to Ottoman Empire).

16.170
gainly, mainly, vainly, ungainly.

16.171
Henley, cleanly, uncleanly.

16.172
keenly, cleanly, queenly.

16.173
only, lonely.

16.174
christianly, maidenly, seamanly, commonly, womanly, humanly, workmanly, matronly, certainly, heavenly, slovenly, unchristianly, uncommonly, gentlemanly.

16.175 [further rhymes may be created by adding -ly to the present participle of appropriate verbs]
kingly, jokingly, seemingly, swimmingly, exceedingly, accordingly, decreasingly, surprisingly.

16.176
wrongly, strongly.

16.177
ripply, triply.

16.178
amply, damply.

16.179
pimply, simply.

16.180
parsley, sparsely.

16.181
bristly, gristly, Sisley (French painter), thistly.

16.182
closely, jocosely, morosely.

16.183
loosely, sprucely, profusely.

16.184
purposely, seriously, previously, obviously.

16.185
fleshly, freshly.

16.186
Attlee, Batley (English town), flatly, rattly.

16.187
Atli (legendary Norse king), Hartley, partly.

16.188
lately, stately.

16.189
fitly, minutely, alternately, definitely, fortunately, immediately.

16.189.1
ultimately, approximately.

16.190
slightly, knightly, nightly, rightly, sprightly, sightly (attractive), fortnightly, unsightly.

16.191
hotly, motley.

16.192
courtly, portly, shortly.

16.193
minutely, absolutely.

16.194
compactly, exactly.

16.195
directly, correctly.

16.196
faintly, saintly.

16.197
Bentley, gently, intently.

16.198
urgently, patiently, patently, instantly, constantly, presently, evidently, consequently.

16.199
ghastly, lastly.

16.200
beastly, priestly, Priestley.

16.201
istle (fibre from tropical trees), modestly, honestly.

16.202
ghostly, mostly.

16.203
deathly, Llanelli.

16.204
earthly, unearthly.

16.205
monthly, bimonthly, trimonthly.

16.206
actively, positively, effectively, respectively, comparatively.

16.207
lovely, unlovely.

16.208
Lesley, Presley, Wesley.

16.209
drizzly, grisly, grizzly.

16.210

gammy, jammy, hammy, clammy, mammy, ramie (shrub yielding fibre), trammie (*Austral* tram driver), chamois, tammy, tamis (cloth for straining), Miami.

16.211

army, barmy, balmy, kami (Japanese divine spirit), smarmy, palmy (prosperous), swami (Hindu title of respect), Zeami (Japanese dramatist), kirigami (art of paper cutting), salami, tsunami (tidal wave), macramé, pastrami, origami.

16.212

Amy, gamy.

16.213

Emmy (US television award), jemmy, semi.

16.214

Fermi, wormy, taxidermy, diathermy, radiothermy (radiation treatment), aluminothermy (chemical process).

16.215

creamy, dreamy, preemie (*US* premature baby), seamy, steamy, steamie (*Scot* public washhouse), polysemy (having many meanings), monosemy (having only one meaning), Aruwimi (Zaîrese river).

16.216

Jimmy, shimmy, blasphemy, elemi (fragrant resin), Ptolemy, synonymy, eponymy (derivation from person's name), toponymy, metonymy (figure of speech).

16.217

limy, limey, blimey, slimy, rimy, grimy, stymie, cor blimey.

16.218

dormie (golf term), horme (psychology term), stormy.

16.219

Komi (Finnish people), foamy, homy, loamy, cleome (tropical plant), Daho-

mey, Salome, anomie (lack of social standards), polychromy (multicoloured decoration), stereochromy (method of wall painting).

16.220

chummy, dummy, gummy, lumme, plummy, mummy, rummy, Brummie, crummy, crumby, tummy, yummy.

16.221

gloomy, plumy, roomy, rheumy.

16.222

Naomi, alchemy, sodomy, infamy, syngamy (sexual reproduction), enemy, gourami, sesame, bosomy, academy, antinomy (contradiction within a law), anatomy, epitome.

16.222.1

bigamy, digamy (second marriage), polygamy.

16.222.2

oogamy (type of sexual reproduction), dichogamy (botany term), endogamy (marriage within social unit), homogamy (botany term), monogamy, misogamy (hatred of marriage), isogamy (botany term), autogamy (biology term), exogamy (marriage outside social unit), heterogamy (botany term), anisogamy (type of sexual reproduction).

16.222.3

bonhomie, economy, agronomy (science of cultivation), gastronomy, astronomy, isonomy (equality before the law), autonomy, taxonomy, pathognomy (study of the emotions), Deuteronomy, cytotaxonomy (classification by cell structure).

16.222.3.1

theonomy (being governed by God), physiognomy.

16.222.4

zootomy (animal dissection), phlebotomy (incision into vein), lobotomy, dichotomy, trichotomy (division into three categories), leucotomy (brain surgery), colotomy (incision into colon), tenotomy (incision into tendon), sclerotomy (eye surgery), neurotomy (surgical cutting of nerve), necrotomy (dissection of corpse), microtomy (cutting of thin sections), nephrotomy (incision into kidney), gastrotomy, autotomy (shedding of body part), cystotomy (incision into bladder), lithotomy (removal of bladder stone), varicotomy, thoracotomy (incision into chest wall), pharyngotomy, laryngotomy, tonsillotomy, laparotomy (investigative abdominal surgery), enterotomy (incision into intestine), hysterotomy (incision into uterus).

16.222.4.1
tracheotomy, craniotomy, stereotomy (cutting three-dimensional solids), osteotomy (surgical cutting of bone), ovariotomy, episiotomy (incision into perineum).

16.222.5
colectomy (surgical removal of colon), splenectomy (removal of spleen), embrectomy (removal of embryo), nephrectomy (removal of kidney), gastrectomy, vasectomy, glossectomy (removal of tongue), mastectomy, cystectomy (removal of bladder), appendectomy, salpingectomy (removal of Fallopian tube), tonsillectomy, pneumonectomy, adenectomy (removal of gland), prostatectomy, appendicectomy, cholecystectomy (removal of gall bladder).

16.222.5.1
thyroidectomy, adenoidectomy, haemorrhoidectomy.

16.222.5.2
hysterectomy, oophorectomy (removal of ovary).

16.222.6
colostomy, gastrostomy (artificial stomach opening), tracheostomy, ileostomy (abdominal operation), gastroenterostomy (intestinal operation).

16.223
Annie, canny, Danny, fanny, nanny, cranny, granny, trannie, shanny (European fish), kokanee (type of salmon), uncanny, hootenanny.

16.224
ani (tropical bird), barney, carny (coax), blarney, Mani (Persian prophet), rani (Indian queen or princess), Mbabane (capital of Swaziland), afghani (Afghan currency), Killarney, sherwani (Indian man's long coat), biriani, Alemanni (4th-century Germanic people), frangipani (fragrant shrub), Pakistani, Hindustani, chilli con carne, Azerbaijani (Iranian people), Mina Hassan Tani (Moroccan port).

16.225
rainy, brainy, grainy, veiny, zany, Na-Dene (language group), Dunsany (Irish writer).

16.226
any, benne (sesame plant), benny (*Slang* amphetamine tablet), fenny (marshy), jenny, Jenny, blenny, many, penny, Kilkenny, catchpenny (designed for instant appeal), pinchpenny (miserly), Asantehene (Ghanaian ruler).

16.227
Ernie, byrnie (coat of mail), journey, attorney.

16.228
beanie (*US* close-fitting hat), genie, meany, teeny, weeny, sweeny (veterinary term), Syene (ancient Egyptian town), bikini, zucchini, Puccini, Houdini, wahine (Polynesian or Maori woman), Irene, Messene (ancient Greek city), Rossini, martini, linguini (type of pasta), Cherubini, fettucine, fantoccini (marionettes), Toscanini, scaloppine (thin slices of meat), Mistassini (Canadian lake).

16.228.1
Cellini (Italian sculptor), Fellini, Mussolini, tortellini (type of pasta).

16.229
skinny, finny, guinea, Guinea, hinny, Linnhe (Scottish loch), linhay (*Dialect* farm building), blini, Pliny, mini, ninny, pinny, spinney, brinny (*Austral* a stone), cine, tinny, whinny, dominie (*Scot* schoolmaster), hominy (*US* coarsely-ground maize), satiny, scrutiny, mutiny, destiny, ignominy, piccaninny.

16.229.1
polygyny (having many female partners), aborigine.

16.229.2
progeny, philogyny (fondness for women), phylogeny (evolution of species), homogeny (similarity through common ancestry), monogyny (having one female partner), ethnogeny (origin of races), orogeny (mountain formation), misogyny, ontogeny (development of organism), embryogeny (development of embryo), epeirogeny (formation of continents).

16.229.3
Rimini, postliminy (legal term), niminy-piminy.

16.229.4
larceny, coparceny (joint heirship).

16.230
piny, spiny, briny, sine (without), shiny, tiny, winy, sunshiny.

16.231
bonny, Johnny, Swanee, yonnie (*Austral* a stone), gironny (heraldic term), Suwannee (US river).

16.232
corny, horny, brawny, scrawny, tawny, thorny, mulligatawny.

16.233
bony, cony, phoney, pony, crony, Tony, stony, yoni (female genitalia in Hinduism).

Marconi, Bodoni (style of type), kongoni (hartebeest), spumone (Italian ice

cream), Oenone (Greek nymph), Benoni (South African city), compony (heraldic term), padrone (Italian innkeeper), Shoshone (American Indian people), tortoni (rich ice cream), canzone (lyrical song).

cannelloni, chitarrone (large lute), Gaborone (capital of Botswana), macaroni, cicerone (tourist guide), minestrone, rigatoni (type of pasta), panettone (Italian spiced bread), zabaglione.

Antonioni (Italian film director), Sierra Leone.

16.233.1
baloney, polony, abalone, provolone (soft cheese).

16.234
downy, brownie, townie.

16.235
bunny, dunny (*Scot* cellar), funny, gunny (*US* coarse fabric), honey, money, runny, sunny, sonny, Sunni (branch of orthodox Islam), tunny, baldmoney (aromatic flowering plant).

16.236
Nguni (language group), loony, Cluny (French town), moony, spoony (foolishly amorous), uni (*short for* university), puny, puisne (of lower rank), Sakyamuni (title of Buddha).

16.237
peony, ebony, Albany, balcony, Gascony, Tuscany, Alderney, euphony, symphony, agony, garganey (Eurasian duck), villainy, colony, scammony, Chamonix, Tammany (US Democratic party organization), harmony, Germany, simony, Romany, fourpenny, twopenny, fivepenny, timpani, tympany (medical term), company, tenpenny, sixpenny, barony, guarani (Paraguayan currency), tyranny, irony, atony, rhatany (South American shrub), betony (Eurasian plant), tetany, dittany (aromatic plant), litany, Brittany, gluttony,

Antony, Bethany, Saxony, saxony (fine yarn), oniony.

chalcedony, diaphony (musical term), telephony, Persephone, telegony (genetics term), Antigone, disharmony, alimony, ceremony, acrimony, agrimony (flowering plant), matrimony, patrimony, parsimony, sanctimony, antimony, testimony, accompany.

16.237.1
irony (resembling iron), bryony, Hesione (Greek mythological princess), Alcyone (Greek mythological character).

16.237.2
tiffany (fine gauzy fabric), polyphony (musical term), epiphany, antiphony (type of choral singing).

16.237.3
Zoffany (British painter), cacophony, colophony (translucent amber substance), homophony (linguistics term), monophony, heterophony (musical term).

16.237.3.1
theophany (manifestation of deity), radiophony (electronic music), stereophony.

16.237.4
theogony (origin of the gods), mahogany, homogony (botany term), cosmogony (origin of universe), schizogony (type of asexual reproduction), heterogony (biology term).

16.237.5
felony, miscellany.

16.237.6
lemony, hegemony (domination by one group), anemone, Gethsemane.

16.237.7
botany, cottony, neoteny (zoology term), monotony, astrobotany, palaeobotany (study of fossil plants).

16.238
acne, hackney, Hackney, chloracne (skin disease), Arachne (Greek mythological character).

16.239
cockney, Hockney, Procne (Greek mythological princess).

16.240
kidney, Sydney, Sidney.

16.241
slangy, tangy.

16.242
dinghy, springy, stringy.

16.243
cappie (*Scot* ice-cream cone), chappie, happy, nappy, snappy, pappy (mushy), crappie (US freshwater fish), scrappy, sappy (full of energy), yappy, unhappy, slaphappy.

16.244
harpy, okapi, syncarpy (botany term), parthenocarpy (fruit development without fertilization).

16.245
peppy, cacoepy (bad pronunciation), orthoepy (study of correct pronunciation).

16.246
chirpy, Euterpe (Greek Muse).

16.247
sleepy, creepy, creepie (*Scot* low stool), weepy, Praesepe (cluster of stars).

16.248
chippy, dippy (*Slang* crazy), gippy, hippie, lippy (*US* insolent), clippie, slippy, nippy, drippy, zippy, recipe, gossipy, Xanthippe (wife of Socrates), Mississippi.

16.249
stripy, stenotypy (form of shorthand), phonotypy (phonetic transcription of speech), stereotypy.

16.250
copy, kopje (small hill), choppy, floppy, sloppy, poppy, stroppy, soppy, jalopy, phenocopy (biology term), microcopy (reduced photographic copy), photocopy.

16.251
dopey, Hopi (American Indian people), ropy, soapy.

16.252
guppy, puppy.

16.253
loopy, droopy, groupie, soupy, NUPE.

16.254
syncope, Agape (Christian love), Alleppey (Indian port), canopy, canapé, therapy, syrupy, satrapy (ancient Persian province), entropy.

calliope (*US* steam-powered organ), apocope (linguistics term), telescopy, Penelope, Parthenope (Greek mythological character), allotropy (chemistry term), lycanthropy (transformation into wolf), philanthropy, misanthropy.

cryotherapy, psychotherapy, chemotherapy, thermotherapy, hypnotherapy, hydrotherapy, massotherapy, phototherapy (medical treatment using light).

radiotherapy, heliotherapy (therapeutic use of sunlight), physiotherapy, immunotherapy, mechanotherapy (treatment using mechanical devices), organotherapy (treatment using gland extracts), roentgenotherapy (therapeutic use of x-rays).

16.254.1
wicopy (US plant), pericope (passage read in church).

16.254.2
cryoscopy (determination of freezing points), endoscopy, rhinoscopy (examination of nasal passages), horoscopy, uroscopy (examination of urine), microscopy, spectroscopy (analysis of spectra), stethoscopy, stereoscopy, ophthalmoscopy, retinoscopy (ophthalmic procedure), ornithoscopy (divination by bird observation).

16.255
impi (Bantu warriors), skimpy, Wimpy (*Trademark*).

16.256
Pompey, swampy.

16.257
bumpy, dumpy, jumpy, humpy (angry or gloomy), lumpy, scrumpy, grumpy, stumpy.

16.258
crispy, wispy.

16.259
colloquy, obloquy (defamatory statement), soliloquy, somniloquy (talking in one's sleep), ventriloquy.

16.260
Barrie, Barry, barye (unit of pressure), carry, Gary, gharry (Indian horse-drawn vehicle), harry, Harry, Larry, marry, parry, tarry, miscarry, glengarry (Scottish woollen cap), remarry, intermarry.

16.261
Bari (Italian port), karri (eucalyptus tree), Chari (African river), sparry (geology term), sari, tarry, starry, ambary (plant yielding fibre), shikari (hunter), safari, Bihari (member of Indian people), Aparri (Philippine port), curare, Ferrari, Vasari (Italian writer and artist), Andvari (Norse mythological character), Cagliari (Sardinian port), zamindari (large Indian agricultural estate), Carbonari (Italian secret political society), Stradivari, charivari.

16.261.1
Pahari (language group), Kalahari, Mata Hari.

16.262
berry, bury, Bury, Kerry (Irish county), skerry (*Scot* small rocky island),

cherry, Derry, derry (*Austral* grudge or dislike), ferry, jerry, Jerry, merry, mere (Maori war club), perry, sherry, Terry, terry (towelling fabric), very, wherry (type of boat), knobkerrie (South African tribesman's stick), chokecherry (US species of cherry), flos ferri (deposit from hot springs), equerry, Owerri (Nigerian town), beriberi, Pondicherry, Londonderry.

16.263
burry (prickly), furry, firry (abounding in fir trees), blurry.

16.264
aery, airy, Carey, scary, chary, dairy, fairy, hairy, lairy (*Austral* gaudy), clary (aromatic plant), glary, Mary, nary (*Dialect* not), prairie, vary, wary, scalare (South American freshwater fish), costmary (aromatic plant), canary, unwary, airy-fairy, Tipperary, cassowary, bersagliere (Italian soldier), condottiere (former European mercenary soldier).

16.265
eyrie, eerie, Erie, beery, cheery, deary, sphery (resembling a sphere), leery, bleary, peri, Peary (US arctic explorer), query, dreary, theory, veery (US thrush), weary, Kediri (Indonesian city), Kashmiri, Guarneri (family of violin-makers), bokmakierie (South African songbird), Dhaulagiri (Nepalese mountain), metatheory (critical study of philosophy).

16.266
daiquiri (iced drink containing rum), Valkyrie, porphyry (type of rock), harakiri.

16.267
fiery, miry, spiry, wiry, expiry, enquiry, inquiry, praemunire (former legal term).

16.268
corrie (circular hollow in hillside), lorry, quarry, sorry, whare (Maori hut).

16.269
dory (spiny-finned fish), gory, hoary, lory (small parrot), flory (heraldic term), glory, saury (tropical fish), Tory, storey, story, John Dory (spiny-finned fish), vainglory, outlawry, furore, centaury (Eurasian plant), clerestory (row of church windows), blindstorey (church storey without windows), signori, hunky-dory, con amore, apospory (botany term), Montessori (Italian educational reformer), cacciatore (Italian cookery term), multistorey, Ruwenzori (African mountain range), Alpha Centauri, viola d'amore (former stringed instrument).

16.270
jury, Jewry, houri, Nuri (Indo-European people), Drury, Curie, fury, Tandoori, potpourri, decury (ten Roman soldiers), Venturi (Italian physicist), Missouri.

16.271
cowry, kauri (New Zealand coniferous tree), dowry, Lowry, Maori.

16.272
curry, scurry, hurry, flurry, slurry, Murray, spurry (low-growing plant), Surrey, surrey, worry.

16.273
mercury, augury, strangury, penury.

16.274
diary, friary, priory, flowery, floury, showery, brewery, Barbary, Burberry (*Trademark*), turbary (peat-cutting area), bribery, Albury (Australian city), daubery, strawberry, snowberry, crowberry, blubbery, rubbery, shrubbery, blueberry, dewberry, Newbury, hackberry, blackberry, cloudberry, Sudbury, dogberry, bilberry, Tilbury, tilbury (horse-drawn carriage), mulberry, anbury (veterinary or botany term), Banbury, cranberry, spiceberry, Shaftesbury, Avebury, Tewkesbury, raspberry, Shrewsbury, gooseberry, Dewsbury, Aylesbury, Salisbury,

Bloomsbury, Queensberry, quackery, Thackeray, Zachary, bakery, peccary (pig-like mammal), succory (chicory), cookery, rookery, piscary (location for fishing), hatchery, archery, lechery, treachery, witchery, butchery, century, spidery, doddery, gaudery (cheap finery), powdery, quandary, boundary, thundery, puffery (exaggerated praise), Nagari (type of Indian script), vagary, beggary, Gregory, roguery, sugary, Calgary, angary (legal term), Sungari (Chinese river), forgery, cudgerie (tropical tree), drudgery, soldiery, alary (relating to wings), raillery, hellery (wild behaviour), celery, sealery, Tuileries, coloury (having colour), scullery, foolery, saddlery, chandlery, burglary, jugglery, butlery (butler's room), cutlery, mammary, gramarye (magic), emery, memory, creamery, primary, flummery, plumbery, mummery, nummary (relating to coins), summary, summery, rosemary, cannery, granary, tannery, stannary (tin mine), swannery, joinery, clownery, gunnery, nunnery, apery (imitative behaviour), papery, drapery, peppery, foppery, coopery (barrel-making), dupery, trumpery, orrery (model of solar system), library, contrary, brasserie, glossary, sorcery, grocery, chancery, tertiary, washery, fishery, luxury, treasury, usury, lingerie, battery, cattery, flattery, artery, martyry (martyr's shrine), Tartary, lottery, pottery, cautery, watery, coterie, notary, rotary, votary, buttery, psaltery (ancient stringed instrument), mastery, blustery, lathery, feathery, leathery, carvery, reverie, every, ovary, Calvary, silvery, Mercury, colliery, misery, causerie (informal talk), rosery, rosary.

zedoary (aromatic ginger-like substance), checkerberry, elderberry, syllabary (list of syllables), chinaberry, Canterbury, huckleberry, whortleberry, loganberry, Glastonbury, boysenberry, serviceberry, grotesquery, debauchery,

solidary (marked by common interests), lapidary (dealer in gemstones), embroidery, prebendary, secondary, legendary, periphery, midwifery, housewifery, menagerie, corollary, tomfoolery, diablerie (devilry), exemplary, Montgomery, customary, chicanery (verbal trickery), reliquary, antiquary, arbitrary, patisserie, greengrocery, illusory, adversary, compulsory, secretory, bijouterie (type of jewellery), perfunctory, emunctory (relating to excretory organ), adultery, desultory, effrontery, peremptory, monastery, upholstery, recovery, discovery.

Devanagari (Indian syllabic script), haberdashery, introductory.

jiggery-pokery, noli-me-tangere (warning against touching).

16.274.1
laniary (tooth adapted for tearing), apiary, topiary, vespiary (wasps' nest), farriery, curriery, furriery, bestiary, vestiary (relating to clothes), ostiary (low-ranking Catholic official), aviary, breviary, hosiery, subsidiary, stipendiary, incendiary, pecuniary, fiduciary (trustee), intermediary.

16.274.1.1
biliary (relating to bile), miliary (resembling millet seeds), ciliary, nobiliary (relating to the nobility), auxiliary, domiciliary, superciliary (relating to the eyebrow).

16.274.1.2
judiciary, officiary (body of officials), justiciary, beneficiary.

16.274.2
mortuary, actuary, February, January, ossuary (receptacle for human bones), statuary, sanctuary, sumptuary (relating to extravagance), estuary, textuary (relating to a text), residuary, obituary, electuary (palatable substance containing drug), voluptuary.

16.274.3
bobbery (pack of hunting dogs), jobbery (corruption in public office), slobbery, snobbery, robbery, corroboree (*Austral* noisy gathering).

16.274.4
chicory, hickory (US nut tree), mickery (pool in river bed), trickery, formicary (ant hill), Terpsichore (Greek Muse), apothecary.

16.274.5
mockery, rockery, crockery, comstockery (*US* excessive censorship).

16.274.6
goliardery (ribald Latin verse), camaraderie.

16.274.7
dromedary, hebdomadary (weekly).

16.274.8
grindery (place for sharpening tools), bookbindery.

16.274.9
piggery, amphigory (piece of nonsense writing), allegory, vinegary, category.

16.274.10
buggery, snuggery, thuggery, skulduggery.

16.274.11
Hungary, ironmongery.

16.274.12
doggery (surly behaviour), toggery (clothes), pettifoggery, demagoguery.

16.274.13
perjury, surgery, psychosurgery, neurosurgery, cryosurgery, electrosurgery.

16.274.14
injury, gingery, orangery.

16.274.15
calorie, gallery, Malory, salary, Valerie, kilocalorie.

16.274.16
Hilary, Hillary, pillory, armillary (relating to bracelets), pupillary, capillary, ancillary, artillery, fritillary, tutelary

(serving as guardian), distillery, axillary (relating to the armpit), maxillary (relating to upper jaw), submaxillary (relating to lower jaw).

16.274.17
drollery, cajolery.

16.274.18
formulary (book of prescribed formulas), cartulary (collection of legal records), vocabulary, constabulary.

16.274.19
chancellery, intercalary (inserted in the calendar), epistolary (relating to letters).

16.274.20
armoury, gendarmerie.

16.274.21
spermary (sperm-producing organ), infirmary.

16.274.22
bloomery (type of ironworks), perfumery.

16.274.23
hennery (place for keeping poultry), venery, millenary (one thousand years), decennary (decade).

16.274.24
fernery, ternary, turnery (objects made on lathe), quaternary (consisting of four).

16.274.25
beanery (cheap restaurant), deanery, denary (based on ten), plenary (complete), greenery, scenery, senary (relating to six), machinery, catenary (type of geometric curve), centenary, duodenary (relating to twelve), bicentenary, tricentenary, quincentenary, quatercentenary.

16.274.26
ordinary, millinery, culinary, seminary, luminary, urinary, parcenary (joint heirship), mercenary, sanguinary, subordinary (heraldic term), extraordinary, imaginary, disciplinary, preliminary,

coparcenary (joint ownership), veterinary, multidisciplinary, interdisciplinary, genitourinary, eleemosynary (dependent on charity).

16.274.27
binary, finery, pinery, quinary (consisting of five), trinary (consisting of three), vinery (place for growing grapes), winery, refinery.

16.274.28
unary (consisting of single element), buffoonery, sublunary (between moon and earth), festoonery.

16.274.29
legionary, pulmonary, coronary, cautionary, dictionary, functionary, pensionary, visionary, antiphonary (collection of biblical passages), precautionary, reactionary, revolutionary, evolutionary.

16.274.29.1
stationery, stationary, inflationary.

16.274.29.2
cessionary (legal term), discretionary, concessionary.

16.274.29.3
missionary, seditionary, expeditionary.

16.274.29.4
lectionary (book of church readings), confectionery, insurrectionary.

16.274.30
slippery, frippery, polypary (base of coral colony).

16.274.31
empery (dominion), extempore.

16.274.32
numerary (relating to numbers), honorary, funerary, vulnerary (relating to a wound), temporary, literary, itinerary, contemporary, supernumerary.

16.274.33
tracery, embracery (attempt to corrupt jury).

16.274.34
pessary, accessory, possessory (relating to possession).

16.274.35
bursary, cursory, nursery, precursory, anniversary.

16.274.36
emissary, dimissory (granting permission to depart), commissary, promissory, janissary (Turkish sovereign's personal guard), necessary, rescissory (having power to rescind), rotisserie, unnecessary.

16.274.37
spicery, derisory.

16.274.38
sensory, dispensary, suspensory, incensory (incense-burner), ostensory (container for displaying Host), extrasensory.

16.274.39
residentiary (officially resident), penitentiary, obedientiary (holder of monastic office), plenipotentiary.

16.274.40 [some words in **16.274.43** may be pronounced to rhyme with this group]
datary (Catholic official), gyratory, natatory (relating to swimming), condemnatory, celebratory, compensatory, anticipatory.

16.274.40.1
judicatory, applicatory, deprecatory, justificatory.

16.274.40.2
ambulatory (relating to walking), circulatory, adulatory, congratulatory.

16.274.41
jittery, glittery, pituri (Australian shrub).

presbytery, auditory, pellitory (European plant), military, solitary, cemetery, limitary, vomitory (causing vomiting), dormitory, fumitory (European plant), planetary, sanitary, monitory (warn-

43

ing), monetary, unitary, dignitary, feretory (Catholic shrine), territory, transitory.

proprietary, pituitary, hereditary, insanitary, premonitory, depository, repository, suppository, expository, paramilitary.

16.274.42

tributary, salutary, statutory, contributory, distributary (stream draining river), executory (not yet effective), noncontributory, interlocutory, circumlocutory.

16.274.43

dietary, placatory, predatory, laudatory (expressing praise), feudatory (relating to feudalism), mandatory, prefatory, offertory, purgatory, nugatory (of little value), fumatory (relating to smoking), chrismatory (receptacle for consecrated oil), signatory, damnatory, repertory, raspatory (surgeon's rasp), juratory (relating to legal oath), vibratory, secretary, migratory, pulsatory, hortatory (urging), lavatory.

masticatory (relating to chewing), educatory, obligatory, consolatory, undulatory, lacrimatory, reformatory, explanatory, cosignatory, declaratory, preparatory, perspiratory, respiratory, inspiratory (relating to inhalation), expiratory (relating to exhalation), procuratory (legal term), dispensatory, invitatory, salutatory, sternutatory (causing sneezing), conservatory, observatory, accusatory, excusatory.

reverberatory, undersecretary.

16.274.43.1

aleatory (dependent on chance), retaliatory, conciliatory, reconciliatory.

16.274.43.2

amendatory (*US* corrective), recommendatory.

16.274.43.3

rogatory (seeking information), derogatory, interrogatory, supererogatory (superfluous).

16.274.43.4

dilatory (time-wasting), depilatory.

16.274.43.5

amatory, defamatory, declamatory, acclamatory, proclamatory, exclamatory, inflammatory.

16.274.43.6

minatory (threatening), discriminatory, hallucinatory.

16.274.43.7

oratory, laboratory, exploratory.

16.274.44

factory, lactary (relating to milk), olfactory, phylactery (case containing Hebrew texts), refractory, calefactory (giving warmth), satisfactory.

16.274.45

nectary (nectar-secreting structure), rectory, sectary (member of a sect), refectory, trajectory, directory, protectory (institution for destitute children).

16.274.46

victory, valedictory, contradictory.

16.274.47

sedimentary, rudimentary, alimentary, elementary, supplementary, complimentary, complementary, documentary, parliamentary, testamentary (relating to a will), unparliamentary.

16.274.48

lientery (medical term), sedentary, voluntary, commentary, promontory, momentary, fragmentary, mesentery (anatomy term), dysentery, inventory, involuntary.

16.274.49

bistoury (long surgical knife), history, mystery, magistery (alchemical substance), prehistory, consistory (diocesan court), psychohistory (psychology term), protohistory.

16.274.50
slavery, knavery, bravery, savoury, unsavoury, antislavery.

16.274.51
livery, quivery, shivery, delivery, olivary (olive-shaped).

16.274.52
ivory, salivary.

16.274.53
revisory, advisory, supervisory.

16.275
gimmickry, mimicry.

16.276
bawdry (obscene language), Cawdrey (English lexicographer), tawdry.

16.277
balladry, bastardry (*Austral* malicious behaviour), wizardry.

16.278
ribaldry, cuckoldry, heraldry.

16.279
husbandry, legendry.

16.280
orphrey (embroidered border on vestment), gallimaufry (*US* hotchpotch).

16.281
comfrey (Eurasian plant), Humphrey.

16.282
imagery, savagery.

16.283
jewellery, riflery (*US* rifle marksmanship), hostelry, cavalry, devilry, revelry, chivalry, rivalry.

16.284
deaconry, falconry, felonry (felons collectively), almonry (house of alms-giver), cannonry (artillery), canonry (office of canon), weaponry, heronry (colony of herons), masonry, blazonry, archdeaconry, freemasonry, citizenry.

16.285
poetry, rabbitry, marquetry, parquetry, circuitry, rocketry, coquetry (flirtation), basketry, musketry, gadgetry, toiletry, summitry (holding summit conferences), puppetry, corsetry, telemetry (measurement of distant events), photogrammetry (making measurements from photographs).

16.285.1
symmetry, planimetry (measurement of plane areas), asymmetry, dissymmetry, altimetry, bathymetry (measurement of ocean depth), acidimetry, oxidimetry (chemistry term), alkalimetry, dolorimetry (measurement of pain).

16.285.2 [further rhymes may be derived from **17.342.3**]
biometry (statistics applied to biology), zoometry (branch of zoology), psychometry (measurement of mental processes), allometry (biology term), thermometry, astrometry (branch of astronomy), isometry (maths term), hypsometry (measurement of altitude), photometry, optometry, iodometry (chemistry term), anemometry (measurement of wind speed), dynamometry (power measurement), anthropometry (measurement of human body).

16.285.2.1
geometry, tacheometry (measurement of distance), stoichiometry (branch of chemistry), craniometry, stereometry (measurement of volume), sociometry (study of social relationships).

16.285.2.2
chronometry, trigonometry.

16.286
bigotry, helotry (serfdom), zealotry (excessive zeal), papeterie (box for papers), barratry (legal term).

16.286.1
psychiatry, podiatry (*US* chiropody), antipsychiatry (psychiatric theory), neuropsychiatry.

16.286.2
zoolatry (worship of animals), bardolatry (excessive admiration for Shake-

speare), idolatry, monolatry (worship of one god), necrolatry (worship of the dead), iconolatry, demonolatry.

16.286.2.1
hagiolatry (veneration of saints), heliolatry (sun worship), bibliolatry (excessive devotion to Bible), Mariolatry (veneration of Virgin Mary), ecclesiolatry (devotion to ecclesiastical traditions).

16.287
gantry, pantry.

16.288
entry, gentry, sentry, re-entry, passementerie (decorative trimming).

16.289
wintry, carpentry.

16.290
country, upcountry.

16.291
pedantry, infantry, pageantry, gallantry, tenantry, errantry, Coventry, pleasantry, peasantry.

16.292
vestry, ancestry.

16.293
sophistry, registry, palmistry, chemistry, ministry, tapestry, forestry, artistry, dentistry, baptistry, casuistry, biochemistry.

16.294
dassie (rodent-like mammal), gassy, lassie, glacé, Plassey, Massey, massé (stroke in billiards), massy (massive), rasse (small catlike mammal), brassie, sassy, chassis, Kumasi (Ghanaian city), Manasseh (Old Testament character), Malagasy (inhabitant of Madagascar), Tallahassee, Haile Selassie.

16.295
farcy (veterinary term), classy, glassy, brassy, grassy, Likasi (Zaîrese city), dalasi (Gambian currency), sannyasi (Brahman mendicant), Adivasi (member of Indian people).

16.296
Basie, lacy, racy, Tracy, O'Casey, Sulawesi (Indonesian islands).

16.297
Jesse, messy, Crécy, dressy, in esse (actually existing).

16.298
mercy, Percy, pursy (short-winded), Circe, gramercy, controversy.

16.298.1
reversi (board game), arsy-versy.

16.299
fleecy, Naoise (Irish mythological character), greasy, Tbilisi (Russian city).

16.300
missy, prissy, sissy, prophecy, Gallice (in French), policy, Anglice (in English), pleurisy, secrecy, courtesy, Eurydice, Chalcidice (Greek peninsula), sub judice, impolicy, discourtesy.

16.300.1
Odyssey, geodesy (measurement of earth), theodicy (branch of theology).

16.301
icy, dicey, spicy, pricey, vice (instead of).

16.302
bossy, lossy (dissipating energy), flossy (US showy), glossy, mossy, mossie (African sparrow), Mossi (African people), posse, in posse (possible).

16.303
horsy, Glauce (Greek mythological character), saucy.

16.304
mousy, Firdausi (Persian epic poet), housey-housey.

16.305
fussy, hussy, pussy.

16.306
goosy, juicy, Lucy, Senussi (member of Muslim sect), Debussy, acey-deucy (type of backgammon).

16.307

abbacy, embassy, argosy (large merchant ship), legacy, fallacy, jealousy, prelacy (office of prelate), Wallasey, pharmacy, primacy, lunacy, papacy, heresy, piracy, oracy (use of speech), curacy (office of curate), euphrasy (flowering plant), leprosy, fantasy, ecstasy, privacy.

idiocy, celibacy, advocacy, candidacy, delegacy (university committee or department), profligacy, supremacy, diplomacy, contumacy (wilful resistance to authority), Varanasi (Indian city), obstinacy, adequacy, conspiracy, accuracy, magistracy, apostasy, isostasy (geological theory).

episcopacy (church government by bishops), inadequacy, inaccuracy, idiosyncrasy.

16.307.1

efficacy, delicacy, intricacy, inefficacy.

16.307.2

intimacy, legitimacy, illegitimacy.

16.307.3

geognosy (study of earth's structure), pharmacognosy (branch of pharmacology).

16.307.4

numeracy, literacy, confederacy, degeneracy, illiteracy.

16.307.5

mobocracy, ptochocracy (government by the poor), ochlocracy (mob rule), democracy, timocracy (political system), nomocracy (government based on law), monocracy, pornocracy (domination by prostitutes), technocracy, hypocrisy, bureaucracy, isocracy (equality of political power), stratocracy (military rule), squattocracy (*Austral* rich farmers collectively), autocracy, plutocracy, slavocracy (domination by slaveholders), gynaecocracy, hierocracy (government by priests), pantisocracy (community ruled by all), meritocracy, gerontocracy, aristocracy.

16.307.5.1

theocracy (government by deity), theocrasy (mingling of deities), hagiocracy (government by holy men).

16.308

Anglesey, minstrelsy.

16.309

fancy, Nancy, geomancy (divination from random dots), theomancy (divination through an oracle), sciomancy (divination through ghosts), rhabdomancy (water divining), chiromancy (palmistry), pyromancy (divination by fire), necromancy (black magic), hydromancy (divination by water), cartomancy (fortune-telling with cards), bibliomancy (divination from random texts), ornithomancy (divination from bird behaviour).

16.310

chancy, Jhansi (Indian city).

16.311

wincey (type of cloth), chaplaincy, De Quincey (English essayist), captaincy.

16.312

buoyancy, fluency, truancy, vacancy, piquancy, cadency (heraldic term), pudency (modesty or prudishness), infancy, agency, regency, valency, clemency, tenancy, pregnancy, frequency, errancy (tendency to err), currency, flagrancy, vagrancy, decency, potency, constancy, solvency, poignancy.

incumbency, presidency, redundancy, exigency, Excellency, inclemency, athermancy (nontransmission of radiant heat), subtenancy, permanency, malignancy, discrepancy, occupancy, infrequency, delinquency, transparency, complacency, indecency, militancy, transmittancy (physics term), hesitancy, prepotency (superiority of power), expectancy, consultancy, accountancy, consistency, conservancy, insolvency.

constituency, diathermancy (transmission of radiant heat), eigenfrequency (physics term), belligerency (being at war), itinerancy, inconsistency, electrovalency (chemistry term).

16.312.1
leniency, expediency.

16.312.2
tendency, dependency, ascendancy, superintendency (office of superintendent).

16.312.3
urgency, surgeoncy (office of surgeon), emergency, insurgency, detergency (cleansing power), counterinsurgency.

16.312.4
stringency, contingency.

16.312.5
efficiency, deficiency, proficiency, sufficiency, inefficiency, insufficiency.

16.312.6
blatancy, patency, dilatancy (physics term).

16.313
epilepsy, narcolepsy (medical term), nympholepsy (state of violent emotion), catalepsy (medical term).

16.314
gypsy, tipsy.

16.315
popsy (*Slang* attractive young woman), dropsy, biopsy, autopsy.

16.316
curtsy, Chertsey.

16.317
ritzy, baronetcy.

16.318
footsie, tootsy, Watutsi (member of African people), tootsy-wootsy.

16.319
ashy, flashy, plashy (wet or marshy), splashy, mashie, brashy (loosely fragmented), trashy, Lubumbashi (Zaîrese city).

16.320
marshy, Ustashi (Yugoslav terrorist organization).

16.321
fleshy, meshy.

16.322
dishy, fishy, rubbishy, maharishi.

16.323
squashy, washy (watery), wishy-washy.

16.324
gushy, slushy, mushy, rushy.

16.325
bushy, cushy, pushy.

16.326
sushi (Japanese food), acouchi (South American rodent).

16.327
batty, catty, scatty, chatty, fatty, platy (freshwater fish), natty, patty, ratty, tatty, Scarlatti, chapatti, Hanratty, Togliatti (Russian city), Cincinnati.

16.328
arty, hearty, lathi (Indian policeman's wooden stick), smartie, party, coati, Masbate (Philippine island), Gauhati (Indian city), Komati (African river), nonparty, ex parte (legal term), Astarte (Phoenician goddess), illuminati (enlightened people).

16.328.1
karate, Marathi (Indian language), Gujarati (Indian people), literati (scholarly people).

16.329
eighty, Ate (Greek goddess), Haiti, platy (geology term), slaty, matey, weighty.

16.330
Getty, jetty, netty (*Dialect* lavatory), petty, sweaty, yeti, confetti, spaghetti, machete, Rossetti, spermaceti (white

waxy substance), Donizetti (Italian operatic composer).

16.331
dirty, shirty, thirty.

16.332
Beatty, meaty, peaty, rete (anatomy term), treaty, sweetie, graffiti, Tahiti, entreaty, Cavite (Philippine port), Papeete (capital of Tahiti), Nefertiti.

16.333
bitty, kitty, ditty, nitty, pity, gritty, smriti (Hindu sacred literature), pretty, city, shitty, witty.

laity, moiety (half), probity, rackety (noisy), crotchety, nudity, crudity, fidgety, nullity, comity (courtesy), samiti (Indian political association), committee, enmity, wapiti (large US deer), uppity, self-pity, equity, rarity, varsity, scarcity, paucity, falsity, sanctity, quantity, chastity, velvety, laxity, fixity.

acerbity, improbity, heredity, absurdity, fidelity, credulity, extremity, Yosemite, infirmity, subcommittee, amenity, indemnity, solemnity, inequity, obliquity, iniquity, antiquity, propinquity (nearness), jequirity (tropical climbing plant), entirety, alacrity, integrity, nitty-gritty, lithotrity (crushing of bladder stone), necessity, caducity (perishableness), intercity, perplexity, complexity, convexity.

infidelity, incredulity, serendipity, mediocrity.

16.333.1
deity, velleity (weakest level of desire), aseity (philosophy term), multeity, haecceity (philosophy term), spontaneity, corporeity, homogeneity, erogeneity, incorporeity.

16.333.2
piety, ubiety (being in particular place), dubiety, impiety, sobriety, propriety, society, satiety, anxiety, inebriety, impropriety.

16.333.2.1
variety, contrariety, notoriety.

16.333.3
congruity, vacuity, acuity, circuity (roundabout quality), tenuity, annuity, fortuity, fatuity, gratuity, superfluity, incongruity, perspicuity, promiscuity, assiduity, ambiguity, contiguity, perpetuity.

16.333.3.1
ingenuity, continuity, discontinuity.

16.333.4
rickety, pernickety.

16.333.5
quiddity (essential nature), fluidity, morbidity, rigidity, frigidity, solidity, validity, timidity, humidity, cupidity, stupidity, rapidity, liquidity, viridity (greenness), aridity, acridity, lucidity, avidity, invalidity, superfluidity (physics term).

16.333.5.1
acidity, placidity, hypoacidity, hyperacidity.

16.333.6
oddity, commodity, incommodity, discommodity (economics term).

16.333.7
fecundity, jocundity, profundity, infecundity.

16.333.8 [further rhymes may be derived from **228**]
locality, rascality, modality, sodality (Catholic religious society), feudality, frugality, molality (chemical concentration), venality, finality, tonality, plurality, neutrality, centrality, natality, vitality, mortality, totality, brutality, fatality, frontality, causality, animality, externality, atonality, hospitality, immortality, polytonality, universality, inhospitality.

16.333.8.1
reality, ideality, cordiality, geniality, unreality, partiality, speciality, social-

ity, bestiality, joviality, congeniality, materiality, impartiality, commerciality, provinciality, territoriality, artificiality, superficiality, extraterritoriality.

16.333.8.1.1
potentiality, confidentiality.

16.333.8.1.2
triviality, conviviality.

16.333.8.2
duality, actuality, punctuality, sensuality, mutuality, sexuality, spirituality, eventuality, individuality, pseudomutuality (psychology term), homosexuality, heterosexuality.

16.333.8.3
technicality, topicality, practicality, whimsicality, illogicality, impracticality.

16.333.8.4
regality, legality, prodigality, illegality.

16.333.8.5
formality, normality, informality, abnormality, subnormality.

16.333.8.6
criminality, originality.

16.333.8.7
banality, commonality (commonness), personality, impersonality, conventionality, constitutionality, unconventionality.

16.333.8.7.1
nationality, rationality, irrationality.

16.333.8.8
principality, municipality.

16.333.8.9
morality, liberality, amorality, immorality, generality, temporality, ephemerality.

16.333.8.10
mentality, sentimentality.

16.333.9
agility, fragility, humility, tranquillity, sterility, virility, febrility (feverishness), gracility (slenderness), docility, facility,

fertility, motility, utility, futility, gentility, hostility, servility, civility, solubility, puerility, imbecility, infertility, versatility, infantility, incivility.

16.333.9.1
mobility, nobility, immobility.

16.333.9.2 [further rhymes may be derived from **228.16**]
ability, debility, stability, probability, credibility, fallibility, gullibility, inability, capability, disability, possibility, sensibility, notability, suitability, flexibility, instability, permeability, improbability, practicability, availability, desirability, impossibility, responsibility, compatibility, unsuitability, susceptibility, suggestibility, manipulability, incompatibility.

16.333.9.2.1
liability, viability, reliability, unreliability.

16.333.9.2.2
risibility, visibility, divisibility, invisibility.

16.333.9.3
senility, juvenility.

16.333.10
jollity, polity (political organization), quality, equality, frivolity, inequality.

16.333.11
amity, calamity.

16.333.12
dimity (cotton fabric), sublimity, proximity, longanimity (patience), anonymity, synonymity, unanimity, magnanimity, equanimity, pusillanimity.

16.333.13
deformity, conformity, enormity, uniformity, nonconformity, unconformity.

16.333.14
sanity, vanity, urbanity, profanity, humanity, inanity, insanity, Christianity, inhumanity.

16.333.15
lenity, serenity, obscenity.

16.333.16
modernity, maternity, paternity, quaternity (group of four), fraternity, confraternity (organized group of men).

16.333.16.1
eternity, coeternity (eternal coexistence), taciturnity.

16.333.17
trinity, affinity, infinity, virginity, vicinity, Latinity, divinity, masculinity, femininity, asininity, consanguinity.

16.333.17.1
salinity, alkalinity.

16.333.18
unity, immunity, community, impunity, disunity, importunity, opportunity.

16.333.19
dignity, indignity, malignity, benignity.

16.333.20
charity, clarity, parity, barbarity, vulgarity, molarity (chemical concentration), polarity, disparity, solidarity, viviparity, oviparity.

16.333.20.1
familiarity, peculiarity, unfamiliarity, multicollinearity (statistics term).

16.333.20.2
hilarity, similarity, capillarity (surface tension), dissimilarity.

16.333.20.3 [further rhymes may be derived from **17.174**]
secularity, jocularity, muscularity, regularity, angularity, singularity, popularity, insularity, irregularity, unpopularity.

16.333.20.3.1
particularity, perpendicularity.

16.333.21
ferity (wildness), verity, celerity (speed), temerity, asperity, prosperity, sincerity, austerity, posterity, dexterity, severity, insincerity, ambidexterity.

16.333.22
priority, majority, minority, sonority, sorority, authority, seniority, inferiority, superiority.

16.333.23
purity, security, obscurity, impurity, futurity, maturity, insecurity, immaturity.

16.333.24
celebrity, muliebrity (womanhood).

16.333.25
audacity, mordacity, mendacity, fugacity (chemistry term), sagacity, tenacity, pugnacity, opacity, loquacity, veracity, voracity, vivacity, pertinacity, inveracity.

16.333.25.1
capacity, rapacity, incapacity.

16.333.26
diversity, perversity, adversity, university.

16.333.27
cecity (blindness), obesity.

16.333.28
felicity, publicity, duplicity, simplicity, complicity, tonicity, sphericity, lubricity (lewdness), basicity (chemistry term), toxicity, infelicity, catholicity, Catholicity, atomicity, historicity (historical authenticity), eccentricity, concentricity, electricity, chromaticity (quality of a colour), authenticity, domesticity, alcoholicity, thermoelectricity, hydroelectricity, photoelectricity.

16.333.28.1
triplicity (group of three), multiplicity.

16.333.28.2
plasticity, elasticity, inelasticity, homoscedasticity (statistics term), photoelasticity (physics term), heteroscedasticity (statistics term).

16.333.29
nicety, benedicite (blessing).

16.333.30
verbosity, viscosity, velocity, villosity (biology term), callosity, pomposity, porosity, atrocity, monstrosity, schistosity (medical term), nebulosity, animosity, tenebrosity, reciprocity.

16.333.30.1
grandiosity, curiosity, preciosity (affectation), speciosity, religiosity (extreme piety), incuriosity.

16.333.30.2
virtuosity, strenuosity, sinuosity, tortuosity, impetuosity, anfractuosity (state of being convoluted).

16.333.30.3
precocity, bellicosity, varicosity.

16.333.30.4
vinosity (distinctive quality of wine), luminosity, voluminosity.

16.333.30.5
ferocity, tuberosity, generosity.

16.333.31
density, immensity, propensity, intensity, extensity (psychology term).

16.333.32
entity, identity, nonentity.

16.333.33
cavity, gravity, suavity, concavity, depravity.

16.333.34
levity, brevity, longevity.

16.333.35
privity (relationship recognized by law), declivity (downward slope), acclivity (upward slope), proclivity, motivity (power of moving), captivity, festivity, expressivity, creativity, permittivity (electrical property), sensitivity, objectivity, subjectivity, selectivity, collectivity, reflectivity (physics term), receptivity, resistivity (electrical property).

16.333.35.1
nativity, negativity, relativity.

16.333.35.2
activity, reactivity, inactivity, hyperactivity, radioactivity.

16.333.35.3
productivity, conductivity, reluctivity (physics term), superconductivity.

16.334
Blighty, flighty, mighty, nightie, almighty, Venite (95th psalm), Aphrodite, Amphitrite (Greek goddess), pendente lite (legal term).

16.335
Scottie, dotty, hottie (*Austral* hot-water bottle), zloty, knotty, snotty, potty, spotty, Menotti (Italian composer), manicotti (large stuffed noodles).

16.336
dorty (*Scot* sullen or haughty), forte, forty, haughty, naughty, sporty, sortie, shortie, warty, pianoforte.

16.337
surety, Trimurti (three Hindu gods).

16.338
dacoity (armed robbery), hoity-toity.

16.339
dhoti (Indian man's long loincloth), floaty, roti (type of unleavened bread), throaty, peyote (cactus), coyote, Don Quixote.

16.340
doughty, grouty.

16.341
butty, cutty, chuttie (*Austral* chewing gum), gutty (*Irish* urchin), smutty, nutty, putty, puttee (cloth wound around leg), rutty (full of ruts), tutty (impure zinc oxide).

16.342
footy, sooty, tutti (musical term), bobotie (South African curried dish), deputy.

16.343
booty, cootie (*US* body louse), snooty, fruity, beauty, cutie, duty, Djibouti

(African republic), agouti, gomuti (East Indian palm), busuuti (Ugandan woman's long garment), tutti-frutti.

16.344
gaiety, liberty, puberty, Hecate (Greek goddess), maggoty, property, champerty (legal term), carroty, poverty, chocolaty, vanaspati (vegetable fat), Amravati (Indian town), Ross and Cromarty.

16.345
crafty, draughty.

16.346
hefty, lefty.

16.347
fifty, nifty, thrifty, shifty, swiftie (*Austral* a trick).

16.348
lofty, softy, toplofty (haughty).

16.349
mufti, Mufti (Muslim legal adviser), tufty.

16.350
guilty, silty.

16.351
faulty, malty, salty.

16.352
fealty, realty, owelty (legal term), cruelty, faculty, penalty, mayoralty, specialty, subtlety, shrievalty (office of sheriff), novelty, casualty, difficulty, commonalty (ordinary people), personalty (personal property), admiralty, severalty (state of being separate).

16.352.1
loyalty, royalty, disloyalty, viceroyalty.

16.353
anti, ante, canty (*Dialect* lively), scanty, Dante, Fanti (Ghanaian people), shanty, Zante (Greek island), chianti, andante, infante (Spanish prince), Ashanti (region of Ghana), Alicante, vigilante, Ypsilanti (Greek revolutionary), diamanté, Rosinante (worn-out old

horse), dilettante, concertante (musical term), pococurante (indifferent).

16.354
dainty, painty.

16.355
kente (brightly-coloured African cloth), plenty, twenty, aplenty, Mindszenty (Hungarian cardinal), lentamente (musical term), cognoscenti (connoisseurs).

16.356
flinty, minty, shinty (form of hockey), teosinte (Central American grass).

16.357
Monty, monte (gambling card game), Brontë.

16.358
jaunty, flaunty (ostentatious).

16.359
bounty, county, Mountie.

16.360
frumenty (sweetened spiced porridge), guaranty, warranty, certainty, seventy, sovereignty, suzerainty, uncertainty.

16.361
Asti, pasty, epinasty (growth of plant part), nyctinasty (botany term), hyponasty (growth of plant part), photonasty (plant's response to light), pederasty.

16.361.1
neoplasty (surgical repair of tissue), zooplasty (transplantation technique), anaplasty (plastic surgery), rhinoplasty (plastic surgery of nose), autoplasty (transplantation from own body), osteoplasty (bone grafting), heteroplasty (transplantation from another body), dermatoplasty (skin grafting), keratoplasty (plastic surgery of cornea).

16.362
nasty, vasty, contrasty (having sharp contrast).

16.363
hasty, pasty, tasty.

16.364
chesty, testy, Tibesti (African mountain range).

16.365
thirsty, bloodthirsty.

16.366
misty, Christie, twisty, modesty, majesty, honesty, amnesty, touristy, sacristy, travesty, immodesty, lese-majesty, dishonesty, Corpus Christi.

16.367
frosty, Anticosti (Canadian island).

16.368
busty, dusty, fusty, gusty, lusty, musty, rusty, crusty, trusty.

16.369
breathy, abernethy.

16.370
pithy, stichomythy (dialogue in Greek drama).

16.371
bothy (*Scot* small shelter), mothy, frothy.

16.372
couthie (*Scot* friendly), toothy.

16.373
Timothy, apathy, empathy, sympathy, telepathy, antipathy.

16.373.1
psychopathy, allopathy, neuropathy (disease of nervous system), hydropathy (water cure), naturopathy.

16.373.1.1
theopathy (religious emotion after meditation), idiopathy (disease of unknown cause), homeopathy, osteopathy.

16.374
healthy, stealthy, wealthy, unhealthy.

16.375
worthy, airworthy, seaworthy, roadworthy, blameworthy, unworthy, noteworthy, trustworthy, praiseworthy, newsworthy, Galsworthy.

16.376
smithy, prithee, stithy (*Dialect* a forge), withy (willow tree).

16.377
navvy, savvy.

16.378
ave, jarvey (coachman), Harvey, grave (musical term), Mohave (American Indian people).

16.379
cavy, cave, cavie (*Scot* hen coop), Davy, slavey (female servant), navy, gravy, wavy, agave (tropical plant).

16.380
bevy, bevvy (*Dialect* alcoholic drink), chevy, heavy, levee, levy, replevy (legal term).

16.381
curvy, scurvy, nervy, topsy-turvy.

16.382
bivvy (*slang* small tent), skivvy, chivy, divvy (*short for* dividend), Livy, privy, civvy (*slang* civilian), tantivy (at full speed), divi-divi (tropical tree).

16.383
covey, lovey, lovey-dovey.

16.384
movie, groovy.

16.385
Muscovy, anchovy, Pahlavi (Middle Persian language).

16.386
maxi, braxy (disease of sheep), taxi, waxy, chronaxie (physiology term), epitaxy (growth on crystal), anthotaxy (flower arrangement on stem).

16.387
sexy, apoplexy.

16.388
dixie (large metal pot), Dixie (southern states of USA), nixie (female water sprite), pixie, pyxie (evergreen shrub), tricksy (mischievous).

16.389
doxy (opinion or doctrine), foxy, moxie (*US* courage), proxy, epoxy, hydroxy (chemical compound), orthodoxy, heterodoxy.

16.390
galaxy, metagalaxy (the universe).

16.391
jazzy, snazzy.

16.392
carzey, ghazi (Muslim fighter against unbelievers), Swazi (African people), Benghazi (Libyan port), Nastase, kamikaze, Ashkenazi.

16.393
daisy, hazy, lazy, mazy (perplexing), crazy, Bel Paese (creamy Italian cheese), upsy-daisy.

16.394
kersey (woollen cloth), jersey, Jersey, Mersey.

16.395
easy, cheesy, sleazy, queasy, breezy, wheezy, Zambezi, speakeasy, pachisi (Indian board game), uneasy.

16.396
busy, dizzy, fizzy, frizzy, tizzy, poesy, tin lizzie, busy Lizzie.

16.397
gauzy, mawsie (*Scot* woollen jersey), Gagauzi (Russian language).

16.398
Boise (US city), noisy, cramoisy (crimson).

16.399
cosy, dozy, Lozi (Zambian language), mosey, nosy, posy, rosy, prosy.

16.400
lousy, blowzy (slovenly), drowsy, frowzy (shabby), Dalhousie (British statesman).

16.401
fuzzy, muzzy.

16.402
boozy, choosy, floozy, woozy, newsy, Pusey (English ecclesiastic), Brancusi, Watusi (member of African people).

16.403
flimsy, slimsy (*US* frail), whimsy.

16.404
gansey (*Dialect* pullover), pansy, tansy (flowering plant).

16.405
frenzy, Mackenzie.

16.406
Kinsey (US zoologist), quinsy.

17 -er [This is the unstressed syllable at the end of such words as *grocer* and *ancestor*. Rhymes dependent on this syllable alone are unsatisfactory and should be avoided. Further rhymes may be created by adding -er to appropriate adjectives and verbs.]
chamber, vodka, polka, Oscar, butcher, scripture, rupture, sculpture, pasture, moisture, Buddha, pilfer, sulphur, Edgar, soldier, chandler, handler, burglar, stapler, sampler, dogma, asthma, Wagner, partner, cobra, extra, pizza, fuchsia, tonsure, azure, sculptor, Ulster, hamster, monster, gangster, youngster, ether, author, premier, Kenya, junior, Windsor, sepulchre.

17.1
layer, player, payer, Freya (Norse goddess), stayer, Malaya, bricklayer, platelayer (railway-track layer), ratepayer, taxpayer, soothsayer, purveyor, surveyor, conveyor, Eritrea (Ethiopian province).

17.2
skier, rhea, Rhea, ria, seer.

Euboea (Greek island), Achaea (region of Greece), trachea, Medea (Greek mythological princess), idea, Judaea, Chaldea (ancient Babylonian region), Hygeia (Greek goddess), Crimea, eupnoea (normal breathing), dyspnoea (difficulty in breathing), spiraea, chorea, sangria, sightseer, tortilla (Mexican pancake), Hosea.

Kampuchea, ratafia, Tanzania, hyperpnoea (increased breathing rate), Nicosia, panacea, overseer, Boadicea, galatea (strong cotton fabric), barathea.

Laodicea, Arimathea.

17.2.1
epopoeia (epic poem), Cassiopeia, pharmacopoeia (list of drugs), prosopopoeia (figure of speech), onomatopoeia.

17.2.2
Korea, Maria, Peraea (ancient Palestinian region), sharia (Islamic doctrines), diarrhoea, pyorrhoea (discharge of pus), leucorrhoea (vaginal discharge), banderilla (bullfighter's assistant), logorrhoea (excessive talkativeness), gonorrhoea, pizzeria, trattoria, Caesarea, Tia Maria (*Trademark*), amenorrhoea, dysmenorrhoea, spermatorrhoea.

17.3
Nubia, hakea (Australian shrub), clarkia, lochia (vaginal discharge), branchia (aquatic animal's gill), bronchia (bronchial tubes), breccia (type of rock), torchier (type of lamp), India, morphia, logia (collection of Christ's sayings), collier, cochlea, trochlea (anatomy term), nuclear, buddleia, Anglia, cattleya (tropical orchid), Antlia (constellation), denier, daphnia, Bosnia (region of Yugoslavia), Napier, rapier, sepia, copier, croupier, barrier, carrier, farrier, garrya (ornamental shrub), harrier, aria, Zaria (Nigerian city), terrier, quarrier (quarryman), warrior, currier, furrier, spurrier (spur maker), fimbria (anatomy term), nutria (coypu fur), Bactria (ancient Asian country), Istria (peninsula in Adriatic Sea), Austria, Mercia, deutzia (flowering shrub), me-

teor, cottier (Irish smallholder), courtier, protea (tropical shrub), Hestia (Greek goddess), Ostia, Parthia, Scythia, clothier, uvea (part of eyeball), clavier, salvia, banksia (Australian shrub), nausea, zoysia (type of grass), woodsia (small fern).

euphorbia (flowering plant), Colombia, Columbia, Slovakia (region of Czechoslovakia), Walachia, rudbeckia (flowering plant), petechia (mark on skin), welwitschia (African desert plant), Cambodia, Hollandia (Indonesian port), montgolfier (hot-air balloon), rauwolfia (tropical tree), Thuringia (region of East Germany), sedilia (group of church seats), saintpaulia (African violet), East Anglia, costumier, arrhythmia, anosmia (inability to smell), petunia, insignia, insomnia, tilapia (African freshwater fish), Olympia, Calabria (region of Italy), anarthria (loss of coherent speech), collinsia (US plant), eupepsia (good digestion), dyspepsia, eclampsia (toxic condition during pregnancy), bilharzia (pathogenic blood fluke), rickettsia (pathogenic microorganism), strelitzia (African plant), opuntia (prickly pear), poinsettia, forsythia, anoxia (lack of oxygen), tillandsia (tropical plant).

Appalachia, Philadelphia, multinuclear, thermonuclear, mononuclear, intranuclear, extranuclear, Ichinomiya (Japanese town), bladder ketmia, pleurodynia (muscular pain between ribs), algolagnia (sexual perversion), photocopier, Alexandria, hypochondria, Cappadocia (ancient Asian region), polydipsia (excessive thirst), preeclampsia (toxic condition during pregnancy), differentia (logic term), hydrometeor (meteorology term), Yugoslavia, Andalusia.

Czechoslovakia, hemianopsia (sight defect), intelligentsia, macula lutea (spot on retina), gynaecomastia (abnormal male breast development), anacoluthia (lack of grammatical sequence).

17.3.1
labia, Swabia (former West German duchy), Arabia, Bessarabia (region of Russia).

17.3.2
Serbia (republic of Yugoslavia), suburbia, ytterbia (chemical compound), exurbia (*US* region outside suburbs).

17.3.3
Libya, tibia, Namibia.

17.3.4
obeah (type of witchcraft), cobia (game fish), phobia, theophobia (fear of God), zoophobia, Francophobia, phagophobia (fear of eating), algophobia (fear of pain), ochlophobia (fear of crowds), Anglophobia, xenophobia, monophobia (fear of being alone), aquaphobia (fear of water), aerophobia, acrophobia, necrophobia, hydrophobia, Negrophobia, astraphobia (fear of thunderstorms), claustrophobia, photophobia, nyctophobia (fear of night), Germanophobia, agoraphobia, triskaidekaphobia (fear of number thirteen).

17.3.5
Gambia, Zambia, Senegambia (region of Africa).

17.3.6
gaillardia (flowering plant), La Guardia (US politician), tachycardia (abnormally rapid heartbeat), bradycardia (abnormally slow heartbeat), megalocardia (abnormal enlargement of heart).

17.3.7
stadia, Arcadia, Acadia (Maritime Provinces of Canada).

17.3.8
media, redia (parasitic larva), acedia (apathy), multimedia (combined use of media), cyclopedia, hypnopaedia, encyclopedia.

17.3.9
Lydia, Numidia (ancient African country).

17.3.10
Mafia, raffia, tafia (West Indian rum), agraphia (loss of writing ability), dysgraphia (impaired writing ability), paragraphia (psychiatric term).

17.3.11
Sofia, dystrophia.

17.3.12 [see also **17.146**]
aphagia (inability to swallow), dysphagia (difficulty in swallowing), polyphagia (abnormal desire to eat), omophagia (eating of raw food), aerophagia (spasmodic swallowing of air), menorrhagia (excessive bleeding during menstruation), metrorrhagia (abnormal bleeding from uterus).

17.3.13 [see also **17.149**]
diplegia, aquilegia (columbine), hemiplegia, quadriplegia, cycloplegia (paralysis of eye muscles), paraplegia, aqua regia (metal-dissolving corrosive mixture).

17.3.14 [see also **17.150**]
Phrygia, steatopygia (excessively fat buttocks).

17.3.15
cambogia (gum resin), apologia.

17.3.16
myalgia (muscular pain), analgia (inability to feel pain), neuralgia, nephralgia, metralgia (pain in the uterus), gastralgia, arthralgia, otalgia (earache), nostalgia, coxalgia (pain in hip joint), causalgia (pathology term), cardialgia, hemialgia (pain on one side), cephalalgia (headache), odontalgia (toothache).

17.3.17
Somalia, Charlotte Amalie (capital of Virgin Islands).

17.3.18 [see also **17.433**]
dahlia, galea (helmet-shaped structure), vedalia (Australian ladybird), Westphalia, regalia, psoralea (tropical plant), Australia, azalea, Lupercalia (Roman fertility festival), echolalia (psychiatric term), glossolalia (gift of tongues), marginalia (marginal notes), penetralia (innermost parts), genitalia.

17.3.18.1
bacchanalia, Saturnalia (ancient Roman festival), paraphernalia.

17.3.19
Saint Helier, hotelier, psychedelia.

17.3.20
Elia, lobelia, grindelia (flowering plant), Rumelia (part of Ottoman empire), camellia, stapelia (cactus-like plant), Karelia (region of Russia), phocomelia (congenital deformity of limbs), syringomyelia (disease of spinal cord).

17.3.21
ILEA, cilia, Pamphylia (ancient Asian region), familiar, Cecilia, conciliar (of ecclesiastical councils), Brasília, sensibilia, unfamiliar, juvenilia, bougainvillea.

17.3.21.1
memorabilia, imponderabilia.

17.3.21.2
zoophilia, paedophilia, Anglophilia, haemophilia, necrophilia, coprophilia (abnormal interest in faeces), Germanophilia, ailurophilia (liking for cats).

17.3.22
foliar (relating to leaves), Grolier (denoting decorative bookbinding style), Mongolia, magnolia, Aetolia (mountainous region of Greece), melancholia, Anatolia (Asian part of Turkey).

17.3.23
Julia, dulia (veneration for saints), abulia (loss of willpower), peculiar,

hyperdulia (veneration for Virgin Mary).

17.3.24
lamia (monster in classical mythology), zamia (tropical plant), macadamia (Australian tree), adynamia (weakness), Mesopotamia.

17.3.25
Urmia (Iranian lake), hypothermia, hyperthermia.

17.3.26
pyaemia (blood poisoning), leukaemia, ischaemia (inadequate blood supply), Bohemia, anaemia, uraemia, sapraemia (blood poisoning), academia, tularaemia (infectious disease), hyperaemia (excess blood in organs), bacteraemia (bacteria in the blood), septicaemia, hypoglycaemia (insufficient blood sugar), hyperglycaemia (excessive blood sugar).

17.3.26.1
toxaemia, anoxaemia (oxygen deficiency in blood).

17.3.27
skimmia (ornamental shrub), bulimia (insatiable hunger).

17.3.28
kalmia (evergreen shrub), ophthalmia (inflammation of the eye), xerophthalmia (eye disease).

17.3.29 [see also **17.434**]
pannier (large basket), Hispania, Britannia.

17.3.30
Sarnia (Canadian port), Goiânia (Brazilian city), Titania, Oceania (Pacific islands), Christiania.

17.3.31
mania, Rainier, Albania, Rumania, leishmania (pathogenic protozoan), Tasmania, Campania (region of Italy), Lithuania, Araucania (region of Chile), miscellanea, Pomerania (region of Eu-

rope), collectanea (miscellany), Transylvania, Pennsylvania.

17.3.31.1
theomania (religious mania), nymphomania, phagomania (compulsive desire to eat), egomania, Anglomania, monomania, hypomania (psychiatric term), pyromania, dipsomania, kleptomania, mythomania (psychiatric term), bibliomania, decalcomania (process of transferring designs), megalomania, balletomania, erotomania (abnormally strong sexual desire).

17.3.31.2
Mauritania, Ruritania, Lusitania, Tripolitania (part of Libya).

17.3.32
hernia, vernier (measuring scale), Hibernia.

17.3.33 [see also **17.435**]
taenia (ancient Greek headband), xenia (botany term), gardenia, Armenia, Ruthenia (region of Russia), asthenia, Slovenia (republic of Yugoslavia), catamenia (menstruation), leucopenia (insufficient white blood cells), hebephrenia (form of schizophrenia), schizophrenia, sarracenia (insectivorous plant), myasthenia (muscular weakness), neurasthenia (nervous breakdown).

17.3.34
linear, tinea (fungal skin disease), zinnia (flowering plant), robinia (tree genus), Sardinia, Virginia, bauhinia (ornamental plant), bilinear, trilinear, collinear (on same straight line), Fourdrinier (paper-making machine), actinia (sea anemone), Bithynia (ancient Asian country), vaccinia (cowpox), gloxinia, rectilinear, curvilinear, interlinear, Abyssinia.

17.3.35
cornea, salicornia (salt-marsh plant), California.

17.3.36
Ionia, zirconia (chemical compound), Snowdonia, aphonia (loss of voice), dysphonia (speech impairment), begonia, mahonia (evergreen shrub), paulownia (Japanese tree), pneumonia, ammonia, bignonia (tropical shrub), boronia (aromatic shrub), claytonia (succulent plant), boltonia (flowering plant), houstonia (flowering plant), Livonia, Slavonia (region of Yugoslavia), Caledonia, Macedonia, Babylonia, eudemonia (happiness), myotonia (lack of muscle tone), catatonia (form of schizophrenia), aniseikonia (visual defect), bronchopneumonia, pleuropneumonia.

17.3.36.1
pogonia (orchid), Paphlagonia (ancient Roman province), Patagonia.

17.3.36.2
valonia (acorns used in tanning), escallonia (ornamental shrub), Cephalonia (Greek island), Catalonia.

17.3.37
myopia, diplopia (double vision), photopia (eye's adaptation to light), Utopia, ectopia (displacement of body part), dystopia (worst possible place), presbyopia, amblyopia (impaired vision), Ethiopia, cornucopia, asthenopia (eyestrain).

17.3.37.1
nyctalopia (night blindness), hemeralopia (day blindness).

17.3.37.2
tritanopia (blue blindness), protanopia (red blindness), deuteranopia (green blindness).

17.3.37.3
scotopia (adjustment for night vision), heterotopia (displacement of body part).

17.3.38
area, Caria (ancient Asian region), varia (collection of literary works), Ica-

ria (Greek island), cercaria (larva of parasitic flatworm), Bulgaria, Dzungaria (region of China), filaria (parasitic roundworm), Samaria, Bavaria, calvaria (top of skull), miliaria (heat rash), araucaria (coniferous tree), adularia (mineral), laminaria (brown seaweed), sanguinaria (plant yielding red dye), cineraria, persicaria (red-stemmed plant), urticaria, alfilaria (flowering plant), Carpentaria (gulf in north Australia).

17.3.38.1
malaria, talaria (winged sandals), calceolaria.

17.3.39
feria (Catholic non-feast day), ceria (chemical compound), Iberia, Liberia, Siberia, inferior, Egeria (female adviser), Nigeria, Algeria, krameria (South American shrub), superior, bacteria, ulterior, anterior, interior, hysteria, wisteria, posterior, exterior, gaultheria (aromatic shrub), diphtheria, latimeria (primitive fish), cryptomeria (coniferous tree), cafeteria, echeveria (tropical plant), sansevieria (cultivated plant), nitrobacteria (soil bacteria).

17.3.40
Syria, Styria (province of Austria), porphyria (hereditary metabolic disease), Illyria, Assyria.

17.3.41
scoria (mass of lava), Gloria, gloria, noria (waterwheel with buckets attached), thoria (chemical compound), euphoria, dysphoria (uneasy feeling), peloria (botany term), Pretoria, Vitória (Brazilian port), Victoria, Astoria, phantasmagoria.

17.3.42
courier, urea, curia, Manchuria, Etruria, pyuria (medical term), Liguria (region of Italy), anuria (suppression of urine production), dysuria (painful urination), polyuria (excessive urine production), thiourea (crystalline substance), ketonuria (medical term), phosphaturia (medical term), haematuria, phenylketonuria (congenital metabolic disorder).

17.3.42.1
albuminuria (urine containing albumin), haemoglobinuria (urine containing haemoglobin).

17.3.42.2
Masuria (region of Poland), glycosuria (excess sugar in urine).

17.3.43
Cambria (Latin name for Wales), Salambria (Greek river).

17.3.44
Umbria (mountainous region of Italy), Cumbria, Northumbria.

17.3.45
Andrea, calandria (part of heat-exchanger).

17.3.46
cassia (tropical plant), glacier, brassiere, Circassia (region of Russia).

17.3.47
mahseer (Indian fish), tarsier, intarsia (mosaic of inlaid wood).

17.3.48
fancier, financier, estancia (Spanish-American ranch).

17.3.49 [see also 17.326]
indicia (distinguishing markings), comitia (Roman legislative assembly), Phoenicia, notitia (register of ecclesiastical districts), adventitia (body organ's external covering).

17.3.50
Numantia (ancient Spanish city), tradescantia, bona vacantia (unclaimed goods).

17.3.51
lithia (chemical compound), Pythia (Greek mythological priestess), stichomythia (dialogue in Greek drama).

17.3.52
Cynthia, Carinthia (Austrian province).

17.3.53 [see also **17.436**]
Xavier (Spanish saint), Moldavia, Moravia, Belgravia, Octavia, Scandinavia.

17.3.54
trivia, Olivia, Bolivia.

17.3.55
fovea (anatomy term), Segovia, synovia (lubricating fluid in joint), Monrovia (capital of Liberia).

17.3.56
apraxia (disorder of nervous system), ataxia (lack of muscular coordination), ataraxia (peace of mind), echopraxia (psychiatric term).

17.3.57
cachexia (weakened condition), alexia (word blindness), dyslexia, anorexia, hyperpyrexia (extremely high fever).

17.3.58
ixia (flowering plant), asphyxia.

17.3.59 [see also **17.332**]
glazier, brazier, grazier, Caucasia, aphasia (disorder of nervous system), dysphasia (impaired coordination of speech), aplasia (congenital absence of organ), dysplasia (abnormal development of organ), Aspasia (ancient Greek courtesan), fantasia, hypoplasia (incomplete development of organ), hyperplasia (enlargement of body part), Anastasia, Australasia, anaplasia (biology term), euthanasia, achondroplasia (skeletal disorder), antonomasia (rhetorical device).

17.3.60 [see also **17.334**]
framboesia (tropical disease), Silesia (central European region), silesia (twill-weave fabric), ecclesia (church congregation), amnesia, aesthesia (normal sensitivity), analgesia, Indonesia, paramnesia (memory disorder), hypermnesia (unusually good memory), telaesthesia (paranormal perception),

thermaesthesia (sensitivity to temperature), anaesthesia, kinaesthesia (sensitivity to movement), synaesthesia (medical term), hypaesthesia (reduced sensibility to touch), cryptaesthesia (extrasensory perception), hyperkinesia (excessive movement), hyperaesthesia (increased sensitivity).

17.3.61
Tunisia, Dionysia (ancient Greek festivals).

17.3.62 [see also **17.335**]
osier, hosier, crosier (bishop's crook), ambrosia, afrormosia (hard teak-like wood).

17.4 [see also **8**]
ayah, buyer, dyer, liar, flyer, maya (Hindu concept), Maia (Greek mythological character), briar, crier, dryer, fryer, friar, prior, stria, via.

Aglaia (Greek goddess), inlier (geology term), supplier, outlier (geology term), papaya, Uriah, greenbrier, sweetbrier, latria (Catholic supreme worship), Messiah, Josiah, Isaiah.

Surabaya (Indonesian port), Zedekiah, Hezekiah, Obadiah, lammergeier (rare vulture), jambalaya (Creole savoury dish), multiplier, Nehemiah, Jeremiah, Biedermeier (conventional), stegomyia (mosquito), Zephaniah, occupier, Araguaia (Brazilian river).

peripeteia (abrupt turn of events), photomultiplier (device measuring electromagnetic radiation).

17.4.1
modifier, qualifier, amplifier, magnifier, purifier, pacifier, rectifier, quantifier (indicator of quantity), humidifier, disqualifier, preamplifier, intensifier, dehumidifier.

17.4.2
pariah, Zachariah, Zechariah, Black Maria.

17.5 [see also **17.430**]
oyer (13th-century assize), coir (coconut fibre), Goya, hoya (Australasian plant), soya, caloyer (Greek Orthodox monk), employer, sequoia (giant redwood tree), destroyer, dianoia (philosophy term), paranoia.

17.6
boa, koa (Hawaian tree), goer, goa (Tibetan gazelle), Goa (district of India), lower, blower, mower, moa, Noah, rower, grower, proa (sailing boat), sower, stoa.

Iowa, jerboa, Balboa (port on Panama Canal), balboa (Panamanian currency), widower, playgoer, churchgoer, racegoer, Alloa, follower, aloha, glass-blower, Samoa, genoa, Genoa, anoa (Indonesian cattle), borrower.

Shenandoah, concertgoer, Krakatoa, Mies van der Rohe (US architect).

17.7
Padua, Joshua, vacua (*plural of* vacuum), rescuer, valuer, Capua (Italian town), Papua, decidua (membrane lining pregnant uterus).

17.7.1
jaguar, Nicaragua.

17.7.2
mantua (loose gown), Mantua (Italian city), Gargantua.

17.8
doer, brewer, sewer, ewer, skewer, skua, Dewar, viewer, wrongdoer, pursuer, reviewer, evildoer, tamandua (tree-living mammal), Porirua (New Zealand city), Rotorua, revenuer (*US* revenue officer), interviewer.

17.9
Abba, dabber (printers' ink pad), jabber, blabber, slabber (*Dialect* slobber), crabber (crab fisherman).

17.10
arbour, barber, harbour, Saba (West Indian island), klangfarbe (musical

term), casaba (melon), Ali Baba, Orizaba (Mexican city).

17.11
caber, labour, neighbour, sabre, ceiba (tropical tree), tabor (small drum), Weber (German composer), belabour (thrash severely).

17.12
Berber, Djerba (Tunisian island), Thurber (US humorist).

17.13
Sheba, amoeba, Kariba (dam on Zambezi river), zareba (enclosure around African village), Beersheba (Israeli town), Bathsheba, entamoeba (parasitic amoeba).

17.14
bibber (drinker), fibber, gibber, calibre, Excalibur.

17.15
Khyber, fibre, briber, scriber (pointed tool), Tiber, copaiba (yellowish resin), subscriber.

17.16
cobber, jobber, clobber, slobber, robber, swabber (*Slang* uncouth fellow), stockjobber (stock exchange dealer).

17.17
dauber, Micawber, absorber, Catawba (American Indian people).

17.18
lobar, sober, October, araroba (Brazilian tree), Manitoba.

17.19
lubber (clumsy person), blubber, rubber, scrubber, grubber (heavy hoe), landlubber.

17.20
goober (peanut), juba (Negro dance), Luba (African people), Cuba, scuba, Nuba (Sudanese people), tuber, tuba, Tshiluba (African language), Aruba (West Indian island), simarouba (tropical tree).

17.21

Aqaba (port of Jordan), cordoba (Nicaraguan currency), dagoba (Buddhist shrine), jellaba (hooded cloak), Annaba (Algerian port), mastaba (pyramid prototype), Addis Ababa.

17.22

Elba, Melba.

17.23

amber, camber, clamber, mamba, samba, sambar (Asian deer), caramba (Asian tree), liquidambar (yellow balsam), viola da gamba.

17.24

ember, Bemba (African people), member, Pemba (Tanzanian island), remember, nonmember, dismember, December, September, November.

17.25

limber, timber, marimba.

17.26

ombre (card game), sombre, Zomba (Malawi city).

17.27

umber, cumber (to hinder), Humber, lumbar, lumber, clumber (type of spaniel), slumber, number, rumba, cucumber, encumber, Columba, outnumber, disencumber.

17.28

backer, Dakar (capital of Senegal), Dacca (capital of Bangladesh), lacquer, slacker, smacker, knacker, packer, cracker, tracker, stacker, hijacker, Malacca (Malaysian state), malacca (walking stick), alpaca, maraca, firecracker, nutcracker, attacker, greywacke (dark rock), bushwhacker (*Austral* travelling woodlander), portulaca (tropical plant).

17.29

barker, kaka (New Zealand parrot), charkha (Indian spinning wheel), marker, parka, Parker, paca (large rodent), bidarka (Eskimo canoe), sifaka (Madagascan mammal), Osaka (Japanese port), moussaka, Lusaka (capital

of Zambia), nosy-parker, anasarca (medical term), koulibiaca (Russian fish pie), Hamilcar Barca (Carthaginian general).

17.30

acre, baker, faker, laker (lake cargo boat), maker, naker (small kettledrum), nacre (mother-of-pearl), Quaker, breaker, saker (large falcon), shaker, taker, weka (New Zealand bird).

cloaca, haymaker, shoemaker, Jamaica, clockmaker, bookmaker, matchmaker, watchmaker, pacemaker, dressmaker, peacemaker, tiebreaker, jawbreaker, lawbreaker, backbreaker, strikebreaker, icebreaker, housebreaker, heartbreaker, moonraker (square sail), boneshaker, caretaker, wiseacre, stavesacre (Eurasian plant).

moneymaker, merrymaker, boilermaker, troublemaker, undertaker.

17.31

chequer, checker, Mecca, pecker, wrecker, trekker, Rebecca, exchequer, woodpecker, oxpecker (African starling), Voortrekker (Afrikaner settler), Rijeka (Yugoslavian port), doubledecker.

17.32

burka (Muslim garment), Gurkha, circa, shirker, worker, tear-jerker, outworker, mazurka, wonder-worker.

17.33

beaker, speaker, Spica (star), squeaker, streaker, seeker, sika (Japanese deer), theca (biology term), Guernica, loudspeaker, eureka, Dominica, Costa Rica, spermatheca (biology term), Tanganyika, Judaica (Jewish literature), bibliotheca (library), Cyrenaica (region of Libya).

17.34

bicker, kicker, dicker (*US* to barter), liquor, clicker (factory foreman), flicker, slicker (*US* sly person), nicker, snicker, picker, pricker (*US* prickle), shicker (*Austral* alcoholic drink), ticker, sticker, vicar, wicker, whicker (whinny).

Baedeker (travel guidebook), Boudicca (Latin name of Boadicea), trafficker, silica, replica, bootlicker, arnica (plant genus), Seneca, picnicker, areca (Asian palm), Africa, paprika, brassica (vegetable genus), Jessica, vesica (bladder), Corsica, Utica (ancient African city), swastika, spitsticker (wood-engraving tool).

angelica, basilica (Roman building), nux vomica (tree yielding poisonous seeds), amphitricha (bacteria), peritricha (bacteria), erotica, exotica, Antarctica, materia medica (study of drugs).

17.34.1
Monica, moniker, Salonika (Greek port), harmonica, japonica (Japanese quince), Veronica, santonica (Oriental plant).

17.34.2
Erica, America.

17.34.3
Attica, sciatica, hepatica (woodland plant).

17.35
duiker (African antelope), hiker, plica (anatomical fold), Micah, mica, pica, piker (*Austral* wild bullock), pika (burrowing mammal), spica (spiral bandage), striker, hitchhiker, Formica (*Trademark*), myrica (medicinal root bark), lorica (protective shell), balalaika.

17.36
ocker (*Austral* boorish person), cocker, chocker (*Austral* full up), docker, Fokker, locker, blocker, mocha, knocker, quokka (small wallaby), rocker, soccer, shocker, stocker, Knickerbocker (*US* New Yorker).

17.37
corker, hawker, porker, talker, stalker, walker, yorker (cricket term), Minorca, deerstalker, jaywalker, sleepwalker, shopwalker, streetwalker, Majorca, kwashiorkor (protein deficiency).

17.38
ochre, oka (Turkish weight), oca (South American plant), coca (Andean shrub), choker, joker, smoker, poker, broker, croaker (tropical fish), stoker, nonsmoker, stockbroker, pawnbroker, Cape Roca (westernmost point of Europe), Asoka (Indian emperor), mediocre, tapioca, carioca (Brazilian dance), Fukuoka (Japanese city), Shizuoka (Japanese city).

17.39
UCCA, chukker (polo term), fucker, mucker (*Slang* friend), pukka, pucker, trucker, succour, sucker, tucker, yucca, felucca (Mediterranean boat), seersucker, bloodsucker, sapsucker (*US* woodpecker), goatsucker (*US* nightjar), motherfucker, honeysucker (nectar-feeding bird).

17.40
cooker, hooker, hookah, looker, onlooker.

17.41
lucre, snooker, euchre (US card game), nucha (nape of neck), palooka (*US* clumsy person), manuka (New Zealand tree), verruca, bazooka, noctiluca (light-emitting organism), melaleuca (Australian shrub), involucre (botany term), Juan de Fuca (US–Canadian strait).

17.42
abaca (Philippine plant), stomacher (decorative piece of material), Hanukkah (Jewish festival), spinnaker, massacre, Whitaker, Ithaca, Karnataka (Indian state).

17.43
anchor, banker, Bangka (Indonesian island), canker, hanker, flanker, spanker,
rancour, ranker, chancre, tanker, tanka
(Japanese verse), Sri Lanka, barranca
(*US* ravine), Casablanca, lingua franca
(common language).

17.44
Inca, Dinka (Sudanese people), blinker, clinker, drinker, sinker, tinker,
stinker, thinker, winker, Treblinka
(Nazi concentration camp), headshrinker, stotinka (Bulgarian coin),
freethinker.

17.45
conquer, conker, concha (shell-shaped
body part), tonka (tree yielding fragrant seeds), Dzongka (Asian language).

17.46
bunker, punka (palm-leaf fan), Junker
(Prussian landowner), mossbunker (US
fish), spelunker (cave explorer).

17.47
lascar (East Indian sailor), Alaska, marasca (European cherry tree), Nebraska, Athabaska (Canadian lake), Madagascar.

17.48
risker, frisker, whisker.

17.49
busker, Musca (constellation), tusker.

17.50
catcher, dacha (Russian country
house), stature, Thatcher, thatcher, viscacha (South American rodent), backscratcher, oystercatcher, baby-snatcher,
body-snatcher, cradle-snatcher, oboe
da caccia (former musical instrument).

17.51
archer, marcher, departure.

17.52
nature, denature, legislature.

17.53
lecher, Fletcher, fletcher (maker of ar-
rows), stretcher.

17.54
lurcher, nurture, searcher, researcher,
gutta-percha (rubbery substance).

17.55
feature, Nietzsche (German philosopher), creature, preacher, teacher,
schoolteacher.

17.56
pitcher, twitcher, dowitcher (arctic
bird), forfeiture, garniture (decoration),
furniture, miniature, Onitsha (Nigerian
port), signature, portraiture, expenditure, discomfiture, literature, temperature, investiture, primogeniture (legal
term).

17.57
botcher, boccia (Italian bowls game),
watcher, topnotcher.

17.58
scorcher, torture.

17.59
cloture (closure in US Senate), poacher, panocha (coarse sugar).

17.60
sloucher, voucher.

17.61
suture, future, cachucha (Spanish
dance).

17.62
cubature (cubic contents), arcature
(small arcade), ligature, filature (silk-
spinning), tablature (form of musical
notation), aperture, quadrature (maths
term), curvature, coverture (legal
term), judicature, musculature, nomenclature.

17.63
fracture, contracture, manufacture.

17.64
lecture, conjecture, architecture.

17.65
picture, stricture.

17.66
structure, substructure, superstructure, infrastructure.

17.67
cincture (surround), tincture.

17.68
juncture, puncture, conjuncture, venipuncture (puncturing of a vein), acupuncture.

17.69
culture, multure (miller's fee), vulture, sepulture (burial), viniculture, sericulture (silkworm rearing), agriculture, viticulture (grape cultivation), horticulture, monoculture (single-crop cultivation), aquaculture (biology term), counterculture (alternative social culture), arboriculture.

17.70
bencher (a judge), denture, trencher (wooden platter), venture, debenture, backbencher, indenture, adventure, peradventure, misadventure.

17.71
lyncher, clincher, flincher, wincher.

17.72
capture, rapture, recapture, enrapture.

17.73
gesture, vesture (garment).

17.74
posture, imposture.

17.75
texture, contexture (weaving).

17.76
fixture, mixture, affixture, admixture, intermixture.

17.77
adder, ladder, bladder, madder, stepladder.

17.78
ardour, khaddar (Indian cotton cloth), cadre (nucleus of trained personnel), Garda (Italian lake), larder, RADA, cicada, Haggadah (part of Jewish literature), armada, monarda (US plant), retarder, Nevada, enchilada (Mexican food), autostrada (Italian motorway).

17.78.1
panada (thick sauce), Granada (Spanish city), promenader.

17.79
aider, Ada, Ede (Dutch city), raider, grader (earth-levelling machine), trader, Seder (Jewish ceremonial meal), Veda (Hindu scriptures), wader, Grenada, crusader, Bethsaida (Israeli town), Rig-Veda (Hindu poetry), invader, alameda (US tree-lined promenade), Ayurveda (Hindu medical treatise).

17.80
Edda (Old Norse poems), bedder (college servant), Kedah (Malaysian state), kheda (elephant enclosure), Cheddar, header, spreader, shredder, shedder (animal that moults), tedder, Vedda (Sri Lankan people), homesteader.

17.81
girder, herder, murder, purdah.

17.82
feeder, leader, Leda (Greek mythological character), bleeder, Blida (Algerian city), pleader, reader, breeder, Breda (Dutch city), cedar, seeder, cheerleader, ringleader, stockbreeder, proofreader, lip-reader, interpleader (legal term), olla podrida (Spanish stew).

17.83
bidder, Jidda (Saudi Arabian port), whydah (African weaverbird), Saida (Lebanese port), Florida, reseda (Mediterranean plant), Cressida, consider, Andromeda, reconsider, spina bifida, asafoetida (foul-smelling resin), primigravida (obstetrics term), multigravida (obstetrics term), camera lucida (microscope attachment).

17.84

eider, Ida, guider, Haida (American Indian people), glider, slider, spider, rider, cider, Oneida (US lake), joyrider, nightrider, outrider, decider, insider, outsider, divider.

17.85

dodder, fodder, plodder.

17.86

order, boarder, border, hoarder, Lauder (Scottish singer), sawder (to flatter), warder, suborder (biology term), recorder, marauder, disorder.

17.87

moider (*Dialect* to bother), embroider.

17.88

odour, Oder (European river), coda, coder, loader, soda, decoder, encoder, Sargodha (Pakistani city), pagoda, Baroda (Indian state), Fashoda (Sudanese town).

17.89

chowder (thick clam soup), Gouda, howdah (seat on elephant), powder, gunpowder.

17.90

udder, chuddar (Indian shawl), judder, rudder, shudder.

17.91

Judah, brooder, Tudor, Barbuda (West Indian island), mouthbrooder (African fish), intruder, Bermuda, draught-excluder, barracuda.

17.92

gelada (African baboon), Canada, Kannada (Indian language), forwarder (bookbinder), ambassador.

17.93

elder, welder.

17.94

fielder, shielder, wielder.

17.95

builder, guilder, Hilda, tilde (phonetic symbol), shipbuilder, Saint Kilda (Hebridean island), Matilda, bewilder.

17.96

alder, Balder (Norse god).

17.97

older, boulder, folder, holder, moulder, smoulder, polder, solder, shoulder, shareholder, freeholder, beholder, stockholder, stadholder (Dutch chief magistrate), smallholder, gasholder, leaseholder, householder.

17.98

candour, dander, gander, panda, pander, sander, vanda (orchid), Luanda (capital of Angola), Rwanda (African republic), Buganda (Ugandan state), Uganda, backhander, right-hander, left-hander, philander, solander (botanical specimen box), outlander (stranger), germander (flowering plant), pomander, Menander (Greek dramatist), expander, Miranda, Lysander, goosander (type of duck), dittander (small plant), bystander, propaganda, gerrymander, calamander (hard wood), salamander, Anaximander (Greek philosopher).

17.98.1

Leander (Greek mythological character), meander, oleander, coriander.

17.98.2

veranda, jacaranda (tropical tree), memoranda.

17.99

Lahnda (Pakistani language), slander, commander, Alexander.

17.100

remainder, attainder (former legal term).

17.101

bender, fender, gender, lender, blender, splendour, slender, mender, spender, render, sender, tender, vendor, Venda (African people), weekender, defender, offender, agenda, engender, suspender, surrender, descender (printing term), ascender (printing term), bartender, pretender, attender, extender, hacienda, moneylender.

17.102
hinder, Pindar (Greek poet), cinder, tinder, calendar, calender (machine for smoothing cloth), cylinder, provender (feed for livestock).

17.103
binder, finder, hinder (at the rear), minder, grinder, winder, bookbinder, viewfinder, rangefinder, pathfinder, reminder, rewinder, sidewinder.

17.104
Fonda, Honda (*Trademark*), ponder, squander, Rhondda, wander, yonder, Golconda (ruined Indian town), transponder (radio transmitter–receiver), anaconda.

17.105
launder, maunder (behave aimlessly).

17.106
joinder (legal term), rejoinder, nonjoinder (legal term), misjoinder (legal term).

17.107
bounder, founder, flounder, rounder, sounder.

17.108
under, chunder, blunder, plunder, sunder, thunder, wonder, osmunda (fern), thereunder, hereunder, asunder, rotunda (circular domed building), floribunda (cultivated rosebush), barramunda (Australian fish).

17.109
seconder, bilander (small cargo ship), islander, Highlander, colander, Jullundur (Indian city), woodlander, Greenlander, Laplander, lavender, New Zealander.

17.110
chaffer (haggle), gaffer, Jaffa, Staffa, zaffer (impure cobalt oxide).

17.111
chafer (beetle), wafer, cockchafer.

17.112
heifer, zephyr.

17.113
ephah (Hebrew unit of measure), FIFA, reefer, Recife (Brazilian port), synalepha (linguistics term).

17.114
differ, conifer, aquifer (water-containing rock), thurifer (incense carrier), Lucifer, crucifer (family of plants), Potiphar (biblical character), rotifer (minute aquatic animal), Apocrypha.

17.115
Haifa (Israeli port), hypha (part of fungus), lifer, cipher, sypher (woodworking term), decipher, encipher.

17.116
offer, Offa (king of Mercia), coffer, scoffer, proffer.

17.117
Ophir (biblical region), gopher, goffer (to crimp), loafer, sofa, chauffeur.

17.118
buffer, duffer, luffa (tropical climbing plant), bluffer, snuffer, puffer, suffer, chufa (tropical sedge).

17.119
loofah, woofer (loudspeaker), tufa (soft rock).

17.120
agrapha (unrecorded sayings of Christ), metaphor, Christopher, telegrapher, philosopher, Pseudepigrapha (Jewish writings).

17.120.1 [further rhymes may be derived from **16.90.2**]
biographer, stenographer (*US* shorthand typist), photographer, radiographer, Hagiographa (section of Old

Testament), choreographer, historiographer (historian).

17.121
alpha, pedalfer (lime-deficient soil), alfalfa, Wadi Halfa (Sudanese town).

17.122
camphor, chamfer.

17.123
dagger, gagger, Jagger, nagger, quagga (extinct horse), bragger, saggar (fireproof box for pottery), stagger, swagger, zigzagger (sewing-machine attachment), carpetbagger.

17.124
aga (Turkish title), laager (African camp), lager, raga (Indian musical term), saga.

17.125
agar, eagre (tidal bore), jaeger, telega (Russian four-wheeled cart), rutabaga (*US* swede).

17.126
egger (moth), beggar, bootlegger.

17.127
burger, burgher, turgor (biology term), virga (meteorology term), beefburger, hamburger, Limburger (strong white cheese).

17.128
eager, meagre, Riga (Russian port), Vega (bright star), bodega (Spanish wine shop), beleaguer, quadriga (chariot), Antigua.

17.129
chigger (mite larva), digger, figure, jigger, snigger, rigour, rigger, trigger, vigour, prefigure, disfigure, transfigure, alegar (malt vinegar), omega, senega (milkwort plant), vinegar, Honegger (French composer), outrigger.

17.130
Eiger, Geiger, liger (lion–tiger hybrid), saiga (Asian antelope), tiger, taiga (coniferous forests), canaigre (US dock plant), Auriga (constellation).

17.131
Dogger, dogger (Dutch fishing vessel), jogger, logger, wagga (*Austral* blanket), pettifogger, Wagga Wagga (Australian city).

17.132
auger (boring tool), augur (predict), sauger (US fish), massasauga (US venomous snake), Mississauga (Canadian town).

17.133
ogre, toga, yoga, Saratoga, Ticonderoga (US battle site).

17.134
bugger, lugger (small boat), slugger (*US* hard-hitting person), mugger, nuggar (Egyptian sailing boat), rugger, Srinagar (Indian city), huggermugger.

17.135
sugar, Yuga (Hindu age of mankind).

17.136
cougar, Luger, ruga (biology term), Kruger (Boer statesman), beluga (large sturgeon), sastruga (ridge on snowfield), Chattanooga.

17.137
realgar (rare mineral), Trafalgar.

17.138
Olga, brolga (Australian bird), Volga.

17.139
mulga (Australian acacia), vulgar.

17.140 [see also **17.245**]
anger, Bangor, languor, clangour, panga (African knife), Tanga (Tanzanian port), Kananga (city in Zaïre), Zamboanga (Philippine port).

17.141 [see also **17.246**]
finger, linger, forefinger, fishfinger, anhinga (aquatic bird), malinger, syringa (flowering shrub), churinga (Aboriginal sacred amulet), cotinga (tropical bird), alcheringa (Aboriginal mythical golden age).

17.142
conger, conga, Tonga, Tsonga (African people), Alba Longa (city of ancient Latium), Rarotonga (Pacific island).

17.143
hunger, munga (*Austral* food), scaremonger, whoremonger, warmonger, fellmonger (dealer in animal skins), fishmonger, costermonger, scandalmonger, ironmonger.

17.144
agger (Roman earthwork), badger, cadger.

17.145
charger, Djaja (Indonesian mountain), rajah, enlarger, turbocharger, supercharger (compressor), maharajah.

17.146 [see also **17.3.12**]
gauger (customs officer), major, stager (experienced person), wager, teenager.

17.147
ledger, dredger, Saint Leger.

17.148
merger, perjure, verger, verdure.

17.149 [see also **17.3.13**]
Ouija, procedure, supersedure.

17.150 [see also **17.3.14**]
voyager, mortgagor, packager, veliger (larva of mollusc), villager, armiger (heraldic term), manager, cottager, integer, vintager (grape harvester).

17.151
Niger, Elijah.

17.152
bodger, codger, dodger, loggia, lodger, Roger.

17.153
Borgia, forger, gorger, Georgia.

17.154
dowager, tanager (US songbird), onager (Iranian wild ass), sockdologer (*US* decisive blow), astrologer.

17.155
grandeur, phalanger (arboreal marsupial).

17.156
danger, manger, ranger, stranger, endanger, arranger, hydrangea, bushranger (person living in bush), moneychanger, autochanger (record-changing device).

17.157
injure, ginger, Jinja (Ugandan town), harbinger, wharfinger (wharf manager), challenger, Salinger (US writer), derringer (US pistol), porringer (small dish), Massinger (English dramatist), passenger, messenger, Kissinger, scavenger.

17.158
lounger, scrounger.

17.159
conjure, blunger (large vat), plunger, sponger.

17.160
Allah, Bala (Welsh lake), calla (African plant), caller (*Scot* fresh food), pallor, valour, Whyalla (Australian port), Valhalla, cavalla (tropical fish), boobialla (Australian shrub), Caracalla (Roman emperor).

17.161
gala, Galle (Sri Lankan port), challah (Jewish plaited loaf), haler (Czech coin), Mahler, parlour, thaler (silver coin), nyala (African antelope), koala, cabbala (ancient Jewish tradition), Ambala (Indian city), trehala (sugary substance), Kampala, impala, Marsala, Uppsala (Swedish city), cantala (tropical plant).

17.161.1
kamala (East Indian tree), Guatemala.

17.162
ala (winglike structure), alar (relating to wings), bailor, baler, scalar, scaler, chela (Hindu religious disciple), jailer, mailer, malar (relating to the cheek),

kwela (South African beat music), trailer, sailor, tailor, Taylor, whaler, Waler (*Austral* saddle horse), Akela, loud-hailer, inhaler, shillelagh, blackmailer, wholesaler, retailer, zarzuela (Spanish operetta), Venezuela.

17.163
Keller, feller, fellah (Arab peasant), heller (old German coin), Pella (ancient Greek city), speller, seller, cellar, cella (room in temple), teller, stellar, dweller.

paella, Viyella (*Trademark*), mabela (African ground corn), rubella, bierkeller, shigella (bacterium), lamella (thin layer), prunella (strong fabric), canella (West Indian spice), Capella (bright star), propeller, chlorella (microscopic plant), umbrella, micella (chemical term), bonsela (African gift), saltcellar, novella, rosella (Australian parrot).

Rockefeller, columella (biology term), villanella (Neapolitan song), salmonella, citronella (Asian grass), gentianella (flowering plant), fustanella (Greek man's white skirt), Cinderella, mozzarella, varicella (chickenpox), vorticella (small animal), storyteller, fortune-teller, tarantella, fenestella (small opening in wall).

17.163.1
glabella (medical term), clarabella (organ stop), Isabella.

17.163.2
patella, panatella.

17.164
curler, pearler (pearl-fishing boat), purler (headlong fall).

17.165
chela (claw), dealer, feeler, healer, kneeler, peeler, spieler (*US* glib talker), sealer, Sheila, tela (web-like structure), vealer (veal calf), velar (linguistics term), wheeler, tequila, candela (unit of luminous intensity), weigela (Asian shrub), sequela (medical term), side-wheeler (paddle-wheeled riverboat), Philomela (Greek mythological princess).

17.166
killer, filler, miller, pillar, squilla (shrimp), thriller, Scylla (Greek sea nymph), scilla (bell-flowered plant), Schiller, schiller (metallic lustre), tiller, villa.

weedkiller, painkiller, chinchilla, spinechiller, cedilla, megillah (Hebrew scroll), mamilla, similar, Aquila (constellation), Priscilla, pteryla (ornithology term), pralltriller (musical term), basilar (anatomy term), Attila, flotilla, mantilla (Spanish scarf), scintilla (minute amount), distiller, Anguilla (West Indian island), axilla (armpit), maxilla (upper jawbone).

sabadilla (tropical plant), granadilla (passion-flower), sapodilla (tropical evergreen tree), drosophila (fruit fly), gypsophila (Mediterranean plant), dissimilar, verisimilar (likely to be true).

17.166.1
manilla, Manila (Philippine port), vanilla, manzanilla (very dry sherry).

17.166.2
papilla (small protuberance), caterpillar.

17.166.3
barilla (salty plant extract), guerrilla, gorilla, zorilla (African mammal), cascarilla (West Indian shrub), camarilla (Spanish cabal), sarsaparilla.

17.167
filar (relating to thread), hyla (tree frog), miler, tiler, Tyler, strobila (body of tapeworm), Delilah, compiler, astylar (architectural term), Rottweiler (breed of dog), amphistylar (architectural term).

17.168
olla (Spanish cooking pot), collar, choler (anger), scholar, dollar, dolour

(grief), holler, squalor, wallah, rix-dollar (former Dutch silver coin), corolla, Eurodollar, petrodollar (money earned exporting petroleum), ayatollah.

17.169
caller, faller (*Austral* lumberjack), mauler, brawler, crawler, trawler, footballer, mandorla (art term).

17.170
oiler, boiler, boyla (Aboriginal witch doctor), spoiler, broiler.

17.171
bowler, bola (South-American Indian weapon), cola, coaler (coal transporter), Ndola (Zambian city), Lola, molar, mola (a fish), poler (*Austral* idler), polar, roller, stroller, solar, tola (Indian weight), volar (anatomy term), Zola (French novelist).

payola (*US* bribe), viola, tombola, Angola, Gongola (Nigerian state), potholer, premolar, bipolar, transpolar, roadroller, steamroller, controller, scagliola (imitation marble).

hemiola (musical term), Carniola (region of Yugoslavia), Moviola (*Trademark*), Coca-Cola (*Trademark*), Pianola (*Trademark*), Hispaniola (West Indian island), Gorgonzola.

17.172
Fowler (English grammarian), howler, growler, prowler, bobowler (*Dialect* large moth).

17.173
colour, mullah (Muslim religious leader), muller (heavy grinding instrument), cruller (US cake), Sulla (Roman dictator), discolour, medulla, Technicolor (*Trademark*), watercolour, nulla-nulla (Aboriginal wooden club), Gujranwala (Pakistani city).

17.174
bulla (seal on papal bull), fuller.

ampulla (flask), ferula (Mediterranean plant), spirula (tropical mollusc), gas-trula (animal embryo), nebula, globular, tubular, vascular, oscular (relating to the mouth), radula (part of mollusc's tongue), modular, nodular, glandular, scrofula, regular, ligula (part of insect's lip), jugular, angular, singular, ungula (maths term), alula (tuft of feathers), cellular, stellular (resembling small stars), primula, formula, nummular (coin-shaped), tumular (mound-like), pinnula, lunula, scapula, scapular (part of monastic habit), morula (biology term), Ursula, consular, spatula, blastula (animal embryo), fistula, Vistula (Polish river), pustular, uvula, valvular.

carbuncular, avuncular, calendula (flowering plant), irregular, Caligula, triangular, rectangular, manipular (relating to manipulation), discipular, bicapsular (botany term), tarantula, equiangular.

17.174.1
tabular, incunabula (book printed before 1500).

17.174.2
fibula, mandibular, vestibular.

17.174.3
facula (bright area on sun), macula, piacular (atonement for sacrilegious act), vernacular, oracular (wise and prophetic), spectacular, tentacular, sustentacular (supporting).

17.174.4
fecula (plant starch extract), specular (having mirror-like properties), secular, nubecula (small galaxy), trabecula (botany term), molecular, vallecula (biology term), Vulpecula (constellation).

17.174.5
furcula (fork-like organ), circular, tubercular, semicircular.

17.174.6
orbicular (circular), corbicula (bee's pollen carrier), pedicular (infested with lice), vehicular, follicular, vermicular

(worm-like), funicular, auricula (cultivated alpine primrose), ventricular (swollen), acicula (needle-shaped structure), articular, cuticula (cuticle), particular, lenticular (lens-shaped), navicular (boat-shaped), appendicular, perpendicular, extravehicular (outside a spacecraft), extracurricular.

17.174.7
ocular, jocular, locular (biology term), binocular, monocular.

17.174.8
muscular, crepuscular, corpuscular, neuromuscular, intramuscular.

17.174.9
annular, cannula (small surgical tube), planula (larval form), granular, campanula.

17.174.10
copula (type of verb), scopula (spider's tuft of hair), popular, unpopular.

17.174.11
insula, insular, peninsula, peninsular.

17.174.12
situla (Iron Age container), titular, capitular (relating to cathedral chapter).

17.175
cooler, kula (Pacific island ceremony), Fula (African people), gular (relating to the throat), hula (Hawaiian dance), ruler, Beulah (biblical name for Israel), Lobengula (Matabele king).

17.176
jeweller, dueller, labeller, falbala (gathered frill), bachelor, modeller, gondola, pergola (framework supporting plants), signaller, cupola, gospeller, quarreller, chancellor, councillor, counsellor, hosteller, traveller, leveller, reveller, shoveler (duck).

rubeola (measles), areola (biology term), alveolar (anatomy term), roseola (red rash), parabola, hyperbola, amygdala (almond-shaped body part), po-

lygala (herbaceous plant), teetotaller, epistoler, Methuselah.

17.176.1
dialler, viola (flowering plant), variola (smallpox).

17.176.2
tricolour, Agricola.

17.176.3
victualler, hospitaller.

17.177
dabbler, gabbler.

17.178
cobbler, gobbler.

17.179
gambler, rambler, scrambler.

17.180
bumbler, fumbler, mumbler, grumbler, tumbler.

17.181
tickler, stickler, chronicler.

17.182
sprinkler, twinkler.

17.183
Adler, paddler, saddler.

17.184
meddler, medlar (fruit), pedlar.

17.185
curdler, hurdler.

17.186
fiddler, tiddler.

17.187
idler, sidler, bridler.

17.188
coddler, toddler, waddler, mollycoddler.

17.189
kindler, swindler.

17.190
riffler (a file), whiffler.

17.191
muffler, ruffler, shuffler.

17.192
haggler, straggler.

17.193
juggler, smuggler, struggler.

17.194
angler, wrangler, strangler.

17.195
Doppler (Austrian physicist), poplar.

17.196
Templar, exemplar (a model).

17.197
nestler, wrestler.

17.198
ostler, jostler.

17.199
bustler, hustler, rustler.

17.200
battler, rattler, prattler, tattler.

17.201
Hitler, whittler.

17.202
butler, cutler, sutler (former army provisions merchant).

17.203
antler, dismantler.

17.204
guzzler, muzzler, puzzler.

17.205
dammar (resin), gammer (*Dialect* old woman), gamma (Greek letter), hammer, clamour, glamour, mamma (breast), crammer, grammar, shammer, stammer, yammer, windjammer, sledgehammer, enamour, programmer, Alabama, yellowhammer.

17.206
armour, amah (Eastern nurse), karma (destiny), Kama (Russian river), charmer, dharma (Hindu custom), farmer, llama, lama (Tibetan priest), Nama (Hottentot people), Parma, Rama (Hindu mythological hero), Brahma (Hindu god), drama, grama (pasture grass), Zama (ancient African city), embalmer, pyjama, Manama (capital of Bahrain), Dalai Lama, diorama (small three-dimensional scene), cyclorama (picture around cylindrical room), panorama, Cinerama (*Trademark*), psychodrama, melodrama, Vasco da Gama.

17.207
squama (scale), framer, tamer, disclaimer, Macías Nguema (Guinean island).

17.208
emmer (variety of wheat), gemma (plant reproductive structure), hemmer, lemma (logic term), tremor, stemma (family tree), dilemma, trilemma (situation presenting three choices), maremma (marshy maritime region), neurolemma (nerve-fibre sheath), analemma (type of sundial).

17.209
Burma, derma (deep inner skin layer), murmur, termor (legal term), Sturmer (eating apple), leucoderma (unpigmented area of skin), scleroderma (skin disease), xeroderma (abnormally dry skin), pyoderma (skin disase), terra firma.

17.210
bema (Athenian speaker's platform), schema, schemer, femur, lemur, Lima, reamer (steel tool), creamer, screamer, dreamer, prima, streamer, Tema (Ghanaian port), steamer.

oedema, redeemer, blasphemer, daydreamer, blastema (biology term).

seriema (South American bird), empyema (accumulation of pus), myxoedema (disease of thyroid gland), Iwo Jima (Pacific island), chromonema (biology term), treponema (bacterium), emphysema, Hiroshima, erotema (rhetorical question), diastema (abnormal fissure), erythema (red patches on skin), exanthema (a rash).

17.211

skimmer, dimmer, glimmer, slimmer, krimmer (Crimean lambswool), trimmer, simmer, shimmer, swimmer.

polymer, ulema (Muslim scholar), anima, enema, minima (*plural of* minimum), cinema, lorimer, dulcimer, Fatima, Mortimer, ultima (final syllable of word), intima (innermost layer of organ), ecthyma (inflammation of skin), nonswimmer, maxima (*plural of* maximum), eczema, Proxima (star).

sclerenchyma (supporting plant tissue), parenchyma (soft plant tissue).

Alma-Tadema (painter), Quinquagesima, Quadragesima, Sexagesima, Septuagesima.

17.212

dimer (chemistry term), lima (US bean), climber, primer, trimer (chemistry term), tryma (hard-shelled fruit), sima (layer of earth's crust), timer, old-timer, full-timer, part-timer, Oppenheimer, Maritimer (inhabitant of Canadian Maritimes), autotimer.

17.213

bomber, comma, homa (sacred plant).

17.214

ormer (edible mollusc), korma (Indian food), dormer, former, Norma, trauma, warmer, reformer, performer, informer, transformer, bedwarmer.

17.215

omer (ancient Hebrew measure), coma, comber, ngoma (East African drum), Homer, homer, noma (inflammation of the mouth), roamer, stroma (biology term), soma, stoma (mouthlike part), vomer (thin flat bone).

glioma (tumour), myoma (muscle tumour), sarcoma, glaucoma, trachoma (eye disease), Tacoma (Washington port), beachcomber, diploma, misnomer, lipoma (fatty tumour), scleroma (patch of hard tissue), aroma, fibroma (fibrous tumour), scotoma (blind spot), xanthoma (yellowish nodule on skin).

angioma (tumour), osteoma (bone tumour), Oklahoma, condyloma (tumour), papilloma (tumour), myeloma (tumour of bone marrow), adenoma (glandular tumour), carcinoma, atheroma (obstruction in artery), haematoma (tumour of clotted blood), encephaloma (brain tumour).

17.216

bummer, gumma (syphilitic tumour), plumber, mummer, rummer (drinking glass), drummer, summer, newcomer, latecomer, midsummer.

17.217

boomer, bloomer, rumour, Nkrumah, struma (a swelling), Sumer (region of Babylon), humour, pneuma (soul), puma, tumour, stumer (*Slang* forgery), satsuma, perfumer, consumer, mazuma (*US* money), empyreuma (burning smell), Montezuma (Aztec emperor).

17.218

agama (small lizard), isomer (chemistry term), gossamer, Latimer, metamer (chemistry term), tautomer (chemistry term), Gautama (early name of Buddha), customer, elastomer (rubbery material), scyphistoma (zoology term), anathema.

17.218.1

monomer (chemistry term), gastronomer, astronomer.

17.219

chacma (baboon), drachma.

17.220

agma (phonetic symbol), magma, syntagma (linguistics term).

17.221

smegma, bregma (part of skull).

17.222

sigma (Greek letter), stigma, enigma, sterigma (botany term).

17.223
plasma, miasma, chiasma (biology term).

17.224
melisma (musical term), charisma.

17.225
Anna, banner, canner, canna (tropical plant), scanner, Hannah, lanner (large falcon), planner, manner, manor, manna, nanna, spanner, tanner, Diana, Guyana (South American republic), goanna (Australian monitor lizard), bandanna, alannah (Irish term of endearment), Fermanagh, Montana, Havana, Savannah (US port), savanna (open grassland), hosanna, Susanna, Susquehanna (US river), ipecacuanha (purgative drug).

17.225.1
Indiana, Pollyanna, Louisiana.

17.226
ana (anecdotes about a person), kana (Japanese syllabic writing), Ghana, garner, mana (power), Tana (Ethiopian lake), tana (Madagascan lemur), varna (Hindu caste), bwana, Tswana (African people).

Tucana (constellation), gymkhana, Fergana (region of Asia), nagana (animal disease), zenana (women's part of house), banana, piranha, Tirana (capital of Albania), Purana (Sanskrit writings), curtana (coronation sword), sultana, nirvana, Tijuana, Botswana, iguana, Ljubljana (Yugoslavian city).

ikebana (Japanese flower-arranging), katakana (Japanese syllabic writing), hiragana (Japanese syllabic writing), pozzuolana (volcanic ash), vox humana, Weimaraner (breed of dog), Lippizaner (breed of horse), Rosh Hashanah (Jewish New Year), marijuana, Mahayana (school of Buddhism), Hinayana (early form of Buddhism), Tell el Amarna (Egyptian ruins).

17.226.1
liana, Ludhiana (Indian city), Juliana, dulciana (organ stop), poinciana (tropical tree), Australiana, Shakespeareana, Victoriana, nicotiana (fragrant flowering plant).

17.226.2
Afrikaner, Americana.

17.227
Cana (biblical town), Gaynor, gainer, planar, planer, drainer, trainer, strainer, arcana (tarot cards), coplanar (in the same plane), Ndjamena (capital of Chad), campaigner, restrainer, detainer, retainer, lantana (tropical shrub), container, sustainer, abstainer, cantilena (musical term), Magdalena (Colombian river), entertainer.

17.228
Jenner (English physician), henna, penna (large feather), senna, tenner, tenor, sienna, Siena, Vienna, duenna, Gehenna (place of torment), antenna, Ravenna (Italian city), Avicenna (Arab philosopher), countertenor.

17.229
earner, burner, learner, Smyrna, turner, cisterna (space containing body fluid), afterburner.

17.230
Lena, cleaner, Nina, Tina, vina (Indian stringed instrument), vena (vein), wiener (*US* smoked sausage), weaner (newly weaned animal), Zena.

hyena, verbena, coquina (soft limestone), kachina (American Indian spirit), Medina (Saudi Arabian city), saphena (leg vein), lagena (narrow-necked bottle), congener (member of category), tahina (sesame-seed paste), dolina (depression in limestone), galena (heavy mineral), euglena (microscopic freshwater organism), demeanour, subpoena, tsarina, Messina, piscina (basin in Catholic church), dracaena (tropical plant), Katsina (Nigerian city), retsina, catena (connected series), phlyctena (small blister), cantina (Spanish bar), sestina (Italian verse form), Christina, Athena, novena (Catholic devotion), convener, rendzina (dark soil).

anabaena (freshwater plant), karabiner (clip used in mountaineering), amphisbaena (worm lizard), hagedena (ulcer), Pasadena, Saint Helena, semolina, Messalina, misdemeanour, Wilhelmina, Agrippina, signorina, orchestrina (musical instrument), scarlatina, sonatina, concertina, cavatina (musical composition), Argentina, Bukovina (region of central Europe).

Herzegovina (region of Yugoslavia), Quezon y Molina (first Philippine president).

17.230.1
arena, Carina (constellation), farina (flour), marina, ocarina, ballerina, Incaparina (high-protein food).

17.231
inner, skinner, dinner, finner (whale), Minna (Nigerian city), pinner (small dainty apron), pinna (biology term), spinner, sinner, Cinna (Roman aristocrat), thinner, winner.

tachina (bristly fly), Kitchener, beginner, bigener (hybrid organism), Eleanor, milliner, mariner, foreigner, parcener (coheir), Porsena (legendary Etruscan king), platina (platinum alloy), patina (shallow Roman dish), retina, breadwinner.

determiner, phenomena, alumina (aluminium oxide), Proserpina (Roman goddess), submariner, Polyxena (Greek mythological princess).

17.231.1
lamina, stamina, examiner.

17.232
China, china, diner, Dinah, liner, miner, mynah, minor, shiner.

trichina (parasitic roundworm), refiner, Aegina (Greek island), Regina, vagina, angina, airliner, eyeliner, salina (salt lake), recliner, headliner, freightliner, jetliner, Lucina (Roman goddess), consignor, moonshiner (*US* whisky smuggler), diviner, designer.

Indochina, Carolina.

casuarina (Australian tree), globigerina (microscopic animal).

17.233
honour, Donna, goner, gonna, wanna, O'Connor, dishonour.

17.233.1
Madonna, belladonna, prima donna.

17.234
corner, fauna, mourner, sauna, avifauna (birds of particular region).

17.235
joiner, amboyna (Indonesian tree), Amboina (Indonesian island).

17.236
owner, boner, donor, Jonah, loner, moaner, Mona, mona (African monkey), krone, trona (greyish mineral), toner, Iona, cinchona (quinine-producing tree bark), Dodona (Greek town), landowner, Bellona (Roman war goddess), Pamplona (Spanish city), Cremona, Pomona (Roman goddess), shipowner, corona, Verona, persona, Daytona, Altona (German port), canzona (musical term), Barcelona, Arizona.

17.237
scunner (*Scot* aversion), dharna (Indian sit-in), gunner, runner, Sunna (Islamic law), stunner, oner (something outstanding), forerunner, Corunna (Spanish port), roadrunner (crested bird), gunrunner, outrunner, frontrunner.

17.238
schooner, lunar, Luna (Roman moon goddess), Poona, crooner, pruner,

sooner, tuna, tuner, Kaduna (Nigerian state), cislunar (between earth and moon), koruna (Czechoslovak currency), vicuña, lacuna (gap), lacunar (ceiling with sunken panels), Fortuna (Roman goddess), semilunar, circumlunar, honeymooner.

17.239
vahana (Indian mythological vehicle), baconer (type of pig), reckoner, thickener, falconer, questioner, Adana (Turkish city), Londoner, stiffener, softener, wagoner, Helena, almoner, Brahmana (Hindu sacred treatise), commoner, sharpener, opener, coroner, fastener, freshener, pensioner, sweetener, lightener, whitener, Westerner, Easterner, strengthener, Northerner, Southerner, taverner, governor, alienor (legal term), prisoner, poisoner.

reversioner (legal term), confectioner, redemptioner (early emigrant to America), Ecbatana (ancient Iranian city).

executioner, paralipomena (supplementary writings).

17.239.1
stationer, probationer, vacationer.

17.239.2
conditioner, commissioner, parishioner, petitioner, practitioner, exhibitioner (scholarship student).

17.240
Gardiner, gardener, hardener, pardner.

17.241
Pydna (ancient Macedonian town), echidna.

17.242
Jumna (Indian river), alumna (*US* female graduate), columnar.

17.243
Mishnah (Jewish precepts), Krishna, Ramakrishna (Hindu religious reformer).

17.244
Etna, Gretna.

17.245 [see also **17.140**]
banger, ganger (foreman of labour gang), hangar, hanger, clanger, franger (*Austral* condom), cliffhanger, straphanger, Selangor (Malaysian state), Tauranga (New Zealand port), paperhanger, Doppelgänger.

17.246 [see also **17.141**]
clinger, pinger, ringer, wringer, springer, stringer (architectural term), singer, stinger (iced whisky and soda), winger, swinger, humdinger, gunslinger, klipspringer (small African antelope), minnesinger (medieval German minstrel), Meistersinger (German poet or musician).

17.247
kappa (Greek letter), dapper, clapper, flapper, napper, nappa (*Slang* head), snapper, wrapper, rapper, grappa, trapper, strapper (*US* strapping person), sapper, schappe (silk yarn or fabric), kidnapper, Harappa (Pakistani city), handicapper (sports handicap assigner), whippersnapper, Phi Beta Kappa (US academic society).

17.248
scarper, Harper, sharper, tapa (paper mulberry bark), cardsharper.

17.249
caper, neper (unit in physics), paper, scraper, draper, shaper, tapir, taper, vapour, flypaper, sandpaper, endpaper, wallpaper, notepaper, newspaper, skyscraper.

17.250
leper, pepper, stepper.

17.251
chirper, Sherpa, usurper.

17.252
keeper, sleeper, nipa (palm tree), Dnieper (Russian river), peeper, pipa (South American toad), reaper, creeper, weeper, sweeper, beekeeper, door-

keeper, storekeeper, book-keeper, goal-keeper, gamekeeper, timekeeper, innkeeper, shopkeeper, housekeeper, gatekeeper, minesweeper, Arequipa (Peruvian city), wicketkeeper.

17.253
kipper, skipper, chipper, dipper, Lippe (German river), clipper, flipper, slipper, nipper, ripper, tripper, stripper, sipper (*US* drinking straw), shipper, tipper, zipper, mudskipper (tropical coastal fish), calliper, juniper, Agrippa (Roman general), day-tripper, worshipper.

17.254
sniper, piper, viper, wiper, sandpiper (bird).

17.255
copper, chopper, Dopper (Afrikaner Church member), Joppa, hopper, popper, cropper, dropper, proper, shopper, topper, stopper, whopper, treehopper (insect), clodhopper, froghopper (small leaping insect), grasshopper, sharecropper (*US* tenant farmer), eavesdropper, improper, gobstopper, teenybopper.

17.256
scorper (fine chisel), pauper, torpor.

17.257
coper (horse dealer), groper, sopor (abnormally deep sleep), toper, L-dopa (natural body substance), landloper (*Scot* vagrant), Europa (satellite of Jupiter), NATSOPA, methyldopa (a drug), interloper.

17.258
upper, cuppa, scupper, crupper (saddle strap), supper.

17.259
Cooper, cooper (barrel-maker), looper (moth larva), blooper (*US* blunder), snooper, grouper (tropical fish), trouper, trooper, super, whooper (white swan), pupa, stupor, mosstrooper (border country raider), peasouper, super-duper.

17.260
walloper (*Austral* policeman), hanaper (wickerwork basket), developer.

17.261
camper, scamper, damper, hamper, clamper (spiked frame on sole), pamper, tamper, Tampa (Florida resort).

17.262
temper, distemper.

17.263
crimper, shrimper, simper, whimper.

17.264
bumper, dumper, jumper, lumper (*US* stevedore), plumper (actor's mouth pad), show-jumper, buckjumper (*Austral* untamed horse).

17.265
asper (Turkish coin), Caspar (one of the Magi), jasper.

17.266
crisper, whisper.

17.267
ROSPA (accident prevention society), prosper.

17.268
Ara (constellation), Harar (Ethiopian city), Nara (Japanese city), para (Yugoslavian coin), vara (Spanish length), cascara, mascara, Bukhara (Russian city), Sahara, Amhara (Ethiopian province), Damara (African people), samara (winged fruit), Asmara (Ethiopian city), Carrara (Italian town), Ferrara, Guevara, gurdwara (Sikh place of worship), capybara, caracara (bird of prey), Tsukahara (Japanese gymnast), Connemara, tuatara, solfatara (sulphurous volcanic vent).

17.268.1
tiara, Honiara (capital of Solomon Islands).

17.269
error, terror, naira (Nigerian currency), Kagera (African river), busera (Ugandan alcoholic drink).

17.270
stirrer, preferrer, conferrer.

17.271
Eire, eyra (feline mammal), bearer, Sarah, wearer, sierra, torchbearer, trainbearer, cupbearer, macebearer, caldera (volcanic crater), wayfarer, seafarer, declarer, Dun Laoghaire, repairer, pareira (medicinal plant root), Riviera, tapadera (US stirrup covering), pintadera (Neolithic decorative stamp), habanera (Cuban dance), demerara, cordillera.

17.272
era, gerah (ancient Hebrew weight), hearer, Hera, lira, sclera (outer covering of eyeball), sera (*plural of* serum), Madeira, chimera (hybrid monster), lempira (Honduran currency), sheepshearer, hetaera (female prostitute), Cythera (Greek island), Gezira (region of Sudan), Hegira (flight of Mohammed), Mufulira (Zambian town), phylloxera (insect that attacks vines).

17.273
mirror, Pyrrha (Greek mythological character), sirrah, wirra (Irish exclamation of sorrow).

17.274
Beira (Mozambique port), hirer, Lyra (constellation), tayra (arboreal mammal), wirer, Sapphira (biblical character), Stagira (ancient Macedonian city), admirer, palmyra (tropical palm), enquirer, spirogyra (freshwater alga).

17.275
horror, begorra, Camorra (Neapolitan secret society), Gomorrah, Illawarra (Australian coastal district).

17.276
aura, borer, bora (violent north wind), Cora, corer, scorer, Dora, hora (traditional circle dance), Laura, flora, Flora, Morar (Scottish loch), Nora, snorer, schnorrer (*US* professional beggar), pourer, sora (US bird).

woodborer (beetle larva), bombora (submerged reef), rasbora (tropical fish), fedora (brimmed hat), Andorra, Pandora, angora, explorer, menorah (Jewish ceremonial candelabrum), aurora, Masora (Hebrew bible text), restorer, signora.

Bora Bora (Pacific island), Tuscarora (American Indian people).

17.277
juror, Jura, pleura (membrane enveloping lungs), crura (leglike structures), surah (twill fabric), tourer, tamboura (Indian musical instrument), Madura (Indonesian island), nonjuror, insurer, Mathura (Indian city), procurer, datura (narcotic plant), bravura, caesura, Kamakura (Japanese city), Djajapura (Indonesian port), El Mansura (Egyptian city), tessitura (musical term), angostura, acciaccatura (musical term), appoggiatura (musical term), coloratura, Bonaventura (Italian saint), camera obscura (optical device).

17.278
borough, durra (cereal grass), thorough, demurrer (objection), kookaburra.

17.279
Scarborough, labourer, Deborah, Berbera (Somalian port), Loughborough, Marlborough, Flamborough, slumberer, Canberra, Farnborough, Atbara (Sudanese town), Gainsborough, Greensboro (US city), Ankara, conqueror, torturer, lecturer, murderer, borderer, solderer, wanderer, plunderer, sufferer, amphora, agora (ancient Greek marketplace), Megara (Greek town), perjurer, conjurer, cellarer (monastic official), cholera, camera, stammerer, armourer, Marmara (Turkish inland sea), Woomera, woomera (Aboriginal spear thrower), genera (*plural of* genus), corpora (*plural of* corpus), emperor, Klemperer (orchestral conductor), tempera (painting medium), whisperer, tessera

(square mosaic tile), sorcerer, treasurer, usurer, chatterer, flatterer, caterer, slaughterer, stutterer, fruiterer, poulterer, tantara (trumpet fanfare), plasterer, plethora, cithara (stringed instrument).

Peterborough, Attenborough, Edinburgh, adventurer, Vadodara (Indian city), philanderer, anaphora (rhetorical device), mandragora (narcotic plant), malingerer, in camera, nullipara (obstetrics term), primipara (obstetrics term), multipara (obstetrics term), Diaspora (Jews' dispersion from Palestine), adulterer, upholsterer, deliverer, discoverer.

manufacturer, sesquialtera (organ stop).

17.279.1
remora (marine fish), ephemera.

17.279.2
Sisera (biblical character), viscera (large internal body organs), chelicera (spider's claw), lonicera (honeysuckle).

17.280
Aldabra (Indian Ocean islands), abracadabra.

17.281
sabra (Israeli-born Jew), macabre.

17.282
zebra, cause célèbre (famous lawsuit).

17.283
Libra, algebra, vertebra.

17.284
timbre, Alhambra, Anambra (Nigerian state).

17.285
umbra, penumbra.

17.286
Phaedra (wife of Theseus), ex cathedra (with authority).

17.287
Alexandra, double entendre.

17.288
tundra, Ramachandra (Hindu mythological character).

17.289
Niagara, podagra (gout), pellagra (vitamin deficiency disease).

17.290
opera, copra (dried coconut kernel).

17.291
quatre (playing card), Cleopatra.

17.292
Chartres, Sumatra, Sinatra.

17.293
Petra (ancient Jordanian city), tetra (tropical fish), et cetera.

17.294
sutra (Sanskrit sayings), Brahmaputra (Asian river), Kamasutra.

17.295
spectra, Electra.

17.296
mantra, Tantra (Sanskrit sacred books).

17.297
orchestra, aspidistra.

17.298
Assur (Assyrian god), gasser, placer (gold-containing sediment), NASA, Mombasa, Makasar (Indonesian port), Cabora Bassa (African dam), antimacassar.

17.299
chaser, facer, mesa (tableland), macer (macebearer), pacer, spacer, racer, bracer, tracer, Hargeisa (Somalian city), embraceor (legal term), steeplechaser.

17.300
lesser, dresser, pressor (producing increased blood pressure), cesser (legal term), Odessa, professor, confessor, hairdresser, aggressor, depressor, oppressor, compressor, processor, asses-

sor, successor, possessor, predecessor, microprocessor.

17.301
bursar, bursa, cursor, mercer, purser, precursor, vice versa.

17.302
kisser, purchaser, officer, Orissa (Indian state), Larisa (Greek city), vibrissa (whisker), abscissa (maths term), mantissa (maths term), artificer (skilled craftsman).

17.303
slicer, Neisse (German–Polish river), ricer (*US* sieve), de-icer.

17.304
Ossa (Greek mountain), dosser, fossa (anatomical depression), glossa (tongue), Canossa (Italian castle), Saragossa (Spanish city), Barbarossa (Holy Roman Emperor).

17.305
courser, Chaucer, Horsa (leader of Jutes), saucer.

17.306
grocer, mucosa (mucous membrane), mimosa, Formosa, serosa (delicate body membrane), greengrocer, Via Dolorosa (road to Calvary), anorexia nervosa.

17.307
douser, Hausa (African people).

17.308
Susa (ancient Iranian city), Teucer (Greek mythological character), anchusa (Eurasian plant), reducer, seducer, producer, transducer, Appaloosa (US breed of horse), Jebel Musa (Moroccan mountain), babirusa.

17.309
trespasser, canvasser.

17.310
balsa, waltzer.

17.311
ulcer, Tulsa.

17.312
cancer, Cancer, merganser (marine diving duck).

17.313
answer, dancer, lancer, enhancer.

17.314
fencer, Mensa, Spencer, censor, sensor, censer (incense burner), tensor (tensing muscle), condenser, dispenser, extensor (extending muscle).

17.315
mincer, pincer, rinser.

17.316
sponsor, responser (radio receiver).

17.317
bouncer, denouncer, announcer.

17.318
balancer, silencer, sequencer (electronic device), encumbrancer (legal term).

17.319
matza (Jewish biscuit), tazza (wine cup), piazza.

17.320
bitser (*Austral* mongrel dog), Switzer (Swiss), howitzer, Pulitzer, tsaritsa (wife of tsar), Amritsar (Indian city).

17.321
Asher, dasher (plunger in a churn), flasher, splasher (protection against splashes), masher, smasher, pasha (Turkish title), rasher, thrasher (US songbird), tamasha (Indian entertainment), gate-crasher, haberdasher.

17.322
Asia, fascia, geisha, Croatia (Yugoslavian republic), acacia, Ilesha (Nigerian town), Galatia, Dalmatia, Laurasia (hypothetical prehistoric land mass), Eurasia, ex gratia, osteomalacia (bone disease).

17.323
flesher (*Scot* butcher), fresher, pressure, tressure (heraldic term), thresher, refresher.

17.324
Persia, inertia.

17.325
Esher, Rhodesia, godetia, Belisha, Portlaoise (Irish town), Venetia (region of ancient Italy), magnesia, aubrietia (trailing plant), montbretia (African plant), Ossetia (region of Russia), Lutetia (ancient name for Paris), Helvetia (Latin name for Switzerland), alopecia.

17.326 [see also **17.3.49**]
fisher, fissure, wisher, Frobisher, kingfisher, militia, polisher, publisher, varnisher, furnisher, finisher, Britisher, well-wisher, extinguisher.

17.327
cosher, quassia (tropical tree), washer, dishwasher.

17.328
kosher, scotia (architectural moulding), Boeotia (region of ancient Greece), Nova Scotia.

17.329
usher, gusher, blusher, Russia, crusher, Prussia.

17.330
censure, dementia (mental deterioration), amentia (congenital mental deficiency).

17.331
affenpinscher (breed of dog), Doberman pinscher.

17.332 [see also **17.3.59**]
erasure, embrasure.

17.333
leisure, pleasure, measure, treasure, displeasure, commeasure (be the same as), admeasure (share out), countermeasure.

17.334 [see also **17.3.60**]
freesia, seizure, nemesia (cultivated plant), Polynesia, Melanesia, Micronesia, Austronesia.

17.335 [see also **17.3.62**]
closure, foreclosure, enclosure, disclosure, exclosure (fenced forest area), composure, exposure, discomposure, underexposure, overexposure.

17.336
attar (oil used in perfume), batter, scatter, chatter, hatter, latter, clatter, flatter, platter, splatter, matter, smatter, natter, patter, spatter, ratter, satyr, shatter, tatter, wildcatter (US oil prospector), regatta, bespatter, Kenyatta, antimatter, pitter-patter.

17.337
barter, Carter, charter, darter (aquatic tropical bird), garter, martyr, Sparta, rata (New Zealand tree), strata, sartor (tailor), tartar, Tartar, starter, riata (a lasso), Djakarta (capital of Indonesia), toccata, Siddhartha (personal name of Buddha), sonata, errata, pro rata, cassata (ice cream), cantata, nonstarter, Magna Carta, alma mater, Stabat Mater (Latin hymn), serenata (18th-century cantata).

17.337.1
chipolata, taramasalata (fish-roe paté).

17.337.2
Maratha (Indian people), desiderata, inamorata.

17.338
eta (Japanese outcast), cater, skater, data, gaiter, hater, later, plater, slater, mater, Meta (Colombian river), pater, crater, freighter, frater (friar), grater, traitor, tater, stater (ancient Greek coin), stator (stationary part of machine), waiter.

debater, abator (legal term), albata (variety of nickel silver), Mercator, dilator, collator, ablator (heat shield), translator, pronator (type of muscle), equator, curator, vibrator, glossator (writer of glosses), peseta, pulsator, rotator, scrutator (examiner), spectator, dictator, testator, dumbwaiter.

incubator, educator, evocator (biology term), liquidator, percolator, escalator, inhalator (device aiding breathing), nomenclator (person who invents names), legislator, collimator (optical device), animator, lacrimator (substance causing tear flow), imprimatur (church licence to publish), pia mater (membrane enclosing brain), dura mater (membrane enclosing brain), exequatur (official authorization), aspirator, procurator, integrator (computer term), perpetrator, illustrator, demonstrator, crux ansata (symbolic cross), commutator, sternutator (substance causing sneezing), commentator, excavator, conservator (custodian).

attenuator, continuator, vasodilator, administrator, totalizator (betting system).

17.338.1
creator, gladiator, radiator, mediator, aviator, caveator (legal term), delineator (tailor's pattern), negotiator, annunciator (location indicator).

17.338.2
judicator (judge), indicator, trafficator (car indicator), applicator, duplicator, lubricator, desiccator (drying apparatus), adjudicator, vinificator (winemaking apparatus), scarificator (surgical instrument), purificator (Communion cloth), divaricator (zoology term).

17.338.3
negator (electronic circuit), alligator, navigator, investigator.

17.338.4
propagator, corrugator (brow-wrinkling muscle), interrogator.

17.338.5
relator (legal term), oscillator, ventilator, scintillator (physics term), invigilator, defibrillator (medical apparatus).

17.338.6
tabulator, speculator, calculator, modulator, regulator, simulator, stimulator,

insulator, postulator (advocate for person's canonization), perambulator, articulator, accumulator.

17.338.7
terminator (dividing line on planet), supinator (muscle of forearm), buccinator (muscle in cheek), coordinator, exterminator, discriminator (electronic circuit), denominator.

17.338.8
detonator, alternator, resonator, impersonator.

17.338.9
narrator, liberator, decorator, moderator, stellarator (physics apparatus), numerator, generator, cinerator (cremation furnace), separator, operator, corporator (member of corporation), respirator, literator (professional writer), collaborator, reverberator (metallurgical furnace), refrigerator, accelerator, enumerator (person taking census), incinerator, recuperator (gun-resetting device).

17.338.10
agitator, imitator, resuscitator.

17.338.11
levator (raising muscle), elevator, activator, cultivator.

17.339
better, betta (fighting fish), debtor, fetter, feta (Greek cheese), getter, letter, Quetta (Pakistani city), setter, tetter (skin eruption), sweater.

Gambetta (French statesman), vendetta, unfetter, go-getter, muleta (matador's small cape), Valletta (capital of Malta), newsletter, biretta (clerical cap), cabretta (soft leather), bonesetter, typesetter, pacesetter, jetsetter, mozzetta (clerical cape), Rosetta.

Damietta (Egyptian town), arietta (short aria), mantelletta (clerical vestment), carburettor, operetta, anchoveta (small anchovy), sinfonietta (short symphony).

17.340

skirter (*Austral* fleece trimmer), hurter (protective object), stertor (laborious noisy breathing), Alberta, frankfurter, Lacerta (constellation), evertor (type of muscle), inverter (electrical circuit), converter, Bizerte (Tunisian port), deserter.

17.341

eater, beater, beta, chaeta (small bristle on worm), cheetah, dita (tropical shrub), fetor (offensive smell), heater, litre, pleater, meter, metre, peter, Peter, pita (fibre-yielding plant), rhetor (teacher of rhetoric), praetor (Roman magistrate), seta (small bristle), teeter, theta, tweeter (loudspeaker).

eggbeater (*US* helicopter), windcheater, beefeater, veleta, Demeter (Greek goddess), Machmeter, ammeter, repeater, saltpetre, ureter, excreta, amrita (Hindu ambrosia), propraetor (Roman exmagistrate), masseter (cheek muscle), receiptor (issuer of receipts), twoseater, Peshitta (version of Bible), partita (musical composition), anteater.

honey-eater (small songbird), millilitre, centilitre, millimetre, centimetre, taximeter, nanometre, kilometre, señorita, margarita (cocktail), Bhagavad-Gita (sacred Hindu text).

17.342

bitter, skitter (scamper), chitter (*US* twitter), fitter, jitter, hitter, litter, lytta (cartilage beneath dog's tongue), flitter, glitter, knitter, pitta (flat Greek bread), quitter, quittor (horse's foot infection), critter, fritter, sitter, shittah (biblical tree), titter, vitta (biology term), twitter.

rabbiter, arbiter, embitter, presbyter, cricketer, traditor (early Christian betrayer), auditor, taffeta, outfitter, Sagitta (constellation), aglitter, transmitter,

janitor, genitor (biological father), monitor, chapiter (upper part of column), Jupiter, trumpeter, heritor, bedsitter, catheter, servitor, Exeter.

inhibitor, exhibitor, counterfeiter, Hippolyta (Greek mythological queen), diameter, parameter, voltameter, pentameter, hexameter, telemeter (distance measurer), hypermeter (verse line), volumeter, progenitor, per capita, accipiter (hawk), non sequitur, apparitor (ecclesiastical court officer), inheritor, interpreter, capacitor, solicitor, competitor, primogenitor.

17.342.1

editor, creditor, subeditor.

17.342.2

emitter, dimeter (verse line), remitter, trimeter (verse line), scimitar, planimeter (plane-area measurer), dosimeter (radiation measurer), tasimeter (temperature-change measurer), pulsimeter, densimeter, altimeter, acidimeter, alkalimeter.

17.342.2.1

perimeter, saccharimeter (sugar-concentration measurer), calorimeter, polarimeter (light-polarization measurer), solarimeter (solar-radiation measurer), colorimeter, vaporimeter (vapour-pressure measurer).

17.342.3

cryometer (low-temperature thermometer), tachometer, viscometer, pedometer, speedometer, odometer, algometer (sensitivity measurer), mileometer, bolometer (radiant-energy measurer), coulometer, cyclometer, atmometer (evaporation measurer), planometer (plate for testing flatness), clinometer, monometer (verse line), pycnometer (bottle for weighing liquids), swingometer, aerometer, sclerometer (mineralhardness measurer), pyrometer, spirometer (lung-capacity measurer), micrometer, hydrometer, hygrometer (humidity measurer), nitrometer, gasometer, optometer, Comptometer (*Trademark*), plastometer (plasticity measurer), bathometer.

cephalometer (head measurer), anemometer (wind-speed measurer), salinometer, inclinometer (aircraft instrument), actinometer (sun-radiation measurer), fluorometer (fluorescence measurer), tellurometer (surveying instrument), magnetometer, densitometer, sensitometer, dilatometer (dimension-change measurer), refractometer, piezometer (pressure measurer), alcoholometer.

17.342.3.1
rheometer (blood-flow measurer), geometer (person who studies geometry), tacheometer (surveying instrument), radiometer, audiometer, eudiometer (chemistry apparatus), heliometer (type of telescope), craniometer, goniometer (angle measurer), variometer, tensiometer, potentiometer.

17.342.3.2
thermometer, dynamometer (power measurer).

17.342.3.3
tonometer, phonometer (sound-intensity measurer), manometer (instrument for comparing pressures), chronometer (nautical timepiece), galvanometer (electric-current measurer).

17.342.3.4
barometer, interferometer, decelerometer, accelerometer.

17.342.3.5
spectrometer (spectrum producer and measurer), electrometer (electrical-potential measurer).

17.342.4
visitor, inquisitor.

17.342.5
prepositor (prefect), depositor, compositor, expositor (person who ex-

pounds), ovipositor (insect's egg-laying organ).

17.343
fighter, lighter, blighter, mitre, nitre, writer, sighter (practice shot in competition), titre, bullfighter, gunfighter, prizefighter, Gauleiter (German governor under Hitler), moonlighter, lamplighter, igniter, songwriter, typewriter, scriptwriter, ghostwriter, exciter (oscillator), excitor (a nerve), amanita (genus of fungi), telewriter, copywriter, underwriter.

17.344
otter, cotter, cotta (clerical surplice), gotta, jotter, blotter, plotter, potter, spotter, squatter, rotter, trotter, totter, stotter (*Scot* good-looking woman), swatter, ricotta (soft white cheese), pelota (Spanish ball game), globetrotter, terra cotta.

17.345
daughter, slaughter, mortar, snorter, porter, quarter, sorter, water.

aorta, goddaughter, granddaughter, stepdaughter, manslaughter, ripsnorter, reporter, supporter, colporteur (book pedlar), importer, transporter, exporter, backwater, breakwater, forequarter, hindquarter, shearwater, firewater (whisky), Bridgwater, freshwater, dishwater, saltwater, Ullswater, kicksorter (physics apparatus).

underwater, Derwentwater.

17.346
Oita (Japanese city), goitre, loiter, Reuter, reconnoitre.

17.347
boater, Kota (Indian city), scoter, lota (brass water container), bloater, floater, motor, notour (Scottish legal term), quota, rota, rotor, voter, iota, biota (biology term), Dakota, promoter, sapota (tropical fruit), acroter (architectural term), nonvoter, locomotor (relating to locomotion), dynamotor

(current-converting machine), Minnesota, sensorimotor (physiology term).

17.348
outer, scouter, doubter, pouter (domestic pigeon), router (cutting tool).

17.349
utter, butter, cutter, scutter (scurry), gutter, gutta (architectural ornament), clutter, flutter, splutter, mutter, nutter, putter, sputter, shutter, stutter, rebutter (legal term), abutter (owner of adjoining property), woodcutter, leafcutter (South American ant), Calcutta, stonecutter, daisycutter (cricket term).

17.350
first-footer, six-footer, shot-putter, coadjutor (bishop's assistant), contributor, distributor, executor, prolocutor (Anglican Church official), interlocutor.

17.351
scooter, hooter, looter, fluter, fruiter, suitor, souter (*Scot* cobbler), neuter, pewter, tutor, freebooter, accoutre, valuta (currency exchange rate), peashooter, crapshooter (*US* craps player), sharpshooter, commuter, computer, barracouta (predatory fish), troubleshooter, persecutor, prosecutor, collocutor (person making conversation), Abeokuta (Nigerian town).

17.352
theatre, predator, comforter, balata (tropical tree, Galata (Turkish port), elater (biology term), amateur, stigmata, senator, orator, waratah (Australian shrub), idolater, automata (*plural of* automaton), Antipater (Macedonian general), declarator (Scottish legal term), comparator (comparing device), conspirator, amphitheatre, Mahabharata (Indian poem).

17.352.1
dieter, rioter, proprietor.

17.353
actor, factor, tractor, reactor, varactor (electronic device), refractor, retractor,

protractor, contractor, extractor, contactor (type of switch), malefactor, benefactor, chiropractor, subcontractor, azotobacter (bacterium).

17.354
hector, nectar, spectre, rector, recta (*plural of* rectum), sector, vector, effector (nerve ending), defector, ejector, ejecta (expelled volcanic material), dejecta (solid body waste), projector, injector, elector, collector, selector, reflector, connector, respecter, prospector, inspector, erector, director, bisector, prosector (person who dissects), detector, protector, convector.

17.355
dicta (*plural of* dictum), lictor (Roman official), victor, predictor, character, constrictor, vasoconstrictor (substance constricting blood vessels).

17.356
okta (meteorological unit), doctor, proctor.

17.357
adductor (type of muscle), inductor (electrical component), conductor, destructor (furnace for burning refuse), instructor, nonconductor, semiconductor.

17.358
after, laughter, rafter, grafter, wafter (fan), thereafter, hereafter.

17.359
snifter, drifter, swifter (nautical term), shoplifter, weightlifter, CARIFTA (Caribbean Free Trade Area).

17.360
kofta (Indian meatballs), lofter (golf club), crofter, softa (Muslim student).

17.361
kelter (condition), delta, smelter, spelter (impure zinc), shelter, Shelta (Irish tinkers' secret language), welter, swelter, helter-skelter.

17.362
filter, philtre (love potion), milter (sexually mature male fish), ultrafilter (filter with tiny pores).

17.363
alter, altar, falter, halter, Malta, palter (be insincere), salter, psalter, defaulter, Gibraltar.

17.364
bolter (*Austral* outsider in race), coulter (plough blade), Volta (Italian physicist).

17.365
antre (cavern), anta (architectural term), banter, canter, plantar, manta (large ray fish), Granta (River Cam), Santa, Tanta (Egyptian city), decanter, trochanter (projection on femur), Vedanta (Hindu school of philosophy), infanta, Atlanta, instanter (without delay), levanter (Mediterranean easterly wind), almucantar (astronomy term), tam-o'-shanter.

17.366
chanter, planter.

17.367
fainter, painter.

17.368
enter, renter, centre, tenter (cloth-stretching frame), venter (belly), scienter (wilfully), magenta, polenta (Italian porridge), tormentor, assentor, placenta, Jobcentre, concentre, preventer (nautical term), inventor, accentor (small songbird), succentor (cathedral cleric), presenter, hypocentre (area below nuclear explosion), orthocentre (maths term), impedimenta.

17.368.1
dissenter, precentor (cathedral cleric), epicentre (area above earthquake origin), barycentre (centre of mass).

17.369
linter (fibre-stripping machine), splinter, Pinter (English dramatist), pinta (skin disease), printer, sprinter, sinter (deposit from hot springs), winter, carpenter, midwinter, calcsinter (porous rock), teleprinter, overwinter (spend the winter).

17.370
saunter, taunter.

17.371
jointer (pointing tool), pointer, appointor (legal term).

17.372
counter, encounter.

17.373
chunter (mutter), junta, hunter, punter, grunter, shunter, pothunter (prize-seeking competitor), marabunta (West Indian wasp).

17.374
captor, chapter, raptor (bird of prey), adapter.

17.375
sceptre, septa (*plural of* septum), receptor, preceptor (teacher), acceptor (electronics term), amboceptor (immune body in blood), interceptor (fighter aircraft), proprioceptor (nerve ending).

17.376
anaglypta, lex non scripta (unwritten law).

17.377
copter (*short for* helicopter), dioptre, helicopter, ornithopter (aircraft with flapping wings).

17.378
tempter, pre-emptor, attempter.

17.379
aster, Astor, pasta, Rasta, raster (electronics term), piastre (South Vietnamese currency), diaster (biology term), Jocasta (mother of Oedipus), cadaster (property register), pilaster (rectangular column in wall), pinaster (Mediterranean pine), canasta, amphiaster (biology term), oleaster (flowering shrub), Zoroaster (Persian prophet), poetaster (inferior poet), cotoneaster,

Antofagasta (Chilean port), verticillaster (botany term).

17.380
castor, caster, plaster, master, pastor, forecaster, broadcaster, newscaster, paymaster, choirmaster, taskmaster, headmaster, bandmaster, grandmaster, schoolmaster, ringmaster, housemaster, scoutmaster, postmaster, toastmaster, quizmaster, disaster, alabaster, quartermaster, stationmaster.

17.381
slaister (*Scot* confused mess), taster, shirtwaister.

17.382
Esther, ester, Chester, fester, jester, Leicester, mester (*Dialect* master), pester, cuesta (long low ridge), tester, testa (outer layer of seed), Vesta, vesta (wooden match), wester (to move towards west).

podesta (Italian magistrate), egesta (body waste), digester, ingesta (food taken by mouth), celesta (keyboard instrument), molester, semester, trimester, sequester, arrester, ancestor, protester, Avesta (Zoroastrian scriptures), investor, sou'wester, Cirencester.

17.382.1
fiesta, siesta, polyester.

17.383
Easter, keister (*US* buttocks), leister (pronged fishing spear), Dniester (Russian river), quaestor (Roman magistrate), autopista (Spanish motorway).

17.384
bistre (drawing pigment), Lister, lister (a plough), blister, clyster (enema), glister, Mr., mister, crista (biology term), sister, vista, twister, xyster (surgical file).

Chichester, Rochester, Dorchester, Colchester, Manchester, Winchester, sophister (second-year undergraduate), register, fillister (adjustable plane),

ballista (ancient catapult), thermistor (electronic component), banister, canister, ganister (sedimentary rock), barrister, thyristor (electronic component), chorister, forester, arista (a bristle), varistor (electronic component), stepsister, harvester, resistor, transistor, deregister.

17.384.1
minister, sinister, administer, maladminister.

17.385
costa (a rib), foster, goster (*Dialect* laugh uncontrollably), hosta (Oriental plant), Gloucester, roster, zoster (shingles), impostor, defroster, paternoster.

17.386
oyster, cloister, roister.

17.387
coaster, poster, throwster (yarn spinner), toaster, four-poster, billposter.

17.388
buster, Custer, duster, lustre, bluster, cluster, fluster, muster, thruster (rocket engine), Worcester, blockbuster, combustor (part of jet engine), Augusta, lacklustre, lincrusta (embossed wallpaper), filibuster, broncobuster, knuckle-duster, Famagusta (Cypriot port).

17.389
booster, rooster.

17.390
Lancaster, Doncaster, baluster, canaster (dried tobacco leaves).

17.391
lobster, mobster.

17.392
bolster, holster, pollster (person who conducts polls), upholster.

17.393
deemster (Manx magistrate), teamster.

17.394
minster, spinster, Westminster, Axminster, Kidderminster.

17.395
Munster, punster.

17.396
hipster, quipster, tipster.

17.397
Arthur, Martha.

17.398
aphtha (small ulceration), naphtha (chemical compound).

17.399
anther, panther, pyracantha (ornamental shrub).

17.400
gather, blather, forgather (assemble), ingather.

17.401
father, farther, lather, slather (large quantity), rather, forefather, godfather, grandfather, stepfather.

17.402
feather, heather, leather, nether, tether, whether, weather, wether (castrated male sheep), together, aweather (nautical term), bellwether (leader of flock), altogether.

17.403
further, murther (murder).

17.404
breather, bequeather.

17.405
dither, hither, slither, thither, whither, wither, swither (*Scot* hesitate), zither.

17.406
either, neither.

17.407
bother, pother (commotion).

17.408
other, mother, smother, brother, godmother, grandmother, stepmother, another, stepbrother.

17.409
carver, kava (Polynesian shrub), Java, larva, lava, laver (seaweed), Drava (European river), Sava (Yugoslavian river), guava, palaver, Delmarva (US peninsula), Morava (Czechoslovakian river), cassava (tropical plant), ottava (octave), Balaclava, Bratislava (Czechoslovakian port), Costa Brava, piassava (South American palm tree).

17.410
deva (Hindu – Buddhist god), favour, haver (dither), laver (baptismal font), claver (*Scot* to gossip), flavour, slaver, quaver, raver, graver (engraving tool), savour, saver, shaver, waiver, waver, cadaver, disfavour, Ungava (region of Canada), engraver, vena cava (large vein), clishmaclaver (*Scot* gossip), semiquaver.

17.411
ever, clever, never, sever, however, whoever, whichever, endeavour, whomever, whenever, wherever, forever, dissever (break off), whatever, howsoever, whatsoever.

17.412
fervour, Nerva (Roman emperor), server, conferva (freshwater alga), Minerva, timeserver, observer, contrayerva (medicinal plant root).

17.413
beaver, kiva (Pueblo Indian underground room), diva, fever, lever, cleaver, Neva (Russian river), Siva (Hindu god), viva (long live!), weaver, weever (marine fish), believer, Geneva, retriever, deceiver, receiver, transceiver (radio transmitter – receiver), unbeliever, cantilever, underachiever.

17.414
giver, liver, flivver (cheap old car), sliver, quiver, river, shiver, lawgiver, gingiva (gum), deliver, Oliver, miniver (fur on ceremonial robes), Nineveh, vetiver (tall Asian grass).

17.415
skiver, diver, fiver, driver, Saiva (Hindu worshipper), stiver (former Dutch

coin), viva (oral examination), Godiva, helldiver (*US* grebe), saliva, co-driver, screwdriver, survivor, conjunctiva.

17.416
bovver, hover, windhover (*Dialect* kestrel).

17.417
ova, over, Dover, clover, nova, rover, drover, trover (legal term), stover (fodder).

flyover, Markova, walkover, Sadowa (battle site in Czechoslovakia), Andover, changeover, Jehovah, pullover, Pavlova, Hanover, ars nova (14th-century music style), hangover, wingover (aircraft manoeuvre), wrapover, slipover, stopover, moreover, Passover, crossover, flashover (electric discharge), pushover, leftover.

supernova, Casanova, bossa nova.

17.418
cover, lover, glover, plover, recover, uncover, discover, undercover, rediscover.

17.419
Hoover (*Trademark*), louvre, mover, Suva (capital of Fiji), Vancouver, remover, manoeuvre, outmanoeuvre, Lietuva.

17.420
salvor (person salvaging boats), salver, quacksalver (quack doctor).

17.421
elver, selva (dense equatorial forest).

17.422
silver, sylva (trees of particular region), quicksilver.

17.423
volva (botany term), revolver.

17.424
culver, vulva.

17.425
Oshawa (Canadian city), Ottawa, pipsissewa (evergreen plant).

17.426
flexor, plexor (medical hammer), indexer.

17.427
fixer, mixer, nixer (*Dialect* spare-time job), elixir.

17.428
boxer, coxa (hip bone or joint), moxa (Oriental medicinal plant substance), bobbysoxer, chionodoxa (Eurasian plant).

17.429
coaxer, hoaxer.

17.430 [see also **17.5**]
lawyer, sawyer.

17.431
bowyer (maker of archery bows), Nagoya (Japanese city), kabaragoya (large monitor lizard).

17.432
thuja (coniferous tree), alleluia.

17.433 [see also **17.3.18**]
failure, derailleur (bicycle gear-changing device).

17.434 [see also **17.3.29**]
Nyanja (African people), lasagne.

17.435 [see also **17.3.33**]
senior, Tigrinya (Ethiopian language), Monsignor.

17.436 [see also **17.3.53**]
paviour (material for paving), saviour, behaviour, misbehaviour.

17.437
lazar (leper), Belshazzar (biblical character), Salmanazar (large wine bottle).

17.438
Gaza, plaza, Kinshasa (capital of Zaïre).

17.439
laser, blazer, maser (microwave laser), razor, Fraser, stargazer, chalaza, trailblazer, eraser, impresa (emblem).

17.440

beezer (*Slang* fellow), geezer, geyser, Pisa, squeezer, freezer, Caesar, teaser, visa, genizah (synagogue storeroom), Theresa, Mona Lisa, Ebenezer.

17.441

Kaiser, miser, riser, sizar (maintained college undergraduate), visor, incisor, devisor (legal term), divisor, adviser, liquidizer, stabilizer, tranquillizer, sterilizer, fertilizer, dialyser, equalizer, neutralizer, totalizer, Breathalyzer (*Trademark*), atomizer, organizer, womanizer, moisturizer, synthesizer, exerciser, appetizer, advertiser, sympathizer, supervisor.

17.441.1

coryza (head cold), mycorrhiza (botany term), tenderizer, vaporizer, pasteurizer, coleorhiza (grass root sheath).

17.442

dozer (*short for* bulldozer), closer, poser, Rosa, bulldozer, Mendoza (Argentine city), Spinoza, composer, sub rosa (in secret), proposer, mariposa (flowering plant), decomposer (organism causing decay).

17.443

bowser (fuel tanker), dowser (water diviner), Mauser, mouser, browser, wowser (*Austral* puritanical person), carouser.

17.444

boozer, loser, bruiser, cruiser, Sousa, user, accuser, medusa (jellyfish), diffuser, infuser (tea-making device), misuser, Lampedusa (Mediterranean island), arethusa (US orchid).

17.445

panzer, kwanza (Angolan currency), stanza, organza, bonanza, extravaganza.

17.446

cleanser, credenza (small sideboard), cadenza, influenza.

18 -ab

cab, scab, dab, fab, gab, jab, lab, blab, flab, slab, Mab (fairy queen), nab, crab, drab, grab, tab, stab.

Joab (biblical character), Moab (biblical kingdom), kebab, vocab, serdab (chamber in Egyptian tomb), prefab, confab, Ahab (biblical king), Skylab, lablab (African bean plant), Chenab (Himalayan river), mihrab (niche in mosque), Cantab.

baobab (African tree), pedicab (Asian passenger-carrying tricycle), minicab.

19 -arb

barb, garb, Saab (*Trademark*), doab (land between converging rivers), rhubarb, bicarb, Punjab, nawab (Muslim prince), inqilab (revolution in India).

20 -abe

babe, astrolabe (former astronomers' instrument).

21 -eb

ebb, deb, bleb (a blister), pleb, neb (*Dialect* projecting part), reb (*US* Confederate soldier), web, cubeb (Asian climbing plant), ardeb (Egyptian unit of measure), Deneb (star), Zagreb, cobweb.

22 -erb

kerb, curb, herb, blurb, Serb (Serbian), verb, suburb, cowherb (flowering plant), potherb (plant used in cooking), superb, perturb, disturb, proverb, adverb, willowherb.

23 -ebe

Beeb, glebe, grebe, ephebe (ancient Greek youth), sungrebe (aquatic bird).

24 -ib

bib, dib, fib, jib, gib (metal bearing), lib, glib, nib, snib (*Scot* door fastening), squib, rib, crib, sib (kin), sahib, ad-lib, Carib (American Indian people), sparerib, corncrib (*US* maize store), midrib (leaf vein), memsahib, Sennacherib (Assyrian king).

25 -ibe
kibe (chilblain), gibe, gybe (nautical term), bribe, scribe, tribe, imbibe, describe, prescribe, proscribe, ascribe, subscribe, transcribe, inscribe, circumscribe, diatribe.

26 -ob
bob, cob, kob (African antelope), fob, gob, job, hob, lob, blob, glob, slob, mob, nob, knob, snob, squab (young pigeon), rob, throb, sob, stob (*Dialect* a stump), swab, yob, nabob (rich person), skibob (vehicle running on skis), corncob, kincob (Indian silk fabric), demob, hobnob, thingumabob.

27 -orb
orb, daub, sorb (tree), warb (*Austral* dirty person), bedaub, desorb (chemistry term), resorb, absorb, adsorb, chemisorb (chemistry term).

28 -obe
daube (meat stew), Job, lobe, globe, robe, probe, strobe, aerobe (organism needing oxygen), microbe, wardrobe, enrobe, saprobe (organism inhabiting foul water), disrobe, bathrobe, Francophobe, Anglophobe, Negrophobe, Russophobe, xenophobe (fearer of strangers), Germanophobe, ailurophobe (fearer of cats).

29 -ub
cub, chub, dub, hub, blub, club, slub, nub, snub, pub, rub, scrub, drub (to beat), grub, shrub, sub, tub, stub, hubbub, nightclub, washtub, bathtub, syllabub, Beelzebub.

30 -ube
boob, jube (church gallery), rube (*US* country bumpkin), cube, tube, jujube, flashcube, Danube, drawtube (telescop-

ic tube), teletube (*short for* television tube).

31 -'b
Jacob, Arab, carob, scarab, cherub, Maghreb (northwest Africa).

32 -ack
back, jack, Jack, hack, lack, lac (resin), black, clack, claque (hired applauders), flak, plaque, slack, mac, smack, knack, snack, pack, quack, rack, wrack (seaweed), crack, track, sac, sack, shack, tack, stack, vac, whack, thwack, yak.

kayak, chiack (*Austral* to tease), Dyak (Malaysian people), playback, greyback (hooded crow), bareback, dieback (tree disease), tieback (*US* curtain fastening), zwieback (toasted rusk), drawback, roorback (*US* false report), throwback, kickback, hatchback, switchback, hunchback, hardback, feedback, halfback, hogback (narrow ridge), tailback, shellback (experienced sailor), fullback, tombac (an alloy), comeback, greenback, thornback (a fish), slingback, humpback, leaseback (property transaction), mossback (*US* conservative person), horseback, flashback, splashback, fatback (pork fat), outback, cutback, fastback (type of car), ack-ack, skyjack, hijack, blackjack, smokejack (spit-turning device), flapjack, slapjack (card game), skipjack, crossjack (type of sail), muntjac (small Asian deer), hardhack (US flowering plant), kulak (Russian peasant), alack, shellac, shoeblack, boneblack (black pigment), lampblack (form of carbon), bootblack, Senlac (Battle of Hastings site), Tarmac (*Trademark*), sumach (shrub), Micmac (American Indian people), knickknack, gopak (Russian dance), mudpack, calpac (brimless hat), woolpack, champac (Indian tree), unpack, hayrack, sérac (ice pinnacle), Dirac (English physicist), tribrach (metrical foot), barn-brack (*Dialect* fruit muffin), rickrack, gimcrack, wisecrack, Shadrach, backtrack, trictrac (board game), sidetrack, soundtrack, racetrack, Barsac (sweet French wine), Cossack, corsac (Asian fox), mailsack, woolsack, ransack, knapsack, hopsack, Meshach, Dvořák, Cuttack (Indian city), ticktack (bookmakers' sign language), hardtack (hard biscuit), thumbtack, haystack, smokestack, Slovak, bushwhack (travel through woods), rucksack, galyak (fur), Cognac, Muzak (*Trademark*), Balzac, Anzac.

Kerouac (US writer), bivouac, piggyback, stickleback, turtleback (part of ship), canvasback (US duck), ipecac (purgative drug), solonchak (type of soil), amberjack (Atlantic fish), lumberjack, crackerjack, natterjack (toad), applejack (apple brandy), steeplejack, supplejack (US vine), Cadillac (*Trademark*), almanac, Sassenach, Pasternak (Russian writer), amphibrach (metrical foot), bric-a-brac, tetrabrach (metrical foot), ovisac (egg sac), Gay-Lussac (French scientist), cul-de-sac, haversack, paddywhack (a smack), Armagnac.

biofeedback (medical term), diamondback (US terrapin), Aniakchak (Alaskan volcanic crater), tacamahac (resinous gum), Apurimac (Peruvian river), Czechoslovak.

32.1
cardiac, Kodiak (large bear), zodiac, coeliac (of the abdomen), umiak (Eskimo boat), maniac, Syriac (former Syrian dialect), Votyak (Finnish people), Pontiac (Indian chief), demoniac (like a demon), simoniac (person who practises simony), ammoniac (gum resin), insomniac, celeriac (vegetable), amnesiac, symposiac (relating to a symposium), nymphomaniac, egomaniac, pyromaniac, dipsomaniac, kleptomaniac, hypochondriac, aphrodisiac,

Dionysiac (relating to Dionysus), megalomaniac.

32.1.1
ileac (relating to the ileum), iliac (relating to the ilium), sacroiliac (joint of pelvis), haemophiliac.

32.2
aback, pickaback, huckaback (coarse fabric), leatherback (turtle), paperback, quarterback, razorback (whale).

32.3
Bacharach, bladderwrack (seaweed), sandarac (tree yielding resin), Skagerrak, tamarack (US larch), anorak, sazerac (US cocktail), azedarach (bark of chinaberry tree).

32.4
attack, nunatak (isolated rock peak), counterattack.

33 -ark
ark, arc, bark, Bach, barque (sailing ship), dark, dhak, hark, haugh (*Dialect* flat valley base), lark, lakh (100 000 Indian rupees), clerk, Clark, Vlach (medieval European people), Mark, mark, marc (remnants of pressed fruit), marque (brand of car), nark, park, spark, quark, Sark, shark, stark.

diarch (botany term), debark (disembark), shagbark (US tree), embark, tanbark (bark producing tannin), soapbark (South American tree), macaque, endarch (botany term), skylark, salesclerk, mudlark, woodlark, seamark, earmark, nomarch (ancient Egyptian administrator), pockmark, bookmark, matchmark (mark on engine components), touchmark (maker's mark on pewter), trademark, tidemark, landmark, hallmark, Denmark, Finnmark (Norwegian county), pressmark (code on library book), sitzmark (skiing term), platemark (hallmark), footmark, ostmark (East German currency), postmark, birthmark, Reichsmark (former German currency), Bismarck, ethnarch (ruler of province), eparch (Orthodox Church bishop), hipparch (ancient Greek cavalry commander), toparch (ruler of small state), ballpark, Arak (Iranian town), xerarch (ecology term), Iraq, Petrarch, tetrarch, Pesach (Passover), mesarch (botany term), Rorschach, landshark (land profiteer), Plutarch, Landtag (German legislative assembly), futhark (phonetic alphabet), aardvark, boschvark (wild pig), exarch (head of Orthodox Church).

paperbark (Australian tree), disembark, ironbark (Australian eucalyptus tree), Offenbach, oligarch, meadowlark, fingermark, monomark (identification mark on goods), watermark, hierarch, perisarc (zoology term), coenosarc (zoology term), ectosarc (ectoplasm of amoeba).

33.1
matriarch, patriarch, gymnasiarch (Greek education magistrate), heresiarch (leader of heretical movement).

33.2
remark, remarque (mark on engraved plate), telemark (skiing term), polemarch (ancient Greek official).

34 -ake
ache, bake, cake, fake, hake, lake, laik (*Dialect* to play), Blake, flake, splake (Canadian hybrid trout), slake, make, snake, spake, quake, rake, brake, break, crake (bird), drake, strake (metal part of wheel), sake, sheik, shake, take, steak, stake, wake.

hardbake (almond toffee), clambake, sunbake (*Austral* sunbathing), backache, teacake, seedcake, beefcake, pancake, queencake, cupcake, shortcake, oatcake, fruitcake, cheesecake, headache, Hoylake, snowflake, remake, unmake, blacksnake (venomous snake), opaque, seaquake (earthquake on seabed), lyke-wake (night vigil over corpse), moonquake (moon tremor),

earthquake, earache, daybreak, firebreak, wordbreak, handbrake, windbreak, jailbreak, canebrake (*US* thicket of canes), heartbreak, outbreak, muckrake, corncrake, firedrake (fire-breathing dragon), sheldrake, mandrake, lapstrake (nautical term), forsake, namesake, keepsake, handshake, heartache, partake, retake, betake, intake, uptake, mistake, beefsteak, sweepstake, toothache, awake.

stomachache, griddlecake, rattlesnake, parabrake (aircraft parachute), undertake, overtake, wapentake (former county subdivision), kittiwake, radiopaque (impervious to radiation).

35 -eck
beck, keck (retch), Czech, check, cheque, deck, heck, Lech (European river), lek (Albanian currency), cleck (*Dialect* gossip), fleck, meck (*Dialect* small coin), neck, nek (mountain pass), sneck (*Dialect* latch), peck, spec, speck, wreck, rec (*short for* recreation), trek, sec.

Purbeck, rebec (former stringed instrument), Seebeck (philately term), xebec (Mediterranean sailing ship), Quebec, Warbeck (pretender to English throne), Brubeck (US jazz musician), pinchbeck (imitation gold), Baalbek (Lebanese town), crombec (African songbird), Steinbeck, Kazbek (Russian volcano), háček (phonetic symbol), raincheck, crosscheck, bedeck, foredeck, cromlech (prehistoric stone structure), fartlek (sports term), fennec, wryneck (woodpecker), crew-neck, breakneck, redneck, roughneck, rollneck, gooseneck (nautical term), OPEC, kopeck (Russian coin), henpeck, flyspeck (small speck), varec (seaweed), tenrec (small mammal), shipwreck, parsec (unit of astronomical distance), cusec (unit of flow), Toltec (American Indian people), Mixtec (American Indian people), Aztec.

bodycheck (sports term), overcheck, quarterdeck, afterdeck, rubberneck (*Slang* sightseer), leatherneck (*Slang* US marine), turtleneck, bottleneck, Chiang Kai-shek, Kohoutek (comet), discotheque, Zapotec (American Indian people), Tehuantepec (region of Mexico).

36 -erk

erk, irk, berk, burke (murder by suffocation), kirk, dirk, jerk, lurk, murk (gloomy darkness), smirk, perk, quirk, cirque (semicircular depression in mountains), shirk, Turk, stirk (heifer), work.

hauberk (long coat of mail), Selkirk, Falkirk, brickwork, clockwork, taskwork (unpleasant work), rework, firework, wirework, cribwork (heavy timber framework), patchwork, coachwork, spadework, roadwork, woodwork, fieldwork, groundwork, legwork, bridgework (small dental plate), framework, teamwork, timework, formwork (wooden mould for concrete), homework, stonework, crownwork (dental crown manufacture), slopwork (manufacture of shoddy goods), glasswork, casework, guesswork, presswork (operation of printing press), piecework, housework, falsework (framework supporting unfinished construction), brushwork, artwork, network, fretwork, brightwork (metal car trimmings), outwork, footwork, breastwork, earthwork, waxwork, berserk.

Atatürk (Turkish general), bodywork, handiwork, fancywork, timberwork, wickerwork, wonderwork (miracle), paperwork, counterwork, overwork, needlework, metalwork, ironwork, openwork, trelliswork, basketwork.

37 -eek

eke, beak, keek (*Scot* peep), cheek, deek (*Dialect* look at), geek (animal-eating sideshow performer), leak, leek, bleak, clique, cleek (golf club), sleek, meek, sneak, pique, peke, peek, peak, speak, squeak, reek, wreak, creek, creak, screak (*Dialect* screech), freak, Greek, shriek, streak, seek, Sikh, chic, teak, week, weak, tweak.

caïque (boat), halfbeak (a fish), grosbeak (bird), Belleek (delicate porcelain), oblique, houseleek (a plant), unique, technique, forepeak (nautical term), bespeak, newspeak, pipsqueak, perique (strong tobacco), tugrik (Mongolian currency), hairstreak (butterfly), cacique (American Indian chief), pratique (permission to use port), critique, boutique, antique, triptyque (permission to import vehicle), mystique, midweek, bezique, physique.

stickybeak (*Austral* inquisitive person), Mozambique, Martinique, ortanique (orange–tangerine hybrid), Chesapeake, fenugreek, hide-and-seek.

38 -ick [further rhymes may be created by removing -al from some adjectives in 228.23]

kick, chick, Dick, hic, hick, lick, click, flick, slick, Mick, nick, snick, pick, quick, rick, brick, crick, prick, trick, strick (unprepared textile fibres), sick, sic, tick, tic, stick, stich (line of poetry), thick, Wick, wick.

spruik (*Austral* speak in public), Bewick (English wood engraver), rhombic, Turkic (language group), psychic, sidekick, dabchick, Dardic (language group), Vedic (relating to Hindu scriptures), medic, medick (a plant), herdic (*US* small carriage), Nordic, dik-dik (small African antelope), Indic (language group), syndic (business agent), asdic (echo sounder), Kufic (early Arabic script), Delphic, georgic (poem about rural life), garlic, Gaelic, cowlick, niblick, public, cyclic, suslik (Eurasian ground squirrel), shashlik (kebab), bootlick, formic (relating to ants), gnomic (relating to aphorisms), bromic (containing bromine), chromic (containing chromium), sphygmic (relating to the pulse), seismic, cosmic, dornick (heavy cloth), runic, Munich, Punic, tunic, picnic, pyknic (having broad squat build), strychnic (relating to strychnine), splanchnic (relating to abdominal organs), Chetnik (Serbian nationalist), beatnik, sputnik, ethnic, epic, unpick, aspic, toothpick, baric (relating to atmospheric pressure), hayrick, xeric (growing in dry conditions), fabric, airbrick, firebrick, rubric, Kubrick (US film director), redbrick, cambric, hydric (containing hydrogen), quadric (maths term), baldric (sash for carrying sword), Ugric (language group), Cymric (Welsh language), cupric (containing copper), pinprick, citric, vitric (relating to glass), nitric, gastric, carsick, basic, airsick, seasick, calcic (containing calcium), homesick, brainsick, heartsick, lovesick, muzhik (Russian peasant), quartic (maths term), deictic (logic term), Celtic, Baltic, haptic (relating to touch), caustic, fustic (tree yielding yellow dye), rustic, crabstick (crab-apple stick), matchstick, swordstick, pigstick (hunt wild boar), maulstick (artist's hand-steadying stick), drumstick, broomstick, greenstick, nonstick, unstick, chapstick (*US* lip salve), slapstick, dipstick, lipstick, ethic, Gothic, Sothic (relating to Sirius), Slavic, Narvik (Norwegian port), pelvic, Lerwick (Scottish town), Brunswick, Keswick, physic, music.

ichthyic (relating to fishes), syllabic, amoebic, acerbic (bitter), Arabic, alembic, anarchic, druidic, bromidic (dull), acidic, fatidic (prophetic), heraldic, malefic, benefic, lethargic, neuralgic, nephralgic, gastralgic, arthralgic, nostalgic, pilgarlic (*Dialect* pitiful person), pashalik (region governed by pasha), catholic, Catholic, republic, acyclic

(chemistry term), bicyclic (forming two circles), ophthalmic, orgasmic, Adonic (type of verse line), arsenic, Dubrovnik, Olympic, epeiric (relating to continental drift), oneiric (relating to dreams), Frederick, bishopric, undertrick (bridge term), gastrotrich (minute aquatic animal), overtrick (bridge term), electric, dioptric, digastric (jaw muscle), silicic (containing silicon), banausic (utilitarian), Tungusic (language group), forensic, intrinsic, extrinsic, cathartic (purgative), elenctic (logic term), acoustic, monostich (single-line poem), tetrastich (four-line poem), pentastich (five-line poem), hexastich (six-line poem), fiddlestick, candlestick, singlestick (wooden sword-substitute), alethic (logic term), helminthic (relating to parasitic worms), Reykjavik, bailiwick, candlewick, dyslexic.

orthorhombic (crystallography term), demagogic, cataclysmic, microcosmic, polytechnic, pyrotechnic (relating to fireworks), archbishopric, dielectric (physics term), pneumogastric (anatomy term), geodesic (maths term), anthelmintic (substance destroying intestinal worms), anacoustic (soundless), ataraxic (calming), analgesic, metaphysic.

polysyllabic, monosyllabic, turbo-electric, thermoelectric (physics term), hydroelectric, isoelectric (having same electric potential), photoelectric, onomatopoeic.

38.1
laic, archaic, trochaic (verse form), Alcaic (verse form), Judaic, Altaic (language group), voltaic, prosaic, mosaic, formulaic, Ptolemaic, Aramaic, Pharisaic, apotropaic (preventing evil), deoxyribonucleic.

38.1.1
Hebraic, algebraic.

38.2
stoic, echoic, heroic, anechoic, amphichroic (producing two colours), polyzoic (zoology term), epizoic (zoology term), Eozoic, Neozoic, holozoic (biology term), Cenozoic, saprozoic (biology term), Mesozoic, entozoic (living inside an animal), cryptozoic (living in dark places), Palaeozoic.

38.3
phobic, strobic (spinning), aerobic (requiring oxygen), xenophobic (afraid of foreigners), aerophobic (afraid of draughts), acrophobic (afraid of heights), necrophobic (afraid of death), hydrophobic, claustrophobic, anaerobic (not requiring oxygen), agoraphobic.

38.4
cubic, pubic, cherubic.

38.5
iambic (metrical foot), galliambic (verse metre), dithyrambic (passionately eloquent).

38.6
Bacchic, Noachic (relating to Noah), stomachic.

38.7
Chadic (language group), dyadic (twofold), dryadic, nomadic, tornadic, faradic (physics term), sporadic.

38.8
comedic (relating to comedy), logaoedic (verse form), orthopaedic, encyclopedic.

38.9
iodic (containing iodine), melodic, psalmodic, spasmodic, synodic, parodic, rhapsodic, periodic, episodic, aperiodic (at irregular intervals), antispasmodic.

38.10
scandic (containing the element scandium), Icelandic.

38.11 [further rhymes may be derived from **16.90.2** and **158.1**]

graphic, traffic, Sapphic (verse form), edaphic (relating to soil), seraphic, telegraphic, epigraphic, pornographic, photographic, epitaphic.

38.12
deific (godlike), morbific (causing disease), prolific, omnific, horrific, febrific (causing fever), specific, Pacific, pacific, calcific (forming lime), conspecific (within the same species), transpacific, beatific, scientific, hieroglyphic, unscientific, stereospecific (chemistry term).

38.12.1
terrific, sudorific (causing sweating), calorific (relating to heat), colorific (relating to colour), honorific, vaporific (producing vapour), soporific.

38.13
trophic (relating to nutrition), strophic (poetry term), eutrophic (ecology term), atrophic, polytrophic (biology term), autotrophic (biology term), prototrophic (biology term), geostrophic (meteorology term), apostrophic, catastrophic, philosophic, oligotrophic (ecology term), heterotrophic (biology term).

38.14
Orphic (mysterious), geomorphic (concerning the earth's surface), endomorphic (having heavy build), monomorphic (having only one form), mesomorphic (having muscular build), metamorphic, protomorphic (primitive), ectomorphic (having thin build), theriomorphic (depicted in animal form), anthropomorphic (depicted in human form), heteromorphic (having different forms).

38.15
magic, tragic, pelagic (relating to open sea), haemorrhagic, anthropophagic (cannibalistic), archipelagic.

38.16
allergic, anergic (lacking energy), lysergic (type of acid), endoergic (energy-

absorbing), exoergic (energy-emitting), metallurgic, cholinergic (biology term), adrenergic (biology term).

38.17
strategic, hemiplegic, quadriplegic, paraplegic.

38.18
logic, choplogic, pedagogic, hypnagogic (psychology term).

38.19
Alec, phallic, Gallic, salic (having high silica content), vocalic (relating to a vowel), alkalic (having high alkali content), medallic, cephalic (relating to the head), Uralic (language group), smart aleck, prevocalic (coming before a vowel), encephalic (relating to the brain), intervocalic (between vowels).

38.19.1
italic, metallic, bimetallic, nonmetallic, genitalic.

38.20
melic (meant to be sung), relic, telic (purposeful), nickelic, Goidelic (language group), angelic, Gadhelic (Gaelic language), scalpellic, psychedelic, philatelic.

38.21
killick (small stone anchor), idyllic, Menelik (Abyssinian emperor), vanillic (relating to vanilla), Cyrillic, acrylic, cresylic (relating to creosote), dactylic (metrical foot), ethylic, methylic, basilic (vein in arm), lyophilic (chemistry term), cryophilic (thriving at low temperatures), zoophilic (fond of animals), haemophilic, thermophilic (thriving in warm conditions), lipophilic (chemistry term), hydrophilic (chemistry term).

38.22
colic, rollick, frolic, Aeolic (ancient Greek dialect), carbolic, ecbolic (inducing labour or abortion), embolic, symbolic, bucolic, Mongolic, petrolic (relating to petroleum), systolic, vitriol-

ic, diabolic, anabolic, hyperbolic, parabolic, catabolic, metabolic, melancholic, hypergolic (spontaneously flammable), alcoholic, diastolic, apostolic.

38.23
aulic (relating to royal court), hydraulic.

38.24
gamic (biology term), agamic (biology term), Islamic, dynamic, ceramic, balsamic, potamic (relating to rivers), panoramic, thermodynamic, aerodynamic, hydrodynamic (physics term), isodynamic (having equal force).

38.25
alchemic, pandemic (widespread epidemic), endemic, polemic, Moslemic, totemic, systemic, polydemic (ecology term), epidemic, academic.

38.26
spermic, endermic (absorbed through skin), taxidermic, hypodermic, diathermic (medical term), endothermic (chemistry term), photothermic (of light and heat), exothermic (chemistry term).

38.27
haemic (relating to blood), anaemic, phonemic (relating to speech sounds), racemic (chemistry term), epistemic (relating to knowledge).

38.28
gimmick, mimic, acronymic, metronymic (relating to maternal name), patronymic.

38.29
comic, syndromic, atomic, entomic (relating to insects), pentomic (dividing into five groups), tragicomic, diatomic (containing two atoms), triatomic (containing three atoms), subatomic, monatomic (containing one atom), physiognomic, intra-atomic, interatomic.

38.29.1
economic, metronomic, astronomic, gastronomic, autonomic (occurring involuntarily), taxonomic, uneconomic, socioeconomic.

38.30
rhythmic, eurhythmic (having pleasing rhythm), logarithmic, isorhythmic (musical term).

38.31
manic, panic, tannic, stannic (containing tin), mechanic, volcanic, Sudanic (language group), organic, Brahmanic, Germanic, tympanic, Hispanic, uranic (containing uranium), Britannic, titanic, satanic, tetanic, sultanic, galvanic, homorganic (linguistics term), inorganic, aldermanic, Alemannic (language group), talismanic, aeromechanic.

38.31.1
messianic (relating to the Messiah), oceanic, suboceanic, transoceanic.

38.32
genic (relating to a gene), splenic (relating to the spleen), phrenic (relating to the diaphragm), sthenic (energetic and strong), sphenic (wedge-shaped), eugenic, Hellenic, asthenic (weak), telegenic (looking good on television), oxygenic, schizophrenic, Saracenic, callisthenic.

38.32.1
myogenic (muscle-forming), psychogenic, oncogenic (tumour-forming), typhogenic (causing typhoid), allergenic, chromogenic (colour-producing), pyrogenic (heat-producing), neurogenic (of nervous origin), androgenic, oestrogenic, allergenic, phytogenic (obtained from plants), photogenic, lactogenic, cryptogenic (of unknown origin), pathogenic, orthogenic (medical term), toxicogenic, immunogenic, hysterogenic, radiogenic (caused by radioactive decay), audiogenic (caused by sound), cariogenic (producing tooth decay),

erotogenic (erogenous), teratogenic (causing fetal deformity).

38.32.1.1
carcinogenic, hallucinogenic.

38.33
scenic, hygienic, irenic (conciliatory), axenic (uncontaminated).

38.34
Finnic (language group), clinic, cynic, rabbinic, albinic, triclinic (crystallography term), Brahminic, Dominic, actinic (denoting type of radiation), succinic (relating to amber), kinnikinnick (mixture for smoking), polyclinic (general hospital), monoclinic (crystallography term), histaminic, nicotinic, haematinic (substance stimulating haemoglobin production), diactinic (physics term).

38.35
conic, phonic, clonic (medical term), chronic, sonic, tonic.

ionic, Ionic, bionic, thionic (relating to sulphur), carbonic, bubonic, iconic, laconic, draconic, obconic (cone-shaped), sardonic, typhonic, euphonic, symphonic, colonic, cyclonic, harmonic, sermonic, demonic, mnemonic, pneumonic, pulmonic, Pharaonic, ironic, Byronic, moronic, vibronic (physics term), synchronic (linguistics term), subsonic, transonic (around the sound barrier), atonic (unstressed), plutonic (geology term), Teutonic, subtonic (musical note), tectonic, planktonic, Miltonic, syntonic (psychology term), gnathonic (deceitfully flattering), Brythonic (language group), pythonic, Slavonic, ozonic.

polyconic (maths term), aniconic (forbidding idol worship), telephonic, polyphonic (musical term), isogonic (maths term), philharmonic, enharmonic (musical term), nonharmonic, geoponic (relating to agricultural science), macaronic (type of verse), diachronic (linguistics term), anachronic (out of date), electronic.

anticyclonic, architectonic (relating to architectural qualities), geotectonic (relating to earth's crust), microelectronic.

38.35.1
thermionic (physics term), embryonic, histrionic, avionic, chameleonic, Napoleonic.

38.35.2
aphonic (voiceless), diaphonic (musical term), megaphonic, xylophonic, homophonic (having identical pronunciation), monophonic, microphonic, quadraphonic, saxophonic, radiophonic, stereophonic, dodecaphonic (musical term).

38.35.3
ammonic, Solomonic, pathognomonic (indicating a particular disease).

38.35.4
masonic, freemasonic, supersonic, infrasonic (below frequency of sound), ultrasonic.

38.35.5
Platonic, diatonic (musical term), hypotonic (lacking tension), hypertonic (having high tension), supertonic (musical note), isotonic (having equal tension), phototonic (responding to light), pentatonic (musical term).

38.36
philippic (speech of bitter denunciation), polytypic (having several different types), monotypic (having only one type), heterotypic (biology term), homeotypic (biology term), stereotypic.

38.37
tropic, topic, myopic, metopic (relating to the forehead), ectopic, entopic (in normal position), Ethiopic, telescopic, periscopic, eurytropic (ecology term), isentropic (physics term), isotopic, radioisotopic.

38.37.1 [further rhymes may be derived from **16.254.2** and **278.1**]
stroboscopic, macroscopic, microscopic, hygroscopic (absorbing moisture from air), orthoscopic (relating to normal vision), stereoscopic, kaleidoscopic.

38.37.2
vagotropic (affecting the vagus nerve), allotropic (existing in several forms), stenotropic (ecology term), inotropic (affecting muscle contraction), hydrotropic (growing towards water), phototropic (growing towards light), thixotropic (becoming thinner when stirred), heliotropic (growing towards sunlight).

38.37.3
philanthropic, misanthropic, palaeanthropic (relating to early man), neoanthropic (resembling modern man), therianthropic (part animal, part human).

38.38
baric (relating to atmospheric pressure), daric (ancient Persian coin), Garrick, stearic (relating to suet), barbaric, Pindaric (type of ode), margaric (resembling pearl), Amharic (Ethiopian official language), tartaric, Balearic, centrobaric (of centre of gravity), isobaric, hyperbaric (relating to high pressures).

38.39
Eric, Berwick, skerrick (*US* small fragment), derrick, Derek, ferric, cleric, steric (chemistry term), valeric (relating to valerian), Homeric, numeric, mesmeric, dineric (chemistry term), generic, glyceric (containing glycerol), enteric, hysteric, hemispheric, atmospheric, stratospheric, polymeric, poromeric (permeable to water vapour), esoteric, exoteric (comprehensible), amphoteric (chemistry term), isosteric (chemistry term), alphanumeric, gastroenteric.

38.40
lyric, pyrrhic, vampiric, empiric, satiric, satyric, panegyric (speech of praise).

38.41
choric (relating to a chorus), Doric (architectural term), Warwick, euphoric, camphoric, phosphoric, caloric, folkloric, historic, meteoric, pyrophoric (igniting spontaneously), semaphoric, metaphoric, allegoric, categoric, prehistoric, phantasmagoric.

38.42
auric (containing gold), boric, chloric, fluoric (relating to fluorine), hydrochloric.

38.43
Rurik (Scandinavian Viking leader), uric, Zürich, mercuric, sulphuric, telluric (terrestrial).

38.44
agaric, Alaric (king of the Visigoths), choleric, turmeric, limerick, Limerick, rhetoric, maverick, Theodoric (king of the Ostrogoths), Ermanaric (king of the Ostrogoths), climacteric.

38.45
Patrick, iatric (relating to medicine), Kirkpatrick, sympatric (biology term), Downpatrick (Irish town), psychiatric, paediatric, geriatric, allopatric (biology term).

38.46 [further rhymes may be derived from **16.285.2** and **17.342.3**]
metric, dimetric (crystallography term), trimetric (relating to verse line), obstetric, asymmetric, bisymmetric, geometric, diametric, kilometric, barometric, isometric.

38.47
centric, acentric, concentric, eccentric, theocentric (theology term), geocentric (having earth at centre), endocentric (linguistics term), egocentric, homocentric (having the same centre), exocentric (linguistics term).

38.48
classic, Liassic, Triassic, thalassic (relating to the sea), thoracic, Jurassic, boracic.

38.49
Attic, attic, batik, phatic (relating to social conversation), static, vatic (relating to a prophet).

sciatic, emphatic, lymphatic, villatic (rustic), spermatic, haematic, climatic, traumatic, komatik (Eskimo sledge), somatic (relating to the body), stomatic (relating to the mouth), pneumatic, rheumatic, magmatic, pragmatic, phlegmatic, dogmatic, dalmatic (tunic-like vestment), asthmatic, Carnatic (region of India), venatic, hepatic, aquatic, erratic, piratic, Socratic, quadratic, astatic (unstable), eustatic (geology term), ecstatic, sylvatic (growing in a wood).

Eleatic (school of philosophy), pancreatic, Adriatic, mydriatic (causing pupil dilation), Hanseatic, Asiatic, acrobatic, aliphatic (chemistry term), subaquatic, hieratic (relating to priests), operatic, biquadratic (maths term), antistatic.

proceleusmatic (metrical foot), semiaquatic, idiosyncratic.

38.49.1
schematic, nematic (chemistry term), sematic (zoology term), thematic, dilemmatic, cinematic, systematic, episematic (zoology term), aposematic (zoology term), athematic (musical term), unsystematic.

38.49.2
chromatic, dramatic, problematic, emblematic, diplomatic, aromatic, achromatic (without colour), dichromatic (having only two colours), trichromatic (relating to three colours), programmatic, automatic, symptomatic, idiomatic, axiomatic (self-evident), iconomatic (representing sounds with pictures), polychromatic, monochro-

matic, apochromatic (physics term), melodramatic, epigrammatic, diagrammatic, anagrammatic, monogrammatic, psychosomatic, asymptomatic, semi-automatic.

38.49.3
stigmatic, enigmatic, astigmatic, paradigmatic (linguistics term), anastigmatic.

38.49.4
prismatic, schismatic, melismatic (musical term), numismatic, charismatic.

38.49.5
fanatic, morganatic, aplanatic (physics term).

38.49.6 [further rhymes may be derived from **16.307.5**]
leucocratic (geology term), democratic, Hippocratic, bureaucratic, mesocratic (geology term), autocratic, plutocratic, aristocratic.

38.49.7
geostatic (geology term), haemostatic (stopping blood flow), thermostatic, hypostatic, gyrostatic (concerned with rotating bodies), hydrostatic (physics term), electrostatic.

38.50
metic (ancient Greek alien), thetic (relating to metrical stress).

hebetic (relating to puberty), eidetic (psychology term), syndetic (linguistics term), prophetic, balletic, phyletic (biology term), athletic, hermetic, emetic, mimetic (imitative), cosmetic, tonetic (linguistics term), magnetic, limnetic (ecology term), pyretic (relating to fever), uretic (relating to urine), ascetic, enthetic (medical term), synthetic, aesthetic, prosthetic, Helvetic (Swiss).

geodetic (geography term), asyndetic (without cross references), exegetic (explanatory), homiletic (relating to a sermon), arithmetic, apyretic (without fe-

ver), diuretic, dietetic, parenthetic, anaesthetic.

antimagnetic, thermomagnetic (physics term), gyromagnetic (physics term), isomagnetic (having equal magnetic force), antipyretic (preventing fever), diaphoretic (causing perspiration), peripatetic, polysynthetic (linguistics term), photosynthetic.

galactopoietic (inducing milk production), electromagnetic.

38.50.1
noetic (relating to the mind), poetic, dianoetic (relating to thought).

38.50.2
diabetic, alphabetic, analphabetic.

38.50.3
energetic, synergetic (acting together), apologetic.

38.50.4
kinetic, phenetic (biology term), genetic, splenetic, frenetic, Venetic (ancient Italian language), telekinetic, hydrokinetic (relating to moving fluids), autokinetic (self-moving), pathogenetic (relating to disease).

38.50.5
phonetic, cybernetic.

38.50.6
bathetic, pathetic, nomothetic (giving laws), apathetic, empathetic, sympathetic, antipathetic, parasympathetic.

38.51
Rhaetic (geology term), cretic (metrical foot), acetic.

38.52
lytic (biology term), clitic (unstressed), critic.

phlebitic, rachitic (having rickets), trachytic (geology term), bronchitic, mephitic (poisonous), graphitic, politic, proclitic (linguistics term), enclitic (linguistics term), Hamitic (language group), Semitic, Sinitic (language group), granitic, neritic (ecology term), Sanskritic, nephritic (relating to the kidneys), Negritic (relating to Negroes), arthritic, Cushitic (language group).

Jesuitic, troglodytic, holophytic (biology term), meningitic, laryngitic, syphilitic, tonsillitic, impolitic, anaclitic (psychology term), stalagmitic, porphyritic (geology term), diacritic, stalactitic.

hermaphroditic, anti-Semitic, Proto-semitic (language group), osteoarthritic.

38.52.1
oolitic, thermolytic (relating to heat loss), analytic, paralytic, hydrolytic (chemistry term), catalytic, electrolytic, sympatholytic (inhibiting nerve impulses), bacteriolytic (destroying bacteria), psychoanalytic.

38.52.2
sybaritic, Ugaritic (extinct Semitic language), Himyaritic (language group), meteoritic.

38.52.3
lymphocytic, parasitic, anthracitic, erythrocytic, semiparasitic.

38.53
glottic (relating to the tongue), chaotic, thrombotic, narcotic, mycotic (relating to fungal infections), psychotic, aphotic (growing without light), Nilotic (relating to the Nile), demotic (of the common people), zymotic (relating to fermentation), osmotic, nepotic, despotic, sclerotic, erotic, cirrhotic, neurotic, parotic (situated near the ear), necrotic (relating to dead tissue), dicrotic (having a double pulse), tricrotic (having a triple pulse), quixotic, azotic (relating to nitrogen), exotic.

idiotic, symbiotic (mutually dependent), semiotic (relating to symbols), amniotic, patriotic, enzootic (veterinary term), creosotic, asymptotic.

epizootic (veterinary term), psychoneurotic.

38.53.1
biotic (relating to living organisms), meiotic, amphibiotic (zoology term), antibiotic, macrobiotic (relating to vegetarian diet).

38.53.2
hypnotic, posthypnotic, agrypnotic (relating to insomnia), autohypnotic.

38.54
aortic, astronautic.

38.55
otic (relating to the ear), photic (relating to light), lotic (inhabiting flowing water), rhotic (linguistics term), euphotic (ecology term), periotic (around the ear).

38.56
maieutic (philosophy term), scorbutic, propaedeutic (preparation before further study), hermeneutic (relating to biblical interpretation), therapeutic, antiscorbutic, radiotherapeutic.

38.57
lunatic, heretic, arithmetic.

38.58
lactic, tactic, didactic, galactic, climactic, atactic (chemistry term), syntactic, prophylactic, parallactic (relating to parallax), ataractic (tranquillizing), chiropractic, anaphylactic, extragalactic, anticlimactic, heliotactic (moving towards sunlight).

38.59
arctic, Nearctic (zoogeographical term), subarctic, Holarctic (zoogeographical term), Antarctic, subantarctic.

38.60
hectic, smectic (chemistry term), eclectic, dyslectic, orectic (relating to desire), eutectic (physics term), cathectic (psychology term), dialectic, catalectic (relating to verse line), apoplectic.

38.61
systaltic (relating to heartbeat), peristaltic.

38.62
antic, mantic (relating to prophecy), frantic, pedantic, gigantic, Atlantic, semantic, romantic, sycophantic, transatlantic.

38.63
lentic (inhabiting still water), argentic (containing silver), crescentic, authentic.

38.64
Pontic (of the Black Sea), quantic (maths term), deontic (logic term), orthodontic.

38.65
sceptic, peptic, septic, dyspeptic, aseptic, epileptic, analeptic (restorative drug), antiseptic.

38.66
diptych, glyptic (relating to engraving), cryptic, triptych, styptic, elliptic, polyptych (altarpiece), ecliptic, procryptic (protectively coloured), apocalyptic.

38.67
optic, Coptic (language group), bioptic, panoptic (taking in all viewpoints), synoptic, orthoptic (relating to binocular vision).

38.68
clastic (geology term), plastic, mastic (aromatic resin), spastic, drastic.

bombastic, sarcastic, stochastic (statistics term), elastic, scholastic, synclastic (maths term), aplastic, euplastic (healing quickly), dynastic, monastic, gymnastic, fantastic, doxastic (logic term).

inelastic, anticlastic (maths term), thromboplastic (forming a blood clot), thermoplastic (becoming soft when heated), anaplastic (relating to plastic surgery), ceroplastic (relating to wax-modelling), esemplastic (unifying), onomastic (relating to proper names),

epispastic (producing a blister), hudibrastic (mock-heroic), periphrastic (circumlocutory).

interscholastic, iconoclastic.

38.68.1
orgiastic, ecclesiastic, enthusiastic.

38.69
majestic, telestich (short poem), domestic, agrestic (rural), isopiestic (having equal atmospheric pressure).

38.70 [further rhymes may be derived from **242.35**]
distich (two-line poem), fistic (relating to boxing), mystic, tristich (three-line poem), cystic.

sadistic, sophistic, stylistic, simplistic, hemistich (half line of verse), eristic (logic term), floristic, touristic, heuristic (helping to learn), juristic, patristic (relating to Church Fathers), artistic, autistic, linguistic.

atheistic, egoistic, jingoistic, altruistic, casuistic, masochistic, Hellenistic (relating to Greek civilization), chauvinistic, communistic, narcissistic, inartistic.

evangelistic, relativistic, sadomasochistic.

38.70.1
logistic, phlogistic (relating to inflammation), syllogistic, eulogistic, synergistic (acting together), antiphlogistic (alleviating inflammation).

38.70.2
ballistic, symbolistic, journalistic, socialistic, fatalistic, novelistic, cannibalistic, nationalistic, rationalistic, naturalistic, commercialistic, capitalistic, sensationalistic, individualistic.

38.70.2.1
realistic, idealistic, surrealistic, materialistic.

38.70.3
euphemistic, pessimistic, optimistic.

38.70.4
mechanistic, modernistic, agonistic (combative), antagonistic, anachronistic, impressionistic.

38.70.5
meristic (biology term), futuristic, aphoristic, humoristic, terroristic, voyeuristic, characteristic, behaviouristic.

38.70.6
statistic, egotistic, chrematistic (relating to money-making).

38.71
gnostic, agnostic, prognostic, acrostic, diagnostic.

38.72
gnathic (relating to the jaw), spathic (resembling the mineral spar), empathic, photobathic (biology term), telepathic, psychopathic, allopathic, idiopathic (medical term), homeopathic, osteopathic, naturopathic.

38.73
lithic (made of stone), ornithic (relating to birds), Eolithic, Neolithic, chalcolithic (archaeology term), megalithic, monolithic, Mesolithic, protolithic (of the Stone Age), Palaeolithic, heliolithic (of sun-worshipping civilization).

38.74
civic, Bolshevik, Menshevik.

38.75
toxic, hypoxic (relating to oxygen deficiency), radiotoxic.

39 -ike
bike, dyke, fyke (*US* fishing net), hike, haik (Arabian outer garment), like, mike, pike, spike, Reich, shrike, trike, strike, psych, sike (*Dialect* small stream), tyke.

Vandyke, Klondike, Thorndike, hitchhike, hairlike, warlike, alike, snakelike, suchlike, godlike, swordlike, childlike, lifelike, shell-like, dreamlike, manlike, swanlike, unlike, apelike, glasslike, cat-like, antlike, Christlike, ghostlike, van Eyck, garpike (freshwater fish), turnpike, handspike (metal lever), alsike (Eurasian clover).

motorbike, ladylike, workmanlike, sportsmanlike.

39.1
dislike, businesslike.

40 -ock
och, bock (beer), cock, chock (wooden wedge), dock, doc, Jock, hock, lock, lough, loch, bloc, block, clock, flock, schlock (*US* inferior goods), mock, smock, knock, nock (notch on arrow), pock, Spock, rock, roc, brock (badger), broch (Scottish circular tower), crock, frock, sock, shock, stock, wok.

blaubok (large antelope), sjambok (heavy whip), Lombok (Indonesian island), steinbok (small antelope), springbok, grysbok (small antelope), gemsbok (large antelope), haycock (small pile of hay), Leacock (Canadian humorist), peacock, seacock, gorcock (male red grouse), moorcock, bibcock (tap with bent nozzle), blackcock (male black grouse), spatchcock, Hitchcock, spitchcock, pinchcock (clamp compressing rubber tube), woodcock, Alcock (British aviator), ball cock, gamecock (fighting cock), Hancock, turncock (Water Authority official), Bangkok, stopcock, petcock (valve on steam boiler), Médoc, burdock, Murdoch, Kodok (Sudanese town), Van Gogh, forehock, Mohock (18th-century aristocratic ruffian), ad hoc, charlock, Belloc, airlock, Shylock, oarlock, forelock, warlock, Moloch, breechblock (metal block in firearm), roadblock, picklock (person who picks locks), o'clock, padlock, deadlock, headlock (wrestling hold), wedlock, elflock (tangled lock of hair), daglock (dung-encrusted sheep's wool), hemlock, unlock, gunlock, Matlock, fet-

lock, wristlock (wrestling hold), havelock (protective cap cover), lovelock
(lock of hair), Enoch, kapok, epoch,
Duroc (US breed of pig), baroque, pibroch, bedrock, defrock, unfrock,
shamrock, rimrock (geology term),
traprock (fine-grained rock), windsock,
foreshock (*US* minor earthquake),
Bartók, ticktock, Gangtok (Indian
city), diestock (screw-cutting tool),
nostoc (blue-green alga), Rostock (East
German port), Vostok (Russian spacecraft), headstock (part of machine
tool), bloodstock, tailstock (part of
machine tool), drillstock (part of
machine tool), penstock (water channel), linstock, gunstock, whipstock
(whip handle), bitstock (handle of
drilling tool), rootstock, livestock.

manioc (tropical plant), Antioch,
poppycock, weathercock, monocoque
(car or aircraft body), shuttlecock, kazachok (Russian folk dance), hollyhock, interlock, antiknock (petrol additive), monadnock (hill of hard rock),
aftershock, alpenstock, Eniwetok (Pacific atoll).

41 -ork
auk, orc (whale), balk, baulk (billiards
term), cork, Cork, calk (metal spike on
shoe), caulk (fill cracks), chalk, fork,
gawk (clumsy person), hawk, nork
(*Austral* female breast), pork, squawk,
talk, torque, stalk, stork, walk, York.

uncork, Dundalk (Irish town), hayfork,
pitchfork, Mohawk, goshawk, nighthawk, newshawk (*US* newspaper reporter), cakewalk, shoptalk, crosstalk,
leafstalk, beanstalk, cornstalk (*Austral*
native Australian), jaywalk, sidewalk,
boardwalk (*US* wooden promenade),
sleepwalk, sheepwalk (land for sheep-
grazing), ropewalk (narrow rope-mak-
ing passage), spacewalk, crosswalk (*US*
pedestrian crossing), catwalk.

sparrowhawk, tomahawk.

42 -oke
oak, coke, choke, folk, joke, hoke
(overact), bloke, cloak, moke, smoke,
poke, spoke, roque (US game resembling croquet), broke, croak, stroke,
soak, soke (former legal term), toque,
stoke, woke, yoke, yolk.

decoke, workfolk, menfolk, tradesfolk,
kinsfolk, slowpoke (*US* slowcoach),
mopoke (Australian owl), bespoke,
keystroke, sidestroke, handstroke (bell-
ringing term), sunstroke, upstroke,
heatstroke, breaststroke, backstroke,
evoke, revoke, provoke, invoke, convoke, awoke, unyoke.

artichoke, okey-doke, gentlefolk,
womenfolk, Roanoke (US island),
masterstroke, Basingstoke.

43 -uck
buck, chuck, duck, fuck, guck (slimy
substance), luck, cluck, pluck, muck,
puck, ruck, cruck (roof timber), truck,
struck, suck, shuck, tuck, stuck, yuk.

roebuck, blackbuck (Indian antelope),
reedbuck (African antelope), jumbuck,
bushbuck (small African antelope),
woodchuck, shelduck, mukluk (Eskimo's sealskin boot), potluck, amok,
Kalmuck (Mongoloid people), dumbstruck, moonstruck, untuck, unstuck.

waterbuck (African antelope), chempaduk (Malaysian fruit tree), mallemuck
(sea bird), thunderstruck.

44 -ook
book, cook, doek (African headscarf),
hook, look, nook, schnook (*US* stupid
person), rook, brook, crook, sook
(coward), shook, took.

daybook, flybook (angler's case for
flies), boobook (Australian owl), bluebook (British government publication),
chequebook, workbook, cookbook,
bankbook, sketchbook, studbook,
handbook, logbook, chapbook (book

of popular ballads), scrapbook, passbook, notebook, textbook, Kirkuk (Iraqi city), billhook, unhook, grasshook (sickle), pothook, boathook, Windhoek (African city), taluk (Indian district), outlook, Sherbrooke (Canadian city), Pembroke, Innsbruck, forsook, nainsook (soft cotton fabric), partook, betook, mistook.

copybook, storybook, pocketbook, overcook, tenterhook, buttonhook (thin hooked instrument), overlook, gerenuk (African antelope), inglenook, Volapuk (artificial language), donnybrook (rowdy brawl), Alanbrooke (British field marshall), Bolingbroke, undertook, overtook.

44.1
Tobruk (Libyan port), Beaverbrook.

45 -uke
kook (*US* eccentric person), douc (Asian monkey), Luke, fluke, snook, spook, tuque (Canadian knitted cap), stook, duke, nuke, puke, chibouk (Turkish tobacco pipe), caoutchouc (rubber material), Seljuk (member of Turkish dynasty), Nanook, Chinook, Farouk, peruke (men's wig), rebuke, archduke, Mameluke (military Egyptian ruler), Pentateuch, Heptateuch, Hexateuch, gobbledegook, bashibazouk (19th-century Turkish soldier).

46 -'ck
Newark, Lubbock (Texan city), Southwark, haddock, paddock, shaddock (tropical fruit tree), piddock (mollusc), ruddock (*Dialect* robin), Norfolk, Suffolk, hillock, lilac, pollack (Atlantic fish), rowlock, mullock (*Dialect* mess), bullock, hammock, mammock (*Dialect* shred), hummock, stomach, bannock (Scottish cake), Cannock, Lanark, Greenock, jonnock (*Dialect* genuine), monarch, dunnock (hedge sparrow), eunuch, arrack (alcoholic spirit), barrack, carrack, borak (*Austral* nonsense), cassock, hassock, tussock, mattock (agricultural tool), buttock, futtock (part of boat), havoc, bulwark, Isaac.

Habakkuk (Old Testament prophet), agalloch (tree yielding fragrant wood), Potomac, Kilmarnock, coronach (*Scot* dirge), laverock (*Dialect* skylark), Sarawak (Malaysian state).

elegiac, paranoiac.

47 -alk
calque (linguistics term), talc, catafalque (platform for coffin).

48 -elk
elk, spelk (*Dialect* wood splinter), whelk.

49 -ilk
ilk, bilk (thwart), milk, silk, Liebfraumilch, buttermilk.

50 -ulk
bulk, skulk, hulk, sulk.

51 -ank
ankh (symbolic cross), bank, banc (legal term), dank, hank, lank, blank, clank, flank, plank, spank, rank, crank, drank, franc, frank, Frank, prank, shrank, sank, shank, tank, stank, thank, wank, swank, yank, Yank.

claybank (*US* dull brownish colour), Clydebank, sandbank, embank, outflank, gangplank, outrank, Cruickshank, redshank (red-stemmed plant), scrimshank (*Slang* shirk work), greenshank (European shore bird), sheepshank.

mountebank, antitank.

52 -ink
ink, kink, skink (tropical lizard), chink, dink (*Scot* neat), fink, gink, jink, link, blink, clink, slink, mink, pink, rink, brink, drink, prink, shrink, sink, sync,

stink, think, wink, swink (*Dialect* to toil), twink, zinc.

ratfink, snowblink (luminosity reflected from snow), iceblink (luminosity reflected from ice), Haitink (Dutch conductor), Bentinck (governor-general of India), rethink, unthink, outthink, hoodwink.

bobolink (US songbird), Maeterlinck (Belgian poet), interlink, countersink, doublethink.

53 -onk
conk, conch, gonk, honk, clonk, plonk, cronk (*Austral* unsound), tonk (*Austral* effeminate man), stonk (bombard with artillery), honky-tonk.

54 -unk
bunk, skunk, chunk, dunk, funk, gunk (*Slang* slimy substance), junk, hunk, clunk, flunk, plunk (to pluck), slunk, monk, punk, spunk, drunk, shrunk, trunk, sunk, stunk, debunk, chipmunk, quidnunc (gossipmonger), preshrunk.

55 -ask
Basque, casque (helmet-like structure), hask (*Dialect* dry cough), Monegasque (citizen of Monaco).

56 -arsk
ask, bask, cask, flask, mask, masque, task, unmask, antimasque (grotesque dance), overtask.

57 -esk
desk, burlesque, Moresque (Moorish decoration), grotesque, Junoesque, statuesque, arabesque, Romanesque (architectural style), picaresque, picturesque, sculpturesque, humoresque.

58 -isk
bisque, disc, disk, risk, brisk, frisk, whisk, obelisk, basilisk (tropical lizard), odalisque (female slave), tamarisk (ornamental tree), asterisk.

59 -osk
bosk (small wood), mosque, kiosk, abelmosk (tropical plant).

60 -usk
Usk (British river), busk, dusk, husk, musk, rusk, brusque, tusk, subfusc (drab), cornhusk.

61 -'sk
mollusc, damask.

62 -atch
batch, catch, hatch, latch, match, natch, snatch, patch, cratch (rack for cattle fodder), scratch, thatch, crosshatch, nuthatch, unlatch, potlatch (American Indian ceremonial activity), rematch, mismatch, dispatch, crosspatch, detach, attach, Saguache (US mountain range).

63 -arch
arch, larch, march, March, parch, starch, frogmarch, routemarch, cornstarch, countermarch, overarch, Dedéagach (Greek port).

64 -etch
etch, ketch, sketch, fetch, lech, fletch (fit with a feather), wretch, retch, stretch, vetch, Dolmetsch (British musician), outstretch.

65 -erch
birch, church, lurch, smirch (to soil), perch, search, unchurch (excommunicate), Christchurch, besmirch, pikeperch (freshwater fish), surfperch (marine fish), research.

66 -eech
each, beach, beech, leech, leach, bleach, pleach (interlace shoots in hedge), peach, speech, reach, breach, breech, screech, preach, teach, horseleech (freshwater leech), impeach, forereach (nautical term), headreach (nau-

tical term), outreach, beseech, unteach, overreach.

67 -itch
itch, bitch, kitsch, ditch, fitch (polecat), hitch, flitch, mitch (*Dialect* play truant), niche, snitch, pitch, quitch (type of grass), rich, stitch, which, witch, switch, twitch.

cowitch (tropical climbing plant), Redditch, orache (herbaceous plant), eldritch (unearthly), enrich, ostrich, hemstitch, backstitch, bewitch, Ipswich, Prestwich, Northwich.

overpitch (cricket term), featherstitch, tsarevitch.

Shostakovich, Rostropovich, Mohorovičić (Yugoslav geologist).

68 -otch
botch, scotch, Scotch, blotch, splotch, notch, potch (*Austral* inferior opal), crotch, watch, swatch, hopscotch, topnotch, hotchpotch, dogwatch, stopwatch, wristwatch, deathwatch, butterscotch, overwatch.

69 -orch
scorch, nautch (traditional Indian dance), porch, torch, debauch, blowtorch.

70 -oach
coach, loach, poach, roach, broach, brooch, slowcoach, stagecoach, mailcoach, cockroach, encroach, reproach, approach, motorcoach.

71 -ouch
ouch, couch, slouch, pouch, crouch, grouch, vouch, debouch (move into larger space).

72 -utch
Kutch (former Indian state), cutch (resinous substance), Dutch, hutch, clutch, much, mutch (close-fitting linen cap), smutch (to smudge), crutch, such, touch, declutch, nonesuch (flowering plant), retouch, insomuch, overmuch, inasmuch, forasmuch.

73 -ootch
butch, cootch (hiding place).

74 -ooch
hooch, mooch, smooch, pooch.

75 -elch
belch, squelch.

76 -ilch
filch, milch (milk-yielding), pilch (infant's outer garment), zilch.

77 -ulch
culch (base of oyster bed), gulch, mulch.

78 -anch
blanch, ranch, branch, stanch, carte blanche, disbranch, avalanche, anabranch (stream branching from river).

79 -ench
bench, blench (shy away), clench, quench, wrench, drench, French, trench, tench, stench, wench, workbench, retrench, entrench.

80 -inch
inch, chinch (*US* bedbug), finch, lynch, clinch, flinch, Minch (Atlantic channel off Scotland), pinch, squinch (supporting arch in tower), cinch, winch, chaffinch, hawfinch, goldfinch, bullfinch, greenfinch, grassfinch.

81 -ornch
haunch, launch, flaunch (slope around chimney top), paunch, craunch (*Dialect* crunch), staunch.

82 -unch
bunch, hunch, lunch, munch, punch, runch (flowering plant), brunch,

crunch, scrunch, sarpanch (Indian village council leader), honeybunch.

83 -ad

ad, add, bad, bade, cad, scad (marine fish), Chad, dad, fad, gad, had, lad, clad, glad, plaid, mad, pad, rad (unit of absorbed radiation), brad (small nail), grad (*short for* graduate), trad, sad, shad, tad (*US* small boy).

forbade, Akkad (ancient Babylonian city), ecad (ecology term), cycad (tropical plant), caudad (towards the tail), Baghdad, granddad, egad, jihad (Islamic holy war), Mashhad (Iranian city), unclad, nomad, maenad (priestess of Bacchus), kneepad, footpad, Arad (Rumanian city), Conrad, tetrad (group of four), dorsad (towards the back), octad, pentad, heptad, hexad.

alidad (surveying instrument), Trinidad, aoudad (wild mountain sheep), Galahad, cephalad (towards the head), ironclad, superadd (add as extra), Petrograd, Stalingrad, Leningrad, Upanishad (ancient Hindu sacred book).

83.1
Iliad, chiliad (group of one thousand), Gilead, ennead (group of nine), gwyniad (freshwater fish), oread (Greek mountain nymph), bromeliad (fleshy-leaved plant), Olympiad.

83.2
dyad (maths term), pleiad (talented group of seven), naiad, dryad, triad, Omayyad (caliph), jeremiad (long mournful lamentation), hamadryad (tree nymph).

83.3
gonad (sex organ), monad (philosophy term), trichomonad (microscopic parasitic animal).

84 -ard [also 1 + -*ed*]

bard, card, chard, guard, hard, lard, nard (aromatic plant), pard, Sade, sard (gemstone), shard, yard.

Liard (Canadian river), liard (former European coin), Fuad (Egyptian king), bombard, Jacquard (fabric with patterned weave), placard, scorecard, filecard, timecard, racecard, discard, falsecard (bridge term), postcard, Goddard, blackguard, rearguard, fireguard, Bogarde, Midgard (Norse mythological place), mudguard, safeguard, lifeguard, vanguard, Asgard (home of Norse gods), Utgard (Norse mythological place), coastguard, die-hard, blowhard (boastful person), ballade (verse form), mallard, foulard (soft light fabric), poulard (spayed hen), roulade, pomade (perfumed hair oil), chamade (former military signal), canard (rumour or hoax), Barnard, spikenard (aromatic Indian plant), Arpád (9th-century Magyar chieftain), Stoppard, charade, estrade (dais), brassard (identifying armband), pesade (dressage term), glissade (ballet step), façade, Hansard, mansard, petard, retard, ill-starred, noyade (execution by drowning), oeillade (suggestive glance), Riyadh (capital of Saudi Arabia), dooryard (*US* yard outside door), foreyard (nautical term), brickyard, dockyard, stockyard, junkyard, churchyard, kaleyard (*Scot* vegetable garden), steelyard, farmyard, barnyard, vineyard, boneyard, shipyard, courtyard, tiltyard (enclosed area for jousting), graveyard.

milliard (thousand million), Savoyard (native of Savoy), Kierkegaard, avantgarde, Abelard, interlard, communard (member of a commune), promenade, leotard, Kristianstad (Swedish town), timberyard, lumberyard, Montagnard (member of mountain people), camelopard (giraffe).

84.1

regard, bodyguard, disregard.

85 -ade [also **2** + *-ed*]

aide, aid, cade (juniper tree), fade, jade, hade (geology term). laid, lade (load cargo), blade, glade, maid, made, paid, spade, raid, braid, grade, trade, shade, staid, they'd, wade, suede.

arcade, decade, cockade, blockade, stockade, brocade, alcaide (Spanish castle commander), cascade, twayblade (orchid), creamlaid, inlaid, unlade (unload), barmaid, mermaid, remade, limeade, milkmaid, handmade, bondmaid (unmarried female slave), self-made, unmade, nursemaid, housemaid, bridesmaid, prepaid, well-paid, unpaid, postpaid, tirade, corrade (geology term), abrade, upbraid, afraid, Belgrade, downgrade, upgrade, comrade, torsade (ornamental twist on hat), crusade, cliché'd, eyeshade, sunshade, nightshade, pervade, evade, invade, unweighed, dissuade, persuade.

El Obeid (Sudanese city), Medicaid (*US* health assistance programme), barricade, autocade (*US* motorcade), motorcade, cavalcade, ambuscade (an ambush), alidade (surveyor's instrument), orangeade, Almohade (former Muslim ruler), Adelaide, defilade (military term), enfilade (military term), fusillade (rapid gunfire), accolade, escalade (scaling walls with ladders), underlaid, marmalade, phylloclade (leaflike plant stem), chambermaid, escapade, underpaid, overpaid, unafraid, overtrade, balustrade, rodomontade (boastful talk).

85.1

brigade, renegade.

85.2

grenade, pasquinade (satire), marinade, serenade, harlequinade.

85.3

carbonade, gasconade (boastful talk), dragonnade (persecution by dragoons), colonnade, esplanade, lemonade, cannonade, carronade (obsolete light cannon), cottonade (coarse fabric), gabionade (construction controlling water flow).

85.4

parade, masquerade.

85.5

degrade, tardigrade (minute segmented animal), taligrade (zoology term), saltigrade (moving by jumps), plantigrade (zoology term), centigrade, unguligrade (walking on hooves), digitigrade (walking on toes).

85.6

aggrade (geology term), retrograde, intergrade (biology term).

86 -ed

bed, dead, fed, head, lead, led, fled, sled, Med, sned (*Dialect* to prune), sped, red, read, redd (*Dialect* to tidy), bread, bred, dread, spread, shred, tread, thread, said, shed, ted, stead, wed, zed.

co-ed, seedbed, roadbed, childbed, embed, hotbed, deathbed, sheep-ked (parasitic fly), airhead (military term), stairhead, spearhead, sorehead (*US* peevish person), warhead, blackhead, blockhead, bulkhead, deadhead, redhead, Godhead, Roundhead, egghead, bighead, nailhead (decorative device), railhead (end of railway), wellhead, steelhead (Pacific trout), bullhead (a fish), drumhead, greenhead (male mallard), bonehead, springhead (source of stream), crosshead, sheepshead (Atlantic fish), Gateshead, cathead (nautical term), fathead, flathead (Pacific fish), pithead, Spithead, hothead, pothead (*Slang* cannabis user), gilthead (Atlantic fish), masthead, hogshead, unlead (printing term), misled, Ahmed, premed, biped, moped, beebread (food for bee larvae), purebred, lowbred, shewbread (Old Testament bread), sowbread (European plant), homebred, inbred, unbred, crispbread, crossbred, sweetbread, shortbread, well-read, unread, bespread, bedspread, widespread, outspread, re-tread, packthread, goldthread (US woodland plant), unthread, unsaid, snowshed (shelter over railway track), bloodshed, woodshed, oersted (unit in physics), bedstead, roadstead, farmstead, homestead, instead, Dyfed, Enzed (New Zealand).

underfed, overfed, knucklehead (foolish person), fiddlehead (nautical term), bufflehead (diving duck), shovelhead (common shark), Birkenhead, maidenhead, Maidenhead, woodenhead (stupid person), dragonhead (flowering plant), quadruped, infrared, underbred (of impure stock), gingerbread, thoroughbred, Ethelred, aforesaid, watershed, Holinshed, newlywed, Samoyed.

86.1
abed, flowerbed, slugabed, riverbed.

86.2
behead, Holyhead, sleepyhead, poppyhead.

86.3
bowhead (arctic whale), towhead (blond-haired person), arrowhead.

86.4
skinhead, pinhead, fountainhead.

86.5
ahead, go-ahead, timberhead (nautical term), Leatherhead, leatherhead (Australian songbird), rudderhead (nautical term), dunderhead, thunderhead (anvil-shaped cloud top), figurehead, loggerhead, hammerhead (shark), copperhead (venomous snake), letterhead, overhead.

86.6
aliped (having wing-like limbs), taliped (having a club foot), pinniped (having flipper-like limbs), fissiped (having separate toes), maxilliped (zoology term), pinnatiped (ornithology term).

87 -erd [also 3 + *-ed*]
urd (bean plant), bird, Byrd, curd, Kurd (nomadic Turkic people), furred, gird, heard, herd, surd, turd, third, word.

firebird, lyrebird, snowbird, bluebird, blackbird, puffbird, jailbird, rainbird, sunbird, songbird, lovebird, potsherd, begird (to surround), cowherd, swineherd, swanherd, unheard, goatherd, absurd, swearword, reword, byword, foreword, catchword, watchword, headword, password, crossword.

ladybird, whirlybird, friarbird, bowerbird, butcherbird, thunderbird, tailorbird, dollarbird, weaverbird, riflebird, wattlebird, mockingbird, hummingbird, undergird, overheard, undeterred, Mesa Verde (high plateau in Colorado), afterword (postscript), overword (repeated phrase or word).

88 -aird [also 4 + *-ed*]
Baird, laird, tow-haired, long-haired, short-haired, unaired, unrepaired, unprepared, unimpaired.

89 -eed [also 5 + *-ed*]
Bede, bead, deed, feed, heed, he'd, lead, lied (type of song), bleed, plead, mead, Mede, knead, need, speed, reed, read, Reid, breed, creed, screed, greed, cede, seed, she'd, steed, weed, we'd, swede, Swede, tweed, Tweed.

indeed, misdeed, handfeed, spoon-feed, fairlead (nautical term), nosebleed, misplead (plead incorrectly), mislead, knock-kneed, stampede, impede, airspeed, Godspeed, groundspeed, jerid (wooden javelin), inbreed, crossbreed, outbreed, proofread, Siegfried, agreed, lip-read, misread, sight-read, birdseed, allseed (plant producing many seeds), wormseed (plant producing medicinal seeds), moonseed (climbing plant), rapeseed, axseed (flowering plant), flaxseed, Jamshid (Persian mythological king), Flamsteed (English astronomer), mayweed, seaweed, fireweed, rockweed (seaweed growing on rocks), pokeweed, duckweed, milkweed, stinkweed, bindweed, pondweed, gulfweed (brown seaweed), ragweed, pigweed, hogweed, knapweed, knotweed, goutweed, accede, exceed, stickseed (plant producing prickly fruits), succeed.

underfeed, winterfeed, overfeed, invalid, interplead (legal term), Ganymede, Runnymede, copyread (*US* subedit), interbreed, beggarweed, waterweed, silverweed, cottonweed.

Harun al-Rashid (8th-century caliph), Berwick-upon-Tweed.

89.1
millipede, cirripede (marine animal), centipede, velocipede (early type of bicycle).

89.2
recede, precede, secede, aniseed, antecede.

89.3
proceed, supersede, retrocede (give back), intercede.

89.4
linseed, pumpkinseed (US fish).

89.5
concede, cottonseed.

89.6
chickweed, stickweed, colicweed.

89.7
thimbleweed, tumbleweed, bugleweed, pickerelweed.

90 -eerd [also **6** + *-ed*]
eared, beard, fyrd (Anglo-Saxon local militia), weird, greybeard (old man), Bluebeard, Blackbeard (English pirate), goatsbeard (plant with woolly stem), lop-eared.

91 -id [Also **16** + *-ed*. Further rhymes may be created by adding *-ed* to appropriate verbs and nouns.]
id, bid, kid, Kidd (Scottish pirate), skid, did, fid (nautical term), gid (disease of sheep), hid, lid, slid, mid, quid, squid, rid, grid, Sid.

sayyid (Muslim title), rabid, crabbed, turbid, verbid (linguistics term), morbid, Irbid (Jordanian town), outbid, naked, wicked, orchid, crooked, tailskid, wretched, bearded, voided (heraldic term), crowded, hooded, wooded, winded, minded, bonded, fronded, undid, wounded, outdid, aphid, syrphid (type of fly), bifid, trifid, jagged, ragged, cragged (*US* craggy), dogged, rugged, pongid (type of ape), aged, turgid, algid (chilly), masjid (Arab mosque), eyelid, cichlid (tropical fish), Euclid, skidlid, timid, humid, tumid, desmid (freshwater alga), phasmid (plant-eating insect), learned, honeyed, moneyed, rapid, sapid (having a pleasant taste), vapid, torpid, Cupid, stupid, limpid, vespid (wasplike), hispid (covered with bristles), cuspid (tooth having one point), liquid, varied, serried, storied, lurid, hurried, hybrid, acrid, sacred, Madrid, kindred, Alfred, hatred, putrid, blessed, cursed, cussed, muscid (type of fly), chalcid (tiny insect), El Cid, fancied, rancid, gifted, tufted, kilted, stilted, tinted, wonted, hunted, stunted, plastid (microscopic cell structure), waisted, frosted, worsted, Hampstead, avid, gravid, David, livid, vivid, ivied, Ovid, bovid, languid, pinguid (fatty or greasy), palsied, frenzied.

noctuid (nocturnal moth), half-naked, unheeded, unseeded, katydid, secluded, included, overdid, long-winded, high-minded, like-minded, broad-minded, quadrifid, multifid, three-legged, bow-legged, cross-legged, carangid (marine fish), nymphalid (brightly-coloured butterfly), annelid (segmented worm), pyralid (tropical moth), Ozalid (*Trademark*), Mohammed, serranid (marine fish), unlearned, hominid, cyprinid (freshwater fish), elapid (venomous snake), bicuspid, tricuspid, illiquid, satyrid (type of butterfly), unwearied, unhurried, dihybrid (genetics term), colubrid (type of snake), eupatrid (ancient Greek landowner), accursed, Abbasid (caliph of Muslim dynasty), assorted, undoubted, sure-footed, club-footed, flat-footed, hydatid (cyst containing tapeworm larva), bigoted, spermatid (immature sperm), chromatid (part of chromosome), propertied, impacted, unbolted, enchanted, unwanted, unwonted, unscripted, adopted, beloved.

disembodied, bloody-minded, narrow-minded, feeble-minded, single-minded, open-minded, prehominid (extinct man-like primate), tertium quid, scolopendrid (type of centipede), geometrid (type of moth), ill-assorted, self-inflicted, unrestricted, anabantid (spiny-finned fish), malimprinted, unadopted, Hemel Hempstead.

antherozoid (botany term), unreconstructed, isoniazid (crystalline compound).

91.1
Aeneid, scarabaeid.

91.2
tracheid (plant cell), tineid (type of moth), clupeid (type of fish), Nereid (Greek nymph), araneid (spider), saturniid (tropical moth), reduviid (type of bug), euphausiid (small shrimp-like animal).

91.3
Clwyd, fluid, druid, semifluid, superfluid (physics term).

91.4
forbid, underbid, carabid (dark-coloured beetle), overbid.

91.5
guarded, unguarded, retarded.

91.6
faded, gadid (marine fish), jaded, braided, unaided, unshaded, colonnaded.

91.7
leaded, wedded, bareheaded, baldheaded, bigheaded, light-headed, unleaded (printing term), interbedded (geology term), muddleheaded, levelheaded.

91.8
misguided, decided, one-sided, lopsided, undecided, undivided.

91.9
corded, sordid, prerecorded, unrewarded.

91.10
loaded, woaded, outmoded, unexploded.

91.11
blooded (of good breeding), studied, blue-blooded, cold-blooded, full-blooded, warm-blooded, hot-blooded, unstudied.

91.12
candid, candied, landed, stranded, barehanded, high-handed, forehanded, backhanded, cack-handed, red-handed, right-handed, left-handed, empty-handed, heavy-handed, underhanded, single-handed.

91.13
splendid, commended, intended, undefended, undescended, unattended.

91.14
rounded, unbounded, unfounded, confounded, astounded.

91.15
rigid, Brigid, frigid, nonrigid, semirigid.

91.16
pallid, valid, invalid.

91.17
jellied, gelid, potbellied.

91.18
olid (foul-smelling), squalid, solid, stolid, semisolid.

91.19
amid, pyramid.

91.20
Enid, sciaenid (type of fish), scorpaenid (spiny-finned fish).

91.21
tabanid (blood-sucking fly), balconied, Sassanid (member of Persian dynasty), oceanid (Greek nymph), Achaemenid (member of Persian dynasty), unaccompanied.

91.22
hackneyed, arachnid.

91.23
tepid, intrepid.

91.24
lipid, insipid, phospholipid.

91.25
arid, married, sparid (tropical fish), subarid, unmarried, semiarid.

91.26
forehead, horrid, florid, torrid, subtorrid (subtropical).

91.27
acarid (tick or mite), ascarid (parasitic worm), salaried, leporid (mammal of hare family), liveried, ephemerid (mayfly), elaterid (click beetle), eurypterid (extinct scorpion-like animal).

91.28
acid, flaccid, placid, triacid (chemistry term), subacid (moderately acid), peracid (type of acid), tetracid (chemistry term), antacid, oxyacid (acid containing oxygen), monoacid (chemistry term).

91.29
viscid, bombycid (type of moth), culicid (mosquito), tortricid (small moth), dytiscid (carnivorous aquatic beetle).

91.30
lucid, deuced, mucid (mouldy), pellucid (translucent), Seleucid (member of ancient dynasty).

91.31
capsid (plant-eating bug), therapsid (extinct reptile).

91.32
fatted, matted, dratted, caryatid.

91.33
uncharted, hardhearted, cold-hearted, kind-hearted, half-hearted, wholehearted, downhearted, light-hearted, stouthearted, softhearted, departed, tenderhearted, chicken-hearted, lionhearted, brokenhearted.

91.34
dated, fated, plated, truncated, outdated, cerated (ornithology term), hydrated (containing water), unabated, educated, calculated, simulated, medullated (anatomy term), mentholated, dissipated, constipated, antiquated, celebrated, fenestrated (having windows), elevated, cultivated, dilapidated, self-opinionated, unpremeditated.

91.34.1
trabeated (architectural term), foliated, floriated (architectural term), asteriated (crystallography term), unappropriated, unsubstantiated.

91.34.2
infatuated, superannuated.

91.34.3
dedicated, complicated, desiccated, alembicated (excessively refined), sophisticated, unsophisticated.

91.34.4
variegated, unmitigated.

91.34.5
belated, related, rutilated (mineralogy term), castellated, pixilated (*US* eccentric).

91.34.6
hyphenated, uncoordinated.

91.34.7
serrated, saturated, perforated, unsaturated, unperforated, exaggerated, incorporated, supersaturated (physics term), unadulterated, polyunsaturated.

91.35
fetid, fretted, sweated, indebted, coroneted.

91.36
concerted, perverted, deserted, miniskirted, disconcerted.

91.37
heated, seated, repeated, conceited.

91.38
fitted, knitted, nitid (bright), limited, helmeted, spirited, turreted, lanceted (architectural term), quick-witted, half-witted, dim-witted, sharp-witted, unedited, unlimited, inherited, unmerited, dispirited, high-spirited, multifaceted.

91.39
sighted, whited, delighted, benighted (ignorant), united, far-sighted, clearsighted, near-sighted, unsighted, longsighted, sharp-sighted, short-sighted, excited, unrequited, uninvited, overexcited.

91.40
dotted, knotted, potted, spotted, unspotted, carotid, parotid, besotted.

91.41
coated, bloated, noted, devoted.

91.42
booted, fluted, reputed, unsuited, undiluted, unpolluted, convoluted, undisputed.

91.43
affected, dejected, collected, unaffected, unreflected, unconnected, unsuspected, unexpected, undirected, undetected.

91.44
malted, salted, vaulted, exalted.

91.45
sainted, unpainted, acquainted, unacquainted.

91.46
rented, scented, demented, lamented, contented, discontented, unprecedented.

91.47
haunted, undaunted.

91.48
jointed, pointed, disjointed, doublejointed, disappointed.

91.49
mounted, uncounted, unmounted.

91.50
talented, unwarranted, uncovenanted (legal term).

91.51
blasted, flabbergasted.

91.52
crested, vested, buprestid (tropical beetle), undigested, unmolested, doublebreasted, unattested.

91.53
listed, tightfisted, unlisted, forested, interested, uninterested, disinterested, unassisted.

91.54
crusted, disgusted, maladjusted.

91.55
fervid, cervid (mammal of deer family), perfervid (extremely ardent).

92 -ide [also 7 + *-ed*]
eyed, I'd, ide (small fish), bide, chide, dyed, guide, hide, Hyde, Clyde, glide, slide, nide (flock of pheasants), snide, pied, ride, bride, gride (to grate), pride, stride, side, tied, tide, wide.

carbide (chemical compound), abide, cockeyed, raphide (needle-shaped crystal), sulphide, confide, phosphide (chemical compound), misguide, waveguide (electronics term), rawhide, cowhide, horsehide, oxhide, halide (chemical compound), walleyed, bolide (large bright meteor), allied, collide, nuclide (type of atomic nucleus), Strathclyde, applied, landslide, backslide, amide (chemical compound), bromide, popeyed, deride, fluoride, hydride (chemical compound), nitride (chemical compound), outride, well-tried, untried, bestride, astride, Tayside, wayside, quayside, seaside, nearside, fireside, cross-eyed, subside, bedside, broadside, landside (part of plough), offside, hillside, Tyneside, onside (sports term), ringside, depside (chemical compound), upside (upper surface), stateside, Port Said, outside, Teesside, betide, Hocktide (former British festival), yuletide, peptide, riptide (turbulent water in sea), Twelfthtide (Epiphany), Shrovetide, divide, worldwide, backside, azide (chemical compound), reside, preside.

ureide (chemical compound), oroide (metal alloy), iodide (chemical compound), athodyd (type of jet engine), disulphide, trisulphide, aldehyde (chemical compound), ophicleide (obsolete wind instrument), actinide (radioactive element), telluride (chemical compound), East Kilbride, anhydride (chemical compound), Ironside, slickenside (polished rock surface), alongside, mercaptide (chemical compound), dipeptide (biochemical compound), Christmastide, subdivide, nationwide.

hydrosulphide, dissatisfied, formaldehyde, benzaldehyde (fragrant oil), polyamide (polymer), preoccupied, unoccupied, Allhallowtide, polypeptide (biochemical compound).

acetaldehyde (colourless volatile liquid), chlorothiazide (drug).

92.1
qualified, dignified, rarefied, countrified, classified, certified, citified, unqualified, undignified, unclassified, unstratified.

92.2
elide, acetylide (chemical compound), acetanilide (crystalline substance).

92.3
sodamide (crystalline substance), thalidomide, cyanamide (crystalline substance), sulphonamide, chlorpropamide (a drug), tolbutamide (medicinal compound), sulphanilamide (crystalline substance), nicotinamide (component of vitamin B).

92.4
cyanide, uranide (type of element), arsenide (chemical compound), lanthanide (type of element), ferrocyanide (chemical compound), isocyanide (chemical compound), platinocyanide (chemical compound).

92.5
boride (chemical compound), chloride, dichloride, trichloride, hydrochloride, tetrachloride.

92.6
saccharide (a sugar), glyceride (chemical compound), deuteride (chemical compound), override, disaccharide, trisaccharide, polysaccharide, monosaccharide.

92.7
beside, decide.

deicide, suicide, herbicide, regicide, algicide, fungicide, filicide, silicide (chemical compound), stillicide (legal term), Barmecide (illusory), germicide, spermicide, vermicide, homicide, parricide (killing of parent), matricide, patricide, fratricide, countryside, feticide, multicide (mass murder), pesticide, larvicide, Heaviside, Merseyside.

tyrannicide, bactericide, sororicide, uxoricide, liberticide (destruction of freedom), aborticide (destruction of fetus), insecticide, infanticide, rodenticide.

92.7.1
miticide (mite-killing substance), parasiticide.

92.8
aside, biocide (chemical for killing organisms), Humberside, ecocide (destruction of natural environment), glycoside (biochemical compound), underside, genocide, waterside, riverside, overside, silverside, nucleoside (biochemical compound), taeniacide (tapeworm-killing substance).

92.9
inside, coincide, Qaboos bin Said (sultan of Oman).

92.10
topside, diopside (type of mineral).

92.11
phosphatide (biochemical compound), Eastertide, nucleotide (biochemical compound), polynucleotide (biochemical compound).

92.12
Whitsuntide, Passiontide, eventide, Ascensiontide.

92.13
provide, Almoravide (member of Islamic people).

92.14
oxide, dioxide, trioxide, monoxide, epoxide (chemical compound), peroxide, hydroxide, methoxide (chemical compound), ethoxide (chemical compound), superoxide, dimethylsulphoxide (medicinal compound).

93 -ired [also **8** + -ed]
oilfired, uninspired, unexpired, overtired.

94 -od
odd, bod, cod, god, hod, Lod (Israeli town), clod, plod, mod, nod, pod, quad, quod (Slang jail), squad, rod, scrod (US young cod), prod, trod, sod, shod, tod, Todd, wad.

lingcod (Pacific fish), ephod (Old Testament priest's vestment), nid-nod (nod repeatedly), bipod, tripod, ramrod, Nimrod, pushrod, roughshod, slipshod, tightwad.

Hesiod (ancient Greek poet), ostracod (tiny freshwater animal), demigod, amphipod (aquatic organism), polypod, unipod, copepod (plankton constituent), goldenrod (yellow-flowered plant).

94.1
decapod, scaphopod (marine mollusc), chilopod (crawling invertebrate), tylopod (type of mammal), diplopod (crawling invertebrate), chenopod (marine mollusc), pteropod (marine mollusc), theropod (dinosaur), sauropod (dinosaur), tetrapod, gastropod, arthropod, chaetopod (type of worm), octopod, hexapod, rhizopod (minute organism), brachiopod (marine invertebrate), branchiopod (freshwater organism), myriapod (crawling invertebrate), cephalopod (marine mollusc), ornithopod (dinosaur).

95 -ord [also **9** + -ed]
oared, board, bawd, baud (unit in computer technology), cord, chord, ford, gaud (cheap trinket), hoard, horde, lord, laud, Maud, maud (Scottish plaid shawl), broad, fraud, sword, ward, sward, fjord, Njord (Norse god).

keyboard, leeboard (board in ship), freeboard (nautical term), seaboard (*US* seashore), scoreboard, floorboard, strawboard (board of compressed straw), backboard, blackboard, blockboard, corkboard, chalkboard (*US* blackboard), buckboard (horse-drawn carriage), duckboard (board covering muddy ground), matchboard, switchboard, cardboard, hardboard, headboard, breadboard, sideboard, surfboard, pegboard, scaleboard (veneer), tailboard, billboard, millboard (strong pasteboard), inboard, signboard, springboard, stringboard (part of staircase), chipboard, clipboard, shipboard, chessboard, dashboard, flashboard (board on dam), splashboard, washboard, dartboard, skateboard, outboard, footboard (foot-operated lever), draughtboard, pasteboard, cheeseboard, record, concord, Concorde, ripcord, whipcord (strong fabric), discord, afford, milord, warlord, landlord, applaud, maraud, abroad, defraud, broadsword, reward, greensward.

shuffleboard, smorgasbord, needlecord, overlord.

95.1
aboard, fibreboard (building material), chequerboard, weatherboard, fingerboard, clapperboard, paperboard (thick cardboard), scraperboard, mortarboard, centreboard (supplementary keel), plasterboard, overboard.

95.2
record, harpsichord, clavichord, misericord.

95.3
accord, monochord (instrument for acoustic analysis), urochord (zoology term), tetrachord (musical term), disaccord, notochord (zoology term), octachord (eight-stringed musical instrument), hexachord (musical term).

95.4
award, toward, untoward.

96 -oord [also **10** + *-ed*]
gourd, Sigurd (Norse mythological hero), assured, insured, self-assured, uninsured, unsecured.

97 -oid [also **11** + *-ed*]
Boyd, Lloyd, Freud, void.

hyoid (bone at tongue base), pyoid (pus-like), zooid (independent animal body), globoid, cuboid, rhomboid, placoid (plate-like), sarcoid (flesh-like), cricoid (cartilage in larynx), trochoid (geometric curve), fucoid (brown seaweed), mucoid, conchoid (geometric curve), discoid, viscoid, gadoid (type of fish), xiphoid (sword-shaped), typhoid, lymphoid, algoid (resembling algae), fungoid, keloid (scar tissue on injury), styloid (stylus-like), xyloid (woody), colloid, tabloid, cycloid (circular), haploid (biology term), diploid (biology term), triploid (biology term), euploid (biology term), dermoid, cymoid (botany term), sphygmoid (pulse-like), sigmoid (S-shaped), desmoid (firm tumour), ethmoid (bone of the face), conoid (geometry term), hypnoid, lipoid (fatty), choroid (membrane of eyeball), toroid (geometry term), labroid (marine fish), fibroid, scombroid (marine fish), cancroid (cancer-like), chancroid (soft venereal ulcer), android, dendroid (tree-like), Negroid, centroid (centre of gravity), astroid (maths term), cissoid (geometric curve), schizoid, deltoid, dentoid (tooth-like), mastoid, cestoid (ribbon-shaped), histoid (resembling normal tissue), cystoid, lithoid (stone-like), devoid, ovoid, avoid, toxoid (toxin used in immunization), rhizoid (root-like plant structure).

gobioid (spiny-finned fish), blennioid (marine fish), scorpioid (scorpion-like), osteoid, ichthyoid, amoeboid, coracoid (zoology term), anthracoid, autacoid (natural internal body secretion), Celluloid (*Trademark*), unemployed, echinoid (marine animal), arachnoid (membrane covering brain), polypoid, anthropoid, porphyroid (geology term), sciuroid (squirrel-like), lemuroid, cylindroid, sinusoid (maths term), emulsoid, suspensoid (chemistry term), ellipsoid, parotoid (poison gland on toad), haematoid, rheumatoid, prismatoid (geometric solid), keratoid (horny), teratoid (monster-like), allantoid (sausage-shaped), acanthoid (spiny), obovoid (egg-shaped), trapezoid, Caucasoid.

paratyphoid, epicycloid (geometric curve), hypocycloid (geometric curve), underemployed, epileptoid.

97.1
geoid (shape of earth), scarabaeoid.

97.2
percoid (type of fish), cysticercoid (tapeworm larva).

97.3
trichoid (hair-like), helicoid (spiral-shaped), gynaecoid (woman-like), lumbricoid (worm-like), cercopithecoid (monkey), mineralocorticoid (steroid hormone).

97.4
meloid (long-legged beetle), varicelloid (resembling chickenpox).

97.5
phylloid (leaf-like), myeloid (anatomy term), condyloid (anatomy term), amyloid (starch-like protein), cotyloid (cup-shaped), nautiloid (mollusc), erysipeloid (type of dermatitis).

97.6
hyaloid (transparent), sialoid (saliva-like), alkaloid, mongoloid, unalloyed, coralloid, metalloid (type of element), petaloid, crystalloid, varioloid (resembling smallpox), paraboloid (geometric surface), hyperboloid (geometric surface), amygdaloid (volcanic rock).

97.7
sphenoid (wedge-shaped), glenoid (having a shallow cavity), ctenoid (comb-like), scorpaenoid (spiny-finned fish).

97.8
crinoid (marine animal), adenoid, solenoid, hominoid, cyprinoid (carp-like), actinoid (having a radiate form), resinoid, albuminoid, carotenoid (red or yellow pigment).

97.8.1
platinoid (platinum-like), gelatinoid.

97.9
annoyed, melanoid (dark-coloured), humanoid, salmonoid, paranoid, bioflavonoid (vitamin).

97.10
spheroid, scleroid (hardened), steroid, theroid (beast-like), hemispheroid, corticosteroid.

97.11
spiroid (spiral), thyroid, parathyroid.

97.12
amberoid (synthetic amber), acaroid (mite- or tick-like), saccharoid, Polaroid (*Trademark*), haemorrhoid, bacteroid, asteroid, hysteroid (resembling hysteria), meteoroid.

98 -ode [also **12** + *-ed*]
ode, bode, code, goad, lode, load, mode, node, Spode, road, rode, strode, toad, woad.

geode (crystal-lined rock cavity), diode, triode (electronic valve), forebode, abode, decode, encode, postcode, cladode (leaflike stem), hallowed, payload, reload, freeload (*US* be a sponger), workload, truckload, unload, shipload, implode (collapse inwards violently), explode, cartload, boatload, anode, dynode (type of electrode), crunode (maths term), acnode (maths term), epode (part of Greek ode), erode, byroad, highroad, corrode, railroad, inroad, tetrode (electronic valve), pentode (electronic valve), cestode, cathode.

Kozhikode (Indian port), unhallowed, overload, wagonload, à la mode, staminode (nonfunctioning stamen), antinode (physics term), internode (part of plant stem), hemipode (quail-like bird), antipode (the exact opposite), megapode (ground-living bird), nesselrode (rich frozen pudding), electrode, episode, nematode, trematode (parasitic flatworm), hydathode (water-secreting plant pore).

98.1
commode, incommode, discommode, alamode (light silk).

99 -oud [also **13** + *-ed*]
Oudh (region of India), loud, cloud, crowd, proud, shroud, stroud (coarse woollen fabric), Saud, showd (*Scot* to rock), unbowed, aloud, becloud (to muddle), enshroud, avowed, well-endowed, overcrowd, ibn-Saud.

99.1
Macleod, thundercloud, overcloud.

100 -ud
bud, cud, scud, dud, blood, flood, mud, spud, rudd (freshwater fish), crud, sudd (floating weed in Nile), stud, thud, redbud (US tree), disbud, rosebud, lifeblood, oxblood (dark reddish-brown colour), m'lud, photoflood (very bright tungsten lamp).

101 -ood
could, good, hood, should, stood, would, wood.

Gielgud, boyhood, monkhood, godhood, childhood, selfhood, girlhood, manhood, nunhood, falsehood, knighthood, sainthood, priesthood, monkshood (poisonous plant), Talmud, Blackwood (bridge term), blackwood (Australian acacia tree), withstood, Larwood (English cricketer), baywood (light soft wood), Heywood, Sherwood, dyewood (wood yielding dye), plywood, firewood, matchwood, touchwood, hardwood, deadwood, redwood, bogwood (wood preserved in bogs), dogwood (European shrub), logwood (tree yielding red dye), Wedgwood, wormwood, greenwood, kingwood (violet-tinted wood), springwood (wood produced in spring), sapwood (wood directly beneath bark), pulpwood (wood used in papermaking), brushwood, heartwood (central core of tree), Fleetwood, whitewood, driftwood, softwood, bentwood, Brentwood, boxwood (close-grained yellow wood), rosewood.

babyhood, hardihood, likelihood, livelihood, widowhood, neighbourhood, sisterhood, fatherhood, motherhood, brotherhood, maidenhood, womanhood, adulthood, parenthood, understood, Hollywood, leatherwood (US flowering shrub), Isherwood, summerwood (late season's wood growth), zebrawood (tree yielding striped wood), bitterwood (tree yielding medicinal bark), orangewood, candlewood (resinous wood), sandalwood, eaglewood (tree yielding aromatic resin), satinwood, ironwood (very hard wood), ribbonwood (New Zealand evergreen tree), southernwood (European wormwood tree), sappanwood (tree yielding red dye), cottonwood (US poplar), buttonwood (US plane tree), misunderstood.

102 -ude [also **15** + *-ed*]
food, Jude, who'd, lewd, mood, snood, pood (Russian unit of weight), rood, rude, brood, crude, prude, shrewd, you'd, dude, feud, hued, nude, pseud.

seafood, wholefood, elude, illude, delude, preclude, seclude, occlude, include, conclude, exclude, postlude (concluding piece of music), detrude (thrust out), protrude, obtrude, intrude, extrude, subdued, prelude, denude, transude, étude, exude.

Safid Rud (Iranian river), unvalued.

102.1
allude, collude, interlude.

102.2
quietude, longitude, solitude, amplitude, plenitude (abundance), magnitude, turpitude (baseness), pulchritude, lassitude, certitude, fortitude, rectitude, sanctitude, altitude, multitude, aptitude, promptitude, servitude, mansuetude (gentleness), consuetude (established custom).

inquietude (restlessness), disquietude (unease), desuetude (state of disuse), similitude, decrepitude, solicitude, vicissitude, incertitude, exactitude, correctitude, ineptitude.

dissimilitude, inexactitude, verisimilitude (appearance of truth).

102.2.1
attitude, latitude, platitude, gratitude, beatitude, colatitude (astronomy coordinate), ingratitude.

103 -'d [also **17** + -ed]
froward (obstinate), coward, Howard, steward, scabbard, tabard, larboard, starboard, cupboard, Hubbard, halberd (spear with axe head), Lombard, acred (having acres of land), chequered, tankard, drunkard, whiskered, Richard, orchard, pochard (diving duck), pilchard, cultured, standard, Stafford, Rockford (US city), Crockford (directory of Anglican clergy), Bradford, Telford, Guildford, Salford, Longford (Irish county), Stratford, Dartford, Hertford, Hartford, Watford, Wexford (Irish county), Oxford, Chelmsford, haggard, laggard, staggard (male red deer), jiggered, niggard, sluggard, ballad, salad, armoured, mannered, Reynard, gurnard (European marine fish), synod, leopard, shepherd, backward,

awkward, farad, Herod, hundred, dotard, sceptred, dastard, bastard, plastered, cloistered, bustard, custard, mustard, method, Harvard, fevered, louvred, wayward, leeward, seaward, Edward, headward (eroding upstream of source), sideward, landward, windward, homeward, inward, onward, downward, upward, outward, westward, eastward, northward, southward, galliard (17th-century dance), halyard, billiard, goliard (medieval European wandering scholar), lanyard, Spaniard, poniard (small dagger), hazard, izard (chamois), gizzard, lizard, blizzard, vizard (a mask), wizard, trousered, buzzard.

unnumbered, good-natured, unstructured, substandard, nonstandard, Hereford, Waterford, Rutherford, Muhammad, enamoured, unanswered, untutored, self-centred, Hereward, northwestward, southwestward, northeastward, southeastward, haphazard, butterfingered.

103.1
period, myriad, photoperiod (period of daylight).

103.2
Bedford, Redford, eisteddfod.

103.3
bollard, collard (variety of cabbage), Lollard, pollard, Bacolod (Philippine town).

103.4
coloured, dullard, varicoloured, particoloured, multicoloured.

103.5
rumoured, good-humoured.

103.6
leisured, measured, treasured, unmeasured.

103.7
uncovered, undiscovered.

103.8
forward, shoreward, henceforward, straightforward.

104 -ebbed
ebbed, webbed, cobwebbed.

105 -erbed [also **22** + *-ed*]
uncurbed, unperturbed, undisturbed.

106 -ogged [also **185** + *-ed*]
fogged (photography term), hogged (nautical term), waterlogged.

107 -inged
stringed, winged, stockinged.

108 -aged [also **193** + *-ed*]
uncaged, engaged, unpaged (having no page numbers), unengaged.

109 -edged [also **194** + *-ed*]
alleged, unfledged, fully-fledged.

110 -idged [also **197** + *-ed*]
privileged, unabridged, disadvantaged, underprivileged.

111 -anged [also **207** + *-ed*]
estranged, prearranged.

112 -aled [also **214** + *-ed*]
veiled, hobnailed, detailed, pigtailed, fan-tailed.

113 -eld [also **215** + *-ed*]
geld, held, meld, weld, fjeld (rocky Scandinavian plateau), Krefeld (West German city), Ziegfeld, Danegeld, beheld, upheld, withheld, self-propelled, unparalleled.

114 -erld [also **216** + *-ed*]
world, unfurled, antiworld (world composed of antimatter), underworld, afterworld.

115 -eeld [also **217** + *-ed*]
bield (*Dialect* refuge), field, heeled, shield, Weald, wield, yield.

Sheffield, airfield, Scofield, snowfield, Nuffield, Wakefield, Lichfield, midfield, oilfield, coalfield, canfield (gambling card game), Enfield, urnfield (cemetery of cremation urns), infield, minefield, cornfield, Springfield (US city), Masefield, Mansfield, Hatfield, outfield, well-heeled, windshield, gumshield.

battlefield, Huddersfield, Macclesfield, Beaconsfield, Sutton Coldfield.

115.1
afield, chesterfield, Chesterfield.

116 -ild [also **218** + *-ed*]
build, skilled, gild, guild, sild, rebuild, upbuild, unskilled, wergild (price on man's life), Brunhild (legendary German queen), self-willed, unwilled, overbuild, semiskilled.

117 -iled [also **219** + *-ed*]
child, Fylde, mild, wild, Wilde, godchild, grandchild, brainchild, stepchild, Rothschild, undefiled.

118 -orld [also **221** + *-ed*]
auld, bald, scald, skald (ancient Scandinavian bard), walled, piebald, skewbald, close-hauled (with the sails flat), Cumbernauld.

119 -oiled [also **222** + *-ed*]
well-oiled, unspoiled, shopsoiled.

120 -oled [also **223** + *-ed*]
old, bold, cold, scold, fold, gold, hold, mould, sold, told, wold.

kobold (German mythological mischievous spirit), threefold, fourfold, twofold, blindfold, billfold, tenfold, enfold, pinfold (cattle pen), ninefold, unfold, sheepfold, eightfold, gatefold (folded oversize page), fivefold, sixfold, freehold, toehold, stokehold (coal bunker in ship), handhold, stronghold, uphold, leasehold, household, foothold, withhold, remould, Detmold (German city), unpolled, unsold, threshold, foretold, untold, Cotswold.

semibold (printing term), manifold, centrefold, overfold (geology term), sevenfold, marigold, stranglehold, buttonmould (core of covered button), Leopold, Hammarskjöld.

120.1
behold, copyhold (legal term).

121 -uled [also **227** + -ed]
Gould, unruled, unschooled, unscheduled.

122 -'ld [also **228** + -ed]
marbled, fabled, gabled, ribald, freckled, pickled, cuckold, raddled, handled, brindled, scaffold, Arnold, pimpled, Harold, titled, gruntled (contented), Tynwald, measled (infested with tapeworm larvae), chiselled, grizzled, sozzled.

spectacled, unbridled, unruffled, bedraggled, newfangled, oldfangled, Macdonald, principled, unequalled, emerald, untitled, disgruntled, untravelled, dishevelled, unrivalled, bespectacled, unprincipled.

122.1
Gerald, herald, Fitzgerald.

122.2
mettled (brave), unsettled.

123 -armed [also **230** + -ed]
armed, becalmed, unharmed, alarmed, unarmed.

124 -amed [also **231** + -ed]
forenamed, unaimed, unnamed, unframed, ashamed, untamed, unacclaimed, unashamed.

125 -ormed [also **238** + -ed]
deformed, reformed, malformed, unformed, uninformed.

126 -imed [also **236** + -ed]
unrhymed, well-timed.

127 -'md [also **242** + -ed]
envenomed, accustomed, unfathomed, unaccustomed.

128 -and [Some -land words in **143** may be pronounced to rhyme with this group. Also **245** + -ed.]
and, band, canned, hand, land, bland, gland, manned, rand, brand, grand, strand, Strand, sand, stand.

proband (person in genealogical study), browband (part of bridle), neckband, headband, sideband (electronics term), fahlband (thin bed of rock), armband, rainband (band in solar spectrum), trainband (16th-century English militia), spaceband (printing term), disband, hatband, sweatband, waistband, waveband, noseband (part of bridle), forehand, backhand, offhand, stagehand, unhand, longhand, shorthand, summand (part of a sum), unmanned, repand (having a wavy margin), expand, firebrand, Streisand, quicksand, greensand (olive-green sandstone), suntanned, headstand, bandstand, handstand, grandstand, washstand, withstand, newsstand, kickstand (stand for bicycle), inkstand.

graduand, bellyband (part of harness), saraband, contraband, Samarkand, deodand (former legal term), beforehand, underhand, overhand, behindhand, second-hand, confirmand, Ferdinand, ordinand, operand (maths term), integrand (mathematical function), ampersand, Kristiansand (Norwegian port), understand.

Witwatersrand (South African region), analysand (person undergoing psychoanalysis), misunderstand.

128.1

radicand (maths term), multiplicand (number multiplied).

129 -arned

darned, demand, remand, command, allemande (musical term), reprimand, countermand.

130 -aned [also **247** + -*ed*]

pained, strained, harebrained, crackbrained, ingrained, close-grained, unstrained, bloodstained, scatterbrained, featherbrained, unrestrained, self-contained.

131 -end

end, bend, fend, lend, blend, mend, pend, penned, spend, rend, friend, trend, send, scend (nautical term), tend, vend, wend.

backbend (gymnastic exercise), unbend, unkenned (*Dialect* unknown), addend (number added to), defend, forfend (*US* protect), offend, augend (number added), pitchblende, hornblende, emend, stipend, upend, append, perpend, impend, misspend, expend, befriend, boyfriend, girlfriend, descend, ascend, godsend, transcend, portend, attend, subtend, intend, contend, distend, Ostend, extend, Southend, Wallsend, Gravesend.

minuend (number subtracted from), dividend, subtrahend (number subtracted), condescend, coextend, Demavend (Iranian volcanic peak), superintend.

131.1

apprehend, reprehend, comprehend, misapprehend.

131.2

amend, commend, recommend, discommend.

131.3

depend, vilipend (treat with contempt).

131.4

suspend, overspend.

131.5

pretend, repetend (repeated digit).

132 -erned [also **249** + -*ed*]

unearned, concerned, unturned, unconcerned.

133 -eened [also **251** + -*ed*]

fiend, archfiend, uncleaned, unscreened.

134 -ind [also **252** + -*ed*]

Ind (poetic name for India), finned, Sind (region of Pakistan), tinned, wind, thick-skinned, thin-skinned, sequined, rescind, destined, spavined (veterinary term), forewind (favourable wind), headwind, woodwind, tailwind, whirlwind, downwind, upwind, crosswind, exscind (cut off), wunderkind (child prodigy), determined, tamarind, undetermined.

135 -ined [also **253** + -*ed*]

bind, kind, find, hind, blind, mind, rind, grind, wind, wynd (*Scot* narrow lane).

cowbind (climbing plant), spellbind, unbind, mankind, unkind, refined, affined (closely related), behind, purblind (partly blind), inclined, streamlined, unlined, remind, unsigned, rewind, enwind, unwind.

gavelkind (former land tenure system), womankind, humankind, unrefined, nonaligned, mastermind, undersigned, overwind.

136 -ond

bond, donned, fond, Gond (former tribal Indian), blonde, blond, pond, frond, Fronde, sonde (device for observing atmosphere), wand, Zond (unmanned Russian spacecraft), second, seconde (fencing position), abscond, keeshond, beau monde, millpond, respond, dropsonde (meteorological device), beyond, vagabond, demimonde, Garamond (typeface), correspond, rawinsonde (meteorological balloon), Trebizond (Turkish port), radiosonde (meteorological device).

137 -orned [also 255 + -ed]

corned, horned, maund (Asian unit of weight), unmourned, unadorned.

138 -oaned [also 257 + -ed]

stoned, rawboned (having bony physique), unboned, unowned, unatoned, unchaperoned.

139 -ound [also 258 + -ed]

bound, found, hound, mound, pound, round, ground, sound, stound (*Dialect* short period), wound, swound (*Dialect* swoon).

rebound, snowbound, abound, strikebound, hidebound, windbound (nautical term), hoofbound (veterinary term), fogbound, spellbound, stormbound, inbound, unbound, brassbound, casebound, icebound, housebound, outbound, westbound, eastbound, earthbound, clothbound, northbound, southbound, redound (have an effect on), profound, dumbfound, confound, greyhound, deerhound, boarhound, horehound (flowering plant), elkhound, bloodhound, wolfhound, draghound, staghound, hellhound (fiend), sleuthhound, foxhound, renowned, geepound (unit of mass), propound, impound, compound, expound, uncrowned, playground, fairground, foreground, background, stoneground, unsound,

astound, unwound, shunt-wound (electrical term), resound.

ironbound (unyielding), decompound (describing type of leaf), ultrasound, series-wound (electrical term).

superabound, merry-go-round.

139.1

around, surround, turnaround.

139.2

aground, underground, overground.

140 -und [also 259 + -ed]

bundh (general strike in India), bund (embankment), fund, secund (botany term), refund, re-fund, rotund, obtund (deaden), moribund, cummerbund, iracund (easily angered), Bundelkhand (region of India), orotund.

141 -oond

Bund (federation), Lund (Swedish city), dachshund.

142 -ooned [also 260 + -ed]

wound, marooned.

143 -'nd [also 261 + -ed]

viand (type of food), prebend (church stipend), riband (ribbon awarded for achievement), roband (nautical term), husband, second, fecund, jocund, hardened, ligand (chemistry term), brigand, legend, taloned, garland, Wayland (character in European folklore), island, highland, Thailand, Ireland, Holland, holland (coarse linen cloth), foreland (headland), Courland (region of Russia), moorland, lowland, Poland, Roland, Dowland (English musician), clubland, scrubland, parkland, Lakeland, dockland, Auckland, Falkland, midland, woodland, England, farmland, homeland, mainland, Greenland, inland, Finland, Vinland (stretch of US coast), Rhineland, gangland, Langland (English poet), Lapland, upland, grassland, Iceland, marshland, heartland, Shetland, Scotland, Gotland (Swedish island), Portland, Jutland, Rutland, wasteland, Cleveland, Friesland (Dutch province), Queensland, Hammond, almond, dromond (medieval sailing vessel), gourmand, Lomond, Richmond, Edmund, Redmond, Sigmund, Dortmund, perpend (large stone in wall), errand, gerund, wizened, thousand.

infecund, rubicund, unquestioned, abandoned, Zululand, Newfoundland, tableland, diamond, Sigismund (Holy Roman Emperor), unopened, reverend, old-fashioned, impassioned, unleavened.

millisecond, nanosecond, microsecond, Sudetenland (region of Czechoslovakia), aforementioned, undermentioned, well-intentioned.

143.1
eland, hieland (*Scot* easily tricked), Zealand, New Zealand.

143.2
Disneyland, fairyland, Maryland, Dixieland, Swaziland, Somaliland, Matabeleland.

143.3
Pondoland (region of South Africa), Togoland, Heligoland (North Sea island).

143.4
Oberland, timberland, borderland, Gelderland (Dutch province), Sunderland, wonderland, Nagaland (Indian state), Westmorland, Switzerland, hinterland, fatherland, motherland, Sutherland, overland, Bechuanaland, Gondwanaland, Nyasaland.

143.4.1
Cumberland, Northumberland.

143.5
conditioned, unconditioned, noncommissioned.

143.6
reasoned, weasand (windpipe), unseasoned.

144 -athed [also **473** + *-ed*]
unscathed, enswathed.

145 -othed [also **478** + *-ed*]
unclothed, betrothed.

146 -aved [also **482** + *-ed*]
unpaved, depraved, unsaved, well-behaved.

147 -erved [also **483** + *-ed*]
decurved (bent downwards), reserved, undeserved, unreserved, well-preserved, unobserved.

148 -eeved [also **484** + *-ed*]
leaved, relieved, well-received, unperceived.

149 -ived [also **486** + *-ed*]
deprived, contrived.

150 -ooved [also **490** + *-ed*]
moved, removed, unmoved, approved, unproved, unimproved.

151 -olved [also **493** + *-ed*]
unsolved, involved, resolved, unresolved, undissolved.

152 -azed [also **509** + *-ed*]
crazed, unglazed.

153 -eezed [also **513** + *-ed*]
pleased, well-pleased, diseased.

154 -ized [also **516** + *-ed*]
sized, pearlized, advised, undisguised, civilized, creolized (linguistics term), undersized, oversized, ill-advised, unadvised, uncivilized, well-organized, disorganized, unauthorized, uncircumcised.

155 -ozed [also **520** + *-ed*]
closed, composed, unposed, disposed, exposed, undisclosed, indisposed, unexposed, undiagnosed.

155.1
supposed, unopposed.

156 -oozed [also **523** + *-ed*]
used, bruised, accused, bemused, amused, disused.

157 -aff
caff, daff, faff, gaff, gaffe, sclaff (golf stroke), raff (*Dialect* rubbish), draff (husks remaining after fermentation), waff (*Dialect* gust), WAAF, piaffe (dressage term), chiffchaff (European warbler), Llandaff, kenaf (jute-like fibre), carafe, riffraff, agraffe (a fastening), bathyscaph, shandygaff.

158 -arf
calf, scarf, chaff, half, haaf (deep-sea fishing ground), laugh, graph, staff, zarf (coffee-cup holder), mooncalf (fool), headscarf, behalf, giraffe, digraph (two-letter sound), trigraph (three-letter sound), distaff, ploughstaff, flagstaff, tipstaff, pikestaff, telegraph, polygraph (lie detector), epigraph (opening quotation in book), serigraph (silk-screen print), shadowgraph, Stevengraph (picture woven in silk), epitaph, cenotaph, quarterstaff (former English weapon).

158.1
myograph (muscular-contraction recorder), tachograph, arcograph (geometric instrument), zincograph (zinc printing-plate), Van de Graaff (US physicist), ondograph (alternating-current recorder), nephograph (cloud-photographing instrument), allograph (signature written for another), stylograph (type of pen), xylograph (wood engraving), holograph (original manu-

script), thermograph, kymograph (medical instrument), homograph, pneumograph, sphygmograph (blood-pressure recorder), seismograph, stenograph, Chinagraph (*Trademark*), monograph, chronograph, barograph, paragraph, spirograph (breathing-movement recorder), macrograph (drawing showing enlarged image), micrograph (picture of microscope image), hygrograph (humidity recorder), autograph, photograph, hectograph (copying process), pictograph, pantograph (instrument for scale drawing), cryptograph (code), lithograph.

oscillograph, Addressograph (*Trademark*), hyetograph (rainfall chart), odontograph (gear-tooth marking aid).

meteorograph, photomicrograph (photograph of microscope image), cinematograph (type of cine-projector), microphotograph (photograph showing reduced image), electroencephalograph.

158.1.1
cardiograph, radiograph, heliograph, oleograph (lithograph imitating oil-painting), Mimeograph (*Trademark*), stereograph (three-dimensional picture), choreograph, phraseograph (phrase representable by symbol), myocardiograph, autoradiograph (photograph of radioactive object), spectroheliograph (instrument for photographing sun), electrocardiograph.

158.1.2
phonograph, coronagraph (optical instrument).

158.1.3
spectrograph (instrument for photographing spectrum), electrograph.

159 -afe
chafe, strafe, safe, waif, vouchsafe, unsafe.

160 -eff

eff, deaf, lev (Bulgarian currency), clef, ref, chef, tef (African grass), ASLEF, Brezhnev, UNICEF.

160.1

Kiev, Prokofiev.

161 -erf

kerf (cut made by saw), scurf, serf, surf, turf.

162 -eef

beef, chief, fief (property granted to vassal), leaf, lief, reef, brief, grief, sheaf, thief, naïf, enfeoff (legal term), flyleaf, thickleaf (succulent plant), broadleaf (tobacco plant), sherif (descendant of Mohammed), debrief, massif, motif, interleaf, overleaf, cloverleaf, leitmotiv, apéritif.

162.1

belief, relief, unbelief, disbelief, misbelief (unorthodox belief), bas-relief, demirelief.

162.2

kharif (autumn-harvested crop), Tenerife.

163 -iff

if, biff, kif (marijuana), skiff, cliff, glyph (groove on frieze), miff, niff, sniff, quiff, Rif (Moroccan people), riff (jazz term), griffe (claw-shaped carved ornament), tiff, stiff, whiff, ziff (*Austral* beard).

kerchief, mischief, Cardiff, Aycliffe (English town), Wycliffe (English religious reformer), Radcliffe, Sutcliffe, triglyph (architectural term), tariff, Er Rif (mountainous region of Morocco), hairif (Eurasian plant), midriff, caitiff (cowardly person), plaintiff, pontiff, mastiff, skewwhiff, Joseph.

neckerchief, handkerchief, anaglyph (stereoscopic picture), hieroglyph, petroglyph (prehistoric rock carving), logogriph (word puzzle), hippogriff (Greek mythological monster), positif (organ keyboard).

163.1

bailiff, caliph, bumbailiff (debt collector).

163.2

serif, sheriff, sanserif, undersheriff.

164 -ife

fife, Fife, life, knife, rife, strife, wife, highlife, wildlife, half-life, nightlife, drawknife (woodcutting tool), jackknife, penknife, wakerife (*Dialect* wakeful), loosestrife, midwife, goodwife, oldwife (long-tailed sea duck), alewife (herring-like fish), housewife, fishwife, afterlife, paperknife, pocketknife, sweetiewife (*Scot* talkative woman).

165 -off

off, cough, coff (*Scot* buy), scoff, doff, quaff, prof, shroff (detector of counterfeit money), trough, toff, takeoff, Chekhov, Khrushchev, sendoff, Wolof (African people), brushoff, liftoff, blastoff, waveoff (signal to aircraft), Nabokov, whooping cough, Godunov (Russian tsar), stroganoff, Romanov (Russian imperial dynasty), Molotov, Rimsky-Korsakov.

165.1

Ustinov, Rachmaninoff.

166 -orf

orfe, Orff (German composer), corf (wagon used in mines), morph (linguistics term), wharf, dwarf, swarf, Waldorf, bimorph (electronics term), dimorph (one of two forms), trimorph (one of three forms), Düsseldorf, polymorph, perimorph (mineral enclosing another).

166.1

pseudomorph (mineral of uncharacteristic form), endomorph, lagomorph

(type of mammal), allomorph, paramorph (mineralogy term), mesomorph,
isomorph (organism with similar
form), ectomorph, rhizomorph (root-
like fungal structure), hystricomorph
(type of rodent), gynandromorph (biology term), enantiomorph (form of
crystal).

167 -oaf
oaf, loaf, limitrophe (near a frontier).

168 -uff
buff, cuff, scuff, chuff, chough, duff,
guff (*Slang* ridiculous talk), huff, luff
(leading edge of sail), bluff, clough
(*Dialect* a gorge), fluff, slough, muff,
snuff, puff, ruff, rough, scruff, gruff,
sough (*Dialect* a drain), tough, tuff
(volcanic rock), stuff.

rebuff, handcuff, earmuff, enough,
woodruff (flowering plant), crossruff
(bridge term), dyestuff, foodstuff,
greenstuff, overstuff.

169 -oof
poof, woof.

170 -ufe
oof (*Slang* money), goof, hoof, kloof
(South African mountain pass), pouffe,
spoof, roof, proof, woof.

shadoof, aloof, sunroof, reproof, wearproof, fireproof, shockproof, skidproof,
soundproof, shellproof, foolproof,
flameproof, stormproof, rainproof, disproof, rustproof, mothproof.

Al Hufuf (Saudi Arabian town),
showerproof, weatherproof, shatterproof, waterproof, counterproof (printing term), bulletproof.

171 -'f
ganef (*US* unscrupulous opportunist),
daraf (unit in physics), paraph (flourish following a signature), seraph, ter-

aph (Old Testament household god),
dandruff.

172 -elf
elf, skelf (*Dialect* wood splinter), pelf
(money), self, shelf, Guelph (Italian
political faction member), thyself, myself, yourself, herself, himself, oneself,
itself.

173 -olf
golf, Rolf, Rudolf, Randolph.

174 -ulf
gulf, engulf.

175 -oolf
wolf, Woolf, Wolfe, werewolf, aardwolf
(nocturnal mammal), Cynewulf (Anglo-Saxon poet), Beowulf (Old English
epic poem), Fenriswolf (Norse mythological wolf).

176 -imph
lymph, nymph, perilymph (fluid in
ear), endolymph (fluid in ear), karyolymph (part of cell nucleus).

177 -umph
bumph, humph, triumph, galumph.

178 -ag
bag, scag (*Dialect* to tear), fag, gag,
jag, hag, lag, flag, slag, mag, nag, knag
(knot in wood), snag, spag (*Welsh*
scratch with claws), rag, brag, crag,
scrag, drag, frag (US military slang
term), sprag (prop used in mining),
sag, shag, tag, stag, vag (*Austral* a vagrant), wag, swag.

debag, fleabag, workbag, feedbag,
handbag, sandbag, windbag, ragbag,
mailbag, beanbag, gasbag, ratbag,
postbag, nosebag, stalag, greylag, Gulag, cagmag (*Dialect* chat idly), washrag (*US* face cloth), ragtag (the
rabble), wigwag (wave flags in signal-
ling), chinwag, zigzag.

saddlebag, lallygag (*US* loiter aimlessly), bullyrag (bully with practical jokes), scallywag.

178.1
kitbag, carpetbag.

179 -arg
bagh (Indian garden), darg (*Dialect* day's work), Prague, Reichstag, Laoag (Philippine city), Bundestag (West German legislative assembly).

180 -aig
Haig, Hague, plague, Craig, vague, stravaig (*Dialect* wander aimlessly).

181 -eg
egg, beg, keg, skeg (nautical term), leg, cleg (horsefly), peg, dreg, teg, muskeg (boggy hollow), foreleg, proleg (larva's abdominal limb), blackleg, dogleg, bootleg, nutmeg, unpeg, Tuareg (member of Berber people), thalweg (geography term), filibeg (Scottish Highlander's kilt), Scanderbeg (Albanian patriot), Winnipeg.

182 -erg
erg, burg (town), berg (*short for* iceberg).

Marburg, Coburg, coburg (type of loaf), Newburg (cookery term), Lindbergh, Strindberg, Bamberg (German town), Hamburg, Limburg, Gomberg (US chemist), homburg, Romberg (US composer), Schoenberg, iceberg, Hapsburg, Vicksburg (American Civil War site), Strasbourg, exergue (inscription on coin).

Magdeburg, Bundaberg (Australian city), osnaburg (coarse cotton fabric), Middelburg (Dutch city), Heidelberg, inselberg (isolated rocky hill), Nuremberg, Württemberg, Luxembourg, Oldenburg (German city), Brandenburg, Hindenburg, Mecklenburg (region of Germany), Orenburg (Russian city),

Battenburg, Gutenberg, Gothenburg (Swedish port), Gettysburg, Petersburg (American Civil War site), Williamsburg (former capital of Virginia), Drakensberg (African mountain range), Saint Petersburg.

182.1
Louisburg (Canadian fortress), Harrisburg (capital of Pennsylvania), Johannesburg.

182.2
Pittsburgh, Pietermaritzburg (capital of Natal).

183 -eeg
league, Grieg, gigue, colleague, renege, blitzkrieg, sitzkrieg, intrigue, squeteague (Atlantic fish), fatigue.

184 -ig
big, dig, fig, gig, jig, pig, rig, brig, frig, grig (*Dialect* lively person), prig, sprig, trig, cig, Whig, wig, swig, twig.

shindig, fishgig (pole for impaling fish), rejig (re-equip), pfennig, bushpig (African wild pig), unrig, Danzig (fancy pigeon), Leipzig, earwig, bagwig (18th-century wig), bigwig.

infra dig, caprifig (wild fig), whirligig, guinea pig, thimblerig (game of chance), periwig, Zagazig (Egyptian city), thingumajig.

185 -og
bog, cog, dog, fog, Gog, jog, Hogg, hog, log, clog, flog, glogg (hot alcoholic drink), slog, mog, smog, nog, snog, pogge (European fish), frog, grog, prog, trog (to stroll), tog.

seadog, firedog, watchdog, fogdog (whitish spot in fog), bulldog, sundog (small rainbow near horizon), hangdog, sheepdog, hot dog, Magog, goosegog, quahog, sandhog (*US* underground worker), hedgehog, prologue, backlog, eclogue, unclog, loglog (logarithm of logarithm), footslog, putlog (beam supporting scaffold floor), eggnog, bullfrog, leapfrog, Hertzog, tautog (Atlantic fish).

underdog, Tagalog, epilogue, antilog, dialogue, duologue, Decalogue, homologue, analogue, monologue, apologue (moral fable), catalogue, travelogue, golliwog, polliwog, Memphremagog (US–Canadian lake).

185.1
befog, pettifog.

185.2
agog, pedagogue, demagogue, haemagogue (promoting blood flow), synagogue, mystagogue (teacher of mystical doctrines), sialagogue (substance stimulating saliva flow), emmenagogue (substance increasing menstrual flow), galactagogue (inducing milk secretion).

186 -org
Borg, morgue, Swedenborg (Swedish scientist and theologian).

187 -oorg
bourg (French market town), Coorg (former province of India), Cherbourg, faubourg.

188 -oag
rogue, brogue, drogue (funnel-shaped device), vogue, collogue (conspire), pirog (large pie), pirogue (canoe), prorogue, pishogue (*Irish* sorcery), disembogue (discharge or flow out).

189 -ug
bug, chug, dug, fug, jug, hug, lug, plug, slug, mug, smug, snug, pug, rug, drug, shrug, trug, tug, thug, vug (mining term).

debug, firebug (arsonist), bedbug, redbug (parasitic larva), humbug, earplug, unplug.

jitterbug, litterbug, doodlebug, spittlebug (leaping insect).

190 -oog
Moog (*Trademark*), fugue.

191 -adge
badge, cadge, fadge (*Dialect* agree), hajj (Muslim pilgrimage to Mecca).

192 -arge
barge, charge, large, marg, marge, sparge (sprinkle), raj, sarge, taj (Muslim's tall cap), surcharge, recharge, discharge, enlarge, Al Marj (ancient Libyan town), swaraj (self-government in India), litharge (lead monoxide), undercharge, supercharge, countercharge, overcharge, lithomarge (type of kaolin).

193 -age
age, cage, phage (virus that destroys bacteria), gauge, gage (a pledge), page, rage, sage, stage, wage, swage (shaped tool).

birdcage, encage, prophage (parasitic virus in bacterium), greengage, engage, teenage, rampage, enrage, outrage, Osage (American Indian people), substage (part of microscope), offstage, downstage, upstage, backstage, assuage.

disengage, archimage (great magician), interpage, underage, overage, saxifrage, multistage.

193.1
macrophage (cell in animal tissue), bacteriophage (virus that destroys bacteria).

194 -edge
edge, kedge (nautical term), hedge, ledge, fledge, pledge, sledge, dredge, sedge, veg, wedge, allege, frankpledge (medieval tithing system), straightedge

(strip used as ruler), featheredge (plank with thin edge).

195 -erge

urge, scourge, dirge, splurge, merge, purge, spurge, serge, surge, verge, emerge, submerge, resurge (rise again), deterge (cleanse), diverge, converge, demiurge (philosophy term), dramaturge, thaumaturge (performer of miracles).

196 -eege

liege, siege, besiege.

197 -idge

midge, ridge, bridge, fridge.

triage (sorting according to priority), buoyage, voyage, flowage, towage, stowage, cowage (tropical climbing plant), brewage, sewage, Babbage (English mathematician), cabbage, garbage, Burbage (English actor), herbage (vegetation for grazing), cribbage, cubage (cubic contents), package, breakage, leakage, dockage (charge for docking ships), lockage (canal lock system), blockage, socage (former legal term), corkage, linkage, shrinkage, boscage (thicket), adage, wordage, cordage (ship's rigging), bandage, blindage (military protective screen), bondage, poundage, groundage (fee for anchorage), roughage, baggage, mortgage, luggage, scalage (*US* percentage price reduction), treillage (trellis), pelage (coat of mammal), mileage, silage, haulage, spoilage, soilage (green fodder), ullage (unfilled part of container), sullage (sewage), Coolidge, Sutlej (Asian river), kentledge (ship's ballast), damage, rummage, scrummage, plumage, carnage, cranage (use of crane), drainage, nonage (being under legal age), dunnage (material for packing cargo), tonnage, seepage, pipage (system of pipes), stoppage, peerage, steer-

age, borage (flowering plant), forage, Norwich, porridge, floorage, storage, moorage, weighbridge, drawbridge, Trowbridge, Stourbridge, abridge, Cambridge, umbrage, Tonbridge, footbridge, Lethbridge (Canadian city), Oxbridge, Uxbridge, suffrage, cartridge, partridge, passage, sausage, dosage, usage, cartage, eatage (*Dialect* grazing rights), metage (official measuring of goods), cottage, pottage, wattage, portage (transport), shortage, outage (missing goods), footage, voltage, vantage, mintage, vintage, frontage, wastage, vestige, hostage, postage, Carthage, lavage (medical procedure), ravage, savage, pavage (tax towards paving streets), cleavage, lovage, salvage, selvage, language, sandwich, messuage (legal term), visage, prisage (customs duty on wine).

verbiage, foliage, lineage, ferriage (transportation by ferry), appendage, diallage (mineral), vassalage, assemblage, endamage, peonage (working to pay debts), orphanage, gallonage, commonage (legal term), baronage, patronage, matronage, parsonage, personage, Stevenage, sewerage, harbourage, acreage, vicarage, brokerage, anchorage, pasturage, plunderage (embezzlement of ship's goods), telpherage (overhead transport system), pilferage, cellarage, Coleridge, haemorrhage, porterage (charge for porter's work), quarterage (quarterly payment), waterage (transportation by ship), fosterage, average, beverage, leverage, coverage, agiotage (business of currency exchange), pilotage, advantage, parentage (ancestry), envisage.

vagabondage, overdosage, disadvantage, protolanguage (reconstructed extinct language), paralanguage (linguistics term), metalanguage (linguistics term).

197.1

pillage, spillage, grillage (arrangement of beams), tillage, stillage (low supporting platform), village, pupillage, sacrilege, mucilage, ensilage (process of storing fodder), cartilage, curtilage (enclosed area of land), sortilege (divination by drawing lots), tutelage, privilege.

197.2

college, knowledge, foreknowledge, acknowledge.

197.3

image, scrimmage, pilgrimage, afterimage.

197.4

homage, West Bromwich.

197.5

manage, pannage (pasturage for pigs), tannage (process of tanning), mismanage.

197.6

ennage (printing term), empennage (rear part of aircraft).

197.7

spinach, Greenwich, concubinage.

197.8

slippage, equipage (horse-drawn carriage).

197.9

carriage, Harwich, marriage, miscarriage, remarriage, disparage, undercarriage, intermarriage.

197.10

courage, encourage, discourage, demurrage (delay of carrier's departure).

197.11

message, presage, expressage (conveyance by express).

197.12

hermitage, maritage (feudal right), heritage, baronetage.

197.13

dotage, flotage, anecdotage.

197.14

tentage (tents), ventage (small hole), percentage.

198 -ige

oblige, disoblige.

199 -odge

bodge, dodge, lodge, plodge (*Dialect* wade), splodge, modge (*Dialect* to botch), stodge, wodge, dislodge, hodgepodge, horologe (timepiece).

200 -orge

forge, gorge, George, regorge (to vomit), engorge, disgorge.

201 -oge

doge, gamboge (gum resin).

202 -ouge

gouge, scrouge (*Dialect* to crowd).

203 -udge

budge, fudge, judge, bludge (*Austral* to scrounge), sludge, smudge, nudge, drudge, grudge, trudge, prejudge, forejudge, forjudge (legal term), adjudge (pronounce formally), misjudge, begrudge.

204 -uge

smoodge (*Austral* smooch), Scrooge, stooge, huge, refuge, deluge, vermifuge (worm-expelling drug), febrifuge (fever-reducing drug), centrifuge, calcifuge (botany term), subterfuge.

205 -ulge

bulge, indulge, divulge.

206 -ange

flange, phalange (finger- or toe-bone), Falange (Spanish Fascist movement).

207 -ainge

change, mange, range, grange, strange, exchange, arrange, estrange, interchange, counterchange, rearrange, disarrange.

207.1

derange, omnirange (radio navigational system).

208 -enge

henge (area with stone circle), Stonehenge, revenge, avenge.

209 -inge

binge, dinge, hinge, cringe, fringe, springe (small snare), singe, tinge, whinge, swinge, twinge, unhinge, challenge, impinge, syringe, orange, infringe, scavenge, lozenge.

210 -ounge

lounge, scrounge.

211 -unge

scunge (*Austral* borrow), gunge, lunge, blunge (ceramics term), plunge, sponge, expunge, muskellunge (US game fish), Narayanganj (Bangladeshi city).

212 -al

gal, pal, sal (salt), shall, cabal, decal (transferred design), coucal (ground-living bird), fallal (showy ornament), formal (chemical compound), grand mal, canal, neral (chemistry term), La Salle (Canadian city), Laval (Canadian city), pedocal (lime-rich soil), caracal (desert lynx), warrigal (*Austral* dingo), methylal (chemical compound), petit mal, rhodinal (fragrant natural oil), falderal (worthless trifle), chaparral (dense growth of trees), acetal (chemical compound), citronellal (fragrant natural oil), Guadalcanal (Pacific island), piperonal (chemical compound), Ashurbanipal (Assyrian king).

213 -arl

Basle, Baal, Carl, dhal (tropical shrub), dal (Indian food), farl (oatmeal cake), marl, gnarl, snarl, rale (medical term), kraal (South African hut village), Vaal (South African river), joual (Canadian French dialect), toile, jarl (medieval Scandinavian chieftain).

Taal (Philippine volcano), real (former Spanish coin), timbale (dish cooked in mould), Baikal (Russian lake), locale, housecarl (medieval Danish household servant), Heimdall (Norse god), Ruisdael (Dutch painter), Imphal (Indian city), halal (Muslim custom), hamal (Oriental servant), unsnarl, Bhopal (Indian city), corral, chorale, morale, Transvaal, riyal (Saudi Arabian currency), khayal (Indian classical vocal music), Chogyal (title of Indian ruler).

Taj Mahal, Ar Rimal (Arabian desert), caporal (strong tobacco), pastorale, Provençal, Nembutal (*Trademark*), Emmenthal, Van der Waal (Dutch chemist).

Escorial (Spanish architectural site), Neanderthal.

213.1

banal, rationale.

214 -ale

ail, ale, bale, bail, kale, scale, dale, fail, faille (soft light fabric), gale, Gael (Gaelic-speaking person), gaol, jail, hail, hale, flail, male, mail, nail, snail, pail, pale, quail, rail, Braille, brail (nautical term), drail (angler's weighted hook), frail, Grail, trail, sail, sale, shale, tale, tail, stale, they'll, veil, vale, wail, whale, wale (weal on skin), dwale (deadly nightshade).

percale (closely-woven cotton fabric), Airedale, Rochdale, Drysdale, Clydesdale, regale, Longueuil (Canadian city), inhale, exhale, Hallel (Jewish chant of praise), camail (part of armour), vermeil (gilded metal), female, blackmail, tenaille (part of fortification), treenail (dowel joining planks), doornail, toenail, hobnail, thumbnail, hangnail, impale, derail, guardrail, handrail, taffrail (rail at ship's stern), engrail (indent edge of), Sangraal (Holy Grail), contrail (vapour trail from aircraft), staysail, resale, skysail, trysail, wassail, foresail, assail, abseil, wholesale, mainsail, topsail, curtail, hairtail (marine fish), detail, retail, hightail, bobtail, cocktail, broadtail (fur from Persian lambs), swordtail (tropical fish), wagtail, pigtail, telltale, fantail, ventail (part of armour), entail, pintail (greyish-brown duck), fishtail (ballroom-dancing step), dovetail, oxtail, foxtail, travail, prevail, avail, unveil, bewail, grisaille (painting technique).

Wensleydale, Corriedale (breed of sheep), amygdale (geology term), Chippendale, Skelmersdale, Abigail, Fine Gael (Irish political party), martingale (strap in horse's harness), galingale (European plant), nightingale, farthingale (framework worn under skirts), fingernail, monorail, ponytail, swallowtail (type of butterfly), tattletale, cottontail, Ebbw Vale, countervail (act with equal force).

215 -ell

ell, bell, belle, bel, dell, fell, jell, gel, hell, Hel (Norse mythological goddess), mel (pure form of honey), smell, knell, spell, quell, cell, sell, shell, tell, well, dwell, swell, yell.

Nowell, gabelle (former French salt tax), barbell, harebell, rebel, doorbell, Nobel, cowbell, bluebell, handbell, dumbbell, chandelle (aeronautics term), Bendel (Nigerian state), Scafell, befell, pell-mell, Parnell, fresnel (unit of frequency), spinel (mineral), Brunel, prunelle (French liqueur), quenelle (meat or fish dumpling), rappel (mountaineer's method of descent), repel, appel (fencing term), lapel, propel, impel, compel, dispel, misspell, expel,

Bakewell, inkwell, morel (edible fungus), jurel (Atlantic fish), marcel (hair style), Purcell, outsell, seashell, eggshell, bombshell, nutshell, artel (Russian cooperative union), cartel, Ravel, Tavel (French rosé wine), farewell, stairwell, speedwell, bridewell (jail), Caldwell, indwell, Cromwell, unwell, excel, Moselle, gazelle.

decibel, Jezebel, Isabel, aludel (vessel used in chemistry), Zinfandel (Californian wine grape), plasmagel (jelly-like protoplasm), aerogel (solid foam), parallel, calomel (purgative powder), philomel (nightingale), oenomel (wine and honey drink), béchamel, organelle (tiny structure inside cell), mangonel (stone-throwing war engine), villanelle (verse form), pimpernel, petronel (17th-century firearm), personnel, fontanelle, amarelle (variety of sour cherry), aquarelle, chanterelle (edible fungus), pipistrelle, radicel (tiny root), pedicel (flower stalk), filoselle (embroidery thread), photocell, cockleshell, tortoiseshell, brocatelle (heavy brocade), moschatel (small flowering plant), muscatel (rich sweet wine), bagatelle, clientele, caravel (sailing ship), Camberwell, demoiselle (small Eurasian crane).

spirituel (having refined wit), materiel (materials and equipment), involucel (botany term), eau de Javelle (bleaching solution), mademoiselle.

215.1
cadelle (small beetle), asphodel.

215.2
nacelle (part of aircraft), undersell, carousel, oversell.

215.3
Courtelle (*Trademark*), foretell, immortelle (everlasting flower).

215.4
boatel, hotel, motel, maître d'hôtel.

216 -erl

earl, burl (small lump in wool), curl, skirl (*Dialect* play bagpipes), churl, furl, girl, hurl, herl (angling term), merle (*Scot* blackbird), knurl (small ridge), purl, pearl, thirl (*Dialect* to drill), whirl, swirl, twirl, uncurl, unfurl, showgirl, cowgirl, switchgirl (*Austral* female switchboard operator), impearl (adorn with pearls), papergirl, mother-of-pearl.

217 -eel

eel, Biel (Swiss town), keel, Kiel (West German port), deal, deil (*Scot* devil), feel, heel, heal, he'll, leal (*Scot* loyal), meal, kneel, Neil, peel, peal, speel (*Dialect* wood splinter), spiel, squeal, reel, creel, seal, seel (falconry term), she'll, teal, steel, steal, veal, we'll, wheel, weal (raised mark on skin), zeal.

abele (white poplar tree), ordeal, misdeal, congeal, selfheal, allheal, allele (genetics term), schlemiel (*US* clumsy), inchmeal (inch by inch), wholemeal, piecemeal, sweetmeal, oatmeal, fistmele (archery term), repeal, appeal, kriegspiel (war game), bonspiel (curling match), newsreel, unseal, conceal, genteel, Bastille, Castile, reveal, Deauville, freewheel, gearwheel, flywheel, sidewheel (riverboat's paddle-wheel), aiguille (needle-shaped mountain peak), cogwheel, millwheel, pinwheel, cartwheel.

dishabille, traymobile (*Austral* trolley), Dormobile (*Trademark*), snowmobile, urodele (type of amphibian), Israfil (archangel in the Koran), cochineal, manchineel (tropical tree), glockenspiel, imbecile, cockatiel, commonweal, automobile.

217.1

anneal, chenille, eau de nil (pale yellowish-green colour).

217.2

underseal, hydrocele, rectocele, blastocoel (embryology term), haemocoel (invertebrate's body cavity), cystocele, haematocele (blood cyst), bubonocele (partial hernia in groin).

218 -ill

ill, bill, kill, skill, chill, dill, fill, gill, hill, mill, mil (unit of length), nil, pill, spill, quill, squill (Mediterranean plant), rill, brill, krill, drill, frill, grill, grille, shrill, trill, thrill, sill, till, still, will, swill, twill.

playbill (poster advertising a play), waybill, Erbil (Iraqi city), gerbil, sibyl (ancient Greek prophetess), wrybill, twibill (agricultural implement), bluebill, shoebill, handbill, bulbil (small bulb-like plant organ), hornbill, thornbill, spoonbill, waxbill, hawksbill (small tropical turtle), storksbill (flowering plant), cranesbill (flowering plant), alkyl (chemical group), Gaitskell, Churchill, idyll, condyle (rounded projection on bone), refill, fulfil, argil (potter's clay), Virgil, strigil (ancient Roman's body-scraper), vigil, Edgehill, molehill, downhill, dunghill, uphill, foothill, allyl (chemical group), amyl (chemical group), Tamil (member of Asian people), sawmill, De Mille, treadmill, windmill, gristmill, anil (West Indian shrub), manille (trump in card game), phenyl (chemical group), vinyl, tranquil, jonquil, fibril (small fibre), nombril (heraldic term), quadrille, mandrill, tendril, nostril, Bovril (*Trademark*), acyl (chemical group), doorsill, groundsill (joist in timber frame), butyl (chemical group), dactyl, dentil (architectural term), lentil, until, pastille, distil, pistil, standstill, instil, ethyl, methyl, chervil, Melville, anvil, Nashville, dullsville, goodwill, pigswill, axil, Brazil, benzyl (chemical group).

razorbill, winterkill (kill by frost exposure), overkill, cacodyl (oily poisonous liquid), daffodil, thionyl (chemical group), uranyl (chemical group), minipill, overspill, escadrille (French aircraft squadron), espadrille, codicil, verticil (biology term), windowsill, uracil (biochemical compound), nitrosyl (chemical group), acetyl, tormentil (Eurasian plant), Bougainville (Pacific island), Jacksonville (US port), whippoorwill, carboxyl (chemical group).

Invercargill, pterodactyl, Merthyr Tydfil.

218.1

sclerophyll (woody evergreen plant), sporophyll (botany term), mesophyll (middle layer of leaf), xanthophyll (plant pigment), cladophyll (botany term), chlorophyll, neutrophil (white blood cell), eosinophil (white blood cell).

218.2

beryl, Beryl, peril, imperil.

218.3

Seville, Baskerville, vaudeville, Stoke Mandeville.

219 -ile

isle, aisle, I'll, bile, chyle (milky fluid in intestine), kyle (*Scot* narrow strait), file, guile, lisle, mile, smile, Nile, pile, spile (heavy timber stake), rile, sile (*Dialect* rain heavily), tile, style, stile, vile, Weill (German composer), wile, while.

labile (unstable), stabile (stationary abstract construction), mobile, nubile, Kabyle (member of Berber people), aedile, defile, profile, nailfile, symphile (entomology term), misfile, Argyll, beguile, agile, fragile, Carlisle, Carlyle, anile (like an old woman), penile, senile, stockpile, woodpile, compile, sterile, virile, febrile, facile, gracile (gracefully slender), sessile (botany term), docile, fertile, quartile (statistics term), motile, protyle (hypothetical sub-

stance), rutile (mineral), futile, fictile (moulded from clay), ductile, pantile, quintile (astrology term), reptile, hairstyle, freestyle, hostile, prostyle (architectural term), turnstile, servile, revile, awhile, meanwhile, erstwhile, worthwhile, resile (spring back), fusile (easily melted), exile.

immobile, crocodile, camomile, Chari-Nile (language group), juvenile, thermopile (radiant energy detector), micropyle (biology term), puerile, afebrile (without fever), indocile, expansile (able to expand), reconcile, infertile, volatile, versatile, pulsatile (beating rhythmically), inductile (not pliant), mercantile, infantile, epistyle (architectural term), peristyle (colonnade surrounding building).

aeolipile (model steam turbine), antifebrile, coleoptile (botany term), acrylonitrile (colourless liquid).

219.1

zoophile (animal lover), Francophile, discophile (collector of gramophone records), paedophile, Anglophile, thermophile (organism thriving in warmth), spermophile (US ground squirrel), xenophile (admirer of foreigners), Negrophile, Russophile, audiophile (hi-fi enthusiast), bibliophile, myrmecophile (animal living with ants), Germanophile, ailurophile (cat lover).

219.2

fissile, missile, scissile (capable of being cut), domicile, antimissile, circumscissile (botany term).

219.3

ensile (store in silo), pensile (ornithology term), tensile, prehensile, thermotensile (physics term).

219.4

tractile (ductile), tactile, retractile (able to be withdrawn), protractile (able to be extended), contractile.

219.5
sectile (easily sliced), projectile, erectile.

219.6
Gentile, percentile (statistics term).

219.7
hypostyle (architectural term), urostyle (zoology term), cyclostyle, amphiprostyle (architectural term).

219.8
sextile, textile, bissextile (relating to leap year).

220 -oll
col, doll, dol (unit of pain intensity), loll, moll.

obol, COBOL, glycol (liquid used as antifreeze), aldol (chemical compound), argol (deposit in wine vats), Gogol, googol (large number), ALGOL, Algol (bright star), Mongol, Jehol (region of China), salol (crystalline substance), xylol (chemical compound), thymol (crystalline compound), enol (chemical compound), phenol (carbolic acid), redpoll (finch), sterol (biochemical compound), cresol (chemical compound), atoll, metol (chemical compound), naphthol (crystalline substance), menthol, AWOL, podzol, benzol (chemical compound).

guaiacol (yellowish oily liquid), protocol, alcohol, mestranol (synthetic hormone), ethanol, methanol (chemical compound), Interpol, cortisol (hormone), creosol (yellow oily liquid), regosol (type of soil), Limassol (Cypriot port), plasmasol (fluid form of protoplasm), planosol (type of soil), parasol, aerosol, girasol (type of opal), entresol (mezzanine floor), lithosol (type of soil), amatol (explosive substance).

dimercaprol (colourless oily liquid), eucalyptol (colourless oily liquid), chloramphenicol (antibiotic).

220.1
borneol (chemical compound), vitriol, oestriol (hormone), geraniol (chemical compound), terpineol (chemical compound), urushiol (poisonous liquid).

220.2
Komsomol (Russian youth association), paracetamol.

220.3
quinol (crystalline substance), eugenol (oily liquid), orcinol (crystalline substance), retinol (biochemical compound), allopurinol (synthetic drug).

220.4
glycerol (syrupy liquid), calciferol (vitamin), tocopherol (vitamin), stigmasterol (biochemical compound), cholesterol, zoosterol (biochemical compound), ergosterol (biochemical compound), sitosterol (extract from soya beans).

221 -orl
awl, all, orle (border around a shield), ball, bawl, caul, call, scall (disease of the scalp), fall, Gaul, gall, hall, haul, maul, mall, small, pall, Paul, pawl (part of ratchet mechanism), spall (rock splinter), squall, brawl, crawl, scrawl, drawl, sprawl, trawl, thrall, Saul, shawl, schorl (black tourmaline), tall, stall, wall, waul (wail like a cat), yawl.

hairball, eyeball, highball, fireball, snowball, screwball, blackball, punchball, oddball, handball, pinball, baseball, netball, meatball, football, mothball, jackal, catcall, withal, bradawl, holdall, befall, snowfall, landfall, windfall, rainfall, downfall, catfall (nautical term), pratfall, pitfall, nightfall, shortfall, footfall, windgall (swelling on horse's fetlock), Bengal, Bohol (Philippine island), guildhall, keelhaul, downhaul (nautical term), townhall, Whitehall, monal (Asian pheasant), Nepal, appal, Blackwall, enthral, Walsall, forestall, thumbstall, install, footstall (base of column), bookstall, sidewall, Cornwall, stonewall.

carryall, Montreal, volleyball, cannonball, basketball, wherewithal, waterfall, Senegal, Donegal, overhaul, overall, disenthral, tattersall (patterned fabric), fingerstall, caterwaul.

221.1
recall, nudicaul (having leafless stems), amplexicaul (botany term).

222 -oil
oil, boil, Boyle, coil, Doyle, foil, noil (short textile fibres), spoil, roil, broil, soil, toil, voile, parboil, gumboil, recoil, uncoil, trefoil, airfoil, cinquefoil (type of plant), milfoil (yarrow), tinfoil, gargoyle, turmoil, despoil, embroil, subsoil, topsoil, multifoil (looped design), disembroil, undersoil.

222.1
aerofoil, hydrofoil, quatrefoil (architectural ornament), counterfoil, Fianna fail (Irish political party).

223 -ole
bowl, boll, bole, coal, kohl, cole (plant of cabbage family), skoal (drinking toast), dole, dhole (fierce canine mammal), foal, goal, whole, hole, mole, knoll, Pole, pole, poll, role, roll, scroll, droll, prole, troll, stroll, soul, sole, Seoul (capital of South Korea), sol (former French coin), shoal, toll, tole (enamelled metal ware), stole, thole (wooden peg in boat), vole.

creole, Sheol (abode of the dead), punchbowl, fishbowl, charcoal, clearcole (size for painting walls), bricole (billiards term), indole (crystalline substance), de Gaulle, cajole, keyhole, kneehole, frijol (variety of French bean), eyehole, blowhole, hellhole, armhole, manhole, pinhole, peephole, loophole, knothole, pothole, porthole, foxhole, anole (small tropical lizard),

maypole, dipole (pair of electric charges), blackpoll (US warbler), catchpole (medieval sheriff's officer), tadpole, flagpole, bargepole, ridgepole, Walpole, beanpole, payroll, pyrrole (colourless toxic liquid), Tyrol, bankroll, bedroll, safrole (plant oil), enrol, unroll, patrol, control, turnsole (plant turning towards sun), insole, console, skatole (crystalline substance), pistole (former European gold coin), extol, azole (chemical compound).

vacuole, amphibole (type of mineral), rocambole (garlic-like plant), caracole (half turn in dressage), pratincole (swallow-like bird), cubbyhole, pigeonhole, buttonhole, Seminole (American Indian), multirole, rock-and-roll, decontrol, self-control, oversoul (spiritual essence of everything), carmagnole (French Revolutionary costume), thiazole (chemical compound), carbazole (chemical compound), bibliopole (dealer in rare books).

223.1
bronchiole, cariole (horse-drawn cart), dariole (mould used in cookery), oriole, aureole (halo), cabriole, capriole (leap), centriole (biology term), petiole (leaf stalk), ostiole (small pore), arteriole (subdivision of artery).

223.2
condole, farandole (lively Provençal dance), girandole (ornamental candleholder).

223.3
parole, barcarole, banderole (long narrow ship's flag), fumarole (vent in volcano), rigmarole, casserole, profiterole.

223.4
rissole, camisole, anisole (colourless fragrant liquid).

224 -owl
owl, cowl, scowl, foul, fowl, jowl, howl, growl, prowl, yowl, peafowl, be-

foul, moorfowl, afoul, wildfowl, water-fowl.

225 -ull

cull, scull, skull, dull, gull, Hull, hull, lull, mull, Mull, null, Tull (English agriculturalist), stull (timber prop in mining), numbskull, annul, caracul (Persian lamb), Solihull, multihull, disannul.

226 -ul [further rhymes may be created by adding *-ful* to appropriate nouns]

bull, full, pull, wool.

Kabul (capital of Afghanistan), bulbul (tropical songbird), playful, careful, prayerful, gleeful, earful, cheerful, fearful, tearful, eyeful, joyful, rueful, wakeful, tankful, thankful, watchful, dreadful, heedful, needful, handful, mindful, changeful, vengeful, baleful, guileful, bowlful, doleful, soulful, armful, harmful, blameful, shameful, brimful, roomful, manful, skinful, sinful, scornful, mournful, spoonful, tuneful, wrongful, songful, hopeful, helpful, graceful, peaceful, blissful, useful, bashful, wishful, artful, cartful, hurtful, fitful, potful, thoughtful, doubtful, fruitful, tactful, restful, wistful, boastful, faithful, mirthful, wrathful, slothful, mouthful, healthful, stealthful, easeful.

Istanbul, bellyful, merciful, fanciful, pitiful, beautiful, dutiful, plentiful, bountiful, powerful, wonderful, colourful, masterful, flavourful, quiverful, reproachful, regardful, remindful, unmindful, revengeful, thimbleful, needleful, meaningful, worshipful, disgraceful, purposeful, deceitful, pocketful, unfaithful.

226.1
awful, lawful, unlawful.

226.2
woeful, sorrowful.

226.3
skilful, wilful, unskilful.

226.4
baneful, gainful, painful, disdainful.

226.5
stressful, successful.

226.6
forceful, remorseful, resourceful.

226.7
fateful, hateful, plateful, grateful, ungrateful.

226.8
fretful, forgetful, regretful.

226.9
spiteful, rightful, frightful, delightful.

226.10
neglectful, respectful, disrespectful.

226.11
eventful, resentful, uneventful.

226.12
tasteful, wasteful, distasteful.

226.13
lustful, trustful, distrustful.

226.14
ruthful, truthful, toothful (small draught of liquor), youthful, untruthful.

227 -ool

boulle (denoting type of marquetry), boule (pear-shaped imitation gemstone), Boole (British mathematician), cool, school, fool, ghoul, Goole (English inland port), joule, who'll, pool, Poole, pul (Afghan coin), spool, rule, drool, shul (synagogue), tool, stool, yule, you'll, mule, mewl, pule (to whimper), tulle.

babul (type of acacia), Stambul (old part of Istanbul), playschool, deschool, preschool, befool (make a fool of), tomfool, cagoule, Banjul (capital of Gambia), Blackpool, whirlpool, ampoule, cesspool, ferrule (metal cap), ferule (flat cane for punishment), spherule (tiny sphere), chondrule (meteorology term), misrule, toadstool, faldstool (bishop's backless seat), close-stool, footstool, lobule, globule, tubule, macule, saccule, locule (biology term), floccule (small mass of particles), bascule (type of bridge), schedule, module, nodule, virgule (printing term), cellule, pilule, granule, venule (small vein), papule (small pimple), cupule (cup-shaped structure), capsule, noctule (insectivorous bat), pustule, frustule (botany term), ovule, valvule.

supercool (cool without freezing), Hartlepool, Pontypool, Liverpool, overrule, vestibule, majuscule, minuscule, gallinule (aquatic bird).

animalcule, hierodule (ancient Greek temple slave).

227.1
spicule (slender pointed structure), ridicule, lodicule (botany term), molecule, fascicule (published instalment of book), graticule (grid), reticule (woman's bag), monticule (small hill).

228 -'l
babble, scabble (shape roughly), dabble, gabble, rabble, scrabble, drabble (make wet or dirty), grabble (grope about), barbel (European fish), garble, marble, Schnabel (US musician), jebel (hill in Arab country), pebble, rebel, treble, burble, herbal, verbal, feeble, Bible, libel, tribal, bobble, cobble, gobble, hobble, nobble, squabble, wobble, bauble, corbel, warble, foible, Jubal (biblical character), rouble, bubal (African antelope), tubal, fimble (male hemp plant), nimble, cymbal, symbol, timbal (type of kettledrum), thimble, wimble (hand tool), umbel (type of inflorescence), bumble, scumble (art term), fumble, jumble, humble, mumble, rumble, crumble, grumble, tumble, stumble, faecal, treacle, faucal (anato-

my term), snorkel, paucal (linguistics term), ducal, ankle, fankle (*Scot* entangle), rankle, Wankel (German engineer), Gaskell (English writer), pascal (unit of pressure), mascle (heraldic term), rascal, fiscal, hatchel (to comb flax), satchel, Rachel, Mitchell, fardel, hadal (relating to ocean depths), ladle, cradle, heddle (part of loom), medal, meddle, pedal, peddle, treadle, curdle, girdle, hurdle, beadle, needle, pedal (relating to the foot), wheedle, caudal, dawdle, modal, nodal, yodel, Kendal, Mendel (Austrian botanist), Grendel (legendary man-eating monster), sendel (fine silk fabric), dirndl, fondle, rondel (type of poem), poundal (unit of force), roundel (circular mark or object), bundle, rundle (ladder rung), trundle, baffle, snaffle, raffle, Eiffel, rifle, trifle, stifle, offal, coffle (line of chained slaves), waffle, gargle, burgle, gurgle, ogle, bogle (*Dialect* bogey), mogul, Vogul (member of Siberian people), juggle, smuggle, snuggle, struggle, mongol, bungle, fungal, jungle, cudgel, angel, dermal, thermal, primal, hummel (*Scot* hornless), pommel (part of saddle), pummel, Brummell, carnal, charnel (sepulchral), darnel (type of grass), tarnal (*US* damned), Chunnel, funnel, gunnel (eel-like fish), gunwale (nautical term), runnel (small stream), tunnel, Bracknell, cracknel, spignel (European plant), signal, hymnal, simnel, grapnel, shrapnel, carpal (wrist bone), carpel (female part of flower), maple, papal, staple, sepal, purple, couple, supple, scruple, cupel (gold-refining vessel), duple, pupil, scalpel, ample, trample, temple, dimple, pimple, crimple (crumple), simple, wimple, rumple, crumple, gospel, rorqual, mayoral, feral (wild), spheral (spherical), squirrel, Cyril, Wirral, gyral (rotating), viral, spiral, timbrel (tambourine), whimbrel (European curlew), sacral, mandrel (spindle in machine tool), spandrel (architectural term), scoundrel, mongrel, April, petrol, petrel, neutral, spectral, astral, wastrel, cloistral, minstrel, hassle, tassel, vassal, basal, chessel (cheese-making mould), nestle, pestle, wrestle, trestle, Cecil, vessel, Faisal, sisal, dorsal, morsel, plimsoll, cancel, handsel (*Dialect* new year gift), spancel (rope for fettering horse), chancel, tinsel, council, counsel, groundsel, Etzel (legendary German king), quetzal (crested bird), pretzel, schnitzel, special, bushel, crucial, nuptial, hurtle, myrtle, turtle, rectal, lintel, pintle (hinge pin), quintal (unit of weight), pastel, coastal, postal, Bethel, lethal, brothel, larval, marvel, navel, naval, serval, hovel, novel, grovel, oval, Lovell, shovel, narwhal (arctic whale), Orwell, lingual, Cromwell, gromwell (flowering plant), Sitwell, Maxwell, Boswell, axle, axel (ice-skating jump), bezel (surface on cutting tool), easel, diesel, teasel, weasel, chisel, fizzle, mizzle (*Dialect* drizzle), drizzle, frizzle, grizzle, sizzle, swizzle, nozzle, schnozzle (*US* nose), causal, guzzle, muzzle, nuzzle, puzzle, damsel.

enfeeble, ensemble, archducal, Arundel, triumphal, conjugal, Portugal, Tintagel, archangel, caramel, communal, tribunal, autumnal, uncouple, quadruple, octuple, quintuple, septuple, sextuple, catarrhal, deferral, referral, palpebral (relating to the eyelid), cerebral, vertebral, sepulchral, integral, urethral, especial, provincial, palatal, pivotal, betrothal, interval, bilingual, trilingual, sublingual, embezzle, reprisal, devisal (act of devising).

chromosomal, metacarpal, thermocouple, episcopal, Sebastopol (Russian port), equinoctial, multilingual, monolingual.

228.1
bael (Indian tree), Jael (biblical character), Raphael, Ishmael (biblical character), betrayal, portrayal, Israel.

228.2
real, ideal, genial (relating to the chin), corneal, surreal, unreal, epigeal (living on soil surface), hypogeal (living below soil surface), pharyngeal, laryngeal, perineal, peroneal (relating to outer leg), oesophageal, peritoneal.

228.3
labial (relating to a lip), brachial (relating to the arm), bronchial, radial, prandial, mondial (of the whole world), Belial (demon), cuneal (wedge-shaped), burial, Gabriel, Umbriel (satellite of Uranus), atrial, patrial, uncial (type of capital letter), lacteal (relating to milk), osteal (relating to bone), bathyal (relating to ocean depths), gavial (Asian crocodile), mesial (in the middle).

proverbial, adverbial, connubial (relating to marriage), Ezekiel, parochial, allodial (former property law term), custodial, postprandial, lymphangial (relating to lymphatic vessel), phalangeal (anatomy term), binomial, trinomial, monomial, biennial, triennial, millennial, perennial, centennial, colloquial, mercurial, industrial, carnassial (type of tooth), popliteal (behind the knee).

myocardial, endocardial, polynomial, entrepreneurial.

228.3.1
medial, predial (relating to land), remedial.

228.3.2
cordial, primordial.

228.3.3
effigial, vestigial, apterygial (zoology term).

228.3.4
filial, familial.

228.3.5
cranial, geranial (chemistry term), intracranial.

228.3.6
genial, menial, venial, congenial.

228.3.7
lineal, pineal, matrilineal, patrilineal.

228.3.8
colonial, baronial, ceremonial, matrimonial, patrimonial, antimonial (containing antimony), testimonial.

228.3.9
troupial (South American songbird), marsupial.

228.3.10
aerial, ariel (Arabian gazelle), Ariel (satellite of Uranus), narial (relating to the nostrils), vicarial, malarial, bursarial, actuarial, estuarial, secretarial, antimalarial.

228.3.11
ferial (relating to weekday), cereal, serial, sidereal, venereal, funereal, imperial, arterial, material, bacterial, ethereal, diphtherial, managerial, presbyterial, immaterial, magisterial, ministerial, monasterial.

228.3.12
oriel, boreal (relating to the north).

arboreal, enchorial (of a particular country), armorial, marmoreal (relating to marble), memorial, manorial, corporeal, gressorial (adapted for walking), cursorial (adapted for running), fossorial (used for burrowing), scansorial (adapted for climbing), sensorial (relating to the senses), tonsorial, sartorial, tutorial, factorial, pictorial, auctorial (relating to an author), tinctorial (relating to dyeing), raptorial (predatory), uxorial.

immemorial, incorporeal, insessorial (adapted for perching), professorial, prefectorial, directorial.

ambassadorial, gladiatorial, multifactorial (genetics term).

228.3.12.1
editorial, territorial, inquisitorial, extraterritorial.

228.3.12.2
piscatorial (relating to fish), purgatorial, grallatorial (ornithology term), clamatorial (ornithology term), senatorial, equatorial, dictatorial, saltatorial (adapted for jumping), legislatorial, gubernatorial (relating to a governor), subequatorial, conspiratorial, visitatorial (relating to official visitation), accusatorial.

228.3.13
bimestrial (lasting for two months), terrestrial, extraterrestrial.

228.3.14
bestial, celestial.

228.3.15
trivial, quadrivial (having four roads meeting), convivial.

228.3.16
jovial, synovial.

228.3.17
fluvial (relating to a river), pluvial (relating to rain), diluvial (produced by a flood), alluvial.

228.3.18
axial, preaxial (anatomy term), biaxial, triaxial, coaxial, abaxial (away from the axis), adaxial (facing towards the axis), uniaxial, epitaxial (electronics term).

228.4
dial, phial, myall (Australian acacia), rial (Iranian currency), trial, sial (part of earth's crust), viol, sundial, denial, espial, retrial, mistrial, self-denial.

228.5
knawel (Eurasian plant), withdrawal.

228.6
loyal, royal, disloyal, pennyroyal (Eurasian plant).

145

228.7
Noel, bestowal.

228.8
bowel, dowel, Powell, rowel (spiked wheel on spur), trowel, towel, vowel, embowel, avowal, disembowel, semi-vowel (phonetics term), disavowal.

228.9
menstrual, gradual, Samuel, sensual, casual, visual, usual, virtual, mutual, punctual, textual, sexual.

premenstrual, continual, consensual (legal term), unusual, perpetual, accentual (rhythmical), eventual, conventual (relating to a convent), perceptual, conceptual, contextual, asexual, bisexual, transsexual.

pari-mutuel (betting system), unisexual, homosexual.

audiovisual, heterosexual.

228.9.1
residual, individual.

228.9.2
annual, manual, biannual, Emmanuel.

228.9.3
ritual, habitual, spiritual.

228.9.4
actual, factual, tactual (caused by touch), contractual.

228.9.5
effectual, aspectual (linguistics term), ineffectual, intellectual.

228.10
jewel, cruel, crewel, gruel, dual, duel, fuel, newel, bejewel, refuel, renewal.

228.11
Abel, able, Babel, cable, fable, gable, label, sable, table, stable, enable, unable, disable, retable (screen behind altar), worktable, timetable, turntable, unstable, disenable.

228.12
kibble (bucket for hoisting material), dibble (small garden tool), nibble, quibble, Ribble, scribble, dribble, fribble (fritter away), gribble (small marine animal), Sybil, mandible, cannibal, Hannibal, thurible (container for burning incense), crucible.

228.13
coble (*Scot* fishing boat), global, noble, ennoble, Grenoble, ignoble.

228.14
bubble, double, nubble (small lump), rubble, trouble, stubble, redouble.

228.15
Hasdrubal (Carthaginian general), soluble, voluble, chasuble, insoluble, resoluble, indissoluble, irresoluble.

228.16 [further rhymes may be created by adding *-able* or *-ible* to appropriate verbs]
playable, payable, probable, placable, peccable (liable to sin), workable, likable, lockable, vocable (vocal sound), bankable, stretchable, touchable, quenchable, readable, affable, laughable, effable, chargeable, legible, changeable, fallible, gullible, tenable, tunable, pregnable, damnable, stoppable, palpable, culpable, equable, arable, parable, sparable (small nail), terrible, horrible, passable, peaceable, possible, forcible, satiable, washable, notable, potable (drinkable), quotable, tractable, liftable, printable, constable, Dunstable, tithable, lovable, taxable, flexible, feasible, plausible.

unknowable, improbable, implacable, remarkable, impeccable, unspeakable, dislikable, educable, revocable, detachable, untouchable, degradable, unreadable, avoidable, refundable, ineffable, illegible, infallible, indelible, redeemable, estimable, conformable, consumable, presumable, fathomable, untenable, amenable, impregnable, unflappable, unstoppable, impalpable, inculpable (guiltless), transferable, desirable, adorable, deplorable, execrable, demonstrable, manoeuvrable, irascible, impassable, impossible, reducible, purchasable, expansible, responsible, pronounceable, collapsible, insatiable, compatible, redoubtable, comfortable, vegetable, palatable, retractable, intractable, perfectible, delectable, respectable, expectable, detectable, predictable, unprintable, adaptable, corruptible, attemptable, contemptible, resistible, exhaustible, observable, forgivable, inflexible, erasable, implausible, opposable, disposable.

imperturbable, ineducable, irrevocable, unavoidable, interchangeable, reconcilable, inviolable, irredeemable, inestimable, unfathomable, undesirable, impenetrable, indemonstrable, irreducible, irresponsible, unpronounceable, incompatible, uncomfortable, unpredictable, incorruptible, irresistible, inexhaustible, unforgivable, irresolvable.

biodegradable, irreconcilable.

228.16.1
agreeable, foreseeable, disagreeable, unforeseeable.

228.16.2
malleable, amiable, permeable, expiable, variable, pitiable, dutiable, leviable, enviable, impermeable, invariable, justiciable (subject to jurisdiction), unenviable, irremediable, semipermeable, differentiable.

228.16.3
liable, pliable, friable, triable, viable, reliable, deniable, inviable, unreliable, undeniable.

228.16.3.1
modifiable, magnifiable, verifiable, classifiable, specifiable, certifiable, notifiable, rectifiable, quantifiable, justifiable, identifiable.

228.16.4
enjoyable, employable, unemployable.

228.16.5
dowable (legal term), allowable.

228.16.6
arguable, valuable, issuable, invaluable.

228.16.7
doable, suable, viewable, renewable.

228.16.8
bribable, describable, indescribable.

228.16.9
breakable, unbreakable, unshakable, mistakable, unmistakable.

228.16.10
medicable, predicable (able to be affirmed), applicable, explicable, amicable, despicable, extricable, practicable, eradicable, inapplicable, inexplicable, communicable, inextricable, impracticable, ineradicable, incommunicable.

228.16.11
drinkable, sinkable, thinkable, undrinkable, unsinkable, unthinkable.

228.16.12
reachable, teachable, impeachable, unteachable, unimpeachable.

228.16.13
approachable, reproachable, irreproachable, unapproachable.

228.16.14
edible, credible, beddable, inedible, incredible.

228.16.15
biddable, formidable.

228.16.16
audible, fordable, laudable, recordable, inaudible, rewardable.

228.16.17
expandable, understandable.

228.16.18
mendable, vendible, unbendable, commendable, dependable, expendable, extendible, recommendable.

147

228.16.19
litigable, mitigable, navigable, indefatigable, circumnavigable.

228.16.20
knowledgeable, negligible, manageable, marriageable, dirigible, corrigible, salvageable, exigible (liable to be demanded), incorrigible.

228.16.20.1
eligible, ineligible, intelligible, unintelligible.

228.16.21
frangible (breakable), tangible, refrangible (able to be refracted), infrangible, intangible, irrefrangible (inviolable).

228.16.22
bailable, scalable, saleable, sailable, resaleable, available, unassailable, unavailable.

228.16.23
syllable, willable, refillable, monosyllable.

228.16.24
controllable, uncontrollable, inconsolable.

228.16.25
calculable, regulable, inoculable, incalculable.

228.16.26
flammable, inflammable, nonflammable, programmable.

228.16.27
explainable, attainable, obtainable, unexplainable, unattainable, unobtainable.

228.16.28
discernible, returnable, indiscernible, nonreturnable.

228.16.29
terminable, imaginable, determinable, interminable, abominable, unimaginable, indeterminable.

228.16.30
finable (liable to a fine), definable, reclinable, inclinable, indefinable, indeclinable.

228.16.31
questionable, pardonable, personable, fashionable, actionable, conscionable, governable, alienable, unquestionable, impressionable, objectionable, unconscionable, ungovernable, inalienable, companionable.

228.16.31.1
pensionable, unmentionable.

228.16.31.2
reasonable, seasonable, unreasonable, unseasonable.

228.16.32
capable, incapable, inescapable.

228.16.33
bearable, tearable, wearable, unbearable, repairable, untearable, unwearable.

228.16.34
curable, durable, insurable, incurable, endurable.

228.16.35
saturable, preferable, tolerable, colourable, memorable, admirable, generable (able to be generated), venerable, honourable, vulnerable, operable, superable, comparable, answerable, mensurable, alterable, favourable, miserable.

considerable, imponderable, insufferable, intolerable, innumerable, dishonourable, invulnerable, inoperable, insuperable, incomparable, unanswerable, commensurable, immensurable, unutterable, inalterable, unfavourable, inexorable.

inconsiderable, indecipherable, irrecoverable.

228.16.35.1
reparable, separable, irreparable, inseparable.

228.16.35.2
pleasurable, measurable, immeasurable.

228.16.36
traceable, effaceable, replaceable, ineffaceable, irreplaceable.

228.16.37
expressible, accessible, irrepressible, inexpressible, inaccessible.

228.16.38
coercible, submersible, reversible, conversable, incoercible, irreversible.

228.16.39
kissable, miscible, immiscible, omissible, permissible, admissible, rescissible (able to be rescinded), noticeable, serviceable, impermissible, inadmissible.

228.16.40
sensible, tensible (able to be stretched), defensible, dispensable, insensible, ostensible, extensible, indefensible, apprehensible, reprehensible, comprehensible, indispensable, incomprehensible.

228.16.41
vincible, invincible, convincible, inconvincible.

228.16.42
depreciable, appreciable, inappreciable.

228.16.43
punishable, perishable, imperishable, distinguishable, extinguishable, indistinguishable, inextinguishable.

228.16.44
sociable, negotiable, dissociable, unsociable.

228.16.45
rateable, debatable, inflatable, untranslatable.

228.16.46
forgettable, regrettable, unforgettable.

228.16.47
convertible, inconvertible, incontrovertible.

228.16.48
eatable, beatable, unbeatable, repeatable.

228.16.49
habitable, dubitable, marketable, creditable, profitable, hospitable, equitable, charitable, heritable, veritable, irritable, indubitable, discreditable, unprofitable, illimitable, inimitable, indomitable, inhospitable, inequitable, inevitable.

228.16.50
indictable, excitable, extraditable.

228.16.51
portable, supportable, insupportable.

228.16.52
reputable, attributable, irrefutable, disreputable.

228.16.53
suitable, mutable, inscrutable, unsuitable, immutable, commutable, imputable, disputable, incommutable, incomputable, indisputable.

228.16.54
deductible, destructible, ineluctable (inescapable), indestructible.

228.16.55
preventable, presentable, unpreventable, unpresentable.

228.16.56
accountable, surmountable, unaccountable, insurmountable.

228.16.57
merchantable, lamentable, warrantable, unwarrantable.

228.16.58
perceptible, susceptible, acceptable, imperceptible, unacceptable.

228.16.59
suggestible, comestible, digestible, arrestable, detestable, contestable, indigestible, incontestable.

228.16.60
combustible, adjustable, incombustible.

228.16.61
achievable, believable, retrievable, conceivable, unbelievable, irretrievable, inconceivable.

228.16.62
movable, provable, immovable, removable, improvable, irremovable.

228.16.63
risible, visible, cognizable (perceptible), divisible, invisible, indivisible.

228.16.64
sizable, devisable, advisable, realizable, recognizable, inadvisable, unrecognizable.

228.16.65
usable, fusible (able to be melted), excusable, infusible, irrecusable (unable to be rejected), inexcusable.

228.17
amble, Campbell, gamble, gambol, ramble, bramble, scramble, shamble, preamble, unscramble.

228.18
Kemble (English acting family), tremble, dissemble, assemble, resemble, disassemble.

228.19
Acol (bridge term), cackle, hackle, mackle (printing term), crackle, grackle (US songbird), shackle, tackle, hamshackle (fetter a horse), ramshackle, tabernacle.

228.20
darkle (grow dark), sparkle, debacle, monarchal.

228.21
deckle, Jekyll, heckle, speckle, freckle, shekel, kenspeckle (*Scot* easily recognized).

228.22
circle, encircle, semicircle, homocercal (zoology term), heterocercal (zoology term).

228.23 [also **38** + *-al*]
chicle (ingredient of chewing-gum), fickle, mickle (*Dialect* much), nickel, pickle, picul (Oriental unit of weight), brickle (*Dialect* brittle), prickle, trickle, strickle, sickle, tickle, stickle (argue about trifles).

vehicle, stoical, cubicle, cubical (relating to volume), radicle (embryonic plant root), radical, nodical (astronomy term), magical, calycle (biology term), caulicle (small plant stalk), biblical, chemical, rhythmical, funicle (botany term), tunicle (Catholic bishop's vestment), technical, apical (at the apex), typical, auricle (heart's upper chamber), curricle (two-wheeled open carriage), metrical, utricle (part of ear), ventricle, fascicle (bundle of branches), classical, farcical, vesical (relating to bladder), vesicle (small cavity), versicle, icicle, bicycle, tricycle, ossicle (small bone in ear), Popsicle (*Trademark*), dropsical, article, particle, vertical, nautical, canticle, sceptical, optical, testicle, ethical, mythical, clavicle, cervical, lexical (relating to vocabulary), musical, whimsical.

veridical (truthful), juridical (relating to law), pontifical, encyclical, inimical, cupronickel, pumpernickel, atypical, cylindrical, theatrical, symmetrical, electrical, nonsensical, elliptical, unmusical.

hierarchical, philosophical, biochemical, aeronautical, dialectical, paradoxical, lackadaisical, ecclesiastical.

228.23.1
medical, pedicle (small plant stalk), premedical, paramedical.

228.23.2
methodical, periodical, immethodical.

228.23.3
graphical, geographical, biographical, typographical, autobiographical.

228.23.4
surgical, liturgical, metallurgical, neurosurgical.

228.23.5 [further rhymes may be derived from **16.108.4**]
logical, illogical, geological, biological, zoological, ecological, psychological, chronological, technological, pathological, mythological.

228.23.6
helical, pellicle (thin surface layer), angelical, evangelical.

228.23.7
silicle (type of fruit), umbilical.

228.23.8
follicle, symbolical, diabolical.

228.23.9
comical, economical, astronomical, gastronomical, anatomical.

228.23.10
panicle (type of inflorescence), sanicle (flowering plant), mechanical, tyrannical, botanical, puritanical.

228.23.11
galenical (pharmacology term), arsenical, ecumenical.

228.23.12
clinical, cynical, rabbinical, dominical (relating to the Lord), adminicle (legal term).

228.23.13
conical, chronicle, canonical, ironical, acronychal (occurring at sunset).

228.23.14
tropical, topical, subtropical.

228.23.15
spherical, clerical, chimerical (fanciful), numerical, hysterical, anticlerical.

228.23.16
lyrical, empirical, satirical.

228.23.17
rhetorical, historical, metaphorical, allegorical, categorical, oratorical.

228.23.18
sabbatical, grammatical, fanatical, mathematical, ungrammatical.

228.23.19
reticle (grid in optical instrument), heretical, alphabetical, catechetical (by question and answer), theoretical, antithetical, hypothetical.

228.23.20
critical, political, analytical, apolitical, diacritical, hypocritical, hypercritical.

228.23.21
cuticle, pharmaceutical.

228.23.22
practical, tactical, impractical.

228.23.23
denticle (small tooth), identical, conventicle (secret group of worshippers).

228.23.24
mystical, statistical, egotistical.

228.23.25
physical, quizzical, metaphysical.

228.24
Michael, cycle, recycle, unicycle, motorcycle.

228.25
cockle, grockle, socle (plinth), corncockle (European wayside plant), streptococcal.

228.26
focal, local, trochal (wheel-shaped), vocal, yokel, bifocal, matrilocal (living with wife's family), patrilocal (living with husband's family).

228.27
buckle, buccal (relating to the cheek), chuckle, muckle (*Scot* much), knuckle, truckle, suckle, parbuckle (rope sling), turnbuckle (device for tightening wire), unbuckle, pinochle (card game), honeysuckle.

228.28
tubercle, manacle, barnacle, cenacle (supper room), binnacle (housing for

ship's compass), pinnacle, monocle, monachal (monastic), miracle, spiracle (respiratory aperture), oracle, coracle, spectacle, pentacle (star-shaped figure), tentacle, obstacle, reciprocal, receptacle, conceptacle (botany term), equivocal, unequivocal.

228.28.1
zodiacal, maniacal, ammoniacal, paradisiacal.

228.29
inkle (linen tape), wrinkle, crinkle, sprinkle, tinkle, winkle, twinkle, besprinkle, periwinkle, Rip Van Winkle.

228.30
uncle, nuncle (*Dialect* uncle), carbuncle, peduncle (flower stalk), furuncle (a boil), caruncle (fleshy outgrowth).

228.31
addle, paddle, raddle, straddle, saddle, staddle, skedaddle, unsaddle, packsaddle, fiddle-faddle.

228.32
kiddle (device for catching fish), diddle, fiddle, middle, piddle, riddle, griddle, twiddle, infidel, unriddle (puzzle out), tarradiddle (nonsense), pyramidal.

228.33 [also 92.7 + -*al*]
idol, idle, Rydal (English village), bridal, bridle, sidle, tidal, unbridle, suicidal, spermicidal, homicidal.

228.34
coddle, doddle, model, noddle, broddle (*Dialect* to poke), toddle, waddle, swaddle, twaddle, remodel, mollycoddle, niddle-noddle (nod rapidly).

228.35
Goidel (Gaelic-speaking Celt), conchoidal (geology term), spheroidal (approximately spherical), adenoidal, sinusoidal (maths term), amygdaloidal (geology term).

228.36
buddle (trough for washing ore), cuddle, fuddle, huddle, muddle, puddle, ruddle (red dye for sheep), befuddle, Tolpuddle.

228.37
boodle, doodle, noodle, poodle, strudel, udal (legal term), feudal, caboodle, flapdoodle (*Slang* foolish talk), canoodle.

228.38
apodal (without feet), citadel, hebdomadal, antipodal.

228.39
candle, scandal, dandle (bounce child on knee), Handel, handle, sandal, vandal, manhandle, panhandle, mishandle.

228.40
kindle, Mindel (European glaciation period), spindle, brindle, Tyndale (English Protestant), dwindle, swindle, rekindle, enkindle.

228.41
skiffle, sniffle, piffle, riffle, whiffle (behave unpredictably), apocryphal.

228.42
scuffle, duffel, muffle, snuffle, ruffle, truffle, shuffle, kerfuffle, reshuffle.

228.43
gaggle, haggle, draggle (hang trailing), straggle, waggle, bedraggle, raggle-taggle (unkempt).

228.44
bagel (Jewish ring-shaped roll), Hegel (German philosopher), plagal (musical term), paigle (cowslip or oxlip), vagal (anatomy term), finagle.

228.45
eagle, beagle, legal, regal, porbeagle, illegal, viceregal, inveigle.

228.46
giggle, jiggle, niggle, sniggle (fish for eels), squiggle, wriggle, wiggle, prodigal, madrigal.

228.47
boggle, goggle, joggle, toggle, woggle, boondoggle (*US* do futile work), hornswoggle (*Slang* to cheat).

228.48
jugal (relating to the cheekbone), frugal, bugle, fugal, centrifugal.

228.49
angle, bangle, dangle, jangle, mangle, spangle, wrangle, strangle, tangle, wangle, triangle, fandangle (elaborate ornament), galangal (Oriental plant), bespangle, quadrangle, rectangle, entangle, untangle, disentangle.

228.50
ingle, bingle (*Austral* minor car crash), dingle (small wooded dell), jingle, mingle, cringle (nautical term), single, shingle, tingle, swingle (flax-beating instrument), commingle (to mix), Kriss Kringle (*US* Santa Claus), surcingle (horse's girth), intermingle.

228.51
camel, mammal, trammel (hindrance), stammel (coarse red woollen cloth), enamel, entrammel.

228.52
gimmal (part of rotating joint), animal, minimal, lacrimal, optimal, maximal, proximal, approximal (situated side by side).

228.52.1
decimal, vigesimal (relating to number twenty), millesimal, centesimal, duodecimal (relating to number twelve), hexadecimal (number system), Quadragesimal (relating to Lent), infinitesimal.

228.53
cormel (tiny new corm), formal, normal, informal, conformal (maths term), abnormal, subnormal, paranormal.

228.54
dismal, abysmal, baptismal, paroxysmal.

228.55
annal, cannel (type of coal), channel, flannel, panel, branle (French country dance), empanel.

228.56
anal, decanal (relating to a dean).

228.57
kennel, fennel, crenel (indentation in battlement), unkennel.

228.58
colonel, kernel, journal, vernal, diurnal, hibernal, infernal, supernal (celestial), eternal, maternal, paternal, fraternal, nocturnal, internal, asternal (unconnected to the sternum), external, sempiternal (everlasting).

228.59
penal, renal, venal, adrenal, duodenal.

228.60
ginnel (*Dialect* passageway between buildings), cardinal, ordinal, marginal, virginal, germinal (embryonic), terminal, Quirinal (hill of ancient Rome), actinal (zoology term), sentinel, Juvenal (Roman satirist), inguinal, vaccinal, original, cacuminal (phonetics term), intestinal, aboriginal.

228.60.1
testudinal (relating to tortoises), longitudinal, latitudinal.

228.60.2
paginal (page-for-page), imaginal (relating to an image).

228.60.3
seminal, trigeminal (anatomy term).

228.60.4
liminal (psychology term), criminal, Viminal (hill of ancient Rome), subliminal.

228.60.5
nominal, abdominal, prenominal (placed before a noun), phenomenal, binominal (biology term), pronominal (relating to a pronoun), adnominal (word modifying a noun).

228.60.6
vicinal (neighbouring), medicinal.

228.61
binal (twofold), final, spinal, rhinal (relating to the nose), vaginal, urinal, doctrinal, semifinal, quarterfinal, periclinal (botany term), anticlinal (botany term), isoclinal (sloping in same direction), anaclinal (geology term), cataclinal (geology term), matutinal (occurring in the morning), cerebrospinal.

228.62
tonal, zonal, hormonal, coronal (anatomy term), atonal.

228.63
regional, ammonal (an explosive), coronal (garland for head), arsenal, personal, factional, fractional, fictional, frictional, functional, optional, seasonal, antiphonal, diagonal, tetragonal (crystallography term), octagonal, hexagonal, orthogonal (relating to right angles), isochronal (having the same duration), impersonal, proportional, instructional, constructional, exceptional, occasional, divisional, provisional, meridional, unexceptional.

228.63.1
bacchanal (drunken celebration), diaconal (relating to a deacon).

228.63.2
national, passional, rational, irrational, multinational, international.

228.63.3
vocational, sensational, recreational, educational, irrigational, congregational, navigational, occupational, inspirational, operational, conversational, gravitational, progestational (before pregnancy), coeducational, denominational, representational.

228.63.4
professional, confessional, congressional, recessional, processional, unprofessional, semiprofessional.

228.63.5
additional, traditional, conditional, salicional (organ stop), nutritional, transitional, unconditional.

228.63.6
notional, emotional, promotional, devotional.

228.63.7
institutional, constitutional, unconstitutional.

228.63.8
sectional, directional.

228.63.9
intentional, conventional, three-dimensional, two-dimensional, unintentional, unconventional.

228.64
apple, chapel, dapple, grapple, crabapple, Whitechapel, pineapple.

228.65
peepul (Indian tree), people, tepal (botany term), steeple, unpeople, townspeople.

228.66
fipple (mouthpiece of wind instrument), nipple, ripple, cripple, triple, tipple, stipple, swipple (part of flail), maniple (unit of Roman soldiers), manciple (steward who buys provisions), principle, principal, multiple, municipal, participle.

228.67
Siple (mountain in Antarctica), stipel (small leaflike structure), disciple, archetypal.

228.68
hopple (hobble), popple, topple, estoppel (legal term).

228.69
opal, copal (hard aromatic resin), nopal (red-flowered cactus), Constantinople.

228.70
sample, example.

228.71
equal, sequel, unequal.

228.72
barrel, Carol, carol, carrel (study cubicle in library), parrel (nautical term), apparel.

228.73
coral, laurel, moral, quarrel, sorrel, amoral, immoral, Balmoral.

228.74
aural, oral, choral, goral (small goat antelope), chloral (oily liquid), floral, aboral (away from the mouth), binaural, monaural.

228.75
jural (relating to law), plural, pleural, rural, crural, Ural, mural, neural, sural (anatomy term), epidural, intramural, extramural.

228.76
liberal, pickerel (US freshwater fish), cockerel, mackerel, natural, structural, cultural, scriptural, sculptural, federal, ruderal (plant growing on wasteland), doggerel, cameral (relating to judicial chamber), humeral, numeral, admiral, general, mineral, funeral, corporal, temporal, nonpareil, vesperal (prayer book), visceral, mensural, lateral, literal, littoral, guttural, doctoral, enteral, apteral (architectural term), dipteral (architectural term), pastoral, several.

illiberal, unnatural, peripheral, bicameral, puerperal, bilateral, trilateral, collateral, postdoctoral, parenteral (medical term), Canaveral, inaugural, behavioural.

supernatural, preternatural, horticultural, unicameral, unilateral, equilateral, quadrilateral, multilateral.

228.76.1
conjectural, architectural.

228.76.2
femoral, ephemeral.

228.76.3
pectoral, electoral.

228.77
tumbrel, adumbral (shadowy).

228.78
dihedral (two-sided), anhedral (aircraft wing's downward inclination), cathedral, polyhedral, hemihedral (crystallography term), rhombohedral, procathedral (church serving as cathedral).

228.79
citral (fragrant plant oil), arbitral (relating to arbitration), diametral (relating to diameter).

228.80
central, ventral, dorsoventral.

228.81
kestrel, orchestral, campestral (relating to fields), ancestral.

228.82
mistral, magistral (pharmacology term), sinistral (relating to left side).

228.83
castle, parcel, tarsal, warsle (*Dialect* wrestle), Newcastle, metatarsal.

228.84
tercel (male falcon or hawk), succursal (subsidiary), rehearsal, demersal (living in deep water), dispersal, reversal, transversal, universal, quaquaversal (geology term).

228.85
kissel (Russian fruit dessert), scissel (waste metal), missal, bristle, gristle, thistle, whistle, abyssal, dismissal, epistle, cacomistle (cat-like mammal).

228.86
dossal (ornamental church hanging), fossil, jostle, throstle, colossal, apostle, hypoglossal (beneath the tongue).

228.87
bustle, justle (jostle), hustle, mussel, muscle, Russell, rustle, tussle, corpuscle.

228.88
pencel (small flag), pencil, stencil, commensal (biology term), utensil.

228.89
consul, tonsil, proconsul.

228.90
martial, marshal, partial, impartial.

228.91
facial, glacial, spatial, racial, abbatial, palatial, preglacial, subglacial, postglacial, multiracial.

228.92
Herschel (English astronomer), tertial (ornithology term), commercial, uncommercial, controversial.

228.93
judicial, official, seneschal (medieval household steward), initial, altricial (ornithology term), prejudicial, beneficial, sacrificial, artificial, unofficial, superficial, interstitial.

228.94
social, precocial (ornithology term), asocial, unsocial, antisocial.

228.95
financial, substantial, insubstantial, circumstantial.

228.96
sciential (knowledgeable), prudential, tangential, sequential, essential, potential, influential, pestilential, exponential, consequential, inessential, nonessential, quintessential, penitential, existential, expediential, experiential, inconsequential.

228.96.1
credential, confidential, precedential, evidential, providential, residential, presidential.

228.96.2
torrential, deferential, preferential, differential, inferential, reverential.

228.97
battle, cattle, chattel, rattle, prattle, tattle, Seattle, embattle, tittle-tattle, Quetzalcoatl (Aztec god).

228.98
startle, Nahuatl (American Indian).

228.99
fatal, natal, ratel (burrowing mammal), ratal (rateable value), prenatal, postnatal, perinatal, antenatal.

228.100
kettle, fettle, metal, mettle, nettle, petal, settle, nonmetal, gunmetal, resettle, unsettle, Citlaltépetl (Mexican volcano), Popocatépetl (Mexican volcano).

228.101
betel, beetle, chital (Asian deer), fetal, decretal (papal edict), centripetal.

228.102
it'll, kittle (*Scot* capricious), skittle, little, spittle, brittle, tittle, victual, whittle.

orbital, cubital (relating to the forearm), sagittal (resembling an arrow), vegetal (relating to plant life), digital, skeletal, belittle, Doolittle, remittal, committal, genital, Capitol, capital, hospital, lickspittle (servile person), acquittal, marital.

parietal (anatomy term), varietal (relating to biological variety), noncommittal, congenital, basipetal (botany term), bicipital (relating to the biceps), occipital (anatomy term), premarital, extramarital.

228.103
title, vital, requital, recital, subtitle, entitle, disentitle.

228.104
bottle, dottle (tobacco remnant in pipe), glottal, mottle, rotl (unit of weight), throttle, wattle, bluebottle, greenbottle (type of fly), axolotl, Aristotle.

228.105
chortle, mortal, portal, immortal.

228.106
total, teetotal, subtotal, sacerdotal (relating to priests), anecdotal.

228.107
cuttle, scuttle, subtle, shuttle, rebuttal.

228.108
Bootle, footle, rootle, brutal, tootle, Kwakiutl (American Indian).

228.109
cantle (part of saddle), mantle, mantel, Fremantle, dismantle, overmantel (shelf over mantlepiece), consonantal.

228.110
dental, gentle, mental, rental, cental (unit of weight), submental (beneath the chin), fragmental, segmental, parental, placental, oriental, transcendental, monumental, departmental, compartmental, continental, developmental, transcontinental, intercontinental.

228.110.1
incidental, accidental, Occidental, coincidental.

228.110.2
sedimental, regimental, elemental, incremental, detrimental, sentimental, experimental.

228.110.3
fundamental, ornamental, sacramental, instrumental, temperamental.

228.110.4
governmental, environmental.

228.111
quantal (physics term), horizontal, periodontal (around a tooth).

228.112
buntal (straw from palm leaves), frontal, prefrontal (zoology term), full-frontal, disgruntle, balibuntal (Philippine straw hat), contrapuntal.

228.113
festal (festive), vestal, agrestal (growing as a weed).

228.114
distal (anatomy term), listel (architectural term), mistal (*Scot* cowshed), pistol, Bristol, crystal, pedestal.

228.115
costal, hostel, Pentecostal, intercostal.

228.116
borstal, Saint Austell.

228.117
cavil, gavel, ravel, gravel, travel, unravel.

228.118
bevel, kevel (nautical term), devil, level, revel, daredevil, bedevil, dishevel.

228.119
evil, shrieval (relating to a sheriff), weevil, coeval (belonging to same age), medieval, upheaval, primeval, retrieval.

228.120
snivel, drivel, frivol (behave frivolously), shrivel, civil, swivel, carnival, Percival, uncivil, festival.

228.121
nival (growing in snow), rival, arrival, aestival (occurring in the summer), revival, survival, adjectival.

228.122
removal, approval, disapproval.

228.123
Daniel, spaniel, Nathaniel.

228.124
basil, Basil, dazzle, frazzle, bedazzle, razzle-dazzle.

228.125
hazel, nasal, phrasal, appraisal.

228.126
kursaal (building at health resort), mangelwurzel (Eurasian beet plant).

157

228.127

losel (*Dialect* worthless person), deposal, proposal, disposal, counterproposal.

228.128

ouzel, foozle (bungle golf shot), fusel (poisonous oily liquid), bamboozle, perusal, accusal, refusal.

228.129

housel (medieval name for Eucharist), spousal (marriage ceremony), tousle, espousal, arousal, carousal.

229 -am

am, Cam, cam, damn, dam, gam (school of whales), jam, jamb, ham, lam, lamb, clam, flam (*Dialect* falsehood), slam, mam, Spam (*Trademark*), ram, cram, scramb (*Dialect* scratch with fingernails), scram, dram, gram, pram, tram, sham, wham, swam, yam.

iamb, Siam, pro-am, ferbam (black powder), Edam, goddamn, milldam, quondam (former), Potsdam (East German city), Corfam (*Trademark*), doorjamb, mallam (West African Islamic scholar), Balaam (Old Testament character), flimflam (nonsense), Annam (part of Vietnam), Menam (Thai river), Hungnam (North Korean port), dirham (Moroccan currency), Ceram (Indonesian island), Bairam (Muslim festival), programme, engram (psychology term), tangram, Assam, cheongsam (Chinese dress), lactam (chemical group), wigwam, nizam (former Turkish soldier), exam.

cofferdam (watertight underwater chamber), Rotterdam, Amsterdam, commendam (temporary Church office), cryptogam (non-flowering plant), Abraham, oriflamme (scarlet medieval French flag), Surinam, Vietnam, dithyramb, epiphragm (part of snail's shell), diaphragm, telegram, milligram, epigram, centigram, cablegram, cocoyam (African food plant), ad nauseam.

229.1

diagram, nephogram (photograph of a cloud), logogram, hologram, nomogram (type of graph), anagram, monogram, chronogram (phrase concealing Roman numerals), phonogram (symbol representing sound), barogram, aerogram, tetragram (four-letter word), cartogram (map showing statistical information), photogram (type of photograph), hectogram, cryptogram (secret symbol), histogram, hexagram (star-shaped figure), roentgenogram (*US* x-ray), hierogram (sacred symbol), parallelogram, encephalogram, pneumoencephalogram, electroencephalogram.

229.1.1

cardiogram, radiogram, ideogram (symbol representing concept), stereogram, phraseogram (symbol representing phrase), electrocardiogram.

229.1.2

kilogram, oscillogram (oscilloscope record), dactylogram (*US* fingerprint).

230 -arm

arm, balm, barm (*Dialect* yeast), calm, charm, farm, harm, malm (greyish limestone), ma'am, smarm, palm, qualm, gram (Indian village), pram (light boat), psalm, Guam (Pacific island).

rearm, embalm, gendarme, Ratlam (Indian city), Islam, imam (Islamic prayer leader), schoolmarm, unarm, napalm, copalm (brown resin), ihram (Muslim pilgrim's white robes), firearm, forearm, disarm, gisarme (battle-axe), Nizam (title of Indian ruler).

Notre Dame, underarm, overarm, Omar Khayyam.

230.1

alarm, salaam, Dar es Salaam (capital of Tanzania).

231 -ame

aim, came, kame (mound formed by glacier), dame, fame, game, hame, lame, blame, claim, flame, maim, name, frame, same, Sejm (Polish legislature), shame, tame, wame (*Dialect* belly or womb).

became, defame, endgame, declaim, reclaim, acclaim, proclaim, disclaim, quitclaim (legal term), exclaim, aflame, inflame, surname, rename, forename, nickname, airframe (part of aircraft), doorframe, selfsame, overcame, counterclaim.

232 -em

em (printer's measure), feme (legal term for woman), gem, hem, clem (*Dialect* be hungry), phlegm, crème, Shem (Noah's eldest son), stem, them.

phloem, proem (preface), Yquem (French vineyard), modem, condemn, mayhem, ahem, xylem, golem (resurrection in Jewish legend), in rem (legal term), item (likewise), contemn (to scorn), millieme (Tunisian coin).

requiem, per diem, diadem, anadem (garland), Bethlehem, periblem (plant tissue), meristem (plant tissue), apothem (geometry term), apophthegm, chernozem (black soil).

233 -erm

berm (narrow ledge), chirm (chirp), firm, germ, perm, sperm, squirm, term, therm, worm.

affirm, infirm, confirm, bookworm, hookworm, silkworm, midterm, inchworm, threadworm, woodworm, blindworm, roundworm, pinworm, ringworm, tapeworm, flatworm, earthworm.

pachyderm, periderm (protective plant layer), endoderm (part of embryo), phelloderm (botany term), mesoderm (part of embryo), ectoderm (part of

embryo), blastoderm (embryology term), reaffirm, disaffirm, endosperm (seed's nutritive tissue), gymnosperm (cone-bearing plant), zoosperm (spermatozoon), isotherm.

234 -eem

beam, scheme, deem, deme (biology term), haem, fleam (blood-letting lancet), gleam, ream, bream, cream, scream, dream, stream, seam, seem, team, teem, steam, theme.

abeam, hornbeam (Eurasian tree), sunbeam, moonbeam, crossbeam, whitebeam (European tree), hakim (Muslim judge), redeem, grapheme (letter), morpheme (grammatical unit), blaspheme, agleam, sememe (unit of meaning), phoneme (distinguishable speech sound), toneme (linguistics term), harem, Tarim (Chinese river), bireme, spireme (tangled mass of chromosomes), trireme, ice cream, daydream, supreme, airstream, headstream, thirdstream (type of jazz), millstream, mainstream, downstream, slipstream, upstream, extreme, berseem (Mediterranean clover), glosseme (linguistics term), raceme, regime, centime, septime (fencing position), esteem, lexeme (minimal unit in vocabulary), oxime (chemical compound).

Hasidim (Jewish sect), academe (place of learning), quinquereme, monotreme, self-esteem, disesteem.

235 -im

Bim (native of Barbados), skim, dim, gym, him, hymn, limb, limn (represent in drawing), glim (*Slang* lamp), slim, mim (*Dialect* prim), nim (a game), quim, rim, brim, crim (*Austral* criminal), scrim (strong fabric), Grimm, grim, prim, trim, shim (thin washer), vim, whim, swim.

poem, Sikkim (Indian state), bedim, forelimb, dislimn (efface), Muslim, paynim, denim, Blenheim, minim, Purim (Jewish holiday), broadbrim (type of hat), megrim, pilgrim, Leitrim, Antrim, Shittim (Old Testament place), victim, maxim.

Ephraim (Old Testament character), cherubim, seraphim, pseudonym, allonym (assumed name), homonym, anonym (pseudonym), synonym, eponym, toponym, acronym, metonym (linguistics term), antonym, exonym (foreigner's version of placename), Kuskokwim (Alaskan river), interim, Abd-el-Krim (Moroccan chief), verbatim.

seriatim (in a series), literatim (letter for letter).

236 -ime

I'm, chyme (digested food in stomach), chime, dime, lime, climb, clime, slime, mime, rime, rhyme, crime, grime, prime, cyme (type of inflorescence), time, thyme.

Trondheim (Norwegian port), Sondheim (US songwriter), Mannheim (West German city), sublime, quicklime, brooklime (trailing plant), birdlime, begrime, daytime, playtime, foretime (the past), wartime, bedtime, halftime, lifetime, ragtime, full-time, sometime, meantime, noontime, springtime, longtime, pastime, peacetime, mistime, part-time, enzyme.

isocheim (line on map), mesenchyme (embryology term), paradigm, Anaheim (Californian city), pantomime, maritime, flexitime, summertime, wintertime, overtime, lysozyme (enzyme), coenzyme (biochemical compound).

237 -om

bomb, dom (title of Catholic monks), hom (ancient Persian sacred plant), mom, pom, from, prom, Tom, tom, firebomb, Syncom (communications satellite), non-com (*short for* noncommissioned officer), sitcom, coulomb, aplomb, pom-pom, therefrom, wherefrom, maelstrom, intercom, abcoulomb.

238 -orm

corm, dorm, form, forme (printing equipment), haulm (thatching material), Maugham, norm, shawm (medieval type of oboe), storm, warm, swarm.

re-form, biform, landform, planform (silhouette viewed from above), inform, conform, transform, platform, waveform, Cairngorm, cairngorm (variety of quartz), lukewarm, snowstorm, sandstorm, windstorm, hailstorm, barnstorm, rainstorm, brainstorm, aswarm.

Cominform (Communist Information Bureau), misinform, thunderstorm.

238.1

deform, reform.

deiform (godlike in form), cubiform, pediform, cordiform (heart-shaped), scyphiform (cup-shaped), fungiform, aliform (wing-shaped), stelliform, cheliform (pincer-like), filiform (threadlike), piliform (hairlike), ramiform (branchlike), vermiform, reniform (kidney-shaped), uniform, cuneiform, ligniform (wood-like), napiform (turnip-shaped), aeriform (gaseous), variform, pyriform (pear-shaped), cribriform (sievelike), fibriform, dendriform (branching), vitriform (resembling glass), gasiform, pisiform (resembling a pea), cruciform, falciform (sickle-shaped), unciform (hook-shaped), scutiform (shield-shaped), multiform, dentiform (tooth-shaped), lentiform (lens-shaped), oviform, linguiform, plexiform (intricate), fusiform (spindle-shaped).

cumuliform, cuculiform (ornithology term), baculiform (rod-shaped), dolabriform (hatchet-shaped), diversiform, digitiform.

238.2

perform, bromoform (chemical compound), chloroform, salverform (botany term), iodoform (crystalline substance), electroform (form by electrolysis), nitrochloroform.

239 -ome

ohm, Om (Hindu sacred syllable), comb, dome, foam, home, heaume (medieval helmet), holm (*Dialect* river island), loam, gnome, nome (modern Greek province), pome (fruit of apple), Rome, roam, brome (type of grass), chrome, tome.

abohm, Beerbohm, trichome (hairlike plant structure), backcomb, cockscomb, radome (radar antenna's protective housing), megohm (one million ohms), Stockholm, phyllome (leaf-like organ), genome (group of chromosomes), Jerome, prodrome (symptom indicating disease), syndrome, rhizome.

honeycomb, currycomb, semidome, astrodome (transparent dome on aircraft), tumblehome (nautical term), metronome, gastronome, polychrome (multicoloured), urochrome (pigment in urine), haemochrome (blood pigment), monochrome, velodrome (cycle-racing arena), cosmodrome (spacecraft launching-site), hippodrome, aerodrome, acrodrome (botany term), palindrome, biostrome (fossil-rich rocky layer), endosome (part of cell nucleus), ribosome (part of living cell), chromosome, monosome (type of chromosome), centrosome (part of living cell), autosome (type of chromosome), leptosome (slender person), schistosome (blood parasite), microtome (biologist's cutting instrument), dermatome (surgical instrument), cyclostome (primitive aquatic vertebrate), monostome (having one mouth).

240 -um

bum, come, scum, chum, dumb, gum, hum, glum, plumb, plum, slum, mum, numb, rum, crumb, scrum, drum, strum, thrum, sum, some, tum, stum (partly fermented wine), thumb, swum.

become, succumb, income, outcome, dumdum, benumb, eardrum, humdrum.

misbecome (be unsuitable for), overcome, Tweedledum, sugarplum, kettledrum.

241 -oom

boom, cwm (valley or hollow), coomb (short valley), doom, whom, loom, bloom, flume (narrow ravine), gloom, glume (botany term), plume, rheum, room, broom, groom, vroom, tomb, womb, fume, Hume, neume (early musical symbol), spume, zoom.

foredoom, heirloom, illume (illuminate), abloom (in flower), broadloom, deplume (deprive of feathers), simoom (desert wind), barroom, playroom, tearoom, storeroom, showroom, darkroom, workroom, stockroom, cloakroom, guardroom, bedroom, headroom, boardroom, wardroom, legroom, bridegroom, saleroom, grillroom, ballroom, greenroom, strongroom, taproom, classroom, houseroom, washroom, mushroom, stateroom, courtroom, bathroom, boxroom, Batum (Russian city), Khartoum, pantoum (verse form), entomb, enwomb, perfume, legume, inhume (to inter), exhume, volume, assume, subsume, consume, costume, resume, presume.

catacomb, checkerbloom (Californian plant), nom de plume, filoplume (hairlike feather), anteroom, elbowroom, hecatomb, disentomb, El Faiyum (Egyptian city).

242 -'m

'em, Graham, Priam, brougham, Newham, sebum, album, plumbum,
Rackham, Shechem (ancient Jordanian
town), caecum, Ockham (English philosopher), Morecambe, oakum (fibre
from unravelled rope), hokum, Malcolm, welcome, dinkum, bunkum,
Beecham, stardom, heirdom, Edom,
freedom, sedum (fleshy-leaved plant),
Sodom, boredom, whoredom, serfdom,
sheikdom, dukedom, seldom, earldom,
Oldham, condom, kingdom, popedom,
princedom, wisdom, begum, Egham,
sorghum, Dodgem (*Trademark*), Belgium, Nahum (Old Testament prophet), alum, Harlem, slalom, Salem,
Elam (ancient Asian kingdom), Caelum (constellation), coelom (body cavity), velum (biology term), column, solemn, solum (upper layer of soil),
problem, emblem, bedlam, hoodlum,
peplum (flared ruffle on garment),
Moslem, Barnum, Arnhem, Farnham,
venom, sphagnum (bog moss), magnum, Clapham, wampum (American
Indian shell money), carom (billiards
term), marram, durum, Durham, labrum (lip), sacrum, buckram, fulcrum,
wolfram, pogrom, grogram (coarse
fabric), ashram (Hindu religious retreat), antrum (anatomy term), tantrum, threesome, fearsome, tiresome,
awesome, dorsum (the back), foursome, noisome, gruesome, twosome,
gladsome, handsome, balsam, toilsome,
wholesome, fulsome, gamesome (merry), hansom, ransom, transom, winsome, lonesome, Epsom, gypsum,
eightsome, jetsam, lightsome, flotsam,
toothsome, lithesome, blithesome,
loathsome, Heysham, Qeshm (island in
Persian Gulf), Gresham, Evesham, atom, Chatham, bottom, scutum, sputum, rectum, dictum, sanctum, bantam, phantom, quantum, septum
(biology term), symptom, system, anthem, fathom, ovum, darksome, Wrexham, irksome, buxom, trillium (three-
leaved plant), William, besom, seism
(earthquake), bosom.

unwelcome, poppadom, martyrdom,
corundum (very hard mineral), Christendom, heathendom, amalgam, stratagem, Brummagem, amylum (starch),
spirillum (type of bacterium), sensillum (insect's sense organ), exemplum,
minimum, optimum, maximum, cardamom, Pergamum (ancient Asian city),
per annum, arcanum (profound secret),
solanum (plant genus), envenom, jejunum, cerebrum, panjandrum, Trivandrum (Indian city), conundrum, pyrethrum, sargassum (floating brown
seaweed), omasum (compartment of
cow's stomach), cumbersome, venturesome, humoursome (capricious), bothersome, Hilversum, unwholesome,
troublesome, meddlesome, cuddlesome,
quarrelsome, nettlesome (causing irritation), burdensome, nasturtium, Lewisham, petersham, cementum (part of a
tooth), omentum (anatomy term), lomentum (plant pod), momentum, tomentum (biology term), Chrysostom
(Greek patriarch), frolicsome, unbosom.

rehoboam, jeroboam, Eboracum (Roman name for York), taraxacum (plant
genus), crinkum-crankum (twisted object), officialdom, duodenum, jus
divinum (divine law), interregnum, hydrargyrum, candelabrum, hippeastrum
(South American plant), ecosystem,
microcosm, macrocosm.

242.1

geum, Te Deum, lyceum, museum, stomodaeum (embryonic mouth cavity),
hypogeum (underground burial vault),
propylaeum (portico forming temple
entrance), mausoleum, perineum, athenaeum (institution promoting learning), gynaeceum (ancient Roman wom-
en's apartments), colosseum,
peritoneum.

242.2

labium, erbium (element), terbium (element), cambium, brachium (arm or armlike part), ischium, scandium, indium (element), allium (plant genus), gallium (element), pallium (vestment or mantle), thallium (element), Valium (*Trademark*), pileum (top of bird's head), thulium (element), fermium (element), cadmium, holmium (element), osmium, hafnium (element), Samnium (ancient Italian city), atrium, yttrium (element), calcium, francium (element), Latium (region of Italy), protium (isotope of hydrogen), Actium, strontium, ostium (biology term), lithium, axiom.

ytterbium (element), aerobium (organism requiring oxygen), rhizobium (rod-shaped bacterium), niobium (element), exordium (beginning of a speech), compendium, patagium (zoology term), contagium (transmission of disease), sporangium (spore-producing plant organ), dentalium (marine mollusc), nobelium (element), triennium, millennium, quinquennium, quadrennium, decennium, septennium, Capernaum, selenium (element), hymenium (fungal tissue), proscenium, ruthenium (element), principium (fundamental principle), marsupium, colloquium, tellurium, masurium (element), anthurium (tropical plant), opprobrium, manubrium (zoology term), potassium, gynoecium (female part of flower), androecium (stamens of flower), technetium (element), lutetium (element), spermatium (reproductive cell in algae), cymatium (architectural moulding), sestertium (ancient Roman currency), consortium, Byzantium, endosteum (membrane within bone), promethium (element), Erechtheum (temple on the Acropolis), quadrivium (medieval branch of learning), lixivium (alkaline solution), eluvium (mass of rock particles), diluvium (geology term), alluvium, colluvium (mixture of rock fragments), effluvium, Elysium, symposium, indusium (enveloping membrane).

epicardium, pericardium, endocardium, myocardium, horologium (clock tower), Verulamium, neodymium (element), californium (element), equilibrium, perichondrium (membrane covering cartilage), hypochondrium (part of abdomen), perinephrium (tissue surrounding kidney), endometrium, epigastrium (part of abdomen), hypogastrium (part of abdomen), corpus luteum (tissue in ovary), periosteum (membrane covering bone), mendelevium (element).

perionychium (skin surrounding fingernail), praseodymium (element), disequilibrium.

242.2.1

radium, stadium, caladium (cultivated tropical plant), palladium, vanadium (element).

242.2.2

medium, tedium, soredium (reproductive organ of lichens), uredium (spore-producing fungal structure), cypripedium (large-flowered orchid).

242.2.3

idiom, oidium (chain of fungal spores), rubidium, glochidium (biology term), ctenidium (mollusc's gill), conidium (fungal spore), gonidium (botany term), iridium, peridium (botany term), nephridium (tubelike excretory organ), clostridium (rod-shaped bacterium), basidium (fungal structure), aecidium (fungal structure), presidium, ascidium (pitcher-shaped plant part), osmiridium (alloy), post meridiem, hesperidium (citrus fruit), antheridium (plant's male sex organ), miracidium (larva of parasitic fluke), ante meridiem.

242.2.4

odium, odeum (building for musical performances), podium, rhodium, sodium, allodium (former property law term), plasmodium (biology term), sympodium (botany term), pseudopodium, lycopodium (non-flowering plant), monopodium (botany term), parapodium (zoology term).

242.2.5
helium, Sealyham, telium (spore-producing fungal structure), berkelium (element), mycelium (fungal body), epithelium, endothelium, mesothelium.

242.2.6
Ilium (ancient Troy), ileum (part of small intestine), ilium (part of hipbone), milium (nodule on skin), cilium, beryllium, penicillium.

242.2.7
scholium (marginal note), folium (geometrical curve), trifolium (clover-like plant), linoleum, petroleum.

242.2.8
premium, gelsemium (climbing shrub).

242.2.9
chromium, encomium, prostomium (zoology term), ferrochromium (iron–chromium alloy).

242.2.10
cranium, germanium, geranium, uranium, titanium, succedaneum (drug substituted for another), Herculaneum (ancient Italian city), pericranium, endocranium, actinouranium (isotope of uranium).

242.2.11
minium (red lead), delphinium, virginium (element), illinium (element), triclinium (ancient Roman dining room), dominium (property law term), actinium, gadolinium, androclinium (cavity in orchid flower), aluminium, condominium, protactinium (element).

242.2.12
conium (hemlock), zirconium (element), meconium, syconium (fig fruit), euphonium, polonium (element), har-

monium, ammonium, stramonium (drug), plutonium, archegonium (plant's female sex organ), sporogonium (spore-bearing plant part), oogonium (biology term), ascogonium (fungal reproductive body), pelargonium, spermogonium (plant reproductive body), carpogonium (plant reproductive body), pandemonium, positronium (physics term).

242.2.13
opium, europium (element).

242.2.14
barium, herbarium (collection of dried plants), sudarium (cloth for wiping face), caldarium (Roman hot-bath room), velarium (awning in Roman theatre), solarium, samarium (element), puparium (entomology term), aquarium, terrarium (container for small organisms), sacrarium (church sanctuary), vivarium, rosarium, columbarium (dovecote), oceanarium, cinerarium (place for cremation ashes), honorarium, leprosarium (hospital for lepers), termitarium (termite nest), planetarium, sanitarium, insectarium, polyzoarium (animal colony), armamentarium (doctor's equipment).

242.2.15
cerium (element), imperium (ancient Roman supreme power), deuterium, bacterium, psalterium (part of cow's stomach), mezereum (fragrant Eurasian shrub), puerperium, elaterium (greenish sediment), ministerium (body of Lutheran ministers), nototherium (extinct marsupial).

242.2.16
Miriam, delirium, collyrium (eye lotion).

242.2.17
corium (deep layer beneath skin), thorium, ciborium (Christian communion vessel), triforium (part of a church), emporium, sensorium (area of the brain), scriptorium (writing room in

monastery), haustorium (organ of parasitic plant), in memoriam, synclinorium (geology term), aspersorium (basin containing holy water), auditorium, sudatorium (Roman steam-bath room), crematorium, fumatorium (airtight fumigation chamber), sanatorium, eupatorium (cultivated tropical plant), moratorium, anticlinorium (geology term).

242.2.18
tritium (isotope of hydrogen), syncytium (zoology term), satellitium (astrology term).

242.2.19
dichasium (type of inflorescence), gymnasium, polychasium (type of inflorescence), monochasium (type of inflorescence).

242.2.20
caesium, magnesium, trapezium.

242.3
menstruum (a solvent), vacuum, residuum, continuum.

242.4
colchicum (Eurasian plant), modicum, Noricum (Celtic Alpine kingdom), capsicum, triticum (cereal grass), High Wycombe, doronicum (Eurasian plant), hypericum (flowering plant), Illyricum (ancient Roman province), viaticum.

242.5
Adam, madam, macadam.

242.6
random, tandem, memorandum, avizandum (Scottish legal term), nil desperandum.

242.7
credendum (Christian article of faith), pudendum, addendum, corrigendum, referendum, definiendum (something to be defined).

242.8
phellem (cork), pelham (horse's bit), vellum, cribellum (spider's spinning organ), labellum (part of orchid flower), flabellum (fan-shaped insect organ), post-bellum, flagellum, clitellum (part of earthworm's body), scutellum (shield-shaped structure), rostellum (beak-like projection), haustellum (entomology term), cerebellum, antebellum.

242.9
phylum, filum (thread-like anatomical part), hilum (botany term), subphylum, asylum.

242.10
Fulham, speculum, vinculum (maths symbol), vasculum (botanist's specimen container), osculum (mouth-like aperture), Tusculum (ancient city near Rome), pendulum, cingulum (girdle-like anatomical part), frenulum (bristle on insect's wing), tenaculum (surgical instrument), vibraculum (type of polyp), operculum (biology term), inoculum (material used for inoculation), coagulum (coagulated mass), Triangulum (constellation), capitulum (biology term), tintinnabulum (small high-pitched bell), acetabulum (cavity in hipbone), infundibulum (funnel-shaped anatomical part).

242.10.1
cubiculum (Roman underground burial chamber), Janiculum (ancient Roman hill), curriculum, aciculum (zoology term), reticulum, diverticulum.

242.11
cimbalom (type of dulcimer), Absalom, tantalum (element), tropaeolum (flowering plant), Jerusalem.

242.12
chrysanthemum, mesembryanthemum.

242.13
Burnham, sternum, viburnum, laburnum, xiphisternum (part of breastbone), episternum (part of breastbone).

242.14
platinum, molybdenum.

242.15

crinum (tropical plant), glucinum (element), antirrhinum, mediastinum (anatomy term).

242.16

galbanum (bitter gum resin), Twickenham, laudanum, labdanum (resinous plant juice), Dagenham, tympanum, Cheltenham, lanthanum (element), olibanum (frankincense), polygonum (plant with jointed stems).

242.17

gingham, Buckingham, Gillingham, Immingham, Sandringham, Altrincham, Walsingham, Nottingham.

242.18

arum, Fareham, Sarum, harum-scarum.

242.19

serum, theorem, disulfiram (a drug), antiserum.

242.20

aurum (gold), forum, jorum (large drinking bowl), quorum, decorum, Mizoram (Indian union territory), variorum (containing scholarly annotations), indecorum, Karakoram (mountain system in Kashmir), cockalorum (self-important person), ad valorem (according to value), pons asinorum (geometry theorem), sanctum sanctorum, schola cantorum.

242.21

labarum (Christian banner), marjoram, asarum (dried wild ginger root), Rotherham, Kanchipuram (Indian city), omnium-gatherum (miscellaneous collection).

242.22

plectrum, spectrum, electrum (gold-silver alloy).

242.23

nostrum, rostrum, colostrum.

242.24

jissom, lissom, crissum (ornithology term), alyssum, wearisome, worrisome, fideicommissum (civil law term).

242.25

blossom, possum, opossum, odontoglossum (tropical orchid).

242.26

stratum, satem (linguistics term), postpartum, erratum, substratum, superstratum, desideratum.

242.27

datum, relatum (logic term), ideatum (philosophy term), petrolatum (petroleum jelly), ultimatum, ageratum (tropical plant), corpus striatum (part of brain).

242.28

pinetum (conifer plantation), tapetum (biology term), acetum (vinegar), Antietam (US battle site), arboretum, equisetum (a plant).

242.29

item, ad infinitum.

242.30

autumn, postmortem.

242.31

notum (entomology term), scrotum, totem, teetotum (spinning top), factotum.

242.32

custom, frustum, accustom, disaccustom.

242.33

rhythm, polyrhythm (style of musical composition), logarithm, algorithm.

242.34

chasm, plasm (type of protoplasm), spasm, sarcasm, orgasm, phantasm, chiliasm (Christian belief), endoplasm, cytoplasm, protoplasm, ectoplasm, pleonasm (use of superfluous words), enthusiasm, iconoclasm (attack on traditional concepts).

242.35

ism, chrism (oil used for anointing), chrisom (baptismal robe), prism, schism.

Maoism, cubism, plumbism (lead poisoning), tychism (philosophy term), sadism, Buddhism, nudism, sophism, Sufism (mystical doctrine), Gaullism, holism (philosophy term), momism (excessive dependence on mother), nomism (theology term), bromism (bromine poisoning), Thomism (doctrine of Thomas Aquinas), Jainism (Hindu sect), monism (philosophy term), bonism (semi-optimistic doctrine), tropism, tsarism, verism (extreme realism), porism (mathematical proposition), tourism, purism, Tantrism (Hindu or Buddhist movement), Graecism, Nazism, fascism, statism (state control), rightism, autism, leftism, baptism, Marxism, sexism.

Dadaism, Bahaism (religious system), fideism (trust placed in faith), Judaism, Hebraism, Mithraism (ancient Persian religion), prosaism (prosaic style), Mazdaism (ancient Persian religion), Lamaism (form of Buddhism), ultraism (extreme philosophy), Sivaism (Hindu cult), Lamarckism, catechism, iodism (iodine poisoning), monadism (philosophical doctrine), faradism (medical use of electricity), Methodism, pacifism, imagism (poetic movement), cataclysm, alarmism, extremism, euphemism, dysphemism (substitution of offensive word), Muslimism, animism (primitive belief), pessimism, optimism, dynamism (philosophical theory), atomism (philosophical theory), totemism, cocainism, communism, escapism, priapism, sinapism, vampirism, tenebrism (style of painting), helichrysum (flowering plant), pentaprism (five-sided prism), erythrism (abnormal red coloration), ostracism, exorcism, solipsism (philosophy term), Englishism, Irishism, fetishism, Britishism, de-

featism, elitism, occultism, gigantism, erethism (high degree of sensitivity), atavism (recurrence of primitive characteristics), paroxysm, Spinozism.

invalidism (being an invalid), diastrophism (movement of earth's crust), catastrophism (geological theory), parallelism, alcoholism, nicotinism, opportunism, malapropism, ventriloquism, polycentrism (political theory), egocentrism, ethnocentrism (belief in race's superiority).

hypothyroidism, hyperthyroidism, Eurocommunism.

242.35.1

deism, Shiism (Islamic belief), theism, misoneism (hatred of anything new), absenteeism.

242.35.2

archaism, Trotskyism, Gandhiism, cockneyism, atheism, ditheism (belief in two gods), tritheism (belief in the Trinity), pantheism, McCarthyism, polytheism, monotheism.

242.35.3

Foism (Chinese Buddhism), Taoism (Chinese philosophy), echoism (linguistics term), locoism (disease of cattle), egoism, jingoism, heroism, dichroism (crystallography term), trichroism (crystallography term), Titoism, xanthochroism (skin condition in goldfish), hylozoism (philosophical doctrine).

242.35.4

truism, Hinduism, altruism, euphuism (Elizabethan prose style).

242.35.5

abysm, syllabism (system of writing).

242.35.6

anarchism, monarchism, masochism, sadomasochism.

242.35.7

Orphism (ancient Greek religion), dwarfism, polymorphism (existence of different forms), endomorphism (geology term), isomorphism (similarity of form), allomorphism (variation in crystalline form), metamorphism, anthropomorphism.

242.35.8
syllogism, synergism (medical term), geophagism (practice of eating earth), dialogism (philosophy term), paralogism (invalid argument), antilogism (philosophy term), neologism, psychologism (belief in psychology).

242.35.9
nihilism, pugilism, virilism (medical term), pointillism, immobilism (reactionary political policy), probabilism (philosophical doctrine), zoophilism (emotional attachment to animals), necrophilism (desire to be dead), evangelism, puerilism (immature behaviour by adult), infantilism, mercantilism (economic theory).

242.35.10
formulism (adherence to formulas), botulism, somnambulism.

242.35.11
myalism (type of witchcraft), ptyalism (excessive excretion of saliva), loyalism, royalism, dualism, verbalism, tribalism, embolism, symbolism, localism, vocalism (exercise of the voice), feudalism, vandalism, Mendelism (science of heredity), legalism (strict adherence to law), mongolism, formalism, finalism (philosophical doctrine), moralism, pluralism, neutralism, centralism, racialism, specialism, socialism, fatalism, vitalism (philosophical doctrine).

diabolism (devil worship), anabolism (metabolic process), metabolism, catabolism (metabolic process), cannibalism, radicalism, syndicalism (workers' revolutionary movement), clericalism (power of the clergy), classicalism (architectural style), physicalism (philosophical doctrine), animalism (preoccupation with physical matters),

liberalism, structuralism, literalism, naturalism, commercialism, provincialism, symmetallism (economic doctrine), bimetallism (economic doctrine), digitalism (digitalis poisoning), capitalism, medievalism, revivalism.

thromboembolism, phenomenalism (philosophy term), universalism (universal characteristic), existentialism, monometallism (economic doctrine), sacerdotalism (principles of the priesthood).

242.35.11.1
realism, idealism, surrealism.

242.35.11.2
colonialism, colloquialism, mercurialism (mercury poisoning), industrialism, territorialism.

242.35.11.2.1
serialism, imperialism, materialism, immaterialism (philosophy term).

242.35.11.3
gradualism (seeking change gradually), sensualism, ritualism, textualism (adherence to text), spiritualism, conceptualism (philosophy term), transsexualism, intellectualism, individualism.

242.35.11.4
journalism, paternalism, externalism (philosophical doctrine).

242.35.11.5
regionalism, personalism (idiosyncrasy), functionalism, professionalism, traditionalism, emotionalism, conventionalism, occasionalism (philosophical theory), institutionalism, constitutionalism.

242.35.11.5.1
nationalism, rationalism, internationalism.

242.35.11.5.2
sensationalism, Congregationalism, operationalism (philosophy of science term), denominationalism, representationalism (philosophy term).

242.35.11.6
mentalism (philosophy term), Orientalism, transcendentalism, sentimentalism, fundamentalism, sacramentalism (theology term), instrumentalism (philosophy term), departmentalism (division into departments), experimentalism, environmentalism (psychology term).

242.35.12
reformism, transformism (theory of evolution), nonconformism.

242.35.13
rabbinism (teachings of rabbis), albinism, morphinism, Stalinism, Galenism (former theory of medicine), Hellenism, feminism, Leninism, strychninism, alpinism, foreignism, Latinism, cretinism, chauvinism, Calvinism, Darwinism, determinism, illuminism (belief in special enlightenment), indeterminism (philosophy term), ultramontanism (Roman Catholic doctrine), hyperinsulinism.

242.35.14
eonism (psychiatry term), pianism (piano-playing skill), Zionism, mechanism, tokenism (doing the minimum necessary), volcanism (formation of volcanoes), hedonism, modernism, paganism, organism, melanism, shamanism (Asian religion), Brahmanism, Germanism, demonism (worship of demons), Mormonism, Romanism (Roman Catholicism), humanism, pelmanism (card game), onanism, prochronism (error in dating), synchronism (simultaneous occurrence), Jansenism, saturnism (lead poisoning), Platonism, Satanism, Titanism (spirit of rebellion), Teutonism, daltonism, westernism, galvanism, unionism.

antagonism, hooliganism, eudemonism (philosophical doctrine), anachronism, parachronism (error in dating), asynchronism (occurrence at different times), immersionism (Christian doctrine), traducianism (theology term),

Confucianism, abstractionism (theory of abstract art), perfectionism, protectionism, expansionism, divisionism (art term), revisionism (deviation from true Marxism), illusionism, infusionism (theology term), charlatanism, Italianism, nonunionism.

servomechanism, Mohammedanism, microorganism, exhibitionism.

242.35.14.1
Fabianism, lesbianism, Canadianism, Pelagianism (heretical Christian doctrine), Australianism, Nestorianism (theological doctrine), Erastianism (state supremacy over church), Swedenborgianism (religious movement), Saint-Simonianism (form of socialism), presbyterianism, Zoroastrianism.

242.35.14.1.1
Arianism (heretical doctrine), Tractarianism, millenarianism (Christian belief), vegetarianism, unitarianism, hereditarianism (psychology term), utilitarianism, humanitarianism, necessitarianism (philosophy term), parliamentarianism, uniformitarianism (geological theory).

242.35.14.2
Gallicanism (French Catholic movement), Anglicanism, Africanism, Vaticanism, republicanism, Americanism.

242.35.14.3
creationism (theological belief), inflationism, deviationism (ideological deviation), isolationism, restorationism (theological belief), presentationism (philosophy term), associationism (psychology term).

242.35.14.4
impressionism, expressionism, postimpressionism, neoimpressionism.

242.35.15
barbarism, labourism, Quakerism, naturism, futurism, aphorism, rigorism (strictness in judgment), algorism (decimal system of counting), vulgarism,

Gongorism (affected literary style), plagiarism, bowdlerism, Hitlerism, mesmerism, mannerism, spoonerism, terrorism, asterism (printing symbol), pasteurism (treatment of rabies), Lutherism, aneurysm, Caesarism (autocratic system of government).

anachorism (geographical misplacement), hypocorism (pet name), adventurism, metamerism (animal's division into segments), euhemerism (historical interpretation of myths), allomerism (chemistry term), isomerism (chemistry term), tautomerism (chemistry term), consumerism, militarism, voluntarism (philosophy term), behaviourism.

adiaphorism (Protestant theological theory), vernacularism, particularism (attention to minority interest).

242.35.16
stoicism, logicism (theory of mathematics), Anglicism, cynicism, classicism, narcissism, Briticism, criticism, witticism, vorticism (English art movement), scepticism, mysticism, Gnosticism, Gothicism, organicism (biological theory), Hispanicism (word borrowed from Spanish), Hibernicism (Irishism), historicism (theory of history), athleticism, asceticism, aestheticism, romanticism, agnosticism, academicism (conventionalism), neoclassicism.

242.35.16.1
phallicism (worship of phallus), Gallicism (word borrowed from French), Italicism.

242.35.16.2
solecism, Catholicism.

242.35.16.3
lyricism, empiricism.

242.35.16.4
Atticism (simple clear expression), fanaticism, dichromaticism (crystallography term).

242.35.16.5
Scotticism, eroticism, neuroticism.

242.35.16.6
scholasticism, monasticism, neoplasticism (style of abstract painting), ecclesiasticism.

242.35.17
Chartism (English reform movement), Bonapartism.

242.35.18
magnetism, syncretism (tendency to combine beliefs), Docetism (early Christian heresy), synthetism (art term), sovietism, Jesuitism, fortuitism (philosophy term), favouritism, anti-Semitism, diamagnetism, geomagnetism, ferromagnetism, paramagnetism, electromagnetism.

242.35.19
mutism, absolutism.

242.35.20
quietism (form of mysticism), narcotism, ergotism, egotism, helotism (sociopolitical system), prelatism (Church government by prelates), schematism (general arrangement), traumatism, rheumatism, pragmatism, stigmatism, dogmatism, hypnotism, nepotism, despotism, teratism (malformed fetus), patriotism, suprematism, animatism, systematism (practice of classifying), automatism, astigmatism, separatism, conservatism, monochromatism (visual defect).

242.35.21
scientism, tarantism (nervous disorder), immanentism (belief in God's omnipresence), Protestantism, indifferentism (indifference to religion).

242.35.22
passivism, nativism (protection of native cultures), activism, recidivism (habitual relapse into crime), primitivism, positivism, negativism, relativism, objectivism, subjectivism, collectivism, Perspectivism (philosophical doctrine),

constructivism (abstract art movement).

243 -elm
elm, helm, realm, wych-elm (Eurasian elm tree), Wilhelm, unhelm (remove the helmet of), Anselm, overwhelm.

244 -ilm
film, microfilm.

245 -an [some -*man* words in 261 may be pronounced to rhyme with this group]
Anne, an, ban, can, Cannes, scan, dan, Dan, fan, gan (*Dialect* to go), Han (Chinese dynasty), clan, flan, plan, man, nan, pan, Pan, panne (velvet fabric), span, ran, bran, cran (measure of fresh herring), scran (*Slang* food), tan, than, van.

cyan (greenish-blue colour), Cheyenne, koan (Buddhist riddle), yuan (Chinese currency), pecan, oilcan, cancan, cooncan (card game), Houdan (breed of domestic fowl), randan (rowing boat), began, Afghan, tolan (crystalline substance), yulan (Chinese magnolia), Gosplan (Russian state planning commission), unman, outman, Hainan (Chinese island), Tainan (Chinese city), honan (silk fabric), Hunan (Chinese province), tarpan (extinct wild horse), claypan (subsurface clay layer), kneepan (kneecap), Saipan (Pacific island), taipan (venomous snake), Chopin, bedpan, deadpan, skidpan, jampan (sedan chair), sampan, brainpan (skull), wingspan, dustpan, pyran (chemical compound), shoran (short-range radar system), furan (flammable toxic liquid), FORTRAN, outran, Pusan (South Korean port), Wonsan (North Korean port), Bashan (biblical region), Anshan (Chinese city), Nan Shan (Chinese mountain range), rattan, kaftan, suntan, divan, Qairwan

(Tunisian city), Lausanne, Kazan (Russian city).

Caliban, billycan, astrakhan, turbofan (fan driven by turbine), Kordofan (Sudanese province), tryptophan (amino acid), Callaghan, Catalan, Ku Klux Klan, overman, cocopan (South African mining wagon), spick-and-span, also-ran, pentosan (biochemical compound), hexosan (biochemical compound), constantan (copper–nickel alloy), mercaptan (chemical compound), caravan.

245.1
redan (type of fortification), sedan, shandrydan (two-wheeled cart).

245.2
Milan, gamelan (East Indian percussion orchestra), Acrilan (*Trademark*).

245.3
trepan (surgical instrument), marzipan.

245.4
Japan, tragopan (Asian pheasant), Belmopan (capital of Belize), Matapan (promontory in southern Greece).

245.5
Oran, saran (resin), Teleran (*Trademark* navigational aid), trimaran, overran, catamaran.

245.6
soutane (Catholic priest's cassock), orang-utan.

245.7
tisane, ptisan (grape juice), Parmesan, artisan, partisan, courtesan, bipartisan, nonpartisan.

246 -arn
Arne (English composer), barn, khan, darn, Han (Chinese imperial dynasty), Marne (French river), San (language group), Shan (Mongoloid people), tarn, Van (Turkish city), guan (South American bird), yarn.

barchan (sand dune), lucarne (dormer window), machan (tiger-hunting platform), maidan (Indian open meeting place), Sudan, goldarn, Tzigane, uhlan (Polish lancer), Kirman (Persian carpet), Oman, Amman, toman (gold coin), Teheran, Iran, Koran, buran (Asian blizzard), Tourane (Vietnamese port), Cwmbran, Khotan (Chinese oasis), Wotan (Germanic god), Bhutan (central Asian kingdom), Multan (Pakistani city), Sevan (Russian lake), pavane, dewan (Indian minister of state), Taiwan, Jawan (Indian soldier), Szechwan (Chinese province), San Juan, Aswan, Dayan, kalian (Oriental pipe), azan (Islamic call to prayer), Fezzan (region of Libya).

skokiaan (South African alcoholic beverage), Vientiane, autobahn, Kublai Khan, Aga Khan, balmacaan (man's knee-length overcoat), Genghis Khan, Abadan (Iranian port), Ramadan (period in Muslim year), Lindisfarne, Abidjan (capital of Ivory Coast), Omdurman (Sudanese city), Suleiman (sultan of Ottoman empire), Hanuman (monkey), Alcoran (Koran), Yucatán (Mexican state), Hindustan, Bantustan, Kwangchowan (region of China), macedoine, Azerbaijan (region of Iran).

246.1
Pakistan, Turkestan (region of Asia), Kurdistan (Asian plateau), Nuristan (region of Afghanistan), Baluchistan (region of Asia), Afghanistan, Waziristan (region of Asia), Kafiristan (region of Afghanistan).

247 -ane
ain (*Scot* own), ane (*Scot* one), bane, Cain, cane, skein, chain, Dane, deign, feign, fain, gain, Jane, lain, lane, blain (blister or sore), plain, plane, slain, Maine, mane, main, pane, pain, Spain, rein, reign, rain, brain, crane, drain, grain, sprain, train, strain, sane, Seine, tain (tinfoil mirror-backing), stain,

Steen (Dutch painter), thane, vein, vain, vane, Wayne, wane, wain, swain, twain, Twain.

cowbane (marsh plant), urbane, fleabane (daisy-like plant), cubane (chemical compound), wolfbane (poisonous plant), bugbane (insect-repelling plant), henbane (poisonous plant), ratsbane (rat poison), arcane, decane (chemical compound), Cockaigne (medieval imaginary land), procaine, alkane (chemical compound), cinquain (five-line poem), enchain, unchain, ordain, lindane (crystalline substance), mundane, disdain, Sinn Fein, regain, Ujjain (Indian city), Elaine, poleyn (armour protecting knee), chilblain, Maclean, airplane, terreplein (top of rampart), skiplane, deplane (disembark from aircraft), seaplane, biplane, triplane, warplane, sailplane (high-performance glider), tailplane (aerofoil at aircraft's tail), volplane (glide without power), emplane (board an aircraft), complain, explain, germane, pearmain, demesne, remain, romaine (*US* cos lettuce), ptomaine (chemical compound), chow mein, humane, mortmain (legal term), propane, Bahrain, terrane, terrain, Lorraine, moraine, borane (chemical compound), forebrain, crackbrain (insane person), midbrain, endbrain, hindbrain, membrane, Ukraine, refrain, migraine, Igraine (King Arthur's mother), grosgrain (heavy ribbed fabric), ingrain, vicereine (viceroy's wife), detrain (disembark from train), vitrain (type of coal), quatrain, entrain (board a train), distrain, restrain, eyestrain, constrain, Bassein (Burmese city), Hussein, insane, butane, obtain, octane, Beltane (ancient Celtic festival), maintain, contain, sustain, abstain, bloodstain, ethane, methane, vervain (flowering plant), dogvane (nautical wind vane), sixain (six-line poem), fusain (fine charcoal pencil).

Tubal-cain (biblical character), preordain, foreordain, transmundane (beyond this world), peneplain (flattish land surface), multiplane (multi-winged aircraft), taxiplane (*US* aircraft for hire), hydroplane (motorboat), aquaplane, aeroplane, gyroplane (self-propelled aircraft), inhumane, frangipane (almond-flavoured pastry), windowpane, counterpane, scatterbrain, featherbrain, Pontchartrain (US lake), hovertrain (hovercraft train), halothane (chemical compound), paravane (device on minesweeper).

cycloalkane (chemical compound), demimondaine, cyclohexane (flammable liquid), polyurethane.

247.1
chicane, hurricane.

247.2
cocaine, lignocaine (local anaesthetic), marocain (ribbed crepe fabric), Novocaine (*Trademark*).

247.3
profane, hydrophane (variety of opal), allophane (mineral), cellophane, cymophane (mineral).

247.4
delaine (wool fabric), Kwajalein (Pacific atoll), Tamerlane (Mongol conqueror), chatelaine (mistress of castle).

247.5
domain, leucomaine (biochemical compound), Charlemagne, legerdemain, El Alamein.

247.6
inane, Dunsinane (Scottish hill), catenane (chemistry term).

247.7
campaign, champagne, elecampane (flowering plant).

247.8
arraign, serein (fine tropical rain), souterrain (underground chamber), suzerain (feudal overlord).

247.9
detain, retain, Aquitaine.

247.10
attain, pertain, appertain, chevrotain (Asian mammal), ascertain, entertain.

247.11
Fonteyn, montane, Bloemfontein (South African city), tramontane (across the mountains), submontane (on lower mountain slopes), ultramontane (beyond the mountains).

248 -en
en (printer's measure), Ben, ben, Ken, ken, sken (*Dialect* to squint), den, fen, gen, hen, Len, glen, men, Penn, pen, wren, Bren, sen (Oriental monetary unit), ten, Sten, then, when, wen (cyst on scalp), yen, Zen.

cayenne, doyenne, Chechen (Russian people), Ardennes, again, greyhen (female black grouse), moorhen, amen, semen, hymen, limen (psychology term), vimen (flexible plant shoot), nomen (ancient Roman's clan name), dolmen, playpen, bullpen (*US* large prison cell), Guienne (former French province), Fukien (Chinese province).

Ogaden (region of Ethiopia), thiophen (chemical compound), tappit-hen, madrilène (tomato-flavoured consommé), regimen, praenomen (ancient Roman's first name), agnomen (ancient Roman's fourth name), cognomen (ancient Roman's family name), acumen, samisen (Japanese stringed instrument), Sun Yat-sen (Chinese statesman), Debrecen (Hungarian city), Longyearbyen (Norwegian island village), Sinhailien (Chinese city).

248.1
julienne (cookery term), tragedienne, comedienne, Tyrolienne (Tyrolean peasant dance), equestrienne, Valenciennes (fine lace).

248.2

flamen (Roman priest), stamen, velamen (enveloping membrane of root),
foramen (hole in a bone), duramen
(woody tissue), putamen (fruit stone),
gravamen (legal term), examen (Catholic examination of conscience).

248.3

rumen, numen (ancient Roman deity),
cerumen (earwax), hegumen (Eastern
Church monastic leader), catechumen
(convert receiving pre-baptismal instruction), energumen (possessed person).

249 -ern

urn, earn, erne (eagle), Bern, burn,
kern (printing term), churn, fern, föhn
(warm Alpine wind), hern (*Dialect* heron), learn, pirn (fishing rod), spurn,
quern (stone hand mill), tern, turn,
terne (metal alloy), stern, Verne, yearn.

lierne (architectural term), Tyburn,
Blackburn, windburn, Swinburne, sunburn, Hepburn, heartburn, sojourn,
adjourn, unlearn, inurn, epergne (din-
ner-table ornament), discern, decern
(Scottish legal term), lucerne, Lucerne,
concern, Saturn, Sauternes, nocturn
(part of Catholic matins), nocturne, intern, upturn, astern, extern, casern
(soldier's billet).

Bannockburn, unconcern, overturn,
Comintern (international Communist
organization).

249.1

gittern (guitar-like instrument), return,
cittern (medieval stringed instrument),
taciturn.

250 -airn

bairn, cairn, Nairn (Scottish Highland
region), Pitcairn (Pacific island), moderne (architectural style), Auvergne
(region of France).

251 -een

been, bean, keen, skean (double-edged
dagger), dene (narrow wooded valley),
dean, sphene (type of mineral), gean
(sweet cherry), Jean, gene, lean, clean,
glean, spleen, mean, mien, mesne (legal term), pean (heraldic term), peen
(part of hammer), queen, reen (*Dialect*
ditch), screen, green, preen, treen
(wooden), seen, scene, sheen, teen, wean, wheen (*Dialect* few).

shebeen (illegal drinking place), buckbean (marsh plant), Azbine (region of
Sahara desert), has-been, takin (large
goatlike mammal), achene (one-seeded
fruit), Tolkien, nankeen, sardine, sourdine (organ stop), codeine, dudeen
(clay pipe), undine (female water spirit), caffeine, trephine (surgical instrument), dauphine (French princess),
morphine, phosphene (physiology
term), beguine (South American
dance), hygiene, phosgene (colourless
poisonous gas), praline, phthalein
(chemical compound), scalene, squalene (biochemical compound), valine
(amino acid), Hellene (a Greek), colleen, choline (biochemical compound),
proline (amino acid), unclean, Crimplene (*Trademark*), Kathleen, Amin,
ammine (chemical compound), gamine
(slim boyish girl), imine (chemical
compound), demean, bromine (dark
red liquid), Benin (African republic),
quinine, strychnine, terpene (chemical
compound), chopine (18th-century
shoe), spalpeen (*Irish* rascal), Mc-
Queen, terrene (relating to the earth),
terrine, serene, moreen (heavy furnishing fabric), dourine (infectious disease
of horses), fluorine, purine (crystalline
compound), windscreen, shagreen
(sharkskin), gangrene, vitrine (glass
display-case), latrine, fascine (bundle
of long sticks), glassine (translucent
book-covering), arsine (colourless poisonous gas), narceine (chemical compound), Essene (member of Jewish

sect), foreseen, obscene, unseen, dasheen (Asian plant), archine (Russian unit of length), ratine (loosely-woven cloth), sateen (glossy fabric resembling satin), eighteen, thirteen, poteen (*Irish* illicit whiskey), fourteen, protein, routine, fifteen, canteen, dentine, pentene (colourless liquid), nineteen, tontine (annuity scheme), umpteen, Christine, pristine, cystine (amino acid), Sistine, sixteen, nervine (soothing the nerves), Slovene, subvene, convene, Salween (Asian river), between, vaccine, cuisine, benzene.

Hallowe'en, toluene (colourless liquid), jellybean, terebene (chemical compound), palanquin (Oriental covered litter), Balanchine (US choreographer), pethidine, brigandine (medieval coat of mail), toxaphene (chemical compound), Josephine, carrageen (edible red seaweed), indigene (native person or organism), epigene (formed at earth's surface), hypogene (formed beneath earth's surface), philhellene (lover of Greece), bellarmine (large earthenware jar), spodumene (greyish-white mineral), mavourneen (Irish term of endearment), cyanine (blue dye), mezzanine, reserpine (medicinal plant extract), Philippine, atropine, Hippocrene (poetic inspiration), multiscreen (type of film presentation), wintergreen (evergreen shrub), evergreen, unforeseen, aubergine, subroutine, velveteen, barquentine (sailing ship), brigantine (sailing ship), Argentine, galantine, clementine, quarantine, seventeen, brilliantine, mangosteen (East Indian tree), polythene, ornithine (amino acid), olivine (mineral), go-between, bombazine, magazine, limousine, organzine (strong silk thread).

piperidine (colourless liquid), tetracycline (antibiotic), physostigmine (medicinal alkaloid), chlorobenzene (colourless liquid), nitrobenzene (chemical compound).

251.1
gradine (step or ledge), iodine, Aberdeen, gaberdine, Engadine (Swiss tourist centre), grenadine.

251.2
Terylene (*Trademark*), Vaseline (*Trademark*), ethylene, methylene, acetylene, polypropylene (plastic), oxyacetylene, polytetrafluoroethylene.

251.3
baleen (whalebone), malines (silk net fabric), Abilene (Texan city), percaline (light cotton fabric), silkaline (fine cotton fabric), mescaline (hallucinogenic drug), Magdalene, bandoline (hairdressing substance), tourmaline (mineral), trampoline, citrulline (amino acid), gasoline, messaline (light silk fabric), naphthalene.

251.4
rhodamine (red dye), melamine, prolamine (plant protein), Dramamine (*Trademark*), protamine (protein), glutamine (amino acid), catecholamine (biochemical compound), pyridoxamine (biochemical compound).

251.5
pyrene (chemical compound), styrene (colourless liquid), polystyrene.

251.6
chlorine, Maureen, taurine (chemical compound), euchlorine (explosive gas mixture), helleborine (type of orchid).

251.7
careen (sway), marine, tureen, tambourine, saccharine, sapphirine (rare blue mineral), gregarine (microscopic parasitic animal), figurine, margarine, algerine (striped woollen cloth), tangerine, pelerine (woman's narrow cape), submarine, curarine (muscle relaxant), butterine (artificial butter), pistareen (18th-century Spanish coin), wolverine (large mammal), Nazarene, aquamarine, ultramarine, nitroglycerine.

251.8
colchicine (medicinal alkaloid), epicene (having bisexual characteristics), Plasticine (*Trademark*), australopithecine.

251.9
Pliocene, Miocene, Eocene, Neocene, Holocene, damascene, ferrocene (crystalline compound), kerosene, tyrosine (amino acid), nigrosine (black pigment), Pleistocene, Oligocene, Palaeocene, adenosine (biochemical compound).

251.10
machine, crepe de Chine.

251.11
lateen (having a triangular sail), creatine (compound found in muscles), libertine, nicotine, tricotine (woollen fabric), gelatine, guillotine, carotene, astatine (chemical element), duvetyn (soft fabric), dessiatine (Russian unit of area).

251.12
ravine, supervene, margravine, landgravine, contravene, intervene.

252 -in
in, inn, bin, kin, skin, chin, din, fin, Finn, gin, hin (Hebrew unit of capacity), Lynn, linn (*Scot* waterfall), Min (Chinese dialect), pin, spin, quin, grin, sin, shin, tin, thin, win, whin (gorse), Gwyn, twin.

zein (protein), ruin, bruin, cabin, sabin (physics unit), Harbin (Chinese city), bobbin, dobbin, robin, dubbin, nubbin (*US* undeveloped fruit), Reuben, dustbin, firkin, gherkin, jerkin, merkin (pubic wig), Pekin, Wrekin, bodkin, lambkin, napkin, pipkin (small cooking pot), limpkin (wading bird), bumpkin, pumpkin, gaskin (part of horse's thigh), bearskin, deerskin, griskin (cut of pork), siskin (Eurasian finch), foreskin, doeskin, buskin (type of boot), Ruskin, redskin, kidskin, calfskin, scarfskin (outermost skin layer), pigskin, sealskin, oilskin, moleskin, wineskin, sheepskin, goatskin, Pushkin, catkin, sharkskin, snakeskin, buckskin, urchin, kitchen, Odin (Norse god), biffin (red cooking apple), griffin, tiffin, boffin, coffin, dauphin, bowfin (US fish), redfin (small fish), threadfin (tropical fish), dolphin, bargain, begin, biggin (close-fitting cap), piggin (small wooden bucket), noggin, Elgin, margin, virgin, engine, carline (Eurasian plant), marlin (tropical fish), marline (nautical rope), Stalin, Berlin, merlin (small falcon), Merlin, purlin (horizontal roof beam), mullein (Mediterranean plant), Boleyn, moulin (vertical shaft in glacier), goblin, Dublin, Brooklyn, franklin, maudlin, Kremlin, gremlin, drumlin, dunlin, Chaplin, chaplain, Joplin, poplin, purslane (trailing weed), porcelain, ratline (nautical term), javelin, ravelin (type of fortification), Evelyn, muslin, King's Lynn, Brahmin, cumin, lumen, admin, Bodmin, jasmine, plasmin (enzyme), tannin, renin (enzyme), lignin (complex plant substance), Turpin, hairpin, pippin, tiepin, lupin, crankpin, linchpin, tenpin, unpin, kingpin, Crispin, tailspin, topspin, hatpin, breastpin (brooch), backspin, Tarquin, sequin, therein, wherein, Erin, herein, stearin, Turin, urine, burin (a chisel), murrain, chagrin, citrin (vitamin), citrine (gemstone), doctrine, oestrin, brethren, sovereign, pepsin, Latin, matin, satin, martin, Martin, marten, cretin, chitin, actin (protein), pectin, plantain, fountain, mountain, Austin, within, Swithin, spavin (growth on horse's hock), savin (juniper bush), flavine (pigment), Irvine, Calvin, Kelvin (British physicist), Darwin, Edwin, Godwin, Goodwin, Baldwin, anguine (resembling a snake), sanguine, penguin, Colwyn, Gershwin, auxin (hormone), fuchsin (red dye), seisin (legal term), rosin.

casein (protein), crocein (red or orange dye), xanthein (plant pigment), Bedouin, genuine, Menuhin, Scriabin (Russian composer), Jacobin, cannabin (cannabis resin), grimalkin (old female cat), Potemkin (Russian statesman), Algonquin (American Indian people), onionskin, capuchin, Aladdin, Dunedin, gliadin (protein), muscadine (US grape plant), paladin (peer of Charlemagne's court), Saladin, Bernardine (Cistercian monk), Borodin, paraffin, Godolphin (English statesman), imagine, tarpaulin, hobgoblin, Dunfermline, discipline, Ho Chi Minh, albumen, bitumen, illumine, legumen (protein), Vietminh, lichenin (chemical compound), melanin, chinquapin (dwarf chestnut tree), underpin, terrapin, thoroughpin (inflammation on horse's hock), harlequin, porphyrin (pigment), aspirin, ephedrine (medicinal alkaloid), Sanhedrin, Benzedrine (*Trademark*), peregrine, Lohengrin, alpestrine, assassin, myosin (protein), niacin, eosin (red dye), moccasin, characin (freshwater fish), Wisconsin, hoatzin (South American bird), freemartin (female twin calf), biotin (vitamin), gelatin, haematin (dark pigment), chromatin (part of cell nucleus), keratin (protein), nystatin (antibiotic), travertine (porous rock), lecithin (biochemical compound), sympathin (hormone), thick-and-thin, Angevin (inhabitant of Anjou), alevin (young salmon or trout).

haemoglobin, myoglobin (protein), bilirubin (bile pigment), Rumpelstiltskin, biliverdin (bile pigment), prostaglandin (hormone-like compound), calamondin (Philippine citrus tree), digitalin (poisonous chemical compound), tatty-peelin (*Scot* pretentious), indiscipline, bacitracin (antibiotic), Taliesin (Welsh bard), vasopressin (hormone), oxytocin (hormone), acriflavine (brownish antiseptic powder), riboflavin (vitamin).

252.1
Owen, heroin, heroine, fibroin (protein), Halesowen (English town), benzoin (gum resin), hydantoin (crystalline substance).

252.2
Larkin, parkin, Suakin (Sudanese port).

252.3
chicken, spillikin, ramekin, cannikin (small can), mannequin (fashion model), manikin (dwarf), pannikin (*Dialect* small cup), henequen (plant yielding rope fibre), larrikin (*Austral* hooligan), lambrequin (ornamental hanging).

252.4
akin, baldachin (silk and gold brocade), manakin (South American bird), dunnakin (*Dialect* lavatory), catechin (chemical compound).

252.5
muffin, puffin, ragamuffin.

252.6
pidgin, origin.

252.7
Helen, Welwyn, Llewellyn, vitellin (protein), Helvellyn, gibberellin (plant hormone).

252.8
myelin, Kerguelen (archipelago in Indian Ocean), aniline (oily liquid), vanillin (crystalline substance), glutelin (protein), Enniskillen (Northern Irish town), podophyllin (bitter yellow resin), penicillin.

252.9
bowline, francolin (partridge), pangolin (scaly anteater).

252.10
globulin, masculine, inulin (chemical compound), lupulin (hop plant extract), insulin, botulin, tuberculin, folliculin (hormone), immunoglobulin.

252.11

kaolin, hyaline (clear and translucent), ptyalin (enzyme), violin, Gobelin, chamberlain, madeleine, magdalen (reformed prostitute), mandolin, cephalin (biochemical compound), formalin (preservative for biological specimens), lanolin (fatty extract from wool), crinoline, capelin (marine fish), zeppelin, cipolin (Italian marble), amygdalin (extract from bitter almonds), encephalin (chemical in the brain), adrenaline, noradrenaline (hormone).

252.12

famine, gamin (street urchin), examine, re-examine.

252.13

ermine, vermin, determine, predetermine.

252.14

women, specimen, maximin (maths term).

252.15

thiamine, Benjamin, jessamine (jasmine), etamin, vitamin, histamine, arsphenamine (drug containing arsenic), amphetamine, provitamin (precursor of vitamin), antihistamine, cyanocobalamin (crystalline substance).

252.16

Lenin, rennin, venin (poisonous part of venom), antivenin.

252.17

linen, feminine, agglutinin (antibody).

252.18

foreign, florin, Ilorin (Nigerian city).

252.19

tambourin (Provençal folk dance), purpurin (crystalline substance), aventurine (dark metal-flecked glass).

252.20

fiorin (perennial grass), suberin (waxy plant substance), saccharin, muscarine (poisonous chemical compound), mandarin, warfarin, gorgerin (architectural term), tamarin (small monkey), coumarin (chemical compound), heparin (biochemical substance), glycerine, bacterin (vaccine prepared from bacteria), nectarine, Catherine, culverin (heavy cannon), luciferin (light-emitting compound), alizarin (crystalline substance), nitroglycerin.

252.21

medicine, salicin (crystalline substance), sericin (protein), ceresin (white wax), capsaicin (crystalline substance), haemolysin (biochemical compound), fibrinolysin (enzyme).

252.22

lysin (substance that destroys cells), ricin (protein), neomycin (antibiotic), streptomycin, tyrothricin (antibiotic), actinomycin (antibiotic).

252.23

bulletin, palmitin (chemical compound), ferritin (protein), quercetin (yellow plant pigment), precipitin (antibody), phenacetin (crystalline substance).

252.24

cutin (waxy plant substance), Rasputin, highfalutin.

252.25

captain, Sahaptin (American Indian).

252.26

destine, predestine, clandestine, progestin (hormone), intestine.

252.27

Justin, Augustine.

252.28

Bevin (British statesman), Previn, replevin (legal term).

252.29

tocsin, toxin, thyroxine (hormone), digitoxin (poisonous chemical compound), antitoxin, zootoxin (toxin produced by animal), phytotoxin (plant poison), autotoxin (medical term).

252.30

resin, muezzin (Islamic mosque official).

253 -ine

bine (climbing stem), kine (cattle), chine, dyne, dine, fine, Jain (member of Hindu sect), line, cline (ecology term), spline, mine, nine, pine, spine, Rhine, brine, shrine, trine (astrology term), sine, sign, syne (*Scot* since), shine, Tyne, tine, stein, thine, vine, whine, wine, swine, twine.

Sabine, carbine, turbine, stibine (poisonous gas), woodbine, combine, alkyne (chemical compound), turdine (relating to thrushes), indign (undeserving), condign (well-deserved), affine (maths term), define, refine, confine, ralline (ornithology term), saline, airline, hairline, beeline, feline, skyline, dyeline (type of blueprint), Pauline (relating to Saint Paul), shoreline, towline, neckline, touchline, deadline, headline, breadline, guideline, sideline, lifeline, tramline, hemline, streamline, pipeline, baseline, dateline, outline, waistline, coastline, clothesline, carmine, canine, Pennine, rapine (forcible seizure of property), repine (be fretful), orpine (succulent plant), opine (hold an opinion), lupine, supine, alpine, vulpine (relating to foxes), vespine (relating to wasps), equine, larine (relating to gulls), taurine, murine (zoology term), murrhine (Roman vase material), eccrine, caprine (relating to goats), enshrine, Petrine (relating to Saint Peter), ursine, hircine (lascivious), quercine (relating to the oak), piscine, porcine, cosine, phocine (relating to seals), calcine (chemistry term), ensign, consign, shoeshine, sunshine, moonshine, outshine, pontine (relating to bridges), Holstein, Bernstein, Einstein, Epstein, cervine (relating to deer), divine, corvine (relating to crows), ovine, bovine, grapevine, entwine, design, resign.

concubine, alcidine (ornithology term), hirundine (relating to swallows), celandine, almandine (violet-red garnet), superfine, trichogyne (botany term), androgyne (bisexual), fringilline (ornithology term), aquiline, musteline (zoology term), induline (blue dye), Ursuline (Catholic teaching nun), vituline (relating to calves), monocline (geology term), microcline (feldspar mineral), isocline (geology term), calcimine (pale wash for walls), sycamine (mulberry tree), undermine, calamine, leonine, falconine (relating to falcons), saturnine, pavonine (relating to peacocks), porcupine, subalpine, cisalpine, transalpine, viverrine (zoology term), platyrrhine (zoology term), sciurine (relating to squirrels), colubrine (relating to snakes), endocrine, holocrine (physiology term), apocrine (physiology term), merocrine (physiology term), exocrine (physiology term), auld lang syne, gegenschein (faint glow in sky), vespertine (occurring in the evening), serotine (biology term), Tridentine (orthodox Roman Catholic), Aventine (ancient Roman hill), transpontine (across a bridge), argentine (relating to silver), valentine, eglantine, serpentine, turpentine, Florentine, Constantine, levantine (silk cloth), Hammerstein, Rubinstein, Frankenstein, Liechtenstein, Eisenstein (Russian film director), Wittgenstein, intertwine, disentwine.

Alexandrine, accipitrine (relating to hawks), internecine, terebinthine, labyrinthine, hyacinthine.

253.1

combine, columbine.

253.2

aerodyne (heavier-than-air machine), anodyne, heterodyne (electronics term).

253.3

align, malign, moline (heraldic term), zibeline (sable fur), alkaline, borderline, underline, opaline, Caroline, coralline, metalline, interline, crystalline, limicoline (ornithology term), Capitoline (ancient Roman hill).

253.4

decline, recline, helicline (spiral-shaped ramp), pericline (white mineral), anticline (rock formation), geanticline (rock formation).

253.5

incline, syncline (rock formation), disincline, geosyncline (depression in earth's crust).

253.6

benign, asinine.

253.7

saccharine, vulturine, leporine (relating to hares), piperine (crystalline substance), passerine, anserine (relating to geese), uterine, riverine, estuarine, adulterine (fake), intrauterine, extrauterine.

253.8

assign, thylacine (Tasmanian wolf), limacine (relating to slugs), psittacine (relating to parrots), countersign, haversine (maths term).

253.9

Byzantine, elephantine, diamantine, adamantine (having diamond-like lustre).

253.10

pristine, Philistine, amethystine.

254 -on

on, Bonn, con, scone, don, Don, phon (unit of loudness), gone, John, shone, wan, won (Korean currency), swan, yon.

kaon (physics particle), rayon, neon, Creon (king of Thebes), gluon (hypothetical particle in physics), Huon (Tasmanian river), muon (elementary particle in physics), Gabon, bonbon, zircon, icon, Yukon, chaconne (musical term), mascon (lunar region), radon (radioactive element), chiffon, argon, Sargon (Assyrian king), bygone, trigon (triangular harp), Saigon, doggone, foregone, trogon (tropical bird), salon, nylon, Orlon (*Trademark*), Teflon (*Trademark*), mouflon (wild mountain sheep), gnomon (part of sundial), xenon, chronon (unit of time), Nippon, coupon, jupon (short sleeveless garment), upon, tampon, pompon, thereon, whereon, Chiron (Greek centaur), giron (heraldic term), fleuron (flower-shaped ornament), pleuron (zoology term), neuron (nerve cell), Hebron (Jordanian city), macron (phonetic symbol), Dacron (*Trademark*), micron, nephron (kidney tubule), neutron, Tucson, baton, cretonne, piton, photon, proton, pluton (geology term), mouton (processed sheepskin), crouton, canton, Canton, won ton (Chinese filled dumpling), lepton (Greek coin), krypton, axon, taxon (biology term), bouillon, meson (elementary particle in physics), boson (elementary particle in physics), Luzon (largest Philippine island), blouson.

Ratisbon (German city), vidicon (small television camera tube), Comecon, orthicon (electronic device), Myrmidon (Greek mythological race), Macedon, stegodon (extinct mammal), celadon (Oriental porcelain), sphenodon (tuatara lizard), mastodon, parergon (additional employment), demijohn, eidolon (apparition), etymon (original form of word), kikumon (Japanese royal emblem), thereupon, whereupon, hereupon, elytron (insect's hard outer wing), positron (physics term), phytotron (experimental plant-growing unit), cyclotron (physics apparatus), electron, limaçon (maths term), cabochon (unfaceted polished gem), feuilleton (part of newspaper), magneton (unit in physics), phlogiston (hypothetical substance causing combustion), trilithon (structure comprising three stones), telethon, elevon (aircraft control surface), sabayon (light foamy dessert), Cro-Magnon, liaison, cabezon (Pacific fish), borazon (chemical compound).

Esdraelon (Israeli plain), sine qua non, Agamemnon, antineutron (physics term), hyperbaton (reversed order of words), automaton, demicanton (part of Swiss canton), anacoluthon (rhetoric term).

254.1
logion (authentic saying of Christ), nucleon, baryon (particle in physics), Sicyon (ancient Greek city), gnathion (point on lower jaw), triskelion (three-legged symbol), Anacreon (Greek poet), himation (ancient Greek cloak), antinucleon (particle in physics).

254.2
Laocoon (Greek mythological priest), entozoon (animal living inside another), protozoon, spermatozoon, haematozoon (microscopic blood parasite).

254.3
colophon (publisher's emblem on book), Bellerophon (Greek mythological hero).

254.4
begone, woebegone, polygon.

254.5
isogon (maths term), decagon, glucagon (hormone), undergone, nonagon, Nipigon (Canadian lake), estragon (tarragon), octagon, pentagon, heptagon, hexagon, dodecagon, undecagon, trimetrogon (method of aerial photography).

254.6
Ceylon, Chillon (Swiss castle), papillon (breed of spaniel), epsilon, upsilon, haematoxylon (thorny tree).

254.7
colon (French colonial farmer), Miquelon (French territorial island group), echelon, etalon (physics device), Avalon, encephalon (the brain).

254.8
anon, guenon (African monkey), argonon (a gas), organon (philosophy term), Parthenon, olecranon (projection behind elbow joint), perispomenon (type of Greek word).

254.9
hereon, interferon.

254.10
boron, moron, thoron (radioisotope of radon), oxymoron (rhetoric term).

254.11
Oberon, Acheron (Greek mythological river), megaron (tripartite rectangular room), aileron, hyperon (elementary particle in physics), operon (genetics term), Percheron (breed of carthorse), enteron (animal's digestive tract), hapteron (botany term), ephemeron (short-lived organism), mesenteron (animal's midgut), hexaemeron (the Creation), diatessaron (musical term).

254.12
chignon, filet mignon, boeuf Bourguignon.

255 -orn
awn, born, borne, bourn, corn, scorn, dawn, fawn, faun, horn, lawn, lorn (forsaken), mourn, morn, Norn (Norse goddess), pawn, spawn, brawn, drawn, prawn, thrawn (*Dialect* crooked), sawn, sorn (*Scot* scrounge hospitality), shorn, Sean, torn, thorn, Vaughan, warn, worn, sworn, yawn.

airborne, chairborne, reborn, freeborn, seaborne, highborn, lowborn, newborn, stillborn, inborn, unborn, baseborn, first-born, Eastbourne, Osborne, earthborn, acorn, bicorn (having two horns), tricorn (cocked hat), einkorn (variety of wheat), Runcorn, popcorn, adorn, dehorn, Gijón (Spanish port), shoehorn, inkhorn (ink container), stinkhorn (foul-smelling fungus), leghorn, foghorn, crumhorn (medieval woodwind instrument), greenhorn (inexperienced person), longhorn (breed of cattle), pronghorn (small US deer), alphorn, shorthorn, althorn (brass instrument), saxhorn (brass instrument), forlorn, lovelorn, frogspawn, withdrawn, indrawn, hawthorn, blackthorn, buckthorn, careworn, forewarn, timeworn, forsworn, Mayon (Philippine volcano), Trabzon (Turkish port).

peppercorn, leprechaun, Apeldoorn (Dutch town), Matterhorn, flugelhorn, alpenhorn, overdrawn, weatherworn, waterworn, Finsteraarhorn (Swiss mountain).

255.1
suborn, waterborne, winterbourne (stream caused by rainfall).

255.2
longicorn (beetle), barleycorn, unicorn, Capricorn, cavicorn (having hollow horns), clavicorn (beetle), lamellicorn (beetle).

256 -oin
Boyne, coin, quoin (external corner of wall), join, loin, groyne, groin, sainfoin (Eurasian plant), rejoin, adjoin, subjoin, enjoin, conjoin, disjoin, purloin, sirloin, Boulogne, tenderloin, frankalmoign (English legal history term), talapoin (small monkey), Assiniboine (Canadian river).

257 -oan
own, bone, Beaune, cone, scone, chon (Korean coin), phone, Joan, hone, loan, lone, blown, clone, flown, Sloane, moan, mown, known, pone (maize bread), rone (*Scot* drainpipe), Rhône, roan, crone, drone, grown, groan, prone, throne, thrown, sewn, sown, sone (unit of loudness), shown, tone, stone, zone.

thighbone, jawbone, backbone, cheekbone, aitchbone (cut of beef), whalebone, trombone, shinbone, hipbone, wishbone, breastbone, dracone (container towed by ship), condone, earphone, sulphone (chemical compound), agon (ancient Greek festival), cogon (tropical grass), chalone (internal secretion), colon (Costa Rican currency), alone, Cologne, cologne, flyblown (contaminated), windblown, full-blown, cyclone, high-flown, bemoan, hormone, unknown, depone (Scottish legal term), repone (Scottish legal term), Capone, postpone, Tyrone, pyrone (chemical compound), neurone, ingrown, oestrone (hormone), dethrone, enthrone, disown, bolson (US desert valley), ketone, tritone (musical term), lactone (chemical compound), halftone, intone, peptone, keystone, freestone (fine-grained stone), kerbstone, touchstone, headstone, lodestone, toadstone (igneous rock), sandstone, grindstone, flagstone, hailstone, millstone, bilestone, milestone, gallstone, gemstone, brimstone, limestone, tombstone, rhinestone, moonstone, copestone, soapstone, whetstone, birthstone, gravestone, flavone (crystalline substance), hexone (chemical compound), ozone, evzone (Greek soldier).

marrowbone, collarbone, knucklebone, anklebone, cuttlebone, herringbone, silicone, methadone (narcotic drug), audiphone (hearing aid), telephone, polyphone (linguistics term), Francophone, chordophone (stringed instrument), megaphone, mellophone (brassband instrument), xylophone, Anglophone, gramophone, homophone (word pronounced like another), vibraphone (percussion instrument), microphone, hydrophone (underwater microphone), Dictaphone (*Trademark*), interphone (telephone system linking rooms), saxophone, sousaphone, heckelphone (bass oboe), overblown, pheromone (chemical substance in animals), unbeknown, rotenone (crystalline substance), ionone (perfumed plant extract), butanone (chemical compound), ethonone (toxic gas), undergrown, overgrown, overthrown, ecdysone (hormone), holystone (sandstone for scrubbing decks), thunderstone (long tapering object), cornerstone, cobblestone, staddlestone, prednisone (steroid drug), cortisone.

radiophone, anticyclone.

enterogastrone (hormone), spironolactone (hormone).

257.1
coumarone (aromatic liquid), chaperon, progesterone, aldosterone, androsterone, testosterone.

257.2
barbitone, semitone, baritone, baryton (bass viol), acetone, phenobarbitone.

257.3
atone, duotone (printing process), sacaton (coarse grass), ecotone (ecology term), undertone, monotone, isotone (chemistry term), overtone.

258 -oun

down, gown, clown, noun, brown, crown, drown, frown, town.

godown (Asian warehouse), hoedown, lowdown, slowdown, showdown, markdown, breakdown, shakedown, touchdown, comedown, sundown, splashdown, shutdown, Piltdown, countdown, nightgown, renown, pronoun, adnoun (adjective used as noun), nutbrown, Motown, midtown, downtown, uptown.

hand-me-down, eiderdown, omadhaun (*Irish* a fool), Portadown, upside-down, tumble-down, thistledown, shantytown, Chinatown, cabbagetown (city slum).

259 -un

bun, dun, done, fun, gun, Hun, none, nun, pun, spun, run, son, sun, sunn (East Indian plant), shun, ton, tonne, tun, stun, one, won.

undone, outdone, begun, handgun, popgun, shotgun, outgun, Falun (Swedish city), Cholon (South Vietnamese city), homespun, finespun, rerun, forerun, millrun, outrun, godson, grandson, stepson, Fushun (Chinese city), someone.

underdone, overdone, overrun, kiloton, megaton, anyone, everyone.

260 -oon

boon, coon, Scone (Scottish parish), goon, June, lune (maths term), loon, moon, noon, poon (Asian tree), spoon, rune, croon, prune, soon, shoon, toon (large tree), swoon, dune, tune.

baboon, tycoon, rockoon (scientifically-equipped rocket), cocoon, puccoon (US plant), raccoon, tuchun (Chinese military governor), cardoon (European plant), bridoon (horse's bit), typhoon, buffoon, lagoon, dragoon, Rangoon, jejune, cohune (US tropical palm), shalloon (light woollen fabric), Walloon, Kowloon, doubloon, forenoon, harpoon, lampoon, teaspoon, gombroon (Oriental pottery), quadroon, Gudrun, gadroon (decorative patterned moulding), poltroon (contemptible coward), Sassoon, gossoon (*Irish* servant boy), bassoon, monsoon, matzoon (fermented milk product), ratoon (crop plant's new growth), cartoon, spittoon, pontoon, spontoon (short pike), festoon, triune (three in one), tribune, immune, commune, repugn, oppugn (to dispute), impugn, Neptune.

rigadoon (old Provençal dance), Dehra Dun (Indian city), demilune (crescent-shaped formation), perilune (point in lunar orbit), honeymoon, tablespoon, dessertspoon, Behistun (Iranian village), picayune (*US* of little value).

Tutankhamun, autoimmune.

260.1
balloon, galloon (decorative cord), saloon, apolune (point in lunar orbit), pantaloon (pantomime character).

260.2
Dunoon, afternoon.

260.3
maroon, macaroon, picaroon (adventurer), Scandaroon (fancy pigeon), Cameroon, octoroon, Iskenderun (Turkish port), vinegarroon (large scorpion-like arachnid).

260.4
platoon, saskatoon (Canadian fruit shrub), Saskatoon (Canadian city).

260.5
fortune, misfortune, importune.

260.6
attune, opportune, inopportune.

261 -'n
ebon, leben (African curdled milk), gibbon, ribbon, auburn, corban (biblical gift), Bourbon, Oban, stubborn, Cuban, Melbourne, Gisborne (New Zealand port), Lisbon, Brisbane, blacken, slacken, bracken, beckon, Deccan, schnecken (*US* bread roll), pekan (US mammal), reckon, Brecon, liken, lichen, silken, Vulcan, Lincoln, Duncan, drunken, shrunken, sunken, scutcheon, scuncheon (part of door jamb), luncheon, puncheon (large cask), truncheon, Christian, Arden, Baden, Dardan (Trojan), garden, harden, lardon (strip of fat), pardon, bourdon (organ stop), hoyden (tomboy), Croydon, loden (thick wool), Snowdon, Woden (Anglo-Saxon god), louden, sudden, wooden, Camden, tendon, linden, Swindon, bounden, London, Hampden, Dresden, deafen, hyphen, siphon, often, soften, orphan, roughen,

druffen (*Dialect* drunk), toughen, lagan (wreckage on sea bed), Skagen (cape in Denmark), Dagan (Babylonian god), jargon, Hagen (German legendary character), Keegan, vegan, tigon (tiger –lion hybrid), bogan (*Canadian* side stream), hogan (American Indian dwelling), Logan, slogan, brogan (heavy boot), roentgen, largen, Georgian, Trojan, Belgian, Injun, St. John, dungeon, Allen, Alan, gallon, talon, Galen (Greek physician), merlon (part of battlement), pylon, fallen, courlan (US wading bird), sullen, woollen, raglan, barman, carman, Raman (Indian physicist), Brahman, Emmen (Dutch city), lemon, German, Herman, merman, sermon, Sherman, pieman, Simon, Cimon (Athenian military commander), fireman, wireman (*US* electrician), common, doorman, foreman, lawman, Mormon, Norman, bowman (oarsman), cowman, ploughman, summon, cabman, kirkman (*Scot* church member), workman, socman (tenant farmer), stockman, milkman, linkman, churchman, Scotchman, watchman, coachman, Dutchman, henchman, Frenchman, adman, badman, madman, Bradman (Australian cricketer), headman, birdman, freedman, goodman, woodman, sandman, bagman (travelling salesman), flagman, ragman, swagman, legman (*US* newspaper reporter), tegmen (insect's leathery forewing), Bergman, dogman (*Austral* crane-driver's assistant), frogman, dolman (long Turkish robe), coalman, oilman, Pullman, penman, gunman, hangman, strongman, apeman, Helpmann (Australian ballet dancer), gasman, baseman (fielder in baseball), spaceman, horseman, Norseman, houseman, batsman, statesman, Scotsman, yachtsman, sportsman, craftsman, draughtsman, huntsman, freshman, bushman, Welshman, batman, atman (Hindu self), hetman (Cossack leader), Pitman, pitman, titman (smallest piglet in litter), Whitman (US poet), boatman, footman, postman, dustman, caveman, marksman, spokesman, Manxman, Tasman, Osman (Turkish sultan), oarsman, tribesman, guardsman, tradesman, herdsman, sidesman (church warden's assistant), swordsman, bandsman, landsman, roundsman, groundsman, bailsman (person who stands bail), dalesman, salesman, clansman, Klansman (Ku Klux Klan member), kinsman, linesman, townsman, Canaan, Lennon, pennon, tenon, happen, sharpen, tarpon (Atlantic fish), weapon, cheapen, deepen, steepen, Ripon, Crippen, ripen, open, dampen, lampern (European lamprey), crampon, hempen, tympan (resonating membrane), lumpen (stupid), aspen, saucepan, Aran, Arran, barren, baron, Karen, marron (chestnut), Sharon, heron, perron (flight of steps), Aaron, Charon (Greek mythological character), sporran, warren, squadron, children, cauldron, chaldron (unit of capacity), pauldron (armour plate protecting shoulder), saffron, apron, matron, natron (a mineral), patron, citron, plectron, chevron, sovran, bison, hyson (Chinese green tea), grison (predatory mammal), coarsen, Dawson, whoreson, hoarsen, Porson (English classical scholar), moisten, Preussen (German name for Prussia), boatswain, bosun, loosen, Ibsen, Gibson, Hudson, Belsen, kelson (strengthening beam on keel), Nelson, telson (zoology term), Wilson, Samson, Jansen, Nansen, Johnson, sponson (ship's outboard gun platform), Bunsen, Simpson, Thompson, stetson, Whitsun, Watson, tutsan (Eurasian woodland shrub), Martian, cushion, auction, sanction, sponsion (sponsorship), Dayton (US city), phaeton (horse-drawn carriage), straighten, straiten (embarrass financially), Satan, oaten (made of oats), croton (tropical shrub), Acton, Clacton, lectern, Stockton, plankton, chieftain, Carlton,

Charlton, Chiltern, Milton, Stilton, Wilton, Dalton (English scientist), saltern (saltworks), Walton, Bolton, molten, sultan, Danton (French revolutionary leader), lantern, Scranton (Pennsylvanian city), Paignton, Denton (English town), lenten, Trenton (US city), wanton, Taunton, hapten (medical term), Clapton (English rock guitarist), Skipton, Hampton, Aston, pastern, eastern, Boston, postern, pleuston (mass of floating microorganisms), Houston, Gladstone, Maidstone, charleston, Princeton, Dunstan (English saint), tungsten, capstan, Ashton, Caxton, Paxton (English architect), sexton (church caretaker), Folkestone, Buxton, Nathan, earthen, python, luthern (dormer window), lengthen, strengthen, heathen, northern, southern, smoothen, cavern, raven (seize prey), tavern, proven, sylvan (relating to woods), Malvern, seawan (shell beads), Jackson, klaxon, flaxen, Saxon, waxen, Texan, Nixon, vixen, oxen, Oxon., coxswain, bullion, Julian, onion, bunion, Bunyan, Runyon (US writer), grunion (Californian fish), trunnion (pivot), Tarzan, cousin, cozen (to trick), dozen, damson, crimson.

Labuan (Malaysian island), Don Juan, Moroccan, Monacan, Faliscan (ancient Italian language), Franciscan, escutcheon, unchristian, exhaustion, combustion, Basildon, Wimbledon, abandon, Ugandan, Clarendon, Abingdon, Hillingdon, Huntingdon, toboggan, Aragon, paragon, tarragon, suffragan (assistant bishop), martagon (Eurasian lily), Monaghan (Irish county), downfallen (dilapidated), chapfallen (dejected), crestfallen, gonfalon (banner), mamelon (small rounded hillock), ortolan (small bird), biathlon, decathlon, pentathlon, uncommon, discommon (legal term), Roscommon (Irish county), husbandman, Orangeman, patrolman, stableman, nobleman, middleman, rifleman, signalman, muscleman, cattleman, gentleman, midshipman, policeman, businessman, serviceman, warehouseman, Englishman, Irishman, aircraftman, merchantman (merchant ship), harvestman (arachnid), talisman, exciseman, ombudsman, backwoodsman, Lebanon, reopen, half-open, Saharan, Anderson, Jefferson, Emerson, Saracen, Paterson, Peterson, Richardson, Nicholson, Mendelssohn, Williamson, Robinson, Dickinson, Atkinson, Stephenson, pincushion, infarction, decoction (medicinal preparation), concoction, intinction (part of Communion), distinction, extinction, emulsion, repulsion, propulsion, impulsion, compulsion, expulsion, revulsion, divulsion (tearing apart), avulsion (forcible separation), convulsion, pre-emption, redemption, exemption, occasion, equation, abrasion, pervasion, evasion, invasion, persuasion, dissuasion, quieten, Pinkerton, charlatan, tarlatan (cotton fabric), Sheraton, Chatterton, Chesterton, doubleton (bridge term), subaltern, Shackleton, Middleton, singleton, Hamilton, simpleton, Edmonton, Bebington, Tarkington (US novelist), Arlington (Virginian county), Darlington, Ellington (US jazz musician), Wellington, Burlington, Islington, Leamington, Lymington, Warrington, Accrington, Washington, Whittington, Lexington (US city), Kensington, Northampton, Southampton, Augustan, Palmerston, autochthon (country's earliest-known inhabitant), Carmarthen, cordovan (fine leather), Donovan, Amazon.

inescutcheon (heraldic term), Muhammadan, solenodon (shrew-like mammal), Tutankhamen, Landeshauptmann (Austrian state governor), polyhedron, rhombohedron, decahedron, tetrahedron, octahedron, hexahedron, rhododendron, philodendron (climbing plant), hobson-jobson (folk etymolo-gy), Wolverhampton, Aldermaston, Saskatchewan, Elizabethan.

261.1

crayon, Malayan, Ghanaian, Pompeian.

261.2

Ian, aeon, Behan (Irish writer), peon (Spanish-American farm labourer), paeon (metrical foot), paean (song of praise), Archaean (geology term), Judaean, Andean, Pandean (relating to Pan), Aegean, Fijian, Augean (very dirty), Crimean, Tarpeian, lyncean (resembling a lynx), protean (variable in form).

amoebaean, Caribbean, Hebridean, Sisyphean (endless and futile), herculean, Coeur de Lion, Ponce de León (Spanish explorer), Pyrenean, Cyclopean (architectural term), European, empyrean (relating to the heavens).

antipodean, epicurean.

261.2.1

plebeian, Jacobean, Maccabean, scarabaean (type of beetle).

261.2.2

spelaean (relating to caves), Achillean, Galilean.

261.2.3

Korean, Terpsichorean, Pythagorean.

261.2.4

Odyssean, Laodicean.

261.3

Ian, lien (legal term).

Serbian (language group), Nubian, Albion, lesbian, guardian, Freudian, Scandian (Scandinavian), Mandaean (member of Iraqi sect), Indian, saffian (tanned leather), Orphean, ruffian, galleon, talion (making punishment fit crime), Caerleon (Welsh town), Bodleian, Anglian, ganglion, Wesleyan, camion (lorry), Samian (relating to Samos), Permian, thermion (high-temperature electron), amnion, Jungian, apian (relating to bees), scorpion, campion, champion, lampion (oil-burning lamp), pampean (relating to pampas), rampion (Eurasian plant), Grampian, tampion (plug for gun's muzzle), Caspian, Thespian, Syrian, Tyrian (relating to ancient Tyre), Zyrian (language group), quarrian (Australian bird), Cambrian, Adrian, Hadrian, Cyprian, Bactrian, Austrian, basion (anatomy term), hessian, Ossian (legendary Irish bard), Lucian (ancient Greek writer), halcyon, Haitian, Gratian (Roman emperor), bastion, Parthian, pantheon, Scythian, Pythian (relating to Delphi), Lothian, Latvian, Marxian.

Columbian, Lamarckian, Noachian (relating to Noah), selachian (zoology term), batrachian (amphibian), Pickwickian, Gulbenkian (British industrialist), Algonquian (language group), Comanchean, accordion, Edwardian, cerulean (deep blue), Bohemian, anthemion (ancient Greek floral design), acromion (part of shoulder blade), Hibernian, quaternion (maths term), Mancunian, Neptunian, Olympian, Tocharian (member of Asian culture), Amphitryon (Greek mythological character), pedestrian, equestrian, Circassian, etesian (relating to Mediterranean winds), Gilbertian, nemertean (ribbon-like marine worm), amphictyon (ancient Greek religious councillor), Atlantean, Carpathian, Promethean (creative or original), Erechtheion (temple on Acropolis), Midlothian, Venusian, Carthusian (Roman Catholic monk), Malthusian (relating to population theory), Dickensian.

ornithischian (zoology term), Appalachian, Amerindian, Christadelphian, theologian, Carolingian (Frankish dynasty), Merovingian (Frankish dynasty), Liverpudlian, epilimnion (upper layer in lake), hypolimnion (bottom layer in lake), Mississippian, Alexandrian, mitochondrion (microscopic structure in cell), salientian (type of amphibian), demibastion (type of fortification), Yugoslavian, Czechoslovakian.

261.3.1
Fabian, gabion (stone-filled cylinder), Arabian.

261.3.2
Gibeon (ancient Palestinian town), Libyan, amphibian.

261.3.3
radian, Arcadian, circadian (relating to biological rhythm), Orcadian (relating to the Orkneys), Acadian (French settler in Canada), gammadion (swastika), Canadian, steradian (unit in geometry).

261.3.4
median, tragedian, comedian, Archimedean.

261.3.5
Gideon, Midian (biblical nation), ophidian (snake-like), viridian (green pigment), meridian, ascidian (tiny marine animal), obsidian (volcanic rock), quotidian, Dravidian (language group), solifidian (relating to religious doctrine), nullifidian (sceptic), postmeridian, proboscidean (zoology term), antemeridian.

261.3.6
Rhodian (relating to Rhodes), melodeon (small accordion), collodion (syrupy liquid), custodian, nickelodeon.

261.3.7 [see also **261.37**]
Phrygian, Stygian (relating to river Styx), Ogygian (extremely ancient), callipygian (having shapely buttocks), Cantabrigian, crossopterygian (bony fish), malacopterygian (soft-finned fish), acanthopterygian (spiny-finned fish).

261.3.8
alien, Salian (relating to Frankish group), Deucalion (Greek mythological character), mammalian, Pygmalion, Australian, bacchanalian, sesquipedalian (using very long words), episcopalian.

261.3.9 [see also **261.119**]
Sabellian (extinct language group), Orwellian, Cromwellian, Machiavellian.

261.3.10
Pelion (Greek mountain), Caelian (ancient Roman hill), parhelion (meteorology term), aphelion (point in planet's orbit), anthelion (meteorology term), chameleon, carnelian (gemstone), Aurelian (Roman emperor), Mingrelian (language group), perihelion (point in planet's orbit), Aristotelian.

261.3.11 [see also **261.120**]
Ilion (Greek name for Troy), skillion (*Austral* lean-to), Gillian, penillion (Welsh sung poetry), epyllion (miniature epic poem), caecilian (limbless amphibian), Sicilian, Quintilian (Roman teacher), reptilian, Castilian (relating to Castile), Abbevillian (archaeological period), Basilian (Eastern Christian monk), Brazilian, crocodilian, Maximilian, lacertilian (lizard), vaudevillian.

261.3.12
Aeolian, Mongolian, Napoleon, Anatolian (language group).

261.3.13
scullion, mullion, Tertullian (Carthaginian Christian theologian), slubberdegullion (slovenly person).

261.3.14
Simeon, simian (resembling a monkey), Endymion, prosimian (zoology term).

261.3.15
Albanian, vulcanian (volcanic), Jordanian, Rumanian, Tasmanian, Iranian, Uranian, Ukrainian, Lithuanian, Panamanian, Transylvanian, Pennsylvanian.

261.3.15.1
Pomeranian, subterranean, Mediterranean.

261.3.16
Fenian (19th-century Irish revolutionary), Armenian, Tyrrhenian (part of Mediterranean), sirenian (zoology term), Ruthenian (language group), Athenian.

261.3.17 [see also **261.122**]
inion (point on skull), Sardinian, Arminian, Socinian (relating to religious doctrine), Justinian (Byzantine emperor), Darwinian, Carthaginian, Valentinian (Roman emperor), Augustinian.

261.3.18
gonion (anatomy term), chthonian (relating to the underworld), aeonian (everlasting), Ionian, Draconian, Franconian (language group), gorgonian (type of coral), chelonian (tortoise or turtle), Johnsonian, Smithsonian, Shoshonean (language group), Etonian, Plutonian (infernal), Newtonian, Miltonian, Estonian (language group), Devonian, favonian (relating to west wind), Oxonian, Caledonian, Macedonian, Aberdonian, Babylonian, Apollonian, Thessalonian, Ciceronian (eloquent), Hambletonian (breed of horse), Amazonian, Lacedaemonian (Spartan).

261.3.19
Fallopian, Utopian, Ethiopian.

261.3.20
carrion, clarion, Marian, orpharion (large lute).

261.3.21
Arian, Darien (part of Panama), Parian (relating to fine marble).

barbarian, Icarian (relating to Icarus), cnidarian (zoology term), Bulgarian, vulgarian (vulgar person), Hungarian, valerian (Eurasian plant), grammarian, planarian (non-parasitic flatworm), riparian, librarian, agrarian, fruitarian (person eating only fruit), Rotarian, sectarian, ovarian, Bavarian, Caesarean, rosarian (person who cultivates roses).

apiarian (relating to beekeeping), Rastafarian, sertularian (zoology term), antiquarian, Sabbatarian (strict observer of Sabbath), libertarian (believer in free thought).

abecedarian (person learning the alphabet), infralapsarian (theology term), supralapsarian (theology term), parliamentarian.

261.3.21.1
millenarian (relating to a thousand), seminarian (student at seminary), centenarian, octogenarian, nonagenarian, quinquagenarian, quadragenarian, sexagenarian, disciplinarian, veterinarian, predestinarian (believer in predestination), valetudinarian (chronically-sick person), latitudinarian (permitting religious freedom), septuagenarian.

261.3.21.2
vegetarian, proletarian, limitarian, sanitarian (relating to sanitation), Trinitarian (believer in the Trinity), unitarian, egalitarian, totalitarian, utilitarian, futilitarian, humanitarian, communitarian (member of communist community), ubiquitarian (believer in Christ's omnipresence), authoritarian.

261.3.22
Pierian (relating to the Muses), Iberian, Siberian, Nigerian, Algerian, Cimmerian (very dark), Sumerian (ancient Babylonian), Wagnerian, Hyperion, Shakespearean, Chaucerian, criterion, eutherian (zoology term), mezereon (Eurasian shrub), presbyterian, prototherian (zoology term), metatherian (marsupial), Hanoverian.

261.3.23
chorion (embryonic membrane), Dorian (ancient Greek), morion (16th-century helmet), saurian (resembling a lizard), Gregorian, Victorian, stento-

rian (extremely loud-voiced), historian, Hyperborean (inhabitant of extreme north), Hypodorian (musical term), prehistorian.

261.3.24
turion (plant bud), durian (Asian tree), Ben-Gurion, tellurian (relating to the earth), tellurion (model showing earth's movement), Silurian, decurion (Roman councillor), pagurian (hermit crab), centurion, Arthurian, Khachaturian (Russian composer), holothurian (sea cucumber).

261.3.25
Umbrian (extinct language group), Cumbrian, Northumbrian.

261.3.26
Lancastrian, Zoroastrian.

261.3.27
fustian, Procrustean (producing conformity ruthlessly).

261.3.28
Corinthian, labyrinthian, pericynthion (point in lunar orbit), apocynthion (point in lunar orbit).

261.3.29
avian, Shavian, subclavian, Moravian, Octavian, Scandinavian.

261.3.30
Vivian, Bolivian, oblivion.

261.3.31
Jovian, Harrovian.

261.3.32
alluvion (overflow), Peruvian, vesuvian (match for lighting cigars), postdiluvian (existing after biblical Flood), antediluvian.

261.3.33
nasion (point on skull), Caucasian, Malaysian, Vespasian, Rabelaisian.

261.3.34 [see also **261.90**]
artesian, Cartesian (relating to Descartes), Polynesian, Indonesian, Melanesian.

261.3.35 [see also **261.91**]
Elysian, Parisian, Dionysian.

261.4
ion, iron, lion, Mayan, Ryan, Brian,
scion, Zion, sadiron (heavy iron), midiron (golf club), gridiron, andiron (log-
stand in fireplace), antlion (tropical insect), anion, cation, flatiron, Hawaiian,
dandelion.

261.4.1
Orion, zwitterion (charged particle).

261.5
doyen, Illinoisan, Iroquoian (American
Indian language).

261.6
lowan (Australian bird), rowan, Caddoan (language group), Minoan, dipnoan (lungfish), bryozoan (colonial
aquatic animal), hydrozoan (small
aquatic animal), sporozoan (microscopic parasitic animal), protozoan (microscopic animal).

261.7
Papuan, gargantuan.

261.8
Schwaben (region of West Germany),
carbon, graben (trough of land),
hydrocarbon, radiocarbon.

261.9
urban, bourbon, Durban, turban, suburban.

261.10
Aachen, darken, hearken, kraken (legendary sea monster), Interlaken.

261.11
bacon, shaken, taken, waken, Jamaican, forsaken, unshaken, mistaken,
awaken, godforsaken, undertaken,
overtaken.

261.12
beacon, deacon, weaken, subdeacon,
archdeacon, Mohican.

261.13
quicken, stricken, sicken, thicken, Barbican, Rubicon, indican (chemical
compound), Helicon (Greek mountain), helicon (bass tuba), pelican, Millikan (US physicist), silicon, publican,
Anglican, pemmican (American Indian
food), salpicon (chopped food in
sauce), hurricane, African, Corsican,
Vatican, lexicon, Mexican, catholicon
(remedy for all diseases), republican,
Dominican, pantechnicon (large van),
American, ferrosilicon (iron–silicon alloy), stereopticon (type of projector).

261.14
oaken, spoken, broken, token, woken,
Hoboken (Belgian city), unspoken,
outspoken, unbroken, heartbroken, betoken, ryokan (traditional Japanese
inn).

261.15
Lucan, toucan, lebkuchen (German
biscuit), Chinookan (American Indian
language).

261.16
Balkan, falcon, gyrfalcon (large rare
falcon).

261.17
Tuscan, Etruscan.

261.18
question, digestion, suggestion, ingestion, congestion, indigestion, autosuggestion.

261.19
gladden, madden, sadden, Ibadan
(Nigerian city), Abaddon (the devil).

261.20
Aden, Aidan, laden, Blaydon (English
town), maiden, menhaden (US fish),
unladen, handmaiden.

261.21
deaden, leaden, redden, Armageddon.

261.22
burden, guerdon (reward), lurdan (stupid), unburden, disburden.

261.23
Eden, Sweden, boustrophedon (relating to writing method), cotyledon, dicotyledon, acotyledon, monocotyledon.

261.24
bidden, hidden, midden (*Dialect* rubbish heap), ridden, forbidden, unbidden, oppidan (urban), harridan, Sheridan, bedridden, Mohammedan, parallelepipedon (geometric solid).

261.25
guidon (small military flag), Haydn, Leiden (Dutch city), Dryden, Sidon (Phoenician city), widen, Poseidon.

261.26
hodden (coarse cloth), Flodden (Northumbrian battlefield), modern, trodden, sodden, Culloden (Scottish battlefield), downtrodden, untrodden, ultramodern.

261.27
Auden, cordon, Gordon, Jordan, broaden, warden, firewarden (*US* fire-prevention officer), churchwarden.

261.28
olden, golden, soldan (archaic word for sultan), embolden, beholden.

261.29
griffon, stiffen, antiphon (response).

261.30
flagon, dragon, wagon, pendragon (leader of ancient Britons), snapdragon, bandwagon.

261.31
pagan, Reagan, Nijmegen (Dutch town), Copenhagen.

261.32
Wigan, cardigan, Milligan, mulligan (*US* a stew), hooligan, ptarmigan, larrigan (leather moccasin boot), perigon (angle of 360°), origan (marjoram), Oregon, balbriggan (unbleached cotton fabric), Michigan, Rattigan (English dramatist), shenanigan.

261.33
organ, Gorgon, Morgan, Glamorgan, Demogorgon (mythological god).

261.34
Trajan (Roman emperor), contagion.

261.35
burgeon, gurjun (Asian tree), surgeon, sturgeon, neurosurgeon.

261.36
legion, region, collegian, subregion, Norwegian, Glaswegian.

261.37 [see also **261.3.7**]
smidgen, pigeon, wigeon (Eurasian duck), religion, florigen (hypothetical plant hormone), Harijan (Indian untouchable), cultigen (cultivated plant), antigen, oxygen, irreligion.

261.38
dudgeon, gudgeon, bludgeon, trudgen (swimming stroke), curmudgeon (surly person).

261.39
biogen (hypothetical protein), cryogen (freezing mixture), habergeon (coat of mail), thrombogen (protein), allergen, halogen, glycogen (biochemical compound), phellogen (cork-producing cells), collagen, zymogen (enzyme precursor), chromogen (chemical compound), pyrogen (substance causing fever), acrogen (type of flowerless plant), hydrogen, androgen, nitrogen, oestrogen, mutagen (substance causing mutation), histogen (plant tissue), pathogen, fibrinogen (blood protein), carcinogen, pepsinogen (enzyme), trypsinogen (enzyme), hallucinogen.

261.40
felon, melon, Magellan, muskmelon (type of melon), pademelon (small wallaby), watermelon.

261.41
billon (alloy used for coins), Dylan, villain, villein, Babylon, Macmillan, castellan (keeper of castle), abutilon (flowering shrub).

261.42
pollen, pollan (whitefish), Hohenzollern (German noble family).

261.43
colon, Nolan, Solon (Athenian statesman), stolen, stollen (rich sweet bread), stolon (horizontal plant stem), swollen, semicolon.

261.44
Ammon (biblical character), gammon, mammon, salmon, shaman (Asian priest), backgammon.

261.45
cayman (US crocodile), layman, Bremen, highwayman, railwayman.

261.46
airman, chairman, repairman.

261.47
demon, he-man, freeman, seaman, eudemon (benevolent spirit), pentstemon (US plant), Lacedaemon (Sparta), cacodemon (evil spirit).

261.48
handyman, bogeyman, clergyman, tallyman, journeyman, dairyman, quarryman, juryman, laundryman, nurseryman, poultryman, countryman, Everyman, persimmon (tropical tree), cavalryman, infantryman, committeeman, artilleryman.

261.49
omen, bowman (archer), foeman, snowman, Roman, showman, yeoman, locoman (engine-driver), dragoman (professional interpreter).

261.50
woman, charwoman, churchwoman, horsewoman, sportswoman, batwoman, townswoman, washerwoman, needlewoman, gentlewoman.

261.51
Truman, Schumann, Yuman (language group), human, Newman, subhuman, inhuman, ichneumon (mongoose), superhuman.

261.52
Turkoman (Asian people), Inkerman (Crimean battle site), Betjeman, trencherman (hearty eater), spiderman, abdomen, ealdorman (Anglo-Saxon judicial official), alderman, landammann (Swiss council chairman), telamon (supporting pillar), Solomon, colourman (person dealing in paints), cyclamen, cinnamon, Chinaman, superman, cameraman, ataman (leader of the Cossacks), peterman (*Slang* safe-breaker), ottoman, slaughterman (slaughterhouse employee), waterman (skilled boatman), motorman (electric-train driver), Ulsterman, weatherman, remainderman (legal term), newspaperman.

261.52.1
fisherman, militiaman.

261.53
chessman, desman (small amphibious mammal), pressman, yes-man, Congressman.

261.54
steersman, frontiersman.

261.55
cannon, canon, fanon (papal vestment), Shannon, Buchanan, colcannon (boiled cabbage and potatoes), Clackmannan.

261.56
finnan, noumenon (philosophy term), phenomenon, prolegomenon (critical introduction).

261.57
capon, unshapen, misshapen.

261.58
Byron, Myron (Greek sculptor), siren, environ, lepidosiren (South American fish).

261.59
Huron, aleurone (protein), macruran (type of crustacean), Van Buren (US president), anuran (tailless amphibian),

brachyuran (type of crustacean), thysanuran (primitive wingless insect).

261.60
longeron (part of aircraft), cateran (former Scottish brigand), Lateran (Roman palace), veteran, Lutheran, Aldebaran (star), poriferan (a sponge), erigeron (flowering plant), cladoceran (tiny freshwater animal), hemipteran (type of insect), chiropteran (relating to bats), orthopteran (type of insect).

261.61
arson, Carson, fasten, parson, sarsen (sandstone boulder), unfasten.

261.62
basin, caisson (watertight structure), chasten, Jason, hasten, mason, washbasin, freemason, stonemason.

261.63
lesson, lessen, delicatessen.

261.64
person, worsen, Macpherson, unperson.

261.65
listen, glisten, Nissen, christen, gambeson (medieval padded garment), Addison, Madison, Edison, Tennyson, venison, unison, Morrison, jettison, cavesson (horse's noseband), diocesan, archdiocesan.

261.65.1
garrison, Harrison, parison (unshaped glass before moulding), warison (bugle note ordering attack), caparison (horse's decorated covering), comparison.

261.66
ashen, fashion, passion, ration, impassion, compassion, dispassion, deration.

261.67
Asian, nation, station.

striation, Croatian (language group), libation, vacation, plication (folding), truncation, laudation (praise), foundation, purgation, lallation (speech defect), dilation, collation, ablation, oblation (religious offering), deflation, reflation, stagflation (economics term), inflation, translation, squamation (formation of scales), formation, summation, Dalmatian, planation (erosion of land surface), vernation (leaf arrangement in bud), venation (arrangement of veins), zonation, lunation (lunar month), damnation, crispation (curling), serration, gyration, oration, libration (oscillating), vibration, migration, titration, filtration, castration, prostration, frustration, cassation (legal term), cessation, Alsatian, pulsation, flirtation, fetation (state of pregnancy), citation, dictation, lactation, saltation (biology term), temptation, gustation (tasting), crustacean, substation, outstation, lavation (washing), starvation, nivation (geology term), privation, ovation, novation (legal term), salvation, solvation (chemistry term), fixation, causation.

conurbation, incubation, titubation, education, inculcation, coruscation (gleam of light), retardation, denudation, exudation, inundation, subjugation, conjugation, promulgation, elongation, prolongation, insolation (exposure to solar radiation), contemplation, legislation, deformation, preformation, malformation, conformation, exhumation, subornation, indignation, assignation, designation, resignation, condemnation, usurpation, occupation, syncopation, aspiration, inspiration, expiration, lucubration (laborious study), desecration, consecration, dehydration, conflagration, arbitration, penetration, infiltration, concentration, orchestration, sequestration, illustration, demonstration, conversation, deportation, importation, transportation, exportation, exhortation, exploitation, affectation, delectation, expectation, eructation (belching), exaltation, exultation, auscultation, consultation, supplantation, implantation, transplantation, confrontation, presentation, coaptation (reuniting two surfaces), acceptation, adaptation, forestation, devastation, salivation, elevation, derivation, deprivation, titivation, motivation, activation, cultivation, captivation, aestivation (biology term), excavation, renovation, innovation, aggravation, depravation, conservation, reservation, preservation, observation, accusation.

coeducation, interlunation (period of moon's invisibility), preoccupation, intermigration, superfetation (medical term), preadaptation (biology term).

261.67.1
creation, radiation, mediation, lineation (outline), expiation, variation, recreation, re-creation, procreation, fasciation (abnormal flattening of stems), aviation.

irradiation, repudiation, retaliation, delineation, columniation (arrangement of architectural columns), inebriation, appropriation, repatriation, expatriation, dissociation, association, expatiation, ingratiation, depreciation, appreciation, negotiation, substantiation, asphyxiation.

transubstantiation, consubstantiation, differentiation.

261.67.1.1
filiation (lineage), affiliation, humiliation, conciliation, disaffiliation, reconciliation.

261.67.1.2
foliation, spoliation, defoliation, despoliation.

261.67.1.3
caseation (formation of cheese), glaciation, emaciation.

261.67.1.4
enunciation, denunciation, renunciation, annunciation, pronunciation, mispronunciation.

261.67.1.5
vitiation, officiation, initiation.

261.67.1.6
deviation, abbreviation, alleviation.

261.67.2
menstruation, arcuation (arrangement of arches), graduation, valuation, situation, fluctuation, punctuation, invultuation (making images for witchcraft), evacuation, evaluation, devaluation, revaluation, attenuation, insinuation, continuation, infatuation, perpetuation, accentuation, superannuation.

261.67.3
probation, approbation, reprobation, perturbation, masturbation, disapprobation, exacerbation.

261.67.4
embarkation, demarcation, disembarkation.

261.67.5
dedication, medication, claudication (lameness), abdication, indication, vindication, defecation, publication, application, replication, supplication, duplication, implication, complication, explication, formication (skin sensation), fornication, fabrication, lubrication, imprecation, metrication, mastication.

eradication, adjudication, multiplication, reduplication, communication, prevarication, domestication, sophistication, prognostication, intoxication.

excommunication, intercommunication, telecommunication.

261.67.5.1 [further rhymes may be derived from 7.3]
modification, qualification, ramification, classification, specification, fortifi-

cation, notification, justification, electrification, identification.

261.67.6
location, vocation, bifurcation, suffocation, allocation, collocation, dislocation, embrocation, altercation, evocation, revocation, provocation, advocation, invocation, convocation, equivocation.

261.67.7
predation, sedation, validation, trepidation, cuspidation (architectural term), liquidation, fluoridation, depredation, oxidation, consolidation, intimidation, dilapidation, elucidation.

261.67.8
gradation, backwardation (stock exchange term), degradation, accommodation, biodegradation.

261.67.9
emendation, commendation, recommendation.

261.67.10
legation (diplomatic mission), negation, allegation, delegation, relegation, obligation, fumigation, denegation (denial), abnegation, irrigation, segregation, congregation, litigation, mitigation, castigation, instigation, navigation, desegregation, investigation, circumnavigation.

261.67.11
rogation, propagation, expurgation, abrogation (official cancellation), subrogation (legal term), interrogation.

261.67.12
elation, gelation (freezing), relation.

strobilation (type of asexual reproduction), jubilation, alkylation (chemistry term), flagellation, congelation, appellation, cupellation (metallurgical process), compilation, correlation, fibrillation, vacillation, tessellation, oscillation, cancellation, titillation, scutellation (arrangement of animal's scales), mutilation, ventilation, scintillation, distillation, constellation.

invigilation, dissimilation, assimilation, horripilation (gooseflesh), interrelation.

malassimilation, hyperventilation.

261.67.13
serrulation (notch), gastrulation (embryology term), tribulation, maculation (spotted pattern), speculation, circulation, calculation, adulation, osculation (maths term), modulation, undulation, regulation, emulation, gemmulation (type of asexual reproduction), formulation, cumulation, annulation (formation of rings), granulation, copulation, population, insulation, postulation, ovulation.

perambulation, ejaculation, vermiculation, matriculation, articulation, denticulation (finely-toothed structure), gesticulation, inoculation, miscalculation, emasculation, demodulation (electronics term), coagulation, accumulation, capitulation, expostulation, recapitulation.

261.67.13.1
tabulation, confabulation, tintinnabulation.

261.67.13.2
angulation, strangulation, triangulation.

261.67.13.3
simulation, stimulation, dissimulation.

261.67.13.4
stipulation, manipulation.

261.67.14
halation (photography term), spallation (nuclear physics reaction), vallation (construction of fortifications), escalation, inhalation, exhalation, immolation, desolation, isolation, consolation, installation, revelation, de-escalation, extrapolation, interpolation, contravallation (fortifications built by besiegers).

261.67.14.1
violation, annihilation.

261.67.15
cremation, sublimation, animation, lacrimation (secretion of tears), decimation, intimation, estimation, approximation, underestimation, overestimation.

261.67.16
affirmation, defamation, reformation, information, confirmation, transformation, acclamation, declamation, reclamation, proclamation, exclamation, inflammation, consummation, automation, misinformation, amalgamation.

261.67.17
carnation, tarnation, incarnation, reincarnation.

261.67.18
crenation (biology term), ruination, combination, machination, pollination, declination, inclination, culmination, fulmination, chlorination, urination, destination, divination, vaccination, recombination, miscegenation (interbreeding of races), desalination, disinclination, insemination, peregrination, indoctrination, hallucination, concatenation (series of interconnected events), agglutination, procrastination, predestination, rejuvenation.

261.67.18.1
ordination, preordination, coordination, subordination, incoordination, insubordination.

261.67.18.2
pagination, imagination, invagination (infolding of tubular structure).

261.67.18.3
lamination, contamination, examination, decontamination, cross-examination.

261.67.18.4
germination, termination, vermination (infestation with vermin), determination, extermination.

261.67.18.5
elimination, recrimination, incrimination, discrimination.

261.67.18.6
commination (threatening vengeance), domination, nomination, abomination, predomination, denomination.

261.67.18.7
rumination, illumination.

261.67.18.8
fascination, assassination.

261.67.19
conation (psychology term), donation, carbonation, eburnation (degenerative condition of bone), hibernation, condonation, profanation, hyphenation, explanation, emanation, coronation, detonation, alternation, intonation, consternation, alienation, impersonation.

261.67.20
obstipation, constipation, emancipation.

261.67.20.1
dissipation, participation, anticipation.

261.67.21
Eurasian, duration, conjuration, carburation, procuration, fulguration (surgical procedure), suppuration, mensuration (measuring), maturation, trituration (grinding into fine powder), transculturation (changing an established culture), prefiguration, configuration, transfiguration, inauguration.

261.67.22
Horatian, narration.

liberation, decoration, saturation, adoration, federation, moderation, perforation, figuration, pejoration (deterioration of word's meaning), toleration, coloration, declaration, exploration, glomeration (cluster), numeration, admiration, reparation, preparation, separation, corporation, desperation, respiration, perspiration, peroration, laceration, ulceration, alteration, restoration, botheration.

melioration (improving), reverberation, deliberation, confederation, consideration, proliferation, exaggeration, refrigeration, deceleration, acceleration, exhilaration, discoloration, commemoration, agglomeration, conglomeration, enumeration, incineration, remuneration, evaporation, recuperation, vituperation, exasperation, trilateration (surveying method), expectoration, perseveration (psychology term), commiseration.

amelioration, deterioration.

261.67.22.1
aberration, collaboration.

261.67.22.2
generation, veneration, degeneration, regeneration.

261.67.22.3
operation, cooperation, disoperation (harmful association between organisms), noncooperation.

261.67.22.4
iteration, literation (representing sounds by letters), reiteration, alliteration, obliteration, transliteration.

261.67.23
calibration, celebration, cerebration (thinking), vertebration, equilibration.

261.67.24
emigration, immigration, integration, redintegration (act of renewal), disintegration.

261.67.25
registration, fenestration (arrangement of windows), ministration, defenestration (throwing person from window), administration, maladministration.

261.67.26
sensation, condensation, compensation, dispensation, aftersensation, overcompensation.

261.67.27
cetacean (whale), habitation, dubitation (doubt), meditation, agitation, vegetation, gurgitation (surging movement), imitation, limitation, sanitation, capitation, palpitation, equitation, irritation, recitation, jactitation (boasting), cavitation (physics term), gravitation, levitation, invitation, excitation, visitation.

cohabitation, premeditation, regurgitation, decapitation, precipitation, interpretation, felicitation, sollicitation, resuscitation.

prestidigitation, rehabilitation, misinterpretation.

261.67.28
dotation (endowment), flotation, notation, potation (drinking), quotation, rotation, annotation, denotation, connotation, misquotation, dextrorotation (rotation to right), laevorotation (rotation to left).

261.67.29
mutation, nutation (nodding), refutation, salutation, permutation, commutation, sternutation (sneezing), deputation, reputation, amputation, imputation, computation, disputation, transmutation.

261.67.30
natation, dilatation, dissertation, constatation (process of establishing truth).

261.67.31
plantation, recantation, incantation.

261.67.32
dentation (tooth-like projections), tentation (method of adjusting machine), indentation, lamentation, fermentation, cementation, fomentation, fragmenta-

tion, segmentation, pigmentation, augmentation, frequentation, assentation (servile agreement), placentation (biology term), ostentation, sustentation (nourishment), orientation, documentation, argumentation, ornamentation, instrumentation, representation, misrepresentation.

261.67.32.1
sedimentation, regimentation, alimentation, implementation, experimentation.

261.67.33
gestation, infestation, molestation, attestation, detestation, protestation, manifestation.

261.67.34
laxation (defecation), taxation, relaxation.

261.67.35
vexation, annexation.

261.67.36 [also **516** + -ation]
sterilization, fertilization, civilization, realization, centralization, organization, dramatization, improvisation, nationalization, generalization.

261.68
freshen, session, cession.

profession, confession, discretion, degression (gradual decrease), regression, digression, aggression, progression, transgression, depression, repression, oppression, suppression, impression, compression, expression, recession, precession, secession, obsession, concession, accession, succession, possession.

indiscretion, reimpression, decompression, repossession, prepossession, self-possession, dispossession.

261.68.1
procession, supersession, intercession.

261.69
Persian, tertian (recurring every other day), version, coercion, recursion (returning), incursion, excursion, emersion (astronomy term), immersion, dispersion, aspersion, assertion, insertion, Cistercian (member of religious order), reversion, diversion, subversion, inversion, conversion, exertion, desertion, animadversion (criticism).

261.69.1
aversion, perversion, introversion, extroversion.

261.70
Rhaetian (language group), Grecian, deletion, depletion, repletion, suppletion (linguistics term), completion, Venetian, Capetian (relating to French dynasty), secretion, accretion, incretion (secretion into bloodstream), concretion, excretion, Helvetian, Diocletian (Roman emperor).

261.71
fission, mission, Titian.

coition, fruition, tuition, ambition, audition, rendition, condition, logician, magician, emission, demission, remission, submission, admission, transmission, monition (warning), munition, technician, ignition, cognition, suspicion, detrition (wearing away by friction), nutrition, contrition, partition, mortician, sortition (casting lots), beautician, tactician, dentition, optician, musician, transition.

intuition, prohibition, imbibition (absorption), inhibition, exhibition, erudition, recondition, precondition, ammunition, premunition (state of immunity), mechanician, premonition, admonition, inanition, precognition (foreknowledge), recognition, parturition, micturition, apparition, rhetorician, preterition (act of omitting), obstetrician, malnutrition, electrician, repartition, tripartition, deglutition, logistician, statistician, acoustician, superstition, Ordovician (geological period).

equipartition, mathematician, diagnostician.

261.71.1
edition, sedition, expedition.

261.71.2
addition, perdition, tradition, extradition.

261.71.3
volition, coalition, abolition, ebullition, demolition.

261.71.4
omission, commission, Domitian (Roman emperor), permission, intromission (insertion or introduction), intermission, academician.

261.71.5
Phoenician, clinician, definition.

261.71.6
attrition, patrician, paediatrician, geriatrician.

261.71.7
petition, dietitian, politician, cosmetician, phonetician, repetition, competition, aesthetician, theoretician.

261.71.8
physician, acquisition, requisition, inquisition, disquisition (formal discourse), metaphysician.

261.71.9
position, apposition, deposition, preposition, reposition, opposition, proposition, supposition, malposition, imposition, composition, disposition, transposition, exposition, presupposition, juxtaposition, decomposition, predisposition, indisposition.

261.72
caution, portion, torsion, abortion, precaution, retortion (retorting), retorsion (reprisal), intorsion (spiral twisting), contortion, distortion, extortion.

261.72.1
apportion, proportion, disproportion.

261.73
ocean, Goshen (region of ancient Egypt), lotion, motion, notion, potion, groschen (Austrian coin), emotion, demotion, devotion.

261.73.1
promotion, commotion, locomotion.

261.74
Russian, Prussian, percussion, concussion, discussion, repercussion, Byelorussian.

261.75
crucian (European fish), dilution, ablution, Confucian, Rosicrucian, attribution, retribution, contribution, distribution, persecution, prosecution, consecution (sequence of events), execution, diminution, Lilliputian, destitution, restitution, prostitution, substitution, institution, constitution.

261.75.1
pollution, solution, volution (spiral motion), dissolution, absolution, revolution, evolution, devolution, involution (complication), convolution, resolution, circumvolution (turning around central axis), irresolution, counterrevolution.

261.75.2
locution, perlocution (philosophy term), allocution (formal speech), elocution, illocution (philosophy term), interlocution (conversation), circumlocution, electrocution.

261.76
action, faction, fraction, traction.

reaction, inaction, diffraction, refraction, detraction, retraction, attraction, protraction, subtraction, contraction, distraction, abstraction, extraction, exaction, transaction.

abreaction (psychiatry term), retroaction, tumefaction (swelling), benefaction, stupefaction, liquefaction, rarefaction, petrifaction, putrefaction, satisfaction, interaction, dissatisfaction.

261.77
lection (variation in text), flexion, section.

defection, refection, affection, perfection, infection, confection, ejection, dejection, rejection, objection, subjection, injection, bolection (architectural term), collection, deflection, reflection, inflection, complexion, connection, inspection, bisection, subsection, midsection, detection, protection, evection (irregularity in moon's motion), advection (heat transfer in air), convection.

imperfection, disinfection, recollection, retroflexion, genuflection, retrospection, introspection, intersection, overprotection.

261.77.1
projection, introjection (psychology term), interjection.

261.77.2
election, selection, re-election, predilection, intellection (thought).

261.77.3
erection, direction, indirection, misdirection.

261.77.4
correction, insurrection, resurrection.

261.77.5
dissection, resection (surgical removal of part), venesection (incision into vein), vivisection.

261.78
diction, fiction, friction, nonfiction, affliction, depiction, restriction, constriction, eviction, conviction, jurisdiction, crucifixion, dereliction, derestriction.

261.78.1
prediction, malediction, valediction, benediction.

261.78.2
addiction, contradiction, interdiction (prohibition).

261.79
fluxion, ruction, suction, eduction (exhaust stroke of engine), deduction, reduction, seduction, abduction, induction, conduction, transduction (genetics term), destruction, obstruction, instruction, construction, solifluction (downhill soil movement), reconstruction, misconstruction (false interpretation).

261.79.1
adduction, production, reproduction, introduction, underproduction.

261.80
unction, function, junction, malfunction, dysfunction, injunction, conjunction, disjunction, inunction (rubbing ointment into skin), compunction.

261.81
scansion, mansion, stanchion (support), expansion.

261.82
gentian, mention, pension, tension.

indention (indentation), declension, dimension, suspension, Lawrentian, ascension, detention, retention, pretension, intention, contention, abstention, extension, prevention, subvention, invention, convention.

hypotension, contravention, intervention, circumvention.

261.82.1
prehension (act of grasping), apprehension, reprehension, comprehension, misapprehension, incomprehension.

261.82.2
dissension, recension (critical literary revision), condescension.

261.82.3
attention, inattention, hypertension.

261.83
caption, recaption (legal term), contraption.

261.84
obreption (obtaining by deceit), subreption (concealment of facts), deception, reception, subception (subliminal perception), inception, conception, exception, self-deception, preconception, misconception.

261.84.1
perception, apperception (psychology term), contraception, intussusception (medical term).

261.85
Egyptian, conniption (*US* fit of rage), description, prescription, proscription, ascription, subscription, transcription, inscription, conscription, circumscription, teletranscription (video recording).

261.86
option, adoption.

261.87
sorption (adsorption or absorption), absorption, adsorption, desorption (chemistry term), chemisorption (chemistry term).

261.88
eruption, corruption, abruption (breaking off), disruption, interruption.

261.89
gumption, assumption, subsumption (inclusion under general heading), consumption, resumption, presumption.

261.90 [see also **261.3.34**]
lesion, Friesian, Ephesian, cohesion, adhesion, inhesion (inherence).

261.91 [see also **261.3.35**]
Frisian (language of Netherlands), scission, vision, elision, collision, derision, misprision (concealment of treasonable act), abscission (shedding of plant parts), incision, concision, envision, excision, circumcision.

261.91.1
decision, recision (cancellation), precision, precisian (strict observer of rules), indecision, imprecision.

261.91.2
division, revision, prevision, subdivision, television.

261.91.3
provision, Eurovision, supervision, stereovision.

261.92
plosion (phonetics term), eclosion (emergence of insect), implosion (collapsing inwards), explosion, erosion, corrosion.

261.93
fusion, allusion, collusion, prolusion (preliminary written exercise), seclusion, occlusion, inclusion, conclusion, exclusion, protrusion, obtrusion, intrusion, extrusion, effusion, diffusion, affusion (method of baptism), profusion, infusion, confusion, transfusion, contusion, malocclusion (dentistry term).

261.93.1
illusion, delusion, disillusion.

261.94
batten, fatten, latten (thin sheet metal), flatten, platan (plane tree), platen (plate in printing press), slattern, pattern, patten (wooden clog), Patton (US general), paten (silver or gold plate), Grattan, Mountbatten, Manhattan, harmattan.

261.95
Barton, carton, hearten, smarten, partan (*Scot* crab), Spartan, tartan, Dumbarton, dishearten, kindergarten, Akhenaten (Egyptian king), sauerbraten (German beef dish).

261.96
jetton (gambling token), Breton, threaten, Tibetan.

261.97
Burton, burton, curtain, Merton, certain, uncertain.

261.98
Eton, eaten, beaten, Keaton, neaten, Cretan, Seaton, wheaten, sweeten, unbeaten, Nuneaton, weather-beaten.

261.99
bittern, bitten, kitten, mitten, smitten, written, Britain, Briton, Britten, witan (Anglo-Saxon advisory council), frostbitten, skeleton, Honiton, puritan, handwritten, unwritten, Mahometan, Samaritan, endoskeleton, exoskeleton, Neapolitan, cosmopolitan, metropolitan.

261.100
chiton (ancient Greek tunic), heighten, lighten, righten (return to normal position), Brighton, brighten, Crichton, frighten, Triton (Greek sea god), triton (marine mollusc), tighten, Titan, whiten, enlighten.

261.101
cotton, gotten, rotten, guncotton, begotten, forgotten, ill-gotten, misbegotten, unforgotten.

261.102
boughten (*Dialect* bought), Laughton, Morton, quartern (measure of weight), quartan (recurring every third day), shorten, tauten, foreshorten.

261.103
button, glutton, mutton, Sutton, unbutton, bellybutton.

261.104
Luton, gluten, Newton, Teuton (member of Germanic people), rambutan (Asian tree).

261.105
Minton, quintan (recurring every fourth day), badminton.

261.106
Preston, teston (former French silver coin), western, Avestan (ancient language).

261.107
piston, Tristan, cistern, Ilkeston (English town), Eddystone, Germiston (South African city), Coniston, sacristan.

261.108
Kingston, Livingstone.

261.109
Phaëthon (Greek mythological character), Jonathan, marathon, leviathan (biblical sea monster).

261.110
carven, Cuxhaven (West German port), Caernarvon.

261.111
Avon, haven, raven, craven, graven, shaven, Newhaven, clean-shaven, unshaven.

261.112
Bevan (British statesman), Devon, heaven, leaven, Severn, seven, Midheaven (astrology term), eleven.

261.113
even, Leven (Scottish loch), Stephen, Genevan, uneven.

261.114
given, Niven, riven, driven, forgiven, Sullivan, unforgiven.

261.115
Ivan, liven, wyvern (heraldic beast), enliven.

261.116
cloven, woven, Eindhoven (Dutch city), Beethoven, interwoven.

261.117
oven, bhavan (large Indian house), coven, govern, sloven, misgovern.

261.118
scallion, stallion, rapscallion, medallion, Italian, battalion.

261.119 [see also **261.3.9**]

hellion (troublesome person), rebellion, Trevelyan.

261.120 [see also **261.3.11**]

billion, jillion (extremely large number), gillion (one thousand million), million, pillion, trillion, zillion, tourbillion (whirlwind), modillion (architectural ornament), vermilion, nonillion (10^{54}), carillon, quadrillion (10^{24}), decillion (10^{60}), cotillion, octillion (10^{48}), centillion (10^{600}), quintillion (10^{30}), septillion (10^{42}), postilion, sextillion (10^{36}), civilian, pavilion.

261.121

banyan, canyon, fanion (surveyor's small flag), companion.

261.122 [see also **261.3.17**]

minion, pinion, dominion, opinion.

261.123

union, reunion, communion, nonunion, intercommunion.

261.124

blazon, raisin, brazen, emblazon, diapason (organ stop).

261.125

reason, treason, season, unreason.

261.126

mizzen, risen, prison, wizen, malison (a curse), benison, denizen, orison, arisen, imprison, bartizan (small turret), partisan (a spear), citizen.

261.127

greisen (light-coloured rock), horizon, spiegeleisen (type of pig iron).

261.128

foison (plentiful supply), poison, empoison.

261.129

chosen, frozen, lederhosen.

262 -iln

kiln, Milne, limekiln.

263 -ang

bang, bhang (narcotic from Indian hemp), cangue (wooden instrument of punishment), dang, fang, gang, gangue (worthless material in ore), hang, Lang, lang (*Scot* long), clang, slang, pang, spang (*US* exactly), rang, prang, sprang, sang, Shang (Chinese dynasty), Tang (Chinese dynasty), tang, stang (*Dialect* throb with pain), vang (nautical term), whang, twang.

kiang (Tibetan wild ass), shebang, gangbang, Nanchang (Chinese city), padang (Malaysian field), Malang (Indonesian city), boomslang (venomous snake), Penang (Malaysian island and state), trepang (Oriental sea cucumber), linsang (forest-dwelling mammal), satang (Thai coin), mustang, Poyang (Chinese lake), Loyang (Chinese city), Shenyang (Chinese city), Pyongyang (capital of North Korea).

overhang, siamang (large black gibbon), navarin, Mazarin, parasang (Persian unit of distance), burrawang (Australian plant).

Heilungkiang (Chinese province), ylang-ylang (aromatic Asian tree), goreng pisang (Malaysian banana fritters), orang-outang.

263.1

probang (surgical instrument), charabanc, interrobang (punctuation mark).

263.2

harangue, meringue, Serang (Indonesian island), boomerang.

264 -eng

Kaifeng (Chinese city), ronggeng (Malay traditional dance), ginseng.

203

265 -ing [further rhymes may be created by adding *-ing* to appropriate verbs]

king, Ching (Chinese dynasty), ding, ling, cling, fling, sling, Ming, ping, wring, ring, bring, spring, string, sing, ting, sting, thing, wing, swing, zing.

gnawing, drawing, webbing, dubbing, rubbing, tubing, backing, blacking, packing, cracking, sacking, whacking, Barking, marking, parking, working, sneaking, Peking, speaking, liking, striking, Viking, smoking, soaking, Woking, ducking, fucking, trucking, sucking, booking, cooking, erlking (mythical malevolent spirit), hulking, Nanking, banking, planking, spanking, ranking, catching, etching, fetching, searching, I Ching (Chinese book of divination), teaching, breeching (harness strap), itching, stitching, witching, coaching, hoatching (*Scot* infested), poaching, scorching, touching, cladding, padding, wording, bidding, sodding, wadding, budding, pudding, gelding, balding, wingding (*US* lively party), surfing, briefing, spiffing, offing, stuffing, roofing, bagging (coarse woven cloth), lagging, flagging, rigging, frigging, wigging, edging, lodging, grudging, swingeing, curling, hurling (Irish game), sterling, Stirling, tiling, hireling, schooling, ruling, tooling, marbling, stabling, sibling, gambling, rambling, brambling (Eurasian finch), crackling, weakling, inkling, sprinkling, twinkling, reedling (Eurasian songbird), seedling, fiddling, middling, piddling, codling (variety of cooking apple), puddling (wrought-iron-making process), worldling (materialist), handling, brandling (small red earthworm), kindling, pindling (*Dialect* peevish), spindling (long and slender), foundling, groundling, rifling (grooves inside gun barrel), trifling, stifling, niggling, juggling, smuggling, angling, gangling, fledgling, changeling, green-

ling (Pacific fish), weanling, grappling, sapling, Kipling, crippling, stripling, coupling, dumpling, nestling, wrestling, nursling, brisling (Norwegian sprat), whistling, princeling, unsling, catling (surgical knife), fatling (fattened young animal), Gatling (machine-gun), rattling, footling, scantling (narrow rafter), mantling (heraldic term), firstling (first offspring), earthling, riesling, quisling (collaborator), gosling, gaming, flaming, lemming, Fleming, slimming, trimming, swimming, priming, timing, canning, planning, awning, mourning, morning, warning, browning, Liaoning (Chinese province), nooning (*US* midday break), tuning, lightning, evening, hanging, longing, mapping, wrapping, strapping, Epping, skipping, chipping, clipping, flipping, ripping, dripping, gripping, shipping, whipping, piping, typing, hopping, sopping, shopping, topping, stopping, whopping, coping, sloping, stoping (geology term), grouping, scalping, helping, camping, tamping (*Welsh* very angry), rasping, grasping, barring, sparring, herring, bullring, hairspring, headspring, handspring, offspring, mainspring, drawstring, bowstring, shoestring, hamstring, unstring, passing, nursing, piercing, icing, crossing, coursing (hunting game by sight), dancing, fencing, bouncing, flouncing (material for making flounces), dashing, lashing, flashing, smashing, crashing, thrashing, Pershing, washing, Flushing (Dutch port), bushing (pipe connector), Cushing, pushing, ruching, batting, matting, tatting, parting, skirting, shirting, beating, heating, fleeting, meeting, greeting, seating, sheeting, boating, coating, floating, outing, Scouting, houting (European whitefish), cutting, nutting, putting, footing, fluting, suiting, shooting, belting, felting, lilting, quilting, halting, malting, vaulting, fainting, painting, printing, wanting, daunting, haunting, pointing, bunting, hunting, tempting, costing, frosting, posting, roasting.

plaything, nothing, something, farthing, bathing, scathing, Worthing, breathing, sheathing (material covering ship's hull), teething, loathing, clothing, soothing, carving, starving, diving, driving, loving, moving, shelving, clearwing (moth), forewing, redwing (European thrush), gull-wing, lapwing, lacewing (insect), batwing, waxwing (songbird), beeswing (crust formed in port), boxing, foxing, pleasing, freezing, seizing (nautical term), dowsing, housing, rousing.

dairying, disturbing, absorbing, woodworking, beseeching, bird-watching, unflinching, regarding, forbidding, unyielding, scaffolding, demanding, commanding, intriguing, obliging, unchanging, towelling, gruelling, sanderling (small sandpiper), underling, fingerling (young fish), panelling, ting-a-ling, snivelling, bitterling (European freshwater fish), fosterling (foster child), hostelling, travelling, bloodcurdling, programming, performing, ausforming (steel-strengthening treatment), brainstorming, adjoining, belonging, galloping, walloping, unceasing, refreshing, brainwashing, first-footing, comforting, shoplifting, weightlifting, revolting, imprinting, excepting, blockbusting, disgusting, anything, everything, revolving, underwing.

pony trekking, overcrowding, corresponding, overwhelming, embarrassing, conveyancing, unrelenting, disappointing, multiplepoinding (Scottish legal term).

265.1
Maying (celebration of May Day), saying, bricklaying, soothsaying, surveying.

265.2
being, skiing, seeing, wellbeing, sightseeing.

265.3
dying, dyeing, flying, spying, crying, trying, undying, outlying, underlying.

265.4
owing, bowing, going, knowing, rowing, sewing, showing, seagoing, foregoing, churchgoing, ingoing, ongoing, outgoing, following, unknowing, harrowing, ingrowing, easy-going, thoroughgoing, overflowing.

265.5
doing, blueing (substance that whitens clothes), brewing, viewing, undoing, wrongdoing, canoeing.

265.6
baking, making, taking, waking, haymaking, dressmaking, lovemaking, backbreaking, housebreaking, heartbreaking, earthshaking, stocktaking, breathtaking, painstaking, merrymaking, undertaking.

265.7
licking, ticking, Mafeking, pigsticking (hunting wild boar), politicking (political canvassing).

265.8
smocking, frocking (coarse material), shocking, stocking, bluestocking.

265.9
corking, Dorking, hawking, walking, sleepwalking.

265.10
blinking, pinking, sinking, stinking, thinking, unblinking, freethinking, unthinking, unwinking.

265.11
fading, lading (cargo), braiding, trading, shading, unfading, degrading.

265.12
bedding, heading, leading (printing term), Reading, wedding, subheading, featherbedding.

265.13
beading, leading, bleeding, pleading, reading, reeding (type of moulding), breeding, sheading (Manx region), mispleading (legal term), misleading, sight-reading, preceding, proceeding, exceeding.

265.14
guiding, hiding, sliding, gliding, riding, siding, abiding, confiding, nitriding (metallurgy term), providing, law-abiding.

265.15
boarding, chording (musical term), hoarding, recording, according, rewarding, unrewarding.

265.16
loading, foreboding.

265.17
building, gilding, shipbuilding, outbuilding.

265.18
scolding, holding, moulding, stockholding, roadholding, smallholding.

265.19
landing, standing, crashlanding, freestanding, upstanding, outstanding, understanding, notwithstanding, misunderstanding.

265.20
ending, mending, pending, spending, unbending, unending, impending, heart-rending, moneylending, condescending.

265.21
binding, finding, blinding, winding, bookbinding.

265.22
grounding, sounding, surrounding, astounding, resounding.

265.23
jogging, logging (lumberjacking), flogging, nogging (building term), frogging (decoration on uniform), pettifogging.

265.24
ageing, staging, engaging.

265.25
bridging, packaging, managing.

265.26
carling (ship's supporting beam), darling, sparling (a fish), starling, rosemaling (Scandinavian decoration).

265.27
ailing, failing, paling, railing, grayling (freshwater fish), sailing, tailing (part of a beam), whaling, unfailing, prevailing, unveiling, unavailing.

265.28
spelling, telling, dwelling, swelling, compelling, misspelling, fortune-telling.

265.29
Ealing, feeling, peeling, ceiling, shieling (*Scot* shepherd's hut), stealing, unfeeling, Darjeeling, revealing, freewheeling.

265.30
billing, killing, skilling (former Scandinavian coin), filling, milling, thrilling, shilling, schilling (Austrian currency), willing, spine-chilling, atheling (Anglo-Saxon prince), unwilling.

265.31
calling, galling, crawling, sprawling, snowballing, appalling, enthralling.

265.32
bowling, polling, rolling, potholing.

265.33
cowling (metal covering), fowling, howling, antifouling (protective paint).

265.34
buckling (bloater), duckling, swashbuckling.

265.35
charming, farming, alarming, disarming.

265.36
scheming, seeming, teeming, redeeming, daydreaming.

265.37
combing, coaming (frame around ship's hatches), homing, gloaming, Wyoming.

265.38
coming, plumbing, becoming, homecoming, incoming, oncoming, shortcoming, forthcoming, unbecoming.

265.39
blooming, grooming, assuming, unassuming.

265.40
caning, graining, training, veining, remaining, entertaining.

265.41
burning, churning, learning, turning, discerning, concerning.

265.42
leaning, cleaning, meaning, greening (variety of cooking apple), Sining (Chinese city), dry-cleaning, demeaning, overweening.

265.43
inning, spinning, winning, beginning, underpinning.

265.44
fining (process of clarifying liquid), lining, mining, refining, divining, designing, interlining.

265.45
cunning, gunning, running, stunning, gunrunning.

265.46
ironing, reckoning, sickening, thickening, questioning, maddening, gardening, happening, opening, fastening, christening, sweetening, frightening, shortening, ravening (voracious), reasoning, seasoning, conditioning.

265.47
springing (architectural term), singing, swinging, mudslinging, upbringing, bell-ringing.

265.48
mapping, wrapping, strapping, overlapping.

265.49
keeping, weeping, sweeping, safekeeping, book-keeping, housekeeping.

265.50
chumping (*Dialect* collecting bonfire wood), thumping, showjumping.

265.51
furring, purring, shirring, stirring, recurring, unerring.

265.52
airing, bearing, daring, fairing, glaring, paring, sparing, raring, tearing, wearing, uncaring, seafaring, unsparing, cheeseparing, overbearing.

265.53
earring, earing (nautical term), gearing, hearing, clearing, searing, steering, endearing, god-fearing, veneering, sheepshearing, engineering, mountaineering, electioneering, orienteering.

265.54
firing, tiring, wiring, aspiring, inspiring, inquiring, retiring, untiring, uninspiring.

265.55
boring, flooring, roaring, warring, skijoring (snow sport), outpouring.

265.56
mooring, during, alluring, enduring, reassuring.

265.57
flowering, towering, overpowering.

265.58
layering (method of plant propagation), neighbouring, timbering, lumbering, doddering, rendering, wandering, thundering, offering, suffering, staggering, fingering, conjuring, colouring, ashlaring (building material), murmuring, scattering, flattering, smattering, catering, Kettering, lettering, guttering, shuttering (wooden mould for con-

crete), factoring (business term), sweltering, plastering, gathering, feathering (plumage), weathering (erosion), blithering, Havering (Greater London borough).

considering, self-catering, woolgathering (daydreaming), manufacturing, mouthwatering.

265.58.1
flavouring, unwavering.

265.59
casing, facing, lacing, placing, spacing, racing, bracing, tracing, interfacing.

265.60
blessing, dressing, pressing, hairdressing, depressing, distressing, prepossessing, unprepossessing.

265.61
kissing, missing, promising, Nipissing (Canadian lake).

265.62
mincing, convincing, unconvincing.

265.63
fishing, furnishing, perishing, brattishing (architectural term), ravishing, astonishing.

265.64
skating, plating, slating, rating, grating, weighting, vacillating, calculating, fulgurating (piercingly painful), penetrating, excruciating, accommodating, unhesitating.

265.64.1
fascinating, discriminating.

265.65
netting, petting, setting, blood-letting, typesetting, upsetting, vignetting (photography term), thermosetting (hardening after heating).

265.66
fitting, splitting, knitting, sitting, bracketing, marketing, spirketting (nautical term), picketing, pipefitting,

hairsplitting, permitting, carpeting, unwitting, unremitting.

265.67
biting, fighting, lighting, slighting, writing, whiting, backbiting, bullfighting, infighting (boxing term), moonlighting, skywriting, handwriting, typewriting, inviting, exciting, uninviting.

265.68
jotting, knotting, potting, rotting, yachting, train-spotting, globetrotting.

265.69
courting, sporting, Storting (Norwegian parliament), supporting.

265.70
acting, distracting, exacting, overacting.

265.71
affecting, respecting, expecting, self-respecting, unsuspecting.

265.72
slanting, enchanting.

265.73
mounting, accounting.

265.74
casting, lasting, blasting, surfcasting (shore-fishing), contrasting, everlasting.

265.75
nesting, resting, cresting (ornamental ridge on building), testing, arresting.

265.76
listing, consisting, harvesting, interesting.

265.77
caving, paving, raving, craving, saving, shaving, engraving, timesaving.

265.78
Irving, nerving (surgical removal of nerve), serving, unnerving, unswerving, deserving, undeserving.

265.79
sleeving (wire insulation), grieving, thieving, weaving, unbelieving.

265.80
living, forgiving, misgiving, thanksgiving.

265.81
glazing, raising, phrasing, grazing, stargazing, amazing, self-raising, double-glazing.

265.82
rising, uprising, surprising, enterprising, appetizing, advertising, uncompromising.

265.83
closing, nosing (projecting edge), supposing, imposing.

265.84
losing, bruising, confusing, amusing.

266 -ong

bong, Caen, dong, gong, hong (Chinese factory), long, flong (printing term), nong (*Austral* stupid person), pong, wrong, prong, strong, throng, song, tong, thong.

Mekong, Hong Kong, quandong (Australian fruit tree), ding-dong, bogong (Australian moth), dugong, mahjong, kalong (fruit bat), élan, daylong, furlong, belong, Shillong (Indian city), oolong, oblong, headlong, sidelong, endlong, lifelong, nightlong, livelong, chaise longue, kampong (Malaysian village), ping-pong (*Trademark*), barong (Philippine knife), headstrong, Armstrong, croissant, plainsong, singsong, souchong (black tea), penchant, diphthong, triphthong (composite vowel sound), morwong (Australian fish), foo yong (Chinese omelette), Qui Nhong (Vietnamese port), bouffant, Kyongsong (capital of South Korea).

billabong, aide-de-camp, Vietcong, wobbegong (shark), Chittagong (Bangladeshi port), Wollongong (Australian city), kurrajong (Australian tree), denouement, scuppernong (US wine), binturong (Asian mammal), cradle-

song, evensong, contretemps, monophthong (simple vowel), currawong (Australian songbird).

266.1
along, prolong, overlong.

266.2
sarong, restaurant.

267 -ung

bung, dung, hung, lung, clung, flung, slung, mung (Australian bean), pung (*US* horse-drawn sleigh), wrung, rung, sprung, strung, sung, tongue, stung, swung, young, among, unstrung, unsung, bluetongue (Australian lizard), Nantung (Chinese city), Shantung (Chinese province), shantung (heavy silk fabric), underhung (protruding from beneath), overhung, aqualung, highly-strung.

268 -ap

bap, cap, chap, dap, gap, Jap, Lapp, lap, clap, flap, slap, map, nap, knap (*Dialect* crest of hill), nappe (rock fold), snap, pap, rap, wrap, crap, scrap, frap (nautical term), trap, strap, sap, tap, yap, zap.

kneecap, recap, snowcap, toecap, mobcap, hubcap, blackcap (European bird), madcap, skullcap, uncap, icecap, nightcap, whitecap (white-crested wave), foolscap, stopgap, mishap, burlap (coarse fabric), dewlap, earflap, genappe (worsted yarn), kidnap, unsnap, catnap, enwrap, unwrap, flytrap, firetrap (building susceptible to burning), giftwrap, mantrap, entrap, suntrap, claptrap, mousetrap, watchstrap, bootstrap, rattrap, deathtrap, jockstrap, heeltap, lagniappe (*US* small gift).

handicap, overlap, thunderclap, photomap (map from aerial photograph), genipap (West Indian tree), rattletrap (broken-down car), wentletrap (marine mollusc), Tonle Sap (Cambodian lake).

269 -arp

carp, scarp, jarp (*Dialect* to smash), harp, sharp, tarp (*Austral* tarpaulin), syncarp (fleshy multiple fruit), escarp (side of fortification ditch), alap (Indian music), cardsharp, watap (American Indian sewing thread), archicarp (fungal reproductive structure), Polycarp (Christian saint), epicarp (outer skin of fruit), pericarp (part of a fruit), ascocarp (part of a fungus), endocarp (inner part of fruit), mesocarp (fleshy part of fruit), cystocarp (reproductive structure of algae), counterscarp (side of fortification ditch), vibraharp (percussion instrument).

270 -ape

ape, cape, scape (leafless stalk bearing flowers), chape (scabbard mounting), gape, jape, nape, rape, crepe, scrape, drape, grape, shape, tape, seascape, escape, cloudscape, landscape, inscape (person's inner nature), townscape, agape, broomrape (plant parasite), reshape, shipshape, misshape, nametape, waterscape, Sellotape (*Trademark*).

271 -ep

kep (*Dialect* to catch), skep (beehive), hep, schlep (*US* to drag), pep, rep, prep, cep (edible fungus), step, steppe, Dieppe, salep (dried orchid tuber), doorstep, sidestep, instep, footstep, quickstep, overstep, Amenhotep (Egyptian pharaoh), Gaziantep (Turkish city).

272 -erp

Earp, burp, chirp, slurp, twerp, Antwerp, usurp.

273 -eep

beep, keep, cheep, cheap, deep, jeep, heap, leap, bleep, sleep, neap, neep (*Dialect* turnip), peep, reap, creep, threap (*Dialect* to scold), seep, sheep, steep, weep, sweep, upkeep, scrapheap, asleep, upsweep, oversleep, cassareep (juice of cassava root), Lakshadweep (islands in Arabian Sea).

274 -ip

kip, skip, chip, dip, gyp, hip, lip, blip, clip, flip, slip, nip, snip, pip, quip, rip, scrip (written certificate), drip, grip, grippe (influenza), trip, strip, sip, ship, tip, whip, zip.

rosehip, harelip, fillip, Philip, polyp, julep (sweet drink), tulip, cowslip, sideslip, gymslip, nonslip, oxlip (woodland plant), genip (West Indian tree), turnip, parsnip, equip, hairgrip, handgrip, unrip, atrip (nautical term), cantrip (magic spell), airstrip, outstrip, gossip, worship, airship, heirship, mayorship, warship, hardship, headship, midship, Lordship, wardship, friendship, flagship, judgeship, steamship, kinship, township, unship, kingship, longship, troopship, spaceship, transship, lightship, courtship, bullwhip (long rawhide whip), horsewhip, bunyip (*Austral* legendary monster), unzip.

paperclip, pillowslip, trusteeship, Ladyship, fellowship, comradeship, battleship, internship, studentship, fingertip, apprenticeship.

274.1

membership, leadership, lectureship, readership, scholarship, ownership, partnership, censorship, sponsorship, authorship, premiership, chancellorship, councillorship, governorship, dictatorship, directorship, receivership (legal term), ambassadorship.

274.2

seamanship, showmanship, workmanship, brinkmanship, penmanship, horsemanship, marksmanship, swordsmanship, salesmanship, gamesmanship, statesmanship, sportsmanship, guardianship, championship, one-upmanship, relationship, musicianship, companionship, citizenship, librarianship.

275 -ipe

hype, clype (*Scot* tell tales), slype (covered passageway in cathedral), snipe, pipe, ripe, gripe, tripe, stripe, type, stipe (plant's reproductive stalk), wipe, swipe.

jacksnipe (Eurasian bird), blowpipe, standpipe, windpipe, bagpipe, tailpipe, drainpipe, hornpipe, downpipe, stovepipe, hawsepipe (nautical term), rareripe (*US* ripening early), unripe, pinstripe, subtype, ectype (a copy), tintype (photographic print), sideswipe.

guttersnipe, liripipe (tip of graduate's hood), underripe, overripe, archetype, Teletype (*Trademark*), antitype (something represented by symbol), antetype (earlier form).

275.1

biotype (biology term), ecotype (ecology term), logotype, collotype (printing process), holotype (original biological type specimen), genotype (organism's genetic constitution), phenotype (biology term), Linotype (*Trademark*), monotype (single print), cerotype (printing process), autotype (photographic process), phototype (photographically-produced printing plate), prototype, countertype (opposite type), heliotype (printing process), karyotype (appearance of organism's chromosomes), stereotype, cyanotype (blueprint), daguerreotype, electrotype (electroplated printing plate), somatotype (classification of physique).

276 -op

bop, cop, kop (prominent isolated African hill), scop (Anglo-Saxon minstrel), chop, fop, hop, lop, clop (sound like horse's hooves), flop, plop, slop, mop, pop, crop, drop, prop, strop, sop, shop, top, stop, whop (to hit), swap.

coop, bebop, Cu-bop (jazz music), Boskop (prehistoric African race), car-

hop (drive-in restaurant waiter), hedgehop (fly near ground level), bellhop, orlop (nautical term), Dunlop, clipclop, flip-flop (type of sandal), slipslop (weak drink), rollmop, coin-op, joypop (*Slang* take drugs), sharecrop (*US* cultivate farmland), stonecrop (fleshy-leaved plant), airdrop (delivery by parachute), eardrop (pendant earring), snowdrop, dewdrop, gumdrop, raindrop, eavesdrop, Aesop, soursop (West Indian tree), sweetsop (West Indian tree), Worksop, milksop, teashop, workshop, bookshop, pawnshop, sweatshop, sweetshop, foretop (platform on ship's foremast), blacktop (*US* bitumen for pavements), hardtop, maintop (platform on ship's mainmast), tiptop, estop (legal term), doorstop, housetop, nonstop, unstop, flattop.

escalope, lollipop, overcrop (cultivate excessively), paradrop (delivery by parachute), turboprop, agitprop (Russian propaganda bureau), barbershop.

276.1

atop, overtop.

277 -orp

scaup (diving duck), dorp (small South African village), gawp, Thorpe, warp, whaup (*Scot* curlew), Scunthorpe, mouldwarp (*Dialect* mole), Krugersdorp (South African city), Australorp (domestic fowl).

278 -ope

cope, scope, dope, hope, lope, slope, mope, nope, pope, rope, roup (*Dialect* auction off), grope, trope (word used figuratively), soap, tope, taupe (brownish-grey colour), stope (mine excavation).

myope, pyrope (yellowish-red garnet), towrope, dragrope, manrope (rope railing on ship), tightrope, sandsoap (gritty soap), metope (architectural term).

radarscope, telescope, episcope (optical projector), periscope, interlope, envelope, antipope, phalarope (aquatic shore bird), lycanthrope (werewolf), misanthrope, isotope, radioisotope.

278.1
stroboscope, bronchoscope, endoscope, thermoscope (temperature-change indicator), seismoscope, chronoscope, snooperscope (US military instrument), baroscope (atmospheric-pressure measurer), gyroscope, horoscope, stauroscope (optical instrument), fluoroscope (x-ray instrument), dichroscope (optical instrument), microscope, hydroscope (instrument for underwater observation), hygroscope (humidity indicator), gastroscope, statoscope (aircraft instrument), otoscope, stethoscope, stereoscope, kaleidoscope, pharyngoscope, laryngoscope, ophthalmoscope, galvanoscope (electric-current detector), urethroscope, tachistoscope (instrument displaying images momentarily).

278.1.1
bioscope (early film projector), skiascope (eye-examining instrument), diascope (optical projector), epidiascope (optical projector).

278.1.2
spectroscope (spectrum-producing instrument), electroscope (electric-charge detector).

278.2
elope, antelope.

278.3
allotrope (chemistry term), thaumatrope (optical illusion toy), heliotrope, azeotrope (chemistry term).

279 -up
up, cup, scup (Atlantic fish), dup (*Dialect* to open), pup, sup, tup, yup, backup, make-up, checkup, teacup, hiccup, eyecup, cockup, kingcup,

roundup, close-up, lash-up (temporary connection of equipment), wickiup (American Indian hut), giddy-up, buttercup.

280 -oop
coop, coupe (shallow glass), scoop, goop (*US* rude person), whoop, hoop, loop, loupe (jeweller's magnifying glass), sloop, snoop, poop, roup (respiratory disease of birds), croup, scroop (*Dialect* make grating sound), droop, drupe (fleshy fruit), group, troupe, troop, soup, stoop, stoup (basin for holy water), swoop, dupe, stupe (hot medicated compress).

recoup, hencoop, regroup, subgroup, Woop Woop (*Austral* backward remote town), nincompoop.

280.1
saloop (infusion of aromatic herbs), Guadeloupe, cantaloupe.

281 -'p
ketchup, gallop, Gallup, galop (19th-century dance), jalap (Mexican plant), Salop, shallop (rowing boat), stanhope (one-seater carriage), larrup (*Dialect* to beat), chirrup, syrup, stirrup, Europe, satrap (Persian governor), caltrop (tropical plant), hyssop (aromatic herb), catsup (*US* ketchup), bishop, tittup (*US* prance), archbishop.

281.1
develop, envelop, redevelop, underdevelop, overdevelop.

281.2
collop (*Dialect* slice of meat), scallop, dollop, gollop (to eat greedily), lollop, trollop, Trollope (British novelist), wallop, codswallop.

282 -alp
alp, scalp, palp, pedipalp (zoology term).

283 -elp
kelp, skelp (*Dialect* to slap), chelp (*Dialect* to chatter), help, whelp, yelp.

284 -ulp
gulp, pulp.

285 -amp
amp, camp, scamp, champ, damp, gamp (umbrella), lamp, clamp, ramp, cramp, tramp, tamp (pat down firmly), stamp, vamp, decamp, encamp, firedamp, blackdamp (gas in mines), whitedamp (gas in mines), blowlamp, revamp, afterdamp (gas in mines).

286 -emp
hemp, temp.

287 -imp
imp, skimp, chimp, gimp (stiffened fabric trimming), guimpe (short blouse), limp, blimp (small airship), pimp, crimp, scrimp, primp, shrimp, simp (*US short for* simpleton).

288 -omp
comp, chomp, clomp, pomp, romp, trompe (apparatus in a forge), stomp, swamp.

289 -ump
bump, chump, dump, jump, hump, lump, clump, plump, slump, pump, rump, crump (to thud), scrump, frump, grump, trump, sump, tump (*Dialect* small mound), stump, thump, mugwump (politically neutral person), gazump, undertrump, overtrump.

290 -asp
gasp, hasp, clasp, rasp, grasp, handclasp, enclasp, unclasp.

291 -isp
lisp, crisp, wisp, will-o'-the-wisp.

292 -osp
wasp, galliwasp (American lizard).

293 -ass
ass, as (ancient Roman unit), bass, gas, lass, mass, wrasse (marine fish), crass, frass (insect excrement), trass (volcanic rock), strass (glass for imitation gemstones), sass, tass (*Dialect* goblet), Tass.

Troas (region of Asia Minor), jackass, ACAS, degas, bagasse (pulp from sugar cane), megass (type of paper), alas, camass (US plant), amass, admass (people susceptible to advertising), landmass, groundmass, en masse, vinasse (residue in a still), Aras (river on Russian border), cuirass, morass, Patras, Mithras (Persian god), Alsace, crevasse.

anabas (freshwater fish), Caiaphas, distringas (legal term), Ladislas (Hungarian saint and king), biomass (biology term), Maecenas (Roman statesman), hippocras (spiced wine), sassafras, demitasse (small coffee cup), tarantass (Russian horse-drawn carriage).

Leonidas (king of Sparta), Epaminondas (ancient Greek general).

293.1
Phidias (Greek sculptor), galleass (type of warship), palliasse, capias (legal term), Lysias (Athenian orator), Herodias (mother of Salome), Asturias (former Spanish kingdom), materfamilias (female head of family), paterfamilias (male head of family).

294 -arse
arse, carse (*Scot* low-lying land), farce, class, glass, pass, sparse, brass, grass, kvass (Russian alcoholic drink).

213

Donbass (Russian industrial region),
volte-face, springhaas (African rodent),
declass, subclass, outclass, eyeglass,
spyglass, hourglass, wineglass, sunglass
(burning glass), surpass, bypass, impasse, Madras, deergrass (bog plant),
bluegrass (folk music), eelgrass (marine
plant), goosegrass, knotgrass (weedy
plant).

superclass (group in classification system), Plexiglass (*Trademark*), galloglass
(Irish chieftain's military retainer),
fibreglass, weatherglass (barometer),
isinglass, underpass, overpass, sparrowgrass (*Dialect* asparagus), peppergrass
(flowering plant).

295 -ace

ace, base, bass, case, chase, dace, face,
lace, place, plaice, mace, pace, space,
race, brace, grace, trace, Thrace.

surbase (architectural term), debase,
subbass (organ stop), subbase (base of
pedestal), wheelbase, staircase, bookcase, crankcase (part of car engine),
watchcase, seedcase, briefcase, encase,
slipcase (protective case for books),
typecase, notecase, nutcase, suitcase,
enchase (engrave metal), vendace
(white fish), wheyface (pale face), reface, pigface (*Austral* creeping plant),
coalface, typeface, outface, shoelace,
enlace, unlace, replace, fireplace, showplace, emplace (put in position), someplace, displace, misplace, birthplace,
bootlace, Lovelace (English poet), grimace, tenace (bridge term), airspace,
footpace (platform before altar), backspace, vambrace (piece of armour),
embrace, mainbrace, unbrace (relax),
headrace, landrace (breed of pig),
scapegrace, disgrace, tailrace, millrace,
retrace, rosace (rose window), ambsace
(lowest throw at dice).

steeplechase, interface, interlace, periclase (mineral), orthoclase (mineral),
commonplace, marketplace, hyper-

space, aerospace, interspace, Samothrace (Greek island).

plagioclase (mineral), oligoclase (mineral).

295.1
abase, rheobase (minimum nerve impulse), diabase (type of rock), contrabass.

295.2
showcase, pillowcase.

295.3
efface, deface, Boniface (Anglo-Saxon
saint).

295.4
apace, carapace.

296 -ess
Bess, Bes (ancient Egyptian god),
chess, fesse (heraldic term), guess, jess
(falconry term), Hesse (West German
state), less, bless, mess, Ness, cress,
dress, press, tress, stress, cess, Tess,
yes.

profess, confess, largess, noblesse, unless, Sheerness, Foulness, Caithness, liquesce, fluoresce, duress, redress, address, headdress, undress, sundress,
nightdress, egress, regress, digress, progress, aggress, ingress, congress, transgress, depress, repress, impress, compress, winepress, express, prestress,
distress, recess, precess, process, assess,
abscess, obsess, princess, access, excess, success, possess.

acquiesce, S.O.S., bouillabaisse, recrudesce, incandesce, otherguess (different), intumesce, deliquesce, effloresce,
pennycress (flowering plant), watercress, maladdress, retrogress, decompress, politesse, effervesce, repossess,
prepossess, dispossess.

296.1
coalesce, recalesce (physics term),
nonetheless, obsolesce, convalesce,
nevertheless.

296.2
finesse, luminesce.

296.3
Lyonnesse (place in Arthurian legend),
Dungeness, pythoness, evanesce, Inver-
ness, rejuvenesce.

296.4
caress, phosphoresce, manageress.

296.5
oppress, suppress, letterpress.

297 -erse
Erse, burse (*Scot* student allowance),
curse, hearse, Merse (Scottish lowland
area), nurse, purse, perse (dark
greyish-blue), terse, thyrse (type of inflorescence), verse, worse.

coerce, disburse, rehearse, immerse,
commerce, disperse, cutpurse, sesterce
(Roman coin), traverse, diverse, covers
(maths term), averse, perverse, obverse,
adverse, inverse, converse, transverse,
reimburse.

297.1
asperse, intersperse.

297.2
reverse, universe.

298 -eece
geese, lease, fleece, niece, Nice, peace,
piece, crease, Greece, grease, cease.

obese, pelisse (fur-trimmed cloak), release, coulisse, police, sublease, hairpiece, earpiece, eyepiece, showpiece,
headpiece, codpiece, fieldpiece (field
gun), tailpiece, timepiece, crownpiece
(part of horse's bridle), crosspiece,
mouthpiece, decrease, increase, Dumfries, degrease, caprice, cassis, decease,
Métis (person of mixed parentage).

chimneypiece, battlepiece (painting
commemorating a battle), mantelpiece,
frontispiece, ambergris, predecease.

298.1
chersonese (peninsula), Peloponnese.

298.2
apiece, altarpiece, centrepiece, masterpiece.

299 -eerse
fierce, pierce, tierce (fencing position),
transpierce.

300 -iss [further rhymes may be
created by adding *-less* to appropriate verbs or *-ness* to appropriate adjectives]
kiss, Dis (Roman god), hiss, bliss,
miss, piss, cuisse (piece of armour),
Riss (European glaciation period), kris
(Malayan knife), sis, this, Swiss.

dais, Saïs (ancient Egyptian city), Thaïs (Athenian courtesan), Powys, prowess, Jewess, Lewes, Lewis, brewis (*Dialect* gravy-soaked bread), abbess, ibis,
rachis (biology term), orchis (orchid),
Colchis (ancient Asian country), purchase, duchess, caddis, Sardis (ancient
Asian city), jaundice, aphis (aphid),
preface, surface, office, Memphis, haggis, Burgess, burgess (citizen of borough), dehisce (burst open), Alice,
chalice, malice, palace, Tallis, starless,
Ellis, trellis, airless, heirless, careless,
hairless, Perlis (Malaysian state), Elis
(ancient Olympic Games site), treeless,
cheerless, fearless, peerless, tearless,
eyeless, tireless, wireless, Aulis (ancient
Greek town), lawless, flawless, shoreless, joyless, jobless, tubeless, backless,
trackless, feckless, necklace, reckless,
smokeless, luckless, thankless, matchless, speechless, headless, wordless,
heedless, needless, seedless, beardless,
lidless, godless, cloudless, cordless,
bloodless, childless, endless, friendless,
kindless (heartless), mindless, boundless, groundless, soundless, lifeless,
selfless, legless, ageless, changeless,
guileless, soulless, goalless, armless,
harmless, aimless, blameless, nameless,
frameless, shameless, dreamless, seamless, limbless, timeless, homeless, form-

less, gormless, anlace (medieval dagger), painless, brainless, stainless, skinless, chinless, sinless, spineless, boneless, toneless, stoneless, sunless, moonless, tuneless, hapless, strapless, shapeless, surplice, sleepless, topless, hopeless, helpless, classless, baseless, faceless, graceless, ceaseless, creaseless, priceless, voiceless, useless, hatless, artless, heartless, stateless, weightless, flightless, sightless, spotless, thoughtless, doubtless, gutless, bootless, rootless, fruitless, tactless, thriftless, shiftless, guiltless, faultless, dauntless, pointless, countless, tasteless, waistless, restless, listless, faithless, breathless, mirthless, worthless, ruthless, toothless, sleeveless, nerveless, loveless, sexless, noiseless, amice (part of priest's vestment), Amis, premiss, Themis (Greek goddess), commis (agent), promise, pumice, pomace, kumiss (drink of fermented milk), submiss (docile), dismiss, anise (Mediterranean plant), greyness, Tanis (ancient Egyptian city), Ennis (Irish town), Denis, menace, tennis, Venice, furnace, Furness, lenis (linguistics term), penis, dearness, clearness, nearness, Highness, slyness, dryness, shyness, coyness, sourness, blueness, newness, Tunis, drabness, blackness, darkness, bleakness, sleekness, meekness, weakness, likeness, frankness, brusqueness, richness, muchness, badness, gladness, madness, sadness, hardness, staidness, deadness, redness, weirdness, oddness, loudness, goodness, lewdness, rudeness, shrewdness, mildness, wildness, baldness, oldness, boldness, coldness, fondness, roundness, soundness, Daphnis (Greek mythological character), deafness, stiffness, roughness, gruffness, toughness, Agnes, vagueness, smugness, strangeness, paleness, staleness, illness, stillness, vileness, smallness, tallness, foulness, dullness, fullness, coolness, calmness, lameness, sameness, tameness, firmness, dimness, slimness, grim-

ness, warmness, dumbness, glumness, numbness, plainness, sternness, keenness, cleanness, meanness, greenness, thinness, fineness, proneness, oneness, sharpness, cheapness, steepness, ripeness, dampness, plumpness, crispness, sparseness, baseness, coarseness, hoarseness, closeness, looseness, rashness, harshness, freshness, fatness, flatness, smartness, lateness, greatness, straightness, wetness, hotness, shortness, stoutness, strictness, deftness, swiftness, softness, scantness, faintness, quaintness, gauntness, bluntness, aptness, promptness, smoothness, braveness, business, lapis, Apis (ancient Egyptian sacred bull), coppice, Puppis (constellation), Thespis (Greek poet), hospice, auspice, marquess, marquis, arris (sharp edge), Harris, Paris, Eris (Greek goddess), derris (Asian climbing plant), Ferris, peeress, orris (iris plant), Boris, Doris, Horace, Maurice, Morris, hubris, indris (large Madagascan mammal), laundress, Negress, Tigris, tigress, ogress, empress, mattress, waitress, traitress, fortress, portress (female porter), buttress, temptress, mistress, seamstress, Persis (ancient Iranian region), cercis (woody plant), tussis (a cough), Francis, apsis (point in planet's orbit), lattice, brattice (mining term), gratis, lettuce, Thetis (Greek goddess), glottis, cutis, poultice, countess, hostess, justice, solstice, pavis (large square shield), Jarvis, parvis (church porch), Davis, Mavis, service, novice, Clovis (Frankish king), pelvis, unguis (claw or hoof), lexis (complete vocabulary), deixis (linguistics term), Zeuxis (ancient Greek painter).

nereis (marine worm), archduchess, druidess, prejudice, Charybdis, edifice, benefice, orifice, artifice, flowerless, powerless, regardless, bottomless, fathomless, accomplice, remorseless, purposeless, effortless, comfortless, relentless, grotesqueness, forwardness, backwardness, awkwardness, aloofness, handsomeness, remoteness, quietness, exactness, pleasantness, abruptness, earnestness, precipice, Serapis (Graeco-Egyptian god), Polaris, ex libris, dentifrice, verdigris, arbitress, monitress, heritress, cockatrice (legendary monster), seductress, conductress, instructress, enchantress, schoolmistress, housemistress, catharsis, pertussis (whooping cough), proglottis (segment of tapeworm), abatis (fortifications term), clematis, apprentice, viscountess, interstice, armistice, injustice, Glenrothes (Scottish town), self-service, disservice.

unpleasantness, ambassadress, Nunc Dimittis (canticle), epiglottis, amphimixis (sexual reproduction), apomixis (type of asexual reproduction), anaptyxis (linguistics term), stylostixis (acupuncture), amanuensis.

300.1
loess, Powys (English writer), allantois (embryology term).

300.2
pubis, Anubis.

300.3
abyss, cannabis.

300.4
bodice, goddess, demigoddess.

300.5
stewardess, cowardice, leopardess, hendiadys (rhetorical device).

300.6
aegis, Lyme Regis, Bognor Regis, Curia Regis (Norman king's court).

300.7
rayless, lumbricalis (worm-like muscle), digitalis, Corona Australis (constellation), aurora australis, Corona Borealis (constellation), aurora borealis.

300.8
cilice (haircloth), bodiless, syphilis, penniless, weariless, merciless, pitiless, amaryllis.

300.9
polis (ancient Greek city-state), solace, Wallace, Cornwallis (British general), torticollis.

300.10
cullis (gutter), Dulles (US statesman), portcullis.

300.11
bullace (damson tree), valueless.

300.12
clueless, viewless, parulis (gumboil).

300.13
Aeolis (Greek god), numberless, featureless, riderless, odourless, Argolis (region of ancient Greece), colourless, humourless, mannerless, chrysalis, pleasureless, measureless, fortalice (small fort), fatherless, motherless, flavourless, driverless, oxalis (flowering plant), corydalis (climbing plant), Persepolis, Hermoupolis (Greek port), Camelopardalis (constellation).

300.13.1
Annapolis (capital of Maryland), Minneapolis, Indianapolis.

300.13.2
propolis (substance collected by bees), cosmopolis, necropolis (burial ground), Acropolis, metropolis, Heliopolis (ancient Egyptian city), megalopolis (complex of adjacent towns).

300.14
questionless, passionless, motionless, expressionless.

300.15
wingless, meaningless.

300.16
senseless, defenceless.

300.17
witless, profitless, limitless, spiritless.

300.18
kermis (Dutch carnival), dermis, vermis (part of brain), epidermis, endodermis (botany term), hypodermis (biology term).

300.19
remiss, Artemis, epididymis (anatomy term).

300.20
amiss, Salamis (Greek island), Semiramis (legendary Assyrian queen).

300.21
harness, unharness, Kiwanis (US community service organization).

300.22
bareness, fairness, unfairness, awareness.

300.23
finis (the end), Guinness, pinnace (small boat).

shabbiness, flabbiness, grubbiness, tubbiness, stickiness, cockiness, silkiness, sulkiness, hardiness, sturdiness, neediness, greediness, giddiness, tidiness, moodiness, rowdiness, dauphiness, fluffiness, stuffiness, earliness, burliness, curliness, surliness, silliness, holiness, lowliness, godliness, worldliness, friendliness, kindliness, ugliness, cleanliness, loneliness, stateliness, ghostliness, liveliness, loveliness, reminisce, gloominess, happiness, sleepiness, sloppiness, airiness, wariness, dreariness, weariness, hungriness, iciness, spiciness, bossiness, sauciness, fussiness, dirtiness, prettiness, naughtiness, daintiness, emptiness, nastiness, thirstiness, healthiness, filthiness, heaviness, laziness, easiness, dizziness, noisiness, cosiness, drowsiness, clumsiness.

foolhardiness, untidiness, orderliness, scholarliness, ungodliness, cowardliness, unworldliness, unfriendliness, unhappiness, unhealthiness.

300.23.1
readiness, steadiness, unsteadiness.

300.24
cornice, rawness, soreness, notornis (rare flightless bird), archaeornis (extinct bird), aepyornis (extinct flightless bird), ichthyornis (extinct sea bird).

300.25
lowness, slowness, Adonis, callowness, shallowness, hollowness, narrowness, lex talionis (law of retaliation).

300.26 [see also **300.31**]
lioness, soberness, deaconess, wilderness, slenderness, tenderness, eagerness, villainess, Romanes (language of gypsies), canoness, baroness, thoroughness, patroness, marchioness, bitterness, otherness, cleverness, governess, togetherness.

300.27
lychnis (flowering plant), sickness, thickness, airsickness, seasickness, homesickness, chromaticness (physics term).

300.28
Widnes, nakedness, wickedness, crookedness, wretchedness, sordidness, raggedness, doggedness, ruggedness, hurriedness, sacredness, cussedness, vividness.

clear-headedness, bigheadedness, pigheadedness, light-headedness, hotheadedness, cold-bloodedness, broadmindedness, kind-heartedness, halfheartedness, downheartedness, lightheartedness, softheartedness, belatedness, quick-wittedness, far-sightedness, near-sightedness, long-sightedness, short-sightedness, sure-footedness, flatfootedness.

level-headedness, narrow-mindedness, feeble-mindedness, single-mindedness, open-mindedness, absent-mindedness, unexpectedness.

300.28.1
candidness, left-handedness, offhandedness, underhandedness.

300.29
kindness, blindness, unkindness.

300.30
feebleness, nimbleness, fickleness, idleness, carefulness, cheerfulness, awfulness, thankfulness, dreadfulness, painfulness, scornfulness, hopefulness, helpfulness, gracefulness, peacefulness, usefulness, gratefulness, spitefulness, thoughtfulness, doubtfulness, boastfulness, faithfulness, truthfulness, suppleness, brittleness, gentleness, evilness.

forgetfulness, unfaithfulness, untruthfulness.

300.31 [see also **300.26**]
stubbornness, drunkenness, suddenness, sullenness, commonness, openness, barrenness, rottenness, evenness, unevenness.

300.32
willingness, nothingness, unwillingness.

300.33
carelessness, cheerlessness, fearlessness, tirelessness, lawlessness, joblessness, recklessness, lucklessness, thanklessness, heedlessness, godlessness, childlessness, friendlessness, mindlessness, lifelessness, selflessness, changelessness, harmlessness, aimlessness, shamelessness, timelessness, homelessness, painlessness, tunelessness, shapelessness, sleeplessness, hopelessness, helplessness, classlessness, pricelessness, uselessness, artlessness, heartlessness, weightlessness, sightlessness, spotlessness, thoughtlessness, fruitlessness, tactlessness, thriftlessness, faultlessness, pointlessness, tastelessness, restlessness, listlessness, breathlessness, worthlessness, ruthlessness.

mercilessness, pitilessness, powerlessness, meaninglessness, remorselessness,

purposelessness, limitlessness, spiritlessness, effortlessness, relentlessness.

300.33.1
senselessness, defencelessness.

300.34
joyousness, righteousness, callousness, zealousness, pompousness, monstrousness, spaciousness, graciousness, preciousness, cautiousness, consciousness, nervousness, biliousness, hazardousness, contagiousness, scrupulousness, dangerousness, boisterousness, facetiousness, infectiousness, subconsciousness, unconsciousness, covetousness, mischievousness, unscrupulousness, semiconsciousness.

300.34.1
dubiousness, tediousness, studiousness, seriousness, deviousness, fastidiousness, melodiousness, lasciviousness.

300.34.2
sensuousness, sumptuousness, conspicuousness, impetuousness, voluptuousness.

300.34.3
viciousness, officiousness, capriciousness, surreptitiousness.

300.34.4
pretentiousness, conscientiousness.

300.35
snobbishness, childishness, selfishness, foolishness, ticklishness, squeamishness, sheepishness, lavishness, peevishness, unselfishness, feverishness.

300.36
curtness, pertness, alertness.

300.37
neatness, sweetness, completeness, incompleteness.

300.38
fitness, witness, unfitness, eyewitness, appropriateness, inappropriateness.

300.39

lightness, rightness, brightness, triteness, tightness, whiteness, politeness, uprightness, impoliteness.

300.40

cuteness, acuteness, astuteness.

300.41

directness, correctness, indirectness, incorrectness.

300.42

fastness, vastness, steadfastness.

300.43

forgiveness, furtiveness, activeness, plaintiveness, impressiveness, possessiveness, decisiveness, explosiveness, impulsiveness, offensiveness, talkativeness, effectiveness, inventiveness, inquisitiveness.

300.44

heiress, mayoress, Seferis (Greek poet), millionairess, Apollinaris (mineral water).

300.45

iris, Iris, Osiris (Egyptian god).

300.46

loris, cantoris (musical term).

300.47

prioress, berberis (cultivated shrub), Sybaris (ancient Greek colony), liquorice, eucharis (South American plant), murderess, sorceress, clitoris, avarice, ephemeris (astronomical table), mons veneris, sui generis (unique), angina pectoris.

300.48

actress, benefactress.

300.49

classis (governing body of church), glacis (a slope), Onassis.

300.50

Acis (Greek mythological character), basis, crasis (linguistics term), stasis, oasis, cataclasis (geology term), haemostasis.

300.51

tmesis (linguistics term), thesis, noesis (functioning of intellect), mimesis, ecesis (ecology term), ascesis (self-discipline), anthesis (flowering process), exegesis, epiclesis (invocation of Holy Spirit), anamnesis (recollection), diuresis, anuresis, enuresis, catachresis (incorrect use of words), erotesis (rhetorical question), leucopoiesis (white blood cell formation), biopoiesis (biology term), diapedesis (medical term), psychokinesis (parapsychology term), cytokinesis (division of cytoplasm), photokinesis (movement towards light), telekinesis, erythropoiesis (red blood cell formation), haematopoiesis (formation of blood), amniocentesis.

300.51.1

paresis (muscular weakness), hysteresis (physics term), diaphoresis, cataphoresis (analytical technique), electrophoresis (analytical technique), iontophoresis (biochemical technique).

300.52

diesis (printing term), ecdysis (shedding of outer layer), symphysis, synesis (linguistics term), synthesis, prosthesis, diaphysis (shaft of long bone), epiphysis (end of long bone), hypophysis (pituitary gland), apophysis (outgrowth), dieresis, aphaeresis (linguistics term), syneresis (contraction of two vowels), haemoptysis (coughing up of blood), diathesis (hereditary susceptibility to disease), metathesis (linguistics term), antithesis, epenthesis (linguistics term), parenthesis, photosynthesis, biosynthesis (biology term), parasynthesis (linguistics term).

300.52.1

dialysis, analysis, paralysis, catalysis, urinalysis, cryptanalysis (study of codes), haemodialysis, psychoanalysis, microanalysis, electrodialysis, electroanalysis.

300.52.2
biolysis (disintegration of organic matter), glycolysis (breakdown of glucose), thermolysis (loss of body heat), haemolysis (red blood cell disintegration), hydrolysis, cytolysis (disintegration of cells), autolysis (self-destruction of cells), histolysis (disintegration of tissues), electrolysis, pneumatolysis (geology term), bacteriolysis (disintegration of bacteria).

300.52.3
emesis, Nemesis, haematemesis (vomiting of blood).

300.52.4
genesis, agenesis (imperfect development), pangenesis (former heredity theory), biogenesis (biological principle), oogenesis (formation of ova), psychogenesis, morphogenesis (development of organism's form), thermogenesis (heat production), sporogenesis (spore formation), histogenesis (tissue and organ formation), pathogenesis (development of a disease), osteogenesis (bone formation), abiogenesis (biological theory), anthropogenesis (study of man's origin), haematogenesis (formation of blood), spermatogenesis (sperm formation).

300.52.5
prothesis (linguistics term), hypothesis.

300.53
Isis, lysis, crisis, epicrisis (pathology term).

300.54
proboscis, salpiglossis (flowering plant).

300.55
Phocis (district in ancient Greece), gnosis (knowledge of spiritual things), ptosis (drooping of the eyelid).

thrombosis, narcosis, mycosis (disease caused by fungus), psychosis, sycosis (inflammation of hair follicles), lordosis, kyphosis, morphosis (biology term), alphosis (absence of skin pigmentation), phimosis (tightness of foreskin), zymosis (any infectious disease), osmosis, prognosis, hypnosis, pyrosis (heartburn), neurosis, fibrosis, necrosis, hidrosis (sweat), nephrosis (kidney disease), mitosis, ostosis (formation of bone).

silicosis, varicosis, toxicosis, psittacosis, acidosis, ankylosis (abnormal immobility of joint), brucellosis (disease of cattle), ecchymosis (skin discoloration through bruising), syndesmosis (type of joint), cyanosis, melanosis (skin condition), telegnosis (parapsychology term), diagnosis, siderosis (lung disease), diarthrosis (freely movable joint), enarthrosis (ball-and-socket joint), synarthrosis (immovable joint), asbestosis.

metempsychosis (migration of soul), Winnipegosis (Canadian lake), anastomosis, autohypnosis, osteoporosis (loss of bony tissue).

300.55.1
symbiosis, scoliosis, ichthyosis, coccidiosis (disease of domestic animals), apotheosis, mononucleosis, pneumoconiosis, endometriosis (pathology term).

300.55.2
meiosis, miosis (constriction of pupil), pyosis (pus formation), abiosis (absence of life), antibiosis, necrobiosis (normal death of cells), anabiosis (resuscitation), parabiosis (union of two individuals).

300.55.3
tuberculosis, pediculosis (infestation with lice), furunculosis (skin condition), diverticulosis.

300.55.4
kenosis (theology term), stenosis, trichinosis (parasitic disease), pollinosis (hay fever), byssinosis (industrial lung disease), hallucinosis (mental disorder), avitaminosis, hypervitaminosis.

300.55.5

sclerosis, cirrhosis, xerosis (abnormal dryness of tissues), phlebosclerosis (hardening of veins), atherosclerosis (disease of arteries), arteriosclerosis.

300.55.6

ketosis (pathology term), halitosis, amitosis (form of cell division), spirochaetosis (disease).

300.55.7

dermatosis, haematosis (oxygenation of blood), keratosis (skin condition), myxomatosis, carcinomatosis.

300.56

Eleusis (Greek town), anacrusis.

300.57

emphasis, protasis (conditional clause), entasis (architectural term), anabasis (ancient Persian military expedition), parabasis (speech of Greek chorus), catabasis (descent), apodosis (main clause), apophasis (rhetorical device), periphrasis, antiphrasis (rhetorical device), diastasis (separation of joined parts), metastasis (spreading of disease), osteoclasis (surgical fracture of bone), bronchiectasis (dilation of bronchial tubes), atelectasis (lung collapse).

300.57.1

diocese, myiasis (infestation by fly larvae), trichiasis (inversion of eyelashes), archdiocese, taeniasis (tapeworm infestation), phthiriasis (infestation with lice), psoriasis, mydriasis (abnormal pupil dilation), lithiasis, amoebiasis (parasitic infection), leishmaniasis (parasitic infection), satyriasis, acariasis (hair infestation), ascariasis (roundworm infestation), filariasis (tropical disease), bilharziasis (tropical disease), schistosomiasis (tropical disease), elephantiasis, trypanosomiasis (sleeping sickness).

300.57.2

paedomorphosis (zoology term), anamorphosis (distorted image), metamorphosis, anthropomorphosis.

300.58

Chalcis (Greek city), peristalsis, diastalsis (medical term).

300.59

sepsis, syllepsis (linguistics term), prolepsis (rhetorical device), asepsis, antisepsis.

300.60

stypsis (medical term), ellipsis.

300.61

synopsis, caryopsis (one-seeded fruit), stereopsis (stereoscopic vision), coreopsis (tropical plant), ampelopsis (tropical vine), thanatopsis (meditation on death).

300.62

mitis (malleable iron), phlebitis, orchitis, rachitis (rickets), bronchitis, carditis, mephitis (foul stench), colitis, typhlitis (intestinal disorder), rhinitis, scleritis (inflammation of eyeball membrane), iritis, neuritis, nephritis, metritis (inflammation of womb), gastritis, arthritis, bursitis, glossitis (inflammation of tongue), otitis, mastitis, cystitis, vulvitis.

tracheitis, ileitis (intestinal disorder), osteitis, uveitis (eye disorder), thyroiditis, mastoiditis (inflammation in ear), meningitis, pharyngitis, laryngitis, ophthalmitis, pneumonitis, urethritis, sinusitis, fibrositis, dermatitis, hepatitis, parotitis (mumps), keratitis (inflammation of cornea), prostatitis, synovitis (inflammation in a joint).

encephalitis, appendicitis, osteoarthritis.

300.62.1

myelitis (inflammation of spinal cord), spondylitis (inflammation of vertebrae), tonsillitis, pyelitis (inflammation of kidney), osteomyelitis (inflammation of bone marrow), poliomyelitis.

300.62.2
cellulitis (inflammation of body tissues), uvulitis, valvulitis (inflammation of heart valve), utriculitis (inflammation of inner ear), diverticulitis.

300.62.3
splenitis, adenitis (inflammation of a gland), vaginitis, retinitis, duodenitis.

300.62.4
colonitis, tympanitis, peritonitis.

300.62.5
blepharitis (inflammation of eyelids), arteritis, enteritis, ovaritis, gastroenteritis.

300.62.6
gingivitis, conjunctivitis.

300.63
fortis (phonetics term), mortise, rigor mortis.

300.64
notice, stephanotis, myosotis.

300.65
factice (soft rubbery material), practice, practise, malpractice.

300.66
mantis, Atlantis.

300.67
pastis, hydrastis (flowering plant).

300.68
testis, Alcestis (Greek mythological queen), ovotestis (snail's reproductive organ).

300.69
clevis (coupling device), crevice, Ben Nevis.

300.70
axis, praxis (practice), taxis (movement), pseudaxis (botany term), prophylaxis, parapraxis (psychology term), geotaxis (biology term), thermotaxis (movement towards heat), phototaxis (movement towards light), epistaxis (nosebleed), anaphylaxis.

301 -ice
ice, bice (medium blue colour), dice, lice, splice, slice, mice, gneiss, nice, pice (former Indian coin), spice, speiss (compound formed after smelting), rice, price, trice, thrice, syce (Indian servant), vice, twice.

de-ice, choc-ice, suffice, allspice, half-price, precise, concise, entice, device, advice.

paradise, merchandise, sacrifice, overnice, underprice, Haltemprice (English township), imprecise, edelweiss, self-sacrifice.

302 -oss
os, boss, coss (Indian unit of distance), Kos (Greek island), cos (variety of lettuce), doss, fosse (ditch), joss (Chinese deity), Jos (Nigerian city), loss, floss, gloss, moss, Ross, cross, crosse (lacrosse stick), dross, toss, stoss (geology term).

chaos, Keos (Greek island), Eos (Greek goddess), speos (ancient Egyptian temple), Chios (Greek island), emboss, Lesbos (Greek island), reredos, kudos, Paphos (village in Cyprus), Argos (ancient Greek city), Lagos, logos (reason), Carlos, Delos (Greek island), Melos (Greek island), tholos (ancient Greek tomb), siglos (ancient Persian coin), bugloss, Amos, Samos (Greek island), demos (nation as political unit), Patmos (Greek island), cosmos, Minos, Lemnos (Greek island), epos (body of poetry), tripos, topos (basic concept), saros (cycle of eclipses), Pharos (ancient Greek lighthouse), Páros (Greek island), Skyros (Greek island), Eros, kaross (African garment), backcross (genetics term), incross (inbreed), uncross, crisscross, outcross, Andros (Greek island), Kinross, non-pros (legal term), Thásos (Greek island), custos (superior in Franciscan order), bathos, pathos, ethos, pithos (ceramic oil container), mythos (beliefs of specific group), Naxos (Greek island), Hyksos (Asian nomad).

Barbados, intrados (inner curve of arch), extrados (outer curve of arch), Tenedos (Greek island), parados (bank behind fortification), Calvados, omphalos (sacred conical object), candyfloss, isogloss (line on map), rallycross, double-cross, Charing Cross, albatross, Thanatos (Greek personification of death), Hephaistos (Greek god).

exophthalmos (abnormal protrusion of eyeball), metanephros (part of kidney).

302.1
Phobos (satellite of Mars), Villa-Lobos (Brazilian composer).

302.2
across, lacrosse, autocross, motocross, intercross (crossbreed).

302.3
Sestos (ancient Turkish town), asbestos.

303 -orse
coarse, course, force, gorse, horse, hoarse, Morse, morse (cloak fastening), Norse, source, sauce.

recourse, forecourse (boat's sail), concourse, dampcourse, racecourse, discourse, endorse, deforce (withhold wrongfully), drayhorse, sawhorse, warhorse, packhorse, workhorse, cockhorse, studhorse, unhorse, racehorse, carthorse, clotheshorse, remorse, premorse (biology term), retrorse (pointing backwards), antrorse (directed upwards), introrse (turned inwards), extrorse (turned outwards), dextrorse (spiralling left to right), divorce, resource.

watercourse, intercourse, hobbyhorse, sinistrorse (spiralling right to left).

303.1
perforce, Wilberforce.

303.2
enforce, reinforce.

304 -oice
Boyce, choice, Joyce, voice, rejoice, Rolls Royce (*Trademark*), devoice (phonetics term), revoice (to echo), invoice, unvoice (phonetics term).

305 -oce
Bose (Indian physicist), kos (Indian unit of distance), dose, close, gross, chausses (medieval garment).

verbose, globose (spherical), thrombose, arkose (type of sandstone), floccose (covered with woolly tufts), jocose, viscose, nodose, strigose (biology term), rugose (wrinkled), filose (thread-like), pilose (covered with fine hairs), ramose (having branches), rimose (having a cracked surface), cymose (botany term), osmose (undergo osmosis), venose, spinose, squarrose (having a rough surface), erose (uneven), Tiros (US weather satellite), torose (biology term), necrose, Negros (Philippine island), engross, setose (bristly).

bellicose, varicose, ventricose (biology term), verrucose (covered with warts), overdose, surculose (bearing suckers), cellulose, squamulose (covered with small scales), ramulose (having small branches), tumulose (mound-like), annulose (segmented), lachrymose (tearful), racemose (botany term), pruinose (covered with waxy bloom), farinose (flour-like), anthracnose (fungal disease), adipose, caespitose (growing in tufts), comatose, keratose (having a horny skeleton), sarmentose (botany term), chaparejos (cowboy's leather overalls).

305.1
grandiose, foliose (leafy), otiose (futile), religiose (sanctimonious).

305.2

morose, suberose (relating to cork), tuberose, acerose (needle-shaped).

306 -ouse

scouse, douse, gauss (unit in physics), house, louse, mouse, nous, spouse, grouse, Strauss, souse, shouse (*Austral* lavatory).

lobscouse, degauss (demagnetize), playhouse, warehouse, teahouse, whorehouse, storehouse, poorhouse, Bauhaus, clubhouse, bakehouse, steakhouse, workhouse, cookhouse, madhouse, guardhouse, birdhouse, roadhouse, Wodehouse, roundhouse, doghouse, alehouse, jailhouse, tollhouse, schoolhouse, farmhouse, henhouse, greenhouse, glasshouse, dosshouse, gatehouse, Statehouse (*US* state capitol), lighthouse, hothouse, pothouse (small pub), courthouse, boathouse, outhouse, penthouse, guesthouse, bathhouse, almshouse, delouse, Nicklaus, booklouse (small wingless insect), woodlouse, reremouse (*Dialect* bat), dormouse, fieldmouse, titmouse, woodgrouse, sandgrouse.

bawdyhouse, powerhouse, summerhouse, Charterhouse, slaughterhouse, porterhouse, chapterhouse (building attached to cathedral), flittermouse (*Dialect* bat).

307 -uss

us, bus, cuss, fuss, Gus, jus (legal right), huss (dogfish), plus, muss (*US* rumple), pus, Russ, crus (lower leg), truss, suss, thus, wus (*Welsh* term of address).

airbus, debus, embus (military term), succuss, percuss, concuss, discuss, cuscus (Australasian marsupial), nonplus, untruss.

minibus, omnibus, blunderbuss, motorbus, overplus.

308 -oos

puss, Grus (constellation), schuss, Tungus (member of Mongoloid people), Anschluss (political or economic union), sourpuss, Vilnius (Russian city), ceteris paribus (other things being equal).

309 -uce

douce (*Scot* sedate), goose, juice, loose, sluice, moose, mousse, noose, Bruce, crouse (*Dialect* saucy), spruce, truce, Sousse (Tunisian port), use, deuce, puce, Zeus.

cayuse (*US* small pony), caboose, camboose (lumberjack's cabin), couscous (North African spicy dish), mongoose, wayzgoose (printing works' annual outing), verjuice (juice of unripe grapes), recluse, unloose, footloose, vamoose, burnoose (Arab's hooded cloak), slipnoose, papoose, ceruse (white lead), Elbrus (Russian mountain), abstruse, abuse, excuse, educe (logic term), deduce, reduce, seduce, produce, induce, conduce, refuse, effuse (spreading out), diffuse, profuse, ill-use, almuce (monk's fur-lined cape), prepuce, disuse, misuse, retuse (botany term), obtuse.

charlotte russe, superinduce (introduce as additional factor).

309.1

adduce (cite as proof), produce, traduce (speak badly of), reproduce, introduce.

310 -'s

joyous, psoas (muscle in loin), Phoebus, rebus, bulbous, nimbus, rhombus, thrombus, Orcus (Roman god), caucus, Dorcas, glaucous (covered with waxy bloom), raucous, ruckus, sulcus (linear groove), incus, rhonchus (rattling breathing sound), bronchus, righteous, gradus (book of musical exercises), nodus (problematic situation), Judas, Indus, Pindus (Greek mountain range), fundus (anatomy term), Dreyfus, scyphus (ancient Greek drinking cup), typhus, Rufus, rufous (reddish brown), Argus, negus (port and lemon drink), bogus, valgus (medical term), Angus, fungus, fungous, gorgeous, balas (red gemstone), Callas, callous, callus, Dallas, phallus, gallous (containing gallium), thallous (containing thallium), thallus (botany term), parlous (dangerous or difficult), talus, Troilus, bolus (ball of chewed food), troublous, windlass, Douglas, surplus, atlas, cutlass, Lammas, spermous (relating to sperm whale), Thermos (*Trademark*), Remus, Mimas (satellite of Saturn), primus, timeous (*Scot* timely), thymus, Thomas, Comus (Roman god), Momus (Greek god), chromous (containing chromium), houmous (Middle Eastern creamy dip), grumous (consisting of granular tissue), humus, dolmas (stuffed vine leaves), isthmus, Christmas, litmus, Xmas, stannous (containing tin), magnus, carpus (wrist), purpose, lupus (skin disease), upas (Javan tree), pompous, trespass, charas (hashish), varus (medical term), scabrous, glabrous (smooth-skinned), cribrous (sieve-like), fibrous, hydrous, Hydrus (constellation), wondrous, walrus, leprous, Cyprus, cypress, cuprous, citrus, nitrous, oestrus, lustrous, monstrous, dextrous, thyrsus (Bacchus' staff), versus, rhesus, Croesus, lapsus (error), Thapsus (ancient town near Carthage), precious, luscious, factious, fractious, noxious, anxious, conscious, captious, bumptious, scrumptious, Plautus (Roman dramatist), tortoise, cactus, Saktas (Hindu sect), ictus (poetry term), rictus (gap of open mouth), Sanctus (hymn in Eucharist), linctus, cantus (medieval church singing), Faustus, favus (fungal skin disease), nervous, fulvous (dull brownish-yellow), canvas, canvass, plexus, nexus, Texas, Jesus, Kansas.

Barabbas, jacobus (former English gold coin), succubus (female demon), incubus (male demon), syllabus, colobus (monkey), Barnabas, Damascus, self-righteous, unrighteous, solidus, Lepidus (ancient Roman statesman), iodous (containing iodine), tremendous, stupendous, horrendous, Josephus (Jewish historian), Sisyphus (Greek mythological king), pemphigus (blistering skin disease), azygous (developing singly), egregious, Tibullus (Roman poet), Lucullus (Roman general), Agulhas (South African headland), Catullus (Roman lyric poet), Wenceslas, enormous, posthumous, nystagmus, Michaelmas, Candlemas, Martinmas, chiasmus (rhetoric term), Erasmus, marasmus (wasting away), alumnus, Vertumnus (Roman god), acarpous (producing no fruit), syncarpous (botany term), Olympus, tenebrous, ludicrous, anhydrous (containing no water), chivalrous, disastrous, excursus (digression from main story), Caucasus, Pegasus, Confucius, infectious, innoxious (harmless), obnoxious, rambunctious, preconscious, subconscious, self-conscious, unconscious, singultus, Hephaestus (Greek god), Augustus, lecythus (ancient Greek vase), calathus (ancient Greek decorative symbol), Oireachtas (Irish parliament), Gustavus (Swedish king), mischievous, abraxas (ancient magic charm).

Menelaus (Greek mythological king), diadelphous (botany term), philadelphus (fragrant shrub), monadelphous (botany term), homozygous (genetics term), creophagous (flesh-eating), zoophagous (feeding on animals), sarcophagus, monophagous (feeding on one food), carpophagous (feeding on fruit), saprophagous (feeding on decaying matter), coprophagous (feeding on dung), oesophagus, analogous, homologous, isologous (chemistry term), Galápagos, asparagus, cunnilingus, gladiolus, nucleolus (part of cell nucleus), alveolus (small cavity), modiolus (part of inner ear), variolous (relating to smallpox), Nostradamus, borborygmus, acrocarpous (botany term), rhizocarpous (producing subterranean flowers), apocarpous (botany term), metacarpus (bones of the hand), multipurpose, idolatrous, ambidextrous, Dionysus (Greek god), Paracelsus (Swiss physician), semiprecious, semiconscious, microdontous (having unusually small teeth), Pocahontas (American Indian woman).

cumulonimbus, Camelopardus (constellation).

310.1

Dias (Portuguese navigator), Aeneas, Linnaeus, Piraeus, uraeus (ancient Egyptian sacred serpent), gluteus (muscle in buttock), scarabaeus (scarab), Manichaeus (Persian prophet), coryphaeus (ancient Greek chorus leader), Ptolemaeus (crater on moon).

310.2

scabious, rubious (dark red), dubious, plumbeous (relating to lead), Roscius (ancient Roman actor), sardius (Old Testament precious stone), radius, tedious, Claudius, studious, Orpheus, Morpheus (Greek god), congius (unit of liquid measure), malleus, Peleus (father of Achilles), pileus (part of mushroom), pileous (relating to hair), coleus, nucleus, nauplius (larva of crustacean), Ennius (Roman poet), corneous (horny), igneous, ligneous, clypeus (part of insect's head), copious, Gropius (US architect), impious, aqueous, ferreous (relating to iron), nacreous, pancreas, cupreous (relating to copper), citreous (greenish-yellow), vitreous, gaseous, caseous, Theseus, osseous, Celsius, Mencius (Chinese philosopher), courteous, piteous, Grotius (Dutch statesman), Proteus (Greek god), luteous (light greenish-yellow),

beauteous, duteous, plenteous, bounteous, struthious (relating to the ostrich), pervious, devious, previous, obvious, envious, nauseous.

Eusebius (early Christian bishop), triphibious, amphibious, Polybius (ancient Greek historian), compendious, dupondius (ancient Roman coin), Pelagius (British monk), rebellious, Equuleus (constellation), aculeus (prickle), abstemious, calumnious, Asclepius (Greek god), subaqueous, obsequious, opprobrious, lugubrious, salubrious, industrious, illustrious, caduceus (Hermes' staff), Lucretius (Roman poet), Helvétius (French philosopher), discourteous, rumbustious, Boethius (Roman philosopher), impervious, trapezius.

impecunious, Aesculapius (Roman god), Belisarius (Byzantine general), Stradivarius.

310.2.1
hideous, perfidious, chlamydeous (having sepals and petals), insidious, fastidious, invidious.

310.2.2
odious, melodious, commodious, Asmodeus (Jewish prince of demons), incommodious.

310.2.3
alias, Sibelius, Vesalius (Flemish anatomist).

310.2.4
Delius, Aurelius (Roman emperor), Berzelius (Swedish chemist), contumelious (insolent).

310.2.5
ileus (obstruction of intestine), bilious, Marsilius (Italian political philosopher), Lucilius (Roman satirist), punctilious, supercilious.

310.2.6
calcaneus (heel bone), Comenius (Czech educational reformer), extra-

neous, Pausanias (Greek geographer and historian), cutaneous, spontaneous, miscellaneous, percutaneous, subcutaneous, simultaneous, instantaneous, contemporaneous, extemporaneous.

310.2.7
genius, splenius (neck muscle), ingenious, arsenious (relating to arsenic), homogeneous, heterogeneous.

310.2.8
Arminius (Dutch theologian), vimineous (producing long flexible shoots), Flaminius (Roman general), gramineous (relating to grasses), sanguineous (relating to blood), ignominious.

310.2.9
euphonious, felonious, harmonious, erroneous, Petronius (Roman satirist), Suetonius (Roman historian), inharmonious.

310.2.9.1
ceremonious, acrimonious, parsimonious, sanctimonious, unceremonious.

310.2.10
Arius (Greek Christian theologian), carious, scarious (botany term), Marius (Roman general), various, Briareus (Greek giant), precarious, vicarious, calcareous, bifarious (botany term), gregarious, hilarious, denarius, Aquarius, retiarius (Roman gladiator), Sagittarius.

310.2.10.1
nefarious, omnifarious (of all sorts), multifarious.

310.2.11
serious, cereus (large cactus), Tiberius, cinereous (greyish), imperious, mysterious, deleterious.

310.2.12
Sirius, delirious.

310.2.13
aureus (Roman coin), Boreas (Greek god), glorious, arboreous (thickly wooded), laborious, inglorious, up-

roarious, censorious, sartorius, Sertorius (Roman soldier), notorious, victorious, Nestorius (Syrian churchman), uxorious, meritorious.

310.2.14
curious, furious, spurious, injurious, usurious, incurious, penurious, luxurious.

310.2.15
Nicias (Athenian statesman), piceous (relating to pitch), griseous (streaked with grey), Odysseus, Dionysius.

310.2.16
Statius (Roman poet), Ignatius (early Christian saint), fieri facias (legal term).

310.2.17
niveous (resembling snow), oblivious, lascivious.

310.2.18
pluvious, Vesuvius.

310.3
eyas (nestling hawk or falcon), bias, Gaius (Roman jurist), lias (blue limestone rock), pious, Pius, bacchius (metrical foot), Elias, Matthias, Ananias, Zacharias, hamadryas (type of baboon), nisi prius (former legal term).

310.4
congruous, menstruous, vacuous, nocuous, arduous, cernuous (drooping), sensuous, fatuous, virtuous, tortuous, fructuous, unctuous, flexuous.

superfluous, mellifluous, circumfluous (surrounded by water), incongruous, innocuous, promiscuous, deciduous, assiduous, ambiguous, contiguous, exiguous (scanty), impetuous, spirituous (containing alcohol), anfractuous (convoluted), tumultuous, voluptuous, contemptuous, tempestuous, incestuous.

310.4.1
perspicuous, transpicuous (transparent), conspicuous, inconspicuous.

310.4.2
strenuous, tenuous, ingenuous, disingenuous.

310.4.3
sinuous, continuous, discontinuous.

310.4.4
sumptuous, presumptuous.

310.5
gibbous, arquebus (long-barrelled gun), Erebus (Greek god), circumbendibus (circumlocution).

310.6
plumbous (containing lead), Columbus.

310.7
Bacchus, Gracchus (Roman tribune), Caracas.

310.8
carcass, sarcous (muscular or fleshy), Hipparchus (Greek astronomer), Aristarchus (crater on moon).

310.9
circus, cercus (zoology term), cysticercus (tapeworm larva).

310.10
muticous (botany term), distichous (arranged in two rows), tristichous (arranged in three rows), Cyzicus (ancient Greek colony), umbilicus, Autolycus, Copernicus, ulotrichous (having curly hair), Leviticus.

310.11
coccus (spherical bacterium), floccus (downy covering on birds), diplococcus (type of bacterium), pneumococcus, gonococcus, micrococcus, streptococcus.

310.12
focus, locus, crocus, hocus-pocus.

310.13
fucus (brown seaweed), mucous, mucus, Seleucus (Macedonian general), caducous (biology term), Ophiuchus (constellation).

310.14
abacus, Spartacus, Antiochus (Syrian king), diplodocus (herbivorous dinosaur), Telemachus (son of Odysseus), Callimachus (Greek poet), Lysimachus (king of Thrace), Caratacus (ancient British chieftain).

310.15
discus, viscous, viscus (large internal organ), hibiscus, meniscus, lemniscus (nerve fibres in brain).

310.16
Midas, Cnidus (ancient Greek city), nidus (insect's nest), Abydos (ancient Egyptian town), Nabonidus (Old Testament character).

310.17
exodus, hazardous, Enceladus (Greek mythological giant), ceratodus (extinct fish).

310.18
dimorphous (chemistry term), amorphous, polymorphous, rhizomorphous (resembling a root), anthropomorphous.

310.19
magus (Zoroastrian priest), tragus (projection in ear), Tagus (European river), vagus, choragus (ancient Greek chorus leader), Las Vegas.

310.20
courageous, umbrageous (shady), outrageous, contagious, advantageous, disadvantageous.

310.21
prodigious, religious, litigious, prestigious, irreligious, sacrilegious.

310.22
jealous, Hellas (ancient name for Greece), zealous, Marcellus (Roman general), ocellus (insect's simple eye), nucellus (botany term), entellus (monkey).

310.23

villus, villous (covered with long hairs), obelus (symbol in text), strobilus (plant cone), trochilus (humming-bird), Aeschylus, aphyllous (having no leaves), Angelus, lapillus (small piece of lava), perilous, scurrilous, bacillus, nautilus, pulvillus (pad on insect's leg), Theophilus (crater on moon), zoophilous (pollinated by animals), Herophilus (Greek anatomist), xerophilous (living in dry conditions), hydrophilous (growing in water), hygrophilous (growing in wet places), coprophilous (growing on dung), stenophyllous (having narrow leaves), aspergillus, adactylous (without fingers or toes), erysipelas, hectocotylus (zoology term).

310.24

hilus (anatomy term), stylus, monostylous (botany term).

310.25

garrulous, fabulous, sabulous (gritty), nebulous, bibulous (addicted to alcohol), tubulous (tube-shaped), flocculus (marking on sun's surface), calculus, modulus, pendulous, scrofulous, Regulus (Roman general), regulus (impure metal), famulus (sorcerer's attendant), hamulus (hooklike projection), emulous (competitive), tremulous, limulus (type of crab), stimulus, Romulus, annulus, populace, populous, scrupulous, patulous (spreading widely), volvulus (abnormal twisting of intestine).

edentulous (toothless), miraculous, tuberculous, homunculus (miniature man), ranunculus (plant genus), unscrupulous, convolvulus.

310.25.1

querulous, glomerulus (anatomy term).

310.25.2

ridiculous, funiculus (anatomy term), ventriculus (bird's gizzard), meticulous, canaliculus (small channel).

310.25.3

credulous, sedulous, incredulous.

310.25.4

stridulous, acidulous.

310.25.5

cumulus, tumulus, cirrocumulus, stratocumulus, altocumulus.

310.26

libellous, embolus, Daedalus, scandalous, carolus (former English coin), Tantalus (Greek mythological king), marvellous, frivolous, malleolus (bony projection on ankle), photophilous (growing in strong light), astragalus (anklebone), anomalous, asepalous (having no sepals), synsepalous (having joined sepals), apetalous (having no petals), sympetalous (having joined petals), Sardanapalus (Assyrian king), Papadopoulos.

310.26.1

obolus (Greek unit of weight), discobolus (discus thrower).

310.26.2

Nicholas, nickelous (relating to nickel), nidicolous (ornithology term), limicolous (living in mud), terricolous (living in soil), saxicolous (living on rocks), arenicolous (living in sandy places), stercoricolous (living in dung).

310.26.3

bicephalous (having two heads), Bucephalus, acephalous (headless), hydrocephalus.

310.27

famous, squamous (biology term), ramus (biology term), mandamus (legal term), uniramous (undivided), ignoramus.

310.28

didymous (in pairs), blasphemous, ginglymus (hinge joint), minimus, mittimus (legal term), maximus, Triptolemus (Greek mythological character).

310.28.1
animus, unanimous, magnanimous, pusillanimous.

310.28.2
onymous (bearing author's name), euonymus (cultivated tree), pseudonymous, synonymous, anonymous, eponymous, antonymous, polyonymous (having several names), Hieronymus, heteronymous (spelt alike).

310.29
infamous, venomous, Pyramus, monogamous, didynamous (botany term), autonomous, anadromous (migrating up river), catadromous (migrating down river), physostomous (zoology term).

310.29.1
bigamous, polygamous.

310.29.2
calamus (Asian palm), thalamus, hypothalamus.

310.29.3
xylotomous (boring into wood), hippopotamus.

310.30
trismus (lockjaw), strabismus, vaginismus (painful vaginal spasm).

310.31
anus, Janus, heinous, manus (wrist and hand), pandanus (palm-like plant), Uranus, Silvanus (Roman god), Coriolanus.

310.32
genus, venous, Venus, Albinus (English scholar), subgenus, Silenus (Greek satyr), scalenus (muscle in neck), Comnenus (Byzantine family), Campinas (Brazilian city), intravenous, arteriovenous.

310.33
ruinous, tendinous (relating to tendons), terminus, verminous, ominous, urinous (relating to urine), gangrenous, acinus (biology term), Circinus (constellation), mountainous, resinous.

libidinous, rubiginous (rust-coloured), indigenous, fuliginous (smoky or sooty), epigenous (growing on the surface), terrigenous (of the earth), perigynous (botany term), vertiginous, vortiginous (whirling), endogenous, homogenous, hypogenous (growing on undersurface), erogenous, urogenous (producing urine), hydrogenous, androgenous (producing only male offspring), nitrogenous, misogynous, autogenous (originating within the body), ferruginous (containing iron), gelatinous.

multitudinous, oleaginous (resembling oil), cartilaginous.

310.33.1
luminous, numinous (awe-inspiring), aluminous (resembling aluminium), voluminous, albuminous (containing albumin), leguminous, bituminous.

310.33.2
glutinous, mutinous, velutinous.

310.34
Minas, minus, Ninus (Assyrian king), spinous (resembling a thorn), sinus, vinous (relating to wine), echinus (sea urchin), Delphinus (constellation), Longinus (Greek writer), Aquinas, Quirinus (Roman god), uncinus (small hooked structure), Plotinus (Roman philosopher), pulvinus (botany term), botulinus (bacterium), matriclinous (resembling female parent), patriclinous (resembling male parent), monoclinous (botany term), Flamininus (Roman general), Antoninus (Roman emperor), laurustinus (flowering shrub).

310.35
onus, bonus, Jonas, clonus (type of convulsion), Cronus, tonus (muscle tone), Tithonus (Greek mythological character), Amazonas (Brazilian state).

310.36

Dardanus (mythological founder of Troy), villainous, uranous (relating to uranium), membranous, synchronous, tetanus, gluttonous, cavernous, ravenous, poisonous, Eridanus (constellation), diaphanous, cacophonous, homophonous (pronounced the same), Telegonus (son of Odysseus), Antigonus (Macedonian king), athermanous (opaque to radiant heat), monotonous, phototonus (botany term), allochthonous (geology term), autochthonous (geology term), diplostemonous (botany term).

310.37

Oedipus, polypus, Lysippus (Greek sculptor), Leucippus (Greek philosopher), platypus, eohippus, Aristippus (Greek philosopher).

310.38

corpus, porpoise, habeas corpus.

310.39

opus, Scopas (Greek sculptor), Canopus.

310.40

octopus, amphitropous (botany term), orthotropous (botany term), pithecanthropus.

310.41

campus, lampas (swelling in horse's mouth), pampas, grampus, hippocampus.

310.42

compass, rumpus, encompass, gyrocompass, astrocompass.

310.43

arras, Arras (French town), harass, embarrass, nonparous (never having given birth), disembarrass.

310.44

ferrous, terrace, nonferrous.

310.45

sclerous (hard or bony), serous, Severus (Roman emperor), Ahasuerus (Old Testament king).

310.46

Pyrrhus, cirrus, scirrhus (cancerous growth), scirrhous (firm), Algeciras (Spanish port).

310.47

gyrus (fold on brain surface), Cyrus, virus, papyrus, Epirus (region of Greece), desirous, echovirus, ultravirus.

310.48

aurous (containing gold), chorus, Horus (Egyptian sun god), chlorous (relating to chlorine), porous, sorus (plant's spore-producing structure), Taurus, torus, pelorus (type of gyrocompass), pylorus (opening in stomach), thesaurus, Centaurus (constellation), Epidaurus (ancient Greek port), Matamoros (Mexican port), Cassiodorus (Roman writer), tubuliflorous (having tubular flowers).

310.48.1

brontosaurus, brachiosaurus, tyrannosaurus.

310.49

Eurus (Greek mythological wind), Honduras, anurous (tailless), coenurus (larva of tapeworm), Arcturus (star), mercurous, Epicurus.

310.50

barbarous, Cerberus (three-headed dog), tuberous, slumberous, acarus (non-parasitic mite), decorous, Icarus, lecherous, treacherous, rapturous, murderous, odorous, Pandarus (Greek mythological character), slanderous, ponderous, chunderous (*Austral* nauseating), thunderous, Zephyrus (Greek god), sulphurous, phosphorus, phosphorous, rigorous, vigorous, languorous, dangerous, valorous, dolorous, amorous, clamorous, glamorous, timorous, humorous, humerus, numerous, generous, onerous, sonorous, vaporous, viperous (relating to a viper), copperas (chemical compound), Hesperus, Bosporus (Turkish strait), prosperous, ulcerous, cancerous, traitorous, tartarous (consisting of tartar), Tartarus (Greek mythological place), stertorous (characterized by heavy snoring), uterus, icterus (jaundice), apterous (wingless), dipterous (having two wings), boisterous, flavorous, Lazarus.

indecorous, adventurous, malodorous, inodorous, Pythagoras, monomerous (botany term), isomerous (botany term), obstreperous, uniparous, multiparous, viviparous, oviparous, dinoceras (extinct mammal), rhinoceros, Monoceros (constellation), adulterous, homopterous (entomology term), macropterous (having large wings), preposterous, cadaverous.

adiaphorous (medical term), electrophorus (apparatus generating static electricity).

310.50.1
cankerous, rancorous, cantankerous.

310.50.2
splendiferous, stelliferous (full of stars), melliferous (producing honey), mammiferous (having breasts), auriferous, ossiferous (containing bones), vociferous, calciferous, lactiferous, fructiferous, umbelliferous, fossiliferous, metalliferous, seminiferous (transporting semen), uriniferous (transporting urine), odoriferous, sudoriferous (producing sweat).

310.50.2.1
coniferous, carboniferous.

310.50.3
herbivorous, frugivorous (fruit-eating), vermivorous (worm-eating), granivorous (grain-eating), carnivorous, omnivorous, apivorous (bee-eating), piscivorous, baccivorous (berry-eating),

graminivorous (grass-eating), insectivorous.

310.51
Lassus (Flemish composer), passus (part of medieval narrative), Crassus, Parnassus, Manassas (US town), Halicarnassus (ancient Greek city).

310.52
Tarsus, tarsus, metatarsus.

310.53
Issus (ancient Turkish battle site), byssus (zoology term), Ephesus, narcissus.

310.54
Knossos, colossus.

310.55
census, consensus.

310.56
spacious, gracious.

herbaceous, sebaceous, bulbaceous (bulb-shaped), audacious, mordacious (bitingly sarcastic), rudaceous (geology term), mendacious, fugacious (passing quickly away), fagaceous (botany term), sagacious, pugnacious, capacious, rapacious, sequacious (following in regular sequence), loquacious, veracious, ceraceous (waxy), voracious, flirtatious, cretaceous (relating to chalk), crustaceous (having a shell), curvaceous, vivacious, vexatious, rosaceous.

alliaceous, liliaceous, tiliaceous (botany term), oleaceous (botany term), foliaceous (resembling a leaf), coriaceous (relating to leather), contumacious (obstinate), saponaceous, carbonaceous, solanaceous (botany term), Athanasius (saint), furfuraceous (relating to bran), arboraceous (resembling a tree), stercoraceous (relating to dung), disputatious, ostentatious, ranunculaceous (botany term).

310.56.1
efficacious, perspicacious, ericaceous (botany term), urticaceous (botany term), inefficacious.

310.56.2

edacious (greedy), predacious (predatory), orchidaceous, iridaceous, hamamelidaceous (botany term), amaryllidaceous.

310.56.3

fallacious, salacious, corollaceous (relating to petals), santalaceous (botany term), polygalaceous (botany term).

310.56.4

minacious (threatening), tenacious, gallinaceous (ornithology term), arenaceous (geology term), farinaceous, erinaceous (relating to hedgehogs), pertinacious.

310.57

specious, synoecious (botany term), facetious, autoecious (botany term), heteroecious (botany term).

310.58

vicious, ambitious, spadiceous (botany term), judicious, officious, flagitious (utterly wicked), delicious, siliceous (relating to silica), malicious, pernicious, propitious, auspicious, suspicious, sericeous (covered with silky hairs), lubricious, capricious, nutritious, factitious, fictitious, injudicious, inofficious (contrary to moral duty), inauspicious, meretricious, repetitious, adscititious (additional), adventitious, surreptitious, superstitious, supposititious.

310.58.1

seditious, expeditious.

310.58.2

Mauritius, avaricious.

310.59

cautious, tortious (legal term), incautious.

310.60

stotious (*Irish* drunk), precocious, ferocious, atrocious.

310.61

Prudentius (Latin Christian poet), tendentious, dissentious, licentious, pretentious, sententious, contentious, conscientious.

310.62

flatus, stratus, status, meatus, hiatus, afflatus (creative power), conatus (striving of natural impulse), saleratus (sodium bicarbonate), apparatus, nimbostratus, cirrostratus, altostratus, cumulostratus.

310.63

fetus, Cetus (constellation), quietus, boletus (brownish fungus), Admetus (Greek mythological king), Servetus (Spanish theologian), Epictetus (Greek philosopher).

310.64

coitus, habitus (physical state), fremitus (medical term), vomitus (vomited matter), crepitus (medical term), impetus, spiritous, acetous (resembling vinegar), Tacitus, covetous, circuitous, fortuitous, gratuitous, Hippolytus (Greek mythological character), calamitous, precipitous, ubiquitous, iniquitous, emeritus, Theocritus (Greek poet), Democritus (Greek philosopher), necessitous, felicitous, solicitous, propositus (legal term).

310.65

situs (location of body part), Titus, tinnitus (ringing in ears), pruritus, detritus, Saint Vitus, Polyclitus (Greek sculptor), Heraclitus (Greek philosopher).

310.66

lotus, Notus (Greek mythological wind), Duns Scotus (Scottish theologian), Polygnotus (Greek painter).

310.67

Brutus, arbutus.

310.68

riotous, Herodotus, eczematous, sclerodermatous (having hard scaly covering), microstomatous (having unusually small mouth).

310.69
rectus (straight muscle), prospectus, conspectus (overall view).

310.70
argentous (relating to silver), momentous, portentous, sedimentous, ligamentous.

310.71
Aegyptus (mythological Egyptian king), eucalyptus.

310.72
canthus (corner of the eye), Xanthus (ancient Asian city), acanthus, acanthous (resembling a thorn), strophanthus (tropical tree), ailanthus (deciduous tree), ananthous (having no flowers), monanthous (one-flowered), helianthus (sunflower), polyanthus, amianthus (variety of asbestos), Erymanthus (Greek mountain), agapanthus (African lily).

310.73
naevus, grievous, longevous (long-lived).

311 -ilse
fils (Middle Eastern coin), grilse.

312 -orlse
false, waltz.

313 -ulse
dulse (red seaweed), pulse, repulse, appulse (astronomy term), impulse, convulse.

314 -ance
hance (architectural term), Hanse (medieval guild of merchants), manse, stance, askance, romance, finance, expanse, Penzance.

315 -arnce
chance, dance, lance, glance, rance (red marble), France, prance, trance,

seance, faïence, nuance, perchance, mumchance (dumbstruck), mischance, enhance, freelance, entrance, advance, Afrikaans, contredanse (Continental dance), fer-de-lance (venomous snake), vraisemblance.

316 -ence
dense, fence, hence, flense (strip blubber from whale), pence, spence (*Dialect* larder), cense (burn incense), sense, tense, thence, whence, condense, defence, offence, immense, commence, prepense (premeditated), dispense, suspense, expense, incense, pretence, intense, self-defence, recommence, recompense, frankincense.

317 -ince
mince, quince, rinse, prince, since, wince, evince, province, convince.

318 -once
bonce, sconce, nonce, ponce, ensconce, response.

319 -ounce
ounce, bounce, jounce (jolt), flounce, pounce, trounce, enounce, denounce, renounce, announce, pronounce, mispronounce.

320 -unce
once, dunce, punce (*Dialect* kick or hit).

321 -'nce [further rhymes may be derived from **420**]
cadence, voidance (annulment), prudence, vengeance, parlance, silence, penance, ordnance, fourpence, sixpence, sequence, Clarence, cumbrance, hindrance, fragrance, entrance, monstrance (receptacle for consecrated Host), license, licence, absence, nonsense, patience, sentience (awareness), conscience, substance, instance, Constance, grievance, brilliance, pleasance

235

(secluded part of garden), presence, usance (commerce term).

abeyance, purveyance, conveyance, flamboyance, annoyance, clairvoyance, allowance, pursuance, disturbance, accordance, concordance, discordance, avoidance, impudence, decadence, abundance, elegance, emergence, resurgence, insurgence, divergence, convergence, allegiance, indulgence, vigilance, pestilence, condolence, virulence, turbulence, ambulance, opulence, corpulence, flatulence, petulance, performance, transhumance (seasonal migration of livestock), ordonnance (systematic arrangement), remanence (physics term), permanence, assonance, dissonance, consonance (agreement), sustenance, governance, resonance, repugnance, subsequence, consequence, eloquence, forbearance, recurrence, occurrence, incurrence, concurrence, remembrance, encumbrance, remonstrance, obeisance, renaissance, innocence, impatience, advertence, importance, inductance (electrical property), conductance (electrical property), reluctance, acquaintance, susceptance (magnetic property), acceptance, circumstance, observance, relevance, connivance, contrivance, ebullience, complaisance, cognizance.

significance, jurisprudence, correspondence, inadvertence, inobservance, omnipresence, recognizance.

overabundance, overindulgence.

321.1
ambience, radiance, audience, permeance, variance, prurience, miscreance, nescience, prescience, transience, irradiance, obedience, clairaudience (psychology term), resilience, convenience, recipience, experience, omniscience, disobedience, inconvenience, inexperience.

321.1.1
dalliance, mésalliance (marriage with social inferior).

321.2
science, defiance, affiance (betroth), reliance, alliance, appliance, compliance, misalliance.

321.3
affluence, effluence, influence, confluence, congruence, issuance, continuance.

321.4
credence, impedance (physics term), antecedence.

321.5
riddance, forbiddance, diffidence, confidence, precedence, incidence, evidence, providence, accidence (linguistics term), residence, self-confidence, coincidence.

321.6
guidance, subsidence.

321.7
resplendence, dependence, attendance, intendance (French public department), independence, condescendence (Scottish legal term).

321.8
arrogance, extravagance.

321.9
diligence, negligence, intelligence, intransigence, counterintelligence.

321.10
balance, valance, imbalance, unbalance, counterbalance.

321.11
valence (chemistry term), surveillance.

321.12
violence, indolence, somnolence, insolence, excellence, nonviolence, ambivalence, equivalence.

321.12.1
prevalence, malevolence, benevolence.

321.13
semblance, resemblance.

321.14
ordinance, eminence, dominance, prominence, chrominance (colour quality of light), luminance (brightness of light), desinence (ending of a word), pertinence, maintenance, countenance, abstinence, provenance, pre-eminence, illuminance (brightness of illumination), appurtenance, impertinence, discountenance, incontinence.

321.15
twopence, comeuppance.

321.16
Terence, aberrance, deterrence.

321.17
clearance, coherence, adherence, inherence, appearance, interference, incoherence, reappearance, nonappearance, disappearance, perseverance.

321.18
Lawrence, Florence, Torrance (Californian city), abhorrence.

321.19
durance (imprisonment), assurance, insurance, endurance, reassurance, coinsurance.

321.20
furtherance, deference, reference, preference, difference, sufferance, inference, conference, transference, tolerance, ignorance, temperance, utterance, protuberance, exuberance, indifference, circumference, belligerence, intolerance, deliverance.

321.20.1
reverence, severance, irreverence.

321.21
essence, quiescence, pubescence, frondescence (leaf-producing process), tumescence, senescence, virescence (process of becoming green), florescence (flowering process), excrescence, vitres-

cence (glass-producing process), quintessence.

acquiescence, erubescence (process of becoming red), iridescence, incandescence, decalescence (heat absorption by metal), recalescence (heat emission by metal), adolescence, opalescence, obsolescence, convalescence, detumescence, intumescence, luminescence, juvenescence, deliquescence, efflorescence, inflorescence, fluorescence, phosphorescence, vaporescence (production of vapour), delitescence (disappearance of disease symptoms), effervescence.

321.22
reticence, beneficence, munificence, magnificence, reminiscence, reconnaissance, resipiscence (acknowledgment of error), concupiscence, reviviscence (revival).

321.23
nuisance, translucence.

321.24
pittance, quittance, remittance, admittance, transmittance, penitence, appetence, competence, acquittance, exitance (measure of radiation emission), concomitance, impenitence, incompetence, inheritance, capacitance (electrical property).

321.25
impotence, omnipotence.

321.26
sentence, repentance.

321.27
distance, outdistance, assistance, persistence, subsistence, insistence, resistance, existence, coexistence.

321.28
brisance (shattering effect of explosion), defeasance (annulment), malfeasance (illegal act), nonfeasance (legal term), misfeasance (legal term).

322 -aps [also **268** + -s]
apse, lapse, schnapps, craps, traps (belongings), taps, perhaps, elapse, relapse, prolapse, collapse, synapse.

323 -apes [also **270** + -s]
gapes (disease of domestic fowl), drapes, traipse, jackanapes.

324 -eps [also **271** + -s]
Steppes, biceps, triceps, anableps (tropical fish), quadriceps, editio princeps (first printed edition).

325 -erps [also **272** + -s]
turps, stirps (line of descendants).

326 -eeps [also **273** + -s]
Pepys, creeps.

327 -ips [also **274** + -s]
snips (small metal-cutting shears), Cripps (British Labour statesman), thrips, Mendips, ellipse, Phillips, eclipse, forceps, midships, amidships, apocalypse.

328 -ipes [also **275** + -s]
cripes, swipes (*Slang* weak beer), bagpipes, panpipes, stovepipes (tight trousers).

329 -ops [also **276** + -s]
Ops (Roman goddess), copse, chops, drops, tops, stops (card game), Cheops (ancient Egyptian king), Pelops (Greek mythological character), stylops (parasitic insect), Cyclops, Cecrops (Greek mythological character), eardrops, muttonchops (side-whiskers), triceratops (rhinoceros-like dinosaur).

330 -orps [also **277** + -s]
corpse, Cleethorpes.

331 -imps [also **287** + -s]
timps (*short for* timpani), glimpse.

332 -umps [also **289** + -s]
dumps, mumps, trumps.

333 -ats [also **365** + -s]
flats, rats, swats (*Dialect* freshly brewed beer), dingbats (*Austral* delirium tremens), congrats, ersatz.

334 -arts [also **366** + -s]
arts, darts, Ghats (Indian mountain range), Harz (German mountain range), clarts (*Dialect* lumps of mud).

335 -aits [also **367** + -s]
Bates, Fates (Greek goddesses controlling destiny), rates, Greats (course at Oxford University), annates (revenue paid to pope), othergates (otherwise).

336 -ets [also **368** + -s]
let's, Metz (French city), Donets (Russian river), assets, pantalets, chervonets (Russian coin), solonetz (salt-rich soil), castanets.

337 -erts [also **369** + -s]
hertz, outskirts, kilohertz.

338 -eets [also **370** + -s]
eats, Keats.

339 -its [also **371** + -s]
its, it's, blitz, splits, spitz (breed of dog), quits, grits (coarsely ground grain), wits, blewits (edible fungus), kibitz (*US* interfere), rackets (game resembling squash), rickets, Saint Kitts (West Indian island), credits, giblets, minutes, Leibnitz, Biarritz, Auschwitz, Austerlitz (Napoleonic battle site), applesnits (Canadian apple dish), Saint Moritz, separates, Horowitz (Russian pianist), slivovitz, Massachusetts.

340 -ites [also **372** + -s]
lights, nights, brights (US car head-
lights), tights, whites, daylights, footlights, Dolomites.

341 -ots [also **373** + -s]
bots (digestive disease of horses),
Scots, lots, Notts., culottes, fleshpots.

342 -orts [also **374** + -s]
orts (Dialect scraps), sports, quartz,
shorts.

343 -oats [also **376** + -s]
Oates, groats (crushed cereal grain),
John o'Groats.

344 -outs [also **377** + -s]
grouts, thereabouts, whereabouts, hereabouts.

345 -oots [also **379** + -s]
foots (dregs), toots (term of endearment), kibbutz.

346 -utes [also **380** + -s]
boots, hoots, gumboots, cahoots.

347 -ants [also **407** + -s]
Hants., pants, Northants., Konstanz
(West German city), underpants.

348 -ints [also **412** + -s]
chintz, Linz (Austrian port), blintz
(thin filled pancake).

349 -ash
ash, bash, cash, cache, dash, fash (Scot
worry), gash, hash, lash, clash, flash,
plash (splash), splash, slash, mash,
smash, gnash, Nash, pash (Slang infatuation), rash, brash, crash, trash,
thrash, sash, tache (short for moustache), stash.

earbash (Austral talk incessantly), Wabash (US river), encash, czardas (Hungarian national dance), slapdash, rehash, eyelash, goulash, calash (horse-

drawn carriage), backlash, unlash,
whiplash, throatlash (bridle strap),
Shamash (Assyrian sun god), quamash
(US plant), mishmash, panache, gate-
crash, midrash (Jewish biblical com-
mentaries), potash, soutache (narrow
braid).

balderdash, pebble-dash, synchroflash
(camera mechanism), photoflash (flash
bulb), callipash (edible part of turtle),
sabretache (cavalryman's leather case),
succotash (US cooked mixed vegetables).

349.1
abash, calabash (US tropical tree).

350 -arsh
harsh, marsh, gouache (art term),
apache (Parisian gangster), moustache,
Chuvash (Russian people).

351 -esh
flesh, mesh, nesh, crèche, fresh, thresh,
tête-bêche (philatelic term), parfleche
(dried rawhide), horseflesh, enmesh,
Mureş (European river), refresh,
afresh, Marrakech, Bangladesh, synchromesh, Gilgamesh (legendary Sumerian king), Andhra Pradesh (Indian
state), Uttar Pradesh (Indian state),
Madhya Pradesh (Indian state).

352 -eesh
quiche, fiche (short for microfiche),
leash, niche, Niš (Yugoslavian town),
babiche (rawhide thongs), unleash,
hashish, maxixe (Brazilian dance), baksheesh, potiche (tall vase), schottische
(19th-century German dance), pastiche,
postiche (architectural term), microfiche, ouananiche (Atlantic salmon),
nouveau riche.

353 -ish [further rhymes may be
created by adding -ish to appropriate adjectives and nouns]
bish (Slang mistake), kish (carbon-rich
graphite), dish, fish, Flysch (Alpine

rock deposits), knish (stuffed dumpling), squish, wish, whish, swish.

Laoighis (Irish county), greyish, boyish, Jewish, bluish, shrewish, newish, furbish, snobbish, rubbish, blackish, brackish, rakish, peckish, Turkish, freakish, stockish (stupid), mawkish, bookish, Frankish, pinkish, monkish, reddish, Kurdish (language group), Swedish, modish, loudish, rudish, prudish, childish, Wendish (language group), fiendish, roundish, raffish, garfish, starfish, crayfish, offish, oarfish, crawfish, sawfish, oafish, blowfish, roughish, jewfish, bluefish, rockfish, stockfish, monkfish, trunkfish, codfish, swordfish, goldfish, dogfish, hogfish, frogfish, batfish, catfish, flatfish, ratfish, whitefish, saltfish, waggish, biggish, piggish, priggish, doggish, hoggish, roguish, sluggish, largish, Salish (American Indian language), churlish, girlish, stylish, Gaulish, smallish, Polish, owlish, bullish, foolish, ghoulish, mulish, publish, ticklish, English, purplish, famish, rammish, blemish, Flemish, skirmish, squeamish, Rhemish (relating to Rheims), warmish, banish, clannish, planish (produce smooth surface on), mannish, Spanish, vanish, garnish, tarnish, varnish, Danish, greenish, burnish, furnish, swinish, Cornish, corniche (coastal road), clownish, brownish, Hunnish (barbarous), punish, longish, apish, sheepish, foppish, popish, uppish, impish, lumpish (clumsy), frumpish, waspish, vanquish, parish, cherish, perish, currish (rude), Irish, boarish, moreish, boorish, Moorish, flattish, rattish, latish, fetish, Lettish, pettish, skittish, British, rightish, whitish, Scottish, goatish, loutish, sluttish, ruttish, Jutish (ancient dialect of Kent), brutish, coltish, Kentish, lavish, ravish, slavish, knavish, dervish, peevish, elvish, anguish, languish, unwish.

babyish, tomboyish, refurbish, Cavendish, jellyfish, killifish, standoffish, silverfish, angelfish, cuttlefish, damselfish, devilish, establish, accomplish, schoolmarmish, Carchemish (ancient Syrian city), womanish, kittenish, heathenish, relinquish, tovarisch (Russian term of address), distinguish, extinguish, disestablish.

353.1
caddish, Kaddish (ancient Jewish prayer), faddish, radish, horseradish.

353.2
blandish, brandish, standish (inkstand), outlandish.

353.3
elfish, selfish, shellfish, unselfish.

353.4
hellish, relish, embellish, disrelish (dislike).

353.5
polish, abolish, demolish.

353.6
Rhenish, replenish.

353.7
finish, Finnish, diminish.

353.8
donnish, admonish, astonish.

353.9
bearish, fairish, garish, squarish, nightmarish.

353.10
flourish, nourish, undernourish.

353.11
gibberish, lickerish, feverish, liverish, amateurish, impoverish.

354 -osh
bosh, Bosch (Dutch painter), cosh, gosh, josh (*US* to tease), cloche, slosh, nosh, posh, quash, squash, tosh, wash, swash (splash noisily).

brioche, kibosh, cohosh (US plant), guilloche (ornamental architectural border), backwash, musquash, caroche (ceremonial carriage), eyewash, siwash

(Canadian knitted sweater), awash, hogwash, brainwash, whitewash, outwash (glacial deposit), mouthwash.

tokoloshe (Bantu mythical malevolent creature), mackintosh.

355 -oshe
gauche, troche (lozenge).

356 -ush
Cush (biblical character), gush, hush, lush, blush, flush, plush, slush, mush, rush, brush, crush, thrush, tush, airbrush (atomizer), hairbrush, sagebrush (US shrub), nailbrush, paintbrush, toothbrush, woodrush (a plant), bulrush, inrush, onrush, uprush, outrush, underbrush (US undergrowth), bottlebrush (Australian shrub).

357 -oosh
bush, Cluj (Rumanian city), mush (Slang face), push, shush, tusche (substance used in lithography), whoosh, swoosh, shadbush (US shrub), ambush, spicebush (US shrub), saltbush (desert shrub), Hindu Kush (Asian mountain range).

358 -ushe
douche, louche (shifty), ruche, tarboosh (brimless Muslim cap), Ingush (Russian people), capuche (friar's large hood), barouche (horse-drawn carriage), cartouche, Kiddush (Jewish traditional blessing).

359 -arzh
plage (mark on sun's surface), bocage (French wooded countryside), sondage (archaeological trench), collage, ménage, barrage, garage, mirage, massage, dressage, corsage, frottage (rubbing), montage, gavage (forced feeding).

fuselage, persiflage, camouflage, badinage, decoupage (decoration with cutouts), entourage, arbitrage (stock exchange term), vernissage (opening of art exhibition), repechage (contest for runners-up), curettage (surgical process), reportage, cabotage (coastal navigation), sabotage, décolletage.

espionage, photomontage, counterespionage.

360 -azhe
beige, greige (undyed), Liège, manège (riding school), cortège.

361 -erzh
concierge, demivierge.

362 -eezh
prestige, noblesse oblige.

363 -ozhe
loge (theatre box), Limoges.

364 -uzhe
luge, rouge, Bruges, vouge (medieval weapon).

365 -at
at, bat, batt (quilt wadding), cat, kat (evergreen shrub), scat, skat (card game), chat, fat, hat, lat (former Latvian currency), blat (US bleat), flat, plait, Platte (US river system), plat (small plot), splat, slat, mat, matt, gnat, pat, Pat, spat, rat, brat, drat, prat, sprat, sat, tat, that, vat, VAT, twat.

Croat, sabbat (period of rest), brickbat, bullbat (American nightjar), combat, wombat, numbat (small Australian marsupial), dingbat, meerkat (South African mongoose), Sno-Cat (Trademark), mudcat (US catfish), wildcat, hellcat, polecat, hepcat, tipcat (a game), muscat, backchat, woodchat, whinchat, stonechat, chitchat, Sadat, SOGAT, sunhat, doormat, format, cowpat, threat, whereat, hereat, jurat (legal term), firebrat (small wingless insect), muskrat, comsat (short for communications satellite), Hallstatt (archaeology term), Darmstadt (West German city), Dumyat (Egyptian town).

Uniat (denoting Eastern Church group), caveat, acrobat, concordat (treaty), butterfat, marrowfat, Astolat (town in Arthurian legend), cervelat (smoked sausage), diplomat, achromat (type of lens), Laundromat (*Trademark*), automat, assignat (former French paper money), pitapat, ziggurat, Ballarat (Australian town), Ararat, dandiprat (16th-century English coin), Intelsat (communications satellite), habitat, aegrotat, ratatat, rheostat (electrical component), chemostat (apparatus for bacteria culture), haemostat (device to stop bleeding), thermostat, clinostat (apparatus for studying plants), barostat (device maintaining constant pressure), aerostat (lighter-than-air craft), pyrostat (fire-alarm activating device), hydrostat (water-detection device), Photostat (*Trademark*), rubáiyát.

Magnificat, requiescat, anastigmat (type of lens), ratatat-tat.

365.1
begat, Kattegat.

365.2 [further rhymes may be derived from **16.307.5**]
democrat, Eurocrat, bureaucrat, autocrat, plutocrat, aristocrat.

365.3
cravat, savate (form of boxing), avadavat (Asian weaverbird).

366 -art
art, baht (Thai currency), cart, chart, dart, fart, ghat (steps leading to river), Jat (Indo-European people), heart, hart, mart, smart, part, tart, start, wat (Thai Buddhist monastery).

kyat (Burmese currency), kiaat (African tree), tuart (eucalyptus tree), Hobart, Rabat (capital of Morocco), jam-bart (piece of armour), Descartes, teacart, go-kart, handcart, dogcart, dustcart, Bogart, Earhart (US aviatrix), blackheart (darkening of woody stems), Bernhardt, greenheart (tropical tree), sweetheart, Eilat (Israeli port), Kalat (division of Pakistan), outsmart, depart, forepart, rampart, impart, mouthpart, Mozart, diktat (imposed decree), redstart, upstart, kick-start.

à la carte, undercart (undercarriage), applecart, Bundesrat (West German federal council).

366.1
apart, Bonaparte, counterpart.

367 -ait
eight, ait (*Dialect* islet), bate, bait, skate, date, fate, fête, gait, gate, hate, late, plate, slate, mate, pate, spate, rate, crate, freight, great, grate, prate, trait, straight, strait, sate, Tate, state, weight, wait.

striate, debate, rebate, tubate (tubular), whitebait, baccate (berry-like), furcate (to fork), plicate (pleated), spicate (having spikes), falcate (sickle-shaped), truncate, cheapskate, predate, chordate (zoology term), caudate (having a tail), cordate (heart-shaped), backdate, mandate, update, misdate, outdate, postdate, sulphate, phosphate, Margate, ligate (constrict with ligature), jugate (having paired parts), floodgate, tailgate, tollgate, Vulgate, sluicegate, Ramsgate, alate (having wings), chelate (having claws), dilate, prolate (spheroidal), bullate (blistered or puckered), ablate, oblate (spheroidal), deflate, reflate, inflate, conflate (combine), drawplate (plate for extruding wire), endplate, nameplate, hotplate, footplate, breastplate, translate, playmate, squamate (scale-like), primate, comate (hairy), bromate, chromate, plumate (having feathers), checkmate, stalemate, schoolmate, roommate, inmate, shipmate, helpmate, classmate, messmate, flatmate, pennate (having feathers or wings), enate (related on mother's side), crenate (having a scalloped edge), binate (occurring in pairs), quinate (composed of five parts), connate (congenital), ornate, phonate (utter speech sounds), pronate, zonate (arranged in zones), lunate (crescent-shaped), agnate (having common male ancestor), magnate, stagnate, cognate (related), pupate, baldpate, palpate, makeweight, ferrate (chemical compound), serrate, aerate, irate, gyrate, orate, borate (chemical compound), chlorate, urate, prorate, librate (to waver), vibrate, third-rate, hydrate, quadrate (make square), migrate, ingrate, disrate (reduce to lower rank), tartrate, nitrate, titrate, filtrate, castrate, first-rate, prostrate, lustrate (purify through religious rituals), frustrate, substrate, clathrate (net-like), pulsate, ansate (having a handle), scutate (covered with bony plates), mutate, lactate, tractate (short tract), dictate, punctate (marked with spots), hastate (botany term), restate, estate, cristate (crested), downstate, upstate, misstate, ovate, flyweight, Kuwait, catchweight, lightweight, fixate, luxate (dislocate).

inchoate (just beginning), benzoate (chemical compound), incubate, intubate (medical term), demarcate, educate, manducate (eat or chew), confiscate, obfuscate (to obscure), infuscate (tinged with brown), coruscate (to sparkle), inundate, fecundate, caliphate, bisulphate, abrogate, subjugate, conjugate, corrugate, promulgate, elongate, Billingsgate, insufflate (blow into), numberplate, boilerplate, copperplate, contemplate, legislate, impregnate, designate, syncopate, extirpate, inculpate, exculpate, lucubrate (to study), adumbrate, dehydrate, second-rate, transmigrate, deflagrate (burn fiercely), infiltrate, concentrate, seques-

trate, illustrate, demonstrate, remonstrate, commutate (reverse electric current), amputate, auscultate, understate, intrastate, interstate, devastate, overstate, reinstate, excavate, enervate, renovate, innovate, aggravate, pennyweight (unit of weight), heavyweight, hundredweight, middleweight, bantamweight, Bassenthwaite.

circumvallate (surround with defensive fortification), interpellate, variolate (inoculate with smallpox virus), capreolate (having tendrils), lanceolate (narrow and tapering), electroplate, carbohydrate, extravasate (exude), tergiversate, methotrexate (a drug).

367.1
create, labiate (aromatic plant), brachiate (swing through trees), radiate, mediate, ideate (imagine), cochleate (shaped like snail's shell), permeate, expiate, re-create, procreate, miscreate (create badly), aviate, obviate, nauseate, roseate.

irradiate, dimidiate (to halve), repudiate, enucleate, delineate, laciniate (jagged), calumniate, excoriate, infuriate, luxuriate, inebriate, appropriate, impropriate (transfer to laity), expropriate, repatriate, expatriate, enunciate, denunciate, annunciate (announce), depreciate, appreciate, excruciate, lixiviate (chemistry term), exuviate (shed outer covering), asphyxiate.

367.1.1
maleate (chemical compound), retaliate.

367.1.2
filiate (fix legal paternity of), affiliate, humiliate, conciliate, disaffiliate.

367.1.3
oleate (chemical compound), spoliate (despoil), defoliate, bifoliate (having two leaves), exfoliate (flake off), linoleate (chemical compound).

367.1.4
caseate (become cheese-like), glaciate, emaciate.

367.1.5
satiate, expatiate, ingratiate.

367.1.6
vitiate, officiate, initiate, propitiate (appease).

367.1.7
negotiate, dissociate, associate, consociate (enter into friendly association), disassociate.

367.1.8
substantiate, instantiate (represent by an example), transubstantiate, circumstantiate.

367.1.9
potentiate (make potent), differentiate.

367.1.10
deviate, alleviate, abbreviate.

367.2
actuate, menstruate, graduate, valuate (*US* value), toluate (chemical compound), fluctuate, punctuate, eventuate (to result), accentuate, evacuate, evaluate, attenuate, extenuate, insinuate, infatuate, perpetuate, effectuate (bring about), individuate (give individuality to), disambiguate, superannuate.

367.2.1
situate, habituate.

367.3
lobate, globate, probate, bilobate, trilobate, conglobate (form into ball).

367.4
abate, cohobate (redistil), stylobate (architectural term), approbate (Scottish legal term), reprobate, acerbate (embitter), masturbate, stereobate (foundation of building), exacerbate.

367.5
dedicate, medicate, predicate, abdicate, indicate, syndicate, vindicate, defecate, spiflicate (*Slang* destroy), triplicate, supplicate, implicate, complicate, explicate (make explicit), fornicate, muricate (having a roughened surface), suricate (South African mongoose), fabricate, lubricate, rubricate (mark with red), imbricate (decorate with overlapping pattern), deprecate, imprecate, metricate, extricate, desiccate, vesicate (to blister), rusticate, exsiccate (dry up).

eradicate, adjudicate, nidificate (build a nest), certificate, pontificate, canonicate (office of canon), communicate, prevaricate, divaricate (diverge at wide angle), prefabricate, decorticate, authenticate, domesticate, sophisticate, prognosticate, hypothecate (legal term), detoxicate (to rid of poison), intoxicate, excommunicate.

367.5.1
duplicate, quadruplicate, reduplicate, centuplicate, quintuplicate.

367.5.2
masticate, elasticate, scholasticate (Jesuit's probation period).

367.6
locate, placate, vacate, bifurcate, suffocate, allocate, collocate, dislocate, translocate (displace), embrocate, altercate, advocate, reciprocate, equivocate.

367.7
sulcate (marked with parallel grooves), inculcate, bisulcate (cleft or cloven).

367.8
sedate, candidate, validate, chlamydate (zoology term), lapidate (pelt with stones), liquidate, fluoridate, depredate, antedate, oxidate, invalidate, consolidate, intimidate, dilapidate, elucidate.

367.9
gradate, vanadate (chemical compound), accommodate.

367.10
negate, delegate, relegate, colligate (join together), obligate, fumigate, ab-

negate, variegate, irrigate, aggregate, segregate, congregate, litigate, mitigate, castigate, instigate, navigate, levigate (grind into powder), suffumigate (fumigate from below), desegregate, investigate, circumnavigate.

367.11
objurgate (scold), propagate, expurgate, arrogate (claim without justification), subrogate (legal term), Watergate, homologate (ratify).

367.11.1
derogate (disparage), interrogate.

367.12
elate, delate (denounce), relate, barbellate (covered with bristles), sibilate (speak with hissing sound), flagellate, mamillate (having nipples), crenellate, depilate, oppilate (to block), correlate, vacillate, tessellate, oscillate, titillate, mutilate, cantillate (to chant), ventilate, scintillate, constellate (form into clusters), ethylate (chemistry term), methylate (chemistry term), assibilate (phonetics term), invigilate, dissimilate, assimilate, interrelate, salicylate (chemical compound), carboxylate (chemical compound).

367.12.1
jubilate, obnubilate (to darken).

367.13
tubulate (form into a tube), ambulate, peculate (embezzle), speculate, circulate, calculate, osculate (to kiss), adulate, modulate, undulate, regulate, lingulate (tongue-shaped), pullulate, ululate, emulate, formulate, cumulate, cannulate (medical term), granulate, cupulate (cup-shaped), sporulate (produce spores), insulate, capsulate (within a capsule), postulate, pustulate, ovulate.

somnambulate, perambulate, ejaculate, miscalculate, emasculate, acidulate (make slightly acid), coagulate, accumulate, encapsulate, congratulate, capitulate, absquatulate (decamp), expostulate.

discombobulate (throw into confusion), circumambulate, recapitulate.

367.13.1
tabulate, confabulate.

367.13.2
vermiculate (decorate with wavy markings), corniculate (having horns), matriculate, articulate, reticulate (covered with a network), gesticulate, disarticulate.

367.13.3
flocculate (form into aggregated mass), deflocculate, inoculate.

367.13.4
angulate, strangulate, triangulate.

367.13.5
simulate, stimulate, dissimulate.

367.13.6
stipulate, manipulate.

367.13.7
copulate, populate, depopulate.

367.14
collate, decollate, cucullate (hood-shaped), escalate, immolate, phenolate (disinfect), desolate, isolate, insolate (expose to sunlight), oxalate (chemical compound), faveolate (honeycombed), machicolate (fortifications term), de-escalate, cardinalate, extrapolate, interpolate.

367.14.1
violate, annihilate.

367.14.2
percolate, intercalate.

367.15
cremate, collimate (adjust optical instrument), sublimate, animate, decimate, intimate, estimate, guesstimate, legitimate, approximate, underestimate.

367.16
carbamate (chemical compound), cyclamate, diplomate (holder of a diploma), desquamate (scale off), consummate, automate, glutamate, meprobamate (tranquillizer), amalgamate.

367.17
innate, pinnate.

cachinnate (laugh loudly), machinate, echinate (covered with spines), pollinate, declinate (drooping), reclinate (bent backwards), culminate, fulminate, supinate, carinate (keel-shaped), marinate, chlorinate, fluorinate, urinate, circinate (botany term), lancinate, pepsinate (medical term), catenate (arrange in rings), Latinate, pectinate (comb-shaped), pulvinate (cushionlike), vaccinate, succinate (chemical compound), resinate.

subordinate, coordinate, originate, oxygenate, hydrogenate, desalinate, disseminate, inseminate, eliminate, recriminate, incriminate, discriminate, peregrinate, indoctrinate, hallucinate, agglutinate, deglutinate (extract gluten from), conglutinate (join together during healing), procrastinate, rejuvenate, ratiocinate (argue logically).

367.17.1
raffinate (chemistry term), decaffeinate.

367.17.2
paginate, evaginate (turn inside out), invaginate.

367.17.3
laminate, deaminate (biochemistry term), delaminate (divide into thin layers), contaminate, interlaminate, decontaminate.

367.17.4
germinate, terminate, exterminate.

367.17.5
dominate, nominate, abominate, predominate, denominate.

367.17.6
ruminate, illuminate, aluminate (chemical compound), acuminate (make pointed).

367.17.7
fascinate, deracinate (uproot), assassinate.

367.18
donate, neonate, carbonate, hibernate, cybernate (control with mechanism), hyphenate, sulphonate (chemistry term), manganate (chemical compound), ammonate (compound containing ammonia), emanate, personate (act the part of), fractionate (separate into constituents), detonate, alternate, sultanate, intonate, consternate, alienate, resonate, decarbonate, permanganate, impersonate.

367.19
constipate, emancipate.

367.19.1
dissipate, participate, anticipate.

367.20
equate, liquate (separate by melting), antiquate.

367.21
berate, cirrate (biology term), aspirate, butyrate (chemical compound).

367.22
mercurate (treat with mercury), pandurate (botany term), sulphurate, fulgurate, depurate (purify), suppurate, maturate, saturate, triturate (grind into fine powder), obturate (block up), micturate, inaugurate.

367.23
narrate, liberate, decorate, federate, moderate, underrate, perforate, biforate (having two openings), camphorate, tolerate, separate, operate, perorate, sororate (marriage custom), acerate (needle-shaped), lacerate, macerate, susurrate (make whispering sound), ulcerate, overrate, exarate (entomology term).

elaborate, collaborate, reverberate, deliberate, corroborate, redecorate, edulcorate (purify by washing), acculturate (assimilate another group's culture), confederate, desiderate (long for), preponderate, proliferate, vociferate, invigorate, exaggerate, refrigerate, decelerate, accelerate, exhilarate, commemorate, agglomerate, conglomerate, enumerate, incinerate, itinerate (travel about), exonerate, remunerate, evaporate, cooperate, incorporate, recuperate, vituperate, exasperate, incarcerate, chelicerate (spider-like animal), eviscerate, expectorate, adulterate, coelenterate, exenterate (remove by surgery), asseverate (declare emphatically), commiserate.

ameliorate, deteriorate, equiponderate (to counterbalance).

367.23.1
generate, venerate, degenerate, regenerate, intenerate (make tender).

367.23.2
iterate, reiterate, alliterate, obliterate, transliterate.

367.24
calibrate, celebrate, cerebrate, concelebrate (celebrate mass together), equilibrate, decerebrate (remove brain).

367.25
picrate (chemical compound), desecrate, consecrate, execrate, deconsecrate.

367.26
regrate (buy up anticipating profit), emigrate, immigrate, denigrate, integrate, redintegrate (make whole again), disintegrate.

367.27
citrate, arbitrate, penetrate, perpetrate, impetrate (obtain by prayer).

367.28
orchestrate, magistrate, administrate.

367.29
sensate, condensate (substance formed by condensation), compensate, insensate.

367.30
hebetate (having a blunt point), meditate, agitate, sagittate (arrow-shaped), vegetate, digitate, cogitate, imitate, capitate (headlike), crepitate (to crackle), palpitate, irritate, nictitate (to blink), gravitate, levitate, hesitate, premeditate, revegetate (grow again), regurgitate, ingurgitate (to gorge), excogitate (devise), decapitate, decrepitate (crackle on heating), precipitate, necessitate, felicitate, resuscitate.

367.30.1
militate, debilitate, habilitate (*US* equip and finance), facilitate, rehabilitate.

367.30.2
acetate, subacetate (crystalline compound), capacitate (make legally competent), incapacitate.

367.31
notate, rotate, annotate, dissertate, tête-à-tête.

367.32
dentate, edentate, bidentate, tridentate, commentate, potentate, orientate, disorientate.

367.33
gestate, testate, intestate.

367.34
costate (having ribs), prostate, apostate.

367.35
nervate (having veins), incurvate (curve inwards), innervate (supply nerves to).

367.36
salivate, elevate, titivate, motivate, activate, cultivate, captivate, aestivate, insalivate (saturate food with saliva), de-

activate, reactivate, inactivate, radioactivate.

367.37
excavate, enervate, renovate, innovate, aggravate.

367.38
await, underweight, paperweight, welterweight, counterweight, featherweight, overweight.

368 -et
ate, bet, sket (*Welsh* to splash), debt, get, jet, het, Lett, let, blet (decay in overripe fruit), met, net, pet, ret (soak textile fibre), fret, tret (commerce term), threat, set, sett (small paving slab), stet, vet, whet, wet, sweat, yet.

layette, barbette (gun platform inside parapet), maquette (sculptor's preliminary model), snackette (snack bar), moquette, coquette, coquet (behave flirtatiously), croquette, banquette, vedette, mofette (opening in volcano), Tophet (Old Testament place), baguette, beget, forget, georgette, ramjet (type of jet engine), fanjet (type of jet engine), Colette, toilette, roulette, inlet, outlet, armet (medieval helmet), Kamet (Indian mountain), roomette (*US* railway sleeping compartment), palmette (ornament resembling palm leaf), kismet, hairnet, dinette, nonet, cornett (old woodwind instrument), lunette, brunette, dragnet, fishnet, pipette, Siret (European river), fleurette (flower-shaped ornament), curet, burette, soubrette (pert girl), aigrette (long feather on hat), regret, chevrette (skin of young goat), asset, cassette, placet (vote of assent), tacet (musical term), reset, fossette (small depression in bone), poussette (country dancing figure), subset, headset, wadset (*Scot* mortgage), handset, offset, filmset, inset, onset, boneset (flowering plant), unset, sunset, typeset, upset, outset, ashet (*Dialect* dish), fléchette (missile

dropped from aircraft), brochette, fourchette (anatomy term), couchette, planchette (board for spirit messages), courgette, quartet, motet, octet, quintet, septet, sestet (six-line verse), sextet, curvet (dressage term), revet (face with stones), corvette (small escort ship), cuvette (shallow dish), quickset (type of hedge), thickset, paillette (sequin), vignette, lorgnette, noisette, rosette.

oubliette (type of dungeon), winceyette, serviette, turbojet, suffragette, superhet (radio receiver), aiguillette (ornament on military uniform), landaulet (small horse-drawn carriage), briolette (pear-shaped jewel), triolet (verse form), rondelet (type of poem), flageolet, flannelette, epaulet, mantelet, novelette, calumet (peace pipe), Antoinette, bobbinet (netted fabric), stockinet, kitchenette, midinette (Parisian salesgirl), clarinet, bassinet, satinet, martinet, alkanet (flowering plant), falconet (small falcon), lansquenet (gambling game), luncheonette (*US* café), wagonette (horse-drawn vehicle), burgonet (16th-century helmet), ballonet (gas compartment in balloon), maisonette, canzonet (short lively song), salopette, imaret (Turkish hospice for pilgrims), vinaigrette, photoset, underset (ocean undercurrent), letterset, avocet, overset (disturb), trebuchet (medieval weapon), epithet, minivet (Asian songbird), vilayet (Turkish administrative division), marquisette (type of fabric), chemisette (underbodice), anisette.

Tafilalet (Moroccan oasis), marionette.

368.1
duet, silhouette, pirouette, minuet, statuette.

368.2
Tibet, quodlibet.

368.3
abet, alphabet.

368.4
piquet (card game), briquette (brick of compressed fuel), etiquette.

368.5
cadet, Bernadette.

368.6
barrette (hair clasp), Leatherette (*Trademark*), Launderette (*Trademark*), cigarette, majorette, cellaret (compartment for wine bottles), collarette, solleret (part of armour), swimmeret (zoology term), bannerette, lanneret (large male falcon), minaret, spinneret, usherette.

368.7
beset, salicet (organ stop), scilicet (that is), videlicet (namely).

368.8
musette (type of bagpipe), crêpe suzette.

368.9
gazette, marmoset.

369 -ert
curt, skirt, chert (variety of quartz), dirt, girt, hurt, blurt, flirt, pert, spurt, quirt (whip with leather thong), squirt, cert, shirt, Sturt (English explorer), vert (former legal term), wort.

seagirt, alert, inert, unhurt, expert, milkwort (flowering plant), assert, insert, concert, outsert (printing term), Blackshirt, nightshirt, pervert, terreverte (painting pigment), divert, overt, obvert (logic term), subvert, advert, invert, convert, stitchwort, woundwort, ragwort, stonewort (green alga), pipewort, soapwort, exsert (protrude), desert, dessert, exert.

miniskirt, underskirt, malapert (saucy), inexpert, navicert (neutral ship's cargo certificate), disconcert, undershirt, reconvert, pennywort, moneywort, gipsywort, bladderwort, slipperwort, liverwort, animadvert (criticize strongly).

369.1
evert, revert, ambivert (psychology term), antevert (displace by tilting forwards).

369.2
avert, pervert, introvert, controvert, extrovert.

370 -eet
eat, beet, beat, skeet, cheat, feet, feat, heat, leet (former manorial court), leat (trench conveying water), bleat, cleat, fleet, gleet (gonorrhoeal discharge), pleat, sleet, meet, meat, mete, neat, peat, Crete, greet, treat, street, seat, cete (group of badgers), sheet, teat, wheat, sweet, suite, tweet.

browbeat, deadbeat, offbeat, drumbeat, downbeat, upbeat, heartbeat, mesquite (small tropical tree), escheat (legal term), dustsheet, effete, defeat, reheat, elite, delete, deplete, replete, complete, athlete, gamete, pigmeat, unmeet (unsuitable), forcemeat, mincemeat, sweetmeat, repeat, compete, buckwheat, terete (cylindrical and tapering), secrete, accrete, concrete, discreet, discrete, excrete, afreet (Arabian mythological monster), retreat, maltreat, entreat, estreat (legal term), mistreat, bystreet, backstreet, reseat, deceit, receipt, unseat, conceit, freesheet (free newspaper), foresheet, broadsheet, groundsheet, mainsheet (nautical term), slipsheet (printing term), petite, aesthete.

polychaete (marine worm), lorikeet (small parrot), parakeet, spirochaete (bacterium), exegete (interpreter of biblical text), superheat (heat above boiling point), overheat, obsolete, paraclete (mediator), incomplete, marguerite, Masorete (Hebrew scholar or rabbi), overeat, indiscreet, meadowsweet, bittersweet.

371 -it

it, bit, bitt (mooring post), kit, skit, chit, dit (short sound in code), fit, git, hit, lit, flit, split, slit, mitt, smit (*Dialect* infection), Schmidt, nit, knit, pit, Pitt, spit, quit, squit (*Slang* insignificant person), writ, Brit, brit (young herring), frit (glaze-making material), grit, sprit (nautical term), sit, shit, tit, wit, Whit, whit, twit.

striate, poet, debit, rarebit, obit (*short for* obituary), Cobbett (English journalist), gobbet (chunk of raw meat), orbit, sorbet, cubit, ambit, gambit, titbit, becket (nautical term), Beckett, banket (gold-bearing rock), blanket, trinket, junket, gasket, lasket (nautical term), basket, casket, flasket (long shallow basket), biscuit, brisket, frisket (printing term), bosket (thicket), musket, hatchet, ratchet, rochet (bishop's white surplice), crotchet, adit, audit, plaudit, bandit, Chindit (World War II soldier), conduit, pundit, surfeit, prophet, profit, soffit (architectural term), forfeit, buffet, tuffet, nymphet, comfit, unfit, outfit, agate, garget (inflammation of cow's udder), target, legate (envoy), Reigate, nugget, drugget (floor-covering fabric), Newgate, Tlingit (American Indian), ringgit (Malaysian currency), gadget, parget (plaster or mortar), pledget (pad used in bandaging), digit, fidget, midget, Bridget, widget, budget, legit, mallet, palate, palette, sallet (15th-century helmet), valet, scarlet, starlet, varlet, playlet, raylet, murrelet (small diving bird), sterlet (small sturgeon), islet, eyelet, stylet (wire in surgical instrument), twilit, collet (claw in jewellery setting), Smollett (Scottish novelist), wallet, toilet, owlet, cullet (waste glass), gullet, mullet, tablet, cablet (small cable), gablet (small gable), driblet (small amount), triblet (spindle used in ringmaking), boblet (two-man bobsleigh), goblet, doublet, circlet, pikelet, spikelet

(small grass flower), booklet, brooklet, anklet, cloudlet, leaflet, pamphlet, eaglet, piglet, singlet, camlet (tough waterproof cloth), hamlet, armlet, gimlet, omelette, veinlet, unlit, sunlit, moonlit, kinglet (small warbler), ringlet, springlet, winglet, chaplet (wreath for head), ripplet (small ripple), triplet, droplet, couplet, drupelet (small fruit), duplet (chemistry term), template, bracelet, corselet (foundation garment), flatlet, Bartlett, martlet (heraldic symbol resembling swallow), partlet (16th-century shawl), tartlet, platelet, notelet, cutlet, nutlet (part of fruit), gauntlet, wristlet (bracelet), wavelet, valvelet, Hazlitt, haslet (meat loaf), emmet (*Dialect* ant), hermit, permit, cermet (high-temperature-resistant material), climate, omit, plummet, summit, submit, admit, helmet, pelmet, transmit, Barnet, garnet, genet (catlike mammal), jennet (female donkey), rennet, senate, sennet (fanfare), sennit (braided cordage), tenet, unit, magnet, unknit, close-knit, tightknit, Capet, lappet (small hanging flap), tappet, carpet, fleapit, skippet (box for preserving document), snippet, pipit, frippet (frivolous young woman), sippet (small piece), tippet (fur cape), whippet, moppet, poppet, puppet, cockpit, chalkpit, sandpit, pulpit, armpit, limpet, crumpet, trumpet, strumpet, respite, acquit, banquet, barret (small cap), caret (symbol indicating insertion), garret, pirate, lyrate (lyreshaped), floret, curate, turret, worrit (*Dialect* tease), secret, Sanskrit, quadrate (cube), pomfret (liquorice sweet), egret, culprit, bowsprit, portrait, basset, facet, tacit, tasset (piece of armour), tercet (three lines of verse), resit, cosset, posset, corset, Dorset, faucet, gusset, russet, dulcet, transit, lancet, Consett, sculpsit (inscription on sculpture), whatsit, freshet (sudden overflowing of river), bullshit, horseshit, bluetit, tomtit, davit (crane-like device), brevet, rivet, grivet (African monkey), privet, trivet, civet, swivet (*Dialect* state of excitement), private, covet, velvet, peewit, godwit (large shore bird), halfwit, dimwit, nitwit, outwit, exit, Tilsit (Russian town).

sobeit, howbeit, albeit, cucurbit (plant of cucumber family), post-obit (legal term), advocate, retrofit (equip with extra parts), Photofit (*Trademark*), counterfeit, discomfit, conjugate, corrugate (wrinkled), Harrogate, surrogate, quadruplet, quintuplet, sextuplet, manumit (free from slavery), decrepit, adequate, priorate (office of prior), floweret, vertebrate, hypocrite, interpret, self-portrait, non licet (unlawful), Somerset, aquavit, margravate, nimblewit (*US* clever person), thimblewit (*US* dunce).

lickety-split (*US* very quickly), predestinate (foreordained), inadequate, invertebrate, haematocrit (medical term), misinterpret, Narraganset (American Indian), affidavit, electromagnet.

371.1

brachiate (botany term), gladiate (sword-shaped), radiate (radiating), ciliate (biology term), pileate (crested), foliate, nucleate (having a nucleus), craniate (having a skull), lineate (streaked), cuneate (wedge-shaped), opiate, seriate (forming a series), fimbriate (fringed), ocreate (sheathed), prussiate (cyanide), cruciate.

chalybeate (containing iron salts), immediate, dimidiate (divided in halves), collegiate, vicariate (rank of vicar), inebriate, appropriate, repatriate, expatriate, initiate (novice), patriciate (rank of patrician), novitiate, associate, licentiate.

intermediate, unifoliate, multifoliate, multinucleate, inappropriate.

371.1.1

Juliet, aculeate (pointed).

371.1.2

aureate (gilded), laureate, baccalaureate, professoriate.

371.2

arcuate (arc-shaped), graduate, Innuit (Eskimo), sinuate (botany term), Jesuit, postgraduate, attenuate (weakened), undergraduate.

371.3

bluet (flowering plant), cruet, suet, intuit (know instinctively).

371.4

babbitt (line with alloy), habit, rabbit, drabbet (coarse yellowish-brown fabric), cohabit, inhabit.

371.5

gibbet, zibet (Asian catlike mammal), prohibit, inhibit, celibate, exhibit, flibbertigibbet.

371.6

jacket, placket (dressmaking term), packet, racquet, racket, bracket, cracket (*Dialect* three-legged stool), tacket (*Dialect* hobnail), bluejacket, straitjacket, lumberjacket, leatherjacket.

371.7

market, Newmarket, matriarchate, patriarchate, Euromarket, hypermarket, supermarket.

371.8

circuit, bifurcate, trifurcate (having three branches), microcircuit.

371.9

snicket (*Dialect* passageway), picket, cricket, pricket (young male deer), ticket, thicket, wicket, predicate, syndicate, forficate (deeply forked), delicate, silicate (chemical compound), triplicate, tunicate (marine animal), imbricate (overlapping), affricate (speech sound), intricate, corticate (having rind or bark), certificate, pontificate, indelicate, umbilicate (having a navel), divaricate (branching), Identikit (*Trademark*), sophisticate, borosilicate (chemical compound).

371.9.1
duplicate, quadruplicate, reduplicate (repeated), centuplicate.

371.10
docket, locket, pocket, rocket, brocket (small deer), crocket (architectural ornament), Crockett, sprocket, socket, pickpocket, skyrocket, retrorocket.

371.11
bucket, tucket (flourish on trumpet), trebucket (medieval weapon), gutbucket (style of jazz-playing), Nantucket.

371.12
edit, credit, coedit, subedit, accredit, discredit, disaccredit.

371.13
befit, benefit.

371.14
frigate, delegate, profligate, aggregate, congregate (assembled).

371.15
pellet, prelate, stellate, flabellate (fan-shaped), appellate (relating to appeals), Marprelate (Puritan author), varicellate (marked with small ridges).

371.16
billet, skillet, fillet, millet, rillet, willet (US shore bird), flagellate (whip-like), distillate, penicillate (having tufts of hairs), verticillate (arranged in whorls).

371.17
bullet, pullet, culet (base of gemstone), tabulate (having a flat surface), undulate, virgulate (rod-shaped), ligulate (strap-shaped), angulate (having angles), ungulate, amulet, cumulate, cumulet (variety of pigeon), annulet (architectural moulding), annulate (having rings), consulate, spatulate, postulate, pustulate, rivulet, vesiculate (biology term), tuberculate (covered with nodules), pedunculate (biology term), avunculate (assigning rights to uncle), coagulate (product of coagulation).

371.17.1
sacculate (biology term), ejaculate (semen), immaculate.

371.17.2
vermiculate (relating to worms), geniculate (bending sharply), auriculate (having ears), articulate, reticulate (in form of network), testiculate (having an oval shape), unguiculate (having claws), inarticulate.

371.18
chocolate, desolate, coverlet, subulate (tapering to a point), amygdalate (relating to almonds), disconsolate, apostolate.

371.18.1
violet, inviolate, ultraviolet.

371.19
emit, limit, remit, delimit, animate, ultimate, intimate, estimate, guesstimate, proximate (nearest or next), inanimate, legitimate, penultimate, approximate, illegitimate, underestimate.

371.20
comet, grommet, vomit, Mahomet.

371.21
commit, permit, recommit, consummate, intermit (suspend activity at intervals).

371.22
Banat (plain in eastern Europe), gannet, Janet, planet, granite, Thanet, pomegranate.

371.23
burnet (flowering plant), gurnet (European marine fish), ternate (consisting of three parts), alternate.

371.24
linnet, minute, spinet, cabinet, rabbinate (office of rabbi), turbinate (scroll-shaped), definite, infinite, laminate, staminate (having stamens), nominate, agminate (gathered together), basinet (medieval helmet), uncinate (hook-shaped), runcinate (botany term), ob-

stinate, indefinite, effeminate, determinate, discriminate, innominate, denominate (maths term), acuminate (narrowing to sharp point), resupinate (reversed or inverted), predeterminate, indeterminate, indiscriminate.

371.24.1
ordinate, coordinate, subordinate, inordinate, incoordinate, insubordinate.

371.24.2
vaginate (having a sheath), Plantagenet, invaginate (folded back on itself).

371.25
bonnet, sonnet, bluebonnet (Scottish brimless hat), unbonnet, sunbonnet.

371.26
cornet, hornet, bicornate.

371.27
punnet, whodunit.

371.28
bayonet, dragonet (spiny-finned fish), pulmonate (having lungs), baronet, coronet, passionate, bicarbonate, diaconate (office of deacon), compassionate, dispassionate, affectionate, subalternate (botany term), Italianate, companionate.

371.28.1
fortunate, unfortunate, importunate.

371.28.2
proportionate, extortionate, disproportionate.

371.29
cygnet, signet, designate.

371.30
parapet, episcopate.

371.31
ferret, merit, serrate, terret (ring on harness), wherrit (to worry), inherit, demerit, disinherit.

371.32
cerate (hard ointment), emirate, vizierate.

371.33
skirret (plant with edible roots), spirit, aspirate, dispirit, inspirit (fill with vigour), levirate (marrying brother's widow), triumvirate.

371.34
accurate, obdurate, indurate (hardened), figurate (musical term), inaccurate, barbiturate.

371.35
federate, moderate, glomerate, numerate, separate, corporate, temperate, desperate, disparate, literate, doctorate, favourite, leveret.

deliberate, confederate, considerate, immoderate, imperforate, agglomerate, conglomerate, innumerate, degenerate, regenerate (restored), subtemperate, intemperate, commensurate, illiterate, electorate, inspectorate, directorate, protectorate, adulterate (impure).

inconsiderate, unregenerate (unrepentant), incommensurate, semiliterate.

371.35.1
tabaret (upholstery fabric), taboret (low stool), elaborate.

371.35.2
preterite, inveterate.

371.36
licit, deficit, elicit, illicit, solicit, implicit, explicit, inexplicit.

371.37
vervet (South African monkey), incurvate (curved inwards), acervate (growing in clusters), enervate (weakened).

371.38
visit, marquisate, marquessate, requisite, perquisite, exquisite, prerequisite.

371.39
closet, posit (postulate), deposit, reposit (put away).

371.40

apposite, opposite, composite, inapposite.

372 -ite

bite, byte (computer term), bight (indentation of shoreline), kite, skite (*Austral* to boast), fight, height, light, blight, flight, flite (*Scot* to scold), plight, sleight, slight, might, mite, smite, knight, night, spite, quite, rite, right, write, Wright, bright, krait (venomous snake), fright, sprite, trite, sight, cite, site, tight, Wight, white, wite (*Dialect* to blame), twite (European finch).

Shiite, fleabite, backbite, snakebite, albite (mineral), frostbite, trachyte (volcanic rock), trichite (slender crystal), Melchite (Eastern Church member), cheddite (an explosive), cordite (an explosive), Luddite, indict, graphite, psephite (type of rock), ophite (type of rock), cockfight, dogfight, sulphite (salt of sulphurous acid), bullfight, gunfight, phosphite (salt of phosphorous acid), prizefight, augite (mineral), halite (rock salt), marlite (type of marl), starlight, daylight, perlite (volcanic rock), skylight, highlight, stylite (pillar-dwelling recluse), twilight, mullite (mineral), searchlight, deadlight (nautical term), headlight, sidelight, floodlight, halflight, taillight, limelight, fanlight, sunlight, moonlight, aplite (type of rock), hoplite (ancient Greek infantryman), droplight (movable electric light), stoplight, gaslight, flashlight, streetlight, spotlight, Hamite (member of African people), samite (heavy silk fabric), Marmite (*Trademark*), Boehmite (mineral), termite, Semite, chromite (mineral), somite (embryology term), stannite (mineral), kainite (mineral), finite, crinite (covered with soft hairs), dunnite (an explosive), dunite (type of rock), Sunnite (orthodox Muslim), unite, stibnite (mineral), weeknight, ichnite (fos-

silized footprint), midnight, good-night, Samnite (ancient Italian), fortnight, despite, requite, playwright, ferrite, pyrite (mineral), chlorite (mineral), norite (type of rock), thorite (mineral), eyebright (flowering plant), Arkwright, dendrite, chondrite (meteorite), nephrite (mineral), tephrite (type of basalt), affright, wheelwright, millwright, alright, wainwright, downright, shipwright, typewrite, upright, cuprite (mineral), Cartwright, outright, contrite, ghostwrite, birthright, forthright, eyesight, foresight, leucite (mineral), hindsight, calcite (mineral), felsite (type of rock), bombsight, insight, incite, quartzite (type of rock), kunzite (gemstone), ratite (flightless bird), partite (divided), airtight, sticktight (plant having barbed fruit), skintight, uptight, proustite (mineral), troostite (mineral), gnathite (zoology term), Levite, cleveite (mineral), sylvite (mineral), invite, bobwhite (US quail), lintwhite (*Scot* linnet), excite, bauxite.

Trotskyite, Karaite (member of Jewish sect), Moabite, coenobite (member of religious order), Jacobite, Rechabite (teetotaller), trilobite, malachite (mineral), blatherskite (foolish talkative person), erudite, recondite (abstruse), heulandite (mineral), pentlandite (mineral), Wycliffite, epiphyte (plant growing on another), geophyte (botany term), neophyte (novice), bryophyte (botany term), cryophyte (plant growing on snow), eclogite (type of rock), Fahrenheit, apartheid, spherulite (crystalline mass in rock), nummulite (fossil), granulite, lazulite, overflight, candlelight, eremite (Christian hermit), Adamite (member of nudist sect), sodomite, calamite (extinct treelike plant), dolomite, dynamite, wolframite (mineral), hellgrammite (US insect larva), catamite, stalagmite, alunite (mineral), disunite, reunite, belemnite, copyright, azurite (gemstone), lazurite (lapis lazuli), achondrite (meteorite), erythrite (mineral), second-sight, bipartite, tripartite, stalactite, transvestite, celestite (mineral), Muscovite, moldavite (natural green glass), Hepplewhite, andesite (volcanic rock), adamsite (poisonous crystalline solid), martensite (metallurgy term).

osteophyte (small bony outgrowth), annabergite (mineral), heteroclite (irregularly formed word), archimandrite (Greek Orthodox monastery head), alexandrite (gemstone), multipartite.

anthropophagite (cannibal), itacolumite (type of sandstone).

372.1
lyddite (an explosive), expedite.

372.2
troglodyte, andradite (gemstone), extradite, hermaphrodite.

372.3
delight, phyllite (type of rock), rubellite (gemstone), tachylyte (black glassy basalt), triphylite (mineral), argillite (type of rock), propylite (geology term), proselyte, apophyllite (mineral), toxophilite (archer), pyrophyllite (mineral), Mutazilite (8th-century liberal Muslim).

372.4
alight, polite.

hyalite (variety of opal), rhyolite (type of rock), cryolite (mineral), zeolite (mineral), oolite (sedimentary rock), kimberlite (rock often containing diamonds), acolyte, Bakelite (*Trademark*), niccolite (mineral), sodalite (mineral), stylolite (geology term), Carmelite, phonolite (volcanic rock), scapolite (mineral), impolite, corallite (fossil coral), uralite (mineral), microlight, coprolite, natrolite (mineral), chrysolite (gemstone), socialite, quarterlight, tantalite (mineral), graptolite (fossil), crystallite (minute crystal in rock).

variolite (type of rock), Israelite, metabolite (substance produced in metabolism), amphibolite (type of rock), lepidolite (mineral), crocidolite (variety of asbestos), theodolite, Pre-Raphaelite, electrolyte, chiastolite (mineral), topazolite (variety of garnet).

372.4.1
satellite, stromatolite (type of rock).

372.5
pinite (mineral), melinite (an explosive), selenite (variety of gypsum), ilmenite (mineral), encrinite (fossil), retinite (resin), nephelinite (type of rock), kaolinite (mineral), gadolinite (mineral), uraninite (mineral).

372.6
tonight, syenite (type of rock), cyanite (mineral), urbanite (*US* city dweller), aconite (poisonous plant), taconite (type of rock), vulcanite (hard rubber), rhodonite (mineral), wulfenite (mineral), morganite (gemstone), melanite (black variety of garnet), ammonite, limonite (mineral), Canaanite, arenite (sandstone), Maronite (Syrian Christian), uranite (mineral), smithsonite (mineral), autunite (mineral), bentonite (clay), austenite (metallurgy term), overnight, sylvanite (mineral), monzonite (type of rock), Midianite, strontianite (mineral), suburbanite, amazonite (gemstone).

372.7
ignite, lignite, gelignite.

372.8
aright, Labourite, sybarite, anchorite, siderite (mineral), underwrite, phosphorite (mineral), margarite (mineral), dolerite (type of rock), tenorite (mineral), Minorite (Franciscan friar), laterite (clay), overwrite, Nazarite (Old Testament ascetic), kieserite (mineral), geyserite (mineral), cordierite (mineral), garnierite (mineral), meteorite, ozocerite (wax), grossularite (gemstone), evaporite (type of rock).

372.9

recite, lewisite (poisonous liquid), plebiscite, scolecite (mineral), magnesite (mineral), variscite (mineral).

372.10

oocyte (immature female germ cell), marcasite, leucocyte, chalcocite (mineral), lymphocyte (type of blood cell), kamacite (iron–nickel alloy), haemocyte (any blood cell), jarosite (mineral), parasite, macrocyte (large red blood cell), microcyte (small red blood cell), anthracite, outasight, oversight, erythrocyte, spermatocyte (immature male germ cell), anorthosite (type of rock).

372.11

Hittite, mimetite (mineral), granitite (type of granite), magnetite (mineral), appetite.

372.12

steatite (variety of talc), biotite (dark-coloured mica), albertite (variety of bitumen), haematite (mineral), apatite (mineral), pyrrhotite (mineral), spessartite (variety of garnet), watertight, goniatite (fossil), peridotite (type of rock).

373 -ot

bot (larva of botfly), cot, Scot, Scott, dot, phot (unit of illumination), got, jot, hot, lot, blot, clot, plot, slot, motte, knot, not, snot, pot, spot, squat, rot, grot (grotto), trot, sot, shott (salt lake in desert), shot, tot, stot (*Scot* to bounce), what, watt, swot, swat, yacht.

robot, boycott, cocotte, dovecot, begot, forgot, inkblot, feedlot (place for fattening livestock), diglot (bilingual), subplot, motmot (tropical bird), cannot, bowknot (decorative knot), slipknot, topknot, whatnot, repot, teapot, jackpot, crackpot, stockpot, stinkpot, hotchpot (legal term), tinpot, despot, tosspot, fusspot, sunspot, nightspot,

cachepot (container for flowerpot), dashpot (mechanism for damping vibration), hotpot, sexpot, Pequot (American Indian), loquat (Oriental fruit tree), kumquat, garotte, dogtrot (gentle trot), foxtrot, earshot, eyeshot, bowshot, buckshot, bloodshot, gunshot, moonshot, slingshot (*US* catapult), slapshot (ice hockey shot), snapshot, grapeshot, upshot, gavotte, abwatt (electrical unit), somewhat.

Candiot (Cretan), carrycot, apricot, massicot (mineral), Sialkot (Pakistani city), peridot (gemstone), microdot, Wyandotte (breed of domestic fowl), Huhehot (Chinese town), melilot (flowering plant), Camelot, ocelot, sans-culotte, polyglot, underplot (subsidiary plot in story), counterplot, guillemot, bergamot, Arbuthnot, monkeypot (tropical tree), coffeepot, gallipot (earthenware pot for ointments), galipot (pine resin), talipot (palm tree), chimneypot, flowerpot, aliquot (maths term), Paraquat (*Trademark*), tommyrot, Aldershot, undershot, overshot, Hottentot, kilowatt, megawatt, forget-me-not.

373.1

allot, calotte (Catholic priest's skullcap), shallot, cachalot (sperm whale), eschalot (shallot).

374 -ort

ought, aught, bought, bort (inferior diamond), caught, court, fought, fort, mort (call on hunting horn), nought, naught, snort, port, sport, quart, rort (*Austral* noisy party), wrought, brought, fraught, sought, sort, short, tort, taut, taught, torte (rich cake), thought, wart, thwart.

abort, forecourt, escort, hillfort, cohort, onslaught, fearnought (heavy woollen fabric), Connaught, dreadnought, carport, purport, airport, seaport, Newport, Stockport, Coalport, import, comport, passport, spaceport, disport (enjoy oneself), Gosport, spoilsport, transport, jetport, outport, Southport, export, inwrought (woven into material), distraught, re-sort, assort, consort, retort, self-taught, untaught, contort, bistort (Eurasian plant), distort, extort, methought, forethought, cavort, athwart, resort, exhort.

Agincourt, Argonaut, juggernaut, cosmonaut, aquanaut, aeronaut, astronaut, reimport, davenport, re-export, overwrought, ultrashort (having very short wavelength), aforethought, afterthought, worrywart (habitual worrier).

374.1
deport, report, heliport, misreport.

374.2
support, hoverport.

375 -oit
coit (*Austral* buttocks), quoit, doit (former Dutch coin), droit, dacoit (armed robber), exploit, adroit, Detroit, maladroit, Massasoit (American Indian chief).

376 -oat
oat, boat, coat, cote, dote, goat, bloat, float, gloat, ploat (*Dialect* thrash), mote, moat, smote, note, quote, rote, wrote, groat, troat (to bellow), throat, shoat (recently-weaned piglet), tote, stoat, vote.

rowboat, showboat, speedboat, lifeboat, whaleboat, steamboat, gunboat, swingboat, longboat, houseboat, surcoat (medieval knight's tunic), redcoat, Rajkot (Indian city), raincoat, turncoat, sheepcote, topcoat, waistcoat, housecoat, greatcoat, dovecote, zygote (fertilized egg cell), afloat, bobfloat (small fishing float), emote, demote, gemot (Anglo-Saxon legal assembly), remote, promote, keynote, denote, connote, woodnote (natural song), footnote, capote (long hooded cloak), com-

pote, unquote, misquote, bluethroat (songbird), whitethroat (songbird), cutthroat, devote, outvote.

powerboat, motorboat, petticoat, undercoat, overcoat, epidote (mineral), lepidote (covered with scaly leaves), antidote, anecdote, table d'hôte, redingote (overcoat), pardalote (Australian songbird), Fomalhaut (star), papillote (paper frill around cutlet), matelote (fish with wine sauce), underquote, creosote, asymptote.

377 -out
out, owt, bout, scout, doubt, gout, lout, clout, flout, nowt, knout (strong whip), snout, pout, spout, rout, drought, grout, sprout, trout, shout, tout, stout.

throughout, blackout, stakeout (*US* police surveillance), lockout, knockout, cookout (*US* barbecue), lookout, redoubt, dugout, mahout (elephant keeper), fallout, ablaut (linguistics term), breechclout (loincloth), umlaut, amaut (Eskimo woman's hood), rainout (radioactive fall-out), brownout (*US* power reduction), dropout, eelpout (marine fish), downspout, without, devout.

waterspout, sauerkraut.

377.1
about, layabout, walkabout, gadabout, roundabout, turnabout, runabout.

378 -ut
butt, but, cut, scut, phut, gut, jut, hut, glut, slut, mutt, smut, nut, putt, rut, strut, shut, tut.

rebut, abut, hackbut (long-barrelled gun), blackbutt (eucalyptus tree), sackbut, haircut, woodcut, uncut, crosscut, foregut, midgut, hindgut, catgut, rotgut, englut (devour ravenously), peanut, doughnut, cobnut, beechnut, groundnut, gallnut (plant gall), walnut, chestnut, half-shut.

scuttlebutt (ship's drinking fountain), Calicut (Indian port), linocut, uppercut, coconut, bladdernut (European shrub), bitternut, butternut, candlenut, hazelnut, sinciput (part of skull), occiput.

379 -oot

foot, put, soot, barefoot, crowfoot (flowering plant), webfoot, Blackfoot (American Indian), finfoot (aquatic bird), goosefoot (weedy plant), coltsfoot (European plant), flatfoot, hotfoot, outfoot (sail faster than), cocksfoot (Eurasian grass), kaput, throughput, Rajput (Hindu military caste member), input, output, pussyfoot, Dasht-i-Lut (Iranian desert plateau), autoput (Yugoslavian motorway), cajuput (Australian shrub).

379.1

afoot, tenderfoot, underfoot.

380 -ute

boot, coot, scoot, jute, hoot, lute, loot, flute, sloot (South African irrigation ditch), moot, snoot (*Slang* nose), root, route, brute, brut, bruit (*US* to report), croute (small piece of toast), fruit, suit, chute, shoot, toot, Ute (American Indian), Bute, beaut, butte (steep-sided hill), cute, scute (zoology term), mute, newt.

freeboot, crowboot (Eskimo boot), jackboot, elute (chemistry term), dilute, Hakluyt (English geographer), folkmoot (medieval district assembly), Beirut, cheroot, snakeroot (US plant), recruit, redroot (bog plant), breadroot (US plant), jackfruit (Asian fruit tree), breadfruit, grapefruit, enroot, en route, unroot, taproot, uproot, beetroot, birthroot (US plant), playsuit, lawsuit, tracksuit, swimsuit, sunsuit, spacesuit, pantsuit, offshoot, outshoot, refute, confute, Salyut, solute, volute, commute, permute, deafmute, transmute, minute, cornute (hornlike), Canute, impute, compute, dispute, Asyut (ancient Egyptian city), hirsute, pursuit, statute, astute.

overboot (protective boot), bandicoot, malamute (Eskimo dog), puttyroot (US orchid), briarroot (wood for tobacco pipes), arrowroot, crinkleroot (flowering plant), coralroot (leafless orchid), Hatshepsut (ancient Egyptian queen), undershoot, parachute, overshoot, persecute, prosecute, execute, comminute (reduce to small fragments).

380.1

galoot (*US* clumsy person), pollute, salute, dissolute, absolute, consolute (chemistry term), evolute (geometric curve), revolute (botany term), involute (intricate), convolute, resolute, irresolute.

380.2

tribute, attribute, contribute, distribute.

380.3

acute, subacute (medical term), electrocute.

380.4

depute, repute, disrepute.

380.5

destitute, prostitute, substitute, institute, constitute, reconstitute.

381 -'t

Fiat (*Trademark*), Stuart, abbot, burbot (freshwater fish), Herbert, sherbet, turbot, nobbut (*Dialect* nothing but), Robert, Schubert, Egbert, Albert, Talbot, filbert, Gilbert, Lambert, Cuthbert, Urquhart, ducat, Alcott, Ascot, mascot, wainscot, effort, Beaufort, Frankfurt, comfort, faggot, maggot, braggart, ergot (crop disease), bigot, Piggott, spigot (cask stopper), boggart (*Dialect* poltergeist), yogurt, ingot, ballot, harlot, Charlotte, Helot (serf), zealot, pilot, Pilate, gamut, marmot, Connacht (Northern Irish province), donnert (*Scot* stunned), caput, Rupert, carat, carrot, claret, parrot, divot, pivot, covert, lovat (colour mixture in tweeds), culvert, stalwart, Quixote, desert.

halibut, Port Talbot, Ethelbert, discomfort, copilot, electret (material with electrical properties), discovert (legal term).

Connecticut, autopilot.

381.1
idiot, galiot (small galley), Eliot, heriot (medieval death duty), Cypriot, patriot, Cheviot, soviet, exeat, compatriot, commissariat, proletariat, secretariat.

381.1.1
chariot, lariat, Marryat, Iscariot.

381.2
diet, fiat (official permission), quiet, ryot (Indian peasant), riot, Wyatt, unquiet, disquiet.

382 -act [also **32** + *-ed*]
act, fact, pact, bract, tract, tact, swacked (*Slang* intoxicated).

react, hunchbacked, unbacked, humpbacked, redact (prepare for publication), enact, impact, compact, infract (violate), detract, retract, attract, protract, subtract, entr'acte, contract, distract, abstract, extract, intact, contact, exact, transact.

abreact (psychology term), retroact, artefact, re-enact, underact, tesseract (four-dimensional figure), cataract, interact, counteract, overact, precontract, subcontract, inexact.

overreact, autodidact (self-taught person).

382.1
diffract, refract, Pontefract.

383 -arct [also **33** + *-ed*]
gedact (organ pipe), infarct (dead tissue), unmarked.

384 -aked [also **34** + *-ed*]
half-baked, unslaked.

385 -ect [also **35** + *-ed*]
sect, unchecked, pandect (comprehensive treatise), defect, prefect, infect, confect (prepare by combining ingredients), eject, deject, reject, project, abject, object, subject, inject, disject (break apart), collect, deflect, reflect, inflect, neglect, connect, landsknecht (mercenary foot soldier), henpecked, aspect, respect, prospect, suspect, inspect, expect, erect, direct, bisect, trisect, transect, insect, protect, obtect (entomology term), exsect (to cut out).

disinfect, genuflect, disconnect, self-respect, disrespect, retrospect, introspect, circumspect, indirect, misdirect, intersect.

interconnect, overprotect.

385.1
effect, defect, aftereffect.

385.2
affect, perfect, disaffect.

385.3
project, traject (to transport), retroject (throw backwards), introject (psychology term), interject.

385.4
elect, prelect (to lecture), select, intellect.

385.5
collect, dialect, recollect, idiolect (individual's language).

385.6
correct, incorrect, resurrect.

385.7
dissect, resect (remove surgically), quadrisect, vivisect.

385.8
detect, architect.

386 -eeked [also **37** + *-ed*]
beaked, peaked, streaked.

387 -ict [also **38** + *-ed*]
Pict, strict, addict, verdict, edict, predict, perfect, object, subject, relict, afflict, inflict, conflict, depict, district, restrict, constrict, evict, convict, maledict (utter a curse), Benedict, pluperfect, imperfect, derelict, apomict (organism produced asexually), derestrict.

387.1
addict, contradict, interdict.

388 -oct [also **40** + *-ed*]
decoct (extract by boiling), concoct, landlocked, unlocked, ectoproct (aquatic animal).

389 -uct [also **43** + *-ed*]
duct, educt (chemistry term), deduct, product, abduct, subduct (draw downwards), induct, conduct, eruct (to belch), destruct, obstruct, instruct, construct, aqueduct, oviduct, viaduct, misconduct, usufruct, superstruct (build on another structure), reconstruct.

390 -ooked [also **44** + *-ed*]
hooked, uncooked.

391 -anct [also **51** + *-ed*]
unthanked, sacrosanct.

392 -inct [also **52** + *-ed*]
tinct (tinted), precinct, distinct, instinct, extinct, succinct, indistinct.

393 -unct [also **54** + *-ed*]
defunct, adjunct, conjunct.

394 -asked [also **56** + *-ed*]
masked, unasked.

395 -atched [also **62** + *-ed*]
well-matched, detached, unscratched, unattached, semidetached.

396 -aft [also **158** + *-ed*]
aft, daft, haft (knife handle), raft, craft, kraft (strong wrapping-paper), draught, draft, graft, shaft, waft.

abaft, aircraft, witchcraft, woodcraft, handcraft, stagecraft, spacecraft, statecraft, redraft, engraft, jackshaft (shaft transmitting engine power), crankshaft, camshaft.

handicraft, hovercraft, needlecraft, overdraft, homograft, autograft, aftershaft (type of feather), countershaft (intermediate shaft in mechanism), understaffed, overstaffed.

anti-aircraft, heterograft.

397 -eft
eft, deft, heft (assess weight of), left, cleft, klepht (Greek brigand), theft, weft, bereft.

398 -ift [also **163** + *-ed*]
gift, lift, rift, drift, shrift, thrift, sift, shift, swift, airlift, uplift, festschrift (commemorative collection of writings), snowdrift, adrift, spindrift (sea spray), spendthrift, gearshift, makeshift.

399 -oft [also **165** + *-ed*]
oft, loft, croft, soft, toft (homestead), aloft, cockloft, Ashcroft, Lowestoft, undercroft (underground chamber).

400 -uft [also **168** + *-ed*]
chuffed, tuft, stuffed, candytuft (flowering plant).

401 -alt
alt (high in pitch), shalt, asphalt, gestalt (overall structure).

402 -elt
belt, Celt, kelt (recently spawned salmon), dealt, felt, gelt (*Slang* money), melt, smelt, knelt, pelt, spelt, celt (ancient axe-like instrument), Scheldt (Eu-

ropean river), veldt, svelte, welt, dwelt, unbelt, backveld (remote rural area), heartfelt, Danegelt, jacksmelt (marine fish), underfelt, Tafilelt (largest oasis in Sahara), Roosevelt.

403 -ilt
built, kilt, guilt, gilt, jilt, hilt, lilt, milt, spilt, quilt, silt, tilt, stilt, wilt, rebuilt, well-built, atilt (tilted), uptilt, Vanderbilt.

404 -orlt
Balt (person from Baltic States), fault, halt, malt, smalt (dark blue glass), salt, vault, cobalt, default, stringhalt (veterinary science term), basalt, persalt (chemical compound), exalt, oxysalt (chemical compound).

404.1
assault, somersault.

405 -oalt
bolt, Boult, colt, dolt, jolt, holt (woodland), moult, smolt (young salmon), poult (young domestic fowl), volt, Humboldt, unbolt, kingbolt (steering bolt on carriage), ringbolt (bolt with ring attached), fishbolt (bolt in railway track), revolt, abvolt (electrical unit), thunderbolt, kilovolt, electronvolt.

406 -ult
cult, occult, adult, indult (Catholic dispensation), tumult, penult (penultimate syllable), insult, consult, result, exult, difficult, catapult, jurisconsult.

407 -ant
ant, bant (*Dialect* string), Kant, cant, scant, pant, rant, Brabant (Belgian province), decant, recant, descant, gallant, Rembrandt, enceinte (enclosure), extant, confidant, commandant, sycophant, hierophant (ancient Greek high priest).

407.1
levant (patterned leather), gallivant.

408 -arnt
aunt, aren't, can't, chant, plant, slant, grant, shan't, plainchant, enchant, supplant, eggplant, implant, transplant, ashplant, waxplant (flowering plant), explant (biology term), aslant, courante (musical term), détente, disenchant, debutante.

409 -aint
ain't, feint, faint, plaint (legal term), paint, quaint, saint, taint, complaint, repaint, greasepaint, acquaint, distraint (legal term), restraint, constraint.

410 -ent
bent, Kent, dent, Ghent, gent, lent, leant, Lent, meant, pent, spent, rent, Brent, brent (small goose), Trent, cent, sent, scent, tent, vent, went, Gwent.

hellbent, unbent, indent, relent, ament (mentally deficient person), fragment, comment, torment, loment (plant pod), augment, unmeant, anent (*Scot* concerning), repent, well-spent, frequent, besprent (sprinkled over), descent, dissent, docent (US lecturer), assent, ascent, per cent, absent, consent, detent (locking device in machine), portent, intent, content, extent, sirvente (Provençal verse form), advent, invent, forwent, forewent, accent.

orient, document, overspent, malcontent, discontent, circumvent, underwent, disorient.

410.1
dement, cement, regiment, aliment, supplement, implement, complement, compliment, experiment, fibrocement.

410.2
foment, ferment, lament, ornament.

410.3
event, prevent, nonevent.

410.4
resent, present, represent, re-present, misrepresent.

411 -ernt

burnt, learnt, weren't, mowburnt (agricultural term), sunburnt, unlearnt.

412 -int

bint (*Slang* girl), skint, dint, hint, lint, flint, Flint, glint, splint, mint, squint, print, sprint, tint, stint.

suint (substance in sheep's wool), skinflint, gunflint, varmint, spearmint, horsemint (European plant), catmint, asquint (glancing furtively), surprint (overprint), reprint, blueprint, woodprint (print from woodcut), offprint (separate reprint of article), imprint, thumbprint, misprint, voiceprint, footprint, newsprint.

calamint (Eurasian plant), peppermint, microprint, fingerprint, mezzotint, undertint (delicate tint), monotint (painting technique), aquatint (copperetching technique), Septuagint.

413 -ynt

pint, cuckoopint.

414 -ont

font, pont (South African river ferry), quant (pole used for punting), want, diplont (biology term), Vermont, Beaumont, piedmont (at foot of mountain), Piedmont (region of Italy), Egmont, schizont (zoology term), symbiont, Negropont (Greek island), Hellespont, halobiont (salt-water organism), Dandie Dinmont.

415 -ornt

daunt, gaunt, jaunt, haunt, flaunt, taunt, vaunt, Broederbond (South African secret society).

416 -oint

joint, point, adjoint (maths term), conjoint, disjoint, anoint, repoint, pourpoint (medieval doublet), viewpoint, breakpoint, checkpoint, knickpoint (break in river profile), midpoint,

standpoint, ballpoint, pinpoint, gunpoint, outpoint (nautical term), needlepoint.

416.1

appoint, disappoint, counterpoint, silverpoint (drawing technique).

417 -oant

don't, wont, won't.

418 -ount

count, fount, mount, re-count, recount, viscount, account, discount, miscount, surmount, demount (remove from mounting), seamount (underwater mountain), dismount.

418.1

amount, paramount, catamount (feline animal), tantamount.

419 -unt

bunt, cunt, dunt (*Dialect* a blow), hunt, blunt, punt, runt, brunt, front, grunt, shunt, stunt, manhunt, seafront, forefront, breakfront (having projecting central section), confront, exeunt.

419.1

affront, waterfront.

420 -'nt [further rhymes may be created by adding *-ment* to appropriate verbs]

mayn't, lambent, bacchant (drunken reveller), vacant, clinquant (tinsel), etchant (acid used for etching), merchant, couchant (heraldic term), trenchant, hadn't, cadent (rhythmic), pedant, verdant, trident, strident, rodent, scandent (climbing), infant, pageant, argent (silver), sergeant, Sargent, agent, regent, sejant (heraldic term), cogent, pungent, sealant, silent, Solent, volant (heraldic term), coolant, ament (catkin), garment, clement, moment, parchment, oddment, fragment, segment, figment, pigment, lodgment, judgment, scarcement (ledge in wall), treatment, vestment, pavement, stagnant, regnant (prevalent), pregnant, remnant, serpent, dopant (chemistry term), rampant, parent, spirant (phonetics term), tyrant, vibrant, hydrant, quadrant, flagrant, fragrant, vagrant, migrant, titrant (chemistry term), entrant, nascent, absent, quotient, Ushant (French island), ancient, potent, octant (eighth part of circle), saltant (biology term), instant, constant, sextant, Havant, haven't, savant, solvent, convent, Derwent, unguent, valiant, brilliant, poignant, hasn't, wisent (European bison), isn't, wasn't.

absorbent, adsorbent, decumbent (lying flat), recumbent, incumbent, impeccant (free from sin), decadent, elephant, triumphant, reagent, newsagent, sibilant, jubilant, flagellant, vigilant, sterilant, pestilent, inclement, deferment, preferment, interment, agreement, requirement, retirement, endowment, embankment, impeachment, enrichment, debouchment (outlet), embranchment, retrenchment, entrenchment, bombardment, débridement (removal of dead tissue), commandment, amendment, intendment (legal term), secondment, enlargement, engagement, infringement, concealment, fulfilment, instalment, enrolment, annulment, enjambment (poetry term), adjournment, discernment, internment, refinement, confinement, alignment, assignment, consignment, adornment, postponement, atonement, escarpment, escapement, encampment, impressment (conscription into government service), assessment, enticement, inducement, advancement, commencement, announcement, pronouncement, refreshment, department, apartment, compartment, revetment (protective facing of stones), maltreatment, indictment, incitement, excitement, allotment, ballottement (medical term), deportment, comportment, assortment, abutment,

recruitment, enactment, enchantment, contentment, resentment, presentment, investment, adjustment, achievement, bereavement, amazement, appeasement, chastisement, amusement, complainant, alternant, indignant, malignant, benignant, repugnant, oppugnant, discrepant, occupant, erumpent (bursting out), delinquent, godparent, grandparent, step-parent, aspirant, figurant, fulgurant, celebrant, emigrant, immigrant, transmigrant, integrant (part of a whole), re-entrant, registrant (person who registers trademark), ministrant, remonstrant, renascent, adjacent, subjacent (forming a foundation), complacent, innocent, dissentient, presentient, consentient (being in agreement), excitant, important, prepotent (greater in power), reactant, surfactant, attractant, reluctant, consultant, resultant, exultant, repentant, accountant, acceptant, inconstant, relevant, pursuivant, connivent, adjuvant (helping), insolvent, dissolvent, resolvent, emollient, ebullient, complaisant, cognizant, recusant (insubordinate).

equipollent (equal in effect), undergarment, overgarment, disagreement, disengagement, development, divertissement, advertisement, disenchantment, maladjustment, misdemeanant, inadvertent, unimportant, idempotent (maths term), executant, irrelevant, incognizant, redevelopment.

420.1

ambient, radiant, gradient, salient, suppliant, fainéant, sapient, variant, orient, miscreant, nutrient, transeunt (philosophy term), sentient, deviant, transient.

resilient, defoliant, recipient, percipient, incipient, excipient (medical term), invariant (maths term), aperient, inebriant, omniscient, insouciant, officiant, negotiant, assentient (approving), insentient, subservient, asphyxiant.

420.1.1
mediant, obedient, submediant (musical term), expedient, ingredient, disobedient, inexpedient.

420.1.2
lenient, prevenient (preceding), convenient, inconvenient.

420.1.3
prurient, esurient (greedy), parturient (relating to childbirth), luxuriant.

420.2
giant, client, pliant, defiant, affiant (US legal term), reliant, compliant, eobiont (biology term), supergiant, incompliant.

420.3
buoyant, flamboyant, foudroyant (sudden and severe), chatoyant (changing in lustre), clairvoyant.

420.4
affluent, effluent, profluent (flowing smoothly), influent (flowing in), confluent, congruent, obstruent (causing obstruction), diluent, issuant, fluctuant, interfluent (flowing together), evacuant (promoting bowel evacuation), attenuant, continuant, substituent, constituent.

420.5
fluent, truant, eluent (chemistry term), pursuant.

420.6
piquant, secant, cosecant.

420.7
predicant (relating to preaching), mendicant, indicant, applicant, supplicant, lubricant, desiccant, vesicant (blistering substance), toxicant (a poison), significant, communicant, intoxicant, insignificant.

420.8
ardent, guardant (heraldic term), regardant (heraldic term), retardant.

420.9
needn't, credent, decedent (deceased person), antecedent.

420.10
didn't, diffident, confident, precedent, dissident, incident, evident, provident, accident, oxidant, occident, self-confident, coincident, improvident, overconfident, antioxidant.

420.10.1
resident, president, nonresident.

420.11
mordant, mordent (melodic ornament), accordant, concordant, discordant.

420.12
couldn't, shouldn't, wouldn't, impudent.

420.13
prudent, student, imprudent, jurisprudent.

420.14
pendant, pendent (dangling), defendant, resplendent, dependant, dependent, appendant (attached), descendant, ascendant, transcendent, attendant, intendant (provincial official), independent, interdependent, superintendent.

420.15
fondant, despondent, respondent (legal term), correspondent, co-respondent.

420.16
abundant, redundant, superabundant.

420.17
elegant, fumigant, congregant, litigant, inelegant.

420.18
termagant, arrogant, extravagant.

420.19
urgent, emergent, resurgent, assurgent (curving upwards), insurgent, detergent, abstergent (cleansing), divergent, convergent.

420.20
indigent, diligent, negligent, exigent (urgent), intelligent, intransigent, unintelligent.

420.21
fulgent (resplendent), indulgent, effulgent (radiant), refulgent (shining), self-indulgent.

420.22
plangent (resonant or plaintive), tangent, cotangent, subtangent.

420.23
ringent (botany term), stringent, refringent (refractive), astringent, contingent.

420.24
gallant, talent, topgallant (ship's mast).

420.25
inhalant, exhalant (emitting a vapour), assailant, bivalent, divalent, trivalent, polyvalent, univalent, monovalent.

420.26
repellent, appellant (person who appeals), propellant, expellant, interpellant (interrupting with question).

420.27
virulent, purulent, turbulent, ambulant, feculent (filthy), flocculent (fleecy), truculent, succulent, esculent (edible), osculant (biology term), fraudulent, undulant, tremulant, simulant, stimulant, crapulent, opulent, corpulent, flatulent, petulant, postulant, pustulant, pulverulent (consisting of dust), avirulent, coagulant, puberulent (covered with down), anticoagulant.

420.28
violent, libellant, redolent, indolent, somnolent, insolent, nonchalant, excellent, nonviolent, sanguinolent (containing blood), equivalent.

420.28.1
prevalent, malevolent, benevolent.

420.29
claimant, clamant (noisy), payment, raiment, repayment.

420.30
cerement (burial clothes), endearment.

420.31
vehement, rudiment, condiment, regiment, aliment, element, supplement, implement, compliment, complement, liniment, muniment, orpiment (mineral), diriment (invalidating), worriment, decrement (diminution), recrement (waste matter), increment, excrement, detriment, nutriment, sentiment, embodiment, habiliment (dress), dissepiment (dividing membrane), presentiment, accompaniment.

420.31.1
pediment, sediment, impediment.

420.31.2
merriment, experiment.

420.32
dormant, informant.

420.33
enjoyment, deployment, employment, redeployment, unemployment.

420.34
document, argument, monument, integument (outer protective layer), emolument.

420.35
adamant, fundament (buttocks), wonderment, parliament, filament, armament, firmament, tenement, ornament, tournament, parament (ecclesiastical vestment), sacrament, instrument, measurement, betterment, testament, lineament, medicament, predicament, bewilderment, disarmament, temperament, arbitrament, accoutrement, hereditament (legal term).

420.35.1
ligament, disfigurement.

420.36
catchment, hatchment (heraldic term), detachment, attachment.

420.37
management, abridgment, acknowledgment, disparagement, encouragement, discouragement.

420.38
derangement, arrangement, estrangement, rearrangement.

420.39
ailment, bailment (legal term), derailment, curtailment.

420.40
battlement, settlement, devilment, puzzlement, entablement (platform supporting statue), entanglement, accouplement (supporting beam), entitlement, embezzlement.

420.41
attainment, containment, entertainment.

420.42
government, abandonment, environment, apportionment, enlightenment, imprisonment.

420.43
shipment, equipment.

420.44
basement, casement, placement, subbasement, replacement, emplacement, displacement.

420.45
endorsement, enforcement, reinforcement.

420.46
harassment, embarrassment.

420.47
garnishment (legal notice), punishment, nourishment, embellishment, establishment, accomplishment, astonishment.

420.48
statement, abatement, affreightment (contract hiring cargo ship), understatement, reinstatement.

420.49
fitment, commitment.

420.50
ointment, anointment, appointment, disappointment.

420.51
movement, improvement.

420.52
pennant, tenant, cotenant, subtenant, lieutenant, sublieutenant.

420.53
eminent, imminent, culminant, fulminant (sudden and violent), urinant (heraldic term), pertinent, continent, revenant, disciplinant (member of Catholic sect), pre-eminent, appurtenant, impertinent, conglutinant (adhesive), subcontinent, incontinent.

420.53.1
germinant, determinant.

420.53.2
dominant, prominent, predominant, subdominant.

420.53.3
ruminant, illuminant.

420.54
sonant (phonetics term), deponent (linguistics term), opponent, proponent, imponent (person imposing a duty), component, exponent.

420.55
permanent, immanent (existing within), assonant, dissonant, consonant, covenant, resonant, impermanent, inconsonant.

420.56
flippant, participant, anticipant.

420.57
frequent, sequent, infrequent.

420.58
aliquant (maths term), subsequent, consequent, inconsequent.

420.59
eloquent, ineloquent, grandiloquent, magniloquent (lofty in style).

420.60
arrant, apparent, transparent.

420.61
errant, gerent (ruler or manager), aberrant, vicegerent, deterrent.

420.62
coherent, adherent, inherent, incoherent.

420.63
torrent, warrant, abhorrent.

420.64
currant, current, decurrent (botany term), recurrent, blackcurrant, redcurrant, incurrent (flowing inwards), concurrent, crosscurrent, excurrent (flowing outwards), transcurrent (running across), photocurrent (current produced by light), undercurrent, intercurrent (occurring between).

420.65
roborant (fortifying), saturant (chemistry term), afferent (conducting inwards), efferent (conducting outwards), deferent, referent, different, tolerant, colorant, cormorant, sonorant (phonetics term), ignorant, operant, lacerant (painfully distressing), cauterant (caustic), reverent.

corroborant, protuberant, exuberant, deodorant, preponderant, indifferent, belligerent, refrigerant, accelerant, exhilarant, intolerant, decolorant, itinerant, expectorant, adulterant, irreverent, antiperspirant.

420.66
penetrant, recalcitrant.

420.67
crescent, quiescent, rubescent, pubescent, tabescent (wasting away), albescent (becoming white), confessant, turgescent, spumescent (producing froth), tumescent, liquescent, decrescent (decreasing in size), increscent (increasing in size), excrescent, nigrescent (blackish), depressant, vitrescent (turning in-

to glass), putrescent, acescent (turning sour), incessant, frutescent, lactescent.

acquiescent, iridescent, viridescent (becoming green), incandescent, adolescent, opalescent, obsolescent, convalescent, deliquescent, fluorescent, arborescent (treelike), phosphorescent, antidepressant.

420.67.1
senescent, juvenescent.

420.67.2
canescent (becoming hoary), evanescent.

420.67.3
flavescent (turning yellow), effervescent, ingravescent (becoming worse).

420.68
versant (mountain side), dispersant, conversant.

420.69
decent, recent, indecent.

420.70
dehiscent, reticent, Stuyvesant (Dutch colonial administrator), maleficent, beneficent, munificent, magnificent, omnificent, indehiscent, reminiscent.

420.71
lucent, translucent, abducent (anatomy term).

420.72
demulcent (soothing), convulsant, anticonvulsant.

420.73
patient, impatient, inpatient, outpatient, sorbefacient (causing absorption), calefacient (causing warmth), stupefacient, liquefacient, abortifacient.

420.74
efficient, deficient, proficient, sufficient, coefficient, inefficient, self-sufficient, insufficient, extinguishant.

420.75
latent, blatant, natant (floating on water), patent, statant (heraldic term),

dilatant, supernatant (floating on the surface).

420.76
militant, volitant (moving rapidly), remittent, penitent, competent, equitant (botany term), irritant, hesitant, visitant, annuitant (person receiving annuity), inhabitant, exorbitant, concomitant, intermittent, impenitent, precipitant, incompetent, abirritant (relieving irritation), omnicompetent, counterirritant.

420.77
mutant, nutant (botany term), pollutant, disputant.

420.78
combatant, adjutant, impotent, noncombatant, coadjutant, armipotent (strong in battle), plenipotent (having full authority), omnipotent, totipotent (zoology term).

420.79
humectant, expectant, disinfectant.

420.80
digestant, contestant, decongestant.

420.81
distant, assistant, persistent, insistent, consistent, Protestant, resistant, existent, equidistant, inconsistent, nonresistant, coexistent, nonexistent.

420.82
fervent, servant, maidservant, bondservant, manservant, observant.

420.83
accent, relaxant.

420.84
bezant (Byzantine gold coin), pheasant, pleasant, peasant, present, unpleasant, omnipresent.

421 -apt [also **268** + -ed]
apt, rapt, snowcapped, adapt, inapt, unapt, periapt (amulet).

422 -ept [also **271** + -ed]
kept, leapt, slept, crept, sept (clan), wept, swept, adept, inept, percept (object of perception), recept (psychology term), precept, transept, incept (ingest), concept, unwept, windswept, backswept, except, accept, nympholept, overslept, intercept.

423 -erpt [also **272** + -ed]
excerpt, usurped.

424 -ipt [also **274** + -ed]
crypt, script, Egypt, decrypt (decode), prescript, subscript, transcript, conscript, typescript, postscript, nondescript, telescript (script for television), manuscript, superscript.

425 -opt [also **276** + -ed]
opt, Copt, coopt, adopt, unstopped.

426 -upt [also **279** + -ed]
erupt, irrupt, abrupt, bankrupt, disrupt.

426.1
corrupt, incorrupt, interrupt.

427 -ulpt
sculpt, gulped, pulped.

428 -empt
empt (*Dialect* to empty), kempt (tidy), tempt, pre-empt, unkempt, attempt, contempt, exempt.

429 -ompt [also **288** + -ed]
prompt, swamped.

430 -ast [also **293** + -ed]
bast (plant tissue), hast, bombast, dicast (Athenian juror), gymnast, peltast (ancient Greek foot soldier), fantast (visionary), trophoblast (embryonic membrane), lymphoblast (immature white blood cell), neuroblast (embryonic nerve cell), mesoblast (embryonic tissue), chloroplast (chlorophyll-con-

taining structure), leucoplast (structure in plant cell), pederast, erythroblast (cell in bone marrow), osteoblast (bone-forming cell), osteoclast (surgical instrument), iconoclast (opponent of established beliefs).

430.1

scholiast (medieval annotator), cineaste (film enthusiast), encomiast (writer of eulogies), gymnasiast (European secondary school student), ecdysiast (striptease artist), enthusiast.

431 -arst [also **294** + *-ed*]

cast, caste, karst, fast, last, blast, mast, past, vast.

precast, die-cast, forecast, broadcast, half-caste, roughcast, wormcast, downcast, typecast, upcast (ventilation shaft in mine), miscast, sportscast, outcast, newscast, makefast (support for securing boat), headfast (ship's mooring rope), holdfast (hook or clamp), Belfast, sunfast (not fading in sunlight), sitfast (sore on horse's back), oblast (Russian administrative division), sandblast, outlast, durmast (oak tree), foremast, half-mast, mainmast, topmast, repast, contrast, avast.

telecast, overcast, simulcast (simultaneous radio–television broadcast), opencast, colourfast, counterblast, jiggermast (small ship's mast), mizzenmast, Elastoplast (*Trademark*).

431.1

aghast, flabbergast.

432 -aste [also **295** + *-ed*]

baste, chaste, haste, paste, taste, waste, waist, lambaste (*Slang* beat severely), barefaced, two-faced, shamefaced, posthaste, unplaced, impaste (apply paint thickly), toothpaste, foretaste, distaste, aftertaste, pantywaist (*US* childish person).

433 -est [also **296** + *-ed*]

best, chest, guest, jest, lest, blest, nest, pest, quest, wrest, rest, Brest, breast, crest, dressed, test, vest, west, zest.

Trieste, gabfest (*US* gathering for conversation), infest, egest (excrete), digest, suggest, ingest, congest, behest, celeste, molest, unblessed, bequest, request, inquest, conquest, abreast, redbreast, goldcrest (small warbler), headrest, well-dressed, kniferest, armrest, unrest, depressed, appressed (pressed closely against), impressed, footrest, unstressed, incest, detest, attest, protest, contest, revest (restore power), divest, invest, northwest, southwest, possessed.

second-best, manifest, disinfest, predigest, Almagest (Ptolemy's treatise on astronomy), alkahest (universal solvent in alchemy), Budapest, rinderpest (disease of cattle), anapaest (metrical foot), overdressed, unimpressed, unexpressed, undervest, self-possessed.

433.1

arrest, Bucharest.

434 -erst [also **297** + *-ed*]

burst, durst, first, Hearst, thirst, versed, worst, wurst, airburst (explosion in the air), cloudburst, sunburst, outburst, headfirst, Pankhurst, Sandhurst, knackwurst (type of sausage), athirst (longing), bratwurst (type of sausage), liverwurst.

435 -eest [also **298** + *-ed*]

east, beast, feast, geest (German heathland), least, piste, priest, yeast, modiste (fashionable milliner or dressmaker), beanfeast, archpriest, deceased, batiste (cotton fabric), artiste, northeast, southeast, wildebeest, hartebeest, arriviste (unscrupulously ambitious person).

436 -ist [Also **300** + *-ed*. Further rhymes may be derived from **242.35** or by adding *-ist* to appropriate adjectives.]
kist (*Dialect* large coffer), fist, gist, hist, list, Liszt, mist, quist (*Dialect* wood pigeon), wrist, grist, tryst, cyst, cist (box holding ritual objects), schist, whist, twist, xyst (long portico).

deist, Maoist, cubist, cambist (foreign-exchange dealer), stockist, Yorkist, sadist, modest, feudist (person involved in feud), nudist, eldest, damnedest, sophist, druggist, fuguist (composer of fugues), Hengist (Jute settler in Britain), legist, cellist, stylist, Gaullist, blacklist, cyclist, enlist, chemist, demist, tanist (heir of Celtic chieftain), earnest, honest, hymnist, Trappist, typist, tempest, Marist (member of Christian sect), aurist (ear specialist), Maurist (16th-century French monk), centrist (person with moderate views), bassist (double bass player), subsist, encyst (biology term), insist, consist, fascist, latticed, artist, chartist, latest, greatest, statist (supporter of state power), rightist, flautist, leftist, dentist, Baptist, farthest, furthest, harvest, linguist, Marxist, sexist, desist, resist, exist.

lobbyist, copyist, atheist, oboist, egoist, soloist, altruist, casuist, Sinarquist (Mexican fascist), anarchist, monarchist, masochist, immodest, pacifist, strategist, violist, extremist, conformist, hygienist, machinist, dishonest, trombonist, communist, columnist, unwitnessed, Decembrist (former Russian revolutionary), Septembrist (former French revolutionary), xenocryst (type of crystal), phenocryst (large crystal), exorcist, defeatist, unpractised, scientist, amethyst, reservist, archivist, Bolshevist, activist, coexist.

propagandist, gymnosophist (member of Indian sect), motorcyclist, biochem-

ist, taxidermist, nonconformist, ventriloquist, equilibrist (person performing balancing acts), optometrist (person treating eye defects), psychiatrist, parachutist, orthodontist, Anabaptist (16th-century Protestant).

encyclopedist, audiotypist.

436.1
Judaist, épéeist, Hebraist (student of Hebrew culture), essayist, Ptolemaist, algebraist.

436.2
Buddhist, Talmudist (Jewish scholar), unprejudiced.

436.3
melodist, rhapsodist, Methodist, chiropodist.

436.4 [further rhymes may be derived from **16.108.4**]
agist (legal term), synergist (medical term), suffragist, liturgist, biologist, zoologist, psychologist, graphologist, technologist, apologist (person defending by argument), archaeologist, radiologist, sociologist, gynaecologist, ornithologist, meteorologist.

436.4.1
allergist, dialogist (contributor to dialogue), metallurgist, genealogist.

436.5
idyllist, pugilist, Familist (member of Christian sect), evangelist.

436.6
fabulist, oculist, Populist (member of People's Party), funambulist, somnambulist.

436.7
loyalist, royalist, arbalest (medieval crossbow), herbalist, verbalist, symbolist, vocalist, medallist, journalist, finalist, moralist, racialist, specialist, socialist, fatalist, metallist (advocate of metal currency), novelist.

minimalist (advocate of minimal policy), maximalist (person favouring direct action), immoralist, generalist (person with broad knowledge), naturalist, capitalist, medievalist, revivalist, removalist (*Austral* furniture remover).

semifinalist, bibliopolist (dealer in rare books), universalist, existentialist.

436.7.1
realist, idealist, surrealist.

436.7.2
aerialist (trapeze artist), glacialist (person studying ice effects), imperialist, materialist, memorialist (writer of memoirs), industrialist.

436.7.3
sensualist, spiritualist, individualist.

436.7.4
analyst, panellist, psychoanalyst.

436.7.5
nationalist, rationalist, sensationalist, educationalist, Congregationalist, conversationalist.

436.7.6
catalyst, philatelist, anticatalyst, biocatalyst (enzyme).

436.7.7
instrumentalist, environmentalist.

436.8
palmist, psalmist, alarmist.

436.9
pessimist, optimist, legitimist (supporter of legitimate ruler).

436.10
alchemist, monogamist, economist, anatomist.

436.10.1
bigamist, polygamist.

436.11
Hellenist (devotee of Greek civilization), feminist, alpinist, Latinist, lutenist (lute player), chauvinist, violinist, determinist.

436.12
balloonist, bassoonist, cartoonist, opportunist.

436.13
hedonist, symphonist, organist, colonist, harmonist, Romanist (supporter of Catholicism), timpanist, Satanist, botanist, alienist (type of psychiatrist), unionist, tobacconist, telephonist, saxophonist, misogynist, accompanist, impressionist, excursionist, abortionist, contortionist, percussionist, destructionist, obstructionist, receptionist, illusionist, exclusionist, coreligionist (adherent of same religion), evolutionist, interventionist.

436.13.1
pianist, Orleanist.

436.13.2
agonist (type of muscle), protagonist, antagonist, deuteragonist (character in Greek drama).

436.13.3
humanist, phillumenist (collector of matchbox labels).

436.13.4
vacationist (*US* holidaymaker), salvationist, segregationist, revelationist (believer in divine revelation), conservationist.

436.13.5
nutritionist, prohibitionist, exhibitionist, abolitionist.

436.13.6
perfectionist, projectionist, protectionist, resurrectionist (body-snatcher), vivisectionist.

436.14
papist, rapist, escapist, landscapist.

436.15
therapist, philanthropist, misanthropist, psychotherapist, radiotherapist, physiotherapist.

436.16
tsarist, guitarist.

436.17
dearest, querist (questioner), careerist.

436.18
forest, florist, deforest, afforest, rainforest, reafforest, disafforest.

436.19
jurist, tourist, purist, manicurist, caricaturist.

436.20
aorist (linguistics term), theorist, diarist, arborist (specialist in tree-cultivation), labourist (supporter of workers' rights), Eucharist, naturist, plagiarist, amorist, humorist, aquarist (aquarium curator), terrorist, satirist, motorist, interest, Everest, apiarist, miniaturist, ocularist (artificial-eye manufacturer), militarist, disinterest, Redemptorist (Catholic missionary), behaviourist, lepidopterist.

436.21
Biblicist (biblical scholar), publicist, Anglicist, lyricist, classicist, physicist, geneticist.

436.22
assist, persist, trichocyst (zoology term), pharmacist, sporocyst (zoology term), macrocyst, statocyst (organ of balance), blastocyst, supremacist, nematocyst (animal's stinging organ).

436.23
cornetist, librettist, clarinetist.

436.24
Semitist (student of Semitic culture), phonetist, portraitist, hereditist (supporter of heredity's influence).

436.25
protist (microscopic organism), unnoticed.

436.26
egotist, dramatist, pragmatist, dogmatist, Donatist (Christian heretic), hypnotist, systematist, numismatist, separatist, anaesthetist.

436.27
dentist, apprenticed, Adventist (member of Christian sect), irredentist.

437 -iced [also **301** + *-ed*]
heist, Kleist (German dramatist), Christ, Zeist (Dutch city), unpriced, poltergeist, Antichrist.

438 -ost [also **302** + *-ed*]
cost, lost, frost, accost, alecost (Asian plant), volost (Russian peasant community), riposte, compost, defrost, hoarfrost, Bifrost (Norse mythological rainbow bridge), teleost (type of fish), Pentecost, permafrost.

439 -orst [also **303** + *-ed*]
horst (ridge of land), exhaust, holocaust, hypocaust (Roman heating system).

440 -oist [also **304** + *-ed*]
foist, joist, hoist, moist, unvoiced.

441 -oast [also **305** + *-ed*]
oast, boast, coast, ghost, host, most, post, roast, toast.

seacoast, rearmost, foremost, backmost, midmost (in the middle), endmost, hindmost, almost, topmost, utmost, doorpost, bedpost, guidepost, soundpost, milepost, impost (customs duty), signpost, lamppost, gatepost, outpost, milquetoast (*US* timid person).

undermost, innermost, uppermost, outermost, farthermost, nethermost, furthermost, bottommost, northernmost, southernmost, westernmost, easternmost.

442 -oust [also **306** + *-ed*]
oust, Faust, joust, roust (rout out), frowst (stuffy atmosphere).

443 -ust [also **307** + *-ed*]
bust, dust, gust, just, lust, must, rust,
crust, trust, thrust, robust, combust,
stardust, sawdust, august, disgust, adjust, unjust, piecrust, encrust, entrust,
distrust, mistrust, upthrust, readjust,
wanderlust, underthrust (geological
fault), overthrust (geological fault).

444 -oost [also **309** + *-ed*]
boost, roost, Proust, langouste (spiny
lobster).

445 -'st [also **310** + *-ed*]
locust, breakfast, steadfast, August,
ballast, Sallust (Roman historian),
dynast, Bathurst (Australian city),
provost, unbiased.

446 -idst
didst, midst.

447 -enst [also **316** + *-ed*]
unfenced, against, fornenst (*Scot* situated against).

448 -'nst [also **321** + *-ed*]
unlicensed, inexperienced.

449 -ished [also **353** + *-ed*]
unfurnished, unfinished, malnourished,
unaccomplished, undernourished, undistinguished.

450 -ext [also **496** + *-ed*]
next, sext (Catholic prayer time), text,
pretext, context, undersexed, oversexed.

451 -ixt [also **498** + *-ed*]
mixed, sixte (fencing position), betwixt.

452 -ath
Gath (biblical city), hath, Plath (US
poet), snath (scythe handle), strath
(*Scot* glen), isobath (line on map),
polymath, aftermath, chaetognath
(wormlike marine animal), plectognath

(spiny-finned fish), psychopath, neuropath (person with nervous disorder),
allopath (orthodox medical practitioner), sociopath (psychiatric term), osteopath, naturopath.

453 -arth
bath, Bath, garth (cloistered courtyard), hearth, lath, path, eyebath, birdbath, Hogarth, bypath (little-used
track), warpath, towpath, footpath.

454 -aith
faith, wraith, saithe (food fish), Galbraith.

455 -eth
Beth, death, breath, Seth, Macbeth, Ja-
peth (biblical character), megadeath
(death of million people), shibboleth,
isopleth (line on map), Ashtoreth (biblical character).

456 -erth
earth, berth, birth, dearth, firth, girth,
mirth, Perth, worth, rebirth, childbirth,
stillbirth, inearth (bury), unearth, afterbirth, pennyworth.

457 -eeth
heath, Leith, Meath, neath, wreath,
Reith, sheath, teeth, beneath, B'nai
B'rith (Jewish fraternal society), monteith (bowl for cooling wineglasses),
underneath.

458 -ith
kith, myth, Smith, pith, grith (place of
safety), withe (twig used for binding).

Hadith (Mohammedan tradition),
Judith, Griffith, tallith (Jewish prayer
shawl), Lilith (biblical demon), goldsmith, gunsmith, tunesmith, whitesmith
(metal polisher), blacksmith, locksmith,
zenith, turpeth (plant yielding purgative), Asquith, Penrith.

sixtieth, eightieth, thirtieth, fortieth, fiftieth, twentieth, ninetieth, Meredith,

eolith (stone tool), neolith (stone tool), laccolith (geology term), coccolith (geology term), megalith, regolith (earth's mantle rock), granolith (paving material), xenolith (geology term), monolith, urolith (stone in urinary tract), acrolith (type of sculpture), microlith (flint tool), gastrolith (stone in the stomach), statolith (biology term), batholith (large mass of granite), Ladysmith, Hammersmith, silversmith.

seventieth, Aberystwyth.

459 -oth
Goth, cloth, moth, wrath, broth, froth, Naboth (biblical character), haircloth, cerecloth (waxed waterproof cloth), backcloth, sackcloth, neckcloth, broadcloth (closely woven fabric), sailcloth, oilcloth, loincloth, dishcloth, cheesecloth, azoth (mercury), Visigoth, Ostrogoth, tablecloth, saddlecloth, behemoth (biblical monster).

460 -orth
Forth, forth, fourth, north, swath (strip of cut grass), henceforth.

461 -oath
oath, both, loath, sloth, quoth, wroth (angry), growth, troth, Thoth (ancient Egyptian deity), Arbroath, ingrowth, upgrowth, outgrowth, undergrowth, overgrowth.

462 -outh
Louth (Irish county), mouth, south, loudmouth, bigmouth, goalmouth, blabbermouth.

463 -ooth
couth, sleuth, Ruth, crwth (ancient stringed instrument), truth, strewth, sooth, tooth, youth, uncouth, Duluth (US port), Redruth, untruth, forsooth, eyetooth, foretooth (front tooth), bucktooth, dogtooth.

464 -'th
Sabbath, Lambeth, mammoth, Yarmouth, Weymouth, vermouth, Plymouth, Falmouth, Monmouth, Bournemouth, Portsmouth, Dartmouth, bismuth, ha'p'orth, Hepworth, Bosworth, Wordsworth, Wandsworth, Goliath, azimuth, Nazareth, Kenilworth, Elizabeth, altazimuth (astronomy instrument).

465 -elth
health, stealth, wealth. Commonwealth.

466 -ilth
filth, tilth (process of tilling land).

467 -anth
hydranth (type of polyp), perianth (part of flower), tragacanth (Asian plant), coelacanth (primitive bony fish), amaranth (flowering plant).

468 -enth
nth, tenth.

469 -eenth
eighteenth, thirteenth, fourteenth, fifteenth, nineteenth, umpteenth, sixteenth, seventeenth.

470 -inth
plinth, helminth (parasitic worm), Corinth, jacinth (gemstone), absinthe, terebinth (small Mediterranean tree), labyrinth, hyacinth, colocynth (climbing plant).

471 -'nth
millionth, billionth, trillionth, thousandth, dozenth.

471.1
seventh, eleventh.

472 -ength
length, strength, wavelength.

473 -athe
bathe, scathe, lathe, spathe (botany term), rathe (blossoming early), swathe, sunbathe, enswathe.

474 -edh
edh (runic character), Gwynedd, Gorsedd (Welsh bardic institution).

475 -eethe
wreathe, breathe, seethe, sheathe, teethe, Westmeath (Irish county), bequeath, enwreath, unsheathe, Pontypridd.

476 -idh
with, therewith, wherewith, herewith, forthwith.

477 -ithe
lithe, blithe, Blyth, writhe, scythe, tithe.

478 -othe
loathe, clothe, reclothe, unclothe, betroth.

479 -oothe
booth, smooth, soothe, tollbooth.

480 -av
have, lav (*short for* lavatory), grav (unit of acceleration).

481 -arve
carve, calve, halve, Slav, Graves (type of wine), starve, varve (geology term), suave, Zouave (French infantryman), Yugoslav.

482 -ave
cave, gave, slave, nave, knave, pave, rave, brave, crave, grave, trave (cage for shoeing horses), save, shave, stave, they've, waive, wave.

concave, forgave, behave, enclave, conclave, exclave, enslave, outbrave, margrave, burgrave (medieval German governor), Redgrave, waldgrave (medieval German forest officer), landgrave, engrave, deprave, spokeshave, palstave (archaeology term).

biconcave, misbehave, autoclave (pressurized container), architrave (moulding), aftershave, microwave, photoengrave.

483 -erve
curve, derv, MIRV (type of missile), nerve, perv (*short for* pervert), serve, verve, swerve, recurve, innerve (stimulate), unnerve, subserve (be helpful), conserve, deserve, reserve, preserve, observe.

484 -eve
Eve, eve, heave, leave, cleave, sleeve, sleave (tangled thread), nieve (*Dialect* fist), peeve, reeve, breve, grieve, greave (piece of armour), sheave, steeve (spar for stowing cargo), thieve, we've, weave.

naive, achieve, khedive (viceroy of Egypt), upheave, shirtsleeve, bereave, aggrieve, Congreve (English dramatist), reprieve, retrieve, perceive, conceive, qui vive, inweave.

interleave, semibreve, apperceive (psychology term), preconceive, misconceive, Genevieve, Tel Aviv, interweave.

underachieve, overachieve, recitative.

484.1
believe, relieve, disbelieve.

484.2
deceive, receive, undeceive.

485 -iv
chiv (*Slang* knife), div, give, live, spiv, sieve, Tiv (member of African people).

forgive, misgive (be apprehensive), relive, olive, unlive, outlive, plausive (ex-

275

pressing approval), octave, plaintive, captive, costive (constipated).

gerundive, abrasive, pervasive, evasive, invasive, dissuasive, persuasive, cohesive, adhesive, purposive, repulsive, impulsive, compulsive, expulsive, revulsive, convulsive, expansive, responsive, expletive, subjunctive, conjunctive, disjunctive, substantive, descriptive, prescriptive, proscriptive, inscriptive, adoptive, absorptive, irruptive, eruptive, disruptive, pre-emptive, consumptive, presumptive, exhaustive, reflexive.

irresponsive, retributive, attributive, contributive, distributive, consecutive, executive, diminutive, substitutive, institutive, constitutive.

485.1
massive, passive, impassive.

485.2
inessive (linguistics term), regressive, digressive, ingressive (phonetics term), depressive, repressive, oppressive, suppressive, impressive, compressive, expressive, recessive, obsessive, concessive, excessive, successive, possessive, inexpressive.

485.2.1
aggressive, progressive, retrogressive.

485.3
cursive, coercive, incursive, discursive, excursive (tending to digress), dispersive, aversive, perversive, subversive.

485.4
missive, permissive, submissive, admissive, dismissive.

485.5
derisive, decisive, incisive, divisive, indecisive.

485.6
plosive (phonetics term), implosive (phonetics term), explosive, erosive, corrosive.

485.7
jussive (linguistics term), percussive (relating to percussion), antitussive (alleviating coughing).

485.8
elusive, illusive, delusive, allusive, reclusive, seclusive, occlusive (phonetics term), inclusive, conclusive, exclusive, protrusive, obtrusive, intrusive, extrusive, abusive, conducive, effusive, diffusive, inconclusive, unobtrusive.

485.9
pensive, tensive (causing tension), defensive, offensive, suspensive, expensive, intensive, ostensive, extensive, inoffensive, apprehensive, comprehensive, inexpensive, coextensive, counteroffensive.

485.10
dative, native, stative (linguistics term), creative, illative (linguistics term), collative, nonstative (linguistics term), concentrative, gravitative.

485.11
furtive, assertive.

485.12
additive, fugitive, volitive (relating to the will), primitive, genitive, lenitive (soothing pain), unitive, punitive, cognitive, secretive, nutritive, transitive, sensitive, partitive, factitive (linguistics term).

intuitive, prohibitive, exhibitive (illustrative), definitive, infinitive, preteritive (linguistics term), interpretive, intransitive, insensitive, repetitive, competitive, acquisitive, inquisitive.

photosensitive, hypersensitive, radiosensitive.

485.12.1
positive, prepositive (linguistics term), appositive (linguistics term), suppositive (involving supposition), postpositive, diapositive, electropositive.

485.13

sportive, abortive, supportive.

485.14

motive, votive, emotive, promotive, locomotive, automotive, electromotive.

485.15 [further rhymes may be derived from **367**]

probative (providing evidence), combative, talkative, sedative, negative, purgative, elative (linguistics term), ablative, conative (linguistics term), calmative, donative (gift), lucrative, portative (portable), optative (expressing a wish), laxative, fixative, causative.

radiative (emitting radiation), rebarbative, reprobative, educative, superlative, contemplative, legislative, affirmative, alternative, imperative, pejorative, restorative, suppurative, illustrative, adversative (linguistics term), appreciative, initiative, associative, consultative, facultative, conservative, preservative, innovative, conciliative, accusative.

continuative (linguistics term), investigative, approximative, administrative, inappreciative.

485.15.1

fricative (phonetics term), siccative (substance causing drying), judicative, indicative, applicative, explicative, affricative (phonetics term), significative, multiplicative, communicative, uncommunicative.

485.15.2

locative, vocative, evocative, provocative.

485.15.3

derogative, prerogative, interrogative.

485.15.4

relative, appellative (name or title), irrelative (unrelated), correlative (mutually related).

485.15.5

speculative, calculative, cumulative, copulative, coagulative, accumulative, manipulative.

485.15.6

formative, normative (establishing a norm), reformative, performative (linguistics term), informative.

485.15.7

combinative, carminative, nominative, ruminative, imaginative, determinative, denominative (naming), agglutinative.

485.15.8

narrative, declarative, preparative, comparative.

485.15.9

curative, durative (linguistics term), depurative (purifying).

485.15.10

decorative, figurative, generative, separative, operative, corporative, ulcerative, alterative (therapeutic drug), deliberative, corroborative, desiderative (expressing desire), alliterative, commemorative, remunerative, cooperative, inoperative, postoperative, vituperative, noncooperative.

485.15.11

demonstrative, remonstrative, undemonstrative.

485.15.12

meditative, vegetative, cogitative, qualitative, imitative, quantitative, authoritative, interpretative.

485.15.13

rotative, denotative.

485.15.14

putative (supposed), commutative (involving substitution).

485.15.15

tentative, augmentative, frequentative (linguistics term), preventative, argumentative, representative.

485.15.16
privative, derivative.

485.16
active, tractive, reactive, inactive, refractive, attractive, subtractive, extractive, retroactive, photoactive (responsive to light), hyperactive, interactive, overactive, unattractive, radioactive.

485.17
effective, defective, affective (arousing emotions), perfective, infective, ejective (phonetics term), projective, objective, subjective, elective, selective, collective, reflective, connective, respective, perspective, prospective, directive, corrective, detective, protective, invective, ineffective, imperfective, irrespective, retrospective, introspective, circumspective.

485.18
fictive, predictive, addictive, vindictive, adjective, conflictive, restrictive, constrictive, convictive, nonrestrictive.

485.19
deductive, seductive, productive, inductive, conductive, destructive, obstructive, instructive, constructive, reproductive, unproductive, counterproductive.

485.20
distinctive, instinctive, extinctive (serving to extinguish), indistinctive.

485.21
pendentive (architectural term), incentive, retentive, attentive, preventive, inventive, disincentive, irretentive, inattentive.

485.22
captive, adaptive.

485.23
deceptive, receptive, preceptive (didactic), perceptive, inceptive (beginning), exceptive (forming an exception), nociceptive (causing pain), imperceptive (lacking in perception), contraceptive.

485.24
festive, restive, digestive, suggestive, congestive, indigestive.

486 -ive
I've, skive, chive, dive, five, jive, hive, live, Clive, rive (split asunder), drive, shrive, strive, thrive, shive (flat cork), wive.

skydive, endive, spoilfive (card game), ogive, beehive, alive, connive, derive, arrive, deprive, contrive, revive, survive, overdrive.

487 -ov
of, Pavlov, thereof, whereof, hereof, Rostov (Russian port), Baal Shem Tov (Jewish religious leader).

488 -ove
cove, Jove, Hove, hove, clove, mauve, rove, drove, grove, shrove, trove, strove, stove, wove, alcove, behove, mangrove, Bromsgrove.

489 -uv
dove, guv, love, glove, shove, above, ringdove, truelove, foxglove, turtledove, ladylove.

490 -oove
move, groove, prove, you've, remove, reprove, approve, improve, disprove, interfluve (land between two rivers), countermove, microgroove (groove in record), disapprove.

491 -alve
salve, valve, bivalve, univalve.

492 -elve
delve, helve (handle of tool), shelve, twelve.

493 -olve
solve, evolve, devolve, revolve, involve, convolve (to coil), dissolve, resolve, absolve.

494 -ax [also **32** + -s]
axe, Bax (English composer), Sfax (Tunisian port), jacks, lax, flax, slacks, pax, sax, tax, wax.

coax, pickaxe, panchax (tropical fish), addax (large antelope), carfax (crossroads), Fairfax, Ajax, relax, smilax (climbing shrub), poleaxe (battle-axe), toadflax, climax, Lomax, larnax (terracotta coffin), Fornax (constellation), hyrax (herbivorous mammal), styrax (tropical tree), borax, storax (tropical plant), thorax, anthrax, surtax, syntax, earwax, paxwax (*Dialect* ligament in neck), beeswax.

Halifax, parallax, minimax, subclimax, disclimax (ecology term), supertax, overtax.

Adirondacks (US mountain range), anticlimax, Astyanax (Greek mythological character).

495 -arx [also **33** + -s]
Berks., Marx.

496 -ex [also **35** + -s]
ex, kex (flowering plant), hex, lex (body of laws), flex, specs, Rex, sex, vex.

ibex, caudex (woody base of stem), codex (volume of ancient manuscripts), index, telex, ilex (evergreen tree), silex (heat-resistant glass), pollex (first digit on forelimb), scolex (head of tapeworm), culex (type of mosquito), reflex, Triplex (*Trademark*), diplex (electronics term), suplex (wrestling hold), duplex, perplex, simplex (electronics term), complex, remex (large flight feather), cimex (bedbug), annex, annexe, Kleenex (*Trademark*), apex, Perspex (*Trademark*), auspex (Roman soothsayer), Pyrex (*Trademark*), Lurex (*Trademark*), Durex (*Trademark*), murex (spiny-shelled mollusc), unsex, latex, vertex, cortex, vortex, dentex

(predatory fish), narthex (portico in church), convex.

subindex, tubifex (small worm), spinifex (Australian grass), pontifex (senior Catholic cleric), isolex (linguistics term), retroflex, circumflex, multiplex (electronics term), quadruplex (fourfold), googolplex (large number), haruspex (ancient Roman priest), interrex (interim ruler), unisex, supersex (genetics term), intersex (zoology term), Middlesex, biconvex.

497 -erx [also **36** + -s]
fireworks, steelworks, gasworks, glassworks, waterworks, ironworks.

498 -ix [also **38** + -s]
fix, mix, nix, Nyx (Greek goddess), pix, pyx (container for Eucharist), six, Styx.

spadix (type of inflorescence), radix, affix, graphics, prefix, suffix, affix, infix, unfix, transfix, postfix (add to the end), calyx, helix, kylix (two-handled drinking vessel), prolix (long and boring), rhythmics, fornix (archlike body structure), technics, tropics, varix (varicose vein), oryx (African antelope), rectrix (tail feather), tectrix (small feather), classics, Essex, Wessex, Sussex, glyptics (engraving precious stones), optics, chopsticks, ethics, cervix, civics (study of citizens' rights), coccyx, physics.

heroics, aerobics, fluidics (use of fluid flow), appendix, superfix (linguistics term), strategics (military strategy), anthelix (cartilage in ear), hydraulics, spondulix, polemics, tagmemics (linguistics term), phonemics (branch of linguistics), eurhythmics, mechanics, sardonyx (gemstone), philippics (bitter invective), subtropics, cicatrix, Bellatrix (star), dioptrics (branch of optics), kinesics (study of body language), forensics (formal debating), politics, Semitics (study of Semitic languages), orthoptics, ekistics (study of human settlements), logistics, sphragistics (study of document seals), ballistics, floristics (branch of botany), statistics, linguistics, acoustics, fiddlesticks.

logopaedics (speech therapy), orthopaedics, pedagogics, isagogics (introductory studies), bionomics (ecology), economics, ergonomics (study of work), agronomics (land economics), loxodromics (navigation technique), pyrotechnics, zootechnics (animal domestication and breeding), metempirics (branch of philosophy), executrix, semiotics (study of symbols), aeronautics, astronautics, hermeneutics (science of scriptural interpretation), therapeutics, pharmaceutics, dialectics, endodontics (branch of dentistry), orthodontics, exodontics (branch of dentistry), prosthodontics, diagnostics, geophysics, astrophysics, biophysics, metaphysics.

498.1
crucifix, antefix (ornament on roof), hieroglyphics.

498.2
dynamics, ceramics, thermodynamics, aerodynamics, electrodynamics.

498.3
eugenics (selective breeding), dysgenics (reducing quality of race), euthenics (study of environment control), cryogenics, callisthenics.

498.4
phoenix, hygienics, irenics (branch of theology).

498.5
onyx, conics (branch of geometry), phonics (phonetic teaching method), bionics, cryonics (freezing corpses for preservation), hedonics (branch of psychology), harmonics, mnemonics, tectonics, nucleonics (application of nuclear energy), thermionics (branch of electronics), histrionics, avionics, quadraphonics, eudemonics (art of happiness), geoponics (science of agriculture), hydroponics (method of plant cultivation), electronics, supersonics, ultrasonics, architectonics (science of architecture), microelectronics.

498.6
spherics, hysterics, atmospherics.

498.7
apteryx (kiwi), Vercingetorix (Gallic chieftain), archaeopteryx.

498.8
theatrics, paediatrics, geriatrics, physiatrics (*US* physiotherapy).

498.9
matrix, testatrix, aviatrix, generatrix (geometry term), separatrix (oblique stroke).

498.10
metrics (use of poetic metre), obstetrics, psychometrics (branch of psychology), isometrics, econometrics (branch of economics).

498.11
statics, chromatics (science of colour), pneumatics (branch of physics), rheumatics, dramatics, dogmatics (study of religious doctrines), aquatics, quadratics (branch of algebra), ecstatics, aerobatics, acrobatics, kinematics (branch of physics), systematics (study of systems), diplomatics, mathematics, numismatics, hydrostatics (study of stationary fluids), biostatics (branch of biology), thermostatics, aerostatics (physics term), electrostatics (branch of physics).

498.12
poetics, athletics, kinetics, genetics, magnetics, aesthetics, prosthetics, exegetics (study of textual interpretation), energetics (science of energy), homiletics (art of preaching sermons), theoretics, dietetics, anaesthetics, apologetics (branch of theology).

498.12.1
phonetics, cybernetics, aerodonetics (study of gliding flight).

498.13
tactics, didactics (science of teaching), syntactics (study of symbol systems), phonotactics (branch of linguistics).

498.14
antics, semantics.

498.15
gymnastics, ceroplastics (wax modelling), onomastics (study of proper names).

499 -ox [also **40** + *-s*]
ox, box, cox, fox, lox (smoked salmon), phlox, Knox, Nox (Roman goddess), pox, stocks, vox (voice).

gearbox, firebox, jukebox, matchbox, soundbox, snuffbox, mailbox, pillbox, strongbox, soapbox, icebox, horsebox, loosebox, hatbox, paintbox, postbox, redox (chemistry term), boondocks (*US* wild desolate country), outfox, cowpox, smallpox, swinepox, Xerox (*Trademark*), aurochs, volvox (microscopic animal).

tinderbox, chatterbox, gogglebox, goldilocks, badderlocks (brownish-green seaweed), equinox, chickenpox.

499.1
paradox, orthodox, heterodox, unorthodox.

500 -orx [also **41** + *-s*]
Fawkes, lawks, Yorks.

501 -oax [also **42** + *-s*]
coax, hoax.

502 -ux [also **43** + *-s*]
ducks, dux (*Scot* best pupil), lux (unit of illumination), flux, crux, shucks, de luxe, afflux (flowing towards), efflux (flowing out), reflux, influx, conflux (merging of rivers), Benelux.

503 -'x [also **46** + *-s*]
hallux (first digit on foot), bollocks, Pollux, lummox (clumsy person), flummox, barracks, Trossachs, Appomattox (US Civil War site).

504 -anx [also **51** + *-s*]
Manx, thanks, Fairbanks, phalanx.

505 -inx [also **52** + *-s*]
sphinx, jinx, Lincs., lynx, links, minx, high jinks, salpinx (anatomy term), pharynx, larynx, syrinx (bird's vocal organ), methinks, androsphinx (sphinx representing man's head), pilliwinks (medieval instrument of torture), tiddlywinks, nasopharynx (region behind nasal cavity), hieracosphinx (hawk-headed sphinx).

506 -unx [also **54** + *-s*]
trunks, quincunx (arrangement of five objects).

507 -az
as, jazz, has, razz (*Slang* deride), Boaz (Old Testament character), Hejaz (Saudi Arabian province), La Paz (Bolivian city), topaz, whereas, Alcatraz, razzmatazz.

508 -arz [also **1** + *-s*]
Mars, parse, vase, Abkhaz (Russian people), Shiraz (Iranian city), Ahwaz (Iranian town), memoirs, handlebars, churidars (Indian long trousers).

509 -aze [also **2** + *-s*]
baize, daze, phase, faze (*US* disconcert), gaze, haze, laze, lase (function as laser), blaze, glaze, maze, maize, smaze (*US* smoky haze), Naze (Essex headland), pes (foot), raise, raze, braise, braze (decorate with brass), craze, fraise (neck ruff), phrase, graze, praise, prase (variety of quartz), chaise (horse-drawn carriage), stays.

ukase (tsar's edict), diphase (physics term), prophase (biology term), stargaze, malaise, ablaze, zymase (enzyme mixture), amaze, manes (Roman minor deities), guanase (enzyme), kinase (biochemical agent), lipase (enzyme), erase, mores, sucrase (enzyme), rephrase, upraise, appraise, dispraise, lactase (enzyme), pectase (enzyme), maltase (enzyme), sideways, endways, edgeways, always, longways, leastways, lengthways.

peptidase (enzyme), oxidase (enzyme), nowadays, hollandaise, polyphase (having alternating voltages), telophase (biology term), anaphase (biology term), metaphase (biology term), amylase (enzyme), cellulase (enzyme), Bordelaise (sauce with red wine), Marseillaise, catalase (enzyme), underglaze (ceramics term), overglaze (ceramics term), lyonnaise (cooked with onions), Béarnaise (rich sauce), mayonnaise, Bolognese, polonaise, paraphrase, metaphrase (literal translation), écossaise, invertase (enzyme), phosphatase (enzyme), anatase (mineral).

histaminase (enzyme), tyrosinase (enzyme), lecithinase (enzyme).

broderie anglaise, enterokinase (enzyme).

509.1

liaise, nuclease (enzyme), urease (enzyme), casease (enzyme), protease (enzyme), ribonuclease (enzyme).

510 -ez

fez, Baez (US folk singer), Boulez (French composer), Cortes.

511 -erz [also 3 + -s]

furze, hers, Meuse, chartreuse, masseuse, mitrailleuse (machine gun), Betelgeuse (star), secateurs.

512 -airz [also 4 + -s]

airs, theirs, stairs, wares, affairs, upstairs, backstairs, downstairs, unawares, Armentières.

513 -eeze [also 5 + -s]

ease, bise (cold northerly wind), cheese, feaze (nautical term), feeze (to beat), he's, lees, lease (*Dialect* open pasture), please, mise (legal term), sneeze, pease (*Dialect* pea), squeeze, breeze, freeze, frieze, seize, seise (legal term), she's, tease, Tees, these, wheeze, tweeze.

scabies, rabies, tabes (wasting of body organ), soubise (onion sauce), pubes, marquise, headcheese (*US* brawn), Hades, Andes, Ganges, tales (legal term), Thales (Greek philosopher), displease, Burmese, Hermes, limes (boundary of Roman empire), Manes (Persian prophet), Menes (ancient Egyptian king), Chinese, stapes (bone in ear), herpes, stipes (zoology term), appease, trapeze, torques (zoology term), Tabriz (Iranian city), refreeze, unfreeze, deepfreeze, reprise, fasces (Roman magistrate's insignia), bases, faeces, fauces (anatomy term), disseise (legal term), heartsease, species, bêtise, Maltese, striptease, Dives (New Testament character), axes, Xerxes, disease.

Celebes (Indonesian island), Caribbees (West Indian islands), Maccabees (Jewish patriotic family), gourmandise, Portuguese, meninges, Hercules, Pericles, Sophocles, Damocles, Heracles, Androcles, johannes (Portuguese gold coin), talipes (club foot), antifreeze, indices, helices (*plural of* helix), Ulysses, Rameses, apices (*plural of* apex), varices (varicose veins), matrices, vertices, vortices, subspecies, consocies (ecology term), penates (Roman household gods), Jaxartes (Russian river), Laertes, expertise, velites (Roman troops), equites (Roman cavalry), pyrites (mineral), sorites (logic term), barytes (mineral), ascites (medical term), Boötes (constellation), litotes (understatement), atlantes (architectural term), Cervantes, Orontes (Asian river).

Diogenes, cheval-de-frise (barrier of spikes), ecospecies, cacoethes (uncontrollable urge).

513.1
sanies (discharge from wound), caries, paries (wall of body organ), facies (biology term), calvities (baldness).

513.2
Héloïse, Genoese, Faeroese, Averroës (Arab philosopher).

513.3
aedes (type of mosquito), heredes (heirs), Archimedes, Diomedes (Greek mythological king).

513.4
Hebrides, Parmenides (Greek philosopher), Eumenides (Greek Furies), Maimonides (Jewish philosopher), Simonides (Greek poet), Pheidippides (Athenian athlete), Euripides, cantharides (former medicine), Hesperides (Greek mythological characters), Pierides (Greek Muses).

513.5
Hyades (cluster of stars), Pleiades, Cyclades, Sporades, antipodes.

513.6
Achilles, Ramillies (Belgian battle site), Antilles, Los Angeles, isosceles, Praxiteles (Greek sculptor).

513.6.1
anopheles (type of mosquito), Mephistopheles.

513.7
valise, vocalise (vocal exercise), legalese, Sinhalese (language of Sri Lanka), journalese, novelese, officialese.

513.8
camise (medieval loose smock), chemise, Siamese, Assamese, Vietnamese.

513.9
Viennese, Lebanese, Pekinese, manganese, Milanese, Japanese, Pyrenees, Cantonese, Dodecanese, Demosthenes (Athenian statesman), Aristophanes (Greek comic dramatist).

513.10
Aries, Ares (Greek god), lares (Roman household gods), nares (nostrils), Antares (star).

513.11
heres (heir), series, Ceres (Roman goddess), congeries (collection).

513.12
cerise, Kanarese (Indian people).

513.13
Pisces, Cambyses (Persian king), Anchises (Trojan prince), Polynices (Greek mythological character).

513.14
menses, Waldenses (members of Catholic sect), Albigenses (medieval French heretics).

513.15
nates (buttocks), Achates (loyal friend), Euphrates, Mithridates (ancient Greek king).

513.16
D.T.s, Aeëtes (Greek mythological king), Sudetes (European mountain range), diabetes.

513.17
Socrates, Xenocrates (Greek philosopher), Hippocrates, Isocrates (Athenian orator).

513.18
cerastes (venomous snake), Ecclesiastes.

513.19
testes, Thyestes (Greek mythological character), Orestes (Greek mythological character).

514 -eerz [also **6** + -*s*]
cheers, shears, Algiers, Pamirs (Asian mountainous region), arrears, Cordeliers (French political club).

515 -iz [Also **16** + -*s*. Further rhymes may be created by adding -*es* to appropriate nouns and verbs.]
is, fizz, phiz (*Slang* face), his, Ms., quiz, squiz (*Austral* inquisitive glance), frizz, 'tis, whizz, swizz (*Slang* disappointment).

Suez, darbies, showbiz, Rockies, laches (legal term), riches, breeches, clutches, crutches, goodies, Cádiz, Indies, undies, hafiz (Islamic title), Kirghiz (Mongoloid people), ages, wages, wellies, Scillies, willies, kermes (dried insect bodies), Orkneys, Jeffreys, glasses, braces, falsies, rushes (film-making term), treatise, panties, civies, blazes, Moses, Menzies.

damages, obsequies, exequies, Benares (Indian city), eyeglasses (*US* spectacles), sunglasses, galluses (*Dialect* braces), galoshes, equities, assizes.

heebie-jeebies, Buenos Aires, elevenses.

515.1
Stannaries, groceries, Potteries, ivories, preliminaries.

515.2
masses, molasses.

515.3
missis, Mrs., premises.

516 -ize [also **7** + -*s*]
guise, pize (*Dialect* to hit), rise, prize, prise, size, wise.

franchise, disguise, stylize, surmise, cognize (perceive), despise, sunrise, moonrise, uprise, comprise, misprize (undervalue), Graecize (imitate ancient Greeks), abscise (to separate), excise, incise, capsize, outsize, pectize (change into jelly), quantize (physics term), baptize, peptize (chemistry term), chastise, Levis (*Trademark*), advise, crabwise, likewise, clockwise, somewise (in some way), unwise, crosswise, slantwise, widthwise.

Judaize, archaize, catechize, affranchise (release from obligation), enfranchise, disfranchise, fluidize, ruggedize (make durable), liquidize, hybridize (to crossbreed), subsidize, oxidize, iodize (treat with iodine), standardize, melodize, anodize, jeopardize, faradize (treat with electricity), sherardize (metallurgy term), rhapsodize, bastardize, methodize, merchandise, gormandize (eat greedily), aggrandize, exorcise, nebulize (atomize), capsulize, butterflies, manyplies (cow's stomach), immunize, communize (nationalize), recognize, solemnize, sulphurize, symmetrize, cicatrize (heal), exorcise, circumcise, amortize, deputize, supervise, improvise, otherwise.

propagandize, apostrophize, philosophize, anticlockwise, counterclockwise, soliloquize, ventriloquize, panegyrize (extol), anthropomorphize (ascribe human form to).

516.1
elegize, syllogize (reason using syllogisms), eulogize, energize, analogize (draw comparisons), geologize (study geology of), neologize (invent new words), theologize, psychologize (make psychological investigations), homologize (be homologous), apologize, mythologize, anthologize (compile an anthology), entomologize (study insects), demythologize.

516.2
stabilize, mobilize, tranquillize, sterilize, fossilize, fertilize, subtilize (refine), utilize, civilize, demobilize, immobilize, lyophilize (freeze-dry), evangelize, volatilize (change into vapour).

516.3

dialyse, symbolize, localize, vocalize, alkalize, idolize, feudalize, scandalize, vandalize, legalize, thermalize (physics term), formalize, normalize, penalize, finalize, signalize, equalize, paralyse, moralize, pluralize, ruralize, hydrolyse, mongrelize, neutralize, centralize, specialize, socialize, catalyse, metallize, vitalize, totalize, brutalize, tantalize, crystallize, breathalyse, novelize (convert into a novel), nasalize.

parabolize (explain by a parable), metabolize, cannibalize, illegalize, animalize, decimalize, caramelize, communalize, monopolize, demoralize, electrolyse, decentralize, commercialize, initialize (computer term), digitalize (treat with digitalis), capitalize, hospitalize, devitalize, revitalize, immortalize, palatalize (phonetics term), recrystallize (chemistry term).

universalize, Orientalize, Occidentalize, sentimentalize, departmentalize, compartmentalize.

516.3.1

realize, idealize.

516.3.2

bestialize, trivialize, mercurialize, industrialize.

516.3.2.1

serialize, arterialize (medical term), materialize, etherealize, immaterialize, dematerialize.

516.3.2.2

memorialize (commemorate), editorialize, territorialize.

516.3.3

actualize, visualize, ritualize, conceptualize, contextualize (put into context), desexualize (castrate or spay), intellectualize, individualize.

516.3.4

verbalize, hyperbolize (exaggerate).

516.3.5

analyse, canalize (provide with canals), channelize, psychoanalyse.

516.3.6

journalize (record in a journal), vernalize (botany term), internalize, externalize.

516.3.7

personalize, nationalize, rationalize, fictionalize, depersonalize, impersonalize, denationalize, conventionalize, internationalize, institutionalize.

516.3.8

liberalize, federalize, generalize, mineralize, gutturalize, naturalize, demineralize, denaturalize.

516.4

demise, remise (legal term), premise (state as a premiss), euphemize (use euphemisms), minimize, racemize (chemistry term), victimize, optimize, maximize, synonymize, legitimize.

516.5

alchemize (alter by alchemy), randomize, infamize (make infamous), Islamize, compromise, atomize, itemize, customize, macadamize, economize, epitomize, phlebotomize (surgical procedure), dichotomize (divide into two), autotomize (zoology term).

516.6

trichinize (infest with parasitic worms), Hellenize (make like ancient Greeks), feminize, scrutinize, divinize (deify), homogenize, nitrogenize, aluminize (cover with aluminium), bituminize, attitudinize (adopt opinion for effect), platitudinize.

516.6.1

Latinize, platinize (coat with platinum), gelatinize (become jelly-like), keratinize (biology term).

516.7

ionize, kyanize (make timber decay-resistant), lionize, carbonize, ebonize (finish to resemble ebony), urbanize, mechanize, preconize (announce publicly), volcanize (subject to volcanic heat), Balkanize (divide into warring states), vulcanize, cinchonize (treat with quinine), Christianize, modernize, euphonize (make pleasant-sounding), jargonize, paganize, organize, colonize, harmonize, Germanize, sermonize, Romanize, womanize, humanize, canonize, tyrannize, ironize (indulge in irony), synchronize, patronize, opsonize (medical term), Russianize, fractionize (divide into fractions), fraternize, Platonize (use Platonic principles), tetanize (induce tetanus), botanize, Teutonize (make German), westernize, heathenize, galvanize, unionize.

decarbonize, suburbanize, reorganize, disorganize, decolonize, dehumanize, skeletonize (reduce to minimum framework), Italianize.

Europeanize, Australianize, pedestrianize, republicanize, Americanize, Mohammedanize, revolutionize.

516.7.1
agonize, antagonize.

516.8
arise, theorize, barbarize, rubberize, suberize (botany term), moisturize, slenderize, tenderize, aphorize (use aphorisms), vulgarize, plagiarize, grangerize (illustrate with borrowed pictures), valorize (fix artificial price for), polarize, solarize (treat with sun's rays), bowdlerize, burglarize (US burgle), glamourize, memorize, summarize, mesmerize, vaporize, pauperize (impoverish), temporize, terrorize, mercerize, pressurize, satirize, cauterize, motorize, notarize (authenticate as notary), factorize, pasteurize, authorize, pulverize.

miniaturize, deodorize, categorize, revalorize (revalue), polymerize (chemistry term), isomerize (chemistry term), containerize, contemporize, extemporize, depressurize, computerize, characterize, transistorize, familiarize.

denuclearize, exteriorize (medical term).

516.8.1
secularize, circularize (distribute circulars to), regularize, singularize, popularize, particularize.

516.8.2
militarize, catheterize, demilitarize.

516.9
apprise, surprise, enterprise.

516.10
laicize (remove ecclesiastical status), Gallicize (make French), publicize, anglicize, plasticize, mythicize, synthesize, italicize, catholicize, Hispanicize (make Spanish), fanaticize, poeticize, romanticize, metathesize (linguistics term), hypothesize, parenthesize, photosynthesize.

516.10.1
criticize, politicize, depoliticize.

516.11
assize, emphasize, ostracize, fantasize, oversize, exercise, metastasize (medical term), apotheosize (glorify).

516.12
digitize, sanitize, monetize (establish as legal tender), magnetize, concretize, syncretize (combine differing beliefs), sensitize, proselytize (convert to another faith), demonetize, remonetize, parasitize, desensitize, hyposensitize (make less sensitive), photosensitize (make sensitive to light), hypersensitize (photography term).

516.13
narcotize, schematize, traumatize, stigmatize, dogmatize, hypnotize, concertize (give concerts), advertise, mediatize (partially annex a state), sovietize, alphabetize, emblematize, acclimatize, automatize, aromatize (make aromatic), achromatize (remove colour from),

demagnetize, dehypnotize, operatize (make into an opera), democratize, bureaucratize, hypostatize (regard as real), apostatize (abandon one's faith), anaesthetize, diazotize (chemistry term).

516.13.1
dramatize, melodramatize, epigrammatize, anagrammatize.

516.13.2
systematize, legitimatize, anathematize (to curse).

516.14
empathize, sympathize, telepathize.

516.15
devise, revise, televise, collectivize.

517 -oz
Oz, Boz (pen name of Dickens), cos, was, 'twas, because, sovkhoz (Russian state farm), Badajoz (Spanish city).

518 -orz [also 9 + -s]
cause, gauze, hawse (nautical term), clause, Mors (Roman god), pause, drawers, tawse, yours, yaws, indoors, outdoors, kolkhoz (Russian collective farm), applause, jackstraws, Azores, Doukhobors (Russian Christian sect), Santa Claus, diapause (period of suspended growth), menopause, mesopause (meteorology term), aeropause (region of upper atmosphere), stratopause (meteorology term).

519 -oize [also 11 + -s]
noise, poise, turquoise, equipoise (equilibrium), centipoise (unit in physics), counterpoise (counterbalancing force), corduroys.

520 -oze [also 12 + -s]
chose, doze, hose, close, nose, pose, rose, brose (*Scot* porridge), croze (recess in barrel), froze, prose, throes, those.

ribose (a sugar), sorbose (a sugar), bilboes (iron bar with shackles), glucose, aldose (a sugar), bulldoze, bellows, xylose (a sugar), parclose (church screen), foreclose, enclose, unclose, disclose, mannose (a sugar), bluenose (*US* puritanical person), hooknose, depose, repose, impose, compose, dispose, transpose, expose, Faeroes, Burroughs, Ambrose, rockrose, sucrose, refroze, unfroze, primrose, Montrose, dextrose, ketose (a sugar), lactose, fructose, maltose, pentose, heptose, hexose.

Berlioz, caseose (biochemical compound), pantihose, ankylose, amylose (component of starch), cellulose, laevulose (a sugar), raffinose (a sugar), dominoes, bladdernose (type of seal), diagnose, bottlenose (type of dolphin), shovelnose (US freshwater sturgeon), decompose, recompose, discompose, predispose, indispose, quelquechose (insignificant thing), pettitoes, galactose (a sugar).

metamorphose, anastomose, superimpose, underexpose, overexpose.

520.1
aloes, gallows, Allhallows, lignaloes (Asian tree).

520.2
appose, oppose, propose, suppose, superpose (maths term), presuppose, interpose, juxtapose.

520.3
arose, tuberose (Mexican plant), saccharose, guelder-rose.

521 -ouze [also 13 + -s]
bouse (nautical term), Cowes, dowse, house, blouse, mouse (hunt mice), rouse, browse, drowse, trouse (close-fitting Irish breeches), rehouse, espouse, arouse, carouse.

522 -uz

buzz, does, fuzz, muzz (make muzzy), abuzz, Hormuz (Iranian island).

523 -ooze [also **15** + -s]

ooze, Ouse, booze, choose, who's, whose, lose, blues, flews (bloodhound's fleshy upper lip), schmooze (US chat), snooze, ruse, roose (Dialect to praise), bruise, cruise, cruse, Druse (religious sect in Lebanon), druse (crystals lining rock cavity), trews, use, fuse, Hughes, muse, mews, news.

Toulouse, peruse, abuse, accuse, incuse (design stamped on coin), excuse, defuse, effuse, diffuse, refuse, infuse, confuse, transfuse, bemuse, amuse, misuse, contuse (to bruise), enthuse.

Veracruz (Mexican state), Santa Cruz (Argentine province), St. Andrews, disabuse, circumfuse (pour around), hypotenuse.

523.1

perfuse (permeate through), suffuse, interfuse (intermingle).

524 -'z [also **17** + -s]

pliers, chequers, sneakers, knickers, blinkers, bonkers, conkers (children's game), Yonkers (US city), withers, waders, glanders, Flanders, rounders, taggers (tin-coated iron sheet), staggers (type of vertigo), cobblers, bloomers, honours, Connors, clippers, jodhpurs, champers, rompers, vespers, horrors, Messrs., lancers (type of dance), pincers, bitters, afters, hipsters, cleavers (goosegrass), peevers (Scot hopscotch), divers, tweezers, scissors, trousers.

Moluccas, dividers, malanders (horse disease), pyjamas, Bahamas, headquarters, estovers (legal term).

Himalayas, camiknickers, knickerbockers, butterfingers, binoculars, Cordilleras (American mountain range).

525 -ads [also **83** + -s]

adze, scads (US lots).

526 -eeds [also **89** + -s]

Leeds, needs, proceeds.

527 -ides [also **92** + -s]

ides, besides, burnsides (US sidewhiskers), ironsides (person with great stamina).

528 -ords [also **95** + -s]

cords, Lords, Broads, sideboards, towards.

529 -odes [also **98** + -s]

Rhodes, crossroads.

530 -uds [also **100** + -s]

buds, suds.

531 -'ds [also **103** + -s]

innards, backwards, seawards, forwards, inwards, onwards, downwards, upwards, outwards, westwards, eastwards, northwards, southwards, billiards, afterwards, heavenwards.

532 -ends [also **131** + -s]

bends, amends, calends (day in Roman calendar).

533 -ounds [also **139** + -s]

bounds, zounds (archaic interjection).

534 -'nds [also **143** + -s]

Highlands, Midlands, Netherlands, Bury St. Edmunds.

535 -egs [also **181** + -s]

dregs, sheerlegs (lifting device), spindlelegs.

536 -ales [also **214** + -*s*]
Dales, tails, Wales, entrails.

537 -els [also **215** + -*s*]
Wells, Seychelles.

538 -ools [also **227** + -*s*]
pools, gules (heraldic term).

539 -'ls [also **228** + -*s*]
Peebles, Gorbals, doubles, shambles, gimbals (device enabling free suspension), hackles, Eccles, oodles, singles, shingles, annals, flannels, finals, Naples, Brussels, nuptials, Beatles, skittles, victuals, bristols, measles, bifocals, spectacles, genitals, incidentals, regimentals (regiment's uniform and insignia), unmentionables.

539.1
cobbles, collywobbles.

539.2
clericals, theatricals, academicals.

539.2.1
Chronicles, canonicals.

540 -arms [also **230** + -*s*]
arms, alms, Brahms, Psalms.

541 -ems [also **232** + -*s*]
hems, Thames.

542 -imes [also **236** + -*s*]
sometimes, betweentimes.

543 -'ms [also **242** + -*s*]
Adams, doldrums, customs, Williams.

544 -ans [also **245** + -*s*]
banns, cans (headphones), glans, Volans (constellation), Octans (constellation), Prestonpans (Scottish battle site), Lytham St. Anne's.

545 -ains [also **247** + -*s*]
pains, reins, Staines, remains, afterpains.

546 -ens [also **248** + -*s*]
ens (metaphysics term), Fens, gens (Roman aristocratic family), lens, cleanse, Valens (Roman emperor), lis pendens (legal term), impatiens (flowering plant), locum tenens, vas deferens, Homo sapiens, delirium tremens.

547 -eens [also **251** + -*s*]
jeans, means, greens, teens, Milton Keynes, Grenadines (West Indian islands), Philippines, smithereens.

548 -ins [also **252** + -*s*]
winze (steeply inclined mining shaft), gubbins (object of little value), Rubens, Dickens, dickens, Hawkins, Wilkins, Jenkins, Hopkins, moleskins, buckskins, Higgins, juggins (silly fellow), muggins, Collins, tenpins, ninepins, matins, Athens, avens (flowering plant), spillikins, candlepins (bowling game), withershins (*Scot* anticlockwise), galligaskins (17th-century men's breeches).

549 -ons [also **254** + -*s*]
bonze (Buddhist priest), pons (bridge of connecting tissue), bronze, frons (entomology term), long johns, nylons.

550 -oans [also **257** + -*s*]
Jones, nones, sawbones, crossbones, headphones, lazybones.

551 -'ns [also **261** + -*s*]
jibbons (*Dialect* spring onions), siemens (unit of electrical conductance), summons, barrens (*US* sparsely-vegetated land), Evans, evens, St. Albans, Gay Gordons, environs, abducens (cranial nerve), munitions, House of Commons.

551.1
relations, Galatians, combinations, congratulations, telecommunications.

552 -ings [also **265** + -*s*]
doings, makings, takings, tidings, leggings, lodgings, dealings, filings, whittlings (wood shavings), earnings, gleanings (useful crop remnants), screenings (refuse separated by sifting), innings, trappings, droppings, heartstrings, Hastings, beestings (first milk from cow), hustings, shavings, leavings, outgoings, surroundings, chitterlings (cooked intestines of pig), belongings, furnishings.

553 -eves [also **484** + -*s* and plurals of some nouns in **162**]
eaves, heaves (disease of horses), greaves (residue of tallow), Hargreaves, Anne of Cleves.

554 -ives [also **486** + -*s* and plurals of some nouns in **164**]
fives (ball game), hives, St. Ives, archives.

555 -elves [also **492** + -*s* and plurals of some nouns in **172**]
ourselves, themselves.

INDEX

A

aa 1
Aachen 261.10
aardvark 33
aardwolf 175
Aaron 261
abaca 17.42
aback 32.2
abacus 310.14
Abadan 246
Abaddon 261.19
abaft 396
abalone 16.233.1
abampere 4
abandon 261
abandoned 143
abandonee 5.14
abandonment 420.42
abase 295.1
abash 349.1
abate 367.4
abatement 420.48
abatis 300
abator 17.338
abattoir 1.17
abaxial 228.3.18
Abba 17.9
abbacy 16.307
Abbasid 91
abbatial 228.91
abbé 2
abbess 300
Abbevillian 261.3.11
abbey 16.5
abbot 381
abbreviate 367.1.10
abbreviation 261.67.1.6
abcoulomb 237
Abd-el-Krim 235
abdicate 367.5

abdication 261.67.5
abdomen 261.52
abdominal 228.60.5
abducens 551
abducent 420.71
abduct 389
abduction 261.79
abeam 234
abecedarian 261.3.21
abed 86.1
Abednego 12.29
Abel 228.11
Abelard 84
abele 217
abelmosk 59
Abeokuta 17.351
Aberdare 4
Aberdeen 251.1
Aberdonian 261.3.18
abernethy 16.369
aberrance 321.16
aberrant 420.61
aberration 261.67.22.1
Aberystwyth 458
abet 368.3
abeyance 321
abhor 9
abhorrence 321.18
abhorrent 420.63
abide 92
abiding 265.14
Abidjan 246
Abigail 214
Abilene 251.3
ability 16.333.9.2
Abingdon 261
abiogenesis 300.52.4
abiosis 300.55.2
abirritant 420.76
abject 385
abjure 10

Abkhaz 508
ablate 367
ablation 261.67
ablative 485.15
ablator 17.338
ablaut 377
ablaze 509
able 228.11
abloom 241
ablution 261.75
abnegate 367.10
abnegation 261.67.10
abnormal 228.53
abnormality 16.333.8.5
Abo 12
aboard 95.1
abode 98
abohm 239
aboideau 12
abolish 353.5
abolition 261.71.3
abolitionist 436.13.5
abominable 228.16.29
abominate 367.17.5
abomination 261.67.18.6
aboral 228.74
aboriginal 228.60
aborigine 16.229.1
abort 374
aborticide 92.7
abortifacient 420.73
abortion 261.72
abortionist 436.13
abortive 485.13
Aboukir 6
abound 139
about 377.1
above 489
abracadabra 17.280

abrade 85
Abraham 229
abrasion 261
abrasive 485
abraxas 310
abreact 382
abreaction 261.76
abreast 433
abridge 197
abridgment 420.37
abroad 95
abrogate 367
abrogation 261.67.11
abrupt 426
abruption 261.88
abruptness 300
Absalom 242.11
abscess 296
abscise 516
abscissa 17.302
abscission 261.91
abscond 136
abseil 214
absence 321
absent 410, 420
absentee 5.24
absenteeism 242.35.1
absente reo 12.2
absent-mindedness 300.28
absinthe 470
absolute 380.1
absolutely 16.193
absolution 261.75.1
absolutism 242.35.19
absolve 493
absorb 27
absorbent 420
absorber 17.17
absorbing 265
absorption 261.87
absorptive 485

absquatulate 367.13
abstain 247
abstainer 17.227
abstemious 310.2
abstention 261.82
abstergent 420.19
abstinence 321.14
abstract 382
abstraction 261.76
abstractionism 242.35.14
abstruse 309
absurd 87
absurdity 16.333
Abu Dhabi 16.6
abulia 17.3.23
abundance 321
abundant 420.16
abuse 309, 523
abusive 485.8
abut 378
abutilon 261.41
abutment 420
abutter 17.349
abuzz 522
abvolt 405
abwatt 373
Abydos 310.16
abysm 242.35.5
abysmal 228.54
abyss 300.3
abyssal 228.85
Abyssinia 17.3.34
acacia 17.322
academe 234
academia 17.3.26
academic 38.25
academicals 539.2
academician 261.71.4
academicism 242.35.16
academy 16.222
Acadia 17.3.7
Acadian 261.3.3
acajou 15
acanthoid 97
acanthopterygian 261.3.7
acanthous 310.72
acanthus 310.72
Acapulco 12
acariasis 300.57.1
acarid 91.27

acaroid 97.12
acarology 16.108.4.13
acarpous 310
acarus 310.50
ACAS 293
accede 89
accelerant 420.65
accelerate 367.23
acceleration 261.67.22
accelerator 17.338.9
accelerometer 17.342.3.4
accent 410, 420.83
accentor 17.368
accentual 228.9
accentuate 367.2
accentuation 261.67.2
accept 422
acceptable 228.16.58
acceptance 321
acceptant 420
acceptation 261.67
acceptor 17.375
access 296
accessible 228.16.37
accession 261.68
accessory 16.274.34
acciaccatura 17.277
accidence 321.5
accident 420.10
accidental 228.110.1
accidie 16.63
accipiter 17.342
accipitrine 253
acclaim 231
acclamation 261.67.16
acclamatory 16.274.43.5
acclimatize 516.13
acclivity 16.333.35
accolade 85
accommodate 367.9
accommodating 265.64
accommodation 261.67.8

accompaniment 420.31
accompanist 436.13
accompany 16.237
accomplice 300
accomplish 353
accomplishment 420.47
accord 95.3
accordance 321
accordant 420.11
according 265.15
accordingly 16.175
accordion 261.3
accost 438
account 418
accountable 228.16.56
accountancy 16.312
accountant 420
accounting 265.73
accouplement 420.40
accoutre 17.351
accoutrement 420.35
Accra 1
accredit 371.12
accrete 370
accretion 261.70
Accrington 261
accrue 15
acculturate 367.23
accumulate 367.13
accumulation 261.67.13
accumulative 485.15.5
accumulator 17.338.6
accuracy 16.307
accurate 371.34
accursed 91
accusal 228.128
accusation 261.67
accusative 485.15
accusatorial 228.3.12.2
accusatory 16.274.43
accuse 523
accused 156
accuser 17.444

accustom 242.32
accustomed 127
ace 295
acedia 17.3.8
acentric 38.47
acephalous 310.26.3
acerate 367.23
acerbate 367.4
acerbic 38
acerbity 16.333
acerose 305.2
acervate 371.37
acescent 420.67
acetabulum 242.10
acetal 212
acetaldehyde 92
acetanilide 92.2
acetate 367.30.2
acetic 38.51
acetify 7.3
acetone 257.2
acetous 310.64
acetum 242.28
acetyl 218
acetylene 251.2
acetylide 92.2
acey-deucy 16.306
Achaea 17.2
Achaemenid 91.21
Achates 513.15
ache 34
achene 251
Achernar 1
Acheron 254.11
achievable 228.16.61
achieve 484
achievement 420
Achillean 261.2.2
Achilles 513.6
achondrite 372
achondroplasia 17.3.59
achromat 365
achromatic 38.49.2
achromatize 516.13
ach-y-fi 5
acicula 17.174.6
aciculum 242.10.1
acid 91.28
acidic 38
acidify 7.3.1
acidimeter 17.342.2

acidimetry
16.285.1
acidity 16.333.5.1
acidosis 300.55
acidulate 367.13
acidulous 310.25.4
acinus 310.33
Acis 300.50
ack-ack 32
ackee 5
acknowledge 197.2
acknowledgment
420.37
acme 16
acne 16.238
acnode 98
Acol 228.19
acolyte 372.4
aconite 372.6
acorn 255
acotyledon 261.23
acouchi 16.326
acoustic 38
acoustician 261.71
acoustics 498
acquaint 409
acquaintance 321
acquainted 91.45
acquiesce 296
acquiescence
321.21
acquiescent 420.67
acquire 8
acquisition
261.71.8
acquisitive 485.12
acquit 371
acquittal 228.102
acquittance 321.24
acre 17.30
acreage 197
acred 103
acrid 91
acridity 16.333.5
acriflavine 252
Acrilan 245.2
acrimonious
310.2.9.1
acrimony 16.237
acrobat 365
acrobatic 38.49
acrobatics 498.11
acrocarpous 310
acrodrome 239
acrogen 261.39

acrolith 458
acromegaly
16.131.2
acromion 261.3
acronychal
228.23.13
acronym 235
acronymic 38.28
acrophobia 17.3.4
acrophobic 38.3
Acropolis 300.13.2
acrospire 8.2
across 302.2
acrostic 38.71
acroter 17.347
acrylic 38.21
acrylonitrile 219
act 382
actin 252
actinal 228.60
acting 265.70
actinia 17.3.34
actinic 38.34
actinide 92
actinium 242.2.11
actinoid 97.8
actinomere 6.3
actinometer
17.342.3
actinomycin 252.22
actinouranium
242.2.10
action 261.76
actionable
228.16.31
Actium 242.2
activate 367.36
activation 261.67
activator 17.338.11
active 485.16
actively 16.206
activeness 300.43
activism 242.35.22
activist 436
activity 16.333.35.2
Acton 261
actor 17.353
actress 300.48
actual 228.9.4
actuality 16.333.8.2
actualize 516.3.3
actually 16.131.1
actuarial 228.3.10
actuary 16.274.2
actuate 367.2

acuity 16.333.3
aculeate 371.1.1
aculeus 310.2
acumen 248
acuminate
367.17.6, 371.24
acupuncture 17.68
acute 380.3
acuteness 300.40
acyclic 38
acyl 218
ad 83
Ada 17.79
adactylous 310.23
adage 197
adagio 12.3
Adam 242.5
adamant 420.35
adamantine 253.9
Adamite 372
Adams 543
adamsite 372
Adana 17.239
adapt 421
adaptable 228.16
adaptation 261.67
adapter 17.374
adaptive 485.22
adaxial 228.3.18
add 83
addax 494
addend 131
addendum 242.7
adder 17.77
addict 387, 387.1
addiction 261.78.2
addictive 485.18
Addis Ababa
17.21
Addison 261.65
addition 261.71.2
additional 228.63.5
additive 485.12
addle 228.31
address 296
addressee 5.19
Addressograph
158.1
adduce 309.1
adduction 261.79.1
adductor 17.357
Adelaide 85
Aden 261.20
adenectomy
16.222.5

adenitis 300.62.3
adenoid 97.8
adenoidal 228.35
adenoidectomy
16.222.5.1
adenoma 17.215
adenosine 251.9
adept 422
adequacy 16.307
adequate 371
adhere 6
adherence 321.17
adherent 420.62
adhesion 261.90
adhesive 485
ad hoc 40
adiaphorism
242.35.15
adiaphorous
310.50
adieu 15.8
ad infinitum
242.29
adipocere 6.7
adipose 305
Adirondacks 494
adit 371
Adivasi 16.295
adjacent 420
adjectival 228.121
adjective 485.18
adjoin 256
adjoining 265
adjoint 416
adjourn 249
adjournment 420
adjudge 203
adjudicate 367.5
adjudication
261.67.5
adjudicator
17.338.2
adjunct 393
adjure 10
adjust 443
adjustable
228.16.60
adjustment 420
adjutant 420.78
adjuvant 420
Adler 17.183
ad-lib 24
adman 261
admass 293
admeasure 17.333

Admetus 310.63
admin 252
adminicle
228.23.12
administer
17.384.1
administrate
367.28
administration
261.67.25
administrative
485.15
administrator
17.338
admirable
228.16.35
admiral 228.76
admiralty 16.352
admiration
261.67.22
admire 8
admirer 17.274
admissible
228.16.39
admission 261.71
admissive 485.4
admit 371
admittance 321.24
admittedly 16.148
admixture 17.76
admonish 353.8
admonition 261.71
ad nauseam 229
adnominal
228.60.5
adnoun 258
ado 15.3
adobe 16.12
adolescence 321.21
adolescent 420.67
Adonic 38
Adonis 300.25
adopt 425
adopted 91
adoption 261.86
adoptive 485
adorable 228.16
adoration
261.67.22
adore 9.4
adorn 255
adornment 420
adrenal 228.59
adrenaline 252.11
adrenergic 38.16

Adrian 261.3
Adriatic 38.49
adrift 398
adroit 375
adscititious 310.58
adsorb 27
adsorbent 420
adsorption 261.87
adularia 17.3.38
adulate 367.13
adulation
261.67.13
adulatory
16.274.40.2
adult 406
adulterant 420.65
adulterate 367.23,
371.35
adulterer 17.279
adulterine 253.7
adulterous 310.50
adultery 16.274
adulthood · 101
adumbral 228.77
adumbrate 367
Aduwa 1
ad valorem 242.20
advance 315
advancement 420
advantage 197
advantageous
310.20
advection 261.77
advent 410
Adventist 436.27
adventitia 17.3.49
adventitious 310.58
adventure 17.70
adventurer 17.279
adventurism
242.35.15
adventurous 310.50
adverb 22
adverbial 228.3
adversary 16.274
adversative 485.15
adverse 297
adversity 16.333.26
advert 369
advertence 321
advertise 516.13
advertisement 420
advertiser 17.441
advertising 265.82
advice 301

advisable 228.16.64
advise 516
advised 154
advisedly 16.148
adviser 17.441
advisory 16.274.53
advocaat 1
advocacy 16.307
advocate 367.6,
371
advocation
261.67.6
adynamia 17.3.24
adze 525
aecidium 242.2.3
aeciospore 9.10
aedes 513.3
aedile 219
Aeëtes 513.16
Aegean 261.2
Aegina 17.232
Aegir 6
aegis 300.6
aegrotat 365
Aegyptus 310.71
Aeneas 310.1
Aeneid 91.1
Aeolian 261.3.12
Aeolic 38.22
aeolipile 219
Aeolis 300.13
aeon 261.2
aeonian 261.3.18
aepyornis 300.24
aerate 367
aerial 228.3.10
aerialist 436.7.2
aeriform 238.1
aerify 7.3
aerobatics 498.11
aerobe 28
aerobic 38.3
aerobics 498
aerobium 242.2
aerodonetics
498.12.1
aerodrome 239
aerodynamic 38.24
aerodynamics
498.2
aerodyne 253.2
aerofoil 222.1
aerogel 215
aerogram 229.1
aerology 16.108.4

aeromechanic
38.31
aerometer 17.342.3
aeronaut 374
aeronautical 228.23
aeronautics 498
aeropause 518
aerophagia 17.3.12
aerophobia 17.3.4
aerophobic 38.3
aeroplane 247
aerosol 220
aerospace 295
aerosphere 6.1
aerostat 365
aerostatics 498.11
aerugo 12.32
aery 16.264
Aeschylus 310.23
Aesculapius 310.2
Aesir 6
Aesop 276
aesthesia 17.3.60
aesthete 370
aesthetic 38.50
aesthetician
261.71.7
aestheticism
242.35.16
aesthetics 498.12
aestival 228.121
aestivate 367.36
aestivation 261.67
aetiology
16.108.4.1
Aetolia 17.3.22
afar 1
afebrile 219
affable 228.16
affair 4.3
affairs 512
affect 385.2
affectation 261.67
affected 91.43
affecting 265.71
affection 261.77
affectionate 371.28
affective 485.17
affenpinscher
17.331
afferent 420.65
affiance 321.2
affiant 420.2
affidavit 371
affiliate 367.1.2

affiliation
261.67.1.1
affine 253
affined 135
affinity 16.333.17
affirm 233
affirmation
261.67.16
affirmative 485.15
affix 498
affixture 17.76
afflatus 310.62
afflict 387
affliction 261.78
affluence 321.3
affluent 420.4
afflux 502
afford 95
afforest 436.18
affranchise 516
affray 2
affreightment
420.48
affricate 371.9
affricative 485.15.1
affright 372
affront 419.1
affusion 261.93
Afghan 245
afghani 16.224
Afghanistan 246.1
aficionado 12.16
afield 115.1
afire 8.1
aflame 231
afloat 376
afoot 379.1
afore 9.6
aforementioned
143
aforesaid 86
aforethought 374
a fortiori 7.11
afoul 224
afraid 85
afreet 370
afresh 351
Africa 17.34
African 261.13
Africanism
242.35.14.2
Afrikaans 315
Afrikaner 17.226.2
Afro 12
afrormosia 17.3.62

aft 396
after 17.358
afterbirth 456
afterbody 16.65
afterburner 17.229
aftercare 4
afterdamp 285
afterdeck 35
aftereffect 385.1
afterglow 12.46
afterimage 197.3
afterlife 164
aftermath 452
afternoon 260.2
afterpains 545
afters 524
aftersensation
261.67.26
aftershaft 396
aftershave 482
aftershock 40
aftertaste 432
afterthought 374
afterwards 531
afterword 87
afterworld 114
aga 17.124
Agadir 6
again 248
against 447
Aga Khan 246
agalloch 46
agama 17.218
Agamemnon 254
agamic 38.24
agapanthus 310.72
Agape 16.254
agape 270
agar 17.125
agaric 38.44
Agartala 1.9
agate 371
agateware 4.9
agave 16.379
age 193
aged 91
agee 5.7
ageing 265.24
ageless 300
agency 16.312
agenda 17.101
agenesis 300.52.4
agent 420
ageratum 242.27
ages 515

agger 17.144
agglomerate
367.23, 371.35
agglomeration
261.67.22
agglutinate 367.17
agglutination
261.67.18
agglutinative
485.15.7
agglutinin 252.17
aggrade 85.6
aggrandize 516
aggravate 367,
367.37
aggravation 261.67
aggregate 367.10,
371.14
aggress 296
aggression 261.68
aggressive 485.2.1
aggressor 17.300
aggrieve 484
aggro 12
aghast 431.1
agile 219
agility 16.333.9
Agincourt 374
agiotage 197
agist 436.4
agitate 367.30
agitation 261.67.27
agitator 17.338.10
agitprop 276
Aglaia 17.4
agleam 234
agley 2
aglitter 17.342
aglow 12.46
agma 17.220
agminate 371.24
agnate 367
Agnes 300
agnomen 248
agnostic 38.71
agnosticism
242.35.16
ago 12.33
agog 185.2
à gogo 12.31
agon 257
agonist 436.13.2
agonistic 38.70.4
agonize 516.7.1
agony 16.237

agora 1.14, 17.279
agoraphobia 17.3.4
agoraphobic 38.3
agouti 16.343
agraffe 157
agrapha 17.120
agraphia 17.3.10
agrarian 261.3.21
agree 5
agreeable 228.16.1
agreed 89
agreement 420
agrestal 228.113
agrestic 38.69
Agricola 17.176.2
agriculture 17.69
agrimony 16.237
Agrippa 17.253
Agrippina 17.230
agrobiology
16.108.4.2
agrology 16.108.4
agronomics 498
agronomy 16.222.3
aground 139.2
agrypnotic 38.53.2
ague 15
Agulhas 310
ah 1
aha 1.5
Ahab 18
Ahasuerus 310.45
ahead 86.5
ahem 232
Ahmed 86
ahoy 11
Ahwaz 508
ai 16.1
aid 85
Aidan 261.20
aide 85
aide-de-camp 266
aider 17.79
aigrette 368
aiguille 217
aiguillette 368
aikido 12.19
ail 214
ailanthus 310.72
aileron 254.11
ailing 265.27
ailment 420.39
ailurophile 219.1
ailurophilia
17.3.21.2

ailurophobe 28
aim 231
aimless 300
aimlessness 300.33
ain 247
ain't 409
aïoli 16.126
air 4
Aïr 6
airborne 255
airbrick 38
airbrush 356
airburst 434
airbus 307
aircraft 396
aircraftman 261
aircrew 15
airdrop 276
Airedale 214
airfield 115
airflow 12
airfoil 222
airframe 231
airhead 86
airiness 300.23
airing 265.52
airless 300
airlift 398
airline 253
airliner 17.232
airlock 40
airman 261.46
airplane 247
airport 374
airs 512
airscrew 15
airship 274
airsick 38
airsickness 300.27
airspace 295
airspeed 89
airstream 234
airstrip 274
airtight 372
airway 2
airworthy 16.375
airy 16.264
airy-fairy 16.264
Aisha 1
aisle 219
ait 367
aitchbone 257
Ajaccio 12.3
ajar 1
Ajax 494

Ajmer 6
Akbar 1
Akela 17.162
akhara 1
Akhenaten 261.95
akimbo 12.6
akin 252.4
Akkad 83
à la 1.7
ala 17.162
Alabama 17.205
alabaster 17.380
à la carte 366
alack 32
alackaday 2.8
alacrity 16.333
Aladdin 252
Alai 7
alameda 17.79
Alamo 12
à la mode 98
alamode 98.1
Alan 261
Alanbrooke 44
alannah 17.225
alap 269
alar 17.162
Alaric 38.44
alarm 230.1
alarmed 123
alarming 265.35
alarmism 242.35
alarmist 436.8
alary 16.274
alas 293
Alaska 17.47
alate 367
albacore 9.2
Alba Longa 17.142
Albania 17.3.31
Albanian 261.3.15
Albans 551
Albany 16.237
albata 17.338
albatross 302
albeit 371
Albert 381
Alberta 17.340
albertite 372.12
albescent 420.67
Albigenses 513.14
albinic 38.34
albinism 242.35.13
albino 12.54
Albinus 310.32

Albion 261.3
albite 372
album 242
albumen 252
albuminoid 97.8
albuminous
  310.33.1
albuminuria
  17.3.42.1
Albuquerque 16.23
Albury 16.274
Alcaic 38.1
alcaide 85
alcalde 16.73
Alcatraz 507
alcazar 1.19
Alcestis 300.68
alchemic 38.25
alchemist 436.10
alchemize 516.5
alchemy 16.222
alcheringa 17.141
alcidine 253
Alcock 40
alcohol 220
alcoholic 38.22
alcoholicity
  16.333.28
alcoholism 242.35
alcoholometer
  17.342.3
Alcoran 246
Alcott 381
alcove 488
Alcyone 16.237.1
Aldabra 17.280
Aldebaran 261.60
aldehyde 92
alder 17.96
alderman 261.52
aldermanic 38.31
Aldermaston 261
Alderney 16.237
Aldershot 373
aldol 220
aldose 520
aldosterone 257.1
ale 214
aleatory
  16.274.43.1
Alec 38.19
alecost 438
alee 5.9
alegar 17.129
alehouse 306

Alemanni 16.224
Alemannic 38.31
alembic 38
alembicated
  91.34.3
Aleppo 12.58
alert 369
alertness 300.36
alethic 38
aleurone 261.59
alevin 252
alewife 164
Alexander 17.99
Alexander Nevski
  16.43
Alexandra 17.287
Alexandria 17.3
Alexandrian 261.3
Alexandrine 253
alexandrite 372
alexia 17.3.57
alfalfa 17.121
alfilaria 17.3.38
Alfred 91
alfresco 12.14
algae 5
algebra 17.283
algebraic 38.1.1
algebraist 436.1
Algeciras 310.46
Algeria 17.3.39
Algerian 261.3.22
algerine 251.7
algicide 92.7
algid 91
Algiers 514
algoid 97
ALGOL 220
Algol 220
algolagnia 17.3
algology 16.108.4
algometer 17.342.3
Algonquian 261.3
Algonquin 252
algophobia 17.3.4
algor 9
algorism 242.35.15
algorithm 242.33
Alhambra 17.284
Al Hufuf 170
alias 310.2.3
Ali Baba 17.10
alibi 7
Alicante 16.353
Alice 300

alidad 83
alidade 85
alien 261.3.8
alienable 228.16.31
alienate 367.18
alienation 261.67.19
alienee 5.14
alienist 436.13
alienor 17.239
aliform 238.1
alight 372.4
align 253.3
alignment 420
alike 39
aliment 410.1, 420.31
alimentary 16.274.47
alimentation 261.67.32.1
alimony 16.237
aliped 86.6
aliphatic 38.49
aliquant 420.58
aliquot 373
aliunde 16.80
alive 486
alizarin 252.20
alkahest 433
alkali 7.7
alkalic 38.19
alkalify 7.3
alkalimeter 17.342.2
alkalimetry 16.285.1
alkaline 253.3
alkalinity 16.333.17.1
alkalize 516.3
alkaloid 97.6
alkane 247
alkanet 368
alkyl 218
alkylation 261.67.12
alkyne 253
all 221
Allah 17.160
allantoid 97
allantois 300.1
allay 2.12
allegation 261.67.10

allege 194
alleged 109
allegedly 16.148
allegiance 321
allegoric 38.41
allegorical 228.23.17
allegory 16.274.9
allegretto 12.75
allegro 12
allele 217
alleluia 17.432
allemande 129
Allen 261
Alleppey 16.254
allergen 261.39
allergenic 38.32.1
allergic 38.16
allergist 436.4.1
allergy 16.108.2
alleviate 367.1.10
alleviation 261.67.1.6
alley 16.112
alleyway 2
Allhallows 520.1
Allhallowtide 92
allheal 217
alliaceous 310.56
alliance 321.2
allied 92
alligator 17.338.3
alliterate 367.23.2
alliteration 261.67.22.4
alliterative 485.15.10
allium 242.2
Alloa 17.6
allocate 367.6
allocation 261.67.6
allochthonous 310.36
allocution 261.75.2
allodial 228.3
allodium 242.2.4
allograph 158.1
allomerism 242.35.15
allometry 16.285.2
allomorph 166.1
allomorphism 242.35.7
allonym 235
allopath 452

allopathic 38.72
allopathy 16.373.1
allopatric 38.45
allophane 247.3
allopurinol 220.3
allot 373.1
allotment 420
allotrope 278.3
allotropic 38.37.2
allotropy 16.254
allottee 5
allow 13
allowable 228.16.5
allowance 321
Alloway 2.28
alloy 11, 11.1
allseed 89
allspice 301
allude 102.1
allure 10.4
alluring 265.56
allusion 261.93
allusive 485.8
alluvial 228.3.17
alluvion 261.3.32
alluvium 242.2
ally 7, 7.7
allyl 218
Almagest 433
alma mater 17.337
almanac 32
almandine 253
Al Marj 192
Alma-Tadema 17.211
almemar 1
almighty 16.334
Almohade 85
almond 143
almoner 17.239
almonry 16.284
Almoravide 92.13
almost 441
alms 540
almshouse 306
almucantar 17.365
almuce 309
aloe 12.38
aloes 520.1
aloft 399
aloha 17.6
alone 257
along 266.1
alongshore 9
alongside 92

aloof 170
aloofness 300
alopecia 17.325
aloud 99
alow 12.45
alp 282
alpaca 17.28
alpenhorn 255
alpenstock 40
alpestrine 252
alpha 17.121
alphabet 368.3
alphabetic 38.50.2
alphabetical 228.23.19
alphabetize 516.13
Alpha Centauri 16.269
alphanumeric 38.39
alphorn 255
alphosis 300.55
alpine 253
alpinism 242.35.13
alpinist 436.11
already 16.60
alright 372
Alsace 293
Alsatian 261.67
alsike 39
also 12
also-ran 245
alt 401
Altaic 38.1
Altair 4
altar 17.363
altarpiece 298.2
altazimuth 464
alter 17.363
alterable 228.16.35
alteration 261.67.22
alterative 485.15.10
altercate 367.6
altercation 261.67.6
alter ego 12.28
alternant 420
alternate 367.18, 371.23
alternately 16.189
alternation 261.67.19
alternative 485.15
alternator 17.338.8

althorn 255
although 12
altimeter 17.342.2
altimetry 16.285.1
altitude 102.2
alto 12.82
altocumulus
310.25.5
altogether 17.402
Altona 17.236
altostratus 310.62
altricial 228.93
Altrincham 242.17
altruism 242.35.4
altruist 436
altruistic 38.70
aludel 215
alula 17.174
alum 242
alumina 17.231
aluminate 367.17.6
aluminium
242.2.11
aluminize 516.6
aluminothermy
16.214
aluminous 310.33.1
alumna 17.242
alumnus 310
alunite 372
alveolar 17.176
alveolus 310
always 509
alyssum 242.24
am 229
amadou 15.3
amah 17.206
amalgam 242
amalgamate 367.16
amalgamation
261.67.16
amanita 17.343
amanuensis 300
amaranth 467
amarelle 215
amaryllidaceous
310.56.2
amaryllis 300.8
amass 293
amateur 17.352
amateurish 353.11
amatol 220
amatory
16.274.43.5
amaut 377

amaze 509
amazement 420
amazing 265.81
Amazon 261
Amazonas 310.35
Amazonian
261.3.18
amazonite 372.6
Ambala 17.161
ambary 16.261
ambassador 17.92
ambassadorial
228.3.12
ambassadorship
274.1
ambassadress 300
amber 17.23
ambergris 298
amberjack 32
amberoid 97.12
ambidexterity
16.333.21
ambidextrous 310
ambience 321.1
ambient 420.1
ambiguity 16.333.3
ambiguous 310.4
ambit 371
ambition 261.71
ambitious 310.58
ambivalence
321.12
ambivert 369.1
amble 228.17
amblyopia 17.3.37
amboceptor 17.375
Amboina 17.235
amboyna 17.235
Ambrose 520
ambrosia 17.3.62
ambsace 295
ambulance 321
ambulant 420.27
ambulate 367.13
ambulatory
16.274.40.2
ambuscade 85
ambush 357
ameliorate 367.23
amelioration
261.67.22
amen 248
amenable 228.16
amend 131.2

amendatory
16.274.43.2
amendment 420
amends 532
Amenhotep 271
amenity 16.333
amenorrhoea
17.2.2
Amen-Ra 1
ament 410
ament 420
amentia 17.330
America 17.34.2
American 261.13
Americana
17.226.2
Americanism
242.35.14.2
Americanize 516.7
Amerindian 261.3
amethyst 436
amethystine 253.10
Amhara 17.268
Amharic 38.38
amiable 228.16.2
amianthus 310.72
amicable 228.16.10
amice 300
amicus curiae 5.2
amid 91.19
amide 92
amidships 327
amigo 12.28
Amin 251
amino 12.54
amir 6.3
Amis 300
amiss 300.20
amitosis 300.55.6
amity 16.333.11
Amman 246
ammeter 17.341
ammine 251
ammo 12
Ammon 261.44
ammonal 228.63
ammonate 367.18
ammonia 17.3.36
ammoniac 32.1
ammoniacal
228.28.1
ammonic 38.35.3
ammonite 372.6
ammonium
242.2.12

ammunition 261.71
amnesia 17.3.60
amnesiac 32.1
amnesty 16.366
amniocentesis
300.51
amnion 261.3
amniotic 38.53
amoeba 17.13
amoebaean 261.2
amoebiasis
300.57.1
amoebic 38
amoeboid 97
amok 43
among 267
amontillado 12.16
amoral 228.73
amorality
16.333.8.9
amoretto 12.75
amorist 436.20
amoroso 12.70
amorous 310.50
amorphous 310.18
amortize 516
Amos 302
amount 418.1
amour 10.1
Amoy 11
amp 285
ampelopsis 300.61
ampere 4
ampersand 128
amphetamine
252.15
amphiaster 17.379
amphibian 261.3.2
amphibiotic
38.53.1
amphibious 310.2
amphibole 223
amphibolite 372.4
amphibology
16.108.4
amphibrach 32
amphichroic 38.2
amphictyon 261.3
amphigory
16.274.9
amphimixis 300
amphipod 94
amphiprostyle
219.7

amphisbaena
17.230
amphistylar 17.167
amphitheatre
17.352
amphitricha 17.34
Amphitrite 16.334
amphitropous
310.40
Amphitryon 261.3
amphora 17.279
amphoteric 38.39
ample 228
amplexicaul 221.1
amplifier 17.4.1
amplify 7.3
amplitude 102.2
amply 16.178
ampoule 227
ampulla 17.174
amputate 367
amputation
261.67.29
amputee 5.23
Amravati 16.344
amrita 17.341
Amritsar 17.320
Amsterdam 229
amulet 371.17
Amur 10.1
amuse 523
amused 156
amusement 420
amusing 265.84
Amy 16.212
amygdala 17.176
amygdalate 371.18
amygdale 214
amygdalin 252.11
amygdaloid 97.6
amygdaloidal
228.35
amyl 218
amylase 509
amyloid 97.5
amylose 520
amylum 242
an 245
ana 17.226
anabaena 17.230
anabantid 91
Anabaptist 436
anabas 293
anabasis 300.57
anabiosis 300.55.2

anableps 324
anabolic 38.22
anabolism
242.35.11
anabranch 78
anachorism
242.35.15
anachronic 38.35
anachronism
242.35.14
anachronistic
38.70.4
anaclinal 228.61
anaclitic 38.52
anacoluthia 17.3
anacoluthon 254
anaconda 17.104
anacoustic 38
Anacreon 254.1
anacrusis 300.56
anadem 232
anadromous
310.29
anaemia 17.3.26
anaemic 38.27
anaerobic 38.3
anaesthesia 17.3.60
anaesthetic 38.50
anaesthetics 498.12
anaesthetist 436.26
anaesthetize 516.13
anaglyph 163
anaglypta 17.376
anagoge 16.106
anagram 229.1
anagrammatic
38.49.2
anagrammatize
516.13.1
Anaheim 236
anal 228.56
analemma 17.208
analeptic 38.65
analgesia 17.3.60
analgesic 38
analgia 17.3.16
analogize 516.1
analogous 310
analogue 185
analogy 16.108.2
analphabetic
38.50.2
analysand 128
analyse 516.3.5
analysis 300.52.1

analyst 436.7.4
analytic 38.52.1
analytical
228.23.20
Anambra 17.284
anamnesis 300.51
anamorphosis
300.57.2
Ananias 310.3
ananthous 310.72
anapaest 433
anaphase 509
anaphora 17.279
anaphylactic 38.58
anaphylaxis 300.70
anaplasia 17.3.59
anaplastic 38.68
anaplasty 16.361.1
anaptyxis 300
anarchic 38
anarchism 242.35.6
anarchist 436
anarchy 16.33
anarthria 17.3
anasarca 17.29
Anastasia 17.3.59
anastigmat 365
anastigmatic
38.49.3
anastomose 520
anastomosis 300.55
anastrophe 16.90
anatase 509
anathema 17.218
anathematize
516.13.2
Anatolia 17.3.22
Anatolian 261.3.12
anatomical
228.23.9
anatomist 436.10
anatomy 16.222
Anaximander
17.98
anbury 16.274
ancestor 17.382
ancestral 228.81
ancestry 16.292
Anchises 513.13
anchor 17.43
anchorage 197
anchorite 372.8
anchoveta 17.339
anchovy 16.385
anchusa 17.308

ancient 420
ancillary 16.274.16
and 128
Andalusia 17.3
andante 16.353
andantino 12.54
Andean 261.2
Anderson 261
Andes 513
andesite 372
Andhra Pradesh
351
andiron 261.4
Andorra 17.276
Andover 17.417
andradite 372.2
Andrea 17.3.45
Andrew 15
Andrews 523
Androcles 513
androclinium
242.2.11
androecium 242.2
androgen 261.39
androgenic 38.32.1
androgenous
310.33
androgyne 253
android 97
Andromache 16.33
Andromeda 17.83
Andros 302
androsphinx 505
androsterone 257.1
Andvari 16.261
Andy 16.77
ane 247
anecdotage 197.13
anecdotal 228.106
anecdote 376
anechoic 38.2
anemochore 9.2
anemography
16.90.2.3
anemology
16.108.4.9
anemometer
17.342.3
anemometry
16.285.2
anemone 16.237.6
anent 410
anergic 38.16
anergy 16.108

aneurysm
242.35.15
anew 15
anfractuosity
16.333.30.2
anfractuous 310.4
angary 16.274
angel 228
angelfish 353
angelic 38.20
angelica 17.34
angelical 228.23.6
angelology
16.108.4
Angelus 310.23
anger 17.140
Angevin 252
angina 17.232
angina pectoris
300.47
angioma 17.215
angle 228.49
angler 17.194
Anglesey 16.308
Anglia 17.3
Anglian 261.3
Anglican 261.13
Anglicanism
242.35.14.2
Anglice 16.300
Anglicism
242.35.16
Anglicist 436.21
anglicize 516.10
angling 265
Anglomania
17.3.31.1
Anglophile 219.1
Anglophilia
17.3.21.2
Anglophobe 28
Anglophobia
17.3.4
Anglophone 257
Angola 17.171
angora 17.276
angostura 17.277
angry 16
Anguilla 17.166
anguine 252
anguish 353
angular 17.174
angularity
16.333.20.3

angulate 367.13.4,
371.17
angulation
261.67.13.2
Angus 310
anhedral 228.78
anhinga 17.141
Anhwei 2
anhydride 92
anhydrous 310
ani 16.224
Aniakchak 32
aniconic 38.35
anil 218
anile 219
aniline 252.8
anima 17.211
animadversion
261.69
animadvert 369
animal 228.52
animalcule 227
animalism
242.35.11
animality 16.333.8
animalize 516.3
animate 367.15,
371.19
animation
261.67.15
animatism
242.35.20
animator 17.338
animé 2
animism 242.35
animosity
16.333.30
animus 310.28.1
anion 261.4
anise 300
aniseed 89.2
aniseikonia 17.3.36
anisette 368
anisogamy
16.222.2
anisole 223.4
Ankara 17.279
ankh 51
ankle 228
anklebone 257
anklet 371
ankylosaur 9.11
ankylose 520
ankylosis 300.55
anlace 300

Anna 17.225
Annaba 17.21
annabergite 372
annal 228.55
annals 539
Annam 229
Annapolis 300.13.1
annates 335
annatto 12.72
Anne 245
anneal 217.1
annelid 91
Anne of Cleves
553
annex 496
annexation
261.67.35
annexe 496
Annie 16.223
annihilate
367.14.1
annihilation
261.67.14.1
anniversary
16.274.35
anno Domini 7.10
annotate 367.31
annotation
261.67.28
announce 319
announcement 420
announcer 17.317
annoy 11
annoyance 321
annoyed 97.9
annual 228.9.2
annuitant 420.76
annuity 16.333.3
annul 225
annular 17.174.9
annulate 371.17
annulation
261.67.13
annulet 371.17
annulment 420
annulose 305
annulus 310.25
annunciate 367.1
annunciation
261.67.1.4
annunciator
17.338.1
anoa 17.6
anode 98
anodize 516

anodyne 253.2
anoint 416
anointment 420.50
anole 223
anomalous 310.26
anomaly 16.131
anomie 16.219
anon 254.8
anonym 235
anonymity
16.333.12
anonymous
310.28.2
anopheles 513.6.1
anorak 32.3
anorexia 17.3.57
anorexia nervosa
17.306
anorthosite 372.10
anosmia 17.3
another 17.408
anoxaemia
17.3.26.1
anoxia 17.3
ansate 367
Anschluss 308
Anselm 243
anserine 253.7
Anshan 245
answer 17.313
answerable
228.16.35
ant 407
anta 17.365
antacid 91.28
antagonism
242.35.14
antagonist 436.13.2
antagonistic
38.70.4
antagonize 516.7.1
antalkali 7.7
Antarctic 38.59
Antarctica 17.34
Antares 513.10
ante 16.353
anteater 17.341
antebellum 242.8
antecede 89.2
antecedence 321.4
antecedent 420.9
antechoir 8.3
antedate 367.8
antediluvian
261.3.32

antefix 498.1
antelope 278.2
antemeridian 261.3.5
ante meridiem 242.2.3
antenatal 228.99
antenna 17.228
anterior 17.3.39
anteroom 241
antetype 275
antevert 369.1
anthelion 261.3.10
anthelix 498
anthelmintic 38
anthem 242
anthemion 261.3
anther 17.399
antheridium 242.2.3
antherozoid 91
anthesis 300.51
anthologize 516.1
anthology 16.108.4
anthotaxy 16.386
anthracite 372.10
anthracitic 38.52.3
anthracnose 305
anthracoid 97
anthrax 494
anthropogenesis 300.52.4
anthropoid 97
anthropology 16.108.4.12
anthropometry 16.285.2
anthropomorphic 38.14
anthropomorphism 242.35.7
anthropomorphize 516
anthropomorphosis 300.57.2
anthropomorphous 310.18
anthropophagi 7.4
anthropophagic 38.15
anthropophagite 372
anthropophagy 16.108.1

anthroposophy 16.90.4
anthurium 242.2
anti 16.353
anti-aircraft 396
antiar 1
antibiosis 300.55.2
antibiotic 38.53.1
antibody 16.65
antic 38.62
anticatalyst 436.7.6
Antichrist 437
anticipant 420.56
anticipate 367.19.1
anticipation 261.67.20.1
anticipatory 16.274.40
anticlastic 38.68
anticlerical 228.23.15
anticlimactic 38.58
anticlimax 494
anticlinal 228.61
anticline 253.4
anticlinorium 242.2.17
anticlockwise 516
anticoagulant 420.27
anticonvulsant 420.72
Anticosti 16.367
antics 498.14
anticyclone 257
anticyclonic 38.35
antidepressant 420.67
antidote 376
Antietam 242.28
antifebrile 219
antifouling 265.33
antifreeze 513
antigen 261.37
Antigone 16.237
Antigonus 310.36
Antigua 17.128
antihero 12.63
antihistamine 252.15
antiknock 40
Antilles 513.6
antilog 185
antilogism 242.35.8
antilogy 16.108.3

antimacassar 17.298
antimagnetic 38.50
antimalarial 228.3.10
antimasque 56
antimatter 17.336
antimere 6.2
antimissile 219.2
antimonial 228.3.8
antimony 16.237
antineutron 254
antinode 98
antinomy 16.222
antinucleon 254.1
Antioch 40
Antiochus 310.14
antioxidant 420.10
Antipater 17.352
antipathetic 38.50.6
antipathy 16.373
antiperspirant 420.65
antiphlogistic 38.70.1
antiphon 261.29
antiphonal 228.63
antiphonary 16.274.29
antiphony 16.237.2
antiphrasis 300.57
antipodal 228.38
antipode 98
antipodean 261.2
antipodes 513.5
antipope 278
antipsychiatry 16.286.1
antipyretic 38.50
antiquarian 261.3.21
antiquary 16.274
antiquate 367.20
antiquated 91.34
antique 37
antiquity 16.333
antirrhinum 242.15
antiscorbutic 38.56
anti-Semitic 38.52
anti-Semitism 242.35.18
antisepsis 300.59
antiseptic 38.65
antiserum 242.19

antislavery 16.274.50
antisocial 228.94
antispasmodic 38.9
antistatic 38.49
antistrophe 16.90.3
antitank 51
antithesis 300.52
antithetical 228.23.19
antitoxin 252.29
antitussive 485.7
antitype 275
antivenin 252.16
antiworld 114
antler 17.203
Antlia 17.3
antlike 39
antlion 261.4
Antofagasta 17.379
Antoinette 368
Antoninus 310.34
Antonio 12.3.4
Antonioni 16.233
antonomasia 17.3.59
Antony 16.237
antonym 235
antonymous 310.28.2
antre 17.365
Antrim 235
antrorse 303
antrum 242
Antwerp 272
Anubis 300.2
anuran 261.59
anuresis 300.51
anuria 17.3.42
anurous 310.49
anus 310.31
anvil 218
anxiety 16.333.2
anxious 310
any 16.226
anybody 16.65
anyhow 13
anyone 259
anything 265
anyway 2
anywhere 4.7
Anzac 32
aorist 436.20
aorta 17.345
aortic 38.54

aoudad 83
apace 295.4
Apache 16.46
apache 350
apagoge 16.106
Aparri 16.261
apart 366.1
apartheid 372
apartment 420
apathetic 38.50.6
apathy 16.373
apatite 372.12
ape 270
Apeldoorn 255
apelike 39
apeman 261
aperient 420.1
aperiodic 38.9
apéritif 162
aperture 17.62
apery 16.274
apetalous 310.26
apex 496
aphaeresis 300.52
aphagia 17.3.12
aphasia 17.3.59
aphelion 261.3.10
aphid 91
aphis 300
aphonia 17.3.36
aphonic 38.35.2
aphorism 242.35.15
aphoristic 38.70.5
aphorize 516.8
aphotic 38.53
aphrodisiac 32.1
Aphrodite 16.334
aphtha 17.398
aphyllous 310.23
apian 261.3
apiarian 261.3.21
apiarist 436.20
apiary 16.274.1
apical 228.23
apices 513
apiece 298.2
Apis 300
apish 353
apivorous 310.50.3
aplanatic 38.49.5
aplanospore 9.10
aplasia 17.3.59
aplastic 38.68
aplenty 16.355
aplite 372

aplomb 237
Apo 12.57
apocalypse 327
apocalyptic 38.66
apocarpous 310
apochromatic
  38.49.2
apocope 16.254
apocrine 253
Apocrypha 17.114
apocryphal 228.41
apocynthion
  261.3.28
apodal 228.38
apodosis 300.57
apogee 5.7
apolitical 228.23.20
Apollinaris 300.44
Apollo 12.43
Apollonian
  261.3.18
apologetic 38.50.3
apologetics 498.12
apologia 17.3.15
apologist 436.4
apologize 516.1
apologue 185
apology
  16.108.4.12
apolune 260.1
apomict 387
apomixis 300
apophasis 300.57
apophthegm 232
apophyge 16.103
apophyllite 372.3
apophysis 300.52
apoplectic 38.60
apoplexy 16.387
aposematic 38.49.1
apospory 16.269
apostasy 16.307
apostate 367.34
apostatize 516.13
a posteriori 7.11
apostle 228.86
apostolate 371.18
apostolic 38.22
apostrophe 16.90
apostrophic 38.13
apostrophize 516
apothecary
  16.274.4
apothem 232
apotheosis 300.55.1

apotheosize 516.11
apotropaic 38.1
appal 221
Appalachia 17.3
Appalachian 261.3
appalling 265.31
Appaloosa 17.308
apparatus 310.62
apparel 228.72
apparent 420.60
apparition 261.71
apparitor 17.342
appeal 217
appear 6.6
appearance 321.17
appease 513
appeasement 420
appel 215
appellant 420.26
appellate 371.15
appellation
  261.67.12
appellative
  485.15.4
appellee 5
append 131
appendage 197
appendant 420.14
appendectomy
  16.222.5
appendicectomy
  16.222.5
appendicitis 300.62
appendicular
  17.174.6
appendix 498
apperceive 484
apperception
  261.84.1
appertain 247.10
appetence 321.24
appetite 372.11
appetizer 17.441
appetizing 265.82
applaud 95
applause 518
apple 228.64
applecart 366
applejack 32
applesnits 339
appliance 321.2
applicable
  228.16.10
applicant 420.7

application
  261.67.5
applicative
  485.15.1
applicator 17.338.2
applicatory
  16.274.40.1
applied 92
appliqué 2.6
apply 7.9
appoggiatura
  17.277
appoint 416.1
appointee 5
appointment
  420.50
appointor 17.371
Appomattox 503
apportion 261.72.1
apportionment
  420.42
appose 520.2
apposite 371.40
apposition 261.71.9
appositive 485.12.1
appraisal 228.125
appraise 509
appreciable
  228.16.42
appreciate 367.1
appreciation
  261.67.1
appreciative 485.15
apprehend 131.1
apprehensible
  228.16.40
apprehension
  261.82.1
apprehensive 485.9
apprentice 300
apprenticed 436.27
apprenticeship 274
appressed 433
apprise 516.9
approach 70
approachable
  228.16.13
approbate 367.4
approbation
  261.67.3
appropriate 367.1,
  371.1
appropriateness
  300.38

appropriation 261.67.1
approval 228.122
approve 490
approved 150
approximal 228.52
approximate 367.15, 371.19
approximately 16.189.1
approximation 261.67.15
approximative 485.15
appulse 313
appurtenance 321.14
appurtenant 420.53
apraxia 17.3.56
après-ski 5
apricot 373
April 228
a priori 7.11
apron 261
apropos 12.59
apse 322
apsis 300
apt 421
apteral 228.76
apterous 310.50
apterygial 228.3.3
apteryx 498.7
aptitude 102.2
aptness 300
Apurimac 32
apyretic 38.50
Aqaba 17.21
aquaculture 17.69
aqualung 267
aquamarine 251.7
aquanaut 374
aquaphobia 17.3.4
aquaplane 247
aqua regia 17.3.13
aquarelle 215
aquarist 436.20
aquarium 242.2.14
Aquarius 310.2.10
aquatic 38.49
aquatics 498.11
aquatint 412
aquavit 371
aqua vitae 7.13
aqueduct 389
aqueous 310.2

aquifer 17.114
Aquila 17.166
aquilegia 17.3.13
aquiline 253
Aquinas 310.34
Aquitaine 247.9
Ara 17.268
Arab 31
arabesque 57
Arabia 17.3.1
Arabian 261.3.1
Arabic 38
arable 228.16
Araby 16.15
Arachne 16.238
arachnid 91.22
arachnoid 97
Arad 83
Aragon 261
Araguaia 17.4
Arak 33
Aramaic 38.1
Aran 261
araneid 91.2
Arapaho 12.37
Ararat 365
araroba 17.18
Aras 293
Araucania 17.3.31
araucaria 17.3.38
arbalest 436.7
arbiter 17.342
arbitrage 359
arbitral 228.79
arbitrament 420.35
arbitrary 16.274
arbitrate 367.27
arbitration 261.67
arbitress 300
arboraceous 310.56
arboreal 228.3.12
arboreous 310.2.13
arborescent 420.67
arboretum 242.28
arboriculture 17.69
arborist 436.20
arbor vitae 7.13
arbour 17.10
Arbroath 461
Arbuthnot 373
arbutus 310.67
arc 33
arcade 85
Arcadia 17.3.7
Arcadian 261.3.3

arcana 17.227
arcane 247
arcanum 242
arcature 17.62
arch 63
Archaean 261.2
archaeologist 436.4
archaeology 16.108.4.1
archaeopteryx 498.7
archaeornis 300.24
archaic 38.1
archaism 242.35.2
archaize 516
archangel 228
archbishop 281
archbishopric 38
archdeacon 261.12
archdeaconry 16.284
archdiocesan 261.65
archdiocese 300.57.1
archducal 228
archduchess 300
archduchy 16.52
archduke 45
archegonium 242.2.12
archer 17.51
archery 16.274
archespore 9
archetypal 228.67
archetype 275
archfiend 133
archicarp 269
archimage 193
archimandrite 372
Archimedean 261.3.4
Archimedes 513.3
archine 251
archipelagic 38.15
archipelago 12.33
architect 385.8
architectonic 38.35
architectonics 498.5
architectural 228.76.1
architecture 17.64
architrave 482
archives 554

archivist 436
archpriest 435
archway 2
arcograph 158.1
arctic 38.59
Arcturus 310.49
arcuate 371.2
arcuation 261.67.2
ardeb 21
Arden 261
Ardennes 248
ardent 420.8
ardour 17.78
arduous 310.4
are 1
area 17.3.38
areaway 2.28
areca 17.34
arena 17.230.1
arenaceous 310.56.4
arenicolous 310.26.2
arenite 372.6
aren't 408
areography 16.90.2.1
areola 17.176
Arequipa 17.252
Ares 513.10
arethusa 17.444
Arezzo 12.71
argali 16.131
argent 420
argentic 38.63
Argentina 17.230
Argentine 251
argentine 253
argentous 310.70
argil 218
argillite 372.3
Argo 12.26
argol 220
Argolis 300.13
argon 254
Argonaut 374
argonon 254.8
Argos 302
argosy 16.307
argot 12.26
arguable 228.16.6
argue 15
argufy 7
argument 420.34

argumentation 261.67.32
argumentative 485.15.15
Argus 310
argy-bargy 16.99
Argyll 219
aria 17.3
Arian 261.3.21
Arianism 242.35.14.1.1
arid 91.25
aridity 16.333.5
ariel 228.3.10
Ariel 228.3.10
Aries 513.10
arietta 17.339
aright 372.8
Arimathea 17.2
arise 516.8
arisen 261.126
arista 17.384
Aristarchus 310.8
Aristippus 310.37
aristocracy 16.307.5
aristocrat 365.2
aristocratic 38.49.6
Aristophanes 513.9
Aristotelian 261.3.10
Aristotle 228.104
arithmetic 38.50, 38.57
Arius 310.2.10
Arizona 17.236
ark 33
Arkansas 9
arkose 305
Arkwright 372
Arlington 261
arm 230
armada 17.78
armadillo 12.42
Armageddon 261.21
Armagh 1.10
Armagnac 32
armament 420.35
armamentarium 242.2.14
armature 10.5
armband 128
armchair 4
armed 123

Armenia 17.3.33
Armenian 261.3.16
Armentières 512
armet 368
armful 226
armhole 223
armiger 17.150
armillary 16.274.16
Arminian 261.3.17
Arminius 310.2.8
armipotent 420.78
armistice 300
armless 300
armlet 371
armoire 1
armorial 228.3.12
armour 17.206
armoured 103
armourer 17.279
armoury 16.274.20
armpit 371
armrest 433
arms 540
Armstrong 266
armure 10
army 16.211
Arne 246
Arnhem 242
arnica 17.34
Arno 12.51
Arnold 122
aroma 17.215
aromatic 38.49.2
aromatize 516.13
arose 520.3
around 139.1
arousal 228.129
arouse 521
Arpád 84
arpeggio 12.3
arquebus 310.5
arrack 46
arraign 247.8
Arran 261
arrange 207
arrangement 420.38
arranger 17.156
arrant 420.60
arras 310.43
Arras 310.43
array 2.19
arrears 514
arrest 433.1

arrestable 228.16.59
arrester 17.382
arresting 265.75
arrhythmia 17.3
Ar Rimal 213
arris 300
arrival 228.121
arrive 486
arriviste 435
arrogance 321.8
arrogant 420.18
arrogate 367.11
arrow 12.60
arrowhead 86.3
arrowroot 380
arse 294
arsenal 228.63
arsenic 38
arsenical 228.23.11
arsenide 92.4
arsenious 310.2.7
arsine 251
ars nova 17.417
arson 261.61
arsphenamine 252.15
arsy-versy 16.298.1
art 366
Art Deco 12.9
artefact 382
artel 215
Artemis 300.19
arterial 228.3.11
arterialize 516.3.2.1
arteriole 223.1
arteriosclerosis 300.55.5
arteriovenous 310.32
arteritis 300.62.5
artery 16.274
artesian 261.3.34
artful 226
arthralgia 17.3.16
arthralgic 38
arthritic 38.52
arthritis 300.62
arthropod 94.1
Arthur 17.397
Arthurian 261.3.24
artichoke 42
article 228.23
articular 17.174.6

articulate 367.13.2, 371.17.2
articulation 261.67.13
articulator 17.338.6
artifice 300
artificer 17.302
artificial 228.93
artificiality 16.333.8.1
artillery 16.274.16
artilleryman 261.48
artisan 245.7
artist 436
artiste 435
artistic 38.70
artistry 16.293
artless 300
artlessness 300.33
arts 334
artwork 36
arty 16.328
Aruba 17.20
arum 242.18
Arundel 228
Aruwimi 16.215
as 293, 507
asafoetida 17.83
Asantehene 16.226
asarum 242.21
asbestos 302.3
asbestosis 300.55
ascariasis 300.57.1
ascarid 91.27
ascend 131
ascendancy 16.312.2
ascendant 420.14
ascender 17.101
ascension 261.82
Ascensiontide 92.12
ascent 410
ascertain 247.10
ascesis 300.51
ascetic 38.50
asceticism 242.35.16
asci 7
ascidian 261.3.5
ascidium 242.2.3
ascites 513
Asclepius 310.2
ascocarp 269

ascogonium
242.2.12
Ascot 381
ascribe 25
ascription 261.85
asdic 38
aseity 16.333.1
asepalous 310.26
asepsis 300.59
aseptic 38.65
asexual 228.9
Asgard 84
ash 349
ashamed 124
ashamedly 16.148
Ashanti 16.353
Ashcroft 399
ashen 261.66
Asher 17.321
ashet 368
Ashkenazi 16.392
ashkey 5
ashlaring 265.58
ashore 9
ashplant 408
ashram 242
Ashton 261
Ashtoreth 455
ashtray 2
Ashurbanipal 212
ashy 16.319
Asia 17.322
Asian 261.67
Asiatic 38.49
aside 92.8
asinine 253.6
asininity 16.333.17
Asir 6
ask 56
askance 314
askew 15
aslant 408
asleep 273
ASLEF 160
Asmara 17.268
Asmodeus 310.2.2
asocial 228.94
Asoka 17.38
asparagus 310
Aspasia 17.3.59
aspect 385
aspectual 228.9.5
aspen 261
asper 17.265
aspergillus 310.23

asperity 16.333.21
asperse 297.1
aspersion 261.69
aspersorium
242.2.17
asphalt 401
asphodel 215.1
asphyxia 17.3.58
asphyxiant 420.1
asphyxiate 367.1
asphyxiation
261.67.1
aspic 38
aspidistra 17.297
aspirant 420
aspirate 367.21,
371.33
aspiration 261.67
aspirator 17.338
aspire 8.2
aspirin 252
aspiring 265.54
asquint 412
Asquith 458
ass 293
assai 7
assail 214
assailant 420.25
Assam 229
Assamese 513.8
assassin 252
assassinate
367.17.7
assassination
261.67.18.8
assault 404.1
assay 2, 2.20
assegai 7.4
assemblage 197
assemble 228.18
assembly 16.138
assent 410
assentation
261.67.32
assentient 420.1
assentor 17.368
assert 369
assertion 261.69
assertive 485.11
assess 296
assessment 420
assessor 17.300
asset 368
assets 336
asseverate 367.23

assibilate 367.12
assiduity 16.333.3
assiduous 310.4
assign 253.8
assignat 365
assignation 261.67
assignee 5.13
assignment 420
assignor 9
assimilate 367.12
assimilation
261.67.12
Assiniboine 256
assist 436.22
assistance 321.27
assistant 420.81
assize 516.11
assizes 515
associate 367.1.7,
371.1
association
261.67.1
associationism
242.35.14.3
associative 485.15
assonance 321
assonant 420.55
assort 374
assorted 91
assortment 420
assuage 193
assume 241
assuming 265.39
assumption 261.89
Assur 17.298
assurance 321.19
assure 10
assured 96
assuredly 16.148
assurgent 420.19
Assyria 17.3.40
Astaire 4
Astarte 16.328
astatic 38.49
astatine 251.11
aster 17.379
asteriated 91.34.1
asterisk 58
asterism 242.35.15
astern 249
asternal 228.58
asteroid 97.12
asthenia 17.3.33
asthenic 38.32
asthenopia 17.3.37

asthma 17
asthmatic 38.49
Asti 16.361
astigmatic 38.49.3
astigmatism
242.35.20
astilbe 16.16
astir 3
Astolat 365
Aston 261
astonish 353.8
astonishing 265.63
astonishment
420.47
Astor 17.379
Astoria 17.3.41
astound 139
astounded 91.14
astounding 265.22
astragalus 310.26
astrakhan 245
astral 228
astraphobia 17.3.4
astray 2
astride 92
astringent 420.23
astrobotany
16.237.7
astrocompass
310.42
astrodome 239
astrogeology
16.108.4.1
astroid 97
astrolabe 20
astrologer 17.154
astrology 16.108.4
astrometry
16.285.2
astronaut 374
astronautic 38.54
astronautics 498
astronomer
17.218.1
astronomic 38.29.1
astronomical
228.23.9
astronomy
16.222.3
astrophotography
16.90.2.6
astrophysics 498
Asturias 293.1
astute 380
astuteness 300.40

Astyanax 494
astylar 17.167
asunder 17.108
Aswan 246
aswarm 238
asylum 242.9
asymmetric 38.46
asymmetry
16.285.1
asymptomatic
38.49.2
asymptote 376
asymptotic 38.53
asynchronism
242.35.14
asyndetic 38.50
Asyut 380
at 365
atactic 38.58
ataman 261.52
ataractic 38.58
ataraxia 17.3.56
ataraxic 38
Atatürk 36
atavism 242.35
ataxia 17.3.56
Atbara 17.279
Ate 16.329
ate 368
atelectasis 300.57
atelier 2
Athabaska 17.47
Athanasius 310.56
atheism 242.35.2
atheist 436
atheistic 38.70
atheling 265.30
athematic 38.49.1
Athena 17.230
athenaeum 242.1
Athenian 261.3.16
Athens 548
athermancy 16.312
athermanous
310.36
atheroma 17.215
atherosclerosis
300.55.5
athirst 434
athlete 370
athletic 38.50
athleticism
242.35.16
athletics 498.12
athodyd 92

athwart 374
atilt 403
Atkinson 261
Atlanta 17.365
Atlantean 261.3
atlantes 513
Atlantic 38.62
Atlantis 300.66
atlas 310
Atli 16.187
atman 261
atmometer
17.342.3
atmosphere 6.1
atmospheric 38.39
atmospherics 498.6
atoll 220
atom 242
atomic 38.29
atomicity 16.333.28
atomism 242.35
atomize 516.5
atomizer 17.441
atonal 228.62
atonality 16.333.8
atone 257.3
atonement 420
atonic 38.35
atony 16.237
atop 276.1
atrial 228.3
atrip 274
atrium 242.2
atrocious 310.60
atrocity 16.333.30
atrophic 38.13
atrophy 16.90
atropine 251
attaboy 11
attach 62
attaché 2.22
attachment 420.36
attack 32.4
attacker 17.28
attain 247.10
attainable
228.16.27
attainder 17.100
attainment 420.41
attar 17.336
attempt 428
attemptable 228.16
attempter 17.378
Attenborough
17.279

attend 131
attendance 321.7
attendant 420.14
attender 17.101
attention 261.82.3
attentive 485.21
attenuant 420.4
attenuate 367.2,
371.2
attenuation
261.67.2
attenuator 17.338
attest 433
attestation
261.67.33
Attic 38.49
attic 38.49
Attica 17.34.3
Atticism
242.35.16.4
Attila 17.166
attire 8
attitude 102.2.1
attitudinize 516.6
Attlee 16.186
attorney 16.227
attract 382
attractant 420
attraction 261.76
attractive 485.16
attributable
228.16.52
attribute 380.2
attribution 261.75
attributive 485
attrition 261.71.6
Attu 15
attune 260.6
atypical 228.23
aubergine 251
aubrietia 17.325
auburn 261
Auckland 143
auction 261
auctioneer 6.5
auctorial 228.3.12
audacious 310.56
audacity 16.333.25
Auden 261.27
audible 228.16.16
audience 321.1
audio 12.3
audiogenic 38.32.1
audiology
16.108.4.1

audiometer
17.342.3.1
audiophile 219.1
audiotypist 436
audiovisual 228.9
audiphone 257
audit 371
audition 261.71
auditor 17.342
auditorium
242.2.17
auditory 16.274.41
au fait 2
Augean 261.2
augend 131
auger 17.132
aught 374
augite 372
augment 410
augmentation
261.67.32
augmentative
485.15.15
augur 17.132
augury 16.273
august 443
August 445
Augusta 17.388
Augustan 261
Augustine 252.27
Augustinian
261.3.17
Augustus 310
auk 41
au lait 2
auld 118
auld lang syne 253
aulic 38.23
Aulis 300
aunt 408
au pair 4
aura 17.276
aural 228.74
aureate 371.1.2
Aurelian 261.3.10
Aurelius 310.2.4
aureole 223.1
aureus 310.2.13
auric 38.42
auricle 228.23
auricula 17.174.6
auriculate 371.17.2
auriferous 310.50.2
Auriga 17.130
aurist 436

aurochs 499
aurora 17.276
aurora australis 300.7
aurora borealis 300.7
aurous 310.48
aurum 242.20
Auschwitz 339
auscultate 367
auscultation 261.67
ausforming 265
auspex 496
auspice 300
auspicious 310.58
austenite 372.6
austere 6
austerity 16.333.21
Austerlitz 339
Austin 252
Australasia 17.3.59
Australia 17.3.18
Australian 261.3.8
Australiana 17.226.1
Australianism 242.35.14.1
Australianize 516.7
australopithecine 251.8
Australorp 277
Austria 17.3
Austrian 261.3
Austronesia 17.334
autacoid 97
autarchy 16.20
autarky 16.20
autecology 16.108.4.4
authentic 38.63
authenticate 367.5
authenticity 16.333.28
author 17
authoritarian 261.3.21.2
authoritative 485.15.12
authority 16.333.22
authorize 516.8
authorship 274.1
autism 242.35
autistic 38.70
auto 12.78
autobahn 246

autobiographical 228.23.3
autobiography 16.90.2
autocade 85
autochanger 17.156
autochthon 261
autochthonous 310.36
autoclave 482
autocracy 16.307.5
autocrat 365.2
autocratic 38.49.6
autocross 302.2
autocue 15
auto-da-fé 2.9
autodidact 382
autoecious 310.57
autogamy 16.222.2
autogenous 310.33
autogiro 12.64
autograft 396
autograph 158.1
autohypnosis 300.55
autohypnotic 38.53.2
autoimmune 260
autokinetic 38.50.4
Autolycus 310.10
autolysis 300.52.2
automat 365
automata 17.352
automate 367.16
automatic 38.49.2
automation 261.67.16
automatism 242.35.20
automatize 516.13
automaton 254
automobile 217
automotive 485.14
autonomic 38.29.1
autonomous 310.29
autonomy 16.222.3
autopilot 381
autopista 17.383
autoplasty 16.361.1
autopsy 16.315
autoput 379
autoradiograph 158.1.1
autosome 239
autostrada 17.78

autosuggestion 261.18
autotimer 17.212
autotomize 516.5
autotomy 16.222.4
autotoxin 252.29
autotrophic 38.13
autotype 275.1
autumn 242.30
autumnal 228
autunite 372.6
Auvergne 250
auxiliary 16.274.1.1
auxin 252
avadavat 365.3
avail 214
availability 16.333.9.2
available 228.16.22
avalanche 78
Avalon 254.7
avant-garde 84
Avar 1
avarice 300.47
avaricious 310.58.2
avast 431
avatar 1
ave 16.378
Avebury 16.274
avenge 208
avens 548
Aventine 253
aventurine 252.19
avenue 15.9
aver 3
average 197
Averroës 513.2
averse 297
aversion 261.69.1
aversive 485.3
avert 369.2
Avesta 17.382
Avestan 261.106
avian 261.3.29
aviary 16.274.1
aviate 367.1
aviation 261.67.1
aviator 17.338.1
aviatrix 498.9
Avicenna 17.228
avid 91
avidity 16.333.5
Aviemore 9
avifauna 17.234
avionic 38.35.1

avionics 498.5
avirulent 420.27
avitaminosis 300.55.4
avizandum 242.6
avocado 12.16
avocet 368
Avogadro 12
avoid 97
avoidable 228.16
avoidance 321
Avon 261.111
avow 13
avowal 228.8
avowed 99
avulsion 261
avuncular 17.174
avunculate 371.17
await 367.38
awake 34
awaken 261.11
award 95.4
aware 4.8
awareness 300.22
awash 354
away 2.28
awe 9
aweather 17.402
aweigh 2.28
awesome 242
awful 226.1
awfully 16.129
awfulness 300.30
awhile 219
awkward 103
awkwardness 300
awl 221
awn 255
awning 265
awoke 42
AWOL 220
awry 7.12
axe 494
axel 228
axenic 38.33
axes 513
axial 228.3.18
axil 218
axilla 17.166
axillary 16.274.16
axiology 16.108.4.1
axiom 242.2
axiomatic 38.49.2
axis 300.70
axle 228

axletree 5
Axminster 17.394
axolotl 228.104
axon 254
axseed 89
ay 2, 7
ayah 17.4
ayatollah 17.168
Aycliffe 163
aye 7
aye-aye 7
Aylesbury 16.274
Aymara 1.14
Ayr 4
Ayrshire 6
Ayurveda 17.79
azalea 17.3.18
azan 246
Azbine 251
azedarach 32.3
azeotrope 278.3
Azerbaijan 246
Azerbaijani 16.224
azide 92
azimuth 464
azole 223
Azores 518
azoth 459
azotic 38.53
azotobacter 17.353
Aztec 35
azure 17
azurite 372
azygous 310

B

Ba 1
baa 1
Baal 213
Baalbek 35
Baal Shem Tov 487
baba 1
Babbage 197
babbitt 371.4
babble 228
babe 20
Babel 228.11
Babi 16.6
babiche 352

babirusa 17.308
baboon 260
babul 227
baby 16.7
babyhood 101
babyish 353
Babylon 261.41
Babylonia 17.3.36
Babylonian 261.3.18
baby-snatcher 17.50
baccalaureate 371.1.2
baccarat 1.14
baccate 367
Bacchae 5
bacchanal 228.63.1
bacchanalia 17.3.18.1
bacchanalian 261.3.8
bacchant 420
Bacchic 38.6
bacchius 310.3
Bacchus 310.7
baccivorous 310.50.3
baccy 16.19
Bach 33
Bacharach 32.3
bachelor 17.176
bacillus 310.23
bacitracin 252
back 32
backache 34
backbencher 17.70
backbend 131
backbite 372
backbiting 265.67
backboard 95
backbone 257
backbreaker 17.30
backbreaking 265.6
backchat 365
backcloth 459
backcomb 239
backcross 302
backdate 367
backer 17.28
backfire 8
backgammon 261.44
background 139
backhand 128

backhanded 91.12
backhander 17.98
backing 265
backlash 349
backless 300
backlog 185
backmost 441
backscratcher 17.50
backside 92
backslide 92
backspace 295
backspin 252
backstage 193
backstairs 512
backstay 2
backstitch 67
backstreet 370
backstroke 42
backswept 422
backtrack 32
backup 279
backveld 402
backward 103
backwardation 261.67.8
backwardness 300
backwards 531
backwash 354
backwater 17.345
backwoodsman 261
Bacolod 103.3
bacon 261.11
baconer 17.239
bacteraemia 17.3.26
bacteria 17.3.39
bacterial 228.3.11
bactericide 92.7
bacterin 252.20
bacteriology 16.108.4.1
bacteriolysis 300.52.2
bacteriolytic 38.52.1
bacteriophage 193.1
bacterium 242.2.15
bacteroid 97.12
Bactria 17.3
Bactrian 261.3
baculiform 238.1
bad 83

Badajoz 517
badderlocks 499
baddie 16.57
bade 83
Baden 261
badge 191
badger 17.144
badinage 359
badly 16.146
badman 261
badminton 261.105
badness 300
Baedeker 17.34
bael 228.1
Baez 510
baffle 228
bag 178
bagasse 293
bagatelle 215
bagel 228.44
baggage 197
bagging 265
baggy 16.91
bagh 179
Baghdad 83
bagman 261
bagpipe 275
bagpipes 328
baguette 368
bagwig 184
Bahai 16.1
Bahaism 242.35
Bahamas 524
Bahrain 247
baht 366
bahuvrihi 5
Baikal 213
bail 214
bailable 228.16.22
bailee 5
bailey 16.114
Bailey 16.114
bailie 16.114
bailiff 163.1
bailiwick 38
bailment 420.39
bailor 17.162
bailsman 261
Bairam 229
Baird 88
bairn 250
bait 367
baize 509
bake 34
bakehouse 306

Bakelite 372.4
baker 17.30
bakery 16.274
Bakewell 215
baking 265.6
baklava 1.15
baksheesh 352
Bala 17.160
Balaam 229
Balaclava 17.409
balalaika 17.35
balance 321.10
balancer 17.318
Balanchine 251
balas 310
balata 17.352
balboa 17.6
Balboa 17.6
balbriggan 261.32
balconied 91.21
balcony 16.237
bald 118
baldachin 252.4
Balder 17.96
balderdash 349
baldheaded 91.7
balding 265
baldmoney 16.235
baldness 300
baldpate 367
baldric 38
Baldwin 252
bale 214
Balearic 38.38
baleen 251.3
baleful 226
baler 17.162
Balfour 9
Bali 16.113
balibuntal 228.112
balk 41
Balkan 261.16
Balkanize 516.7
balky 16.28
ball 221
ballad 103
ballade 84
balladeer 6
balladry 16.277
Ballarat 365
ballast 445
ball cock 40
ballerina 17.230.1
ballet 2
balletic 38.50

balletomania
 17.3.31.1
ballista 17.384
ballistic 38.70.2
ballistics 498
ballonet 368
balloon 260.1
balloonist 436.12
ballot 381
ballottement 420
ballpark 33
ballpoint 416
ballroom 241
bally 16.112
ballyhoo 15
balm 230
balmacaan 246
Balmoral 228.73
balmy 16.211
balneology
 16.108.4.1
baloney 16.233.1
balsa 17.310
balsam 242
balsamic 38.24
Balt 404
Balthazar 1.19
Baltic 38
Baltimore 9
Baluchi 16.53
Baluchistan 246.1
baluster 17.390
balustrade 85
Balzac 32
Bamberg 182
bambino 12.54
bamboo 15
bamboozle 228.128
ban 245
banal 213.1
banality 16.333.8.7
banana 17.226
Banat 371.22
banausic 38
Banbury 16.274
banc 51
band 128
bandage 197
bandanna 17.225
bandeau 12.23
banderilla 17.2.2
banderillero 12.62
banderole 223.3
bandicoot 380
bandit 371

bandmaster 17.380
bandoleer 6
bandoline 251.3
bandore 9
bandsman 261
bandstand 128
bandwagon 261.30
bandy 16.77
bandy-bandy 16.77
bane 247
baneful 226.4
bang 263
Bangalore 9.8
banger 17.245
Bangka 17.43
Bangkok 40
Bangladesh 351
bangle 228.49
Bangor 17.140
banish 353
banister 17.384
banjo 12
Banjul 227
bank 51
bankable 228.16
bankbook 44
banker 17.43
banket 371
banking 265
bankroll 223
bankrupt 426
bankruptcy 16
banksia 17.3
banner 17.225
bannerette 368.6
bannock 46
Bannockburn 249
banns 544
banquet 371
banquette 368
banshee 5
bant 407
bantam 242
bantamweight 367
banter 17.365
Bantu 15
Bantustan 246
banyan 261.121
banzai 7
bap 268
baptism 242.35
baptismal 228.54
Baptist 436
baptistry 16.293
baptize 516

bar 1
Barabbas 310
barathea 17.2
barb 19
Barbados 302
barbarian 261.3.21
barbaric 38.38
barbarism
 242.35.15
barbarity 16.333.20
barbarize 516.8
Barbarossa 17.304
barbarous 310.50
Barbary 16.274
barbecue 15
barbel 228
barbell 215
barbellate 367.12
barber 17.10
barbershop 276
barbette 368
Barbican 261.13
Barbirolli 16.122
barbitone 257.2
barbiturate 371.34
Barbuda 17.91
barcarole 223.3
Barcelona 17.236
barchan 246
bard 84
bardolatry 16.286.2
bare 4
bareback 32
barefaced 432
barefoot 379
barehanded 91.12
bareheaded 91.7
Bareilly 16.114
barely 16.117
bareness 300.22
bargain 252
barge 192
bargepole 223
Bari 16.261
baric 38, 38.38
barilla 17.166.3
baritone 257.2
barium 242.2.14
bark 33
barker 17.29
Barking 265
barley 16.113
barleycorn 255.2
barm 230
barmaid 85

barman 261
Barmecide 92.7
barmy 16.211
barn 246
Barnabas 310
barnacle 228.28
Barnard 84
Barnardo 12.16
barn-brack 32
Barnet 371
barney 16.224
barnstorm 238
Barnum 242
barnyard 84
Baroda 17.88
barogram 229.1
barograph 158.1
barometer
 17.342.3.4
barometric 38.46
baron 261
baronage 197
baroness 300.26
baronet 371.28
baronetage 197.12
baronetcy 16.317
barong 266
baronial 228.3.8
barony 16.237
baroque 40
baroscope 278.1
barostat 365
barouche 358
barque 33
barquentine 251
barrack 46
barracks 503
barracouta 17.351
barracuda 17.91
barrage 359
barramunda 17.108
barranca 17.43
barratry 16.286
barré 2.16
barrel 228.72
barren 261
barrenness 300.31
barrens 551
barret 371
barrette 368.6
barricade 85
Barrie 16.260
barrier 17.3
barring 265
barrister 17.384

barroom 241
barrow 12.60
Barry 16.260
Barrymore 9
Barsac 32
bartender 17.101
barter 17.337
Bartholomew 15
bartizan 261.126
Bartlett 371
Bartók 40
Barton 261.95
barycentre
 17.368.1
barye 16.260
baryon 254.1
barysphere 6
barytes 513
baryton 257.2
basal 228
basalt 404
basaltware 4
bascule 227
base 295
baseball 221
baseborn 255
baseless 300
baseline 253
baseman 261
basement 420.44
baseness 300
bases 513
bash 349
Bashan 245
bashaw 9
bashful 226
bashibazouk 45
Bashkir 6
basic 38
basically 16.142
basicity 16.333.28
basidium 242.2.3
Basie 16.296
basify 7.3
Basil 228.124
basil 228.124
basilar 17.166
Basildon 261
Basilian 261.3.11
basilic 38.21
basilica 17.34
basilisk 58
basin 261.62
basinet 371.24
Basingstoke 42

basion 261.3
basipetal 228.102
basis 300.50
bask 56
Baskerville 218.3
basket 371
basketball 221
basketry 16.285
basketwork 36
Basle 213
Basque 55
bas-relief 162.1
bass 293, 295
Bassein 247
Bassenthwaite 367
basset 371
Basse-Terre 4
bassinet 368
bassist 436
basso 12.68
bassoon 260
bassoonist 436.12
bast 430
bastard 103
bastardize 516
bastardry 16.277
bastardy 16.72
baste 432
Bastille 217
bastinado 12.17
bastion 261.3
bat 365
batch 62
bate 367
bateau 12.72
Bates 335
batfish 353
bath 453
Bath 453
bathe 473
bathetic 38.50.6
bathhouse 306
bathing 265
batholith 458
bathometer
 17.342.3
bathos 302
bathrobe 28
bathroom 241
Bathsheba 17.13
bathtub 29
Bathurst 445
bathyal 228.3
bathymetry
 16.285.1

bathyscaph 157
bathysphere 6
batik 38.49
batiste 435
Batley 16.186
batman 261
baton 254
batrachian 261.3
batsman 261
batt 365
battalion 261.118
batten 261.94
Battenburg 182
batter 17.336
battery 16.274
batting 265
battle 228.97
battledore 9
battlefield 115
battlement 420.40
battlepiece 298
battler 17.200
battleship 274
battue 15
batty 16.327
Batum 241
batwing 265
batwoman 261.50
bauble 228
Bauchi 16.51
baud 95
Bauhaus 306
bauhinia 17.3.34
baulk 41
bauxite 372
Bavaria 17.3.38
Bavarian 261.3.21
bawbee 5
bawd 95
bawdry 16.276
bawdy 16.66
bawdyhouse 306
bawl 221
Bax 494
bay 2
bayadere 6
bayonet 371.28
bayou 15
baywood 101
bazaar 1.19
bazoo 15.10
bazooka 17.41
be 5
beach 66

beachcomber 17.215
Beach-la-Mar 1.12
beacon 261.12
Beaconsfield 115
bead 89
beading 265.13
beadle 228
beady 16.62
beagle 228.45
beak 37
beaked 386
beaker 17.33
beam 234
bean 251
beanbag 178
beanery 16.274.25
beanfeast 435
beanie 16.228
beano 12.54
beanpole 223
beanstalk 41
bear 4
bearable 228.16.33
beard 90
bearded 91
beardless 300
bearer 17.271
bearing 265.52
bearish 353.9
Béarnaise 509
bearskin 252
beast 435
beastly 16.200
beat 370
beatable 228.16.48
beaten 261.98
beater 17.341
beatific 38.12
beatify 7.3.8
beating 265
beatitude 102.2.1
Beatles 539
beatnik 38
Beatty 16.332
beau 12
Beaufort 381
beaujolais 2.12
beau monde 136
Beaumont 414
Beaune 257
beaut 380
beauteous 310.2
beautician 261.71
beautiful 226

beautify 7.3
beauty 16.343
beaux-arts 1
beaver 17.413
Beaverbrook 44.1
Bebington 261
bebop 276
becalmed 123
became 231
because 517
beccafico 12.10
béchamel 215
bêche-de-mer 4.4
Bechuanaland 143.4
beck 35
becket 371
Beckett 371
beckon 261
becloud 99
become 240
becoming 265.38
bed 86
bedaub 27
bedazzle 228.124
bedbug 189
beddable 228.16.14
bedder 17.80
bedding 265.12
Bede 89
bedeck 35
bedevil 228.118
bedew 15.7
bedfellow 12.40
Bedford 103.2
Bedfordshire 6
bedim 235
Bedivere 6.11
bedlam 242
Bedouin 252
bedpan 245
bedpost 441
bedraggle 228.43
bedraggled 122
bedridden 261.24
bedrock 40
bedroll 223
bedroom 241
bedside 92
bedsitter 17.342
bedsore 9
bedspread 86
bedstead 86
bedstraw 9
bedtime 236

bedwarmer 17.214
bee 5
Beeb 23
beebread 86
beech 66
Beecham 242
beechnut 378
beef 162
beefburger 17.127
beefcake 34
beefeater 17.341
beefsteak 34
beefy 16.84
beehive 486
beekeeper 17.252
beeline 253
Beelzebub 29
been 251
beep 273
beer 6
Beerbohm 239
Beersheba 17.13
beery 16.265
beestings 552
beeswax 494
beeswing 265
beet 370
Beethoven 261.116
beetle 228.101
beetroot 380
beezer 17.440
befall 221
befell 215
befit 371.13
befog 185.1
befool 227
before 9.5
beforehand 128
befoul 224
befriend 131
befuddle 228.36
beg 181
began 245
begat 365.1
beget 368
beggar 17.126
beggarly 16.131.2
beggarweed 89
beggary 16.274
begin 252
beginner 17.231
beginning 265.43
begird 87
begone 254.4
begonia 17.3.36

begorra 17.275
begot 373
begotten 261.101
begrime 236
begrudge 203
beguile 219
beguine 251
begum 242
begun 259
behalf 158
Behan 261.2
behave 482
behaviour 17.436
behavioural 228.76
behaviourism 242.35.15
behaviourist 436.20
behaviouristic 38.70.5
behead 86.2
beheld 113
behemoth 459
behest 433
behind 135
behindhand 128
Behistun 260
behold 120.1
beholden 261.28
beholder 17.97
behove 488
beige 360
being 265.2
Beira 17.274
Beirut 380
bejewel 228.10
bel 215
belabour 17.11
belah 1
belated 91.34.5
belatedness 300.28
belay 2.11
belch 75
beleaguer 17.128
belemnite 372
Belfast 431
belfry 16
Belgae 5
Belgian 261
Belgium 242
Belgrade 85
Belgravia 17.3.53
Belial 228.3
belie 7.5
belief 162.1

believable
228.16.61
believe 484.1
believer 17.413
Belisarius 310.2
Belisha 17.325
belittle 228.102
bell 215
belladonna
17.233.1
bellarmine 251
Bellatrix 498
bellboy 11
belle 215
Belleek 37
Bellerophon 254.3
bellhop 276
bellicose 305
bellicosity
16.333.30.3
belligerence 321.20
belligerency 16.312
belligerent 420.65
Belloc 40
Bellona 17.236
bellow 12.40
bellows 520
bell-ringing 265.47
bellwether 17.402
belly 16.115
bellyband 128
bellybutton
261.103
bellyful 226
Belmopan 245.4
belong 266
belonging 265
belongings 552
beloved 91
below 12.42
Bel Paese 16.393
Belsen 261
Belshazzar 17.437
belt 402
Beltane 247
belting 265
beltway 2
beluga 17.136
belvedere 6
bema 17.210
Bemba 17.24
bemire 8
bemoan 257
bemuse 523
bemused 156

ben 248
Ben 248
Benares 515
bench 79
bencher 17.70
bend 131
Bendel 215
bender 17.101
Bendigo 12.29
bends 532
bendy 16.78
beneath 457
benedicite
16.333.29
Benedict 387
benediction
261.78.1
benefaction 261.76
benefactor 17.353
benefactress 300.48
benefic 38
benefice 300
beneficence 321.22
beneficent 420.70
beneficial 228.93
beneficiary
16.274.1.2
benefit 371.13
Benelux 502
Benevento 12.84
benevolence
321.12.1
benevolent
420.28.1
Bengal 221
Bengali 16.123
Benghazi 16.392
Ben-Gurion
261.3.24
benighted 91.39
benign 253.6
benignant 420
benignity 16.333.19
Benin 251
benison 261.126
Benjamin 252.15
benne 16.226
Ben Nevis 300.69
benny 16.226
Benoni 16.233
bent 410
Bentinck 52
Bentley 16.197
bentonite 372.6
bentwood 101

Benue 2.3
benumb 240
benzaldehyde 92
Benzedrine 252
benzene 251
benzoate 367
benzoin 252.1
benzol 220
benzyl 218
Beowulf 175
bequeath 475
bequeather 17.404
bequest 433
Berar 1
berate 367.21
Berber 17.12
Berbera 17.279
berberis 300.47
bereave 484
bereavement 420
bereft 397
beret 2
berg 182
bergamot 373
Bergman 261
beriberi 16.262
berk 36
Berkeley 16.140
berkelium 242.2.5
Berks. 495
Berkshire 6
Berlin 252
Berlioz 520
berm 233
Bermuda 17.91
Bern 249
Bernadette 368.5
Bernardine 252
Bernhardt 366
Bernstein 253
berry 16.262
bersagliere 16.264
berseem 234
berserk 36
berth 456
Berwick 38.39
Berwick-upon-
Tweed 89
beryl 218.2
Beryl 218.2
beryllium 242.2.6
Berzelius 310.2.4
Bes 296
beseech 66
beseeching 265

beset 368.7
beside 92.7
besides 527
besiege 196
besmear 6
besmirch 65
besom 242
besotted 91.40
bespangle 228.49
bespatter 17.336
bespeak 37
bespectacled 122
bespoke 42
bespread 86
besprent 410
besprinkle 228.29
Bess 296
Bessarabia 17.3.1
best 433
bestial 228.3.14
bestiality
16.333.8.1
bestialize 516.3.2
bestiary 16.274.1
bestir 3
bestow 12
bestowal 228.7
bestrew 15
bestride 92
bet 368
beta 17.341
betake 34
betel 228.101
Betelgeuse 511
Beth 455
Bethany 16.237
Bethel 228
Bethlehem 232
Bethsaida 17.79
betide 92
bêtise 513
Betjeman 261.52
betoken 261.14
betony 16.237
betook 44
betray 2
betrayal 228.1
betroth 478
betrothal 228
betrothed 145
betta 17.339
better 17.339
betterment 420.35
between 251
betweentimes 542

betwixt 451
Beulah 17.175
Bevan 261.112
bevel 228.118
beverage 197
Beverly 16.131
Bevin 252.28
bevvy 16.380
bevy 16.380
bewail 214
beware 4.7
Bewick 38
bewilder 17.95
bewilderment
　420.35
bewitch 67
bey 2
beyond 136
bezant 420.84
bezel 228
bezique 37
bezoar 9
Bhagalpur 10
Bhagavad-Gita
　17.341
bhang 263
bhavan 261.117
bhindi 16.79
Bhopal 213
Bhutan 246
biannual 228.9.2
Biarritz 339
bias 310.3
biathlon 261
biaxial 228.3.18
bib 24
bibber 17.14
bibcock 40
bibelot 12
Bible 228
biblical 228.23
Biblicist 436.21
bibliography
　16.90.2.1
bibliolatry
　16.286.2.1
bibliomancy
　16.309
bibliomania
　17.3.31.1
bibliophile 219.1
bibliopole 223
bibliopolist 436.7
bibliotheca 17.33
bibulous 310.25

bicameral 228.76
bicapsular 17.174
bicarb 19
bicarbonate 371.28
bice 301
bicentenary
　16.274.25
bicephalous
　310.26.3
biceps 324
bicipital 228.102
bicker 17.34
biconcave 482
biconvex 496
bicorn 255
bicornate 371.26
bicuspid 91
bicycle 228.23
bicyclic 38
bid 91
bidarka 17.29
bidarkee 5.3
biddable 228.16.15
bidden 261.24
bidder 17.83
bidding 265
biddy 16.63
bide 92
bidentate 367.32
bidet 2
Biedermeier 17.4
Biel 217
bield 115
biennial 228.3
bier 6
bierkeller 17.163
bifarious 310.2.10
biff 163
biffin 252
bifid 91
bifocal 228.26
bifocals 539
bifoliate 367.1.3
biforate 367.23
biform 238
Bifrost 438
bifurcate 367.6,
　371.8
bifurcation
　261.67.6
big 184
bigamist 436.10.1
bigamous 310.29.1
bigamy 16.222.1
bigener 17.231

bigeye 7
biggin 252
biggish 353
bighead 86
bigheaded 91.7
bigheadedness
　300.28
bight 372
bigmouth 462
bignonia 17.3.36
bigot 381
bigoted 91
bigotry 16.286
bigwig 184
Bihar 1.6
Bihari 16.261
bijou 15
bijouterie 16.274
Bikaner 6.5
bike 39
bikini 16.228
bilander 17.109
bilateral 228.76
Bilbao 12
bilberry 16.274
bilboes 520
bile 219
bilestone 257
bilharzia 17.3
bilharziasis
　300.57.1
biliary 16.274.1.1
bilinear 17.3.34
bilingual 228
bilious 310.2.5
biliousness 300.34
bilirubin 252
biliverdin 252
bilk 49
bill 218
billabong 266
billboard 95
billet 371.16
billet-doux 15.2
billfold 120
billhook 44
billiard 103
billiards 531
billing 265.30
Billingsgate 367
billion 261.120
billionaire 4.5
billionth 471
billon 261.41
billow 12.42

billowy 16.3
billposter 17.387
billy 16.120
billycan 245
billyo 12.3.2
bilobate 367.3
Bim 235
bimbo 12.6
bimestrial 228.3.13
bimetallic 38.19.1
bimetallism
　242.35.11
bimonthly 16.205
bimorph 166
bin 252
binal 228.61
binary 16.274.27
binate 367
binaural 228.74
bind 135
binder 17.103
bindi-eye 7.1
binding 265.21
bindweed 89
bine 253
binge 209
bingey 16.110
bingle 228.50
bingo 12.36
binnacle 228.28
binocular 17.174.7
binoculars 524
binomial 228.3
binominal 228.60.5
bint 412
binturong 266
bio-assay 2.20
biocatalyst 436.7.6
biocenology
　16.108.4.10
biochemical 228.23
biochemist 436
biochemistry
　16.293
biocide 92.8
biodegradable
　228.16
biodegradation
　261.67.8
biofeedback 32
bioflavonoid 97.9
biogen 261.39
biogenesis 300.52.4
biogeography
　16.90.2.1

313

biographer
17.120.1
biographical
228.23.3
biography 16.90.2
biological 228.23.5
biologist 436.4
biology 16.108.4.2
biolysis 300.52.2
biomass 293
biometry 16.285.2
bionic 38.35
bionics 498.5
bionomics 498
biophysics 498
biopoiesis 300.51
biopsy 16.315
bioptic 38.67
bioscope 278.1.1
biosphere 6.1
biostatics 498.11
biostrome 239
biosynthesis 300.52
biota 17.347
biotic 38.53.1
biotin 252
biotite 372.12
biotype 275.1
bipartisan 245.7
bipartite 372
biped 86
biplane 247
bipod 94
bipolar 17.171
biquadratic 38.49
birch 65
bird 87
birdbath 453
birdcage 193
birdhouse 306
birdie 16.61
birdlime 236
birdman 261
birdseed 89
bird-watching 265
bireme 234
biretta 17.339
biriani 16.224
Birkenhead 86
Biro 12.64
birr 3
birth 456
birthday 2
birthmark 33
birthplace 295

birthright 372
birthroot 380
birthstone 257
Biscay 2
biscuit 371
bise 513
bisect 385
bisection 261.77
bisector 17.354
bisexual 228.9
bish 353
bishop 281
bishopric 38
Biskra 1
Bismarck 33
bismuth 464
bison 261
bisque 58
bissextile 219.8
bistort 374
bistoury 16.274.49
bistre 17.384
bistro 12
bisulcate 367.7
bisulphate 367
bisymmetric 38.46
bit 371
bitch 67
bitchy 16.49
bite 372
Bithynia 17.3.34
biting 265.67
bitser 17.320
bitstock 40
bitt 371
bitten 261.99
bitter 17.342
bitterling 265
bittern 261.99
bitterness 300.26
bitternut 378
bitters 524
bittersweet 370
bitterwood 101
bitty 16.333
bitumen 252
bituminize 516.6
bituminous
310.33.1
bivalent 420.25
bivalve 491
bivouac 32
bivvy 16.382
biweekly 16.141
biyearly 16.119

bizarre 1
Bizerte 17.340
Bizet 2.30
blab 18
blabber 17.9
blabbermouth 462
black 32
blackball 221
Blackbeard 90
blackberry 16.274
blackbird 87
blackboard 95
blackbuck 43
Blackburn 249
blackbutt 378
blackcap 268
blackcock 40
blackcurrant
420.64
blackdamp 285
blacken 261
blackfly 7
Blackfoot 379
blackguard 84
blackhead 86
blackheart 366
blacking 265
blackish 353
blackjack 32
blackleg 181
blacklist 436
blackmail 214
blackmailer 17.162
Black Maria 17.4.2
blackness 300
blackout 377
blackpoll 223
Blackpool 227
Blackshirt 369
blacksmith 458
blacksnake 34
blackthorn 255
blacktop 276
Blackwall 221
Blackwood 101
blackwood 101
bladder 17.77
bladder ketmia
17.3
bladdernose 520
bladdernut 378
bladderwort 369
bladderwrack 32.3
blade 85
blah 1

blain 247
Blake 34
blame 231
blameful 226
blameless 300
blameworthy
16.375
blanch 78
bland 128
blandish 353.2
blank 51
blanket 371
blankly 16.144
blare 4
blarney 16.224
blasé 2
blaspheme 234
blasphemer 17.210
blasphemous
310.28
blasphemy 16.216
blast 431
blasted 91.51
blastema 17.210
blasting 265.74
blastocoel 217.2
blastocyst 436.22
blastoderm 233
blastoff 165
blastomere 6.3
blastopore 9
blastula 17.174
blat 365
blatancy 16.312.6
blatant 420.75
blather 17.400
blatherskite 372
blaubok 40
Blaydon 261.20
blaze 509
blazer 17.439
blazes 515
blazon 261.124
blazonry 16.284
bleach 66
bleak 37
bleakness 300
bleary 16.265
bleat 370
bleb 21
bleed 89
bleeder 17.82
bleeding 265.13
bleep 273
blemish 353

blench 79
blend 131
blender 17.101
Blenheim 235
blennioid 97
blenny 16.226
blepharitis
300.62.5
bless 296
blessed 91
blessing 265.60
blest 433
blet 368
blew 15
blewits 339
Blida 17.82
Bligh 7
blight 372
blighter 17.343
Blighty 16.334
blimey 16.217
blimp 287
blind 135
blindage 197
blindfold 120
blinding 265.21
blindly 16.155
blindness 300.29
blindstorey 16.269
blindworm 233
blini 16.229
blink 52
blinker 17.44
blinkers 524
blinking 265.10
blintz 348
blip 274
bliss 300
blissful 226
blister 17.384
blithe 477
blithering 265.58
blithesome 242
blitz 339
blitzkrieg 183
blizzard 103
bloat 376
bloated 91.41
bloater 17.347
blob 26
bloc 40
block 40
blockade 85
blockage 197
blockboard 95

blockbuster 17.388
blockbusting 265
blocker 17.36
blockhead 86
Bloemfontein
247.11
bloke 42
blond 136
blonde 136
blood 100
bloodcurdling 265
blooded 91.11
bloodhound 139
bloodless 300
blood-letting
265.65
bloodshed 86
bloodshot 373
bloodstain 247
bloodstained 130
bloodstock 40
bloodsucker 17.39
bloodthirsty 16.365
bloody 16.69
bloody-minded 91
bloom 241
bloomer 17.217
bloomers 524
bloomery
16.274.22
blooming 265.39
Bloomsbury 16.274
blooper 17.259
blossom 242.25
blot 373
blotch 68
blotchy 16.50
blotter 17.344
blotto 12.77
blouse 521
blouson 254
blow 12
blower 17.6
blowfish 353
blowfly 7
blowhard 84
blowhole 223
blowlamp 285
blown 257
blowpipe 275
blowtorch 69
blowy 16.3
blowzy 16.400
blub 29
blubber 17.19

blubbery 16.274
bludge 203
bludgeon 261.38
blue 15
Bluebeard 90
bluebell 215
blueberry 16.274
bluebill 218
bluebird 87
blue-blooded 91.11
bluebonnet 371.25
bluebook 44
bluebottle 228.104
bluefish 353
bluegrass 294
blueing 265.5
bluejacket 371.6
blueness 300
bluenose 520
blueprint 412
blues 523
bluestocking 265.8
bluet 371.3
bluethroat 376
bluetit 371
bluetongue 267
bluey 16.4
bluff 168
bluffer 17.118
bluish 353
blunder 17.108
blunderbuss 307
blunge 211
blunger 17.159
blunt 419
bluntness 300
blur 3
blurb 22
blurry 16.263
blurt 369
blush 356
blusher 17.329
bluster 17.388
blustery 16.274
Blyth 477
B'nai B'rith 457
boa 17.6
Boadicea 17.2
boar 9
board 95
boarder 17.86
boarding 265.15
boardroom 241
boardwalk 41
boarhound 139

boarish 353
boast 441
boastful 226
boastfulness 300.30
boat 376
boatel 215.4
boater 17.347
boathook 44
boathouse 306
boating 265
boatload 98
boatman 261
boatswain 261
Boaz 507
bob 26
bobbery 16.274.3
bobbin 252
bobbinet 368
bobble 228
bobby 16.11
bobbysoxer 17.428
bobfloat 376
boblet 371
bobolink 52
bobotie 16.342
bobowler 17.172
bobsleigh 2
bobtail 214
bobwhite 372
bocage 359
boccia 17.57
bock 40
bod 94
bode 98
bodega 17.128
bodge 199
bodger 17.152
bodgie 16.104
bodice 300.4
bodiless 300.8
bodily 16.120
bodkin 252
Bodleian 261.3
Bodmin 252
Bodoni 16.233
body 16.65
bodycheck 35
bodyguard 84.1
body-snatcher
17.50
bodywork 36
Boehmite 372
Boeotia 17.328
Boer 10
Boethius 310.2

boeuf Bourguignon
  254.12
boffin 252
bog 185
bogan 261
Bogarde 84
Bogart 366
bogey 16.96
bogeyman 261.48
boggart 381
boggle 228.47
boggy 16.94
bogie 16.96
bogle 228
Bognor Regis
  300.6
bogong 266
Bogor 9
Bogotá 1
bogus 310
bogwood 101
Bohemia 17.3.26
Bohemian 261.3
Bohol 221
boil 222
boiler 17.170
boilermaker 17.30
boilerplate 367
Boise 16.398
boisterous 310.50
boisterousness
  300.34
bokmakierie
  16.265
bola 17.171
bold 120
boldness 300
bole 223
bolection 261.77
bolero 12.62
boletus 310.63
Boleyn 252
bolide 92
Bolingbroke 44
bolivar 1
Bolivia 17.3.54
Bolivian 261.3.30
boll 223
bollard 103.3
bollocks 503
bolo 12.44
Bolognese 509
bolometer 17.342.3
Bolshevik 38.74
Bolshevist 436

bolson 257
bolster 17.392
bolt 405
bolter 17.364
Bolton 261
boltonia 17.3.36
bolus 310
bomb 237
bombard 84
bombardier 6
bombardment 420
bombast 430
bombastic 38.68
Bombay 2
bombazine 251
bombé 2
bomber 17.213
bombora 17.276
bombshell 215
bombsight 372
bombycid 91.29
bona fide 16.64
Bonaire 4
bonanza 17.445
Bonaparte 366.1
Bonapartism
  242.35.17
bona vacantia
  17.3.50
Bonaventura
  17.277
bonbon 254
bonce 318
bond 136
bondage 197
bonded 91
bondmaid 85
bondservant
  420.82
bone 257
boneblack 32
bonehead 86
boneless 300
boner 17.236
boneset 368
bonesetter 17.339
boneshaker 17.30
boneyard 84
bonfire 8
bong 266
bongo 12
bonhomie 16.222.3
Boniface 295.3
bonism 242.35
bonito 12.76

bonkers 524
Bonn 254
bonnet 371.25
bonny 16.231
bonsai 7
bonsela 17.163
bonspiel 217
bonus 310.35
bony 16.233
bonze 549
boo 15
boob 30
boobialla 17.160
boobook 44
booby 16.14
boodle 228.37
boogie 16.98
boogie-woogie
  16.98
boohoo 15
book 44
bookbinder 17.103
bookbindery
  16.274.8
bookbinding
  265.21
bookcase 295
bookie 16.31
booking 265
bookish 353
book-keeper
  17.252
book-keeping
  265.49
booklet 371
booklouse 306
bookmaker 17.30
bookmark 33
bookshop 276
bookstall 221
bookworm 233
Boole 227
boom 241
boomer 17.217
boomerang 263.2
boomslang 263
boon 260
boondocks 499
boondoggle 228.47
boor 10
boorish 353
boost 444
booster 17.389
boot 380
bootblack 32

booted 91.42
bootee 5
Boötes 513
booth 479
bootlace 295
Bootle 228.108
bootleg 181
bootlegger 17.126
bootless 300
bootlick 38
bootlicker 17.34
boots 346
bootstrap 268
booty 16.343
booze 523
boozer 17.444
boozy 16.402
bop 276
bora 17.276
Bora Bora 17.276
boracic 38.48
borage 197
borak 46
borane 247
borate 367
borax 494
borazon 254
borborygmus 310
Bordeaux 12
Bordelaise 509
bordello 12.40
border 17.86
bordereau 12
borderer 17.279
borderland 143.4
borderline 253.3
bordure 10
bore 9
boreal 228.3.12
Boreas 310.2.13
boredom 242
boree 5
borer 17.276
Borg 186
Borgia 17.153
boric 38.42
boride 92.5
boring 265.55
Boris 300
born 255
borne 255
Borneo 12.3
borneol 220.1
Borodin 252
Borodino 12.54

boron 254.10
boronia 17.3.36
borosilicate 371.9
borough 17.278
borrow 12.65
borrower 17.6
borstal 228.116
bort 374
borzoi 11
boscage 197
Bosch 354
boschvark 33
Bose 305
bosh 354
bosk 59
bosket 371
Boskop 276
Bosnia 17.3
bosom 242
bosomy 16.222
boson 254
Bosporus 310.50
boss 302
bossa nova 17.417
bossiness 300.23
bossy 16.302
Boston 261
bosun 261
Boswell 228
Bosworth 464
bot 373
botanical 228.23.10
botanist 436.13
botanize 516.7
botany 16.237.7
botargo 12.26
botch 68
botcher 17.57
botchy 16.50
botfly 7
both 461
bother 17.407
botheration 261.67.22
bothersome 242
bothy 16.371
bots 341
Botswana 17.226
bottle 228.104
bottlebrush 356
bottleneck 35
bottlenose 520
bottom 242
bottomless 300
bottommost 441

botulin 252.10
botulinus 310.34
botulism 242.35.10
bouchée 2
bouclé 2
bouclée 2
Boudicca 17.34
boudoir 1
bouffant 266
Bougainville 218
bougainvillea 17.3.21
bough 13
bought 374
boughten 261.102
bougie 5
bouillabaisse 296
bouillon 254
boulder 17.97
boule 227
boulevard 1
boulevardier 2.1
Boulez 510
boulle 227
Boulogne 256
Boult 405
bounce 319
bouncer 17.317
bouncing 265
bound 139
boundary 16.274
bounden 261
bounder 17.107
boundless 300
bounds 533
bounteous 310.2
bountiful 226
bounty 16.359
bouquet 2
bouquet garni 5.10
Bourbon 261
bourbon 261.9
bourdon 261
bourg 187
bourgeois 1
bourgeoisie 5
bourn 255
Bournemouth 464
bourrée 2.18
bouse 521
boustrophedon 261.23
bout 377
boutique 37
boutonniere 4.1

bouzouki 16.32
bovid 91
bovine 253
Bovril 218
bovver 17.416
bow 12, 13
bowdlerism 242.35.15
bowdlerize 516.8
bowel 228.8
bower 14
bowerbird 87
bowfin 252
bowhead 86.3
bowing 265.4
bowknot 373
bowl 223
bow-legged 91
bowler 17.171
bowlful 226
bowline 252.9
bowling 265.32
bowman 261, 261.49
bowsaw 9
bowser 17.443
bowshot 373
bowsprit 371
bowstring 265
bow-wow 13
bowyer 17.431
box 499
boxcar 1
boxer 17.428
boxing 265
boxroom 241
boxwood 101
boy 11
Boyce 304
boycott 373
Boyd 97
boyfriend 131
boyhood 101
boyish 353
boyla 17.170
Boyle 222
Boyne 256
boysenberry 16.274
Boz 517
bra 1
Brabant 407
brace 295
bracelet 371
bracer 17.299
braces 515

brachial 228.3
brachiate 367.1, 371.1
brachiopod 94.1
brachiosaurus 310.48.1
brachium 242.2
brachylogy 16.108.3
brachyuran 261.59
bracing 265.59
bracken 261
bracket 371.6
bracketing 265.66
brackish 353
Bracknell 228
bract 382
brad 83
bradawl 221
Bradford 103
Bradley 16.146
Bradman 261
Bradshaw 9
bradycardia 17.3.6
brae 2
brag 178
braggadocio 12.3
braggart 381
bragger 17.123
Brahma 17.206
Brahman 261
Brahmana 17.239
Brahmanic 38.31
Brahmanism 242.35.14
Brahmaputra 17.294
Brahmin 252
Brahminic 38.34
Brahms 540
Brahui 16.4
braid 85
braided 91.6
braiding 265.11
brail 214
Braille 214
brain 247
brainchild 117
brainless 300
brainpan 245
brainsick 38
brainstorm 238
brainstorming 265
brainwash 354
brainwashing 265

brainy 16.225
braise 509
brake 34
bramble 228.17
brambling 265
bran 245
branch 78
branchia 17.3
branchiopod 94.1
Brancusi 16.402
brand 128
Brandenburg 182
brandish 353.2
brandling 265
Brando 12.23
brandy 16.77
branle 228.55
brash 349
brashy 16.319
Brasília 17.3.21
brass 294
brassard 84
brassbound 139
brasserie 16.274
brassica 17.34
brassie 16.294
brassiere 17.3.46
brassy 16.295
brat 365
Bratislava 17.409
brattice 300
brattishing 265.63
bratwurst 434
bravado 12.16
brave 482
braveness 300
bravery 16.274.50
bravissimo 12.48
bravo 12
bravura 17.277
braw 9
brawl 221
brawler 17.169
brawn 255
brawny 16.232
braxy 16.386
bray 2
braze 509
brazen 261.124
brazier 17.3.59
Brazil 218
Brazilian 261.3.11
breach 66
bread 86
breadboard 95

breadfruit 380
breadline 253
breadroot 380
breadwinner
17.231
break 34
breakable 228.16.9
breakage 197
breakaway 2.28
breakdown 258
breaker 17.30
breakfast 445
breakfront 419
breakneck 35
breakpoint 416
breakwater 17.345
bream 234
breast 433
breastbone 257
breastpin 252
breastplate 367
breaststroke 42
breastwork 36
breath 455
breathalyse 516.3
Breathalyzer
17.441
breathe 475
breather 17.404
breathing 265
breathless 300
breathlessness
300.33
breathtaking 265.6
breathy 16.369
breccia 17.3
Brecknockshire 6
Brecon 261
Breconshire 6.8
bred 86
Breda 17.82
bree 5
breech 66
breechblock 40
breechclout 377
breeches 515
breeching 265
breed 89
breeder 17.82
breeding 265.13
breeze 513
breezy 16.395
bregma 17.221
Bremen 261.45
Bren 248

Brent 410
brent 410
Brentwood 101
br'er 3
Brest 433
brethren 252
Breton 261.96
breve 484
brevet 371
breviary 16.274.1
brevity 16.333.34`
brew 15
brewage 197
brewer 17.8
brewery 16.274
brewing 265.5
brewis 300
Brezhnev 160
Brian 261.4
Brian Boru 15.6
briar 17.4
Briareus 310.2.10
briarroot 380
bribable 228.16.8
bribe 25
briber 17.15
bribery 16.274
bric-a-brac 32
brick 38
brickbat 365
bricklayer 17.1
bricklaying 265.1
brickle 228.23
brickwork 36
brickyard 84
bricole 223
bridal 228.33
bride 92
bridegroom 241
bridesmaid 85
bridewell 215
bridge 197
Bridget 371
bridgework 36
bridging 265.25
Bridgwater 17.345
bridie 16.64
bridle 228.33
bridler 17.187
bridoon 260
Brie 5
brief 162
briefcase 295
briefing 265
briefly 16.158

brig 184
brigade 85.1
brigadier 6
brigalow 12.45
brigand 143
brigandine 251
brigantine 251
bright 372
brighten 261.100
brightness 300.39
Brighton 261.100
brights 340
brightwork 36
Brigid 91.15
brill 218
brilliance 321
brilliant 420
brilliantine 251
brim 235
brimful 226
brimstone 257
brindle 228.40
brindled 122
brine 253
bring 265
brink 52
brinkmanship
274.2
brinny 16.229
briny 16.230
brioche 354
briolette 368
briquette 368.4
brisance 321.28
Brisbane 261
brise-soleil 2.12
brisk 58
brisket 371
brisling 265
bristle 228.85
bristly 16.181
Bristol 228.114
bristols 539
Brit 371
brit 371
Britain 261.99
Britannia 17.3.29
Britannic 38.31
Briticism 242.35.16
British 353
Britisher 17.326
Britishism 242.35
Briton 261.99
Brittany 16.237
Britten 261.99

brittle 228.102
brittleness 300.30
broach 70
broad 95
broadbrim 235
broadcast 431
broadcaster 17.380
broadcloth 459
broaden 261.27
broadleaf 162
broadloom 241
broadly 16.150
broad-minded 91
broad-mindedness 300.28
Broadmoor 9
Broads 528
broadsheet 370
broadside 92
broadsword 95
broadtail 214
Broadway 2
brocade 85
brocatelle 215
broccoli 16.131
broch 40
broché 2
brochette 368
brochure 10
brock 40
brocket 371.10
broddle 228.34
broderie anglaise 509
Broederbond 415
brogan 261
brogue 188
broil 222
broiler 17.170
broke 42
broken 261.14
brokenhearted 91.33
broker 17.38
brokerage 197
brolga 17.138
brolly 16.122
bromate 367
brome 239
bromeliad 83.1
bromic 38
bromide 92
bromidic 38
bromine 251
bromism 242.35

bromoform 238.2
Bromsgrove 488
bronchi 7
bronchia 17.3
bronchial 228.3
bronchiectasis 300.57
bronchiole 223.1
bronchitic 38.52
bronchitis 300.62
bronchopneumonia 17.3.36
bronchoscope 278.1
bronchus 310
bronco 12
broncobuster 17.388
Brontë 16.357
brontosaurus 310.48.1
bronze 549
brooch 70
brood 102
brooder 17.91
broody 16.71
brook 44
brooklet 371
brooklime 236
Brooklyn 252
broom 241
broomrape 270
broomstick 38
brose 520
broth 459
brothel 228
brother 17.408
brotherhood 101
brother-in-law 9
brotherly 16.131
brougham 242
brought 374
brouhaha 1.5
brow 13
browband 128
browbeat 370
brown 258
brownie 16.234
browning 265
brownish 353
brownout 377
browse 521
browser 17.443
Brubeck 35
Bruce 309

brucellosis 300.55
Bruges 364
bruin 252
bruise 523
bruised 156
bruiser 17.444
bruising 265.84
bruit 380
Brummagem 242
Brummell 228
Brummie 16.220
brunch 82
Brunei 7
Brunel 215
brunette 368
Brunhild 116
Brunswick 38
brunt 419
brush 356
brushoff 165
brushwood 101
brushwork 36
brusque 60
brusqueness 300
Brussels 539
brut 380
brutal 228.108
brutality 16.333.8
brutalize 516.3
brute 380
brutify 7.3
brutish 353
Brutus 310.67
bryology 16.108.4.2
bryony 16.237.1
bryophyte 372
bryozoan 261.6
Brythonic 38.35
bubal 228
bubble 228.14
bubbly 16.136
bubo 12
bubonic 38.35
bubonocele 217.2
buccal 228.27
buccaneer 6.5
buccinator 17.338.7
bucentaur 9.12
Bucephalus 310.26.3
Buchanan 261.55
Bucharest 433.1
buck 43
buckaroo 15.6

buckbean 251
buckboard 95
bucket 371.11
buckeye 7
Buckingham 242.17
Buckinghamshire 6
buckjumper 17.264
buckle 228.27
buckling 265.34
bucko 12
buckram 242
bucksaw 9
buckshee 5
buckshot 373
buckskin 252
buckskins 548
buckthorn 255
bucktooth 463
buckwheat 370
bucolic 38.22
bud 100
Budapest 433
Buddha 17
Buddhism 242.35
Buddhist 436.2
budding 265
buddle 228.36
buddleia 17.3
buddy 16.69
budge 203
budgerigar 1.4
budget 371
budgie 16.107
buds 530
Buenos Aires 515
buff 168
buffalo 12.45
buffer 17.118
buffet 2, 371
bufflehead 86
buffoon 260
buffoonery 16.274.28
bug 189
bugaboo 15.1
Buganda 17.98
bugbane 247
bugger 17.134
buggery 16.274.10
buggy 16.97
bugle 228.48
bugleweed 89.7
bugloss 302
build 116

builder

builder 17.95
building 265.17
built 403
Bukhara 17.268
Bukovina 17.230
Bulawayo 12.1
bulbaceous 310.56
bulbil 218
bulbous 310
bulbul 226
Bulgaria 17.3.38
Bulgarian 261.3.21
bulge 205
bulimia 17.3.27
bulk 50
bulkhead 86
bulky 16.35
bull 226
bulla 17.174
bullace 300.11
bullate 367
bullbat 365
bulldog 185
bulldoze 520
bulldozer 17.442
bullet 371.17
bulletin 252.23
bulletproof 170
bullfight 372
bullfighter 17.343
bullfighting 265.67
bullfinch 80
bullfrog 185
bullhead 86
bullion 261
bullish 353
bullock 46
bullpen 248
bullring 265
bullshit 371
bullwhip 274
bully 16.129
bullyrag 178
bulrush 356
bulwark 46
bum 240
bumbailiff 163.1
bumble 228
bumblebee 5
bumbler 17.180
bummalo 12.45
bummer 17.216
bump 289
bumper 17.264
bumph 177

bumpkin 252
bumptious 310
bumpy 16.257
bun 259
bunch 82
bunchy 16.56
bund 140
Bund 141
Bundaberg 182
Bundelkhand 140
Bundesrat 366
Bundestag 179
bundh 140
bundle 228
bung 267
bungalow 12.45
bungle 228
bunion 261
bunk 54
bunker 17.46
bunkum 242
bunny 16.235
bunraku 15
Bunsen 261
bunt 419
buntal 228.112
bunting 265
Bunyan 261
bunyip 274
buoy 11
buoyage 197
buoyancy 16.312
buoyant 420.3
buprestid 91.52
bur 3
buran 246
Burbage 197
Burberry 16.274
burble 228
burbot 381
burden 261.22
burdensome 242
burdock 40
bureau 12.66
bureaucracy
    16.307.5
bureaucrat 365.2
bureaucratic
    38.49.6
bureaucratize
    516.13
burette 368
burg 182
burgee 5
burgeon 261.35

burger 17.127
burgess 300
Burgess 300
burgher 17.127
Burghley 16.116
burglar 17
burglarize 516.8
burglary 16.274
burgle 228
burgonet 368
burgrave 482
Burgundy 16.81
burial 228.3
burin 252
burka 17.32
burke 36
burl 216
burlap 268
burlesque 57
burley 16.116
burliness 300.23
Burlington 261
burly 16.116
Burma 17.209
Burmese 513
burn 249
burner 17.229
burnet 371.23
Burnham 242.13
burning 265.41
burnish 353
burnoose 309
burnsides 527
burnt 411
buroo 15.6
burp 272
burr 3
burrawang 263
Burroughs 520
burrow 12
burry 16.263
bursa 17.301
bursar 17.301
bursarial
    228.3.10
bursary 16.274.35
burse 297
bursitis 300.62
burst 434
burton 261.97
Burton 261.97
bury 16.262
Bury 16.262
bus 307
busbar 1

busby 16
busera 17.269
bush 357
bushbaby 16.7
bushbuck 43
bushel 228
Bushido 12.19
bushing 265
Bushire 8
bushman 261
bushpig 184
bushranger 17.156
bushwhack 32
bushwhacker 17.28
bushy 16.325
business 300
businesslike 39.1
businessman 261
busk 60
busker 17.49
buskin 252
bust 443
bustard 103
buster 17.388
bustle 228.87
bustler 17.199
busty 16.368
busuuti 16.343
busy 16.396
busybody 16.65
busy Lizzie 16.396
but 378
butane 247
butanone 257
butch 73
butcher 17
butcherbird 87
butchery 16.274
Bute 380
butler 17.202
butlery 16.274
butt 378
butte 380
butter 17.349
butterbur 3
buttercup 279
butterfat 365
butterfingered 103
butterfingers 524
butterflies 516
butterfly 7
butterine 251.7
Buttermere 6.3
buttermilk 49
butternut 378

butterscotch 68
buttery 16.274
buttock 46
button 261.103
buttonhole 223
buttonhook 44
buttonmould 120
buttonwood 101
buttress 300
butty 16.341
butyl 218
butyrate 367.21
buxom 242
Buxton 261
buy 7
buyer 17.4
buzz 522
buzzard 103
bwana 17.226
by 7
bye 7
Byelorussian
 261.74
bygone 254
bylaw 9
bypass 294
bypath 453
Byrd 87
byre 8
byrnie 16.227
byroad 98
Byron 261.58
Byronic 38.35
byssinosis 300.55.4
byssus 310.53
bystander 17.98
bystreet 370
byte 372
byway 2.26
byword 87
Byzantine 253.9
Byzantium 242.2

C

cab 18
cabal 212
caballero 12.62
cabaret 2.19
cabbage 197
cabbagetown 258

cabbala 17.161
cabby 16.5
caber 17.11
cabezon 254
cabin 252
cabinet 371.24
cable 228.11
cablegram 229
cablet 371
cableway 2
cabman 261
cabochon 254
caboodle 228.37
caboose 309
Cabora Bassa
 17.298
cabotage 359
cabretta 17.339
cabriole 223.1
cabriolet 2.12
cacao 12
cacciatore 16.269
cachalot 373.1
cache 349
cachepot 373
cachet 2.22
cachexia 17.3.57
cachinnate 367.17
cachou 15
cachucha 17.61
cacique 37
cack-handed 91.12
cackle 228.19
cacodemon 261.47
cacodyl 218
cacoepy 16.245
cacoethes 513
cacography 16.90.2
cacology 16.108.4.6
cacomistle 228.85
cacophonous
 310.36
cacophony
 16.237.3
cactus 310
cacuminal 228.60
cad 83
cadaster 17.379
cadaver 17.410
cadaverous 310.50
caddie 16.57
caddis 300
caddish 353.1
Caddoan 261.6
caddy 16.57

cade 85
cadelle 215.1
cadence 321
cadency 16.312
cadent 420
cadenza 17.446
cadet 368.5
cadge 191
cadger 17.144
cadi 16.58
Cadillac 32
Cádiz 515
cadmium 242.2
cadre 17.78
caduceus 310.2
caducity 16.333
caducous 310.13
caecilian 261.3.11
caecum 242
Caelian 261.3.10
Caelum 242
Caen 266
Caerleon 261.3
Caernarvon
 261.110
Caernarvonshire
 6.8
Caerphilly 16.120
Caesar 17.440
Caesarea 17.2.2
Caesarean 261.3.21
Caesarism
 242.35.15
caesium 242.2.20
caespitose 305
caesura 17.277
café 2
cafeteria 17.3.39
caff 157
caffeine 251
cage 193
cagey 16.100
Cagliari 16.261
cagmag 178
cagoule 227
cahoots 346
Caiaphas 293
Cain 247
caïque 37
cairn 250
Cairngorm 238
cairngorm 238
Cairo 12.64
caisson 261.62
Caithness 296

caitiff 163
cajole 223
cajolery 16.274.17
cajuput 379
cake 34
cakewalk 41
Calabar 1.2
calabash 349.1
Calabria 17.3
caladium 242.2.1
Calais 2
calalu 15.5
calamander 17.98
calamine 253
calamint 412
calamite 372
calamitous 310.64
calamity 16.333.11
calamondin 252
calamus 310.29.2
calandria 17.3.45
calash 349
calathus 310
calcaneus 310.2.6
calcar 1
calcareous 310.2.10
calceolaria
 17.3.38.1
calcic 38
calciferol 220.4
calciferous
 310.50.2
calcific 38.12
calcifuge 204
calcify 7.3
calcimine 253
calcine 253
calcite 372
calcium 242.2
calcsinter 17.369
calculable
 228.16.25
calculate 367.13
calculated 91.34
calculating 265.64
calculation
 261.67.13
calculative 485.15.5
calculator 17.338.6
calculus 310.25
Calcutta 17.349
caldarium 242.2.14
caldera 17.271
Caldwell 215
Caledonia 17.3.36

Caledonian
    261.3.18
calefacient   420.73
calefactory
    16.274.44
calendar   17.102
calender   17.102
calends   532
calendula   17.174
calenture   10
calf   158
calfskin   252
Calgary   16.274
calibrate   367.24
calibration
    261.67.23
calibre   17.14
calico   12.11
Calicut   378
California   17.3.35
californium   242.2
Caligula   17.174
calipee   5
caliph   163.1
caliphate   367
calk   41
call   221
calla   17.160
Callaghan   245
callais   2
Callas   310
callboy   11
caller   17.160,
    17.169
calligraphy   16.90
Callimachus   310.14
calling   265.31
calliope   16.254
callipash   349
calliper   17.253
callipygian   261.3.7
callisthenic   38.32
callisthenics   498.3
callosity   16.333.30
callous   310
callousness   300.34
callow   12.38
callowness   300.25
callus   310
calm   230
calmative   485.15
calmness   300
calomel   215
caloric   38.41
calorie   16.274.15

calorific   38.12.1
calorimeter
    17.342.2.1
calotte   373.1
caloyer   17.5
calpac   32
calque   47
caltrop   281
calumet   368
calumniate   367.1
calumnious   310.2
calumny   16
Calvados   302
calvaria   17.3.38
Calvary   16.274
calve   481
Calvin   252
Calvinism
    242.35.13
calvities   513.1
calycle   228.23
calypso   12
calyx   498
Cam   229
cam   229
Camagüey   2
camail   214
camaraderie
    16.274.6
camarilla   17.166.3
camass   293
camber   17.23
Camberwell   215
cambist   436
cambium   242.2
Cambodia   17.3
cambogia   17.3.15
camboose   309
Cambria   17.3.43
Cambrian   261.3
cambric   38
Cambridge   197
Cambridgeshire   6
Cambyses   513.13
Camden   261
came   231
camel   228.51
cameleer   6
camellia   17.3.20
camelopard   84
Camelopardalis
    300.13
Camelopardus   310
Camelot   373
cameo   12.3

camera   17.279
cameral   228.76
camera lucida
    17.83
cameraman   261.52
camera obscura
    17.277
Cameroon   260.3
camiknickers   524
camion   261.3
camise   513.8
camisole   223.4
camlet   371
camomile   219
camoodi   16.71
Camorra   17.275
camouflage   359
camp   285
campaign   247.7
campaigner   17.227
Campania   17.3.31
campanile   16.118
campanology
    16.108.4.11
campanula
    17.174.9
Campbell   228.17
camper   17.261
campestral   228.81
camphire   8
camphor   17.122
camphorate   367.23
camphoric   38.41
Campinas   310.32
camping   265
campion   261.3
camporee   5.17
campus   310.41
camshaft   396
can   245
Cana   17.227
Canaan   261
Canaanite   372.6
Canada   17.92
Canadian   261.3.3
Canadianism
    242.35.14.1
canaigre   17.130
canal   212
canaliculus
    310.25.2
canalize   516.3.5
canapé   16.254
canard   84
canary   16.264

canasta   17.379
canaster   17.390
Canaveral   228.76
Canberra   17.279
cancan   245
cancel   228
cancellation
    261.67.12
Cancer   17.312
cancer   17.312
cancerous   310.50
cancroid   97
candela   17.165
candelabrum   242
candid   91.12
candidacy   16.307
candidate   367.8
candidness
    300.28.1
candied   91.12
Candiot   373
candle   228.39
candlelight   372
Candlemas   310
candlenut   378
candlepins   548
candlestick   38
candlewick   38
candlewood   101
candour   17.98
candy   16.77
candyfloss   302
candytuft   400
cane   247
canebrake   34
canella   17.163
canescent   420.67.2
canfield   115
cangue   263
canine   253
caning   265.40
canister   17.384
canker   17.43
cankerous   310.50.1
canna   17.225
cannabin   252
cannabis   300.3
Cannae   5
canned   128
cannel   228.55
cannelloni   16.233
cannelure   10.4
canner   17.225
cannery   16.274
Cannes   245

cannibal 228.12
cannibalism
242.35.11
cannibalistic
38.70.2
cannibalize 516.3
cannikin 252.3
canning 265
Cannock 46
cannon 261.55
cannonade 85.3
cannonball 221
cannoneer 6.5
cannonry 16.284
cannot 373
cannula 17.174.9
cannulate 367.13
canny 16.223
canoe 15
canoeing 265.5
canon 261.55
canoness 300.26
canonical
228.23.13
canonicals 539.2.1
canonicate 367.5
canonize 516.7
canonry 16.284
canoodle 228.37
Canopus 310.39
canopy 16.254
Canossa 17.304
cans 544
cant 407
can't 408
Cantab. 18
cantabile 16.120
Cantabrigian
261.3.7
cantala 17.161
cantaloupe 280.1
cantankerous
310.50.1
cantata 17.337
canteen 251
canter 17.365
Canterbury 16.274
cantharides 513.4
canthus 310.72
canticle 228.23
cantilena 17.227
cantilever 17.413
cantillate 367.12
cantina 17.230
cantle 228.109

canto 12.83
canton 254
Canton 254
Cantonese 513.9
cantor 9
cantoris 300.46
cantrip 274
Cantuar. 1
cantus 310
canty 16.353
Canute 380
canvas 310
canvasback 32
canvass 310
canvasser 17.309
canyon 261.121
canzona 17.236
canzone 16.233
canzonet 368
caoutchouc 45
cap 268
capability
16.333.9.2
capable 228.16.32
capacious 310.56
capacitance 321.24
capacitate 367.30.2
capacitor 17.342
capacity
16.333.25.1
cap-a-pie 5
caparison 261.65.1
cape 270
capelin 252.11
Capella 17.163
caper 17.249
Capernaum 242.2
Cape Roca 17.38
Capet 371
Capetian 261.70
capias 293.1
capillarity
16.333.20.2
capillary 16.274.16
capital 228.102
capitalism
242.35.11
capitalist 436.7
capitalistic 38.70.2
capitalize 516.3
capitate 367.30
capitation
261.67.27
Capitol 228.102
Capitoline 253.3

capitular 17.174.12
capitulate 367.13
capitulation
261.67.13
capitulum 242.10
capo 12
capon 261.57
Capone 257
caporal 213
capote 376
Cappadocia 17.3
cappie 16.243
cappuccino 12.54
capreolate 367
Capri 5
capriccio 12.3
capriccioso 12.70
caprice 298
capricious 310.58
capriciousness
300.34.3
Capricorn 255.2
caprifig 184
caprine 253
capriole 223.1
capsaicin 252.21
capsicum 242.4
capsid 91.31
capsize 516
capstan 261
capsulate 367.13
capsule 227
capsulize 516
captain 252.25
captaincy 16.311
caption 261.83
captious 310
captivate 367.36
captivation 261.67
captive 485, 485.22
captivity 16.333.35
captor 17.374
capture 17.72
Capua 17.7
capuche 358
capuchin 252
caput 381
capybara 17.268
car 1
carabao 12.1
carabid 91.4
carabineer 6.4
caracal 212
Caracalla 17.160
caracara 17.268

Caracas 310.7
caracole 223
caracul 225
carafe 157
caramba 17.23
caramel 228
caramelize 516.3
carangid 91
carapace 295.4
carat 381
Caratacus 310.14
caravan 245
caravanserai 7.12
caravel 215
caraway 2.28
carbamate 367.16
carbazole 223
carbide 92
carbine 253
carbohydrate 367
carbolic 38.22
carbon 261.8
carbonaceous
310.56
carbonade 85.3
carbonado 12.17
Carbonari 16.261
carbonate 367.18
carbonation
261.67.19
carbonic 38.35
carboniferous
310.50.2.1
carbonize 516.7
carboxyl 218
carboxylate 367.12
carboy 11
carbuncle 228.30
carbuncular 17.174
carburation
261.67.21
carburettor 17.339
carby 16.6
carcass 310.8
Carchemish 353
carcinogen 261.39
carcinogenic
38.32.1.1
carcinoma 17.215
carcinomatosis
300.55.7
card 84
cardamom 242
cardboard 95
cardiac 32.1

cardialgia 17.3.16
Cardiff 163
cardigan 261.32
Cardiganshire 6.8
cardinal 228.60
cardinalate 367.14
cardiogram 229.1.1
cardiograph
  158.1.1
cardiography
  16.90.2.1
cardiomegaly
  16.131.2
carditis 300.62
cardoon 260
cardsharp 269
cardsharper 17.248
care 4
careen 251.7
career 6
careerist 436.17
carefree 5
careful 226
carefulness 300.30
careless 300
carelessness 300.33
caress 296.4
caret 371
caretaker 17.30
careworn 255
Carey 16.264
carfare 4.2
carfax 494
cargo 12.26
carhop 276
Caria 17.3.38
Carib 24
Caribbean 261.2
Caribbees 513
caribou 15
caricature 10.5
caricaturist 436.19
caries 513.1
CARIFTA 17.359
carillon 261.120
carillonneur 3
Carina 17.230.1
carinate 367.17
Carinthia 17.3.52
carioca 17.38
cariogenic 38.32.1
cariole 223.1
carious 310.2.10
Carl 213
carline 252

carling 265.26
Carlisle 219
Carlos 302
Carlow 12.39
Carlton 261
Carlyle 219
carmagnole 223
carman 261
Carmarthen 261
Carmarthenshire
  6.8
Carmelite 372.4
carminative
  485.15.7
carmine 253
carnage 197
carnal 228
carnassial 228.3
Carnatic 38.49
carnation
  261.67.17
carnelian 261.3.10
carnet 2.14
carnify 7.3
Carniola 17.171
carnival 228.120
carnivore 9.13
carnivorous
  310.50.3
Carnot 12.51
carny 16.224
carob 31
caroche 354
carol 228.72
Carol 228.72
Carolina 17.232
Caroline 253.3
Carolingian 261.3
carolus 310.26
carom 242
carotene 251.11
carotenoid 97.8
carotid 91.40
carousal 228.129
carouse 521
carousel 215.2
carouser 17.443
carp 269
carpal 228
Carpathian 261.3
carpel 228
Carpentaria
  17.3.38
carpenter 17.369
carpentry 16.289

carpet 371
carpetbag 178.1
carpetbagger
  17.123
carpeting 265.66
carpogonium
  242.2.12
carpology 16.108.4
carpophagous 310
carpophore 9.6
carport 374
carpus 310
carrack 46
carrageen 251
Carrara 17.268
carrefour 9.6
carrel 228.72
carriage 197.9
carriageway 2.29
carrier 17.3
carrion 261.3.20
carronade 85.3
carrot 381
carroty 16.344
carry 16.260
carryall 221
carrycot 373
carse 294
carsick 38
Carson 261.61
cart 366
cartage 197
carte blanche 78
cartel 215
Carter 17.337
Cartesian 261.3.34
cartful 226
Carthage 197
Carthaginian
  261.3.17
carthorse 303
Carthusian 261.3
cartilage 197.1
cartilaginous
  310.33
cartload 98
cartogram 229.1
cartography
  16.90.2
cartomancy 16.309
carton 261.95
cartoon 260
cartoonist 436.12
cartouche 358
cartridge 197

cartulary 16.274.18
cartwheel 217
Cartwright 372
caruncle 228.30
carve 481
carven 261.110
carver 17.409
carvery 16.274
carving 265
caryatid 91.32
caryopsis 300.61
carzey 16.392
casaba 17.10
Casablanca 17.43
Casanova 17.417
cascade 85
cascara 17.268
cascarilla 17.166.3
case 295
casease 509.1
caseate 367.1.4
caseation
  261.67.1.3
casebound 139
casefy 7.3
casein 252
casement 420.44
caseose 520
caseous 310.2
casern 249
casework 36
cash 349
cashew 15
cashier 6
cashmere 6
casing 265.59
casino 12.54
cask 56
casket 371
Caspar 17.265
Caspian 261.3
casque 55
cassareep 273
cassata 17.337
cassation 261.67
cassava 17.409
casserole 223.3
cassette 368
cassia 17.3.46
cassimere 6.2
Cassiodorus 310.48
Cassiopeia 17.2.1
cassis 298
cassock 46
cassoulet 2

cassowary 16.264
cast 431
castanets 336
castaway 2.28
caste 431
castellan 261.41
castellated 91.34.5
caster 17.380
castigate 367.10
castigation 261.67.10
Castile 217
Castilian 261.3.11
casting 265.74
castle 228.83
Castlereagh 2
castor 17.380
castrate 367
castration 261.67
castrato 12.73
Castro 12
casual 228.9
casualty 16.352
casuarina 17.232
casuist 436
casuistic 38.70
casuistry 16.293
cat 365
catabasis 300.57
catabolic 38.22
catabolism 242.35.11
catachresis 300.51
cataclasis 300.50
cataclinal 228.61
cataclysm 242.35
cataclysmic 38
catacomb 241
catadromous 310.29
catafalque 47
Catalan 245
catalase 509
catalectic 38.60
catalepsy 16.313
catalogue 185
Catalonia 17.3.36.2
catalyse 516.3
catalysis 300.52.1
catalyst 436.7.6
catalytic 38.52.1
catamaran 245.5
catamenia 17.3.33
catamite 372
catamount 418.1

cataphoresis 300.51.1
catapult 406
cataract 382
catarrhal 228
catastrophe 16.90
catastrophic 38.13
catastrophism 242.35
catatonia 17.3.36
Catawba 17.17
catcall 221
catch 62
catcher 17.50
catchfly 7
catching 265
catchment 420.36
catchpenny 16.226
catchpole 223
catchweight 367
catchword 87
catchy 16.46
catechetical 228.23.19
catechin 252.4
catechism 242.35
catechize 516
catecholamine 251.4
catechumen 248.3
categoric 38.41
categorical 228.23.17
categorize 516.8
category 16.274.9
catena 17.230
catenane 247.6
catenary 16.274.25
catenate 367.17
cater 17.338
cateran 261.60
caterer 17.279
catering 265.58
caterpillar 17.166.2
caterwaul 221
catfall 221
catfish 353
catgut 378
catharsis 300
cathartic 38
Cathay 2
cathead 86
cathectic 38.60
cathedral 228.78
Catherine 252.20

catheter 17.342
catheterize 516.8.2
cathode 98
Catholic 38
catholic 38
Catholicism 242.35.16.2
Catholicity 16.333.28
catholicity 16.333.28
catholicize 516.10
catholicon 261.13
cation 261.4
catkin 252
catlike 39
catling 265
catmint 412
catnap 268
Cato 12.74
catsup 281
cattalo 12.45
cattery 16.274
cattle 228.97
cattleman 261
cattleya 17.3
catty 16.327
Catullus 310
catwalk 41
Caucasia 17.3.59
Caucasian 261.3.33
Caucasoid 97
Caucasus 310
caucus 310
caudad 83
caudal 228
caudate 367
caudex 496
caught 374
caul 221
cauldron 261
caulicle 228.23
cauliflower 14
caulk 41
causal 228
causalgia 17.3.16
causality 16.333.8
causation 261.67
causative 485.15
cause 518
cause célèbre 17.282
causerie 16.274
causeway 2
caustic 38

cauterant 420.65
cauterize 516.8
cautery 16.274
caution 261.72
cautionary 16.274.29
cautious 310.59
cautiousness 300.34
cavalcade 85
cavalier 6
cavalla 17.160
cavalry 16.283
cavalryman 261.48
cavatina 17.230
cave 16.379, 482
caveat 365
caveat emptor 9
caveator 17.338.1
caveman 261
Cavendish 353
cavern 261
cavernous 310.36
cavesson 261.65
cavetto 12.75
caviar 1
cavicorn 255.2
cavie 16.379
cavil 228.117
caving 265.77
cavitation 261.67.27
Cavite 16.332
cavity 16.333.33
cavort 374
cavy 16.379
caw 9
Cawdrey 16.276
Cawnpore 9
Caxton 261
cay 2
cayenne 248
cayman 261.45
cayuse 309
cease 298
ceaseless 300
Cecil 228
Cecilia 17.3.21
cecity 16.333.27
Cecrops 329
cedar 17.82
cede 89
cedi 16.59
cedilla 17.166
ceiba 17.11

ceilidh 16.114
ceiling 265.29
celadon 254
celandine 253
Celebes 513
celebrant 420
celebrate 367.24
celebrated 91.34
celebration
261.67.23
celebratory
16.274.40
celebrity 16.333.24
celeriac 32.1
celerity 16.333.21
celery 16.274
celesta 17.382
celeste 433
celestial 228.3.14
celestite 372
celibacy 16.307
celibate 371.5
cell 215
cella 17.163
cellar 17.163
cellarage 197
cellarer 17.279
cellaret 368.6
Cellini 16.228.1
cellist 436
cello 12.40
cellophane 247.3
cellular 17.174
cellulase 509
cellule 227
cellulitis 300.62.2
Celluloid 97
cellulose 305, 520
Celsius 310.2
celt 402
Celt 402
Celtic 38
cembalo 12.45
cement 410.1
cementation
261.67.32
cementum 242
cemetery 16.274.41
cenacle 228.28
cenotaph 158
cenote 2.24
Cenozoic 38.2
cense 316
censer 17.314
censor 17.314

censorious 310.2.13
censorship 274.1
censure 17.330
census 310.55
cent 410
cental 228.110
centaur 9.12
Centaurus 310.48
centaury 16.269
centenarian
261.3.21.1
centenary
16.274.25
centennial 228.3
centesimal 228.52.1
centesimo 12.48
centigrade 85.5
centigram 229
centilitre 17.341
centillion 261.120
centime 234
centimetre 17.341
centipede 89.1
centipoise 519
cento 12.84
central 228.80
centralism
242.35.11
centrality 16.333.8
centralization
261.67.36
centralize 516.3
centre 17.368
centreboard 95.1
centrefold 120
centrepiece 298.2
centric 38.47
centrifugal 228.48
centrifuge 204
centriole 223.1
centripetal 228.101
centrist 436
centrobaric 38.38
centroid 97
centromere 6.3
centrosome 239
centrosphere 6.1
centuplicate
367.5.1, 371.9.1
centurion 261.3.24
century 16.274
cep 271
cephalad 83
cephalalgia 17.3.16
cephalic 38.19

cephalin 252.11
cephalometer
17.342.3
Cephalonia
17.3.36.2
cephalopod 94.1
ceraceous 310.56
Ceram 229
ceramic 38.24
ceramics 498.2
cerastes 513.18
cerate 371.32
cerated 91.34
ceratodus 310.17
Cerberus 310.50
cercaria 17.3.38
cercis 300
cercopithecoid 97.3
cercus 310.9
cere 6
cereal 228.3.11
cerebellum 242.8
cerebral 228
cerebrate 367.24
cerebration
261.67.23
cerebrospinal
228.61
cerebrum 242
cerecloth 459
cerement 420.30
ceremonial 228.3.8
ceremonious
310.2.9.1
ceremony 16.237
Ceres 513.11
ceresin 252.21
cereus 310.2.11
ceria 17.3.39
cerise 513.12
cerium 242.2.15
cermet 371
cernuous 310.4
cero 12.63
cerography 16.90.2
ceroplastic 38.68
ceroplastics 498.15
cerotype 275.1
cert 369
certain 261.97
certainly 16.174
certainty 16.360
certifiable
228.16.3.1

certificate 367.5,
371.9
certified 92.1
certify 7.3
certiorari 7
certitude 102.2
cerulean 261.3
cerumen 248.3
ceruse 309
Cervantes 513
cervelat 365
cervical 228.23
cervid 91.55
cervine 253
cervix 498
cess 296
cessation 261.67
cesser 17.300
cession 261.68
cessionary
16.274.29.2
cesspool 227
cestode 98
cestoid 97
cetacean 261.67.27
cete 370
ceteris paribus 308
cetology 16.108.4
Cetus 310.63
Ceylon 254.6
chablis 16.132
cha-cha 1
chacma 17.219
chaconne 254
Chad 83
Chadic 38.7
chaeta 17.341
chaetognath 452
chaetopod 94.1
chafe 159
chafer 17.111
chaff 158
chaffer 17.110
chaffinch 80
chagrin 252
chain 247
chair 4
chairborne 255
chairman 261.46
chaise 509
chaise longue 266
chalaza 17.439
chalcedony 16.237
chalcid 91
Chalcidice 16.300

Chalcis 300.58
chalcocite 372.10
chalcography 16.90.2
chalcolithic 38.73
Chaldea 17.2
Chaldee 5
chaldron 261
chalet 2
chalice 300
chalicothere 6.10
chalk 41
chalkboard 95
chalkpit 371
chalky 16.28
challah 17.161
challenge 209
challenger 17.157
challis 16.112
chalone 257
chalybeate 371.1
chamade 84
chamber 17
chamberlain 252.11
chambermaid 85
chambray 2
chameleon 261.3.10
chameleonic 38.35.1
chamfer 17.122
chamois 16.210
Chamonix 16.237
champ 285
champac 32
champagne 247.7
champers 524
champerty 16.344
champion 261.3
championship 274.2
Champs Elysées 2.30
chance 315
chancel 228
chancellery 16.274.19
chancellor 17.176
chancellorship 274.1
chancery 16.274
chancre 17.43
chancroid 97
chancy 16.310

chandelier 6
chandelle 215
Chandernagore 9.7
Chandigarh 1.4
chandler 17
chandlery 16.274
Changchow 13
change 207
changeable 228.16
changeful 226
changeless 300
changelessness 300.33
changeling 265
changeover 17.417
Changteh 2
channel 228.55
channelize 516.3.5
chant 408
chanter 17.366
chanterelle 215
chanticleer 6
Chantilly 16.120
chaos 302
chaotic 38.53
chap 268
chaparejos 305
chaparral 212
chapatti 16.327
chapbook 44
chape 270
chapeau 12
chapel 228.64
chaperon 257.1
chapfallen 261
chapiter 17.342
chaplain 252
chaplaincy 16.311
chaplet 371
Chaplin 252
chappie 16.243
chapstick 38
chapter 17.374
chapterhouse 306
char 1
charabanc 263.1
characin 252
character 17.355
characteristic 38.70.5
characterize 516.8
charade 84
charas 310
charcoal 223
chard 84

charge 192
chargeable 228.16
chargé d'affaires 4
charger 17.145
Chari 16.261
Charing Cross 302
Chari-Nile 219
chariot 381.1.1
charioteer 6.9
charisma 17.224
charismatic 38.49.4
charitable 228.16.49
charity 16.333.20
charivari 16.261
charkha 17.29
charlady 16.59
charlatan 261
charlatanism 242.35.14
Charlemagne 247.5
charleston 261
Charlie 16.113
charlock 40
Charlotte 381
Charlotte Amalie 17.3.17
charlotte russe 309
Charlton 261
charm 230
charmer 17.206
Charminar 1
charming 265.35
charnel 228
Charollais 2.12
Charon 261
charpai 7
charpoy 11
charqui 16.20
chart 366
charter 17.337
Charterhouse 306
Chartism 242.35.17
chartist 436
Chartres 17.292
chartreuse 511
charwoman 261.50
chary 16.264
Charybdis 300
chase 295
chaser 17.299
chasm 242.34
chassé 2.20
chasseur 3
chassis 16.294

chaste 432
chasten 261.62
chastise 516
chastisement 420
chastity 16.333
chasuble 228.15
chat 365
chateau 12.72
chatelaine 247.4
Chatham 242
chatoyant 420.3
Chattanooga 17.136
chattel 228.97
chatter 17.336
chatterbox 499
chatterer 17.279
Chatterton 261
chatty 16.327
Chaucer 17.305
Chaucerian 261.3.22
chauffeur 17.117
chausses 305
chauvinism 242.35.13
chauvinist 436.11
chauvinistic 38.70
chaw 9
chayote 2.24
cheap 273
cheapen 261
cheapness 300
cheapskate 367
cheat 370
Chechen 248
check 35
checker 17.31
checkerberry 16.274
checkerbloom 241
checkmate 367
checkpoint 416
checkup 279
checky 16.22
Cheddar 17.80
cheddite 372
cheek 37
cheekbone 257
cheeky 16.24
cheep 273
cheer 6
cheerful 226
cheerfulness 300.30
cheerio 12.3

cheerleader 17.82
cheerless 300
cheerlessness
   300.33
cheers 514
cheery 16.265
cheese 513
cheeseboard 95
cheesecake 34
cheesecloth 459
cheeseparing
   265.52
cheesy 16.395
cheetah 17.341
chef 160
Chekhov 165
chela 17.162,
   17.165
chelate 367
chelicera 17.279.2
chelicerate 367.23
cheliform 238.1
Chelmsford 103
chelonian 261.3.18
chelp 283
Chelsea 16
Cheltenham 242.16
chemical 228.23
chemin de fer 4.3
chemise 513.8
chemisette 368
chemisorb 27
chemisorption
   261.87
chemist 436
chemistry 16.293
chemostat 365
chemotherapy
   16.254
chempaduk 43
chemurgy 16.102
Chenab 18
Chengteh 2
chenille 217.1
chenopod 94.1
cheongsam 229
Cheops 329
cheque 35
chequebook 44
chequer 17.31
chequerboard 95.1
chequered 103
chequers 524
Cherbourg 187
cherish 353

chernozem 232
Cherokee 5
cheroot 380
cherry 16.262
chersonese 298.1
chert 369
Chertsey 16.316
cherub 31
cherubic 38.4
cherubim 235
Cherubini 16.228
chervil 218
chervonets 336
Chesapeake 37
Cheshire 6
chess 296
chessboard 95
chessel 228
chessman 261.53
chest 433
Chester 17.382
chesterfield 115.1
Chesterfield 115.1
Chesterton 261
chestnut 378
chesty 16.364
Chetnik 38
cheval-de-frise 513
chevet 2
Cheviot 381.1
chevrette 368
chevron 261
chevrotain 247.10
chevy 16.380
chew 15
chewy 16.4
Cheyenne 245
chiack 32
Chiang Kai-shek
   35
chianti 16.353
chiaroscuro 12.66
chiasma 17.223
chiasmus 310
chiastolite 372.4
chibouk 45
chic 37
Chicago 12.26
chicalote 2.24
chicane 247.1
chicanery 16.274
Chichester 17.384
chichi 5
chick 38
chickabiddy 16.63

chickadee 5.4
chickaree 5.17
Chickasaw 9.11
chicken 252.3
chicken-hearted
   91.33
chickenpox 499
chickpea 5
chickweed 89.6
chicle 228.23
chico 12.10
chicory 16.274.4
chide 92
chief 162
chiefly 16.158
chieftain 261
chiffchaff 157
chiffon 254
chiffonier 6.5
chigetai 7
chigger 17.129
chignon 254.12
chigoe 12.29
chihuahua 1
chilblain 247
child 117
childbed 86
childbirth 456
childhood 101
childish 353
childishness 300.35
childless 300
childlessness
   300.33
childlike 39
children 261
Chile 16.120
chiliad 83.1
chiliasm 242.34
chill 218
chilli 16.120
chilli con carne
   16.224
Chillon 254.6
chilly 16.120
chilopod 94.1
Chiltern 261
chime 236
chimera 17.272
chimere 6.2
chimerical
   228.23.15
chimney 16
chimneypiece 298
chimneypot 373

chimp 287
chimpanzee 5
chin 252
china 17.232
China 17.232
chinaberry 16.274
Chinagraph 158.1
Chinaman 261.52
Chinatown 258
chinaware 4.8
chinch 80
chincherinchee 5
chinchilla 17.166
Chindit 371
chiné 2
chine 253
Chinee 5.13
Chinese 513
Ching 265
chink 52
chinless 300
chino 12.54
chinoiserie 5.17
Chinook 45
Chinookan 261.15
chinquapin 252
chintz 348
chinwag 178
chionodoxa 17.428
Chios 302
chip 274
chipboard 95
chipmunk 54
chipolata 17.337.1
Chippendale 214
chipper 17.253
chipping 265
chippy 16.248
chirm 233
chiromancy 16.309
Chiron 254
chiropodist 436.3
chiropody 16.72
chiropractic 38.58
chiropractor
   17.353
chiropteran 261.60
chirp 272
chirper 17.251
chirpy 16.246
chirr 3
chirrup 281
chisel 228
chiselled 122
chit 371

chital 228.101
chitarrone 16.233
chitchat 365
chitin 252
chiton 261.100
Chittagong 266
chitter 17.342
chitterlings 552
chiv 485
chivalrous 310
chivalry 16.283
chive 486
chivy 16.382
chlamydate 367.8
chlamydeous
310.2.1
chlamydospore
9.10
Chloe 16.3
chloracne 16.238
chloral 228.74
chloramphenicol
220
chlorate 367
chlorella 17.163
chloric 38.42
chloride 92.5
chlorinate 367.17
chlorination
261.67.18
chlorine 251.6
chlorite 372
chlorobenzene 251
chloroform 238.2
chlorophyll 218.1
chloroplast 430
chlorothiazide 92
chlorous 310.48
chlorpropamide
92.3
choc-ice 301
chock 40
chocker 17.36
chocolate 371.18
chocolaty 16.344
Choctaw 9
Chogyal 213
choice 304
choir 8
choirboy 11
choirmaster 17.380
choke 42
chokebore 9
chokecherry 16.262
choker 17.38

cholecystectomy
16.222.5
choler 17.168
cholera 17.279
choleric 38.44
cholesterol 220.4
choli 16.126
choline 251
cholinergic 38.16
cholla 1
Cholon 259
chomp 288
chon 257
chondrify 7.3
chondrite 372
chondrule 227
choose 523
choosy 16.402
chop 276
Chopin 245
chopine 251
choplogic 38.18
chopper 17.255
choppy 16.250
chops 329
chopsticks 498
choragus 310.19
choral 228.74
chorale 213
chord 95
chordate 367
chording 265.15
chordophone 257
chore 9
chorea 17.2
choreograph
158.1.1
choreographer
17.120.1
choreography
16.90.2.1
choric 38.41
chorion 261.3.23
chorister 17.384
Chorley 16.123
chorography
16.90.2
choroid 97
chorology
16.108.4.13
chortle 228.105
chorus 310.48
chose 520
chosen 261.129
Chota Nagpur 10

Chou 12
chou 15
chough 168
choux 15
chow 13
chowder 17.89
chow mein 247
chrematistic
38.70.6
chrism 242.35
chrismatory
16.274.43
chrisom 242.35
Christ 437
Christadelphian
261.3
Christchurch 65
christen 261.65
Christendom 242
christening 265.46
Christian 261
Christiania 17.3.30
Christianity
16.333.14
Christianize 516.7
christianly 16.174
Christie 16.366
Christina 17.230
Christine 251
Christlike 39
Christmas 310
Christmastide 92
Christology
16.108.4
Christopher 17.120
chromate 367
chromatic 38.49.2
chromaticity
16.333.28
chromaticness
300.27
chromatics 498.11
chromatid 91
chromatin 252
chromatography
16.90.2.6
chromatophore 9.6
chrome 239
chromic 38
chrominance
321.14
chromite 372
chromium 242.2.9
chromogen 261.39

chromogenic
38.32.1
chromolithography
16.90.2
chromonema
17.210
chromosomal 228
chromosome 239
chromous 310
chronaxie 16.386
chronic 38.35
chronicle 228.23.13
chronicler 17.181
Chronicles 539.2.1
chronogram 229.1
chronograph 158.1
chronological
228.23.5
chronology
16.108.4.11
chronometer
17.342.3.3
chronometry
16.285.2.2
chronon 254
chronoscope 278.1
chrysalis 300.13
chrysanthemum
242.12
chrysolite 372.4
Chrysostom 242
chthonian 261.3.18
chub 29
chubby 16.13
chuck 43
chuckle 228.27
chuddar 17.90
chufa 17.118
chuff 168
chuffed 400
chuffy 16.88
chug 189
chukar 1
chukker 17.39
chum 240
chummy 16.220
chump 289
chumping 265.50
chunder 17.108
chunderous 310.50
chunk 54
chunky 16.39
Chunnel 228
chunter 17.373
church 65

churchgoer 17.6
churchgoing 265.4
Churchill 218
churchman 261
churchwarden
  261.27
churchwoman
  261.50
churchyard 84
churidars 508
churinga 17.141
churl 216
churlish 353
churn 249
churning 265.41
chute 380
chutney 16
chuttie 16.341
Chuvash 350
chyle 219
chyme 236
ciao 13
ciborium 242.2.17
cicada 17.78
cicatrix 498
cicatrize 516
cicely 16.131
Cicero 12
cicerone 16.233
Ciceronian
  261.3.18
cichlid 91
cider 17.84
cig 184
cigar 1.4
cigarette 368.6
cigarillo 12.42
ciggy 16.93
cilia 17.3.21
ciliary 16.274.1.1
ciliate 371.1
cilice 300.8
cilium 242.2.6
cimbalom 242.11
cimex 496
Cimmerian
  261.3.22
Cimon 261
cinch 80
cinchona 17.236
cinchonize 516.7
Cincinnati 16.327
cincture 17.67
cinder 17.102
Cinderella 17.163

cine 16.229
cineaste 430.1
cinema 17.211
cinematic 38.49.1
cinematograph
  158.1
cinematography
  16.90.2.6
Cinerama 17.206
cineraria 17.3.38
cinerarium
  242.2.14
cinerator 17.338.9
cinereous 310.2.11
cingulum 242.10
Cinna 17.231
cinnabar 1.2
cinnamon 261.52
cinquain 247
cinquefoil 222
Cinzano 12.51
cipher 17.115
cipolin 252.11
circa 17.32
circadian 261.3.3
Circassia 17.3.46
Circassian 261.3
Circe 16.298
circinate 367.17
Circinus 310.33
circle 228.22
circlet 371
circuit 371.8
circuitous 310.64
circuitry 16.285
circuity 16.333.3
circular 17.174.5
circularize 516.8.1
circulate 367.13
circulation
  261.67.13
circulatory
  16.274.40.2
circumambulate
  367.13
circumbendibus
  310.5
circumcise 516
circumcision
  261.91
circumference
  321.20
circumflex 496
circumfluous 310.4
circumfuse 523

circumlocution
  261.75.2
circumlocutory
  16.274.42
circumlunar 17.238
circumnavigable
  228.16.19
circumnavigate
  367.10
circumnavigation
  261.67.10
circumscissile
  219.2
circumscribe 25
circumscription
  261.85
circumspect 385
circumspective
  485.17
circumstance 321
circumstantial
  228.95
circumstantiate
  367.1.8
circumvallate 367
circumvent 410
circumvention
  261.82
circumvolution
  261.75.1
circus 310.9
ciré 36
Cirencester 17.382
cirque 36
cirrate 367.21
cirrhosis 300.55.5
cirrhotic 38.53
cirripede 89.1
cirrocumulus
  310.25.5
cirrostratus 310.62
cirrus 310.46
cisalpine 253
cisco 12.15
cislunar 17.238
cissoid 97
cist 436
Cistercian 261.69
cistern 261.107
cisterna 17.229
citadel 228.38
citation 261.67
cite 372
cithara 17.279
cithered 92.1

citify 7.3
citizen 261.126
citizenry 16.284
citizenship 274.2
Citlaltépetl 228.100
citral 228.79
citrate 367.27
citreous 310.2
citric 38
citrin 252
citrine 252
citron 261
citronella 17.163
citronellal 212
citrulline 251.3
citrus 310
cittern 249.1
city 16.333
civet 371
civic 38.74
civics 498
civies 515
civil 228.120
civilian 261.120
civility 16.333.9
civilization
  261.67.36
civilize 516.2
civilized 154
civvy 16.382
clack 32
Clackmannan
  261.55
Clacton 261
clad 83
cladding 265
cladoceran 261.60
cladode 98
cladophyll 218.1
claim 231
claimant 420.29
clairaudience 321.1
clair-obscure 10
clairvoyance 321
clairvoyant 420.3
clam 229
clamant 420.29
clamatorial
  228.3.12.2
clambake 34
clamber 17.23
clammy 16.210
clamorous 310.50
clamour 17.205
clamp 285

clamper 17.261
clan 245
clandestine 252.26
clang 263
clanger 17.245
clangour 17.140
clank 51
clannish 353
clansman 261
clap 268
Clapham 242
clapper 17.247
clapperboard 95.1
Clapton 261
claptrap 268
claque 32
clarabella 17.163.1
Clare 4
Clarence 321
Clarendon 261
claret 381
clarify 7.3.4
clarinet 368
clarinetist 436.23
clarion 261.3.20
clarity 16.333.20
Clark 33
clarkia 17.3
claro 12.61
clarts 334
clary 16.264
clash 349
clasp 290
class 294
classic 38.48
classical 228.23
classicalism
  242.35.11
classicism
  242.35.16
classicist 436.21
classics 498
classifiable
  228.16.3.1
classification
  261.67.5.1
classified 92.1
classify 7.3.6
classis 300.49
classless 300
classlessness
  300.33
classmate 367
classroom 241
classy 16.295

clastic 38.68
clathrate 367
clatter 17.336
claudication
  261.67.5
Claudius 310.2
clause 518
claustrophobia
  17.3.4
claustrophobic
  38.3
claver 17.410
clavichord 95.2
clavicle 228.23
clavicorn 255.2
clavier 17.3
claw 9
clay 2
claybank 51
claymore 9
claypan 245
claytonia 17.3.36
clean 251
cleaner 17.230
cleaning 265.42
cleanliness 300.23
cleanly 16.171,
  16.172
cleanness 300
cleanse 546
cleanser 17.446
clean-shaven
  261.111
clear 6
clearance 321.17
clearcole 223
clear-headedness
  300.28
clearing 265.53
clearness 300
clear-sighted 91.39
clearway 2
clearwing 265
cleat 370
cleavage 197
cleave 484
cleaver 17.413
cleavers 524
cleck 35
cleek 37
Cleethorpes 330
clef 160
cleft 397
cleg 181
clem 232

clematis 300
clemency 16.312
clement 420
clementine 251
clench 79
Cleo 12.2
cleome 16.219
Cleopatra 17.291
clerestory 16.269
clergy 16.102
clergyman 261.48
cleric 38.39
clerical 228.23.15
clericalism
  242.35.11
clericals 539.2
clerihew 15
clerk 33
clerkly 16.140
cleruchy 16.31
cleveite 372
Cleveland 143
clever 17.411
cleverness 300.26
clevis 300.69
clew 15
cliché 2
cliché'd 85
Clichy 5
click 38
clicker 17.34
client 420.2
clientele 215
cliff 163
cliffhanger 17.245
climacteric 38.44
climactic 38.58
climate 371
climatic 38.49
climatology
  16.108.4.15.1
climax 494
climb 236
climber 17.212
clime 236
clinch 80
clincher 17.71
cline 253
cling 265
clinger 17.246
clinic 38.34
clinical 228.23.12
clinician 261.71.5
clink 52
clinker 17.44

clinometer 17.342.3
clinostat 365
clinquant 420
clip 274
clipboard 95
clip-clop 276
clipper 17.253
clippers 524
clippie 16.248
clipping 265
clique 37
cliquey 16.24
clishmaclaver
  17.410
clitellum 242.8
clitic 38.52
clitoris 300.47
Clive 486
cloaca 17.30
cloak 42
cloakroom 241
clobber 17.16
cloche 354
clock 40
clockmaker 17.30
clockwise 516
clockwork 36
clod 94
clodhopper 17.255
clog 185
cloisonné 2
cloister 17.386
cloistered 103
cloistral 228
clomp 288
clone 257
clonic 38.35
clonk 53
clonus 310.35
clop 276
close 305, 520
closed 155
close-grained 130
close-hauled 118
close-knit 371
closely 16.182
closeness 300
closer 17.442
close-stool 227
closet 371.39
close-up 279
closing 265.83
clostridium 242.2.3
closure 17.335
clot 373

cloth 459
clothbound 139
clothe 478
clotheshorse 303
clothesline 253
clothier 17.3
clothing 265
cloture 17.59
cloud 99
cloudberry 16.274
cloudburst 434
cloudless 300
cloudlet 371
cloudscape 270
cloudy 16.68
clough 168
clout 377
clove 488
cloven 261.116
clover 17.417
cloverleaf 162
Clovis 300
clown 258
clownery 16.274
clownish 353
cloy 11
club 29
clubby 16.13
club-footed 91
clubhouse 306
clubland 143
cluck 43
clucky 16.30
clue 15
clueless 300.12
Cluj 357
clumber 17.27
clump 289
clumsiness 300.23
clumsy 16
clung 267
clunk 54
Cluny 16.236
clupeid 91.2
cluster 17.388
clutch 72
clutches 515
clutter 17.349
Clwyd 91.3
Clyde 92
Clydebank 51
Clydesdale 214
clype 275
clypeus 310.2
clyster 17.384

cnidarian 261.3.21
Cnidus 310.16
coach 70
coaching 265
coachman 261
coachwork 36
coadjutant 420.78
coadjutor 17.350
coagulant 420.27
coagulate 367.13,
    371.17
coagulation
    261.67.13
coagulative
    485.15.5
coagulum 242.10
coal 223
coaler 17.171
coalesce 296.1
coalface 295
coalfield 115
coalition 261.71.3
coalman 261
Coalport 374
coaming 265.37
coaptation 261.67
coarse 303
coarsen 261
coarseness 300
coast 441
coastal 228
coaster 17.387
coastguard 84
coastline 253
coat 376
coated 91.41
coatee 5
coati 16.328
coating 265
coax 494, 501
coaxer 17.429
coaxial 228.3.18
cob 26
cobalt 404
cobber 17.16
Cobbett 371
cobble 228
cobbler 17.178
cobblers 524
cobbles 539.1
cobblestone 257
cobia 17.3.4
coble 228.13
cobnut 378
COBOL 220

cobra 17
Coburg 182
coburg 182
cobweb 21
cobwebbed 104
coca 17.38
Coca-Cola 17.171
cocaine 247.2
cocainism 242.35
cocci 7
coccidiosis
    300.55.1
coccolith 458
coccus 310.11
coccyx 498
cochineal 217
cochlea 17.3
cochleate 367.1
cock 40
cockade 85
cock-a-doodle-doo
    15
Cockaigne 247
cock-a-leekie 16.24
cockalorum 242.20
cockatiel 217
cockatoo 15
cockatrice 300
cockchafer 17.111
cocker 17.36
cockerel 228.76
cockeye 7
cockeyed 92
cockfight 372
cockhorse 303
cockiness 300.23
cockle 228.25
cocklebur 3
cockleshell 215
cockloft 399
cockney 16.239
cockneyfy 7.3
cockneyism
    242.35.2
cockpit 371
cockroach 70
cockscomb 239
cocksfoot 379
cockshy 7
cockspur 3
cocksure 10
cocktail 214
cockup 279
cocky 16.27
coco 12.12

cocoa 12.12
coco de mer 4.4
coconut 378
cocoon 260
cocopan 245
cocotte 373
cocoyam 229
cod 94
coda 17.88
coddle 228.34
coddler 17.188
code 98
codeine 251
coder 17.88
codex 496
codfish 353
codger 17.152
codicil 218
codicology
    16.108.4.4
codify 7.3
codling 265
codpiece 298
co-driver 17.415
codswallop 281.2
Cody 16.67
co-ed 86
coedit 371.12
coeducation 261.67
coeducational
    228.63.3
coefficient 420.74
coelacanth 467
coelenterate 367.23
coeliac 32.1
coelom 242
coenobite 372
coenosarc 33
coenurus 310.49
coenzyme 236
coerce 297
coercible 228.16.38
coercion 261.69
coercive 485.3
coeternity
    16.333.16.1
Coeur de Lion
    261.2
coeval 228.119
coexist 436
coexistence 321.27
coexistent 420.81
coextend 131
coextensive 485.9
coff 165

coffee 16.86
coffeepot 373
coffer 17.116
cofferdam 229
coffin 252
coffle 228
cog 185
cogent 420
cogitate 367.30
cogitative 485.15.12
Cognac 32
cognate 367
cognition 261.71
cognitive 485.12
cognizable 228.16.63
cognizance 321
cognizant 420
cognize 516
cognomen 248
cognoscenti 16.355
cogon 257
cogwheel 217
cohabit 371.4
cohabitation 261.67.27
cohere 6
coherence 321.17
coherent 420.62
cohesion 261.90
cohesive 485
coho 12
cohobate 367.4
cohort 374
cohosh 354
cohune 260
coiffeur 3
coil 222
coin 256
coincide 92.9
coincidence 321.5
coincident 420.10
coincidental 228.110.1
coin-op 276
coinsurance 321.19
coinsure 10.2
Cointreau 12
coir 17.5
coit 375
coition 261.71
coitus 310.64
coke 42
col 220

cola 17.171
colander 17.109
colatitude 102.2.1
colcannon 261.55
Colchester 17.384
colchicine 251.8
colchicum 242.4
Colchis 300
colcothar 1
cold 120
cold-blooded 91.11
cold-bloodedness 300.28
cold-hearted 91.33
coldness 300
cole 223
colectomy 16.222.5
coleoptile 219
coleorhiza 17.441.1
Coleridge 197
coleslaw 9
Colette 368
coleus 310.2
coley 16.126
colic 38.22
colicweed 89.6
colitis 300.62
collaborate 367.23
collaboration 261.67.22.1
collaborator 17.338.9
collage 359
collagen 261.39
collapsar 1
collapse 322
collapsible 228.16
collar 17.168
collarbone 257
collard 103.3
collarette 368.6
collate 367.14
collateral 228.76
collation 261.67
collative 485.10
collator 17.338
colleague 183
collect 385, 385.5
collectanea 17.3.31
collected 91.43
collection 261.77
collective 485.17
collectivism 242.35.22

collectivity 16.333.35
collectivize 516.15
collector 17.354
colleen 251
college 197.2
collegian 261.36
collegiate 371.1
collet 371
collide 92
collie 16.122
collier 17.3
colliery 16.274
colligate 367.10
collimate 367.15
collimator 17.338
collinear 17.3.34
Collins 548
collinsia 17.3
collision 261.91
collocate 367.6
collocation 261.67.6
collocutor 17.351
collodion 261.3.6
collogue 188
colloid 97
collop 281.2
colloquial 228.3
colloquialism 242.35.11.2
colloquium 242.2
colloquy 16.259
collotype 275.1
collude 102.1
collusion 261.93
colluvium 242.2
colly 16.122
collyrium 242.2.16
collywobbles 539.1
colobus 310
colocynth 470
Cologne 257
cologne 257
Colombia 17.3
Colombo 12.7
colon 254.7, 257, 261.43
colonel 228.58
colonial 228.3.8
colonialism 242.35.11.2
colonic 38.35
colonist 436.13
colonitis 300.62.4

colonize 516.7
colonnade 85.3
colonnaded 91.6
Colonsay 2
colony 16.237
colophon 254.3
colophony 16.237.3
Colorado 12.16
colorant 420.65
coloration 261.67.22
coloratura 17.277
colorific 38.12.1
colorimeter 17.342.2.1
colossal 228.86
colosseum 242.1
colossus 310.54
colostomy 16.222.6
colostrum 242.23
colotomy 16.222.4
colour 17.173
colourable 228.16.35
coloured 103.4
colourfast 431
colourful 226
colouring 265.58
colourless 300.13
colourman 261.52
coloury 16.274
colporteur 17.345
colt 405
coltish 353
coltsfoot 379
colubrid 91
colubrine 253
colugo 12.32
Columba 17.27
columbarium 242.2.14
Columbia 17.3
Columbian 261.3
columbine 253.1
Columbus 310.6
columella 17.163
column 242
columnar 17.242
columniation 261.67.1
columnist 436
colure 10.4
Colwyn 252
coly 16.126
coma 17.215

Comanche 16.54
Comanchean 261.3
comate 367
comatose 305
comb 239
combat 365
combatant 420.78
combative 485.15
comber 17.215
combination
  261.67.18
combinations 551.1
combinative
  485.15.7
combine 253,
  253.1
combing 265.37
combo 12
combust 443
combustible
  228.16.60
combustion 261
combustor 17.388
come 240
comeback 32
Comecon 254
comedian 261.3.4
comedic 38.8
comedienne 248.1
comedo 12.19
comedown 258
comedy 16.63
comely 16.168
Comenius 310.2.6
comestible
  228.16.59
comet 371.20
comeuppance
  321.15
comfit 371
comfort 381
comfortable 228.16
comforter 17.352
comforting 265
comfortless 300
comfrey 16.281
comic 38.29
comical 228.23.9
Cominform 238
coming 265.38
Comintern 249
comitia 17.3.49
comity 16.333
comma 17.213
command 129

commandant 407
commandeer 6
commander 17.99
commanding 265
commandment 420
commando 12
commeasure
  17.333
commemorate
  367.23
commemoration
  261.67.22
commemorative
  485.15.10
commence 316
commencement
  420
commend 131.2
commendable
  228.16.18
commendam 229
commendation
  261.67.9
commended 91.13
commensal 228.88
commensurable
  228.16.35
commensurate
  371.35
comment 410
commentary
  16.274.48
commentate 367.32
commentator
  17.338
commerce 297
commercial 228.92
commercialism
  242.35.11
commercialistic
  38.70.2
commerciality
  16.333.8.1
commercialize
  516.3
commère 4
commination
  261.67.18.6
commingle 228.50
comminute 380
commis 300
commiserate
  367.23
commiseration
  261.67.22

commissar 1
commissariat 381.1
commissary
  16.274.36
commission
  261.71.4
commissionaire 4.5
commissioner
  17.239.2
commissure 10
commit 371.21
commitment
  420.49
committal 228.102
committee 16.333
committeeman
  261.48
commode 98.1
commodious
  310.2.2
commodity
  16.333.6
commodore 9.4
common 261
commonage 197
commonality
  16.333.8.7
commonalty
  16.352
commoner 17.239
commonly 16.174
commonness
  300.31
commonplace 295
commonweal 217
Commonwealth
  465
commotion
  261.73.1
communal 228
communalize 516.3
communard 84
commune 260
communicable
  228.16.10
communicant
  420.7
communicate 367.5
communication
  261.67.5
communicative
  485.15.1
communion
  261.123
communiqué 2.7

communism 242.35
communist 436
communistic 38.70
communitarian
  261.3.21.2
community
  16.333.18
communize 516
commutable
  228.16.53
commutate 367
commutation
  261.67.29
commutative
  485.15.14
commutator 17.338
commute 380
commuter 17.351
Comnenus 310.32
Como 12.49
comp 288
compact 382
compactly 16.194
companion 261.121
companionable
  228.16.31
companionate
  371.28
companionship
  274.2
companionway 2
company 16.237
comparable
  228.16.35
comparative
  485.15.8
comparatively
  16.206
comparator 17.352
compare 4
comparison
  261.65.1
compartment 420
compartmental
  228.110
compartmentalize
  516.3
compass 310.42
compassion 261.66
compassionate
  371.28
compatibility
  16.333.9.2
compatible 228.16
compatriot 381.1

compeer 6
compel 215
compelling 265.28
compendious 310.2
compendium 242.2
compensate 367.29
compensation
261.67.26
compensatory
16.274.40
compere 4
compete 370
competence 321.24
competent 420.76
competition
261.71.7
competitive 485.12
competitor 17.342
compilation
261.67.12
compile 219
compiler 17.167
complacency
16.312
complacent 420
complain 247
complainant 420
complaint 409
complaisance 321
complaisant 420
complement 410.1,
420.31
complementary
16.274.47
complete 370
completeness
300.37
completion 261.70
complex 496
complexion 261.77
complexity 16.333
compliance 321.2
compliant 420.2
complicate 367.5
complicated
91.34.3
complication
261.67.5
complicity
16.333.28
compliment 410.1,
420.31
complimentary
16.274.47
comply 7

component 420.54
compony 16.233
comport 374
comportment 420
compose 520
composed 155
composer 17.442
composite 371.40
composition
261.71.9
compositor
17.342.5
compost 438
composure 17.335
compote 376
compound 139
comprador 9.4
comprehend 131.1
comprehensible
228.16.40
comprehension
261.82.1
comprehensive
485.9
compress 296
compression
261.68
compressive 485.2
compressor 17.300
comprise 516
compromise 516.5
Comptometer
17.342.3
compulsion 261
compulsive 485
compulsory 16.274
compunction
261.80
computation
261.67.29
compute 380
computer 17.351
computerize 516.8
comrade 85
comradeship 274
comsat 365
comstockery
16.274.5
Comus 310
con 254
con amore 16.269
conation 261.67.19
conative 485.15
conatus 310.62
con brio 12.2

concatenation
261.67.18
concave 482
concavity
16.333.33
conceal 217
concealment 420
concede 89.5
conceit 370
conceited 91.37
conceivable
228.16.61
conceive 484
concelebrate
367.24
concentrate 367
concentration
261.67
concentrative
485.10
concentre 17.368
concentric 38.47
concentricity
16.333.28
concept 422
conceptacle 228.28
conception 261.84
conceptual 228.9
conceptualism
242.35.11.3
conceptualize
516.3.3
concern 249
concerned 132
concernedly 16.148
concerning 265.41
concert 369
concertante 16.353
concerted 91.36
concertgoer 17.6
concertina 17.230
concertino 12.54
concertize 516.13
concerto 12
concession 261.68
concessionaire 4.5
concessionary
16.274.29.2
concessive 485.2
conch 53
concha 17.45
conchoid 97
conchoidal 228.35
conchology
16.108.4

concierge 361
conciliar 17.3.21
conciliate 367.1.2
conciliation
261.67.1.1
conciliative 485.15
conciliatory
16.274.43.1
concise 301
concision 261.91
conclave 482
conclude 102
conclusion 261.93
conclusive 485.8
concoct 388
concoction 261
concomitance
321.24
concomitant
420.76
concord 95
concordance 321
concordant 420.11
concordat 365
Concorde 95
concourse 303
concrete 370
concretion 261.70
concretize 516.12
concubinage 197.7
concubine 253
concupiscence
321.22
concur 3
concurrence 321
concurrent 420.64
concuss 307
concussion 261.74
condemn 232
condemnation
261.67
condemnatory
16.274.40
condensate 367.29
condensation
261.67.26
condense 316
condenser 17.314
condescend 131
condescendence
321.7
condescending
265.20
condescension
261.82.2

condign 253
condiment 420.31
condition 261.71
conditional
228.63.5
conditioned 143.5
conditioner
17.239.2
conditioning
265.46
condole 223.2
condolence 321
condom 242
condominium
242.2.11
condonation
261.67.19
condone 257
condor 9
condottiere 16.264
conduce 309
conducive 485.8
conduct 389
conductance 321
conduction 261.79
conductive 485.19
conductivity
16.333.35.3
conductor 17.357
conductress 300
conduit 371
condyle 218
condyloid 97.5
condyloma 17.215
cone 257
confab 18
confabulate
367.13.1
confabulation
261.67.13.1
confect 385
confection 261.77
confectioner
17.239
confectionery
16.274.29.4
confederacy
16.307.4
confederate 367.23,
371.35
confederation
261.67.22
confer 3
conferee 5
conference 321.20

conferrer 17.270
conferva 17.412
confess 296
confessant 420.67
confessedly 16.148
confession 261.68
confessional
228.63.4
confessor 17.300
confetti 16.330
confidant 407
confide 92
confidence 321.5
confident 420.10
confidential
228.96.1
confidentiality
16.333.8.1.1
confiding 265.14
configuration
261.67.21
confine 253
confinement 420
confirm 233
confirmand 128
confirmation
261.67.16
confiscate 367
Confiteor 9.1
confiture 10
conflagration
261.67
conflate 367
conflict 387
conflictive 485.18
confluence 321.3
confluent 420.4
conflux 502
conform 238
conformable
228.16
conformal 228.53
conformation
261.67
conformist 436
conformity
16.333.13
confound 139
confounded 91.14
confraternity
16.333.16
confrère 4
confront 419
confrontation
261.67

Confucian 261.75
Confucianism
242.35.14
Confucius 310
con fuoco 12.12
confuse 523
confusedly 16.148
confusing 265.84
confusion 261.93
confute 380
conga 17.142
congé 2
congeal 217
congelation
261.67.12
congener 17.230
congenial 228.3.6
congeniality
16.333.8.1
congenital 228.102
conger 17.142
congeries 513.11
congest 433
congestion 261.18
congestive 485.24
congius 310.2
conglobate 367.3
conglomerate
367.23, 371.35
conglomeration
261.67.22
conglutinant
420.53
conglutinate
367.17
Congo 12
congrats 333
congratulate
367.13
congratulations
551.1
congratulatory
16.274.40.2
congregant 420.17
congregate 367.10,
371.14
congregation
261.67.10
congregational
228.63.3
Congregationalism
242.35.11.5.2
Congregationalist
436.7.5
congress 296

congressional
228.63.4
Congressman
261.53
Congreve 484
congruence 321.3
congruent 420.4
congruity 16.333.3
congruous 310.4
conic 38.35
conical 228.23.13
conics 498.5
conidium 242.2.3
conifer 17.114
coniferous
310.50.2.1
Coniston 261.107
conium 242.2.12
conjectural
228.76.1
conjecture 17.64
conjoin 256
conjoint 416
conjugal 228
conjugate 367, 371
conjugation 261.67
conjunct 393
conjunction 261.80
conjunctiva 17.415
conjunctive 485
conjunctivitis
300.62.6
conjuncture 17.68
conjuration
261.67.21
conjure 10, 17.159
conjurer 17.279
conjuring 265.58
conk 53
conker 17.45
conkers 524
con moto 12.79
Connacht 381
connate 367
Connaught 374
connect 385
Connecticut 381
connection 261.77
connective 485.17
connector 17.354
Connemara 17.268
conniption 261.85
connivance 321
connive 486
connivent 420

336

connoisseur 3
Connors 524
connotation
261.67.28
connote 376
connubial 228.3
conoid 97
conquer 17.45
conqueror 17.279
conquest 433
conquistador 9.4
Conrad 83
consanguinity
16.333.17
conscience 321
conscientious
310.61
conscientiousness
300.34.4
conscionable
228.16.31
conscious 310
consciousness
300.34
conscript 424
conscription
261.85
consecrate 367.25
consecration
261.67
consecution 261.75
consecutive 485
consensual 228.9
consensus 310.55
consent 410
consentient 420
consequence 321
consequent 420.58
consequential
228.96
consequently
16.198
conservancy 16.312
conservation
261.67
conservationist
436.13.4
conservatism
242.35.20
conservative 485.15
conservatoire 1.17
conservator 17.338
conservatory
16.274.43
conserve 483

Consett 371
consider 17.83
considerable
228.16.35
considerate 371.35
consideration
261.67.22
considering 265.58
consign 253
consignee 5.13
consignment 420
consignor 17.232
consist 436
consistency 16.312
consistent 420.81
consisting 265.76
consistory
16.274.49
consociate 367.1.7
consocies 513
consolation
261.67.14
consolatory
16.274.43
console 223
consolidate 367.8
consolidation
261.67.7
consolute 380.1
consommé 2
consonance 321
consonant 420.55
consonantal
228.109
consort 374
consortium 242.2
conspecific 38.12
conspectus 310.69
conspicuous
310.4.1
conspicuousness
300.34.2
conspiracy 16.307
conspirator 17.352
conspiratorial
228.3.12.2
conspire 8
constable 228.16
constabulary
16.274.18
Constance 321
constancy 16.312
constant 420
constantan 245
Constantine 253

Constantinople
228.69
constantly 16.198
constatation
261.67.30
constellate 367.12
constellation
261.67.12
consternate 367.18
consternation
261.67.19
constipate 367.19
constipated 91.34
constipation
261.67.20
constituency
16.312
constituent 420.4
constitute 380.5
constitution 261.75
constitutional
228.63.7
constitutionalism
242.35.11.5
constitutionality
16.333.8.7
constitutive 485
constrain 247
constraint 409
constrict 387
constriction 261.78
constrictive 485.18
constrictor 17.355
construct 389
construction
261.79
constructional
228.63
constructive 485.19
constructivism
242.35.22
construe 15
consubstantiation
261.67.1
consuetude 102.2
consul 228.89
consular 17.174
consulate 371.17
consult 406
consultancy 16.312
consultant 420
consultation 261.67
consultative 485.15
consumable 228.16
consume 241

consumer 17.217
consumerism
242.35.15
consummate
367.16, 371.21
consummation
261.67.16
consumption
261.89
consumptive 485
contact 382
contactor 17.353
contagion 261.34
contagious 310.20
contagiousness
300.34
contagium 242.2
contain 247
container 17.227
containerize 516.8
containment
420.41
contaminate
367.17.3
contamination
261.67.18.3
contango 12.35
conté 2
contemn 232
contemplate 367
contemplation
261.67
contemplative
485.15
contemporaneous
310.2.6
contemporary
16.274.32
contemporize 516.8
contempt 428
contemptible
228.16
contemptuous
310.4
contend 131
content 410
contented 91.46
contention 261.82
contentious 310.61
contentment 420
contest 433
contestable
228.16.59
contestant 420.80
context 450

337

contextual 228.9
contextualize
516.3.3
contexture 17.75
contiguity 16.333.3
contiguous 310.4
continent 420.53
continental
228.110
contingency
16.312.4
contingent 420.23
continual 228.9
continuance 321.3
continuant 420.4
continuation
261.67.2
continuative
485.15
continuator 17.338
continue 15.9
continuity
16.333.3.1
continuo 12
continuous 310.4.3
continuum 242.3
conto 12.85
contort 374
contortion 261.72
contortionist
436.13
contour 10
contraband 128
contrabass 295.1
contraception
261.84.1
contraceptive
485.23
contract 382
contractile 219.4
contraction 261.76
contractor 17.353
contractual 228.9.4
contracture 17.63
contradict 387.1
contradiction
261.78.2
contradictory
16.274.46
contrail 214
contralto 12.82
contraption 261.83
contrapuntal
228.112

contrariety
16.333.2.1
contrary 16.274
contrast 431
contrasting 265.74
contrasty 16.362
contravallation
261.67.14
contravene 251.12
contravention
261.82
contrayerva 17.412
contredanse 315
contretemps 266
contribute 380.2
contribution
261.75
contributive 485
contributor 17.350
contributory
16.274.42
contrite 372
contrition 261.71
contrivance 321
contrive 486
contrived 149
control 223
controllable
228.16.24
controller 17.171
controversial
228.92
controversy 16.298
controvert 369.2
contumacious
310.56
contumacy 16.307
contumelious
310.2.4
contuse 523
contusion 261.93
conundrum 242
conurbation 261.67
conure 10
convalesce 296.1
convalescence
321.21
convalescent
420.67
convection 261.77
convector 17.354
convene 251
convener 17.230
convenience 321.1
convenient 420.1.2

convent 420
conventicle
228.23.23
convention 261.82
conventional
228.63.9
conventionalism
242.35.11.5
conventionality
16.333.8.7
conventionalize
516.3.7
conventual 228.9
converge 195
convergence 321
convergent 420.19
conversable
228.16.38
conversant 420.68
conversation
261.67
conversational
228.63.3
conversationalist
436.7.5
converse 297
conversion 261.69
convert 369
converter 17.340
convertible
228.16.47
convex 496
convexity 16.333
convey 2
conveyance 321
conveyancing 265
conveyor 17.1
convict 387
conviction 261.78
convictive 485.18
convince 317
convincible
228.16.41
convincing 265.62
convivial 228.3.15
conviviality
16.333.8.1.2
convocation
261.67.6
convoke 42
convolute 380.1
convoluted 91.42
convolution
261.75.1
convolve 493

convolvulus 310.25
convoy 11
convulsant 420.72
convulse 313
convulsion 261
convulsive 485
Conway 2
cony 16.233
coo 15
Cooch Behar 1.6
cooee 5
cook 44
cookbook 44
cooker 17.40
cookery 16.274
cookhouse 306
cookie 16.31
cooking 265
cookout 377
cool 227
coolabah 1.2
coolant 420
cooler 17.175
Coolidge 197
coolie 16.130
coolness 300
coomb 241
coon 260
cooncan 245
coop 276, 280
cooper 17.259
Cooper 17.259
cooperate 367.23
cooperation
261.67.22.3
cooperative
485.15.10
coopery 16.274
coopt 425
coordinate 367.17,
371.24.1
coordination
261.67.18.1
coordinator
17.338.7
Coorg 187
coot 380
cootch 73
cootie 16.343
cop 276
copaiba 17.15
copal 228.69
copalm 230
coparcenary
16.274.26

coparceny 16.229.4
cope 278
Copenhagen
261.31
copepod 94
coper 17.257
Copernicus 310.10
copestone 257
copier 17.3
copilot 381
coping 265
copious 310.2
coplanar 17.227
copper 17.255
copperas 310.50
copperhead 86.5
copperplate 367
coppice 300
copra 17.290
coprolite 372.4
coprophagous 310
coprophilia
17.3.21.2
coprophilous
310.23
copse 329
Copt 425
copter 17.377
Coptic 38.67
copula 17.174.10
copulate 367.13.7
copulation
261.67.13
copulative 485.15.5
copy 16.250
copybook 44
copyhold 120.1
copyist 436
copyread 89
copyright 372
copywriter 17.343
coquelicot 12.11
coquet 368
coquetry 16.285
coquette 368
coquina 17.230
coquito 12.76
Cora 17.276
coracle 228.28
coracoid 97
coral 228.73
coralline 253.3
corallite 372.4
coralloid 97.6
coralroot 380

cor anglais 2
corban 261
corbel 228
corbicula 17.174.6
cor blimey 16.217
cord 95
cordage 197
cordate 367
corded 91.9
Cordelier 6
Cordeliers 514
cordial 228.3.2
cordiality
16.333.8.1
cordierite 372.8
cordiform 238.1
cordillera 17.271
Cordilleras 524
cordite 372
cordless 300
cordoba 17.21
cordon 261.27
cordovan 261
cords 528
corduroy 11
corduroys 519
core 9
coreligionist 436.13
coreopsis 300.61
corer 17.276
co-respondent
420.15
corf 166
Corfam 229
Corfu 15
corgi 16.95
coriaceous 310.56
coriander 17.98.1
Corinth 470
Corinthian
261.3.28
Coriolanus 310.31
corium 242.2.17
cork 41
Cork 41
corkage 197
corkboard 95
corker 17.37
corking 265.9
corkscrew 15
corm 238
cormel 228.53
cormorant 420.65
corn 255
corncob 26

corncockle 228.25
corncrake 34
corncrib 24
cornea 17.3.35
corneal 228.2
corned 137
corneous 310.2
corner 17.234
cornerstone 257
cornet 371.26
cornetist 436.23
cornett 368
cornfield 115
cornflour 14
cornflower 14
cornhusk 60
cornice 300.24
corniche 353
corniculate
367.13.2
Cornish 353
cornstalk 41
cornstarch 63
cornucopia 17.3.37
cornute 380
Cornwall 221
Cornwallis 300.9
corny 16.232
corolla 17.168
corollaceous
310.56.3
corollary 16.274
corona 17.236
Corona Australis
300.7
Corona Borealis
300.7
coronach 46
coronagraph
158.1.2
coronal 228.62,
228.63
coronary 16.274.29
coronation
261.67.19
coroner 17.239
coronet 371.28
coroneted 91.35
corpora 17.279
corporal 228.76
corporate 371.35
corporation
261.67.22
corporative
485.15.10

corporator
17.338.9
corporeal 228.3.12
corporeity 16.333.1
corps 9
corpse 330
corpulence 321
corpulent 420.27
corpus 310.38
Corpus Christi
16.366
corpuscle 228.87
corpuscular
17.174.8
corpus delicti 7
corpus luteum
242.2
corpus striatum
242.27
corpus vile 16.121
corrade 85
corral 213
correct 385.6
correction 261.77.4
correctitude 102.2
corrective 485.17
correctly 16.195
correctness 300.41
Corregidor 9.3
correlate 367.12
correlation
261.67.12
correlative 485.15.4
correspond 136
correspondence
321
correspondent
420.15
corresponding 265
corridor 9.3
corrie 16.268
Corriedale 214
corrigendum 242.7
corrigible
228.16.20
corroborant 420.65
corroborate 367.23
corroborative
485.15.10
corroboree
16.274.3
corrode 98
corrosion 261.92
corrosive 485.6
corrugate 367, 371

corrugator
17.338.4
corrupt 426.1
corruptible 228.16
corruption 261.88
corsac 32
corsage 359
corsair 4
corselet 371
corset 371
corsetier 6
corsetry 16.285
Corsica 17.34
Corsican 261.13
cortège 360
Cortes 510
cortex 496
corticate 371.9
corticosteroid
97.10
cortisol 220
cortisone 257
corundum 242
Corunna 17.237
coruscate 367
coruscation 261.67
corvée 2
corvette 368
corvine 253
corydalis 300.13
coryphaeus 310.1
coryphée 2
coryza 17.441.1
cos 302, 517
cosecant 420.6
cosh 354
cosher 17.327
cosignatory
16.274.43
cosine 253
cosiness 300.23
cosmetic 38.50
cosmetician
261.71.7
cosmic 38
cosmodrome 239
cosmogony
16.237.4
cosmography
16.90.2
cosmology 16.108.4
cosmonaut 374
cosmopolis
300.13.2

cosmopolitan
261.99
cosmos 302
COSPAR 1
coss 302
Cossack 32
cosset 371
cost 438
costa 17.385
Costa Brava
17.409
costal 228.115
Costa Rica 17.33
costate 367.34
costermonger
17.143
costing 265
costive 485
costly 16
costmary 16.264
costume 241
costumier 17.3
cosy 16.399
cot 373
cotangent 420.22
cote 376
cotenant 420.52
coterie 16.274
cotillion 261.120
cotinga 17.141
cotoneaster 17.379
Cotswold 120
cotta 17.344
cottage 197
cottager 17.150
cotter 17.344
cottier 17.3
cotton 261.101
cottonade 85.3
cottonseed 89.5
cottontail 214
cottonweed 89
cottonwood 101
cottony 16.237.7
cotyledon 261.23
cotyloid 97.5
coucal 212
couch 71
couchant 420
couchette 368
coudé 2
cougar 17.136
cough 165
could 101
couldn't 420.12

coulee 2
coulisse 298
couloir 1
coulomb 237
coulometer
17.342.3
coulter 17.364
coumarin 252.20
coumarone 257.1
council 228
councillor 17.176
councillorship
274.1
counsel 228
counsellor 17.176
count 418
countdown 258
countenance
321.14
counter 17.372
counteract 382
counterattack 32.4
counterbalance
321.10
counterblast 431
counterchange 207
countercharge 192
counterclaim 231
counterclockwise
516
counterculture
17.69
counterespionage
359
counterfeit 371
counterfeiter
17.342
counterfoil 222.1
counterglow 12.46
counterinsurgency
16.312.3
counterintelligence
321.9
counterirritant
420.76
countermand 129
countermarch 63
countermeasure
17.333
countermove 490
counteroffensive
485.9
counterpane 247
counterpart 366.1
counterplot 373

counterpoint 416.1
counterpoise 519
counterproductive
485.19
counterproof 170
counterproposal
228.127
counter-revolution
261.75.1
counterscarp 269
countershaft 396
countersign 253.8
countersink 52
counterspy 7
countertenor
17.228
countertype 275.1
countervail 214
counterweigh 2.28
counterweight
367.38
counterwork 36
countess 300
countless 300
countrified 92.1
countrify 7.3
country 16.290
countryman 261.48
countryside 92.7
county 16.359
coup 15
coup d'état 1
coupé 2
coupe 280
couple 228
couplet 371
coupling 265
coupon 254
courage 197.10
courageous 310.20
courante 408
courgette 368
courier 17.3.42
courlan 261
Courland 143
course 303
courser 17.305
coursing 265
court 374
Courtelle 215.3
courteous 310.2
courtesan 245.7
courtesy 16.300
courthouse 306
courtier 17.3

courting 265.69
courtly 16.192
courtroom 241
courtship 274
courtyard 84
couscous 309
cousin 261
couteau 12.80
couth 463
couthie 16.372
couture 10
couturier 2.1
cove 488
coven 261.117
covenant 420.55
covenantee 5.24
Coventry 16.291
cover 17.418
coverage 197
coverlet 371.18
covers 297
covert 381
coverture 17.62
covet 371
covetous 310.64
covetousness
  300.34
covey 16.383
cow 13
cowage 197
coward 103
cowardice 300.5
cowardliness
  300.23
cowardly 16.152
cowbane 247
cowbell 215
cowbind 135
cowboy 11
cower 14
Cowes 521
cowgirl 216
cowherb 22
cowherd 87
cowhide 92
cowitch 67
cowl 224
cowlick 38
cowling 265.33
cowman 261
cowpat 365
cowpea 5
cowpox 499
cowry 16.271
cowslip 274

cox 499
coxa 17.428
coxalgia 17.3.16
coxswain 261
coy 11
coyness 300
coyote 16.339
coypu 15
cozen 261
crab 18
crab-apple 228.64
crabbed 91
crabber 17.9
crabby 16.5
crabstick 38
crabwise 516
crack 32
crackbrain 247
crackbrained 130
cracker 17.28
crackerjack 32
cracket 371.6
cracking 265
crackjaw 9
crackle 228.19
crackling 265
cracknel 228
crackpot 373
Cracow 13
cradle 228
cradle-snatcher
  17.50
cradlesong 266
craft 396
craftsman 261
crafty 16.345
crag 178
cragged 91
craggy 16.91
Craig 180
crake 34
cram 229
crambo 12
crammer 17.205
cramoisy 16.398
cramp 285
crampon 261
cran 245
cranage 197
cranberry 16.274
crane 247
cranesbill 218
cranial 228.3.5
craniate 371.1

craniology
  16.108.4.1
craniometer
  17.342.3.1
craniometry
  16.285.2.1
craniotomy
  16.222.4.1
cranium 242.2.10
crank 51
crankcase 295
crankpin 252
crankshaft 396
cranky 16.36
cranny 16.223
crap 268
crappie 16.243
craps 322
crapshooter 17.351
crapulent 420.27
craquelure 10.4
crash 349
crashing 265
crashlanding
  265.19
crasis 300.50
crass 293
Crassus 310.51
cratch 62
crate 367
crater 17.338
craunch 81
cravat 365.3
crave 482
craven 261.111
craving 265.77
craw 9
crawfish 353
crawl 221
crawler 17.169
Crawley 16.123
crawling 265.31
cray 2
crayfish 353
crayon 261.1
craze 509
crazed 152
crazy 16.393
creak 37
creaky 16.24
cream 234
creamer 17.210
creamery 16.274
creamlaid 85
creamy 16.215

crease 298
creaseless 300
create 367.1
creatine 251.11
creation 261.67.1
creationism
  242.35.14.3
creative 485.10
creativity 16.333.35
creator 17.338.1
creature 17.55
crèche 351
Crécy 16.297
credence 321.4
credendum 242.7
credent 420.9
credential 228.96.1
credenza 17.446
credibility
  16.333.9.2
credible 228.16.14
credit 371.12
creditable
  228.16.49
creditor 17.342.1
credits 339
credo 12.18
credulity 16.333
credulous 310.25.3
Cree 5
creed 89
creek 37
creel 217
creep 273
creeper 17.252
creepie 16.247
creeps 326
creepy 16.247
creepy-crawly
  16.123
cremate 367.15
cremation
  261.67.15
crematorium
  242.2.17
crème 232
Cremona 17.236
crenate 367
crenation 261.67.18
crenature 10.5
crenel 228.57
crenellate 367.12
creole 223
creolized 154
Creon 254

creophagous 310
creosol 220
creosote 376
creosotic 38.53
crepe 270
crepe de Chine 251.10
crêpe suzette 368.8
crepitate 367.30
crepitus 310.64
crept 422
crepuscular 17.174.8
crescendo 12.24
crescent 420.67
crescentic 38.63
cresol 220
cress 296
Cressida 17.83
crest 433
crested 91.52
crestfallen 261
cresting 265.75
cresylic 38.21
cretaceous 310.56
Cretan 261.98
Crete 370
cretic 38.51
cretin 252
cretinism 242.35.13
cretonne 254
crevasse 293
crevice 300.69
crew 15
Crewe 15
crewel 228.10
crew-neck 35
crib 24
cribbage 197
cribellum 242.8
cribriform 238.1
cribrous 310
cribwork 36
Crichton 261.100
crick 38
cricket 371.9
cricketer 17.342
cricoid 97
crier 17.4
crikey 16.26
crim 235
crime 236
Crimea 17.2
Crimean 261.2
criminal 228.60.4

criminality 16.333.8.6
criminology 16.108.4.10
crimp 287
crimper 17.263
crimple 228
Crimplene 251
crimson 261
cringe 209
cringle 228.50
crinite 372
crinkle 228.29
crinkleroot 380
crinkly 16.145
crinkum-crankum 242
crinoid 97.8
crinoline 252.11
crinum 242.15
criollo 12.44
cripes 328
Crippen 261
cripple 228.66
crippling 265
Cripps 327
crisis 300.53
crisp 291
crispation 261.67
crispbread 86
crisper 17.266
Crispin 252
crispness 300
crispy 16.258
crisscross 302
crissum 242.24
crista 17.384
cristate 367
criterion 261.3.22
critic 38.52
critical 228.23.20
criticism 242.35.16
criticize 516.10.1
critique 37
critter 17.342
croak 42
croaker 17.38
croaky 16.29
Croat 365
Croatia 17.322
Croatian 261.67
crocein 252
crochet 2
crocidolite 372.4
crock 40

crockery 16.274.5
crocket 371.10
Crockett 371.10
Crockford 103
crocodile 219
crocodilian 261.3.11
crocus 310.12
Croesus 310
croft 399
crofter 17.360
croissant 266
Cro-Magnon 254
crombec 35
cromlech 35
Cromwell 215, 228
Cromwellian 261.3.9
crone 257
cronk 53
Cronus 310.35
crony 16.233
crook 44
crooked 91
crookedness 300.28
croon 260
crooner 17.238
crop 276
cropper 17.255
croquet 2
croquette 368
crosier 17.3.62
cross 302
crossbar 1
crossbeam 234
crossbones 550
crossbow 12
crossbred 86
crossbreed 89
crosscheck 35
crosscurrent 420.64
crosscut 378
crosse 302
cross-examination 261.67.18.3
cross-eyed 92
crossfire 8
crosshatch 62
crosshead 86
crossing 265
crossjack 32
cross-legged 91
crossopterygian 261.3.7
crossover 17.417

crosspatch 62
crosspiece 298
crossroads 529
crossruff 168
crosstalk 41
crosstree 5
crosswalk 41
crosswind 134
crosswise 516
crossword 87
crotch 68
crotchet 371
crotchety 16.333
croton 261
crouch 71
croup 280
croupier 17.3
crouse 309
croute 380
crouton 254
crow 12
crowbar 1
crowberry 16.274
crowboot 380
crowd 99
crowded 91
crowfoot 379
crown 258
crownpiece 298
crownwork 36
Croydon 261
croze 520
cru 15
crucial 228
crucian 261.75
cruciate 371.1
crucible 228.12
crucifer 17.114
crucifix 498.1
crucifixion 261.78
cruciform 238.1
crucify 7.3
cruck 43
crud 100
crude 102
crudity 16.333
cruel 228.10
cruelty 16.352
cruet 371.3
Cruickshank 51
cruise 523
cruiser 17.444
cruiseway 2
cruller 17.173
crumb 240

crumble 228
crumbly 16.139
crumby 16.220
crumhorn 255
crummy 16.220
crump 289
crumpet 371
crumple 228
crunch 82
crunchy 16.56
crunode 98
crupper 17.258
crura 17.277
crural 228.75
crus 307
crusade 85
crusader 17.79
cruse 523
crush 356
crusher 17.329
crust 443
crustacean 261.67
crustaceous 310.56
crusted 91.54
crusty 16.368
crutch 72
crutches 515
crux 502
crux ansata 17.338
cruzeiro 12.62
crwth 463
cry 7
crybaby 16.7
crying 265.3
cryobiology
16.108.4.2
cryogen 261.39
cryogenics 498.3
cryolite 372.4
cryometer 17.342.3
cryonics 498.5
cryophilic 38.21
cryophyte 372
cryoscopy 16.254.2
cryosurgery
16.274.13
cryotherapy 16.254
crypt 424
cryptaesthesia
17.3.60
cryptanalysis
300.52.1
cryptic 38.66
cryptogam 229
cryptogenic 38.32.1

cryptogram 229.1
cryptograph 158.1
cryptography
16.90.2
cryptology
16.108.4.17
cryptomeria
17.3.39
cryptozoic 38.2
crystal 228.114
crystalline 253.3
crystallite 372.4
crystallize 516.3
crystallography
16.90.2.2
crystalloid 97.6
ctenidium 242.2.3
ctenoid 97.7
ctenophore 9.6
cub 29
Cuba 17.20
cubage 197
Cuban 261
cubane 247
cubature 17.62
cubbyhole 223
cube 2, 30
cubeb 21
cubic 38.4
cubical 228.23
cubicle 228.23
cubiculum 242.10.1
cubiform 238.1
cubism 242.35
cubist 436
cubit 371
cubital 228.102
cuboid 97
Cu-bop 276
cuckold 122
cuckoldry 16.278
cuckoo 15
cuckoopint 413
cuculiform 238.1
cucullate 367.14
cucumber 17.27
cucurbit 371
cud 100
cuddle 228.36
cuddlesome 242
cuddly 16.151
cuddy 16.69
cudgel 228
cudgerie 16.274
cue 15

cuesta 17.382
cuff 168
cuirass 293
cuirassier 6.7
cuir-bouilli 5
cuisine 251
cuisse 300
culch 77
cul-de-sac 32
culet 371.17
culex 496
culicid 91.29
culinary 16.274.26
cull 225
cullet 371
cullis 300.10
Culloden 261.26
cully 16.128
culminant 420.53
culminate 367.17
culmination
261.67.18
culottes 341
culpa 1
culpable 228.16
culprit 371
cult 406
cultigen 261.37
cultivar 1
cultivate 367.36
cultivated 91.34
cultivation 261.67
cultivator
17.338.11
cultural 228.76
culture 17.69
cultured 103
culver 17.424
culverin 252.20
culvert 381
cumber 17.27
Cumberland
143.4.1
Cumbernauld 118
cumbersome 242
cumbrance 321
Cumbria 17.3.44
Cumbrian 261.3.25
cumin 252
cummerbund 140
cumshaw 9
cumulate 367.13,
371.17
cumulation
261.67.13

cumulative
485.15.5
cumulet 371.17
cumuliform 238.1
cumulonimbus 310
cumulostratus
310.62
cumulus 310.25.5
cuneal 228.3
cuneate 371.1
cuneiform 238.1
cunjevoi 11
cunnilingus 310
cunning 265.45
cunt 419
cup 279
cupbearer 17.271
cupboard 103
cupcake 34
cupel 228
cupellation
261.67.12
Cupid 91
cupidity 16.333.5
cupola 17.176
cuppa 17.258
cupreous 310.2
cupric 38
cuprite 372
cupronickel 228.23
cuprous 310
cupulate 367.13
cupule 227
cur 3
curable 228.16.34
Curacao 12
curacy 16.307
curare 16.261
curarine 251.7
curate 371
curative 485.15.9
curator 17.338
curb 22
curd 87
curdle 228
curdler 17.185
cure 10
curet 368
curettage 359
curfew 15
curia 17.3.42
Curia Regis 300.6
Curie 16.270
curio 12.3

343

curiosity
16.333.30.1
curious 310.2.14
curl 216
curler 17.164
curlew 15
curlicue 15
curliness 300.23
curling 265
curly 16.116
curmudgeon
261.38
currant 420.64
currawong 266
currency 16.312
current 420.64
curricle 228.23
curriculum
242.10.1
curriculum vitae
7.13
currier 17.3
curriery 16.274.1
currish 353
curry 16.272
currycomb 239
curse 297
cursed 91
cursive 485.3
cursor 17.301
cursorial 228.3.12
cursory 16.274.35
curt 369
curtail 214
curtailment 420.39
curtain 261.97
curtana 17.226
curtilage 197.1
curtness 300.36
curtsy 16.316
curvaceous 310.56
curvature 17.62
curve 483
curvet 368
curvilinear 17.3.34
curvy 16.381
cuscus 307
cusec 35
Cush 356
Cushing 265
cushion 261
Cushitic 38.52
cushy 16.325
CUSO 12
cuspid 91

cuspidation
261.67.7
cuspidor 9.3
cuss 307
cussed 91
cussedness 300.28
custard 103
Custer 17.388
custodial 228.3
custodian 261.3.6
custody 16.72
custom 242.32
customary 16.274
customer 17.218
customize 516.5
customs 543
custos 302
cut 378
cutaneous 310.2.6
cutaway 2.28
cutback 32
cutch 72
cute 380
cuteness 300.40
Cuthbert 381
cuticle 228.23.21
cuticula 17.174.6
cutie 16.343
cutin 252.24
cutis 300
cutlass 310
cutler 17.202
cutlery 16.274
cutlet 371
cutpurse 297
Cuttack 32
cutter 17.349
cutthroat 376
cutting 265
cuttle 228.107
cuttlebone 257
cuttlefish 353
cutty 16.341
cuvette 368
Cuxhaven 261.110
cwm 241
Cwmbran 246
cyan 245
cyanamide 92.3
cyanide 92.4
cyanine 251
cyanite 372.6
cyanocobalamin
252.15
cyanosis 300.55

cyanotype 275.1
Cybele 16.120
cybernate 367.18
cybernetic 38.50.5
cybernetics
498.12.1
cycad 83
Cyclades 513.5
cyclamate 367.16
cyclamen 261.52
cycle 228.24
cyclic 38
cyclist 436
cycloalkane 247
cyclohexane 247
cycloid 97
cyclometer
17.342.3
cyclone 257
cyclonic 38.35
Cyclopean 261.2
cyclopedia 17.3.8
cycloplegia 17.3.13
Cyclops 329
cyclorama 17.206
cyclostome 239
cyclostyle 219.7
cyclotron 254
cygnet 371.29
cylinder 17.102
cylindrical 228.23
cylindroid 97
cymar 1.11
cymatium 242.2
cymbal 228
cymbalo 12.45
cyme 236
cymoid 97
cymophane 247.3
cymose 305
Cymric 38
Cynewulf 175
cynic 38.34
cynical 228.23.12
cynicism 242.35.16
cynosure 10
Cynthia 17.3.52
cy pres 2
cypress 310
Cyprian 261.3
cyprinid 91
cyprinoid 97.8
Cypriot 381.1
cypripedium
242.2.2

Cyprus 310
Cyrenaica 17.33
Cyril 228
Cyrillic 38.21
Cyrus 310.47
cyst 436
cystectomy
16.222.5
cystic 38.70
cysticercoid 97.2
cysticercus 310.9
cystine 251
cystitis 300.62
cystocarp 269
cystocele 217.2
cystoid 97
cystotomy 16.222.4
Cythera 17.272
cytokinesis 300.51
cytology
16.108.4.14
cytolysis 300.52.2
cytoplasm 242.34
cytotaxonomy
16.222.3
Cyzicus 310.10
czardas 349
Czech 35
Czechoslovak 32
Czechoslovakia
17.3
Czechoslovakian
261.3

D

dab 18
dabber 17.9
dabble 228
dabbler 17.177
dabchick 38
da capo 12.57
Dacca 17.28
dace 295
dacha 17.50
dachshund 141
dacoit 375
dacoity 16.338
Dacron 254
dactyl 218
dactylic 38.21

dactylogram 229.1.2
dactylography 16.90.2.2
dactylology 16.108.4.8
dad 83
Dada 1
Dadaism 242.35
daddy 16.57
dado 12.17
Daedalus 310.26
daff 157
daffodil 218
daffy 16.82
daft 396
Dagan 261
Dagenham 242.16
dagger 17.123
daglock 40
dagoba 17.21
daguerreotype 275.1
dah 1
dahlia 17.3.18
Dahna 1
Dahomey 16.219
daily 16.114
daintiness 300.23
dainty 16.354
daiquiri 16.266
dairy 16.264
dairying 265
dairyman 261.48
dais 300
daisy 16.393
daisycutter 17.349
Dakar 17.28
Dakota 17.347
dal 213
Dalai Lama 17.206
dalasi 16.295
dale 214
Dales 536
dalesman 261
Dalhousie 16.400
Dali 16.113
Dallas 310
dalliance 321.1.1
dally 16.112
Dalmatia 17.322
Dalmatian 261.67
dalmatic 38.49
Dalton 261

daltonism 242.35.14
dam 229
damage 197
damages 515
Damanhûr 10
Damara 17.268
damascene 251.9
Damascus 310
damask 61
dame 231
Damietta 17.339
dammar 17.205
damn 229
damnable 228.16
damnation 261.67
damnatory 16.274.43
damnedest 436
damnify 7.3
Damocles 513
damp 285
dampcourse 303
dampen 261
damper 17.261
damply 16.178
dampness 300
damsel 228
damselfish 353
damselfly 7
damson 261
dan 245
Dan 245
Danaë 5.1
dance 315
dancer 17.313
dancing 265
dandelion 261.4
dander 17.98
Dandie Dinmont 414
dandify 7.3
dandiprat 365
dandle 228.39
dandruff 171
dandruffy 16.88
dandy 16.77
Dane 247
Danegeld 113
Danegelt 402
Danelaw 9
dang 263
danger 17.156
dangerous 310.50

dangerousness 300.34
dangle 228.49
Daniel 228.123
Danish 353
dank 51
Danny 16.223
Dante 16.353
Danton 261
Danube 30
Danzig 184
dap 268
daphnia 17.3
Daphnis 300
dapper 17.247
dapple 228.64
daraf 171
darbies 515
Dardan 261
Dardanus 310.36
Dardic 38
dare 4
daredevil 228.118
Dar es Salaam 230.1
Darfur 10
darg 179
daric 38.38
Darien 261.3.21
daring 265.52
dariole 223.1
Darjeeling 265.29
dark 33
darken 261.10
darkle 228.20
darkly 16.140
darkness 300
darkroom 241
darksome 242
darling 265.26
Darlington 261
Darmstadt 365
darn 246
darned 129
darnel 228
dart 366
dartboard 95
darter 17.337
Dartford 103
Dartmoor 10
Dartmouth 464
darts 334
Darwin 252
Darwinian 261.3.17

Darwinism 242.35.13
dash 349
dashboard 95
dasheen 251
dasher 17.321
dashiki 16.24
dashing 265
dashpot 373
Dasht-i-Lut 379
dassie 16.294
dastard 103
dastardly 16.152
dasyure 10
data 17.338
date 367
dated 91.34
dateline 253
dative 485.10
dato 12.73
datum 242.27
datura 17.277
daub 27
daube 28
dauber 17.17
daubery 16.274
daughter 17.345
daughter-in-law 9
daunt 415
daunting 265
dauntless 300
dauphin 252
dauphine 251
dauphiness 300.23
davenport 374
David 91
Davis 300
davit 371
Davy 16.379
daw 9
dawdle 228
dawn 255
Dawson 261
day 2
Dayan 246
daybook 44
dayboy 11
daybreak 34
daydream 234
daydreamer ·17.210
daydreaming 265.36
daylight 372
daylights 340
daylong 266

daystar 1
daytime 236
Dayton 261
Daytona 17.236
day-tripper 17.253
daze 509
dazzle 228.124
deacon 261.12
deaconess 300.26
deaconry 16.284
deactivate 367.36
dead 86
deadbeat 370
deaden 261.21
deadeye 7
deadhead 86
deadlight 372
deadline 253
deadlock 40
deadly 16.147
deadness 300
deadpan 245
deadwood 101
deaf 160
deafen 261
deafmute 380
deafness 300
deal 217
dealer 17.165
dealings 552
dealt 402
deaminate 367.17.3
dean 251
deanery 16.274.25
dear 6
dearest 436.17
dearly 16.119
dearness 300
dearth 456
deary 16.265
death 455
deathbed 86
deathblow 12
deathly 16.203
deathtrap 268
deathwatch 68
Deauville 217
deb 21
debacle 228.20
debag 178
debar 1.1
debark 33
debase 295
debatable
    228.16.45

debate 367
debater 17.338
debauch 69
debauchee 5
debauchery 16.274
debenture 17.70
debilitate 367.30.1
debility 16.333.9.2
debit 371
debonair 4.5
Deborah 17.279
debouch 71
debouchment 420
Debrecen 248
débridement 420
debrief 162
debris 16
debt 368
debtor 17.339
debug 189
debunk 54
debus 307
Debussy 16.306
debut 15
debutante 408
decade 85
decadence 321
decadent 420
decaffeinate
    367.17.1
decagon 254.5
decahedron 261
decal 212
decalcomania
    17.3.31.1
decalescence
    321.21
Decalogue 185
decamp 285
decanal 228.56
decane 247
decani 7
decant 407
decanter 17.365
decapitate 367.30
decapitation
    261.67.27
decapod 94.1
decarbonate 367.18
decarbonize 516.7
decathlon 261
decay 2.7
Deccan 261
decease 298
deceased 435

decedent 420.9
deceit 370
deceitful 226
deceive 484.2
deceiver 17.413
decelerate 367.23
deceleration
    261.67.22
decelerometer
    17.342.3.4
December 17.24
Decembrist 436
decency 16.312
decennary
    16.274.23
decennium 242.2
decent 420.69
decentralize 516.3
deception 261.84
deceptive 485.23
decerebrate 367.24
decern 249
decibel 215
decide 92.7
decided 91.8
decidedly 16.148
decider 17.84
decidua 17.7
deciduous 310.4
decillion 261.120
decimal 228.52.1
decimalize 516.3
decimate 367.15
decimation
    261.67.15
decipher 17.115
decision 261.91.1
decisive 485.5
decisiveness 300.43
deck 35
deckle 228.21
declaim 231
declamation
    261.67.16
declamatory
    16.274.43.5
declaration
    261.67.22
declarative
    485.15.8
declarator 17.352
declaratory
    16.274.43
declare 4
declarer 17.271

declass 294
declassify 7.3.6
declension 261.82
declinate 367.17
declination
    261.67.18
decline 253.4
declivity 16.333.35
declutch 72
decoct 388
decoction 261
decode 98
decoder 17.88
decoke 42
decollate 367.14
décolletage 359
décolleté 2
decolonize 516.7
decolorant 420.65
decompose 520
decomposer 17.442
decomposition
    261.71.9
decompound 139
decompress 296
decompression
    261.68
decongestant
    420.80
deconsecrate
    367.25
decontaminate
    367.17.3
decontamination
    261.67.18.3
decontrol 223
décor 9
decorate 367.23
decoration
    261.67.22
decorative
    485.15.10
decorator 17.338.9
decorous 310.50
decorticate 367.5
decorum 242.20
decoupage 359
decoy 11
decrease 298
decreasingly 16.175
decree 5
decree nisi 7
decrement 420.31
decrepit 371
decrepitate 367.30

decrepitude 102.2
decrescent 420.67
decretal 228.101
decry 7
decrypt 424
decumbent 420
decurion 261.3.24
decurrent 420.64
decurved 147
decury 16.270
Dedéagach 63
dedicate 367.5
dedicated 91.34.3
dedication 261.67.5
deduce 309
deduct 389
deductible
  228.16.54
deduction 261.79
deductive 485.19
Dee 5
deed 89
deejay 2
deek 37
deem 234
deemster 17.393
deep 273
deepen 261
deepfreeze 513
deer 6
deergrass 294
deerhound 139
deerskin 252
deerstalker 17.37
de-escalate 367.14
de-escalation
  261.67.14
deface 295.3
de facto 12
defamation
  261.67.16
defamatory
  16.274.43.5
defame 231
default 404
defaulter 17.363
defeasance 321.28
defeat 370
defeatism 242.35
defeatist 436
defecate 367.5
defecation
  261.67.5
defect 385, 385.1
defection 261.77

defective 485.17
defector 17.354
defence 316
defenceless 300.16
defencelessness
  300.33.1
defend 131
defendant 420.14
defender 17.101
defenestration
  261.67.25
defensible
  228.16.40
defensive 485.9
defer 3
deference 321.20
deferent 420.65
deferential
  228.96.2
deferment 420
deferral 228
defiance 321.2
defiant 420.2
defibrillator
  17.338.5
deficiency 16.312.5
deficient 420.74
deficit 371.36
defilade 85
defile 219
definable 228.16.30
define 253
definiendum 242.7
definite 371.24
definitely 16.189
definition 261.71.5
definitive 485.12
deflagrate 367
deflate 367
deflation 261.67
deflect 385
deflection 261.77
deflocculate
  367.13.3
deflower 14
Defoe 12
defoliant 420.1
defoliate 367.1.3
defoliation
  261.67.1.2
deforce 303
deforest 436.18
deform 238.1
deformation 261.67
deformed 125

deformity
  16.333.13
defraud 95
defray 2
defrock 40
defrost 438
defroster 17.385
deft 397
deftness 300
defunct 393
defuse 523
defy 7.3
Degas 1
degas 293
de Gaulle 223
degauss 306
degeneracy
  16.307.4
degenerate
  367.23.1, 371.35
degeneration
  261.67.22.2
deglutinate 367.17
deglutition 261.71
degradable 228.16
degradation
  261.67.8
degrade 85.5
degrading 265.11
degrease 298
degree 5.18
degression 261.68
dehisce 300
dehiscent 420.70
dehorn 255
Dehra Dun 260
dehumanize 516.7
dehumidifier 17.4.1
dehumidify 7.3.1
dehydrate 367
dehydration 261.67
dehypnotize 516.13
de-ice 301
de-icer 17.303
deicide 92.7
deictic 38
deific 38.12
deiform 238.1
deify 7.3
deign 247
deil 217
deism 242.35.1
deist 436
deity 16.333.1
deixis 300

deject 385
dejecta 17.354
dejected 91.43
dejection 261.77
de jure 2.18
dekko 12.9
delaine 247.4
De la Mare 4
delaminate
  367.17.3
delate 367.12
Delaware 4.8
delay 2.11
dele 16.118
delectable 228.16
delectation 261.67
delegacy 16.307
delegate 367.10,
  371.14
delegation
  261.67.10
delete 370
deleterious
  310.2.11
deletion 261.70
Delhi 16.115
deli 16.115
deliberate 367.23,
  371.35
deliberation
  261.67.22
deliberative
  485.15.10
delicacy 16.307.1
delicate 371.9
delicatessen 261.63
delicious 310.58
delight 372.3
delighted 91.39
delightful 226.9
Delilah 17.167
delimit 371.19
delineate 367.1
delineation
  261.67.1
delineator 17.338.1
delinquency 16.312
delinquent 420
deliquesce 296
deliquescence
  321.21
deliquescent 420.67
delirious 310.2.12
delirium 242.2.16

delirium tremens
546
delitescence 321.21
Delius 310.2.4
deliver 17.414
deliverance 321.20
deliverer 17.279
delivery 16.274.51
dell 215
Delmarva 17.409
Delos 302
delouse 306
Delphic 38
delphinium
242.2.11
Delphinus 310.34
delta 17.361
deltiology
16.108.4.1
deltoid 97
delude 102
deluge 204
delusion 261.93.1
delusive 485.8
de luxe 502
delve 492
demagnetize
516.13
demagogic 38
demagogue 185.2
demagoguery
16.274.12
demagogy 16.94
demand 129
demanding 265
demarcate 367
demarcation
261.67.4
dematerialize
516.3.2.1
Demavend 131
deme 234
demean 251
demeaning 265.42
demeanour 17.230
dement 410.1
demented 91.46
dementia 17.330
demerara 17.271
demerit 371.31
demersal 228.84
demesne 247
Demeter 17.341
demibastion 261.3
demicanton 254

demigod 94
demigoddess 300.4
demijohn 254
demilitarize 516.8.2
De Mille 218
demilune 260
demimondaine 247
demimonde 136
demineralize
516.3.8
demirelief 162.1
demise 516.4
demission 261.71
demist 436
demitasse 293
demiurge 195
demivierge 361
demo 12
demob 26
demobilize 516.2
democracy
16.307.5
democrat 365.2
democratic 38.49.6
democratize 516.13
Democritus 310.64
demodulation
261.67.13
Demogorgon
261.33
demography
16.90.2.3
demoiselle 215
demolish 353.5
demolition
261.71.3
demon 261.47
demonetize 516.12
demoniac 32.1
demonic 38.35
demonism
242.35.14
demonolatry
16.286.2
demonology
16.108.4.11
demonstrable
228.16
demonstrate 367
demonstration
261.67
demonstrative
485.15.11
demonstrator
17.338

demoralize 516.3
demos 302
Demosthenes 513.9
demote 376
demotic 38.53
demotion 261.73
demount 418
demulcent 420.72
demulsify 7.3.7
demur 3
demure 10
demurrage 197.10
demurrer 17.278
demy 7
demystify 7.3
demythologize
516.1
den 248
denarius 310.2.10
denary 16.274.25
denationalize
516.3.7
denaturalize
516.3.8
denature 17.52
denazify 7.3
Denbighshire 6
dendriform 238.1
dendrite 372
dendrochronology
16.108.4.11
dendroid 97
dendrology
16.108.4
dene 251
Deneb 21
denegation
261.67.10
deniable 228.16.3
denial 228.4
denier 17.3
denigrate 367.26
denim 235
Denis 300
denizen 261.126
Denmark 33
denominate
367.17.5, 371.24
denomination
261.67.18.6
denominational
228.63.3
denominationalism
242.35.11.5.2

denominative
485.15.7
denominator
17.338.7
denotation
261.67.28
denotative
485.15.13
denote 376
denouement 266
denounce 319
denouncer 17.317
dense 316
densimeter
17.342.2
densitometer
17.342.3
density 16.333.31
dent 410
dental 228.110
dentalium 242.2
dentate 367.32
dentation
261.67.32
dentex 496
denticle 228.23.23
denticulation
261.67.13
dentiform 238.1
dentifrice 300
dentil 218
dentine 251
dentist 436, 436.27
dentistry 16.293
dentition 261.71
dentoid 97
Denton 261
denture 17.70
denuclearize 516.8
denudation 261.67
denude 102
denunciate 367.1
denunciation
261.67.1.4
deny 7.10
deodand 128
deodar 1
deodorant 420.65
deodorize 516.8
deontic 38.64
deontology
16.108.4.16
deoxyribonucleic
38.1
depart 366

departed 91.33
department 420
departmental 228.110
departmentalism 242.35.11.6
departmentalize 516.3
departure 17.51
depend 131.3
dependable 228.16.18
dependant 420.14
dependence 321.7
dependency 16.312.2
dependent 420.14
depersonalize 516.3.7
depict 387
depiction 261.78
depilate 367.12
depilatory 16.274.43.4
deplane 247
deplete 370
depletion 261.70
deplorable 228.16
deplore 9
deploy 11
deployment 420.33
deplume 241
depoliticize 516.10.1
depone 257
deponent 420.54
depopulate 367.13.7
deport 374.1
deportation 261.67
deportee 5
deportment 420
deposal 228.127
depose 520
deposit 371.39
deposition 261.71.9
depositor 17.342.5
depository 16.274.41
depot 12.58
depravation 261.67
deprave 482
depraved 146
depravity 16.333.33

deprecate 367.5
deprecatory 16.274.40.1
depreciable 228.16.42
depreciate 367.1
depreciation 261.67.1
depredate 367.8
depredation 261.67.7
depress 296
depressant 420.67
depressed 433
depressing 265.60
depression 261.68
depressive 485.2
depressor 17.300
depressurize 516.8
deprivation 261.67
deprive 486
deprived 149
depside 92
depurate 367.22
depurative 485.15.9
deputation 261.67.29
depute 380.4
deputize 516
deputy 16.342
De Quincey 16.311
deracinate 367.17.7
derail 214
derailleur 17.433
derailment 420.39
derange 207.1
derangement 420.38
deration 261.66
Derby 16.6
Derbyshire 6
deregister 17.384
Derek 38.39
derelict 387
dereliction 261.78
derestrict 387
derestriction 261.78
deride 92
derision 261.91
derisive 485.5
derisory 16.274.37
derivation 261.67
derivative 485.15.16

derive 486
derma 17.209
dermal 228
dermatitis 300.62
dermatology 16.108.4.15
dermatome 239
dermatoplasty 16.361.1
dermatosis 300.55.7
dermis 300.18
dermoid 97
derogate 367.11.1
derogative 485.15.3
derogatory 16.274.43.3
derrick 38.39
derrière 4.1
derring-do 15
derringer 17.157
derris 300
Derry 16.262
derry 16.262
derv 483
dervish 353
Derwent 420
Derwentwater 17.345
desalinate 367.17
desalination 261.67.18
descant 407
Descartes 366
descend 131
descendant 420.14
descender 17.101
descent 410
deschool 227
describable 228.16.8
describe 25
description 261.85
descriptive 485
descry 7
desecrate 367.25
desecration 261.67
desegregate 367.10
desegregation 261.67.10
desensitize 516.12
desert 369, 381
deserted 91.36
deserter 17.340
desertion 261.69

deserve 483
deservedly 16.148.1
deserving 265.78
desexualize 516.3.3
desiccant 420.7
desiccate 367.5
desiccated 91.34.3
desiccator 17.338.2
desiderata 17.337.2
desiderate 367.23
desiderative 485.15.10
desideratum 242.26
design 253
designate 367, 371.29
designation 261.67
designer 17.232
designing 265.44
desinence 321.14
desirability 16.333.9.2
desirable 228.16
desire 8
desirous 310.47
desist 436
desk 57
desman 261.53
desmid 91
desmoid 97
desolate 367.14, 371.18
desolation 261.67.14
desorb 27
desorption 261.87
despair 4
desperado 12.16
desperate 371.35
desperation 261.67.22
despicable 228.16.10
despise 516
despite 372
despoil 222
despoliation 261.67.1.2
despondent 420.15
despot 373
despotic 38.53
despotism 242.35.20
desquamate 367.16
dessert 369

dessertspoon 260
dessiatine 251.11
destination
261.67.18
destine 252.26
destined 134
destiny 16.229
destitute 380.5
destitution 261.75
destroy 11
destroyer 17.5
destruct 389
destructible
228.16.54
destruction 261.79
destructionist
436.13
destructive 485.19
destructor 17.357
desuetude 102.2
desultory 16.274
detach 62
detachable 228.16
detached 395
detachment 420.36
detail 214
detailed 112
detain 247.9
detainee 5.11
detainer 17.227
detect 385.8
detectable 228.16
detection 261.77
detective 485.17
detector 17.354
detent 410
détente 408
detention 261.82
deter 3
deterge 195
detergency
16.312.3
detergent 420.19
deteriorate 367.23
deterioration
261.67.22
determinable
228.16.29
determinant
420.53.1
determinate 371.24
determination
261.67.18.4
determinative
485.15.7

determine 252.13
determined 134
determiner 17.231
determinism
242.35.13
determinist 436.11
deterrence 321.16
deterrent 420.61
detest 433
detestable
228.16.59
detestation
261.67.33
dethrone 257
detinue 15.9
Detmold 120
detonate 367.18
detonation
261.67.19
detonator 17.338.8
detour 10
detoxicate 367.5
detoxify 7.3
detract 382
detraction 261.76
detrain 247
detriment 420.31
detrimental
228.110.2
detrition 261.71
detritus 310.65
Detroit 375
de trop 12
detrude 102
detumescence
321.21
Deucalion 261.3.8
deuce 309
deuced 91.30
deuteragonist
436.13.2
deuteranopia
17.3.37.2
deuteride 92.6
deuterium 242.2.15
Deuteronomy
16.222.3
deutzia 17.3
deva 17.410
devaluation
261.67.2
devalue 15
Devanagari 16.274
devastate 367
devastation 261.67

develop 281.1
developer 17.260
development 420
developmental
228.110
deviant 420.1
deviate 367.1.10
deviation
261.67.1.6
deviationism
242.35.14.3
device 301
devil 228.118
devilish 353
devilment 420.40
devilry 16.283
devious 310.2
deviousness
300.34.1
devisable 228.16.64
devisal 228
devise 516.15
devisee 5
devisor 17.441
devitalize 516.3
devoice 304
devoid 97
devoirs 1.18
devolution
261.75.1
devolve 493
Devon 261.112
Devonian 261.3.18
devote 376
devoted 91.41
devotee 5
devotion 261.73
devotional 228.63.6
devour 14
devout 377
dew 15
dewan 246
Dewar 17.8
dewberry 16.274
dewclaw 9
dewdrop 276
Dewey 16.4
dewlap 268
Dewsbury 16.274
dewy 16.4
dexterity 16.333.21
dextrorotation
261.67.28
dextrorse 303
dextrose 520

dextrous 310
dey 2
dhak 33
dhal 213
dharma 17.206
dharna 17.237
Dhaulagiri 16.265
dhobi 16.12
dhole 223
dhoti 16.339
dhow 13
diabase 295.1
diabetes 513.16
diabetic 38.50.2
diablerie 16.274
diabolic 38.22
diabolical 228.23.8
diabolism
242.35.11
diabolo 12.45
diachronic 38.35
diaconal 228.63.1
diaconate 371.28
diacritic 38.52
diacritical
228.23.20
diactinic 38.34
diadelphous 310
diadem 232
diagnose 520
diagnosis 300.55
diagnostic 38.71
diagnostician
261.71
diagnostics 498
diagonal 228.63
diagram 229.1
diagrammatic
38.49.2
dial 228.4
dialect 385.5
dialectic 38.60
dialectical 228.23
dialectics 498
dialectology
16.108.4
diallage 197
dialler 17.176.1
dialogism 242.35.8
dialogist 436.4.1
dialogue 185
dialyse 516.3
dialyser 17.441
dialysis 300.52.1

diamagnetism
242.35.18
diamanté 16.353
diamantine 253.9
diameter 17.342
diametral 228.79
diametric 38.46
diametrically
16.142
diamond 143
diamondback 32
Diana 17.225
dianoetic 38.50.1
dianoia 17.5
diapason 261.124
diapause 518
diapedesis 300.51
diaphanous 310.36
diaphonic 38.35.2
diaphony 16.237
diaphoresis
300.51.1
diaphoretic 38.50
diaphragm 229
diaphysis 300.52
diapir 6.6
diapositive
485.12.1
diarch 33
diarchy 16.20
diarist 436.20
diarrhoea 17.2.2
diarthrosis 300.55
diary 16.274
Dias 310.1
diascope 278.1.1
Diaspora 17.279
diaspore 9.10
diastalsis 300.58
diastasis 300.57
diastema 17.210
diaster 17.379
diastole 16.131
diastolic 38.22
diastrophism
242.35
diatessaron 254.11
diathermancy
16.312
diathermic 38.26
diathermy 16.214
diathesis 300.52
diatomic 38.29
diatonic 38.35.5
diatribe 25

diazotize 516.13
dib 24
dibble 228.12
dicast 430
dice 301
dicey 16.301
dichasium 242.2.19
dichloride 92.5
dichogamy
16.222.2
dichotomize 516.5
dichotomy
16.222.4
dichroism 242.35.3
dichromatic
38.49.2
dichromaticism
242.35.16.4
dichroscope 278.1
Dick 38
Dickens 548
dickens 548
Dickensian 261.3
dicker 17.34
Dickinson 261
dicky 16.25
dicotyledon 261.23
dicrotic 38.53
dicta 17.355
Dictaphone 257
dictate 367
dictation 261.67
dictator 17.338
dictatorial
228.3.12.2
dictatorship 274.1
diction 261.78
dictionary
16.274.29
dictum 242
did 91
Didache 5
didactic 38.58
didactics 498.13
diddle 228.32
Diderot 12
didgeridoo 15.2
didicoy 11
didn't 420.10
Dido 12.20
didst 446
didymous 310.28
didynamous 310.29
die 7
dieback 32

die-cast 431
die-hard 84
dielectric 38
Dien Bien Phu 15
Dieppe 271
dieresis 300.52
diesel 228
diesis 300.52
diestock 40
diet 381.2
dietary 16.274.43
dieter 17.352.1
dietetic 38.50
dietetics 498.12
dietitian 261.71.7
differ 17.114
difference 321.20
different 420.65
differentia 17.3
differentiable
228.16.2
differential
228.96.2
differentiate
367.1.9
differentiation
261.67.1
difficult 406
difficulty 16.352
diffidence 321.5
diffident 420.10
diffract 382.1
diffraction 261.76
diffuse 309, 523
diffuser 17.444
diffusion 261.93
diffusive 485.8
dig 184
digamy 16.222.1
digastric 38
digest 433
digestant 420.80
digester 17.382
digestible
228.16.59
digestion 261.18
digestive 485.24
digger 17.129
digit 371
digital 228.102
digitalin 252
digitalis 300.7
digitalism
242.35.11
digitalize 516.3

digitate 367.30
digitiform 238.1
digitigrade 85.5
digitize 516.12
digitoxin 252.29
diglot 373
dignified 92.1
dignify 7.3.3
dignitary 16.274.41
dignity 16.333.19
digraph 158
digress 296
digression 261.68
digressive 485.2
dihedral 228.78
dihybrid 91
dik-dik 38
diktat 366
dilapidate 367.8
dilapidated 91.34
dilapidation
261.67.7
dilatancy 16.312.6
dilatant 420.75
dilatation
261.67.30
dilate 367
dilation 261.67
dilatometer
17.342.3
dilator 17.338
dilatory
16.274.43.4
dildo 12
dilemma 17.208
dilemmatic 38.49.1
dilettante 16.353
diligence 321.9
diligent 420.20
dill 218
dilly 16.120
dilly-dally 16.112
diluent 420.4
dilute 380
dilution 261.75
diluvial 228.3.17
diluvium 242.2
dim 235
dime 236
dimension 261.82
dimer 17.212
dimercaprol 220
dimeter 17.342.2
dimethylsulphoxide
92.14

dimetric 38.46
dimidiate 367.1
dimidiate 371.1
diminish 353.7
diminuendo 12.24
diminution 261.75
diminutive 485
dimissory
16.274.36
dimity 16.333.12
dimmer 17.211
dimness 300
dimorph 166
dimorphous 310.18
dimple 228
dimwit 371
dim-witted 91.38
din 252
Dinah 17.232
dinar 1
dine 253
diner 17.232
dineric 38.39
dinette 368
ding 265
dingbat 365
dingbats 333
ding-dong 266
dinge 209
dinghy 16.242
dingle 228.50
dingo 12.36
dingy 16.110
dink 52
Dinka 17.44
dinkum 242
dinky 16.37
dinner 17.231
dinoceras 310.50
dinosaur 9.11
dinothere 6.10
dint 412
diocesan 261.65
diocese 300.57.1
Diocletian 261.70
diode 98
Diogenes 513
Diomedes 513.3
Dionysia 17.3.61
Dionysiac 32.1
Dionysian 261.3.35
Dionysius 310.2.15
Dionysus 310
diopside 92.10
dioptre 17.377

dioptric 38
dioptrics 498
Dior 9.1
diorama 17.206
dioxide 92.14
dip 274
dipeptide 92
diphase 509
diphtheria 17.3.39
diphtherial
228.3.11
diphthong 266
diplegia 17.3.13
diplex 496
diplococcus 310.11
diplodocus 310.14
diploë 5
diploid 97
diploma 17.215
diplomacy 16.307
diplomat 365
diplomate 367.16
diplomatic 38.49.2
diplomatics 498.11
diplont 414
diplopia 17.3.37
diplopod 94.1
diplostemonous
310.36
dipnoan 261.6
dipody 16.72
dipole 223
dipper 17.253
dippy 16.248
dipsomania
17.3.31.1
dipsomaniac 32.1
dipstick 38
dipteral 228.76
dipterous 310.50
diptych 38.66
Dirac 32
dire 8
direct 385
direction 261.77.3
directional
228.63.8
directive 485.17
directly 16.195
directness 300.41
director 17.354
directorate 371.35
directorial 228.3.12
directorship 274.1
directory 16.274.45

dirge 195
dirham 229
dirigible 228.16.20
diriment 420.31
dirk 36
dirndl 228
dirt 369
dirtiness 300.23
dirty 16.331
Dis 300
disability
16.333.9.2
disable 228.11
disabuse 523
disaccharide 92.6
disaccord 95.3
disaccredit 371.12
disaccustom 242.32
disadvantage 197
disadvantaged 110
disadvantageous
310.20
disaffect 385.2
disaffiliate 367.1.2
disaffiliation
261.67.1.1
disaffirm 233
disafforest 436.18
disagree 5
disagreeable
228.16.1
disagreement 420
disallow 13
disambiguate 367.2
disannul 225
disappear 6.6
disappearance
321.17
disappoint 416.1
disappointed 91.48
disappointing 265
disappointment
420.50
disapprobation
261.67.3
disapproval
228.122
disapprove 490
disarm 230
disarmament
420.35
disarming 265.35
disarrange 207
disarray 2.19

disarticulate
367.13.2
disassemble 228.18
disassociate 367.1.7
disaster 17.380
disastrous 310
disavow 13
disavowal 228.8
disband 128
disbar 1
disbelief 162.1
disbelieve 484.1
disbranch 78
disbud 100
disburden 261.22
disburse 297
disc 58
discard 84
discern 249
discernible
228.16.28
discerning 265.41
discernment 420
discharge 192
disciple 228.67
disciplinant 420.53
disciplinarian
261.3.21.1
disciplinary
16.274.26
discipline 252
discipular 17.174
disclaim 231
disclaimer 17.207
disclimax 494
disclose 520
disclosure 17.335
disco 12.15
discobolus 310.26.1
discography
16.90.2
discoid 97
discoloration
261.67.22
discolour 17.173
discombobulate
367.13
discomfit 371
discomfiture 17.56
discomfort 381
discommend 131.2
discommode 98.1
discommodity
16.333.6
discommon 261

discompose 520
discomposure 17.335
disconcert 369
disconcerted 91.36
disconnect 385
disconsolate 371.18
discontent 410
discontented 91.46
discontinue 15.9
discontinuity 16.333.3.1
discontinuous 310.4.3
discophile 219.1
discord 95
discordance 321
discordant 420.11
discotheque 35
discount 418
discountenance 321.14
discourage 197.10
discouragement 420.37
discourse 303
discourteous 310.2
discourtesy 16.300
discover 17.418
discoverer 17.279
discovert 381
discovery 16.274
discredit 371.12
discreditable 228.16.49
discreet 370
discrepancy 16.312
discrepant 420
discrete 370
discretion 261.68
discretionary 16.274.29.2
discriminate 367.17, 371.24
discriminating 265.64.1
discrimination 261.67.18.5
discriminator 17.338.7
discriminatory 16.274.43.6
discursive 485.3
discus 310.15
discuss 307

discussion 261.74
disdain 247
disdainful 226.4
disease 513
diseased 153
disembark 33
disembarkation 261.67.4
disembarrass 310.43
disembodied 91
disembody 16.65
disembogue 188
disembowel 228.8
disembroil 222
disenable 228.11
disenchant 408
disenchantment 420
disencumber 17.27
disendow 13
disengage 193
disengagement 420
disentangle 228.49
disenthral 221
disentitle 228.103
disentomb 241
disentwine 253
disequilibrium 242.2
disestablish 353
disesteem 234
disfavour 17.410
disfigure 17.129
disfigurement 420.35.1
disfranchise 516
disgorge 200
disgrace 295
disgraceful 226
disgruntle 228.112
disgruntled 122
disguise 516
disgust 443
disgusted 91.54
disgusting 265
dish 353
dishabille 217
disharmony 16.237
dishcloth 459
dishearten 261.95
dishevel 228.118
dishevelled 122
dishonest 436
dishonesty 16.366

dishonour 17.233
dishonourable 228.16.35
dishwasher 17.327
dishwater 17.345
dishy 16.322
disillusion 261.93.1
disincentive 485.21
disinclination 261.67.18
disincline 253.5
disinfect 385
disinfectant 420.79
disinfection 261.77
disinfest 433
disingenuous 310.4.2
disinherit 371.31
disintegrate 367.26
disintegration 261.67.24
disinter 3
disinterest 436.20
disinterested 91.53
disject 385
disjoin 256
disjoint 416
disjointed 91.48
disjunction 261.80
disjunctive 485
disk 58
dislikable 228.16
dislike 39.1
dislimn 235
dislocate 367.6
dislocation 261.67.6
dislodge 199
disloyal 228.6
disloyalty 16.352.1
dismal 228.54
dismantle 228.109
dismantler 17.203
dismay 2
dismember 17.24
dismiss 300
dismissal 228.85
dismissive 485.4
dismount 418
Disneyland 143.2
disobedience 321.1
disobedient 420.1.1
disobey 2.4
disoblige 198

disoperation 261.67.22.3
disorder 17.86
disorderly 16.131
disorganize 516.7
disorganized 154
disorient 410
disorientate 367.32
disown 257
disparage 197.9
disparagement 420.37
disparate 371.35
disparity 16.333.20
dispassion 261.66
dispassionate 371.28
dispatch 62
dispel 215
dispensable 228.16.40
dispensary 16.274.38
dispensation 261.67.26
dispensatory 16.274.43
dispense 316
dispenser 17.314
dispersal 228.84
dispersant 420.68
disperse 297
dispersion 261.69
dispersive 485.3
dispirit 371.33
dispirited 91.38
displace 295
displacement 420.44
display 2
displease 513
displeasure 17.333
disport 374
disposable 228.16
disposal 228.127
dispose 520
disposed 155
disposition 261.71.9
dispossess 296
dispossession 261.68
dispraise 509
disproof 170

disproportion
261.72.1
disproportionate
371.28.2
disprove 490
disputable
228.16.53
disputant 420.77
disputation
261.67.29
disputatious 310.56
dispute 380
disqualifier 17.4.1
disqualify 7.3.2
disquiet 381.2
disquietude 102.2
disquisition
261.71.8
Disraeli 16.114
disrate 367
disregard 84.1
disrelish 353.4
disrepair 4.6
disreputable
228.16.52
disrepute 380.4
disrespect 385
disrespectful
226.10
disrobe 28
disrupt 426
disruption 261.88
disruptive 485
dissatisfaction
261.76
dissatisfied 92
dissatisfy 7
dissect 385.7
dissection 261.77.5
disseise 513
dissemble 228.18
disseminate 367.17
dissension 261.82.2
dissent 410
dissenter 17.368.1
dissentient 420
dissentious 310.61
dissepiment 420.31
dissertate 367.31
dissertation
261.67.30
disservice 300
dissever 17.411
dissident 420.10
dissimilar 17.166

dissimilarity
16.333.20.2
dissimilate 367.12
dissimilation
261.67.12
dissimilitude 102.2
dissimulate
367.13.5
dissimulation
261.67.13.3
dissipate 367.19.1
dissipated 91.34
dissipation
261.67.20.1
dissociable
228.16.44
dissociate 367.1.7
dissociation
261.67.1
dissolute 380.1
dissolution
261.75.1
dissolve 493
dissolvent 420
dissonance 321
dissonant 420.55
dissuade 85
dissuasion 261
dissuasive 485
dissymmetry
16.285.1
distaff 158
distal 228.114
distance 321.27
distant 420.81
distaste 432
distasteful 226.12
distemper 17.262
distend 131
distich 38.70
distichous 310.10
distil 218
distillate 371.16
distillation
261.67.12
distiller 17.166
distillery 16.274.16
distinct 392
distinction 261
distinctive 485.20
distinguish 353
distinguishable
228.16.43
distort 374
distortion 261.72

distract 382
distracting 265.70
distraction 261.76
distrain 247
distrainee 5.11
distraint 409
distrait 2
distraught 374
distress 296
distressing 265.60
distributary
16.274.42
distribute 380.2
distributee 5.23
distribution 261.75
distributive 485
distributor 17.350
district 387
distringas 293
distrust 443
distrustful 226.13
disturb 22
disturbance 321
disturbing 265
disulfiram 242.19
disulphide 92
disunite 372
disunity 16.333.18
disuse 309
disused 156
dit 371
dita 17.341
ditch 67
ditheism 242.35.2
dither 17.405
dithyramb 229
dithyrambic 38.5
dittander 17.98
dittany 16.237
ditto 12
dittography
16.90.2.5
ditty 16.333
diuresis 300.51
diuretic 38.50
diurnal 228.58
div 485
diva 17.413
divalent 420.25
divan 245
divaricate 367.5,
371.9
divaricator
17.338.2
dive 486

diver 17.415
diverge 195
divergence 321
divergent 420.19
divers 524
diverse 297
diversiform 238.1
diversify 7.3
diversion 261.69
diversity 16.333.26
divert 369
diverticulitis
300.62.2
diverticulosis
300.55.3
diverticulum
242.10.1
divertimento 12.84
divertissement 420
Dives 513
divest 433
divide 92
dividend 131
divider 17.84
dividers 524
divi-divi 16.382
divination
261.67.18
divine 253
diviner 17.232
diving 265
divining 265.44
divinity 16.333.17
divinize 516.6
divisibility
16.333.9.2.2
divisible 228.16.63
division 261.91.2
divisional 228.63
divisionism
242.35.14
divisive 485.5
divisor 17.441
divorcé 2
divorce 303
divorcee 5.21
divot 381
divulge 205
divulsion 261
divvy 16.382
Dixie 16.388
dixie 16.388
Dixieland 143.2
Diyarbakir 6
dizziness 300.23

dizzy 16.396
Djaja 17.145
Djajapura 17.277
Djakarta 17.337
Djambi 16.17
Djerba 17.12
Djibouti 16.343
Dnieper 17.252
Dniester 17.383
do 15
doab 19
doable 228.16.7
dobbin 252
dobby 16.11
Doberman pinscher
 17.331
dobla 1
dobsonfly 7
doc 40
docent 410
Docetism
 242.35.18
docile 219
docility 16.333.9
dock 40
dockage 197
docker 17.36
docket 371.10
dockland 143
dockyard 84
doctor 17.356
doctoral 228.76
doctorate 371.35
doctrinaire 4
doctrinal 228.61
doctrine 252
document 410,
 420.34
documentary
 16.274.47
documentation
 261.67.32
dodder 17.85
doddering 265.58
doddery 16.274
doddle 228.34
dodecagon 254.5
Dodecanese 513.9
dodecaphonic
 38.35.2
dodge 199
Dodgem 242
dodger 17.152
dodgy 16.104
dodo 12.21

Dodona 17.236
doe 12
doek 44
doer 17.8
does 522
doeskin 252
doff 165
dog 185
dogberry 16.274
dogcart 366
doge 201
dogfight 372
dogfish 353
dogged 91
doggedness 300.28
Dogger 17.131
dogger 17.131
doggerel 228.76
doggery 16.274.12
doggish 353
doggo 12
doggone 254
doggy 16.94
doghouse 306
dogie 16.96
dogleg 181
dogma 17
dogman 261
dogmatic 38.49
dogmatics 498.11
dogmatism
 242.35.20
dogmatist 436.26
dogmatize 516.13
dogsbody 16.65
dogtooth 463
dogtrot 373
dogvane 247
dogwatch 68
dogwood 101
doh 12
Doha 1
doily 16.125
doing 265.5
doings 552
doit 375
dol 220
dolabriform 238.1
doldrums 543
dole 223
doleful 226
dolerite 372.8
dolina 17.230
doll 220
dollar 17.168

dollarbird 87
dollop 281.2
dolly 16.122
dolman 261
dolmas 310
dolmen 248
Dolmetsch 64
dolomite 372
Dolomites 340
dolorimetry
 16.285.1
doloroso 12.70
dolorous 310.50
dolour 17.168
dolphin 252
dolt 405
dom 237
domain 247.5
dome 239
domestic 38.69
domesticate 367.5
domestication
 261.67.5
domesticity
 16.333.28
domicile 219.2
domiciliary
 16.274.1.1
dominance 321.14
dominant 420.53.2
dominate 367.17.5
domination
 261.67.18.6
domineer 6.4
Dominic 38.34
Dominica 17.33
dominical
 228.23.12
Dominican 261.13
dominie 16.229
dominion 261.122
dominium 242.2.11
domino 12.55
dominoes 520
Domitian 261.71.4
don 254
Don 254
Donar 1
donate 367.18
donation 261.67.19
Donatist 436.26
donative 485.15
Donbass 294
Doncaster 17.390
done 259

donee 5
Donegal 221
Donets 336
dong 266
Donizetti 16.330
Don Juan 261
donkey 16.38
Donna 17.233
donned 136
donnert 381
donnish 353.8
donnybrook 44
donor 17.236
Donovan 261
Don Quixote
 16.339
don't 417
doodah 1.3
doodle 228.37
doodlebug 189
Doolittle 228.102
doom 241
doomsday 2
door 9
doorbell 215
doorframe 231
doorjamb 229
doorkeeper 17.252
doorman 261
doormat 365
doornail 214
doorpost 441
doorsill 218
doorstep 271
doorstop 276
doorway 2
dooryard 84
dopant 420
dope 278
dopey 16.251
Doppelgänger
 17.245
Dopper 17.255
Doppler 17.195
dor 9
Dora 17.276
Dorado 12.16
Dorcas 310
Dorchester 17.384
Dorian 261.3.23
Doric 38.41
Doris 300
Dorking 265.9
dorm 238
dormant 420.32

dormer 17.214
dormie 16.218
dormitory
 16.274.41
Dormobile 217
dormouse 306
dornick 38
doronicum 242.4
dorp 277
dorsad 83
dorsal 228
Dorset 371
dorsoventral
 228.80
dorsum 242
Dortmund 143
dorty 16.336
dory 16.269
dosage 197
dose 305
do-si-do 12.19
dosimeter 17.342.2
doss 302
dossal 228.86
dosser 17.304
dosshouse 306
dossier 2.1
Dostoevsky 16.43
dot 373
dotage 197.13
dotard 103
dotation 261.67.28
dote 376
dotted 91.40
dottle 228.104
dotty 16.335
Dou 13
Douai 2.2
double 228.14
double-breasted
 91.52
double-cross 302
double-decker
 17.31
double entendre
 17.287
double-glazing
 265.81
double-jointed
 91.48
doubles 539
doublet 371
doublethink 52
doubleton 261
doubletree 5

doubloon 260
doublure 10
doubly 16.136
doubt 377
doubter 17.348
doubtful 226
doubtfulness
 300.30
doubtless 300
douc 45
douce 309
douceur 3
douche 358
dough 12
doughboy 11
doughnut 378
doughty 16.340
doughy 16.3
Douglas 310
Doukhobors 518
dour 10
dourine 251
Douro 12.66
douroucouli 16.130
douse 306
douser 17.307
dove 489
dovecot 373
dovecote 376
Dover 17.417
dovetail 214
dowable 228.16.5
dowager 17.154
dowdy 16.68
dowel 228.8
dower 14
dowitcher 17.56
Dowland 143
down 258
downbeat 370
downcast 431
downfall 221
downfallen 261
downgrade 85
downhaul 221
downhearted 91.33
downheartedness
 300.28
downhill 218
Downpatrick 38.45
downpipe 275
downpour 9
downright 372
downspout 377
downstage 193

downstairs 512
downstate 367
downstream 234
downtown 258
downtrodden
 261.26
downward 103
downwards 531
downwind 134
downy 16.234
dowry 16.271
dowse 521
dowser 17.443
dowsing 265
doxastic 38.68
doxology 16.108.4
doxy 16.389
doyen 261.5
doyenne 248
Doyle 222
doze 520
dozen 261
dozenth 471
dozer 17.442
dozy 16.399
drab 18
drabbet 371.4
drabble 228
drably 16.132
drabness 300
dracaena 17.230
drachma 17.219
dracone 257
Draconian
 261.3.18
draconic 38.35
draff 157
draft 396
draftee 5
drag 178
dragée 2
draggle 228.43
draghound 139
dragnet 368
dragoman 261.49
dragon 261.30
dragonet 371.28
dragonfly 7
dragonhead 86
dragonnade 85.3
dragoon 260
dragrope 278
drail 214
drain 247
drainage 197

drainer 17.227
drainpipe 275
drake 34
Drakensberg 182
dram 229
drama 17.206
Dramamine 251.4
dramatic 38.49.2
dramatically
 16.142
dramatics 498.11
dramatis personae
 7
dramatist 436.26
dramatization
 261.67.36
dramatize 516.13.1
dramaturge 195
dramaturgy 16.102
Drambuie 16.4
drank 51
drape 270
draper 17.249
drapery 16.274
drapes 323
drastic 38.68
drastically 16.142
drat 365
dratted 91.32
draught 396
draughtboard 95
draught-excluder
 17.91
draughtsman 261
draughty 16.345
Drava 17.409
Dravidian 261.3.5
draw 9
drawback 32
drawbar 1
drawbridge 197
drawee 5
drawer 9
drawers 518
drawing 265
drawknife 164
drawl 221
drawn 255
drawplate 367
drawstring 265
drawtube 30
dray 2
drayhorse 303
dread 86
dreadful 226

dreadfully 16.129
dreadfulness 300.30
dreadnought 374
dream 234
dreamer 17.210
dreamless 300
dreamlike 39
dreamy 16.215
dreariness 300.23
dreary 16.265
dredge 194
dredger 17.147
dree 5
dreg 181
dreggy 16.92
dregs 535
drench 79
Dresden 261
dress 296
dressage 359
dressed 433
dresser 17.300
dressing 265.60
dressmaker 17.30
dressmaking 265.6
dressy 16.297
drew 15
Dreyfus 310
dribble 228.12
driblet 371
drift 398
drifter 17.359
driftwood 101
drill 218
drillstock 40
drink 52
drinkable 228.16.11
drinker 17.44
drip 274
dripping 265
drippy 16.248
drive 486
drivel 228.120
driven 261.114
driver 17.415
driverless 300.13
driveway 2
driving 265
drizzle 228
drizzly 16.209
drogue 188
droit 375
droll 223

drollery 16.274.17
dromedary 16.274.7
dromond 143
drone 257
drongo 12
drool 227
droop 280
droopy 16.253
drop 276
droplet 371
droplight 372
dropout 377
dropper 17.255
droppings 552
drops 329
dropsical 228.23
dropsonde 136
dropsy 16.315
drosophila 17.166
dross 302
drought 377
drove 488
drover 17.417
drown 258
drowse 521
drowsiness 300.23
drowsy 16.400
drub 29
drudge 203
drudgery 16.274
druffen 261
drug 189
drugget 371
druggist 436
drugstore 9
druid 91.3
druidess 300
druidic 38
drum 240
drumbeat 370
drumhead 86
drumlin 252
drummer 17.216
drumstick 38
drunk 54
drunkard 103
drunken 261
drunkenness 300.31
drupe 280
drupelet 371
Drury 16.270
druse 523
Druse 523

dry 7
dryad 83.2
dryadic 38.7
dry-cleaning 265.42
Dryden 261.25
dryer 17.4
dryness 300
Drysdale 214
D.T.s 513.16
dual 228.10
dualism 242.35.11
duality 16.333.8.2
dub 29
Dubai 7
dubbin 252
dubbing 265
dubiety 16.333.2
dubious 310.2
dubiousness 300.34.1
dubitable 228.16.49
dubitation 261.67.27
Dublin 252
Dubonnet 2
Dubrovnik 38
ducal 228
ducat 381
duce 16.53
duchess 300
duchy 16.52
duck 43
duckboard 95
ducking 265
duckling 265.34
ducks 502
duckweed 89
ducky 16.30
duct 389
ductile 219
dud 100
dude 102
dudeen 251
dudgeon 261.38
Dudley 16.151
due 15
duel 228.10
dueller 17.176
duello 12.40
duenna 17.228
duet 368.1
duff 168
duffel 228.42

duffer 17.118
dug 189
dugong 266
dugout 377
duiker 17.35
duke 45
dukedom 242
dulcet 371
dulciana 17.226.1
dulcify 7.3.7
dulcimer 17.211
dulia 17.3.23
dull 225
dullard 103.4
Dulles 300.10
dullness 300
dullsville 218
dulse 313
Duluth 463
duly 16.130
Du Maurier 2.1
dumb 240
Dumbarton 261.95
dumbbell 215
dumbfound 139
dumbness 300
dumbstruck 43
dumbwaiter 17.338
dumdum 240
Dumfries 298
dummy 16.220
dump 289
dumper 17.264
dumpling 265
dumps 332
dumpy 16.257
Dumyat 365
dun 259
Dunbar 1
Duncan 261
dunce 320
Dundalk 41
Dundee 5
dunderhead 86.5
dune 260
Dunedin 252
Dunfermline 252
dung 267
dungaree 5.17
Dungeness 296.3
dungeon 261
dunghill 218
dunite 372
dunk 54

Dun Laoghaire
17.271
dunlin 252
Dunlop 276
dunnage 197
dunnakin 252.4
dunnite 372
dunno 12
dunnock 46
dunny 16.235
Dunoon 260.2
Dunsany 16.225
Dunsinane 247.6
Duns Scotus
310.66
Dunstable 228.16
Dunstan 261
dunt 419
duo 12
duodecimal
228.52.1
duodenal 228.59
duodenary
16.274.25
duodenitis 300.62.3
duodenum 242
duologue 185
duomo 12.49
duotone 257.3
dup 279
dupe 280
dupery 16.274
duple 228
duplet 371
duplex 496
duplicate 367.5.1
duplicate 371.9.1
duplication
261.67.5
duplicator 17.338.2
duplicity 16.333.28
dupondius 310.2
durable 228.16.34
dura mater 17.338
duramen 248.2
durance 321.19
Durango 12.35
duration 261.67.21
durative 485.15.9
Durban 261.9
durbar 1
duress 296
Durex 496
durgah 1
Durham 242

durian 261.3.24
during 265.56
durmast 431
duro 12.66
Duroc 40
durra 17.278
durst 434
durum 242
dusk 60
dusky 16.42
Düsseldorf 166
dust 443
dustbin 252
dustcart 366
duster 17.388
dustman 261
dustpan 245
dustsheet 370
dusty 16.368
Dutch 72
Dutchman 261
duteous 310.2
dutiable 228.16.2
dutiful 226
duty 16.343
duvet 2
duvetyn 251.11
dux 502
dvandva 1
Dvořák 32
dwale 214
dwarf 166
dwarfism 242.35.7
dwell 215
dweller 17.163
dwelling 265.28
dwelt 402
dwindle 228.40
dyad 83.2
dyadic 38.7
Dyak 32
dye 7
dyed 92
dyeing 265.3
dyeline 253
dyer 17.4
dyestuff 168
dyewood 101
Dyfed 86
dying 265.3
dyke 39
Dylan 261.41
dynamic 38.24
dynamics 498.2
dynamism 242.35

dynamite 372
dynamo 12
dynamometer
17.342.3.2
dynamometry
16.285.2
dynamotor 17.347
dynast 445
dynastic 38.68
dynasty 16
dyne 253
dynode 98
dysentery
16.274.48
dysfunction 261.80
dysgenics 498.3
dysgraphia 17.3.10
dyslectic 38.60
dyslexia 17.3.57
dyslexic 38
dysmenorrhoea
17.2.2
dyspepsia 17.3
dyspeptic 38.65
dysphagia 17.3.12
dysphasia 17.3.59
dysphemism
242.35
dysphonia 17.3.36
dysphoria 17.3.41
dysplasia 17.3.59
dyspnoea 17.2
dysteleology
16.108.4.1
dystopia 17.3.37
dystrophia 17.3.11
dystrophy 16.90.3
dysuria 17.3.42
dytiscid 91.29
Dzongka 17.45
Dzungaria 17.3.38

E

each 66
eager 17.128
eagerness 300.26
eagle 228.45
eaglet 371
eaglewood 101
eagre 17.125

ealdorman 261.52
Ealing 265.29
ear 6
earache 34
earbash 349
eardrop 276
eardrops 329
eardrum 240
eared 90
earflap 268
earful 226
Earhart 366
earing 265.53
earl 216
earldom 242
earliness 300.23
early 16.116
earmark 33
earmuff 168
earn 249
earner 17.229
earnest 436
earnestness 300
earnings 552
Earp 272
earphone 257
earpiece 298
earplug 189
earring 265.53
earshot 373
earth 456
earthborn 255
earthbound 139
earthen 261
earthenware 4
earthling 265
earthly 16.204
earthquake 34
earthshaking 265.6
earthstar 1
earthwork 36
earthworm 233
earthy 16
earwax 494
earwig 184
ease 513
easeful 226
easel 228
easiness 300.23
east 435
East Anglia 17.3
eastbound 139
Eastbourne 255
Easter 17.383
easterly 16.131

eastern 261
Easterner 17.239
easternmost 441
Eastertide 92.11
East Kilbride 92
Eastleigh 5
eastward 103
eastwards 531
easy 16.395
easy-going 265.4
eat 370
eatable 228.16.48
eatage 197
eaten 261.98
eater 17.341
eats 338
eau de Javelle 215
eau de nil 217.1
eau de vie 5
eaves 553
eavesdrop 276
eavesdropper
17.255
ebb 21
ebbed 104
Ebbw Vale 214
Ebenezer 17.440
ebon 261
ebonize 516.7
ebony 16.237
Eboracum 242
ebullience 321
ebullient 420
ebullition 261.71.3
eburnation
261.67.19
ecad 83
écarté 2.23
Ecbatana 17.239
ecbolic 38.22
eccentric 38.47
eccentricity
16.333.28
ecchymosis 300.55
Eccles 539
ecclesia 17.3.60
Ecclesiastes 513.18
ecclesiastic 38.68.1
ecclesiastical
228.23
ecclesiasticism
242.35.16.6
ecclesiolatry
16.286.2.1

ecclesiology
16.108.4.1
eccrine 253
ecdysiast 430.1
ecdysis 300.52
ecdysone 257
ecesis 300.51
echelon 254.7
echeveria 17.3.39
echidna 17.241
echinate 367.17
echinoid 97
echinus 310.34
echo 12.9
echoic 38.2
echoism 242.35.3
echolalia 17.3.18
echopraxia 17.3.56
echovirus 310.47
éclair 4
eclampsia 17.3
éclat 1
eclectic 38.60
eclipse 327
ecliptic 38.66
eclogite 372
eclogue 185
eclosion 261.92
ecocide 92.8
ecological 228.23.5
ecology 16.108.4
econometrics
498.10
economic 38.29.1
economical
228.23.9
economics 498
economist 436.10
economize 516.5
economy 16.222.3
écorché 2
ecospecies 513
ecosphere 6.1
écossaise 509
ecosystem 242
ecotone 257.3
ecotype 275.1
écraseur 3
ecru 15
ecstasy 16.307
ecstatic 38.49
ecstatics 498.11
ecthyma 17.211
ectoderm 233
ectomorph 166.1

ectomorphic 38.14
ectopia 17.3.37
ectopic 38.37
ectoplasm 242.34
ectoproct 388
ectosarc 33
ectype 275
Ecuador 9.4
ecumenical
228.23.11
eczema 17.211
eczematous 310.68
edacious 310.56.2
Edam 229
edaphic 38.11
Edda 17.80
eddo 12
eddy 16.60
Eddystone 261.107
Ede 17.79
edelweiss 301
Eden 261.23
edentate 367.32
edentulous 310.25
Edgar 17
edge 194
Edgehill 218
edgeways 509
edging 265
edgy 16.101
edh 474
edible 228.16.14
edict 387
edifice 300
edify 7.3
Edinburgh 17.279
Edison 261.65
edit 371.12
edition 261.71.1
editio princeps 324
editor 17.342.1
editorial 228.3.12.1
editorialize
516.3.2.2
Edmonton 261
Edmund 143
Edmunds 534
Edom 242
educable 228.16
educate 367
educated 91.34
education 261.67
educational
228.63.3

educationalist
436.7.5
educative 485.15
educator 17.338
educatory
16.274.43
educe 309
educt 389
eduction 261.79
edulcorate 367.23
Edward 103
Edwardian 261.3
Edwin 252
eel 217
eelgrass 294
eelpout 377
e'er 4
eerie 16.265
eff 160
effable 228.16
efface 295.3
effaceable
228.16.36
effect 385.1
effective 485.17
effectively 16.206
effectiveness
300.43
effector 17.354
effectual 228.9.5
effectually 16.131.1
effectuate 367.2
effeminate 371.24
effendi 16.78
efferent 420.65
effervesce 296
effervescence
321.21
effervescent
420.67.3
effete 370
efficacious 310.56.1
efficacy 16.307.1
efficiency 16.312.5
efficient 420.74
effigial 228.3.3
effigy 16.103
effloresce 296
efflorescence
321.21
effluence 321.3
effluent 420.4
effluvium 242.2
efflux 502
effort 381

effortless 300
effortlessness
  300.33
effrontery 16.274
effulgent 420.21
effuse 309, 523
effusion 261.93
effusive 485.8
eft 397
egad 83
egalitarian
  261.3.21.2
Egbert 381
Egeria 17.3.39
egest 433
egesta 17.382
egg 181
eggbeater 17.341
egger 17.126
egghead 86
eggnog 185
eggplant 408
eggshell 215
Egham 242
eglantine 253
Egmont 414
ego 12.28
egocentric 38.47
egocentrism 242.35
egoism 242.35.3
egoist 436
egoistic 38.70
egomania 17.3.31.1
egomaniac 32.1
egotism 242.35.20
egotist 436.26
egotistic 38.70.6
egotistical
  228.23.24
egregious 310
egress 296
egret 371
Egypt 424
Egyptian 261.85
Egyptology
  16.108.4.17
eh 2
eider 17.84
eiderdown 258
eidetic 38.50
eidolon 254
Eiffel 228
eigenfrequency
  16.312
Eiger 17.130

eight 367
eighteen 251
eighteenth 469
eightfold 120
eightieth 458
eightsome 242
eighty 16.329
Eilat 366
Eindhoven 261.116
einkorn 255
Einstein 253
Eire 17.271
Eisenhower 14
Eisenstein 253
eisteddfod 103.2
either 17.406
ejaculate 367.13,
  371.17.1
ejaculation
  261.67.13
eject 385
ejecta 17.354
ejection 261.77
ejective 485.17
ejector 17.354
eke 37
ekistics 498
elaborate 367.23,
  371.35.1
Elaine 247
El Alamein 247.5
Elam 242
élan 266
eland 143.1
elapid 91
elapse 322
elasmosaur 9.11
elastic 38.68
elasticate 367.5.2
elasticity
  16.333.28.2
elastomer 17.218
Elastoplast 431
elate 367.12
elater 17.352
elaterid 91.27
elaterium 242.2.15
elation 261.67.12
elative 485.15
Elba 17.22
elbow 12
elbowroom 241
Elbrus 309
El Cid 91
elder 17.93

elderberry 16.274
elderly 16.131
eldest 436
El Dorado 12.16
eldritch 67
Eleanor 17.231
Eleatic 38.49
elecampane 247.7
elect 385.4
election 261.77.2
electioneer 6.5
electioneering
  265.53
elective 485.17
elector 17.354
electoral 228.76.3
electorate 371.35
Electra 17.295
electret 381
electric 38
electrical 228.23
electrician 261.71
electricity
  16.333.28
electrification
  261.67.5.1
electrify 7.3
electroanalysis
  300.52.1
electrocardiogram
  229.1.1
electrocardiograph
  158.1.1
electrocardiography
  16.90.2.1
electrocute 380.3
electrocution
  261.75.2
electrode 98
electrodialysis
  300.52.1
electrodynamics
  498.2
electroencephalo-
  gram 229.1
electroencephalo-
  graph 158.1
electroform 238.2
electrograph
  158.1.3
electrolyse 516.3
electrolysis
  300.52.2
electrolyte 372.4
electrolytic 38.52.1

electromagnet 371
electromagnetic
  38.50
electromagnetism
  242.35.18
electrometallurgy
  16.108.2
electrometer
  17.342.3.5
electromotive
  485.14
electron 254
electronic 38.35
electronics 498.5
electronvolt 405
electrophoresis
  300.51.1
electrophorus
  310.50
electroplate 367
electropositive
  485.12.1
electroscope
  278.1.2
electrostatic
  38.49.7
electrostatics
  498.11
electrosurgery
  16.274.13
electrotype 275.1
electrovalency
  16.312
electrum 242.22
electuary 16.274.2
eleemosynary
  16.274.26
elegance 321
elegant 420.17
elegiac 46
elegize 516.1
elegy 16.103
element 420.31
elemental
  228.110.2
elementary
  16.274.47
elemi 16.216
elenctic 38
elephant 420
elephantiasis
  300.57.1
elephantine 253.9
Eleusis 300.56
elevate 367.36

elevated 91.34
elevation 261.67
elevator 17.338.11
eleven 261.112
elevenses 515
eleventh 471.1
elevon 254
elf 172
El Faiyum 241
elfish 353.3
elflock 40
Elgar 1
Elgin 252
El Greco 12.9
Eli 7
Elia 17.3.20
Elias 310.3
elicit 371.36
elide 92.2
eligible 228.16.20.1
Elijah 17.151
eliminate 367.17
elimination
 261.67.18.5
Eliot 381.1
Elis 300
elision 261.91
elite 370
elitism 242.35
elixir 17.427
Elizabeth 464
Elizabethan 261
elk 48
elkhound 139
ell 215
Ellington 261
ellipse 327
ellipsis 300.60
ellipsoid 97
elliptic 38.66
elliptical 228.23
Ellis 300
elm 243
El Mansura 17.277
El Misti 5
El Obeid 85
elocution 261.75.2
elongate 367
elongation 261.67
elope 278.2
eloquence 321
eloquent 420.59
El Paso 12.68
El Salvador 9.4
elsewhere 4

Elsinore 9
elucidate 367.8
elucidation
 261.67.7
elude 102
eluent 420.5
elusive 485.8
elute 380
eluvium 242.2
elver 17.421
elvish 353
Ely 16.118
Elysian 261.3.35
Elysium 242.2
elytron 254
em 232
'em 242
emaciate 367.1.4
emaciation
 261.67.1.3
emanate 367.18
emanation
 261.67.19
emancipate 367.19
emancipation
 261.67.20
emasculate 367.13
emasculation
 261.67.13
embalm 230
embalmer 17.206
embank 51
embankment 420
embargo 12.26
embark 33
embarkation
 261.67.4
embarrass 310.43
embarrassing 265
embarrassment
 420.46
embassy 16.307
embattle 228.97
embed 86
embellish 353.4
embellishment
 420.47
ember 17.24
embezzle 228
embezzlement
 420.40
embitter 17.342
emblazon 261.124
emblem 242
emblematic 38.49.2

emblematize
 516.13
embodiment
 420.31
embody 16.65
embolden 261.28
embolic 38.22
embolism
 242.35.11
embolus 310.26
emboly 16.131
emboss 302
embouchure 10
embowel 228.8
embower 14
embrace 295
embraceor 17.299
embracery
 16.274.33
embranchment 420
embrasure 17.332
embrectomy
 16.222.5
embrocate 367.6
embrocation
 261.67.6
embroider 17.87
embroidery 16.274
embroil 222
embryo 12.3
embryogeny
 16.229.2
embryology
 16.108.4.1
embryonic 38.35.1
embus 307
emcee 5
emend 131
emendation
 261.67.9
emerald 122
emerge 195
emergence 321
emergency
 16.312.3
emergent 420.19
emeritus 310.64
emersion 261.69
Emerson 261
emery 16.274
emesis 300.52.3
emetic 38.50
emigrant 420
emigrate 367.26

emigration
 261.67.24
émigré 2
eminence 321.14
eminent 420.53
emir 6
emirate 371.32
emissary 16.274.36
emission 261.71
emit 371.19
emitter 17.342.2
Emmanuel 228.9.2
Emmen 261
emmenagogue
 185.2
Emmenthal 213
emmer 17.208
emmet 371
Emmy 16.213
emollient 420
emolument 420.34
emote 376
emotion 261.73
emotional 228.63.6
emotionalism
 242.35.11.5
emotive 485.14
empanel 228.55
empathetic 38.50.6
empathic 38.72
empathize 516.14
empathy 16.373
empennage 197.6
emperor 17.279
empery 16.274.31
emphasis 300.57
emphasize 516.11
emphatic 38.49
emphatically
 16.142
emphysema 17.210
empire 8
empiric 38.40
empirical 228.23.16
empiricism
 242.35.16.3
emplace 295
emplacement
 420.44
emplane 247
employ 11
employable
 228.16.4
employee 5
employer 17.5

employment
420.33
empoison 261.128
emporium 242.2.17
empower 14
empress 300
empt 428
emptiness 300.23
empty 16
empty-handed
91.12
empyema 17.210
empyrean 261.2
empyreuma 17.217
emu 15
emulate 367.13
emulation
261.67.13
emulous 310.25
emulsify 7.3.7
emulsion 261
emulsoid 97
emunctory 16.274
en 248
enable 228.11
enact 382
enactment 420
enamel 228.51
enamour 17.205
enamoured 103
enantiomorph
166.1
enarthrosis 300.55
enate 367
encage 193
encamp 285
encampment 420
encapsulate 367.13
encase 295
encash 349
enceinte 407
Enceladus 310.17
encephalic 38.19
encephalin 252.11
encephalitis 300.62
encephalogram
229.1
encephalography
16.90.2.2
encephaloma
17.215
encephalon 254.7
enchain 247
enchant 408
enchanted 91

enchanting 265.72
enchantment 420
enchantress 300
enchase 295
enchilada 17.78
enchorial 228.3.12
encipher 17.115
encircle 228.22
enclasp 290
enclave 482
enclitic 38.52
enclose 520
enclosure 17.335
encode 98
encoder 17.88
encomiast 430.1
encomium 242.2.9
encompass 310.42
encore 9
encounter 17.372
encourage 197.10
encouragement
420.37
encrinite 372.5
encroach 70
encrust 443
encumber 17.27
encumbrance 321
encumbrancer
17.318
encyclical 228.23
encyclopedia
17.3.8
encyclopedic 38.8
encyclopedist 436
encyst 436
end 131
endamage 197
endanger 17.156
endarch 33
endbrain 247
endear 6
endearing 265.53
endearment 420.30
endeavour 17.411
endemic 38.25
endermic 38.26
endgame 231
ending 265.20
endive 486
endless 300
endlong 266
endmost 441
endocardial 228.3
endocardium 242.2

endocarp 269
endocentric 38.47
endocranium
242.2.10
endocrine 253
endoderm 233
endodermis 300.18
endodontics 498
endoergic 38.16
endogamy 16.222.2
endogenous 310.33
endolymph 176
endometriosis
300.55.1
endometrium 242.2
endomorph 166.1
endomorphic 38.14
endomorphism
242.35.7
endoplasm 242.34
endorse 303
endorsee 5.21
endorsement
420.45
endoscope 278.1
endoscopy 16.254.2
endoskeleton
261.99
endosome 239
endosperm 233
endospore 9.10
endosteum 242.2
endothelium
242.2.5
endothermic 38.26
endow 13
endowment 420
endpaper 17.249
endplate 367
endplay 2
endue 15
endurable
228.16.34
endurance 321.19
endure 10
enduring 265.56
endways 509
Endymion 261.3.14
enema 17.211
enemy 16.222
energetic 38.50.3
energetics 498.12
energize 516.1
energumen 248.3
energy 16.108

enervate 367,
371.37
enervate 371.37
Enesco 12.14
enfeeble 228
enfeoff 162
Enfield 115
enfilade 85
enfold 120
enforce 303.2
enforcement
420.45
enfranchise 516
Engadine 251.1
engage 193
engaged 108
engagement 420
engaging 265.24
engender 17.101
engine 252
engineer 6.4
engineering 265.53
England 143
English 353
Englishism 242.35
Englishman 261
englut 378
engorge 200
engraft 396
engrail 214
engram 229
engrave 482
engraver 17.410
engraving 265.77
engross 305
engulf 174
enhance 315
enhancer 17.313
enharmonic 38.35
Enid 91.20
enigma 17.222
enigmatic 38.49.3
Eniwetok 40
enjambment 420
enjoin 256
enjoy 11
enjoyable 228.16.4
enjoyment 420.33
enkindle 228.40
enlace 295
enlarge 192
enlargement 420
enlarger 17.145
enlighten 261.100

enlightenment 420.42
enlist 436
enliven 261.115
en masse 293
enmesh 351
enmity 16.333
ennage 197.6
ennead 83.1
Ennis 300
Enniskillen 252.8
Ennius 310.2
ennoble 228.13
ennui 5
Enoch 40
enol 220
enormity 16.333.13
enormous 310
enough 168
enounce 319
enquire 8
enquirer 17.274
enquiry 16.267
enrage 193
enrapture 17.72
enrich 67
enrichment 420
enrobe 28
enrol 223
enrolment 420
enroot 380
en route 380
ens 546
ensconce 318
ensemble 228
enshrine 253
enshroud 99
ensign 253
ensilage 197.1
ensile 219.3
enslave 482
ensnare 4
ensphere 6
ensue 15
ensure 10.2
enswathe 473
enswathed 144
entablement 420.40
entail 214
entamoeba 17.13
entangle 228.49
entanglement 420.40
entasis 300.57
Entebbe 16.8

entelechy 16.25
entellus 310.22
enter 17.368
enteral 228.76
enteric 38.39
enteritis 300.62.5
enterogastrone 257
enterokinase 509
enteron 254.11
enterotomy 16.222.4
enterprise 516.9
enterprising 265.82
entertain 247.10
entertainer 17.227
entertaining 265.40
entertainment 420.41
enthetic 38.50
enthral 221
enthralling 265.31
enthrone 257
enthuse 523
enthusiasm 242.34
enthusiast 430.1
enthusiastic 38.68.1
entice 301
enticement 420
entire 8
entirety 16.333
entitle 228.103
entitlement 420.40
entity 16.333.32
entomb 241
entomic 38.29
entomologize 516.1
entomology 16.108.4
entopic 38.37
entourage 359
entozoic 38.2
entozoon 254.2
entr'acte 382
entrails 536
entrain 247
entrammel 228.51
entrance 315, 321
entrant 420
entrap 268
entreat 370
entreaty 16.332
entrée 2
entrench 79
entrenchment 420

entrepreneur 3
entrepreneurial 228.3
entresol 220
entropy 16.254
entrust 443
entry 16.288
entwine 253
enucleate 367.1
enumerate 367.23
enumeration 261.67.22
enumerator 17.338.9
enunciate 367.1
enunciation 261.67.1.4
enuresis 300.51
envelop 281.1
envelope 278
envenom 242
envenomed 127
enviable 228.16.2
envious 310.2
environ 261.58
environment 420.42
environmental 228.110.4
environmentalism 242.35.11.6
environmentalist 436.7.7
environs 551
envisage 197
envision 261.91
envoy 11
envy 16
enwind 135
enwomb 241
enwrap 268
enwreath 475
Enzed 86
enzootic 38.53
enzyme 236
enzymology 16.108.4
eobiont 420.2
Eocene 251.9
eohippus 310.37
eolith 458
Eolithic 38.73
eonism 242.35.14
Eos 302
eosin 252

eosinophil 218.1
Eozoic 38.2
Epaminondas 293
eparch 33
eparchy 16.20
epaulet 368
épée 2
épéeist 436.1
epeiric 38
epeirogeny 16.229.2
epenthesis 300.52
epergne 249
ephah 17.113
ephebe 23
ephedrine 252
ephemera 17.279.1
ephemeral 228.76.2
ephemerality 16.333.8.9
ephemerid 91.27
ephemeris 300.47
ephemeron 254.11
Ephesian 261.90
Ephesus 310.53
ephod 94
ephor 9
Ephraim 235
epiboly 16.131
epic 38
epicardium 242.2
epicarp 269
epicene 251.8
epicentre 17.368.1
epiclesis 300.51
epicrisis 300.53
Epictetus 310.63
epicure 10.3
epicurean 261.2
Epicurus 310.49
epicycloid 97
Epidaurus 310.48
epidemic 38.25
epidemiology 16.108.4.1
epidermis 300.18
epidiascope 278.1.1
epididymis 300.19
epidote 376
epidural 228.75
epigastrium 242.2
epigeal 228.2
epigene 251
epigenous 310.33
epiglottis 300

epigram 229
epigrammatic 38.49.2
epigrammatize 516.13.1
epigraph 158
epigraphic 38.11
epigraphy 16.90
epilepsy 16.313
epileptic 38.65
epileptoid 97
epilimnion 261.3
epilogue 185
epimere 6.2
epinasty 16.361
epiphany 16.237.2
epiphragm 229
epiphysis 300.52
epiphyte 372
Epirus 310.47
episcopacy 16.307
episcopal 228
episcopalian 261.3.8
episcopate 371.30
episcope 278
episematic 38.49.1
episiotomy 16.222.4.1
episode 98
episodic 38.9
epispastic 38.68
epistaxis 300.70
epistemic 38.27
epistemology 16.108.4.9
episternum 242.13
epistle 228.85
epistolary 16.274.19
epistoler 17.176
epistrophe 16.90.3
epistyle 219
epitaph 158
epitaphic 38.11
epitaxial 228.3.18
epitaxy 16.386
epithelium 242.2.5
epithet 368
epitome 16.222
epitomize 516.5
epizoic 38.2
epizootic 38.53
epoch 40
epode 98

eponym 235
eponymous 310.28.2
eponymy 16.216
épopée 5.16
epopoeia 17.2.1
epos 302
epoxide 92.14
epoxy 16.389
Epping 265
epsilon 254.6
Epsom 242
Epstein 253
epyllion 261.3.11
equable 228.16
equal 228.71
equality 16.333.10
equalize 516.3
equalizer 17.441
equally 16.131
equanimity 16.333.12
equate 367.20
equation 261
equator 17.338
equatorial 228.3.12.2
equerry 16.262
equestrian 261.3
equestrienne 248.1
equiangular 17.174
equidistant 420.81
equilateral 228.76
equilibrate 367.24
equilibration 261.67.23
equilibrist 436
equilibrium 242.2
equine 253
equinoctial 228
equinox 499
equip 274
equipage 197.8
equipartition 261.71
equipment 420.43
equipoise 519
equipollent 420
equiponderate 367.23
equisetum 242.28
equitable 228.16.49
equitant 420.76
equitation 261.67.27

equites 513
equities 515
equity 16.333
equivalence 321.12
equivalent 420.28
equivocal 228.28
equivocate 367.6
equivocation 261.67.6
Equuleus 310.2
era 17.272
eradicable 228.16.10
eradicate 367.5
eradication 261.67.5
erasable 228.16
erase 509
eraser 17.439
Erasmus 310
Erastianism 242.35.14.1
erasure 17.332
Erbil 218
erbium 242.2
ere 4
Erebus 310.5
Erechtheion 261.3
Erechtheum 242.2
erect 385
erectile 219.5
erection 261.77.3
erector 17.354
eremite 372
erethism 242.35
erg 182
ergo 12
ergonomics 498
ergosterol 220.4
ergot 381
ergotism 242.35.20
Eric 38.39
Erica 17.34.2
ericaceous 310.56.1
Eridanus 310.36
Erie 16.265
erigeron 261.60
Erin 252
erinaceous 310.56.4
Eris 300
eristic 38.70
Eritrea 17.1
erk 36
erlking 265
Ermanaric 38.44

ermine 252.13
erne 249
Ernie 16.227
erode 98
erogeneity 16.333.1
erogenous 310.33
Eros 302
erose 305
erosion 261.92
erosive 485.6
erotema 17.210
erotesis 300.51
erotic 38.53
erotica 17.34
eroticism 242.35.16.5
erotogenic 38.32.1
erotology 16.108.4.15
erotomania 17.3.31.1
err 3
errancy 16.312
errand 143
errant 420.61
errantry 16.291
errata 17.337
erratic 38.49
erratum 242.26
Er Rif 163
erroneous 310.2.9
error 17.269
ersatz 333
Erse 297
erstwhile 219
erubescence 321.21
eruct 389
eructation 261.67
erudite 372
erudition 261.71
erumpent 420
erupt 426
eruption 261.88
eruptive 485
Erymanthus 310.72
eryngo 12.36
erysipelas 310.23
erysipeloid 97.5
erythema 17.210
erythrism 242.35
erythrite 372
erythroblast 430
erythrocyte 372.10
erythrocytic 38.52.3

erythropoiesis
300.51
Esau 9
escadrille 218
escalade 85
escalate 367.14
escalation
261.67.14
escalator 17.338
escallonia 17.3.36.2
escalope 276
escapade 85
escape 270
escapee 5.15
escapement 420
escapism 242.35
escapist 436.14
escapology
16.108.4.12
escarp 269
escarpment 420
eschalot 373.1
eschar 1
eschatology
16.108.4.15
escheat 370
eschew 15
escolar 1.9
Escorial 213
escort 374
escritoire 1
escrow 12
escudo 12.22
esculent 420.27
escutcheon 261
Esdraelon 254
esemplastic 38.68
Esher 17.325
Eskimo 12.48
esoteric 38.39
espadrille 218
esparto 12.73
especial 228
especially 16.131
Esperanto 12.83
espial 228.4
espionage 359
Espiritu Santo
12.83
esplanade 85.3
espousal 228.129
espouse 521
esprit 5
esprit de corps 9.2
espy 7

esquire 8
essay 2
essayist 436.1
essence 321.21
Essene 251
essential 228.96
Essequibo 12.5
Essex 498
establish 353
establishment
420.47
estancia 17.3.48
estate 367
esteem 234
ester 17.382
esterify 7.3.5
Esther 17.382
estimable 228.16
estimate 367.15,
371.19
estimation
261.67.15
Estonian 261.3.18
estop 276
estoppel 228.68
estovers 524
estrade 84
estragon 254.5
estrange 207
estranged 111
estrangement
420.38
estray 2
estreat 370
estuarial 228.3.10
estuarine 253.7
estuary 16.274.2
esurient 420.1.3
eta 17.338
etaerio 12.3
etalon 254.7
etamin 252.15
et cetera 17.293
etch 64
etchant 420
etching 265
eternal 228.58
eternity
16.333.16.1
etesian 261.3
ethane 247
ethanol 220
Ethelbert 381
Ethelred 86
ether 17

ethereal 228.3.11
etherealize
516.3.2.1
ethic 38
ethical 228.23
ethics 498
Ethiopia 17.3.37
Ethiopian 261.3.19
Ethiopic 38.37
ethmoid 97
ethnarch 33
ethnic 38
ethnocentrism
242.35
ethnogeny 16.229.2
ethnography
16.90.2
ethnology 16.108.4
ethology 16.108.4
ethonone 257
ethos 302
ethoxide 92.14
ethyl 218
ethylate 367.12
ethylene 251.2
ethylic 38.21
etiquette 368.4
Etna 17.244
Eton 261.98
Etonian 261.3.18
Etruria 17.3.42
Etruscan 261.17
étude 102
étui 5
etymology
16.108.4.9
etymon 254
Etzel 228
Euboea 17.2
eucalyptol 220
eucalyptus 310.71
eucharis 300.47
Eucharist 436.20
euchlorine 251.6
euchre 17.41
Euclid 91
eudemon 261.47
eudemonia 17.3.36
eudemonics 498.5
eudemonism
242.35.14
eudiometer
17.342.3.1
eugenic 38.32
eugenics 498.3

eugenol 220.3
euglena 17.230
euhemerism
242.35.15
eulogistic 38.70.1
eulogize 516.1
eulogy 16.108
Eumenides 513.4
eunuch 46
euonymus 310.28.2
eupatorium
242.2.17
eupatrid 91
eupepsia 17.3
euphausiid 91.2
euphemism 242.35
euphemistic
38.70.3
euphemize 516.4
euphonic 38.35
euphonious 310.2.9
euphonium
242.2.12
euphonize 516.7
euphony 16.237
euphorbia 17.3
euphoria 17.3.41
euphoric 38.41
euphotic 38.55
euphrasy 16.307
Euphrates 513.15
Euphrosyne 5.12
euphuism 242.35.4
euplastic 38.68
euploid 97
eupnoea 17.2
Eurasia 17.322
Eurasian 261.67.21
eureka 17.33
eurhythmic 38.30
eurhythmics 498
Euripides 513.4
Eurocommunism
242.35
Eurocrat 365.2
Eurodollar 17.168
Euromarket 371.7
Europa 17.257
Europe 281
European 261.2
Europeanize 516.7
europium 242.2.13
Eurovision
261.91.3
Eurus 310.49

Eurydice 16.300
eurypterid 91.27
eurytropic 38.37
Eusebius 310.2
eustatic 38.49
eutectic 38.60
Euterpe 16.246
euthanasia 17.3.59
euthenics 498.3
eutherian 261.3.22
eutrophic 38.13
evacuant 420.4
evacuate 367.2
evacuation
   261.67.2
evacuee 5
evade 85
evaginate 367.17.2
evaluate 367.2
evaluation 261.67.2
evanesce 296.3
evanescent
   420.67.2
evangelical
   228.23.6
evangelism
   242.35.9
evangelist 436.5
evangelistic 38.70
evangelize 516.2
Evans 551
evaporate 367.23
evaporation
   261.67.22
evaporite 372.8
evasion 261
evasive 485
eve 484
Eve 484
evection 261.77
Evelyn 252
even 261.113
evening 265
evenness 300.31
evens 551
evensong 266
event 410.3
eventful 226.11
eventide 92.12
eventual 228.9
eventuality
   16.333.8.2
eventually 16.131.1
eventuate 367.2
ever 17.411

Everest 436.20
evergreen 251
everlasting 265.74
evermore 9.9
evert 369.1
evertor 17.340
every 16.274
everybody 16.65
everyday 2
Everyman 261.48
everyone 259
everything 265
everywhere 4.7
Evesham 242
evict 387
eviction 261.78
evidence 321.5
evident 420.10
evidential 228.96.1
evidently 16.198
evil 228.119
evildoer 17.8
evilness 300.30
evince 317
eviscerate 367.23
evocation 261.67.6
evocative 485.15.2
evocator 17.338
evoke 42
evolute 380.1
evolution 261.75.1
evolutionary
   16.274.29
evolutionist 436.13
evolve 493
evzone 257
ewe 15
ewer 17.8
ex 496
exacerbate 367.4
exacerbation
   261.67.3
exact 382
exacting 265.70
exaction 261.76
exactitude 102.2
exactly 16.194
exactness 300
exaggerate 367.23
exaggerated
   91.34.7
exaggeration
   261.67.22
exalt 404
exaltation 261.67

exalted 91.44
exam 229
examen 248.2
examination
   261.67.18.3
examine 252.12
examinee 5.12
examiner 17.231.1
example 228.70
exanthema 17.210
exarate 367.23
exarch 33
exasperate 367.23
exasperation
   261.67.22
Excalibur 17.14
ex cathedra 17.286
excavate 367,
   367.37
excavation 261.67
excavator 17.338
exceed 89
exceeding 265.13
exceedingly 16.175
excel 215
excellence 321.12
Excellency 16.312
excellent 420.28
excelsior 9.1
except 422
excepting 265
exception 261.84
exceptional 228.63
exceptive 485.23
excerpt 423
excess 296
excessive 485.2
exchange 207
exchequer 17.31
excipient 420.1
excise 516
exciseman 261
excision 261.91
excitable 228.16.50
excitant 420
excitation
   261.67.27
excite 372
excited 91.39
excitement 420
exciter 17.343
exciting 265.67
excitor 17.343
exclaim 231

exclamation
   261.67.16
exclamatory
   16.274.43.5
exclave 482
exclosure 17.335
exclude 102
exclusion 261.93
exclusionist 436.13
exclusive 485.8
excogitate 367.30
excommunicate
   367.5
excommunication
   261.67.5
excoriate 367.1
excrement 420.31
excrescence 321.21
excrescent 420.67
excreta 17.341
excrete 370
excretion 261.70
excruciate 367.1
excruciating 265.64
exculpate 367
excurrent 420.64
excursion 261.69
excursionist 436.13
excursive 485.3
excursus 310
excusable
   228.16.65
excusatory
   16.274.43
excuse 309, 523
exeat 381.1
execrable 228.16
execrate 367.25
executant 420
execute 380
execution 261.75
executioner 17.239
executive 485
executor 17.350
executory
   16.274.42
executrix 498
exegesis 300.51
exegete 370
exegetic 38.50
exegetics 498.12
exemplar 17.196
exemplary 16.274
exemplify 7.3
exemplum 242

exempt 428
exemption 261
exenterate 367.23
exequatur 17.338
exequies 515
exercise 516.11
exerciser 17.441
exergue 182
exert 369
exertion 261.69
Exeter 17.342
exeunt 419
exfoliate 367.1.3
ex gratia 17.322
exhalant 420.25
exhalation
261.67.14
exhale 214
exhaust 439
exhaustible 228.16
exhaustion 261
exhaustive 485
exhibit 371.5
exhibition 261.71
exhibitioner
17.239.2
exhibitionism
242.35.14
exhibitionist
436.13.5
exhibitive 485.12
exhibitor 17.342
exhilarant 420.65
exhilarate 367.23
exhilaration
261.67.22
exhort 374
exhortation 261.67
exhumation 261.67
exhume 241
exigency 16.312
exigent 420.20
exigible 228.16.20
exiguous 310.4
exile 219
exist 436
existence 321.27
existent 420.81
existential 228.96
existentialism
242.35.11
existentialist 436.7
exit 371
exitance 321.24
ex libris 300

Exmoor 10
exocentric 38.47
exocrine 253
exodontics 498
exodus 310.17
exoergic 38.16
ex officio 12.3
exogamy 16.222.2
exonerate 367.23
exonym 235
exophthalmos 302
exorbitant 420.76
exorcise 516
exorcism 242.35
exorcist 436
exordium 242.2
exoskeleton 261.99
exosphere 6.1
exospore 9.10
exoteric 38.39
exothermic 38.26
exotic 38.53
exotica 17.34
expand 128
expandable
228.16.17
expander 17.98
expanse 314
expansible 228.16
expansile 219
expansion 261.81
expansionism
242.35.14
expansive 485
ex parte 16.328
expatiate 367.1.5
expatiation
261.67.1
expatriate 367.1,
371.1
expatriation
261.67.1
expect 385
expectable 228.16
expectancy 16.312
expectant 420.79
expectation 261.67
expecting 265.71
expectorant 420.65
expectorate 367.23
expectoration
261.67.22
expediency
16.312.1
expedient 420.1.1

expediential 228.96
expedite 372.1
expedition 261.71.1
expeditionary
16.274.29.3
expeditious
310.58.1
expel 215
expellant 420.26
expend 131
expendable
228.16.18
expenditure 17.56
expense 316
expensive 485.9
experience 321.1
experiential 228.96
experiment 410.1,
420.31.2
experimental
228.110.2
experimentalism
242.35.11.6
experimentation
261.67.32.1
expert 369
expertise 513
expiable 228.16.2
expiate 367.1
expiation 261.67.1
expiration 261.67
expiratory
16.274.43
expire 8
expiry 16.267
explain 247
explainable
228.16.27
explanation
261.67.19
explanatory
16.274.43
explant 408
expletive 485
explicable
228.16.10
explicate 367.5
explication
261.67.5
explicative
485.15.1
explicit 371.36
explode 98
exploit 375
exploitation 261.67

exploration
261.67.22
exploratory
16.274.43.7
explore 9
explorer 17.276
explosion 261.92
explosive 485.6
explosiveness
300.43
exponent 420.54
exponential 228.96
export 374
exportation 261.67
exporter 17.345
exposé 2.31
expose 520
exposed 155
exposition 261.71.9
expositor 17.342.5
expository
16.274.41
expostulate 367.13
expostulation
261.67.13
exposure 17.335
expound 139
express 296
expressage 197.11
expressible
228.16.37
expression 261.68
expressionism
242.35.14.4
expressionless
300.14
expressive 485.2
expressivity
16.333.35
expresso 12.69
expressway 2
expropriate 367.1
expulsion 261
expulsive 485
expunge 211
expurgate 367.11
expurgation
261.67.11
exquisite 371.38
exscind 134
exsect 385
exsert 369
exsiccate 367.5
exstrophy 16.90
extant 407

extemporaneous
310.2.6
extempore
16.274.31
extemporize 516.8
extend 131
extender 17.101
extendible
228.16.18
extensible
228.16.40
extension 261.82
extensity 16.333.31
extensive 485.9
extensor 17.314
extent 410
extenuate 367.2
exterior 17.3.39
exteriorize 516.8
exterminate
367.17.4
extermination
261.67.18.4
exterminator
17.338.7
extern 249
external 228.58
externalism
242.35.11.4
externality
16.333.8
externalize 516.3.6
extinct 392
extinction 261
extinctive 485.20
extinguish 353
extinguishable
228.16.43
extinguishant
420.74
extinguisher 17.326
extirpate 367
extol 223
extort 374
extortion 261.72
extortionate
371.28.2
extra 17
extract 382
extraction 261.76
extractive 485.16
extractor 17.353
extracurricular
17.174.6

extraditable
228.16.50
extradite 372.2
extradition
261.71.2
extrados 302
extragalactic 38.58
extramarital
228.102
extramural 228.75
extraneous 310.2.6
extranuclear 17.3
extraordinary
16.274.26
extrapolate 367.14
extrapolation
261.67.14
extrasensory
16.274.38
extraterrestrial
228.3.13
extraterritorial
228.3.12.1
extraterritoriality
16.333.8.1
extrauterine 253.7
extravagance 321.8
extravagant 420.18
extravaganza
17.445
extravasate 367
extravehicular
17.174.6
extreme 234
extremely 16.166
extremism 242.35
extremist 436
extremity 16.333
extricable
228.16.10
extricate 367.5
extrinsic 38
extrorse 303
extroversion
261.69.1
extrovert 369.2
extrude 102
extrusion 261.93
extrusive 485.8
exuberance 321.20
exuberant 420.65
exudation 261.67
exude 102
exult 406
exultant 420

exultation 261.67
exurbia 17.3.2
exuviae 5.2
exuviate 367.1
eyas 310.3
eye 7
eyeball 221
eyebath 453
eyebright 372
eyebrow 13
eyecup 279
eyed 92
eyeful 226
eyeglass 294
eyeglasses 515
eyehole 223
eyelash 349
eyeless 300
eyelet 371
eyelid 91
eyeliner 17.232
eyepiece 298
eyeshade 85
eyeshot 373
eyesight 372
eyesore 9
eyestrain 247
eyetooth 463
eyewash 354
eyewitness 300.38
eyra 17.271
eyrie 16.265
eyrir 6
Ezekiel 228.3

F

fa 1
fab 18
Fabergé 2
Fabian 261.3.1
Fabianism
242.35.14.1
fable 228.11
fabled 122
fabric 38
fabricate 367.5
fabrication
261.67.5
fabulist 436.6
fabulous 310.25

facade 84
face 295
facebar 1
faceless 300
facer 17.299
facet 371
facetiae 5.2
facetious 310.57
facetiousness
300.34
facial 228.91
facies 513.1
facile 219
facilitate 367.30.1
facility 16.333.9
facing 265.59
facsimile 16.120
fact 382
factice 300.65
faction 261.76
factional 228.63
factious 310
factitious 310.58
factitive 485.12
factor 17.353
factorial 228.3.12
factoring 265.58
factorize 516.8
factory 16.274.44
factotum 242.31
factual 228.9.4
facula 17.174.3
facultative 485.15
faculty 16.352
fad 83
faddish 353.1
fade 85
faded 91.6
fadge 191
fading 265.11
faecal 228
faeces 513
Faeroes 520
Faeroese 513.2
faff 157
fag 178
fagaceous 310.56
faggot 381
fahlband 128
Fahrenheit 372
faïence 315
fail 214
failing 265.27
faille 214
failure 17.433

fain 247
fainéant 420.1
faint 409
fainter 17.367
fainting 265
faintly 16.196
faintness 300
fair 4
Fairbanks 504
Fairfax 494
fairground 139
fairing 265.52
fairish 353.9
fairlead 89
fairly 16.117
fairness 300.22
fairway 2
fairy 16.264
fairyland 143.2
Faisal 228
faith 454
faithful 226
faithfulness 300.30
faithless 300
fake 34
faker 17.30
fakir 6
fa-la 1.7
Falange 206
falbala 17.176
falcate 367
falciform 238.1
falcon 261.16
falconer 17.239
falconet 368
falconine 253
falconry 16.284
falderal 212
faldstool 227
Falerii 7.1
Faliscan 261
Falkirk 36
Falkland 143
fall 221
fallacious 310.56.3
fallacy 16.307
fallal 212
fallen 261
faller 17.169
fallibility
  16.333.9.2
fallible 228.16
Fallopian 261.3.19
fallout 377
fallow 12.38

Falmouth 464
false 312
false-card 84
falsehood 101
falsetto 12.75
falsework 36
falsies 515
falsify 7.3
falsity 16.333
falter 17.363
Falun 259
Famagusta 17.388
fame 231
familial 228.3.4
familiar 17.3.21
familiarity
  16.333.20.1
familiarize 516.8
Familist 436.5
family 16.120
famine 252.12
famish 353
famous 310.27
famulus 310.25
fan 245
fanatic 38.49.5
fanatical 228.23.18
fanaticism
  242.35.16.4
fanaticize 516.10
fancied 91
fancier 17.3.48
fanciful 226
fancy 16.309
fancywork 36
fandangle 228.49
fandango 12.35
fanfare 4
fang 263
fanion 261.121
fanjet 368
fankle 228
fanlight 372
fanny 16.223
fanon 261.55
fantail 214
fan-tailed 112
fantasia 17.3.59
fantasize 516.11
fantast 430
fantastic 38.68
fantasy 16.307
Fanti 16.353
fantoccini 16.228
far 1

farad 103
Faraday 2.8
faradic 38.7
faradism 242.35
faradize 516
farandole 223.2
faraway 2.28
farce 294
farci 5
farcical 228.23
farcy 16.295
fardel 228
fare 4
Fareham 242.18
farewell 215
farina 17.230.1
farinaceous
  310.56.4
farinose 305
farl 213
farm 230
farmer 17.206
farmhouse 306
farming 265.35
farmland 143
farmstead 86
farmyard 84
Farnborough
  17.279
Farnham 242
faro 12.62
Farouk 45
farrago 12.26
farrier 17.3
farriery 16.274.1
farrow 12.60
far-sighted 91.39
far-sightedness
  300.28
fart 366
farther 17.401
farthermost 441
farthest 436
farthing 265
farthingale 214
fartlek 35
fasces 513
fascia 17.322
fasciation 261.67.1
fascicle 228.23
fascicule 227.1
fascinate 367.17.7
fascinating
  265.64.1

fascination
  261.67.18.8
fascine 251
fascism 242.35
fascist 436
fash 349
fashion 261.66
fashionable
  228.16.31
Fashoda 17.88
fast 431
fastback 32
fasten 261.61
fastener 17.239
fastening 265.46
fastidious 310.2.1
fastidiousness
  300.34.1
fastness 300.42
fat 365
fatal 228.99
fatalism 242.35.11
fatalist 436.7
fatalistic 38.70.2
fatality 16.333.8
fatback 32
fate 367
fated 91.34
fateful 226.7
Fates 335
fathead 86
father 17.401
fatherhood 101
father-in-law 9
fatherland 143.4
fatherless 300.13
fatherly 16.131
fathom 242
fathomable 228.16
fathomless 300
fatidic 38
fatigue 183
Fatima 17.211
fatling 265
fatness 300
fatso 12
fatted 91.32
fatten 261.94
fatty 16.327
fatuity 16.333.3
fatuous 310.4
faubourg 187
faucal 228
fauces 513
faucet 371

369

fault 404
faultless 300
faultlessness 300.33
faulty 16.351
faun 255
fauna 17.234
Fauré 2
Faust 442
Faustus 310
faux pas 1
faveolate 367.14
favonian 261.3.18
favour 17.410
favourable
 228.16.35
favourite 371.35
favouritism
 242.35.18
favus 310
Fawkes 500
fawn 255
fay 2
faze 509
fealty 16.352
fear 6
fearful 226
fearfully 16.129
fearless 300
fearlessness 300.33
fearnought 374
fearsome 242
feasible 228.16
feast 435
feat 370
feather 17.402
featherbedding
 265.12
featherbrain 247
featherbrained 130
featheredge 194
feathering 265.58
featherstitch 67
featherweight
 367.38
feathery 16.274
feature 17.55
featureless 300.13
feaze 513
febrific 38.12
febrifuge 204
febrile 219
febrility 16.333.9
February 16.274.2
feckless 300
fecula 17.174.4

feculent 420.27
fecund 143
fecundate 367
fecundity 16.333.7
fed 86
fedayee 5
federal 228.76
federalize 516.3.8
federate 367.23,
 371.35
federation
 261.67.22
fedora 17.276
fee 5
feeble 228
feeble-minded 91
feeble-mindedness
 300.28
feebleness 300.30
feed 89
feedback 32
feedbag 178
feeder 17.82
feedlot 373
feel 217
feeler 17.165
feeling 265.29
feet 370
feeze 513
feign 247
feint 409
feldspar 1
felicitate 367.30
felicitation
 261.67.27
felicitous 310.64
felicity 16.333.28
feline 253
fell 215
fellah 17.163
fellatio 12.3.6
feller 17.163
Fellini 16.228.1
fellmonger 17.143
felloe 12.40
fellow 12.40
fellowship 274
felo de se 5.20
felon 261.40
felonious 310.2.9
felonry 16.284
felony 16.237.5
felsite 372
felt 402
felting 265

felucca 17.39
female 214
feme 232
feminine 252.17
femininity
 16.333.17
feminism 242.35.13
feminist 436.11
feminize 516.6
femoral 228.76.2
femur 17.210
fen 248
fence 316
fencer 17.314
fencing 265
fend 131
fender 17.101
fenestella 17.163
fenestrated 91.34
fenestration
 261.67.25
Fenian 261.3.16
fennec 35
fennel 228.57
fenny 16.226
Fenrir 6
Fenriswolf 175
Fens 546
fenugreek 37
feral 228
ferbam 229
fer-de-lance 315
Ferdinand 128
feretory 16.274.41
Fergana 17.226
feria 17.3.39
ferial 228.3.11
ferity 16.333.21
Fermanagh 17.225
ferment 410.2
fermentation
 261.67.32
Fermi 16.214
fermium 242.2
fern 249
fernery 16.274.24
ferocious 310.60
ferocity 16.333.30.5
Ferrara 17.268
Ferrari 16.261
ferrate 367
ferreous 310.2
ferret 371.31
ferriage 197
ferric 38.39

Ferris 300
ferrite 372
ferritin 252.23
ferrocene 251.9
ferrochromium
 242.2.9
ferrocyanide 92.4
ferromagnetism
 242.35.18
ferrosilicon 261.13
ferrous 310.44
ferruginous 310.33
ferrule 227
ferry 16.262
fertile 219
fertility 16.333.9
fertilization
 261.67.36
fertilize 516.2
fertilizer 17.441
ferula 17.174
ferule 227
fervent 420.82
fervid 91.55
fervour 17.412
fescue 15
fesse 296
festal 228.113
fester 17.382
festival 228.120
festive 485.24
festivity 16.333.35
festoon 260
festoonery
 16.274.28
festschrift 398
feta 17.339
fetal 228.101
fetation 261.67
fetch 64
fetching 265
fête 367
feticide 92.7
fetid 91.35
fetish 353
fetishism 242.35
fetlock 40
fetor 17.341
fetter 17.339
fettle 228.100
fettucine 16.228
fetus 310.63
feud 102
feudal 228.37

feudalism 242.35.11
feudality 16.333.8
feudalize 516.3
feudatory 16.274.43
feudist 436
feuilleton 254
fever 17.413
fevered 103
feverfew 15
feverish 353.11
feverishness 300.35
few 15
fey 2
fez 510
Fezzan 246
fiancé 2
Fianna fail 222.1
fiasco 12
Fiat 381
fiat 381.2
fib 24
fibber 17.14
fibre 17.15
fibreboard 95.1
fibreglass 294
fibriform 238.1
fibril 218
fibrillation 261.67.12
fibrinogen 261.39
fibrinolysin 252.21
fibrocement 410.1
fibroid 97
fibroin 252.1
fibroma 17.215
fibrosis 300.55
fibrositis 300.62
fibrous 310
fibula 17.174.2
fiche 352
fichu 15
fickle 228.23
fickleness 300.30
fictile 219
fiction 261.78
fictional 228.63
fictionalize 516.3.7
fictitious 310.58
fictive 485.18
fid 91
fiddle 228.32
fiddle-de-dee 5

fiddle-faddle 228.31
fiddlehead 86
fiddler 17.186
fiddlestick 38
fiddlesticks 498
fiddling 265
fideicommissum 242.24
fideism 242.35
fidelity 16.333
fidget 371
fidgety 16.333
fiduciary 16.274.1
fie 7
fief 162
field 115
fielder 17.94
fieldfare 4
fieldmouse 306
fieldpiece 298
fieldwork 36
fiend 133
fiendish 353
fierce 299
fieri facias 310.2.16
fiery 16.267
fiesta 17.382.1
FIFA 17.113
Fife 164
fife 164
fifteen 251
fifteenth 469
fiftieth 458
fifty 16.347
fig 184
fight 372
fighter 17.343
fighting 265.67
figment 420
figurant 420
figurate 371.34
figuration 261.67.22
figurative 485.15.10
figure 17.129
figurehead 86.5
figurine 251.7
Fijian 261.2
filament 420.35
filar 17.167
filaria 17.3.38
filariasis 300.57.1
filature 17.62

filbert 381
filch 76
file 219
filecard 84
filet mignon 254.12
filial 228.3.4
filiate 367.1.2
filiation 261.67.1.1
filibeg 181
filibuster 17.388
filicide 92.7
filiform 238.1
filigree 5.18
filings 552
Filipino 12.54
fill 218
filler 17.166
fillet 371.16
filling 265.30
fillip 274
fillister 17.384
filly 16.120
film 244
filmography 16.90.2
filmset 368
filoplume 241
filose 305
filoselle 215
fils 311
filter 17.362
filth 466
filthiness 300.23
filthy 16
filtrate 367
filtration 261.67
filum 242.9
fimble 228
fimbria 17.3
fimbriate 371.1
fin 252
finable 228.16.30
finagle 228.44
final 228.61
finale 16.113
finalism 242.35.11
finalist 436.7
finality 16.333.8
finalize 516.3
finally 16.131
finals 539
finance 314
financial 228.95
financier 17.3.48

finch 80
find 135
finder 17.103
finding 265.21
fine 2
fine 253
Fine Gael 214
fineness 300
finery 16.274.27
finespun 259
finesse 296.2
finfoot 379
finger 17.141
fingerboard 95.1
fingering 265.58
fingerling 265
fingermark 33
fingernail 214
fingerprint 412
fingerstall 221
fingertip 274
finicky 16.25
fining 265.44
finis 300.23
finish 353.7
finisher 17.326
Finistère 4
Finisterre 4
finite 372
fink 52
Finland 143
Finn 252
finnan 261.56
finnan haddie 16.57
finned 134
finner 17.231
Finnic 38.34
Finnish 353.7
Finnmark 33
finny 16.229
fino 12.54
Finsteraarhorn 255
fiorin 252.20
fipple 228.66
fir 3
Firdausi 16.304
fire 8
firearm 230
fireball 221
firebird 87
firebomb 237
firebox 499
firebrand 128
firebrat 365

firebreak 34
firebrick 38
firebug 189
firecracker 17.28
firedamp 285
firedog 185
firedrake 34
firefly 7
fireguard 84
fireman 261
fireplace 295
fireproof 170
fireside 92
firetrap 268
firewarden 261.27
firewater 17.345
fireweed 89
firewood 101
firework 36
fireworks 497
firing 265.54
firkin 252
firm 233
firmament 420.35
firmness 300
firmware 4
firry 16.263
first 434
first-born 255
first-footer 17.350
first-footing 265
firstling 265
first-rate 367
firth 456
fiscal 228
fish 353
fishbolt 405
fishbowl 223
fisher 17.326
fisherman 261.52.1
fishery 16.274
fishfinger 17.141
fishgig 184
fishing 265.63
fishmonger 17.143
fishnet 368
fishtail 214
fishwife 164
fishy 16.322
fissile 219.2
fission 261.71
fissiped 86.6
fissure 17.326
fist 436
fistic 38.70

fistmele 217
fistula 17.174
fit 371
fitch 67
fitful 226
fitly 16.189
fitment 420.49
fitness 300.38
fitted 91.38
fitter 17.342
fitting 265.66
Fittipaldi 16.73
Fitzgerald 122.1
five 486
fivefold 120
fivepenny 16.237
fiver 17.415
fives 554
fix 498
fixate 367
fixation 261.67
fixative 485.15
fixedly 16.148
fixer 17.427
fixity 16.333
fixture 17.76
fizz 515
fizzle 228
fizzy 16.396
fjeld 113
fjord 95
flab 18
flabbergast 431.1
flabbergasted 91.51
flabbiness 300.23
flabby 16.5
flabellate 371.15
flabellum 242.8
flaccid 91.28
flag 178
flagellant 420
flagellate 367.12,
 371.16
flagellation
 261.67.12
flagellum 242.8
flageolet 368
flagging 265
flaggy 16.91
flagitious 310.58
flagman 261
flagon 261.30
flagpole 223
flagrancy 16.312
flagrant 420

flagship 274
flagstaff 158
flagstone 257
flail 214
flair 4
flak 32
flake 34
flaky 16.21
flam 229
flambé 2.5
flambeau 12
Flamborough
 17.279
flamboyance 321
flamboyant 420.3
flame 231
flamen 248.2
flamenco 12.13
flameproof 170
flaming 265
flamingo 12.36
Flamininus 310.34
Flaminius 310.2.8
flammable
 228.16.26
Flamsteed 89
flan 245
Flanders 524
flange 206
flank 51
flanker 17.43
flannel 228.55
flannelette 368
flannels 539
flap 268
flapdoodle 228.37
flapjack 32
flapper 17.247
flare 4
flash 349
flashback 32
flashboard 95
flashcube 30
flasher 17.321
flashing 265
flashlight 372
flashover 17.417
flashy 16.319
flask 56
flasket 371
flat 365
flatfish 353
flatfoot 379
flat-footed 91

flat-footedness
 300.28
flathead 86
flatiron 261.4
flatlet 371
flatly 16.186
flatmate 367
flatness 300
flats 333
flatten 261.94
flatter 17.336
flatterer 17.279
flattering 265.58
flattery 16.274
flattish 353
flattop 276
flatulence 321
flatulent 420.27
flatus 310.62
flatworm 233
Flaubert 4
flaunch 81
flaunt 415
flaunty 16.358
flautist 436
flavescent 420.67.3
flavine 252
flavone 257
flavorous 310.50
flavour 17.410
flavourful 226
flavouring 265.58.1
flavourless 300.13
flaw 9
flawless 300
flax 494
flaxen 261
flaxseed 89
flay 2
flea 5
fleabag 178
fleabane 247
fleabite 372
fleam 234
fleapit 371
fléchette 368
fleck 35
fled 86
fledge 194
fledgling 265
fledgy 16.101
flee 5
fleece 298
fleecy 16.299
fleet 370

fleeting 265
Fleetwood 101
Fleming 265
Flemish 353
flense 316
flesh 351
flesher 17.323
fleshly 16.185
fleshpots 341
fleshy 16.321
fletch 64
Fletcher 17.53
fletcher 17.53
fleur-de-lis 5.9
fleurette 368
fleuron 254
flew 15
flews 523
flex 496
flexibility
   16.333.9.2
flexible 228.16
flexion 261.77
flexitime 236
flexor 17.426
flexuous 310.4
fley 2
flibbertigibbet
   371.5
flick 38
flicker 17.34
flight 372
flightless 300
flighty 16.334
flimflam 229
flimsy 16.403
flinch 80
flincher 17.71
fling 265
Flint 412
flint 412
Flintshire 6
flinty 16.356
flip 274
flip-flop 276
flippant 420.56
flipper 17.253
flipping 265
flirt 369
flirtation 261.67
flirtatious 310.56
flit 371
flitch 67
flite 372
flitter 17.342

flittermouse 306
flivver 17.414
float 376
floater 17.347
floating 265
floaty 16.339
floccose 305
flocculate 367.13.3
floccule 227
flocculent 420.27
flocculus 310.25
floccus 310.11
flock 40
Flodden 261.26
floe 12
flog 185
flogging 265.23
flong 266
flood 100
floodgate 367
floodlight 372
floor 9
floorage 197
floorboard 95
flooring 265.55
floozy 16.402
flop 276
floppy 16.250
Flora 17.276
flora 17.276
floral 228.74
Florence 321.18
Florentine 253
florescence 321.21
floret 371
floriated 91.34.1
floribunda 17.108
florid 91.26
Florida 17.83
florigen 261.37
florin 252.18
florist 436.18
floristic 38.70
floristics 498
flory 16.269
flos ferri 16.262
floss 302
flossy 16.302
flotage 197.13
flotation 261.67.28
flotilla 17.166
flotsam 242
flounce 319
flouncing 265
flounder 17.107

flour 14
flourish 353.10
floury 16.274
flout 377
flow 12
flowage 197
flower 14
flowerbed 86.1
floweret 371
flowering 265.57
flowerless 300
flowerpot 373
flowery 16.274
flown 257
flu 15
fluctuant 420.4
fluctuate 367.2
fluctuation
   261.67.2
flue 15
fluency 16.312
fluent 420.5
fluff 168
fluffiness 300.23
fluffy 16.88
flugelhorn 255
fluid 91.3
fluidics 498
fluidity 16.333.5
fluidize 516
fluke 45
fluky 16.32
flume 241
flummery 16.274
flummox 503
flung 267
flunk 54
flunky 16.39
fluoresce 296
fluorescence 321.21
fluorescent 420.67
fluoric 38.42
fluoridate 367.8
fluoridation
   261.67.7
fluoride 92
fluorinate 367.17
fluorine 251
fluorometer
   17.342.3
fluoroscope 278.1
fluorspar 1
flurry 16.272
flush 356
Flushing 265

fluster 17.388
flute 380
fluted 91.42
fluter 17.351
fluting 265
flutter 17.349
fluvial 228.3.17
flux 502
fluxion 261.79
fly 7
flyaway 2.28
flyblown 257
flybook 44
flyby 7
flyer 17.4
flying 265.3
flyleaf 162
flyover 17.417
flypaper 17.249
Flysch 353
flyspeck 35
flytrap 268
flyweight 367
flywheel 217
foal 223
foam 239
foamy 16.219
fob 26
focal 228.26
focus 310.12
fodder 17.85
foe 12
foeman 261.49
fog 185
fogbound 139
fogdog 185
fogged 106
foggy 16.94
foghorn 255
fogy 16.96
föhn 249
foible 228
foil 222
Foism 242.35.3
foison 261.128
foist 440
Fokker 17.36
fold 120
foldaway 2.28
folder 17.97
foliaceous 310.56
foliage 197
foliar 17.3.22
foliate 371.1
foliated 91.34.1

foliation

foliation 261.67.1.2
folio 12.3.3
foliose 305.1
folium 242.2.7
folk 42
Folkestone 261
folklore 9
folkloric 38.41
folkmoot 380
follicle 228.23.8
follicular 17.174.6
folliculin 252.10
follow 12.43
follower 17.6
following 265.4
folly 16.122
Fomalhaut 376
foment 410.2
fomentation
261.67.32
fond 136
Fonda 17.104
fondant 420.15
fondle 228
fondness 300
fondue 15
font 414
Fontainebleau 12
fontanelle 215
Fonteyn 247.11
Foochow 13
food 102
foodstuff 168
fool 227
foolery 16.274
foolhardiness
300.23
foolhardy 16.58
foolish 353
foolishness 300.35
foolproof 170
foolscap 268
foot 379
footage 197
football 221
footballer 17.169
footboard 95
footboy 11
footbridge 197
footfall 221
footgear 6
foothill 218
foothold 120
footing 265
footle 228.108

footlights 340
footling 265
footloose 309
footman 261
footmark 33
footnote 376
footpace 295
footpad 83
footpath 453
footplate 367
footprint 412
footrest 433
foots 345
footsie 16.318
footslog 185
footsore 9
footstall 221
footstep 271
footstool 227
footway 2
footwear 4
footwork 36
footy 16.342
foo yong 266
foozle 228.128
fop 276
foppery 16.274
foppish 353
for 9
forage 197
foramen 248.2
forasmuch 72
foray 2
forbade 83
forbear 4
forbearance 321
forbid 91.4
forbiddance 321.5
forbidden 261.24
forbidding 265
forbore 9
forby 7
force 303
forceful 226.6
force majeure 3
forcemeat 370
forceps 327
forcible 228.16
ford 95
fordable 228.16.16
fore 9
forearm 230
forebear 4
forebode 98
foreboding 265.16

forebrain 247
forecast 431
forecaster 17.380
foreclose 520
foreclosure 17.335
forecourse 303
forecourt 374
foredeck 35
foredoom 241
forefather 17.401
forefinger 17.141
forefront 419
forego 12
foregoing 265.4
foregone 254
foreground 139
foregut 378
forehand 128
forehanded 91.12
forehead 91.26
forehock 40
foreign 252.18
foreigner 17.231
foreignism
242.35.13
forejudge 203
foreknew 15
foreknow 12
foreknowledge
197.2
foreland 143
foreleg 181
forelimb 235
forelock 40
foreman 261
foremast 431
foremost 441
forename 231
forenamed 124
forenoon 260
forensic 38
forensics 498
foreordain 247
forepart 366
forepaw 9
forepeak 37
foreplay 2
forequarter 17.345
forereach 66
forerun 259
forerunner 17.237
foresail 214
foresaw 9
foresee 5.21

foreseeable
228.16.1
foreseen 251
foreshadow 12
foresheet 370
foreshock 40
foreshore 9
foreshorten
261.102
foresight 372
foreskin 252
forest 436.18
forestall 221
forestation 261.67
forested 91.53
forester 17.384
forestry 16.293
foretaste 432
foretell 215.3
forethought 374
foretime 236
foretold 120
foretooth 463
foretop 276
forever 17.411
forevermore 9.9
forewarn 255
forewent 410
forewind 134
forewing 265
foreword 87
foreyard 84
forfeit 371
forfeiture 17.56
forfend 131
forficate 371.9
forgather 17.400
forgave 482
forge 200
forger 17.153
forgery 16.274
forget 368
forgetful 226.8
forgetfulness
300.30
forget-me-not 373
forgettable
228.16.46
forgivable 228.16
forgive 485
forgiven 261.114
forgiveness 300.43
forgiving 265.80
forgot 373
forgotten 261.101

374

forjudge 203
fork 41
forlorn 255
form 238
formal 212
formal 228.53
formaldehyde 92
formalin 252.11
formalism
242.35.11
formality
16.333.8.5
formalize 516.3
format 365
formation 261.67
formative 485.15.6
forme 238
former 17.214
formerly 16.131
formic 38
Formica 17.35
formicary 16.274.4
formication
261.67.5
formidable
228.16.15
formless 300
Formosa 17.306
formula 17.174
formulaic 38.1
formulary
16.274.18
formulate 367.13
formulation
261.67.13
formulism
242.35.10
formwork 36
Fornax 494
fornenst 447
fornicate 367.5
fornication
261.67.5
fornix 498
forsake 34
forsaken 261.11
forsook 44
forsooth 463
forswear 4
forsworn 255
forsythia 17.3
fort 374
fortalice 300.13
forte 16.336
fortepiano 12

forth 460
Forth 460
forthcoming 265.38
forthright 372
forthwith 476
fortieth 458
fortification
261.67.5.1
fortify 7.3
fortis 300.63
fortissimo 12.48
fortitude 102.2
fortnight 372
fortnightly 16.190
FORTRAN 245
fortress 300
fortuitism
242.35.18
fortuitous 310.64
fortuity 16.333.3
Fortuna 17.238
fortunate 371.28.1
fortunately 16.189
fortune 260.5
fortune-teller
17.163
fortune-telling
265.28
forty 16.336
forum 242.20
forward 103.8
forwarder 17.92
forwardness 300
forwards 531
forwent 410
fossa 17.304
fosse 302
fossette 368
fossil 228.86
fossiliferous
310.50.2
fossilize 516.2
fossorial 228.3.12
foster 17.385
fosterage 197
fosterling 265
Fotheringhay 2.10
foudroyant 420.3
fought 374
foul 224
foulard 84
Foulness 296
foulness 300
found 139
foundation 261.67

founder 17.107
foundling 265
foundry 16
fount 418
fountain 252
fountainhead 86.4
four 9
fourchette 368
Fourdrinier 17.3.34
fourfold 120
Fourier 2.1
fourpence 321
fourpenny 16.237
four-poster 17.387
fourragère 4
fourscore 9
foursome 242
foursquare 4
fourteen 251
fourteenth 469
fourth 460
fovea 17.3.55
Fowey 11
fowl 224
Fowler 17.172
fowling 265.33
fox 499
foxfire 8
foxglove 489
foxhole 223
foxhound 139
foxing 265
foxtail 214
foxtrot 373
foxy 16.389
foyer 2
Fra 1
fracas 1
fraction 261.76
fractional 228.63
fractionate 367.18
fractionize 516.7
fractious 310
fracture 17.63
frae 2
frag 178
fragile 219
fragility 16.333.9
fragment 410
fragment 420
fragmental 228.110
fragmentary
16.274.48
fragmentation
261.67.32

fragrance 321
fragrant 420
frail 214
fraise 509
framboesia 17.3.60
frame 231
frameless 300
framer 17.207
framework 36
franc 51
France 315
franchise 516
Francis 300
Franciscan 261
francium 242.2
francolin 252.9
Franconian
261.3.18
Francophile 219.1
Francophobe 28
Francophobia
17.3.4
Francophone 257
franger 17.245
frangible 228.16.21
frangipane 247
frangipani 16.224
frank 51
Frank 51
frankalmoign 256
Frankenstein 253
Frankfurt 381
frankfurter 17.340
frankincense 316
Frankish 353
franklin 252
frankly 16.144
frankness 300
frankpledge 194
frantic 38.62
frap 268
frappé 2
Fraser 17.439
frass 293
fratchy 16.46
frater 17.338
fraternal 228.58
fraternity
16.333.16
fraternize 516.7
fratricide 92.7
Frau 13
fraud 95
fraudulent 420.27
fraught 374

fray 2
frazzle 228.124
freak 37
freakish 353
freaky 16.24
freckle 228.21
freckled 122
Frederick 38
free 5
freebie 16.10
freeboard 95
freeboot 380
freebooter 17.351
freeborn 255
freedman 261
freedom 242
freehold 120
freeholder 17.97
freelance 315
freeload 98
freely 16.118
freeman 261.47
freemartin 252
freemason 261.62
freemasonic
  38.35.4
freemasonry 16.284
freesheet 370
freesia 17.334
freestanding 265.19
freestone 257
freestyle 219
freethinker 17.44
freethinking 265.10
freeway 2
freewheel 217
freewheeling
  265.29
freeze 513
freezer 17.440
freezing 265
freight 367
freighter 17.338
freightliner 17.232
Fremantle 228.109
fremitus 310.64
French 79
Frenchify 7.3
Frenchman 261
frenetic 38.50.4
frenulum 242.10
frenzied 91
frenzy 16.405
frequency 16.312
frequent 410

frequent 420.57
frequentation
  261.67.32
frequentative
  485.15.15
fresco 12.14
fresh 351
freshen 261.68
freshener 17.239
fresher 17.323
freshet 371
freshly 16.185
freshman 261
freshness 300
freshwater 17.345
fresnel 215
fret 368
fretful 226.8
fretted 91.35
fretwork 36
Freud 97
Freudian 261.3
Frey 2
Freya 17.1
friable 228.16.3
friar 17.4
friarbird 87
friary 16.274
fribble 228.12
fricassee 5
fricative 485.15.1
friction 261.78
frictional 228.63
Friday 2
fridge 197
friend 131
friendless 300
friendlessness
  300.33
friendliness 300.23
friendly 16.154
friendship 274
Friesian 261.90
Friesland 143
frieze 513
frig 184
frigate 371.14
frigging 265
fright 372
frighten 261.100
frightening 265.46
frightful 226.9
frightfully 16.129
frigid 91.15
frigidity 16.333.5

frijol 223
frill 218
frilly 16.120
fringe 209
fringilline 253
frippery 16.274.30
frippet 371
Frisbee 5
Frisco 12.15
frisé 2.30
Frisian 261.91
frisk 58
frisker 17.48
frisket 371
frisky 16.41
frit 371
fritillary 16.274.16
fritter 17.342
frivol 228.120
frivolity 16.333.10
frivolous 310.26
frizz 515
frizzle 228
frizzy 16.396
fro 12
Frobisher 17.326
frock 40
frocking 265.8
froe 12
frog 185
frogfish 353
frogging 265.23
froggy 16.94
froghopper 17.255
frogman 261
frogmarch 63
frogspawn 255
frolic 38.22
frolicsome 242
from 237
frond 136
Fronde 136
fronded 91
frondescence
  321.21
Frondeur 3
frons 549
front 419
frontage 197
frontal 228.112
frontality 16.333.8
frontier 6
frontiersman
  261.54
frontispiece 298

frontrunner 17.237
frost 438
frostbite 372
frostbitten 261.99
frosted 91
frosting 265
frosty 16.367
froth 459
frothy 16.371
frottage 359
froward 103
frown 258
frowst 442
frowzy 16.400
froze 520
frozen 261.129
fructiferous
  310.50.2
fructify 7.3
fructose 520
fructuous 310.4
frugal 228.48
frugality 16.333.8
frugivorous
  310.50.3
fruit 380
fruitarian 261.3.21
fruitcake 34
fruiter 17.351
fruiterer 17.279
fruitful 226
fruition 261.71
fruitless 300
fruitlessness 300.33
fruity 16.343
frumenty 16.360
frump 289
frumpish 353
frustrate 367
frustration 261.67
frustule 227
frustum 242.32
frutescent 420.67
fry 7
fryer 17.4
Fuad 84
fuchsia 17
fuchsin 252
fuck 43
fucker 17.39
fucking 265
fucoid 97
fucus 310.13
fuddle 228.36
fuddy-duddy 16.69

G

fudge 203
fuel 228.10
fug 189
fugacious 310.56
fugacity 16.333.25
fugal 228.48
fugitive 485.12
fugue 190
fuguist 436
Fuji 5
Fukien 248
Fukuoka 17.38
Fula 17.175
fulcrum 242
fulfil 218
fulfilment 420
fulgent 420.21
fulgurant 420
fulgurate 367.22
fulgurating 265.64
fulguration
 261.67.21
Fulham 242.10
fuliginous 310.33
full 226
fullback 32
full-blooded 91.11
full-blown 257
fuller 17.174
full-frontal 228.112
fullness 300
full-time 236
full-timer 17.212
fully 16.129
fully-fledged 109
fulminant 420.53
fulminate 367.17
fulmination
 261.67.18
fulsome 242
fulvous 310
fumarole 223.3
fumatorium
 242.2.17
fumatory 16.274.43
fumble 228
fumbler 17.180
fume 241
fumigant 420.17
fumigate 367.10
fumigation
 261.67.10
fumitory 16.274.41
fun 259
funambulist 436.6

function 261.80
functional 228.63
functionalism
 242.35.11.5
functionary
 16.274.29
fund 140
fundament 420.35
fundamental
 228.110.3
fundamentalism
 242.35.11.6
fundi 5
fundus 310
Fundy 16.80
funeral 228.76
funerary 16.274.32
funereal 228.3.11
funfair 4
fungal 228
fungi 7
fungicide 92.7
fungiform 238.1
fungoid 97
fungous 310
fungus 310
funicle 228.23
funicular 17.174.6
funiculus 310.25.2
funk 54
funky 16.39
funnel 228
funny 16.235
fur 3
furan 245
furbelow 12.42
furbish 353
furcate 367
furcula 17.174.5
furfuraceous
 310.56
furious 310.2.14
furl 216
furlong 266
furlough 12
furnace 300
Furness 300
furnish 353
furnisher 17.326
furnishing 265.63
furnishings 552
furniture 17.56
furor 9
furore 16.269
furphy 16.83

furred 87
furrier 17.3
furriery 16.274.1
furring 265.51
furrow 12
furry 16.263
further 17.403
furtherance 321.20
furthermore 9.9
furthermost 441
furthest 436
furtive 485.11
furtiveness 300.43
furuncle 228.30
furunculosis
 300.55.3
fury 16.270
furze 511
fusain 247
fuse 523
fusee 5
fusel 228.128
fuselage 359
Fushun 259
fusible 228.16.65
fusiform 238.1
fusile 219
fusilier 6
fusillade 85
fusion 261.93
fuss 307
fussiness 300.23
fusspot 373
fussy 16.305
fustanella 17.163
fustian 261.3.27
fustic 38
fusty 16.368
futhark 33
futile 219
futilitarian
 261.3.21.2
futility 16.333.9
futtock 46
future 17.61
futurism 242.35.15
futuristic 38.70.5
futurity 16.333.23
futurology
 16.108.4.13
fuzz 522
fuzzy 16.401
fyke 39
Fylde 117
fyrd 90

Ga 1
gab 18
gabble 228
gabbler 17.177
gabby 16.5
gabelle 215
gaberdine 251.1
gabfest 433
gabion 261.3.1
gabionade 85.3
gable 228.11
gabled 122
gablet 371
Gabon 254
Gabor 9
Gaborone 16.233
Gabriel 228.3
gaby 16.7
gad 83
gadabout 377.1
gadfly 7
gadget 371
gadgeteer 6
gadgetry 16.285
Gadhelic 38.20
gadid 91.6
gadoid 97
gadolinite 372.5
gadolinium
 242.2.11
gadroon 260
Gael 214
Gaelic 38
gaff 157
gaffe 157
gaffer 17.110
gag 178
gaga 1
Gagauzi 16.397
gage 193
gagger 17.123
gaggle 228.43
gaiety 16.344
gaillardia 17.3.6
gaily 16.114
gain 247
gainer 17.227
gainful 226.4
gainly 16.170
gainsay 2

Gainsborough
 17.279
gait 367
gaiter 17.338
Gaitskell 218
Gaius 310.3
gal 212
gala 17.161
galactagogue 185.2
galactic 38.58
galactopoietic
 38.50
galactose 520
galago 12.26
galah 1.9
Galahad 83
galangal 228.49
galantine 251
Galápagos 310
galatea 17.2
Galatia 17.322
Galatians 551.1
galaxy 16.390
galbanum 242.16
Galbraith 454
gale 214
galea 17.3.18
Galen 261
galena 17.230
galenical 228.23.11
Galenism
 242.35.13
Galibi 16.10
Galilean 261.2.2
Galilee 5.8
galilee 5.8
Galileo 12.1
galingale 214
galiot 381.1
galipot 373
gall 221
gallant 407, 420.24
gallantry 16.291
Galle 17.161
galleass 293.1
galleon 261.3
gallery 16.274.15
galley 16.112
gallfly 7
galliambic 38.5
galliard 103
Gallic 38.19
Gallicanism
 242.35.14.2
Gallice 16.300

Gallicism
 242.35.16.1
Gallicize 516.10
galligaskins 548
gallimaufry 16.280
gallinaceous
 310.56.4
galling 265.31
gallinule 227
Gallipoli 16.131.5
gallipot 373
gallium 242.2
gallivant 407.1
galliwasp 292
gallnut 378
galloglass 294
gallon 261
gallonage 197
galloon 260.1
gallop 281
galloping 265
gallous 310
Galloway 2.28
gallows 520.1
gallstone 257
Gallup 281
galluses 515
galoot 380.1
galop 281
galore 9.8
galoshes 515
Galsworthy 16.375
galumph 177
galvanic 38.31
galvanism
 242.35.14
galvanize 516.7
galvanometer
 17.342.3.3
galvanoscope 278.1
galvo 12
Galway 2
galyak 32
gam 229
gambado 12.17
gambeson 261.65
Gambetta 17.339
Gambia 17.3.5
gambier 6
gambit 371
gamble 228.17
gambler 17.179
gambling 265
gamboge 201
gambol 228.17

game 231
gamecock 40
gamekeeper 17.252
gamelan 245.2
gamely 16.165
gamesmanship
 274.2
gamesome 242
gamete 370
gametophore 9.6
gamic 38.24
gamin 252.12
gamine 251
gaming 265
gamma 17.205
gammadion
 261.3.3
gammer 17.205
gammon 261.44
gammy 16.210
gamp 285
gamut 381
gamy 16.212
gan 245
gander 17.98
Gandhi 16.77
Gandhiism
 242.35.2
ganef 171
gang 263
gangbang 263
ganger 17.245
Ganges 513
gangland 143
gangling 265
ganglion 261.3
gangplank 51
gangrene 251
gangrenous 310.33
gangster 17
Gangtok 40
gangue 263
gangway 2
ganister 17.384
gannet 371.22
gansey 16.404
gantry 16.287
Ganymede 89
gaol 214
gap 268
gape 270
gapes 323
gar 1
garage 359
Garamond 136

garb 19
garbage 197
garble 228
Garbo 12
Garda 17.78
garden 261
gardener 17.240
gardenia 17.3.33
gardening 265.46
Gardiner 17.240
garfish 353
garganey 16.237
Gargantua 17.7.2
gargantuan 261.7
garget 371
gargle 228
gargoyle 222
Garibaldi 16.75
garibaldi 16.75
garish 353.9
garland 143
garlic 38
garlicky 16.25
garment 420
garner 17.226
garnet 371
garnierite 372.8
garnish 353
garnishee 5
garnishment
 420.47
garniture 17.56
garotte 373
garpike 39
garret 371
Garrick 38.38
garrison 261.65.1
garrulous 310.25
garrya 17.3
garter 17.337
garth 453
Gary 16.260
gas 293
gasbag 178
gasconade 85.3
Gascony 16.237
gaseous 310.2
gash 349
gasholder 17.97
gasiform 238.1
gasify 7.3.6
Gaskell 228
gasket 371
gaskin 252
gaslight 372

gasman 261
gasolier 6
gasoline 251.3
gasometer 17.342.3
gasp 290
Gaspé 2
gasser 17.298
gassy 16.294
gastralgia 17.3.16
gastralgic 38
gastrectomy
16.222.5
gastric 38
gastritis 300.62
gastroenteric 38.39
gastroenteritis
300.62.5
gastroenterology
16.108.4.13
gastroenterostomy
16.222.6
gastrolith 458
gastrology 16.108.4
gastronome 239
gastronomer
17.218.1
gastronomic
38.29.1
gastronomical
228.23.9
gastronomy
16.222.3
gastropod 94.1
gastroscope 278.1
gastrostomy
16.222.6
gastrotomy
16.222.4
gastrotrich 38
gastrula 17.174
gastrulation
261.67.13
gasworks 497
gate 367
gateau 12.72
gate-crash 349
gate-crasher 17.321
gatefold 120
gatehouse 306
gatekeeper 17.252
gatepost 441
Gateshead 86
gateway 2
Gath 452
gather 17.400

gathering 265.58
Gatling 265
gauche 355
gaucherie 5.17
gaucho 12
gaud 95
gaudery 16.274
Gaudi 16.68
gaudy 16.66
gauge 193
gauger 17.146
Gauhati 16.328
Gaul 221
Gauleiter 17.343
Gaulish 353
Gaullism 242.35
Gaullist 436
gaultheria 17.3.39
gaunt 415
gauntlet 371
gauntness 300
gaur 14
gauss 306
Gautama 17.218
gauze 518
gauzy 16.397
gavage 359
gave 482
gavel 228.117
gavelkind 135
gavial 228.3
gavotte 373
gawk 41
gawky 16.28
gawp 277
gay 2
Gay Gordons 551
Gay-Lussac 32
Gaynor 17.227
Gaza 17.438
Gazankulu 15.4
gaze 509
gazebo 12.5
gazelle 215
gazette 368.9
gazetteer 6
Gaziantep 271
gazpacho 12
gazump 289
gean 251
geanticline 253.4
gear 6
gearbox 499
gearing 265.53
gearshift 398

gearwheel 217
gecko 12.9
gedact 383
gee 5
gee-gee 5
geek 37
geepound 139
geese 298
geest 435
geezer 17.440
gegenschein 253
Gehenna 17.228
Geiger 17.130
geisha 17.322
gel 215
gelada 17.92
gelatin 252
gelatine 251.11
gelatinize 516.6.1
gelatinoid 97.8.1
gelatinous 310.33
gelation 261.67.12
geld 113
Gelderland 143.4
gelding 265
gelid 91.17
gelignite 372.7
gelsemium 242.2.8
gelt 402
gem 232
Gemini 7.10
gemma 17.208
gemmulation
261.67.13
gemology 16.108.4
gemot 376
gemsbok 40
gemstone 257
gen 248
genappe 268
gendarme 230
gendarmerie
16.274.20
gender 17.101
gene 251
genealogist 436.4.1
genealogy 16.108.2
genera 17.279
generable
228.16.35
general 228.76
generalissimo 12.48
generalist 436.7
generality
16.333.8.9

generalization
261.67.36
generalize 516.3.8
generally 16.131
generate 367.23.1
generation
261.67.22.2
generative
485.15.10
generator 17.338.9
generatrix 498.9
generic 38.39
generosity
16.333.30.5
generous 310.50
genesis 300.52.4
genet 371
genetic 38.50.4
geneticist 436.21
genetics 498.12
Geneva 17.413
Genevan 261.113
Genevieve 484
Genghis Khan 246
genial 228.2,
228.3.6
geniality 16.333.8.1
genic 38.32
geniculate 371.17.2
genie 16.228
genii 7.1
genip 274
genipap 268
genital 228.102
genitalia 17.3.18
genitalic 38.19.1
genitals 539
genitive 485.12
genitor 17.342
genitourinary
16.274.26
genius 310.2.7
genizah 17.440
Genoa 17.6
genoa 17.6
genocide 92.8
Genoese 513.2
genome 239
genotype 275.1
gens 546
gent 410
genteel 217
gentian 261.82
gentianella 17.163
Gentile 219.6

gentility 16.333.9
gentle 228.110
gentlefolk 42
gentleman 261
gentlemanly 16.174
gentleness 300.30
gentlewoman
    261.50
gently 16.197
gentry 16.288
genu 15
genuflect 385
genuflection 261.77
genuine 252
genus 310.32
geocentric 38.47
geochronology
    16.108.4.11
geode 98
geodesic 38
geodesy 16.300.1
geodetic 38.50
geognosy 16.307.3
geographical
    228.23.3
geography
    16.90.2.1
geoid 97.1
geological 228.23.5
geologize 516.1
geology 16.108.4.1
geomagnetism
    242.35.18
geomancy 16.309
geometer
    17.342.3.1
geometric 38.46
geometrid 91
geometry
    16.285.2.1
geomorphic 38.14
geomorphology
    16.108.4
geophagism
    242.35.8
geophagy 16.108.1
geophysics 498
geophyte 372
geoponic 38.35
geoponics 498.5
Geordie 16.66
George 200
georgette 368
Georgia 17.153
Georgian 261

georgic 38
Georgie 16.105
geostatic 38.49.7
geostrophic 38.13
geosyncline 253.5
geotaxis 300.70
geotectonic 38.35
gerah 17.272
Gerald 122.1
geranial 228.3.5
geraniol 220.1
geranium 242.2.10
geratology
    16.108.4.15
gerbil 218
gerent 420.61
gerenuk 44
geriatric 38.45
geriatrician
    261.71.6
geriatrics 498.8
germ 233
German 261
germander 17.98
germane 247
Germanic 38.31
Germanism
    242.35.14
germanium
    242.2.10
Germanize 516.7
Germanophile
    219.1
Germanophilia
    17.3.21.2
Germanophobe 28
Germanophobia
    17.3.4
Germany 16.237
germicide 92.7
germinal 228.60
germinant 420.53.1
germinate 367.17.4
germination
    261.67.18.4
Germiston 261.107
Geronimo 12.48
gerontocracy
    16.307.5
gerontology
    16.108.4.16
gerrymander 17.98
Gershwin 252
gerund 143
gerundive 485

gesso 12.69
gestalt 401
Gestapo 12.57
gestate 367.33
gestation 261.67.33
gesticulate 367.13.2
gesticulation
    261.67.13
gesture 17.73
get 368
Gethsemane
    16.237.6
getter 17.339
Getty 16.330
Gettysburg 182
geum 242.1
gewgaw 9
geyser 17.440
geyserite 372.8
Gezira 17.272
Ghana 17.226
Ghanaian 261.1
gharry 16.260
ghastly 16.199
ghat 366
Ghats 334
ghazi 16.392
ghee 5
Ghent 410
gherkin 252
ghetto 12.75
ghibli 16.134
ghillie 16.120
ghost 441
ghostlike 39
ghostliness 300.23
ghostly 16.202
ghostwrite 372
ghostwriter 17.343
ghoul 227
ghoulish 353
giant 420.2
gib 24
gibber 17.14
gibberellin 252.7
gibberish 353.11
gibbet 371.5
gibbon 261
gibbous 310.5
gibe 25
Gibeon 261.3.2
giblets 339
Gibraltar 17.363
Gibson 261
gid 91

giddiness 300.23
giddy 16.63
giddy-up 279
Gideon 261.3.5
gidgee 5.6
gie 5
Gielgud 101
gift 398
gifted 91
giftwrap 268
gig 184
gigantic 38.62
gigantism 242.35
gigantomachy
    16.33
giggle 228.46
giggly 16.160
gigolo 12.45
gigot 12.28
gigue 183
Gijón 255
Gilbert 381
Gilbertian 261.3
gild 116
gilding 265.17
Gilead 83.1
gilet 2.11
gilgai 7
Gilgamesh 351
gill 218
Gillian 261.3.11
gillie 16.120
Gillingham 242.17
gillion 261.120
gillyflower 14
gilt 403
gilthead 86
gimbals 539
gimcrack 32
gimlet 371
gimmal 228.52
gimme 5
gimmick 38.28
gimmickry 16.275
gimmicky 16.25
gimp 287
gin 252
ginger 17.157
gingerbread 86
gingerly 16.131
gingery 16.274.14
gingham 242.17
gingili 16.120
gingiva 17.414
gingivitis 300.62.6

ginglymus 310.28
gink 52
ginnel 228.60
ginseng 264
Giotto 12.77
gippy 16.248
gipsywort 369
giraffe 158
girandole 223.2
girasol 220
gird 87
girder 17.81
girdle 228
girl 216
girlfriend 131
girlhood 101
girlie 16.116
girlish 353
giro 12.64
giron 254
gironny 16.231
girt 369
girth 456
gisarme 230
Gisborne 261
gist 436
git 371
gittern 249.1
give 485
given 261.114
giver 17.414
gizzard 103
glabella 17.163.1
glabrous 310
glacé 16.294
glacial 228.91
glacialist 436.7.2
glaciate 367.1.4
glaciation
  261.67.1.3
glacier 17.3.46
glaciology
  16.108.4.1
glacis 300.49
glad 83
gladden 261.19
glade 85
gladiate 371.1
gladiator 17.338.1
gladiatorial
  228.3.12
gladiolus 310
gladly 16.146
gladness 300
gladsome 242

Gladstone 261
glair 4
Glamorgan 261.33
glamorous 310.50
glamour 17.205
glamourize 516.8
glance 315
gland 128
glanders 524
glandular 17.174
glans 544
glare 4
glaring 265.52
glary 16.264
Glasgow 12
glass 294
glass-blower 17.6
glasses 515
glasshouse 306
glassine 251
glasslike 39
glassware 4
glasswork 36
glassworks 497
glassy 16.295
Glastonbury
  16.274
Glaswegian 261.36
Glauce 16.303
glaucoma 17.215
glaucous 310
glaze 509
glazier 17.3.59
glazing 265.81
gleam 234
glean 251
gleanings 552
glebe 23
glee 5
gleeful 226
gleet 370
glen 248
Glencoe 12
Glendower 14
glengarry 16.260
glenoid 97.7
Glenrothes 300
gley 2
gliadin 252
glib 24
glibly 16.134
glide 92
glider 17.84
gliding 265.14
glim 235

glimmer 17.211
glimpse 331
glint 412
glioma 17.215
glissade 84
glissando 12.23
glisten 261.65
glister 17.384
glitter 17.342
glittery 16.274.41
gloaming 265.37
gloat 376
glob 26
global 228.13
globate 367.3
globe 28
globetrotter 17.344
globetrotting
  265.68
globigerina 17.232
globoid 97
globose 305
globular 17.174
globule 227
globulin 252.10
glochidium 242.2.3
glockenspiel 217
glogg 185
glomerate 371.35
glomeration
  261.67.22
glomerulus
  310.25.1
gloom 241
gloominess 300.23
gloomy 16.221
Gloria 17.3.41
gloria 17.3.41
glorify 7.3
glorious 310.2.13
glory 16.269
gloss 302
glossa 17.304
glossary 16.274
glossator 17.338
glossectomy
  16.222.5
glosseme 234
glossitis 300.62
glossolalia 17.3.18
glossy 16.302
glottal 228.104
glottic 38.53
glottis 300
Gloucester 17.385

Gloucestershire 6
glove 489
glover 17.418
glow 12
glower 14
gloxinia 17.3.34
glucagon 254.5
glucinum 242.15
glucose 520
glue 15
gluey 16.4
glum 240
glume 241
glumly 16.168
glumness 300
gluon 254
glut 378
glutamate 367.16
glutamine 251.4
glutelin 252.8
gluten 261.104
gluteus 310.1
glutinous 310.33.2
glutton 261.103
gluttonous 310.36
gluttony 16.237
glyceric 38.39
glyceride 92.6
glycerine 252.20
glycerol 220.4
glycogen 261.39
glycol 220
glycolysis 300.52.2
glycoside 92.8
glycosuria
  17.3.42.2
glyph 163
glyphography
  16.90.2
glyptic 38.66
glyptics 498
glyptography
  16.90.2
gnarl 213
gnash 349
gnat 365
gnathic 38.72
gnathion 254.1
gnathite 372
gnathonic 38.35
gnaw 9
gnawing 265
gneiss 301
gnocchi 16.27
gnome 239

gnomic 38
gnomon 254
gnosis 300.55
gnostic 38.71
Gnosticism 242.35.16
gnu 15
go 12
Goa 17.6
goa 17.6
goad 98
go-ahead 86.5
goal 223
goalie 16.126
goalkeeper 17.252
goalless 300
goalmouth 462
goanna 17.225
goat 376
goatee 5
goatherd 87
goatish 353
goatsbeard 90
goatskin 252
goatsucker 17.39
gob 26
gobbet 371
gobble 228
gobbledegook 45
gobbler 17.178
Gobelin 252.11
go-between 251
Gobi 16.12
gobioid 97
goblet 371
goblin 252
gobstopper 17.255
goby 16.12
god 94
godchild 117
goddamn 229
Goddard 84
goddaughter 17.345
goddess 300.4
godetia 17.325
godfather 17.401
god-fearing 265.53
godforsaken 261.11
Godhead 86
godhood 101
Godiva 17.415
godless 300
godlessness 300.33
godlike 39

godliness 300.23
godly 16.149
godmother 17.408
Godolphin 252
godown 258
godparent 420
godsend 131
godson 259
Godspeed 89
Godunov 165
Godwin 252
godwit 371
goer 17.6
goffer 17.117
Gog 185
go-getter 17.339
goggle 228.47
gogglebox 499
Gogol 220
Goiânia 17.3.30
Goidel 228.35
Goidelic 38.20
going 265.4
goitre 17.346
go-kart 366
Golconda 17.104
gold 120
goldarn 246
goldcrest 433
golden 261.28
goldeneye 7
goldenrod 94
goldeye 7
goldfinch 80
goldfish 353
goldilocks 499
goldsmith 458
goldthread 86
golem 232
golf 173
goliard 103
goliardery 16.274.6
Goliath 464
golliwog 185
gollop 281.2
golly 16.122
Gomberg 182
gombroon 260
Gomorrah 17.275
gomuti 16.343
gonad 83.3
Gond 136
Gondar 1
gondola 17.176
gondolier 6

Gondwanaland 143.4
gone 254
goner 17.233
gonfalon 261
gonfalonier 6.5
gong 266
Gongola 17.171
Gongorism 242.35.15
goniatite 372.12
gonidium 242.2.3
goniometer 17.342.3.1
gonion 261.3.18
gonk 53
gonna 17.233
gonococcus 310.11
gonophore 9.6
gonorrhoea 17.2.2
goo 15
goober 17.20
good 101
goodbye 7
good-humoured 103.5
goodies 515
goodman 261
good-natured 103
goodness 300
good-night 372
goodwife 164
goodwill 218
Goodwin 252
goody 16.70
Goodyear 6
goody-goody 16.70
gooey 16.4
goof 170
goofy 16.89
googly 16.162
googol 220
googolplex 496
Goole 227
goon 260
goop 280
goosander 17.98
goose 309
gooseberry 16.274
goosefoot 379
goosegog 185
goosegrass 294
gooseneck 35
goosy 16.306
gopak 32

gopher 17.117
goral 228.74
Gorbals 539
gorcock 40
Gordon 261.27
gore 9
goreng pisang 263
gorge 200
gorgeous 310
gorger 17.153
gorgerin 252.20
Gorgon 261.33
gorgonian 261.3.18
Gorgonzola 17.171
gorilla 17.166.3
Gorky 16.28
gormandize 516
gormless 300
gorse 303
Gorsedd 474
gory 16.269
gosh 354
goshawk 41
Goshen 261.73
gosling 265
gospel 228
gospeller 17.176
Gosplan 245
Gosport 374
gossamer 17.218
gossip 274
gossipy 16.248
gossoon 260
goster 17.385
got 373
Goth 459
Gothenburg 182
Gothic 38
Gothicism 242.35.16
Gotland 143
gotta 17.344
gotten 261.101
gouache 350
Gouda 17.89
gouge 202
goulash 349
Gould 121
Gounod 12
gourami 16.222
gourd 96
gourmand 143
gourmandise 513
gourmet 2
gout 377

goutweed 89
govern 261.117
governable
228.16.31
governance 321
governess 300.26
government 420.42
governmental
228.110.4
governor 17.239
governorship 274.1
Gower 14
gown 258
Goya 17.5
grab 18
grabble 228
graben 261.8
Gracchus 310.7
grace 295
graceful 226
gracefulness 300.30
graceless 300
gracile 219
gracility 16.333.9
gracious 310.56
graciousness
300.34
grackle 228.19
grad 83
gradate 367.9
gradation 261.67.8
grade 85
grader 17.79
gradient 420.1
gradine 251.1
gradual 228.9
gradualism
242.35.11.3
graduand 128
graduate 367.2,
371.2
graduation
261.67.2
gradus 310
Graecism 242.35
Graecize 516
graffiti 16.332
graffito 12.76
graft 396
grafter 17.358
Graham 242
Grail 214
grain 247
graining 265.40
grainy 16.225

grallatorial
228.3.12.2
gram 229, 230
grama 17.206
gramarye 16.274
gramercy 16.298
gramineous 310.2.8
graminivorous
310.50.3
grammar 17.205
grammarian
261.3.21
grammatical
228.23.18
grammatology
16.108.4.15
gramophone 257
Grampian 261.3
grampus 310.41
Granada 17.78.1
granadilla 17.166
granary 16.274
grand 128
grandchild 117
Grand Coulee
16.130
granddad 83
granddaughter
17.345
grandee 5
grandeur 17.155
grandfather 17.401
grandiloquent
420.59
grandiose 305.1
grandiosity
16.333.30.1
grandioso 12.70
grandma 1
grand mal 212
grandmama 1.12
grandmaster
17.380
grandmother
17.408
grandpa 1
grandpapa 1
grandparent 420
grandson 259
grandstand 128
grange 207
grangerize 516.8
granite 371.22
graniteware 4.9
granitic 38.52

granitite 372.11
granivorous
310.50.3
granny 16.223
granolith 458
granophyre 8.1
grant 408
Granta 17.365
grantee 5
grantor 9
gran turismo 12.50
granular 17.174.9
granulate 367.13
granulation
261.67.13
granule 227
granulite 372
grape 270
grapefruit 380
grapeshot 373
grapevine 253
graph 158
grapheme 234
graphic 38.11
graphical 228.23.3
graphics 498
graphite 372
graphitic 38.52
graphologist 436.4
graphology
16.108.4
grapnel 228
grappa 17.247
Grappelli 16.115
grapple 228.64
grappling 265
graptolite 372.4
Grasmere 6
grasp 290
grasping 265
grass 294
grassfinch 80
grasshook 44
grasshopper 17.255
grassland 143
grassy 16.295
grate 367
grateful 226.7
gratefulness 300.30
grater 17.338
Gratian 261.3
graticule 227.1
gratify 7.3.8
grating 265.64
gratis 300

gratitude 102.2.1
Grattan 261.94
gratuitous 310.64
gratuity 16.333.3
grav 480
gravamen 248.2
grave 16.378, 482
gravel 228.117
gravelly 16.131
graven 261.111
graver 17.410
Graves 481
Gravesend 131
gravestone 257
graveyard 84
gravid 91
gravitate 367.30
gravitation
261.67.27
gravitational
228.63.3
gravitative 485.10
gravity 16.333.33
gravure 10
gravy 16.379
Gray 2
grayling 265.27
graze 509
grazier 17.3.59
grazing 265.81
grease 298
greasepaint 409
greasy 16.299
great 367
greatcoat 376
greatest 436
greatness 300
Greats 335
greave 484
greaves 553
grebe 23
Grecian 261.70
Greece 298
greed 89
greediness 300.23
greedy 16.62
Greek 37
Greeley 16.118
green 251
greenback 32
greenbottle
228.104
greenbrier 17.4
greenery 16.274.25
greenfinch 80

greenfly 7
greengage 193
greengrocer 17.306
greengrocery 16.274
greenhead 86
greenheart 366
greenhorn 255
greenhouse 306
greening 265.42
greenish 353
Greenland 143
Greenlander 17.109
greenling 265
greenness 300
Greenock 46
greenroom 241
greens 547
greensand 128
Greensboro 17.279
greenshank 51
greenstick 38
greenstuff 168
greensward 95
Greenwich 197.7
greenwood 101
greet 370
greeting 265
gregarine 251.7
gregarious 310.2.10
Gregorian 261.3.23
Gregory 16.274
greige 360
greisen 261.127
gremlin 252
Grenada 17.79
grenade 85.2
grenadier 6
grenadine 251.1
Grenadines 547
Grendel 228
Grenoble 228.13
Gresham 242
gressorial 228.3.12
Gretna 17.244
grew 15
grey 2
greyback 32
greybeard 90
greyhen 248
greyhound 139
greyish 353
greylag 178
greyness 300

greywacke 17.28
gribble 228.12
grid 91
griddle 228.32
griddlecake 34
gride 92
gridiron 261.4
grief 162
Grieg 183
grievance 321
grieve 484
grieving 265.79
grievous 310.73
griffe 163
griffin 252
Griffith 458
griffon 261.29
grig 184
grigri 5
grill 218
grillage 197.1
grille 218
grillroom 241
grilse 311
grim 235
grimace 295
Grimaldi 16.75
grimalkin 252
grime 236
Grimm 235
grimness 300
Grimsby 16
grimy 16.217
grin 252
grind 135
grindelia 17.3.20
grinder 17.103
grindery 16.274.8
grindstone 257
gringo 12.36
grip 274
gripe 275
grippe 274
gripping 265
grisaille 214
griseous 310.2.15
griskin 252
grisly 16.209
grison 261
grist 436
gristle 228.85
gristly 16.181
gristmill 218
grit 371
grith 458

grits 339
gritty 16.333
grivet 371
grizzle 228
grizzled 122
grizzly 16.209
groan 257
groat 376
groats 343
grocer 17.306
groceries 515.1
grocery 16.274
grockle 228.25
grog 185
groggy 16.94
grogram 242
groin 256
Grolier 17.3.22
grommet 371.20
gromwell 228
groom 241
grooming 265.39
groove 490
groovy 16.384
grope 278
groper 17.257
Gropius 310.2
grosbeak 37
groschen 261.73
grosgrain 247
gross 305
grossularite 372.8
grot 373
grotesque 57
grotesqueness 300
grotesquery 16.274
Grotius 310.2
grotto 12.77
grouch 71
grouchy 16.51
ground 139
groundage 197
grounding 265.22
groundless 300
groundling 265
groundmass 293
groundnut 378
groundsel 228
groundsheet 370
groundsill 218
groundsman 261
groundspeed 89
groundwork 36
group 280
grouper 17.259

groupie 16.253
grouping 265
grouse 306
grout 377
grouts 344
grouty 16.340
grove 488
grovel 228
grow 12
grower 17.6
growl 224
growler 17.172
grown 257
growth 461
groyne 256
grub 29
grubber 17.19
grubbiness 300.23
grubby 16.13
grudge 203
grudging 265
gruel 228.10
gruelling 265
gruesome 242
gruff 168
gruffness 300
grumble 228
grumbler 17.180
grumbly 16.139
grumous 310
grump 289
grumpy 16.257
Grundy 16.80
grunion 261
grunt 419
grunter 17.373
gruntled 122
Grus 308
Gruyère 4
grysbok 40
guacamole 16.126
Guadalcanal 212
Guadalquivir 6.11
Guadeloupe 280.1
guaiacol 220
Guam 230
guan 246
guanase 509
guano 12.51
guarani 16.237
Guarani 5.14
guarantee 5.24
guarantor 9
guaranty 16.360
guard 84

guardant 420.8
guarded 91.5
guardhouse 306
guardian 261.3
guardianship 274.2
guardrail 214
guardroom 241
guardsman 261
Guarneri 16.265
Guatemala 17.161.1
guava 17.409
guayule 16.130
gubbins 548
gubernatorial 228.3.12.2
guck 43
gudgeon 261.38
Gudrun 260
guelder-rose 520.3
Guelph 172
guenon 254.8
guerdon 261.22
Guernica 17.33
guerrilla 17.166.3
guess 296
guesstimate 367.15, 371.19
guesswork 36
guest 433
guesthouse 306
Guevara 17.268
guff 168
guffaw 9
guidance 321.6
guide 92
guideline 253
guidepost 441
guider 17.84
guiding 265.14
guidon 261.25
Guienne 248
guild 116
guilder 17.95
Guildford 103
guildhall 221
guile 219
guileful 226
guileless 300
guillemot 373
guilloche 354
guillotine 251.11
guilt 403
guiltless 300

guilty 16.350
guimpe 287
Guinea 16.229
guinea 16.229
guinea pig 184
Guinevere 6.11
Guinness 300.23
guipure 10
guise 516
guitar 1
guitarist 436.16
Gujarati 16.328.1
Gujranwala 17.173
Gulag 178
gular 17.175
Gulbenkian 261.3
gulch 77
gules 538
gulf 174
gulfweed 89
gull 225
gullet 371
gullibility 16.333.9.2
gullible 228.16
gull-wing 265
gully 16.128
gulp 284
gulped 427
gum 240
gumbo 12.7
gumboil 222
gumboots 346
gumdrop 276
gumma 17.216
gummy 16.220
gumption 261.89
gumshield 115
gumshoe 15
gumtree 5
gun 259
gunboat 376
guncotton 261.101
gunfight 372
gunfighter 17.343
gunfire 8
gunflint 412
gunge 211
gungy 16.111
gunk 54
gunlock 40
gunman 261
gunmetal 228.100

gunnel 228
gunner 17.237
gunnery 16.274
gunning 265.45
gunny 16.235
gunplay 2
gunpoint 416
gunpowder 17.89
gunrunner 17.237
gunrunning 265.45
gunshot 373
gunslinger 17.246
gunsmith 458
gunstock 40
Guntur 10
gunwale 228
gunyah 1
guppy 16.252
Gur 10
gurdwara 17.268
gurgitation 261.67.27
gurgle 228
gurjun 261.35
Gurkha 17.32
Gurkhali 16.113
Gurmukhi 16.31
gurnard 103
gurnet 371.23
guru 15
Gus 307
gush 356
gusher 17.329
gushy 16.324
gusset 371
gust 443
gustation 261.67
Gustavus 310
gusto 12
gusty 16.368
gut 378
gutbucket 371.11
Gutenberg 182
gutless 300
gutta 17.349
gutta-percha 17.54
gutter 17.349
guttering 265.58
guttersnipe 275
guttural 228.76
gutturalize 516.3.8
gutty 16.341
guv 489

guy 7
Guyana 17.225
guyot 12.2
guzzle 228
guzzler 17.204
Gwalior 9.1
Gwelo 12
Gwent 410
Gwyn 252
Gwynedd 474
gwyniad 83.1
gybe 25
gym 235
gymkhana 17.226
gymnasiarch 33.1
gymnasiast 430.1
gymnasium 242.2.19
gymnast 430
gymnastic 38.68
gymnastics 498.15
gymnosophist 436
gymnosperm 233
gymslip 274
gynaeceum 242.1
gynaecocracy 16.307.5
gynaecoid 97.3
gynaecologist 436.4
gynaecology 16.108.4.4
gynaecomastia 17.3
gynandromorph 166.1
gynarchy 16.20
gynoecium 242.2
gyp 274
gypsophila 17.166
gypsum 242
gypsy 16.314
gyral 228
gyrate 367
gyration 261.67
gyratory 16.274.40
gyre 8
gyrfalcon 261.16
gyrocompass 310.42
gyromagnetic 38.50
gyroplane 247
gyroscope 278.1
gyrostatic 38.49.7
gyrus 310.47

H

ha 1
haaf 158
haar 1
Habakkuk 46
habanera 17.271
habeas corpus
310.38
haberdasher 17.321
haberdashery
16.274
habergeon 261.39
habiliment 420.31
habilitate 367.30.1
habit 371.4
habitable 228.16.49
habitat 365
habitation
261.67.27
habitual 228.9.3
habituate 367.2.1
habitué 2.3
habitus 310.64
háček 35
hachure 10
hacienda 17.101
hack 32
hackamore 9.9
hackberry 16.274
hackbut 378
hackle 228.19
hackles 539
Hackney 16.238
hackney 16.238
hackneyed 91.22
hacksaw 9
had 83
hadal 228
haddock 46
hade 85
Hades 513
Hadith 458
hadn't 420
Hadrian 261.3
hadrosaur 9.11
hae 2
haecceity 16.333.1
haem 234
haemagogue 185.2
haematemesis
300.52.3
haematic 38.49

haematin 252
haematinic 38.34
haematite 372.12
haematocele 217.2
haematocrit 371
haematogenesis
300.52.4
haematoid 97
haematology
16.108.4.15
haematoma 17.215
haematopoiesis
300.51
haematosis
300.55.7
haematoxylon
254.6
haematozoon 254.2
haematuria 17.3.42
haemic 38.27
haemochrome 239
haemocoel 217.2
haemocyte 372.10
haemodialysis
300.52.1
haemoglobin 252
haemoglobinuria
17.3.42.1
haemolysin 252.21
haemolysis
300.52.2
haemophilia
17.3.21.2
haemophiliac
32.1.1
haemophilic 38.21
haemoptysis
300.52
haemorrhage 197
haemorrhagic
38.15
haemorrhoid 97.12
haemorrhoidectomy
16.222.5.1
haemostasis 300.50
haemostat 365
haemostatic
38.49.7
haeremai 7
hafiz 515
hafnium 242.2
haft 396
hag 178
Hagar 1
hagedena 17.230

Hagen 261
Haggadah 17.78
Haggai 7
haggard 103
haggis 300
haggle 228.43
haggler 17.192
hagiarchy 16.20
hagiocracy
16.307.5.1
Hagiographa
17.120.1
hagiography
16.90.2.1
hagiolatry
16.286.2.1
hagiology
16.108.4.1
Hague 180
ha-ha 1.5
Haida 17.84
Haifa 17.115
Haig 180
haik 39
hail 214
Haile Selassie
16.294
hailstone 257
hailstorm 238
Hainan 245
hair 4
hairball 221
hairbrush 356
haircloth 459
haircut 378
hairdo 15
hairdresser 17.300
hairdressing 265.60
hairgrip 274
hairif 163
hairless 300
hairlike 39
hairline 253
hairnet 368
hairpiece 298
hairpin 252
hairsplitting 265.66
hairspring 265
hairstreak 37
hairstyle 219
hairtail 214
hairy 16.264
Haiti 16.329
Haitian 261.3
Haitink 52

hajj 191
hake 34
hakea 17.3
hakim 234
Hakluyt 380
Hakodate 2.23
Halakah 1
halal 213
halation 261.67.14
halberd 103
halcyon 261.3
hale 214
Haleakala 1.7
haler 17.161
Halesowen 252.1
half 158
halfback 32
half-baked 384
halfbeak 37
half-caste 431
half-day 2
half-hearted 91.33
half-heartedness
300.28
half-life 164
half-light 372
half-mast 431
half-naked 91
half-open 261
half-price 301
half-shut 378
half-time 236
halftone 257
halfway 2
halfwit 371
halfwitted 91.38
halibut 381
Halicarnassus
310.51
halide 92
Halifax 494
halite 372
halitosis 300.55.6
hall 221
Hallel 214
Halley 16.112
hallo 12.45
halloo 15.5
hallow 12.38
hallowed 98
Hallowe'en 251
Hallstatt 365
hallucinate 367.17

hallucination
261.67.18
hallucinatory
16.274.43.6
hallucinogen
261.39
hallucinogenic
38.32.1.1
hallucinosis
300.55.4
hallux 503
hallway 2
halo 12
halobiont 414
halogen 261.39
halothane 247
halt 404
Haltemprice 301
halter 17.363
haltere 6
halting 265
halvah 1
halve 481
halyard 103
ham 229
Hama 1.10
hamadryad 83.2
hamadryas 310.3
hamal 213
hamamelidaceous
310.56.2
Hambletonian
261.3.18
Hamburg 182
hamburger 17.127
hame 231
Hamilcar Barca
17.29
Hamilton 261
Hamite 372
Hamitic 38.52
hamlet 371
Hammarskjöld 120
hammer 17.205
hammerhead 86.5
Hammersmith 458
Hammerstein 253
hammertoe 12
hammock 46
Hammond 143
Hammurabi 16.6
hammy 16.210
Hampden 261
hamper 17.261
Hampshire 6

Hampstead 91
Hampton 261
hamshackle 228.19
hamster 17
hamstring 265
hamulus 310.25
Han 245, 246
hanaper 17.260
hance 314
Hancock 40
hand 128
handbag 178
handball 221
handbarrow 12.60
handbell 215
handbill 218
handbook 44
handbrake 34
handcart 366
handclasp 290
handcraft 396
handcuff 168
Handel 228.39
handfeed 89
handful 226
handgrip 274
handgun 259
handhold 120
handicap 268
handicapper
17.247
handicraft 396
handiwork 36
handkerchief 163
handle 228.39
handlebar 1
handlebars 508
handled 122
handler 17
handling 265
handmade 85
handmaiden
261.20
hand-me-down
258
handrail 214
handsaw 9
handsel 228
handset 368
handshake 34
handsome 242
handsomeness 300
handspike 39
handspring 265
handstand 128

handstroke 42
handwriting 265.67
handwritten 261.99
handy 16.77
handyman 261.48
hang 263
hangar 17.245
Hangchow 13
hangdog 185
hanger 17.245
hanging 265
hangman 261
hangnail 214
hangover 17.417
hank 51
hanker 17.43
hanky 16.36
hanky-panky 16.36
Hannah 17.225
Hannibal 228.12
Hanoi 11
Hanover 17.417
Hanoverian
261.3.22
Hanratty 16.327
Hansard 84
Hanse 314
Hanseatic 38.49
hansom 242
Hants. 347
Hanukkah 17.42
Hanuman 246
haphazard 103
hapless 300
haploid 97
haplology 16.108.4
ha'p'orth 464
happen 261
happening 265.46
happiness 300.23
happy 16.243
Hapsburg 182
hapten 261
hapteron 254.11
haptic 38
harakiri 16.266
harambee 2.5
harangue 263.2
Harappa 17.247
Harar 17.268
harass 310.43
harassment 420.46
Harbin 252
harbinger 17.157
harbour 17.10

harbourage 197
hard 84
hardback 32
hardbake 34
hardboard 95
harden 261
hardened 143
hardener 17.240
hardhack 32
hardhearted 91.33
hardihood 101
hardiness 300.23
hardly 16
hardness 300
hardship 274
hardtack 32
hardtop 276
hardware 4
hardwood 101
hardy 16.58
hare 4
harebell 215
harebrained 130
harelip 274
harem 234
Hargeisa 17.299
Hargreaves 553
haricot 12.11
Harijan 261.37
Haringey 2.10
hark 33
Harlem 242
harlequin 252
harlequinade 85.2
harlot 381
Harlow 12.39
harm 230
harmattan 261.94
harmful 226
harmless 300
harmlessness
300.33
harmonic 38.35
harmonica 17.34.1
harmonics 498.5
harmonious
310.2.9
harmonist 436.13
harmonium
242.2.12
harmonize 516.7
harmony 16.237
harness 300.21
Harold 122
harp 269

Harper 17.248
harpoon 260
harpsichord 95.2
harpy 16.244
harridan 261.24
harrier 17.3
Harris 300
Harrisburg 182.1
Harrison 261.65.1
Harrogate 371
Harrovian 261.3.31
Harrow 12.60
harrow 12.60
harrowing 265.4
Harry 16.260
harry 16.260
harsh 350
harshness 300
hart 366
hartebeest 435
Hartford 103
Hartlepool 227
Hartley 16.187
harum-scarum
    242.18
Harun al-Rashid
    89
haruspex 496
Harvard 103
harvest 436
harvester 17.384
harvesting 265.76
harvestman 261
Harvey 16.378
Harwich 197.9
Harz 334
has 507
has-been 251
Hasdrubal 228.15
hash 349
hashish 352
Hasidim 234
hask 55
haslet 371
hasn't 420
hasp 290
hassle 228
hassock 46
hast 430
hastate 367
haste 432
hasten 261.62
Hastings 552
hasty 16.363
hat 365

hatband 128
hatbox 499
hatch 62
hatchback 32
hatchel 228
hatchery 16.274
hatchet 371
hatchment 420.36
hatchway 2
hate 367
hateful 226.7
hater 17.338
Hatfield 115
hath 452
Hathaway 2.28
hatless 300
hatpin 252
hatred 91
Hatshepsut 380
hatter 17.336
hauberk 36
haugh 33
haughty 16.336
haul 221
haulage 197
haulm 238
haunch 81
haunt 415
haunted 91.47
haunting 265
Hausa 17.307
hausfrau 13
haustellum 242.8
haustorium
    242.2.17
hautboy 11
hauteur 3
Havana 17.225
Havant 420
have 480
havelock 40
haven 261.111
haven't 420
haver 17.410
Havering 265.58
haversack 32
haversine 253.8
havildar 1
havoc 46
haw 9
Hawaii 16.2
Hawaiian 261.4
hawfinch 80
Hawhaw 9
hawk 41

hawker 17.37
hawking 265.9
Hawkins 548
hawksbill 218
hawse 518
hawsepipe 275
hawthorn 255
hay 2
haycock 40
Haydn 261.25
hayfork 41
haymaker 17.30
haymaking 265.6
hayrack 32
hayrick 38
haystack 32
haywire 8
hazard 103
hazardous 310.17
hazardousness
    300.34
haze 509
hazel 228.125
hazelnut 378
Hazlitt 371
hazy 16.393
he 5
head 86
headache 34
headachy 16.21
headband 128
headboard 95
headcheese 513
headdress 296
header 17.80
headfast 431
headfirst 434
headgear 6
heading 265.12
headless 300
headlight 372
headline 253
headliner 17.232
headlock 40
headlong 266
headman 261
headmaster 17.380
headphones 550
headpiece 298
headquarters 524
headrace 295
headreach 66
headrest 433
headroom 241
headscarf 158

headset 368
headship 274
headshrinker 17.44
headspring 265
headsquare 4
headstand 128
headstock 40
headstone 257
headstream 234
headstrong 266
headward 103
headway 2
headwind 134
headword 87
heady 16.60
heal 217
healer 17.165
Healey 16.118
health 465
healthful 226
healthiness 300.23
healthy 16.374
heap 273
hear 6
heard 87
hearer 17.272
hearing 265.53
hearken 261.10
hearsay 2
hearse 297
Hearst 434
heart 366
heartache 34
heartbeat 370
heartbreak 34
heartbreaker 17.30
heartbreaking
    265.6
heartbroken 261.14
heartburn 249
hearten 261.95
heartfelt 402
hearth 453
heartland 143
heartless 300
heartlessness
    300.33
heart-rending
    265.20
heartsease 513
heartsick 38
heartstrings 552
heartwood 101
hearty 16.328
heat 370

heated 91.37
heater 17.341
heath 457
heathen 261
heathendom 242
heathenish 353
heathenize 516.7
heather 17.402
heating 265
heatstroke 42
heaume 239
heave 484
heaven 261.112
heavenly 16.174
heavenwards 531
heaves 553
heaviness 300.23
Heaviside 92.7
heavy 16.380
heavy-handed
 91.12
heavyweight 367
hebdomadal 228.38
hebdomadary
 16.274.7
Hebe 16.10
hebephrenia
 17.3.33
hebetate 367.30
hebetic 38.50
Hebraic 38.1.1
Hebraism 242.35
Hebraist 436.1
Hebrew 15
Hebridean 261.2
Hebrides 513.4
Hebron 254
Hecate 16.344
hecatomb 241
heck 35
heckelphone 257
heckle 228.21
hectare 1
hectic 38.60
hectocotylus
 310.23
hectogram 229.1
hectograph 158.1
hector 17.354
he'd 89
heddle 228
hedge 194
hedgehog 185
hedgehop 276
hedgerow 12

hedonics 498.5
hedonism
 242.35.14
hedonist 436.13
heebie-jeebies 515
heed 89
heedful 226
heedless 300
heedlessness
 300.33
heehaw 9
heel 217
heeled 115
heeltap 268
heft 397
hefty 16.346
Hegel 228.44
hegemony 16.237.6
Hegira 17.272
hegumen 248.3
Heidelberg 182
heifer 17.112
heigh-ho 12
height 372
heighten 261.100
Heilungkiang 263
Heimdall 213
heinous 310.31
heir 4
heirdom 242
heiress 300.44
heirless 300
heirloom 241
heirship 274
heist 437
heitiki 5
Hejaz 507
Hel 215
held 113
Helen 252.7
Helena 17.239
helianthus 310.72
helical 228.23.6
helices 513
helichrysum 242.35
helicline 253.4
helicoid 97.3
Helicon 261.13
helicon 261.13
helicopter 17.377
Heligoland 143.3
heliograph 158.1.1
heliolatry
 16.286.2.1
heliolithic 38.73

heliometer
 17.342.3.1
Heliopolis 300.13.2
heliotactic 38.58
heliotherapy
 16.254
heliotrope 278.3
heliotropic 38.37.2
heliotype 275.1
heliport 374.1
helium 242.2.5
helix 498
hell 215
he'll 217
Hellas 310.22
hellbent 410
hellcat 365
helldiver 17.415
hellebore 9
helleborine 251.6
Hellene 251
Hellenic 38.32
Hellenism
 242.35.13
Hellenist 436.11
Hellenistic 38.70
Hellenize 516.6
heller 17.163
hellery 16.274
Hellespont 414
hellfire 8
hellgrammite 372
hellhole 223
hellhound 139
hellion 261.119
hellish 353.4
hello 12.40
helm 243
helmet 371
helmeted 91.38
helminth 470
helminthic 38
helminthology
 16.108.4
Hélot 381
helotism 242.35.20
helotry 16.286
help 283
helpful 226
helpfulness 300.30
helping 265
helpless 300
helplessness 300.33
Helpmann 261

helpmate 367
Helsinki 16.37
helter-skelter
 17.361
helve 492
Helvellyn 252.7
Helvetia 17.325
Helvetian 261.70
Helvetic 38.50
Helvetii 7.1
Helvétius 310.2
hem 232
he-man 261.47
Hemel Hempstead
 91
hemeralopia
 17.3.37.1
hemialgia 17.3.16
hemianopsia 17.3
hemihedral 228.78
Hemingway 2
hemiola 17.171
hemiplegia 17.3.13
hemiplegic 38.17
hemipode 98
hemipteran 261.60
hemisphere 6
hemispheric 38.39
hemispheroid 97.10
hemistich 38.70
hemline 253
hemlock 40
hemmer 17.208
hemp 286
hempen 261
hems 541
hemstitch 67
hen 248
henbane 247
hence 316
henceforth 460
henceforward
 103.8
henchman 261
hencoop 280
hendiadys 300.5
henequen 252.3
henge 208
Hengist 436
henhouse 306
Henley 16.171
henna 17.228
hennery 16.274.23
henpeck 35
henpecked 385

389

hep 271
heparin 252.20
hepatic 38.49
hepatica 17.34.3
hepatitis 300.62
Hepburn 249
hepcat 365
Hephaestus 310
Hephaistos 302
Hepplewhite 372
heptad 83
heptagon 254.5
heptarchy 16.20
Heptateuch 45
heptose 520
Hepworth 464
her 3
Hera 17.272
Heracles 513
Heraclitus 310.65
herald 122.1
heraldic 38
heraldry 16.278
herb 22
herbaceous 310.56
herbage 197
herbal 228
herbalist 436.7
herbarium 242.2.14
Herbert 381
herbicide 92.7
herbivore 9.13
herbivorous
 310.50.3
herby 16.9
Herculaneum
 242.2.10
herculean 261.2
Hercules 513
herd 87
herder 17.81
herdic 38
herdsman 261
here 6
hereabouts 344
hereafter 17.358
hereat 365
hereby 7
heredes 513.3
hereditament
 420.35
hereditarianism
 242.35.14.1.1
hereditary
 16.274.41

hereditist 436.24
heredity 16.333
Hereford 103
herein 252
hereinbefore 9.5
hereinto 15
hereof 487
hereon 254.9
Herero 12.62
heres 513.11
heresiarch 33.1
heresy 16.307
heretic 38.57
heretical 228.23.19
hereto 15
heretofore 9
hereunder 17.108
hereupon 254
Hereward 103
herewith 476
heriot 381.1
heritable 228.16.49
heritage 197.12
heritor 17.342
heritress 300
herl 216
Herman 261
hermaphrodite
 372.2
hermaphroditic
 38.52
hermeneutic 38.56
hermeneutics 498
Hermes 513
hermetic 38.50
hermit 371
hermitage 197.12
Hermoupolis
 300.13
hern 249
hernia 17.3.32
herniorrhaphy
 16.90.1
hero 12.63
Herod 103
Herodias 293.1
Herodotus 310.68
heroic 38.2
heroics 498
heroin 252.1
heroine 252.1
heroism 242.35.3
heron 261
heronry 16.284
Herophilus 310.23

herpes 513
herpetology
 16.108.4
herring 265
herringbone 257
hers 511
Herschel 228.92
herself 172
Hertford 103
Hertfordshire 6
hertz 337
Hertzog 185
Herzegovina
 17.230
he's 513
Hesiod 94
Hesione 16.237.1
hesitancy 16.312
hesitant 420.76
hesitate 367.30
Hesperides 513.4
hesperidium
 242.2.3
Hesperus 310.50
Hesse 296
hessian 261.3
Hestia 17.3
het 368
hetaera 17.272
heterocercal 228.22
heteroclite 372
heterodox 499.1
heterodoxy 16.389
heterodyne 253.2
heteroecious
 310.57
heterogamy
 16.222.2
heterogeneous
 310.2.7
heterogony
 16.237.4
heterograft 396
heteromorphic
 38.14
heteronymous
 310.28.2
heterophony
 16.237.3
heteroplasty
 16.361.1
heteroscedasticity
 16.333.28.2
heterosexual 228.9

heterosexuality
 16.333.8.2
heterostyly 16.121
heterotopia
 17.3.37.3
heterotrophic 38.13
heterotypic 38.36
hetman 261
heulandite 372
heuristic 38.70
hew 15
hex 496
hexachord 95.3
hexad 83
hexadecimal
 228.52.1
hexaemeron 254.11
hexagon 254.5
hexagonal 228.63
hexagram 229.1
hexahedron 261
hexameter 17.342
hexapod 94.1
hexastich 38
Hexateuch 45
hexone 257
hexosan 245
hexose 520
hey 2
heyday 2
Heysham 242
Heywood 101
Hezekiah 17.4
hi 7
hiatus 310.62
hibachi 16.47
hibernal 228.58
hibernate 367.18
hibernation
 261.67.19
Hibernia 17.3.32
Hibernian 261.3
Hibernicism
 242.35.16
hibiscus 310.15
hic 38
hiccup 279
hick 38
hickey 16.25
hickory 16.274.4
hid 91
hidalgo 12.34
hidden 261.24
hide 92
hide-and-seek 37

hideaway 2.28
hidebound 139
hideous 310.2.1
hiding 265.14
hidrosis 300.55
hie 7
hieland 143.1
hieracosphinx 505
hierarch 33
hierarchical 228.23
hierarchy 16.20
hieratic 38.49
hierocracy 16.307.5
hierodule 227
hieroglyph 163
hieroglyphic 38.12
hieroglyphics 498.1
hierogram 229.1
hierology 16.108.4
Hieronymus
 310.28.2
hierophant 407
hi-fi 7
Higgins 548
high 7
highball 221
highborn 255
highboy 11
highbrow 13
highchair 4
highfalutin 252.24
high-flown 257
high-handed 91.12
high jinks 505
highland 143
Highlander 17.109
Highlands 534
highlife 164
highlight 372
highly 16.121
highly-strung 267
high-minded 91
Highness 300
highroad 98
high-spirited 91.38
hightail 214
highway 2.26
highwayman
 261.45
High Wycombe
 242.4
hijack 32
hijacker 17.28
hike 39
hiker 17.35

hilarious 310.2.10
hilarity 16.333.20.2
Hilary 16.274.16
Hilda 17.95
hill 218
Hillary 16.274.16
hillbilly 16.120
hillfort 374
Hillingdon 261
hillock 46
hillside 92
hilly 16.120
hilt 403
hilum 242.9
hilus 310.24
Hilversum 242
him 235
Himalayas 524
himation 254.1
Himeji 5.5
himself 172
Himyaritic 38.52.2
hin 252
Hinayana 17.226
Hinckley 16.145
hind 135
hindbrain 247
Hindenburg 182
hinder 17.102
hinder 17.103
hindgut 378
Hindi 16.79
hindmost 441
hindquarter 17.345
hindrance 321
hindsight 372
Hindu 15
Hinduism 242.35.4
Hindu Kush 357
Hindustan 246
Hindustani 16.224
hinge 209
hinny 16.229
hint 412
hinterland 143.4
hip 274
hipbone 257
hipparch 33
Hipparchus 310.8
hippeastrum 242
hippie 16.248
hippo 12
hippocampus
 310.41
hippocras 293

Hippocrates 513.17
Hippocratic
 38.49.6
Hippocrene 251
hippodrome 239
hippogriff 163
Hippolyta 17.342
Hippolyte 5.22
Hippolytus 310.64
hippopotamus
 310.29.3
hipster 17.396
hipsters 524
hiragana 17.226
hircine 253
hire 8
hireling 265
hirer 17.274
Hirohito 12.76
Hiroshige 2
Hiroshima 17.210
hirsute 380
hirundine 253
his 515
Hispania 17.3.29
Hispanic 38.31
Hispanicism
 242.35.16
Hispanicize 516.10
Hispaniola 17.171
hispid 91
hiss 300
hist 436
histaminase 509
histamine 252.15
histaminic 38.34
histogen 261.39
histogenesis
 300.52.4
histogram 229.1
histoid 97
histology 16.108.4
histolysis 300.52.2
historian 261.3.23
historic 38.41
historical 228.23.17
historicism
 242.35.16
historicity
 16.333.28
historiographer
 17.120.1
historiography
 16.90.2.1
history 16.274.49

histrionic 38.35.1
histrionics 498.5
hit 371
hitch 67
Hitchcock 40
hitchhike 39
hitchhiker 17.35
hither 17.405
hitherto 15
Hitler 17.201
Hitlerism
 242.35.15
hitter 17.342
Hittite 372.11
hive 486
hives 554
ho 12
hoar 9
hoard 95
hoarder 17.86
hoarding 265.15
hoarfrost 438
hoarse 303
hoarsen 261
hoarseness 300
hoary 16.269
hoatching 265
hoatzin 252
hoax 501
hoaxer 17.429
hob 26
Hobart 366
hobble 228
hobbledehoy 11
hobby 16.11
hobbyhorse 303
hobgoblin 252
hobnail 214
hobnailed 112
hobnob 26
hobo 12
Hoboken 261.14
hobson-jobson 261
Ho Chi Minh 252
hock 40
hockey 16.27
Hockney 16.239
Hocktide 92
hocus-pocus 310.12
hod 94
hodden 261.26
hodgepodge 199
hoe 12
hoedown 258
Hofei 2

hog 185
hogan 261
Hogarth 453
hogback 32
hogfish 353
Hogg 185
hogged 106
hoggish 353
Hogmanay 2
hogshead 86
hogtie 7
hogwash 354
hogweed 89
Hohenzollern 261.42
hoi polloi 11.1
hoist 440
hoity-toity 16.338
hoke 42
hokey cokey 16.29
Hokkaido 12.20
hokum 242
Hokusai 7
Holarctic 38.59
hold 120
holdall 221
holder 17.97
holdfast 431
holding 265.18
hole 223
holey 16.126
holiday 2
holiness 300.23
Holinshed 86
holism 242.35
Holland 143
holland 143
hollandaise 509
Hollandia 17.3
holler 17.168
hollow 12.43
hollowness 300.25
holly 16.122
hollyhock 40
Hollywood 101
holm 239
holmium 242.2
holocaust 439
Holocene 251.9
holocrine 253
hologram 229.1
holograph 158.1
holography 16.90.2
holophytic 38.52

holothurian 261.3.24
holotype 275.1
holozoic 38.2
Holstein 253
holster 17.392
holt 405
holy 16.126
Holyhead 86.2
holystone 257
hom 237
homa 17.213
homage 197.4
hombre 2
homburg 182
home 239
homebred 86
homecoming 265.38
homeland 143
homeless 300
homelessness 300.33
homely 16
homeopathic 38.72
homeopathy 16.373.1.1
homeotypic 38.36
Homer 17.215
homer 17.215
Homeric 38.39
homesick 38
homesickness 300.27
homespun 259
homestead 86
homesteader 17.80
homeward 103
homework 36
homicidal 228.33
homicide 92.7
homiletic 38.50
homiletics 498.12
homily 16.120
homing 265.37
hominid 91
hominoid 97.8
hominy 16.229
homo 12.49
homocentric 38.47
homocercal 228.22
homogamy 16.222.2
homogeneity 16.333.1

homogeneous 310.2.7
homogenize 516.6
homogenous 310.33
homogeny 16.229.2
homogony 16.237.4
homograft 396
homograph 158.1
homologate 367.11
homologize 516.1
homologous 310
homologue 185
homology 16.108.4
homonym 235
homophone 257
homophonic 38.35.2
homophonous 310.36
homophony 16.237.3
homopterous 310.50
homorganic 38.31
Homo sapiens 546
homoscedasticity 16.333.28.2
homosexual 228.9
homosexuality 16.333.8.2
homozygous 310
homunculus 310.25
homy 16.219
honan 245
Honda 17.104
Honduras 310.49
hone 257
Honegger 17.129
honest 436
honestly 16.201
honesty 16.366
honey 16.235
honeybee 5
honeybunch 82
honeycomb 239
honeydew 15.7
honey-eater 17.341
honeyed 91
honeymoon 260
honeymooner 17.238
honeysucker 17.39
honeysuckle 228.27
hong 266

Hong Kong 266
Honiara 17.268.1
Honiton 261.99
honk 53
honky-tonk 53
Honolulu 15.4
honorarium 242.2.14
honorary 16.274.32
honorific 38.12.1
honour 17.233
honourable 228.16.35
honours 524
Honshu 15
hooch 74
hood 101
hooded 91
hoodlum 242
hoodoo 15
hoodwink 52
hooey 16.4
hoof 170
hoofbound 139
Hooghly 16.162
hoo-ha 1
hook 44
hookah 17.40
hooked 390
hooker 17.40
hooknose 520
hookworm 233
hooky 16.31
hooligan 261.32
hooliganism 242.35.14
hoop 280
hoopla 1
hoopoe 15
hoorah 1.13
hooray 2
hoosegow 13
hoot 380
hootenanny 16.223
hooter 17.351
hoots 346
Hoover 17.419
hop 276
hope 278
hopeful 226
hopefully 16.129
hopefulness 300.30
Hopeh 2
hopeless 300

hopelessness 300.33
Hopi 16.251
Hopkins 548
hoplite 372
hoplology 16.108.4
hopper 17.255
hopping 265
hopple 228.68
hopsack 32
hopscotch 68
hora 17.276
Horace 300
Horae 5
Horatian 261.67.22
horde 95
horehound 139
horizon 261.127
horizontal 228.111
horme 16.218
hormonal 228.62
hormone 257
Hormuz 522
horn 255
hornbeam 234
hornbill 218
hornblende 131
horned 137
hornet 371.26
hornpipe 275
hornswoggle 228.47
horny 16.232
horologe 199
horologium 242.2
horology 16.108.4
horoscope 278.1
horoscopy 16.254.2
Horowitz 339
horrendous 310
horrible 228.16
horribly 16.137
horrid 91.26
horrific 38.12
horrify 7.3
horripilation 261.67.12
horror 17.275
horrors 524
Horsa 17.305
horse 303
horseback 32

horsebox 499
horseflesh 351
horsefly 7
horsehair 4
horsehide 92
horseleech 66
horseman 261
horsemanship 274.2
horsemint 412
horseplay 2
horsepower 14
horseradish 353.1
horseshit 371
horseshoe 15
horsewhip 274
horsewoman 261.50
horst 439
horsy 16.303
hortatory 16.274.43
horticultural 228.76
horticulture 17.69
Horus 310.48
hosanna 17.225
hose 520
Hosea 17.2
hosier 17.3.62
hosiery 16.274.1
hospice 300
hospitable 228.16.49
hospital 228.102
hospitality 16.333.8
hospitalize 516.3
hospitaller 17.176.3
host 441
hosta 17.385
hostage 197
hostel 228.115
hosteller 17.176
hostelling 265
hostelry 16.283
hostess 300
hostile 219
hostility 16.333.9
hot 373
hotbed 86
hot-blooded 91.11
hotchpot 373
hotchpotch 68

hot dog 185
hotel 215.4
hotelier 17.3.19
hotfoot 379
hothead 86
hot-headedness 300.28
hothouse 306
hotly 16.191
hotness 300
hotplate 367
hotpot 373
Hotspur 3
hotspur 3
Hottentot 373
hottie 16.335
Houdan 245
Houdini 16.228
houmous 310
hound 139
Hounslow 12
hour 14
hourglass 294
houri 16.270
hourly 16.127
house 306, 521
houseboat 376
housebound 139
houseboy 11
housebreaker 17.30
housebreaking 265.6
housecarl 213
housecoat 376
housefly 7
household 120
householder 17.97
housekeeper 17.252
housekeeping 265.49
housel 228.129
houseleek 37
housemaid 85
houseman 261
housemaster 17.380
housemistress 300
House of Commons 551
houseroom 241
housetop 276
housewife 164

housewifery 16.274
housework 36
housey-housey 16.304
housing 265
Houston 261
houstonia 17.3.36
houting 265
Hove 488
hove 488
hovel 228
hover 17.416
hovercraft 396
hoverport 374.2
hovertrain 247
how 13
Howard 103
howbeit 371
howdah 17.89
howdy 16.68
howe'er 4
however 17.411
howitzer 17.320
howl 224
howler 17.172
howling 265.33
howsoever 17.411
howtowdie 16.68
hoy 11
hoya 17.5
hoyden 261
Hoylake 34
Hsi 5
hub 29
Hubbard 103
hubbub 29
hubby 16.13
hubcap 268
hubris 300
huckaback 32.2
huckleberry 16.274
Huddersfield 115
huddle 228.36
hudibrastic 38.68
Hudson 261
hue 15
hued 102
huff 168
huffy 16.88
hug 189
huge 204
huggermugger 17.134

Hughes 523
Hugo 12.32
Huguenot 12
Huhehot 373
hula 17.175
hulk 50
hulking 265
Hull 225
hull 225
hullabaloo 15.5
hum 240
human 261.51
humane 247
humanism
 242.35.14
humanist 436.13.3
humanitarian
 261.3.21.2
humanitarianism
 242.35.14.1.1
humanity
 16.333.14
humanize 516.7
humankind 135
humanly 16.174
humanoid 97.9
Humber 17.27
Humberside 92.8
humble 228
humbly 16.139
Humboldt 405
humbug 189
humdinger 17.246
humdrum 240
Hume 241
humectant 420.79
humeral 228.76
humerus 310.50
humid 91
humidifier 17.4.1
humidify 7.3.1
humidity 16.333.5
humidor 9.3
humiliate 367.1.2
humiliation
 261.67.1.1
humility 16.333.9
hummel 228
hummingbird 87
hummock 46
humoresque 57
humorist 436.20
humoristic 38.70.5
humorous 310.50
humour 17.217

humourless 300.13
humoursome 242
hump 289
humpback 32
humpbacked 382
humph 177
Humphrey 16.281
humpy 16.257
humus 310
Hun 259
Hunan 245
hunch 82
hunchback 32
hunchbacked 382
hundred 103
hundredweight
 367
hung 267
Hungarian
 261.3.21
Hungary
 16.274.11
hunger 17.143
Hungnam 229
hungriness 300.23
hungry 16
hunk 54
hunky-dory
 16.269
Hunnish 353
hunt 419
hunted 91
hunter 17.373
hunting 265
Huntingdon 261
Huntingdonshire
 6.8
huntsman 261
Huon 254
Hupeh 2
hurdle 228
hurdler 17.185
hurdy-gurdy 16.61
hurl 216
hurley 16.116
hurling 265
hurly-burly 16.116
Huron 261.59
hurrah 1
hurricane 247.1,
 261.13
hurried 91
hurriedness 300.28
hurry 16.272
hurt 369

hurter 17.340
hurtful 226
hurtle 228
husband 143
husbandman 261
husbandry 16.279
hush 356
husk 60
husky 16.42
huss 307
hussar 1
Hussein 247
hussy 16.305
hustings 552
hustle 228.87
hustler 17.199
hut 378
hutch 72
Hutu 15
hyacinth 470
hyacinthine 253
Hyades 513.5
hyaline 252.11
hyalite 372.4
hyaloid 97.6
hybrid 91
hybridize 516
hydantoin 252.1
hydathode 98
hydatid 91
Hyde 92
hydrangea 17.156
hydrant 420
hydranth 467
hydrargyrum 242
hydrastis 300.67
hydrate 367
hydrated 91.34
hydraulic 38.23
hydraulics 498
hydric 38
hydride 92
hydro 12
hydrocarbon 261.8
hydrocele 217.2
hydrocephalus
 310.26.3
hydrocephaly
 16.131
hydrochloric 38.42
hydrochloride 92.5
hydrodynamic
 38.24
hydroelectric 38

hydroelectricity
 16.333.28
hydrofoil 222.1
hydrogen 261.39
hydrogenate
 367.17
hydrogenous
 310.33
hydrography
 16.90.2
hydrokinetic
 38.50.4
hydrology
 16.108.4
hydrolyse 516.3
hydrolysis
 300.52.2
hydrolytic 38.52.1
hydromancy
 16.309
hydrometeor 17.3
hydrometer
 17.342.3
hydropathy
 16.373.1
hydrophane 247.3
hydrophilic 38.21
hydrophilous
 310.23
hydrophobia
 17.3.4
hydrophobic 38.3
hydrophone 257
hydroplane 247
hydroponics 498.5
hydropower 14
hydroscope 278.1
hydroski 5
hydrosphere 6.1
hydrostat 365
hydrostatic
 38.49.7
hydrostatics
 498.11
hydrosulphide 92
hydrotherapy
 16.254
hydrotropic
 38.37.2
hydrous 310
hydroxide 92.14
hydroxy 16.389
hydrozoan 261.6
Hydrus 310
hyena 17.230

hyetograph 158.1
hyetography
16.90.2.5
Hygeia 17.2
hygiene 251
hygienic 38.33
hygienics 498.4
hygienist 436
hygrograph 158.1
hygrometer
17.342.3
hygrophilous
310.23
hygroscope 278.1
hygroscopic
38.37.1
Hyksos 302
hyla 17.167
hylozoism
242.35.3
hymen 248
hymenium 242.2
hymn 235
hymnal 228
hymnist 436
hymnody 16.72
hymnology
16.108.4
hyoid 97
hypaesthesia
17.3.60
hype 275
hyperacidity
16.333.5.1
hyperactive 485.16
hyperactivity
16.333.35.2
hyperaemia
17.3.26
hyperaesthesia
17.3.60
hyperbaric 38.38
hyperbaton 254
hyperbola 17.176
hyperbole 16.131
hyperbolic 38.22
hyperbolize
516.3.4
hyperboloid 97.6
Hyperborean
261.3.23
hypercritical
228.23.20
hyperdulia 17.3.23

hyperglycaemia
17.3.26
hypergolic 38.22
hypericum 242.4
hyperinsulinism
242.35.13
Hyperion 261.3.22
hyperkinesia
17.3.60
hypermarket 371.7
hypermeter
17.342
hypermnesia
17.3.60
hyperon 254.11
hyperplasia
17.3.59
hyperpnoea 17.2
hyperpyrexia
17.3.57
hypersensitive
485.12
hypersensitize
516.12
hyperspace 295
hypertension
261.82.3
hyperthermia
17.3.25
hyperthyroidism
242.35
hypertonic 38.35.5
hypertrophy 16.90
hyperventilation
261.67.12
hypervitaminosis
300.55.4
hypha 17.115
hyphen 261
hyphenate 367.18
hyphenated
91.34.6
hyphenation
261.67.19
hypnagogic 38.18
hypnoid 97
hypnology
16.108.4
hypnopaedia
17.3.8
hypnosis 300.55
hypnotherapy
16.254
hypnotic 38.53.2

hypnotism
242.35.20
hypnotist 436.26
hypnotize 516.13
hypo 12
hypoacidity
16.333.5.1
hypocaust 439
hypocentre 17.368
hypochondria 17.3
hypochondriac
32.1
hypochondrium
242.2
hypocorism
242.35.15
hypocrisy 16.307.5
hypocrite 371
hypocritical
228.23.20
hypocycloid 97
hypodermic 38.26
hypodermis
300.18
Hypodorian
261.3.23
hypogastrium
242.2
hypogeal 228.2
hypogene 251
hypogenous
310.33
hypogeum 242.1
hypoglossal
228.86
hypoglycaemia
17.3.26
hypolimnion 261.3
hypomania
17.3.31.1
hyponasty 16.361
hypophysis 300.52
hypoplasia 17.3.59
hyposensitize
516.12
hypostatic 38.49.7
hypostatize 516.13
hypostyle 219.7
hypotension
261.82
hypotenuse 523
hypothalamus
310.29.2

hypothecate 367.5
hypothermia
17.3.25
hypothesis
300.52.5
hypothesize
516.10
hypothetical
228.23.19
hypothyroidism
242.35
hypotonic 38.35.5
hypoxic 38.75
hypsometry
16.285.2
hyrax 494
hyson 261
hyssop 281
hysterectomy
16.222.5.2
hysteresis 300.51.1
hysteria 17.3.39
hysteric 38.39
hysterical
228.23.15
hysterics 498.6
hysterogenic
38.32.1
hysteroid 97.12
hysterotomy
16.222.4
hystricomorph
166.1

I

I 7
iamb 229
iambic 38.5
Ian 261.2, 261.3
iatric 38.45
Ibadan 261.19
Iberia 17.3.39
Iberian 261.3.22
ibex 496
ibis 300
ibn-Saud 99
Ibo 12.5

Ibsen 261
Icaria 17.3.38
Icarian 261.3.21
Icarus 310.50
ice 301
iceberg 182
iceblink 52
icebound 139
icebox 499
icebreaker 17.30
icecap 268
ice cream 234
Iceland 143
Icelandic 38.10
Iceni 7
I Ching 265
Ichinomiya 17.3
ichneumon 261.51
ichnite 372
ichnology 16.108.4
ichor 9
ichthyic 38
ichthyoid 97
ichthyology
   16.108.4.1
ichthyornis 300.24
ichthyosaur 9.11
ichthyosis 300.55.1
icicle 228.23
iciness 300.23
icing 265
icon 254
iconic 38.35
iconoclasm 242.34
iconoclast 430
iconoclastic 38.68
iconography
   16.90.2
iconolatry 16.286.2
iconology 16.108.4
iconomatic 38.49.2
icterus 310.50
ictus 310
icy 16.301
id 91
I'd 92
Ida 17.84
Idaho 12.37
ide 92
idea 17.2
ideal 228.2
idealism
   242.35.11.1
idealist 436.7.1
idealistic 38.70.2.1

ideality 16.333.8.1
idealize 516.3.1
ideate 367.1
ideatum 242.27
idempotent 420
identical 228.23.23
identifiable
   228.16.3.1
identification
   261.67.5.1
identify 7.3
Identikit 371.9
identity 16.333.32
ideogram 229.1.1
ideography
   16.90.2.1
ideology 16.108.4.1
ides 527
idiocy 16.307
idiolect 385.5
idiom 242.2.3
idiomatic 38.49.2
idiopathic 38.72
idiopathy
   16.373.1.1
idiosyncrasy
   16.307
idiosyncratic 38.49
idiot 381.1
idiotic 38.53
idle 228.33
idleness 300.30
idler 17.187
idol 228.33
idolater 17.352
idolatrous 310
idolatry 16.286.2
idolize 516.3
idyll 218
idyllic 38.21
idyllist 436.5
if 163
Ife 16.84
igloo 15
Ignatius 310.2.16
igneous 310.2
ignite 372.7
igniter 17.343
ignition 261.71
ignoble 228.13
ignominious
   310.2.8
ignominy 16.229
ignoramus 310.27
ignorance 321.20

ignorant 420.65
ignore 9
Igraine 247
iguana 17.226
ihram 230
ikebana 17.226
ILEA 17.3.21
ileac 32.1.1
ileitis 300.62
ileostomy 16.222.6
Ilesha 17.322
ileum 242.2.6
ileus 310.2.5
ilex 496
iliac 32.1.1
Iliad 83.1
Ilion 261.3.11
Ilium 242.2.6
ilium 242.2.6
ilk 49
Ilkeston 261.107
ill 218
I'll 219
ill-advised 154
ill-assorted 91
illative 485.10
Illawarra 17.275
illegal 228.45
illegality 16.333.8.4
illegalize 516.3
illegible 228.16
illegitimacy
   16.307.2
illegitimate 371.19
ill-gotten 261.101
illiberal 228.76
illicit 371.36
illimitable
   228.16.49
illinium 242.2.11
Illinois 11
Illinoisan 261.5
illiquid 91
illiteracy 16.307.4
illiterate 371.35
illness 300
illocution 261.75.2
illogical 228.23.5
illogicality
   16.333.8.3
ill-starred 84
illude 102
illume 241
illuminance 321.14
illuminant 420.53.3

illuminate 367.17.6
illuminati 16.328
illumination
   261.67.18.7
illumine 252
illuminism
   242.35.13
ill-use 309
illusion 261.93.1
illusionism
   242.35.14
illusionist 436.13
illusive 485.8
illusory 16.274
illustrate 367
illustration 261.67
illustrative 485.15
illustrator 17.338
illustrious 310.2
Illyria 17.3.40
Illyricum 242.4
ilmenite 372.5
Iloilo 12.41
Ilorin 252.18
I'm 236
image 197.3
imagery 16.282
imaginable
   228.16.29
imaginal 228.60.2
imaginary
   16.274.26
imagination
   261.67.18.2
imaginative
   485.15.7
imagine 252
imagism 242.35
imago 12.27
imam 230
imaret 368
imbalance 321.10
imbecile 217
imbecility 16.333.9
imbibe 25
imbibition 261.71
imbricate 367.5,
   371.9
imbroglio 12.3.3
imbue 15
imine 251
imitate 367.30
imitation 261.67.27
imitative 485.15.12
imitator 17.338.10

immaculate 371.17.1
immanent 420.55
immanentism 242.35.21
immaterial 228.3.11
immaterialism 242.35.11.2.1
immaterialize 516.3.2.1
immature 10.5
immaturity 16.333.23
immeasurable 228.16.35.2
immediate 371.1
immediately 16.189
immemorial 228.3.12
immense 316
immensity 16.333.31
immensurable 228.16.35
immerse 297
immersion 261.69
immersionism 242.35.14
immethodical 228.23.2
immigrant 420
immigrate 367.26
immigration 261.67.24
imminent 420.53
Immingham 242.17
immiscible 228.16.39
immobile 219
immobilism 242.35.9
immobility 16.333.9.1
immobilize 516.2
immoderate 371.35
immodest 436
immodesty 16.366
immolate 367.14
immolation 261.67.14
immoral 228.73
immoralist 436.7
immorality 16.333.8.9

immortal 228.105
immortality 16.333.8
immortalize 516.3
immortelle 215.3
immovable 228.16.62
immune 260
immunity 16.333.18
immunize 516
immunoassay 2.20
immunogenic 38.32.1
immunoglobulin 252.10
immunology 16.108.4
immunotherapy 16.254
immure 10
immutable 228.16.53
Imo 12.47
imp 287
impact 382
impacted 91
impair 4
impala 17.161
impale 214
impalpable 228.16
impart 366
impartial 228.90
impartiality 16.333.8.1
impassable 228.16
impasse 294
impassion 261.66
impassioned 143
impassive 485.1
impaste 432
impatience 321
impatiens 546
impatient 420.73
impeach 66
impeachable 228.16.12
impeachment 420
impearl 216
impeccable 228.16
impeccant 420
impecunious 310.2
impedance 321.4
impede 89

impediment 420.31.1
impedimenta 17.368
impel 215
impend 131
impending 265.20
impenetrable 228.16
impenitence 321.24
impenitent 420.76
imperative 485.15
imperator 9
imperceptible 228.16.58
imperceptive 485.23
imperfect 387
imperfection 261.77
imperfective 485.17
imperforate 371.35
imperial 228.3.11
imperialism 242.35.11.2.1
imperialist 436.7.2
imperil 218.2
imperious 310.2.11
imperishable 228.16.43
imperium 242.2.15
impermanent 420.55
impermeable 228.16.2
impermissible 228.16.39
impersonal 228.63
impersonality 16.333.8.7
impersonalize 516.3.7
impersonate 367.18
impersonation 261.67.19
impersonator 17.338.8
impertinence 321.14
impertinent 420.53
imperturbable 228.16
impervious 310.2
impetigo 12.30
impetrate 367.27

impetuosity 16.333.30.2
impetuous 310.4
impetuousness 300.34.2
impetus 310.64
Imphal 213
impi 16.255
impiety 16.333.2
impinge 209
impious 310.2
impish 353
implacable 228.16
implant 408
implantation 261.67
implausible 228.16
implement 410.1, 420.31
implementation 261.67.32.1
implicate 367.5
implication 261.67.5
implicit 371.36
implode 98
implore 9
implosion 261.92
implosive 485.6
imply 7
impolicy 16.300
impolite 372.4
impoliteness 300.39
impolitic 38.52
imponderabilia 17.3.21.1
imponderable 228.16.35
imponent 420.54
import 374
importance 321
important 420
importation 261.67
importer 17.345
importunate 371.28.1
importune 260.5
importunity 16.333.18
impose 520
imposing 265.83
imposition 261.71.9

impossibility
16.333.9.2
impossible 228.16
impost 441
impostor 17.385
imposture 17.74
impotence 321.25
impotent 420.78
impound 139
impoverish 353.11
impracticable
228.16.10
impractical
228.23.22
impracticality
16.333.8.3
imprecate 367.5
imprecation
261.67.5
imprecise 301
imprecision
261.91.1
impregnable
228.16
impregnate 367
impresa 17.439
impresario 12.3.5
impress 296
impressed 433
impression 261.68
impressionable
228.16.31
impressionism
242.35.14.4
impressionist
436.13
impressionistic
38.70.4
impressive 485.2
impressiveness
300.43
impressment 420
imprimatur 17.338
imprint 412
imprinting 265
imprison 261.126
imprisonment
420.42
improbability
16.333.9.2
improbable 228.16
improbity 16.333
impromptu 15
improper 17.255
impropriate 367.1

impropriety
16.333.2
improvable
228.16.62
improve 490
improvement
420.51
improvident 420.10
improvisation
261.67.36
improvise 516
imprudent 420.13
impudence 321
impudent 420.12
impugn 260
impulse 313
impulsion 261
impulsive 485
impulsiveness
300.43
impunity 16.333.18
impure 10
impurity 16.333.23
imputable
228.16.53
imputation
261.67.29
impute 380
in 252
inability 16.333.9.2
inaccessible
228.16.37
inaccuracy 16.307
inaccurate 371.34
inaction 261.76
inactivate 367.36
inactive 485.16
inactivity
16.333.35.2
inadequacy 16.307
inadequate 371
inadmissible
228.16.39
inadvertence 321
inadvertent 420
inadvisable
228.16.64
inalienable
228.16.31
inalterable
228.16.35
inamorata 17.337.2
inamorato 12.73
inane 247.6
inanimate 371.19

inanition 261.71
inanity 16.333.14
inapplicable
228.16.10
inapposite 371.40
inappreciable
228.16.42
inappreciative
485.15
inappropriate
371.1
inappropriateness
300.38
inapt 421
inarticulate
371.17.2
inartistic 38.70
inasmuch 72
inattention
261.82.3
inattentive 485.21
inaudible 228.16.16
inaugural 228.76
inaugurate 367.22
inauguration
261.67.21
inauspicious
310.58
inboard 95
inborn 255
inbound 139
inbred 86
inbreed 89
Inca 17.44
incalculable
228.16.25
in camera 17.279
incandesce 296
incandescence
321.21
incandescent
420.67
incantation
261.67.31
incapable
228.16.32
incapacitate
367.30.2
incapacity
16.333.25.1
Incaparina
17.230.1
incarcerate 367.23
incarnation
261.67.17

incautious 310.59
incendiary 16.274.1
incense 316
incensory
16.274.38
incentive 485.21
incept 422
inception 261.84
inceptive 485.23
incertitude 102.2
incessant 420.67
incest 433
incestuous 310.4
inch 80
inchmeal 217
inchoate 367
inchworm 233
incidence 321.5
incident 420.10
incidental
228.110.1
incidentally 16.131
incidentals 539
incinerate 367.23
incineration
261.67.22
incinerator
17.338.9
incipient 420.1
incise 516
incision 261.91
incisive 485.5
incisor 17.441
incite 372
incitement 420
incivility 16.333.9
inclemency 16.312
inclement 420
inclinable
228.16.30
inclination
261.67.18
incline 253.5
inclined 135
inclinometer
17.342.3
include 102
included 91
inclusion 261.93
inclusive 485.8
incoercible
228.16.38
incognito 12.76
incognizant 420
incoherence 321.17

incoherent 420.62
incombustible
228.16.60
income 240
incoming 265.38
incommensurate
371.35
incommode 98.1
incommodious
310.2.2
incommodity
16.333.6
incommunicable
228.16.10
incommunicado
12.16
incommutable
228.16.53
incomparable
228.16.35
incompatibility
16.333.9.2
incompatible
228.16
incompetence
321.24
incompetent
420.76
incomplete 370
incompleteness
300.37
incompliant 420.2
incomprehensible
228.16.40
incomprehension
261.82.1
incomputable
228.16.53
inconceivable
228.16.61
inconclusive 485.8
incongruity
16.333.3
incongruous 310.4
inconsequent
420.58
inconsequential
228.96
inconsiderable
228.16.35
inconsiderate
371.35
inconsistency
16.312
inconsistent 420.81

inconsolable
228.16.24
inconsonant 420.55
inconspicuous
310.4.1
inconstant 420
incontestable
228.16.59
incontinence
321.14
incontinent 420.53
incontrovertible
228.16.47
inconvenience
321.1
inconvenient
420.1.2
inconvertible
228.16.47
inconvincible
228.16.41
incoordinate
371.24.1
incoordination
261.67.18.1
incorporate 367.23
incorporated
91.34.7
incorporeal
228.3.12
incorporeity
16.333.1
incorrect 385.6
incorrectness
300.41
incorrigible
228.16.20
incorrupt 426.1
incorruptible
228.16
increase 298
incredible
228.16.14
incredulity 16.333
incredulous
310.25.3
increment 420.31
incremental
228.110.2
increscent 420.67
incretion 261.70
incriminate 367.17
incrimination
261.67.18.5
incross 302

incubate 367
incubation 261.67
incubator 17.338
incubus 310
inculcate 367.7
inculcation 261.67
inculpable 228.16
inculpate 367
incumbency 16.312
incumbent 420
incunabula
17.174.1
incur 3
incurable 228.16.34
incuriosity
16.333.30.1
incurious 310.2.14
incurrence 321
incurrent 420.64
incursion 261.69
incursive 485.3
incurvate 367.35,
371.37
incus 310
incuse 523
Ind 134
indebted 91.35
indecency 16.312
indecent 420.69
indecipherable
228.16.35
indecision 261.91.1
indecisive 485.5
indeclinable
228.16.30
indecorous 310.50
indecorum 242.20
indeed 89
indefatigable
228.16.19
indefensible
228.16.40
indefinable
228.16.30
indefinite 371.24
indehiscent 420.70
indelible 228.16
indelicate 371.9
indemnify 7.3
indemnity 16.333
indemonstrable
228.16
indent 410
indentation
261.67.32

indention 261.82
indenture 17.70
independence
321.7
independent
420.14
indescribable
228.16.8
indestructible
228.16.54
indeterminable
228.16.29
indeterminate
371.24
indeterminism
242.35.13
index 496
indexer 17.426
India 17.3
Indian 261.3
Indiana 17.225.1
Indianapolis
300.13.1
Indic 38
indican 261.13
indicant 420.7
indicate 367.5
indication 261.67.5
indicative 485.15.1
indicator 17.338.2
indices 513
indicia 17.3.49
indict 372
indictable
228.16.50
indictment 420
Indies 515
indifference 321.20
indifferent 420.65
indifferentism
242.35.21
indigene 251
indigenous 310.33
indigent 420.20
indigestible
228.16.59
indigestion 261.18
indigestive 485.24
indign 253
indignant 420
indignation 261.67
indignity 16.333.19
indigo 12.29
indirect 385

indirection
261.77.3
indirectness 300.41
indiscernible
228.16.28
indiscipline 252
indiscreet 370
indiscretion 261.68
indiscriminate
371.24
indispensable
228.16.40
indispose 520
indisposed 155
indisposition
261.71.9
indisputable
228.16.53
indissoluble 228.15
indistinct 392
indistinctive 485.20
indistinguishable
228.16.43
indium 242.2
individual 228.9.1
individualism
242.35.11.3
individualist
436.7.3
individualistic
38.70.2
individuality
16.333.8.2
individualize
516.3.3
individuate 367.2
indivisible
228.16.63
Indochina 17.232
indocile 219
indoctrinate 367.17
indoctrination
261.67.18
indole 223
indolence 321.12
indolent 420.28
indomitable
228.16.49
Indonesia 17.3.60
Indonesian
261.3.34
indoor 9
indoors 518
Indore 9
indrawn 255

indris 300
indubitable
228.16.49
induce 309
inducement 420
induct 389
inductance 321
inductee 5
inductile 219
induction 261.79
inductive 485.19
inductor 17.357
indulge 205
indulgence 321
indulgent 420.21
induline 253
indult 406
indurate 371.34
Indus 310
indusium 242.2
industrial 228.3
industrialism
242.35.11.2
industrialist
436.7.2
industrialize
516.3.2
industrious 310.2
industry 16
indwell 215
inearth 456
inebriant 420.1
inebriate 367.1,
371.1
inebriation
261.67.1
inebriety 16.333.2
inedible 228.16.14
ineducable 228.16
ineffable 228.16
ineffaceable
228.16.36
ineffective 485.17
ineffectual 228.9.5
inefficacious
310.56.1
inefficacy 16.307.1
inefficiency
16.312.5
inefficient 420.74
inelastic 38.68
inelasticity
16.333.28.2
inelegant 420.17

ineligible
228.16.20.1
ineloquent 420.59
ineluctable
228.16.54
inept 422
ineptitude 102.2
inequality
16.333.10
inequitable
228.16.49
inequity 16.333
ineradicable
228.16.10
inert 369
inertia 17.324
inescapable
228.16.32
inescutcheon 261
in esse 16.297
inessential 228.96
inessive 485.2
inestimable 228.16
inevitable
228.16.49
inexact 382
inexactitude 102.2
inexcusable
228.16.65
inexhaustible
228.16
inexorable
228.16.35
inexpedient 420.1.1
inexpensive 485.9
inexperience 321.1
inexperienced 448
inexpert 369
inexplicable
228.16.10
inexplicit 371.36
inexpressible
228.16.37
inexpressive 485.2
inextinguishable
228.16.43
inextricable
228.16.10
infallible 228.16
infamize 516.5
infamous 310.29
infamy 16.222
infancy 16.312
infant 420
infanta 17.365

infante 16.353
infanticide 92.7
infantile 219
infantilism
242.35.9
infantility 16.333.9
infantry 16.291
infantryman
261.48
infarct 383
infarction 261
infare 4
infatuate 367.2
infatuated 91.34.2
infatuation
261.67.2
infect 385
infection 261.77
infectious 310
infectiousness
300.34
infective 485.17
infecund 143
infecundity
16.333.7
infelicity 16.333.28
infer 3
inference 321.20
inferential 228.96.2
inferior 17.3.39
inferiority
16.333.22
infernal 228.58
inferno 12.53
infertile 219
infertility 16.333.9
infest 433
infestation
261.67.33
infidel 228.32
infidelity 16.333
infield 115
infighting 265.67
infiltrate 367
infiltration 261.67
infinite 371.24
infinitesimal
228.52.1
infinitive 485.12
infinity 16.333.17
infirm 233
infirmary 16.274.21
infirmity 16.333
infix 498
inflame 231

inflammable
228.16.26
inflammation
261.67.16
inflammatory
16.274.43.5
inflatable 228.16.45
inflate 367
inflation 261.67
inflationary
16.274.29.1
inflationism
242.35.14.3
inflect 385
inflection 261.77
inflexible 228.16
inflict 387
inflorescence
321.21
inflow 12
influence 321.3
influent 420.4
influential 228.96
influenza 17.446
influx 502
info 12
inform 238
informal 228.53
informality
16.333.8.5
informant 420.32
information
261.67.16
informative
485.15.6
informer 17.214
infract 382
infra dig 184
infralapsarian
261.3.21
infrangible
228.16.21
infrared 86
infrasonic 38.35.4
infrastructure
17.66
infrequency 16.312
infrequent 420.57
infringe 209
infringement 420
infulae 5
infundibulum
242.10
infuriate 367.1
infuscate 367

infuse 523
infuser 17.444
infusible 228.16.65
infusion 261.93
infusionism
242.35.14
ingather 17.400
ingenious 310.2.7
ingénue 15
ingenuity
16.333.3.1
ingenuous 310.4.2
ingest 433
ingesta 17.382
ingestion 261.18
ingle 228.50
inglenook 44
inglorious 310.2.13
ingoing 265.4
ingot 381
ingrain 247
ingrained 130
ingrate 367
ingratiate 367.1.5
ingratiation
261.67.1
ingratitude 102.2.1
ingravescent
420.67.3
ingredient 420.1.1
ingress 296
ingressive 485.2
ingrowing 265.4
ingrown 257
ingrowth 461
inguinal 228.60
ingurgitate 367.30
Ingush 358
inhabit 371.4
inhabitant 420.76
inhalant 420.25
inhalation
261.67.14
inhalator 17.338
inhale 214
inhaler 17.162
inharmonious
310.2.9
inhere 6
inherence 321.17
inherent 420.62
inherit 371.31
inheritance 321.24
inherited 91.38
inheritor 17.342

inhesion 261.90
inhibit 371.5
inhibition 261.71
inhibitor 17.342
inhospitable
228.16.49
inhospitality
16.333.8
inhuman 261.51
inhumane 247
inhumanity
16.333.14
inhume 241
inimical 228.23
inimitable
228.16.49
inion 261.3.17
iniquitous 310.64
iniquity 16.333
initial 228.93
initialize 516.3
initially 16.131
initiate 367.1.6,
371.1
initiation
261.67.1.5
initiative 485.15
inject 385
injection 261.77
injector 17.354
injudicious 310.58
Injun 261
injunction 261.80
injure 17.157
injurious 310.2.14
injury 16.274.14
injustice 300
ink 52
inkblot 373
Inkerman 261.52
inkhorn 255
inkle 228.29
inkling 265
inkstand 128
inkwell 215
inky 16.37
inlaid 85
inland 143
inlay 2
inlet 368
inlier 17.4
inmate 367
in memoriam
242.2.17
inn 252

innards 531
innate 367.17
inner 17.231
innermost 441
innervate 367.35
innerve 483
inning 265.43
innings 552
innkeeper 17.252
innocence 321
innocent 420
innocuous 310.4
innominate 371.24
in nomine 2.15
innovate 367,
367.37
innovation 261.67
innovative 485.15
innoxious 310
Innsbruck 44
innuendo 12.24
Innuit 371.2
innumerable
228.16.35
innumerate 371.35
inobservance 321
inoculable
228.16.25
inoculate 367.13.3
inoculation
261.67.13
inoculum 242.10
inodorous 310.50
inoffensive 485.9
inofficious 310.58
inoperable
228.16.35
inoperative
485.15.10
inopportune 260.6
inordinate 371.24.1
inorganic 38.31
inotropic 38.37.2
inpatient 420.73
in posse 16.302
input 379
inqilab 19
inquest 433
inquietude 102.2
inquire 8
inquiring 265.54
inquiry 16.267
inquisition
261.71.8
inquisitive 485.12

401

inquisitiveness 300.43
inquisitor 17.342.4
inquisitorial 228.3.12.1
in re 2
in rem 232
inroad 98
inrush 356
insalivate 367.36
insane 247
insanitary 16.274.41
insanity 16.333.14
insatiable 228.16
inscape 270
inscribe 25
inscription 261.85
inscriptive 485
inscrutable 228.16.53
insect 385
insectarium 242.2.14
insecticide 92.7
insectivore 9.13
insectivorous 310.50.3
insecure 10.3
insecurity 16.333.23
inselberg 182
inseminate 367.17
insemination 261.67.18
insensate 367.29
insensible 228.16.40
insensitive 485.12
insentient 420.1
inseparable 228.16.35.1
insert 369
insertion 261.69
insessorial 228.3.12
inset 368
inshore 9
inside 92.9
insider 17.84
insidious 310.2.1
insight 372
insignia 17.3
insignificant 420.7
insincere 6

insincerity 16.333.21
insinuate 367.2
insinuation 261.67.2
insipid 91.24
insist 436
insistence 321.27
insistent 420.81
insolate 367.14
insolation 261.67
insole 223
insolence 321.12
insolent 420.28
insoluble 228.15
insolvency 16.312
insolvent 420
insomnia 17.3
insomniac 32.1
insomuch 72
insouciant 420.1
inspect 385
inspection 261.77
inspector 17.354
inspectorate 371.35
inspiration 261.67
inspirational 228.63.3
inspiratory 16.274.43
inspire 8
inspiring 265.54
inspirit 371.33
instability 16.333.9.2
install 221
installation 261.67.14
instalment 420
instance 321
instant 420
instantaneous 310.2.6
instanter 17.365
instantiate 367.1.8
instantly 16.198
instar 1
instead 86
instep 271
instigate 367.10
instigation 261.67.10
instil 218
instinct 392
instinctive 485.20

institute 380.5
institution 261.75
institutional 228.63.7
institutionalism 242.35.11.5
institutionalize 516.3.7
institutive 485
instruct 389
instruction 261.79
instructional 228.63
instructive 485.19
instructor 17.357
instructress 300
instrument 420.35
instrumental 228.110.3
instrumentalism 242.35.11.6
instrumentalist 436.7.7
instrumentation 261.67.32
insubordinate 371.24.1
insubordination 261.67.18.1
insubstantial 228.95
insufferable 228.16.35
insufficiency 16.312.5
insufficient 420.74
insufflate 367
insula 17.174.11
insular 17.174.11
insularity 16.333.20.3
insulate 367.13
insulation 261.67.13
insulator 17.338.6
insulin 252.10
insult 406
insuperable 228.16.35
insupportable 228.16.51
insurable 228.16.34
insurance 321.19
insure 10.2
insured 96

insurer 17.277
insurgence 321
insurgency 16.312.3
insurgent 420.19
insurmountable 228.16.56
insurrection 261.77.4
insurrectionary 16.274.29.4
intact 382
intaglio 12.3
intake 34
intangible 228.16.21
intarsia 17.3.47
integer 17.150
integral 228
integrand 128
integrant 420
integrate 367.26
integration 261.67.24
integrator 17.338
integrity 16.333
integument 420.34
intellect 385.4
intellection 261.77.2
intellectual 228.9.5
intellectualism 242.35.11.3
intellectualize 516.3.3
intelligence 321.9
intelligent 420.20
intelligentsia 17.3
intelligible 228.16.20.1
Intelsat 365
intemperate 371.35
intend 131
intendance 321.7
intendant 420.14
intended 91.13
intendment 420
intenerate 367.23.1
intense 316
intensifier 17.4.1
intensify 7.3
intensity 16.333.31
intensive 485.9
intent 410
intention 261.82

intentional
228.63.9
intently 16.197
inter 3
interact 382
interaction 261.76
interactive 485.16
interatomic 38.29
interbedded 91.7
interbreed 89
intercalary
16.274.19
intercalate 367.14.2
intercede 89.3
intercept 422
interceptor 17.375
intercession
261.68.1
interchange 207
interchangeable
228.16
intercity 16.333
intercom 237
intercommunication
261.67.5
intercommunion
261.123
interconnect 385
intercontinental
228.110
intercostal 228.115
intercourse 303
intercross 302.2
intercurrent 420.64
interdependent
420.14
interdict 387.1
interdiction
261.78.2
interdisciplinary
16.274.26
interest 436.20
interested 91.53
interesting 265.76
interface 295
interfacing 265.59
interfere 6
interference 321.17
interferometer
17.342.3.4
interferon 254.9
interfluent 420.4
interfluve 490
interfuse 523.1
intergrade 85.6

interim 235
interior 17.3.39
interject 385.3
interjection
261.77.1
interlace 295
Interlaken 261.10
interlaminate
367.17.3
interlard 84
interlay 2.12
interleaf 162
interleave 484
interline 253.3
interlinear 17.3.34
interlining 265.44
interlink 52
interlock 40
interlocution
261.75.2
interlocutor 17.350
interlocutory
16.274.42
interlope 278
interloper 17.257
interlude 102.1
interlunation
261.67
intermarriage 197.9
intermarry 16.260
intermediary
16.274.1
intermediate 371.1
interment 420
intermezzo 12.71
intermigration
261.67
interminable
228.16.29
intermingle 228.50
intermission
261.71.4
intermit 371.21
intermittent 420.76
intermixture 17.76
intern 249
internal 228.58
internalize 516.3.6
international
228.63.2
internationalism
242.35.11.5.1
internationalize
516.3.7
internecine 253

internee 5
internment 420
internode 98
internship 274
interpage 193
interpellant 420.26
interpellate 367
interphone 257
interplay 2
interplead 89
interpleader 17.82
Interpol 220
interpolate 367.14
interpolation
261.67.14
interpose 520.2
interpret 371
interpretation
261.67.27
interpretative
485.15.12
interpreter 17.342
interpretive 485.12
interregnum 242
interrelate 367.12
interrelation
261.67.12
interrex 496
interrobang 263.1
interrogate
367.11.1
interrogation
261.67.11
interrogative
485.15.3
interrogator
17.338.4
interrogatory
16.274.43.3
interrupt 426.1
interruption 261.88
interscholastic
38.68
intersect 385
intersection 261.77
intersex 496
interspace 295
intersperse 297.1
interstate 367
interstice 300
interstitial 228.93
interstratify 7.3.8
intertrigo 12.30
intertwine 253
interval 228

intervene 251.12
intervention 261.82
interventionist
436.13
interview 15
interviewee 5
interviewer 17.8
intervocalic 38.19
interweave 484
interwoven 261.116
intestate 367.33
intestinal 228.60
intestine 252.26
intima 17.211
intimacy 16.307.2
intimate 367.15,
371.19
intimation
261.67.15
intimidate 367.8
intimidation
261.67.7
intinction 261
into 15
intolerable
228.16.35
intolerance 321.20
intolerant 420.65
intonate 367.18
intonation
261.67.19
intone 257
intorsion 261.72
in toto 12.79
intoxicant 420.7
intoxicate 367.5
intoxication
261.67.5
intra-atomic 38.29
intracranial 228.3.5
intractable 228.16
intrados 302
intramural 228.75
intramuscular
17.174.8
intransigence 321.9
intransigent 420.20
intransitive 485.12
intranuclear 17.3
intrastate 367
intrauterine 253.7
intravenous 310.32
intrepid 91.23
intricacy 16.307.1
intricate 371.9

intrigue 183
intriguing 265
intrinsic 38
intro 12
introduce 309.1
introduction
261.79.1
introductory
16.274
introject 385.3
introjection
261.77.1
intromission
261.71.4
introrse 303
introspect 385
introspection
261.77
introspective
485.17
introversion
261.69.1
introvert 369.2
intrude 102
intruder 17.91
intrusion 261.93
intrusive 485.8
intubate 367
intuit 371.3
intuition 261.71
intuitive 485.12
intumesce 296
intumescence
321.21
intussusception
261.84.1
inulin 252.10
inunction 261.80
inundate 367
inundation 261.67
inure 10
inurn 249
invade 85
invader 17.79
invaginate
367.17.2, 371.24.2
invagination
261.67.18.2
invalid 89
invalid 91.16
invalidate 367.8
invalidism 242.35
invalidity 16.333.5
invaluable 228.16.6
invariable 228.16.2

invariant 420.1
invasion 261
invasive 485
invective 485.17
inveigh 2
inveigle 228.45
invent 410
invention 261.82
inventive 485.21
inventiveness
300.43
inventor 17.368
inventory
16.274.48
inveracity
16.333.25
Invercargill 218
Inverness 296.3
inverse 297
inversion 261.69
invert 369
invertase 509
invertebrate 371
inverter 17.340
invest 433
investigate 367.10
investigation
261.67.10
investigative
485.15
investigator
17.338.3
investiture 17.56
investment 420
investor 17.382
inveterate 371.35.2
inviable 228.16.3
invidious 310.2.1
invigilate 367.12
invigilation
261.67.12
invigilator 17.338.5
invigorate 367.23
invincible
228.16.41
inviolable 228.16
inviolate 371.18.1
invisibility
16.333.9.2.2
invisible 228.16.63
invitation
261.67.27
invitatory
16.274.43
invite 372

inviting 265.67
in vitro 12
invocation 261.67.6
invoice 304
invoke 42
involucel 215
involucre 17.41
involuntary
16.274.48
involute 380.1
involution 261.75.1
involve 493
involved 151
invulnerable
228.16.35
invultuation
261.67.2
inward 103
inwardly 16.152
inwards 531
inweave 484
inwrought 374
Io 12.4
iodic 38.9
iodide 92
iodine 251.1
iodism 242.35
iodize 516
iodoform 238.2
iodometry 16.285.2
iodous 310
ion 261.4
Iona 17.236
Ionesco 12.14
Ionia 17.3.36
Ionian 261.3.18
ionic 38.35
Ionic 38.35
ionize 516.7
ionone 257
ionosphere 6.1
iontophoresis
300.51.1
iota 17.347
I.O.U 15
Iowa 17.6
ipecac 32
ipecacuanha
17.225
Ipswich 67
iracund 140
Iran 246
Iranian 261.3.15
Iraq 33
Iraqi 16.20

irascible 228.16
irate 367
Irbid 91
ire 8
Ireland 143
Irene 16.228
irenic 38.33
irenics 498.4
iridaceous 310.56.2
iridescence 321.21
iridescent 420.67
iridium 242.2.3
Iris 300.45
iris 300.45
Irish 353
Irishism 242.35
Irishman 261
iritis 300.62
irk 36
irksome 242
iron 261.4
ironbark 33
ironbound 139
ironclad 83
ironic 38.35
ironical 228.23.13
ironing 265.46
ironize 516.7
ironmonger 17.143
ironmongery
16.274.11
Ironside 92
ironsides 527
ironware 4
ironwood 101
ironwork 36
ironworks 497
irony 16.237,
16.237.1
Iroquoian 261.5
Iroquois 11
irradiance 321.1
irradiate 367.1
irradiation
261.67.1
irrational 228.63.2
irrationality
16.333.8.7.1
Irrawaddy 16.65
irreconcilable
228.16
irrecoverable
228.16.35
irrecusable
228.16.65

irredeemable
228.16
irredentist 436.27
irreducible 228.16
irrefrangible
228.16.21
irrefutable
228.16.52
irregular 17.174
irregularity
16.333.20.3
irrelative 485.15.4
irrelevant 420
irreligion 261.37
irreligious 310.21
irremediable
228.16.2
irremovable
228.16.62
irreparable
228.16.35.1
irreplaceable
228.16.36
irrepressible
228.16.37
irreproachable
228.16.13
irresistible 228.16
irresoluble 228.15
irresolute 380.1
irresolution
261.75.1
irresolvable 228.16
irrespective 485.17
irresponsible
228.16
irresponsive 485
irretentive 485.21
irretrievable
228.16.61
irreverence
321.20.1
irreverent 420.65
irreversible
228.16.38
irrevocable 228.16
irrigate 367.10
irrigation 261.67.10
irrigational
228.63.3
irritable 228.16.49
irritant 420.76
irritate 367.30
irritation 261.67.27
irrupt 426

irruptive 485
Irvine 252
Irving 265.78
is 515
Isaac 46
Isabel 215
Isabella 17.163.1
isagoge 16.106
isagogics 498
Isaiah 17.4
isallobar 1.2
Isar 1
Iscariot 381.1.1
ischaemia 17.3.26
ischium 242.2
isentropic 38.37
Isherwood 101
Ishmael 228.1
isinglass 294
Isis 300.53
Iskander Bey 2.4
Iskenderun 260.3
Islam 230
Islamic 38.24
Islamize 516.5
island 143
islander 17.109
Islay 2
isle 219
islet 371
Islington 261
ism 242.35
Ismaili 16.118
isn't 420
isobar 1.2
isobaric 38.38
isobath 452
isocheim 236
isochor 9.2
isochronal 228.63
isoclinal 228.61
isocline 253
isocracy 16.307.5
Isocrates 513.17
isocyanide 92.4
isodiaphere 6
isodynamic 38.24
isoelectric 38
isogamy 16.222.2
isogloss 302
isogon 254.5
isogonic 38.35
isolate 367.14
isolation 261.67.14

isolationism
242.35.14.3
isolex 496
isologous 310
isomagnetic 38.50
isomer 17.218
isomerism
242.35.15
isomerize 516.8
isomerous 310.50
isometric 38.46
isometrics 498.10
isometry 16.285.2
isomorph 166.1
isomorphism
242.35.7
isoniazid 91
isonomy 16.222.3
isopiestic 38.69
isopleth 455
isorhythmic 38.30
isosceles 513.6
isostasy 16.307
isosteric 38.39
isothere 6.10
isotherm 233
isotone 257.3
isotonic 38.35.5
isotope 278
isotopic 38.37
Israel 228.1
Israeli 16.114
Israelite 372.4
Israfil 217
issuable 228.16.6
issuance 321.3
issuant 420.4
issue 15
Issus 310.53
Istanbul 226
isthmus 310
istle 16.201
Istria 17.3
it 371
itacolumite 372
Italian 261.118
Italianate 371.28
Italianism
242.35.14
Italianize 516.7
italic 38.19.1
Italicism
242.35.16.1
italicize 516.10
Italy 16.131

itch 67
itching 265
itchy 16.49
item 232, 242.29
itemize 516.5
iterate 367.23.2
iteration
261.67.22.4
Ithaca 17.42
itinerancy 16.312
itinerant 420.65
itinerary 16.274.32
itinerate 367.23
it'll 228.102
it's 339
its 339
itself 172
Ivan 261.115
I've 486
Ives 554
ivied 91
ivories 515.1
ivory 16.274.52
ivy 16
Iwo Jima 17.210
ixia 17.3.58
izard 103
Izmir 6

J

jab 18
Jabalpur 10
jabber 17.9
jabberwocky 16.27
jaborandi 16.77
jabot 12
jacamar 1.12
jacana 1
jacaranda 17.98.2
jacinth 470
Jack 32
jack 32
jackal 221
jackanapes 323
jackass 293
jackboot 380
jackdaw 9
jackeroo 15.6
jacket 371.6
jackfruit 380

jackknife 164
jackpot 373
jacks 494
jackshaft 396
jacksmelt 402
jacksnipe 275
Jackson 261
Jacksonville 218
jackstay 2
jackstraws 518
Jacob 31
Jacobean 261.2.1
Jacobin 252
Jacobite 372
jacobus 310
Jacquard 84
jactitation
 261.67.27
jade 85
jaded 91.6
jaeger 17.125
Jael 228.1
Jaffa 17.110
jag 178
jagged 91
Jagger 17.123
jaggy 16.91
jaguar 17.7.1
jaguarundi 16.80
jai alai 7
jail 214
jailbird 87
jailbreak 34
jailer 17.162
jailhouse 306
Jain 253
Jainism 242.35
Jaipur 10
jalap 281
jalopy 16.250
jalousie 5
jam 229
Jamaica 17.30
Jamaican 261.11
jamb 229
jambalaya 17.4
jambart 366
jamboree 5.17
jammy 16.210
jampan 245
Jamshedpur 10
Jamshid 89
Janata 1
Jane 247
Janet 371.22

jangle 228.49
Janiculum 242.10.1
janissary 16.274.36
janitor 17.342
Jansen 261
Jansenism
 242.35.14
January 16.274.2
Janus 310.31
Jap 268
Japan 245.4
Japanese 513.9
jape 270
Japheth 455
japonica 17.34.1
jar 1
jardinière 4.1
jargon 261
jargonize 516.7
jarl 213
jarosite 372.10
jarp 269
Jarrow 12.60
jarvey 16.378
Jarvis 300
jasmine 252
Jason 261.62
jaspé 2
jasper 17.265
Jat 366
jato 12.74
jaundice 300
jaunt 415
jaunty 16.358
Java 17.409
javelin 252
jaw 9
Jawan 246
jawbone 257
jawbreaker 17.30
Jaxartes 513
jay 2
jaywalk 41
jaywalker 17.37
jazz 507
jazzy 16.391
jealous 310.22
jealousy 16.307
Jean 251
jeans 547
jebel 228
Jebel Musa 17.308
jeep 273
jeer 6
Jefferson 261

Jeffreys 515
Jehol 220
Jehovah 17.417
jejune 260
jejunum 242
Jekyll 228.21
jell 215
jellaba 17.21
jellied 91.17
jellify 7.3
jello 12.40
jelly 16.115
jellybean 251
jellyfish 353
jemmy 16.213
Jenkins 548
Jenner 17.228
jennet 371
Jenny 16.226
jenny 16.226
jeopardize 516
jeopardy 16.72
jequirity 16.333
jerboa 17.6
jeremiad 83.2
Jeremiah 17.4
Jericho 12.11
jerid 89
jerk 36
jerkin 252
jerky 16.23
jeroboam 242
Jerome 239
Jerry 16.262
jerry 16.262
Jersey 16.394
jersey 16.394
Jerusalem 242.11
jess 296
jessamine 252.15
Jesse 16.297
Jessica 17.34
jest 433
jester 17.382
Jesu 15
Jesuit 371.2
Jesuitic 38.52
Jesuitism 242.35.18
Jesus 310
jet 368
jeté 2
Jethro 12
jetliner 17.232
jetport 374
jetsam 242

jetsetter 17.339
jettison 261.65
jetton 261.96
jetty 16.330
Jew 15
jewel 228.10
jeweller 17.176
jewellery 16.283
Jewess 300
jewfish 353
Jewish 353
Jewry 16.270
Jezebel 215
Jhansi 16.310
jib 24
jibbons 551
Jidda 17.83
jiffy 16.85
jig 184
jigger 17.129
jiggered 103
jiggermast 431
jiggery-pokery
 16.274
jiggle 228.46
jigsaw 9
jihad 83
jillion 261.120
jilt 403
Jimmy 16.216
jingle 228.50
jingo 12.36
jingoism 242.35.3
jingoistic 38.70
Jinja 17.157
jink 52
jinni 5.12
jinx 505
jissom 242.24
jitter 17.342
jitterbug 189
jittery 16.274.41
jive 486
Joab 18
Joan 257
Job 26
job 28
jobber 17.16
jobbery 16.274.3
Jobcentre 17.368
jobless 300
joblessness 300.33
Jocasta 17.379
Jock 40
jockey 16.27

jockstrap 268
jocose 305
jocosely 16.182
jocular 17.174.7
jocularity
  16.333.20.3
jocund 143
jocundity 16.333.7
jocundly 16.157
jodhpurs 524
Jodo 12.21
Joe 12
joey 16.3
jog 185
jogger 17.131
jogging 265.23
joggle 228.47
Jogjakarta 1
johannes 513
Johannesburg
  182.1
John 254, 261
John Dory 16.269
Johnny 16.231
John o'Groats 343
Johnson 261
Johnsonian
  261.3.18
Johore 9
join 256
joinder 17.106
joiner 17.235
joinery 16.274
joint 416
jointed 91.48
jointer 17.371
joist 440
joke 42
joker 17.38
jokingly 16.175
jollify 7.3.2
jollity 16.333.10
jolly 16.122
Jolo 12.44
jolt 405
Jonah 17.236
Jonas 310.35
Jonathan 261.109
Jones 550
jonnock 46
jonquil 218
Joplin 252
Joppa 17.255
Jordan 261.27
Jordanian 261.3.15

jorum 242.20
Jos 302
Joseph 163
Josephine 251
Josephus 310
josh 354
Joshua 17.7
Josiah 17.4
joss 302
jostle 228.86
jostler 17.198
jot 373
jotter 17.344
jotting 265.68
joual 213
joule 227
jounce 319
journal 228.58
journalese 513.7
journalism
  242.35.11.4
journalist 436.7
journalistic 38.70.2
journalize 516.3.6
journey 16.227
journeyman 261.48
journo 12.53
joust 442
Jove 488
jovial 228.3.16
joviality 16.333.8.1
Jovian 261.3.31
jowl 224
joy 11
Joyce 304
joyful 226
joyless 300
joyous 310
joyousness 300.34
joypop 276
joyrider 17.84
Juan de Fuca
  17.41
juba 17.20
Jubal 228
jube 16.14, 30
jubilant 420
jubilate 367.12.1
jubilation
  261.67.12
jubilee 5.8
Judaea 17.2
Judaean 261.2
Judah 17.91
Judaic 38.1

Judaica 17.33
Judaism 242.35
Judaist 436.1
Judaize 516
Judas 310
judder 17.90
Jude 102
judge 203
judgeship 274
judgment 420
judicative 485.15.1
judicator 17.338.2
judicatory
  16.274.40.1
judicature 17.62
judicial 228.93
judiciary 16.274.1.2
judicious 310.58
Judith 458
judo 12.22
judogi 16.96
judoka 1
Judy 16.71
jug 189
jugal 228.48
jugate 367
juggernaut 374
juggins 548
juggle 228
juggler 17.193
jugglery 16.274
juggling 265
jugular 17.174
juice 309
juicy 16.306
jujitsu 15
juju 15
jujube 30
jukebox 499
julep 274
Julia 17.3.23
Julian 261
Juliana 17.226.1
Julie 16.130
julienne 248.1
Juliet 371.1.1
Jullundur 17.109
July 7.6
jumble 228
jumbo 12.7
jumbuck 43
Jumna 17.242
jump 289
jumper 17.264
jumpy 16.257

junction 261.80
juncture 17.68
June 260
Jungian 261.3
jungle 228
junior 17
juniper 17.253
junk 54
Junker 17.46
junket 371
junkie 16.39
junkyard 84
Juno 12
Junoesque 57
junta 17.373
Jupiter 17.342
jupon 254
Jura 17.277
jural 228.75
Jurassic 38.48
jurat 365
juratory 16.274.43
jurel 215
juridical 228.23
jurisconsult 406
jurisdiction 261.78
jurisprudence 321
jurisprudent 420.13
jurist 436.19
juristic 38.70
juror 17.277
jury 16.270
juryman 261.48
jus 307
jus civile 16.118
jus divinum 242
jus naturale 16.114
jussive 485.7
jus soli 7
just 443
justice 300
justiciable 228.16.2
justiciar 1
justiciary
  16.274.1.2
justifiable
  228.16.3.1
justification
  261.67.5.1
justificatory
  16.274.40.1
justify 7.3
Justin 252.27
Justinian 261.3.17
justle 228.87

jut 378
jute 380
Jutish 353
Jutland 143
Juvenal 228.60
juvenescence
321.21
juvenescent
420.67.1
juvenile 219
juvenilia 17.3.21
juvenility
16.333.9.3
juxtapose 520.2
juxtaposition
261.71.9

K

kabaragoya 17.431
kabuki 16.32
Kabul 226
Kabyle 219
kachang puteh
2.25
kachina 17.230
Kaddish 353.1
Kaduna 17.238
Kafiristan 246.1
kaftan 245
Kagera 17.269
Kaifeng 264
kainite 372
Kaiser 17.441
kaka 17.29
kakapo 12.59
kakemono 12.56
kaki 16.20
kala-azar 1.19
Kalahari 16.261.1
Kalamazoo 15.10
Kalat 366
kale 214
kaleidoscope 278.1
kaleidoscopic
38.37.1
kaleyard 84
Kalgoorlie 16.124
Kali 16.112
kali 16.113
kalian 246

kalmia 17.3.28
Kalmuck 43
kalong 266
Kama 17.206
kamacite 372.10
Kamakura 17.277
kamala 17.161.1
Kamasutra 17.294
kame 231
Kamet 368
kami 16.211
kamikaze 16.392
Kampala 17.161
kampong 266
Kampuchea 17.2
kana 17.226
Kananga 17.140
Kanarese 513.12
Kanchipuram
242.21
Kandahar 1
Kandy 16.77
kanga 1
kangaroo 15.6
KaNgwane 2.14
Kannada 17.92
Kano 12.51
Kanpur 10
Kansas 310
Kant 407
kantar 1
kaolin 252.11
kaolinite 372.5
kaon 254
kapok 40
kappa 17.247
kaput 379
karabiner 17.230
Karachi 16.47
Karaite 372
Karakoram 242.20
karate 16.328.1
Karelia 17.3.20
Karen 261
Kariba 17.13
karma 17.206
Karnataka 17.42
Karoo 15.6
kaross 302
karri 16.261
karst 431
karyolymph 176
karyotype 275.1
Kasai 7
kasbah 1

Kashmir 6
Kashmiri 16.265
kat 365
katakana 17.226
Kathiawar 1
Kathleen 251
Katmai 7
Katmandu 15
Katsina 17.230
Kattegat 365.1
katydid 91
Kauai 5
kauri 16.271
kava 17.409
Kawasaki 16.20
Kay 2
kayak 32
Kayseri 5
kazachok 40
Kazan 245
Kazbek 35
kazoo 15.10
Keaton 261.98
Keats 338
kebab 18
keck 35
Kedah 17.80
kedge 194
kedgeree 5.17
Kediri 16.265
Keegan 261
keek 37
keel 217
keelhaul 221
keen 251
keenly 16.172
keenness 300
keep 273
keeper 17.252
keeping 265.49
keepsake 34
keeshond 136
keg 181
keister 17.383
Keller 17.163
Kelly 16.115
keloid 97
kelp 283
kelson 261
kelt 402
kelter 17.361
Kelvin 252
Kemble 228.18
kempt 428
Ken 248

ken 248
kenaf 157
Kendal 228
kendo 12.24
Kenilworth 464
Kennedy 16.63
kennel 228.57
keno 12.54
kenosis 300.55.4
Kensington 261
kenspeckle 228.21
Kent 410
kente 16.355
Kentish 353
kentledge 197
Kentucky 16.30
Kenya 17
Kenyatta 17.336
Keos 302
kep 271
kepi 5.15
kept 422
keratin 252
keratinize 516.6.1
keratitis 300.62
keratoid 97
keratoplasty
16.361.1
keratose 305
keratosis 300.55.7
kerb 22
kerbstone 257
kerchief 163
kerf 161
kerfuffle 228.42
Kerguelen 252.8
kermes 515
kermis 300.18
kern 249
kernel 228.58
kerosene 251.9
Kerouac 32
Kerr 3
Kerry 16.262
kersey 16.394
kerseymere 6.2
kestrel 228.81
Keswick 38
ketch 64
ketchup 281
keto 12.76
ketone 257
ketonuria 17.3.42
ketose 520
ketosis 300.55.6

Kettering 265.58
kettle 228.100
kettledrum 240
kevel 228.118
Kew 15
kex 496
key 5
keyboard 95
keyhole 223
keynote 376
keystone 257
keystroke 42
Khachaturian
 261.3.24
khaddar 17.78
khadi 16.58
khaki 16.20
khan 246
kharif 162.2
Khartoum 241
khayal 213
kheda 17.80
khedive 484
Khmer 4
Khoikhoi 11
Khotan 246
Khrushchev 165
Khyber 17.15
kiaat 366
kiang 263
Kiangsi 5
kibble 228.12
kibbutz 345
kibe 25
kibitz 339
kiblah 1
kibosh 354
kick 38
kickback 32
kicker 17.34
kickshaw 9
kicksorter 17.345
kickstand 128
kick-start 366
kid 91
Kidd 91
Kidderminster
 17.394
kiddle 228.32
Kiddush 358
kiddy 16.63
kidnap 268
kidnapper 17.247
kidney 16.240
kidskin 252

Kiel 217
kier 6
Kierkegaard 84
kieselguhr 10
kieserite 372.8
Kiev 160.1
kif 163
kikoi 11
kikumon 254
Kildare 4
Kilimanjaro 12.61
Kilkenny 16.226
kill 218
Killarney 16.224
killdeer 6
killer 17.166
killick 38.21
Killiecrankie 16.36
killifish 353
killing 265.30
Kilmarnock 46
kiln 262
kilo 12.41
kilocalorie
 16.274.15
kilogram 229.1.2
kilohertz 337
kilometre 17.341
kilometric 38.46
kiloton 259
kilovolt 405
kilowatt 373
kilt 403
kilted 91
Kimberley 16.131
kimberlite 372.4
kimono 12.56
kin 252
Kinabalu 15.5
kinaesthesia
 17.3.60
kinase 509
kincob 26
kind 135
kindergarten
 261.95
kind-hearted 91.33
kind-heartedness
 300.28
kindle 228.40
kindler 17.189
kindless 300
kindliness 300.23
kindling 265
kindly 16.155

kindness 300.29
kindred 91
kine 253
kinematics 498.11
kinesics 498
kinetic 38.50.4
kinetics 498.12
king 265
kingbolt 405
kingcup 279
kingdom 242
kingfisher 17.326
kinglet 371
kingpin 252
kingship 274
King's Lynn 252
Kingston 261.108
kingwood 101
kink 52
kinkajou 15
kinky 16.37
kinnikinnick 38.34
kino 12.54
Kinross 302
Kinsey 16.406
kinsfolk 42
Kinshasa 17.438
kinship 274
kinsman 261
kiosk 59
kip 274
Kipling 265
kipper 17.253
Kirghiz 515
kirigami 16.211
kirk 36
Kirkby 16.9
kirkman 261
Kirkpatrick 38.45
Kirkuk 44
Kirman 246
kish 353
kismet 368
kiss 300
kissable 228.16.39
kissel 228.85
kisser 17.302
kissing 265.61
Kissinger 17.157
kist 436
kit 371
kitbag 178.1
kitchen 252
Kitchener 17.231
kitchenette 368

kitchenware 4
kite 372
kith 458
kitsch 67
kitten 261.99
kittenish 353
kittiwake 34
kittle 228.102
kitty 16.333
kiva 17.413
Kiwanis 300.21
klangfarbe 17.10
Klansman 261
klaxon 261
Kleenex 496
Kleist 437
Klemperer 17.279
klepht 397
kleptomania
 17.3.31.1
kleptomaniac 32.1
klipspringer 17.246
Klondike 39
kloof 170
knack 32
knacker 17.28
knackwurst 434
knag 178
knap 268
knapsack 32
knapweed 89
knar 1
knave 482
knavery 16.274.50
knavish 353
knawel 228.5
knead 89
knee 5
kneecap 268
kneehole 223
kneel 217
kneeler 17.165
kneepad 83
kneepan 245
knell 215
knelt 402
knew 15
Knickerbocker
 17.36
knickerbockers 524
knickers 524
knickknack 32
knickpoint 416
knife 164
kniferest 433

knight 372
knighthood 101
knightly 16.190
knish 353
knit 371
knitted 91.38
knitter 17.342
knitting 265.66
knitwear 4.9
knob 26
knobbly 16.135
knobkerrie 16.262
knock 40
knocker 17.36
knock-kneed 89
knockout 377
knoll 223
Knossos 310.54
knot 373
knotgrass 294
knothole 223
knotted 91.40
knotting 265.68
knotty 16.335
knotweed 89
knout 377
know 12
know-how 13
knowing 265.4
knowledge 197.2
knowledgeable
 228.16.20
known 257
Knox 499
knuckle 228.27
knucklebone 257
knuckle-duster
 17.388
knucklehead 86
knur 3
knurl 216
K.O. 12.1
koa 17.6
koala 17.161
koan 245
kob 26
Kobe 16.12
kobold 120
Kochi 5
Kodiak 32.1
Kodok 40
kofta 17.360
koftgar 1
Kohima 1.11
Kohinoor 10

kohl 223
kohlrabi 16.6
Kohoutek 35
koine 5
kokanee 16.223
Koko Nor 9
kolinsky 16.45
kolkhoz 518
Kol Nidre 2
kolo 12.44
Komati 16.328
komatik 38.49
Komi 16.219
Komodo 12.21
Komsomol 220.2
kongoni 16.233
Konstanz 347
Konya 1
kook 45
kookaburra 17.278
kooky 16.32
Kootenay 5.14
kop 276
kopeck 35
kopje 16.250
Koran 246
Kordofan 245
Korea 17.2.2
Korean 261.2.3
korma 17.214
koruna 17.238
Kos 302
kos 305
kosher 17.328
Kota 17.347
koto 12.79
koulibiaca 17.29
kowhai 7
Kowloon 260
kowtow 13
Kozhikode 98
Kra 1
kraal 213
kraft 396
krait 372
Krakatoa 17.6
kraken 261.10
krameria 17.3.39
Krefeld 113
Kremlin 252
kriegspiel 217
krill 218
krimmer 17.211
Krio 12.2
kris 300

Krishna 17.243
Kriss Kringle
 228.50
Kristiansand 128
Kristianstad 84
kromesky 16.40
krone 17.236
Kruger 17.136
Krugersdorp 277
krypton 254
Kuala Lumpur 10
Kublai Khan 246
Kubrick 38
kudos 302
kudu 15
Kufic 38
Ku Klux Klan 245
kula 17.175
kulak 32
Kumamoto 12.79
Kumasi 16.294
kumbaloi 11.1
kumiss 300
kumquat 373
kung fu 15
Kungur 10
kunzite 372
Kura 1
Kurd 87
Kurdish 353
Kurdistan 246.1
Kure 2
kurrajong 266
kursaal 228.126
Kuskokwim 235
Kutch 72
Kuwait 367
kvass 294
Kwa 1
kwacha 1
Kwajalein 247.4
Kwakiutl 228.108
Kwangchowan 246
kwanza 17.445
kwashiorkor 17.37
Kweisui 2
kwela 17.162
kyanize 516.7
kyat 366
kyle 219
kylix 498
kyloe 12
kymograph 158.1
Kyongsong 266
Kyoto 12.79

kyphosis 300.55
kyu 15

L

laager 17.124
lab 18
labarum 242.21
labdanum 242.16
label 228.11
labeller 17.176
labellum 242.8
labia 17.3.1
labial 228.3
labiate 367.1
labile 219
labium 242.2
lablab 18
laboratory
 16.274.43.7
laborious 310.2.13
labour 17.11
labourer 17.279
labourism
 242.35.15
labourist 436.20
Labourite 372.8
Labrador 9.4
labroid 97
labrum 242
Labuan 261
laburnum 242.13
labyrinth 470
labyrinthian
 261.3.28
labyrinthine 253
lac 32
laccolith 458
lace 295
Lacedaemon
 261.47
Lacedaemonian
 261.3.18
lacerant 420.65
lacerate 367.23
laceration
 261.67.22
Lacerta 17.340
lacertilian 261.3.11
lacewing 265
laches 515

lachrymose 305
lacing 265.59
laciniate 367.1
lack 32
lackadaisical
  228.23
lackey 16.19
lacklustre 17.388
laconic 38.35
lacquer 17.28
lacrimal 228.52
lacrimation
  261.67.15
lacrimator 17.338
lacrimatory
  16.274.43
lacrosse 302.2
lactam 229
lactary 16.274.44
lactase 509
lactate 367
lactation 261.67
lacteal 228.3
lactescent 420.67
lactic 38.58
lactiferous 310.50.2
lactogenic 38.32.1
lactone 257
lactose 520
lacuna 17.238
lacunar 17.238
lacy 16.296
lad 83
ladder 17.77
laddie 16.57
lade 85
laden 261.20
la-di-da 1
lading 265.11
ladino 12.54
Ladislas 293
ladle 228
lady 16.59
ladybird 87
ladyfy 7.3
ladylike 39
ladylove 489
Ladyship 274
Ladysmith 458
Laertes 513
laevorotation
  261.67.28
laevulose 520
lag 178
lagan 261

lagena 17.230
lager 17.124
laggard 103
lagging 265
lagniappe 268
lagomorph 166.1
lagoon 260
Lagos 302
La Guardia 17.3.6
lah 1
Lahnda 17.99
Lahore 9
laic 38.1
laicize 516.10
laid 85
laik 34
lain 247
lair 4
laird 88
lairy 16.264
laity 16.333
lake 34
Lakeland 143
laker 17.30
lakh 33
Lakshadweep 273
laky 16.21
Lala 1.7
lallation 261.67
lallygag 178
lam 229
lama 17.206
Lamaism 242.35
Lamarckian 261.3
Lamarckism
  242.35
lamb 229
lambaste 432
lambent 420
Lambert 381
Lambeth 464
lambkin 252
lambrequin 252.3
lamé 2
lame 231
lamella 17.163
lamellicorn 255.2
lamely 16.165
lameness 300
lament 410.2
lamentable
  228.16.57
lamentation
  261.67.32
lamented 91.46

lamia 17.3.24
lamina 17.231.1
laminaria 17.3.38
laminate 367.17.3,
  371.24
lamination
  261.67.18.3
Lammas 310
lammergeier 17.4
lamp 285
lampas 310.41
lampblack 32
Lampedusa 17.444
lampern 261
lampion 261.3
lamplighter 17.343
lampoon 260
lamppost 441
lamprophyre 8.1
Lanai 16.1
lanai 16.1
Lanark 46
Lancashire 6
Lancaster 17.390
Lancastrian
  261.3.26
lance 315
lanceolate 367
lancer 17.313
lancers 524
lancet 371
lanceted 91.38
lancinate 367.17
land 128
landammann
  261.52
landau 9
landaulet 368
landed 91.12
Landeshauptmann
  261
landfall 221
landform 238
landgrave 482
landgravine 251.12
landing 265.19
landlady 16.59
landlocked 388
landloper 17.257
landlord 95
landlubber 17.19
landmark 33
landmass 293
landowner 17.236
landrace 295

landscape 270
landscapist 436.14
Landseer 6
landshark 33
landside 92
landsknecht 385
landslide 92
landsman 261
Landtag 33
landward 103
lane 247
Lang 263
lang 263
Langland 143
langouste 444
language 197
langue de chat 1
languid 91
languish 353
languor 17.140
languorous 310.50
langur 10
laniary 16.274.1
lank 51
lanky 16.36
lanner 17.225
lanneret 368.6
lanolin 252.11
lansquenet 368
lantana 17.227
lantern 261
lanthanide 92.4
lanthanum 242.16
lanugo 12.32
lanyard 103
Lao 13
Laoag 179
Laocoon 254.2
Laodicea 17.2
Laodicean 261.2.4
Laoighis 353
Laotze 2
lap 268
laparotomy
  16.222.4
La Paz 507
lapel 215
lapidary 16.274
lapidate 367.8
lapidify 7.3.1
lapillus 310.23
lapis 300
lapis lazuli 7.6
Lapland 143
Laplander 17.109

411

Lapp 268
lappet 371
lapse 322
lapstrake 34
lapsus 310
lapwing 265
larboard 103
larceny 16.229.4
larch 63
lard 84
larder 17.78
lardon 261
lares 513.10
large 192
largen 261
largess 296
largish 353
largo 12.26
lariat 381.1.1
larine 253
Larisa 17.302
lark 33
Larkin 252.2
larkspur 3
larnax 494
La Rochefoucauld 12
larrigan 261.32
larrikin 252.3
larrup 281
Larry 16.260
larva 17.409
larval 228
larvicide 92.7
Larwood 101
laryngeal 228.2
laryngitic 38.52
laryngitis 300.62
laryngology 16.108.4.7
laryngoscope 278.1
laryngotomy 16.222.4
larynx 505
lasagne 17.434
La Salle 212
lascar 17.47
lascivious 310.2.17
lasciviousness 300.34.1
lase 509
laser 17.439
lash 349
lashing 265
Lashio 12.3

lash-up 279
lasket 371
lass 293
lassie 16.294
lassitude 102.2
lasso 15
Lassus 310.51
last 431
lasting 265.74
lastly 16.199
Las Vegas 310.19
lat 365
latch 62
latchkey 5
late 367
latecomer 17.216
lateen 251.11
lately 16.188
lateness 300
latent 420.75
later 17.338
lateral 228.76
Lateran 261.60
laterite 372.8
latest 436
latex 496
lath 453
lathe 473
lather 17.401
lathery 16.274
lathi 16.328
Latimer 17.218
latimeria 17.3.39
Latin 252
Latinate 367.17
Latinism 242.35.13
Latinist 436.11
Latinity 16.333.17
Latinize 516.6.1
Latino 12.54
latish 353
latitude 102.2.1
latitudinal 228.60.1
latitudinarian 261.3.21.1
Latium 242.2
latria 17.4
latrine 251
latten 261.94
latter 17.336
latterly 16.131.7
lattice 300
latticed 436
Latvian 261.3
laud 95

laudable 228.16.16
laudanum 242.16
laudation 261.67
laudatory 16.274.43
Lauder 17.86
laugh 158
laughable 228.16
laughter 17.358
Laughton 261.102
launch 81
launder 17.105
Launderette 368.6
laundress 300
Laundromat 365
laundry 16
laundryman 261.48
Laura 17.276
Laurasia 17.322
laureate 371.1.2
laurel 228.73
laurustinus 310.34
Lausanne 245
lav 480
lava 17.409
lavage 197
Laval 212
lavation 261.67
lavatory 16.274.43
lavender 17.109
laver 17.409, 17.410
laverock 46
lavish 353
lavishness 300.35
law 9
law-abiding 265.14
lawbreaker 17.30
lawful 226.1
lawgiver 17.414
lawks 500
lawless 300
lawlessness 300.33
lawman 261
lawn 255
Lawrence 321.18
Lawrentian 261.82
lawsuit 380
lawyer 17.430
lax 494
laxation 261.67.34
laxative 485.15
laxity 16.333
lay 2
layabout 377.1

layer 17.1
layering 265.58
layette 368
layman 261.45
lazar 17.437
lazaretto 12.75
Lazarus 310.50
laze 509
laziness 300.23
lazulite 372
lazurite 372
lazy 16.393
lazybones 550
L-dopa 17.257
lea 5
leach 66
Leacock 40
lead 86, 89
Leadbelly 16.115
leaded 91.7
leaden 261.21
leader 17.82
leadership 274.1
leading 265.12, 265.13
leaf 162
leafcutter 17.349
leaflet 371
leafstalk 41
leafy 16.84
league 183
Leah 6
leak 37
leakage 197
leaky 16.24
leal 217
Leamington 261
lean 251
Leander 17.98.1
leaning 265.42
leant 410
leap 273
leapfrog 185
leapt 422
Lear 6
learn 249
learned 91
learner 17.229
learning 265.41
learnt 411
lease 298, 513
leaseback 32
leasehold 120
leaseholder 17.97
leash 352

least 435
leastways 509
leat 370
leather 17.402
leatherback 32.2
Leatherette 368.6
Leatherhead 86.5
leatherhead 86.5
leatherjacket 371.6
leatherneck 35
leatherwood 101
leathery 16.274
leave 484
leaved 148
leaven 261.112
leavings 552
Lebanese 513.9
Lebanon 261
leben 261
lebkuchen 261.15
Le Carré 2.16
Lech 35
lech 64
lecher 17.53
lecherous 310.50
lechery 16.274
lecithin 252
lecithinase 509
lectern 261
lection 261.77
lectionary
  16.274.29.4
lector 9
lecture 17.64
lecturer 17.279
lectureship 274.1
lecythus 310
led 86
Leda 17.82
lederhosen 261.129
ledge 194
ledger 17.147
lee 5
leeboard 95
leech 66
Leeds 526
leek 37
leer 6
leery 16.265
lees 513
leet 370
leeward 103
leeway 2
left 397
left-handed 91.12

left-handedness
  300.28.1
left-hander 17.98
leftism 242.35
leftist 436
leftover 17.417
lefty 16.346
leg 181
legacy 16.307
legal 228.45
legalese 513.7
legalism 242.35.11
legality 16.333.8.4
legalize 516.3
legate 371
legatee 5
legation 261.67.10
legato 12.73
legator 9
legend 143
legendary 16.274
legendry 16.279
legerdemain 247.5
leggings 552
leggy 16.92
leghorn 255
legible 228.16
legion 261.36
legionary 16.274.29
legionnaire 4.5
legislate 367
legislation 261.67
legislative 485.15
legislator 17.338
legislatorial
  228.3.12.2
legislature 17.52
legist 436
legit 371
legitimacy 16.307.2
legitimate 367.15,
  371.19
legitimatize
  516.13.2
legitimist 436.9
legitimize 516.4
legless 300
legman 261
legroom 241
legume 241
legumen 252
leguminous
  310.33.1
legwork 36
Lehár 1

lei 5.1
Leibnitz 339
Leicester 17.382
Leicestershire 6
Leiden 261.25
Leigh 5
Leipzig 184
leishmania 17.3.31
leishmaniasis
  300.57.1
leister 17.383
leisure 17.333
leisured 103.6
leisurely 16.131
Leith 457
leitmotiv 162
Leitrim 235
lek 35
Lely 16.118
lemma 17.208
lemming 265
lemniscus 310.15
Lemnos 302
lemon 261
lemonade 85.3
lemony 16.237.6
lempira 17.272
lemur 17.210
lemuroid 97
Len 248
Lena 17.230
lend 131
lender 17.101
length 472
lengthen 261
lengthways 509
lengthy 16
leniency 16.312.1
lenient 420.1.2
Lenin 252.16
Leningrad 83
Leninism 242.35.13
lenis 300
lenitive 485.12
lenity 16.333.15
Lennon 261
leno 12.54
lens 546
Lent 410
lent 410
lentamente 16.355
lenten 261
lentic 38.63
lenticular 17.174.6
lentiform 238.1

lentigo 12.30
lentil 218
lento 12.84
Leo 12.2
Leonidas 293
leonine 253
leopard 103
leopardess 300.5
Leopold 120
leotard 84
leper 17.250
lepidolite 372.4
lepidopterist
  436.20
lepidosiren 261.58
lepidote 376
Lepidus 310
leporid 91.27
leporine 253.7
leprechaun 255
leprosarium
  242.2.14
leprosy 16.307
leprous 310
lepton 254
leptosome 239
lequear 6
Lerwick 38
lesbian 261.3
lesbianism
  242.35.14.1
Lesbos 302
Les Cayes 2
lese-majesty 16.366
lesion 261.90
Lesley 16.208
less 296
lessee 5.19
lessen 261.63
lesser 17.300
lesson 261.63
lessor 9
lest 433
let 368
lethal 228
lethargic 38
lethargy 16.108
Lethbridge 197
Leto 12.76
let's 336
Lett 368
letter 17.339
letterhead 86.5
lettering 265.58
letterpress 296.5

413

letterset 368
Lettish 353
lettuce 300
Leucippus 310.37
leucite 372
leucocratic 38.49.6
leucocyte 372.10
leucoderma 17.209
leucomaine 247.5
leucopenia 17.3.33
leucoplast 430
leucopoiesis 300.51
leucorrhoea 17.2.2
leucotomy 16.222.4
leukaemia 17.3.26
lev 160
levant 407.1
levanter 17.365
levantine 253
levator 17.338.11
levee 16.380
level 228.118
level-headed 91.7
level-headedness
 300.28
leveller 17.176
Leven 261.113
lever 17.413
leverage 197
leveret 371.35
Levi 7
leviable 228.16.2
leviathan 261.109
levigate 367.10
levirate 371.33
Levis 516
levitate 367.30
levitation 261.67.27
Levite 372
Leviticus 310.10
levity 16.333.34
levy 16.380
lewd 102
lewdness 300
Lewes 300
Lewis 300
Lewisham 242
lewisite 372.9
lex 496
lexeme 234
lexical 228.23
lexicography
 16.90.2
lexicology
 16.108.4.4

lexicon 261.13
lexigraphy 16.90
Lexington 261
lexis 300
lex loci 7
lex non scripta
 17.376
lex talionis 300.25
ley 5
Leyte 2
li 5
liability
 16.333.9.2.1
liable 228.16.3
liaise 509.1
liaison 254
liana 17.226.1
Liaoning 265
liar 17.4
Liard 84
liard 84
lias 310.3
Liassic 38.48
lib 24
libation 261.67
libel 228
libellant 420.28
libellee 5.9
libellous 310.26
liberal 228.76
liberalism
 242.35.11
liberality
 16.333.8.9
liberalize 516.3.8
liberate 367.23
liberation
 261.67.22
liberator 17.338.9
Liberia 17.3.39
libertarian 261.3.21
liberticide 92.7
libertine 251.11
liberty 16.344
libidinous 310.33
libido 12.18
Libra 17.283
librarian 261.3.21
librarianship 274.2
library 16.274
librate 367
libration 261.67
librettist 436.23
libretto 12.75
Libya 17.3.3

Libyan 261.3.2
lice 301
licence 321
license 321
licensee 5
licentiate 371.1
licentious 310.61
lichen 261
lichenin 252
lichenology
 16.108.4.11
Lichfield 115
licit 371.36
lick 38
lickerish 353.11
lickety-split 371
licking 265.7
lickspittle 228.102
lictor 17.355
lid 91
lidless 300
lido 12.18
lie 7
Liebfraumilch 49
Liechtenstein 253
lied 89
lief 162
liege 196
Liège 360
lien 261.3
lientery 16.274.48
lierne 249
Lietuva 17.419
lieu 15
lieutenant 420.52
life 164
lifeblood 100
lifeboat 376
lifeguard 84
lifeless 300
lifelessness 300.33
lifelike 39
lifeline 253
lifelong 266
lifer 17.115
lifetime 236
Liffey 16.85
lift 398
liftable 228.16
liftboy 11
liftoff 165
ligament 420.35.1
ligamentous 310.70
ligand 143
ligate 367

ligature 17.62
liger 17.130
light 372
lighten 261.100
lightener 17.239
lighter 17.343
light-headed 91.7
light-headedness
 300.28
light-hearted 91.33
light-heartedness
 300.28
lighthouse 306
lighting 265.67
lightness 300.39
lightning 265
lights 340
lightship 274
lightsome 242
lightweight 367
lignaloes 520.1
ligneous 310.2
ligniform 238.1
lignify 7.3.3
lignin 252
lignite 372.7
lignocaine 247.2
ligula 17.174
ligulate 371.17
ligure 10
Liguria 17.3.42
likable 228.16
Likasi 16.295
like 39
likelihood 101
likely 16.143
like-minded 91
liken 261
likeness 300
likewise 516
liking 265
lilac 46
liliaceous 310.56
Lilith 458
Liliuokalani 5.10
Lilliputian 261.75
lilly-pilly 16.120
Lilo 12
lilt 403
lilting 265
lily 16.120
Lima 17.210
lima 17.212
limacine 253.8
limacon 254

Limassol 220
limb 235
limber 17.25
limbless 300
limbo 12.6
Limburg 182
Limburger 17.127
lime 236
limeade 85
limekiln 262
limelight 372
limen 248
Limerick 38.44
limerick 38.44
limes 513
limestone 257
limey 16.217
limicoline 253.3
limicolous 310.26.2
liminal 228.60.4
limit 371.19
limitarian
  261.3.21.2
limitary 16.274.41
limitation
  261.67.27
limited 91.38
limitless 300.17
limitlessness
  300.33
limitrophe 167
limn 235
limnetic 38.50
limnology 16.108.4
Limoges 363
limonite 372.6
limousine 251
limp 287
limpet 371
limpid 91
limpkin 252
Limpopo 12
limulus 310.25
limy 16.217
linchpin 252
Lincoln 261
Lincolnshire 6.8
lincrusta 17.388
Lincs. 505
linctus 310
lindane 247
Lindbergh 182
linden 261
Lindisfarne 246
line 253

lineage 197
lineal 228.3.7
lineament 420.35
linear 17.3.34
lineate 371.1
lineation 261.67.1
linen 252.17
liner 17.232
linesman 261
ling 265
lingcod 94
linger 17.141
lingerie 16.274
lingo 12.36
lingua franca
  17.43
lingual 228
linguiform 238.1
linguini 16.228
linguist 436
linguistic 38.70
linguistics 498
lingulate 367.13
linhay 16.229
liniment 420.31
lining 265.44
link 52
linkage 197
linkboy 11
linkman 261
links 505
linn 252
Linnaeus 310.1
linnet 371.24
Linnhe 16.229
lino 12
linocut 378
linoleate 367.1.3
linoleum 242.2.7
Linotype 275.1
linsang 263
linseed 89.4
linstock 40
lint 412
lintel 228
linter 17.369
lintwhite 372
Linz 348
lion 261.4
lioness 300.26
lion-hearted 91.33
lionize 516.7
lip 274
lipase 509
lipid 91.24

lipoid 97
lipoma 17.215
lipophilic 38.21
Lippe 17.253
Lippizaner 17.226
lippy 16.248
lip-read 89
lip-reader 17.82
lipstick 38
liquate 367.20
liquefacient 420.73
liquefaction 261.76
liquefy 7.3
liquesce 296
liquescent 420.67
liqueur 10.3
liquid 91
liquidambar 17.23
liquidate 367.8
liquidation
  261.67.7
liquidator 17.338
liquidity 16.333.5
liquidize 516
liquidizer 17.441
liquor 17.34
liquorice 300.47
lira 17.272
liripipe 275
Lisbon 261
lisle 219
lisp 291
lis pendens 546
Lissajous 15
lissom 242.24
list 436
listed 91.53
listel 228.114
listen 261.65
Lister 17.384
lister 17.384
listing 265.76
listless 300
listlessness 300.33
Liszt 436
lit 371
litany 16.237
literacy 16.307.4
literal 228.76
literalism 242.35.11
literally 16.131
literary 16.274.32
literate 371.35
literati 16.328.1
literatim 235

literation
  261.67.22.4
literator 17.338.9
literature 17.56
litharge 192
lithe 477
lithesome 242
lithia 17.3.51
lithiasis 300.57.1
lithic 38.73
lithium 242.2
lithograph 158.1
lithography 16.90.2
lithoid 97
lithology
  16.108.4.18
lithomarge 192
lithosol 220
lithosphere 6.1
lithotomy 16.222.4
lithotrity 16.333
Lithuania 17.3.31
Lithuanian
  261.3.15
litigable 228.16.19
litigant 420.17
litigate 367.10
litigation 261.67.10
litigious 310.21
litmus 310
litotes 513
litre 17.341
litter 17.342
littérateur 3.1
litterbug 189
little 228.102
littoral 228.76
liturgical 228.23.4
liturgist 436.4
liturgy 16.108
live 485, 486
livelihood 101
liveliness 300.23
livelong 266
lively 16
liven 261.115
liver 17.414
liveried 91.27
liverish 353.11
Liverpool 227
Liverpudlian 261.3
liverwort 369
liverwurst 434
livery 16.274.51
livestock 40

liveware 4
livid 91
living 265.80
Livingstone
  261.108
Livonia 17.3.36
Livy 16.382
lixiviate 367.1
lixivium 242.2
lizard 103
Ljubljana 17.226
llama 17.206
Llandaff 157
Llandudno 12
Llanelli 16.203
llano 12.51
Llano Estacado
  12.16
Llewellyn 252.7
Lloyd 97
lo 12
loach 70
load 98
loaded 91.10
loader 17.88
loading 265.16
loaf 167
loafer 17.117
loam 239
loamy 16.219
loan 257
loath 461
loathe 478
loathing 265
loathsome 242
lob 26
lobar 17.18
lobate 367.3
lobby 16.11
lobbyist 436
lobe 28
lobelia 17.3.20
Lobengula 17.175
loblolly 16.122
lobotomy 16.222.4
lobscouse 306
lobster 17.391
lobster thermidor
  9.3
lobule 227
local 228.26
locale 213
localism 242.35.11
locality 16.333.8
localize 516.3

locate 367.6
location 261.67.6
locative 485.15.2
loch 40
lochia 17.3
loci 7
lock 40
lockable 228.16
lockage 197
locker 17.36
locket 371.10
lockjaw 9
lockout 377
locksmith 458
loco 12.12
locoism 242.35.3
locoman 261.49
locomotion
  261.73.1
locomotive 485.14
locomotor 17.347
locular 17.174.7
locule 227
locum tenens 546
locus 310.12
locus sigilli 7.5
locus standi 7
locust 445
locution 261.75.2
Lod 94
lode 98
lodestar 1
lodestone 257
lodge 199
lodger 17.152
lodging 265
lodgings 552
lodgment 420
lodicule 227.1
loess 300.1
loft 399
lofter 17.360
lofty 16.348
log 185
Logan 261
loganberry 16.274
logaoedic 38.8
logarithm 242.33
logarithmic 38.30
logbook 44
loge 363
logger 17.131
loggerhead 86.5
loggia 17.152

logging 265.23
logia 17.3
logic 38.18
logical 228.23.5
logician 261.71
logicism 242.35.16
logion 254.1
logistic 38.70.1
logistician 261.71
logistics 498
loglog 185
logo 12.31
logogram 229.1
logogriph 163
logomachy 16.33
logopaedics 498
logorrhoea 17.2.2
logos 302
logotype 275.1
logwood 101
logy 16.96
Lohengrin 252
loin 256
loincloth 459
loiter 17.346
Loki 16.29
Lola 17.171
loll 220
Lollard 103.3
lollipop 276
lollop 281.2
lolly 16.122
Lomax 494
Lombard 103
Lombardy 16.72
Lombok 40
loment 410
lomentum 242
Lomond 143
London 261
Londonderry
  16.262
Londoner 17.239
lone 257
loneliness 300.23
lonely 16.173
loner 17.236
lonesome 242
long 266
longanimity
  16.333.12
longboat 376
longbow 12
longeron 261.60
longevity 16.333.34

longevous 310.73
Longfellow 12.40
Longford 103
long-haired 88
longhand 128
longhorn 255
longicorn 255.2
longing 265
Longinus 310.34
longish 353
longitude 102.2
longitudinal
  228.60.1
long johns 549
longship 274
longshore 9
long-sighted 91.39
long-sightedness
  300.28
longspur 3
longtime 236
Longueuil 214
longways 509
long-winded 91
Longyearbyen 248
lonicera 17.279.2
loo 15
looby 16.14
loofah 17.119
look 44
looker 17.40
lookout 377
loom 241
loon 260
loony 16.236
loop 280
looper 17.259
loophole 223
loopy 16.253
loose 309
loosebox 499
loosely 16.183
loosen 261
looseness 300
loosestrife 164
loot 380
looter 17.351
lop 276
lope 278
lop-eared 90
lophophore 9.6
lopsided 91.8
loquacious 310.56
loquacity 16.333.25
loquat 373

lor 9
lord 95
lordly 16.150
lordosis 300.55
Lords 528
Lordship 274
lordy 16.66
lore 9
Lorelei 7.7
lorgnette 368
lorica 17.35
lorikeet 370
lorimer 17.211
loris 300.46
lorn 255
Lorraine 247
lorry 16.268
lory 16.269
Los Angeles 513.6
lose 523
losel 228.127
loser 17.444
losing 265.84
loss 302
lossy 16.302
lost 438
lot 373
lota 17.347
Lothair 4
Lothario 12.3.5
Lothian 261.3
lotic 38.55
lotion 261.73
lots 341
lottery 16.274
lotto 12.77
lotus 310.66
louche 358
loud 99
louden 261
loud-hailer 17.162
loudish 353
loudmouth 462
loudness 300
loudspeaker 17.33
lough 40
Loughborough
17.279
Louis 16.4
louis 16.4
Louisburg 182.1
louis d'or 9.3
Louisiana 17.225.1
lounge 210
lounger 17.158

loupe 280
lour 14
louse 306
lousy 16.400
lout 377
Louth 462
loutish 353
louvar 1
louvre 17.419
louvred 103
lovable 228.16
lovage 197
lovat 381
love 489
lovebird 87
Lovelace 295
loveless 300
loveliness 300.23
Lovell 228
lovelock 40
lovelorn 255
lovely 16.207
lovemaking 265.6
lover 17.418
lovesick 38
lovey 16.383
lovey-dovey 16.383
loving 265
low 12
lowan 261.6
lowborn 255
lowboy 11
lowbred 86
lowbrow 13
lowdown 258
lower 17.6
Lowestoft 399
lowland 143
lowliness 300.23
lowly 16.126
lowness 300.25
Lowry 16.271
lox 499
loxodromics 498
loyal 228.6
loyalism 242.35.11
loyalist 436.7
loyalty 16.352.1
Loyang 263
lozenge 209
lozengy 16.110
Lozi 16.399
Luanda 17.98
Luba 17.20
lubber 17.19

Lubbock 46
lubricant 420.7
lubricate 367.5
lubrication
261.67.5
lubricator 17.338.2
lubricious 310.58
lubricity 16.333.28
Lubumbashi
16.319
Lucan 261.15
lucarne 246
lucent 420.71
Lucerne 249
lucerne 249
Lucian 261.3
lucid 91.30
lucidity 16.333.5
Lucifer 17.114
luciferin 252.20
Lucilius 310.2.5
Lucina 17.232
luck 43
luckless 300
lucklessness 300.33
lucky 16.30
lucrative 485.15
lucre 17.41
Lucretius 310.2
lucubrate 367
lucubration 261.67
Lucullus 310
Lucy 16.306
Luddite 372
Ludhiana 17.226.1
ludicrous 310
ludo 12.22
luff 168
luffa 17.118
lug 189
luge 364
Luger 17.136
luggage 197
lugger 17.134
lugubrious 310.2
Luke 45
lukewarm 238
lull 225
lullaby 7
Lulu 15.4
lumbago 12.27
lumbar 17.27
lumber 17.27
lumbering 265.58
lumberjack 32

lumberjacket 371.6
lumberyard 84
lumbricalis 300.7
lumbricoid 97.3
lumen 252
luminance 321.14
luminary 16.274.26
luminesce 296.2
luminescence
321.21
luminosity
16.333.30.4
luminous 310.33.1
lumme 16.220
lummox 503
lump 289
lumpen 261
lumper 17.264
lumpish 353
lumpy 16.257
Luna 17.238
lunacy 16.307
lunar 17.238
lunate 367
lunatic 38.57
lunation 261.67
lunch 82
luncheon 261
luncheonette 368
Lund 141
Lundy 16.80
lune 260
lunette 368
lung 267
lunge 211
lungi 5
lunula 17.174
Lupercalia 17.3.18
lupin 252
lupine 253
lupulin 252.10
lupus 310
lur 10
lurch 65
lurcher 17.54
lurdan 261.22
lure 10
Lurex 496
lurid 91
lurk 36
Lusaka 17.29
luscious 310
lush 356
Lusitania 17.3.31.2
lust 443

417

lustful 226.13
lustrate 367
lustre 17.388
lustreware 4.8
lustrous 310
lusty 16.368
lute 380
lutenist 436.11
luteous 310.2
Lutetia 17.325
lutetium 242.2
Lutheran 261.60
Lutherism
242.35.15
luthern 261
Luton 261.104
lux 502
luxate 367
Luxembourg 182
Luxor 9
luxuriant 420.1.3
luxuriate 367.1
luxurious 310.2.14
luxury 16.274
Luzon 254
Lyallpur 10
lycanthrope 278
lycanthropy 16.254
lycée 2
lyceum 242.1
lychee 5
lychnis 300.27
lycopodium
242.2.4
lyddite 372.1
Lydia 17.3.9
lye 7
lyke-wake 34
Lyme Regis 300.6
Lymington 261
lymph 176
lymphangial 228.3
lymphatic 38.49
lymphoblast 430
lymphocyte 372.10
lymphocytic
38.52.3
lymphoid 97
lyncean 261.2
lynch 80
lyncher 17.71
Lynn 252
lynx 505
lyonnaise 509
Lyonnesse 296.3

lyophilic 38.21
lyophilize 516.2
Lyra 17.274
lyrate 371
lyre 8
lyrebird 87
lyric 38.40
lyrical 228.23.16
lyricism
242.35.16.3
lyricist 436.21
Lysander 17.98
Lysenko 12.13
lysergic 38.16
Lysias 293.1
Lysimachus 310.14
lysin 252.22
Lysippus 310.37
lysis 300.53
lysozyme 236
lytic 38.52
lytta 17.342

M

ma 1
ma'am 230
maar 1
Mab 18
mabela 17.163
mac 32
macabre 17.281
macadam 242.5
macadamia 17.3.24
macadamize 516.5
macaque 33
macaroni 16.233
macaronic 38.35
macaroon 260.3
Macaulay 16.123
macaw 9.2
Macbeth 455
Maccabean 261.2.1
Maccabees 513
maccaboy 11
Macclesfield 115
Macdonald 122
mace 295
macebearer 17.271
macedoine 246
Macedon 254

Macedonia 17.3.36
Macedonian
261.3.18
macer 17.299
macerate 367.23
machan 246
machete 16.330
Machiavelli 16.115
Machiavellian
261.3.9
machicolate 367.14
machinate 367.17
machination
261.67.18
machine 251.10
machinery
16.274.25
machinist 436
machismo 12.50
Machmeter 17.341
machree 5
Machu Picchu 15
Macías Nguema
17.207
Mackay 7.2
Mackenzie 16.405
mackerel 228.76
Mackinaw 9
mackintosh 354
mackle 228.19
Maclean 247
Macleod 99.1
Macmillan 261.41
Macpherson
261.64
macramé 16.211
macrencephaly
16.131
macrobiotic
38.53.1
macrocephaly
16.131
macrocosm 242
macrocyst 436.22
macrocyte 372.10
macrograph 158.1
macron 254
macrophage 193.1
macropterous
310.50
macroscopic
38.37.1
macruran 261.59
macula 17.174.3
macula lutea 17.3

maculation
261.67.13
macule 227
mad 83
Madagascar 17.47
madam 242.5
madcap 268
madden 261.19
maddening 265.46
madder 17.77
made 85
Madeira 17.272
madeleine 252.11
mademoiselle 215
madhouse 306
Madhya Pradesh
351
Madison 261.65
madly 16.146
madman 261
madness 300
Madonna 17.233.1
Madras 294
madrepore 9
Madrid 91
madrigal 228.46
madrilène 248
Madura 17.277
Madurai 7
maduro 12.66
Maebashi 5
Maecenas 293
maelstrom 237
maenad 83
maestoso 12.70
maestro 12
Maeterlinck 52
Mafeking 265.7
Mafia 17.3.10
mafioso 12.70
mag 178
magazine 251
magdalen 252.11
Magdalena 17.227
Magdalene 251.3
Magdeburg 182
Magellan 261.40
magenta 17.368
maggot 381
maggoty 16.344
Maghreb 31
magi 7
magic 38.15
magical 228.23
magician 261.71

Maginot 12.55
magisterial
228.3.11
magistery
16.274.49
magistracy 16.307
magistral 228.82
magistrate 367.28
magistrature 10.5
magma 17.220
magmatic 38.49
Magna Carta
17.337
magnanimity
16.333.12
magnanimous
310.28.1
magnate 367
magnesia 17.325
magnesite 372.9
magnesium
242.2.20
magnet 371
magnetic 38.50
magnetics 498.12
magnetism
242.35.18
magnetite 372.11
magnetize 516.12
magneto 12.76
magnetometer
17.342.3
magneton 254
magnetosphere 6.1
magnifiable
228.16.3.1
Magnificat 365
magnificence
321.22
magnificent 420.70
magnifico 12.11
magnifier 17.4.1
magnify 7.3
magniloquent
420.59
magnitude 102.2
magnolia 17.3.22
magnum 242
magnus 310
Magog 185
magot 12.26
magpie 7
maguey 2
magus 310.19
Magyar 1

Mahabharata
17.352
Mahanadi 16.72
maharajah 17.145
maharani 5.10
maharishi 16.322
Mahayana 17.226
Mahdi 16.58
Mahé 2
mahjong 266
Mahler 17.161
mahogany 16.237.4
Mahomet 371.20
Mahometan 261.99
mahonia 17.3.36
mahout 377
mahseer 17.3.47
Maia 17.4
maid 85
maidan 246
maiden 261.20
maidenhair 4
Maidenhead 86
maidenhead 86
maidenhood 101
maidenly 16.174
maidservant 420.82
Maidstone 261
maieutic 38.56
mail 214
mailbag 178
mailbox 499
mailcoach 70
mailer 17.162
mailsack 32
maim 231
Maimonides 513.4
main 247
mainbrace 295
Maine 247
mainland 143
mainly 16.170
mainmast 431
mainsail 214
mainsheet 370
mainspring 265
mainstay 2
mainstream 234
maintain 247
maintenance
321.14
maintop 276
maisonette 368
maître d'hôtel
215.4

maize 509
majestic 38.69
majesty 16.366
major 17.146
Majorca 17.37
major-domo 12.49
majorette 368.6
majority 16.333.22
majuscule 227
Makasar 17.298
make 34
makefast 431
maker 17.30
makeshift 398
make-up 279
makeweight 367
making 265.6
makings 552
Makurdi 16.61
Malabar 1.2
Malacca 17.28
malacca 17.28
Malachi 7.2
malachite 372
malacology
16.108.4.6
malacopterygian
261.3.7
maladdress 296
maladjusted 91.54
maladjustment 420
maladminister
17.384.1
maladministration
261.67.25
maladroit 375
malady 16.72
mala fide 16.64
Malagasy 16.294
malaise 509
malamute 380
malanders 524
Malang 263
malapert 369
malapropism
242.35
malapropos 12.59
malar 17.162
malaria 17.3.38.1
malarial 228.3.10
malarkey 16.20
malassimilation
261.67.12
Malay 2.12
Malaya 17.1

Malayan 261.1
Malaysian 261.3.33
Malcolm 242
malcontent 410
Male 2
male 214
maleate 367.1.1
maledict 387
malediction
261.78.1
malefactor 17.353
malefic 38
maleficent 420.70
malevolence
321.12.1
malevolent
420.28.1
malfeasance 321.28
malformation
261.67
malformed 125
malfunction 261.80
Mali 16.113
malice 300
malicious 310.58
malign 253.3
malignancy 16.312
malignant 420
malignity
16.333.19
malimprinted 91
malines 251.3
malinger 17.141
malingerer 17.279
Malinke 16.37
Malinowski 16.44
malison 261.126
mall 221
mallam 229
mallard 84
malleable 228.16.2
mallee 5
mallemuck 43
malleolus 310.26
mallet 371
malleus 310.2
mallow 12.38
malm 230
Malmö 12
malnourished 449
malnutrition
261.71
malocclusion
261.93
malodorous 310.50

Malory 16.274.15
malposition
261.71.9
malpractice 300.65
malt 404
Malta 17.363
maltase 509
malted 91.44
Maltese 513
Malthusian 261.3
malting 265
maltose 520
maltreat 370
maltreatment 420
malty 16.351
Malvern 261
mam 229
mama 1.12
mamba 17.23
mambo 12
mamelon 261
Mameluke 45
mamey 5
mamilla 17.166
mamillate 367.12
mamma 17.205
mammal 228.51
mammalian
261.3.8
mammalogy
16.108.2
mammary 16.274
mammiferous
310.50.2
mammock 46
mammon 261.44
mammoth 464
mammy 16.210
man 245
mana 17.226
manacle 228.28
manage 197.5
manageable
228.16.20
management
420.37
manager 17.150
manageress 296.4
managerial
228.3.11
managing 265.25
manakin 252.4
Manama 17.206
Manassas 310.51
Manasseh 16.294

manatee 5
Manchester 17.384
manchineel 217
Manchu 15
Manchuria 17.3.42
manciple 228.66
Mancunian 261.3
Mandaean 261.3
Mandalay 2.12
mandamus 310.27
mandarin 252.20
mandate 367
mandatory
16.274.43
Mande 2
mandi 16.80
mandible 228.12
mandibular
17.174.2
mandir 6
mandolin 252.11
mandorla 17.169
mandragora 17.279
mandrake 34
mandrel 228
mandrill 218
manducate 367
mane 247
manège 360
Manes 513
manes 509
manful 226
mangabey 2.4
Mangalore 9.8
manganate 367.18
manganese 513.9
mange 207
mangelwurzel
228.126
manger 17.156
mangle 228.49
mango 12.35
mangonel 215
mangosteen 251
mangrove 488
mangy 16.109
manhandle 228.39
Manhattan 261.94
manhole 223
manhood 101
manhunt 419
Mani 16.224
mania 17.3.31
maniac 32.1
maniacal 228.28.1

manic 38.31
Manichaeus 310.1
manicotti 16.335
manicure 10.3
manicurist 436.19
manifest 433
manifestation
261.67.33
manifesto 12.86
manifold 120
manikin 252.3
Manila 17.166.1
manilla 17.166.1
manille 218
manioc 40
maniple 228.66
manipulability
16.333.9.2
manipular 17.174
manipulate
367.13.6
manipulation
261.67.13.4
manipulative
485.15.5
Manisa 1
Manitoba 17.18
mankind 135
manky 16.36
manlike 39
manly 16.169
manna 17.225
manned 128
mannequin 252.3
manner 17.225
mannered 103
mannerism
242.35.15
mannerless 300.13
mannerly 16.131
Mannheim 236
mannish 353
mannose 520
manoeuvrable
228.16
manoeuvre 17.419
man-of-war 9
manometer
17.342.3.3
manor 17.225
manorial 228.3.12
manpower 14
manrope 278
mansard 84
manse 314

manservant 420.82
Mansfield 115
mansion 261.81
manslaughter
17.345
mansuetude 102.2
manta 17.365
manteau 12.83
mantel 228.109
mantelet 368
mantelletta 17.339
mantelpiece 298
manteltree 5
mantic 38.62
mantilla 17.166
mantis 300.66
mantissa 17.302
mantle 228.109
mantling 265
Mantoux 15
mantra 17.296
mantrap 268
Mantua 17.7.2
mantua 17.7.2
manual 228.9.2
manubrium 242.2
manufacture 17.63
manufacturer
17.279
manufacturing
265.58
manuka 17.41
manumit 371
manure 10
manus 310.31
manuscript 424
Manx 504
Manxman 261
many 16.226
manyplies 516
manzanilla
17.166.1
Maoism 242.35
Maoist 436
Maori 16.271
map 268
maple 228
mapping 265,
265.48
Maputo 12.80
maquette 368
maquis 5.3
mar 1
mara 1.14
marabou 15.1

marabout 15.1
marabunta 17.373
maraca 17.28
marasca 17.47
maraschino 12.54
marasmus 310
Maratha 17.337.2
Marathi 16.328.1
marathon 261.109
maraud 95
marauder 17.86
maravedi 16.59
marble 228
marbled 122
marbling 265
Marburg 182
marc 33
marcasite 372.10
marcel 215
Marcellus 310.22
March 63
march 63
marcher 17.51
marchioness 300.26
Marconi 16.233
Marco Polo 12.44
mardy 16.58
mare 2.17, 4
maremma 17.208
marg 192
margaric 38.38
margarine 251.7
margarita 17.341
margarite 372.8
Margate 367
margay 2
marge 192
margin 252
marginal 228.60
marginalia 17.3.18
marginally
16.131.3
margravate 371
margrave 482
margravine 251.12
marguerite 370
Maria 17.2.2
mariachi 16.47
Marian 261.3.20
Maribor 9
Marie 5.17
marigold 120
marijuana 17.226
marimba 17.25
marina 17.230.1

marinade 85.2
marinate 367.17
Marinduque 2
marine 251.7
mariner 17.231
Mariolatry
16.286.2.1
Mariology
16.108.4.1
marionette 368
mariposa 17.442
Marist 436
maritage 197.12
marital 228.102
maritime 236
Maritimer 17.212
Marius 310.2.10
marjoram 242.21
Mark 33
mark 33
markdown 258
markedly 16.148
marker 17.29
market 371.7
marketable
228.16.49
marketing 265.66
marketplace 295
markhor 9
marking 265
markka 1
Markova 17.417
marksman 261
marksmanship
274.2
marl 213
Marlborough
17.279
marlin 252
marline 252
marlite 372
Marlowe 12.39
marmalade 85
Marmara 17.279
Marmite 372
marmoreal
228.3.12
marmoset 368.9
marmot 381
Marne 246
marocain 247.2
Maronite 372.6
maroon 260.3
marooned 142
Marprelate 371.15

marque 33
marquee 5.3
marquess 300
marquessate 371.38
marquetry 16.285
marquis 300
marquisate 371.38
marquise 513
marquisette 368
Marrakech 351
marram 242
marriage 197.9
marriageable
228.16.20
married 91.25
marron 261
marrow 12.60
marrowbone 257
marrowfat 365
marry 16.260
Marryat 381.1.1
Mars 508
Marsala 17.161
Marseillaise 509
marsh 350
marshal 228.90
Marshalsea 5
marshland 143
marshmallow 12.38
marshy 16.320
Marsilius 310.2.5
marsupial 228.3.9
marsupium 242.2
mart 366
martagon 261
Martello 12.40
marten 252
martensite 372
Martha 17.397
martial 228.90
Martian 261
Martin 252
martin 252
martinet 368
martingale 214
martini 16.228
Martinique 37
Martinmas 310
martlet 371
martyr 17.337
martyrdom 242
martyrology
16.108.4.13
martyry 16.274
marvel 228

marvellous 310.26
Marx 495
Marxian 261.3
Marxism 242.35
Marxist 436
Mary 16.264
Maryland 143.2
marzipan 245.3
Masai 7
Masbate 16.328
mascara 17.268
mascle 228
mascon 254
mascot 381
masculine 252.10
masculinity
16.333.17
Masefield 115
maser 17.439
mash 349
masher 17.321
Mashhad 83
mashie 16.319
masjid 91
mask 56
masked 394
masochism
242.35.6
masochist 436
masochistic 38.70
mason 261.62
masonic 38.35.4
masonry 16.284
Masora 17.276
Masorete 370
masque 56
masquerade 85.4
mass 293
Massachusetts 339
massacre 17.42
massage 359
massasauga 17.132
Massasoit 375
massé 16.294
Massenet 2
masses 515.2
masseter 17.341
masseur 3
masseuse 511
Massey 16.294
massicot 373
massif 162
Massinger 17.157
massive 485.1

massotherapy
16.254
massy 16.294
mast 431
mastaba 17.21
mastectomy
16.222.5
master 17.380
masterful 226
masterly 16.131
mastermind 135
masterpiece 298.2
masterstroke 42
mastery 16.274
masthead 86
mastic 38.68
masticate 367.5.2
mastication
261.67.5
masticatory
16.274.43
mastiff 163
mastitis 300.62
mastodon 254
mastoid 97
mastoiditis 300.62
masturbate 367.4
masturbation
261.67.3
Masuria 17.3.42.2
masurium 242.2
mat 365
Matabele 16.118
Matabeleland
143.2
Matadi 16.58
matador 9.4
Mata Hari
16.261.1
Matamoros 310.48
Matapan 245.4
match 62
matchboard 95
matchbox 499
matchless 300
matchmaker 17.30
matchmark 33
matchstick 38
matchwood 101
maté 2.23
mate 367
matelote 376
mater 17.338
materfamilias
293.1

material 228.3.11
materialism
242.35.11.2.1
materialist 436.7.2
materialistic
38.70.2.1
materiality
16.333.8.1
materialize
516.3.2.1
materially 16.131
materia medica
17.34
materiel 215
maternal 228.58
maternity
16.333.16
matey 16.329
mathematical
228.23.18
mathematician
261.71
mathematics
498.11
Mathura 17.277
Matilda 17.95
matin 252
matinée 2.15
matins 548
Matlock 40
matriarch 33.1
matriarchate 371.7
matriarchy 16.20
matrices 513
matricide 92.7
matriclinous
310.34
matriculate
367.13.2
matriculation
261.67.13
matrilineal 228.3.7
matrilocal 228.26
matrimonial
228.3.8
matrimony 16.237
matrix 498.9
matron 261
matronage 197
matronly 16.174
matt 365
mattamore 9.9
matted 91.32
matter 17.336
Matterhorn 255

Matthew 15
Matthias 310.3
matting 265
mattock 46
mattress 300
maturate 367.22
maturation
261.67.21
mature 10.5
maturity 16.333.23
matutinal 228.61
matza 17.319
matzoon 260
Maud 95
maud 95
maudlin 252
Maugham 238
maul 221
mauler 17.169
maulstick 38
Mau Mau 13
Mauna Kea 1
Mauna Loa 1
maund 137
maunder 17.105
Maureen 251.6
Maurice 300
Maurist 436
Mauritania
17.3.31.2
Mauritius 310.58.2
Mauser 17.443
mausoleum 242.1
mauve 488
maverick 38.44
Mavis 300
mavourneen 251
maw 9
mawkish 353
mawsie 16.397
maxi 16.386
maxilla 17.166
maxillary 16.274.16
maxilliped 86.6
maxim 235
maxima 17.211
maximal 228.52
maximalist 436.7
Maximilian
261.3.11
maximin 252.14
maximize 516.4
maximum 242
maximus 310.28
maxixe 352

Maxwell 228
May 2
may 2
maya 17.4
Mayan 261.4
maybe 16.7
Mayday 2
Mayfair 4
Mayflower 14
mayfly 7
mayhem 232
Maying 265.1
mayn't 420
Mayo 12.1
Mayon 255
mayonnaise 509
mayor 4
mayoral 228
mayoralty 16.352
mayoress 300.44
mayorship 274
maypole 223
mayweed 89
Mazarin 263
Mazdaism 242.35
maze 509
mazuma 17.217
mazurka 17.32
mazy 16.393
Mbabane 16.224
McCarthyism
242.35.2
McCoy 11
McQueen 251
me 5
mead 89
meadow 12
meadowlark 33
meadowsweet 370
meagre 17.128
meal 217
mealy 16.118
mean 251
meander 17.98.1
meaning 265.42
meaningful 226
meaningless 300.15
meaninglessness
300.33
meanness 300
means 547
meant 410
meantime 236
meanwhile 219
meany 16.228

measled 122
measles 539
measurable
  228.16.35.2
measure 17.333
measured 103.6
measureless 300.13
measurement
  420.35
meat 370
meatball 221
Meath 457
meatus 310.62
meaty 16.332
Mecca 17.31
Meccano 12.51
mechanic 38.31
mechanical
  228.23.10
mechanician
  261.71
mechanics 498
mechanism
  242.35.14
mechanistic
  38.70.4
mechanize 516.7
mechanotherapy
  16.254
meck 35
Mecklenburg 182
meconium 242.2.12
Med 86
medal 228
medallic 38.19
medallion 261.118
medallist 436.7
meddle 228
meddler 17.184
meddlesome 242
Mede 89
Medea 17.2
media 17.3.8
medial 228.3.1
median 261.3.4
mediant 420.1.1
mediastinum
  242.15
mediate 367.1
mediation 261.67.1
mediatize 516.13
mediator 17.338.1
medic 38
medicable
  228.16.10

Medicaid 85
medical 228.23.1
medicament 420.35
Medicare 4
medicate 367.5
medication
  261.67.5
medicinal 228.60.6
medicine 252.21
medick 38
medico 12.11
medieval 228.119
medievalism
  242.35.11
medievalist 436.7
Medina 17.230
mediocre 17.38
mediocrity 16.333
meditate 367.30
meditation
  261.67.27
meditative
  485.15.12
Mediterranean
  261.3.15.1
medium 242.2.2
medlar 17.184
medley 16.147
Médoc 40
medulla 17.173
medullated 91.34
medusa 17.444
Medway 2
mee 5
meek 37
meekly 16.141
meekness 300
meerkat 365
meet 370
meeting 265
megadeath 455
megalith 458
megalithic 38.73
megalocardia
  17.3.6
megalomania
  17.3.31.1
megalomaniac 32.1
megalopolis
  300.13.2
megalosaur 9.11
megaphone 257
megaphonic
  38.35.2
megapode 98

Megara 17.279
megaron 254.11
megaspore 9.10
megass 293
megathere 6.10
megaton 259
megawatt 373
megillah 17.166
megohm 239
megrim 235
Meiji 5
meiosis 300.55.2
meiotic 38.53.1
Meir 6
Meistersinger
  17.246
Mekong 266
mel 215
melaleuca 17.41
melamine 251.4
melancholia
  17.3.22
melancholic 38.22
melancholy 16.131
Melanesia 17.334
Melanesian
  261.3.34
melanin 252
melanism
  242.35.14
melanite 372.6
melanoid 97.9
melanosis 300.55
melaphyre 8.1
Melba 17.22
Melbourne 261
Melchior 9.1
Melchite 372
meld 113
melee 2
melic 38.20
melilot 373
melinite 372.5
melioration
  261.67.22
melisma 17.224
melismatic 38.49.4
melliferous
  310.50.2
mellifluous 310.4
mellophone 257
mellow 12.40
melodeon 261.3.6
melodic 38.9
melodious 310.2.2

melodiousness
  300.34.1
melodist 436.3
melodize 516
melodrama 17.206
melodramatic
  38.49.2
melodramatize
  516.13.1
melody 16.72
meloid 97.4
melon 261.40
Melos 302
melt 402
Melville 218
member 17.24
membership 274.1
membrane 247
membranous
  310.36
memento 12.84
memento mori
  7.11
memo 12
memoir 1
memoirs 508
memorabilia
  17.3.21.1
memorable
  228.16.35
memoranda
  17.98.2
memorandum
  242.6
memorial 228.3.12
memorialist
  436.7.2
memorialize
  516.3.2.2
memorize 516.8
memory 16.274
Memphis 300
Memphremagog
  185
memsahib 24
men 248
menace 300
ménage 359
menagerie 16.274
Menai 7
Menam 229
Menander 17.98
menarche 16.20
Mencius 310.2
mend 131

423

mendable
228.16.18
mendacious 310.56
mendacity
16.333.25
Mendel 228
mendelevium 242.2
Mendelism
242.35.11
Mendelssohn 261
mender 17.101
mendicant 420.7
mending 265.20
Mendips 327
Mendoza 17.442
Menelaus 310
Menelik 38.21
Menes 513
menfolk 42
menhaden 261.20
menhir 6
menial 228.3.6
meninges 513
meningitic 38.52
meningitis 300.62
meniscus 310.15
meno 12.52
menology 16.108.4
menopause 518
menorah 17.276
menorrhagia
17.3.12
Menotti 16.335
Mensa 17.314
menses 513.14
Menshevik 38.74
menstrual 228.9
menstruate 367.2
menstruation
261.67.2
menstruous 310.4
menstruum 242.3
mensurable
228.16.35
mensural 228.76
mensuration
261.67.21
menswear 4
mental 228.110
mentalism
242.35.11.6
mentality
16.333.8.10
menthol 220
mentholated 91.34

mention 261.82
mentor 9.12
menu 15
Menuhin 252
Menzies 515
meow 13
Mephistopheles
513.6.1
mephitic 38.52
mephitis 300.62
meprobamate
367.16
mercantile 219
mercantilism
242.35.9
mercaptan 245
mercaptide 92
Mercator 17.338
mercenary
16.274.26
mercer 17.301
mercerize 516.8
merchandise 301,
516
merchant 420
merchantable
228.16.57
merchantman 261
Mercia 17.3
merciful 226
merciless 300.8
mercilessness
300.33
mercurate 367.22
mercurial 228.3
mercurialism
242.35.11.2
mercurialize
516.3.2
mercuric 38.43
mercurous 310.49
mercury 16.273
Mercury 16.274
mercy 16.298
mere 16.262, 6
Meredith 458
merely 16.119
merengue 2
meretricious 310.58
merganser 17.312
merge 195
merger 17.148
meridian 261.3.5
meridional 228.63
meringue 263.2

merino 12.54
Merionethshire 6
meristem 232
meristic 38.70.5
merit 371.31
meritocracy
16.307.5
meritorious
310.2.13
merkin 252
merle 216
Merlin 252
merlin 252
merlon 261
mermaid 85
merman 261
merocrine 253
Meroë 5
Merovingian 261.3
merrily 16.120
merriment 420.31.2
merry 16.262
merry-go-round
139
merrymaker 17.30
merrymaking 265.6
Merse 297
Mersey 16.394
Merseyside 92.7
Merthyr Tydfil
218
Merton 261.97
mesa 17.299
mésalliance 321.1.1
mesarch 33
Mesa Verde 87
mescaline 251.3
mesembryanthemum
242.12
mesenchyme 236
mesenteron 254.11
mesentery
16.274.48
mesh 351
Meshach 32
meshy 16.321
mesial 228.3
mesmeric 38.39
mesmerism
242.35.15
mesmerize 516.8
mesne 251
mesoblast 430
mesocarp 269
mesocratic 38.49.6

mesoderm 233
Mesolithic 38.73
mesomorph 166.1
mesomorphic 38.14
meson 254
mesopause 518
mesophyll 218.1
Mesopotamia
17.3.24
mesosphere 6.1
mesothelium
242.2.5
Mesozoic 38.2
mesquite 370
mess 296
message 197.11
Messalina 17.230
messaline 251.3
Messene 16.228
messenger 17.157
Messiah 17.4
messianic 38.31.1
Messina 17.230
messmate 367
Messrs. 524
messuage 197
messy 16.297
mester 17.382
mestranol 220
met 368
Meta 17.338
metabolic 38.22
metabolism
242.35.11
metabolite 372.4
metabolize 516.3
metacarpal 228
metacarpus 310
metagalaxy 16.390
metage 197
metal 228.100
metalanguage 197
metallic 38.19.1
metalliferous
310.50.2
metalline 253.3
metallist 436.7
metallize 516.3
metallography
16.90.2.2
metalloid 97.6
metallurgic 38.16
metallurgical
228.23.4

metallurgist
436.4.1
metallurgy
16.108.2
metalwork 36
metamer 17.218
metamere 6.3
metamerism
242.35.15
metamorphic 38.14
metamorphism
242.35.7
metamorphose 520
metamorphosis
300.57.2
metanephros 302
metaphase 509
metaphor 17.120
metaphoric 38.41
metaphorical
228.23.17
metaphrase 509
metaphysic 38
metaphysical
228.23.25
metaphysician
261.71.8
metaphysics 498
metapsychology
16.108.4.5
metastasis 300.57
metastasize 516.11
metatarsal 228.83
metatarsus 310.52
metatheory 16.265
metatherian
261.3.22
metathesis 300.52
metathesize 516.10
mete 370
metempirics 498
metempsychosis
300.55
meteor 17.3
meteoric 38.41
meteorite 372.8
meteoritic 38.52.2
meteorograph
158.1
meteoroid 97.12
meteorologist
436.4
meteorology
16.108.4.13
meter 17.341

methadone 257
methane 247
methanol 220
methinks 505
method 103
methodical
228.23.2
Methodism 242.35
Methodist 436.3
methodize 516
methodology
16.108.4
methotrexate 367
methought 374
methoxide 92.14
Methuselah 17.176
methyl 218
methylal 212
methylate 367.12
methyldopa 17.257
methylene 251.2
methylic 38.21
metic 38.50
meticulous
310.25.2
métier 2.1
Métis 298
metol 220
metonym 235
metonymy 16.216
metope 278
metopic 38.37
metralgia 17.3.16
metre 17.341
metric 38.46
metrical 228.23
metricate 367.5
metrication
261.67.5
metrics 498.10
metrify 7.3
metritis 300.62
metro 12
metrology 16.108.4
metronome 239
metronomic
38.29.1
metronymic 38.28
metropolis
300.13.2
metropolitan
261.99
metrorrhagia
17.3.12
mettle 228.100

mettled 122.2
Metz 336
meunière 4
Meuse 511
mew 15
mewl 227
mews 523
Mexicali 16.113
Mexican 261.13
Mexico 12.11
mezereon 261.3.22
mezereum 242.2.15
mezzanine 251
mezzo 12.71
mezzotint 412
mi 5
Miami 16.210
miasma 17.223
mica 17.35
Micah 17.35
Micawber 17.17
mice 301
micella 17.163
Michael 228.24
Michaelmas 310
Michelangelo 12.42
Michigan 261.32
Mick 38
mickery 16.274.4
mickle 228.23
Micmac 32
microanalysis
300.52.1
microbe 28
microbiology
16.108.4.2
microcephaly
16.131
microcircuit 371.8
microclimatology
16.108.4.15.1
microcline 253
micrococcus 310.11
microcopy 16.250
microcosm 242
microcosmic 38
microcyte 372.10
microdontous 310
microdot 373
microelectronic
38.35
microelectronics
498.5
microfiche 352
microfilm 244

micrograph 158.1
micrography
16.90.2
microgroove 490
microlight 372.4
microlith 458
micrometer
17.342.3
micron 254
Micronesia 17.334
microorganism
242.35.14
micropalaeontology
16.108.4.16
microphone 257
microphonic
38.35.2
microphotograph
158.1
microprint 412
microprocessor
17.300
micropyle 219
microscope 278.1
microscopic
38.37.1
microscopy
16.254.2
microsecond 143
microspore 9.10
microstomatous
310.68
microtome 239
microtomy
16.222.4
microwave 482
micrurgy 16.102
micturate 367.22
micturition 261.71
mid 91
midair 4
Midas 310.16
midbrain 247
midday 2
Middelburg 182
midden 261.24
middle 228.32
middlebrow 13
middleman 261
Middlesex 496
Middleton 261
middleweight 367
middling 265
middy 16.63
midfield 115

Midgard 84
midge 197
midget 371
midgut 378
Midheaven 261.112
midi 16.63
Midian 261.3.5
Midianite 372.6
midinette 368
midiron 261.4
midland 143
Midlands 534
Midlothian 261.3
midmost 441
midnight 372
midpoint 416
midrash 349
midrib 24
midriff 163
midsection 261.77
midship 274
midshipman 261
midships 327
midst 446
midsummer 17.216
midterm 233
midtown 258
midway 2
midweek 37
midwife 164
midwifery 16.274
midwinter 17.369
mien 251
Mies van der Rohe
    17.6
miff 163
miffy 16.85
might 372
mighty 16.334
migraine 247
migrant 420
migrate 367
migration 261.67
migratory
    16.274.43
mihrab 18
mikado 12.16
mike 39
mil 218
milady 16.59
Milan 245.2
Milanese 513.9
milch 76
mild 117
mildew 15

mildness 300
mile 219
mileage 197
mileometer
    17.342.3
milepost 441
miler 17.167
milestone 257
milfoil 222
miliaria 17.3.38
miliary 16.274.1.1
milieu 3
militancy 16.312
militant 420.76
militarism
    242.35.15
militarist 436.20
militarize 516.8.2
military 16.274.41
militate 367.30.1
militia 17.326
militiaman
    261.52.1
milium 242.2.6
milk 49
milkmaid 85
milkman 261
milko 12
milksop 276
milkweed 89
milkwort 369
milky 16.34
Milky Way 2
mill 218
Millais 2.11
millboard 95
milldam 229
millefleurs 3
millenarian
    261.3.21.1
millenarianism
    242.35.14.1.1
millenary
    16.274.23
millennial 228.3
millennium 242.2
millepore 9
miller 17.166
millesimal 228.52.1
millet 371.16
milliard 84
millibar 1.1
millieme 232
Milligan 261.32
milligram 229

Millikan 261.13
millilitre 17.341
millimetre 17.341
milliner 17.231
millinery 16.274.26
milling 265.30
million 261.120
millionaire 4.5
millionairess
    300.44
millionth 471
millipede 89.1
millisecond 143
millpond 136
millrace 295
millrun 259
millstone 257
millstream 234
millwheel 217
millwright 372
Milne 262
milord 95
milquetoast 441
milt 403
milter 17.362
Milton 261
Miltonian 261.3.18
Miltonic 38.35
Milton Keynes
    547
Milwaukee 16.28
mim 235
Mimas 310
mime 236
Mimeograph
    158.1.1
mimesis 300.51
mimetic 38.50
mimetite 372.11
mimic 38.28
mimicry 16.275
Mimir 6
mimosa 17.306
Min 252
minacious 310.56.4
Mina Hassan Tani
    16.224
minaret 368.6
Minas 310.34
minatory
    16.274.43.6
mince 317
mincemeat 370
mincer 17.315
Minch 80

mincing 265.62
mind 135
minded 91
Mindel 228.40
minder 17.103
mindful 226
mindless 300
mindlessness
    300.33
Mindszenty 16.355
mine 253
minefield 115
miner 17.232
mineral 228.76
mineralize 516.3.8
mineralocorticoid
    97.3
mineralogy
    16.108.2
Minerva 17.412
minestrone 16.233
minesweeper
    17.252
Ming 265
mingle 228.50
Mingrelian
    261.3.10
mingy 16.110
mini 16.229
miniature 17.56
miniaturist 436.20
miniaturize 516.8
minibus 307
minicab 18
minim 235
minima 17.211
minimal 228.52
minimalist 436.7
minimax 494
minimize 516.4
minimum 242
minimus 310.28
mining 265.44
minion 261.122
minipill 218
miniskirt 369
miniskirted 91.36
minister 17.384.1
ministerial
    228.3.11
ministerium
    242.2.15
ministrant 420
ministration
    261.67.25

ministry 16.293
minium 242.2.11
miniver 17.414
minivet 368
mink 52
Minna 17.231
Minneapolis 300.13.1
minnesinger 17.246
Minnesota 17.347
minnow 12.55
Minoan 261.6
minor 17.232
Minorca 17.37
Minorite 372.8
minority 16.333.22
Minos 302
Minotaur 9
minster 17.394
minstrel 228
minstrelsy 16.308
mint 412
mintage 197
Minton 261.105
minty 16.356
minuend 131
minuet 368.1
minus 310.34
minuscule 227
minute 371.24, 380
minutely 16.189, 16.193
minutes 339
minutiae 5.2
minx 505
Miocene 251.9
miosis 300.55.2
Miquelon 254.7
Mira Ceti 7.13
miracidium 242.2.3
miracle 228.28
miraculous 310.25
mirador 9.4
mirage 359
Miranda 17.98
mire 8
mirepoix 1
Miriam 242.2.16
mirror 17.273
mirth 456
mirthful 226
mirthless 300
MIRV 483
miry 16.267
misadventure 17.70

misalliance 321.2
misanthrope 278
misanthropic 38.37.3
misanthropist 436.15
misanthropy 16.254
misapply 7.9
misapprehend 131.1
misapprehension 261.82.1
misbecome 240
misbegotten 261.101
misbehave 482
misbehaviour 17.436
misbelief 162.1
miscalculate 367.13
miscalculation 261.67.13
miscarriage 197.9
miscarry 16.260
miscast 431
miscegenation 261.67.18
miscellanea 17.3.31
miscellaneous 310.2.6
miscellany 16.237.5
mischance 315
mischief 163
mischievous 310
mischievousness 300.34
miscible 228.16.39
misconceive 484
misconception 261.84
misconduct 389
misconstruction 261.79
misconstrue 15
miscount 418
miscreance 321.1
miscreant 420.1
miscreate 367.1
miscue 15
misdate 367
misdeal 217
misdeed 89
misdemeanant 420

misdemeanour 17.230
misdirect 385
misdirection 261.77.3
mise 513
miser 17.441
miserable 228.16.35
misère 4
misericord 95.2
miserly 16.131
misery 16.274
misfeasance 321.28
misfile 219
misfire 8
misfortune 260.5
misgive 485
misgiving 265.80
misgovern 261.117
misguide 92
misguided 91.8
mishandle 228.39
mishap 268
mishear 6
mishmash 349
Mishnah 17.243
misinform 238
misinformation 261.67.16
misinterpret 371
misinterpretation 261.67.27
misjoinder 17.106
misjudge 203
mislay 2
mislead 89
misleading 265.13
misled 86
mismanage 197.5
mismatch 62
misnomer 17.215
misogamy 16.222.2
misogynist 436.13
misogynous 310.33
misogyny 16.229.2
misology 16.108.4
misoneism 242.35.1
misplace 295
misplay 2
misplead 89
mispleading 265.13
misprint 412
misprision 261.91
misprize 516

mispronounce 319
mispronunciation 261.67.1.4
misquotation 261.67.28
misquote 376
misread 89
misreport 374.1
misrepresent 410.4
misrepresentation 261.67.32
misrule 227
miss 300
missal 228.85
misshape 270
misshapen 261.57
missile 219.2
missing 265.61
mission 261.71
missionary 16.274.29.3
missis 515.3
Mississauga 17.132
Mississippi 16.248
Mississippian 261.3
missive 485.4
Missouri 16.270
misspell 215
misspelling 265.28
misspend 131
misstate 367
missy 16.300
mist 436
mistakable 228.16.9
mistake 34
mistaken 261.11
mistal 228.114
Mistassini 16.228
mister 17.384
mistigris 5.18
mistime 236
mistletoe 12
mistook 44
mistral 228.82
mistreat 370
mistress 300
mistrial 228.4
mistrust 443
misty 16.366
misunderstand 128
misunderstanding 265.19
misunderstood 101

427

misuse 309, 523
misuser 17.444
mitch 67
Mitchell 228
mite 372
Mithraism 242.35
Mithras 293
Mithridates 513.15
miticide 92.7.1
mitigable 228.16.19
mitigate 367.10
mitigation
 261.67.10
mitis 300.62
mitochondrion
 261.3
mitosis 300.55
mitrailleuse 511
mitre 17.343
mitt 371
mitten 261.99
mittimus 310.28
mix 498
mixed 451
mixer 17.427
Mixtec 35
mixture 17.76
Mizar 1
Mizoguchi 16.53
Mizoram 242.20
mizzen 261.126
mizzenmast 431
mizzle 228
m'lud 100
mnemonic 38.35
mnemonics 498.5
Mnemosyne 5.12
mo 12
moa 17.6
Moab 18
Moabite 372
moan 257
moaner 17.236
moat 376
mob 26
mobcap 268
mobile 219
mobility 16.333.9.1
mobilize 516.2
mobocracy
 16.307.5
mobster 17.391
moccasin 252
mocha 17.36
mock 40

mockery 16.274.5
mockingbird 87
mod 94
modal 228
modality 16.333.8
mode 98
model 228.34
modeller 17.176
modem 232
moderate 367.23,
 371.35
moderation
 261.67.22
moderato 12.73
moderator 17.338.9
modern 261.26
moderne 250
modernism
 242.35.14
modernistic 38.70.4
modernity
 16.333.16
modernize 516.7
modest 436
modestly 16.201
modesty 16.366
modge 199
modicum 242.4
modifiable
 228.16.3.1
modification
 261.67.5.1
modifier 17.4.1
modify 7.3
modillion 261.120
modiolus 310
modish 353
modiste 435
modular 17.174
modulate 367.13
modulation
 261.67.13
modulator 17.338.6
module 227
modulus 310.25
mofette 368
mog 185
Mogadishu 15
Mogador 9.4
mogul 228
mohair 4
Mohammed 91
Mohammedan
 261.24

Mohammedanism
 242.35.14
Mohammedanize
 516.7
Mohave 16.378
Mohawk 41
Mohican 261.12
Mohock 40
Mohorovičić 67
moider 17.87
moidore 9
moiety 16.333
moire 1
moiré 2.17
moist 440
moisten 261
moisture 17
moisturize 516.8
moisturizer 17.441
moke 42
mola 17.171
molality 16.333.8
molar 17.171
molarity 16.333.20
molasses 515.2
Moldau 13
Moldavia 17.3.53
moldavite 372
mole 223
molecular 17.174.4
molecule 227.1
molehill 218
moleskin 252
moleskins 548
molest 433
molestation
 261.67.33
molester 17.382
moline 253.3
moll 220
mollify 7.3.2
mollusc 61
Molly 16.122
molly 16.122
mollycoddle 228.34
mollycoddler
 17.188
Molly Maguire 8
Moloch 40
Molokai 16.1
Molotov 165
molten 261
Moluccas 524
moly 16.126

molybdenum
 242.14
mom 237
Mombasa 17.298
moment 420
momentarily
 16.120.1
momentary
 16.274.48
momentous 310.70
momentum 242
momism 242.35
Momus 310
Mona 17.236
mona 17.236
Monacan 261
monachal 228.28
Monaco 12
monad 83.3
monadelphous 310
monadism 242.35
monadnock 40
Monaghan 261
monal 221
Mona Lisa 17.440
monanthous
 310.72
monarch 46
monarchal 228.20
monarchism
 242.35.6
monarchist 436
monarchy 16.33
monarda 17.78
monasterial
 228.3.11
monastery 16.274
monastic 38.68
monasticism
 242.35.16.6
monatomic 38.29
monaural 228.74
Monday 2
mondial 228.3
Monegasque 55
monetary
 16.274.41
monetize 516.12
money 16.235
moneychanger
 17.156
moneyed 91
moneylender
 17.101

moneylending 265.20
moneymaker 17.30
moneywort 369
mongo 12
Mongol 220
mongol 228
Mongolia 17.3.22
Mongolian 261.3.12
Mongolic 38.22
mongolism 242.35.11
mongoloid 97.6
mongoose 309
mongrel 228
mongrelize 516.3
Monica 17.34.1
moniker 17.34.1
monism 242.35
monition 261.71
monitor 17.342
monitory 16.274.41
monitress 300
monk 54
monkey 16.39
monkeypot 373
monkfish 353
monkhood 101
monkish 353
monkshood 101
Monmouth 464
Monmouthshire 6
mono 12
monoacid 91.28
Monoceros 310.50
monochasium 242.2.19
monochord 95.3
monochromatic 38.49.2
monochromatism 242.35.20
monochrome 239
monocle 228.28
monocline 253
monoclinic 38.34
monoclinous 310.34
monocoque 40
monocotyledon 261.23
monocracy 16.307.5

monocular 17.174.7
monoculture 17.69
monody 16.72
monogamist 436.10
monogamous 310.29
monogamy 16.222.2
monogram 229.1
monogrammatic 38.49.2
monograph 158.1
monogyny 16.229.2
monolatry 16.286.2
monolingual 228
monolith 458
monolithic 38.73
monologue 185
monomania 17.3.31.1
monomark 33
monomer 17.218.1
monomerous 310.50
monometallism 242.35.11
monometer 17.342.3
monomial 228.3
monomorphic 38.14
mononuclear 17.3
mononucleosis 300.55.1
monophagous 310
monophobia 17.3.4
monophonic 38.35.2
monophony 16.237.3
monophthong 266
monopodium 242.2.4
monopolize 516.3
monopoly 16.131.6
monorail 214
monosaccharide 92.6
monosemy 16.215
monosome 239
monostich 38
monostome 239
monostrophe 16.90

monostylous 310.24
monosyllabic 38
monosyllable 228.16.23
monotheism 242.35.2
monotint 412
monotone 257.3
monotonous 310.36
monotony 16.237.7
monotreme 234
monotype 275.1
monotypic 38.36
monovalent 420.25
monoxide 92.14
Monroe 12
Monrovia 17.3.55
Monsignor 17.435
monsoon 260
monster 17
monstrance 321
monstrosity 16.333.30
monstrous 310
monstrousness 300.34
mons veneris 300.47
montage 359
Montagnard 84
Montague 15
Montana 17.225
montane 247.11
montbretia 17.325
monte 16.357
Monte Carlo 12.39
Montego 12.28
monteith 457
Montenegro 12.67
Monterey 2.19
Monterrey 2.19
Montessori 16.269
Montezuma 17.217
montgolfier 17.3
Montgomery 16.274
monthly 16.205
monticule 227.1
Montreal 221
Montrose 520
Monty 16.357
monument 420.34

monumental 228.110
monzonite 372.6
moo 15
mooch 74
mood 102
moodiness 300.23
moody 16.71
Moog 190
moolah 1
moolvie 5
moon 260
moonbeam 234
mooncalf 158
mooneye 7
moonflower 14
moonless 300
moonlight 372
moonlighter 17.343
moonlighting 265.67
moonlit 371
moonquake 34
moonraker 17.30
moonrise 516
moonseed 89
moonshine 253
moonshiner 17.232
moonshot 373
moonstone 257
moonstruck 43
moony 16.236
Moor 10
moor 10
moorage 197
moorcock 40
Moore 10
moorfowl 224
moorhen 248
mooring 265.56
Moorish 353
moorland 143
moose 309
moot 380
mop 276
mope 278
moped 86
mopoke 42
moppet 371
moquette 368
mor 9
moraine 247
moral 228.73
morale 213
moralism 242.35.11

moralist 436.7
morality 16.333.8.9
moralize 516.3
Morar 17.276
morass 293
moratorium
  242.2.17
Morava 17.409
Moravia 17.3.53
Moravian 261.3.29
moray 2
morbid 91
morbidity 16.333.5
morbific 38.12
morbilli 7.5
morcha 1
mordacious 310.56
mordacity
  16.333.25
mordant 420.11
Mordecai 16.2
mordent 420.11
more 9
Morecambe 242
moreen 251
moreish 353
morel 215
morello 12.40
moreover 17.417
mores 509
Moresque 57
Morgan 261.33
morganatic 38.49.5
morganite 372.6
Morgan le Fay 2.9
morgue 186
moribund 140
morion 261.3.23
Morisco 12.15
Morley 16.123
Mormon 261
Mormonism
  242.35.14
morn 255
mornay 2
morning 265
Moroccan 261
Morocco 12
morocco 12
moron 254.10
moronic 38.35
morose 305.2
morosely 16.182
morph 166
morpheme 234

Morpheus 310.2
morphia 17.3
morphine 251
morphinism
  242.35.13
morphogenesis
  300.52.4
morphology
  16.108.4
morphosis 300.55
Morris 300
Morrison 261.65
morro 12.65
morrow 12.65
Mors 518
Morse 303
morse 303
morsel 228
mort 374
mortal 228.105
mortality 16.333.8
mortar 17.345
mortarboard 95.1
mortgage 197
mortgagee 5.6
mortgagor 17.150
mortician 261.71
mortify 7.3
Mortimer 17.211
mortise 300.63
mortmain 247
Morton 261.102
mortuary 16.274.2
morula 17.174
morwong 266
mosaic 38.1
moschatel 215
Moscow 12
Moselle 215
Moses 515
mosey 16.399
Moslem 242
Moslemic 38.25
mosque 59
mosquito 12.76
moss 302
mossback 32
mossbunker 17.46
Mossi 16.302
mossie 16.302
mosstrooper
  17.259
mossy 16.302
most 441
mostly 16.202

mot 12
mote 376
motel 215.4
motet 368
moth 459
mothball 221
mother 17.408
motherfucker 17.39
motherhood 101
mother-in-law 9
motherland 143.4
motherless 300.13
motherly 16.131
mother-of-pearl
  216
mothproof 170
mothy 16.371
motif 162
motile 219
motility 16.333.9
motion 261.73
motionless 300.14
motivate 367.36
motivation 261.67
motive 485.14
motivity 16.333.35
motley 16.191
motmot 373
motocross 302.2
motor 17.347
motorbike 39
motorboat 376
motorbus 307
motorcade 85
motorcar 1
motorcoach 70
motorcycle 228.24
motorcyclist 436
motorist 436.20
motorize 516.8
motorman 261.52
motorway 2.28
Motown 258
motte 373
mottle 228.104
motto 12.77
mouflon 254
mouillé 2
mould 120
moulder 17.97
moulding 265.18
mouldwarp 277
mouldy 16.76
moulin 252
moult 405

mound 139
mount 418
mountain 252
mountaineer 6.4
mountaineering
  265.53
mountainous
  310.33
Mountbatten
  261.94
mountebank 51
mounted 91.49
Mountie 16.359
mounting 265.73
Mount Rushmore
  9
mourn 255
mourner 17.234
mournful 226
mourning 265
mouse 306, 521
mouser 17.443
mousetrap 268
moussaka 17.29
mousse 309
moustache 350
mousy 16.304
mouth 462
mouthbrooder
  17.91
mouthful 226
mouthpart 366
mouthpiece 298
mouthwash 354
mouthwatering
  265.58
mouton 254
movable 228.16.62
move 490
moved 150
movement 420.51
mover 17.419
movie 16.384
moving 265
Moviola 17.171
mow 12, 13
mowburnt 411
mower 17.6
mown 257
moxa 17.428
moxie 16.389
Mozambique 37
Mozart 366
mozzarella 17.163
mozzetta 17.339

Mr. 17.384
Mrs. 515.3
Ms. 515
much 72
muchness 300
mucid 91.30
mucilage 197.1
muck 43
mucker 17.39
muckle 228.27
muckrake 34
mucky 16.30
mucoid 97
mucosa 17.306
mucous 310.13
mucus 310.13
mud 100
mudcat 365
muddle 228.36
muddleheaded 91.7
muddy 16.69
mudguard 84
mudir 6
mudlark 33
mudpack 32
mudra 1
mudskipper 17.253
mudslinging 265.47
muezzin 252.30
muff 168
muffin 252.5
muffle 228.42
muffler 17.191
Mufti 16.349
mufti 16.349
Mufulira 17.272
mug 189
Mugabe 16.6
mugger 17.134
muggins 548
muggy 16.97
mugwump 289
Muhammad 103
Muhammadan 261
Muir 10
mukluk 43
mulatto 12.72
mulberry 16.274
mulch 77
mule 227
muleta 17.339
muleteer 6
muley 16.130
mulga 17.139

muliebrity
16.333.24
mulish 353
Mull 225
mull 225
mullah 17.173
mullein 252
muller 17.173
mullet 371
mulley 16.128
mulligan 261.32
mulligatawny
16.232
mullion 261.3.13
mullite 372
mullock 46
mulloway 2.28
Multan 246
multeity 16.333.1
multicide 92.7
multicollinearity
16.333.20.1
multicoloured
103.4
multidisciplinary
16.274.26
multifaceted 91.38
multifactorial
228.3.12
multifarious
310.2.10.1
multifid 91
multifoil 222
multifoliate 371.1
multiform 238.1
multigravida 17.83
multihull 225
multilateral 228.76
multilingual 228
multimedia 17.3.8
multimillionaire
4.5
multinational
228.63.2
multinuclear 17.3
multinucleate
371.1
multipara 17.279
multiparous 310.50
multipartite 372
multiplane 247
multiple 228.66
multiplepoinding
265
multiplex 496

multiplicand 128.1
multiplication
261.67.5
multiplicative
485.15.1
multiplicity
16.333.28.1
multiplier 17.4
multiply 7.8
multipurpose 310
multiracial 228.91
multirole 223
multiscreen 251
multistage 193
multistorey 16.269
multitude 102.2
multitudinous
310.33
multure 17.69
mum 240
mumble 228
mumbler 17.180
mumbo jumbo
12.7
mumchance 315
mummer 17.216
mummery 16.274
mummify 7.3
mummy 16.220
mumps 332
munch 82
mundane 247
mung 267
munga 17.143
Munich 38
municipal 228.66
municipality
16.333.8.8
munificence 321.22
munificent 420.70
muniment 420.31
munition 261.71
munitions 551
Munster 17.395
muntjac 32
muon 254
mural 228.75
murder 17.81
murderer 17.279
murderess 300.47
murderous 310.50
Murdoch 40
Mures 351
murex 496
muricate 367.5

Murillo 12.42
murine 253
murk 36
murky 16.23
murmur 17.209
murmuring 265.58
Murphy 16.83
murrain 252
Murray 16.272
murre 3
murrelet 371
murrhine 253
Murrumbidgee
16.103
murther 17.403
Musca 17.49
muscadine 252
muscarine 252.20
muscat 365
muscatel 215
muscid 91
muscle 228.87
muscleman 261
muscovado 12.16
Muscovite 372
Muscovy 16.385
muscular 17.174.8
muscularity
16.333.20.3
musculature 17.62
muse 523
museology
16.108.4.1
musette 368.8
museum 242.1
mush 356, 357
mushroom 241
mushy 16.324
music 38
musical 228.23
musician 261.71
musicianship 274.2
musicology
16.108.4.4
musk 60
muskeg 181
muskellunge 211
musket 371
musketeer 6
musketry 16.285
muskmelon 261.40
muskrat 365
musky 16.42
Muslim 235
Muslimism 242.35

muslin 252
muso 12
musquash 354
muss 307
mussel 228.87
Mussolini 16.228.1
must 443
mustachio 12.3
mustang 263
mustard 103
mustee 5
musteline 253
muster 17.388
musty 16.368
mutable 228.16.53
mutagen 261.39
mutant 420.77
mutate 367
mutation 261.67.29
Mutazilite 372.3
mutch 72
mute 380
muticous 310.10
mutilate 367.12
mutilation
  261.67.12
mutineer 6.4
mutinous 310.33.2
mutiny 16.229
mutism 242.35.19
mutt 378
mutter 17.349
mutton 261.103
muttonchops 329
mutual 228.9
mutuality
  16.333.8.2
Muzak 32
muzhik 38
muzz 522
muzzle 228
muzzler 17.204
muzzy 16.401
my 7
myalgia 17.3.16
myalism 242.35.11
myall 228.4
myasthenia 17.3.33
mycelium 242.2.5
Mycenae 5
mycology
  16.108.4.5
mycorrhiza
  17.441.1
mycosis 300.55

mycotic 38.53
mydriasis 300.57.1
mydriatic 38.49
myelin 252.8
myelitis 300.62.1
myeloid 97.5
myeloma 17.215
myiasis 300.57.1
mynah 17.232
myocardial 228.3
myocardiograph
  158.1.1
myocardium 242.2
myogenic 38.32.1
myoglobin 252
myograph 158.1
myology 16.108.4.2
myoma 17.215
myope 278
myopia 17.3.37
myopic 38.37
myosin 252
myosotis 300.64
myotonia 17.3.36
myriad 103.1
myriapod 94.1
myrica 17.35
myrmecology
  16.108.4.4
myrmecophile
  219.1
Myrmidon 254
Myron 261.58
myrrh 3
myrtle 228
myself 172
Mysore 9
mystagogue 185.2
mysterious
  310.2.11
mystery 16.274.49
mystic 38.70
mystical 228.23.24
mysticism
  242.35.16
mystify 7.3
mystique 37
myth 458
mythical 228.23
mythicize 516.10
mythological
  228.23.5
mythologize 516.1
mythology
  16.108.4.18

mythomania
  17.3.31.1
mythos 302
myxoedema 17.210
myxomatosis
  300.55.7

N

NAAFI 16.82
nab 18
nabob 26
Nabokov 165
Nabonidus 310.16
Naboth 459
nacelle 215.2
nacre 17.30
nacreous 310.2
Na-Dene 16.225
nadir 6
nae 2
naevus 310.73
nag 178
Nagaland 143.4
nagana 17.226
Nagano 12.51
Nagari 16.274
Nagasaki 16.20
nagger 17.123
nagor 9
Nagoya 17.431
Nagpur 10
Nahuatl 228.98
Nahum 242
naiad 83.2
naïf 162
nail 214
nailbrush 356
nailfile 219
nailhead 86
nainsook 44
naira 17.269
Nairn 250
Nairobi 16.12
naive 484
naiveté 2
naked 91
nakedness 300.28
naker 17.30
NALGO 12.34
Nama 17.206

namby-pamby
  16.17
name 231
nameless 300
namely 16.165
nameplate 367
namesake 34
nametape 270
Namhoi 11
Namibia 17.3.3
Namur 10
nan 245
Nanchang 263
Nancy 16.309
nankeen 251
Nanking 265
nanna 17.225
nanny 16.223
nanometre 17.341
Nanook 45
nanosecond 143
Nansen 261
Nan Shan 245
Nantucket 371.11
Nantung 267
Naoise 16.299
Naomi 16.222
nap 268
napalm 230
nape 270
naphtha 17.398
naphthalene 251.3
naphthol 220
Napier 17.3
napiform 238.1
napkin 252
Naples 539
Napoleon 261.3.12
Napoleonic 38.35.1
nappa 17.247
nappe 268
napper 17.247
nappy 16.243
Nara 17.268
Narayanganj 211
narceine 251
narcissism
  242.35.16
narcissistic 38.70
narcissus 310.53
narcolepsy 16.313
narcosis 300.55
narcotic 38.53
narcotism
  242.35.20

narcotize 516.13
nard 84
nares 513.10
narial 228.3.10
nark 33
Narraganset 371
narrate 367.23
narration 261.67.22
narrative 485.15.8
narrator 17.338.9
narrow 12.60
narrow-minded 91
narrow-mindedness 300.28
narrowness 300.25
narthex 496
Narvik 38
narwhal 228
nary 16.264
NASA 17.298
nasal 228.125
nasalize 516.3
nascent 420
Nash 349
Nashville 218
nasion 261.3.33
nasopharynx 505
Nastase 16.392
nastiness 300.23
nasturtium 242
nasty 16.362
natal 228.99
natality 16.333.8
natant 420.75
natation 261.67.30
natatory 16.274.40
natch 62
nates 513.15
Nathan 261
Nathaniel 228.123
nation 261.67
national 228.63.2
nationalism 242.35.11.5.1
nationalist 436.7.5
nationalistic 38.70.2
nationality 16.333.8.7.1
nationalization 261.67.36
nationalize 516.3.7
nationwide 92
native 485.10
nativism 242.35.22

nativity 16.333.35.1
NATO 12.74
natrolite 372.4
natron 261
NATSOPA 17.257
natter 17.336
natterjack 32
natty 16.327
natural 228.76
naturalism 242.35.11
naturalist 436.7
naturalistic 38.70.2
naturalize 516.3.8
naturally 16.131
nature 17.52
naturism 242.35.15
naturist 436.20
naturopath 452
naturopathic 38.72
naturopathy 16.373.1
naught 374
naughtiness 300.23
naughty 16.336
nauplius 310.2
nausea 17.3
nauseate 367.1
nauseous 310.2
nautch 69
nautical 228.23
nautiloid 97.5
nautilus 310.23
Navaho 12.37
naval 228
navar 1
navarin 263
Navarre 1.15
nave 482
navel 228
navicert 369
navicular 17.174.6
navigable 228.16.19
navigate 367.10
navigation 261.67.10
navigational 228.63.3
navigator 17.338.3
navvy 16.377
navy 16.379
nawab 19
Naxos 302
nay 2

Nazarene 251.7
Nazareth 464
Nazarite 372.8
Naze 509
Nazi 16
Nazify 7.3
Nazism 242.35
Ndjamena 17.227
Ndola 17.171
Neagh 2
Neanderthal 213
Neapolitan 261.99
near 6
nearby 7
Nearctic 38.59
nearly 16.119
nearness 300
nearside 92
near-sighted 91.39
near-sightedness 300.28
neat 370
neaten 261.98
neath 457
neatness 300.37
neb 21
Nebraska 17.47
nebula 17.174
nebulize 516
nebulosity 16.333.30
nebulous 310.25
necessarily 16.120.1
necessary 16.274.36
necessitarianism 242.35.14.1.1
necessitate 367.30
necessitous 310.64
necessity 16.333
neck 35
Neckar 1
neckband 128
neckcloth 459
neckerchief 163
necklace 300
neckline 253
necktie 7
neckwear 4
necrobiosis 300.55.2
necrolatry 16.286.2
necrology 16.108.4

necromancy 16.309
necrophilia 17.3.21.2
necrophilism 242.35.9
necrophobia 17.3.4
necrophobic 38.3
necropolis 300.13.2
necrose 305
necrosis 300.55
necrotic 38.53
necrotomy 16.222.4
nectar 17.354
nectarine 252.20
nectary 16.274.45
neddy 16.60
née 2
need 89
needful 226
neediness 300.23
needle 228
needlecord 95
needlecraft 396
needleful 226
needlepoint 416
needless 300
needlewoman 261.50
needlework 36
needn't 420.9
needs 526
needy 16.62
neep 273
ne'er 4
nefarious 310.2.10.1
Nefertiti 16.332
negate 367.10
negation 261.67.10
negative 485.15
negativism 242.35.22
negativity 16.333.35.1
negator 17.338.3
neglect 385
neglectful 226.10
negligee 2
negligence 321.9
negligent 420.20
negligible 228.16.20
negotiable 228.16.44

negotiant 420.1
negotiate 367.1.7
negotiation
261.67.1
negotiator 17.338.1
Negress 300
Negritic 38.52
Negrito 12.76
Negro 12.67
Negroid 97
Negrophile 219.1
Negrophobe 28
Negrophobia
17.3.4
Negropont 414
Negros 305
negus 310
Nehemiah 17.4
Nehru 15
neigh 2
neighbour 17.11
neighbourhood 101
neighbouring
265.58
neighbourly 16.131
Neil 217
Neisse 17.303
neither 17.406
nek 35
nelly 16.115
Nelson 261
nelumbo 12.7
nematic 38.49.1
nematocyst 436.22
nematode 98
Nembutal 213
nemertean 261.3
nemesia 17.334
Nemesis 300.52.3
nene 2
neoanthropic
38.37.3
Neocene 251.9
neoclassicism
242.35.16
neodymium 242.2
neoimpressionism
242.35.14.4
neolith 458
Neolithic 38.73
neologism 242.35.8
neologize 516.1
neomycin 252.22
neon 254
neonate 367.18

neophyte 372
neoplasticism
242.35.16.6
neoplasty 16.361.1
neoteny 16.237.7
Neozoic 38.2
Nepal 221
Nepali 16.123
neper 17.249
nephelinite 372.5
nephew 15
nephogram 229.1
nephograph 158.1
nephology 16.108.4
nephralgia 17.3.16
nephralgic 38
nephrectomy
16.222.5
nephridium 242.2.3
nephrite 372
nephritic 38.52
nephritis 300.62
nephron 254
nephrosis 300.55
nephrotomy
16.222.4
nepotic 38.53
nepotism 242.35.20
Neptune 260
Neptunian 261.3
neral 212
Nereid 91.2
nereis 300
neritic 38.52
Nero 12.63
neroli 16.131
Nerva 17.412
nervate 367.35
nerve 483
nerveless 300
nervine 251
nerving 265.78
nervous 310
nervousness 300.34
nervure 10
nervy 16.381
nescience 321.1
nesh 351
Ness 296
nesselrode 98
nest 433
nesting 265.75
nestle 228
nestler 17.197
nestling 265

Nestor 9
Nestorianism
242.35.14.1
Nestorius 310.2.13
net 368
netball 221
nether 17.402
Netherlands 534
nethermost 441
netting 265.65
nettle 228.100
nettlesome 242
netty 16.330
network 36
neume 241
neural 228.75
neuralgia 17.3.16
neuralgic 38
neurasthenia
17.3.33
neuritis 300.62
neuroblast 430
neurogenic 38.32.1
neurolemma
17.208
neurology 16.108.4
neuromuscular
17.174.8
neuron 254
neurone 257
neuropath 452
neuropathology
16.108.4
neuropathy
16.373.1
neuropsychiatry
16.286.1
neurosis 300.55
neurosurgeon
261.35
neurosurgery
16.274.13
neurosurgical
228.23.4
neurotic 38.53
neuroticism
242.35.16.5
neurotomy
16.222.4
neuter 17.351
neutral 228
neutralism
242.35.11
neutrality 16.333.8
neutralize 516.3

neutralizer 17.441
neutretto 12.75
neutrino 12.54
neutron 254
neutrophil 218.1
Neva 17.413
Nevada 17.78
névé 2
never 17.411
nevermore 9.9
nevertheless 296.1
new 15
Newark 46
newborn 255
Newburg 182
Newbury 16.274
Newcastle 228.83
newcomer 17.216
newel 228.10
newfangled 122
Newfie 16.89
Newfoundland 143
Newgate 371
Newham 242
Newhaven 261.111
newish 353
newly 16.130
newlywed 86
Newman 261.51
Newmarket 371.7
newness 300
Newport 374
news 523
newsagent 420
newscast 431
newscaster 17.380
newshawk 41
newsletter 17.339
newspaper 17.249
newspaperman
261.52
newspeak 37
newsprint 412
newsreel 217
newsstand 128
newsworthy 16.375
newsy 16.402
newt 380
Newton 261.104
Newtonabbey 16.5
Newtonian
261.3.18
New Zealand
143.1

New Zealander 17.109
next 450
nexus 310
ngaio 12.4
ngoma 17.215
Nguni 16.236
ngwee 2
niacin 252
Niagara 17.289
Niamey 2
nib 24
nibble 228.12
niblick 38
Nicaragua 17.7.1
niccolite 372.4
Nice 298
nice 301
nicety 16.333.29
niche 67, 352
Nicholas 310.26.2
Nicholson 261
Nicias 310.2.15
nick 38
nickel 228.23
nickelic 38.20
nickelodeon 261.3.6
nickelous 310.26.2
nicker 17.34
Nicklaus 306
nickname 231
Nicosia 17.2
nicotiana 17.226.1
nicotinamide 92.3
nicotine 251.11
nicotinic 38.34
nicotinism 242.35
nictitate 367.30
niddle-noddle 228.34
nide 92
nidicolous 310.26.2
nidificate 367.5
nidify 7.3.1
nid-nod 94
nidus 310.16
Niebuhr 10
niece 298
niello 12.40
Nietzsche 17.55
nieve 484
niff 163
nifty 16.347
Niger 17.151

Nigeria 17.3.39
Nigerian 261.3.22
niggard 103
niggardly 16.152
niggle 228.46
niggling 265
niggly 16.160
nigh 7
night 372
nightcap 268
nightclub 29
nightdress 296
nightfall 221
nightgown 258
nighthawk 41
nightie 16.334
nightingale 214
nightjar 1
nightlife 164
nightlong 266
nightly 16.190
nightmare 4
nightmarish 353.9
nightrider 17.84
nights 340
nightshade 85
nightshirt 369
nightspot 373
nightwear 4
nigrescent 420.67
nigrosine 251.9
nihilism 242.35.9
Nijinsky 16.45
Nijmegen 261.31
Nikko 12.10
nil 218
nil desperandum 242.6
Nile 219
nilgai 7
Nilotic 38.53
nim 235
nimble 228
nimbleness 300.30
nimblewit 371
nimbostratus 310.62
nimbus 310
niminy-piminy 16.229.3
Nimrod 94
Nina 17.230
nincompoop 280
nine 253
ninefold 120

ninepins 548
nineteen 251
nineteenth 469
ninetieth 458
ninety 16
Nineveh 17.414
ninny 16.229
Ninus 310.34
niobium 242.2
nip 274
nipa 17.252
Nipigon 254.5
Nipissing 265.61
nipper 17.253
nipple 228.66
Nippon 254
Nippur 10
nippy 16.248
nirvana 17.226
Niš 352
Nishapur 10
nisi 7
nisi prius 310.3
Nissen 261.65
nit 371
nitid 91.38
nitrate 367
nitre 17.343
nitric 38
nitride 92
nitriding 265.14
nitrify 7.3
nitrobacteria 17.3.39
nitrobenzene 251
nitrochloroform 238.2
nitrogen 261.39
nitrogenize 516.6
nitrogenous 310.33
nitroglycerin 252.20
nitroglycerine 251.7
nitrometer 17.342.3
nitroso 12.70
nitrosyl 218
nitrous 310
nitty 16.333
nitty-gritty 16.333
nitwit 371
Niue 2.2
nival 228.121
nivation 261.67
Niven 261.114

niveous 310.2.17
nix 498
nixer 17.427
nixie 16.388
Nixon 261
nizam 229
Nizam 230
Njord 95
Nkomo 12.49
Nkrumah 17.217
no 12
Noachian 261.3
Noachic 38.6
Noah 17.6
nob 26
nobble 228
nobbut 381
Nobel 215
nobelium 242.2
nobiliary 16.274.1.1
nobility 16.333.9.1
noble 228.13
nobleman 261
noblesse 296
noblesse oblige 362
nobody 16.72
nociceptive 485.23
nock 40
noctiluca 17.41
noctuid 91
noctule 227
nocturn 249
nocturnal 228.58
nocturne 249
nocuous 310.4
nod 94
nodal 228
noddle 228.34
noddy 16.65
node 98
nodical 228.23
nodose 305
nodular 17.174
nodule 227
nodus 310
Noel 228.7
noesis 300.51
noetic 38.50.1
nog 185
noggin 252
nogging 265.23
noil 222
noise 519

noiseless 300
noisette 368
noisiness 300.23
noisome 242
noisy 16.398
Nolan 261.43
noli-me-tangere 16.274
noma 17.215
nomad 83
nomadic 38.7
nomarch 33
nomarchy 16.20
nombril 218
nom de guerre 4
nom de plume 241
nome 239
nomen 248
nomenclator 17.338
nomenclature 17.62
nominal 228.60.5
nominate 367.17.5, 371.24
nomination 261.67.18.6
nominative 485.15.7
nominee 5.12
nomism 242.35
nomocracy 16.307.5
nomogram 229.1
nomology 16.108.4
nomothetic 38.50.6
nonage 197
nonagenarian 261.3.21.1
nonagon 254.5
nonaligned 135
nonappearance 321.17
nonce 318
nonchalant 420.28
non-com 237
noncombatant 420.78
noncommissioned 143.5
noncommittal 228.102
nonconductor 17.357

nonconformism 242.35.12
nonconformist 436
nonconformity 16.333.13
noncontributory 16.274.42
noncooperation 261.67.22.3
noncooperative 485.15.10
nondescript 424
none 259
nonentity 16.333.32
nones 550
nonessential 228.96
nonesuch 72
nonet 368
nonetheless 296.1
nonevent 410.3
nonexistent 420.81
nonfeasance 321.28
nonferrous 310.44
nonfiction 261.78
nonflammable 228.16.26
nong 266
nonharmonic 38.35
nonillion 261.120
nonjoinder 17.106
nonjuror 17.277
non licet 371
nonmember 17.24
nonmetal 228.100
nonmetallic 38.19.1
nonpareil 228.76
nonparous 310.43
nonpartisan 245.7
nonparty 16.328
nonplus 307
non-pros 302
nonresident 420.10.1
nonresistant 420.81
nonrestrictive 485.18
nonreturnable 228.16.28
nonrigid 91.15
nonsense 321
nonsensical 228.23
non sequitur 17.342
nonslip 274

nonsmoker 17.38
nonstandard 103
nonstarter 17.337
nonstative 485.10
nonstick 38
nonstop 276
nonswimmer 17.211
non-U 15
nonunion 261.123
nonunionism 242.35.14
nonviolence 321.12
nonviolent 420.28
nonvoter 17.347
noodle 228.37
nook 44
noon 260
noonday 2
nooning 265
noontime 236
noose 309
nopal 228.69
nope 278
nor 9
Nora 17.276
noradrenaline 252.11
Nordic 38
Norfolk 46
noria 17.3.41
Noricum 242.4
norite 372
nork 41
norm 238
Norma 17.214
normal 228.53
normality 16.333.8.5
normalize 516.3
normally 16.131
Norman 261
Normandy 16.81
normative 485.15.6
Norn 255
Norse 303
Norseman 261
north 460
Northampton 261
Northamptonshire 6.8
Northants. 347
northbound 139
northeast 435

northeasterly 16.131
northeastward 103
northerly 16.131
northern 261
Northerner 17.239
northernmost 441
Northumberland 143.4.1
Northumbria 17.3.44
Northumbrian 261.3.25
northward 103
northwards 531
northwest 433
northwesterly 16.131
northwestward 103
Northwich 67
Norway 2
Norwegian 261.36
Norwich 197
nose 520
nosebag 178
noseband 128
nosebleed 89
nosegay 2
nosh 354
nosing 265.83
nosography 16.90.2
nosology 16.108.4
nostalgia 17.3.16
nostalgic 38
nostoc 40
Nostradamus 310
nostril 218
nostrum 242.23
nosy 16.399
nosy-parker 17.29
not 373
notability 16.333.9.2
notable 228.16
notarize 516.8
notary 16.274
notate 367.31
notation 261.67.28
notch 68
note 376
notebook 44
notecase 295
noted 91.41
notelet 371
notepaper 17.249

noteworthy 16.375
nothing 265
nothingness 300.32
notice 300.64
noticeable
228.16.39
notifiable
228.16.3.1
notification
261.67.5.1
notify 7.3
notion 261.73
notional 228.63.6
notitia 17.3.49
notochord 95.3
notoriety
16.333.2.1
notorious 310.2.13
notornis 300.24
nototherium
242.2.15
notour 17.347
Notre Dame 230
Nottingham 242.17
Nottinghamshire 6
Notts. 341
notum 242.31
Notus 310.66
notwithstanding
265.19
nougat 1
nought 374
noumenon 261.56
noun 258
nourish 353.10
nourishment
420.47
nous 306
nouveau riche 352
nova 17.417
Nova Scotia
17.328
novation 261.67
novel 228
novelese 513.7
novelette 368
novelist 436.7
novelistic 38.70.2
novelize 516.3
novella 17.163
Novello 12.40
novelty 16.352
November 17.24
novena 17.230
novice 300

novitiate 371.1
Novocaine 247.2
now 13
nowadays 509
noway 2.27
Nowell 215
nowhere 4
nowt 377
Nox 499
noxious 310
noyade 84
noyau 12.4
nozzle 228
nth 468
nuance 315
nub 29
Nuba 17.20
nubbin 252
nubble 228.14
nubecula 17.174.4
Nubia 17.3
Nubian 261.3
nubile 219
nucellus 310.22
nucha 17.41
nuclear 17.3
nuclease 509.1
nucleate 371.1
nuclei 7.1
nucleolus 310
nucleon 254.1
nucleonics 498.5
nucleoside 92.8
nucleotide 92.11
nucleus 310.2
nuclide 92
nuddy 16.69
nude 102
nudge 203
nudicaul 221.1
nudism 242.35
nudist 436
nudity 16.333
Nuffield 115
nugatory 16.274.43
nuggar 17.134
nugget 371
nuisance 321.23
nuke 45
null 225
nullah 1
nulla-nulla 17.173
nullifidian 261.3.5
nullify 7.3

nullipara 17.279
nullipore 9
nullity 16.333
Numantia 17.3.50
numb 240
numbat 365
number 17.27
numberless 300.13
numberplate 367
numbness 300
numbskull 225
numdah 1
numen 248.3
numeracy 16.307.4
numeral 228.76
numerary
16.274.32
numerate 371.35
numeration
261.67.22
numerator 17.338.9
numeric 38.39
numerical
228.23.15
numerology
16.108.4.13
numerous 310.50
Numidia 17.3.9
numinous 310.33.1
numismatic 38.49.4
numismatics
498.11
numismatist 436.26
nummary 16.274
nummular 17.174
nummulite 372
nun 259
nunatak 32.4
Nunc Dimittis 300
nuncio 12.3
nuncle 228.30
Nuneaton 261.98
nunhood 101
nunnery 16.274
NUPE 16.253
Nupe 2
nuptial 228
nuptials 539
Nuremberg 182
Nuri 16.270
Nuristan 246.1
nurse 297
nursemaid 85
nursery 16.274.35

nurseryman 261.48
nursing 265
nursling 265
nurture 17.54
nut 378
nutant 420.77
nutation 261.67.29
nutbrown 258
nutcase 295
nutcracker 17.28
nuthatch 62
nutlet 371
nutmeg 181
nutria 17.3
nutrient 420.1
nutriment 420.31
nutrition 261.71
nutritional
228.63.5
nutritionist
436.13.5
nutritious 310.58
nutritive 485.12
nutshell 215
nutter 17.349
nutting 265
nutty 16.341
nux vomica 17.34
nuzzle 228
nyala 17.161
Nyanja 17.434
Nyasaland 143.4
nyctalopia
17.3.37.1
nyctinasty 16.361
nyctophobia 17.3.4
nye 7
nylghau 9
nylon 254
nylons 549
nymph 176
nymphalid 91
nymphet 371
nympho 12
nympholepsy
16.313
nympholept 422
nymphomania
17.3.31.1
nymphomaniac
32.1
nystagmus 310
nystatin 252
Nyx 498

O

oaf 167
oafish 353
oak 42
oaken 261.14
oakum 242
oar 9
oared 95
oarfish 353
oarlock 40
oarsman 261
oasis 300.50
oast 441
oat 376
oatcake 34
oaten 261
Oates 343
oath 461
oatmeal 217
oba 1
Obadiah 17.4
Oban 261
obbligato 12.73
obconic 38.35
obdurate 371.34
obeah 17.3.4
obedience 321.1
obedient 420.1.1
obedientiary
 16.274.39
obeisance 321
obelisk 58
obelus 310.23
Oberland 143.4
Oberon 254.11
obese 298
obesity 16.333.27
obey 2.4
obfuscate 367
obi 16.12
obit 371
obituary 16.274.2
object 385, 387
objectify 7.3.9
objection 261.77
objectionable
 228.16.31
objective 485.17
objectivism
 242.35.22
objectivity
 16.333.35

objurgate 367.11
oblast 431
oblate 367
oblation 261.67
obligate 367.10
obligation
 261.67.10
obligatory
 16.274.43
oblige 198
obligee 5.6
obliging 265
obligor 9
oblique 37
obliquity 16.333
obliterate 367.23.2
obliteration
 261.67.22.4
oblivion 261.3.30
oblivious 310.2.17
oblong 266
obloquy 16.259
obnoxious 310
obnubilate
 367.12.1
oboe 12
oboe da caccia
 17.50
oboist 436
obol 220
obolus 310.26.1
Obote 2.24
obovoid 97
obreption 261.84
obscene 251
obscenity
 16.333.15
obscure 10
obscurity 16.333.23
obsequies 515
obsequious 310.2
observable 228.16
observance 321
observant 420.82
observation 261.67
observatory
 16.274.43
observe 483
observer 17.412
obsess 296
obsession 261.68
obsessive 485.2
obsidian 261.3.5
obsolesce 296.1

obsolescence
 321.21
obsolescent 420.67
obsolete 370
obstacle 228.28
obstetric 38.46
obstetrician 261.71
obstetrics 498.10
obstinacy 16.307
obstinate 371.24
obstipation
 261.67.20
obstreperous
 310.50
obstruct 389
obstruction 261.79
obstructionist
 436.13
obstructive 485.19
obstruent 420.4
obtain 247
obtainable
 228.16.27
obtect 385
obtrude 102
obtrusion 261.93
obtrusive 485.8
obtund 140
obturate 367.22
obtuse 309
obverse 297
obvert 369
obviate 367.1
obvious 310.2
obviously 16.184
oca 17.38
ocarina 17.230.1
O'Casey 16.296
occasion 261
occasional 228.63
occasionalism
 242.35.11.5
occasionally
 16.131.4
occident 420.10
Occidental
 228.110.1
Occidentalize 516.3
occipital 228.102
occiput 378
occlude 102
occlusion 261.93
occlusive 485.8
occult 406
occultism 242.35

occupancy 16.312
occupant 420
occupation 261.67
occupational
 228.63.3
occupier 17.4
occupy 7
occur 3
occurrence 321
ocean 261.73
oceanarium
 242.2.14
Oceania 17.3.30
oceanic 38.31.1
oceanid 91.21
oceanography
 16.90.2.4
oceanology
 16.108.4.11
ocellus 310.22
ocelot 373
och 40
ochlocracy
 16.307.5
ochlophobia 17.3.4
ochre 17.38
ocker 17.36
Ockham 242
o'clock 40
O'Connor 17.233
ocreate 371.1
octachord 95.3
octad 83
octagon 254.5
octagonal 228.63
octahedron 261
octane 247
Octans 544
octant 420
octave 485
Octavia 17.3.53
Octavian 261.3.29
octavo 12
octet 368
octillion 261.120
October 17.18
octogenarian
 261.3.21.1
octopod 94.1
octopus 310.40
octoroon 260.3
octroi 1
octuple 228
ocular 17.174.7
ocularist 436.20

438

oculist 436.6
odalisque 58
odd 94
oddball 221
oddity 16.333.6
oddly 16.149
oddment 420
oddness 300
ode 98
Oder 17.88
Odessa 17.300
odeum 242.2.4
Odin 252
odious 310.2.2
odium 242.2.4
odometer 17.342.3
odontalgia 17.3.16
odontoglossum
242.25
odontograph 158.1
odoriferous
310.50.2
odorous 310.50
odour 17.88
odourless 300.13
Odyssean 261.2.4
Odysseus 310.2.15
Odyssey 16.300.1
oedema 17.210
Oedipus 310.37
oeillade 84
oenology 16.108.4
oenomel 215
Oenone 16.233
o'er 9
oersted 86
oesophageal 228.2
oesophagus 310
oestrin 252
oestriol 220.1
oestrogen 261.39
oestrogenic 38.32.1
oestrone 257
oestrus 310
of 487
off 165
Offa 17.116
offal 228
offbeat 370
Offenbach 33
offence 316
offend 131
offender 17.101
offensive 485.9

offensiveness
300.43
offer 17.116
offering 265.58
offertory 16.274.43
offhand 128
offhandedness
300.28.1
office 300
officer 17.302
official 228.93
officialdom 242
officialese 513.7
officially 16.131
officiant 420.1
officiary 16.274.1.2
officiate 367.1.6
officiation
261.67.1.5
officious 310.58
officiousness
300.34.3
offing 265
offish 353
offprint 412
offset 368
offshoot 380
offshore 9
offside 92
offspring 265
offstage 193
oft 399
often 261
Ogaden 248
ogee 5
ogive 486
ogle 228
Ogooué 2.27
ogre 17.133
ogress 300
Ogygian 261.3.7
oh 12
Ohio 12.4
ohm 239
oidium 242.2.3
oil 222
oilcan 245
oilcloth 459
oiler 17.170
oilfield 115
oilfired 93
oilman 261
oilskin 252
oily 16.125
ointment 420.50

Oireachtas 310
Oita 17.346
oka 17.38
okapi 16.244
okay 2
Okeechobee 16.12
okey-doke 42
okey-dokey 16.29
Oklahoma 17.215
okta 17.356
old 120
Old Bailey 16.114
olden 261.28
Oldenburg 182
older 17.97
oldfangled 122
old-fashioned 143
Oldham 242
oldie 16.76
oldness 300
old-timer 17.212
oldwife 164
olé 2
oleaceous 310.56
oleaginous 310.33
oleander 17.98.1
oleaster 17.379
oleate 367.1.3
olecranon 254.8
oleograph 158.1.1
olfactory 16.274.44
Olga 17.138
olibanum 242.16
olid 91.18
oligarch 33
oligarchy 16.20
Oligocene 251.9
oligoclase 295
oligopoly 16.131.6
oligotrophic 38.13
olio 12.3.3
olivary 16.274.51
olive 485
Oliver 17.414
Olivia 17.3.54
Olivier 2.1
olivine 251
olla 17.168
olla podrida 17.82
ology 16.108.4
oloroso 12.70
Olympia 17.3
Olympiad 83.1
Olympian 261.3
Olympic 38

Olympus 310
Om 239
omadhaun 258
Omagh 1
Omaha 1
Oman 246
Omar Khayyam
230
omasum 242
Omayyad 83.2
ombre 17.26
ombudsman 261
Omdurman 246
omega 17.129
omelette 371
omen 261.49
omentum 242
omer 17.215
ominous 310.33
omissible 228.16.39
omission 261.71.4
omit 371
ommatophore 9.6
omnibus 307
omnicompetent
420.76
omnifarious
310.2.10.1
omnific 38.12
omnificent 420.70
omnipotence
321.25
omnipotent 420.78
omnipresence 321
omnipresent
420.84
omnirange 207.1
omniscience 321.1
omniscient 420.1
omnium-gatherum
242.21
omnivore 9.13
omnivorous
310.50.3
omophagia 17.3.12
omophagy 16.108.1
Omphale 5.9
omphalos 302
on 254
onager 17.154
onanism 242.35.14
Onassis 300.49
once 320
oncogenic 38.32.1
oncology 16.108.4

oncoming 265.38
ondograph 158.1
one 259
Oneida 17.84
oneiric 38
oneness 300
oner 17.237
onerous 310.50
oneself 172
one-sided 91.8
one-upmanship 274.2
ongoing 265.4
onion 261
onionskin 252
oniony 16.237
Onitsha 17.56
onlooker 17.40
only 16.173
onomastic 38.68
onomastics 498.15
onomatopoeia 17.2.1
onomatopoeic 38
onrush 356
onset 368
onshore 9
onside 92
onslaught 374
Ontario 12.3
onto 15
ontogeny 16.229.2
ontology 16.108.4.16
onus 310.35
onus probandi 16.77
onward 103
onwards 531
onymous 310.28.2
onyx 498.5
oocyte 372.10
oodles 539
oof 170
oogamy 16.222.2
oogenesis 300.52.4
oogonium 242.2.12
ooh 15
oolite 372.4
oolitic 38.52.1
oology 16.108.4.3
oolong 266
oompah 1
oophorectomy 16.222.5.2

ooze 523
opacity 16.333.25
opal 228.69
opalescence 321.21
opalescent 420.67
opaline 253.3
opaque 34
OPEC 35
open 261
opencast 431
opener 17.239
opening 265.46
open-minded 91
open-mindedness 300.28
openness 300.31
openwork 36
opera 17.290
operable 228.16.35
operand 128
operant 420.65
operate 367.23
operatic 38.49
operation 261.67.22.3
operational 228.63.3
operationalism 242.35.11.5.2
operative 485.15.10
operatize 516.13
operator 17.338.9
operculum 242.10
operetta 17.339
operon 254.11
ophicleide 92
ophidian 261.3.5
ophiology 16.108.4.1
Ophir 17.117
ophite 372
Ophiuchus 310.13
ophthalmia 17.3.28
ophthalmic 38
ophthalmitis 300.62
ophthalmology 16.108.4
ophthalmoscope 278.1
ophthalmoscopy 16.254.2
opiate 371.1
opine 253
opinion 261.122

opium 242.2.13
Oporto 12.78
opossum 242.25
Oppenheimer 17.212
oppidan 261.24
oppilate 367.12
opponent 420.54
opportune 260.6
opportunism 242.35
opportunist 436.12
opportunity 16.333.18
opposable 228.16
oppose 520.2
opposite 371.40
opposition 261.71.9
oppress 296.5
oppression 261.68
oppressive 485.2
oppressor 17.300
opprobrious 310.2
opprobrium 242.2
oppugn 260
oppugnant 420
Ops 329
opsonize 516.7
opt 425
optative 485.15
optic 38.67
optical 228.23
optician 261.71
optics 498
optimal 228.52
optimism 242.35
optimist 436.9
optimistic 38.70.3
optimize 516.4
optimum 242
option 261.86
optional 228.63
optometer 17.342.3
optometrist 436
optometry 16.285.2
opulence 321
opulent 420.27
opuntia 17.3
opus 310.39
or 9
orache 67
oracle 228.28
oracular 17.174.3
oracy 16.307

oral 228.74
Oran 245.5
orange 209
orangeade 85
Orangeman 261
orangery 16.274.14
orangewood 101
orang-outang 263
orang-utan 245.6
orate 367
oration 261.67
orator 17.352
oratorical 228.23.17
oratorio 12.3
oratory 16.274.43.7
orb 27
orbicular 17.174.6
orbit 371
orbital 228.102
orc 41
Orcadian 261.3.3
orchard 103
orchestra 17.297
orchestral 228.81
orchestrate 367.28
orchestration 261.67
orchestrina 17.230
orchid 91
orchidaceous 310.56.2
orchis 300
orchitis 300.62
orcinol 220.3
Orcus 310
ordain 247
ordeal 217
order 17.86
orderliness 300.23
orderly 16.131
ordinal 228.60
ordinance 321.14
ordinand 128
ordinarily 16.120.1
ordinary 16.274.26
ordinate 371.24.1
ordination 261.67.18.1
ordnance 321
ordonnance 321
Ordovician 261.71
ordure 10
ore 9
oread 83.1

orectic 38.60
oregano 12.51
Oregon 261.32
Orenburg 182
Orestes 513.19
orfe 166
Orff 166
organ 261.33
organdie 16.81
organelle 215
organic 38.31
organicism 242.35.16
organism 242.35.14
organist 436.13
organization 261.67.36
organize 516.7
organizer 17.441
organography 16.90.2.4
organology 16.108.4.11
organon 254.8
organotherapy 16.254
organza 17.445
organzine 251
orgasm 242.34
orgasmic 38
orgeat 1
orgiastic 38.68.1
orgy 16.105
oriel 228.3.12
orient 410
orient 420.1
oriental 228.110
Orientalism 242.35.11.6
Orientalize 516.3
orientate 367.32
orientation 261.67.32
Oriente 2
orienteering 265.53
orifice 300
oriflamme 229
origami 16.211
origan 261.32
origin 252.6
original 228.60
originality 16.333.8.6
originally 16.131.3
originate 367.17

Orinoco 12.12
oriole 223.1
Orion 261.4.1
orison 261.126
Orissa 17.302
Orizaba 17.10
Orkneys 515
Orlando 12.23
orle 221
Orleanist 436.13.1
Orlon 254
orlop 276
Orly 5
Ormandy 16.81
ormer 17.214
ormolu 15.5
ornament 410.2, 420.35
ornamental 228.110.3
ornamentation 261.67.32
ornate 367
ornithic 38.73
ornithine 251
ornithischian 261.3
ornithologist 436.4
ornithology 16.108.4.18
ornithomancy 16.309
ornithopod 94.1
ornithopter 17.377
ornithoscopy 16.254.2
orogeny 16.229.2
orography 16.90.2
oroide 92
orology 16.108.4
Orontes 513
orotund 140
orphan 261
orphanage 197
orpharion 261.3.20
Orphean 261.3
Orpheus 310.2
Orphic 38.14
Orphism 242.35.7
orphrey 16.280
orpiment 420.31
orpine 253
orrery 16.274
orris 300
ortanique 37
orthicon 254

orthocentre 17.368
orthoclase 295
orthodontic 38.64
orthodontics 498
orthodontist 436
orthodox 499.1
orthodoxy 16.389
orthoepy 16.245
orthogenic 38.32.1
orthogonal 228.63
orthography 16.90.2
orthopaedic 38.8
orthopaedics 498
orthopteran 261.60
orthoptic 38.67
orthoptics 498
orthorhombic 38
orthoscopic 38.37.1
orthostichy 16.25
orthotropous 310.40
ortolan 261
orts 342
Orwell 228
Orwellian 261.3.9
oryx 498
os 302
Osage 193
Osaka 17.29
Osborne 255
Oscar 17
oscillate 367.12
oscillation 261.67.12
oscillator 17.338.5
oscillogram 229.1.2
oscillograph 158.1
osculant 420.27
oscular 17.174
osculate 367.13
osculation 261.67.13
osculum 242.10
Oshawa 17.425
osier 17.3.62
Osiris 300.45
Oslo 12
Osman 261
Osmanli 16.169
osmiridium 242.2.3
osmium 242.2
osmose 305
osmosis 300.55
osmotic 38.53

osmunda 17.108
osnaburg 182
Ossa 17.304
osseous 310.2
Ossetia 17.325
Ossian 261.3
ossicle 228.23
ossiferous 310.50.2
ossify 7.3
ossuary 16.274.2
osteal 228.3
osteitis 300.62
Ostend 131
ostensible 228.16.40
ostensive 485.9
ostensory 16.274.38
ostentation 261.67.32
ostentatious 310.56
osteoarthritic 38.52
osteoarthritis 300.62
osteoblast 430
osteoclasis 300.57
osteoclast 430
osteogenesis 300.52.4
osteoid 97
osteology 16.108.4.1
osteoma 17.215
osteomalacia 17.322
osteomyelitis 300.62.1
osteopath 452
osteopathic 38.72
osteopathy 16.373.1.1
osteophyte 372
osteoplasty 16.361.1
osteoporosis 300.55
osteotomy 16.222.4.1
Ostia 17.3
ostiary 16.274.1
ostinato 12.73
ostiole 223.1
ostium 242.2
ostler 17.198
ostmark 33

ostosis 300.55
ostracism 242.35
ostracize 516.11
ostracod 94
ostrich 67
Ostrogoth 459
otalgia 17.3.16
Othello 12.40
other 17.408
othergates 335
otherguess 296
otherness 300.26
otherwhere 4.8
otherwise 516
otherworldly
16.153
otic 38.55
otiose 305.1
otitis 300.62
otolaryngology
16.108.4.7
otology 16.108.4
otoscope 278.1
ottava 17.409
Ottawa 17.425
otter 17.344
Otto 12.77
ottoman 261.52
Ouachita 9
ouananiche 352
oubliette 368
ouch 71
Oudh 99
ought 374
Ouija 17.149
ounce 319
our 14
ourselves 555
Ouse 523
oust 442
out 377
outage 197
outasight 372.10
outback 32
outbid 91
outboard 95
outbound 139
outbrave 482
outbreak 34
outbreed 89
outbuilding 265.17
outburst 434
outcast 431
outclass 294
outcome 240

outcross 302
outdate 367
outdated 91.34
outdid 91
outdistance 321.27
outdo 15
outdone 259
outdoor 9
outdoors 518
outer 17.348
outermost 441
outface 295
outfield 115
outfit 371
outfitter 17.342
outflank 51
outflow 12
outfoot 379
outfox 499
outgo 12
outgoing 265.4
outgoings 552
outgrow 12
outgrowth 461
outgun 259
outhouse 306
outing 265
outjockey 16.27
outlander 17.98
outlandish 353.2
outlast 431
outlaw 9
outlawry 16.269
outlay 2
outlet 368
outlier 17.4
outline 253
outlive 485
outlook 44
outlying 265.3
outman 245
outmanoeuvre
17.419
outmoded 91.10
outnumber 17.27
outpatient 420.73
outpoint 416
outport 374
outpost 441
outpouring 265.55
output 379
outrage 193
outrageous 310.20
outran 245
outrank 51

outreach 66
outride 92
outrider 17.84
outrigger 17.129
outright 372
outrun 259
outrunner 17.237
outrush 356
outsell 215
outsert 369
outset 368
outshine 253
outshoot 380
outside 92
outsider 17.84
outsize 516
outskirts 337
outsmart 366
outspoken 261.14
outspread 86
outstanding 265.19
outstation 261.67
outstay 2
outstretch 64
outstrip 274
outthink 52
outvote 376
outward 103
outwardly 16.152
outwards 531
outwash 354
outweigh 2
outwit 371
outwork 36
outworker 17.32
ouzel 228.128
ouzo 12
ova 17.417
oval 228
ovarian 261.3.21
ovariotomy
16.222.4.1
ovaritis 300.62.5
ovary 16.274
ovate 367
ovation 261.67
oven 261.117
ovenware 4
over 17.417
overabundance 321
overachieve 484
overact 382
overacting 265.70
overactive 485.16
overage 193

overall 221
overarch 63
overarm 230
overawe 9
overbear 4
overbearing 265.52
overbid 91.4
overblown 257
overboard 95.1
overboot 380
overbuild 116
overcame 231
overcast 431
overcharge 192
overcheck 35
overcloud 99.1
overcoat 376
overcome 240
overcompensation
261.67.26
overconfident
420.10
overcook 44
overcrop 276
overcrowd 99
overcrowding 265
overdevelop 281.1
overdid 91
overdo 15.3
overdone 259
overdosage 197
overdose 305
overdraft 396
overdraw 9
overdrawn 255
overdressed 433
overdrive 486
overdue 15.8
overdye 7
overeat 370
overestimation
261.67.15
overexcited 91.39
overexpose 520
overexposure
17.335
overfed 86
overfeed 89
overflight 372
overflow 12
overflowing 265.4
overfly 7
overfold 120
overgarment 420
overglaze 509.

overground 139.2
overgrow 12
overgrown 257
overgrowth 461
overhand 128
overhang 263
overhaul 221
overhead 86.5
overhear 6
overheard 87
overheat 370
overhung 267
overindulgence 321
overjoy 11
overkill 218
overland 143.4
overlap 268
overlapping 265.48
overlay 2.12
overleaf 162
overlie 7.7
overload 98
overlong 266.1
overlook 44
overlord 95
overly 16.131
overman 245
overmantel 228.109
overmuch 72
overnice 301
overnight 372.6
overpaid 85
overpass 294
overpay 2
overpitch 67
overplay 2
overplus 307
overpower 14
overpowering 265.57
overprotect 385
overprotection 261.77
overran 245.5
overrate 367.23
overreach 66
overreact 382
override 92.6
overripe 275
overrule 227
overrun 259
overscore 9
oversee 5
overseer 17.2
oversell 215.2

overset 368
oversew 12
oversexed 450
overshadow 12
overshoe 15
overshoot 380
overshot 373
overside 92.8
oversight 372.10
oversimplify 7.3
oversize 516.11
oversized 154
overslaugh 9
oversleep 273
overslept 422
oversoul 223
overspend 131.4
overspent 410
overspill 218
overstaffed 396
overstate 367
overstay 2
oversteer 6
overstep 271
overstuff 168
overt 369
overtake 34
overtaken 261.11
overtask 56
overtax 494
overthrew 15
overthrow 12
overthrown 257
overthrust 443
overtime 236
overtired 93
overtone 257.3
overtook 44
overtop 276.1
overtrade 85
overtrick 38
overtrump 289
overture 10.5
overturn 249
overview 15
overwatch 68
overweening 265.42
overweigh 2.28
overweight 367.38
overwhelm 243
overwhelming 265
overwind 135
overwinter 17.369
overword 87

overwork 36
overwrite 372.8
overwrought 374
Ovid 91
oviduct 389
oviform 238.1
ovine 253
oviparity 16.333.20
oviparous 310.50
ovipositor 17.342.5
ovisac 32
ovoid 97
ovotestis 300.68
ovulate 367.13
ovulation 261.67.13
ovule 227
ovum 242
ow 13
owe 12
owelty 16.352
Owen 252.1
Owerri 16.262
owing 265.4
owl 224
owlet 371
owlish 353
own 257
owner 17.236
ownership 274.1
owt 377
ox 499
oxalate 367.14
oxalis 300.13
oxblood 100
oxbow 12
Oxbridge 197
oxen 261
oxeye 7
Oxford 103
Oxfordshire 6
oxhide 92
oxidant 420.10
oxidase 509
oxidate 367.8
oxidation 261.67.7
oxide 92.14
oxidimetry 16.285.1
oxidize 516
oxime 234
oxlip 274
Oxon. 261
Oxonian 261.3.18
oxpecker 17.31

oxtail 214
oxyacetylene 251.2
oxyacid 91.28
oxygen 261.37
oxygenate 367.17
oxygenic 38.32
oxymoron 254.10
oxysalt 404
oxytocin 252
oyer 17.5
Oyo 12
oyster 17.386
oystercatcher 17.50
Oz 517
Ozalid 91
ozocerite 372.8
ozone 257
ozonic 38.35
ozonosphere 6.1

P

pa 1
paca 17.29
pace 295
pacemaker 17.30
pacer 17.299
pacesetter 17.339
paceway 2
pachisi 16.395
pachyderm 233
Pacific 38.12
pacific 38.12
pacifier 17.4.1
pacifism 242.35
pacifist 436
pacify 7.3.6
pack 32
package 197
packager 17.150
packaging 265.25
packer 17.28
packet 371.6
packhorse 303
packing 265
packsaddle 228.31
packthread 86
pact 382
pad 83
padang 263
padding 265

paddle

paddle 228.31
paddler 17.183
paddock 46
Paddy 16.57
paddy 16.57
paddywhack 32
pademelon 261.40
padlock 40
padrone 16.233
Padua 17.7
paduasoy 11
paean 261.2
paediatric 38.45
paediatrician
  261.71.6
paediatrics 498.8
paedology 16.108.4
paedomorphosis
  300.57.2
paedophile 219.1
paedophilia
  17.3.21.2
paella 17.163
paeon 261.2
pagan 261.31
paganism
  242.35.14
paganize 516.7
page 193
pageant 420
pageantry 16.291
pageboy 11
paginal 228.60.2
paginate 367.17.2
pagination
  261.67.18.2
pagoda 17.88
pagurian 261.3.24
Pahari 16.261.1
Pahlavi 16.385
paid 85
paigle 228.44
Paignton 261
pail 214
paillette 368
pain 247
pained 130
painful 226.4
painfulness 300.30
painkiller 17.166
painless 300
painlessness 300.33
pains 545
painstaking 265.6
paint 409

paintbox 499
paintbrush 356
painter 17.367
painting 265
painty 16.354
pair 4
paisa 1
paisley 16
pakeha 1.6
Pakistan 246.1
Pakistani 16.224
pal 212
palace 300
paladin 252
palaeanthropic
  38.37.3
palaeethnology
  16.108.4
palaeoanthropology
  16.108.4.12
palaeobotany
  16.237.7
Palaeocene 251.9
palaeoclimatology
  16.108.4.15.1
palaeography
  16.90.2.1
Palaeolithic 38.73
palaeontography
  16.90.2
palaeontology
  16.108.4.16
Palaeozoic 38.2
palaeozoology
  16.108.4.3
palais 2
palanquin 251
palatable 228.16
palatal 228
palatalize 516.3
palate 371
palatial 228.91
palaver 17.409
pale 214
paleness 300
palette 371
palindrome 239
paling 265.27
pall 221
palladium 242.2.1
palliasse 293.1
pallid 91.16
pallium 242.2
pallor 17.160
pally 16.112

palm 230
Palmerston 261
palmette 368
palmetto 12.75
palmist 436.8
palmistry 16.293
palmitin 252.23
palmy 16.211
palmyra 17.274
palolo 12.44
Palomar 1.12
palomino 12.54
palooka 17.41
palp 282
palpable 228.16
palpate 367
palpebral 228
palpitate 367.30
palpitation
  261.67.27
palsied 91
palstave 482
palter 17.363
paltry 16
paly 16.114
palynology
  16.108.4.10
Pamirs 514
pampas 310.41
pampean 261.3
pamper 17.261
pampero 12.62
pamphlet 371
pamphleteer 6
Pamphylia 17.3.21
Pamplona 17.236
Pan 245
pan 245
panacea 17.2
panache 349
panada 17.78.1
Panama 1.12
Panamanian
  261.3.15
panatella 17.163.2
Panay 7
pancake 34
panchax 494
pancreas 310.2
pancreatic 38.49
panda 17.98
pandanus 310.31
Pandarus 310.50
Pandean 261.2
pandect 385

pandemic 38.25
pandemonium
  242.2.12
pander 17.98
Pandora 17.276
pandour 10
pandowdy 16.68
pandurate 367.22
pandy 16.77
pane 247
panegyric 38.40
panegyrize 516
panel 228.55
panelling 265
panellist 436.7.4
panettone 16.233
pang 263
panga 17.140
pangenesis
  300.52.4
pangolin 252.9
panhandle 228.39
panic 38.31
panicky 16.25
panicle 228.23.10
panjandrum 242
Pankhurst 434
pannage 197.5
panne 245
pannier 17.3.29
pannikin 252.3
panocha 17.59
panoply 16
panoptic 38.67
panorama 17.206
panoramic 38.24
panpipes 328
pansophy 16.90
pansy 16.404
pant 407
pantalets 336
pantaloon 260.1
pantechnicon
  261.13
pantheism 242.35.2
pantheon 261.3
panther 17.399
panties 515
pantihose 520
pantile 219
pantisocracy
  16.307.5
panto 12.83
pantograph 158.1
pantomime 236

pantoum 241
pantry 16.287
pants 347
pantsuit 380
pantywaist 432
panzer 17.445
Paotow 13
pap 268
papa 1
papacy 16.307
Papadopoulos
  310.26
papal 228
papaya 17.4
Papeete 16.332
paper 17.249
paperback 32.2
paperbark 33
paperboard 95.1
paperboy 11
paperclip 274
papergirl 216
paperhanger
  17.245
paperknife 164
paperweight 367.38
paperwork 36
papery 16.274
papeterie 16.286
Paphlagonia
  17.3.36.1
Paphos 302
papier-mâché 2.22
papilla 17.166.2
papilloma 17.215
papillon 254.6
papillote 376
papist 436.14
papoose 309
pappy 16.243
paprika 17.34
Papua 17.7
Papuan 261.7
papule 227
papyrus 310.47
par 1
Pará 1.14
para 17.268
parabasis 300.57
parabiosis 300.55.2
parable 228.16
parabola 17.176
parabolic 38.22
parabolize 516.3
paraboloid 97.6

parabrake 34
Paracelsus 310
paracetamol 220.2
parachronism
  242.35.14
parachute 380
parachutist 436
paraclete 370
parade 85.4
paradigm 236
paradigmatic
  38.49.3
paradise 301
paradisiacal
  228.28.1
parados 302
paradox 499.1
paradoxical 228.23
paradrop 276
paraffin 252
paragoge 16.106
paragon 261
paragraph 158.1
paragraphia
  17.3.10
Paraguay 7
parakeet 370
paralanguage 197
paralipomena
  17.239
parallactic 38.58
parallax 494
parallel 215
parallelepipedon
  261.24
parallelism 242.35
parallelogram
  229.1
paralogism
  242.35.8
paralyse 516.3
paralysis 300.52.1
paralytic 38.52.1
paramagnetism
  242.35.18
paramedical
  228.23.1
parament 420.35
parameter 17.342
paramilitary
  16.274.41
paramnesia 17.3.60
paramorph 166.1
paramount 418.1
paramour 10.1

paranoia 17.5
paranoiac 46
paranoid 97.9
paranormal 228.53
parapet 371.30
paraph 171
paraphernalia
  17.3.18.1
paraphrase 509
paraplegia 17.3.13
paraplegic 38.17
parapodium
  242.2.4
parapraxis 300.70
parapsychology
  16.108.4.5
Paraquat 373
parasang 263
Parashah 1
parasite 372.10
parasitic 38.52.3
parasiticide 92.7.1
parasitize 516.12
parasitology
  16.108.4.14
parasol 220
parastichy 16.25
parasympathetic
  38.50.6
parasynthesis
  300.52
parathyroid 97.11
paratyphoid 97
paravane 247
parboil 222
parbuckle 228.27
parcel 228.83
parcenary
  16.274.26
parcener 17.231
parch 63
parchment 420
parclose 520
pard 84
pardalote 376
pardner 17.240
pardon 261
pardonable
  228.16.31
pare 4
pareira 17.271
parenchyma 17.211
parent 420
parentage 197
parental 228.110

parenteral 228.76
parenthesis 300.52
parenthesize
  516.10
parenthetic 38.50
parenthood 101
parergon 254
paresis 300.51.1
parfait 2
parfleche 351
parget 371
parhelion 261.3.10
pariah 17.4.2
Parian 261.3.21
paries 513.1
parietal 228.102
pari-mutuel 228.9
paring 265.52
Paris 300
parish 353
parishioner
  17.239.2
Parisian 261.3.35
parison 261.65.1
parity 16.333.20
park 33
parka 17.29
Parker 17.29
parkin 252.2
parking 265
parkland 143
parkway 2
parky 16.20
parlance 321
parley 16.113
parliament 420.35
parliamentarian
  261.3.21
parliamentarianism
  242.35.14.1.1
parliamentary
  16.274.47
parlour 17.161
parlous 310
Parma 17.206
Parmenides 513.4
Parmentier 2
Parmesan 245.7
Parnassus 310.51
Parnell 215
parochial 228.3
parodic 38.9
parody 16.72
parole 223.3
parolee 5

Páros 302
parotic 38.53
parotid 91.40
parotitis 300.62
parotoid 97
paroxysm 242.35
paroxysmal 228.54
parquet 2
parquetry 16.285
parr 1
parrel 228.72
parricide 92.7
parrot 381
parry 16.260
parse 508
parsec 35
Parsee 5
parsimonious
    310.2.9.1
parsimony 16.237
parsley 16.180
parsnip 274
parson 261.61
parsonage 197
part 366
partake 34
partan 261.95
parterre 4
parthenocarpy
    16.244
Parthenon 254.8
Parthenope 16.254
Parthia 17.3
Parthian 261.3
partial 228.90
partiality
    16.333.8.1
partially 16.131
participant 420.56
participate
    367.19.1
participation
    261.67.20.1
participle 228.66
particle 228.23
parti-coloured
    103.4
particular 17.174.6
particularism
    242.35.15
particularity
    16.333.20.3.1
particularize
    516.8.1
parting 265

partisan 245.7,
    261.126
partita 17.341
partite 372
partition 261.71
partitive 485.12
partlet 371
partly 16.187
partner 17
partnership 274.1
partook 44
partridge 197
part-time 236
part-timer 17.212
parturient 420.1.3
parturition 261.71
party 16.328
parulis 300.12
parure 10
parvis 300
Pasadena 17.230
Pasargadae 5.4
Pasay 7
pascal 228
pash 349
pasha 17.321
pashalik 38
paso doble 2.13
pasquinade 85.2
pass 294
passable 228.16
passably 16.137
passage 197
passageway 2.29
passbook 44
passé 2
passementerie
    16.288
passenger 17.157
passe-partout 15
passepied 2
passer-by 7
passerine 253.7
passing 265
passion 261.66
passional 228.63.2
passionate 371.28
passionflower 14
passionless 300.14
Passiontide 92.12
passive 485.1
passivism
    242.35.22
passkey 5
Passover 17.417

passport 374
passus 310.51
password 87
past 431
pasta 17.379
paste 432
pasteboard 95
pastel 228
pastern 261
Pasternak 32
pasteurism
    242.35.15
pasteurize 516.8
pasteurizer
    17.441.1
pastiche 352
pastille 218
pastime 236
pastis 300.67
pastor 17.380
pastoral 228.76
pastorale 213
pastrami 16.211
pastry 16
pasturage 197
pasture 17
pasty 16.361,
    16.363
pat 365
Pat 365
patagium 242.2
Patagonia
    17.3.36.1
patch 62
patchouli 16.129
patchwork 36
patchy 16.46
pâté 2
pate 367
patella 17.163.2
paten 261.94
patency 16.312.6
patent 420.75
patentee 5.24
patently 16.198
patentor 9
pater 17.338
paterfamilias 293.1
paternal 228.58
paternalism
    242.35.11.4
paternity 16.333.16
paternoster 17.385
Paterson 261
path 453

pathetic 38.50.6
pathfinder 17.103
pathogen 261.39
pathogenesis
    300.52.4
pathogenetic
    38.50.4
pathogenic 38.32.1
pathognomonic
    38.35.3
pathognomy
    16.222.3
pathological
    228.23.5
pathology 16.108.4
pathos 302
pathway 2
patience 321
patient 420.73
patiently 16.198
patina 17.231
patio 12.3
patisserie 16.274
Patmos 302
patois 1
Patras 293
patrial 228.3
patriarch 33.1
patriarchate 371.7
patriarchy 16.20
patrician 261.71.6
patriciate 371.1
patricide 92.7
Patrick 38.45
patriclinous 310.34
patrilineal 228.3.7
patrilocal 228.26
patrimonial 228.3.8
patrimony 16.237
patriot 381.1
patriotic 38.53
patriotism
    242.35.20
patristic 38.70
patrol 223
patrolman 261
patrology 16.108.4
patron 261
patronage 197
patroness 300.26
patronize 516.7
patronymic 38.28
pattée 2
patten 261.94
patter 17.336

pattern 261.94
Patton 261.94
patty 16.327
patulous 310.25
paua 14
paucal 228
paucity 16.333
Paul 221
pauldron 261
Pauline 253
paulownia 17.3.36
paunch 81
paunchy 16.55
pauper 17.256
pauperize 516.8
Pausanias 310.2.6
pause 518
pavage 197
pavane 246
pavé 2
pave 482
pavement 420
pavilion 261.120
paving 265.77
paviour 17.436
pavis 300
Pavlov 487
Pavlova 17.417
pavonine 253
paw 9
pawky 16.28
pawl 221
pawn 255
pawnbroker 17.38
Pawnee 5
pawnshop 276
pawpaw 9
pax 494
Paxton 261
paxwax 494
pay 2
payable 228.16
payday 2
payee 5.1
payer 17.1
payload 98
paymaster 17.380
payment 420.29
paynim 235
payola 17.171
payroll 223
pea 5
peace 298
peaceable 228.16
peaceful 226

peacefulness
  300.30
peacemaker 17.30
peacetime 236
peach 66
peacock 40
peafowl 224
peak 37
peaked 386
peaky 16.24
peal 217
pean 251
peanut 378
pear 4
pearl 216
pearler 17.164
pearlized 154
pearly 16.116
pearmain 247
Peary 16.265
peasant 420.84
peasantry 16.291
pease 513
peashooter 17.351
peasouper 17.259
peat 370
peaty 16.332
peau de soie 1
pebble 228
pebble-dash 349
pebbly 16.133
pecan 245
peccable 228.16
peccadillo 12.42
peccary 16.274
peccavi 5
peck 35
pecker 17.31
Peckinpah 1
peckish 353
pectase 509
pectin 252
pectinate 367.17
pectize 516
pectoral 228.76.3
peculate 367.13
peculiar 17.3.23
peculiarity
  16.333.20.1
pecuniary 16.274.1
pedagogic 38.18
pedagogics 498
pedagogue 185.2
pedagogy 16.104
pedal 228

pedalfer 17.121
pedalo 12.45
pedant 420
pedantic 38.62
pedantry 16.291
peddle 228
pederast 430
pederasty 16.361
pedestal 228.114
pedestrian 261.3
pedestrianize 516.7
Pedi 16.60
pedicab 18
pedicel 215
pedicle 228.23.1
pedicular 17.174.6
pediculosis
  300.55.3
pedicure 10.3
pediform 238.1
pedigree 5.18
pediment 420.31.1
pedipalp 282
pedlar 17.184
pedocal 212
pedology 16.108.4
pedometer 17.342.3
peduncle 228.30
pedunculate 371.17
pee 5
Peebles 539
peek 37
peekaboo 15.1
peel 217
peeler 17.165
peelie-wally 16.112
peeling 265.29
peen 251
peep 273
peeper 17.252
peephole 223
peepshow 12
peepul 228.65
peer 6
peerage 197
peeress 300
peerless 300
peeve 484
peevers 524
peevish 353
peevishness 300.35
peewee 5
peewit 371
peg 181
Pegasus 310

pegboard 95
peignoir 1.16
pejoration
  261.67.22
pejorative 485.15
pekan 261
peke 37
Pekin 252
Pekinese 513.9
Peking 265
pekoe 12.10
pelage 197
Pelagianism
  242.35.14.1
pelagic 38.15
Pelagius 310.2
pelargonium
  242.2.12
Pelé 2
Pelée 2.12
pelerine 251.7
Peleus 310.2
pelf 172
pelham 242.8
pelican 261.13
Pelion 261.3.10
pelisse 298
Pella 17.163
pellagra 17.289
pellet 371.15
pellicle 228.23.6
pellitory 16.274.41
pell-mell 215
pellucid 91.30
pelmanism
  242.35.14
pelmet 371
Peloponnese 298.1
Pelops 329
peloria 17.3.41
pelorus 310.48
pelota 17.344
pelt 402
peltast 430
pelvic 38
pelvis 300
Pemba 17.24
Pembroke 44
Pembrokeshire 6
pemmican 261.13
pemphigus 310
pen 248
penal 228.59
penalize 516.3
penalty 16.352

penance 321
Penang 263
penates 513
pence 316
pencel 228.88
penchant 266
Penchi 5
pencil 228.88
pend 131
pendant 420.14
pendent 420.14
pendente lite
16.334
pendentive 485.21
pending 265.20
pendragon 261.30
pendulous 310.25
pendulum 242.10
Penelope 16.254
peneplain 247
penetralia 17.3.18
penetrant 420.66
penetrate 367.27
penetrating 265.64
penetration 261.67
penguin 252
penicillate 371.16
penicillin 252.8
penicillium 242.2.6
penile 219
penillion 261.3.11
peninsula
17.174.11
peninsular
17.174.11
penis 300
penitence 321.24
penitent 420.76
penitential 228.96
penitentiary
16.274.39
penknife 164
penman 261
penmanship 274.2
Penn 248
penna 17.228
pennant 420.52
pennate 367
penned 131
penniless 300.8
Pennine 253
pennon 261
Pennsylvania
17.3.31

Pennsylvanian
261.3.15
penny 16.226
pennycress 296
pennyroyal 228.6
pennyweight 367
pennywort 369
pennyworth 456
penology 16.108.4
Penrith 458
pensile 219.3
pension 261.82
pensionable
228.16.31.1
pensionary
16.274.29
pensioner 17.239
pensive 485.9
penstock 40
pent 410
pentacle 228.28
pentad 83
pentagon 254.5
pentameter 17.342
pentaprism 242.35
pentarchy 16.20
pentastich 38
Pentateuch 45
pentathlon 261
pentatonic 38.35.5
Pentecost 438
Pentecostal
228.115
pentene 251
penthouse 306
pentimento 12.84
pentlandite 372
pentode 98
pentomic 38.29
pentosan 245
pentose 520
pentstemon 261.47
penuche 16.53
penult 406
penultimate 371.19
penumbra 17.285
penurious 310.2.14
penury 16.273
Penzance 314
peon 261.2
peonage 197
peony 16.237
people 228.65
pep 271
peplum 242

pepper 17.250
peppercorn 255
peppergrass 294
peppermint 412
peppery 16.274
peppy 16.245
pepsin 252
pepsinate 367.17
pepsinogen 261.39
peptic 38.65
peptidase 509
peptide 92
peptize 516
peptone 257
Pepys 326
Pequot 373
per 3
peracid 91.28
peradventure 17.70
Peraea 17.2.2
perambulate
367.13
perambulation
261.67.13
perambulator
17.338.6
per annum 242
percale 214
percaline 251.3
per capita 17.342
perceive 484
per cent 410
percentage 197.14
percentile 219.6
percept 422
perceptible
228.16.58
perception
261.84.1
perceptive 485.23
perceptual 228.9
perch 65
perchance 315
Percheron 254.11
percipient 420.1
Percival 228.120
percoid 97.2
percolate 367.14.2
percolator 17.338
percuss 307
percussion 261.74
percussionist
436.13
percussive 485.7

percutaneous
310.2.6
Percy 16.298
per diem 232
perdition 261.71.2
peregrinate 367.17
peregrination
261.67.18
peregrine 252
peremptory 16.274
perennial 228.3
perfect 385.2, 387
perfectible 228.16
perfection 261.77
perfectionism
242.35.14
perfectionist
436.13.6
perfective 485.17
perfecto 12.81
perfervid 91.55
perfidious 310.2.1
perfidy 16.63
perforate 367.23
perforated 91.34.7
perforation
261.67.22
perforce 303.1
perform 238.2
performance 321
performative
485.15.6
performer 17.214
performing 265
perfume 241
perfumer 17.217
perfumery
16.274.22
perfunctory 16.274
perfuse 523.1
Pergamum 242
pergola 17.176
perhaps 322
peri 16.265
perianth 467
periapt 421
periblem 232
pericardium 242.2
pericarp 269
perichondrium
242.2
periclase 295
Pericles 513
periclinal 228.61
pericline 253.4

pericope 16.254.1
pericranium 242.2.10
pericynthion 261.3.28
periderm 233
peridium 242.2.3
peridot 373
peridotite 372.12
perigee 5.6
perigon 261.32
perigynous 310.33
perihelion 261.3.10
peril 218.2
perilous 310.23
perilune 260
perilymph 176
perimeter 17.342.2.1
perimorph 166
perinatal 228.99
perineal 228.2
perinephrium 242.2
perineum 242.1
period 103.1
periodic 38.9
periodical 228.23.2
periodontal 228.111
perionychium 242.2
periosteum 242.2
periotic 38.55
peripatetic 38.50
peripeteia 17.4
peripheral 228.76
periphery 16.274
periphrasis 300.57
periphrastic 38.68
perique 37
perisarc 33
periscope 278
periscopic 38.37
perish 353
perishable 228.16.43
perishing 265.63
perispomenon 254.8
peristalsis 300.58
peristaltic 38.61
peristyle 219
peritoneal 228.2
peritoneum 242.1

peritonitis 300.62.4
peritricha 17.34
periwig 184
periwinkle 228.29
perjure 17.148
perjurer 17.279
perjury 16.274.13
perk 36
perky 16.23
Perlis 300
perlite 372
perlocution 261.75.2
perm 233
permafrost 438
permalloy 11
permanence 321
permanency 16.312
permanent 420.55
permanganate 367.18
permeability 16.333.9.2
permeable 228.16.2
permeance 321.1
permeate 367.1
Permian 261.3
permissible 228.16.39
permission 261.71.4
permissive 485.4
permit 371, 371.21
permitting 265.66
permittivity 16.333.35
permutation 261.67.29
permute 380
pernicious 310.58
pernickety 16.333.4
Pernod 12.53
peroneal 228.2
perorate 367.23
peroration 261.67.22
peroxide 92.14
perpend 131, 143
perpendicular 17.174.6
perpendicularity 16.333.20.3.1
perpetrate 367.27
perpetrator 17.338
perpetual 228.9

perpetuate 367.2
perpetuation 261.67.2
perpetuity 16.333.3
perplex 496
perplexity 16.333
perquisite 371.38
perron 261
perry 16.262
persalt 404
per se 2
perse 297
persecute 380
persecution 261.75
persecutor 17.351
Persephone 16.237
Persepolis 300.13
perseverance 321.17
perseveration 261.67.22
persevere 6.11
Pershing 265
Persia 17.324
Persian 261.69
persicaria 17.3.38
persiflage 359
persimmon 261.48
Persis 300
persist 436.22
persistence 321.27
persistent 420.81
person 261.64
persona 17.236
personable 228.16.31
personage 197
personal 228.63
personalism 242.35.11.5
personality 16.333.8.7
personalize 516.3.7
personally 16.131.4
personalty 16.352
personate 367.18
personify 7.3
personnel 215
perspective 485.17
Perspectivism 242.35.22
Perspex 496
perspicacious 310.56.1

perspicuity 16.333.3
perspicuous 310.4.1
perspiration 261.67.22
perspiratory 16.274.43
perspire 8.2
persuade 85
persuasion 261
persuasive 485
pert 369
pertain 247.10
Perth 456
pertinacious 310.56.4
pertinacity 16.333.25
pertinence 321.14
pertinent 420.53
pertness 300.36
perturb 22
perturbation 261.67.3
pertussis 300
Peru 15.6
peruke 45
perusal 228.128
peruse 523
Peruvian 261.3.32
perv 483
pervade 85
pervasion 261
pervasive 485
perverse 297
perversion 261.69.1
perversity 16.333.26
perversive 485.3
pervert 369, 369.2
perverted 91.36
pervious 310.2
pes 509
Pesach 33
pesade 84
peseta 17.338
pesewa 1
Peshitta 17.341
pesky 16.40
peso 12
pessary 16.274.34
pessimism 242.35
pessimist 436.9
pessimistic 38.70.3

pest 433
pester 17.382
pesticide 92.7
pestilence 321
pestilent 420
pestilential 228.96
pestle 228
pet 368
petal 228.100
petalody 16.67
petaloid 97.6
petard 84
petcock 40
petechia 17.3
Peter 17.341
peter 17.341
Peterborough
 17.279
Peterlee 5.9
Peterloo 15.5
peterman 261.52
Petersburg 182
petersham 242
Peterson 261
pethidine 251
petiole 223.1
petit bourgeois 1
petite 370
petit four 9.5
petition 261.71.7
petitioner 17.239.2
petit mal 212
Petra 17.293
Petrarch 33
petrel 228
petrifaction 261.76
petrify 7.3
Petrine 253
petrodollar 17.168
petroglyph 163
Petrograd 83
petrography
 16.90.2
petrol 228
petrolatum 242.27
petroleum 242.2.7
petrolic 38.22
petrology 16.108.4
petronel 215
Petronius 310.2.9
petticoat 376
pettifog 185.1
pettifogger 17.131
pettifoggery
 16.274.12

pettifogging 265.23
petting 265.65
pettish 353
pettitoes 520
petty 16.330
petulance 321
petulant 420.27
petunia 17.3
pew 15
pewter 17.351
peyote 16.339
pfennig 184
Phaedra 17.286
Phaëthon 261.109
phaeton 261
phage 193
phagomania
 17.3.31.1
phagophobia
 17.3.4
phalange 206
phalangeal 228.3
phalanger 17.155
phalanx 504
phalarope 278
phallic 38.19
phallicism
 242.35.16.1
phallus 310
phantasm 242.34
phantasmagoria
 17.3.41
phantasmagoric
 38.41
phantom 242
Pharaoh 12.62
Pharaonic 38.35
Pharisaic 38.1
Pharisee 5.20
pharmaceutical
 228.23.21
pharmaceutics 498
pharmacist 436.22
pharmacognosy
 16.307.3
pharmacology
 16.108.4.6
pharmacopoeia
 17.2.1
pharmacy 16.307
Pharos 302
pharyngeal 228.2
pharyngitis 300.62
pharyngology
 16.108.4.7

pharyngoscope
 278.1
pharyngotomy
 16.222.4
pharynx 505
phase 509
phasmid 91
phatic 38.49
pheasant 420.84
Pheidippides 513.4
phellem 242.8
phelloderm 233
phellogen 261.39
phenacetin 252.23
phenetic 38.50.4
phenobarbitone
 257.2
phenocopy 16.250
phenocryst 436
phenol 220
phenolate 367.14
phenology
 16.108.4.10
phenomena 17.231
phenomenal
 228.60.5
phenomenalism
 242.35.11
phenomenology
 16.108.4.10
phenomenon
 261.56
phenotype 275.1
phenyl 218
phenylketonuria
 17.3.42
pheromone 257
phew 15
phial 228.4
Phi Beta Kappa
 17.247
Phidias 293.1
Philadelphia 17.3
philadelphus 310
Philae 5
philander 17.98
philanderer 17.279
philanthropic
 38.37.3
philanthropist
 436.15
philanthropy
 16.254
philatelic 38.20
philatelist 436.7.6

philately 16.131.7
Philby 16.16
philharmonic 38.35
philhellene 251
Philip 274
Philippi 7
philippic 38.36
philippics 498
Philippine 251
Philippines 547
Philistine 253.10
Phillips 327
phillumenist
 436.13.3
philodendron 261
philogyny 16.229.2
philology
 16.108.4.8
philomel 215
Philomela 17.165
philosopher 17.120
philosophic 38.13
philosophical
 228.23
philosophize 516
philosophy 16.90.4
philtre 17.362
phimosis 300.55
phiz 515
phlebitic 38.52
phlebitis 300.62
phlebosclerosis
 300.55.5
phlebotomize 516.5
phlebotomy
 16.222.4
phlegm 232
phlegmatic 38.49
phloem 232
phlogistic 38.70.1
phlogiston 254
phlox 499
phlyctena 17.230
phobia 17.3.4
phobic 38.3
Phobos 302.1
phocine 253
Phocis 300.55
phocomelia 17.3.20
Phoebe 16.10
phoebe 16.10
Phoebus 310
Phoenicia 17.3.49
Phoenician
 261.71.5

phoenix 498.4
phon 254
phonate 367
phone 257
phoneme 234
phonemic 38.27
phonemics 498
phonetic 38.50.5
phonetician
  261.71.7
phonetics 498.12.1
phonetist 436.24
phoney 16.233
phonic 38.35
phonics 498.5
phonogram 229.1
phonograph
  158.1.2
phonography
  16.90.2
phonolite 372.4
phonology
  16.108.4.11
phonometer
  17.342.3.3
phonotactics
  498.13
phonotypy 16.249
phooey 16.4
phosgene 251
phosphatase 509
phosphate 367
phosphatide 92.11
phosphaturia
  17.3.42
phosphene 251
phosphide 92
phosphite 372
phospholipid 91.24
phosphoresce 296.4
phosphorescence
  321.21
phosphorescent
  420.67
phosphoric 38.41
phosphorite 372.8
phosphorous
  310.50
phosphorus 310.50
phot 373
photic 38.55
photo 12.79
photoactive 485.16
photobathic 38.72
photocell 215

photocopier 17.3
photocopy 16.250
photocurrent
  420.64
photoelasticity
  16.333.28.2
photoelectric 38
photoelectricity
  16.333.28
photoengrave 482
Photofit 371
photoflash 349
photoflood 100
photogenic 38.32.1
photogram 229.1
photogrammetry
  16.285
photograph 158.1
photographer
  17.120.1
photographic 38.11
photography
  16.90.2.6
photogravure 10
photokinesis
  300.51
photolithography
  16.90.2
photomap 268
photometry
  16.285.2
photomicrograph
  158.1
photomontage 359
photomultiplier
  17.4
photon 254
photonasty 16.361
photoperiod 103.1
photophilous
  310.26
photophobia 17.3.4
photophore 9.6
photopia 17.3.37
photosensitive
  485.12
photosensitize
  516.12
photoset 368
photosphere 6.1
Photostat 365
photosynthesis
  300.52
photosynthesize
  516.10

photosynthetic
  38.50
phototaxis 300.70
phototelegraphy
  16.90
phototherapy
  16.254
photothermic 38.26
phototonic 38.35.5
phototonus 310.36
phototropic 38.37.2
prototype 275.1
phototypography
  16.90.2
phrasal 228.125
phrase 509
phraseogram
  229.1.1
phraseograph
  158.1.1
phraseology
  16.108.4.1
phrasing 265.81
phrenic 38.32
phrenology
  16.108.4.10
Phrygia 17.3.14
Phrygian 261.3.7
phthalein 251
phthiriasis 300.57.1
phut 378
phycology
  16.108.4.5
phylactery
  16.274.44
phyle 16.121
phyletic 38.50
phyllite 372.3
phylloclade 85
phylloid 97.5
phyllome 239
phylloxera 17.272
phylogeny 16.229.2
phylum 242.9
physiatrics 498.8
physic 38
physical 228.23.25
physicalism
  242.35.11
physically 16.142
physician 261.71.8
physicist 436.21
physics 498
physiognomic
  38.29

physiognomy
  16.222.3.1
physiography
  16.90.2.1
physiology
  16.108.4.1
physiotherapist
  436.15
physiotherapy
  16.254
physique 37
physostigmine 251
physostomous
  310.29
phytogenic 38.32.1
phytology
  16.108.4.14
phytopathology
  16.108.4
phytosociology
  16.108.4.1
phytotoxin 252.29
phytotron 254
pi 7
piacular 17.174.3
piaffe 157
pia mater 17.338
pianism 242.35.14
pianissimo 12.48
pianist 436.13.1
piano 12
pianoforte 16.336
Pianola 17.171
piassava 17.409
piastre 17.379
piazza 17.319
pibroch 40
pica 17.35
picador 9.4
Picardy 16.72
picaresque 57
picaroon 260.3
Picasso 12.68
picayune 260
Piccadilly 16.120
piccalilli 16.120
piccaninny 16.229
piccolo 12.45
pice 301
piceous 310.2.15
pichiciego 12.27
pick 38
pickaback 32.2
pickaxe 494
picker 17.34

pickerel 228.76
pickerelweed 89.7
picket 371.9
picketing 265.66
pickle 228.23
pickled 122
picklock 40
pickpocket 371.10
Pickwickian 261.3
picnic 38
picnicker 17.34
picot 12.10
picotee 5
picrate 367.25
Pict 387
pictograph 158.1
pictorial 228.3.12
picture 17.65
picturesque 57
picul 228.23
piddle 228.32
piddling 265
piddock 46
pidgin 252.6
pie 7
piebald 118
piece 298
piecemeal 217
piecework 36
piecrust 443
pied 92
Piedmont 414
piedmont 414
pieman 261
pier 6
pierce 299
piercing 265
Pierian 261.3.22
Pierides 513.4
Pierrot 12.63
pietà 1
Pietermaritzburg 182.2
piety 16.333.2
piezometer 17.342.3
piffle 228.41
pig 184
pigeon 261.37
pigeonhole 223
pigface 295
piggery 16.274.9
piggin 252
piggish 353
Piggott 381

piggy 16.93
piggyback 32
pig-headedness 300.28
piglet 371
pigmeat 370
pigment 420
pigmentation 261.67.32
pigskin 252
pigstick 38
pigsticking 265.7
pigsty 7
pigswill 218
pigtail 214
pigtailed 112
pigweed 89
pika 17.35
pike 39
pikelet 371
pikeperch 65
piker 17.35
pikestaff 158
pilaster 17.379
Pilate 381
pilau 13
pilch 76
pilchard 103
pile 219
pileate 371.1
pileous 310.2
pileum 242.2
pileus 310.2
pilfer 17
pilferage 197
pilgarlic 38
pilgrim 235
pilgrimage 197.3
pili 5.8
piliform 238.1
pill 218
pillage 197.1
pillar 17.166
pillbox 499
pillion 261.120
pilliwinks 505
pillory 16.274.16
pillow 12.42
pillowcase 295.2
pillowslip 274
pilose 305
pilot 381
pilotage 197
Piltdown 258
pilule 227

pimento 12.84
pimp 287
pimpernel 215
pimple 228
pimpled 122
pimply 16.179
pin 252
pinafore 9.6
pinaster 17.379
pinball 221
pince-nez 2
pincer 17.315
pincers 524
pinch 80
pinchbeck 35
pinchcock 40
pinchpenny 16.226
pincushion 261
Pindar 17.102
Pindaric 38.38
pindling 265
Pindus 310
pine 253
pineal 228.3.7
pineapple 228.64
Pinero 12.63
pinery 16.274.27
pinetum 242.28
pinfold 120
ping 265
pinger 17.246
ping-pong 266
pinguid 91
pinhead 86.4
pinhole 223
pinion 261.122
pinite 372.5
pink 52
Pinkerton 261
pinkeye 7
pinkie 16.37
pinking 265.10
pinkish 353
pinna 17.231
pinnace 300.23
pinnacle 228.28
pinnate 367.17
pinnatiped 86.6
pinner 17.231
pinniped 86.6
pinnula 17.174
pinny 16.229
Pinocchio 12.3
pinochle 228.27
pinole 16.126

pinpoint 416
pinprick 38
pinstripe 275
pint 413
pinta 17.369
pintadera 17.271
pintail 214
Pinter 17.369
pintle 228
pinwheel 217
pinworm 233
piny 16.230
piolet 2
pioneer 6.5
pious 310.3
pip 274
pipa 17.252
pipage 197
pipe 275
pipeclay 2
pipefitting 265.66
pipeline 253
piper 17.254
piperidine 251
piperine 253.7
piperonal 212
pipette 368
pipewort 369
piping 265
pipistrelle 215
pipit 371
pipkin 252
pippin 252
pipsissewa 17.425
pipsqueak 37
piquancy 16.312
piquant 420.6
piqué 2.6
pique 37
piquet 368.4
piracy 16.307
Piraeus 310.1
piranha 17.226
pirate 371
piratic 38.49
pirn 249
pirog 188
pirogue 188
pirouette 368.1
Pisa 17.440
piscary 16.274
piscatorial 228.3.12.2
Pisces 513.13
piscina 17.230

452

piscine 253
piscivorous
310.50.3
pishogue 188
pisiform 238.1
pismire 8
piss 300
Pissarro 12.61
pistachio 12.3
pistareen 251.7
piste 435
pistil 218
pistol 228.114
pistole 223
pistoleer 6
piston 261.107
pit 371
pita 17.341
pitapat 365
Pitcairn 250
pitch 67
pitchblende 131
pitcher 17.56
pitchfork 41
pitchy 16.49
piteous 310.2
pitfall 221
pith 458
pithead 86
pithecanthropus
310.40
pithos 302
pithy 16.370
pitiable 228.16.2
pitiful 226
pitiless 300.8
pitilessness 300.33
Pitman 261
pitman 261
piton 254
Pitot 12.76
Pitt 371
pitta 17.342
pittance 321.24
pitter-patter 17.336
Pittsburgh 182.2
pituitary 16.274.41
pituri 16.274.41
pity 16.333
Pius 310.3
pivot 381
pivotal 228
pix 498
pixie 16.388
pixilated 91.34.5

Pizarro 12.61
pize 516
pizza 17
pizzeria 17.2.2
pizzicato 12.73
placable 228.16
placard 84
placate 367.6
placatory 16.274.43
place 295
placebo 12.5
placement 420.44
placenta 17.368
placental 228.110
placentation
261.67.32
placer 17.298
placet 368
placid 91.28
placidity 16.333.5.1
placing 265.59
placket 371.6
placoid 97
plagal 228.44
plage 359
plagiarism
242.35.15
plagiarist 436.20
plagiarize 516.8
plagioclase 295
plague 180
plaice 295
plaid 83
plain 247
plainchant 408
plainness 300
plainsong 266
plaint 409
plaintiff 163
plaintive 485
plaintiveness
300.43
plait 365
plan 245
planar 17.227
planarian 261.3.21
planation 261.67
planchette 368
plane 247
planer 17.227
planet 371.22
planetarium
242.2.14
planetary
16.274.41

planform 238
plangent 420.22
planimeter
17.342.2
planimetry
16.285.1
planish 353
plank 51
planking 265
plankton 261
planktonic 38.35
planner 17.225
planning 265
planography
16.90.2.4
planometer
17.342.3
planosol 220
plant 408
Plantagenet
371.24.2
plantain 252
plantar 17.365
plantation
261.67.31
planter 17.366
plantigrade 85.5
planula 17.174.9
plaque 32
plash 349
plashy 16.319
plasm 242.34
plasma 17.223
plasmagel 215
plasmasol 220
plasmin 252
plasmodium
242.2.4
Plassey 16.294
plaster 17.380
plasterboard 95.1
plastered 103
plasterer 17.279
plastering 265.58
plastic 38.68
Plasticine 251.8
plasticity
16.333.28.2
plasticize 516.10
plastid 91
plastometer
17.342.3
plat 365
platan 261.94
plat du jour 10

plate 367
plateau 12.72
plated 91.34
plateful 226.7
platelayer 17.1
platelet 371
platemark 33
platen 261.94
plater 17.338
platform 238
Plath 452
platina 17.231
plating 265.64
platinize 516.6.1
platinocyanide
92.4
platinoid 97.8.1
platinum 242.14
platitude 102.2.1
platitudinize 516.6
Plato 12.74
Platonic 38.35.5
Platonism
242.35.14
Platonize 516.7
platoon 260.4
Platte 365
platter 17.336
platy 16.327,
16.329
platypus 310.37
platyrrhine 253
plaudit 371
plausible 228.16
plausive 485
Plautus 310
play 2
playable 228.16
playback 32
playbill 218
playboy 11
player 17.1
playful 226
playgoer 17.6
playground 139
playhouse 306
playlet 371
playmate 367
playpen 248
playroom 241
playschool 227
playsuit 380
plaything 265
playtime 236
playwright 372

plaza 17.438
plea 5
pleach 66
plead 89
pleader 17.82
pleading 265.13
pleasance 321
pleasant 420.84
pleasantness 300
pleasantry 16.291
please 513
pleased 153
pleasing 265
pleasurable
 228.16.35.2
pleasure 17.333
pleasureless 300.13
pleat 370
pleater 17.341
pleb 21
plebby 16.8
plebeian 261.2.1
plebiscite 372.9
plectognath 452
plectron 261
plectrum 242.22
pledge 194
pledgee 5.5
pledget 371
pledgor 9
pleiad 83.2
Pleiades 513.5
plein-air 4
Pleistocene 251.9
plenary 16.274.25
plenipotent 420.78
plenipotentiary
 16.274.39
plenitude 102.2
plenteous 310.2
plentiful 226
plenty 16.355
pleonasm 242.34
plesiosaur 9.11
plethora 17.279
pleura 17.277
pleural 228.75
pleurisy 16.300
pleurodynia 17.3
pleuron 254
pleuropneumonia
 17.3.36
pleuston 261
plew 15
plexiform 238.1

Plexiglass 294
plexor 17.426
plexus 310
pliable 228.16.3
pliant 420.2
plica 17.35
plicate 367
plication 261.67
plié 2
pliers 524
plight 372
plimsoll 228
plinth 470
Pliny 16.229
Pliocene 251.9
plissé 2
ploat 376
plod 94
plodder 17.85
plodge 199
plonk 53
plonko 12
plop 276
plosion 261.92
plosive 485.6
plot 373
Plotinus 310.34
plotter 17.344
plough 13
ploughboy 11
ploughman 261
ploughshare 4
ploughstaff 158
plover 17.418
ploy 11
pluck 43
plucky 16.30
plug 189
plum 240
plumage 197
plumate 367
plumb 240
plumbago 12.27
plumbeous 310.2
plumber 17.216
plumbery 16.274
plumbing 265.38
plumbism 242.35
plumbous 310.6
plumbum 242
plume 241
plummet 371
plummy 16.220
plump 289
plumper 17.264

plumpness 300
plumy 16.221
plunder 17.108
plunderage 197
plunderer 17.279
plunge 211
plunger 17.159
plunk 54
pluperfect 387
plural 228.75
pluralism 242.35.11
plurality 16.333.8
pluralize 516.3
plus 307
plush 356
Plutarch 33
Pluto 12.80
plutocracy 16.307.5
plutocrat 365.2
plutocratic 38.49.6
pluton 254
Plutonian 261.3.18
plutonic 38.35
plutonium 242.2.12
pluvial 228.3.17
pluvious 310.2.18
ply 7
Plymouth 464
plywood 101
pneuma 17.217
pneumatic 38.49
pneumatics 498.11
pneumatology
 16.108.4.15
pneumatolysis
 300.52.2
pneumatophore 9.6
pneumococcus
 310.11
pneumoconiosis
 300.55.1
pneumoencephalo-
 gram 229.1
pneumogastric 38
pneumograph
 158.1
pneumonectomy
 16.222.5
pneumonia 17.3.36
pneumonic 38.35
pneumonitis
 300.62
Po 12
po 12
poach 70

poacher 17.59
poaching 265
Pocahontas 310
pochard 103
pock 40
pocket 371.10
pocketbook 44
pocketful 226
pocketknife 164
pockmark 33
poco 12.12
pococurante 16.353
pod 94
podagra 17.289
poddy 16.65
podesta 17.382
podgy 16.104
podiatry 16.286.1
podium 242.2.4
podophyllin 252.8
podzol 220
Poe 12
poem 235
poesy 16.396
poet 371
poetaster 17.379
poetic 38.50.1
poeticize 516.10
poetics 498.12
poetry 16.285
pogge 185
pogonia 17.3.36.1
pogrom 242
Pohai 7
poi 11
poignancy 16.312
poignant 420
poinciana 17.226.1
poinsettia 17.3
point 416
pointed 91.48
pointer 17.371
pointillism
 242.35.9
pointing 265
pointless 300
pointlessness
 300.33
poise 519
poison 261.128
poisoner 17.239
poisonous 310.36
poke 42
poker 17.38
pokeweed 89

poky 16.29
Poland 143
polar 17.171
polarimeter
17.342.2.1
Polaris 300
polarity 16.333.20
polarize 516.8
Polaroid 97.12
polder 17.97
Pole 223
pole 223
poleaxe 494
polecat 365
polemarch 33.2
polemic 38.25
polemics 498
polenta 17.368
poler 17.171
poleyn 247
police 298
policeman 261
policy 16.300
polio 12.3.3
poliomyelitis
300.62.1
polis 300.9
Polish 353
polish 353.5
polisher 17.326
Politburo 12.66
polite 372.4
politeness 300.39
politesse 296
politic 38.52
political 228.23.20
politician 261.71.7
politicize 516.10.1
politicking 265.7
politico 12.11
politics 498
polity 16.333.10
polka 17
poll 223
pollack 46
pollan 261.42
pollard 103.3
pollen 261.42
pollex 496
pollinate 367.17
pollination
261.67.18
polling 265.32
pollinosis 300.55.4
polliwog 185

pollster 17.392
pollutant 420.77
pollute 380.1
pollution 261.75.1
Pollux 503
Polly 16.122
Pollyanna 17.225.1
polo 12.44
polonaise 509
polonium 242.2.12
polony 16.233.1
poltergeist 437
poltroon 260
poly 16.122
polyamide 92
polyanthus 310.72
Polybius 310.2
Polycarp 269
polycentrism
242.35
polychaete 370
polychasium
242.2.19
polychromatic
38.49.2
polychrome 239
polychromy 16.219
polyclinic 38.34
Polyclitus 310.65
polyconic 38.35
polydemic 38.25
polydipsia 17.3
polyester 17.382.1
polygala 17.176
polygalaceous
310.56.3
polygamist
436.10.1
polygamous
310.29.1
polygamy 16.222.1
polyglot 373
Polygnotus 310.66
polygon 254.4
polygonum 242.16
polygraph 158
polygyny 16.229.1
polyhedral 228.78
polyhedron 261
polymath 452
polymer 17.211
polymeric 38.39
polymerize 516.8
polymorph 166

polymorphism
242.35.7
polymorphous
310.18
Polynesia 17.334
Polynesian
261.3.34
Polynices 513.13
polynomial 228.3
polynucleotide
92.11
polynya 1
polyonymous
310.28.2
polyp 274
polypary 16.274.30
polypeptide 92
polyphagia 17.3.12
polyphase 509
polyphone 257
polyphonic 38.35
polyphony
16.237.2
polypod 94
polypody 16.67
polypoid 97
polypropylene
251.2
polyptych 38.66
polypus 310.37
polyrhythm 242.33
polysaccharide
92.6
polysemy 16.215
polystyrene 251.5
polysyllabic 38
polysynthetic 38.50
polytechnic 38
polytetrafluoroethy-
lene 251.2
polytheism
242.35.2
polythene 251
polytonality
16.333.8
polytrophic 38.13
polytypic 38.36
polyunsaturated
91.34.7
polyurethane 247
polyuria 17.3.42
polyvalent 420.25
Polyxena 17.231
polyzoarium
242.2.14

polyzoic 38.2
pom 237
pomace 300
pomade 84
pomander 17.98
pome 239
pomegranate
371.22
pomelo 12.42
Pomerania 17.3.31
Pomeranian
261.3.15.1
pomfret 371
pommel 228
pomology 16.108.4
Pomona 17.236
pomp 288
pompadour 10
pompano 12
Pompeii 5.1
Pompeiian 261.1
Pompey 16.256
pom-pom 237
pompon 254
pomposity
16.333.30
pompous 310
pompousness
300.34
ponce 318
Ponce de León
261.2
poncho 12
pond 136
ponder 17.104
ponderous 310.50
Pondicherry 16.262
Pondoland 143.3
pondweed 89
pone 257
pong 266
pongee 5
pongid 91
poniard 103
pons 549
pons asinorum
242.20
pons Varolii 7.1
pont 414
Pontchartrain 247
Pontefract 382.1
Pontiac 32.1
Pontic 38.64
pontifex 496
pontiff 163

455

pontifical 228.23
pontificate 367.5,
    371.9
pontine 253
pontonier 6.5
pontoon 260
Pontypool 227
Pontypridd 475
pony 16.233
ponytail 214
pony trekking 265
pooch 74
pood 102
poodle 228.37
poof 169
pooh 15
Pooh-Bah 1
pooh-pooh 15
pool 227
Poole 227
pools 538
poon 260
Poona 17.238
poop 280
poor 10
poorhouse 306
poorly 16.124
pop 276
popcorn 255
pope 278
popedom 242
popeyed 92
popgun 259
popinjay 2
popish 353
poplar 17.195
poplin 252
popliteal 228.3
Popocatépetl
    228.100
poppadom 242
popper 17.255
poppet 371
popple 228.68
poppy 16.250
poppycock 40
poppyhead 86.2
Popsicle 228.23
popsy 16.315
populace 310.25
popular 17.174.10
popularity
    16.333.20.3
popularize 516.8.1
populate 367.13.7

population
    261.67.13
Populist 436.6
populous 310.25
porbeagle 228.45
porcelain 252
porch 69
porcine 253
porcupine 253
pore 9
porgy 16.95
poriferan 261.60
Porirua 17.8
porism 242.35
pork 41
porker 17.37
porkpie 7
porky 16.28
pornocracy
    16.307.5
pornographic 38.11
pornography
    16.90.2
poromeric 38.39
porosity 16.333.30
porous 310.48
porphyria 17.3.40
porphyrin 252
porphyritic 38.52
porphyroid 97
porphyry 16.266
porpoise 310.38
porridge 197
porringer 17.157
Porsena 17.231
Porson 261
port 374
portable 228.16.51
Portadown 258
portage 197
portal 228.105
portative 485.15
portcullis 300.10
porte-cochere 4
portend 131
portent 410
portentous 310.70
porter 17.345
porterage 197
porterhouse 306
portfire 8
portfolio 12.3.3
porthole 223
portico 12.11
portière 4.1

portion 261.72
Portland 143
Portlaoise 17.325
portly 16.192
portmanteau 12.83
portrait 371
portraitist 436.24
portraiture 17.56
portray 2
portrayal 228.1
portress 300
Port Said 92
Port-Salut 15.5
Portsmouth 464
Port Talbot 381
Portugal 228
Portuguese 513
portulaca 17.28
pose 520
Poseidon 261.25
poser 17.442
poseur 3
posh 354
posit 371.39
positif 163
position 261.71.9
positive 485.12.1
positively 16.206
positivism
    242.35.22
positron 254
positronium
    242.2.12
posse 16.302
possess 296
possessed 433
possession 261.68
possessive 485.2
possessiveness
    300.43
possessor 17.300
possessory
    16.274.34
posset 371
possibility
    16.333.9.2
possible 228.16
possibly 16.137
possum 242.25
post 441
postage 197
postal 228
postbag 178
post-bellum 242.8
postbox 499

postboy 11
postcard 84
postcode 98
postdate 367
postdiluvian
    261.3.32
postdoctoral
    228.76
poster 17.387
posterior 17.3.39
posterity 16.333.21
postern 261
postfix 498
postglacial 228.91
postgraduate 371.2
posthaste 432
posthumous 310
posthypnotic
    38.53.2
postiche 352
postilion 261.120
postimpressionism
    242.35.14.4
posting 265
postliminy
    16.229.3
postlude 102
postman 261
postmark 33
postmaster 17.380
postmeridian
    261.3.5
post meridiem
    242.2.3
postmortem 242.30
postnatal 228.99
post-obit 371
postoperative
    485.15.10
postpaid 85
postpartum 242.26
postpone 257
postponement 420
postpositive
    485.12.1
postprandial 228.3
postscript 424
postulant 420.27
postulate 367.13,
    371.17
postulation
    261.67.13
postulator 17.338.6
posture 17.74
postwar 9

posy 16.399
pot 373
potable 228.16
potamic 38.24
potamology
16.108.4
potash 349
potassium 242.2
potation 261.67.28
potato 12.74
potbellied 91.17
potbelly 16.115
potboy 11
potch 68
poteen 251
Potemkin 252
potency 16.312
potent 420
potentate 367.32
potential 228.96
potentiality
16.333.8.1.1
potentiate 367.1.9
potentiometer
17.342.3.1
potful 226
pothead 86
pother 17.407
potherb 22
pothole 223
potholer 17.171
potholing 265.32
pothook 44
pothouse 306
pothunter 17.373
potiche 352
potion 261.73
Potiphar 17.114
potlatch 62
potluck 43
Potomac 46
potpie 7
potpourri 16.270
Potsdam 229
potsherd 87
pottage 197
potted 91.40
potter 17.344
Potteries 515.1
pottery 16.274
potting 265.68
potto 12.77
potty 16.335
pouch 71
pouffe 170

poulard 84
poult 405
poulterer 17.279
poultice 300
poultry 16
poultryman 261.48
pounce 319
pound 139
poundage 197
poundal 228
pour 9
pourer 17.276
pourpoint 416
poussette 368
pout 377
pouter 17.348
poverty 16.344
pow 13
powder 17.89
powdery 16.274
Powell 228.8
power 14
powerboat 376
powerful 226
powerhouse 306
powerless 300
powerlessness
300.33
powwow 13
Powys 300, 300.1
pox 499
Poyang 263
pozzuolana 17.226
practicability
16.333.9.2
practicable
228.16.10
practical 228.23.22
practicality
16.333.8.3
practice 300.65
practise 300.65
practitioner
17.239.2
praemunire 16.267
praenomen 248
Praesepe 16.247
praetor 17.341
pragmatic 38.49
pragmatism
242.35.20
pragmatist 436.26
Prague 179
prairie 16.264
praise 509

praiseworthy
16.375
praline 251
pralltriller 17.166
pram 229, 230
prance 315
prandial 228.3
prang 263
prank 51
prase 509
praseodymium
242.2
prat 365
prate 367
pratfall 221
pratincole 223
pratique 37
prattle 228.97
prattler 17.200
prawn 255
praxis 300.70
Praxiteles 513.6
prayer 4
prayerful 226
preach 66
preacher 17.55
preachify 7.3
preadaptation
261.67
preamble 228.17
preamplifier 17.4.1
prearranged 111
preaxial 228.3.18
prebend 143
prebendary 16.274
precarious 310.2.10
precast 431
precaution 261.72
precautionary
16.274.29
precede 89.2
precedence 321.5
precedent 420.10
precedential
228.96.1
preceding 265.13
precentor 17.368.1
precept 422
preceptive 485.23
preceptor 17.375
precess 296
precession 261.68
precinct 392
preciosity
16.333.30.1

precious 310
preciousness
300.34
precipice 300
precipitant 420.76
precipitate 367.30
precipitation
261.67.27
precipitin 252.23
precipitous 310.64
precis 5
precise 301
precisian 261.91.1
precision 261.91.1
preclude 102
precocial 228.94
precocious 310.60
precocity
16.333.30.3
precognition
261.71
preconceive 484
preconception
261.84
precondition
261.71
preconize 516.7
preconscious 310
precontract 382
precursor 17.301
precursory
16.274.35
predacious
310.56.2
predate 367
predation 261.67.7
predator 17.352
predatory
16.274.43
predecease 298
predecessor 17.300
predestinarian
261.3.21.1
predestinate 371
predestination
261.67.18
predestine 252.26
predeterminate
371.24
predetermine
252.13
predial 228.3.1
predicable
228.16.10

predicament 420.35
predicant 420.7
predicate 367.5, 371.9
predict 387
predictable 228.16
prediction 261.78.1
predictive 485.18
predictor 17.355
predigest 433
predilection 261.77.2
predispose 520
predisposition 261.71.9
prednisone 257
predominant 420.53.2
predominate 367.17.5
predomination 261.67.18.6
pre-eclampsia 17.3
preemie 16.215
pre-eminence 321.14
pre-eminent 420.53
pre-empt 428
pre-emption 261
pre-emptive 485
pre-emptor 17.378
preen 251
prefab 18
prefabricate 367.5
preface 300
prefatory 16.274.43
prefect 385
prefectorial 228.3.12
prefecture 10
prefer 3
preferable 228.16.35
preference 321.20
preferential 228.96.2
preferment 420
preferrer 17.270
prefiguration 261.67.21
prefigure 17.129
prefix 498
preformation 261.67

prefrontal 228.112
preglacial 228.91
pregnable 228.16
pregnancy 16.312
pregnant 420
prehensile 219.3
prehension 261.82.1
prehistorian 261.3.23
prehistoric 38.41
prehistory 16.274.49
prehominid 91
prejudge 203
prejudice 300
prejudicial 228.93
prelacy 16.307
prelate 371.15
prelatism 242.35.20
prelect 385.4
preliminaries 515.1
preliminary 16.274.26
prelude 102
premarital 228.102
premature 10.5
premed 86
premedical 228.23.1
premeditate 367.30
premeditation 261.67.27
premenstrual 228.9
premier 17
premiere 4.1
premiership 274.1
premise 516.4
premises 515.3
premiss 300
premium 242.2.8
premolar 17.171
premonition 261.71
premonitory 16.274.41
premorse 303
premunition 261.71
prenatal 228.99
prenominal 228.60.5
preoccupation 261.67
preoccupied 92
preoccupy 7

preordain 247
preordination 261.67.18.1
prep 271
prepaid 85
preparation 261.67.22
preparative 485.15.8
preparatory 16.274.43
prepare 4.6
prepay 2
prepense 316
preponderant 420.65
preponderate 367.23
preposition 261.71.9
prepositive 485.12.1
prepositor 17.342.5
prepossess 296
prepossessing 265.60
prepossession 261.68
preposterous 310.50
prepotency 16.312
prepotent 420
prepuce 309
Pre-Raphaelite 372.4
prerecorded 91.9
prerequisite 371.38
prerogative 485.15.3
presa 1
presage 197.11
presbyopia 17.3.37
presbyter 17.342
presbyterial 228.3.11
presbyterian 261.3.22
presbyterianism 242.35.14.1
presbytery 16.274.41
preschool 227
prescience 321.1
prescribe 25
prescript 424

prescription 261.85
prescriptive 485
presence 321
present 410.4, 420.84
presentable 228.16.55
presentation 261.67
presentationism 242.35.14.3
presenter 17.368
presentient 420
presentiment 420.31
presently 16.198
presentment 420
preservation 261.67
preservative 485.15
preserve 483
preshrunk 54
preside 92
presidency 16.312
president 420.10.1
presidential 228.96.1
presidio 12.3.1
presidium 242.2.3
presignify 7.3.3
Presley 16.208
press 296
pressing 265.60
pressman 261.53
pressmark 33
pressor 17.300
pressure 17.323
pressurize 516.8
presswork 36
prestidigitation 261.67.27
prestige 362
prestigious 310.21
presto 12.86
Preston 261.106
Prestonpans 544
prestress 296
Prestwich 67
presumable 228.16
presumably 16.137
presume 241
presumption 261.89
presumptive 485
presumptuous 310.4.4

presuppose 520.2
presupposition
261.71.9
pretence 316
pretend 131.5
pretender 17.101
pretension 261.82
pretentious 310.61
pretentiousness
300.34.4
preterite 371.35.2
preterition 261.71
preteritive 485.12
preternatural
228.76
pretext 450
Pretoria 17.3.41
prettify 7.3
prettiness 300.23
pretty 16.333
pretzel 228
Preussen 261
prevail 214
prevailing 265.27
prevalence
321.12.1
prevalent 420.28.1
prevaricate 367.5
prevarication
261.67.5
prevenient 420.1.2
prevent 410.3
preventable
228.16.55
preventative
485.15.15
preventer 17.368
prevention 261.82
preventive 485.21
preview 15
Previn 252.28
previous 310.2
previously 16.184
prevision 261.91.2
prevocalic 38.19
prewar 9
Priam 242
priapism 242.35
price 301
priceless 300
pricelessness
300.33
pricey 16.301
prick 38
pricker 17.34

pricket 371.9
prickle 228.23
prickly 16.142
pride 92
prie-dieu 3
priest 435
priesthood 101
Priestley 16.200
priestly 16.200
prig 184
priggish 353
prim 235
prima 17.210
primacy 16.307
prima donna
17.233.1
primal 228
primarily 16.120.1
primary 16.274
primate 367
primatology
16.108.4.15.1
prime 236
primer 17.212
primero 12.62
primeval 228.119
primigravida 17.83
priming 265
primipara 17.279
primitive 485.12
primitivism
242.35.22
primo 12.47
primogenitor
17.342
primogeniture
17.56
primordial 228.3.2
primp 287
primrose 520
primula 17.174
primus 310
prince 317
princedom 242
princeling 265
princess 296
Princeton 261
principal 228.66
principality
16.333.8.8
Principe 5
principium 242.2
principle 228.66
principled 122
prink 52

print 412
printable 228.16
printer 17.369
printing 265
prior 17.4
priorate 371
prioress 300.47
priority 16.333.22
priory 16.274
prisage 197
Priscilla 17.166
prise 516
prism 242.35
prismatic 38.49.4
prismatoid 97
prison 261.126
prisoner 17.239
prissy 16.300
pristine 251
pristine 253.10
prithee 16.376
privacy 16.307
private 371
privateer 6.9
privation 261.67
privative 485.15.16
privet 371
privilege 197.1
privileged 110
privity 16.333.35
privy 16.382
prize 516
prizefight 372
prizefighter 17.343
pro 12
proa 17.6
pro-am 229
probabilism
242.35.9
probability
16.333.9.2
probable 228.16
probably 16.137
proband 128
probang 263.1
probate 367.3
probation 261.67.3
probationer
17.239.1
probative 485.15
probe 28
probity 16.333
problem 242
problematic
38.49.2

proboscidean
261.3.5
proboscis 300.54
procaine 247
procathedral
228.78
procedure 17.149
proceed 89.3
proceeding 265.13
proceeds 526
proceleusmatic
38.49
process 296
procession 261.68.1
processional
228.63.4
processor 17.300
prochronism
242.35.14
proclaim 231
proclamation
261.67.16
proclamatory
16.274.43.5
proclitic 38.52
proclivity
16.333.35
Procne 16.239
proconsul 228.89
procrastinate
367.17
procrastination
261.67.18
procreate 367.1
procreation
261.67.1
Procrustean
261.3.27
procryptic 38.66
proctology
16.108.4
proctor 17.356
procuration
261.67.21
procurator 17.338
procuratory
16.274.43
procure 10
procurer 17.277
prod 94
prodigal 228.46
prodigality
16.333.8.4
prodigious 310.21
prodigy 16.103

459

prodrome 239
produce 309, 309.1
producer 17.308
product 389
production 261.79.1
productive 485.19
productivity 16.333.35.3
proem 232
prof 165
profanation 261.67.19
profane 247.3
profanity 16.333.14
profess 296
profession 261.68
professional 228.63.4
professionalism 242.35.11.5
professor 17.300
professorial 228.3.12
professoriate 371.1.2
proffer 17.116
proficiency 16.312.5
proficient 420.74
profile 219
profit 371
profitable 228.16.49
profiteer 6
profiterole 223.3
profitless 300.17
profligacy 16.307
profligate 371.14
profluent 420.4
profound 139
profoundly 16.156
profundity 16.333.7
profuse 309
profusely 16.183
profusion 261.93
prog 185
progenitor 17.342
progeny 16.229.2
progestational 228.63.3
progesterone 257.1
progestin 252.26
proglottis 300

prognosis 300.55
prognostic 38.71
prognosticate 367.5
prognostication 261.67.5
programmable 228.16.26
programmatic 38.49.2
programme 229
programmer 17.205
programming 265
progress 296
progression 261.68
progressive 485.2.1
prohibit 371.5
prohibition 261.71
prohibitionist 436.13.5
prohibitive 485.12
project 385, 385.3
projectile 219.5
projection 261.77.1
projectionist 436.13.6
projective 485.17
projector 17.354
projet 2
Prokofiev 160.1
prolamine 251.4
prolapse 322
prolate 367
prole 223
proleg 181
prolegomenon 261.56
prolepsis 300.59
proletarian 261.3.21.2
proletariat 381.1
proliferate 367.23
proliferation 261.67.22
prolific 38.12
proline 251
prolix 498
prolocutor 17.350
prologue 185
prolong 266.1
prolongation 261.67
prolusion 261.93
prom 237
promenade 84

promenader 17.78.1
Promethean 261.3
promethium 242.2
prominence 321.14
prominent 420.53.2
promiscuity 16.333.3
promiscuous 310.4
promise 300
promisee 5.20
promising 265.61
promisor 9
promissory 16.274.36
promontory 16.274.48
promote 376
promoter 17.347
promotion 261.73.1
promotional 228.63.6
promotive 485.14
prompt 429
promptitude 102.2
promptness 300
promulgate 367
promulgation 261.67
pronate 367
pronator 17.338
prone 257
proneness 300
prong 266
pronghorn 255
pronominal 228.60.5
pronoun 258
pronounce 319
pronounceable 228.16
pronouncement 420
pronto 12.85
pronunciamento 12.84
pronunciation 261.67.1.4
proof 170
proofread 89
proof-reader 17.82
prop 276
propaedeutic 38.56
propaganda 17.98
propagandist 436

propagandize 516
propagate 367.11
propagation 261.67.11
propagator 17.338.4
propane 247
propel 215
propellant 420.26
propeller 17.163
propensity 16.333.31
proper 17.255
properly 16.131.6
propertied 91
property 16.344
prophage 193
prophase 509
prophecy 16.300
prophesy 7
prophet 371
prophetic 38.50
prophylactic 38.58
prophylaxis 300.70
propinquity 16.333
propitiate 367.1.6
propitious 310.58
propolis 300.13.2
proponent 420.54
proportion 261.72.1
proportional 228.63
proportionate 371.28.2
proposal 228.127
propose 520.2
proposer 17.442
proposition 261.71.9
propositus 310.64
propound 139
propraetor 17.341
proprietary 16.274.41
proprietor 17.352.1
propriety 16.333.2
proprioceptor 17.375
propulsion 261
propylaeum 242.1
propylite 372.3
pro rata 17.337
prorate 367
prorogue 188

prosaic 38.1
prosaism 242.35
proscenium 242.2
prosciutto 12.80
proscribe 25
proscription 261.85
proscriptive 485
prose 520
prosector 17.354
prosecute 380
prosecution 261.75
prosecutor 17.351
proselyte 372.3
proselytize 516.12
Proserpina 17.231
prosimian 261.3.14
prosody 16.72
prosopopoeia 17.2.1
prospect 385
prospective 485.17
prospector 17.354
prospectus 310.69
prosper 17.267
prosperity 16.333.21
prosperous 310.50
prostaglandin 252
prostate 367.34
prostatectomy 16.222.5
prostatitis 300.62
prosthesis 300.52
prosthetic 38.50
prosthetics 498.12
prosthodontics 498
prostitute 380.5
prostitution 261.75
prostomium 242.2.9
prostrate 367
prostration 261.67
prostyle 219
prosy 16.399
protactinium 242.2.11
protagonist 436.13.2
protamine 251.4
protanopia 17.3.37.2
protasis 300.57
protea 17.3
protean 261.2
protease 509.1

protect 385
protection 261.77
protectionism 242.35.14
protectionist 436.13.6
protective 485.17
protector 17.354
protectorate 371.35
protectory 16.274.45
protégé 2
protein 251
protest 433
Protestant 420.81
Protestantism 242.35.21
protestation 261.67.33
protester 17.382
Proteus 310.2
prothesis 300.52.5
protist 436.25
protium 242.2
protocol 220
protohistory 16.274.49
protolanguage 197
protolithic 38.73
protomorphic 38.14
proton 254
protoplasm 242.34
Protosemitic 38.52
prototherian 261.3.22
prototrophic 38.13
prototype 275.1
protozoan 261.6
protozoology 16.108.4.3
protozoon 254.2
protract 382
protractile 219.4
protraction 261.76
protractor 17.353
protrude 102
protrusion 261.93
protrusive 485.8
protuberance 321.20
protuberant 420.65
protyle 219
proud 99
Proust 444

proustite 372
provable 228.16.62
prove 490
proven 261
provenance 321.14
Provencal 213
provender 17.102
proverb 22
proverbial 228.3
provide 92.13
providence 321.5
provident 420.10
providential 228.96.1
providing 265.14
province 317
provincial 228
provincialism 242.35.11
provinciality 16.333.8.1
provision 261.91.3
provisional 228.63
proviso 12
provitamin 252.15
Provo 12
provocation 261.67.6
provocative 485.15.2
provoke 42
provolone 16.233.1
provost 445
prow 13
prowess 300
prowl 224
prowler 17.172
Proxima 17.211
proximal 228.52
proximate 371.19
proximity 16.333.12
proximo 12.48
proxy 16.389
prude 102
prudence 321
prudent 420.13
prudential 228.96
Prudentius 310.61
prudish 353
pruinose 305
prune 260
prunella 17.163
prunelle 215
pruner 17.238

prurience 321.1
prurient 420.1.3
prurigo 12.30
pruritus 310.65
Prussia 17.329
Prussian 261.74
prussiate 371.1
pry 7
psalm 230
psalmist 436.8
psalmodic 38.9
psalmody 16.72
Psalms 540
psalter 17.363
psalterium 242.2.15
psaltery 16.274
psephite 372
psephology 16.108.4
pseud 102
pseudaxis 300.70
Pseudepigrapha 17.120
pseudo 12.22
pseudomorph 166.1
pseudomutuality 16.333.8.2
pseudonym 235
pseudonymous 310.28.2
pseudopodium 242.2.4
pshaw 9
psittacine 253.8
psittacosis 300.55
psoas 310
psoralea 17.3.18
psoriasis 300.57.1
psych 39
Psyche 16.26
psyche 16.26
psychedelia 17.3.19
psychedelic 38.20
psychiatric 38.45
psychiatrist 436
psychiatry 16.286.1
psychic 38
psycho 12
psychoanalyse 516.3.5
psychoanalysis 300.52.1
psychoanalyst 436.7.4

psychoanalytic 38.52.1
psychobiology 16.108.4.2
psychodrama 17.206
psychogenesis 300.52.4
psychogenic 38.32.1
psychohistory 16.274.49
psychokinesis 300.51
psychological 228.23.5
psychologism 242.35.8
psychologist 436.4
psychologize 516.1
psychology 16.108.4.5
psychometrics 498.10
psychometry 16.285.2
psychoneurotic 38.53
psychopath 452
psychopathic 38.72
psychopathology 16.108.4
psychopathy 16.373.1
psychosis 300.55
psychosomatic 38.49.2
psychosurgery 16.274.13
psychotherapist 436.15
psychotherapy 16.254
psychotic 38.53
Ptah 1
ptarmigan 261.32
pteridology 16.108.4
pterodactyl 218
pteropod 94.1
pterosaur 9.11
pteryla 17.166
ptisan 245.7
ptochocracy 16.307.5

Ptolemaeus 310.1
Ptolemaic 38.1
Ptolemaist 436.1
Ptolemy 16.216
ptomaine 247
ptosis 300.55
ptyalin 252.11
ptyalism 242.35.11
pub 29
puberty 16.344
puberulent 420.27
pubes 513
pubescence 321.21
pubescent 420.67
pubic 38.4
pubis 300.2
public 38
publican 261.13
publication 261.67.5
publicist 436.21
publicity 16.333.28
publicize 516.10
publicly 16.142
publish 353
publisher 17.326
Puccini 16.228
puccoon 260
puce 309
puck 43
pucker 17.39
pudding 265
puddle 228.36
puddling 265
pudency 16.312
pudendum 242.7
pudgy 16.107
pueblo 12
puerile 219
puerilism 242.35.9
puerility 16.333.9
puerperal 228.76
puerperium 242.2.15
Puerto Rico 12.10
puff 168
puffbird 87
puffer 17.118
puffery 16.274
puffin 252.5
puffy 16.88
pug 189
pugilism 242.35.9
pugilist 436.5
pugnacious 310.56

pugnacity 16.333.25
puisne 16.236
puke 45
pukka 17.39
pul 227
pulchritude 102.2
pule 227
Pulitzer 17.320
pull 226
pullet 371.17
pulley 16.129
Pullman 261
pullover 17.417
pullulate 367.13
pulmonary 16.274.29
pulmonate 371.28
pulmonic 38.35
pulp 284
pulped 427
pulpit 371
pulpwood 101
pulsar 1
pulsate 367
pulsatile 219
pulsation 261.67
pulsator 17.338
pulsatory 16.274.43
pulse 313
pulsimeter 17.342.2
pulverize 516.8
pulverulent 420.27
pulvillus 310.23
pulvinate 367.17
pulvinus 310.34
puma 17.217
pumice 300
pummel 228
pump 289
pumpernickel 228.23
pumpkin 252
pumpkinseed 89.4
pun 259
punce 320
punch 82
punchball 221
punchbowl 223
puncheon 261
Punchinello 12.40
punchy 16.56
punctate 367
punctilio 12.3.2
punctilious 310.2.5

punctual 228.9
punctuality 16.333.8.2
punctuate 367.2
punctuation 261.67.2
puncture 17.68
pundit 371
pung 267
pungent 420
Punic 38
punish 353
punishable 228.16.43
punishment 420.47
punitive 485.12
Punjab 19
Punjabi 16.6
punk 54
punka 17.46
punnet 371.27
punster 17.395
punt 419
punter 17.373
puny 16.236
pup 279
pupa 17.259
puparium 242.2.14
pupate 367
pupil 228
pupillage 197.1
pupillary 16.274.16
puppet 371
puppeteer 6
puppetry 16.285
Puppis 300
puppy 16.252
Purana 17.226
Purbeck 35
purblind 135
Purcell 215
purchasable 228.16
purchase 300
purchaser 17.302
purdah 17.81
pure 10
purebred 86
purée 2.18
purely 16.124
purgation 261.67
purgative 485.15
purgatorial 228.3.12.2
purgatory 16.274.43

purge 195
Puri 5
purificator 17.338.2
purifier 17.4.1
purify 7.3
Purim 235
purine 251
purism 242.35
purist 436.19
puritan 261.99
puritanical
228.23.10
purity 16.333.23
purl 216
purler 17.164
purlieu 15
purlin 252
purloin 256
purple 228
purplish 353
purport 374
purpose 310
purposeful 226
purposeless 300
purposelessness
300.33
purposely 16.184
purposive 485
purpure 10
purpurin 252.19
purr 3
purring 265.51
purse 297
purser 17.301
purslane 252
pursuance 321
pursuant 420.5
pursue 15
pursuer 17.8
pursuit 380
pursuivant 420
pursy 16.298
purulent 420.27
purvey 2
purveyance 321
purveyor 17.1
purview 15
pus 307
Pusan 245
Pusey 16.402
push 357
pushchair 4
pushing 265
Pushkin 252
pushover 17.417

pushrod 94
pushy 16.325
pusillanimity
16.333.12
pusillanimous
310.28.1
puss 308
pussy 16.305
pussyfoot 379
pustulant 420.27
pustular 17.174
pustulate 367.13,
371.17
pustule 227
put 379
putamen 248.2
putative 485.15.14
putlog 185
putrefaction 261.76
putrefy 7.3
putrescent 420.67
putrid 91
putt 378
puttee 16.341
putter 17.349
putting 265
putty 16.341
puttyroot 380
puzzle 228
puzzlement 420.40
puzzler 17.204
pya 1
pyaemia 17.3.26
pycnometer
17.342.3
Pydna 17.241
pyelitis 300.62.1
pyelography
16.90.2.2
Pygmalion 261.3.8
pygmy 16
pyjama 17.206
pyjamas 524
pyknic 38
pylon 261
pylorus 310.48
pyoderma 17.209
pyoid 97
Pyongyang 263
pyorrhoea 17.2.2
pyosis 300.55.2
pyracantha 17.399
pyralid 91
pyramid 91.19
pyramidal 228.32

Pyramus 310.29
pyran 245
pyre 8
pyrene 251.5
Pyrenean 261.2
Pyrenees 513.9
pyrethrum 242
pyretic 38.50
Pyrex 496
pyridoxamine
251.4
pyriform 238.1
pyrite 372
pyrites 513
pyrogen 261.39
pyrogenic 38.32.1
pyrography 16.90.2
pyromancy 16.309
pyromania
17.3.31.1
pyromaniac 32.1
pyrometallurgy
16.108.2
pyrometer 17.342.3
pyrone 257
pyrope 278
pyrophoric 38.41
pyrophyllite 372.3
pyrosis 300.55
pyrostat 365
pyrotechnic 38
pyrotechnics 498
Pyrrha 17.273
pyrrhic 38.40
pyrrhotite 372.12
Pyrrhus 310.46
pyrrole 223
Pythagoras 310.50
Pythagorean
261.2.3
Pythia 17.3.51
Pythian 261.3
python 261
pythoness 296.3
pythonic 38.35
pyuria 17.3.42
pyx 498
pyxie 16.388

Q

Qaboos bin Said
92.9
Qairwan 245
Qatar 1
Qeshm 242
qintar 1
qua 2
quack 32
quackery 16.274
quacksalver 17.420
quad 94
quadragenarian
261.3.21.1
Quadragesima
17.211
Quadragesimal
228.52.1
quadrangle 228.49
quadrant 420
quadraphonic
38.35.2
quadraphonics
498.5
quadrate 367, 371
quadratic 38.49
quadratics 498.11
quadrature 17.62
quadrennium 242.2
quadric 38
quadriceps 324
quadrifid 91
quadriga 17.128
quadrilateral
228.76
quadrille 218
quadrillion 261.120
quadriplegia
17.3.13
quadriplegic 38.17
quadrisect 385.7
quadrivial 228.3.15
quadrivium 242.2
quadroon 260
quadruped 86
quadruple 228
quadruplet 371
quadruplex 496
quadruplicate
367.5.1, 371.9.1
quaestor 17.383
quaff 165

quagga 17.123
quaggy 16.91
quagmire 8
quahog 185
quail 214
quaint 409
quaintness 300
quake 34
Quaker 17.30
Quakerism 242.35.15
quaky 16.21
quale 16.113
qualification 261.67.5.1
qualified 92.1
qualifier 17.4.1
qualify 7.3.2
qualitative 485.15.12
quality 16.333.10
qualm 230
quamash 349
quandary 16.274
quandong 266
quango 12.35
quant 414
quantal 228.111
quantic 38.64
quantifiable 228.16.3.1
quantifier 17.4.1
quantify 7.3
quantitative 485.15.12
quantity 16.333
quantize 516
quantum 242
quaquaversal 228.84
quarantine 251
quare 4
quark 33
quarrel 228.73
quarreller 17.176
quarrelsome 242
quarrian 261.3
quarrier 17.3
quarry 16.268
quarryman 261.48
quart 374
quartan 261.102
quarter 17.345
quarterage 197
quarterback 32.2

quarterdeck 35
quarterfinal 228.61
quarterlight 372.4
quarterly 16.131
quartermaster 17.380
quartern 261.102
quarterstaff 158
quartet 368
quartic 38
quartile 219
quarto 12.78
quartz 342
quartzite 372
quasar 1
quash 354
Quasimodo 12.21
quassia 17.327
quatercentenary 16.274.25
quaternary 16.274.24
quaternion 261.3
quaternity 16.333.16
quatrain 247
quatre 17.291
quatrefoil 222.1
quaver 17.410
quay 5
quayside 92
queasy 16.395
Quebec 35
quebracho 12
queen 251
queencake 34
queenly 16.172
Queensberry 16.274
Queensland 143
queer 6
quell 215
quelquechose 520
quench 79
quenchable 228.16
quenelle 215
quercetin 252.23
quercine 253
querist 436.17
quern 249
querulous 310.25.1
query 16.265
quest 433
question 261.18

questionable 228.16.31
questioner 17.239
questioning 265.46
questionless 300.14
questionnaire 4.5
Quetta 17.339
quetzal 228
Quetzalcoatl 228.97
queue 15
Quezon y Molina 17.230
quibble 228.12
quiche 352
quick 38
quicken 261.13
quickie 16.25
quicklime 236
quickly 16.142
quicksand 128
quickset 368
quicksilver 17.422
quickstep 271
quick-witted 91.38
quick-wittedness 300.28
quid 91
quiddity 16.333.5
quidnunc 54
quid pro quo 12
quiescence 321.21
quiescent 420.67
quiet 381.2
quieten 261
quietism 242.35.20
quietness 300
quietude 102.2
quietus 310.63
quiff 163
quill 218
quillai 7.5
quilt 403
quilting 265
quim 235
quin 252
quinary 16.274.27
quinate 367
quince 317
quincentenary 16.274.25
quincunx 506
Qui Nhong 266
quinine 251
quinol 220.3

quinquagenarian 261.3.21.1
Quinquagesima 17.211
quinquennium 242.2
quinquereme 234
quinsy 16.406
quintal 228
quintan 261.105
quintessence 321.21
quintessential 228.96
quintet 368
quintile 219
Quintilian 261.3.11
quintillion 261.120
quintuple 228
quintuplet 371
quintuplicate 367.5.1
quip 274
quipster 17.396
quire 8
Quirinal 228.60
Quirinus 310.34
quirk 36
quirky 16.23
quirt 369
quisling 265
quist 436
quit 371
quitch 67
quitclaim 231
quite 372
Quito 12.76
quits 339
quittance 321.24
quitter 17.342
quittor 17.342
quiver 17.414
quiverful 226
quivery 16.274.51
qui vive 484
Quixote 381
quixotic 38.53
quiz 515
quizmaster 17.380
quizzical 228.23.25
quod 94
quodlibet 368.2
quoin 256
quoit 375
quokka 17.36

quondam 229
quorum 242.20
quota 17.347
quotable 228.16
quotation
 261.67.28
quote 376
quoth 461
quotidian 261.3.5
quotient 420
quo warranto
 12.83

R

Ra 1
Rabat 366
rabbi 7
rabbinate 371.24
rabbinic 38.34
rabbinical
 228.23.12
rabbinism
 242.35.13
rabbit 371.4
rabbiter 17.342
rabbitry 16.285
rabble 228
Rabelais 2.12
Rabelaisian
 261.3.33
rabi 16.13
rabid 91
rabies 513
raccoon 260
race 295
racecard 84
racecourse 303
racegoer 17.6
racehorse 303
raceme 234
racemic 38.27
racemize 516.4
racemose 305
racer 17.299
racetrack 32
Rachel 228
rachis 300
rachitic 38.52
rachitis 300.62

Rachmaninoff
 165.1
racial 228.91
racialism 242.35.11
racialist 436.7
racing 265.59
rack 32
racket 371.6
racketeer 6
rackets 339
rackety 16.333
Rackham 242
raconteur 3
racquet 371.6
racy 16.296
rad 83
RADA 17.78
radar 1
radarscope 278
Radcliffe 163
raddle 228.31
raddled 122
radial 228.3
radian 261.3.3
radiance 321.1
radiant 420.1
radiate 367.1,
 371.1
radiation 261.67.1
radiative 485.15
radiator 17.338.1
radical 228.23
radicalism
 242.35.11
radically 16.142
radicand 128.1
radicel 215
radicle 228.23
radii 7.1
radio 12.3
radioactivate
 367.36
radioactive 485.16
radioactivity
 16.333.35.2
radiobiology
 16.108.4.2
radiocarbon 261.8
radiogenic 38.32.1
radiogram 229.1.1
radiograph 158.1.1
radiographer
 17.120.1
radiography
 16.90.2.1

radioisotope 278
radioisotopic 38.37
radiologist 436.4
radiology
 16.108.4.1
radiometer
 17.342.3.1
radiopaque 34
radiophone 257
radiophonic
 38.35.2
radiophony
 16.237.3.1
radiosensitive
 485.12
radiosonde 136
radiotelegraphy
 16.90
radiotherapeutic
 38.56
radiotherapist
 436.15
radiotherapy
 16.254
radiothermy 16.214
radiotoxic 38.75
radish 353.1
radium 242.2.1
radius 310.2
radix 498
Radnorshire 6
radome 239
radon 254
radula 17.174
raff 157
raffia 17.3.10
raffinate 367.17.1
raffinose 520
raffish 353
raffle 228
raft 396
rafter 17.358
rag 178
raga 17.124
ragamuffin 252.5
ragbag 178
rage 193
ragged 91
raggedness 300.28
raggedy 16.63
raggle-taggle
 228.43
ragi 16.91
raglan 261
ragman 261

ragout 15
ragtag 178
ragtime 236
ragweed 89
ragwort 369
raid 85
raider 17.79
rail 214
railcar 1
railhead 86
railing 265.27
raillery 16.274
railroad 98
railway 2
railwayman 261.45
raiment 420.29
rain 247
rainband 128
rainbird 87
rainbow 12
raincheck 35
raincoat 376
raindrop 276
rainfall 221
rainforest 436.18
Rainier 17.3.31,
 2.1
rainout 377
rainproof 170
rainstorm 238
rainy 16.225
raise 509
raisin 261.124
raising 265.81
raj 192
rajah 17.145
Rajkot 376
Rajput 379
rake 34
raki 5.3
rakish 353
rale 213
rallentando 12.23
ralline 253
rally 16.112
rallycross 302
ram 229
Rama 17.206
Ramachandra
 17.288
Ramadan 246
Ramakrishna
 17.243
Raman 261
Rambert 4

ramble 228.17
rambler 17.179
rambling 265
Rambouillet 2
rambunctious 310
rambutan 261.104
ramekin 252.3
Rameses 513
ramie 16.210
ramification
  261.67.5.1
ramiform 238.1
ramify 7.3
Ramillies 513.6
ramjet 368
rammish 353
ramose 305
ramp 285
rampage 193
rampant 420
rampart 366
rampion 261.3
ramrod 94
Ramsgate 367
ramshackle 228.19
ramulose 305
ramus 310.27
ran 245
rance 315
ranch 78
ranchero 12.62
Ranchi 16.54
rancid 91
rancorous 310.50.1
rancour 17.43
rand 128
randan 245
Randolph 173
random 242.6
randomize 516.5
randy 16.77
rang 263
range 207
rangefinder 17.103
ranger 17.156
Rangoon 260
rangy 16.109
rani 16.224
rank 51
ranker 17.43
ranking 265
rankle 228
ransack 32
ransom 242
rant 407

ranunculaceous
  310.56
ranunculus 310.25
rap 268
rapacious 310.56
rapacity
  16.333.25.1
Rapa Nui 16.4
rape 270
rapeseed 89
Raphael 228.1
raphide 92
rapid 91
rapidity 16.333.5
rapier 17.3
rapine 253
rapist 436.14
rapparee 5.17
rappee 5
rappel 215
rapper 17.247
rapport 9
rapporteur 3
rapscallion 261.118
rapt 421
raptor 17.374
raptorial 228.3.12
rapture 17.72
rapturous 310.50
rare 4
rarebit 371
rarefaction 261.76
rarefied 92.1
rarefy 7.3
rarely 16.117
rareripe 275
raring 265.52
rarity 16.333
Rarotonga 17.142
rasbora 17.276
rascal 228
rascality 16.333.8
rascally 16.131
rash 349
rasher 17.321
rashness 300
rasp 290
raspatory
  16.274.43
raspberry 16.274
rasping 265
Rasputin 252.24
rasse 16.294
Rasta 17.379

Rastafarian
  261.3.21
raster 17.379
rat 365
rata 17.337
ratafia 17.2
ratal 228.99
ratatat 365
ratatat-tat 365
ratatouille 5
ratbag 178
ratchet 371
rate 367
rateable 228.16.45
ratel 228.99
ratepayer 17.1
rates 335
ratfink 52
ratfish 353
rathe 473
rather 17.401
ratify 7.3.8
ratiné 2.15
ratine 251
rating 265.64
ratio 12.3.6
ratiocinate 367.17
ration 261.66
rational 228.63.2
rationale 213.1
rationalism
  242.35.11.5.1
rationalist 436.7.5
rationalistic
  38.70.2
rationality
  16.333.8.7.1
rationalize 516.3.7
Ratisbon 254
ratite 372
Ratlam 230
ratline 252
ratoon 260
rats 333
ratsbane 247
rattan 245
ratter 17.336
Rattigan 261.32
rattish 353
rattle 228.97
rattler 17.200
rattlesnake 34
rattletrap 268
rattling 265
rattly 16.186

rattrap 268
ratty 16.327
raucous 310
raunchy 16.55
rauwolfia 17.3
ravage 197
rave 482
Ravel 215
ravel 228.117
ravelin 252
raven 261, 261.111
ravening 265.46
Ravenna 17.228
ravenous 310.36
raver 17.410
ravine 251.12
raving 265.77
ravioli 16.126
ravish 353
ravishing 265.63
raw 9
Rawalpindi 16.79
rawboned 138
rawhide 92
rawinsonde 136
rawness 300.24
ray 2
rayless 300.7
raylet 371
rayon 254
raze 509
razee 5
razoo 15.10
razor 17.439
razorback 32.2
razorbill 218
razz 507
razzle-dazzle
  228.124
razzmatazz 507
re 2, 5
reach 66
reachable
  228.16.12
react 382
reactant 420
reaction 261.76
reactionary
  16.274.29
reactivate 367.36
reactive 485.16
reactivity
  16.333.35.2
reactor 17.353
read 86, 89

466

readable 228.16
reader 17.82
readership 274.1
readily 16.120
readiness 300.23.1
Reading 265.12
reading 265.13
readjust 443
ready 16.60
reaffirm 233
reafforest 436.18
Reagan 261.31
reagent 420
real 213, 228.2
realgar 17.137
realism 242.35.11.1
realist 436.7.1
realistic 38.70.2.1
reality 16.333.8.1
realizable 228.16.64
realization 261.67.36
realize 516.3.1
really 16.119
realm 243
realty 16.352
ream 234
reamer 17.210
reap 273
reaper 17.252
reappear 6.6
reappearance 321.17
rear 6
rearguard 84
rearm 230
rearmost 441
rearrange 207
rearrangement 420.38
reason 261.125
reasonable 228.16.31.2
reasoned 143.6
reasoning 265.46
reassurance 321.19
reassure 10
reassuring 265.56
Réaumur 10
reb 21
rebarbative 485.15
rebate 367
rebec 35
Rebecca 17.31

rebel 215, 228
rebellion 261.119
rebellious 310.2
rebirth 456
reborn 255
rebound 139
rebuff 168
rebuild 116
rebuilt 403
rebuke 45
rebus 310
rebut 378
rebuttal 228.107
rebutter 17.349
rec 35
recalcitrant 420.66
recalesce 296.1
recalescence 321.21
recall 221.1
recant 407
recantation 261.67.31
recap 268
recapitulate 367.13
recapitulation 261.67.13
recaption 261.83
recapture 17.72
recce 16.22
recede 89.2
receipt 370
receiptor 17.341
receive 484.2
receiver 17.413
receivership 274.1
recension 261.82.2
recent 420.69
recept 422
receptacle 228.28
reception 261.84
receptionist 436.13
receptive 485.23
receptivity 16.333.35
receptor 17.375
recess 296
recession 261.68
recessional 228.63.4
recessive 485.2
Rechabite 372
recharge 192
recherché 2
recidivism 242.35.22

Recife 17.113
recipe 16.248
recipience 321.1
recipient 420.1
reciprocal 228.28
reciprocate 367.6
reciprocity 16.333.30
recision 261.91.1
recital 228.103
recitation 261.67.27
recitative 484
recite 372.9
reckless 300
recklessness 300.33
reckon 261
reckoner 17.239
reckoning 265.46
reclaim 231
reclamation 261.67.16
reclinable 228.16.30
reclinate 367.17
recline 253.4
recliner 17.232
reclothe 478
recluse 309
reclusive 485.8
recognition 261.71
recognizable 228.16.64
recognizance 321
recognize 516
recognizee 5
recognizor 9
recoil 222
recollect 385.5
recollection 261.77
recombination 261.67.18
recommence 316
recommend 131.2
recommendable 228.16.18
recommendation 261.67.9
recommendatory 16.274.43.2
recommit 371.21
recompense 316
recompose 520
reconcilable 228.16
reconcile 219

reconciliation 261.67.1.1
reconciliatory 16.274.43.1
recondite 372
recondition 261.71
reconnaissance 321.22
reconnoitre 17.346
reconsider 17.83
reconstitute 380.5
reconstruct 389
reconstruction 261.79
reconvert 369
record 95, 95.2
recordable 228.16.16
recorder 17.86
recording 265.15
recount 418
recoup 280
recourse 303
recover 17.418
recovery 16.274
re-create 367.1
recreation 261.67.1
recreational 228.63.3
recrement 420.31
recriminate 367.17
recrimination 261.67.18.5
recrudesce 296
recruit 380
recruitment 420
recrystallize 516.3
recta 17.354
rectal 228
rectangle 228.49
rectangular 17.174
recti 7
rectifiable 228.16.3.1
rectifier 17.4.1
rectify 7.3.9
rectilinear 17.3.34
rectitude 102.2
recto 12.81
rectocele 217.2
rector 17.354
rectory 16.274.45
rectrix 498
rectum 242
rectus 310.69

recumbent 420
recuperate 367.23
recuperation
261.67.22
recuperator
17.338.9
recur 3
recurrence 321
recurrent 420.64
recurring 265.51
recursion 261.69
recurve 483
recusant 420
recycle 228.24
red 86
redact 382
redan 245.1
redbreast 433
redbrick 38
redbud 100
redbug 189
redcoat 376
redcurrant 420.64
redd 86
redden 261.21
reddish 353
Redditch 67
redecorate 367.23
redeem 234
redeemable 228.16
redeemer 17.210
redeeming 265.36
redemption 261
redemptioner
17.239
Redemptorist
436.20
redeploy 11
redeployment
420.33
redevelop 281.1
redevelopment 420
redeye 7
redfin 252
Redford 103.2
Redgrave 482
red-handed 91.12
redhead 86
redia 17.3.8
redingote 376
redintegrate 367.26
redintegration
261.67.24
rediscover 17.418
Redmond 143

redneck 35
redness 300
redo 15
redolent 420.28
redouble 228.14
redoubt 377
redoubtable 228.16
redound 139
redox 499
redpoll 220
redraft 396
redress 296
redroot 380
Redruth 463
redshank 51
redskin 252
redstart 366
reduce 309
reducer 17.308
reducible 228.16
reduction 261.79
redundancy 16.312
redundant 420.16
reduplicate 367.5.1,
371.9.1
reduplication
261.67.5
reduviid 91.2
redware 4
redwing 265
redwood 101
re-echo 12.9
reed 89
reedbuck 43
reeding 265.13
reedling 265
reedy 16.62
reef 162
reefer 17.113
reek 37
reel 217
re-election 261.77.2
reen 251
re-enact 382
re-entrant 420
re-entry 16.288
reeve 484
re-examine 252.12
re-export 374
ref 160
reface 295
refection 261.77
refectory 16.274.45
refer 3
referee 5.17

reference 321.20
referendum 242.7
referent 420.65
referral 228
refill 218
refillable 228.16.23
refine 253
refined 135
refinement 420
refiner 17.232
refinery 16.274.27
refining 265.44
reflate 367
reflation 261.67
reflect 385
reflection 261.77
reflective 485.17
reflectivity
16.333.35
reflector 17.354
reflet 2
reflex 496
reflexive 485
reflux 502
re-form 238, 238.1
reformation
261.67.16
reformative
485.15.6
reformatory
16.274.43
reformed 125
reformer 17.214
reformism
242.35.12
refract 382.1
refraction 261.76
refractive 485.16
refractometer
17.342.3
refractor 17.353
refractory
16.274.44
refrain 247
refrangible
228.16.21
refreeze 513
refresh 351
refresher 17.323
refreshing 265
refreshment 420
refrigerant 420.65
refrigerate 367.23
refrigeration
261.67.22

refrigerator
17.338.9
refringent 420.23
refroze 520
refuel 228.10
refuge 204
refugee 5
refulgent 420.21
re-fund 140
refundable 228.16
refurbish 353
refusal 228.128
refuse 309, 523
refutation
261.67.29
refute 380
regain 247
regal 228.45
regale 214
regalia 17.3.18
regality 16.333.8.4
regard 84.1
regardant 420.8
regardful 226
regarding 265
regardless 300
regatta 17.336
regency 16.312
regenerate
367.23.1, 371.35
regeneration
261.67.22.2
regent 420
reggae 2
regicide 92.7
regime 234
regimen 248
regiment 410.1,
420.31
regimental
228.110.2
regimentals 539
regimentation
261.67.32.1
Regina 17.232
region 261.36
regional 228.63
regionalism
242.35.11.5
register 17.384
registrant 420
registrar 1
registration
261.67.25
registry 16.293

regnant 420
regolith 458
regorge 200
regosol 220
regrate 367.26
regress 296
regression 261.68
regressive 485.2
regret 368
regretful 226.8
regrettable 228.16.46
regroup 280
regulable 228.16.25
regular 17.174
regularity 16.333.20.3
regularize 516.8.1
regulate 367.13
regulation 261.67.13
regulator 17.338.6
Regulus 310.25
regulus 310.25
regurgitate 367.30
regurgitation 261.67.27
rehabilitate 367.30.1
rehabilitation 261.67.27
rehash 349
rehearsal 228.84
rehearse 297
reheat 370
rehoboam 242
rehouse 521
Reich 39
Reichsmark 33
Reichstag 179
Reid 89
reify 7.3
Reigate 371
reign 247
reimburse 297
reimport 374
reimpression 261.68
rein 247
reincarnation 261.67.17
reindeer 6
reinforce 303.2
reinforcement 420.45

reins 545
reinstate 367
reinstatement 420.48
reinsure 10.2
reiterate 367.23.2
reiteration 261.67.22.4
Reith 457
reject 385
rejection 261.77
rejig 184
rejoice 304
rejoin 256
rejoinder 17.106
rejuvenate 367.17
rejuvenation 261.67.18
rejuvenesce 296.3
rekindle 228.40
relapse 322
relate 367.12
related 91.34.5
relation 261.67.12
relations 551.1
relationship 274.2
relative 485.15.4
relativism 242.35.22
relativistic 38.70
relativity 16.333.35.1
relator 17.338.5
relatum 242.27
relax 494
relaxant 420.83
relaxation 261.67.34
relay 2, 2.11
release 298
relegate 367.10
relegation 261.67.10
relent 410
relentless 300
relentlessness 300.33
relevance 321
relevant 420
reliability 16.333.9.2.1
reliable 228.16.3
reliance 321.2
reliant 420.2
relic 38.20

relict 387
relief 162.1
relieve 484.1
relieved 148
religion 261.37
religiose 305.1
religiosity 16.333.30.1
religious 310.21
relinquish 353
reliquary 16.274
reliquiae 5.2
relish 353.4
relive 485
reload 98
reluctance 321
reluctant 420
reluctivity 16.333.35.3
rely 7.5
remade 85
remain 247
remainder 17.100
remainderman 261.52
remaining 265.40
remains 545
remake 34
remand 129
remanence 321
remark 33.2
remarkable 228.16
remarque 33.2
remarriage 197.9
remarry 16.260
rematch 62
Rembrandt 407
remedial 228.3.1
remedy 16.63
remember 17.24
remembrance 321
remex 496
remind 135
reminder 17.103
remindful 226
reminisce 300.23
reminiscence 321.22
reminiscent 420.70
remise 516.4
remiss 300.19
remission 261.71
remit 371.19
remittal 228.102
remittance 321.24

remittee 5.22
remittent 420.76
remitter 17.342.2
remnant 420
remodel 228.34
remonetize 516.12
remonstrance 321
remonstrant 420
remonstrate 367
remonstrative 485.15.11
remontoir 1
remora 17.279.1
remorse 303
remorseful 226.6
remorseless 300
remorselessness 300.33
remote 376
remoteness 300
remould 120
removable 228.16.62
removal 228.122
removalist 436.7
remove 490
removed 150
remover 17.419
remunerate 367.23
remuneration 261.67.22
remunerative 485.15.10
Remus 310
renaissance 321
renal 228.59
rename 231
renascent 420
Renault 12.52
rend 131
render 17.101
rendering 265.58
rendezvous 15
rendition 261.71
rendzina 17.230
renegade 85.1
renege 183
renew 15.9
renewable 228.16.7
renewal 228.10
Renfrew 15
reniform 238.1
renin 252
rennet 371
rennin 252.16

Reno 12.54
Renoir 1
renounce 319
renovate 367,
  367.37
renovation 261.67
renown 258
renowned 139
rent 410
rental 228.110
rented 91.46
renter 17.368
renunciation
  261.67.1.4
renvoi 11
reopen 261
reorganize 516.7
rep 271
repaint 409
repair 4.6
repairable
  228.16.33
repairer 17.271
repairman 261.46
repand 128
reparable
  228.16.35.1
reparation
  261.67.22
repartee 5
repartition 261.71
repast 431
repatriate 367.1,
  371.1
repatriation
  261.67.1
repay 2
repayment 420.29
repeal 217
repeat 370
repeatable
  228.16.48
repeated 91.37
repeatedly 16.148
repeater 17.341
repechage 359
repel 215
repellent 420.26
repent 410
repentance 321.26
repentant 420
repercussion
  261.74
repertoire 1.17
repertory 16.274.43

repetend 131.5
repetition 261.71.7
repetitious 310.58
repetitive 485.12
rephrase 509
repine 253
replace 295
replaceable
  228.16.36
replacement 420.44
replay 2
replenish 353.6
replete 370
repletion 261.70
replevin 252.28
replevy 16.380
replica 17.34
replication
  261.67.5
reply 7.8
repoint 416
repone 257
report 374.1
reportage 359
reportedly 16.148
reporter 17.345
repose 520
reposit 371.39
reposition 261.71.9
repository
  16.274.41
repossess 296
repossession
  261.68
repot 373
repoussé 2.21
reprehend 131.1
reprehensible
  228.16.40
reprehension
  261.82.1
represent 410.4
re-present 410.4
representation
  261.67.32
representational
  228.63.3
representationalism
  242.35.11.5.2
representative
  485.15.15
repress 296
repression 261.68
repressive 485.2
reprieve 484

reprimand 129
reprint 412
reprisal 228
reprise 513
repro 12
reproach 70
reproachable
  228.16.13
reproachful 226
reprobate 367.4
reprobation
  261.67.3
reprobative 485.15
reproduce 309.1
reproduction
  261.79.1
reproductive
  485.19
reprography
  16.90.2
reproof 170
reprove 490
reptile 219
reptilian 261.3.11
republic 38
republican 261.13
republicanism
  242.35.14.2
republicanize 516.7
repudiate 367.1
repudiation
  261.67.1
repugn 260
repugnance 321
repugnant 420
repulse 313
repulsion 261
repulsive 485
reputable
  228.16.52
reputation
  261.67.29
repute 380.4
reputed 91.42
request 433
requiem 232
requiescat 365
require 8.3
requirement 420
requisite 371.38
requisition
  261.71.8
requital 228.103
requite 372
reredos 302

reremouse 306
rerun 259
resale 214
resaleable
  228.16.22
rescind 134
rescissible
  228.16.39
rescissory
  16.274.36
rescue 15
rescuer 17.7
research 65
researcher 17.54
reseat 370
resect 385.7
resection 261.77.5
reseda 17.83
resemblance 321.13
resemble 228.18
resent 410.4
resentful 226.11
resentment 420
reserpine 251
reservation 261.67
reserve 483
reserved 147
reservedly 16.148.1
reservist 436
reservoir 1.18
reset 368
resettle 228.100
reshape 270
reshuffle 228.42
reside 92
residence 321.5
resident 420.10.1
residential 228.96.1
residentiary
  16.274.39
residual 228.9.1
residuary 16.274.2
residue 15.7
residuum 242.3
resign 253
resignation 261.67
resignedly 16.148
resile 219
resilience 321.1
resilient 420.1
resin 252.30
resinate 367.17
resinoid 97.8
resinous 310.33
resipiscence 321.22

resist 436
resistance 321.27
resistant 420.81
resistible 228.16
resistivity
16.333.35
resistor 17.384
resit 371
resoluble 228.15
resolute 380.1
resolution 261.75.1
resolve 493
resolved 151
resolvent 420
resonance 321
resonant 420.55
resonate 367.18
resonator 17.338.8
resorb 27
resort 374
resound 139
resounding 265.22
resource 303
resourceful 226.6
respect 385
respectable 228.16
respecter 17.354
respectful 226.10
respecting 265.71
respective 485.17
respectively 16.206
respiration
261.67.22
respirator 17.338.9
respiratory
16.274.43
respire 8
respite 371
resplendence 321.7
resplendent 420.14
respond 136
respondent 420.15
response 318
responser 17.316
responsibility
16.333.9.2
responsible 228.16
responsive 485
respray 2
rest 433
restate 367
restaurant 266.2
restaurateur 3.1
restful 226
restharrow 12.60

resting 265.75
restitution 261.75
restive 485.24
restless 300
restlessness 300.33
restoration
261.67.22
restorationism
242.35.14.3
restorative 485.15
restore 9
restorer 17.276
restrain 247
restrainer 17.227
restraint 409
restrict 387
restriction 261.78
restrictive 485.18
result 406
resultant 420
résumé 2
resume 241
resumption 261.89
resupinate 371.24
resurge 195
resurgence 321
resurgent 420.19
resurrect 385.6
resurrection
261.77.4
resurrectionist
436.13.6
resuscitate 367.30
resuscitation
261.67.27
resuscitator
17.338.10
ret 368
retable 228.11
retail 214
retailer 17.162
retain 247.9
retainer 17.227
retake 34
retaliate 367.1.1
retaliation 261.67.1
retaliatory
16.274.43.1
retard 84
retardant 420.8
retardation 261.67
retarded 91.5
retarder 17.78
retch 64
rete 16.332

retention 261.82
retentive 485.21
rethink 52
retiarius 310.2.10
reticence 321.22
reticent 420.70
reticle 228.23.19
reticulate 367.13.2
reticulate 371.17.2
reticule 227.1
reticulum 242.10.1
retina 17.231
retinite 372.5
retinitis 300.62.3
retinol 220.3
retinoscopy
16.254.2
retinue 15.9
retire 8
retirement 420
retiring 265.54
retorsion 261.72
retort 374
retortion 261.72
retouch 72
retrace 295
retract 382
retractable 228.16
retractile 219.4
retraction 261.76
retractor 17.353
re-tread 86
retreat 370
retrench 79
retrenchment 420
retrial 228.4
retribution 261.75
retributive 485
retrievable
228.16.61
retrieval 228.119
retrieve 484
retriever 17.413
retro 12
retroact 382
retroaction 261.76
retroactive 485.16
retrocede 89.3
retrochoir 8
retrofire 8
retrofit 371
retroflex 496
retroflexion 261.77
retrograde 85.6
retrogress 296

retrogressive
485.2.1
retroject 385.3
retrorocket 371.10
retrorse 303
retrospect 385
retrospection
261.77
retrospective
485.17
retroussé 2.21
retry 7
retsina 17.230
return 249.1
returnable
228.16.28
retuse 309
Reuben 252
reunify 7.3
reunion 261.123
reunite 372
Reuter 17.346
revalorize 516.8
revaluation
261.67.2
revalue 15
revamp 285
reveal 217
revealing 265.29
revegetate 367.30
reveille 16.112
revel 228.118
revelation
261.67.14
revelationist
436.13.4
reveller 17.176
revelry 16.283
revenant 420.53
revenge 208
revengeful 226
revenue 15.9
revenuer 17.8
reverberate 367.23
reverberation
261.67.22
reverberator
17.338.9
reverberatory
16.274.43
revere 6.11
reverence 321.20.1
reverend 143
reverent 420.65
reverential 228.96.2

reverie 16.274
revers 6.11
reversal 228.84
reverse 297.2
reversi 16.298.1
reversible 228.16.38
reversion 261.69
reversioner 17.239
revert 369.1
revest 433
revet 368
revetment 420
review 15
reviewer 17.8
revile 219
revise 516.15
revision 261.91.2
revisionism 242.35.14
revisory 16.274.53
revitalize 516.3
revival 228.121
revivalism 242.35.11
revivalist 436.7
revive 486
revivify 7.3
reviviscence 321.22
revocable 228.16
revocation 261.67.6
revoice 304
revoke 42
revolt 405
revolting 265
revolute 380.1
revolution 261.75.1
revolutionary 16.274.29
revolutionize 516.7
revolve 493
revolver 17.423
revolving 265
revue 15
revulsion 261
revulsive 485
reward 95
rewardable 228.16.16
rewarding 265.15
rewind 135
rewinder 17.103
rewire 8
reword 87
rework 36

Rex 496
Reykjavik 38
Reynard 103
rhabdomancy 16.309
Rhaetian 261.70
Rhaetic 38.51
rhapsodic 38.9
rhapsodist 436.3
rhapsodize 516
rhapsody 16.72
rhatany 16.237
Rhea 17.2
rhea 17.2
Rhemish 353
Rhenish 353.6
rheobase 295.1
rheology 16.108.4.1
rheometer 17.342.3.1
rheostat 365
rhesus 310
rhetor 17.341
rhetoric 38.44
rhetorical 228.23.17
rhetorician 261.71
rheum 241
rheumatic 38.49
rheumatics 498.11
rheumatism 242.35.20
rheumatoid 97
rheumatology 16.108.4.15
rheumy 16.221
rhinal 228.61
Rhine 253
Rhineland 143
rhinestone 257
rhinitis 300.62
rhino 12
rhinoceros 310.50
rhinology 16.108.4
rhinoplasty 16.361.1
rhinoscopy 16.254.2
rhizobium 242.2
rhizocarpous 310
rhizoid 97
rhizome 239
rhizomorph 166.1
rhizomorphous 310.18

rhizopod 94.1
rhizosphere 6.1
rhodamine 251.4
Rhodes 529
Rhodesia 17.325
Rhodian 261.3.6
rhodinal 212
rhodium 242.2.4
rhododendron 261
rhodonite 372.6
rhombic 38
rhombohedral 228.78
rhombohedron 261
rhomboid 97
rhombus 310
rhonchus 310
Rhondda 17.104
Rhône 257
rhotic 38.55
rhubarb 19
rhyme 236
rhyolite 372.4
rhythm 242.33
rhythmic 38.30
rhythmical 228.23
rhythmics 498
ria 17.2
rial 228.4
Rialto 12.82
riata 17.337
rib 24
ribald 122
ribaldry 16.278
riband 143
Ribble 228.12
ribbon 261
ribbonwood 101
riboflavin 252
ribonuclease 509.1
ribose 520
ribosome 239
rice 301
ricer 17.303
ricercare 2.17
rich 67
Richard 103
Richardson 261
Richelieu 3
riches 515
Richmond 143
richness 300
ricin 252.22
rick 38
rickets 339

rickettsia 17.3
rickety 16.333.4
rickrack 32
rickshaw 9
ricochet 2
ricotta 17.344
rictus 310
rid 91
riddance 321.5
ridden 261.24
riddle 228.32
ride 92
rider 17.84
riderless 300.13
ridge 197
ridgepole 223
ridgetree 5
ridgeway 2.29
ridicule 227.1
ridiculous 310.25.2
riding 265.14
Ridley 16.148
ridotto 12.77
riesling 265
Rif 163
rife 164
riff 163
riffle 228.41
riffler 17.190
riffraff 157
rifle 228
riflebird 87
rifleman 261
riflery 16.283
rifling 265
rift 398
rig 184
Riga 17.128
rigadoon 260
rigatoni 16.233
rigger 17.129
rigging 265
right 372
righten 261.100
righteous 310
righteousness 300.34
rightful 226.9
right-handed 91.12
right-hander 17.98
rightish 353
rightism 242.35
rightist 436
rightly 16.190
rightness 300.39

rigid 91.15
rigidify 7.3.1
rigidity 16.333.5
rigmarole 223.3
rigor 9
rigorism 242.35.15
rigor mortis 300.63
rigorous 310.50
rigour 17.129
Rig-Veda 17.79
Rijeka 17.31
rile 219
Riley 16.121
rill 218
rillet 371.16
rim 235
rime 236
Rimini 16.229.3
rimose 305
rimrock 40
Rimsky-Korsakov 165
rimy 16.217
rind 135
rinderpest 433
ring 265
ringbolt 405
ringdove 489
ringent 420.23
ringer 17.246
ringgit 371
ringleader 17.82
ringlet 371
ringmaster 17.380
ringside 92
ringworm 233
rink 52
rinse 317
rinser 17.315
Rio 12.2
Rio de Janeiro 12.63
riot 381.2
rioter 17.352.1
riotous 310.68
rip 274
riparian 261.3.21
ripcord 95
ripe 275
ripen 261
ripeness 300
ripieno 12.52
Ripon 261
riposte 438
ripper 17.253

ripping 265
ripple 228.66
ripplet 371
ripply 16.177
ripsnorter 17.345
riptide 92
Rip Van Winkle 228.29
rise 516
risen 261.126
riser 17.441
risibility 16.333.9.2.2
risible 228.16.63
rising 265.82
risk 58
risker 17.48
risky 16.41
Risorgimento 12.84
risotto 12.77
risqué 2
Riss 300
rissole 223.4
ritardando 12.23
rite 372
ritenuto 12.80
ritornello 12.40
ritual 228.9.3
ritualism 242.35.11.3
ritualize 516.3.3
ritzy 16.317
rival 228.121
rivalry 16.283
rive 486
riven 261.114
river 17.414
riverbed 86.1
riverine 253.7
riverside 92.8
rivet 371
Riviera 17.271
rivière 4.1
rivulet 371.17
rix-dollar 17.168
Riyadh 84
riyal 213
roach 70
road 98
roadbed 86
roadblock 40
roadholding 265.18
roadhouse 306
roadroller 17.171

roadrunner 17.237
roadstead 86
roadway 2
roadwork 36
roadworthy 16.375
roam 239
roamer 17.215
roan 257
Roanoke 42
roar 9
roaring 265.55
roast 441
roasting 265
rob 26
roband 143
robber 17.16
robbery 16.274.3
robe 28
Robert 381
Robespierre 4
robin 252
robinia 17.3.34
Robinson 261
roble 2.13
roborant 420.65
robot 373
Rob Roy 11
robust 443
roc 40
rocaille 7
rocambole 223
Rochdale 214
Rochester 17.384
rochet 371
rock 40
rockabilly 16.120
rock-and-roll 223
Rockefeller 17.163
rocker 17.36
rockery 16.274.5
rocket 371.10
rocketeer 6
rocketry 16.285
rockfish 353
Rockford 103
Rockies 515
rockoon 260
rockrose 520
rockweed 89
rocky 16.27
rococo 12.12
rod 94
rode 98
rodent 420
rodenticide 92.7

rodeo 12.3
rodomontade 85
roe 12
roebuck 43
roentgen 261
roentgenogram 229.1
roentgenotherapy 16.254
rogation 261.67.11
rogatory 16.274.43.3
Roger 17.152
Roget 2
rogue 188
roguery 16.274
roguish 353
roil 222
roily 16.125
roister 17.386
Roland 143
role 223
Rolf 173
roll 223
rollaway 2.28
rollbar 1
roller 17.171
rollick 38.22
rolling 265.32
rollmop 276
rollneck 35
Rolls Royce 304
roly-poly 16.126
romaine 247
romaji 16.99
Roman 261.49
romance 314
Romanes 300.26
Romanesque 57
Romanism 242.35.14
Romanist 436.13
Romanize 516.7
Romano 12.51
Romanov 165
romantic 38.62
romanticism 242.35.16
romanticize 516.10
Romany 16.237
Romberg 182
Rome 239
Romeo 12.3
romp 288
rompers 524

Romulus 310.25
rondeau 12
rondel 228
rondelet 368
rondo 12
rondure 10
rone 257
Roneo 12.3.4
ronggeng 264
roo 15
rood 102
roof 170
roofing 265
rook 44
rookery 16.274
rookie 16.31
room 241
roomette 368
roomful 226
roommate 367
roomy 16.221
roorback 32
roose 523
Roosevelt 402
roost 444
rooster 17.389
root 380
rootle 228.108
rootless 300
rootstock 40
rope 278
ropewalk 41
ropy 16.251
roque 42
Roquefort 9
roquelaure 9.8
rorqual 228
Rorschach 33
rort 374
Rosa 17.442
rosace 295
rosaceous 310.56
rosarian 261.3.21
Rosario 12.3.5
rosarium 242.2.14
rosary 16.274
Roscius 310.2
Roscommon 261
rosé 2.31
rose 520
roseate 367.1
rosebay 2
rosebud 100
rosehip 274
rosella 17.163

rosemaling 265.26
rosemary 16.274
roseola 17.176
rosery 16.274
Rosetta 17.339
rosette 368
rosewood 101
Rosh Hashanah
  17.226
Rosicrucian 261.75
Rosie Lee 5.8
rosin 252
Rosinante 16.353
ROSPA 17.267
Ross 302
Ross and Cromarty
  16.344
Rossetti 16.330
Rossini 16.228
rostellum 242.8
roster 17.385
Rostock 40
Rostov 487
Rostropovich 67
rostrum 242.23
rosy 16.399
rot 373
rota 17.347
Rotarian 261.3.21
rotary 16.274
rotate 367.31
rotation 261.67.28
rotative 485.15.13
rotator 17.338
rote 376
rotenone 257
rotgut 378
Rotherham 242.21
Rothermere 6.3
Rothschild 117
roti 16.339
rotifer 17.114
rotisserie 16.274.36
rotl 228.104
rotogravure 10
rotor 17.347
Rotorua 17.8
rotten 261.101
rottenness 300.31
rotter 17.344
Rotterdam 229
rotting 265.68
Rottweiler 17.167
rotund 140
rotunda 17.108

Rouault 12
rouble 228
roué 2.2
rouge 364
rouge et noir 1.16
rough 168
roughage 197
roughcast 431
roughen 261
roughish 353
roughly 16.159
roughneck 35
roughness 300
roughshod 94
roulade 84
rouleau 12
roulette 368
round 139
roundabout 377.1
rounded 91.14
roundel 228
roundelay 2.11
rounder 17.107
rounders 524
Roundhead 86
roundhouse 306
roundish 353
roundly 16.156
roundness 300
roundsman 261
roundup 279
roundworm 233
roup 278, 280
rouse 521
rousing 265
Rousseau 12
roust 442
rout 377
route 380
routemarch 63
router 17.348
routine 251
roux 15
rove 488
rover 17.417
row 12, 13
rowan 261.6
rowboat 376
rowdiness 300.23
rowdy 16.68
rowel 228.8
rower 17.6
rowing 265.4
rowlock 46
Roy 11

royal 228.6
royalism 242.35.11
royalist 436.7
royalty 16.352.1
rub 29
rubáiyát 365
Rub' al Khali
  16.113
rubato 12.73
rubber 17.19
rubberize 516.8
rubberneck 35
rubbery 16.274
rubbing 265
rubbish 353
rubbishy 16.322
rubble 228.14
rube 30
rubefy 7.3
rubella 17.163
rubellite 372.3
Rubens 548
rubeola 17.176
rubescent 420.67
Rubicon 261.13
rubicund 143
rubidium 242.2.3
rubiginous 310.33
Rubinstein 253
rubious 310.2
rubric 38
rubricate 367.5
ruby 16.14
ruche 358
ruching 265
ruck 43
rucksack 32
ruckus 310
ruction 261.79
rudaceous 310.56
rudbeckia 17.3
rudd 100
rudder 17.90
rudderhead 86.5
ruddle 228.36
ruddock 46
ruddy 16.69
rude 102
rudeness 300
ruderal 228.76
rudiment 420.31
rudimentary
  16.274.47
rudish 353
Rudolf 173

rue 15
rueful 226
ruff 168
ruffian 261.3
ruffle 228.42
ruffler 17.191
rufous 310
Rufus 310
rug 189
ruga 17.136
rugby 16
rugged 91
ruggedize 516
ruggedness 300.28
rugger 17.134
rugose 305
Ruhr 10
ruin 252
ruination 261.67.18
ruinous 310.33
Ruisdael 213
rule 227
ruler 17.175
ruling 265
rum 240
Rumania 17.3.31
Rumanian 261.3.15
rumba 17.27
rumble 228
rumbustious 310.2
Rumelia 17.3.20
rumen 248.3
ruminant 420.53.3
ruminate 367.17.6
rumination
  261.67.18.7
ruminative
  485.15.7
rummage 197
rummer 17.216
rummy 16.220
rumour 17.217
rumoured 103.5
rump 289
Rumpelstiltskin
  252
rumple 228
rumpus 310.42
run 259
runabout 377.1
runch 82
runcinate 371.24
Runcorn 255
rundle 228
rune 260

rung 267
runic 38
runnel 228
runner 17.237
running 265.45
runny 16.235
Runnymede 89
runt 419
runway 2
Runyon 261
rupee 5
Rupert 381
rupture 17
rural 228.75
ruralize 516.3
Rurik 38.43
Ruritania 17.3.31.2
Ruse 2.21
ruse 523
rush 356
rushes 515
rushy 16.324
rusk 60
Ruskin 252
Russ 307
Russell 228.87
russet 371
Russia 17.329
Russian 261.74
Russianize 516.7
Russky 16.42
Russophile 219.1
Russophobe 28
rust 443
rustic 38
rusticate 367.5
rustle 228.87
rustler 17.199
rustproof 170
rusty 16.368
rut 378
rutabaga 17.125
Ruth 463
Ruthenia 17.3.33
Ruthenian 261.3.16
ruthenium 242.2
Rutherford 103
ruthful 226.14
ruthless 300
ruthlessness 300.33
rutilated 91.34.5
rutile 219
Rutland 143
ruttish 353
rutty 16.341

Ruwenzori 16.269
Rwanda 17.98
Ryan 261.4
Rydal 228.33
rye 7
ryokan 261.14
ryot 381.2

S

Saab 19
Saar 1
Saba 17.10
sabadilla 17.166
Sabah 1
sabayon 254
sabbat 365
Sabbatarian
  261.3.21
Sabbath 464
sabbatical
  228.23.18
Sabellian 261.3.9
sabin 252
Sabine 253
sable 228.11
sabotage 359
saboteur 3.1
sabra 17.281
sabre 17.11
sabretache 349
sabulous 310.25
sac 32
sacaton 257.3
saccharide 92.6
saccharify 7.3.4
saccharimeter
  17.342.2.1
saccharin 252.20
saccharine 251.7,
  253.7
saccharoid 97.12
saccharose 520.3
sacculate 371.17.1
saccule 227
sacerdotal 228.106
sacerdotalism
  242.35.11
sachet 2.22
sack 32
sackbut 378

sackcloth 459
sacking 265
sacral 228
sacrament 420.35
sacramental
  228.110.3
sacramentalism
  242.35.11.6
Sacramento 12.84
sacrarium 242.2.14
sacred 91
sacredness 300.28
sacrifice 301
sacrificial 228.93
sacrilege 197.1
sacrilegious 310.21
sacristan 261.107
sacristy 16.366
sacroiliac 32.1.1
sacrosanct 391
sacrum 242
sad 83
Sadat 365
sadden 261.19
saddle 228.31
saddlebag 178
saddlecloth 459
saddler 17.183
saddlery 16.274
saddletree 5
Sadducee 5
Sade 84
sadiron 261.4
sadism 242.35
sadist 436
sadistic 38.70
sadly 16.146
sadness 300
sadomasochism
  242.35.6
sadomasochistic
  38.70
Sadowa 17.417
safari 16.261
safe 159
safeguard 84
safekeeping 265.49
safety 16
saffian 261.3
safflower 14
saffron 261
Safid Rud 102
safrole 223
sag 178
saga 17.124

sagacious 310.56
sagacity 16.333.25
sagamore 9.9
sage 193
sagebrush 356
saggar 17.123
Sagitta 17.342
sagittal 228.102
Sagittarius
  310.2.10
sagittate 367.30
sago 12.27
Saguache 62
saguaro 12.61
Sahaptin 252.25
Sahara 17.268
Saharan 261
sahib 24
said 86
Saida 17.83
saiga 17.130
Saigon 254
sail 214
sailable 228.16.22
sailcloth 459
sailing 265.27
sailor 17.162
sailplane 247
sainfoin 256
saint 409
Saint Austell
  228.116
sainted 91.45
Sainte Foy 11
Saint Helena
  17.230
Saint Helier
  17.3.19
sainthood 101
Saint Kilda 17.95
Saint Kitts 339
Saint Leger 17.147
saintly 16.196
Saint Moritz 339
saintpaulia 17.3
Saint Petersburg
  182
Saint-Simonianism
  242.35.14.1
Saint Vitus 310.65
Saipan 245
Saïs 300
saithe 454
Saiva 17.415
Sakai 7

sake 16.20, 34
saker 17.30
Saki 16.20
saki 16.20
Saktas 310
Sakyamuni 16.236
sal 212
salaam 230.1
salacious 310.56.3
salad 103
Saladin 252
salamander 17.98
Salambria 17.3.43
salami 16.211
Salamis 300.20
salaried 91.27
salary 16.274.15
salchow 12
sale 214
saleable 228.16.22
Salem 242
salep 271
saleratus 310.62
saleroom 241
salesclerk 33
salesman 261
salesmanship 274.2
Salford 103
Salian 261.3.8
salic 38.19
salicet 368.7
salicin 252.21
salicional 228.63.5
salicornia 17.3.35
salicylate 367.12
salient 420.1
salientian 261.3
salify 7.3
salina 17.232
saline 253
Salinger 17.157
salinity 16.333.17.1
salinometer
  17.342.3
Salisbury 16.274
Salish 353
saliva 17.415
salivary 16.274.52
salivate 367.36
salivation 261.67
sallee 16.112
sallet 371
sallow 12.38
Sallust 445
Sally 16.112

sally 16.112
salmagundi 16.80
Salmanazar 17.437
salmon 261.44
salmonella 17.163
salmonoid 97.9
salol 220
Salome 16.219
salon 254
Salonika 17.34.1
saloon 260.1
saloop 280.1
Salop 281
salopette 368
salpicon 261.13
salpiglossis 300.54
salpingectomy
  16.222.5
salpinx 505
salsify 16.85
salt 404
saltant 420
saltarello 12.40
saltation 261.67
saltatorial
  228.3.12.2
saltbush 357
saltcellar 17.163
salted 91.44
salter 17.363
saltern 261
saltfish 353
saltigrade 85.5
saltire 8
saltpetre 17.341
saltwater 17.345
salty 16.351
salubrious 310.2
Saluki 16.32
salutary 16.274.42
salutation
  261.67.29
salutatory
  16.274.43
salute 380.1
Salvador 9.4
salvage 197
salvageable
  228.16.20
salvation 261.67
salvationist
  436.13.4
salve 491
salver 17.420
salverform 238.2

salvia 17.3
salvo 12
sal volatile 16.120
salvor 17.420
Salween 251
Salyut 380
samara 17.268
Samaria 17.3.38
Samaritan 261.99
samarium 242.2.14
Samarkand 128
samba 17.23
sambar 17.23
same 231
sameness 300
Samian 261.3
samisen 248
samite 372
samiti 16.333
Samnite 372
Samnium 242.2
Samoa 17.6
Samos 302
Samothrace 295
samovar 1.15
Samoyed 86
sampan 245
samphire 8
sample 228.70
sampler 17
Samson 261
Samuel 228.9
samurai 7
San 246
sanatorium
  242.2.17
sanbenito 12.76
San Bernardino
  12.54
sanctify 7.3
sanctimonious
  310.2.9.1
sanctimony 16.237
sanction 261
sanctitude 102.2
sanctity 16.333
sanctuary 16.274.2
sanctum 242
sanctum sanctorum
  242.20
Sanctus 310
sand 128
sandal 228.39
sandalwood 101
sandarac 32.3

sandbag 178
sandbank 51
sandblast 431
sander 17.98
sanderling 265
sandfly 7
sandgrouse 306
sandhi 16.77
sandhog 185
Sandhurst 434
San Diego 12.27
sandman 261
sandpaper 17.249
sandpiper 17.254
sandpit 371
Sandringham
   242.17
sandsoap 278
sandstone 257
sandstorm 238
sandwich 197
sandy 16.77
sane 247
San Fernando
   12.23
San Francisco
   12.15
sang 263
sangaree 5.17
Sangraal 214
sangria 17.2
sanguinaria 17.3.38
sanguinary
   16.274.26
sanguine 252
sanguineous
   310.2.8
sanguinolent
   420.28
Sanhedrin 252
sanicle 228.23.10
sanies 513.1
sanitarian
   261.3.21.2
sanitarium
   242.2.14
sanitary 16.274.41
sanitation
   261.67.27
sanitize 516.12
sanity 16.333.14
San Jose 2.31
San Juan 246
sank 51
San Marino 12.54

sannyasi 16.295
San Salvador 9.4
sans-culotte 373
sanserif 163.2
sansevieria 17.3.39
Sanskrit 371
Sanskritic 38.52
San Stefano 12.51
Santa 17.365
Santa Claus 518
Santa Cruz 523
Santa Fe 2.9
santalaceous
   310.56.3
Santee 5
Santiago 12.26
Santo Domingo
   12.36
santonica 17.34.1
sap 268
sapajou 15
sapele 16.118
saphena 17.230
sapid 91
sapient 420.1
sapling 265
sapodilla 17.166
saponaceous
   310.56
saponify 7.3
sapota 17.347
sappanwood 101
sapper 17.247
Sapphic 38.11
Sapphira 17.274
sapphire 8
sapphirine 251.7
Sappho 12
sappy 16.243
sapraemia 17.3.26
saprobe 28
saprophagous 310
saprozoic 38.2
sapsago 12.33
sapsucker 17.39
sapwood 101
saraband 128
Saracen 261
Saracenic 38.32
Saragossa 17.304
Sarah 17.271
saran 245.5
Saratoga 17.133
Sarawak 46
sarcasm 242.34

sarcastic 38.68
sarcoid 97
sarcoma 17.215
sarcophagus 310
sarcous 310.8
sard 84
Sardanapalus
   310.26
sardine 251
Sardinia 17.3.34
Sardinian 261.3.17
Sardis 300
sardius 310.2
sardonic 38.35
sardonyx 498
sargasso 12.68
sargassum 242
sarge 192
Sargent 420
Sargodha 17.88
Sargon 254
sari 16.261
Sark 33
sarmentose 305
Sarnia 17.3.30
sarong 266.2
saros 302
sarpanch 82
sarracenia 17.3.33
sarsaparilla
   17.166.3
sarsen 261.61
sartor 17.337
sartorial 228.3.12
sartorius 310.2.13
Sarum 242.18
sash 349
Saskatchewan 261
Saskatoon 260.4
saskatoon 260.4
sass 293
sassaby 16.15
sassafras 293
Sassanid 91.21
Sassenach 32
Sassoon 260
sassy 16.294
sastruga 17.136
sat 365
satai 2
Satan 261
satang 263
satanic 38.31
Satanism 242.35.14
Satanist 436.13

satchel 228
sate 367
sateen 251
satellite 372.4.1
satellitium 242.2.18
satem 242.26
satiable 228.16
satiate 367.1.5
satiety 16.333.2
satin 252
satinet 368
satinwood 101
satiny 16.229
satire 8
satiric 38.40
satirical 228.23.16
satirist 436.20
satirize 516.8
satisfaction 261.76
satisfactory
   16.274.44
satisfy 7
satrap 281
satrapy 16.254
satsuma 17.217
saturable 228.16.35
saturant 420.65
saturate 367.22
saturated 91.34.7
saturation
   261.67.22
Saturday 2.8
Saturn 249
Saturnalia
   17.3.18.1
saturniid 91.2
saturnine 253
saturnism
   242.35.14
satyagrahi 5
satyr 17.336
satyriasis 300.57.1
satyric 38.40
satyrid 91
sauce 303
saucepan 261
saucer 17.305
sauciness 300.23
saucy 16.303
Saud 99
Saudi 16.68
sauerbraten 261.95
sauerkraut 377
sauger 17.132
Saul 221

Sault Sainte Marie
  5.17
sauna 17.234
saunter 17.370
saurian 261.3.23
sauropod 94.1
saury 16.269
sausage 197
sauté 2.24
Sauternes 249
Sava 17.409
savage 197
savagery 16.282
Savaii 5
savanna 17.225
Savannah 17.225
savant 420
savate 365.3
save 482
saveloy 11.1
saver 17.410
savin 252
saving 265.77
saviour 17.436
savoir-faire 4.2
savour 17.410
savoury 16.274.50
Savoy 11
savoy 11
Savoyard 84
savvy 16.377
saw 9
sawbones 550
sawder 17.86
sawdust 443
sawfish 353
sawhorse 303
sawmill 218
sawn 255
sawyer 17.430
sax 494
saxhorn 255
saxicolous 310.26.2
saxifrage 193
Saxon 261
Saxony 16.237
saxony 16.237
saxophone 257
saxophonic 38.35.2
saxophonist 436.13
say 2
saying 265.1
sayyid 91
sazerac 32.3
scab 18

scabbard 103
scabble 228
scabby 16.5
scabies 513
scabious 310.2
scabrous 310
scad 83
scads 525
Scafell 215
scaffold 122
scaffolding 265
scag 178
scagliola 17.171
scalable 228.16.22
scalage 197
scalar 17.162
scalare 16.264
scald 118
scale 214
scaleboard 95
scalene 251
scalenus 310.32
scaler 17.162
scall 221
scallion 261.118
scallop 281.2
scallywag 178
scaloppine 16.228
scalp 282
scalpel 228
scalpellic 38.20
scalping 265
scaly 16.114
scammony 16.237
scamp 285
scamper 17.261
scampi 16
scan 245
scandal 228.39
scandalize 516.3
scandalmonger
  17.143
scandalous 310.26
Scandaroon 260.3
scandent 420
Scanderbeg 181
Scandian 261.3
scandic 38.10
Scandinavia
  17.3.53
Scandinavian
  261.3.29
scandium 242.2
scanner 17.225
scansion 261.81

scansorial 228.3.12
scant 407
scantling 265
scantness 300
scanty 16.353
scape 270
scapegrace 295
scaphopod 94.1
scapolite 372.4
scapula 17.174
scapular 17.174
scar 1
scarab 31
scarabaean 261.2.1
scarabaeid 91.1
scarabaeoid 97.1
scarabaeus 310.1
Scarborough
  17.279
scarcely 16
scarcement 420
scarcity 16.333
scare 4
scarecrow 12
scaremonger
  17.143
scarf 158
scarfskin 252
scarificator
  17.338.2
scarify 7.3
scarious 310.2.10
scarlatina 17.230
Scarlatti 16.327
scarlet 371
scarp 269
scarper 17.248
scary 16.264
scat 365
scathe 473
scathing 265
scatology 16.108.4
scatter 17.336
scatterbrain 247
scatterbrained 130
scattering 265.58
scatty 16.327
scaup 277
scavenge 209
scavenger 17.157
scenario 12.3.5
scend 131
scene 251
scenery 16.274.25
scenic 38.33

scenography
  16.90.2
scent 410
scented 91.46
sceptic 38.65
sceptical 228.23
scepticism
  242.35.16
sceptre 17.375
sceptred 103
schappe 17.247
schedule 227
Scheldt 402
schema 17.210
schematic 38.49.1
schematism
  242.35.20
schematize 516.13
scheme 234
schemer 17.210
scheming 265.36
scherzando 12.23
scherzo 12
schiller 17.166
Schiller 17.166
schilling 265.30
schipperke 16.33
schism 242.35
schismatic 38.49.4
schist 436
schistosity
  16.333.30
schistosome 239
schistosomiasis
  300.57.1
schizo 12
schizogony
  16.237.4
schizoid 97
schizont 414
schizophrenia
  17.3.33
schizophrenic
  38.32
schlemiel 217
schlep 271
schlock 40
Schmidt 371
schmooze 523
Schnabel 228
schnapps 322
schnecken 261
schnitzel 228
schnook 44
schnorrer 17.276

schnozzle 228
Schoenberg 182
schola cantorum
242.20
scholar 17.168
scholarliness
300.23
scholarly 16.131
scholarship 274.1
scholastic 38.68
scholasticate
367.5.2
scholasticism
242.35.16.6
scholiast 430.1
scholium 242.2.7
school 227
schoolboy 11
schoolhouse 306
schoolie 16.130
schooling 265
schoolmarm 230
schoolmarmish 353
schoolmaster
17.380
schoolmate 367
schoolmistress 300
schoolteacher
17.55
schooner 17.238
schorl 221
schottische 352
Schubert 381
Schumann 261.51
schuss 308
schwa 1
Schwaben 261.8
sciaenid 91.20
sciamachy 16.33
sciatic 38.49
sciatica 17.34.3
science 321.2
scienter 17.368
sciential 228.96
scientific 38.12
scientism 242.35.21
scientist 436
Scientology
16.108.4
sci-fi 7
scilicet 368.7
scilla 17.166
Scillies 515
Scilly 16.120
scimitar 17.342.2

scintigraphy 16.90
scintilla 17.166
scintillate 367.12
scintillation
261.67.12
scintillator
17.338.5
sciomancy 16.309
scion 261.4
Scipio 12.3
scirrhous 310.46
scirrhus 310.46
scissel 228.85
scissile 219.2
scission 261.91
scissors 524
sciurine 253
sciuroid 97
sclaff 157
sclera 17.272
sclerenchyma
17.211
scleritis 300.62
scleroderma 17.209
sclerodermatous
310.68
scleroid 97.10
scleroma 17.215
sclerometer
17.342.3
sclerophyll 218.1
sclerosis 300.55.5
sclerotic 38.53
sclerotomy
16.222.4
sclerous 310.45
scoff 165
scoffer 17.116
scofflaw 9
Scofield 115
scold 120
scolding 265.18
scolecite 372.9
scolex 496
scoliosis 300.55.1
scolopendrid 91
scombroid 97
sconce 318
scone 254, 257
Scone 260
scoop 280
scoot 380
scooter 17.351
scop 276
Scopas 310.39

scope 278
scopula 17.174.10
scorbutic 38.56
scorch 69
scorcher 17.58
scorching 265
score 9
scoreboard 95
scorecard 84
scorer 17.276
scoria 17.3.41
scorify 7.3
scorn 255
scornful 226
scornfulness 300.30
scorpaenid 91.20
scorpaenoid 97.7
scorper 17.256
Scorpio 12.3
scorpioid 97
scorpion 261.3
Scot 373
Scotch 68
scotch 68
Scotchman 261
scoter 17.347
scotia 17.328
Scotland 143
scotoma 17.215
scotopia 17.3.37.3
Scots 341
Scotsman 261
Scott 373
Scotticism
242.35.16.5
Scottie 16.335
Scottish 353
scoundrel 228
scour 14
scourge 195
scouse 306
scout 377
scouter 17.348
Scouting 265
scoutmaster 17.380
scow 13
scowl 224
scrabble 228
scrag 178
scraggy 16.91
scram 229
scramb 229
scramble 228.17
scrambler 17.179
scran 245

Scranton 261
scrap 268
scrapbook 44
scrape 270
scraper 17.249
scraperboard 95.1
scrapheap 273
scrappy 16.243
scratch 62
scratchy 16.46
scrawl 221
scrawny 16.232
screak 37
scream 234
screamer 17.210
scree 5
screech 66
screed 89
screen 251
screenings 552
screenplay 2
screw 15
screwball 221
screwdriver 17.415
screwy 16.4
Scriabin 252
scribble 228.12
scribbly 16.134
scribe 25
scriber 17.15
scrim 235
scrimmage 197.3
scrimp 287
scrimshank 51
scrimshaw 9
scrip 274
script 424
scriptorium
242.2.17
scriptural 228.76
scripture 17
scriptwriter 17.343
scrod 94
scrofula 17.174
scrofulous 310.25
scroll 223
Scrooge 204
scroop 280
scrotum 242.31
scrouge 202
scrounge 210
scrounger 17.158
scrub 29
scrubber 17.19
scrubby 16.13

scrubland 143
scruff 168
scruffy 16.88
scrum 240
scrummage 197
scrump 289
scrumptious 310
scrumpy 16.257
scrunch 82
scruple 228
scrupulous 310.25
scrupulousness
  300.34
scrutator 17.338
scrutineer 6.4
scrutinize 516.6
scrutiny 16.229
scry 7
scuba 17.20
scud 100
scuff 168
scuffle 228.42
scull 225
scullery 16.274
scullion 261.3.13
sculpsit 371
sculpt 427
sculptor 17
sculptural 228.76
sculpture 17
sculpturesque 57
scum 240
scumble 228
scuncheon 261
scunge 211
scungy 16.111
scunner 17.237
Scunthorpe 277
scup 279
scupper 17.258
scuppernong 266
scurf 161
scurrilous 310.23
scurry 16.272
scurvy 16.381
scut 378
scutate 367
scutcheon 261
scute 380
scutellation
  261.67.12
scutellum 242.8
scutiform 238.1
scutter 17.349
scuttle 228.107

scuttlebutt 378
scutum 242
Scylla 17.166
scyphiform 238.1
scyphistoma
  17.218
scyphus 310
scythe 477
Scythia 17.3
Scythian 261.3
sea 5
seaboard 95
seaborne 255
seacoast 441
seacock 40
seadog 185
seafarer 17.271
seafaring 265.52
seafood 102
seafront 419
seagirt 369
seagoing 265.4
seal 217
sealant 420
sealer 17.165
sealery 16.274
sealskin 252
Sealyham 242.2.5
seam 234
seaman 261.47
seamanly 16.174
seamanship 274.2
seamark 33
seamless 300
seamount 418
seamstress 300
seamy 16.215
Sean 255
seance 315
seaplane 247
seaport 374
seaquake 34
sear 6
search 65
searcher 17.54
searching 265
searchlight 372
searing 265.53
seascape 270
seashell 215
seashore 9
seasick 38
seasickness 300.27
seaside 92
season 261.125

seasonable
  228.16.31.2
seasonal 228.63
seasoning 265.46
seat 370
seated 91.37
seating 265
Seaton 261.98
Seattle 228.97
seawan 261
seaward 103
seawards 531
seaware 4
seaway 2
seaweed 89
seaworthy 16.375
sebaceous 310.56
Sebastopol 228
sebum 242
sec 35
secant 420.6
secateurs 511
secco 12.9
secede 89.2
secession 261.68
seclude 102
secluded 91
seclusion 261.93
seclusive 485.8
second 136
second 143
secondary 16.274
second-best 433
seconde 136
seconder 17.109
second-hand 128
secondly 16.157
secondment 420
second-rate 367
second-sight 372
secrecy 16.300
secret 371
secretarial 228.3.10
secretariat 381.1
secretary 16.274.43
secrete 370
secretion 261.70
secretive 485.12
secretory 16.274
sect 385
sectarian 261.3.21
sectary 16.274.45
sectile 219.5
section 261.77
sectional 228.63.8

sector 17.354
secular 17.174.4
secularity
  16.333.20.3
secularize 516.8.1
secund 140
secure 10.3
security 16.333.23
sedan 245.1
sedate 367.8
sedation 261.67.7
sedative 485.15
sedentary
  16.274.48
Seder 17.79
sedge 194
Sedgemoor 10
sedilia 17.3
sediment 420.31.1
sedimental
  228.110.2
sedimentary
  16.274.47
sedimentation
  261.67.32.1
sedimentous
  310.70
sedition 261.71.1
seditionary
  16.274.29.3
seditious 310.58.1
seduce 309
seducer 17.308
seduction 261.79
seductive 485.19
seductress 300
sedulous 310.25.3
sedum 242
see 5
Seebeck 35
seed 89
seedbed 86
seedcake 34
seedcase 295
seeder 17.82
seedless 300
seedling 265
seedy 16.62
seeing 265.2
seek 37
seeker 17.33
seel 217
seem 234
seeming 265.36
seemingly 16.175

seemly 16.166
seen 251
seep 273
seepage 197
seer 17.2
seersucker 17.39
seesaw 9
seethe 475
Seferis 300.44
segment 420
segmental 228.110
segmentation 261.67.32
Segovia 17.3.55
segregate 367.10
segregation 261.67.10
segregationist 436.13.4
seigneur 3
Seine 247
seise 513
seisin 252
seism 242
seismic 38
seismograph 158.1
seismography 16.90.2
seismology 16.108.4
seismoscope 278.1
seize 513
seizing 265
seizure 17.334
sejant 420
Sejm 231
Sekondi 5
selachian 261.3
Selangor 17.245
seldom 242
select 385.4
selection 261.77.2
selective 485.17
selectivity 16.333.35
selector 17.354
selenite 372.5
selenium 242.2
selenography 16.90.2
selenology 16.108.4.10
Seleucid 91.30
Seleucus 310.13
self 172

self-assured 96
self-catering 265.58
self-centred 103
self-confidence 321.5
self-confident 420.10
self-conscious 310
self-contained 130
self-control 223
self-deception 261.84
self-defence 316
self-denial 228.4
self-esteem 234
selfheal 217
selfhood 101
self-indulgent 420.21
self-inflicted 91
selfish 353.3
selfishness 300.35
selfless 300
selflessness 300.33
self-made 85
self-opinionated 91.34
self-pity 16.333
self-portrait 371
self-possessed 433
selfpossession 261.68
self-propelled 113
self-raising 265.81
self-respect 385
self-respecting 265.71
self-righteous 310
self-sacrifice 301
selfsame 231
self-service 300
self-sufficient 420.74
self-taught 374
self-willed 116
Seljuk 45
Selkirk 36
sell 215
seller 17.163
Sellotape 270
selva 17.421
selvage 197
semantic 38.62
semantics 498.14
semaphore 9.6

semaphoric 38.41
sematic 38.49.1
semblance 321.13
semé 2
sememe 234
semen 248
semester 17.382
semi 16.213
semiaquatic 38.49
semiarid 91.25
semiautomatic 38.49.2
semibold 120
semibreve 484
semicircle 228.22
semicircular 17.174.5
semicolon 261.43
semiconductor 17.357
semiconscious 310
semiconsciousness 300.34
semidetached 395
semidome 239
semifinal 228.61
semifinalist 436.7
semifluid 91.3
semiliterate 371.35
semilunar 17.238
seminal 228.60.3
seminar 1
seminarian 261.3.21.1
seminary 16.274.26
seminiferous 310.50.2
Seminole 223
semiotic 38.53
semiotics 498
semiparasitic 38.52.3
semipermeable 228.16.2
semiprecious 310
semipro 12
semiprofessional 228.63.4
semiquaver 17.410
Semiramis 300.20
semirigid 91.15
semiskilled 116
semisolid 91.18
Semite 372
Semitic 38.52

Semitics 498
Semitist 436.24
semitone 257.2
semivowel 228.8
semolina 17.230
sempiternal 228.58
semplice 16.49
sen 248
senary 16.274.25
senate 371
senator 17.352
senatorial 228.3.12.2
send 131
Sendai 7
sendel 228
sender 17.101
sendoff 165
Seneca 17.34
senega 17.129
Senegal 221
Senegambia 17.3.5
senescence 321.21
senescent 420.67.1
seneschal 228.93
senile 219
senility 16.333.9.3
senior 17.435
seniority 16.333.22
Senlac 32
senna 17.228
Sennacherib 24
Sennar 1
sennet 371
sennit 371
señor 9
señorita 17.341
sensate 367.29
sensation 261.67.26
sensational 228.63.3
sensationalism 242.35.11.5.2
sensationalist 436.7.5
sensationalistic 38.70.2
sense 316
senseless 300.16
senselessness 300.33.1
sensibilia 17.3.21
sensibility 16.333.9.2
sensible 228.16.40

481

sensillum 242
sensitive 485.12
sensitivity 16.333.35
sensitize 516.12
sensitometer 17.342.3
sensor 17.314
sensorial 228.3.12
sensorimotor 17.347
sensorium 242.2.17
sensory 16.274.38
sensual 228.9
sensualism 242.35.11.3
sensualist 436.7.3
sensuality 16.333.8.2
sensuous 310.4
sensuousness 300.34.2
sent 410
sentence 321.26
sententious 310.61
sentience 321
sentient 420.1
sentiment 420.31
sentimental 228.110.2
sentimentalism 242.35.11.6
sentimentality 16.333.8.10
sentimentalize 516.3
sentinel 228.60
sentry 16.288
Senussi 16.306
Seoul 223
sepal 228
separable 228.16.35.1
separate 367.23, 371.35
separates 339
separation 261.67.22
separatism 242.35.20
separatist 436.26
separative 485.15.10
separator 17.338.9
separatrix 498.9

sepia 17.3
sepoy 11
sepsis 300.59
sept 422
septa 17.375
September 17.24
Septembrist 436
septennium 242.2
septet 368
septic 38.65
septicaemia 17.3.26
septillion 261.120
septime 234
septuagenarian 261.3.21.1
Septuagesima 17.211
Septuagint 412
septum 242
septuple 228
sepulchral 228
sepulchre 17
sepulture 17.69
sequacious 310.56
sequel 228.71
sequela 17.165
sequence 321
sequencer 17.318
sequent 420.57
sequential 228.96
sequester 17.382
sequestrate 367
sequestration 261.67
sequin 252
sequined 134
sequoia 17.5
ser 6
sera 17.272
sérac 32
seraglio 12.3
serail 7.12
Serang 263.2
seraph 171
seraphic 38.11
seraphim 235
Serapis 300
Serb 22
Serbia 17.3.2
Serbian 261.3
serdab 18
sere 6
serein 247.8
serenade 85.2
serenata 17.337

serendipity 16.333
serene 251
serenity 16.333.15
serf 161
serfdom 242
serge 195
sergeant 420
serial 228.3.11
serialism 242.35.11.2.1
serialize 516.3.2.1
seriate 371.1
seriatim 235
sericeous 310.58
sericin 252.21
sericulture 17.69
seriema 17.210
series 513.11
series-wound 139
serif 163.2
serigraph 158
serious 310.2.11
seriously 16.184
seriousness 300.34.1
sermon 261
sermonic 38.35
sermonize 516.7
serology 16.108.4
serosa 17.306
serotine 253
serous 310.45
serpent 420
serpentine 253
serpigo 12.30
serranid 91
serrate 367, 371.31
serrated 91.34.7
serration 261.67
serried 91
serrulation 261.67.13
Sertorius 310.2.13
sertularian 261.3.21
serum 242.19
serval 228
servant 420.82
serve 483
server 17.412
Servetus 310.63
service 300
serviceable 228.16.39
serviceberry 16.274

serviceman 261
serviette 368
servile 219
servility 16.333.9
serving 265.78
servitor 17.342
servitude 102.2
servo 12
servomechanism 242.35.14
sesame 16.222
sesquialtera 17.279
sesquipedalian 261.3.8
sessile 219
session 261.68
sesterce 297
sestertium 242.2
sestet 368
sestina 17.230
Sestos 302.3
set 368
seta 17.341
Seth 455
setose 305
sett 368
settee 5
setter 17.339
setting 265.65
settle 228.100
settlement 420.40
Sevan 246
seven 261.112
sevenfold 120
seventeen 251
seventeenth 469
seventh 471.1
seventieth 458
seventy 16.360
sever 17.411
several 228.76
severally 16.131
severalty 16.352
severance 321.20.1
severe 6.11
severity 16.333.21
Severn 261.112
Severus 310.45
Seville 218.3
sew 12
sewage 197
sewer 17.8
sewerage 197
sewing 265.4
sewn 257

sex 496
sexagenarian
  261.3.21.1
Sexagesima 17.211
sexism 242.35
sexist 436
sexless 300
sexology 16.108.4
sexpot 373
sext 450
sextant 420
sextet 368
sextile 219.8
sextillion 261.120
sexton 261
sextuple 228
sextuplet 371
sexual 228.9
sexuality 16.333.8.2
sexy 16.387
Seychelles 537
Seymour 9
Sfax 494
sforzando 12.23
sfumato 12.73
shabbiness 300.23
shabby 16.5
shack 32
shackle 228.19
Shackleton 261
shad 83
shadbush 357
shaddock 46
shade 85
shading 265.11
shadoof 170
shadow 12
shadowgraph 158
shadowy 16.3
Shadrach 32
shady 16.59
shaft 396
Shaftesbury 16.274
shag 178
shagbark 33
shaggy 16.91
shagreen 251
shah 1
shake 34
shakedown 258
shaken 261.11
shaker 17.30
Shakespeare 6
Shakespearean
  261.3.22

Shakespeareana
  17.226.1
shako 12.8
shaky 16.21
shale 214
shall 212
shalloon 260
shallop 281
shallot 373.1
shallow 12.38
shallowness 300.25
shalt 401
sham 229
shaman 261.44
shamanism
  242.35.14
Shamash 349
shamble 228.17
shambles 539
shame 231
shamefaced 432
shameful 226
shameless 300
shamelessness
  300.33
shammer 17.205
shampoo 15
shamrock 40
Shan 246
shandrydan 245.1
shandy 16.77
shandygaff 157
Shang 263
Shanghai 7
shanghai 7
Shangri-la 1.8
shank 51
Shankar 1
Shannon 261.55
shanny 16.223
Shansi 5
shan't 408
Shantung 267
shantung 267
shanty 16.353
shantytown 258
shape 270
shapeless 300
shapelessness
  300.33
shaper 17.249
shard 84
share 4
sharecrop 276

sharecropper
  17.255
shareholder 17.97
sharia 17.2.2
shark 33
sharkskin 252
Sharon 261
sharp 269
sharpen 261
sharpener 17.239
sharper 17.248
sharpness 300
sharpshooter
  17.351
sharp-sighted 91.39
sharp-witted 91.38
shashlik 38
shatter 17.336
shatterproof 170
shave 482
shaven 261.111
shaver 17.410
Shavian 261.3.29
shaving 265.77
shavings 552
Shaw 9
shawl 221
shawm 238
Shawnee 5
she 5
sheading 265.13
sheaf 162
shear 6
shears 514
shearwater 17.345
sheath 457
sheathe 475
sheathing 265
sheave 484
Sheba 17.13
shebang 263
shebeen 251
Shechem 242
shed 86
she'd 89
shedder 17.80
sheen 251
sheep 273
sheepcote 376
sheepdog 185
sheepfold 120
sheepish 353
sheepishness
  300.35
sheep-ked 86

sheepshank 51
sheepshead 86
sheepshearer
  17.272
sheepshearing
  265.53
sheepskin 252
sheepwalk 41
sheer 6
sheerlegs 535
Sheerness 296
sheet 370
sheeting 265
Sheffield 115
sheik 34
sheikdom 242
Sheila 17.165
shekel 228.21
sheldrake 34
shelduck 43
shelf 172
shell 215
she'll 217
shellac 32
shellback 32
Shelley 16.115
shellfire 8
shellfish, 353.3
shell-like 39
shellproof 170
Shelta 17.361
shelter 17.361
shelve 492
shelving 265
Shem 232
Shema 1.12
Shenandoah 17.6
shenanigan 261.32
Shensi 5
Shenyang 263
Sheol 223
shepherd 103
sherardize 516
Sheraton 261
sherbet 381
Sherbrooke 44
Sheridan 261.24
sherif 162
sheriff 163.2
Sherman 261
Sherpa 17.251
sherry 16.262
sherwani 16.224
Sherwood 101
she's 513

Shetland   143
shewbread   86
shiai   7
shibboleth   455
shicker   17.34
shield   115
shielder   17.94
shieling   265.29
shift   398
shiftless   300
shifty   16.347
shigella   17.163
shih-tzu   15
Shiism   242.35.1
Shiite   372
shikar   1
shikari   16.261
shillelagh   17.162
shilling   265.30
Shillong   266
shillyshally   16.112
Shiloh   12
shim   235
shimmer   17.211
shimmy   16.216
Shimonoseki   16.22
shin   252
shinbone   257
shindig   184
shindy   16.79
shine   253
shiner   17.232
shingle   228.50
shingles   539
shingly   16.163
Shinto   12
shinty   16.356
shiny   16.230
ship   274
shipboard   95
shipbuilder   17.95
shipbuilding
   265.17
shipload   98
shipmate   367
shipment   420.43
shipowner   17.236
shipper   17.253
shipping   265
shipshape   270
shipway   2
shipwreck   35
shipwright   372
shipyard   84
shiralee   5.9

Shiraz   508
Shiré   2
shire   8
shirk   36
shirker   17.32
shirr   3
shirring   265.51
shirt   369
shirting   265
shirtsleeve   484
shirtwaister   17.381
shirty   16.331
shit   371
shittah   17.342
Shittim   235
shitty   16.333
shive   486
shiver   17.414
shivery   16.274.51
Shizuoka   17.38
Shluh   15
shoal   223
shoat   376
shock   40
shocker   17.36
shocking   265.8
shockproof   170
shod   94
shoddy   16.65
shoe   15
shoebill   218
shoeblack   32
shoehorn   255
shoelace   295
shoemaker   17.30
shoeshine   253
shoestring   265
shoetree   5
shofar   1
shoji   5
shone   254
shoo   15
shoofly   7
shook   44
shoon   260
shoot   380
shooting   265
shop   276
shopkeeper   17.252
shoplifter   17.359
shoplifting   265
shopper   17.255
shopping   265
shopsoiled   119
shoptalk   41

shopwalker   17.37
shoran   245
shore   9
shoreless   300
shoreline   253
shoreward   103.8
shorn   255
short   374
shortage   197
shortbread   86
shortcake   34
shortcoming
   265.38
shorten   261.102
shortening   265.46
shortfall   221
short-haired   88
shorthand   128
shorthorn   255
shortie   16.336
shortly   16.192
shortness   300
shorts   342
short-sighted   91.39
short-sightedness
   300.28
Shoshone   16.233
Shoshonean
   261.3.18
Shostakovich   67
shot   373
shotgun   259
shot-putter   17.350
shott   373
should   101
shoulder   17.97
shouldn't   420.12
shouse   306
shout   377
shove   489
shovel   228
shoveler   17.176
shovelhead   86
shovelnose   520
show   12
showbiz   515
showboat   376
showcase   295.2
showd   99
showdown   258
shower   14
showerproof   170
showery   16.274
showgirl   216
showing   265.4

show-jumper
   17.264
showjumping
   265.50
showman   261.49
showmanship
   274.2
shown   257
showpiece   298
showplace   295
showroom   241
showy   16.3
shrank   51
shrapnel   228
shred   86
shredder   17.80
shrew   15
shrewd   102
shrewdie   16.71
shrewdness   300
shrewish   353
Shrewsbury   16.274
shriek   37
shrieval   228.119
shrievalty   16.352
shrift   398
shrike   39
shrill   218
shrimp   287
shrimper   17.263
shrine   253
shrink   52
shrinkage   197
shrive   486
shrivel   228.120
shroff   165
Shropshire   6
shroud   99
shrove   488
Shrovetide   92
shrub   29
shrubbery   16.274
shrubby   16.13
shrug   189
shrunk   54
shrunken   261
shuck   43
shucks   502
shudder   17.90
shuffle   228.42
shuffleboard   95
shuffler   17.191
shuggy   16.97
shul   227
shun   259

shunt 419
shunter 17.373
shunt-wound 139
shush 357
shut 378
shutdown 258
shuteye 7
shutter 17.349
shuttering 265.58
shuttle 228.107
shuttlecock 40
shy 7
Shylock 40
shyness 300
sial 228.4
sialagogue 185.2
Sialkot 373
sialoid 97.6
Siam 229
siamang 263
Siamese 513.8
sib 24
Sibelius 310.2.3
Siberia 17.3.39
Siberian 261.3.22
sibilant 420
sibilate 367.12
sibling 265
sibyl 218
sic 38
siccative 485.15.1
Sicilian 261.3.11
Sicily 16.120
sick 38
sickbay 2
sicken 261.13
sickening 265.46
sickle 228.23
sickly 16.142
sickness 300.27
Sicyon 254.1
Sid 91
Siddhartha 17.337
side 92
sideband 128
sideboard 95
sideboards 528
sidecar 1
sidekick 38
sidelight 372
sideline 253
sidelong 266
sidereal 228.3.11
siderite 372.8
siderosis 300.55

sideshow 12
sideslip 274
sidesman 261
sidestep 271
sidestroke 42
sideswipe 275
sidetrack 32
sidewalk 41
sidewall 221
sideward 103
sideways 509
sidewheel 217
sidewheeler 17.165
sidewinder 17.103
siding 265.14
sidle 228.33
sidler 17.187
Sidney 16.240
Sidon 261.25
siege 196
Siegfried 89
siemens 551
Siena 17.228
sienna 17.228
sierra 17.271
Sierra Leone
  16.233
siesta 17.382.1
sieve 485
sifaka 17.29
sift 398
sigh 7
sight 372
sighted 91.39
sighter 17.343
sightless 300
sightlessness
  300.33
sightly 16.190
sight-read 89
sight-reading
  265.13
sightsee 5
sightseeing 265.2
sightseer 17.2
Sigismund 143
siglos 302
sigma 17.222
sigmoid 97
Sigmund 143
sign 253
signal 228
signalize 516.3
signaller 17.176
signally 16.131

signalman 261
signatory 16.274.43
signature 17.56
signboard 95
signet 371.29
significance 321
significant 420.7
significative
  485.15.1
signify 7.3.3
signor 9
signora 17.276
signori 16.269
signorina 17.230
signpost 441
Sigurd 96
sika 17.33
sike 39
Sikh 37
Sikkim 235
silage 197
sild 116
sile 219
silence 321
silencer 17.318
silent 420
Silenus 310.32
Silesia 17.3.60
silesia 17.3.60
silex 496
silhouette 368.1
silica 17.34
silicate 371.9
siliceous 310.58
silicic 38
silicide 92.7
silicle 228.23.7
silicon 261.13
silicone 257
silicosis 300.55
silk 49
silkaline 251.3
silken 261
silkiness 300.23
silkworm 233
silky 16.34
sill 218
silliness 300.23
silly 16.120
silo 12
silt 403
silty 16.350
Silurian 261.3.24
Silvanus 310.31
silver 17.422

silverfish 353
silverpoint 416.1
silverside 92.8
silversmith 458
silverware 4.8
silverweed 89
silvery 16.274
sima 17.212
simarouba 17.20
Simeon 261.3.14
simian 261.3.14
similar 17.166
similarity
  16.333.20.2
simile 16.120
similitude 102.2
simmer 17.211
simnel 228
Simon 261
simoniac 32.1
Simonides 513.4
simony 16.237
simoom 241
simp 287
simpatico 12.11
simper 17.263
simple 228
simpleton 261
simplex 496
simplicity
  16.333.28
simplify 7.3
simplistic 38.70
simply 16.179
Simpson 261
simulant 420.27
simulate 367.13.5
simulated 91.34
simulation
  261.67.13.3
simulator 17.338.6
simulcast 431
simultaneous
  310.2.6
sin 252
Sinai 7
sinapism 242.35
Sinarquist 436
Sinatra 17.292
since 317
sincere 6
sincerely 16.119
sincerity 16.333.21
sinciput 378
Sinclair 4

Sind 134
Sindhi 16.79
sine 16.230
sine 253
sinecure 10.3
sine qua non 254
sinew 15.9
sinfonietta 17.339
sinful 226
sing 265
Singapore 9
singe 209
singer 17.246
singing 265.47
single 228.50
single-handed
  91.12
single-minded 91
single-mindedness
  300.28
singles 539
singlestick 38
singlet 371
singleton 261
singly 16.163
singsong 266
singular 17.174
singularity
  16.333.20.3
singularize 516.8.1
singultus 310
Sinhailien 248
Sinhalese 513.7
Sining 265.42
sinister 17.384.1
sinistral 228.82
sinistrorse 303
Sinitic 38.52
sink 52
sinkable 228.16.11
sinker 17.44
sinking 265.10
sinless 300
sinner 17.231
Sinn Fein 247
Sinology 16.108.4
sinter 17.369
sinuate 371.2
sinuosity
  16.333.30.2
sinuous 310.4.3
sinus 310.34
sinusitis 300.62
sinusoid 97
sinusoidal 228.35

Sioux 15
sip 274
siphon 261
siphonophore 9.6
Siple 228.67
sipper 17.253
sippet 371
sir 3
sirdar 1
sire 8
siren 261.58
sirenian 261.3.16
Siret 368
Sirius 310.2.12
sirloin 256
sirocco 12
sirrah 17.273
sirree 5.17
sirvente 410
sis 300
sisal 228
Sisera 17.279.2
siskin 252
Sisley 16.181
sissy 16.300
sister 17.384
sisterhood 101
sister-in-law 9
sisterly 16.131
Sistine 251
Sisyphean 261.2
Sisyphus 310
sit 371
sitar 1
sitcom 237
site 372
sitfast 431
sitology
  16.108.4.14
sitosterol 220.4
sitter 17.342
sitting 265.66
situate 367.2.1
situation 261.67.2
situla 17.174.12
situs 310.65
Sitwell 228
sitzkrieg 183
sitzmark 33
Siva 17.413
Sivaism 242.35
siwash 354
six 498
sixain 247
sixfold 120

six-footer 17.350
sixpence 321
sixpenny 16.237
sixte 451
sixteen 251
sixteenth 469
sixtieth 458
sixty 16
sizable 228.16.64
sizar 17.441
size 516
sized 154
sizzle 228
sjambok 40
Skagen 261
Skagerrak 32.3
skald 118
skat 365
skate 367
skateboard 95
skater 17.338
skating 265.64
skatole 223
skean 251
skedaddle 228.31
skeet 370
skeg 181
skein 247
skeletal 228.102
skeleton 261.99
skeletonize 516.7
skelf 172
skelly 16.115
Skelmersdale 214
skelp 283
sken 248
skep 271
skerrick 38.39
skerry 16.262
sket 368
sketch 64
sketchbook 44
sketchy 16.48
skew 15
skewbald 118
skewer 17.8
skewwhiff 163
ski 5
skiascope 278.1.1
skibob 26
skid 91
skidlid 91
skidpan 245
skidproof 170
skidway 2

skier 17.2
skiff 163
skiffle 228.41
skiing 265.2
skijoring 265.55
skilful 226.3
skill 218
skilled 116
skillet 371.16
skilling 265.30
skillion 261.3.11
skilly 16.120
skim 235
skimmer 17.211
skimmia 17.3.27
skimp 287
skimpy 16.255
skin 252
skinflint 412
skinful 226
skinhead 86.4
skink 52
skinless 300
skinner 17.231
skinny 16.229
skint 412
skintight 372
skip 274
skipjack 32
skiplane 247
skipper 17.253
skippet 371
skipping 265
Skipton 261
skirl 216
skirmish 353
skirr 3
skirret 371.33
skirt 369
skirter 17.340
skirting 265
skit 371
skite 372
skitter 17.342
skittish 353
skittle 228.102
skittles 539
skive 486
skiver 17.415
skivvy 16.382
skoal 223
skokiaan 246
skua 17.8
skulduggery
  16.274.10

skulk 50
skull 225
skullcap 268
skunk 54
sky 7
skydive 486
Skye 7
skyjack 32
Skylab 18
skylark 33
skylight 372
skyline 253
skyrocket 371.10
Skyros 302
skysail 214
skyscraper 17.249
skywriting 265.67
slab 18
slabber 17.9
slack 32
slacken 261
slacker 17.28
slacks 494
slag 178
slain 247
slaister 17.381
slake 34
slalom 242
slam 229
slander 17.99
slanderous 310.50
slang 263
slangy 16.241
slant 408
slanting 265.72
slantwise 516
slap 268
slapdash 349
slaphappy 16.243
slapjack 32
slapshot 373
slapstick 38
slash 349
slat 365
slate 367
slater 17.338
slather 17.401
slating 265.64
slattern 261.94
slaty 16.329
slaughter 17.345
slaughterer 17.279
slaughterhouse 306
slaughterman
   261.52

Slav 481
slave 482
slaver 17.410
slavery 16.274.50
slavey 16.379
Slavic 38
slavish 353
slavocracy 16.307.5
Slavonia 17.3.36
Slavonic 38.35
slay 2
sleave 484
sleazy 16.395
sled 86
sledge 194
sledgehammer
   17.205
sleek 37
sleekness 300
sleep 273
sleeper 17.252
sleepiness 300.23
sleepless 300
sleeplessness
   300.33
sleepwalk 41
sleepwalker 17.37
sleepwalking 265.9
sleepy 16.247
sleepyhead 86.2
sleet 370
sleeve 484
sleeveless 300
sleeving 265.79
sleigh 2
sleight 372
slender 17.101
slenderize 516.8
slenderness 300.26
slept 422
sleuth 463
sleuthhound 139
slew 15
slice 301
slicer 17.303
slick 38
slickenside 92
slicker 17.34
slid 91
slide 92
slider 17.84
sliding 265.14
slight 372
slighting 265.67
slightly 16.190

Sligo 12.30
slim 235
slime 236
slimmer 17.211
slimming 265
slimness 300
slimsy 16.403
slimy 16.217
sling 265
slingback 32
slingshot 373
slink 52
slinky 16.37
slip 274
slipcase 295
slipknot 373
slipnoose 309
slipover 17.417
slippage 197.8
slipper 17.253
slipperwort 369
slippery 16.274.30
slippy 16.248
slipsheet 370
slipshod 94
slipslop 276
slipstream 234
slipway 2
slit 371
slither 17.405
sliver 17.414
slivovitz 339
Sloane 257
slob 26
slobber 17.16
slobbery 16.274.3
sloe 12
slog 185
slogan 261
sloganeer 6.5
sloop 280
sloot 380
slop 276
slope 278
sloping 265
sloppiness 300.23
sloppy 16.250
slopwork 36
slosh 354
slot 373
sloth 461
slothful 226
slouch 71
sloucher 17.60
Slough 13

slough 13, 168
Slovak 32
Slovakia 17.3
sloven 261.117
Slovene 251
Slovenia 17.3.33
slovenly 16.174
slow 12
slowcoach 70
slowdown 258
slowly 16.126
slowness 300.25
slowpoke 42
slub 29
slubberdegullion
   261.3.13
sludge 203
slug 189
slugabed 86.1
sluggard 103
slugger 17.134
sluggish 353
sluice 309
sluicegate 367
slum 240
slumber 17.27
slumberer 17.279
slumberous 310.50
slump 289
slung 267
slunk 54
slur 3
slurp 272
slurry 16.272
slush 356
slushy 16.324
slut 378
sluttish 353
sly 7
slyness 300
slype 275
smack 32
smacker 17.28
small 221
smallboy 11
smallholder 17.97
smallholding
   265.18
smallish 353
smallness 300
smallpox 499
smalt 404
smarm 230
smarmy 16.211
smart 366

smart aleck 38.19
smarten 261.95
smartie 16.328
smartness 300
smash 349
smasher 17.321
smashing 265
- smatter 17.336
smattering 265.58
smaze 509
smear 6
smectic 38.60
smegma 17.221
smell 215
smelly 16.115
smelt 402
smelter 17.361
smew 15
smidgen 261.37
smilax 494
smile 219
smirch 65
smirk 36
smit 371
smite 372
Smith 458
smithereens 547
Smithsonian
  261.3.18
smithsonite 372.6
smithy 16.376
smitten 261.99
smock 40
smocking 265.8
smog 185
smoke 42
smokejack 32
smokeless 300
smoker 17.38
smokestack 32
smoking 265
smoko 12.12
smoky 16.29
Smollett 371
smolt 405
smooch 74
smoodge 204
smooth 479
smoothbore 9
smoothen 261
smoothness 300
smorgasbord 95
smote 376
smother 17.408
smoulder 17.97

smriti 16.333
smudge 203
smudgy 16.107
smug 189
smuggle 228
smuggler 17.193
smuggling 265
smugly 16.161
smugness 300
smut 378
smutch 72
smutty 16.341
Smyrna 17.229
snack 32
snackette 368
snaffle 228
snafu 15
snag 178
snail 214
snake 34
snakebite 372
snakelike 39
snakeroot 380
snakeskin 252
snaky 16.21
snap 268
snapdragon 261.30
snapper 17.247
snappy 16.243
snapshot 373
snare 4
snarl 213
snatch 62
snatchy 16.46
snath 452
snazzy 16.391
sneak 37
sneakers 524
sneaking 265
sneaky 16.24
sneck 35
sned 86
sneer 6
sneeze 513
snib 24
snick 38
snicker 17.34
snicket 371.9
snide 92
sniff 163
sniffle 228.41
sniffy 16.85
snifter 17.359
snigger 17.129
sniggle 228.46

snip 274
snipe 275
sniper 17.254
snippet 371
snips 327
snitch 67
snivel 228.120
snivelling 265
snob 26
snobbery 16.274.3
snobbish 353
snobbishness
  300.35
Sno-Cat 365
snog 185
snood 102
snook 45
snooker 17.41
snoop 280
snooper 17.259
snooperscope 278.1
snoot 380
snooty 16.343
snooze 523
snore 9
snorer 17.276
snorkel 228
snort 374
snorter 17.345
snot 373
snotty 16.335
snout 377
snow 12
snowball 221
snowballing 265.31
snowberry 16.274
snowbird 87
snowblink 52
snowbound 139
snowcap 268
snowcapped 421
Snowdon 261
Snowdonia 17.3.36
snowdrift 398
snowdrop 276
snowfall 221
snowfield 115
snowflake 34
snowman 261.49
snowmobile 217
snowplough 13
snowshed 86
snowshoe 15
snowstorm 238
snowy 16.3

snub 29
snuff 168
snuffbox 499
snuffer 17.118
snuffle 228.42
snuffly 16.159
snuffy 16.88
snug 189
snuggery 16.274.10
snuggle 228
snye 7
so 12
soak 42
soaking 265
so-and-so 12
soap 278
soapbark 33
soapbox 499
soapolallie 16.112
soapstone 257
soapwort 369
soapy 16.251
soar 9
sob 26
sobeit 371
sober 17.18
soberness 300.26
sobriety 16.333.2
sobriquet 2.7
socage 197
soccer 17.36
sociable 228.16.44
social 228.94
socialism 242.35.11
socialist 436.7
socialistic 38.70.2
socialite 372.4
sociality 16.333.8.1
socialize 516.3
society 16.333.2
Socinian 261.3.17
sociobiology
  16.108.4.2
socioeconomic
  38.29.1
sociologist 436.4
sociology
  16.108.4.1
sociometry
  16.285.2.1
sociopath 452
sock 40
sockdologer 17.154
socket 371.10
sockeye 7

socle 228.25
socman 261
Socrates 513.17
Socratic 38.49
sod 94
soda 17.88
sodalite 372.4
sodality 16.333.8
sodamide 92.3
sodden 261.26
sodding 265
sodium 242.2.4
Sodom 242
sodomite 372
sodomy 16.222
sofa 17.117
sofar 1
soffit 371
Sofia 17.3.11
soft 399
softa 17.360
soften 261
softener 17.239
softhearted 91.33
softheartedness
 300.28
softness 300
software 4
softwood 101
softy 16.348
SOGAT 365
soggy 16.94
soh 12
Soho 12
soignée 2
soil 222
soilage 197
soiree 2.17
sojourn 249
soke 42
sol 223
solace 300.9
solanaceous 310.56
solander 17.98
solanum 242
solar 17.171
solarimeter
 17.342.2.1
solarium 242.2.14
solarize 516.8
sold 120
soldan 261.28
solder 17.97
solderer 17.279
soldier 17

soldierly 16.131
soldiery 16.274
sole 223
solecism
 242.35.16.2
solely 16.164
solemn 242
solemnify 7.3
solemnity 16.333
solemnize 516
solenodon 261
solenoid 97.8
Solent 420
sol-fa 1
solfatara 17.268
solfeggio 12.3
solferino 12.54
soli 16.126
solicit 371.36
solicitor 17.342
solicitous 310.64
solicitude 102.2
solid 91.18
solidago 12.27
solidarity 16.333.20
solidary 16.274
solidify 7.3.1
solidity 16.333.5
solidus 310
solifidian 261.3.5
solifluction 261.79
Solihull 225
soliloquize 516
soliloquy 16.259
solipsism 242.35
solitaire 4
solitary 16.274.41
solitude 102.2
solleret 368.6
sollicitation
 261.67.27
solo 12.44
soloist 436
Solomon 261.52
Solomonic 38.35.3
Solon 261.43
solonchak 32
solonetz 336
solstice 300
solubility 16.333.9
soluble 228.15
solum 242
solute 380
solution 261.75.1
solvation 261.67

solve 493
solvency 16.312
solvent 420
Solway 2
soma 17.215
Somali 16.113,
 17.3.17
Somaliland 143.2
somatic 38.49
somatology
 16.108.4.15
somatopleure 10
somatotype 275.1
sombre 17.26
sombrero 12.62
some 240
somebody 16.72
someday 2
somehow 13
someone 259
someplace 295
somersault 404.1
Somerset 371
something 265
sometime 236
sometimes 542
someway 2
somewhat 373
somewhere 4
somewise 516
somite 372
sommelier 2
somnambulate
 367.13
somnambulism
 242.35.10
somnambulist
 436.6
somniloquy 16.259
somnolence 321.12
somnolent 420.28
son 259
sonant 420.54
sonar 1
sonata 17.337
sonatina 17.230
sondage 359
sonde 136
Sondheim 236
sone 257
son et lumière 4.1
song 266
songbird 87
songful 226
Songhai 7

songwriter 17.343
sonic 38.35
son-in-law 9
sonnet 371.25
sonneteer 6
sonny 16.235
sonobuoy 11
sonorant 420.65
sonority 16.333.22
sonorous 310.50
Soochow 13
sook 44
soon 260
sooner 17.238
soot 379
sooth 463
soothe 479
soothing 265
soothsay 2
soothsayer 17.1
soothsaying 265.1
sooty 16.342
sop 276
Sophie 16.87
sophism 242.35
sophist 436
sophister 17.384
sophistic 38.70
sophisticate 367.5,
 371.9
sophisticated
 91.34.3
sophistication
 261.67.5
sophistry 16.293
Sophocles 513
sophomore 9.9
Sophy 16.87
sopor 17.257
soporific 38.12.1
sopping 265
soppy 16.250
soprano 12.51
sora 17.276
sorb 27
sorbefacient 420.73
sorbet 371
sorbose 520
sorcerer 17.279
sorceress 300.47
sorcery 16.274
sordid 91.9
sordidness 300.28
sore 9
soredium 242.2.2

sorehead 86
sorely 16.123
soreness 300.24
sorghum 242
sorgo 12
sori 7.11
sorites 513
sorn 255
sororate 367.23
sororicide 92.7
sorority 16.333.22
sorption 261.87
sorrel 228.73
Sorrento 12.84
sorrow 12.65
sorrowful 226.2
sorry 16.268
sort 374
sorter 17.345
sortie 16.336
sortilege 197.1
sortition 261.71
sorus 310.48
S.O.S. 296
so-so 12.70
sostenuto 12.80
sot 373
soteriology
  16.108.4.1
Sothic 38
sotto voce 16.50
sou 15
soubise 513
soubrette 368
souchong 266
soufflé 2
sough 13, 168
sought 374
soul 223
soulful 226
soulless 300
sound 139
soundbox 499
sounder 17.107
sounding 265.22
soundless 300
soundly 16.156
soundness 300
soundpost 441
soundproof 170
soundtrack 32
soup 280
soupy 16.253
sour 14
source 303

sourdine 251
sourly 16.127
sourness 300
sourpuss 308
soursop 276
Sousa 17.444
sousaphone 257
souse 306
Sousse 309
soutache 349
soutane 245.6
souter 17.351
souterrain 247.8
south 462
Southampton 261
southbound 139
southeast 435
southeasterly
  16.131
southeastward 103
Southend 131
southerly 16.131
southern 261
Southerner 17.239
southernmost 441
southernwood 101
southpaw 9
Southport 374
southward 103
southwards 531
Southwark 46
southwest 433
southwesterly
  16.131
southwestward 103
souvenir 6.5
sou'wester 17.382
sovereign 252
sovereignty 16.360
soviet 381.1
sovietism 242.35.18
sovietize 516.13
sovkhoz 517
sovran 261
sow 12, 13
sowbread 86
sower 17.6
sown 257
soy 11
soya 17.5
sozzled 122
spa 1
space 295
spaceband 128
spacecraft 396

spaceman 261
spaceport 374
spacer 17.299
spaceship 274
spacesuit 380
spacewalk 41
spacing 265.59
spacious 310.56
spaciousness
  300.34
spade 85
spadework 36
spadiceous 310.58
spadix 498
spae 2
spag 178
spaghetti 16.330
Spain 247
spake 34
spall 221
spallation
  261.67.14
spalpeen 251
Spam 229
span 245
spancel 228
spandrel 228
spang 263
spangle 228.49
Spaniard 103
spaniel 228.123
Spanish 353
spank 51
spanker 17.43
spanking 265
spanner 17.225
spar 1
sparable 228.16
spare 4
sparerib 24
sparge 192
sparid 91.25
sparing 265.52
spark 33
sparkle 228.20
sparling 265.26
sparring 265
sparrow 12.60
sparrowgrass 294
sparrowhawk 41
sparry 16.261
sparse 294
sparsely 16.180
sparseness 300
Sparta 17.337

Spartacus 310.14
Spartan 261.95
spasm 242.34
spasmodic 38.9
spastic 38.68
spat 365
spatchcock 40
spate 367
spathe 473
spathic 38.72
spatial 228.91
spatter 17.336
spatula 17.174
spatulate 371.17
spavin 252
spavined 134
spawn 255
spay 2
speak 37
speakeasy 16.395
speaker 17.33
speaking 265
spear 6
spearhead 86
spearmint 412
spec 35
special 228
specialism
  242.35.11
specialist 436.7
speciality
  16.333.8.1
specialize 516.3
specially 16.131
specialty 16.352
specie 5
species 513
specifiable
  228.16.3.1
specific 38.12
specifically 16.142
specification
  261.67.5.1
specify 7.3
specimen 252.14
speciosity
  16.333.30.1
specious 310.57
speck 35
speckle 228.21
specs 496
spectacle 228.28
spectacled 122
spectacles 539

spectacular 17.174.3
spectator 17.338
spectra 17.295
spectral 228
spectre 17.354
spectrograph 158.1.3
spectroheliograph 158.1.1
spectrometer 17.342.3.5
spectroscope 278.1.2
spectroscopy 16.254.2
spectrum 242.22
specular 17.174.4
speculate 367.13
speculation 261.67.13
speculative 485.15.5
speculator 17.338.6
speculum 242.10
sped 86
speech 66
speechify 7.3
speechless 300
speed 89
speedboat 376
speedo 12.18
speedometer 17.342.3
speedway 2
speedwell 215
speedy 16.62
speel 217
speiss 301
spelaean 261.2.2
speleology 16.108.4.1
spelk 48
spell 215
spellbind 135
spellbound 139
speller 17.163
spelling 265.28
spelt 402
spelter 17.361
spelunker 17.46
spence 316
Spencer 17.314
spend 131
spender 17.101

spending 265.20
spendthrift 398
spent 410
speos 302
sperm 233
spermaceti 16.330
spermary 16.274.21
spermatheca 17.33
spermatic 38.49
spermatid 91
spermatium 242.2
spermatocyte 372.10
spermatogenesis 300.52.4
spermatorrhoea 17.2.2
spermatozoon 254.2
spermic 38.26
spermicidal 228.33
spermicide 92.7
spermogonium 242.2.12
spermophile 219.1
spermous 310
spessartite 372.12
spew 15
Spey 2
sphagnum 242
sphene 251
sphenic 38.32
sphenodon 254
sphenoid 97.7
spheral 228
sphere 6
spherical 228.23.15
sphericity 16.333.28
spherics 498.6
spheroid 97.10
spheroidal 228.35
spherule 227
spherulite 372
sphery 16.265
sphinx 505
sphragistics 498
sphygmic 38
sphygmograph 158.1
sphygmoid 97
Spica 17.33
spica 17.35
spicate 367
spiccato 12.73

spice 301
spiceberry 16.274
spicebush 357
spicery 16.274.37
spiciness 300.23
spick-and-span 245
spicule 227.1
spicy 16.301
spider 17.84
spiderman 261.52
spidery 16.274
spiegeleisen 261.127
spiel 217
spieler 17.165
spiffing 265
spiffy 16.85
spiflicate 367.5
spignel 228
spigot 381
spike 39
spikelet 371
spikenard 84
spiky 16.26
spile 219
spill 218
spillage 197.1
spillikin 252.3
spillikins 548
spillway 2
spilt 403
spin 252
spina bifida 17.83
spinach 197.7
spinal 228.61
spindle 228.40
spindlelegs 535
spindling 265
spindrift 398
spine 253
spine-chiller 17.166
spine-chilling 265.30
spinel 215
spineless 300
spinet 371.24
spinifex 496
spinnaker 17.42
spinner 17.231
spinneret 368.6
spinney 16.229
spinning 265.43
spinose 305
spinous 310.34
Spinoza 17.442

Spinozism 242.35
spinster 17.394
spiny 16.230
spiracle 228.28
spiraea 17.2
spiral 228
spirant 420
spire 8
spireme 234
spirillum 242
spirit 371.33
spirited 91.38
spiritless 300.17
spiritlessness 300.33
spiritous 310.64
spiritual 228.9.3
spiritualism 242.35.11.3
spiritualist 436.7.3
spirituality 16.333.8.2
spirituel 215
spirituous 310.4
spirketting 265.66
spirochaete 370
spirochaetosis 300.55.6
spirograph 158.1
spirogyra 17.274
spiroid 97.11
spirometer 17.342.3
spironolactone 257
spirula 17.174
spiry 16.267
spit 371
spitchcock 40
spite 372
spiteful 226.9
spitefulness 300.30
spitfire 8
Spithead 86
spitsticker 17.34
spittle 228.102
spittlebug 189
spittoon 260
spitz 339
spiv 485
splake 34
splanchnic 38
splash 349
splashback 32
splashboard 95
splashdown 258

splasher 17.321
splashy 16.319
splat 365
splatter 17.336
splay 2
spleen 251
splendid 91.13
splendiferous
  310.50.2
splendour 17.101
splenectomy
  16.222.5
splenetic 38.50.4
splenic 38.32
splenitis 300.62.3
splenius 310.2.7
splenomegaly
  16.131.2
splice 301
spline 253
splint 412
splinter 17.369
split 371
splits 339
splitting 265.66
splodge 199
splodgy 16.104
splore 9
splotch 68
splurge 195
splutter 17.349
Spock 40
Spode 98
spodumene 251
spoil 222
spoilage 197
spoiler 17.170
spoilfive 486
spoilsport 374
spoke 42
spoken 261.14
spokeshave 482
spokesman 261
spoliate 367.1.3
spoliation
  261.67.1.2
spondee 5
spondulix 498
spondylitis
  300.62.1
sponge 211
sponger 17.159
spongy 16.111
sponsion 261
sponson 261

sponsor 17.316
sponsorship 274.1
spontaneity
  16.333.1
spontaneous
  310.2.6
spontoon 260
spoof 170
spook 45
spooky 16.32
spool 227
spoon 260
spoonbill 218
spoonerism
  242.35.15
spoon-feed 89
spoonful 226
spoony 16.236
spoor 10
Sporades 513.5
sporadic 38.7
sporangium 242.2
spore 9
sporocyst 436.22
sporogenesis
  300.52.4
sporogonium
  242.2.12
sporophore 9.6
sporophyll 218.1
sporozoan 261.6
sporran 261
sport 374
sporting 265.69
sportive 485.13
sports 342
sportscast 431
sportsman 261
sportsmanlike 39
sportsmanship
  274.2
sportswear 4
sportswoman
  261.50
sporty 16.336
sporulate 367.13
spot 373
spotless 300
spotlessness 300.33
spotlight 372
spotted 91.40
spotter 17.344
spotty 16.335
spousal 228.129
spouse 306

spout 377
sprag 178
sprain 247
sprang 263
sprat 365
sprawl 221
sprawling 265.31
spray 2
spread 86
spreader 17.80
spree 5
sprig 184
sprightly 16.190
spring 265
springboard 95
springbok 40
springe 209
springer 17.246
Springfield 115
springhaas 294
springhead 86
springing 265.47
springlet 371
springtime 236
springwood 101
springy 16.242
sprinkle 228.29
sprinkler 17.182
sprinkling 265
sprint 412
sprinter 17.369
sprit 371
sprite 372
sprocket 371.10
sprout 377
spruce 309
sprucely 16.183
sprue 15
spruik 38
sprung 267
spry 7
spud 100
spume 241
spumescent 420.67
spumone 16.233
spun 259
spunk 54
spunky 16.39
spur 3
spurge 195
spurious 310.2.14
spurn 249
spurrier 17.3
spurry 16.272
spurt 369

sputnik 38
sputter 17.349
sputum 242
spy 7
spyglass 294
spying 265.3
squab 26
squabble 228
squacco 12.8
squad 94
squadron 261
squalene 251
squalid 91.18
squall 221
squally 16.123
squalor 17.168
squama 17.207
squamate 367
squamation 261.67
squamous 310.27
squamulose 305
squander 17.104
square 4
squarely 16.117
squarish 353.9
squarrose 305
squash 354
squashy 16.323
squat 373
squatter 17.344
squattocracy
  16.307.5
squaw 9
squawk 41
squeak 37
squeaker 17.33
squeaky 16.24
squeal 217
squeamish 353
squeamishness
  300.35
squeegee 5
squeeze 513
squeezer 17.440
squelch 75
squeteague 183
squib 24
squid 91
squiffy 16.85
squiggle 228.46
squill 218
squilla 17.166
squinch 80
squint 412
squire 8

squirearchy 16.20
squirm 233
squirrel 228
squirt 369
squish 353
squit 371
squiz 515
Sri Lanka 17.43
Srinagar 17.134
St. Anne's
   554
stab 18
Stabat Mater
   17.337
stabile 219
stability 16.333.9.2
stabilize 516.2
stabilizer 17.441
stable 228.11
stableboy 11
stableman 261
stabling 265
staccato 12.73
stack 32
stacker 17.28
stacte 5
staddle 228.31
staddlestone 257
stadholder 17.97
stadia 17.3.7
stadium 242.2.1
staff 158
Staffa 17.110
Stafford 103
Staffordshire 6
stag 178
stage 193
stagecoach 70
stagecraft 396
stagehand 128
stager 17.146
stagflation 261.67
staggard 103
stagger 17.123
staggering 265.58
staggers 524
staghound 139
staging 265.24
Stagira 17.274
stagnant 420
stagnate 367
stagy 16.100
staid 85
staidness 300
stain 247

Staines 545
stainless 300
stair 4
staircase 295
stairhead 86
stairs 512
stairway 2
stairwell 215
stake 34
stakeout 377
stalactite 372
stalactitic 38.52
stalag 178
stalagmite 372
stalagmitic 38.52
stale 214
stalemate 367
staleness 300
Stalin 252
Stalingrad 83
Stalinism 242.35.13
stalk 41
stalker 17.37
stalky 16.28
stall 221
stallion 261.118
stalwart 381
Stambul 227
stamen 248.2
stamina 17.231.1
staminate 371.24
staminode 98
staminody 16.67
stammel 228.51
stammer 17.205
stammerer 17.279
stamp 285
stampede 89
stance 314
stanch 78
stanchion 261.81
stand 128
standard 103
standardize 516
standee 5
standing 265.19
standish 353.2
standoffish 353
standpipe 275
standpoint 416
standstill 218
stang 263
stanhope 281
stank 51
Stanley 16.169

Stannaries 515.1
stannary 16.274
stannic 38.31
stannite 372
stannous 310
stanza 17.445
stapelia 17.3.20
stapes 513
staphylorrhaphy
   16.90.1
staple 228
stapler 17
star 1
starboard 103
starch 63
starchy 16.47
stardom 242
stardust 443
stare 4
starfish 353
stargaze 509
stargazer 17.439
stargazing 265.81
stark 33
starless 300
starlet 371
starlight 372
starling 265.26
starry 16.261
start 366
starter 17.337
startle 228.98
starvation 261.67
starve 481
starving 265
stash 349
stasis 300.50
statant 420.75
state 367
statecraft 396
Statehouse 306
stateless 300
stateliness 300.23
stately 16.188
statement 420.48
stater 17.338
stateroom 241
stateside 92
statesman 261
statesmanship
   274.2
static 38.49
statics 498.11
station 261.67

stationary
   16.274.29.1
stationer 17.239.1
stationery
   16.274.29.1
stationmaster
   17.380
statism 242.35
statist 436
statistic 38.70.6
statistical
   228.23.24
statistician 261.71
statistics 498
Statius 310.2.16
stative 485.10
statocyst 436.22
statolith 458
stator 17.338
statoscope 278.1
statuary 16.274.2
statue 15
statuesque 57
statuette 368.1
stature 17.50
status 310.62
status quo 12
statute 380
statutory 16.274.42
staunch 81
stauroscope 278.1
stave 482
stavesacre 17.30
stay 2
stayer 17.1
stays 509
staysail 214
stead 86
steadfast 445
steadfastness
   300.42
steadily 16.120
steadiness 300.23.1
steady 16.60
steak 34
steakhouse 306
steal 217
stealing 265.29
stealth 465
stealthful 226
stealthy 16.374
steam 234
steamboat 376
steamer 17.210
steamie 16.215

steamroller 17.171
steamship 274
steamy 16.215
stearic 38.38
stearin 252
steatite 372.12
steatopygia 17.3.14
steed 89
steel 217
steelhead 86
steelworks 497
steely 16.118
steelyard 84
Steen 247
steep 273
steepen 261
steeple 228.65
steeplechase 295
steeplechaser
  17.299
steeplejack 32
steepness 300
steer 6
steerage 197
steerageway 2.29
steering 265.53
steersman 261.54
steeve 484
stegodon 254
stegomyia 17.4
stegosaur 9.11
stein 253
Steinbeck 35
steinbok 40
stele 16.118
stellar 17.163
stellarator 17.338.9
stellate 371.15
stelliferous
  310.50.2
stelliform 238.1
stellify 7.3
stellular 17.174
stem 232
stemma 17.208
stemware 4
Sten 248
stench 79
stencil 228.88
steno 12.52
stenograph 158.1
stenographer
  17.120.1
stenography
  16.90.2.4

stenophyllous
  310.23
stenosis 300.55.4
stenotropic 38.37.2
stenotypy 16.249
stentor 9.12
stentorian 261.3.23
step 271
stepbrother 17.408
stepchild 117
stepdaughter
  17.345
stepfather 17.401
stephanotis 300.64
Stephen 261.113
Stephenson 261
stepladder 17.77
stepmother 17.408
step-parent 420
steppe 271
stepper 17.250
Steppes 324
stepsister 17.384
stepson 259
steradian 261.3.3
stercoraceous
  310.56
stercoricolous
  310.26.2
stere 6
stereo 12.3
stereobate 367.4
stereochromy
  16.219
stereogram 229.1.1
stereograph 158.1.1
stereography
  16.90.2.1
stereometry
  16.285.2.1
stereophonic
  38.35.2
stereophony
  16.237.3.1
stereopsis 300.61
stereopticon 261.13
stereoscope 278.1
stereoscopic
  38.37.1
stereoscopy
  16.254.2
stereospecific 38.12
stereotomy
  16.222.4.1
stereotype 275.1

stereotypic 38.36
stereotypy 16.249
stereovision
  261.91.3
steric 38.39
sterigma 17.222
sterilant 420
sterile 219
sterility 16.333.9
sterilization
  261.67.36
sterilize 516.2
sterilizer 17.441
sterlet 371
sterling 265
stern 249
sternness 300
sternum 242.13
sternutation
  261.67.29
sternutator 17.338
sternutatory
  16.274.43
sternway 2
steroid 97.10
sterol 220
stertor 17.340
stertorous 310.50
stet 368
stethoscope 278.1
stethoscopy
  16.254.2
stetson 261
stevedore 9.3
Stevenage 197
Stevengraph 158
stew 15
steward 103
stewardess 300.5
sthenic 38.32
stibine 253
stibnite 372
stich 38
stichomythia
  17.3.51
stichomythy 16.370
stick 38
sticker 17.34
stickiness 300.23
stickle 228.23
stickleback 32
stickler 17.181
stickseed 89
sticktight 372
stickweed 89.6

sticky 16.25
stickybeak 37
stiff 163
stiffen 261.29
stiffener 17.239
stiffness 300
stifle 228
stifling 265
stigma 17.222
stigmasterol 220.4
stigmata 17.352
stigmatic 38.49.3
stigmatism
  242.35.20
stigmatize 516.13
stile 219
stiletto 12.75
still 218
stillage 197.1
stillbirth 456
stillborn 255
stillicide 92.7
stillness 300
stilt 403
stilted 91
Stilton 261
stimulant 420.27
stimulate 367.13.5
stimulation
  261.67.13.3
stimulator 17.338.6
stimulus 310.25
sting 265
stinger 17.246
stingo 12.36
stingray 2
stingy 16.110
stink 52
stinker 17.44
stinkhorn 255
stinking 265.10
stinkpot 373
stinkweed 89
stint 412
stipe 275
stipel 228.67
stipend 131
stipendiary
  16.274.1
stipes 513
stipple 228.66
stipulate 367.13.6
stipulation
  261.67.13.4
stir 3

stirk 36
Stirling 265
stirps 325
stirrer 17.270
stirring 265.51
stirrup 281
stitch 67
stitching 265
stitchwort 369
stithy 16.376
stiver 17.415
stoa 17.6
stoat 376
stob 26
stochastic 38.68
stock 40
stockade 85
stockbreeder 17.82
stockbroker 17.38
stocker 17.36
stockfish 353
stockholder 17.97
stockholding
  265.18
Stockholm 239
stockinet 368
stocking 265.8
stockinged 107
stockish 353
stockist 436
stockjobber 17.16
stockman 261
stockpile 219
Stockport 374
stockpot 373
stockroom 241
stocks 499
stocktaking 265.6
Stockton 261
stocky 16.27
stockyard 84
stodge 199
stodgy 16.104
stogy 16.96
stoic 38.2
stoical 228.23
stoichiology
  16.108.4.1
stoichiometry
  16.285.2.1
stoicism 242.35.16
stoke 42
stokehold 120
Stoke Mandeville
  218.3

stoker 17.38
Stokowski 16.44
stole 223
stolen 261.43
stolid 91.18
stollen 261.43
stolon 261.43
stoma 17.215
stomach 46
stomachache 34
stomacher 17.42
stomachic 38.6
stomachy 16.33
stomatic 38.49
stomatology
  16.108.4.15
stomodaeum 242.1
stomp 288
stone 257
stonechat 365
stonecrop 276
stonecutter 17.349
stoned 138
stoneground 139
Stonehenge 208
stoneless 300
stonemason 261.62
stonewall 221
stoneware 4
stonework 36
stonewort 369
stonk 53
stony 16.233
stood 101
stooge 204
stook 45
stool 227
stoop 280
stop 276
stopcock 40
stope 278
stopgap 268
stoping 265
stoplight 372
stopover 17.417
stoppable 228.16
stoppage 197
Stoppard 84
stopper 17.255
stopping 265
stops 329
stopwatch 68
storage 197
storax 494
store 9

storehouse 306
storekeeper 17.252
storeroom 241
storey 16.269
storied 91
stork 41
storksbill 218
storm 238
stormbound 139
stormproof 170
stormy 16.218
Stornoway 2.28
Storting 265.69
story 16.269
storybook 44
storyteller 17.163
stoss 302
stot 373
stotinka 17.44
stotious 310.60
stotter 17.344
stound 139
stoup 280
stour 14
Stourbridge 197
stout 377
stouthearted 91.33
stoutness 300
stove 488
stovepipe 275
stovepipes 328
stover 17.417
stow 12
stowage 197
stowaway 2.28
strabismus 310.30
straddle 228.31
Stradivari 16.261
Stradivarius 310.2
strafe 159
straggle 228.43
straggler 17.192
straight 367
straightaway 2.28
straightedge 194
straighten 261
straightforward
  103.8
straightness 300
strain 247
strained 130
strainer 17.227
strait 367
straiten 261
straitjacket 371.6

strake 34
stramonium
  242.2.12
Strand 128
strand 128
stranded 91.12
strange 207
strangeness 300
stranger 17.156
strangle 228.49
stranglehold 120
strangler 17.194
strangulate
  367.13.4
strangulation
  261.67.13.2
strangury 16.273
Stranraer 1
strap 268
straphanger 17.245
strapless 300
strappado 12.17
strapper 17.247
strapping 265
strapping 265.48
Strasbourg 182
strass 293
strata 17.337
stratagem 242
strategic 38.17
strategically 16.142
strategics 498
strategist 436
strategy 16.103
Stratford 103
strath 452
Strathclyde 92
strathspey 2
stratify 7.3.8
stratigraphy 16.90
stratocracy
  16.307.5
stratocumulus
  310.25.5
stratopause 518
stratosphere 6.1
stratospheric 38.39
stratum 242.26
stratus 310.62
Strauss 306
stravaig 180
straw 9
strawberry 16.274
strawboard 95
stray 2

streak 37
streaked 386
streaker 17.33
streaky 16.24
stream 234
streamer 17.210
streamline 253
streamlined 135
street 370
streetcar 1
streetlight 372
streetwalker 17.37
Streisand 128
strelitzia 17.3
strength 472
strengthen 261
strengthener
 17.239
strenuosity
 16.333.30.2
strenuous 310.4.2
streptococcal
 228.25
streptococcus
 310.11
streptomycin
 252.22
stress 296
stressful 226.5
stretch 64
stretchable 228.16
stretcher 17.53
stretchy 16.48
stretto 12.75
strew 15
strewth 463
stria 17.4
striate 367
striate 371
striation 261.67
strick 38
stricken 261.13
strickle 228.23
strict 387
strictness 300
stricture 17.65
stride 92
strident 420
stridor 9
stridulous 310.25.4
strife 164
strigil 218
strigose 305
strike 39
strikebound 139

strikebreaker 17.30
striker 17.35
striking 265
Strindberg 182
string 265
stringboard 95
stringed 107
stringency 16.312.4
stringent 420.23
stringer 17.246
stringhalt 404
stringy 16.242
strip 274
stripe 275
stripling 265
stripper 17.253
striptease 513
stripy 16.249
strive 486
strobe 28
strobic 38.3
strobila 17.167
strobilation
 261.67.12
strobilus 310.23
stroboscope 278.1
stroboscopic
 38.37.1
strode 98
stroganoff 165
stroke 42
stroll 223
stroller 17.171
stroma 17.215
stromatolite
 372.4.1
Stromboli 16.131
strong 266
strongbox 499
stronghold 120
strongly 16.176
strongman 261
strongroom 241
strontianite 372.6
strontium 242.2
strop 276
strophanthus
 310.72
strophe 16.87
strophic 38.13
stroppy 16.250
stroud 99
strove 488
struck 43
structural 228.76

structuralism
 242.35.11
structure 17.66
strudel 228.37
struggle 228
struggler 17.193
strum 240
struma 17.217
strumpet 371
strung 267
strut 378
struthious 310.2
strychnic 38
strychnine 251
strychninism
 242.35.13
Stuart 381
stub 29
stubble 228.14
stubbly 16.136
stubborn 261
stubbornness
 300.31
stubby 16.13
stucco 12
stuck 43
stud 100
studbook 44
student 420.13
studentship 274
studhorse 303
studied 91.11
studio 12.3
studious 310.2
studiousness
 300.34.1
study 16.69
stuff 168
stuffed 400
stuffiness 300.23
stuffing 265
stuffy 16.88
stull 225
stultify 7.3
stum 240
stumble 228
stumer 17.217
stump 289
stumpy 16.257
stun 259
stung 267
stunk 54
stunner 17.237
stunning 265.45
stunt 419

stunted 91
stupe 280
stupefacient 420.73
stupefaction 261.76
stupefy 7.3
stupendous 310
stupid 91
stupidity 16.333.5
stupor 17.259
sturdiness 300.23
sturdy 16.61
sturgeon 261.35
Sturmer 17.209
Sturt 369
stutter 17.349
stutterer 17.279
Stuyvesant 420.70
sty 7
Stygian 261.3.7
style 219
stylet 371
stylish 353
stylist 436
stylistic 38.70
stylite 372
stylize 516
stylobate 367.4
stylograph 158.1
stylography 16.90.2
styloid 97
stylolite 372.4
stylops 329
stylostixis 300
stylus 310.24
stymie 16.217
stypsis 300.60
styptic 38.66
styrax 494
styrene 251.5
Styria 17.3.40
Styx 498
suable 228.16.7
Suakin 252.2
suave 481
suavity 16.333.33
sub 29
subacetate 367.30.2
subacid 91.28
subacute 380.3
subah 1
subalpine 253
subaltern 261
subalternate 371.28
subantarctic 38.59
subaquatic 38.49

subaqueous 310.2
subarctic 38.59
subarid 91.25
subassembly
16.138
subatomic 38.29
subbase 295
subbasement
420.44
subbass 295
subception 261.84
subclass 294
subclavian 261.3.29
subclimax 494
subcommittee
16.333
subconscious 310
subconsciousness
300.34
subcontinent
420.53
subcontract 382
subcontractor
17.353
subcutaneous
310.2.6
subdeacon 261.12
subdivide 92
subdivision
261.91.2
subdominant
420.53.2
subduct 389
subdue 15
subdued 102
subedit 371.12
subeditor 17.342.1
subequatorial
228.3.12.2
suberin 252.20
suberize 516.8
suberose 305.2
subfamily 16.120
subfusc 60
subgenus 310.32
subglacial 228.91
subgroup 280
subheading 265.12
subhuman 261.51
subindex 496
subjacent 420
subject 385, 387
subjectify 7.3.9
subjection 261.77
subjective 485.17

subjectivism
242.35.22
subjectivity
16.333.35
subjoin 256
sub judice 16.300
subjugate 367
subjugation 261.67
subjunctive 485
sublease 298
sublieutenant
420.52
sublimate 367.15
sublimation
261.67.15
sublime 236
sublimely 16.167
subliminal 228.60.4
sublimity 16.333.12
sublingual 228
sublunary
16.274.28
submarine 251.7
submariner 17.231
submaxillary
16.274.16
submediant 420.1.1
submental 228.110
submerge 195
submersible
228.16.38
submiss 300
submission 261.71
submissive 485.4
submit 371
submontane 247.11
subnormal 228.53
subnormality
16.333.8.5
suboceanic 38.31.1
suborder 17.86
subordinary
16.274.26
subordinate 367.17
subordinate
371.24.1
subordination
261.67.18.1
suborn 255.1
subornation 261.67
subphylum 242.9
subplot 373
subpoena 17.230
subregion 261.36
subreption 261.84

subrogate 367.11
subrogation
261.67.11
sub rosa 17.442
subroutine 251
subscribe 25
subscriber 17.15
subscript 424
subscription 261.85
subsection 261.77
subsequence 321
subsequent 420.58
subserve 483
subservient 420.1
subset 368
subside 92
subsidence 321.6
subsidiary 16.274.1
subsidize 516
subsidy 16.63
subsist 436
subsistence 321.27
subsoil 222
subsonic 38.35
subspecies 513
substage 193
substance 321
substandard 103
substantial 228.95
substantiate
367.1.8
substantiation
261.67.1
substantive 485
substation 261.67
substituent 420.4
substitute 380.5
substitution 261.75
substitutive 485
substrate 367
substratum 242.26
substructure 17.66
subsume 241
subsumption
261.89
subtangent 420.22
subtemperate
371.35
subtenancy 16.312
subtenant 420.52
subtend 131
subterfuge 204
subterranean
261.3.15.1
subtilize 516.2

subtitle 228.103
subtle 228.107
subtlety 16.352
subtonic 38.35
subtorrid 91.26
subtotal 228.106
subtract 382
subtraction 261.76
subtractive 485.16
subtrahend 131
subtropical
228.23.14
subtropics 498
subtype 275
subulate 371.18
suburb 22
suburban 261.9
suburbanite 372.6
suburbanize 516.7
suburbia 17.3.2
subvene 251
subvention 261.82
subversion 261.69
subversive 485.3
subvert 369
subway 2
subzero 12.63
succedaneum
242.2.10
succeed 89
succentor 17.368
success 296
successful 226.5
succession 261.68
successive 485.2
successor 17.300
succinate 367.17
succinct 392
succinic 38.34
succory 16.274
succotash 349
succour 17.39
succubus 310
succulent 420.27
succumb 240
succursal 228.84
succuss 307
such 72
suchlike 39
suck 43
sucker 17.39
sucking 265
suckle 228.27
sucrase 509
sucrose 520

suction 261.79
Sudan 246
Sudanic 38.31
sudarium 242.2.14
sudatorium 242.2.17
Sudbury 16.274
sudd 100
sudden 261
suddenness 300.31
Sudetenland 143
Sudetes 513.16
sudor 9
sudoriferous 310.50.2
sudorific 38.12.1
suds 530
sue 15
suede 85
suet 371.3
Suetonius 310.2.9
Suez 515
suffer 17.118
sufferance 321.20
sufferer 17.279
suffering 265.58
suffice 301
sufficiency 16.312.5
sufficient 420.74
suffix 498
suffocate 367.6
suffocation 261.67.6
Suffolk 46
suffragan 261
suffrage 197
suffragette 368
suffragist 436.4
suffumigate 367.10
suffuse 523.1
Sufi 16.89
Sufism 242.35
sugar 17.135
sugar daddy 16.57
sugarplum 240
sugary 16.274
suggest 433
suggestibility 16.333.9.2
suggestible 228.16.59
suggestion 261.18
suggestive 485.24
suicidal 228.33
suicide 92.7

sui generis 300.47
suint 412
suit 380
suitability 16.333.9.2
suitable 228.16.53
suitcase 295
suite 370
suiting 265
suitor 17.351
sukiyaki 16.20
Sulawesi 16.296
sulcate 367.7
sulcus 310
Suleiman 246
sulk 50
sulkiness 300.23
sulky 16.35
Sulla 17.173
sullage 197
sullen 261
sullenness 300.31
Sullivan 261.114
sully 16.128
sulphanilamide 92.3
sulphate 367
sulphide 92
sulphite 372
sulphonamide 92.3
sulphonate 367.18
sulphone 257
sulphur 17
sulphurate 367.22
sulphuric 38.43
sulphurize 516
sulphurous 310.50
sultan 261
sultana 17.226
sultanate 367.18
sultanic 38.31
sultry 16
Sulu 15.4
sum 240
sumach 32
Sumatra 17.292
Sumer 17.217
Sumerian 261.3.22
summa 1
summa cum laude 2
summand 128
summarize 516.8
summary 16.274
summation 261.67

summer 17.216
summerhouse 306
summertime 236
summerwood 101
summery 16.274
summit 371
summitry 16.285
summon 261
summons 551
Sumo 12
sump 289
sumptuary 16.274.2
sumptuous 310.4.4
sumptuousness 300.34.2
sun 259
sunbake 34
sunbathe 473
sunbeam 234
sunbird 87
sunbonnet 371.25
sunburn 249
sunburnt 411
sunburst 434
sundae 2
Sunday 2
sunder 17.108
Sunderland 143.4
sundew 15
sundial 228.4
sundog 185
sundown 258
sundress 296
sundry 16
sunfast 431
sunflower 14
sung 267
Sungari 16.274
sunglass 294
sunglasses 515
sungrebe 23
sunhat 365
sunk 54
sunken 261
sunless 300
sunlight 372
sunlit 371
sunn 259
Sunna 17.237
Sunni 16.235
Sunnite 372
sunny 16.235
sunray 2
sunrise 516

sunroof 170
sunset 368
sunshade 85
sunshine 253
sunshiny 16.230
sunspot 373
sunstar 1
sunstroke 42
sunsuit 380
suntan 245
suntanned 128
suntrap 268
Sun Yat-sen 248
sup 279
super 17.259
superable 228.16.35
superabound 139
superabundant 420.16
superadd 83
superannuate 367.2
superannuated 91.34.2
superannuation 261.67.2
superb 22
superbazaar 1.19
supercharge 192
supercharger 17.145
superciliary 16.274.1.1
supercilious 310.2.5
superclass 294
superconductivity 16.333.35.3
supercool 227
super-duper 17.259
superego 12.28
supererogatory 16.274.43.3
superfamily 16.120
superfetation 261.67
superficial 228.93
superficiality 16.333.8.1
superfine 253
superfix 498
superfluid 91.3
superfluidity 16.333.5

superfluity 16.333.3
superfluous 310.4
supergiant 420.2
superheat 370
superhero 12.63
superhet 368
superhighway 2.26
superhuman 261.51
superimpose 520
superinduce 309
superintend 131
superintendency 16.312.2
superintendent 420.14
superior 17.3.39
superiority 16.333.22
superlative 485.15
superman 261.52
supermarket 371.7
supernal 228.58
supernatant 420.75
supernatural 228.76
supernova 17.417
supernumerary 16.274.32
superoxide 92.14
superpose 520.2
superpower 14
supersaturated 91.34.7
superscript 424
supersede 89.3
supersedure 17.149
supersession 261.68.1
supersex 496
supersonic 38.35.4
supersonics 498.5
superstar 1
superstition 261.71
superstitious 310.58
superstratum 242.26
superstruct 389
superstructure 17.66
supertax 494
supertonic 38.35.5
supervene 251.12
supervise 516

supervision 261.91.3
supervisor 17.441
supervisory 16.274.53
supinate 367.17
supinator 17.338.7
supine 253
suplex 496
supper 17.258
supplant 408
supplantation 261.67
supple 228
supplejack 32
supplement 410.1
supplement 420.31
supplementary 16.274.47
suppleness 300.30
suppletion 261.70
suppliant 420.1
supplicant 420.7
supplicate 367.5
supplication 261.67.5
supplier 17.4
supply 7.9
support 374.2
supportable 228.16.51
supporter 17.345
supporting 265.69
supportive 485.13
suppose 520.2
supposed 155.1
supposedly 16.148
supposing 265.83
supposition 261.71.9
suppositious 310.58
suppositive 485.12.1
suppository 16.274.41
suppress 296.5
suppression 261.68
suppressive 485.2
suppurate 367.22
suppuration 261.67.21
suppurative 485.15
supralapsarian 261.3.21

supremacist 436.22
supremacy 16.307
suprematism 242.35.20
supreme 234
supremo 12.47
Surabaya 17.4
surah 17.277
sural 228.75
surbase 295
surcharge 192
surcingle 228.50
surcoat 376
surculose 305
surd 87
sure 10
sure-footed 91
sure-footedness 300.28
surely 16.124
surety 16.337
surf 161
surface 300
surfactant 420
surfboard 95
surfcasting 265.74
surfeit 371
surfie 16.83
surfing 265
surfperch 65
surge 195
surgeon 261.35
surgeoncy 16.312.3
surgery 16.274.13
surgical 228.23.4
suricate 367.5
Surinam 229
surliness 300.23
surly 16.116
surmise 516
surmount 418
surmountable 228.16.56
surname 231
surpass 294
surplice 300
surplus 310
surprint 412
surprise 516.9
surprising 265.82
surprisingly 16.175
surreal 228.2
surrealism 242.35.11.1
surrealist 436.7.1

surrealistic 38.70.2.1
surrender 17.101
surreptitious 310.58
surreptitiousness 300.34.3
Surrey 16.272
surrey 16.272
surrogate 371
surround 139.1
surrounding 265.22
surroundings 552
surtax 494
surveillance 321.11
survey 2
surveying 265.1
surveyor 17.1
survival 228.121
survive 486
survivor 17.415
Susa 17.308
Susanna 17.225
susceptance 321
susceptibility 16.333.9.2
susceptible 228.16.58
sushi 16.326
suslik 38
suspect 385
suspend 131.4
suspender 17.101
suspense 316
suspension 261.82
suspensive 485.9
suspensoid 97
suspensory 16.274.38
suspicion 261.71
suspicious 310.58
suspire 8.2
Susquehanna 17.225
suss 307
Sussex 498
sustain 247
sustainer 17.227
sustenance 321
sustentacular 17.174.3
sustentation 261.67.32
susurrate 367.23
Sutcliffe 163

Sutherland 143.4
Sutlej 197
sutler 17.202
sutra 17.294
suttee 5
Sutton 261.103
Sutton Coldfield
115
suture 17.61
Suva 17.419
Suwannee 16.231
suzerain 247.8
suzerainty 16.360
svelte 402
swab 26
swabber 17.16
Swabia 17.3.1
swacked 382
swaddle 228.34
swag 178
swage 193
swagger 17.123
swagman 261
Swahili 16.118
swain 247
swallow 12.43
swallowtail 214
swam 229
swami 16.211
swamp 288
swamped 429
swampy 16.256
swan 254
Swanee 16.231
swanherd 87
swank 51
swanky 16.36
swanlike 39
swannery 16.274
Swansea 16
swap 276
swaraj 192
sward 95
swarf 166
swarm 238
swarthy 16
swash 354
swashbuckling
265.34
swastika 17.34
swat 373
swatch 68
swath 460
swathe 473
swats 333

swatter 17.344
sway 2
Swazi 16.392
Swaziland 143.2
swear 4
swearword 87
sweat 368
sweatband 128
sweated 91.35
sweater 17.339
sweatshop 276
sweaty 16.330
Swede 89
swede 89
Sweden 261.23
Swedenborg 186
Swedenborgianism
242.35.14.1
Swedish 353
sweeny 16.228
sweep 273
sweeper 17.252
sweeping 265.49
sweepstake 34
sweet 370
sweetbread 86
sweetbrier 17.4
sweeten 261.98
sweetener 17.239
sweetening 265.46
sweetheart 366
sweetie 16.332
sweetiewife 164
sweetmeal 217
sweetmeat 370
sweetness 300.37
sweetshop 276
sweetsop 276
swell 215
swelling 265.28
swelter 17.361
sweltering 265.58
swept 422
swerve 483
swift 398
swifter 17.359
swiftie 16.347
swiftness 300
swig 184
swill 218
swim 235
swimmer 17.211
swimmeret 368.6
swimming 265
swimmingly 16.175

swimsuit 380
Swinburne 249
swindle 228.40
swindler 17.189
Swindon 261
swine 253
swineherd 87
swinepox 499
swing 265
swingboat 376
swinge 209
swingeing 265
swinger 17.246
swinging 265.47
swingle 228.50
swingometer
17.342.3
swinish 353
swink 52
swipe 275
swipes 328
swipple 228.66
swirl 216
swish 353
Swiss 300
switch 67
switchback 32
switchboard 95
switcheroo 15.6
switchgirl 216
swither 17.405
Swithin 252
Switzer 17.320
Switzerland 143.4
swivel 228.120
swivet 371
swizz 515
swizzle 228
swollen 261.43
swoon 260
swoop 280
swoosh 357
sword 95
swordfish 353
swordlike 39
swordplay 2
swordsman 261
swordsmanship
274.2
swordstick 38
swordtail 214
swore 9
sworn 255
swot 373
swound 139

swum 240
swung 267
swy 7
Sybaris 300.47
sybarite 372.8
sybaritic 38.52.2
Sybil 228.12
sycamine 253
sycamore 9.9
syce 301
sycee 5
syconium 242.2.12
sycophant 407
sycophantic 38.62
sycosis 300.55
Sydney 16.240
Syene 16.228
syenite 372.6
syllabary 16.274
syllabi 7
syllabic 38
syllabify 7.3
syllabism 242.35.5
syllable 228.16.23
syllabub 29
syllabus 310
syllepsis 300.59
syllogism 242.35.8
syllogistic 38.70.1
syllogize 516.1
sylva 17.422
sylvan 261
sylvanite 372.6
sylvatic 38.49
sylvite 372
symbiont 414
symbiosis 300.55.1
symbiotic 38.53
symbol 228
symbolic 38.22
symbolical
228.23.8
symbolism
242.35.11
symbolist 436.7
symbolistic 38.70.2
symbolize 516.3
symbology
16.108.4
symmetallism
242.35.11
symmetrical 228.23
symmetrize 516
symmetry 16.285.1

sympathetic 38.50.6
sympathin 252
sympathize 516.14
sympathizer 17.441
sympatholytic 38.52.1
sympathy 16.373
sympatric 38.45
sympetalous 310.26
symphile 219
symphonic 38.35
symphonist 436.13
symphony 16.237
symphysis 300.52
sympodium 242.2.4
symposiac 32.1
symposium 242.2
symptom 242
symptomatic 38.49.2
symptomatology 16.108.4.15
synaesthesia 17.3.60
synagogue 185.2
synalepha 17.113
synapse 322
synarchy 16.33
synarthrosis 300.55
sync 52
syncarp 269
syncarpous 310
syncarpy 16.244
synchroflash 349
synchromesh 351
synchronic 38.35
synchronism 242.35.14
synchronize 516.7
synchronous 310.36
synclastic 38.68
syncline 253.5
synclinorium 242.2.17
Syncom 237
syncopate 367
syncopation 261.67
syncope 16.254
syncretism 242.35.18
syncretize 516.12
syncytium 242.2.18

syndesmosis 300.55
syndetic 38.50
syndic 38
syndicalism 242.35.11
syndicate 367.5, 371.9
syndrome 239
syndromic 38.29
syne 253
synecdoche 16.33
synecology 16.108.4.4
syneresis 300.52
synergetic 38.50.3
synergism 242.35.8
synergist 436.4
synergistic 38.70.1
synergy 16.108
synesis 300.52
syngamy 16.222
synod 103
synodic 38.9
synoecious 310.57
synonym 235
synonymity 16.333.12
synonymize 516.4
synonymous 310.28.2
synonymy 16.216
synopsis 300.61
synoptic 38.67
synovia 17.3.55
synovial 228.3.16
synovitis 300.62
synsepalous 310.26
syntactic 38.58
syntactics 498.13
syntagma 17.220
syntax 494
synthesis 300.52
synthesize 516.10
synthesizer 17.441
synthetic 38.50
synthetism 242.35.18
syntonic 38.35
sypher 17.115
syphilis 300.8
syphilitic 38.52
syphilology 16.108.4.8
Syria 17.3.40
Syriac 32.1

Syrian 261.3
syringa 17.141
syringe 209
syringomyelia 17.3.20
syrinx 505
syrphid 91
syrup 281
syrupy 16.254
systaltic 38.61
system 242
systematic 38.49.1
systematics 498.11
systematism 242.35.20
systematist 436.26
systematize 516.13.2
systematology 16.108.4.15
systemic 38.25
systole 16.131
systolic 38.22
syzygy 16.103
Szechwan 246

T

ta 1
Taal 213
tab 18
tabanid 91.21
tabard 103
tabaret 371.35.1
Tabasco 12
tabby 16.5
tabernacle 228.19
tabes 513
tabescent 420.67
tablature 17.62
table 228.11
tableau 12
tablecloth 459
table d'hôte 376
tableland 143
tablespoon 260
tablet 371
tableware 4
tabloid 97
taboo 15.1
tabor 17.11

taboret 371.35.1
Tabriz 513
tabular 17.174.1
tabulate 367.13.1, 371.17
tabulation 261.67.13.1
tabulator 17.338.6
tacamahac 32
tacet 368
tache 349
tacheometer 17.342.3.1
tacheometry 16.285.2.1
tachina 17.231
tachistoscope 278.1
tachograph 158.1
tachometer 17.342.3
tachycardia 17.3.6
tachygraphy 16.90
tachylyte 372.3
tacit 371
taciturn 249.1
taciturnity 16.333.16.1
Tacitus 310.64
tack 32
tacket 371.6
tackle 228.19
tacky 16.19
Tacoma 17.215
taconite 372.6
tact 382
tactful 226
tactic 38.58
tactical 228.23.22
tactician 261.71
tactics 498.13
tactile 219.4
tactless 300
tactlessness 300.33
tactual 228.9.4
tad 83
tadpole 223
taenia 17.3.33
taeniacide 92.8
taeniasis 300.57.1
taffeta 17.342
taffrail 214
Taffy 16.82
taffy 16.82
tafia 17.3.10
Tafilalet 368

Tafilelt 402
tag 178
Tagalog 185
taggers 524
tagliatelle 16.115
tagmemics 498
Tagore 9.7
Tagus 310.19
tahina 17.230
Tahiti 16.332
tahr 1
tahsildar 1
taiga 17.130
tail 214
tailback 32
tailboard 95
tailgate 367
tailing 265.27
taille 7
taillight 372
tailor 17.162
tailorbird 87
tailpiece 298
tailpipe 275
tailplane 247
tailrace 295
tails 536
tailskid 91
tailspin 252
tailstock 40
tailwind 134
tain 247
Tainan 245
taint 409
taipan 245
Taipei 2
Taiwan 246
taj 192
Taj Mahal 213
taka 1
takahe 5
take 34
takeaway 2.28
taken 261.11
takeoff 165
taker 17.30
takin 251
taking 265.6
takings 552
Takoradi 16.58
talapoin 256
talaria 17.3.38.1
Talbot 381
talc 47
tale 214

talent 420.24
talented 91.50
tales 513
Taliesin 252
taligrade 85.5
talion 261.3
taliped 86.6
talipes 513
talipot 373
talisman 261
talismanic 38.31
talk 41
talkative 485.15
talkativeness
    300.43
talker 17.37
talkie 16.28
tall 221
Tallahassee 16.294
tallboy 11
Tallis 300
tallith 458
tallness 300
tallow 12.38
tally 16.112
tally-ho 12
tallyman 261.48
Talmud 101
Talmudist 436.2
talon 261
taloned 143
taluk 44
talus 310
tamale 16.113
tamandua 17.8
tamarack 32.3
tamarin 252.20
tamarind 134
tamarindo 12.25
tamarisk 58
tamasha 17.321
Tambora 1.14
tambour 10
tamboura 17.277
tambourin 252.19
tambourine 251.7
tame 231
tameness 300
tamer 17.207
Tamerlane 247.4
Tamil 218
tamis 16.210
Tammany 16.237
tammy 16.210

tam-o'-shanter
    17.365
tamp 285
Tampa 17.261
tamper 17.261
tamping 265
tampion 261.3
tampon 254
tan 245
Tana 17.226
tana 17.226
tanager 17.154
Tanana 1
tanbark 33
tandem 242.6
Tandoori 16.270
Tang 263
tang 263
Tanga 17.140
Tanganyika 17.33
tangelo 12.45
tangent 420.22
tangential 228.96
tangerine 251.7
tangible 228.16.21
Tangier 6
tangle 228.49
tango 12.35
tangram 229
tangy 16.241
Tanis 300
tanist 436
Tanjore 9
tank 51
tanka 17.43
tankard 103
tanker 17.43
tankful 226
tannage 197.5
tanner 17.225
tannery 16.274
tannic 38.31
tannin 252
tansy 16.404
Tanta 17.365
tantalite 372.4
tantalize 516.3
tantalum 242.11
Tantalus 310.26
tantamount 418.1
tantara 17.279
tantivy 16.382
Tantra 17.296
Tantrism 242.35
tantrum 242

Tanzania 17.2
Taoism 242.35.3
tap 268
tapa 17.248
tapadera 17.271
tape 270
taper 17.249
tapestry 16.293
tapetum 242.28
tapeworm 233
tapioca 17.38
tapir 17.249
tapis 5
tappet 371
tappit-hen 248
taproom 241
taproot 380
taps 322
tar 1
taramasalata
    17.337.1
tarantass 293
tarantella 17.163
tarantism
    242.35.21
Taranto 12.83
tarantula 17.174
taraxacum 242
tarboosh 358
tardigrade 85.5
tardy 16.58
tare 4
target 371
tariff 163
Tarim 234
Tarkington 261
tarlatan 261
Tarmac 32
tarn 246
tarnal 228
tarnation 261.67.17
tarnish 353
taro 12.61
tarot 12.60
tarp 269
tarpan 245
tarpaulin 252
Tarpeian 261.2
tarpon 261
Tarquin 252
tarradiddle 228.32
tarragon 261
tarry 16.260,
    16.261
tarsal 228.83

tarsier 17.3.47
Tarsus 310.52
tarsus 310.52
tart 366
tartan 261.95
Tartar 17.337
tartar 17.337
tartaric 38.38
tartarous 310.50
Tartarus 310.50
Tartary 16.274
tartlet 371
tartrate 367
Tarzan 261
tasimeter 17.342.2
task 56
taskmaster 17.380
taskwork 36
Tasman 261
Tasmania 17.3.31
Tasmanian
  261.3.15
Tass 293
tass 293
tassel 228
tasset 371
taste 432
tasteful 226.12
tasteless 300
tastelessness
  300.33
taster 17.381
tasty 16.363
tat 365
ta-ta 1
Tate 367
tater 17.338
tatouay 2.3
tatter 17.336
tattersall 221
tatting 265
tattle 228.97
tattler 17.200
tattletale 214
tattoo 15
tatty 16.327
tatty-peelin 252
taught 374
taunt 415
taunter 17.370
Taunton 261
taupe 278
Tauranga 17.245
taurine 251.6, 253
tauromachy 16.33

Taurus 310.48
taut 374
tauten 261.102
tautog 185
tautology 16.108.4
tautomer 17.218
tautomerism
  242.35.15
Tavel 215
tavern 261
taverner 17.239
taw 9
tawdry 16.276
tawny 16.232
tawse 518
tax 494
taxable 228.16
taxation 261.67.34
taxi 16.386
taxidermic 38.26
taxidermist 436
taxidermy 16.214
taximeter 17.341
taxiplane 247
taxis 300.70
taxiway 2
taxon 254
taxonomic 38.29.1
taxonomy 16.222.3
taxpayer 17.1
Tay 2
tay 2
Taylor 17.162
tayra 17.274
Tayside 92
tazza 17.319
Tbilisi 16.299
Tchaikovsky 16.44
te 5
tea 5
teacake 34
teacart 366
teach 66
teachable
  228.16.12
teacher 17.55
teaching 265
teacup 279
teahouse 306
teak 37
teal 217
team 234
teamster 17.393
teamwork 36
teapot 373

teapoy 11
tear 4, 6
tearable 228.16.33
tearful 226
tearing 265.52
tear-jerker 17.32
tearless 300
tearoom 241
tease 513
teasel 228
teaser 17.440
teashop 276
teaspoon 260
teat 370
technetium 242.2
technical 228.23
technicality
  16.333.8.3
technician 261.71
Technicolor 17.173
technics 498
technique 37
technocracy
  16.307.5
technological
  228.23.5
technologist 436.4
technology
  16.108.4
tectonic 38.35
tectonics 498.5
tectrix 498
ted 86
tedder 17.80
Te Deum 242.1
tedious 310.2
tediousness
  300.34.1
tedium 242.2.2
tee 5
teem 234
teeming 265.36
teen 251
teenage 193
teenager 17.146
teens 547
teeny 16.228
teenybopper
  17.255
Tees 513
Teesside 92
teeter 17.341
teeth 457
teethe 475
teething 265

teetotal 228.106
teetotaller 17.176
teetotum 242.31
tef 160
Teflon 254
teg 181
tegmen 261
Teheran 246
Tehuantepec 35
tela 17.165
telaesthesia 17.3.60
telamon 261.52
Tel Aviv 484
telecast 431
telecommunication
  261.67.5
telecommunications
  551.1
teledu 15.2
telega 17.125
telegenic 38.32
telegnosis 300.55
Telegonus 310.36
telegony 16.237
telegram 229
telegraph 158
telegrapher 17.120
telegraphic 38.11
telegraphy 16.90
telekinesis 300.51
telekinetic 38.50.4
Telemachus 310.14
telemark 33.2
telemeter 17.342
telemetry 16.285
teleology
  16.108.4.1
teleost 438
telepathic 38.72
telepathize 516.14
telepathy 16.373
telephone 257
telephonic 38.35
telephonist 436.13
telephony 16.237
telephoto 12.79
telephotography
  16.90.2.6
teleplay 2
teleprinter 17.369
Teleran 245.5
telescope 278
telescopic 38.37
telescopy 16.254
telescript 424

telestich

telestich 38.69
telethon 254
teletranscription
261.85
teletube 30
Teletype 275
televise 516.15
television 261.91.2
telewriter 17.343
telex 496
Telford 103
telic 38.20
teliospore 9.10
telium 242.2.5
tell 215
Tell el Amarna
17.226
teller 17.163
telling 265.28
telltale 214
tellurian 261.3.24
telluric 38.43
telluride 92
tellurion 261.3.24
tellurium 242.2
tellurometer
17.342.3
telly 16.115
telophase 509
telpherage 197
telson 261
Telstar 1
Tema 17.210
temerity 16.333.21
temp 286
temper 17.262
tempera 17.279
temperament
420.35
temperamental
228.110.3
temperance 321.20
temperate 371.35
temperature 17.56
tempest 436
tempestuous 310.4
Templar 17.196
template 371
temple 228
tempo 12
temporal 228.76
temporality
16.333.8.9
temporary
16.274.32

temporize 516.8
tempt 428
temptation 261.67
tempter 17.378
tempting 265
temptress 300
tempura 1.13
ten 248
tenable 228.16
tenace 295
tenacious 310.56.4
tenacity 16.333.25
tenaculum 242.10
tenaille 214
tenancy 16.312
tenant 420.52
tenantry 16.291
tench 79
tend 131
tendency 16.312.2
tendentious 310.61
tender 17.101
tenderfoot 379.1
tenderhearted
91.33
tenderize 516.8
tenderizer 17.441.1
tenderloin 256
tenderness 300.26
tendinous 310.33
tendon 261
tendril 218
tenebrism 242.35
tenebrosity
16.333.30
tenebrous 310
Tenedos 302
tenement 420.35
Tenerife 162.2
tenet 371
tenfold 120
Tengri Nor 9
tenner 17.228
Tennessee 5.20
tennis 300
tenno 12.52
Tennyson 261.65
tenon 261
tenor 17.228
tenorite 372.8
tenorrhaphy
16.90.1
tenotomy 16.222.4
tenpenny 16.237
tenpin 252

tenpins 548
tenrec 35
tense 316
tensible 228.16.40
tensile 219.3
tensiometer
17.342.3.1
tension 261.82
tensive 485.9
tensor 17.314
tent 410
tentacle 228.28
tentacular 17.174.3
tentage 197.14
tentation 261.67.32
tentative 485.15.15
tenter 17.368
tenterhook 44
tenth 468
tenuity 16.333.3
tenuous 310.4.2
tenure 10
tenuto 12.80
Tenzing Norgay 2
teocalli 16.112
teosinte 16.356
tepal 228.65
tepee 5
tepefy 7.3
tephrite 372
tepid 91.23
tequila 17.165
Terai 7.12
teraph 171
teratism 242.35.20
teratogenic 38.32.1
teratoid 97
teratology
16.108.4.15
terbium 242.2
tercel 228.84
tercet 371
terebene 251
terebinth 470
terebinthine 253
teredo 12.18
Terence 321.16
terete 370
tergiversate 367
teriyaki 16.20
term 233
termagant 420.18
terminable
228.16.29
terminal 228.60

terminate 367.17.4
termination
261.67.18.4
terminator
17.338.7
terminology
16.108.4.10
terminus 310.33
termitarium
242.2.14
termite 372
termor 17.209
tern 249
ternary 16.274.24
ternate 371.23
terne 249
terpene 251
terpineol 220.1
Terpsichore
16.274.4
Terpsichorean
261.2.3
terrace 310.44
terra cotta 17.344
terra firma 17.209
terrain 247
terrane 247
terrapin 252
terrarium 242.2.14
terrene 251
terreplein 247
terrestrial 228.3.13
terret 371.31
terre-verte 369
terrible 228.16
terribly 16.137
terricolous
310.26.2
terrier 17.3
terrific 38.12.1
terrify 7.3.5
terrigenous 310.33
terrine 251
territorial
228.3.12.1
territorialism
242.35.11.2
territoriality
16.333.8.1
territorialize
516.3.2.2
territory 16.274.41
terror 17.269
terrorism 242.35.15
terrorist 436.20

504

terroristic 38.70.5
terrorize 516.8
Terry 16.262
terry 16.262
terse 297
tertial 228.92
tertian 261.69
tertiary 16.274
tertium quid 91
Tertullian 261.3.13
Terylene 251.2
terzetto 12.75
Tess 296
tessellate 367.12
tessellation
  261.67.12
tessera 17.279
tesseract 382
tessitura 17.277
test 433
testa 17.382
testament 420.35
testamentary
  16.274.47
testate 367.33
testator 17.338
testatrix 498.9
tester 17.382
testes 513.19
testicle 228.23
testiculate 371.17.2
testify 7.3
testimonial 228.3.8
testimony 16.237
testing 265.75
testis 300.68
teston 261.106
testosterone 257.1
testudinal 228.60.1
testudo 12.22
testy 16.364
tetanic 38.31
tetanize 516.7
tetanus 310.36
tetany 16.237
tetchy 16.48
tête-à-tête 367.31
tête-bêche 351
tether 17.402
tetra 17.293
tetrabrach 32
tetrachloride 92.5
tetrachord 95.3
tetracid 91.28
tetracycline 251

tetrad 83
tetragonal 228.63
tetragram 229.1
tetrahedron 261
tetralogy 16.108.2
tetrapod 94.1
tetrapody 16.72
tetrarch 33
tetraspore 9.10
tetrastich 38
tetrode 98
tetter 17.339
Teucer 17.308
Teuton 261.104
Teutonic 38.35
Teutonism
  242.35.14
Teutonize 516.7
Tewkesbury 16.274
Texan 261
Texas 310
text 450
textbook 44
textile 219.8
textual 228.9
textualism
  242.35.11.3
textuary 16.274.2
texture 17.75
Thackeray 16.274
Thai 7
Thailand 143
Thaïs 300
thalamus 310.29.2
thalassic 38.48
thaler 17.161
Thales 513
thalidomide 92.3
thallium 242.2
thallous 310
thallus 310
thalweg 181
Thames 541
than 245
thanatopsis 300.61
Thanatos 302
thane 247
Thanet 371.22
Thanjavur 10
thank 51
thankful 226
thankfulness
  300.30
thankless 300

thanklessness
  300.33
thanks 504
thanksgiving
  265.80
Thapsus 310
Thásos 302
that 365
thatch 62
thatcher 17.50
Thatcher 17.50
thaumatology
  16.108.4.15
thaumatrope 278.3
thaumaturge 195
thaw 9
thearchy 16.20
theatre 17.352
theatrical 228.23
theatricals 539.2
theatrics 498.8
theca 17.33
thee 5
theft 397
their 4
theirs 512
theism 242.35.1
them 232
thematic 38.49.1
theme 234
Themis 300
themselves 555
then 248
thenar 1
thence 316
theocentric 38.47
theocracy
  16.307.5.1
theocrasy
  16.307.5.1
Theocritus 310.64
theodicy 16.300.1
theodolite 372.4
Theodoric 38.44
theogony 16.237.4
theologian 261.3
theologize 516.1
theology 16.108.4.1
theomachy 16.33
theomancy 16.309
theomania
  17.3.31.1
theonomy
  16.222.3.1

theopathy
  16.373.1.1
theophagy 16.108.1
theophany
  16.237.3.1
Theophilus 310.23
theophobia 17.3.4
theorem 242.19
theoretical
  228.23.19
theoretician
  261.71.7
theoretics 498.12
theorist 436.20
theorize 516.8
theory 16.265
theosophy 16.90.4
therapeutic 38.56
therapeutics 498
therapist 436.15
therapsid 91.31
therapy 16.254
there 4
thereabouts 344
thereafter 17.358
thereat 365
thereby 7
therefore 9
therefrom 237
therein 252
thereinto 15
thereof 487
thereon 254
Theresa 17.440
thereto 15
theretofore 9
thereunder 17.108
thereupon 254
therewith 476
therianthropic
  38.37.3
theriomorphic
  38.14
therm 233
thermae 5
thermaesthesia
  17.3.60
thermal 228
thermalize 516.3
thermion 261.3
thermionic 38.35.1
thermionics 498.5
thermistor 17.384
thermocouple 228

thermodynamic 38.24
thermodynamics 498.2
thermoelectric 38
thermoelectricity 16.333.28
thermogenesis 300.52.4
thermograph 158.1
thermography 16.90.2
thermolysis 300.52.2
thermolytic 38.52.1
thermomagnetic 38.50
thermometer 17.342.3.2
thermometry 16.285.2
thermonuclear 17.3
thermophile 219.1
thermophilic 38.21
thermopile 219
thermoplastic 38.68
Thermopylae 5.9
Thermos 310
thermoscope 278.1
thermosetting 265.65
thermosphere 6.1
thermostat 365
thermostatic 38.49.7
thermostatics 498.11
thermotaxis 300.70
thermotensile 219.3
thermotherapy 16.254
theroid 97.10
theropod 94.1
thesaurus 310.48
these 513
Theseus 310.2
thesis 300.51
Thespian 261.3
Thespis 300
Thessalonian 261.3.18
Thessaly 16.131
theta 17.341

thetic 38.50
Thetis 300
theurgy 16.102
thew 15
they 2
they'd 85
they'll 214
they're 4
they've 482
thiamine 252.15
thiazole 223
thick 38
thick-and-thin 252
thicken 261.13
thickener 17.239
thickening 265.46
thicket 371.9
thickleaf 162
thickly 16.142
thickness 300.27
thickset 368
thick-skinned 134
thief 162
thieve 484
thieving 265.79
thigh 7
thighbone 257
thimble 228
thimbleful 226
thimblerig 184
thimbleweed 89.7
thimblewit 371
thin 252
thine 253
thing 265
thingumabob 26
thingumajig 184
think 52
thinkable 228.16.11
thinker 17.44
thinking 265.10
thinner 17.231
thinness 300
thin-skinned 134
thionic 38.35
thionyl 218
thiophen 248
thiourea 17.3.42
third 87
third-rate 367
thirdstream 234
thirl 216
Thirlmere 6
thirst 434
thirstiness 300.23

thirsty 16.365
thirteen 251
thirteenth 469
thirtieth 458
thirty 16.331
this 300
thistle 228.85
thistledown 258
thistly 16.181
thither 17.405
thitherto 15
thixotropic 38.37.2
thole 223
tholos 302
Thomas 310
Thomism 242.35
Thompson 261
thong 266
Thor 9
thoracic 38.48
thoracotomy 16.222.4
thorax 494
thoria 17.3.41
thorite 372
thorium 242.2.17
thorn 255
thornback 32
thornbill 218
Thorndike 39
thorny 16.232
thoron 254.10
thorough 17.278
thoroughbred 86
thoroughfare 4.3
thoroughgoing 265.4
thoroughly 16.131
thoroughness 300.26
thoroughpin 252
Thorpe 277
those 520
Thoth 461
thou 13
though 12
thought 374
thoughtful 226
thoughtfulness 300.30
thoughtless 300
thoughtlessness 300.33
thousand 143
thousandth 471

Thrace 295
thrall 221
thrash 349
thrasher 17.321
thrashing 265
thrawn 255
thread 86
threadbare 4
threadfin 252
threadworm 233
thready 16.60
threap 273
threat 368
threaten 261.96
three 5
three-dimensional 228.63.9
threefold 120
three-legged 91
threescore 9
threesome 242
threnody 16.72
thresh 351
thresher 17.323
threshold 120
threw 15
thrice 301
thrift 398
thriftless 300
thriftlessness 300.33
thrifty 16.347
thrill 218
thriller 17.166
thrilling 265.30
thrips 327
thrive 486
throat 376
throatlash 349
throaty 16.339
throb 26
throes 520
thromboembolism 242.35.11
thrombogen 261.39
thromboplastic 38.68
thrombose 305
thrombosis 300.55
thrombotic 38.53
thrombus 310
throne 257
throng 266
throstle 228.86
throttle 228.104

through 15
throughout 377
throughput 379
throughway 2
throw 12
throwaway 2.28
throwback 32
thrown 257
throwster 17.387
thrum 240
thrush 356
thrust 443
thruster 17.388
thud 100
thug 189
thuggee 5
thuggery 16.274.10
thuja 17.432
Thule 5
thulium 242.2
thumb 240
thumbnail 214
thumbprint 412
thumbscrew 15
thumbstall 221
thumbtack 32
thump 289
thumping 265.50
thunder 17.108
thunderbird 87
thunderbolt 405
thunderclap 268
thundercloud 99.1
thunderhead 86.5
thundering 265.58
thunderous 310.50
thunderstone 257
thunderstorm 238
thunderstruck 43
thundery 16.274
Thurber 17.12
thurible 228.12
thurifer 17.114
Thuringia 17.3
Thursday 2
thus 307
thwack 32
thwart 374
thy 7
Thyestes 513.19
thylacine 253.8
thyme 236
thymol 220
thymus 310
thyristor 17.384

thyroid 97.11
thyroidectomy
  16.222.5.1
thyroiditis 300.62
thyroxine 252.29
thyrse 297
thyrsus 310
thysanuran 261.59
thyself 172
Tia Maria 17.2.2
tiara 17.268.1
Tiber 17.15
Tiberius 310.2.11
Tibesti 16.364
Tibet 368.2
Tibetan 261.96
tibia 17.3.3
Tibullus 310
tic 38
tick 38
ticker 17.34
ticket 371.9
ticking 265.7
tickle 228.23
tickler 17.181
ticklish 353
ticklishness 300.35
ticktack 32
tick-tack-toe 12
ticktock 40
Ticonderoga
  17.133
tidal 228.33
tiddler 17.186
tiddly 16.148
tiddlywinks 505
tide 92
tidemark 33
tideway 2
tidiness 300.23
tidings 552
tidy 16.64
tie 7
tieback 32
tiebreaker 17.30
tied 92
tiepin 252
tier 6
tierce 299
tiff 163
tiffany 16.237.2
tiffin 252
tiger 17.130
tiger's-eye 7
tight 372

tighten 261.100
tightfisted 91.53
tightknit 371
tightness 300.39
tightrope 278
tights 340
tightwad 94
tigon 261
Tigré 2
tigress 300
Tigrinya 17.435
Tigris 300
Tijuana 17.226
tiki 16.24
tilapia 17.3
Tilbury 16.274
tilbury 16.274
tilde 17.95
tile 219
tiler 17.167
tiliaceous 310.56
tiling 265
till 218
tillage 197.1
tillandsia 17.3
tiller 17.166
Tilly 16.120
Tilsit 371
tilt 403
tilth 466
tiltyard 84
Timaru 15.6
timbal 228
timbale 213
timber 17.25
timberhead 86.5
timbering 265.58
timberland 143.4
timberwork 36
timberyard 84
timbre 17.284
timbrel 228
Timbuktu 15
time 236
timecard 84
timekeeper 17.252
timeless 300
timelessness 300.33
timely 16.167
timeous 310
timepiece 298
timer 17.212
timesaving 265.77
timeserver 17.412
timetable 228.11

timework 36
timeworn 255
timid 91
timidity 16.333.5
timing 265
timocracy 16.307.5
Timor 9
timorous 310.50
Timoshenko 12.13
Timothy 16.373
timpani 16.237
timpanist 436.13
timps 331
tin 252
Tina 17.230
tinct 392
tinctorial 228.3.12
tincture 17.67
tinder 17.102
tinderbox 499
tine 253
tinea 17.3.34
tineid 91.2
tinfoil 222
ting 265
ting-a-ling 265
tinge 209
tingle 228.50
tingly 16.163
tinker 17.44
tinkle 228.29
tin lizzie 16.396
tinned 134
tinnitus 310.65
tinny 16.229
tinpot 373
tinsel 228
tint 412
Tintagel 228
tinted 91
tintinnabulation
  261.67.13.1
tintinnabulum
  242.10
Tintoretto 12.75
tintype 275
tinware 4
tiny 16.230
tip 274
tipcat 365
tipper 17.253
Tipperary 16.264
tippet 371
tipple 228.66
tipstaff 158

tipster 17.396
tipsy 16.314
tiptoe 12
tiptop 276
tirade 85
Tirana 17.226
tire 8
tireless 300
tirelessness 300.33
tiresome 242
Tirich Mir 6
tiring 265.54
Tiros 305
Tirunelveli 16.115
'tis 515
tisane 245.7
tissue 15
tit 371
Titan 261.100
Titania 17.3.30
titanic 38.31
Titanism 242.35.14
titanium 242.2.10
titanosaur 9.11
titanothere 6.10
titbit 371
tithable 228.16
tithe 477
Tithonus 310.35
titi 5
Titian 261.71
titillate 367.12
titillation 261.67.12
titivate 367.36
titivation 261.67
title 228.103
titled 122
titman 261
titmouse 306
Tito 12.76
Titoism 242.35.3
titrant 420
titrate 367
titration 261.67
titre 17.343
titter 17.342
tittle 228.102
tittle-tattle 228.97
tittup 281
titubation 261.67
titular 17.174.12
Titus 310.65
Tiv 485
Tivoli 16.131
tizzy 16.396

Tlingit 371
tmesis 300.51
to 15
toad 98
toadflax 494
toadstone 257
toadstool 227
toady 16.67
toast 441
toaster 17.387
toastmaster 17.380
tobacco 12.8
tobacconist 436.13
Tobago 12.27
toboggan 261
Tobruk 44.1
Toby 16.12
toccata 17.337
Tocharian 261.3
tocology 16.108.4
tocopherol 220.4
tocsin 252.29
tod 94
today 2.8
Todd 94
toddle 228.34
toddler 17.188
toddy 16.65
to-do 15.3
tody 16.67
toe 12
toea 1
toecap 268
toehold 120
toenail 214
toey 16.3
toff 165
toffee 16.86
toft 399
tog 185
toga 17.133
together 17.402
togetherness
  300.26
toggery 16.274.12
toggle 228.47
Togliatti 16.327
Togo 12.31
Togoland 143.3
toil 222
toile 213
toilet 371
toiletry 16.285
toilette 368
toilsome 242

tokay 2
Tokay 7
token 261.14
tokenism 242.35.14
tokoloshe 354
Tokyo 12
tola 17.171
tolan 245
tolbutamide 92.3
told 120
tole 223
Toledo 12.17,
  12.18
tolerable 228.16.35
tolerance 321.20
tolerant 420.65
tolerate 367.23
toleration
  261.67.22
Tolkien 251
toll 223
tollbooth 479
tollgate 367
tollhouse 306
Tolpuddle 228.36
Tolstoy 11
Toltec 35
toluate 367.2
toluene 251
Tom 237
tom 237
tomahawk 41
tomalley 16.112
toman 246
tomato 12.73
tomb 241
tombac 32
tombola 17.171
tomboy 11
tomboyish 353
tombstone 257
tome 239
tomentum 242
tomfool 227
tomfoolery 16.274
tommyrot 373
tomography
  16.90.2
tomorrow 12.65
tomtit 371
ton 259
tonal 228.62
tonality 16.333.8
Tonbridge 197
tone 257

toneless 300
toneme 234
toner 17.236
tonetic 38.50
tong 266
Tonga 17.142
tongue 267
tonic 38.35
tonicity 16.333.28
tonight 372.6
tonk 53
tonka 17.45
Tonle Sap 268
tonnage 197
tonne 259
tonneau 12
tonometer
  17.342.3.3
tonsil 228.89
tonsillectomy
  16.222.5
tonsillitic 38.52
tonsillitis 300.62.1
tonsillotomy
  16.222.4
tonsorial 228.3.12
tonsure 17
tontine 251
tonus 310.35
Tony 16.233
too 15
toodle-oo 15.5
took 44
tool 227
tooling 265
toon 260
toot 380
tooth 463
toothache 34
toothbrush 356
toothful 226.14
toothless 300
toothpaste 432
toothpick 38
toothsome 242
toothy 16.372
tootle 228.108
toots 345
tootsy 16.318
tootsy-wootsy
  16.318
top 276
toparch 33
topaz 507
topazolite 372.4

508

topcoat 376
tope 278
topee 5.16
toper 17.257
topgallant 420.24
Tophet 368
topiary 16.274.1
topic 38.37
topical 228.23.14
topicality
16.333.8.3
topknot 373
topless 300
toplofty 16.348
topmast 431
topminnow 12.55
topmost 441
topnotch 68
topnotcher 17.57
topography 16.90.2
topology
16.108.4.12
toponym 235
toponymy 16.216
topos 302
topper 17.255
topping 265
topple 228.68
tops 329
topsail 214
topside 92.10
topsoil 222
topspin 252
topsy-turvy 16.381
toque 42
tor 9
Torbay 2
torch 69
torchbearer 17.271
torchère 4
torchier 17.3
tore 9
toreador 9.4
torero 12.62
tori 7.11
torii 5.2
torment 410
tormentil 218
tormentor 17.368
torn 255
tornadic 38.7
tornado 12.17
toroid 97
Toronto 12.85
torose 305

torpedo 12.18
torpid 91
torpor 17.256
Torquay 5
torque 41
torques 513
torr 9
Torrance 321.18
torrefy 7.3
torrent 420.63
torrential 228.96.2
torrid 91.26
torsade 85
torsion 261.72
torso 12
tort 374
torte 374
tortellini 16.228.1
torticollis 300.9
tortilla 17.2
tortious 310.59
tortoise 310
tortoiseshell 215
tortoni 16.233
tortricid 91.29
tortuosity
16.333.30.2
tortuous 310.4
torture 17.58
torturer 17.279
torus 310.48
Tory 16.269
Toscanini 16.228
tosh 354
toss 302
tosspot 373
tot 373
total 228.106
totalitarian
261.3.21.2
totality 16.333.8
totalizator 17.338
totalize 516.3
totalizer 17.441
tote 376
totem 242.31
totemic 38.25
totemism 242.35
totipotent 420.78
totter 17.344
toucan 261.15
touch 72
touchable 228.16
touchdown 258
touché 2

touching 265
touchline 253
touchmark 33
touchstone 257
touchwood 101
touchy 16.52
tough 168
toughen 261
toughie 16.88
toughness 300
Toulouse 523
toupee 2
tour 10
touraco 12
Tourane 246
tourbillion 261.120
tourer 17.277
tourism 242.35
tourist 436.19
touristic 38.70
touristy 16.366
tourmaline 251.3
tournament 420.35
tournedos 12
tourniquet 2.7
tousle 228.129
tous-les-mois 1
tout 377
tovarisch 353
tow 12
towage 197
toward 95.4
towards 528
towbar 1
towel 228.8
towelling 265
tower 14
towering 265.57
tow-haired 88
towhead 86.3
towline 253
town 258
townee 5
townhall 221
townie 16.234
townscape 270
township 274
townsman 261
townspeople
228.65
townswoman
261.50
towpath 453
towrope 278
toxaemia 17.3.26.1

toxaphene 251
toxic 38.75
toxicant 420.7
toxicity 16.333.28
toxicogenic 38.32.1
toxicology
16.108.4.4
toxicosis 300.55
toxin 252.29
toxoid 97
toxophilite 372.3
toy 11
Toyama 1.10
trabeated 91.34.1
trabecula 17.174.4
Trabzon 255
trace 295
traceable 228.16.36
tracer 17.299
tracery 16.274.33
trachea 17.2
tracheid 91.2
tracheitis 300.62
tracheostomy
16.222.6
tracheotomy
16.222.4.1
trachoma 17.215
trachyte 372
trachytic 38.52
tracing 265.59
track 32
tracker 17.28
trackless 300
tracksuit 380
tract 382
tractable 228.16
Tractarianism
242.35.14.1.1
tractate 367
tractile 219.4
traction 261.76
tractive 485.16
tractor 17.353
Tracy 16.296
trad 83
trade 85
trademark 33
trader 17.79
tradescantia
17.3.50
tradesfolk 42
tradesman 261
trading 265.11
tradition 261.71.2

traditional 228.63.5
traditionalism 242.35.11.5
traditor 17.342
traduce 309.1
traducianism 242.35.14
Trafalgar 17.137
traffic 38.11
trafficator 17.338.2
trafficker 17.34
tragacanth 467
tragedian 261.3.4
tragedienne 248.1
tragedy 16.63
tragic 38.15
tragically 16.142
tragicomedy 16.63
tragicomic 38.29
tragopan 245.4
tragus 310.19
trail 214
trailblazer 17.439
trailer 17.162
train 247
trainband 128
trainbearer 17.271
trainee 5.11
trainer 17.227
training 265.40
train-spotting 265.68
traipse 323
trait 367
traitor 17.338
traitorous 310.50
traitress 300
Trajan 261.34
traject 385.3
trajectory 16.274.45
tra-la 1.7
Tralee 5.9
tram 229
tramline 253
trammel 228.51
trammie 16.210
tramontane 247.11
tramp 285
trample 228
trampoline 251.3
tramway 2
trance 315
trannie 16.223
tranquil 218

tranquillity 16.333.9
tranquillize 516.2
tranquillizer 17.441
transact 382
transaction 261.76
transalpine 253
transatlantic 38.62
transceiver 17.413
transcend 131
transcendent 420.14
transcendental 228.110
transcendentalism 242.35.11.6
transcontinental 228.110
transcribe 25
transcript 424
transcription 261.85
transculturation 261.67.21
transcurrent 420.64
transducer 17.308
transduction 261.79
transect 385
transept 422
transeunt 420.1
transfer 3
transferable 228.16
transferee 5.17
transference 321.20
transfiguration 261.67.21
transfigure 17.129
transfix 498
transform 238
transformation 261.67.16
transformer 17.214
transformism 242.35.12
transfuse 523
transfusion 261.93
transgress 296
transgression 261.68
transhumance 321
transience 321.1
transient 420.1
transistor 17.384
transistorize 516.8

transit 371
transition 261.71
transitional 228.63.5
transitive 485.12
transitory 16.274.41
translate 367
translation 261.67
translator 17.338
transliterate 367.23.2
transliteration 261.67.22.4
translocate 367.6
translucence 321.23
translucent 420.71
transmigrant 420
transmigrate 367
transmission 261.71
transmit 371
transmittance 321.24
transmittancy 16.312
transmitter 17.342
transmogrify 7.3
transmundane 247
transmutation 261.67.29
transmute 380
transoceanic 38.31.1
transom 242
transonic 38.35
transpacific 38.12
transparency 16.312
transparent 420.60
transpicuous 310.4.1
transpierce 299
transpire 8
transplant 408
transplantation 261.67
transpolar 17.171
transponder 17.104
transpontine 253
transport 374
transportation 261.67
transporter 17.345

transpose 520
transposition 261.71.9
transsexual 228.9
transsexualism 242.35.11.3
transship 274
transubstantiate 367.1.8
transubstantiation 261.67.1
transude 102
Transvaal 213
transversal 228.84
transverse 297
transvestite 372
Transylvania 17.3.31
Transylvanian 261.3.15
trap 268
trapeze 513
trapezium 242.2.20
trapezius 310.2
trapezoid 97
trapper 17.247
trappings 552
Trappist 436
traprock 40
traps 322
trash 349
trashy 16.319
trass 293
trattoria 17.2.2
trauma 17.214
traumatic 38.49
traumatism 242.35.20
traumatize 516.13
travail 214
trave 482
travel 228.117
traveller 17.176
travelling 265
travelogue 185
traverse 297
travertine 252
travesty 16.366
travois 11
trawl 221
trawler 17.169
tray 2
traymobile 217
treacherous 310.50
treachery 16.274

treacle 228
treacly 16.141
tread 86
treadle 228
treadmill 218
treason 261.125
treasure 17.333
treasured 103.6
treasurer 17.279
treasury 16.274
treat 370
treatise 515
treatment 420
treaty 16.332
Trebizond 136
treble 228
Treblinka 17.44
trebly 16.133
trebuchet 368
trebucket 371.11
tree 5
treehopper 17.255
treeless 300
treen 251
treenail 214
treenware 4
trefoil 222
trehala 17.161
treillage 197
trek 35
trekker 17.31
trellis 300
trelliswork 36
trematode 98
tremble 228.18
trembly 16.138
tremendous 310
tremolo 12.45
tremor 17.208
tremulant 420.27
tremulous 310.25
trench 79
trenchant 420
trencher 17.70
trencherman
  261.52
trend 131
trendy 16.78
Trent 410
Trenton 261
trepan 245.3
trepang 263
trephine 251
trepidation
  261.67.7

treponema 17.210
trespass 310
trespasser 17.309
tress 296
tressure 17.323
trestle 228
trestletree 5
tret 368
trevally 16.112
Trevelyan 261.119
Trevino 12.54
trews 523
trey 2
triable 228.16.3
triacid 91.28
triad 83.2
triage 197
trial 228.4
triangle 228.49
triangular 17.174
triangulate
  367.13.4
triangulation
  261.67.13.2
Triangulum 242.10
triarchy 16.20
Triassic 38.48
triatomic 38.29
triaxial 228.3.18
tribal 228
tribalism 242.35.11
tribe 25
tribesman 261
triblet 371
tribrach 32
tribulation
  261.67.13
tribunal 228
tribune 260
tributary 16.274.42
tribute 380.2
trice 301
tricentenary
  16.274.25
triceps 324
triceratops 329
trichiasis 300.57.1
trichina 17.232
trichinize 516.6
Trichinopoly
  16.131.6
trichinosis 300.55.4
trichite 372
trichloride 92.5
trichocyst 436.22

trichogyne 253
trichoid 97.3
trichology
  16.108.4.4
trichome 239
trichomonad 83.3
trichotomy
  16.222.4
trichroism 242.35.3
trichromatic
  38.49.2
trick 38
trickery 16.274.4
trickle 228.23
tricksy 16.388
tricky 16.25
triclinic 38.34
triclinium 242.2.11
tricolour 17.176.2
tricorn 255
tricot 12.11
tricotine 251.11
tricrotic 38.53
trictrac 32
tricuspid 91
tricycle 228.23
trident 420
tridentate 367.32
Tridentine 253
triennial 228.3
triennium 242.2
trierarchy 16.20
Trieste 433
trifid 91
trifle 228
trifling 265
trifolium 242.2.7
triforium 242.2.17
trifurcate 371.8
trig 184
trigeminal 228.60.3
trigger 17.129
triglyph 163
trigon 254
trigonometry
  16.285.2.2
trigraph 158
trike 39
trilateral 228.76
trilateration
  261.67.22
trilby 16.16
trilemma 17.208
trilinear 17.3.34
trilingual 228

trilithon 254
trill 218
trillion 261.120
trillionth 471
trillium 242
trilobate 367.3
trilobite 372
trilogy 16.108.3
trim 235
trimaran 245.5
trimer 17.212
trimester 17.382
trimeter 17.342.2
trimetric 38.46
trimetrogon 254.5
trimmer 17.211
trimming 265
trimonthly 16.205
trimorph 166
Trimurti 16.337
trinary 16.274.27
Trincomalee 5.9
trine 253
Trinidad 83
Trinitarian
  261.3.21.2
trinity 16.333.17
trinket 371
trinomial 228.3
trio 12.2
triode 98
triolet 368
trioxide 92.14
trip 274
tripartite 372
tripartition 261.71
tripe 275
triphibious 310.2
triphthong 266
triphylite 372.3
triplane 247
triple 228.66
triplet 371
Triplex 496
triplicate 367.5,
  371.9
triplicity
  16.333.28.1
triploid 97
triply 16.177
tripod 94
tripody 16.72
Tripoli 16.131.5
tripoli 16.131.5

Tripolitania
  17.3.31.2
tripos 302
tripper 17.253
Triptolemus 310.28
triptych 38.66
triptyque 37
tripwire 8
trireme 234
trisaccharide 92.6
trisect 385
triskaidekaphobia
  17.3.4
triskelion 254.1
trismus 310.30
Tristan 261.107
tristich 38.70
tristichous 310.10
trisulphide 92
tritanopia 17.3.37.2
trite 372
triteness 300.39
tritheism 242.35.2
triticale 16.113
triticum 242.4
tritium 242.2.18
Triton 261.100
triton 261.100
tritone 257
triturate 367.22
trituration
  261.67.21
triumph 177
triumphal 228
triumphant 420
triumvirate 371.33
triune 260
trivalent 420.25
Trivandrum 242
trivet 371
trivia 17.3.54
trivial 228.3.15
triviality
  16.333.8.1.2
trivialize 516.3.2
triweekly 16.141
Troas 293
troat 376
trocar 1
trochaic 38.1
trochal 228.26
trochanter 17.365
troche 355
trochee 5
trochilus 310.23

trochlea 17.3
trochoid 97
trochophore 9.6
trod 94
trodden 261.26
trog 185
troglodyte 372.2
troglodytic 38.52
trogon 254
Troilus 310
Trojan 261
troll 223
trolley 16.122
trollop 281.2
Trollope 281.2
trombone 257
trombonist 436
trompe 288
trona 17.236
Trondheim 236
troop 280
trooper 17.259
troopship 274
troostite 372
tropaeolum 242.11
trope 278
trophic 38.13
trophoblast 430
trophy 16.87
tropic 38.37
tropical 228.23.14
tropics 498
tropism 242.35
tropology 16.108.4
troposphere 6.1
Trossachs 503
trot 373
troth 461
Trotsky 16
Trotskyism
  242.35.2
Trotskyite 372
trotter 17.344
troubadour 10
trouble 228.14
troublemaker 17.30
troubleshooter
  17.351
troublesome 242
troublous 310
trou-de-loup 15.5
trough 165
trounce 319
troupe 280
trouper 17.259

troupial 228.3.9
trouse 521
trousered 103
trousers 524
trousseau 12
trout 377
trouvère 4
trove 488
trover 17.417
Trowbridge 197
trowel 228.8
Troy 11
truancy 16.312
truant 420.5
truce 309
truck 43
trucker 17.39
truckie 16.30
trucking 265
truckle 228.27
truckload 98
truculent 420.27
Trudeau 12.22
trudge 203
trudgen 261.38
true 15
truelove 489
truffle 228.42
trug 189
truism 242.35.4
truly 16.130
Truman 261.51
trumeau 12
trump 289
trumpery 16.274
trumpet 371
trumpeter 17.342
trumps 332
truncate 367
truncated 91.34
truncation 261.67
truncheon 261
trundle 228
trunk 54
trunkfish 353
trunks 506
trunnion 261
Truro 12.66
truss 307
trust 443
trustee 5
trusteeship 274
trustful 226.13
trustworthy 16.375
trusty 16.368

truth 463
truthful 226.14
truthfulness 300.30
try 7
trying 265.3
tryma 17.212
trypanosomiasis
  300.57.1
trypsinogen 261.39
tryptophan 245
trysail 214
tryst 436
tsar 1
tsarevitch 67
tsarina 17.230
tsarism 242.35
tsarist 436.16
tsaritsa 17.320
Tshiluba 17.20
Tshombe 16.18
Tsinghai 7
Tsonga 17.142
Tsukahara 17.268
tsunami 16.211
Tsushima 1
Tswana 17.226
Tuareg 181
tuart 366
tuatara 17.268
tub 29
tuba 17.20
tubal 228
Tubal-cain 247
tubate 367
tubbiness 300.23
tubby 16.13
tube 30
tubeless 300
tuber 17.20
tubercle 228.28
tubercular 17.174.5
tuberculate 371.17
tuberculin 252.10
tuberculosis
  300.55.3
tuberculous 310.25
tuberose 305.2,
  520.3
tuberosity
  16.333.30.5
tuberous 310.50
tubifex 496
tubing 265
tubular 17.174
tubulate 367.13

tubule 227
tubuliflorous 310.48
tubulous 310.25
Tucana 17.226
tuchun 260
tuck 43
tucker 17.39
tucket 371.11
Tucson 254
Tudor 17.91
Tuesday 2
tufa 17.119
tuff 168
tuffet 371
tuft 400
tufted 91
tufty 16.349
tug 189
tugrik 37
tui 16.4
Tuileries 16.274
tuition 261.71
tularaemia 17.3.26
tulip 274
Tull 225
tulle 227
Tulsa 17.311
tum 240
tumble 228
tumble-down 258
tumblehome 239
tumbler 17.180
tumbleweed 89.7
tumbrel 228.77
tumefaction 261.76
tumefy 7.3
tumescence 321.21
tumescent 420.67
tumid 91
tummy 16.220
tumour 17.217
tump 289
tumular 17.174
tumulose 305
tumult 406
tumultuous 310.4
tumulus 310.25.5
tun 259
tuna 17.238
tunable 228.16
tundra 17.288
tune 260
tuneful 226
tuneless 300

tunelessness 300.33
tuner 17.238
tunesmith 458
tungsten 261
Tungus 308
Tungusic 38
tunic 38
tunicate 371.9
tunicle 228.23
tuning 265
Tunis 300
Tunisia 17.3.61
tunnel 228
tunny 16.235
tup 279
tupelo 12.42
Tupi 5
tuque 45
turban 261.9
turbary 16.274
turbid 91
turbinate 371.24
turbine 253
turbocar 1
turbocharger 17.145
turbo-electric 38
turbofan 245
turbojet 368
turboprop 276
turbot 381
turbulence 321
turbulent 420.27
turd 87
turdine 253
tureen 251.7
turf 161
turfy 16.83
turgescent 420.67
turgid 91
turgor 17.127
Turin 252
turion 261.3.24
Turk 36
Turkestan 246.1
Turkey 16.23
turkey 16.23
Turkic 38
Turkish 353
Turkoman 261.52
turmeric 38.44
turmoil 222
turn 249
turnabout 377.1
turnaround 139.1

turnbuckle 228.27
turncoat 376
turncock 40
turner 17.229
turnery 16.274.24
turning 265.41
turnip 274
turnkey 5
turnpike 39
turnsole 223
turnstile 219
turntable 228.11
turpentine 253
turpeth 458
Turpin 252
turpitude 102.2
turps 325
turquoise 519
turret 371
turreted 91.38
turtle 228
turtleback 32
turtledove 489
turtleneck 35
Tuscan 261.17
Tuscany 16.237
Tuscarora 17.276
tusche 357
Tusculum 242.10
tush 356
tusk 60
tusker 17.49
Tussaud 12
tussis 300
tussle 228.87
tussock 46
tussore 9
tut 378
Tutankhamen 261
Tutankhamun 260
tutee 5
tutelage 197.1
tutelary 16.274.16
tutor 17.351
tutorial 228.3.12
tutsan 261
tutti 16.342
tutti-frutti 16.343
tutty 16.341
tutu 15
Tuvalu 15.5
tu-whit tu-whoo 15
tuxedo 12.18
tuyère 4

twaddle 228.34
Twain 247
twain 247
twang 263
'twas 517
twat 365
twayblade 85
tweak 37
twee 5
Tweed 89
tweed 89
Tweedledee 5
Tweedledum 240
tweedy 16.62
tweet 370
tweeter 17.341
tweeze 513
tweezers 524
Twelfthtide 92
twelve 492
twentieth 458
twenty 16.355
'twere 3
twerp 272
Twi 5
twibill 218
twice 301
Twickenham 242.16
twiddle 228.32
twig 184
twiggy 16.93
twilight 372
twilit 371
twill 218
twin 252
twine 253
twinge 209
twink 52
twinkle 228.29
twinkler 17.182
twinkling 265
twirl 216
twist 436
twister 17.384
twisty 16.366
twit 371
twitch 67
twitcher 17.56
twite 372
twitter 17.342
two 15
two-dimensional 228.63.9
two-faced 432

twofold 120
twopence 321.15
twopenny 16.237
two-seater 17.341
twosome 242
Tyburn 249
Tyche 16.26
tychism 242.35
Tycho 12
tycoon 260
tyke 39
Tyler 17.167
tylopod 94.1
tympan 261
tympanic 38.31
tympanitis
 300.62.4
tympanum 242.16
tympany 16.237
Tyndale 228.40
Tyne 253
Tyneside 92
Tynwald 122
type 275
typecase 295
typecast 431
typeface 295
typescript 424
typeset 368
typesetter 17.339
typesetting 265.65
typewrite 372
typewriter 17.343
typewriting 265.67
typhlitis 300.62
typhlology
 16.108.4
typhogenic 38.32.1
typhoid 97
typhonic 38.35
typhoon 260
typhus 310
typical 228.23
typically 16.142
typify 7.3
typing 265
typist 436
typo 12
typographical
 228.23.3
typography 16.90.2
typology 16.108.4
typothetae 5.22
tyrannical
 228.23.10

tyrannicide 92.7
tyrannize 516.7
tyrannosaur 9.11
tyrannosaurus
 310.48.1
tyranny 16.237
tyrant 420
Tyre 8
tyre 8
Tyrian 261.3
tyro 12.64
Tyrol 223
Tyrolienne 248.1
Tyrone 257
tyrosinase 509
tyrosine 251.9
tyrothricin 252.22
Tyrrhenian
 261.3.16
Tzigane 246

U

ubiety 16.333.2
ubiquitarian
 261.3.21.2
ubiquitous 310.64
UCCA 17.39
udal 228.37
udder 17.90
udo 12.22
UFO 12
ufology 16.108.4
Uganda 17.98
Ugandan 261
Ugaritic 38.52.2
ugli 16.161
uglify 7.3
ugliness 300.23
ugly 16.161
Ugric 38
uhlan 246
Uigur 10
uintathere 6.10
Ujjain 247
ukase 509
ukiyoe 2
Ukraine 247
Ukrainian 261.3.15
ukulele 16.114
ulcer 17.311

ulcerate 367.23
ulceration
 261.67.22
ulcerative
 485.15.10
ulcerous 310.50
ulema 17.211
ullage 197
Ullswater 17.345
ulotrichous 310.10
Ulster 17
Ulsterman 261.52
ulterior 17.3.39
ultima 17.211
ultimate 371.19
ultimately 16.189.1
ultimatum 242.27
ultimo 12.48
ultrafilter 17.362
ultrahigh 7
ultraism 242.35
ultramarine 251.7
ultramodern
 261.26
ultramontane
 247.11
ultramontanism
 242.35.13
ultrashort 374
ultrasonic 38.35.4
ultrasonics 498.5
ultrasound 139
ultraviolet 371.18.1
ultravirus 310.47
ululate 367.13
Ulysses 513
umbel 228
umbelliferous
 310.50.2
umber 17.27
umbilical 228.23.7
umbilicate 371.9
umbilicus 310.10
umbo 12.7
umbra 17.285
umbrage 197
umbrageous 310.20
umbrella 17.163
Umbria 17.3.44
Umbrian 261.3.25
Umbriel 228.3
umiak 32.1
umlaut 377
umpire 8
umpteen 251

umpteenth 469
Umtali 16.113
unabated 91.34
unable 228.11
unabridged 110
unacceptable
 228.16.58
unacclaimed 124
unaccompanied
 91.21
unaccomplished
 449
unaccountable
 228.16.56
unaccustomed 127
unacquainted
 91.45
unadopted 91
unadorned 137
unadulterated
 91.34.7
unadvised 154
unadvisedly 16.148
unaffected 91.43
unafraid 85
unaided 91.6
unaimed 124
unaired 88
unalloyed 97.6
unanimity
 16.333.12
unanimous
 310.28.1
unanswerable
 228.16.35
unanswered 103
unapproachable
 228.16.13
unappropriated
 91.34.1
unapt 421
unarm 230
unarmed 123
unary 16.274.28
unashamed 124
unashamedly
 16.148
unasked 394
unassailable
 228.16.22
unassisted 91.53
unassuming 265.39
unatoned 138
unattached 395

unattainable 228.16.27
unattended 91.13
unattested 91.52
unattractive 485.16
unauthorized 154
unavailable 228.16.22
unavailing 265.27
unavoidable 228.16
unaware 4.8
unawares 512
unbacked 382
unbalance 321.10
unbar 1
unbearable 228.16.33
unbeatable 228.16.48
unbeaten 261.98
unbecoming 265.38
unbeknown 257
unbelief 162.1
unbelievable 228.16.61
unbeliever 17.413
unbelieving 265.79
unbelt 402
unbend 131
unbendable 228.16.18
unbending 265.20
unbent 410
unbiased 445
unbidden 261.24
unbind 135
unbirthday 2
unblessed 433
unblinking 265.10
unbolt 405
unbolted 91
unboned 138
unbonnet 371.25
unborn 255
unbosom 242
unbound 139
unbounded 91.14
unbowed 99
unbrace 295
unbreakable 228.16.9
unbred 86
unbridle 228.33
unbridled 122
unbroken 261.14

unbuckle 228.27
unburden 261.22
unbutton 261.103
uncaged 108
uncanny 16.223
uncap 268
uncaring 265.52
unceasing 265
unceremonious 310.2.9.1
uncertain 261.97
uncertainty 16.360
unchain 247
unchanging 265
unchaperoned 138
uncharted 91.33
unchecked 385
unchristian 261
unchristianly 16.174
unchurch 65
uncial 228.3
unciform 238.1
uncinate 371.24
uncinus 310.34
uncircumcised 154
uncivil 228.120
uncivilized 154
unclad 83
unclasp 290
unclassified 92.1
uncle 228.30
unclean 251
uncleaned 133
uncleanly 16.171
unclear 6
unclog 185
unclose 520
unclothe 478
unclothed 145
uncoil 222
uncomfortable 228.16
uncommercial 228.92
uncommon 261
uncommonly 16.174
uncommunicative 485.15.1
uncompromising 265.82
unconcern 249
unconcerned 132

unconcernedly 16.148
unconditional 228.63.5
unconditioned 143.5
unconformity 16.333.13
unconnected 91.43
unconscionable 228.16.31
unconscious 310
unconsciousness 300.34
unconstitutional 228.63.7
uncontrollable 228.16.24
unconventional 228.63.9
unconventionality 16.333.8.7
unconvincing 265.62
uncooked 390
uncoordinated 91.34.6
uncork 41
uncounted 91.49
uncouple 228
uncouth 463
uncovenanted 91.50
uncover 17.418
uncovered 103.7
uncross 302
uncrowned 139
unction 261.80
unctuous 310.4
uncurbed 105
uncurl 216
uncut 378
undaunted 91.47
undecagon 254.5
undeceive 484.2
undecided 91.8
undefended 91.13
undefiled 117
undemonstrative 485.15.11
undeniable 228.16.3
under 17.108
underachieve 484

underachiever 17.413
underact 382
underage 193
underarm 230
underbelly 16.115
underbid 91.4
underbody 16.65
underbred 86
underbrush 356
undercarriage 197.9
undercart 366
undercharge 192
underclay 2
undercoat 376
undercover 17.418
undercroft 399
undercurrent 420.64
underdevelop 281.1
underdog 185
underdone 259
underemployed 97
underestimate 367.15, 371.19
underestimation 261.67.15
underexpose 520
underexposure 17.335
underfed 86
underfeed 89
underfelt 402
underfloor 9
underfoot 379.1
underfur 3
undergarment 420
undergird 87
underglaze 509
undergo 12.33
undergone 254.5
undergraduate 371.2
underground 139.2
undergrown 257
undergrowth 461
underhand 128
underhanded 91.12
underhandedness 300.28.1
underhung 267
underlaid 85
underlay 2.12

underlie 7.7
underline 253.3
underling 265
underlying 265.3
undermentioned 143
undermine 253
undermost 441
underneath 457
undernourish 353.10
undernourished 449
underpaid 85
underpants 347
underpass 294
underpay 2
underpin 252
underpinning 265.43
underplay 2
underplot 373
underprice 301
underprivileged 110
underproduction 261.79.1
underquote 376
underrate 367.23
underripe 275
underscore 9
undersea 5
underseal 217.2
undersecretary 16.274.43
undersell 215.2
underset 368
undersexed 450
undersheriff 163.2
undershirt 369
undershoot 380
undershot 373
underside 92.8
undersigned 135
undersized 154
underskirt 369
undersoil 222
understaffed 396
understand 128
understandable 228.16.17
understanding 265.19
understate 367

understatement 420.48
understood 101
understudy 16.69
undertake 34
undertaken 261.11
undertaker 17.30
undertaking 265.6
underthrust 443
undertint 412
undertone 257.3
undertook 44
undertow 12
undertrick 38
undertrump 289
undervalue 15
undervest 433
underwater 17.345
underwear 4.8
underweight 367.38
underwent 410
underwing 265
underworld 114
underwrite 372.8
underwriter 17.343
undescended 91.13
undeserved 147
undeserving 265.78
undesirable 228.16
undetected 91.43
undetermined 134
undeterred 87
undiagnosed 155
undid 91
undies 515
undigested 91.52
undignified 92.1
undiluted 91.42
undine 251
undirected 91.43
undisclosed 155
undiscovered 103.7
undisguised 154
undisputed 91.42
undissolved 151
undistinguished 449
undisturbed 105
undivided 91.8
undo 15
undoing 265.5
undone 259
undoubted 91
undress 296

undrinkable 228.16.11
undue 15
undulant 420.27
undulate 367.13, 371.17
undulation 261.67.13
undulatory 16.274.43
unduly 16.130
undying 265.3
unearned 132
unearth 456
unearthly 16.204
uneasy 16.395
uneconomic 38.29.1
unedited 91.38
unemployable 228.16.4
unemployed 97
unemployment 420.33
unending 265.20
unengaged 108
unenviable 228.16.2
unequal 228.71
unequalled 122
unequivocal 228.28
unerring 265.51
UNESCO 12.14
uneven 261.113
unevenness 300.31
uneventful 226.11
unexceptional 228.63
unexpected 91.43
unexpectedness 300.28
unexpired 93
unexplainable 228.16.27
unexploded 91.10
unexposed 155
unexpressed 433
unfading 265.11
unfailing 265.27
unfair 4
unfairness 300.22
unfaithful 226
unfaithfulness 300.30
unfamiliar 17.3.21

unfamiliarity 16.333.20.1
unfasten 261.61
unfathomable 228.16
unfathomed 127
unfavourable 228.16.35
unfeeling 265.29
unfenced 447
unfetter 17.339
unfinished 449
unfit 371
unfitness 300.38
unfix 498
unflappable 228.16
unfledged 109
unflinching 265
unfold 120
unforeseeable 228.16.1
unforeseen 251
unforgettable 228.16.46
unforgivable 228.16
unforgiven 261.114
unforgotten 261.101
unformed 125
unfortunate 371.28.1
unfounded 91.14
unframed 124
unfreeze 513
unfriendliness 300.23
unfriendly 16.154
unfrock 40
unfroze 520
unfurl 216
unfurled 114
unfurnished 449
ungainly 16.170
Ungava 17.410
unglazed 152
ungodliness 300.23
ungodly 16.149
ungovernable 228.16.31
ungrammatical 228.23.18
ungrateful 226.7
unguarded 91.5
unguent 420

unguiculate 371.17.2
unguis 300
ungula 17.174
ungulate 371.17
unguligrade 85.5
unhair 4
unhallowed 98
unhand 128
unhappiness 300.23
unhappy 16.243
unharmed 123
unharness 300.21
unhealthiness 300.23
unhealthy 16.374
unheard 87
unheeded 91
unhelm 243
unhesitating 265.64
unhinge 209
unholy 16.126
unhook 44
unhorse 303
unhurried 91
unhurt 369
uni 16.236
Uniat 365
uniaxial 228.3.18
unicameral 228.76
UNICEF 160
unicorn 255.2
unicycle 228.24
unifoliate 371.1
uniform 238.1
uniformitarianism 242.35.14.1.1
uniformity 16.333.13
unify 7.3
unilateral 228.76
unimaginable 228.16.29
unimpaired 88
unimpeachable 228.16.12
unimportant 420
unimpressed 433
unimproved 150
uninformed 125
uninspired 93
uninspiring 265.54
uninsured 96

unintelligent 420.20
unintelligible 228.16.20.1
unintentional 228.63.9
uninterested 91.53
uninvited 91.39
uninviting 265.67
union 261.123
unionism 242.35.14
unionist 436.13
unionize 516.7
uniparous 310.50
unipod 94
unique 37
uniramous 310.27
unisex 496
unisexual 228.9
unison 261.65
unit 371
unitarian 261.3.21.2
unitarianism 242.35.14.1.1
unitary 16.274.41
unite 372
united 91.39
unitive 485.12
unity 16.333.18
univalent 420.25
univalve 491
universal 228.84
universalism 242.35.11
universalist 436.7
universality 16.333.8
universalize 516.3
universally 16.131
universe 297.2
university 16.333.26
unjust 443
unkempt 428
unkenned 131
unkennel 228.57
unkind 135
unkindness 300.29
unknit 371
unknowable 228.16
unknowing 265.4
unknown 257
unlace 295
unlade 85

unladen 261.20
unlash 349
unlatch 62
unlawful 226.1
unlay 2
unlead 86
unleaded 91.7
unlearn 249
unlearned 91
unlearnt 411
unleash 352
unleavened 143
unless 296
unlicensed 448
unlike 39
unlikely 16.143
unlimited 91.38
unlined 135
unlisted 91.53
unlit 371
unlive 485
unload 98
unlock 40
unlocked 388
unloose 309
unlovely 16.207
unlucky 16.30
unmade 85
unmake 34
unman 245
unmanly 16.169
unmanned 128
unmannerly 16.131
unmarked 383
unmarried 91.25
unmask 56
unmeant 410
unmeasured 103.6
unmeet 370
unmentionable 228.16.31.1
unmentionables 539
unmerited 91.38
unmindful 226
unmistakable 228.16.9
unmitigated 91.34.4
unmolested 91.52
unmoor 10
unmounted 91.49
unmourned 137
unmoved 150
unmusical 228.23

unnamed 124
unnatural 228.76
unnecessary 16.274.36
unnerve 483
unnerving 265.78
unnoticed 436.25
unnumbered 103
unobserved 147
unobtainable 228.16.27
unobtrusive 485.8
unoccupied 92
unofficial 228.93
unopened 143
unopposed 155.1
unorthodox 499.1
unowned 138
unpack 32
unpaged 108
unpaid 85
unpainted 91.45
unparalleled 113
unparliamentary 16.274.47
unpaved 146
unpeg 181
unpeople 228.65
unperceived 148
unperforated 91.34.7
unperson 261.64
unperturbed 105
unpick 38
unpin 252
unplaced 432
unpleasant 420.84
unpleasantness 300
unplug 189
unpolled 120
unpolluted 91.42
unpopular 17.174.10
unpopularity 16.333.20.3
unposed 155
unpractised 436
unprecedented 91.46
unpredictable 228.16
unprejudiced 436.2
unpremeditated 91.34
unprepared 88

unprepossessing
265.60
unpresentable
228.16.55
unpreventable
228.16.55
unpriced 437
unprincipled 122
unprintable 228.16
unproductive
485.19
unprofessional
228.63.4
unprofitable
228.16.49
unpronounceable
228.16
unproved 150
unqualified 92.1
unquestionable
228.16.31
unquestioned 143
unquiet 381.2
unquote 376
unravel 228.117
unread 86
unreadable 228.16
unready 16.60
unreal 228.2
unreality
16.333.8.1
unreason 261.125
unreasonable
228.16.31.2
unrecognizable
228.16.64
unreconstructed 91
unrefined 135
unreflected 91.43
unregenerate
371.35
unrelenting 265
unreliability
16.333.9.2.1
unreliable 228.16.3
unremitting 265.66
unrepaired 88
unrequited 91.39
unreserved 147
unreservedly
16.148.1
unresolved 151
unrest 433
unrestrained 130
unrestricted 91

unrewarded 91.9
unrewarding
265.15
unrhymed 126
unriddle 228.32
unrig 184
unrighteous 310
unrip 274
unripe 275
unrivalled 122
unroll 223
unroot 380
unruffled 122
unruled 121
unruly 16.130
unsaddle 228.31
unsafe 159
unsaid 86
unsaturated
91.34.7
unsaved 146
unsavoury
16.274.50
unsay 2
unscathed 144
unscheduled 121
unschooled 121
unscientific 38.12
unscramble 228.17
unscratched 395
unscreened 133
unscrew 15
unscripted 91
unscrupulous
310.25
unscrupulousness
300.34
unseal 217
unseasonable
228.16.31.2
unseasoned 143.6
unseat 370
unsecured 96
unseeded 91
unseemly 16.166
unseen 251
unselfish 353.3
unselfishness
300.35
unset 368
unsettle 228.100
unsettled 122.2
unsex 496
unshaded 91.6

unshakable
228.16.9
unshaken 261.11
unshapen 261.57
unshaven 261.111
unsheathe 475
unship 274
unsighted 91.39
unsightly 16.190
unsigned 135
unsinkable
228.16.11
unskilful 226.3
unskilled 116
unslaked 384
unsling 265
unsnap 268
unsnarl 213
unsociable
228.16.44
unsocial 228.94
unsold 120
unsolved 151
unsophisticated
91.34.3
unsound 139
unsparing 265.52
unspeakable
228.16
unspoiled 119
unspoken 261.14
unspotted 91.40
unstable 228.11
unsteadiness
300.23.1
unsteady 16.60
unstick 38
unstop 276
unstoppable 228.16
unstopped 425
unstrained 130
unstratified 92.1
unstressed 433
unstring 265
unstructured 103
unstrung 267
unstuck 43
unstudied 91.11
unsubstantiated
91.34.1
unsuitability
16.333.9.2
unsuitable
228.16.53
unsuited 91.42

unsung 267
unsure 10
unsuspected 91.43
unsuspecting
265.71
unswear 4
unswerving 265.78
unsystematic
38.49.1
untamed 124
untangle 228.49
untaught 374
unteach 66
unteachable
228.16.12
untearable
228.16.33
untenable 228.16
unthanked 391
unthink 52
unthinkable
228.16.11
unthinking 265.10
unthread 86
untidiness 300.23
untidy 16.64
untie 7
until 218
untimely 16.167
untiring 265.54
untitled 122
unto 15
untold 120
untouchable 228.16
untoward 95.4
untranslatable
228.16.45
untravelled 122
untried 92
untrodden 261.26
untrue 15
untruss 307
untruth 463
untruthful 226.14
untruthfulness
300.30
untuck 43
unturned 132
untutored 103
unusual 228.9
unutterable
228.16.35
unvalued 102
unveil 214
unveiling 265.27

unvoice 304
unvoiced 440
unwanted 91
unwarrantable 228.16.57
unwarranted 91.50
unwary 16.264
unwavering 265.58.1
unwearable 228.16.33
unwearied 91
unweighed 85
unwelcome 242
unwell 215
unwept 422
unwholesome 242
unwieldy 16.74
unwilled 116
unwilling 265.30
unwillingness 300.32
unwind 135
unwinking 265.10
unwise 516
unwish 353
unwitnessed 436
unwitting 265.66
unwonted 91
unworldliness 300.23
unworldly 16.153
unworthy 16.375
unwound 139
unwrap 268
unwritten 261.99
unyielding 265
unyoke 42
unzip 274
up 279
Upanishad 83
upas 310
upbeat 370
upbraid 85
upbringing 265.47
upbuild 116
upcast 431
upcountry 16.290
update 367
upend 131
upgrade 85
upgrowth 461
upheaval 228.119
upheave 484
upheld 113

uphill 218
uphold 120
upholster 17.392
upholsterer 17.279
upholstery 16.274
upkeep 273
upland 143
uplift 398
upon 254
upper 17.258
uppercut 378
uppermost 441
uppish 353
uppity 16.333
Uppsala 17.161
upraise 509
uprear 6
upright 372
uprightness 300.39
uprise 516
uprising 265.82
uproar 9
uproarious 310.2.13
uproot 380
uprush 356
upset 368
upsetting 265.65
upshot 373
upside 92
upside-down 258
upsilon 254.6
upstage 193
upstairs 512
upstanding 265.19
upstart 366
upstate 367
upstream 234
upstroke 42
upsweep 273
upsy-daisy 16.393
uptake 34
upthrust 443
uptight 372
uptilt 403
uptown 258
upturn 249
upward 103
upwards 531
upwind 134
Ur 3
uracil 218
uraemia 17.3.26
uraeus 310.1
Ural 228.75

Uralic 38.19
uralite 372.4
Uranian 261.3.15
uranic 38.31
uranide 92.4
uraninite 372.5
uranite 372.6
uranium 242.2.10
uranography 16.90.2.4
uranous 310.36
Uranus 310.31
uranyl 218
urate 367
urban 261.9
urbane 247
urbanite 372.6
urbanity 16.333.14
urbanize 516.7
urchin 252
urd 87
urdé 2
Urdu 15
urea 17.3.42
urease 509.1
uredium 242.2.2
ureide 92
ureter 17.341
urethral 228
urethritis 300.62
urethroscope 278.1
uretic 38.50
urge 195
urgency 16.312.3
urgent 420.19
urgently 16.198
Uriah 17.4
uric 38.43
urinal 228.61
urinalysis 300.52.1
urinant 420.53
urinary 16.274.26
urinate 367.17
urination 261.67.18
urine 252
uriniferous 310.50.2
urinous 310.33
Urmia 17.3.25
urn 249
urnfield 115
urochord 95.3
urochrome 239
urodele 217
urogenous 310.33

urolith 458
urology 16.108.4
uroscopy 16.254.2
urostyle 219.7
Urquhart 381
ursine 253
Ursula 17.174
Ursuline 253
urticaceous 310.56.1
urticaria 17.3.38
Uruguay 7
urushiol 220.1
us 307
usable 228.16.65
usage 197
usance 321
use 309, 523
used 156
useful 226
usefulness 300.30
useless 300
uselessness 300.33
user 17.444
Ushant 420
usher 17.329
usherette 368.6
Usk 60
Üsküdar 1.3
usquebaugh 9
Ustashi 16.320
Ustinov 165.1
usual 228.9
usually 16.131
usufruct 389
usurer 17.279
usurious 310.2.14
usurp 272
usurpation 261.67
usurped 423
usurper 17.251
usury 16.274
Utah 9
Utamaro 12.61
Ute 380
utensil 228.88
uterine 253.7
uterus 310.50
Utgard 84
Utica 17.34
utilitarian 261.3.21.2
utilitarianism 242.35.14.1.1
utility 16.333.9

utilize 516.2
utmost 441
Utopia 17.3.37
Utopian 261.3.19
utricle 228.23
utriculitis 300.62.2
Uttar Pradesh 351
utter 17.349
utterance 321.20
utterly 16.131
uvea 17.3
uveitis 300.62
uvula 17.174
uvulitis 300.62.2
Uxbridge 197
uxorial 228.3.12
uxoricide 92.7
uxorious 310.2.13

V

Vaal 213
vac 32
vacancy 16.312
vacant 420
vacate 367.6
vacation 261.67
vacationer 17.239.1
vacationist
    436.13.4
vaccinal 228.60
vaccinate 367.17
vaccination
    261.67.18
vaccine 251
vaccinia 17.3.34
vacillate 367.12
vacillating 265.64
vacillation
    261.67.12
vacua 17.7
vacuity 16.333.3
vacuole 223
vacuous 310.4
vacuum 242.3
Vadodara 17.279
vag 178
vagabond 136
vagabondage 197
vagal 228.44
vagary 16.274

vagina 17.232
vaginal 228.61
vaginate 371.24.2
vaginismus 310.30
vaginitis 300.62.3
vagotropic 38.37.2
vagrancy 16.312
vagrant 420
vague 180
vagueness 300
vagus 310.19
vahana 17.239
vain 247
vainglory 16.269
vainly 16.170
vair 4
valance 321.10
vale 2, 214
valediction
    261.78.1
valedictory
    16.274.46
valence 321.11
Valenciennes 248.1
valency 16.312
Valens 546
valentine 253
Valentinian
    261.3.17
Valentino 12.54
valerian 261.3.21
valeric 38.39
Valerie 16.274.15
valet 371
valetudinarian
    261.3.21.1
valgus 310
Valhalla 17.160
valiant 420
valid 91.16
validate 367.8
validation 261.67.7
validity 16.333.5
valine 251
valise 513.7
Valium 242.2
Valkyrie 16.266
vallation 261.67.14
vallecula 17.174.4
Valletta 17.339
valley 16.112
valonia 17.3.36.2
valorize 516.8
valorous 310.50
valour 17.160

valuable 228.16.6
valuate 367.2
valuation 261.67.2
value 15
valueless 300.11
valuer 17.7
valuta 17.351
valve 491
valvelet 371
valvular 17.174
valvule 227
valvulitis 300.62.2
vambrace 295
vamoose 309
vamp 285
vampire 8
vampiric 38.40
vampirism 242.35
Van 246
van 245
vanadate 367.9
vanadium 242.2.1
vanaspati 16.344
Van Buren 261.59
Vancouver 17.419
vanda 17.98
vandal 228.39
vandalism
    242.35.11
vandalize 516.3
Van de Graaff
    158.1
Vanderbilt 403
Van der Waal 213
Vandyke 39
vane 247
van Eyck 39
vang 263
Van Gogh 40
vanguard 84
vanilla 17.166.1
vanillic 38.21
vanillin 252.8
vanish 353
vanity 16.333.14
vanquish 353
vantage 197
vapid 91
vaporescence
    321.21
vaporetto 12.75
vaporific 38.12.1
vaporimeter
    17.342.2.1
vaporize 516.8

vaporizer 17.441.1
vaporous 310.50
vapour 17.249
var 1
vara 17.268
varactor 17.353
Varanasi 16.307
varec 35
varia 17.3.38
variable 228.16.2
variance 321.1
variant 420.1
variation 261.67.1
varicella 17.163
varicellate 371.15
varicelloid 97.4
varices 513
varicoloured 103.4
varicose 305
varicosis 300.55
varicosity
    16.333.30.3
varicotomy
    16.222.4
varied 91
variegate 367.10
variegated 91.34.4
varietal 228.102
variety 16.333.2.1
variform 238.1
variola 17.176.1
variolate 367
variolite 372.4
varioloid 97.6
variolous 310
variometer
    17.342.3.1
variorum 242.20
various 310.2.10
variscite 372.9
varistor 17.384
varix 498
varlet 371
varmint 412
varna 17.226
varnish 353
varnisher 17.326
varsity 16.333
varus 310
varve 481
vary 16.264
Vasari 16.261
Vasco da Gama
    17.206
vascular 17.174

vasculum 242.10
vas deferens 546
vase 508
vasectomy 16.222.5
Vaseline 251.2
vasoconstrictor
17.355
vasodilator 17.338
vasopressin 252
vassal 228
vassalage 197
vast 431
vastness 300.42
vasty 16.362
VAT 365
vat 365
vatic 38.49
Vatican 261.13
Vaticanism
242.35.14.2
Vaud 12
vaudeville 218.3
vaudevillian
261.3.11
Vaughan 255
vault 404
vaulted 91.44
vaulting 265
vaunt 415
vavasor 9.11
veal 217
vealer 17.165
vector 17.354
Veda 17.79
vedalia 17.3.18
Vedanta 17.365
Vedda 17.80
vedette 368
Vedic 38
veer 6
veery 16.265
veg 194
Vega 17.128
vegan 261
vegetable 228.16
vegetal 228.102
vegetarian
261.3.21.2
vegetarianism
242.35.14.1.1
vegetate 367.30
vegetation
261.67.27
vegetative
485.15.12

vehement 420.31
vehicle 228.23
vehicular 17.174.6
Veii 7
veil 214
veiled 112
vein 247
veining 265.40
veinlet 371
veiny 16.225
velamen 248.2
velar 17.165
velarium 242.2.14
Velcro 12
veldt 402
veleta 17.341
veliger 17.150
velites 513
velleity 16.333.1
Vellore 9.8
vellum 242.8
veloce 16.50
velocipede 89.1
velocity 16.333.30
velodrome 239
velours 10
velouté 2.25
velum 242
velure 10.4
velutinous 310.33.2
velvet 371
velveteen 251
velvety 16.333
vena 17.230
vena cava 17.410
venal 228.59
venality 16.333.8
venatic 38.49
venation 261.67
vend 131
Venda 17.101
vendace 295
vendee 5
vendetta 17.339
vendible 228.16.18
vendor 9, 17.101
vendue 15
veneer 6.4
veneering 265.53
venerable
228.16.35
venerate 367.23.1
veneration
261.67.22.2
venereal 228.3.11

venereology
16.108.4.1
venery 16.274.23
venesection
261.77.5
Venetia 17.325
Venetian 261.70
Venetic 38.50.4
Venezuela 17.162
vengeance 321
vengeful 226
venial 228.3.6
Venice 300
venin 252.16
venipuncture 17.68
venison 261.65
Venite 16.334
venom 242
venomous 310.29
venose 305
venous 310.32
vent 410
ventage 197.14
ventail 214
venter 17.368
ventilate 367.12
ventilation
261.67.12
ventilator 17.338.5
ventral 228.80
ventricle 228.23
ventricose 305
ventricular
17.174.6
ventriculus
310.25.2
ventriloquism
242.35
ventriloquist 436
ventriloquize 516
ventriloquy 16.259
venture 17.70
venturesome 242
Venturi 16.270
venue 15
venule 227
Venus 310.32
Venusian 261.3
veracious 310.56
veracity 16.333.25
Veracruz 523
veranda 17.98.2
verb 22
verbal 228

verbalism
242.35.11
verbalist 436.7
verbalize 516.3.4
verbatim 235
verbena 17.230
verbiage 197
verbid 91
verbose 305
verbosity 16.333.30
Vercingetorix 498.7
verdant 420
verdict 387
verdigris 300
verdure 17.148
verge 195
verger 17.148
verglas 1
veridical 228.23
verifiable
228.16.3.1
verify 7.3.5
verily 16.120
verisimilar 17.166
verisimilitude
102.2
verism 242.35
verismo 12.50
veritable 228.16.49
verity 16.333.21
verjuice 309
Vermeer 6
vermeil 214
vermicelli 16.115
vermicide 92.7
vermicular
17.174.6
vermiculate
367.13.2, 371.17.2
vermiculation
261.67.13
vermiform 238.1
vermifuge 204
vermilion 261.120
vermin 252.13
vermination
261.67.18.4
verminous 310.33
vermis 300.18
vermivorous
310.50.3
Vermont 414
vermouth 464
vernacular 17.174.3

vernacularism
    242.35.15
vernal 228.58
vernalize 516.3.6
vernation 261.67
Verne 249
vernier 17.3.32
vernissage 359
Verona 17.236
Veronica 17.34.1
verruca 17.41
verrucose 305
Versailles 7
versant 420.68
versatile 219
versatility 16.333.9
verse 297
versed 434
versicle 228.23
versify 7.3
version 261.69
verso 12
versus 310
vert 369
vertebra 17.283
vertebral 228
vertebrate 371
vertebration
    261.67.23
vertex 496
vertical 228.23
vertices 513
verticil 218
verticillaster 17.379
verticillate 371.16
vertiginous 310.33
vertigo 12.29
Vertumnus 310
Verulamium 242.2
vervain 247
verve 483
vervet 371.37
very 16.262
Vesalius 310.2.3
vesica 17.34
vesical 228.23
vesicant 420.7
vesicate 367.5
vesicle 228.23
vesiculate 371.17
Vespasian 261.3.33
vesperal 228.76
vespers 524
vespertine 253
vespiary 16.274.1

vespid 91
vespine 253
Vespucci 16.53
vessel 228
vest 433
Vesta 17.382
vesta 17.382
vestal 228.113
vested 91.52
vestiary 16.274.1
vestibular 17.174.2
vestibule 227
vestige 197
vestigial 228.3.3
vestment 420
vestry 16.292
vesture 17.73
vesuvian 261.3.32
Vesuvius 310.2.18
vet 368
vetch 64
veteran 261.60
veterinarian
    261.3.21.1
veterinary
    16.274.26
vetiver 17.414
veto 12.76
vex 496
vexation 261.67.35
vexatious 310.56
vexillology
    16.108.4.8
via 17.4
viability
    16.333.9.2.1
viable 228.16.3
Via Dolorosa
    17.306
viaduct 389
viand 143
viaticum 242.4
vibraculum 242.10
vibraharp 269
vibrant 420
vibraphone 257
vibrate 367
vibration 261.67
vibrato 12.73
vibrator 17.338
vibratory 16.274.43
vibrio 12.3
vibrissa 17.302
vibronic 38.35
viburnum 242.13

vicar 17.34
vicarage 197
vicarial 228.3.10
vicariate 371.1
vicarious 310.2.10
vice 16.301, 301
vicegerent 420.61
viceregal 228.45
vicereine 247
viceroy 11
viceroyalty
    16.352.1
vice versa 17.301
vicinal 228.60.6
vicinity 16.333.17
vicious 310.58
viciousness
    300.34.3
vicissitude 102.2
Vicksburg 182
victim 235
victimize 516.4
victor 17.355
Victoria 17.3.41
Victorian 261.3.23
Victoriana 17.226.1
victorious 310.2.13
victory 16.274.46
victual 228.102
victualler 17.176.3
victuals 539
vicuña 17.238
vide 16.64
videlicet 368.7
video 12.3.1
vidicon 254
vie 7
Vienna 17.228
Viennese 513.9
Vientiane 246
Vietcong 266
Vietminh 252
Vietnam 229
Vietnamese 513.8
view 15
viewable 228.16.7
viewer 17.8
viewfinder 17.103
viewing 265.5
viewless 300.12
viewpoint 416
vigesimal 228.52.1
vigil 218
vigilance 321
vigilant 420

vigilante 16.353
vignette 368
vignetting 265.65
Vigo 12.28
vigorous 310.50
vigour 17.129
Viking 265
vilayet 368
vile 219
vileness 300
vilify 7.3
vilipend 131.3
villa 17.166
village 197.1
villager 17.150
villain 261.41
villainess 300.26
villainous 310.36
villainy 16.237
Villa-Lobos 302.1
villanella 17.163
villanelle 215
villatic 38.49
villein 261.41
villi 7.5
villosity 16.333.30
villous 310.23
villus 310.23
Vilnius 308
vim 235
vimen 248
Viminal 228.60.4
vimineous 310.2.8
vina 17.230
vinaigrette 368
vinasse 293
vincible 228.16.41
vinculum 242.10
vindicate 367.5
vindication
    261.67.5
vindictive 485.18
vine 253
vinegar 17.129
vinegarroon 260.3
vinegary 16.274.9
vinery 16.274.27
vineyard 84
viniculture 17.69
vinificator 17.338.2
Vinland 143
vino 12.54
vinosity
    16.333.30.4
vinous 310.34

vintage 197
vintager 17.150
vinyl 218
viol 228.4
viola 17.171,
  17.176.1
viola da gamba
  17.23
viola d'amore
  16.269
violate 367.14.1
violation
  261.67.14.1
violence 321.12
violent 420.28
violet 371.18.1
violin 252.11
violinist 436.11
violist 436
violoncello 12.40
viper 17.254
viperous 310.50
virago 12.26
viral 228
virelay 2.11
virescence 321.21
virga 17.127
Virgil 218
virgin 252
virginal 228.60
Virginia 17.3.34
virginity 16.333.17
virginium 242.2.11
Virgo 12
virgulate 371.17
virgule 227
viridescent 420.67
viridian 261.3.5
viridity 16.333.5
virile 219
virilism 242.35.9
virility 16.333.9
virology 16.108.4
virtual 228.9
virtually 16.131.1
virtue 15
virtuosity
  16.333.30.2
virtuoso 12.70
virtuous 310.4
virulence 321
virulent 420.27
virus 310.47
visa 17.440
visage 197

vis-à-vis 5
viscacha 17.50
viscera 17.279.2
visceral 228.76
viscid 91.29
viscoid 97
viscometer
  17.342.3
viscose 305
viscosity 16.333.30
viscount 418
viscountess 300
viscous 310.15
viscus 310.15
Vishnu 15
visibility
  16.333.9.2.2
visible 228.16.63
Visigoth 459
vision 261.91
visionary 16.274.29
visit 371.38
visitant 420.76
visitation 261.67.27
visitatorial
  228.3.12.2
visitor 17.342.4
visor 17.441
vista 17.384
Vistula 17.174
visual 228.9
visualize 516.3.3
vital 228.103
vitalism 242.35.11
vitality 16.333.8
vitalize 516.3
vitamin 252.15
vitellin 252.7
vitiate 367.1.6
vitiation 261.67.1.5
viticulture 17.69
Vitória 17.3.41
vitrain 247
vitreous 310.2
vitrescence 321.21
vitrescent 420.67
vitric 38
vitriform 238.1
vitrify 7.3
vitrine 251
vitriol 220.1
vitriolic 38.22
vitta 17.342
vituline 253
vituperate 367.23

vituperation
  261.67.22
vituperative
  485.15.10
viva 17.413, 17.415
vivace 16.47
vivacious 310.56
vivacity 16.333.25
Vivaldi 16.73
vivarium 242.2.14
viva voce 16.50
viverrine 253
Vivian 261.3.30
vivid 91
vividness 300.28
vivify 7.3
viviparity
  16.333.20
viviparous 310.50
vivisect 385.7
vivisection 261.77.5
vivisectionist
  436.13.6
vixen 261
Viyella 17.163
vizard 103
vizier 6
vizierate 371.32
Vlach 33
Vladimir 6.2
vocab 18
vocable 228.16
vocabulary
  16.274.18
vocal 228.26
vocalic 38.19
vocalise 513.7
vocalism 242.35.11
vocalist 436.7
vocalize 516.3
vocation 261.67.6
vocational 228.63.3
vocative 485.15.2
vociferate 367.23
vociferous 310.50.2
vodka 17
vogue 188
Vogul 228
voice 304
voiceless 300
voiceprint 412
void 97
voidance 321
voided 91
voile 222

voir dire 6
Volans 544
volant 420
Volapuk 44
volar 17.171
volatile 219
volatilize 516.2
volcanic 38.31
volcanism
  242.35.14
volcanize 516.7
volcano 12
volcanology
  16.108.4.11
vole 223
Volga 17.138
volitant 420.76
volition 261.71.3
volitive 485.12
volley 16.122
volleyball 221
volost 438
volplane 247
Volsci 5
volt 405
Volta 17.364
voltage 197
voltaic 38.1
Voltaire 4
voltameter 17.342
volte-face 294
voluble 228.15
volume 241
volumeter 17.342
voluminosity
  16.333.30.4
voluminous
  310.33.1
voluntarism
  242.35.15
voluntary
  16.274.48
volunteer 6
voluptuary
  16.274.2
voluptuous 310.4
voluptuousness
  300.34.2
volute 380
volution 261.75.1
volva 17.423
Volvo 12
volvox 499
volvulus 310.25
vomer 17.215

vomit 371.20
vomitory 16.274.41
vomitus 310.64
voodoo 15
Voortrekker 17.31
voracious 310.56
voracity 16.333.25
vortex 496
vorticella 17.163
vortices 513
vorticism 242.35.16
vortiginous 310.33
Vostok 40
votary 16.274
vote 376
voter 17.347
votive 485.14
Votyak 32.1
vouch 71
voucher 17.60
vouchsafe 159
vouge 364
voussoir 1
Vouvray 2
vow 13
vowel 228.8
vox 499
vox humana
   17.226
vox populi 7.6
voyage 197
voyager 17.150
voyageur 3
voyeur 3
voyeuristic 38.70.5
vraisemblance 315
vroom 241
vug 189
Vulcan 261
vulcanian 261.3.15
vulcanite 372.6
vulcanize 516.7
vulgar 17.139
vulgarian 261.3.21
vulgarism
   242.35.15
vulgarity 16.333.20
vulgarize 516.8
Vulgate 367
vulnerable
   228.16.35
vulnerary
   16.274.32
Vulpecula 17.174.4
vulpine 253

vulture 17.69
vulturine 253.7
vulva 17.424
vulvitis 300.62

W

WAAF 157
Wabash 349
wacky 16.19
wad 94
wadding 265
waddle 228.34
waddler 17.188
waddy 16.65
wade 85
wader 17.79
waders 524
wadi 16.65
Wadi Halfa 17.121
Wad Medani 5.10
wadset 368
wae 2
wafer 17.111
waff 157
waffle 228
waft 396
wafter 17.358
wag 178
wage 193
wager 17.146
wages 515
wagga 17.131
Wagga Wagga
   17.131
waggish 353
waggle 228.43
Wagner 17
Wagnerian
   261.3.22
wagon 261.30
wagoner 17.239
wagonette 368
wagonload 98
wagtail 214
Wahhabi 16.6
wahine 16.228
waif 159
Waikato 12.73
Waikiki 5
wail 214

wain 247
wainscot 381
wainwright 372
waist 432
waistband 128
waistcoat 376
waisted 91
waistless 300
waistline 253
wait 367
waiter 17.338
waitress 300
waive 482
waiver 17.410
wake 34
Wakefield 115
wakeful 226
waken 261.11
wakerife 164
waking 265.6
Walachia 17.3
Waldemar 1.11
Waldenses 513.14
waldgrave 482
Waldorf 166
wale 214
Waler 17.162
Wales 536
walk 41
walkabout 377.1
walker 17.37
walkie-talkie 16.28
walking 265.9
walkover 17.417
walkway 2
wall 221
wallaby 16.15
Wallace 300.9
wallah 17.168
wallaroo 15.6
Wallasey 16.307
walled 118
wallet 371
walleye 7
walleyed 92
wallflower 14
Walloon 260
wallop 281.2
walloper 17.260
walloping 265
wallow 12.43
wallpaper 17.249
Wallsend 131
wally 16.112,
   16.122

walnut 378
Walpole 223
walrus 310
Walsall 221
Walsingham
   242.17
Walton 261
waltz 312
waltzer 17.310
wame 231
wampum 242
wan 254
wand 136
wander 17.104
wanderer 17.279
wandering 265.58
wanderlust 443
wanderoo 15.6
Wandsworth 464
wane 247
Wanganui 16.4
wangle 228.49
wank 51
Wankel 228
wanna 17.233
want 414
wanting 265
wanton 261
wapentake 34
wapiti 16.333
wappenshaw 9
war 9
waratah 17.352
warb 27
Warbeck 35
warble 228
ward 95
warden 261.27
warder 17.86
wardrobe 28
wardroom 241
wardship 274
ware 4
warehouse 306
warehouseman 261
wares 512
warfare 4
warfarin 252.20
warhead 86
warhorse 303
wariness 300.23
warison 261.65.1
Warley 16.123
warlike 39
warlock 40

warlord 95
warm 238
warm-blooded
91.11
warmer 17.214
warmish 353
warmness 300
warmonger 17.143
warn 255
warning 265
warp 277
warpath 453
warplane 247
warrant 420.63
warrantable
228.16.57
warrantee 5.24
warrantor 9
warranty 16.360
warren 261
warrigal 212
warring 265.55
Warrington 261
warrior 17.3
Warsaw 9
warship 274
warsle 228.83
wart 374
wartime 236
warty 16.336
Warwick 38.41
Warwickshire 6
wary 16.264
was 517
wash 354
washable 228.16
washbasin 261.62
washboard 95
washday 2
washer 17.327
washerwoman
261.50
washery 16.274
washing 265
Washington 261
washrag 178
washroom 241
washstand 128
washtub 29
washy 16.323
wasn't 420
wasp 292
waspish 353
wassail 214
wastage 197

waste 432
wasteful 226.12
wasteland 143
wasteweir 6
wastrel 228
wat 366
watap 269
watch 68
watchcase 295
watchdog 185
watcher 17.57
watchful 226
watchmaker 17.30
watchman 261
watchstrap 268
watchtower 14
watchword 87
water 17.345
waterage 197
waterborne 255.1
waterbuck 43
watercolour 17.173
watercourse 303
watercress 296
waterfall 221
Waterford 103
waterfowl 224
waterfront 419.1
Watergate 367.11
waterlogged 106
Waterloo 15.5
waterman 261.52
watermark 33
watermelon 261.40
waterproof 170
waterscape 270
watershed 86
waterside 92.8
waterspout 377
watertight 372.12
waterway 2.28
waterweed 89
waterworks 497
waterworn 255
watery 16.274
Watford 103
Watson 261
watt 373
wattage 197
Watteau 12.77
wattle 228.104
wattlebird 87
Watusi 16.402
Watutsi 16.318
Waugh 9

waul 221
wave 482
waveband 128
waveform 238
waveguide 92
wavelength 472
wavelet 371
waveoff 165
waver 17.410
wavy 16.379
wax 494
waxbill 218
waxen 261
waxplant 408
waxwing 265
waxwork 36
waxy 16.386
way 2
waybill 218
wayfarer 17.271
Wayland 143
waylay 2
Wayne 247
wayside 92
wayward 103
wayzgoose 309
Waziristan 246.1
we 5
weak 37
weaken 261.12
weakling 265
weakly 16.141
weakness 300
weal 217
Weald 115
wealth 465
wealthy 16.374
wean 251
weaner 17.230
weanling 265
weapon 261
weaponry 16.284
wear 4
Wear 6
wearable 228.16.33
wearer 17.271
weariless 300.8
weariness 300.23
wearing 265.52
wearisome 242.24
wearproof 170
weary 16.265
weasand 143.6
weasel 228
weather 17.402

weather-beaten
261.98
weatherboard 95.1
weathercock 40
weatherglass 294
weathering 265.58
weatherly 16.131
weatherman 261.52
weatherproof 170
weatherworn 255
weave 484
weaver 17.413
weaverbird 87
weaving 265.79
web 21
webbed 104
webbing 265
webby 16.8
Weber 17.11
webfoot 379
wed 86
we'd 89
wedded 91.7
wedding 265.12
wedge 194
Wedgwood 101
wedlock 40
Wednesday 2
wee 5
weed 89
weedkiller 17.166
weedy 16.62
week 37
weekday 2
weekender 17.101
weekly 16.141
weeknight 372
weeny 16.228
weep 273
weeper 17.252
weeping 265.49
weepy 16.247
weever 17.413
weevil 228.119
weft 397
weigela 17.165
weigh 2
weighbridge 197
weight 367
weighting 265.64
weightless 300
weightlessness
300.33
weightlifter 17.359
weightlifting 265

weighty 16.329
Weihai 7
Weill 219
Weimaraner 17.226
weir 6
weird 90
weirdness 300
weka 17.30
welcome 242
weld 113
welder 17.93
welfare 4
well 215
we'll 217
well-aware 4.8
well-behaved 146
wellbeing 265.2
well-built 403
well-dressed 433
well-endowed 99
wellhead 86
well-heeled 115
wellies 515
Wellington 261
well-intentioned 143
well-matched 395
well-oiled 119
well-organized 154
well-paid 85
well-pleased 153
well-preserved 147
well-read 86
well-received 148
Wells 537
well-spent 410
well-timed 126
well-to-do 15.3
well-tried 92
well-wisher 17.326
Welshman 261
welt 402
welter 17.361
welterweight 367.38
welwitschia 17.3
Welwyn 252.7
Wembley 16.138
wen 248
Wenceslas 310
wench 79
wend 131
Wendish 353
Wendy 16.78
Wensleydale 214

went 410
wentletrap 268
wept 422
were 3
we're 6
weren't 411
werewolf 175
wergild 116
Wesley 16.208
Wesleyan 261.3
Wessex 498
west 433
westbound 139
West Bromwich 197.4
wester 17.382
westerly 16.131
western 261.106
Westerner 17.239
westernism 242.35.14
westernize 516.7
westernmost 441
Westmeath 475
Westminster 17.394
Westmorland 143.4
Weston-super-Mare 4.4
Westphalia 17.3.18
westward 103
westwards 531
wet 368
wether 17.402
wetness 300
we've 484
Wexford 103
Weymouth 464
whack 32
whacking 265
whacko 12.8
whale 214
whaleboat 376
whalebone 257
whaler 17.162
whaling 265.27
wham 229
whang 263
Whangarei 2.17
whangee 5
whare 16.268
wharf 166
wharfinger 17.157
what 373
whatever 17.411

whatnot 373
whatsit 371
whatsoever 17.411
whaup 277
wheat 370
wheatear 6
wheaten 261.98
wheedle 228
wheel 217
wheelbarrow 12.60
wheelbase 295
wheelchair 4
wheeler 17.165
wheelie 16.118
wheelwright 372
wheen 251
wheeze 513
wheezy 16.395
whelk 48
whelp 283
when 248
whence 316
whene'er 4
whenever 17.411
where 4
whereabouts 344
whereas 507
whereat 365
whereby 7
where'er 4
wherefore 9
wherefrom 237
wherein 252
whereinto 15
whereof 487
whereon 254
whereto 15
whereupon 254
wherever 17.411
wherewith 476
wherewithal 221
wherrit 371.31
wherry 16.262
whet 368
whether 17.402
whetstone 257
whey 2
wheyface 295
which 67
whichever 17.411
whicker 17.34
whiff 163
whiffle 228.41
whiffler 17.190
whiffletree 5

Whig 184
while 219
whim 235
whimbrel 228
whimper 17.263
whimsical 228.23
whimsicality 16.333.8.3
whimsy 16.403
whin 252
whinchat 365
whine 253
whinge 209
whinny 16.229
whip 274
whipcord 95
whiplash 349
whippersnapper 17.247
whippet 371
whipping 265
whippoorwill 218
whipsaw 9
whipstock 40
whirl 216
whirligig 184
whirlpool 227
whirlwind 134
whirlybird 87
whirr 3
whish 353
whisk 58
whisker 17.48
whiskered 103
whisky 16.41
whisper 17.266
whisperer 17.279
whist 436
whistle 228.85
whistling 265
whit 371
Whit 371
Whitaker 17.42
white 372
whitebait 367
whitebeam 234
whitecap 268
Whitechapel 228.64
whited 91.39
whitedamp 285
whitefish 353
Whitehall 221
whiten 261.100
whitener 17.239

whiteness 300.39
whites 340
whitesmith 458
whitethroat 376
whitewash 354
whitewood 101
whither 17.405
whiting 265.67
whitish 353
whitlow 12
Whitman 261
Whitsun 261
Whitsuntide 92.12
Whittington 261
whittle 228.102
whittler 17.201
whittlings 552
whizz 515
who 15
whoa 12
who'd 102
whodunit 371.27
whoever 17.411
whole 223
wholefood 102
wholehearted 91.33
wholemeal 217
wholesale 214
wholesaler 17.162
wholesome 242
who'll 227
wholly 16.164
whom 241
whomever 17.411
whoop 280
whooper 17.259
whooping cough
165
whoosh 357
whop 276
whopper 17.255
whopping 265
whore 9
whoredom 242
whorehouse 306
whoremonger
17.143
whoreson 261
whortleberry
16.274
who's 523
whose 523
whoso 12
why 7
Whyalla 17.160

whydah 17.83
Wichita 9
Wick 38
wick 38
wicked 91
wickedness 300.28
wicker 17.34
wickerwork 36
wicket 371.9
wicketkeeper
17.252
wickiup 279
wicopy 16.254.1
wide 92
widen 261.25
widespread 86
widget 371
widgie 16.103
Widnes 300.28
widow 12.19
widower 17.6
widowhood 101
widthwise 516
wield 115
wielder 17.94
wieldy 16.74
wiener 17.230
wife 164
wig 184
Wigan 261.32
wigeon 261.37
wigging 265
wiggle 228.46
wiggly 16.160
Wight 372
wigwag 178
wigwam 229
Wilberforce 303.1
wilco 12
wild 117
wildcat 365
wildcatter 17.336
Wilde 117
wildebeest 435
wilderness 300.26
wildfire 8
wildfowl 224
wildlife 164
wildness 300
wile 219
wilful 226.3
Wilhelm 243
Wilhelmina 17.230
Wilkins 548
will 218

willable 228.16.23
willet 371.16
William 242
Williams 543
Williamsburg 182
Williamson 261
willies 515
willing 265.30
willingness 300.32
williwaw 9
will-o'-the-wisp
291
willow 12.42
willowherb 22
willowy 16.3
willpower 14
willy-nilly 16.120
Wilson 261
wilt 403
Wilton 261
Wiltshire 6
wily 16.121
wimble 228
Wimbledon 261
wimple 228
Wimpy 16.255
win 252
wince 317
wincey 16.311
winceyette 368
winch 80
wincher 17.71
Winchester 17.384
wind 134, 135
windbag 178
windblown 257
windbound 139
windbreak 34
windburn 249
windcheater 17.341
winded 91
winder 17.103
Windermere 6.3
windfall 221
windgall 221
Windhoek 44
windhover 17.416
winding 265.21
windjammer
17.205
windlass 310
windlestraw 9
windmill 218
window 12.25
windowpane 247

windowsill 218
windpipe 275
windscreen 251
windshield 115
windsock 40
Windsor 17
windstorm 238
windswept 422
windward 103
windy 16.79
wine 253
wineglass 294
winepress 296
winery 16.274.27
wineskin 252
wing 265
wingding 265
winged 107
winger 17.246
wingless 300.15
winglet 371
wingover 17.417
wingspan 245
wink 52
winker 17.44
winkle 228.29
Winnebago 12.27
winner 17.231
winning 265.43
Winnipeg 181
Winnipegosis
300.55
winnow 12.55
wino 12
winsome 242
winter 17.369
winterbourne 255.1
winterfeed 89
wintergreen 251
winterkill 218
wintertime 236
wintry 16.289
winy 16.230
winze 548
wipe 275
wiper 17.254
wire 8
wireless 300
wireman 261
wirer 17.274
wirework 36
wiring 265.54
wirra 17.273
Wirral 228
wiry 16.267

527

Wisconsin 252
wisdom 242
wise 516
wiseacre 17.30
wisecrack 32
wisent 420
wish 353
wishbone 257
wisher 17.326
wishful 226
wishy-washy
16.323
wisp 291
wispy 16.258
wisteria 17.3.39
wistful 226
wit 371
witan 261.99
witch 67
witchcraft 396
witchery 16.274
witching 265
wite 372
with 476
withal 221
withdraw 9
withdrawal 228.5
withdrawn 255
withdrew 15
withe 458
wither 17.405
withers 524
withershins 548
withheld 113
withhold 120
within 252
without 377
withstand 128
withstood 101
withy 16.376
witless 300.17
witness 300.38
wits 339
Wittgenstein 253
witticism 242.35.16
witty 16.333
Witwatersrand 128
wive 486
wizard 103
wizardry 16.277
wizen 261.126
wizened 143
woad 98
woaded 91.10
wobbegong 266

wobble 228
wobbly 16.135
Wodehouse 306
Woden 261
wodge 199
woe 12
woebegone 254.4
woeful 226.2
woggle 228.47
wok 40
woke 42
woken 261.14
Woking 265
wold 120
wolf 175
wolfbane 247
Wolfe 175
wolfhound 139
wolfram 242
wolframite 372
Wollongong 266
wolly 16.122
Wolof 165
Wolverhampton
261
wolverine 251.7
woman 261.50
womanhood 101
womanish 353
womanize 516.7
womanizer 17.441
womankind 135
womanly 16.174
womb 241
wombat 365
women 252.14
womenfolk 42
won 254, 259
wonder 17.108
wonderful 226
wonderland 143.4
wonderment
420.35
wonderwork 36
wonder-worker
17.32
wondrous 310
wonky 16.38
Wonsan 245
won't 417
wont 417
wonted 91
won ton 254
woo 15
wood 101

woodbine 253
woodborer 17.276
woodchat 365
woodchuck 43
woodcock 40
woodcraft 396
woodcut 378
woodcutter 17.349
wooded 91
wooden 261
woodenhead 86
woodgrouse 306
woodland 143
woodlander 17.109
woodlark 33
woodlouse 306
woodman 261
woodnote 376
woodpecker 17.31
woodpile 219
woodprint 412
woodruff 168
woodrush 356
woodscrew 15
woodshed 86
woodsia 17.3
woodwind 134
woodwork 36
woodworking 265
woodworm 233
woody 16.70
woof 169, 170
woofer 17.119
wool 226
Woolf 175
woolgathering
265.58
woollen 261
woolly 16.129
woolpack 32
woolsack 32
Woomera 17.279
woomera 17.279
Woop Woop 280
woozy 16.402
Worcester 17.388
Worcestershire 6
word 87
wordage 197
wordbreak 34
wording 265
wordless 300
wordplay 2
Wordsworth 464
wordy 16.61

wore 9
work 36
workable 228.16
workaday 2.8
workbag 178
workbench 79
workbook 44
workday 2
worker 17.32
workfolk 42
workhorse 303
workhouse 306
working 265
workload 98
workman 261
workmanlike 39
workmanly 16.174
workmanship
274.2
workroom 241
workshop 276
workshy 7
Worksop 276
worktable 228.11
world 114
worldliness 300.23
worldling 265
worldly 16.153
worldwide 92
worm 233
wormcast 431
wormseed 89
wormwood 101
wormy 16.214
worn 255
worriment 420.31
worrisome 242.24
worrit 371
worry 16.272
worrywart 374
worse 297
worsen 261.64
worship 274
worshipful 226
worshipper 17.253
worst 434
worsted 91
wort 369
worth 456
Worthing 265
worthless 300
worthlessness
300.33
worthwhile 219
worthy 16.375

Wotan 246
would 101
wouldn't 420.12
wound 139, 142
wounded 91
woundwort 369
wove 488
woven 261.116
wow 13
wowser 17.443
wrack 32
wraith 454
wrangle 228.49
wrangler 17.194
wrap 268
wrapover 17.417
wrapper 17.247
wrapping 265
wrapping 265.48
wrasse 293
wrath 459
wrathful 226
wreak 37
wreath 457
wreathe 475
wreck 35
wrecker 17.31
Wrekin 252
wren 248
wrench 79
wrest 433
wrestle 228
wrestler 17.197
wrestling 265
wretch 64
wretched 91
wretchedness
  300.28
Wrexham 242
wriggle 228.46
Wright 372
wring 265
wringer 17.246
wrinkle 228.29
wrinkly 16.145
wrist 436
wristlet 371
wristlock 40
wristwatch 68
writ 371
write 372
writer 17.343
writhe 477
writing 265.67
written 261.99

wrong 266
wrongdoer 17.8
wrongdoing 265.5
wrongful 226
wrongly 16.176
wrote 376
wroth 461
wrought 374
wrung 267
wry 7
wrybill 218
wryneck 35
Wu 15
Wuhu 15
wulfenite 372.6
Wu-lu-mu-ch'i 5
wunderkind 134
wurley 16.116
wurst 434
Württemberg 182
wus 307
Wyandotte 373
Wyatt 381.2
wych-elm 243
Wycherley 16.131
Wycliffe 163
Wycliffite 372
Wye 7
wynd 135
Wyoming 265.37
wyvern 261.115

X

xanthein 252
Xanthippe 16.248
xanthochroism
  242.35.3
xanthoma 17.215
xanthophyll 218.1
Xanthus 310.72
Xavier 17.3.53
xebec 35
xenia 17.3.33
Xenocrates 513.17
xenocryst 436
xenolith 458
xenon 254
xenophile 219.1
xenophobe 28
xenophobia 17.3.4

xenophobic 38.3
xerarch 33
xeric 38
xeroderma 17.209
xerography 16.90.2
xerophilous 310.23
xerophthalmia
  17.3.28
xerosere 6.7
xerosis 300.55.5
Xerox 499
Xerxes 513
xiphisternum
  242.13
xiphoid 97
Xmas 310
x-ray 2
xylem 232
xylograph 158.1
xylography 16.90.2
xyloid 97
xylol 220
xylophone 257
xylophonic 38.35.2
xylose 520
xylotomous
  310.29.3
xyst 436
xyster 17.384

Y

yacht 373
yachting 265.68
yachtsman 261
yahoo 15
yak 32
yam 229
yammer 17.205
Yank 51
yank 51
yap 268
yappy 16.243
yard 84
Yarmouth 464
yarn 246
yarrow 12.60
yaw 9
yawl 221
yawn 255
yaws 518

ye 5
yea 2
year 6
yearly 16.119
yearn 249
yeast 435
yell 215
yellow 12.40
yellowhammer
  17.205
yelp 283
yen 248
yeoman 261.49
yes 296
yes-man 261.53
yesterday 2.8
yet 368
yeti 16.330
yew 15
yield 115
yippee 5
ylang-ylang 263
yob 26
yodel 228
yoga 17.133
yogi 16.96
yogurt 381
yoke 42
yokel 228.26
yolk 42
yon 254
yonder 17.104
yoni 16.233
Yonkers 524
yonnie 16.231
yoo-hoo 15
yore 9
York 41
yorker 17.37
Yorkist 436
Yorks 500
Yorkshire 6
Yosemite 16.333
you 15
you'd 102
you'll 227
young 267
youngster 17
your 9
you're 10
yours 518
yourself 172
youth 463
youthful 226.14
you've 490

yowl 224
yo-yo 12
Ypsilanti 16.353
Yquem 232
ytterbia 17.3.2
ytterbium 242.2
yttrium 242.2
yuan 245
Yucatán 246
yucca 17.39
Yuga 17.135
Yugoslav 481
Yugoslavia 17.3
Yugoslavian 261.3
yuk 43
yukky 16.30
Yukon 254
yulan 245
yule 227
yuletide 92
Yuman 261.51
yummy 16.220
yup 279

Z

zabaglione 16.233
Zachariah 17.4.2
Zacharias 310.3
Zachary 16.274
zaffer 17.110
Zagazig 184
Zagreb 21
Zaïre 6
Zama 17.206
Zambezi 16.395
Zambia 17.3.5
Zamboanga 17.140
zamia 17.3.24
zamindar 1
zamindari 16.261
Zante 16.353

zany 16.225
Zanzibar 1.1
zap 268
Zapotec 35
zareba 17.13
zarf 158
Zaria 17.3
zarzuela 17.162
zeal 217
Zealand 143.1
zealot 381
zealotry 16.286
zealous 310.22
zealousness 300.34
Zeami 16.211
Zebedee 16.63
zebra 17.282
zebrawood 101
zebu 15
zecchino 12.54
Zechariah 17.4.2
zed 86
Zedekiah 17.4
zedoary 16.274
zee 5
zein 252
Zeist 437
Zen 248
Zena 17.230
zenana 17.226
zenith 458
zeolite 372.4
Zephaniah 17.4
zephyr 17.112
Zephyrus 310.50
zeppelin 252.11
zero 12.63
zest 433
Zeus 309
Zeuxis 300
zibeline 253.3
zibet 371.5
Ziegfeld 113
ziff 163
ziggurat 365

zigzag 178
zigzagger 17.123
zila 1.8
zilch 76
zillion 261.120
zinc 52
zincograph 158.1
zincography
  16.90.2
Zinfandel 215
zing 265
zinnia 17.3.34
Zion 261.4
Zionism 242.35.14
zip 274
zipper 17.253
zippy 16.248
zircon 254
zirconia 17.3.36
zirconium 242.2.12
zither 17.405
zloty 16.335
zo 12
zodiac 32.1
zodiacal 228.28.1
Zoffany 16.237.3
Zohar 1
Zola 17.171
Zomba 17.26
zombie 16.18
zonal 228.62
zonate 367
zonation 261.67
Zond 136
zone 257
zoo 15
zoochore 9.2
zoogeography
  16.90.2.1
zoography 16.90.2
zooid 97
zoolatry 16.286.2
zoological 228.23.5
zoologist 436.4

zoology 16.108.4.3
zoom 241
zoometry 16.285.2
zoophagous 310
zoophile 219.1
zoophilia 17.3.21.2
zoophilic 38.21
zoophilism
  242.35.9
zoophilous 310.23
zoophobia 17.3.4
zooplasty 16.361.1
zoosperm 233
zoospore 9.10
zoosterol 220.4
zootechnics 498
zootomy 16.222.4
zootoxin 252.29
zorilla 17.166.3
Zoroaster 17.379
Zoroastrian
  261.3.26
Zoroastrianism
  242.35.14.1
zoster 17.385
Zouave 481
zounds 533
zoysia 17.3
zucchetto 12.75
zucchini 16.228
Zuider Zee 5
Zulu 15.4
Zululand 143
Zürich 38.43
zwieback 32
zwitterion 261.4.1
zygote 376
zymase 509
zymogen 261.39
zymology 16.108.4
zymosis 300.55
zymotic 38.53
zymurgy 16.102
Zyrian 261.3